UNDERSTANDING COPYRIGHT LAW

LexisNexis Law School Publishing Advisory Board

UNDERSTANDING COPYRIGHT LAW

Sixth Edition

Marshall A. Leaffer
Distinguished Scholar in Intellectual Property Law and University Fellow
Mauer School of Law, Indiana University

Print ISBN: 978-0-7698-6902-5
eBook ISBN: 978-0-7698-9629-8

Library of Congress Cataloging-in-Publication Data

Leaffer, Marshall A., 1943- e author.

Understanding copyright law / Marshall A. Leaffer, Distinguished Scholar in Intellectual Property Law and University Fellow Mauer School of Law, Indiana University. -- 6th ed.

pages cm

Includes index.

ISBN 978-0-7698-6902-5

1. Copyright--United States. I. Title.

KF2994.L43 2014

346.7304'82--dc23

2014031300

NOTE TO USERS

To ensure that you are using the latest materials available in this area, please be sure to periodically check the LexisNexis Law School web site for downloadable updates and supplements at www.lexisnexis.com/lawschool.

Editorial Offices
630 Central Ave., New Providence, NJ 07974 (908) 464-6800
201 Mission St., San Francisco, CA 94105-1831 (415) 908-3200
www.lexisnexis.com

MATTHEW BENDER

(2014–Pub.839)

Preface

The changes during the past four years have been incremental but significant as Congress and the courts try to adapt copyright to inexorable pressures of digital technologies. These past four years have not seen blockbuster legislation such as the Digital Millennium Copyright Act of 1998. If Congress has been relatively dormant in copyright during this time frame, the Supreme Court, by comparison, has been active in field during the past four years. I have incorporated into this treatise important Supreme Court cases such as *Golan v. Holder*, sustaining the constitutionality of restoration of copyright; *Kirstaeng v. Harper and Row*, internationalizing the first sale doctrine; and *ABC v. Aereo*, attempting to reconcile a "troublesome" digital technology with the public performance right. As always, I have included commentary on the most important cases decided by the federal courts.

As I have said in each of my prefaces to previous editions, I am privileged to have collaborated on a related project as co-author with Craig Joyce, Peter Jaszi, Tyler Ochoa, and Michael Carroll on *Copyright Law*, now its Ninth Edition (2013). Their insights on the subject matter of copyright have enriched my knowledge enormously.

My special thanks to Cristina Gegenschatz for her professional editorial skills, and to Anna Wortham, third year student at Indiana University, Maurer School of Law, who tirelessly worked with me to update materials for this new edition.

Table of Contents

Chapter 10 FAIR USE AND OTHER DEFENSES TO COPYRIGHT INFRINGEMENT . . . 495

Chapter 1

INTRODUCTION TO COPYRIGHT AND INTELLECTUAL PROPERTY LAW

INTRODUCTION

"The general rule of law is, that the noblest of human productions — knowledge, truths ascertained, conceptions and ideas — become after voluntary communication to others, free as the air to common use." *International News Service v. Associated Press*, 248 U.S. 215, 250 (1918) (Justice Brandeis, dissenting).

"No man but a blockhead ever wrote, except for money." Samuel Johnson, as quoted in III James Boswell, Boswell's Life of Johnson 19 (G. B. Hill ed., 1934).

§ 1.01 INTRODUCTION AND CHAPTER OVERVIEW

In a surprisingly short period of time, the United States has evolved from an industrial to an information and services-based society. Our post-industrial era is marked by rapid technological change in which our ability to reproduce and receive information grows exponentially. It is hard to believe that motion pictures first appeared little more than seventy-five years ago; many of us can remember a time when cable and satellite communications belonged to a hazy future. Who can predict what new information-based technologies lie ahead? From all indications, the communications revolution is only in its infancy.

As the value of communicative expression grows, so does the legal structure that governs the rules concerning its ownership. Products of the mind — informational products — are protected under three areas of "Intellectual Property" law. *Patent law* provides a limited monopoly for new and inventive products, processes, and designs. *Trademark law* prohibits product imitators from passing off their goods or services as the products of others. *Copyright law* protects "original works of authorship." A separate body of state-created law provides additional protection.

The information industries are critically important to the American economy in its post-industrial stage.[1] The numbers are staggering, as a study released in 2013 demonstrates.[2] In 2012, the copyright industries (including prerecorded music, motion pictures, home videos, books, periodicals, newspapers, and computer

---

[1] For a discussion of the broader impact of intellectual property rights on society and copyright's expansive role in particular, see John Tehranian, *Towards a Critical IP Theory: Copyright, Consecration, and Control*, 2012 B.Y.U. L. Rev. 1237.

[2] Stephen E. Siwek, Economists Incorporated, Copyright Industries in the U.S. Economy: The 2013 Report (Nov. 2013) (prepared for the International Intellectual Property Alliance), *available at* http://www.iipa.com/pdf/2013_Copyright_Industries_Full_Report.PDF.

software) accounted for 6.48%, or $1,015.6 billion, of U.S. Gross Domestic Product (GDP). The "total" copyright industries employed 8.35% of U.S. workers in 2012, a level approaching the total employment levels of the entire health care industry, social security sector, and the entire manufacturing sector. The increase in their share of American trade has been similarly dramatic. While the U.S. continues to experience large and growing trade deficits, the copyright industries continue to thrive in overseas sales and exports. In 2012, select U.S. copyright industries achieved foreign sales and exports of $142 billion, surpassing the foreign sales of other major U.S. sectors, including aerospace, agriculture, food, and pharmaceuticals and medicines. These figures are sure to grow in coming years.

Such developments indicate the growing importance of intellectual property. The transfer of information has become an ever greater component of international trade and the centerpiece of U.S. competitiveness. Unlike other areas of the economy, the intellectual property sector is one where the United States is a net exporter — indeed, the world's largest exporter by far. Whether old media (motion pictures, music) or new (computer software), this nation is preeminent in the production and distribution of copyrighted works. But there is a dark side to this success. American copyright owners are increasingly vulnerable to piracy and expropriation abroad and subject to inadequate protection of their interests under foreign laws. Accordingly, the international aspects of copyright law can no longer be given secondary consideration in a serious study of the subject.[3]

In the broadest sense, copyright law creates a system of property rights for certain kinds of intangible products, generally called "works of authorship." Initiated in 18th century England, the first copyright act gave authors the exclusive right to make copies of their books. Today, copyright law covers much broader ground, including not only most artistic, literary, and musical works, but computer software and some kinds of databases as well.

The term *copyright* is a highly descriptive term: the right to make copies. It reflects the basic Anglo-American notion that undesirable economic results will occur if unimpeded copying is allowed for those intangible products whose production we wish to encourage. The focus of copyright law is on the benefits derived by the public from the labors of authors. By this view, reward to the copyright owner or author is a secondary concern.[4]

Although the term "copyright" is highly descriptive in one sense, it is a misnomer in another. Contemporary copyright law copyright goes much further than just protecting works against copying in the strict sense of the word. Much of what we protect in copyright law today, such as performance rights, display rights, and derivative works rights, are more akin to rights to *use* a work rather than to *copy* it.[5]

---

[3] *See infra* chapter 12. For an overview of U.S. intellectual property law policy in a changing world order, see Marshall A. Leaffer, *Protecting American Intellectual Property Abroad: Toward a New Multilateralism*, 76 Iowa L. Rev. 273 (1991).

[4] *But cf.* Jessica Litman, *Real Copyright Reform*, 96 Iowa L. Rev. 1 (2010) (urging a reallocation of copyright's benefits to give more rights to creators and less control to copyright intermediaries).

[5] For a development of this idea, see John M. Kernochan, *Imperatives for Enforcing Author's Rights*,

The analog of copyright in the civil law world is known as *droit d'auteur* (France), *derecho de autor* (Spain), *Urheberrecht* (Germany), all of which can be translated as *author's rights*. The difference in terminology between the common law *copyright* and the civil law *author's rights* is more than linguistic coincidence: it reveals a fundamental difference in attitude between the two legal traditions about works of authorship. The term "copyright" is an impersonal one, removed from the author. It connotes a negative right, the right of the owner to prevent copying of his work. The general philosophy of copyright in the common law world is to provide material support to one who invests in producing the work, whether an individual author or corporate entity. The ultimate goal of copyright is to enhance public welfare, an essentially economic value.[6]

By comparison, the civil law tradition views the author's work as an extension of his or her personality, which springs into existence by a personal act of creation. This view reflects a more sympathetic attitude toward the author.[7] In the civil law world, an author is deemed to have a moral entitlement to control and exploit the product of his or her intellect. Under a principle of natural justice, the author, whose work is identified with his or her name throughout its existence, is given the right to publish that work as he or she sees fit and to prevent its injury or mutilation.[8]

This introductory chapter is divided into three parts. Part I treats copyright from a historical viewpoint, beginning with developments in 16th century England to the passage of the 1976 Act — our current federal copyright statute. Part II examines the nature of intangible property and the economic rationale for copyright law. Part III provides a broad overview of other forms of intellectual property protection such as federal patent and trademark law as well as state trade secret and unfair competition law.

---

131 Revue Internationale du Droit D'Auteur [R.I.D.A.] 181 (1987).

[6] *But cf.* Michael J. Madison, *Knowledge Curation*, 86 Notre Dame L. Rev. 141 (2011) (exploring to what extent intellectual property law should focus on the durability of information and knowledge instead of merely producing new knowledge and offering access to it).

[7] *See* Jeremy Phillips, Robyn Durie & Ian Karet, Whale on Copyright 13 (5th ed. 1997).

[8] The significance of this difference in attitude between the common law and civil law world will be discussed later in connection with 1990 amendments to U.S. copyright law providing certain "moral rights" protection for visual artists. These amendments to American copyright law suggest that the line between the two approaches — "copyright" versus "moral right" may not be as sharp as it once was. In fact, there seems to be an increasing convergence between the common law and civil law systems. Despite this convergence, however, the civil law still affords a wider scope of protection than traditional common law has been willing to allow. For example, although the 1990 amendments to the Copyright Act established a moral right for visual artists, the scope of this right is limited compared to moral rights recognition in certain civil law countries like France — a country whose moral rights protection extends to a broad range of works. *See infra* § 8.28.

Part I. HISTORICAL OVERVIEW OF COPYRIGHT[9]

§ 1.02 FROM THE BEGINNINGS TO THE STATUTE OF ANNE (1710)

The development of copyright law has been a continuing response to the challenges posed by new technologies that reproduce and distribute human expression. Since the late 19th Century, for example, copyright in the United States has adapted to assimilate photography, motion pictures, and sound recordings. In today's world technological change is relentless. At this moment and for the foreseeable future, the debate centers on how to best modify copyright law to regulate use of digital information technology in general and digital networks (such as the Internet) in particular. The connection between technological change and copyright is nothing new. Indeed, the first copyright statute was a reaction to a new technology of the fifteenth century: the printing press.[10]

Introduced into England in 1476 by William Caxton, the printing press allowed large-scale reproduction of books for the first time. This new technology enriched publishers and booksellers (although not necessarily authors) and threatened the Crown, which shuddered at the thought of widespread dissemination of works advocating religious heresy and political upheaval. The Crown's solution to the problem was a system of regulation designed to control this "dangerous art." In 1534, a royal decree prohibited anyone from publishing without a license and without approval from official censors. In 1557, the Crown conferred a publishing monopoly on the Stationer's Company, a group of London printers and booksellers, who were expected to do the Crown's bidding while handsomely lining their own pockets.[11]

After a controversial and checkered career, during which the Stationer's copyright was used as an instrument of both monopoly and press control, the exclusive license to publish expired in 1695, leaving the Stationer's Company unsheltered by regulation and vulnerable to competition from "upstart" publishers. Parliament heeded the Company's predictions of economic disaster and anarchy, and, in response to these lobbying efforts, passed the first copyright act — the Statute of Anne — in 1710.[12]

Until 1731, the Statute of Anne maintained Stationer's rights in works already printed. But the Stationers' expectation of a continued monopoly over book

---

[9] For an excellent overview of the early development of copyright law, see L. Ray Patterson, Copyright in Historical Perspective (1968).

[10] For an argument that the tension between competing economic interests and different business models is not a novel contemporary concept but rather existed before 1710 when the Statute of Anne was enacted, see Isabella Alexander, *All Change for the Digital Economy: Copyright and Business Models in the Early Eighteenth Century*, 25 Berkeley Tech. L.J. 1351 (2010).

[11] *See* Benjamin Kaplan, An Unhurried View of Copyright 5 (1967).

[12] Statute of Anne, 1710, 8 Ann., c. 19 (Eng.). For a discussion regarding the Statute of Anne as a legal transplant and its adaptation over time, see Oren Bracha, *The Adventures of the Statute of Anne in the Land of Unlimited Possibilities: The Life of a Legal Transplant*, 25 Berkeley Tech. L.J. 1427 (2010).

publishing never materialized. In effect, the Statute of Anne undermined the Stationers' stranglehold on the book trade by recognizing for the first time the rights of authors to their works. The stated purpose of the Statute, as revealed in its enactment clause, was ". . . the encouragement of learned men to compose and write useful work."[13] Thus, the Statute of Anne shifted the emphasis from the Stationer's Company to authors in general and declared that its ultimate purpose was to enhance public welfare by encouraging the dissemination of knowledge.[14]

The Statute of Anne rewarded authors for their creations but at the same time recognized the public domain by limiting the duration of authors' rights to a specific number of years.[15] For existing works, the Statute provided that "authors and their assigns" should have the sole right of publication for twenty-one years. New books enjoyed a different term of protection. They were given a first term of protection of fourteen years for authors and their assigns, measured from the date of first publication, plus a second term of fourteen years, which reverted to the author if he lived to its commencement. Although the Statute appeared on its face to create a limited term of protection, the Stationer's Company claimed perpetual rights over their works and asserted that the statute was merely designed to provide them with expedited recovery against piracy. The lower courts sustained the Stationer's Company's position for more than a half century until the famous case of *Donaldson v. Beckett*.[16] In rejecting the plaintiffs' argument for a common law right in copyright that would exist in perpetuity, the House of Lords in *Donaldson* established that the term of copyright is finite. And once that copyright term is exhausted, a work will (in today's parlance) fall into the "public domain."

The Statute of Anne defined a "copy" as being "the sale, liberty of printing, and reprinting of a book." Infringement occurred when a third party printed, reprinted, or imported the book without consent. The protection granted was basically no more than a prohibition against literal copying.[17] To enforce one's rights, one had to register the title of the book with the Stationer's Company before publication.

On the whole, the Statute of Anne, which became the model for copyright law in the United States, articulated a series of mixed and contradictory messages about the purposes of copyright.[18] On the one hand, the Statute, as interpreted by the House of Lords in *Donaldson*, vindicated the consumer interest in creating a public domain and allowing free access to previously protected works. On the other hand, the Stationer's Company's argument for perpetual protection was favorably re-

---

13 *Id.* at c. 19 § 1.

14 *See* Bernard A. Grossman, *Cycles in Copyright*, 22 N.Y.L. Sch. L. Rev. 653, 657 (1977).

15 *See* Howard B. Abrams, *The Historic Foundation of American Copyright Law: Exploding the Myth of Common Law Copyright*, 29 Wayne L. Rev. 1119, 1141 (1983).

16 2 Bro. P.C. 129, 1 Eng. Rep. 837 Burr. (4th ed.) 2408, 98 Eng. Rep. 257 (H.L. 1774). In *Donaldson*, the House of Lords overruled *Millar v. Taylor*, 4 Burr. (4th ed.) 2303, 98 Eng. Rep. 201 (K.B. 1789), decided just five years before.

17 *See generally* L. Ray Patterson & Craig Joyce, *Monopolizing the Law: The Scope of Copyright Protection for Law Reports and Statutory Compilations*, 36 UCLA L. Rev. 719, Part IV (1989).

18 *See* Diane Leenheer Zimmerman, *The Statute of Anne and Its Progeny: Variations Without a Theme*, 47 Hous. L. Rev. 965 (2010) (discussing the instability that came from introducing the Statute of Anne into the American copyright system and the statute's lingering effects).

ceived by "natural rights" advocates who view authorship as a privileged category of human activity.[19] As we will see, these two foundational approaches to copyright, one based on the natural rights of the author and the other on utilitarian principles (the economic rationale of copyright), are sometimes at cross purposes. These approaches will be discussed in a later section.[20]

§ 1.03 FROM THE CONSTITUTION TO THE COPYRIGHT ACT OF 1909

Although the colonies already had their own forms of copyright laws,[21] the Framers of the Constitution recognized the need for a uniform law for copyright and patents.[22] The United States Constitution, Article I, Section 8, Clause 8, which empowers Congress to legislate copyright and patent statutes, reads as follows: "To promote the Progress of Science and the useful Arts, by securing for limited Times, to Authors and Inventors, the exclusive Right to their respective Writings and Discoveries."

The Patent and Copyright Clause was adopted in final form without debate in a secret proceeding on September 5, 1787. As a result, little is known about what the Framers had in mind in drafting this particular constitutional clause or about the scope of the various terms of the constitutional language.[23] Consequently, one is left with the language of the Clause itself, which does not even use the term "copyright." As revealed in the constitutional language, the dominant idea is to promote the dissemination of knowledge to enhance public welfare. This goal is to be accomplished by giving authors an *economic incentive* in the form of a monopoly right over their writings for limited times. But it would be inaccurate to conclude that the Framers rejected entirely the notions of author's rights based on natural rights reasoning. Why, one may ask, does the Copyright Clause speak of "securing" the rights of authors if those rights were not recognized as being preexistent?[24] Moreover, what are we to make of statements of various Framers seeming to endorse notions of "author's rights?"[25] In the end, the ambiguity of the constitu-

---

[19] *See generally* Peter Jaszi, *Toward a Theory of Copyright: The Metamorphoses of "Authorship,"* 1991 DUKE L.J. 455.

[20] *See infra* §§ 1.07–1.08.

[21] Twelve states had adopted copyright statutes on the eve of the first federal copyright law of 1790. Abrams, *supra* note 11, at 1173.

[22] *See generally* Francine Crawford, *Pre-Constitutional Copyright Statutes*, 23 BULL. COPYRIGHT SOC'Y 11 (1975).

[23] *See* Ralph Oman, *The Copyright Clause: "A Charter For A Living People,"* 17 U. BALT. L. REV. 99, 103 (1987).

[24] *See generally* Barbara Ringer, *Two Hundred Years of American Copyright Law*, *in* TWO HUNDRED YEARS OF ENGLISH AND AMERICAN PATENT, TRADEMARK AND COPYRIGHT LAW 117, 126 (1977) (discussing The Federalist No. 143).

[25] *See generally*, EDWARD C. WALTERSCHEID, THE NATURE OF THE INTELLECTUAL PROPERTY CLAUSE: A STUDY IN HISTORICAL PERSPECTIVE 133–139 (2002). *See also* Tyler T. Ochoa & Mark Rose, *The Anti-Monopoly Origins of the Patent and Copyright Clause*, 49 J. COPYRIGHT SOC'Y 675 (2002); Dotan Oliar, *Making Sense of the Intellectual Property Clause: Promotion of Progress as a Limitation on Congress's Intellectual Property Power*, 94 GEO. L.J. 1771 (2006).

tional language is probably nothing more than a reflection of the divided character of American thought, which continues to this day, about the purposes of the copyright system.

The first Copyright Act of 1790[26] was passed pursuant to this constitutional authority and its provisions, modeled on the Statute of Anne, set the tone for future statutes. Like the Statute of Anne, the Act of 1790 gave protection to the author or his assigns of maps, charts, and books for two fourteen-year terms, an original and a renewal term. Judicial constructions, including most notably *Wheaton v. Peters* in 1834,[27] followed *Donaldson v. Beckett* in insisting on the primacy of federal law. From 1790 until the 1909 Act, copyright law underwent two general revisions,[28] in addition to several important amendments, which greatly elaborated many aspects of copyrightable subject matter, rights, remedies, and administration.[29]

Although copyright protection expanded in scope in the nineteenth century, that protection was limited to American authors. Like most countries during the pre-Berne Convention era, the United States excluded the works of foreign authors from copyright protection. As a net importer of copyrighted works, discrimination against works of foreign origin resulted in an economic benefit to the United States and allowed its publishers to pirate popular British works such as those of Wordsworth, Dickens, and Thackeray. It was not until 1891, with the passage of the Chace Act, that American law even gave a semblance of protection to foreign works.[30]

---

[26] Act of May 31, 1790, ch. 15, 1 Stat. 124.

[27] 33 U.S. (8 Pet.) 591 (1834). The case is discussed at length in Craig Joyce, *The Rise of the Supreme Court Reporter: An Institutional Perspective on Marshall Court Ascendency*, 83 Mich. L. Rev. 1291, Part III (1985).

[28] The general revisions took place in 1831 and 1870.

[29] Some of the more important changes occurred as follows: 1819, federal jurisdiction for copyright cases; 1831, addition of musical compositions as copyrightable subject matter and extension of the copyright term from 14 to 28 years; 1846, deposit requirements for the Library of Congress; 1856, public performance right for dramatic works; 1865, photographs as copyrightable subject matter; 1870, Copyright Office created and Library of Congress given principal responsibility for copyright; 1874, notice provisions required. For a more detailed look at the changes in the law between 1790 and 1909, see William F. Patry, Copyright Law and Practice, Ch. 1 (2014).

[30] Act of March 3, 1891, ch. 565, 26 Stat. 1106. The Chace Act empowered the president to extend copyright to works of foreign nationals but imposed formalities as a prerequisite to protection, as well as the "manufacturing clause," which required all copies of foreign literary works to be printed from type set in the U.S. *See* Paul Goldstein, Copyright's Highway: From Gutenberg to the Celestial Jukebox 148–152 (2003) (describing the evolution of the U.S. from a net importer to a net exporter of copyrighted works and the corresponding change in attitude toward the protection of foreign works and pressure to enter into international copyright agreements); *See also* Peter K. Yu, *The Copyright Divide*, 25 Cardozo L. Rev. 331 (2003) (reviewing nineteenth century attitudes about copyright and the status of the U.S. as a pirate nation).

§ 1.04 THE 1909 ACT

[A] General Provisions of the 1909 Act

In December 1905, President Theodore Roosevelt called for a complete revision of the copyright law to meet modern conditions. The result was the Copyright Act of 1909 which lasted for 68 years, until the enactment of the current law — the Copyright Act of 1976. Despite the four-year revision process, the 1909 Act was hardly a model of clarity, coherence, or precision. But it did contain important innovations. For instance, copyrightable subject matter was expanded to include "all the writings of an author." [31] The Act included a bifurcated durational system, a first term of twenty-eight years and a second twenty-eight-year renewal term, conferring copyright protection for a possible fifty-six years.[32] Under the Act, federal copyright began at the moment of publication[33] rather than the time the title of the work was filed for registration, as had been previously required. Except for works not intended for reproduction (such as motion pictures and speeches), unpublished works were not covered by the Act, and a dual system of state common law copyright for unpublished works and federal protection for published works existed. Because of its various provisions, the 1909 Act did not solve the problems, which excluded the United States from joining the principal treaty governing international copyright relations — the Berne Convention for the Protection of Literary and Artistic Works.

[B] United States's Exclusion from the Berne Convention

One particularly unfortunate feature of the 1909 Act was its failure to amend U.S. law to conform to the then relatively new Berne Convention for the Protection of Literary and Artistic Works. Concluded in 1886, the Berne Convention was the first, and has for over 100 years remained the principal, international copyright convention.[34] Since its inception, the Berne Convention has been revised five times, most recently in the 1971 Paris revision. Its success as an international agreement is reflected by its large number of adherents, which by the mid-1980s included every major country in the world except China, the Soviet Union, and the United States.

The 1909 Act retained several aspects of U.S. copyright law, which constituted major stumbling blocks for United States entry into the Berne Convention. Two of the more prominent impediments were the Act's insistence on compliance with certain formalities as a prerequisite for copyright protection and its shorter term of copyright.[35] The 1909 Act required notice on all published copies of a work;

---

[31] *See* 17 U.S.C. § 4 (1909 Act).

[32] *See* 17 U.S.C. § 24 (1909 Act).

[33] *See* 17 U.S.C. § 10 (1909 Act).

[34] For an overview on the Berne Convention, see Stephen M. Stewart, International Copyright and Neighboring Rights 86–132 (1983).

[35] There were other 1909 Act provisions impeding U.S. entry into Berne. This subject is discussed in fuller detail in *infra* § 12.05.

failure to include the required notice could inject the work into the public domain.[36] This aspect of American law was clearly in conflict with the Berne requirement that copyright protection be granted absent compliance with formalities. In addition, the 1909 Act's bifurcated durational system was not in accord with Berne's minimum durational requirement of the life of the author plus fifty years.[37] Consequently, these and other provisions of the 1909 Act prevented U.S. entry into the Berne Convention.

[C] Legislative Attempts to Re-tool the 1909 Act

From 1909 until the passage of the 1976 Act, changing times and technologies forced Congress to amend the 1909 Act. For example, motion pictures were added to copyrightable subject matter in 1912, and, in 1952, a performance right for profit was provided for nondramatic literary works. In 1954, the United States ratified the Universal Copyright Convention,[38] which provides nondiscriminatory protection to nationals of all member nations for works published within their borders. No formalities are required for unpublished works. Published works, however, must bear a prescribed notice. A nation can require other formalities for its own nationals or for works first published within its borders, as long as these further requirements are imposed without discrimination against nationals of foreign member states.

With the passage of time, it became apparent that the 1909 Act was beyond repair and should be replaced by new legislation.[39] In 1955, Congress authorized a copyright revision project. Twenty years of reports and extensive hearings ensued, culminating in the passage of the Copyright Act of 1976.[40]

§ 1.05 THE COPYRIGHT ACT OF 1976

[A] Important Changes in the 1976 Act

The 1976 Act made innovative changes in addition to clarifying certain aspects of existing law. The more important aspects of the Act include:

(1) *Preemption of Common Law Copyright.* Section 301 of the 1976 Act preempts common law copyright, which had bedeviled the administration of the 1909 Act.[41] No longer is there a dual system of copyright, *i.e.*, federal protection for published works and state common law protection for unpublished works. Now all works fixed in a tangible medium of expression are protected under the federal Act from the moment of creation.

---

[36] *See* 17 U.S.C. § 10 (1909 Act).

[37] Berne Convention art. 7.

[38] Universal Copyright Convention, Sept. 6, 1962.

[39] For an overview of the 1909 and 1976 Acts, see Robert A. Gorman, *An Overview of the Copyright Act of 1976*, 126 U. Pa. L. Rev. 856 (1978).

[40] H.R. Rep. No. 94-1476, at 47–50 (1976).

[41] *See* 17 U.S.C. § 301.

(2) *Duration.* The Act eliminated the dual twenty-eight year terms for copyright and replaced them with a single, extended term of the life of the author plus 50 years.[42] Publication is no longer the measuring point for most works. However, an alternate term of seventy-five years from publication or 100 years from creation, whichever is less, was given for anonymous and pseudonymous works and works made for hire.[43] Even here, the term is much longer than under the 1909 Act.

(3) *Formalities.* Formalities continued to be important under the 1976 Act. Notice was still required for all published works, and it was possible to forfeit copyright by failure to affix notice.[44] Registration of copyright and recordation of transfers of copyright were also conditions to bringing suits for infringement of these works until amendments, which took effect in 1989, eliminated the latter requirement and modified the former.[45] The Berne Convention Implementation Act of 1988modified these formalities.[46] A requirement mandating the domestic manufacture of copies of copyrighted works was maintained in the Act but expired in 1986.

(4) *Subject Matter.* The 1976 Act established broad categories of subject matter that, according to the legislative history, are to be construed liberally. These are: (1) literary works; (2) musical works; (3) dramatic works; [47] (4) pantomimes and choreographic works; (5) pictorial, graphic, and sculptural works; (6) motion pictures and other audiovisual works; (7) sound recordings; and (8) architectural works.[48] The subject matter is broad but Congress fell short of including all the writings of an author as it could have done under its constitutional authority. Rather, the subject matter of copyright includes *original* works of authorship, set forth in eight broad and overlapping categories. What constitutes sufficient originality for a valid copyright is a matter of judicial precedent.

(5) *The Exclusive Rights and Their Limitations.* Originally, § 106 of the 1976 Act enumerated five exclusive rights of copyright ownership: the rights to reproduce and adapt the copyrighted work, and to distribute, perform, and display it publicly. A new provision, § 106A, was added in 1990 to delineate rights in works of visual art. In 1995, Congress added a sixth exclusive right, a performance right for sound recordings by digital audio transmission. The sections immediately following § 106A[49] impose various limitations on these exclusive rights. Section 107,

---

[42] *See* 17 U.S.C. § 302(a). In 1998, the basic term was extended to life-plus-seventy-years. *See* Pub. L. 105298, 112 Stat. 2827 (1998).

[43] *See* 17 U.S.C. § 302(c). In 1998, the term for these works was extended to ninety-five years from publication or 120 from creation. *See* Pub. L. 105298, 112 Stat. 2827 (1998).

[44] *See* 17 U.S.C. §§ 401(a), 405.

[45] *See* 17 U.S.C. § 411.

[46] *See* 17 U.S.C. §§ 411, 205.

[47] *See generally* Jessica D. Litman, *The Invention of the Common Law Play Right*, 25 BERKELEY TECH. L.J. 1381 (2010) (discussing the history of the rights of playwrights and how the attribution and integrity rights claimed by playwrights today arose primarily from customs and contracts rather than copyright law).

[48] *See* 17 U.S.C. § 102(a). In 1990, § 102(a) was amended to include architectural works. *See* 17 U.S.C. § 102(a)(8).

[49] *See* 17 U.S.C. §§ 107–121.

the first of those limitations, codifies the judicially developed "fair use" privilege.[50] The 1976 Act has tried to codify the privilege of fair use, the broadest exception to the exclusive rights under § 106, by setting forth criteria to be used in determining what constitutes fair use.[51]

(6) *Compulsory Licenses and the Copyright Royalty Administration.* The 1976 Act has increased to six the number of compulsory licenses in copyright, allowing access to copyrighted works on payment of the statutory fees and compliance with certain formalities. Under the 1976 Act as originally passed, there were only four compulsory licenses:[52] the cable television license, the mechanical recording license, [53] the jukebox license, and the public broadcasting license. A new license for satellite home viewing, the satellite retransmission license, was added in 1988.[54] In 1995, Congress added another compulsory license for certain digital audio transmissions.[55] The compulsory licenses had been administered by the Copyright Royalty Tribunal ("CRT"), an administrative agency established by the 1976 Act.[56] Constantly under fire, the CRT was abolished in 1993 and replaced by Copyright Arbitration Royalty Panels ("CARPs").[57]

(7) *Ownership.* Ownership of copyright is divisible under the 1976 Act; the copyright owner can now license or assign parts of the copyright to third parties, who can bring suits for infringement of their ownership rights.[59] The Act also specifies that ownership of the material object does not entail ownership of the copyright in the work.[60]

(8) *Entry into Berne.* Although some progress had been made toward entry into the Berne Convention, such as extending the term of copyright, other stumbling blocks impeding entry, such as the formalities of notice and registration, had not been removed. It was not until the Berne Act amendments of 1988 that these impediments to U.S. adherence were overcome.

(9) *Legislative Developments from 1978 to 1988.* Major developments in copyright have occurred since passage of the 1976 Act. In 1980, a new § 117 was added to the Act, involving the protection and scope of rights in computer programs.[61] Other amendments have been added as well,[62] including the passage

---

[50] For a discussion of the uncertainty of the scope of fair use exemptions to copyright law on the Internet and the roll of copyright trolls, see Ian Polonsky, *You Can't Go Home Again: The Righthaven Cases and Copyright Trolling on the Internet*, 36 Colum. J.L. & Arts 71 (2012).

[51] *See* 17 U.S.C. § 107.

[52] *See* 17 U.S.C. §§ 111, 115, 116, 118.

[53] For a history of the compulsory license for making phonorecords of nondramatic musical works and an argument for why it should be repealed, see Howard B. Abrams, *Copyright's First Compulsory License*, 26 Santa Clara Computer & High Tech L.J. 215 (2010).

[54] 17 U.S.C. § 119.

[55] *See* 17 U.S.C. § 114(d).

[56] *See* 17 U.S.C. §§ 801–810.

[57] The Copyright Royalty Tribunal Act of 1993, Pub. L. No. 103-198 (1993).

[59] *See* 17 U.S.C. § 201(d).

[60] *See* 17 U.S.C. § 202.

[61] *See* 17 U.S.C. § 117.

of the Semiconductor Chip Protection Act of 1984.[63] Affording protection to semiconductor mask works, this Act is a legislative response to the need to protect a new technology that is vital to our economic well-being.

[B] The Berne Convention Implementation Act of 1988[64]

Effective March 1, 1988, the United States entered into the Berne Union, the largest and most important international copyright convention. Among the principal motivating factors for entry at this time were the United States' withdrawal from UNESCO, the United Nations agency, which administers the Universal Copyright Convention ("UCC"); the growing importance of intellectual property in world trade; and the systematic piracy of American works in certain foreign countries. To have a say in the development of international copyright policy and establish copyright relations with twenty-four more countries, it was felt that the United States should join the world copyright community as soon as possible.[65]

The Berne Convention Implementation Act of 1988 ("BCIA") amended several aspects of the 1976 Copyright Act in conflict with Berne requirements. The Implementation Act reflects a *minimalist* approach whereby Congress attempted to amend the 1976 Copyright Act only where there was a direct conflict with the provisions of the Berne Convention.[66]

The most significant changes brought about by the Berne Amendments are the modification of formalities such as notice, registration, and recordation as conditions of copyright protection. These changes were necessitated by Berne requirements that copyright protection not be based on compliance with formalities.[67] Accordingly, the 1988 amendments have abrogated the notice requirement.[68] For works published on or after March 1, 1989, notice is permissive, and a copyright owner can no longer forfeit copyright by omitting notice of publicly distributed copies of the work.[69] The registration requirement has also been modified. For works originating from a Berne country, registration is no longer required as a prerequisite for bringing a suit for copyright infringement.[70] Finally, recordation in the Copyright Office of an interest in copyright is no longer required as a prerequisite to bringing a suit for infringement.[71]

---

62 See the Record Rental Amendment of 1984, Pub. L. No. 98-450, 98 Stat. 1727 (1984) and the Satellite Home Viewer Act of 1988, Pub. L. No. 100-667, 104 Stat. 3949 (1988).

63 Pub. L. No. 98-620, 98 Stat. 3347 (1984). For a discussion of the Act and the technology of semiconductor mask works, see *infra* § 3.09.

64 Pub. L. No. 100-568, 102 Stat. 2853 (1988).

65 H.R. Rep. No. 100-609, 100th Cong., 2d Sess. 7 (1988).

66 *See id.* at 20.

67 *See* Berne Convention art. 5(2).

68 *See* 17 U.S.C. § 401. For a discussion of notice, see *infra* § 4.08.

69 *See* 17 U.S.C. § 405. For a discussion of omission of notice, see *infra* § 4.11.

70 *See* 17 U.S.C. § 411. For a discussion of copyright registration, see *infra* §§ 7.01–7.08.

71 *See* 17 U.S.C. § 205(d), requiring recordation to bring an infringement suit, which was deleted by the BCIA. For a discussion of recordation, see *infra* § 5.14.

In addition to relaxing certain formalities, the 1988 amendments include an express recognition of architectural plans in the definition of pictorial, graphic, and sculptural works,[72] a modification of the jukebox license,[73] and a doubling of the limits for statutory damages.[74]

[C] Amendments to the Copyright Since 1978

Technology — and copyright law — have continued to develop since 1978. Revisions to the newly enacted law began as early as 1980, when a completely amended § 117 was added to the Act, establishing protection for, and the scope of rights in, computer programs. Congress has created a new exclusive right under § 106, that is the right to perform publicly a sound recording by means of a digital audio transmission, as well as enacting new limitations, in favor of such worthy enterprises as educational and nonprofit organizations, on rights already recognized. Existing statutory licenses have been revised, and new ones added. New technologies have been accommodated. Renewals, to the extent that they remain relevant under the present law of duration, have been made automatic. Copyright infringement has been criminalized to a degree heretofore unknown. And Congress has busied itself legislating *outside the Copyright Act*, in an area that has come to be called "paracopyright" in acknowledgment of the reality that it is based on practical concerns and constitutional powers other than those found in Art. I, § 8, cl. 8. These, and many more highlights — and "lowlights" — of copyright law revision, will receive treatment in the chapters that follow. Three sets of developments, however, deserve special mention. The first is United States entry into the Berne Convention.

Effective March 1, 1989, the United States entered into the Berne Union, the largest and most important international copyright convention. Among the principal motivating factors for entry at this time were the United States' withdrawal from UNESCO, the United Nations agency, which administers the Universal Copyright Convention ("UCC"); the growing importance of intellectual property in world trade; and the systematic piracy of American works in certain foreign countries. To have a say in the development of international copyright policy, and establish copyright relations with 24 more countries, it was felt that the United States should join the world copyright community as soon as possible.[75]

The Berne Convention Implementation Act of 1988 ("BCIA") amended several aspects of the 1976 Copyright Act in conflict with Berne requirements. The Implementation Act reflects a *minimalist* approach whereby Congress attempted to amend the 1976 Copyright Act only where there was a direct conflict with the provisions of the Berne Convention.[76]

---

[72] *See* 17 U.S.C. § 101. For a discussion of architectural works, see *infra* § 3.16.

[73] *See* 17 U.S.C. § 116 (as amended by the BCIA). For a discussion of the jukebox license, see *infra* § 8.21.

[74] *See* 17 U.S.C. § 504(c). This increase in statutory damages is unrelated to the requirements of Berne adherence.

[75] H.R. Rep. No. 100-609, 100th Cong., 2d Sess. 7 (1988).

[76] *See id.* at 20.

The most significant changes brought about by the Berne Amendments are the modification of formalities such as notice, registration, and recordation as conditions of copyright protection. These changes were necessitated by Berne requirements that copyright protection not be based on compliance with formalities.[77] Accordingly, the 1988 amendments have abrogated the notice requirement.[78] For works published on or after March 1, 1989, notice is permissive and a copyright owner can no longer forfeit copyright by omitting notice of publicly distributed copies of the work.[79] The registration requirement has also been modified. For works originating from a Berne country, registration is no longer required as a prerequisite for bringing a suit for copyright infringement.[80] Finally, recordation in the Copyright Office of an interest in copyright is no longer required as a prerequisite to bringing a suit for infringement.[81]

In addition to relaxing certain formalities, the 1988 amendments include an express recognition of architectural plans in the definition of pictorial, graphic, and sculptural works,[82] a modification of the jukebox license,[83] and a doubling of the limits for statutory damages.[84]

Second, Congress has advanced swiftly in revising U.S. copyright law to better serve the nation's international trade interests. Early in 1994, as part of the implementation of the North American Free Trade Agreement ("NAFTA"), Congress added to Title 17 a new § 104A, permitting foreign copyright owners to obtain "restoration" of their copyrights in certain Mexican and Canadian films which had fallen into the public domain in the United States for failure to comply with the notice provisions of the 1976 Act. This modest experiment in retroactivity soon was subsumed in the more dramatic developments which followed the conclusion of the Final Act of the Uruguay Round of the General Agreement on Tariffs and Trade ("GATT"). In December 1994, Congress enacted the Uruguay Round Agreements Act ("URAA"), that provides retroactive protection for large numbers of works of foreign origin in the U.S. public domain under a wide range of circumstances.[85]

Third, on consecutive days in late 1998, Congress enacted two landmark pieces of legislation. The "Sonny Bono Copyright Term Extension Act" or "CTEA" (October 27, 1998), extended the term of copyright protection by 20 years for works created by an individual on or after January 1, 1978, a term measured by the

---

[77] *See* Berne Convention art. 5(2).

[78] *See* 17 U.S.C. § 401. For a discussion of notice, see *infra* § 4.08.

[79] *See* 17 U.S.C. § 405. For a discussion of omission of notice, see *infra* § 4.11.

[80] *See* 17 U.S.C. § 411. For a discussion of copyright registration, see *infra* §§ 7.01–7.08.

[81] *See* 17 U.S.C. § 205(d), requiring recordation to bring an infringement suit, which was deleted by the BCIA. For a discussion of recordation, see *infra* § 5.14.

[82] *See* 17 U.S.C. § 101. For a discussion of architectural works, see *infra* § 3.16.

[83] *See* 17 U.S.C. § 116 (as amended by the BCIA). For a discussion of the jukebox license, see *infra* § 8.21.

[84] *See* 17 U.S.C. § 504(c). This increase in statutory damages is unrelated to the requirements of Berne adherence.

[85] 17 U.S.C. § 104A. See the discussion in *infra* §§ 6.18–6.19.

life of the author plus 70 years.[86] In addition, the "Digital Millennium Copyright Act" or "DMCA" (October 28, 1998),[87] enacted an astonishing number of disparate measures. Most important, the DMCA implemented the two treaties, on copyright, and on performances and phonograms, adopted by the World Intellectual Property Organization in 1996. The result is a schema of "technological protections" for digitized information. The importance of this development, viewed from the perspective of traditional copyright law, would be difficult to overstate.

All in all, prodded by practical politics, technological changes and international pressures, Congress has hardly been idle since enacting the Copyright Act of 1976.

[D] The Continuing Importance of the 1909 Act and the 1976 Act as Originally Enacted

Both the 1909 Act and the provisions of the 1976 Act as originally enacted remain relevant for several reasons. Most importantly, works whose source country is the United States[88] and that have gone into the public domain under the 1909 Act and the original provisions of the 1976 Act remain in the public domain. For example, if a work was published without notice under the 1909 Act, it could be injected into the public domain.[89] Such a work cannot be revived by the less harsh forfeiture provisions of the 1976 Act[90] or the total abrogation of the notice requirement under the Berne Amendments of 1988.[91] In addition, the 1976 Act has specifically incorporated provisions of the prior law, and has retained standards developed in case law decided under the 1909 Act for important issues such as the standards of originality and copyright infringement.

A copyright scholar has a complicated task. She must be conversant with the provisions of the 1909 Act, the 1976 Act as originally enacted, and subsequent amendments to the 1976 Act to be able to determine which piece of legislation is applicable in a particular situation.

[E] Copyright Legislation In Perspective

One salient trend, reflected in copyright legislation from the 1976 Act to the present day, is the increasingly international dimension of copyright. Much copyright legislation passed over the last thirty years is a function of the pressures of operating in an increasingly interconnected world. Global markets for

---

[86] *See* The Sonny Bono Copyright Term Extension Act, Pub. L. 105298, 112 Stat. 2827 (1998

[87] *See* The Digital Millennium Copyright Act, Pub. L. 105304, 112 Stat. 2860 (1998).

[88] Section 104A, passed pursuant to U.S. obligations under the WTO TRIPs Agreement, restores copyright in works whose source country is a member of the World Trade Organization or an adherent of the Berne Convention. It does not restore copyright for works in the public domain whose source country is the United States. *See* 17 U.S.C. § 104A. Copyright restoration is discussed in *infra* §§ 4.18–4.19.

[89] For a discussion of notice under the 1909 Act, see *infra* § 4.14. For an argument that proponents of the public domain should embrace the rhetoric of physical property, see David Fagundes, *Property Rhetoric and the Public Domain*, 94 Minn. L. Rev. 652 (2010).

[90] *See* 17 U.S.C. Trans. & Supp. Prov. § 103.

[91] *See* Berne Convention Implementation Act of 1988, Pub. L. No. 100-568 § 12 (1988).

information and the preeminent role of the United States in the export of informational products has forced Congress to make fundamental changes in the law of copyright. The Berne Convention, NAFTA, the TRIPS Agreement, and the 1996 WIPO Copyright Treaties have required major changes in U.S law. The effect of these international agreements on U.S. copyright law has resulted in the Berne Convention Implementation Act, recognition of moral rights for visual artists, restoration of copyright for certain foreign works, and the Digital Millennium Copyright Act. Other changes to U.S law resulting from various international pressures and obligations will surely take place.

Another trend in U.S. copyright law is its increasing complexity, which results more from domestic politics than from international pressures. As any examination of the current Act will reveal, U. S. copyright law has become increasingly complex over the last thirty years. The Copyright Act of 1909, in most editions, takes up barely twenty-five pages, while the 1976 Act, as amended to date, sprawls over 200. In part, this dramatic difference in the length of the two statutes is attributable to the fact that the 1976 Act goes into significantly more detail than its predecessor on almost every topic it covers. An important fraction of the additional bulk can be traced to the various sets of provisions dealing with cable television, secondary transmissions by satellite carriers, secondary transmissions by superstations and network stations (all of which are lodged within the body of the Copyright Act), and to the provisions governing such matters as statutory royalties for digital audio recordings, copyright management information systems, and protection of certain original designs. Each of these latter subject matters, although not within the Act itself, lies in the "neighboring provisions" of Title 17. This complexity in copyright law reflects the increasingly regulatory nature[92] of copyright, a visible by-product of compromises struck between representatives of industry groups who have direct financial stakes in the outcome.

If this trend toward "Balkanization" in copyright legislation continues, it will only become more and more difficult for anyone — let alone a non-specialist — to make coherent sense of the overall statutory scheme.[93] How Congress responds to these pressures will be an indication of whether our copyright law can continue to grow by accretion, or whether it will soon require another general revision beginning from first principles.

---

[92] *See* Joseph P. Liu, *Regulatory Copyright*, 83 N.C. L. Rev. 87, 91 (2003) (specifying the ways that copyright law has become "increasingly more detailed and industry-specific, relying more on compulsory licenses and, in some cases, mandating adoption of certain technologies and banning others").

[93] *See generally* Jessica Litman, *Revising Copyright Law in the Information Age*, 75 Or. L. Rev. 19 (1996). For a discussion of the extant problems in copyright law due to an increase in proliferation of works granted copyright protection; distribution of copyrights to more people; and fragmentation of the number, type, and size of separately-owned rights within a copyright bundle, see Molly Shaffer Van Houweling, *Author Autonomy and Atomism in Copyright Law*, 96 Va. L. Rev. 549 (2010).

Part II. JUSTIFICATIONS FOR COPYRIGHT LAW

§ 1.06 GENERALLY

Whether property rights should be recognized in products of the mind is a matter of longstanding debate and challenges fundamental assumptions about why society creates a system of property rights.[94] Few question the correctness of granting property rights in land or chattels, but when the subject turns to intangible property, the consensus breaks down. There continues to be a lively debate about the nature and scope of protection for intellectual products.[95]

Discomfort with recognizing property rights in products of the mind runs through the common law, under which property rights arose from possession. But intellectual products were quite unlike land or chattels because once disseminated publicly, ideas and other intangibles were not subject to exclusive possession. Justice Brandeis reflected this view in a famous dissent: "The general rule of law is, that the noblest of human productions — knowledge, truths ascertained, conceptions, and ideas — become, after voluntary communication to others, free as the air to common use."[96]

Despite common law resistance, however, property rights for intellectual property always have had vigorous support. In general, arguments for establishing property rights in anything (land, chattels, or intangibles) are justified on two fundamental grounds: first, a person's moral right to reap the fruits of his or her own labor (an idea based on natural law philosophy); and second, a utilitarian rationale that views copyright law as an incentive system designed to produce an optimal quantity of works of authorship, and thereby enhance public welfare.[97] The emphasis of natural rights theory, characteristic of Continental European states, focuses on the author as an individual who deserves, on moral principles, to be compensated for work done. By comparison, the utilitarian justification, historically more common in the United States and Great Britain, places consumer welfare in

---

[94] For an analysis of the argument that "copyright is policy, not property" and its application to the digital revolution. *see* Adam Mosoff, *Is Copyright Property?*, 42 San Diego L. Rev. 29 (2005).

[95] *See, e.g.*, Shuhba Ghosh, *Deprivatizing Copyright*, 54 Case W. Res. L. Rev. 1 (2004); Tom Bell, *Authors Welfare: Copyright as a Statutory Mechanism for Redistributing Rights*, 69 Brook L. Rev. 229 (2003); Lloyd Weinreb, *Copyright for Functional Expression*, 111 Harv. L. Rev. 1149 (1998); Neil Weinstock Netanel, *Copyright in a Democratic Civil Society*, 106 Yale L.J. 283 (1996); Stewart E. Sterk, *Rehetoric and Reality in Copyright Law*, 94 Mich. L. Rev. 1197 (1995–1996); Glynn S. Lunney, Jr., *Reexamining Copyright's Incentive Access Paradigm*, 49 Vand. L. Rev. 483 (1996); James Boyle, *A Theory of Law and Information: Copyright, Spleens, Blackmail, and Insider Trading*, 80 Cal. L. Rev. 1413 (1992); Jessica Litman, *The Public Domain*, 39 Emory L.J. 965 (1990); David Vaver, *Intellectual Property Today: Of Myths and Paradoxes*, 69 Can. Bar Rev. 98 (1990); Tom G. Palmer, *Intellectual Property: A Non-Posnerian Law and Economics Approach*, 12 Hamline L. Rev. 261 (1989); Wendy J. Gordon, *An Inquiry Into the Merits of Copyright: The Challenges of Consistency, Consent, and Encouragement Theory*, 41 Stan. L. Rev. 1343 (1989).

[96] *International News Service v. Associated Press*, 248 U.S. 215, 250 (1918).

[97] For an argument that author-centeredness is not the correct baseline assumption for copyright law but rather that participants of the copyright policy process should adopt the presumption that copyright centers on the proper industrial policy for creative industries, see Julie E. Cohen, *Copyright as Property in the Post-Industrial Economy: A Research Agenda*, 2011 Wis. L. Rev. 141.

the forefront, treating reward to authors primarily as a means to that end. In this country, the debate between advocates of these positions is of more than mere historical interest. It continues today.

§ 1.07 THE NATURAL LAW JUSTIFICATION

[A] Natural Law and the Author

Competing with the "utilitarian" rhetoric in American copyright discourse, from the earliest era of the Republic down to the present day, is the alternative rhetoric of "natural rights" or "inherent entitlement." The natural law justification for recognizing property rights in works of authorship is based on the rights of authors to reap the fruits of their creations, to obtain rewards for their contributions to society, and to protect the integrity of their creations as an entitlement based on their individual efforts or as extensions of their personalities.

[B] Locke and the Labor Model

The proposition that a person is entitled to the fruits of his labor is a compelling argument in favor of property rights of any kind, tangible or intangible. The most famous proponent of this natural rights theory was John Locke, the eighteenth century English philosopher, who reasoned that persons have a natural right of property in their bodies. In owning their bodies, people also own the labor of their bodies and, by extension, the fruits of their labor.[98]

In England itself, Lockean reasoning had little prominence in the campaign to establish the new law of copyright, which culminated in the Statute of Anne in 1710. Across the English Channel, however, the emphasis on "authorship" and "authors' rights" provided the primary ideological justification for the recognition of new legal interests in literary and artistic creations in 18th Century European intellectual property law, and this emphasis provided a convenient basis on which those interests could be allocated. Both of these developments were urgently required if the new statutes were to serve the needs of the emerging commercial marketplace in works of the imagination. Ultimately, the belief in the paramount importance of "authorship" was to take on a significance of its own, marking the doctrinal landscapes of national law systems which emerged in countries such as France and Germany.[99]

The natural law justification for copyright continues to enjoy considerable currency throughout the world. Perhaps most importantly, it has animated

---

[98] *See* JOHN LOCKE, SECOND TREATISE OF GOVERNMENT Ch. 5 (1960). For an overview of Lockean natural law theory as applied to intellectual property, see Wendy J. Gordon, *A Property Right in Self Expression: Equality and Individualism in the Natural Law of Intellectual Property*, 102 YALE L.J. 1533 (1993).

[99] For a general discussion of "authorship" as a legal concept, see Peter Jaszi, *Toward a Theory of Copyright: The Metamorphoses of "Authorship,"* 41 DUKE L.J. 455 (1991). *See also* Roger Chartier, *Figures of the Author*, *in* OF AUTHORS AND ORIGINS: ESSAYS ON COPYRIGHT LAW 7 (B. Sherman & A. Strowel eds., 1994); Oren Bracha, *The Ideology of Authorship Revisited: Authors, Markets, and Liberal Values in Early American Copyright*, 118 YALE L.J. 186 (2008).

successive revisions of the Berne Convention for the Protection of Literary and Artistic Property, up to and including the 1971 Paris Revision[100] to which the United States adhered in 1989.

It would be wrong, however, to regard the "natural rights" conception of copyright as a recent European import into British and U.S. copyright law. The claims of "authorship" exerted a shaping influence in late 18th and 19th Century British copyright law. Even before the 1790 Federal Copyright Act, Lockean rhetoric has been part of the discourse of American copyright law in tension with the utilitarian conception discussed above.[101]

Lockean rhetoric remains a crucial part of the discourse in copyright jurisprudence today. In its present-day form, this view holds that an individual who has created a piece of music or a work of art should have the right to control its use and be compensated for its sale, no less than a farmer reaps the benefits of his crop. In addition, because the author has enriched society through his creation, the author has a fundamental right to obtain a reward commensurate with the value of her contribution. Thus, copyright law, which confers an exclusive property right in an author's work, vindicates the natural right of individuals to control their works and to be justly compensated for their contributions to society.[102]

The Lockean justification for copyright law provides a useful vocabulary but is indeterminate insofar as its specific implications are concerned. First, Lockean natural law theory maintains that the author should have control over his work but indicates little about how much control the author should have, how long that control should last, and who should benefit from the copyrighted work. The reality of positive law thus conflicts with the natural rights ideal. The United States has adopted a positive law approach, under which rights are granted solely as a matter of statute. The content of such rights is to be determined as the legislature sees fit, in accordance with the constitutional goal of promoting the progress of science.

Second, some have questioned whether copyright law satisfies the ideal of just compensation for the author's contribution to society. Empirically, copyright law has not particularly rewarded works of enduring social value; the contrary has more often occurred. Again, the reality of positive law departs from the abstractions of natural rights theory. As a theoretical matter, the goal of fair compensation is at best a vague concept. No one can show what is the "fair" price for any commodity, service, or work of authorship. Normally, for most endeavors, we prefer to allow the market to set its price and believe the consumer is benefited when competition pushes that price toward the marginal cost of production. But even if it were possible to determine "just" compensation, society generally seems unconcerned about ensuring compensation in a sum equal to what any given

---

[100] *See supra* § 1.04. Nor should one overlook the 1948 Universal Declaration of Human Rights, which at Article 27(2) reads: "Everyone has the right to the protections of the moral and material interests resulting from any scientific, literary, or artistic production of which he is the author."

[101] "Bracketing the slavery issue, there was perhaps no debate more insistent for writers in antebellum American than the issue of literary property." G. Rice, The Transformation of Authorship in America 77 (1997).

[102] For an overview of natural rights theory, see Alfred C. Yen, *Restoring the Natural Law: Copyright as Labor and Possession*, 51 Ohio St. L.J. 517 (1990).

individual — whether schoolteacher, farmer, auto worker, or nurse — contributes. Indeed, virtually all salaried workers and entrepreneurs are rewarded in lesser measure than the value they contribute — the difference being profit.

[C] Hegel and the Personality Model

The most influential alternative to the labor-based Lockean model of natural law is one based on a personality justification.[103] Associated with the German philosopher Hegel, and embodied in "moral rights" legislation, the personality model advances the idea that property provides a means for self-actualization, for personal expression, and for the dignity of the individual. Putting to one side Hegel's difficult concepts of human will and freedom, the personality theory of intellectual property has an immediate intuitive appeal. After all, is an idea not a manifestation of the creator's personality or self? As such, should it not belong to its creator?

One celebrated formulation of personality rights can be found in Article 6*bis* of the Berne Convention, which requires that member states protect an author's rights of "integrity" and "attribution." Despite the fact that Berne 6*bis* makes no distinction between literary, artistic, or musical works, the personality justification applies better to some categories of copyrighted works than others. The arts are a prime example. In a work of art, the personality traits of the author are materialized in an external object. Personality-based natural rights are inscribed in the rights of "attribution" and "integrity" for certain visual artists, which are now specifically recognized in § 106A of the Copyright Act of 1976, as amended following U.S. admission to Berne in 1989. In addition to § 106A, U.S. law, at the state level, recognizes personality interests in various bodies of law that overlap with copyright, such as unfair competition law, defamation, privacy, and right of publicity.

In contrast to the arts, the personality justification is difficult to apply to intellectual products that appear to reflect little or no personality from individual creators. An intellectual property system based on personality interests will have trouble finding reliable indicia for an individual who has little or no real personality stake in a particular object. Unlike Lockean labor theory, which may be applied across the range of intellectual property, a personality justification works less well when applied to intellectual products that are not suffused with what society would call "personal expression." Thus, a labor justification may be applied equally well to patent protection for a new chemical compound, a database, or a poem. On the other hand, personality theory cannot be conveniently applied to works of utility, computer programs, maps, or highly collaborative works, where individual personality is subsumed in a collective effort. In short, personality theory would exclude categories of works now recognized as integral parts of copyright law.

In addition to the category problems, personality theory shares some of the same conceptual problems found in a labor theory of property. Personality (or

---

[103] *Cf.* Jeanne C. Fromer, *Expressive Incentives in Intellectual Property*, 98 Va. L. Rev. 1745 (2012) (arguing that incentives favoring personality and labor interests can still support underlying utilitarian notions of providing limited incentives to create socially valuable works).

labor, for that matter) is not an on/off proposition but is found in varying amounts, depending on the particular work under consideration. Suppose one could say that a particular painting manifests the personality of the artist to a greater degree than another painting. If we accept this to be the case, should works be protected according to the amount of personality they manifest? If so, how should one make this measurement? In truth, Lockean labor theory also suffers from this conceptual dilemma, given that different works result from varying degrees of labor input.[104]

In summary, then, the utilitarian and natural law views (both of Locke and of Hegel) raise a good many questions to which they do not offer definitive answers. However, recognition of the ultimately indeterminate character of natural law theory has not detracted from its popularity in the discourse of copyright law and policy. It is fair to say that, throughout the history of Anglo-American copyright law, the natural law justification has been successfully deployed to explain or justify virtually every extension of the scope or intensity of copyright protection. In addition, it has motivated the successive revisions of the Berne Convention, which has continued to attract additional adherents including the United States.[105] Despite its appeal to many, natural law theory provides no more than a starting point and limited justification for copyright law. As an alternative to natural law propositions, one must turn to a utilitarian justification for the protection of intangible property rights. Based on economic principles, the utilitarian approach vindicates copyright law as an incentive system for authors to create works of authorship and thereby enhances the public welfare.[106] As the next section shows, this view of copyright is deeply ingrained in U.S. law.

§ 1.08 THE UTILITARIAN CONCEPTION OF COPYRIGHT LAW

[A] The Economic Rationale of the Copyright Clause[107]

Without specifying the form of protection, art. 1, § 8, cl. 8 of the United States Constitution empowers Congress to legislate copyright and patent statutes, conferring a limited monopoly on writings and inventions.[108] By implication, the

---

[104] For those wishing to brush up on their Hegel, see G. Hegel, Philiosphy of Right, (T.M. Knox trans., Oxford: Clarendon Press, 1965) (1820) at pp. 40–57; and Neil Netanel, *Copyright, Alienability Restrictions and the Enhancement of Author Autonomy: A Normative Evaluation*, 24 Rutgers L.J. 347 (1993). Hegelian property theory is examined in Radin, *Property and Personhood*, 34 Stan. L. Rev. 957 (1982). For application of the theory to intellectual property, see Justin Hughes, *The Philosophy of Intellectual Property*, 77 Geo. L.J. 287, 330–65 (1988).

[105] See also the 1948 Universal Declaration of Human Rights, Article 27(2), which gives the rights of authors a dignity coequal with that afforded to the most basic entitlements of humankind. The Article reads: "Everyone has the right to the protections of the moral and material interests resulting from any scientific, literary, or artistic creation of which he is the author."

[106] For a historical overview of the public welfare rationale of copyright and its deep roots in American law, see Craig Dallon, *The Problem with Congress and Copyright Law: Forgetting the Past and Ignoring the Public Interest*, 44 Santa Clara L. Rev. 365 (2004).

[107] *See generally* Stephen G. Breyer, *"The Uneasy Case for Copyright": A Look Back Across Four*

Constitution recognizes that copyright law plays an important role in our market economy. Rather than encouraging production of works by government subsidy, or awards or prizes, the author is given, through the limited monopoly of copyright law, a private property right over his creation, the worth of which will ultimately be determined by the market. The underlying policy of this constitutional provision is to promote the public welfare through private market incentives. The U.S. Supreme Court, in *Mazer v. Stein*,[109] stated the rationale underlying the Copyright Clause as follows: "The economic philosophy behind the clause empowering Congress to grant patents and copyrights is the conviction that encouragement of individual effort by personal gain is the best way to advance the public welfare through the talents of authors and inventors in science and the useful arts."[110]

[B] Why Should Property Rights Be Created for Information?

The law confers property rights on most things of value that we normally think of as being tangible things that occupy physical space, such as land or movable objects. The law, however, also recognizes property rights in information, an intangible product. This is hardly surprising. Information can be of great value as well as costly to produce, and without a legal regime protecting certain informational products, we would not produce the optimal amount of information for the public welfare. For this reason, copyright law recognizes property rights in certain kinds of expressive information called "works of authorship."

Protecting informational products presents special difficulties for the law because of the inherent intangible nature of these products. Products of information, for example, a piece of music, a computer program, or a radio signal, have characteristics that differentiate them from tangible products, such as a chair, an apple, or a television set. Once information is created, it can never be used up, and it can be used at little cost. A song can be sung endlessly or a computer program reproduced over and over, without ever using it up or depriving anyone else of its use. Information does not present the allocation problems that physical property does. If someone steals my automobile, I am deprived of it. My automobile is finite and exhaustible, whereas my song is infinite and inexhaustible.

This characteristic of intellectual property leads to an economic dilemma. Creating property rights in information imposes costs on the public. Why confer a life-plus-70-years monopoly for a work of art, a computer program, or a piece of music, if each of these products can be used infinitely and simultaneously without depriving anyone else of their use? Free market economics would prohibit creation of monopolies without an economic justification. As a monopolist, the owner of the

---

Decades, 79 GEO. WASH. L. REV. 1635 (2011) (summarizing the importance of economics to copyright law and that its importance is just as relevant today as when his original article by the same title was published in 1970).

[108] *But cf.* Jeanne C. Fromer, *The Intellectual Property Clause's External Limitations*, 61 DUKE L.J. 1329 (2012) (arguing that the IP Clause limits the ways that Congress can promote the progress of science and arts but that Congress has increasingly reached beyond its specified powers).

[109] 347 U.S. 201 (1954).

[110] *Id.* at 219.

copyright can charge a higher than competitive price for his or her product, causing people to buy less of it and to seek less useful substitutes for it. In economic terms, consumer welfare is distorted by this property right (copyright), which results in a less than maximum diffusion of information.

The above analysis is not entirely accurate because it applies only to information already created.[111] "If it can be copied by a free rider who has none of the development costs, a producer, for example, will not invest the millions of dollars it takes to create a movie because she will not receive a proper return on her investment. The creator who cannot recoup his investment will not create. Thus, if the author cannot exclude others from his work, the result will be either nonproduction or nondisclosure. Viewed in this way, copyright law represents an economic tradeoff between optimal creation of works of authorship and their optimal use.[112]

Informational products, as one learns from economic theory, have *public goods* characteristics, whose basic attributes can be summarized as nonrivalrous consumption and nonappropriability. For example, a television signal carrying a copyrighted movie can be consumed nonrivalrously (one person's use of the signal does not deprive another consumer's use of the same signal). In addition, the signal is nonappropriable because it is difficult for its producer to appropriate its value through its sale. Consumers will tend to become "free riders" of the signal, which can be easily captured and used at little or no cost. Because the producer cannot appropriate its true value through its sale, a suboptimal amount of information will be produced. The solution to the public goods problem (to encourage optimal production) is either direct government subsidy or giving limited monopoly rights

---

[111] *See* Frank H. Easterbrook, *The Supreme Court and the Economic System*, 98 Harv. L. Rev. 4 (1984) (Judge Easterbrook takes the position that intellectual property cases often reflect a tradeoff between optimal creation of information and its optimal use. As a result, he advocates an *ex ante* approach as opposed to an *ex post* approach in deciding intellectual property cases. The *ex ante* approach is forward looking and is concerned with making rules, which encourage the optimal creation and use of information. By comparison, the *ex post* approach is one that is solely concerned with settling a dispute between the parties).

[112] *Id.* at 25. Another way of putting it: a system of copyright that promotes economic efficiency will be one in which its principal doctrines "maximize the benefits from creating additional works, minus both the losses from limiting access and the costs of administering copyright protection." *See* William M. Landes & Richard A. Posner, *An Economic Analysis of Copyright Law*, 28 J. Legal Stud. 325, 326 (1989). For other views concerning the economics of intellectual property and copyright law, see Raymond Shih Kay Ku, Jiayang Sun, and Yiying Fan, *Does Copyright Law Promote Creativity? An Empirical Analysis*, 62 Vand. L. Rev. 1669 (2009) (finding little empirical support that legal changes in copyright protection will affect the number of works produced); Dotan Oliar and Christopher Sprigman, *There's No Free Laugh (Anymore)* 94 Va. L. Rev. 1787 (2008) (using stand-up comedy to illustrate that social norms can sometimes serve as an alternative to copyright); Sara Stadler, *Incentive and Expectation in Copyright*, 58 Hastings L.J. 433 (2007) (arguing that defining rights in terms of incentive causes a cycle of ever-increasing expectations and rights); Mark A. Lemley, *Property, Intellectual Property, and Free Riding*, 83 Tex. L. Rev. 1031 (2005) (criticizing the application of real property rhetoric to intellectual property); Christopher Yoo, *Copyright and Product Differentiation*, 79 N.Y.U. L. Rev. 212 (2004) (providing an economic model of copyright, based on the theory of product differentiation, that emphasizes the stimulation of market entrants resulting in greater public access due to lower prices); and Christopher Yoo, *Public Goods Economics: A Misunderstood Relation*, 155 U. Pa. L. Rev. 635 (2007) (questioning the application of pure public goods analysis to copyright).

to authors through copyright law.[113]

In the absence of copyright protection, self-help through market headstart is the traditional means by which an author or inventor can obtain a return on investment. By being the first to print and sell a book, could the creator earn enough profit to justify his investment and induce his or her continued creation? If so, headstart is a sufficient incentive for continued production; as a result, granting a copyright monopoly is unnecessary and harms the consumer.[114] A headstart advantage may adequately reward some inventors and authors, particularly when the costs of reproduction are significantly less than the costs of creation. But a headstart advantage is only as good as the length of time it takes another to copy your product. A company spending millions in developing a computer operating system program or motion picture could hardly compete with an imitator, which has no development costs and is able to copy the program quickly and cheaply and enter the market immediately thereafter. Consequently, market headstart may be inadequate to encourage the optimal creation of works of authorship and inventions.

In place of an unregulated market, copyright law confers a limited monopoly on works of authorship. On the one hand, copyright law provides the incentive to create information and a shelter to develop and protect it. On the other hand, the copyright monopoly is a limited one — limited in time and scope by such doctrines as idea/expression, originality, and fair use. Viewed in this way, copyright law represents an economic tradeoff between encouraging the optimal creation of works of authorship through monopoly incentives and providing for their optimal access, use, and distribution through limiting doctrines. As Justice Stewart, in *Twentieth Century Music Corporation v. Aiken*, said:

> The immediate effect of our copyright law is to secure a fair return for an author's creative labor. But the ultimate aim is, by this incentive, to stimulate artistic creativity for the public good. "The sole interest of the United States and the primary object in conferring the monopoly," the Supreme Court has said, "lie in the general benefits derived by the public from the labors of authors."[115]

---

[113] *See* Armen Alchian & William Allen, Exchange and Production: Competition, Coordination and Control 99–101 (3d ed. 1983). For a basic overview of the economics of property rights in information and the public goods problem, see Robert Cooter & Thomas Ulen, Law and Economics 135–68 (1988); *see also* Mark Lemley, *Economics of Improvement in Intellectual Property Law*, 75 Tex. L. Rev. 989 (1997) (discussing both copyright and patent, with a focus on works and inventions that build on the past — as all do).

[114] This argument is elaborately made in a famous article, Stephen Breyer, *The Uneasy Case for Copyright: A Study in Copyright of Books, Photocopies and Computer Programs*, 84 Harv. L. Rev. 281 (1970). *Compare* Barry W. Tyerman, *The Economic Rationale for Copyright Protection for Published Books: A Reply to Professor Breyer*, 18 UCLA L. Rev. 1100 (1971), *with* Stephen Breyer, *Copyright: A Rejoinder*, 20 UCLA L. Rev. 75 (1972). For a discussion of the strengths and weaknesses of the economic theory of copyright, see Wendy J. Gordon, *An Inquiry into the Merits of Copyright: The Challenges of Consistency, Consent, and Encouragement Theory*, 41 Stan. L. Rev. 1343 (1989).

[115] 422 U.S. 151, 156 (1975). For an argument that treating copyright as a government-sponsored mechanism for encouraging creativity ignores the importance of copyright's private law architecture, see

The "utilitarian" concept of copyright provides a powerful explanation of the ways in which our collective life may be affected by changes in the law. Whether or not the scope of copyright protection significantly affects the behavior of individual poets, painters or computer programmers can be endlessly debated. One can say, however, that changes in the scope of copyright protection affect the investment in the production and dissemination of works of authorship, from a societal standpoint. This insight, of course, does not in itself provide a practical way by which to determine the desirability of particular changes in copyright law, nor can it assess their impact on public welfare. Presumably, some level of protection exists that would provide for optimal incentives to create works of authorship, yet allows for an optimal dissemination of those same works and their access by the consuming public.[116] This normative goal is easy to state, but to quantify that level of optimal protection raises difficult and probably insoluble methodological questions.

§ 1.09 THE FUTURE OF COPYRIGHT AND THE DIGITAL CHALLENGE

[A] From Gutenberg to the Internet

Just as the printing press gave rise to the need for copyright law, new technologies have created the further need for legislative response. After a twenty-year revision process, the Copyright Act of 1976 was passed with the hope that the law could meet the challenges of new technologies. But what seemed to be a far-sighted, intelligently drafted statute quickly became obsolete in some ways. The reason for this partial obsolescence is the time lag between technological and legal change. Technological change always seems to outstrip the law's ability for adaptation. This is no better exemplified than in the law of copyright, a victim of the inexorable march of technological progress.

Over its several centuries of existence, copyright law has successfully negotiated a series of "crises" precipitated by changes in information distribution by adapting itself to new technological circumstances.[117] In the last century or so, for example, copyright has proved flexible enough to deal effectively with the new media of photography, motion pictures, and sound recordings. The crisis of the moment, however, may pose a greater challenge by far to the adaptability of the copyright system.

As copyright and the world move into the Third Millennium, a development in information technology, which may have as much potential for social

---

Shyamkrishna Balganesh, *The Obligatory Structure of Copyright Law: Unbundling the Wrong of Copying*, 125 Harv. L. Rev. 1664 (2012).

[116] *But see* Abraham Bell & Gideon Parchomovsky, *The Case for Imperfect Enforcement of Property Rights*, 160 U. Pa. L. Rev. 1927 (2012) (challenging the view that perfect protection of private property rights would provide owners with an optimal incentive to invest in their assets).

[117] For a discussion regarding whether copyright owners should be free to control new technological uses of their works or whether the law should allow technological innovators free to explore and exploit such uses, see Dotan Oliar, *The Copyright-Innovation Tradeoff: Property Rules, Liability Rules, and Intentional Infliction of Harm*, 64 Stan. L. Rev. 951 (2012).

transformation as did movable type, is leading some to question the continued relevance of traditional copyright law. That development is the digitization of information — *i.e.*, its description by means of strings of binary code — which was ushered in by the invention and popularization of digital computers. On paper, digital code is expressed symbolically as zeros and ones; electronically, it is embodied in a series of on or off settings. A variety of different media may be used to fix information in electronic form: magnetic tape, floppy disks, silicon chips, CDs, and DVDs. Whatever the medium, it is in this so-called machine-readable form that digital code can be recognized by electronic devices, such as computers, which in turn may be programmed to respond in various ways to digital signals.

One consequence of digitization was to introduce an entirely new category of information products — computer programs — into the marketplace, with disquieting consequences for schemes of legal protection developed in response to earlier technologies. Yet another consequence of the advent of digital code was to create a powerful new means by which to store large amounts of information of all kinds. In fact, all the varieties of "works" previously known to human culture (and to the law of copyright) can be — and, increasingly, are being — expressed in digital form. Such records, of course, can be retransformed (with the help of a properly programmed machine) into recognizable text, image, or sound.

Digital information technology is to be contrasted with analog technology, which preceded it and which still persists.[118] Take the example of a photographic image. Prints, negatives, screen projections, and cathode tube displays are all alternative potential analog embodiments of an image. What they have in common is that they represent that image — its shape, density, color, and so forth — directly to the human sense of sight. Now consider an image encoded on a digital medium — for example, a CD-ROM. No matter how hard one studies the surface of the disk, no matter at what magnification, and no matter how bright the light, no representation of the image can be discerned there. What the CD-ROM contains is not a representation but an extraordinarily detailed description of the image, from which it can be rapidly reconstructed by electronic means.

It is precisely because they are descriptions rather than representations that images recorded in digital formats can be manipulated with such relative ease. Altering the texture of the background or the shape of a foreground object in an analog record of a photographic image might take a skilled retoucher hours or days, involving as it does the painstaking alteration of every affected portion of the picture. Beginning with a digitized image, the same result may be achieved with photo processing software in minutes by changing the descriptive parameters of the digital record. That such digital records describe rather than represent information gives rise to some of the most important implications of the new technology for the law of intellectual property.

If digitalization allows us to store and manipulate data in ways never thought of, it has radically changed the way we transmit data. In a network environment,

---

[118] For an analysis of the characteristics of the digital media and its implications for copyright law, see Pamela Samuelson, *Digital Media and the Changing Face of Intellectual Property Law*, 16 RUTGERS COMPUTER & TECH. L.J. 323 (1990). For a comprehensive overview of digital age issues affecting copyright, see Fred H. Cate, *The Technological Transformation of Copyright Law*, 81 IOWA L. REV. 1395 (1996).

"packets" of information are routed from the memory of the sender's computer to that of the receiver's, either directly or, more commonly, by way of a series of electronic waystations ("servers" and "routers"). The existence of these networks depends on the wide acceptance of common standards governing how information is to be broken down, sent, and reassembled. Collectively, these linked networks form what is called the "Internet."

The Internet is made possible through the acceptance of common standards — such as the Transmission Control Protocol ("TCP") and the Internet Protocol ("IP").[119] These developments have been accelerated dramatically by the creation of the multimedia branch of the Internet, the World Wide Web ("the Web"), by a researcher at the CERN physical laboratory in Geneva, Switzerland, in 1990 — and by the popularization of the Web, which followed the development of "web browser" software. Today, use of the Internet grows exponentially. What was not that long ago an obscure (albeit powerful) communication system patronized by a small number of computer scientists and other devotees of digital technology has been transformed into the newest mass medium.

With the phenomenal development in communications networking, transmission of data is no longer limited to one-to-one communication (*e.g.*, telephone communication) or one-to-many communication (*e.g.*, broadcasting). The networking of communications facilities allows transmission of data from everyone to anywhere. Physical limits do not restrict the number of copies of a work that can be transmitted by electronic means. Similarly, no ceiling exists as to the number of recipients that can receive the work or where they may receive it. We are well into the era of "Web 2.0," the current jargon commonly associated with interactive information sharing, interoperability, and user-centered design. Whatever term we use to describe the current trends in Internet development and design, today's web, with its rich user-generated material,[120] metadata, and dynamic content, allows users to do more than retrieve information, and it promotes innovative ways to create, exploit, and preserve copyrighted works.[121]

[B] The Digital Challenge and Copyright Law

The digital revolution has allowed access to works and their reproduction and dissemination in once unimaginable ways.[122] Data storage, transmission, and manipulability seriously challenge the control of the copyright owner over his

---

[119] By now, a distinction has emerged between "internet" with a small *i*, and "Internet" with a capital *I*. Officially, the distinction was simple: "internet" meant any network using TCP/IP, while "Internet" meant the public, federally subsidized network that was made up of many linked networks all running the TCP/IP protocols. K. Hafner & M. Lyon, Where Wizards Stay Up Late: The Origins of the Internet 244 (1996).

[120] *See* Daniel Gervais, *The Tangled Web of UGC: Making Sense of User Generated Content*, 11 Vand, J. of Ent. and Tech. Law 841 (2009).

[121] *See* Peter S. Menel, *Knowledge Accessibility and Preservation Policy for the Digital Age*, 44 Hous. L. Rev. 1013 (2007) (discussing preservation policy) and Diane Zimmerman, *Can Our Culture Be Saved? The Future of Digital Archiving*, 91 Minn. L. Rev. 989 (2007) (discussing the possibility of digitizing works before they enter the public domain).

[122] For a discussion of communities devoted to providing more access to intellectual property-

work.[123]

While changes in copying technologies may dramatically affect incentives to produce works of authorship, other current changes in technology call into question the very notion of authorship and of copyright law itself. Traditionally, a reference to the "author" of a work calls to mind a person, such as a novelist, composer, or artist. This "individualistic" notion of authorship (also called the "romantic" model of authorship) is ingrained in popular thinking and inscribed in the law of copyright.[124] But is this individualistic model of creation, on which so much of copyright law is based, appropriate to the world of digital electronic technologies where sounds, images, and words are duplicated, rearranged, and disseminated over vast, reticulated electronic networks?[125]

Some assert that traditional copyright law based on protecting a static printed text is ill suited to today's world. In short, we need a copyright paradigm for the protection of informational products to meet the digital challenge. Without the ability to exclude others in the networked environment, information providers will have little incentive to disseminate works that take a heavy investment in time and effort. The fear is that we may be left with these wonderful digital copying and transmission technologies with less and less worth copying.

In particular, corporate providers of copyrighted content — the so-called "copyright industries" that produce motion pictures, make sound recordings, publish books, and distribute software — have had a mixed response to the growth trend in Internet usage.[126] In their view, the network environment is a place of both great opportunity and tremendous risk. On the one hand, they have identified the Internet as a potential future source of vast profits: a distribution medium with the potential of delivering content of all kinds, on demand, to consumers without the high overhead associated with conventional distribution systems. On the other hand, they perceive the Internet as a present danger to their valuable intangible assets. Their aim, then, is to make the network environment "safe" for digital commerce in information and entertainment products.

---

protected goods and their use of rhetoric in trying to enact change, see Jessica M. Silbey, *Comparative Tales of Origins and Access: Intellectual Property and the Rhetoric of Social Change*, 61 Case W. Res. L. Rev. 195 (2010).

[123] A case in point is the Google Book Search initiative which has made agreements to scan, archive, and digitize the contents of all books in major libraries such as the University of Michigan, Harvard University, and the New York Public library. The goal is to provide a searchable online database of all printed works that is accessible to the public. The Google project is discussed at greater length at *infra* § 6.03(c).

[124] The history, meaning, and ideology of authorship are examined comprehensively in Peter Jaszi, *Toward a Theory of Copyright: The Metamorphoses of "Authorship"* , 1991 Duke L.J. 455. *See also* Jessica Litman, *Copyright as Myth*, 53 U. Pitt. L. Rev. 235 (1991); Robert H. Rotstein, *Beyond Metaphor: Copyright Infringement and the Fiction of the Work*, 68 Chi. Kent L. Rev. 725 (1993); Martha Woodmansee, The Author, the Arts, and the Market: Rereading the History of Aesthetics (1993).

[125] Because digitization has called into question so many of the sacred notions of copyright, one might ask what role copyright law will play in protecting the creative output of authors. This issue is explored in Marshall Leaffer, *Protecting Author's Rights in a Digital Age*, 27 U. Tol. L. Rev. 1 (1996).

[126] *See generally* Niva Elkin-Koren, *The Changing Nature of Books and "The Uneasy Case for Copyright,"* 79 Geo. Wash. L. Rev. 1712 (2011) (discussing the emergence of eBooks and the implications for copyright law of these changes in digital publishing).

To some extent, this goal can be achieved through self-help by means of "technological safeguards" that create barriers to infringement: scrambling, encryption, watermarking, use of secure passwords, and so forth. But content providers are quick to argue that any technological security measures can eventually be "hacked," and that, therefore, new legal protections for copyrighted works in the network environment are also required.

In August 1995, a working group of a special Clinton Administration Task Force issued its report, the so-called "White Paper" on Intellectual Property and the National Information Infrastructure.[127] Although many of the White Paper proposals proved too controversial for legislative approval, its provisions against the circumvention of technological protection systems became the focus of a Diplomatic Conference of the World Intellectual Property Organization. The final treaties incorporated the "digital agenda" in calling on states to adopt legal measures to prevent "circumvention" of the technological protection system. On October 27, 1998, President Clinton signed into law the Digital Millennium Copyright Act ("DCMA"), which implemented the WIPO Copyright Treaties. As its centerpiece, the Act provides civil and criminal remedies against those who circumvent technological safeguards and tamper with copyright management information.[128]

In addition to the anticircumvention provisions, copyright owners have looked to other bodies of law, most importantly contract law, to protect their creations. We are all aware of the ubiquitous "shrink wrap" and "click on" licenses that the purchaser or user is required to accept as a condition of installing and using the software. Often these licenses include terms that run contrary to copyright law, restricting use of the program in ways copyright doctrine does not.

The state of the law on the enforceability of such terms is still unsettled, both as a matter of contract doctrine and its relation to the law of copyright preemption. The currently stalled drive to enact the Uniform Computer Information Transactions Act represented an attempt to address this issue through state-by-state legislation. Ultimately, it may be for the courts to sort out this thorny issue.[129]

One way or the other, the emergence of restrictive information licensing focuses new attention on the relationship between contract and copyright and on the question of the extent to which our legal system should enable or abet the displacement of copyright rules by private arrangements.

---

[127] *See* Information Infrastructure Task Force, Intellectual Property and the National Information Infrastructure: The Report of the Working Group on Intellectual Property Rights (1995).

[128] The DMCA is discussed at *infra* § 8.31. For a comprehensive background and analysis of the issues, see Jessica Litman, Digital Copyright: Protecting Intellectual Property on the Internet (2001).

[129] The copyright/contract intersection and the issue of preemption is discussed at *infra* § 11.07[B].

[C] The Future of Copyright

The emergent business model for the distribution of copyrighted works in the network environment seems to challenge the survival of an "informational commons."[130] The day may soon be upon us when copyrighted works reside predominately in electronic networks, rather than in material form, and when owners of these informational products will no longer have to look to traditional copyright law for protection. The trend is that readers, listeners, and viewers of copyrighted works are having less and less unencumbered lawful personal use of books, films, or music in a technological and legal environment in which those uses are easier to trace and charge for.[131] In place of traditional copyright law, a combination of technological restrictions, contractual arrangements, and criminal sanctions may well provide sufficient protection to copyright owners who will largely ignore traditional copyright law as the basis of enforcing their rights. In the coming world of the celestial jukebox, box office, or library, there may come a time that online access to a work will be allowed only to those who agree to conditions of payment and terms of use. Accordingly, copyright owners will negotiate for the kind of access license the user desires, such as read-only access for viewing or copying access. In short, technology may make it possible for information proprietors to treat every use as a new instance of "access." The fear is that such proprietors could maximize profits while continuing to withhold their works from general scrutiny, including fair use.[132]

In response to this dark vision, information proprietors assert that consumers need not worry about being deprived of access to copyrighted works. They argue that because profit maximization is their essential motivation to disseminate works in digital networks, a pay-per-use information environment will enhance access in a more universal fashion and at a lower cost than ever before. In this view, copyrighted content will become ever more plentiful and readily accessible though efficient distribution, characterized by ubiquitous electronic licensing and the payment of fees.[133] A pay-per-use information environment may represent a utopia or its opposite, depending on one's perspective.

Whatever view one has about the new information environment, copyright policymakers face issues radically different than those of the past. Previously, it was enough to ask how traditional copyright principles applied to new media.

---

[130] For a discussion of this concept, see Lawrence Lessig, The Future of Ideas: The Fate of Commons in a Connected World (2001); Yohai Benkler, *Free as the Air to Common Use: First Amendment Constraints on Enclosure of the Public Domain*, 74 N.Y.U. L. Rev. 354 (1999); Glynn S. Lunney Jr., *The Death of Copyright: Digital Technology, Private Copying and the Digital Millennium Copyright Act*, 87 Va. L. Rev. 813 (2001); James Boyle, *The Second Enclosure Movement and the Constriction of the Public Domain*, 66 L. & Contemp. Probs. 33 (2003).

[131] The idea that ambit of personal use of copyrighted work is shrinking is elegantly developed in Jessica Litman, *Law Personal Use*, 85 Tex. L. Rev. 1871 (2007) (arguing against the approach that presupposes that all uses are unlawful unless specifically exempted by the Copyright Act).

[132] The issues regarding fair use in a digital network environment are discussed at *infra* § 10.17.

[133] For a discussion of both the necessary and counterproductive nature of government intervention in reaching licensing deals, see Peter C. DiCola & Matthew Sag, *An Information-Gathering Approach to Copyright Policy*, 34 Cardoza L. Rev. 173 (2012).

Digital technology in general and digital networks in particular pose a more fundamental inquiry;[134] Even if traditional copyright doctrines may not apply comfortably in cyberspace, we could work to install their functional equivalents.[135] The challenge, though, remains the same: how to enhance public welfare with some balance between the interests of copyright owners and those of users.[136] Striking this balance has never been easy from a theoretical or political standpoint. But the struggle to do so must continue because its goal is a social imperative and worth the fight.

Part III. COPYRIGHT, PATENT, AND TRADEMARK COMPARED

§ 1.10 GENERALLY

Anyone who seeks a thorough understanding of copyright law should be well acquainted with the other major bodies of intellectual property protection, particularly patent and trademark law. Although based on different statutes, goals, and theories, these three forms of intellectual property law protection (copyright, patent, and trademark) are interrelated and often overlap in the same subject matter.[137] The purpose of the next section is to paint these relationships with a broad brush, starting first with the federal intellectual property law and then proceeding to an analogous body of law arising out of state causes of action.

Copyright, patent, and trademark law share basic similarities. First, by their nature, all three major areas of intellectual property law recognize property rights in differing forms of information: copyright (expressive information); patent (technological information); and trademark (symbolic information). Second, because

---

[134] *See* Diane Zimmerman, *Living Without Copyright in a Digital World*, 70 Alb. L. Rev. 1375 (2007) (arguing that copyright offers little practical significance and is simply not up the task in cyberspace); *see also*, Graeme Austin, *Metamorphosis of Artists Rights in the Digital Age*, 28 Colum. J.L. & Arts 397 (2005); Molly Van Houwelling, *Distributive Values in Copyright*, 83 Tex. L. Rev. 1535 (2005).

[135] Ann Bartow, *Electrifying Copyright Norms and Making Cyberspace More Like a Book*, 48 Vill. L. Rev. 13 (2003) (focusing on how legal rules written with the offline world in mind have not translated well to the digital world).

[136] For a balanced overview, see World Intellectual Property Organization, Intellectual Property on the Internet: A Survey of Issues (2002). For an analysis of various reform proposals, *see* Pamela Samuelson, *Is Copyright Reform Possible?*, 126 Harv. L. Rev. 740 (2013) (analyzing copyright reform proposals by William Patry and Jason Mazzone, arguing that their proposals are incomplete, and setting forth more substantive reform proposals); Greg Lastowka, *Innovative Copyright*, 109 Mich. L. Rev. 1011 (2011) (summarizing Michael A. Carrier's proposals for copyright reform and arguing that much more radical reforms are necessary in order to resolve the conflicts with innovative technologies); Pamela Samuelson, *The Copyright Principles Project: Directions for Reform*, 25 Berkeley Tech. L.J. 1175 (2010) (setting forth copyright reform proposed by the Copyright Principles Project).

[137] For a discussion of the development of intellectual property since the 19th century and its relationship with copyright law, see Justin Hughes, *A Short History of "Intellectual Property" in Relation to Copyright*, 33 Cardozo L. Rev. 1293 (2012). For an in-depth discussion of contemporary intellectual property perspectives and how intellectual property law, culture, and the production of material intersect, see Mario Biagioli, Peter Jaszi & Martha Woodmansee (eds.), Making and Unmaking Intellectual Property: Creative Production in Legal and Cultural Perspective (2011).

these bodies of law concern federally recognized rights, they are governed by federal statutes and administered by federal agencies. Third, from an international perspective, intellectual property is found in its most developed form in Western industrialized countries, and rights in such property frequently are the subjects of international conventions.

§ 1.11 PATENT LAW

[A] Generally

Compared with copyright, patent law is a form of intellectual property protection that is harder to secure, more difficult to maintain, and shorter in duration. Once obtained, however, a patent can be a more powerful form of protection than copyright. The patent grant encourages investment in research and development to produce valuable technological information. It creates a limited monopoly over this information in return for its public disclosure. Once issued, the patent becomes a public record, accessible to those wishing to use the information to improve or invent around the invention and to those wishing to use the patent once its term expires.

Patent law is the only branch of intellectual property in which the claimant's rights are dependent on a governmental grant — one made by the U.S. Patent and Trademark Office. In contrast, a copyright does not spring into existence by an official act of government, but by the creative act of an author in fixing the work in a tangible medium of expression. Subsequent registration of a copyright with the Copyright Office enhances the value of the owner's right but is not the source of it. Similarly, trademark rights do not begin with registration of the mark in the U.S. Patent and Trademark Office but rather by the use of the mark on a product or service. Certainly, important procedural and substantive ramifications result from trademark registration. Moreover, an application for trademark before actual use may provide significant advantages. Despite these benefits, the basic fact remains: the substantive right to preclude others from using the mark vests only when use has been demonstrated.

Not surprisingly, the differing roles of the various federal and state bureaucracies in the regulation of intellectual property rights is often a source of confusion to the non-specialist.

[B] Procedures for Obtaining a Patent

To prosecute patent applications before the PTO, a practitioner must have a technical background and must pass a special PTO examination. These special qualifications are intended ensure that the patent application is drafted properly and that its prosecution will be guided competently through the PTO's administrative procedures.

A patent lasts from issuance to an expiration date twenty years from the date of filing, provided that the required maintenance fees are paid.[138] In the case of ornamental design patents, the patent lasts for fourteen years from issuance.[139] The decision to grant the patent is made after the patent examiner evaluates the application to determine whether it meets the standards of patentability.

The patent application consists of four parts:[140] (1) the specification, including a summary of the invention often accompanied by drawings; (2) one or more claims at the end of the specification; (3) an oath, declaring that the inventor or inventors actually invented the invention described in the specification; and (4) the filing fees. The specification shows the preferred embodiment of the invention and discloses the best means of making and using it. The numbered claims, found at the end of the patent document, determine the scope of the patent and are critical in deciding if the patent has been infringed.

The administrative process leading to issuance of a patent can take years and thousands of dollars in legal fees.[141] Thus, a patent should be sought only after careful consideration as to the chances of its successful issuance and its eventual validity if challenged in a court of law.

In 2011, Congress passed a major patent reform bill, the America Invents Act ("AIA"). Among other goals, the AIA aims to reduce the disparity between the invention-date-related provisions of the prior United States law and the "first-to-file" systems of the rest of the world. Before the passage of the AIA, U.S. patent conferred rights to the first inventor, whereas the rest of world conferred the patent on the basis of first to file. Revised 35 U.S.C. § 102 provides that the first person to file a patent application is entitled to patent it, unless he or she derived the information from another inventor, or another person publicly disclosed the invention first and filed an application within one year of such disclosure.[142] The new provisions apply only to applications filed on or after March 16, 2013. Applications filed before that date, and patents granted on such applications are governed by the provisions of the previous statute.

[C] Kinds of Patents

A patent confers a legal right to exclude others for a limited time from making, using, or selling the patented invention throughout the United States. There are three kinds of patents: a utility patent with a term running from the date of issuance, which expires twenty years from the date of application; a plant patent

---

[138] *See* 35 U.S.C. § 154. Legislation related to obligations under the GATT changed the term to 20 years from the date of application. Previously, patents lasted 17 years from the moment of issuance.

[139] The duration for design patents was extended to 15 years by the Patent Law Implementation act of 2012, Pub. Law 112-211 (December 19, 2012).

[140] *See* 35 U.S.C. §§ 111–115.

[141] *But cf.* Jonathan S. Mazur & David Fagundes, *Costly Intellectual Property*, 64 Vand. L. Rev. 677 (2012) (arguing that despite the criticisms aimed at both patent and copyright vesting systems, the systems are socially beneficial).

[142] In most other countries, a prior public disclosure before filing destroys patentability, *i.e.*, there is no grace period.

having the same term; and a design patent with a fourteen-year term measured from the date of the grant.

Utility patents are granted for new, useful, and nonobvious products and processes.[143] Plant patents may be given for discovering and asexually reproducing new and distinct plant varieties.[144] Design patents are granted for new, original, and ornamental designs for articles of manufacture.[145] Utility patents are those most often referred to when patents are discussed, and, overall, the most important from an economic standpoint.

[D] Utility Patents: Requirements for Validity

The patent statute sets forth the requirements for patentability in § 101.[146] A patent is conferred on one who ". . . invents or discovers any new and useful process, machine, manufacture or composition of matter, or any new improvement thereof."[147] To obtain a patent one must show (1) patentable subject matter, (2) novelty, (3) usefulness, and (4) nonobviousness.

Patentable subject matter covers the full range of technological innovations that can be physically implemented in a product or process. Products are things: machines, chemical compounds, or objects. A process is a method of achieving a result. In addition to the more familiar patents covering mechanical, electrical, and chemical products or processes, patents have been granted for inventions in biotechnology (*e.g.*, manmade microbes)[148] and processes using computer software.[149] Patents, however, may *not* be granted for abstract ideas,[150] mathematical algorithms, or laws of nature.[151] Generally speaking, the subject matter of utility patents and that of copyrights do not overlap. But copyright law has extended significant protection to software, creating the potential that a given program may be protected under both intellectual property schemes.

Only *novel* products or processes are patentable. Under the "novelty requirement," an invention must be something truly new, above and beyond what already exists. Thus, consistent with the novelty requirement, one cannot patent a preexisting natural substance, although one may be able to claim rights in an improved version of such a substance or in a process for its extraction. Transcending the novelty requirement, there are real limits on the patentability of fundamental "laws of nature" even if newly discovered. Even so, recent debates about the patent eligibility of genetic sequences isolated through recombinant DNA technology and mathematical algorithms underlying computer programs

[143] 35 U.S.C. § 101.

[144] 35 U.S.C. § 161.

[145] 35 U.S.C. § 171. For a discussion of design patents, see *infra* § 3.15.

[146] *See* 35 U.S.C. § 101.

[147] *Id.*

[148] *See Diamond v. Chakrabarty*, 447 U.S. 303 (1980).

[149] *See Diamond v. Diehr*, 450 U.S. 175 (1981).

[150] *See Bilski v. Kappos*, 130 S. Ct. 3218 (2010).

[151] *See Mayo Collaborative Servs. v. Prometheus Labs., Inc.*, 132 S. Ct. 1289 (2012).

have created questions about the exact scope of such restrictions.[152]

The novelty requirement also reveals a fundamental difference between patent law and the law of copyright, which requires only that a protected work be original — the author's own, not something copied from another work. Theoretically at least, two people who independently created identical works could both hold copyrights, and neither one's use would infringe the other's rights. Thus, in order to recover for copyright infringement, a plaintiff must always prove that the defendant actually copied. By contrast, independent origination is not a defense in a patent infringement action. One who obtains a valid patent is entitled to enforce it against all who make, sell, or use the invention, whether or not they know about the work or the patent.[153]

By the same token, however, an invention may also be found to lack novelty if its inventor (or someone else) publicly used it before filing to patent it.[154] Moreover, an invention is not considered novel if an application for it is not filed in the Patent Office within a year from the time the invention is used, placed on sale in the United States, or described in a printed publication or patent anywhere in the world.[155] In this way, the patent statute encourages early disclosure of the invention through application in the Patent Office.

In the Patent Office, examiners scrutinize the record of "prior art" to assess an invention's novelty. But the statute requires them to look to this source for other determinations as well. Even if the subject matter is new, patentability is precluded if the invention would be obvious to one with ordinary skill in the art. In other words, the invention sought to be patented must be nonobvious.[156] Applying the nonobviousness standard is one of the most troublesome tasks in patent law. Determination of obviousness is ultimately a question of law based on several factual conclusions. The leading case on this issue, *Graham v. John Deere Co.*,[157] sets forth the process of inquiry to determine nonobviousness. First, the scope and content of the "prior art" must be determined. Next, the differences between the "prior art" and the claim must be ascertained. Finally, the level of ordinary skill of the practitioner in the pertinent art must be resolved. Secondary considerations such as commercial success and the failure of others to make the discovery are also taken into account. It is easy to see why obviousness determinations in courtroom settings are often lengthy proceedings involving battles of technical experts testifying why a certain invention is obvious or not.

Nothing in copyright or trademark approximates the nonobviousness standard. The same can be said for the utility requirement in patent law, requiring that the invention be useful.[158] "Utility" means that the invention must work as described in

---

[152] *See, e.g.*, John A. Burtis, *Towards a Rational Jurisprudence of Computer-Related Patentability in Light of In Re Alappat*, 79 Minn. L. Rev. 1129 (1995).

[153] *See* 35 U.S.C. § 271(a).

[154] *See* 35 U.S.C. § 102(a).

[155] *See* 35 U.S.C. § 102(b).

[156] *See* 35 U.S.C. § 103.

[157] 383 U.S. 1 (1966).

[158] *See* 35 U.S.C. § 101.

the patent application. Utility also means that the invention must confer some benefit upon mankind.[159]

[E] Patent Infringement

The patentee can enforce the patent against those who make, use, offer to sell, and sell the patented invention.[160] A patent is the most exclusive right in intellectual property law, and, as noted above, original creation and innocent infringement cannot be asserted as defenses to patent infringement. The Patent Act allows for injunctive relief and up to three times actual damages for certain infringements.[161] Patent infringement suits brought in federal district court can be appealed to the Court of Appeals for the Federal Circuit, a special appeals court created in 1982 in large part to handle the technicalities of patent litigation and to add a rational uniformity to patent law. Although the patentee enjoys a legislative presumption of validity of the patent, some courts have become notorious for appearing eager to strike down patents as being invalid. Thus, in litigation, the patentee runs the risk of having the patent invalidated after incurring the expense of obtaining the patent and defending it in the patent litigation. The effect can be economically devastating to a patentee who made these substantial expenditures in expectation that the patent would be validated.

§ 1.12 TRADEMARK LAW

[A] Generally

Unlike copyright and patent law, which are exclusively creatures of statute, the origins of trademark law are in the common law. Indeed, the earliest British trademark decisions seem very distant from our modern notions of intellectual property. At its origins, trademark was a kind of consumer protection law, designed to prevent merchants from passing off inferior goods by using well-established signs or labels.

Today, trademark law has come a long way from its beginnings, and federal statutes confer on proprietors of marks a broad range of property-like rights in symbolic features that identify the origin of products or services. A trademark can be a word, symbol, or device so long as it is used by a business to distinguish its goods from those of others.[162] Trademarks — brand names and other symbols of identity — such as Coca-Cola, the Pillsbury Dough Boy, and the golden arches of McDonald's surround us. These trade symbols are valuable to businesses and consumers. To their owners, a trade symbol is a marketing device, a focus of brand loyalty. To consumers, trade symbols allow the saving of time in deciding which product to buy and where to buy it. On the negative side, critics of trademark law

---

[159] *See Brenner v. Manson*, 383 U.S. 519 (1966).

[160] *See* 35 U.S.C. § 271.

[161] *See* 35 U.S.C. §§ 281–294.

[162] *See* 15 U.S.C. § 1127; *see generally* Restatement (Third) of Unfair Competition § 9 (Tent. Draft No. 2, Mar. 23, 1990).

believe that trade symbols create irrational brand loyalty, permitting the owner of a well-known mark to set his price for the product above the competitive price. As such, an overly strong trademark law creates entry barriers to new competition from lower priced products and more efficient competitors. Whatever the merits of these arguments, trademark law, like other branches of intellectual property law, is strongest and most developed in the Western countries.

Trademarks, unlike patents and copyrights, can theoretically last forever so long as they are used to distinguish goods or services. Trademarks can be abandoned by nonuse or can fall into the public domain — become the generic name of a product — if they no longer distinguish the goods or services. But ownership of a trademark is not subject to a specific duration and can theoretically endure in perpetuity.

Unlike copyright and patent law, trademark law is not the exclusive domain of federal law. Whereas a federal statute is the only source of copyright and patent law, trademark rights arise out of the state common law. The first trademark statutes in the United States were state laws, and even today the federal role is a coordinate (and theoretically) limited one.[163] Specifically, Congress' power to legislate is limited to interstate or foreign trade transactions. Meanwhile, the states continue to apply their own independent trademark systems locally. Where appropriate, federal courts may consider state law based trademark claims along with federal ones under the principle of pendant jurisdiction. In addition, the states and federal government both offer facilities for trademark registration, and these (especially the latter) are important from a practical standpoint.

[B] Federal Registration of Trademarks

The Lanham Act[164] establishes a registration system administered by the U.S. Patent and Trademark Office. Trademark registration is important from a practical standpoint. The registrant enjoys substantial procedural and substantive advantages beyond common law rights, as well as access to enhanced remedies in cases of infringement. Among these benefits are that: (1) the certificate of registration is *prima facie* evidence of the validity of the registration;[165] (2) registration is constructive notice to others of the claim of ownership;[166] (3) registration confers federal jurisdiction without regard to diversity of citizenship or amount in controversy;[167] (4) registration can become incontestable after five years of continuous use of the mark and will constitute the exclusive right to use of the mark;[168] (5) registration provides the right to treble damages, attorney's fees, and other remedies in an action for infringement;[169] and (6) registration provides the right to request customs officials to bar importation of goods bearing infringing

---

163 *See Trademark Cases*, 100 U.S. 82 (1879).

164 *See* 15 U.S.C. §§ 1051–1127.

165 *See* 15 U.S.C. § 1057(b).

166 *See* 15 U.S.C. § 1072.

167 *See* 15 U.S.C. § 1111.

168 *See* 15 U.S.C. § 1065.

169 *See* 15 U.S.C. §§ 1116–1120.

trademarks.[170] Taken as a whole, these advantages are a powerful inducement to register.

Federal trademark registration is obtained by filing an application in the Trademark Office. Once filed, an application is reviewed by a trademark examiner who verifies, among other things, that: (1) the mark is not deceptive; (2) the mark is not confusingly similar to another mark; and (3) the mark is not merely descriptive of the goods or misdescriptive of them, geographically descriptive or misdescriptive, or primarily merely a surname.[171] Although an applicant can base his application on an *intent to use* the mark in commerce as well as on *actual use*, registration will not issue until actual use of the mark is proven.[172]

The trademark examination process is neither as lengthy nor as costly as an examination of a patent. The trademark application is relatively simple to complete as compared with the patent application. Further, in contrast to pursuing a patent, prosecution before the Trademark Office does not require the aid of a special attorney admitted to practice before the agency. The trademark registration process, however, can be much more intricate and costly than filing for copyright registration.

[C] Federal Unfair Competition Law: Section 43(a) of the Lanham Act

Under both federal and state law, the first user of a distinctive mark may have an action against one who offers goods or services marked in a confusingly similar manner. Section 43(a) of the Lanham Act[173] specifically provides for relief in cases where there has been a so-called "false designation of origin," and state laws provide general relief against "passing off" as a form of "unfair competition." As the doctrine is understood, passing off takes place when a business makes a false representation likely to cause consumer confusion.

The classic example of passing off is infringement of trademark, which has been applied to protect names, words, and symbols associated with particular firms or their products. The notion of passing off is applied more broadly to other indicia of commercial identity such as packaging, product configuration, and labeling and may include the total image, advertising materials, and marketing techniques by which the product or service is presented to customers. Many of these commercial attributes, collectively known as "trade dress," do not qualify for federal trademark registration. Trade dress, however, may be protected under section 43(a) of the Lanham Act, which has enjoyed increasing vitality since the 1960s. The last several years have seen a vast increase in the number of suits brought under section 43(a) and in the scope of the holdings they have produced.[174]

---

170 *See* 15 U.S.C. § 1124.

171 *See* 15 U.S.C. § 1052(a), (d), (e).

172 *See* 15 U.S.C. § 1051(b)(1)(A).

173 15 U.S.C. §§ 1051–1127.

174 *See Two Pesos, Inc. v. Taco Cabana, Inc.*, 505 U.S. 763 (1992) (holding that a Mexican restaurant's total image is protectable trade dress based on a finding of inherent distinctiveness without proof that

Claims of passing off under section 43(a) and copyright infringement often overlap. For example, the plaintiff may have a copyright on a label or advertising material on its product. If the defendant closely imitates the label by creating a substantially similar label, an action can be brought for copyright infringement. In addition, if the defendant sells goods under the same or similar label, causing consumer confusion about the origin of the defendant's goods or services, an action for trademark and/or trade dress infringement may arise. Such protection goes further than copyright protection. First, protectable trademarks and trade dress may enjoy perpetual protection, so long as they are used and maintain their ability to indicate source. Second, unlike the situation in copyright, a third party user may not claim independent creation as a defense to an action in the nature of passing off. Conversely, trademark and trade dress protection is limited in some ways in which copyright is not. For example, distinctive trade dress will only be protected when third party use creates a likelihood of confusion.

[D] Trademark Infringement

A trademark is infringed when a third party without authorization uses a confusingly similar mark on similar goods or services.[175] The ultimate test is whether the concurrent use of the two marks would cause consumers to be mistaken or confused about the source of origin or sponsorship of the goods or services. Thus, the marks neither have to be identical nor used on identical products to be confusingly similar.

[E] Trademark Dilution

Generally speaking, a successful action for trademark infringement requires that the defendant's use of the plaintiff's mark causes confusion about the origin of products or services. Thus, if the trademark TIDE is used by a third party on another detergent or related product, such as a dishrag, the consumer would be confused as to the origin of the product. Alternatively, confusion would not take place if TIDE were used on an unrelated product such as apple juice or dog food. Owners of strong marks, ones widely recognized by consumers, *e.g.*, TIDE, have often argued that third party use on related products could dilute the distinctive quality of their mark and detract from their positive image. Antidilution laws found in about half the states have reflected these concerns and have been enforced to protect strong (if not always famous) marks[176] against third party use that would lead to the blurring of the distinctive character or tarnishment of the mark. In

the trade dress has secondary meaning). The Supreme Court somewhat cut back the scope of protection under section 43(a) in *Wal-Mart Stores, Inc. v. Samara Bros., Inc.*, 529 U.S. 205 (2000), holding that for a product design, as opposed to trade dress and packaging, a showing of acquired distinctiveness by secondary meaning is necessary.

[175] *See* 15 U.S.C. § 1052(d).

[176] *See, e.g., Wedgwood Homes, Inc. v. Lund*, 659 P.2d 377 (Or. 1993); *Deere & Co. v. MTD Products, Inc.*, 41 F.3d 39 (2d Cir. 1994) (finding that the use of altered, animated form of John Deere logo in advertisement constituted dilution under New York law).

1996,[177] Congress enacted the first federal cause of action for dilution to provide relief against the blurring or tarnishment of a *famous* mark.[178] The Federal Statute — commonly referred to as § 43(c) — limits antidilution protection to famous marks only and establishes criteria to determine whether a mark is famous.[179]

---

[177] The 1996 Act was substantially amended by the Trademark Dilution Revision Act of 2006, Pub. L. No. 109-312, 120 Stat. 1730 (2006).

[178] 15 U.S.C. § 1125(c).

[179] 15 U.S.C. § 1125(c)(2)(i)–(vi).

§ 1.13 CHART COMPARING COPYRIGHT, PATENT, AND TRADEMARK

	COPYRIGHT	PATENT[180]	TRADEMARK
SUBJECT MATTER	Literary, dramatic, and musical works; pantomimes and choreography; pictorial, graphic, and sculptural works; audiovisual works; sound recordings; architectural works	Utility patent: Functional features of products and processes Design patent: Ornamental designs for manufactured goods	Words, names, symbols, or devices
STANDARDS FOR VALIDITY	Originality and fixation in a tangible medium of expression	Utility patent: Novelty, nonobviousness, and utility Design patent: What is obvious to ordinary designer	Use of mark to distinguish one's goods or services
WHEN PROTECTION BEGINS	Upon fixation of original expression	When granted by U.S. Patent and Trademark Office	Upon use of mark
DURATION OF PROTECTION	Life of the author (or longest lived joint author) plus 70 years; or 95 years from publication or 120 years from creation, whichever expires first	Utility patent: Until 20 years from date filed Design patent: 14 years from date issued[181]	So long as properly used as trademark
STANDARDS FOR INFRINGE-MENT	Copying and improper appropriation	Utility patent: Mainly by making, using, or selling something covered by the claim language Design patent: Similarity of the designs to the ordinary observer[182]	Likelihood of confusion

[180] Summary omits patents for distinct and new plant varieties asexually reproduced, *i.e.*, without using seeds (same term of protection as utility patents). *See* 35 U.S.C. §§ 161–164.

[181] Extended to 15 years by the Patent Law Treaties Implementation Act of 2012, Pub. Law 112-211 (December 19, 2012).

[182] Extended to 15 years by the Patent Law Treaties Implementation Act of 2012, Pub. Law 112-211 (December 19, 2012).

§ 1.14 STATE INTELLECTUAL PROPERTY LAW

A diverse system of state intellectual property law plays a significant role in protecting intangible property. These areas of state law are variously known as: trade secret, unfair competition, common law copyright, right to publicity, and misappropriation. Two of the more important areas of traditional state protection are trade secret and unfair competition, which are analogous to patent and trademark law, respectively. Of less practical importance is common law copyright, which is almost entirely preempted by federal law. In addition to these traditional forms of state law protection, the right to publicity represents a relatively new body of law having similarities to both copyright and trademark law. Finally, an older form of state law, misappropriation law, is still available in appropriate cases. State protection of intangible property interests supplements federal protection and fills in gaps unattended by federal law.

[A] Trade Secrets

The Uniform Trade Secrets Act, adopted in various versions in a majority of states, defines a trade secret as follows:

> "Trade Secret" means information, including a formula, pattern, compilation, program, device, method, technique, or process, that: derives independent economic value, actual or potential, from not being generally known to, and not being readily ascertainable by proper means by, other persons who can obtain economic value from its disclosure or use, and is the subject of efforts that are reasonable under the circumstances.[183]

Trade secret law protects much the same technological information as does patent law, but trade secret subject matter is even broader, extending to customer lists, marketing plans, and other information not included within patentable subject matter.[184] In addition, a trade secret does not have to meet the rigorous standards of inventiveness required by patent law. For these reasons, some businesses decide not to seek patent protection if the risk of being rejected for lack of patentable subject matter or inventiveness is substantial and/or does not justify the time and expense of the patent application process.

Trade secrecy is, however, no general substitute for patent protection. One crucial difference is that a valid trade secret exists only if it is substantially "secret" within the trade secret owner's industry. Absolute secrecy is not required, but if the trade secret is widely used within the industry, it is less likely that it can be

[183] Uniform Trade Secrets Act, with 1985 Amendments § 1(4). The still influential Restatement of Torts § 757, Comment b (1939), defines a trade secret as consisting of: ". . . any formula, pattern, device or compilation of information which is used in one's business, which gives him an opportunity to obtain an advantage over competitors who do not know or use it. [A trade secret] may be a formula for a chemical compound; a process of manufacturing, treating or preserving materials; a pattern for a machine or other device; or a list of customers." *See also* Restatement (Third) of Unfair Competition § 39 (1995); *Metallurgical Industries, Inc. v. Fourtek, Inc.*, 790 F.2d 1195 (5th Cir. 1996).

[184] *See id.*

protected as a property right. Other factors that courts consider in determining whether secrecy exists are the following: the extent to which the subject matter is known by the employees in the trade secret owner's business and the extent of measures taken to guard the secrecy of the subject matter.[185]

Trade secrets have the attributes of property and can be licensed, taxed, and inherited.[186] But if an attribute of property is the right to exclude others from using it, the trade secret is a weak form of property protection. A trade secret can only be enforced against improper appropriation, such as theft by an industrial spy[187] or a breach of a confidential relationship not to divulge the trade secret. This is why it is often said that trade secret law protects a relationship rather than a property interest.

Trade secrets are a particularly appropriate form of protection for processes. By its nature, a process, such as the formula for making Coca-Cola, can be practiced secretly by a few people and is often difficult to determine by reverse engineering. Compared with the twenty-year patent monopoly, a trade secret may exist forever, so long as substantial secrecy exists. Thus, instead of seeking a patent for a process that will have to be publicly disclosed in the patent grant and whose patent protection will last only twenty years, many businesses prefer the trade secret status of their information in a gamble for a much longer term of protection.

[B] Unfair Competition Law

The term "unfair competition" is defined in two ways. It is sometimes used in the broadest sense as covering any cause of action against acts of "commercial immorality" among competitors. This would include actions for trade secret misappropriation, interference with contractual relations, predatory pricing, trademark infringement, product disparagement, and any other activity contrary to our notions of fair competitive practices.

"Unfair competition law" is most commonly used in referring to an action for "passing off," that is, an action against an individual that passes off its goods or services as someone else's. An action for unfair competition may involve trademark infringement; use of confusingly similar corporate names; use of similar titles of literary works, products, or containers; and trade dress similarities. False representations and false advertising would fall under this definition of unfair competition as well.[188]

---

[185] *See* Roger M. Milgrim, Trade Secrets § 2.01 (1988); *see also Rockwell Graphic Sys., Inc. v. DEV Industries, Inc.*, 925 F.2d 174 (7th Cir. 1991).

[186] The Supreme Court adopted this view in *Ruckelshaus v. Monsanto Co.*, 467 U.S. 986, 1001–04 (1984).

[187] *See, e.g.*, *E.I. du Pont de Nemours & Co. v. Christopher*, 431 F.2d 1012 (5th Cir. 1970) (stating aerial photography of a plant undergoing construction was an improper means of appropriating a trade secret).

[188] *See generally* Restatement (Third) of Unfair Competition §§ 2–6 (Tent. Draft No. 1, Apr., 12, 1988).

[C] Common Law Copyright

Under the 1909 Act, federal copyright protection began when an author published his work. Unpublished works were given protection, if at all, under state common law copyright. In contrast, the 1976 Act now protects works from the moment of creation — that is, when they are fixed in a tangible medium of expression.[189] In so doing, the 1976 Act specifically preempts state common law copyright.[190] Federal preemption will occur for a work *fixed in a tangible medium of expression* if the state law covers the subject matter of copyright and confers the same kinds of exclusive rights found in the federal Copyright Act.

Although federal preemption casts a long shadow, state common law copyright might play a role when a work is not fixed in a tangible medium of expression. Examples would include an oral interview or jazz improvisation. The states would not be precluded from protecting these nonfixed works under their own copyright laws. The underlying authority lies in the United States Constitution, which allows Congress to pass laws protecting "writings of authors."[191] Writings are generally recognized as works embodied in some kind of material form, the opposite of a purely oral or other nonfixed work.[192] Falling outside the constitutional authority of Congress, protection of oral or other nonfixed works could validly be regulated by state law. In practice, however, few courts have even considered copyright protection for oral works, but they have recognized its possibility.[193]

[D] The Right of Publicity

In 1953, a court[194] recognized for the first time an intangible property right called the "right of publicity."[195] A body of law had already developed around the right of privacy, prohibiting appropriation for commercial benefit of a person's name or likeness. If a private person's name or likeness is used to advertise a commercial product,[196] for example, the law would allow issuance of an injunction and would award appropriate damages for this invasion of private life, as well as the right to be let alone as a private citizen. However, when the persona of an athlete, a movie star, or other celebrity is exploited in this way, one cannot argue as persuasively that a privacy interest is invaded. Celebrities, by implication, have waived aspects of their privacy. The harm that occurs in these circumstances is a commercial one because the celebrity has been deprived of a property right in the fruit of his labors — *i.e.*, the ability to exploit commercially his name or picture.

---

[189] *See* 17 U.S.C. § 102(a).

[190] *See* 17 U.S.C. § 301(a).

[191] U.S. Const. art. I, § 8, cl. 8.

[192] *See Goldstein v. California*, 412 U.S. 546, 567–68 (1973).

[193] *See, e.g., Estate of Hemingway v. Random House, Inc.*, 244 N.E.2d 250 (N.Y. 1968). For a discussion of this case, see *infra* § 2.05.

[194] *Haelan Labs., Inc. v. Topps Chewing Gum, Inc.*, 202 F.2d 866 (2d Cir.), *cert. denied*, 346 U.S. 816 (1953).

[195] The leading treatise on the subject is J. THOMAS MCCARTHY, THE RIGHTS OF PUBLICITY AND PRIVACY (2d ed. 2008).

[196] *See Pavesich v. New England Life Ins.* 50 S.E. 68 (Ga. 1905).

The right to privacy relates to dignitary harm, whereas the right to publicity involves commercial harm. The two rights rest on distinct legal theories.

Some states have statutes protecting the right of publicity;[197] in others, the right is protected under the common law.[198] Whatever its form, the right of publicity is a more absolute right than either trademark or unfair competition rights and is based on a theory of unjust enrichment. To prevail in an action for the right of publicity, one does not have to show confusion of source of sponsorship or falsity as in an action for trademark infringement. Rather, the aggrieved plaintiff in an action for right of publicity must only show the appropriation of goodwill in the use of his or her name or likeness.

The right of publicity has continued to expand beyond its traditional domain of names and likenesses. Recent case law has used the publicity doctrine to protect attributes concerning other aspects of the identity and image of a celebrity. These have included prohibitions against a Bette Midler sound-alike in a commercial,[199] the use of the phrase "Here's Johnny" by a seller of portable toilets,[200] and an advertisement showing a robot resembling Vanna White in a game show.[201]

In addition to the ever-expanding scope of the publicity right, the duration of the right is another controversial area. Whether the right of publicity survives the death of a celebrity varies from state to state.[202] Some courts[203] and state statutes[204] have recognized its descendibility, while others have declared that it ends on death,[205] like the right to privacy. A number of state statutes recognize its descendibility but, like copyright law, limit its duration to prevent distant generations from claiming the right. The policy favoring the right of publicity,

---

197 *See* Cal. Civ. Code § 3344.

198 *See Hirsch v. S.C. Johnson & Son, Inc.*, 280 N.W.2d 129 (Wis. 1979).

199 *Midler v. Ford Motor Co.*, 849 F.2d 460 (9th Cir. 1988).

200 *Carson v. Here's Johnny Portable Toilets, Inc.*, 698 F.2d 831 (6th Cir. 1983).

201 *White v. Samsung Elecs. Am., Inc.*, 971 F.2d 1395 (9th Cir. 1992), *pet. for reh'g and reh'g en banc denied*, 989 F.2d 1512 (9th Cir. 1993). Worthy of particular attention is Judge Alex Kozinski's dissenting opinion questioning the overprotection of celebrity image under an ever expanding cause of action for right of publicity: "Overprotecting intellectual property is as harmful as underprotecting it. Creativity is impossible without a rich public domain." 989 F.2d at 1513.

202 A fascinating battle has erupted over the post-mortem rights to exploit Marilyn Monroe's image. Two federal district courts initially held that CMG did not have standing to sue because Monroe could not devise property in her will that did not exist at the time of her death in 1962. *See Shaw Family Archives, Ltd. v. CMG Worldwide, Inc.*, 486 F. Supp. 2d 309 (S.D.N.Y. 2007). After California amended its statute to expressly make its post-mortem right retroactive, both courts ruled that Monroe was domiciled in New York, rather than California, at the time of her death. *See Milton H. Greene Archives, Inc. v. CMG Worldwide, Inc.*, 568 F. Supp. 2d 1152 (C.D. Cal. 2008). Because New York does not recognize a post-mortem right of publicity, the rulings (if upheld on appeal) will cast Monroe's image into the public domain.

203 *See, e.g., Martin Luther King, Jr. Ctr. for Soc. Change, Inc. v. American Heritage Prods., Inc.*, 694 F.2d 674 (11th Cir. 1983).

204 *See, e.g.*, Cal. Civ. Code § 990.

205 *See, e.g., Memphis Dev. Found. v. Factors, Etc.*, 616 F.2d 956 (6th Cir. 1980) (declining to recognize a post-mortem right of publicity in Elvis Presley's persona).

much less its descendibility, is dubious at best.[206] Supporters of the right and its descendibility maintain that it encourages artistic creativity, as does federal copyright law. Those opposing the right argue that, even if it encourages commercial exploitation of celebrity persona, other branches of intellectual property, such as trademark and unfair competition, rest on sounder assumptions, which support many of the same interests as the right of publicity.[207]

[E] Misappropriation

The misappropriation doctrine is the broadest, if not the vaguest, theory protecting intangibles under state law. The doctrine traces its name to the United States Supreme Court decision in *International News Service v. Associated Press*.[208] In this case, the INS, a news gathering organization, systematically gathered "hot" news stories from the AP's publicly distributed newspapers and bulletin boards, which it was able to send to its subscribers on the West Coast, sometimes actually beating AP newspapers to publication. The activity engaged in by INS, the appropriation of news, did not fit into the traditional areas of intellectual property. Gathering the news from public sources involved no breach of trust on which to base an action for theft of trade secrets; there was no passing off to justify an action for unfair competition; nor did the INS engage in copyright infringement. Despite this lack of traditional intellectual property protection, the Supreme Court held that the INS activities constituted a new variety of unfair competition called "misappropriation." It enjoined the INS from using AP news reports until the commercial value of the news (its "hotness") had dissipated. The Court recognized not a general property right in the news, but a quasi-property right in "hot, breaking news," which protected the originator from its competitor. In his dissent, Justice Brandeis stated that the majority was conferring monopoly rights in an idea that should be in the public domain and that protection of intangibles should be left to traditional forms of intellectual property protection.

The decision in *Erie Railroad Co. v. Tompkins*[209] effectively invalidated many prior exercises in federal judicial law making, including that in *INS*. But the misappropriation doctrine continues to exist on the fringes of intellectual property law. Applied equitably, causes of action for misappropriation have been successful where the traditional forms of intellectual property protection do not apply but where a need for protection exists. The strong cases have typically arisen when: (1) A, by substantial investment, has created an intangible of value not protected by patent, trademark, or copyright law, or breach of confidence, which is (2) appropriated by B, a free rider, at little cost, (3) thereby injuring A and

---

206 For an overview of these critiques see Marshall Leaffer, *The Right of Publicity, A Comparative View*, 70 Alb. L. Rev. 1357 (2008).

207 *Cf.* David Lange, *Recognizing the Public Domain*, 44 Law & Contemp. Probs. 147 (1981). *But see* Peter L. Felcher & Edward L. Rubin, *The Descendibility of the Right of Publicity: Is There Commercial Life After Death?*, 89 Yale L.J. 1125 (1980).

208 248 U.S. 215 (1918). For an overview of the doctrine, see Leo Raskind, *The Misappropriation Doctrine as a Competitive Norm of Intellectual Property Law*, 75 Minn. L. Rev. 875 (1991). For further discussion of this case in the context of federal preemption, see *infra* § 11.02[B].

209 304 U.S. 64 (1938).

jeopardizing A's continued production of the intangible.[210] Under this theory, the Metropolitan Opera was able to enjoin the unauthorized recording of its broadcasts.[211] Similarly, before sound recordings were given protection by a federal law in 1971, tape piracy was attacked under the misappropriation doctrine.[212] Although the plaintiffs were unable to base their claim on traditional bodies of intellectual property law, they succeeded under the misappropriation doctrine in both situations.

Some courts have expressed a hostility toward the misappropriation doctrine, claiming that it conflicts with the policy underlying federal patent and copyright law and is therefore preempted under the Supremacy Clause of the Constitution. In 1929, Judge Learned Hand refused to apply the doctrine to dress design piracy on this ground.[213] And in the 1964 *Sears, Roebuck and Co. v. Stiffel Co.*[214] and *Compco Corp. v. DayBrite Lighting, Inc.*[215] cases, the Supreme Court struck down Illinois unfair competition law as clashing with the policies of federal patent law. In addition to case law hostile to the doctrine, § 301 of the 1976 Copyright Act expressly preempts state laws that cover the same ground as federal copyright.[216] Despite these contrary trends, the misappropriation doctrine still appears to be alive and has occasionally been applied.[217] In what form misappropriation will survive into the next millennium remains, for now, unsettled.[218]

---

[210] *See also* J. Thomas McCarthy, Trademarks and Unfair Competition § 10.51 (4th ed. 2009).

[211] *Metropolitan Opera Ass'n v. Wagner-Nichols Recorder Corp.*, 199 Misc. 787 (N.Y. Sup. Ct. 1950), *aff'd*, 279 A.D. 632 (N.Y. App. Div. 1951).

[212] *See Goldstein v. California*, 412 U.S. 546 (1973).

[213] *Cheney Bros. v. Doris Silk Corp.*, 35 F.2d 279 (2d Cir. 1929).

[214] 376 U.S. 225 (1964).

[215] 376 U.S. 234 (1964).

[216] For a full discussion of the misappropriation doctrine and the preemptive effect of 17 U.S.C. § 301(a), see *infra* Chapter 11.

[217] For example, misappropriation was the theory used to enjoin the Chicago Board of Trade when it proposed the sale of stock market index contracts based on the Dow Jones Average. The intangible value was the valuable information embodied in the Dow Jones Average. *See Board of Trade v. Dow Jones & Co.*, 439 N.E.2d 526 (Ill. 1982); *Standard & Poor's Corp. v. Commodities Exch., Inc.*, 683 F.2d 704 (2d Cir. 1982). In 1997, the vitality of the misappropriation doctrine was strongly confirmed in *National Basketball Ass'n, Inc. v. Motorola*, 105 F.3d 841 (2d Cir. 1997) (discussing the misappropriation doctrine at length, although ultimately finding preemption on the specific facts). *See also Associated Press v. All Headline News*, 608 F. Supp. 2d 454 (S.D.N.Y. 2009) (holding that a distributor of breaking news on the Internet is subject to a "hot news misappropriate claim under New York state law).

[218] The continued vitality of the misappropriation doctrine apparently was confirmed in *Barclay's Capital, Inc. v. Theflyonthewall.com, Inc.*, 650 F.3d 876 (2d Cir. 2011) (discussing misappropriation at length, although ultimately finding preemption on specific facts).

Chapter 2

SUBJECT MATTER OF COPYRIGHT: GENERAL STANDARDS

§ 2.01 INTRODUCTION AND CHAPTER OVERVIEW

The threshold requirement for copyrightability is set forth in § 102(a) of the Copyright Act: "Copyright protection subsists, in accordance with this title, in original works of authorship fixed in any tangible medium of expression, now known or later developed, from which they can be perceived, reproduced, or otherwise communicated, either directly or with the aid of a machine or device."[1]

Section 102(a) establishes two fundamental requirements for copyright protection: originality and fixation. By comparison, § 102(b) denies protection to any "idea, procedure, process, system, method of operation, concept, principle, or discovery . . . ."[2] This chapter examines the meaning of these statutory provisions to understand what Congress can do pursuant to its constitutional authority "To Promote the Progress of Science . . ., by securing for limited Times to Authors . . . the exclusive Right to their . . . Writings . . . ."[3]

Additionally, this chapter — which is divided into four parts — examines the basic standards for copyrightability. Parts I and II examine the meaning of fixation and originality. Part III involves the copyrightability of derivative works and compilations, and primarily focuses on what constitutes originality for works that are substantially based on other copyrighted works or public domain materials. Part IV addresses the noncopyrightable subject matter set forth in § 102(b) and other related topics, including the copyrightability of "immoral" works and governmental works.

---

[1] 17 U.S.C. § 102(a).

[2] 17 U.S.C. § 102(b).

[3] As to whether the writings of authors constitute "Science" or "useful Arts," even the Supreme Court has seemed uncertain. In *Bleistein v. Donaldson Lithographing Co.*, 188 U.S. 239 (1903), the Court assumed the latter. But more recently, in *Graham v. John Deere Co.*, 383 U.S. 1 (1966), the Court proceeded on the view that, in eighteenth century usage, "Science" referred to the products of authors and "useful Arts" to the works of inventors. In light of the order in which the Framers placed both "Authors and Inventors" and "Writings and Discoveries," the better view probably is that "Science and useful Arts" have the meanings attributed to them in *Graham*. Hence, the usage in the text above.

Part I. FIXATION

§ 2.02 FIXATION AND THE DISTINCTION BETWEEN THE MATERIAL OBJECT AND THE COPYRIGHT

Under the Copyright Clause of the U.S. Constitution, Congress may make laws to protect the "Writings" of Authors. The "writings" requirement has been construed by the Supreme Court to mean any "physical rendering" of the fruits of the author's creativity.[4] The fixation requirement arises in two portions of the Copyright Act. First, under § 102(a) of the Act, a work is incapable of protection under federal law unless it is "fixed" in a "tangible medium of expression." Second, fixation also plays a role in determining whether a defendant has infringed a copyright. Section 106(1) of the Act provides that the copyright owner has the exclusive right to "reproduce the copyrighted work in copies or phonorecords."[5] The Act defines "copies" as "material objects . . . in which a work is fixed . . . ." Accordingly, a defendant does not infringe the right to reproduce unless he or she has reproduced the copyrighted work in fixed form.

As the statutory language indicates, copyright subsists in "works of authorship." An "author" in the constitutional sense means *the person to whom anything owes its origin*. The creator of a work is its author.[6] Thus, a copyright comes into existence when an author takes the affirmative step of placing his or her work on a material object such as a piece of paper, digital media (*e.g.*, a CD), or a block of marble. Unlike a patent, which is conferred by the act of the government, a copyright is created by the act of an author in fixing the work in a tangible medium of expression.[7] After creating the work in this manner, the author may register[8] his or her claim to copyright in the Copyright Office; however, the act of registration does not *create* the copyright.

An important preliminary distinction must be made between the copyright and the material object.[9] Copyright is an interest in an intangible property right called a work of authorship that, to qualify for statutory protection, must be fixed in a material object. A copyright springs into existence when both a work of authorship and a material object merge through the act of fixation. The Copyright Act enumerates seven broad categories of works of authorship,[10] each of which may be

---

[4] *Goldstein v. California*, 412 U.S. 546 (1973).

[5] *See* 17 U.S.C. § 101 (copies).

[6] *See Burrow-Giles Lithographic Co. v. Sarony*, 111 U.S. 53, 58 (1884). It can be assumed that the term "author" means human author. For a discussion of computer authored works, see *infra* § 3.07.

[7] *See* 17 U.S.C. § 102(a).

[8] *See* 17 U.S.C. § 408.

[9] *See* 17 U.S.C. § 202. The Copyright Act establishes that:

> Ownership of the material object or any of the exclusive rights under a copyright is distinct from ownership of any material object in which the work is embodied. Transfer of ownership of any material object . . . does not in itself convey rights in the copyrighted work embodied in the object.

[10] These are: (1) literary works, (2) musical works (including words), (3) dramatic works, (4)

embodied in a variety of material objects. Suppose, for example, that A writes a novel. For copyright purposes, A's novel would fall under the category of a literary work,[11] one composed of words or symbols. A's novel could be embodied on paper, printed on microfiche, or recorded on digital media, such as an audio CD. There is but a single work of authorship, the literary work, no matter how numerous or diverse the material objects on which the work is placed.[12]

Although fixation of a work may take place on an infinite variety of material objects, the Copyright Act defines all material objects in terms of two broad categories: copies and phonorecords. Phonorecords are objects in which sounds are fixed, whereas copies are a residual category consisting of all material objects that are not phonorecords.[13] Thus, copies and phonorecords comprise all the material objects in which works are capable of being fixed.

§ 2.03 TANGIBLE MEDIUM OF EXPRESSION

[A] The Fixation Requirement: Generally

For the purpose of the Copyright Act, "[a] work is fixed in a tangible medium of expression when its embodiment in a copy of phonorecord, by or under the authority of the author, is sufficiently permanent or stable to permit it to be perceived, reproduced, or otherwise communicated for more than a transitory duration".[14] Thus, work is fixed in a tangible form when it is placed in a relatively stable and permanent embodiment for more than a transitory duration so that it can be recorded or written in some way. Thus, mere performance of a work does not qualify under this provision. No matter how innovative, ingenious, or beautiful a performance by an improvisational theater group or jazz musician, the basic standard of fixation would not be met, and statutory copyright protection could not be obtained without a recordation in some form. As the House Report states: "the definition of fixation would exclude from the concept purely evanescent or transient reproductions such as those projected briefly on a screen, shown electronically on a television or other cathode ray tube, or captured momentarily in the memory of a computer.[15]

---

pantomimes and choreographic works, (5) pictorial works, (6) motion pictures and other audiovisual works, and (7) sound recordings. *See* 17 U.S.C. § 102. Included as well are compilations and derivative works. *See* 17 U.S.C. § 103.

[11] "Literary works are works . . . expressed in words, numbers, or other verbal or numerical symbols or indicia, regardless of the nature of the material objects, such as books, periodicals, manuscripts, phonorecords, film, tapes, disks, or cards, in which they are embodied." 17 U.S.C. § 101 (literary works). The term "literary works" also includes computer databases. *See* H.R. Rep. No. 94-1476, at 54 (1976).

[12] *See* H.R. Rep. No. 94-1476, at 53 (1976).

[13] Professor Nimmer argues that "an unnecessary complexity in a necessarily complex statute could have been avoided by defining copies to include all material objects in which works of authorship are fixed, regardless of whether or not the work itself consists of sound." Nimmer on Copyright § 2.03[C] (2014).

[14] 17 U.S.C. § 101(fixed).

[15] *See* H.R. Rep. No. 94-1476, at 53 (1976).

The fixation requirement directly relates to the Copyright Clause of the Constitution, which limits the grant of copyright to writings of authors.[16] Only works that qualify as writings may claim federal copyright protection. The Supreme Court has construed the "writings" requirement to mean any physical rendering of the fruits of intellectual activity.[17] Thus, the physical rendering should take some material form capable of identification and have a more or less permanent endurance.

In construing the fixation requirement courts have emphasized the stability of the media in work is embodied or the duration of the embodiment without taking into account the second part of the definition, that is whether the duration of the work existed long enough so that it could be 'perceived, reproduced, or otherwise communicated." For example, in *Kelly v. Chicago Park District*[18] the court held that plaintiff's ambitious wildflower display in Chicago's Grant Park was not fixed in a tangible medium of expression. It acknowledged that the pictorial design of a garden may be "fixed" when printed on paper or stored in a computer, and that the living plants constituting the garden are "tangible and can be perceived to be perceived, reproduced, or otherwise communicated for more than a transitory duration." Nonetheless, the court held that the garden itself was "not stable or permanent enough to be called 'fixed'" within the meaning of § 101, because "[s]eeds and plants in a garden are naturally in a state of perpetual change; they germinate, grow, bloom, become dormant, and eventually die. . . . [A garden] may endure from season to season, but its nature is one of dynamic change."[19] In similar fashion another court held that a video stream[20] would be too evanescent or transient to meet the requirement of tangibility.

[B] "Fixed Under the Authority of the Author"

To obtain copyright, the author herself or someone under her authorization[21] must reduce the work to a relatively stable form. Only then may an author control the performance of her work by third parties. Suppose that A, a performance artist, recites a spontaneous poetic monologue, which is recorded by B, a member of the audience. The recordation would not constitute a "fixation" for the purpose of copyright because the author did not authorize it. Thus, A would not be able to control B's exploitation of the piece. What should A do to avoid this "non-fixation" problem? A should record the poetic work on magnetic tape *before* the performance. The work would then be fixed and third parties would infringe the copyright if they reproduced the work or performed it without permission.

---

[16] U.S. Const. art. I, § 8, cl. 8: "To promote the Progress of Science and useful Arts, by securing for limited Times to Authors and Inventors the exclusive Right to their respective Writings and Discoveries."

[17] *Goldstein v. California*, 412 U.S. 546 (1973).

[18] 635 F.3d 290 (7th Cir. 2011).

[19] *Id.* at 305.

[20] *Cartoon Network v. CSC Holdings, Inc.*, 536 F.3d 121 (2d Cir. 2008) that a buffer copy of a video stream that lasted for only 1.2 seconds was not fixed because it did not last for "a period of more than a transitory duration." This case and discussion of the role of "fixation" for copyright law on the Internet is discussed in more detail in § 8.04 [A].

[21] *See* H.R. Rep. No. 94-1476, at 53 (1976).

Obviously, the author should "fix" her work beforehand. This is not always possible for works that are created spontaneously, but would a simultaneous fixation of the work as it is being performed qualify for copyright? For live broadcasts, the Copyright Act provides protection when the work is being simultaneously recorded. Customarily, a simultaneous recording is carried out for most broadcasts. There is, however, a gap in the law for non-broadcasted works, that is, for works that are not being simultaneously transmitted[22] beyond the place where they are being performed. Even though they may be simultaneously recorded, they are not covered by this provision, which requires transmission. Non-broadcasted works would thus be in jeopardy of appropriation by someone in the audience making an unauthorized recording. One solution to this problem is to have the performance telephoned to another location, thereby meeting the transmission requirement.[23]

[C] Perception by Machine or Device

The fixation requirement will be satisfied if the work as fixed can be perceived either directly or with the aid of a machine or device.[24] The fixation can take place in any manner, form, or medium. It makes no difference if the work is written in words, numbers, notes, sounds, pictures, or other symbols, so long as they can be perceived either directly or by any machine or device existing now or developed at a later time. The broad language of the Copyright Act is intended to overturn a famous and much criticized case under the 1909 Act, *White-Smith Music Publishing Co. v. Apollo Co.*,[25] which held that a piano roll was not a copy of the musical composition embodied on it and therefore did not qualify for copyright protection because there must be a printed record in intelligible notation, readable to the eye. The *White-Smith* doctrine was applied to both phonorecords and magnetic tape, neither of which embody intelligible, human eye-readable written notation. Today, under the Copyright Act, the *White-Smith* doctrine is completely overruled, allowing copyrightability for sound recordings, computer programs, motion pictures, and other works embodied on objects that cannot be read without a machine or device.[26]

---

[22] To transmit is to communicate a performance "by any device or process whereby images or sounds are received beyond the place from which they are sent." 17 U.S.C. § 101.

[23] *See* Nimmer on Copyright § 1.08[C][2] (2014).

[24] *See* 17 U.S.C. § 102(a).

[25] 209 U.S. 1 (1908).

[26] The House Report makes this clear: "This broad language is intended to avoid the artificial and largely unjustifiable distinctions, derived from cases such as *White-Smith Music Publishing Co. v. Apollo Co.*, 209 U.S. 1 (1908)." H.R. Rep. No. 94-1476, at 52 (1976).

[D] Fixation and the Digital Challenge: RAM Copies and Videogames

[1] RAM Copies

The digital age has challenged the doctrine of fixation as never before. In today's world we are able to reproduce works in ways not contemplated by the Copyright Act. For example, how the law treat RAM copies or buffer copies that our computer's make every time we open an image on the internet by placing it in temporary, Random-Access memory (RAM) so that it can be viewed on the computer screen. Whether RAM copies or buffer copies are fixed has received more attention in the infringement context. Initially, in *MAI Systems Corp. v. Peak Computer Inc.*,[27] the court held that the loading of the plaintiff's copyrighted software into RAM constituted a fixation and qualified as a "copy" under the Copyright Act for purposes of infringement analysis because the copy could be "perceived, reproduced or communicated." Although the specific result of *MAI* was overturned in 1998 by Title III of the Digital Millennium Copyright Act,[28] the court's reasoning was not rejected by Congress. To the contrary, Congress appeared to accept implicitly the holding of *MAI* in drafting other portions of the DMCA. Despite academic criticism of the *MAI* decision, courts have consistently accepted it's holding that a work can be electronically "fixed" in RAM for purposes of the Act.[29]

[2] Videogames

The fixation requirement has been extensively analyzed in cases involving actions for infringement of copyrighted videogames.[30] For this kind of entertainment, visual images and sounds are produced by computer programs stored in various memory devices. When the game is not being played, the images are repetitive, but during play, they are subject to variation by human intervention.[31] The defendants in several cases have claimed that they were free to copy the plaintiffs' games because the games were not fixed in a tangible medium of expression but were rather ephemeral projections on a cathode ray tube. In addition, the variations of image patterns due to the different skills of those playing the games prevented a sufficiently consistent pattern to constitute a fixation of the work. The case law has universally renounced this reasoning.

---

27 991 F.2d 511 (9th Cir. 1993),

28 Codified at 17 U.S.C. § 117(c).

29 The RAM copy issue is discussed more extensively in

30 *Tandy Corp. v. Personal Micro Computers, Inc.*, 524 F. Supp. 171 (N.D. Cal. 1981); *Stern Elecs., Inc. v. Kaufman*, 523 F. Supp. 635 (E.D.N.Y. 1981); *Atari, Inc. v. Amusement World, Inc.*, 547 F. Supp. 222 (D. Md. 1981); *Atari, Inc. v. North Am. Philips Consumer Elecs. Corp.*, 672 F.2d. 607 (7th Cir. 1982); *Williams Elec., Inc. v. Arctic Int'l, Inc.*, 685 F.2d 870 (3d Cir. 1982).

31 "Video games . . . can roughly be described as computers programmed to create on a television screen cartoons in which some of the action is controlled by the player." *Stern Elec.*, 669 F.2d at 853.

In *Stern Electronics., Inc. v. Kaufman*,[32] the question whether the statutory fixation requirement was met arose since the audiovisual images were transient and could not be fixed. The court held that the audiovisual game was "permanently embodied in a material object, the memory devices, from which it could be perceived with the aid of the other components of the game."[33] These memory devices, called ROMs (read only memory), are tiny computer chips containing thousands of pieces of data, which store the instructions of the computer program. A microprocessor executes the program, causing the game to operate. The fixation requirement is met when the computer program is embodied in the ROM device. There is nothing startling about the holding in *Stern* once it is understood that the ROM is the material object, and the copyrighted work is the computer program embodied in it.

Another issue litigated in the videogame cases is whether the player's participation prevents the fixing of the audiovisual patterns. In *Williams Electronics Inc. v. Artic International, Inc.*,[34] the court rejected this claim, concluding that there is always a repetitive sequence of a substantial portion of the sights and sounds of the game, whether in the play mode or the attract mode. In other words, many aspects of the display remain constant from game to game regardless of how the player operates the controls. The fixation requirement does not require that the work be written down or recorded somewhere exactly as the eye perceives it. Rather, all that is necessary is that the work is capable of being perceived with the aid of a machine or device.[35]

§ 2.04 THE ANTI-BOOTLEG PROVISIONS: AN EXCEPTION TO THE FIXATION REQUIREMENT?

The American requirement of "fixation" as a precondition for copyright protection is not characteristic of "authors' rights" laws around the world. Many countries protect fixed and unfixed works without differentiation. Neither the Berne Convention, to which the United States acceded effective March 1, 1989, nor the Universal Copyright Convention, to which the United States has been a party since 1955, limits member states to protecting fixed works. Until the passage of the anti-bootleg provisions under the Uruguay Round Agreements Act,[36] the fixation requirement constituted a major obstacle to an effective remedy for the unauthorized fixation of live performances. Effective December 8, 1994, the unauthorized fixation of sound recordings and music videos of live *musical* performances is rendered illegal.

The practice of bootlegging live musical performances of U.S. artists has presented a legal quandary for performers of music. As discussed above, federal copyright's fixation requirement has deprived performing artists of an effective cause of action against the unauthorized fixation of live performances. As already stated, a work is fixed only when embodied in a tangible medium "by or under the

[32] 669 F.2d 852 (2d Cir. 1982).

[33] *Id.* at 856.

[34] 685 F.2d 870 (3d Cir. 1982).

[35] *See Midway Mfg. Co. v. Artic Int'l, Inc.*, 547 F. Supp. 999 (N.D. Ill. 1982).

[36] Pub. L. No. 103-465, 108 Stat. 4809 (1994).

authority of the author." As a result, there are commercially valuable types of cultural artifacts — notably, live musical performances — which are not fixed when recorded without authorization but which the United States has an interest in protecting against unauthorized exploitation. For example, suppose an unauthorized recording (or "bootleg") of a live musical performance by a U.S. performer is made in a foreign country. A mechanical compulsory license fee might be paid for the musical composition, but no permission is sought from, nor royalties paid to, the performers. The reason is that performances are not "works" within the meaning of the Berne Convention, and although the Rome Convention does protect performers, the United States is not a party to the latter.

The problem was addressed in the past through various state anti-bootlegging and unfair competition laws, and by common law copyright. Performers have sought relief against acts taking place in individual states, with varying success; however, recourse against international trade in bootleg sound recordings has been largely elusive. Effective copyright enforcement against international bootlegging depends on the U.S. Customs Service stopping entry of the recording at the border. The Customs Service does not, as a rule, enforce rights under state law. Once bootleg recordings make their way into the stream of commerce, from a practical standpoint, their further sale and distribution become impossible to curtail. Consequently, lack of effective border enforcement, pursuant to a uniform federal law, has led to a vibrant international trade in bootleg recordings.

The Uruguay Round Agreements Act, designed to implement U.S. obligations under the new World Trade Organization (previously known as the GATT), has provided civil and criminal remedies to combat the bootleg trade. A new Chapter 11 of the Copyright Act grants performers a civil cause of action for the unauthorized making, fixation, and trafficking[37] in sound recordings and music videos. Section 1101 of the Act makes it illegal to fix the sounds or sounds and images of a live musical performance in a copy or phonorecord, or to reproduce copies or phonorecords of such a performance from an unauthorized fixation.[38] It is also illegal to transmit to the public or distribute any copy or phonorecord embodying the unauthorized recording. Persons who engage in such activities are subject to all the remedies for infringement under copyright.[39] Supplementing the civil cause of action are criminal provisions that subject the unauthorized fixation of and trafficking in sound recordings, music videos, or live musical performances to criminal penalties.[40]

The anti-bootleg provisions in the new Chapter 11 of the Copyright Act represent a departure from a basic tenet of U.S copyright law. For the first time, a remedy is given for works that are not fixed by the author in a tangible medium of expression. This and other aspects of the enactment raise some difficult issues of constitutionality. One fundamental question is whether the "anti-bootlegging" provisions are

[37] "[T]he term 'traffic in' means transport, transfer, or otherwise dispose of, to another, as consideration for anything of value, or make or obtain control of with intent to transport, transfer or dispose of." *Id.*

[38] 17 U.S.C. § 1101(a)(1).

[39] For infringement remedies, see 17 U.S.C. §§ 502–505.

[40] *See* 18 U.S.C. § 2319A.

rights under copyright or whether they fall into a *sui generis* category outside the realm of copyright.

Section 1101 (3) provides that those who violate a performer's rights "shall be subject to the remedies provided in §§ 502 through 505, to the same extent as an infringer of copyright." The language of the enactment suggests that the anti-bootleg provisions were intended to fall under copyright. But this is hardly clear because the anti-bootlegging right is not subject to a specific duration. As such, one may question whether they are consistent with the "limited times" provisions embodied in the Copyright Clause of the Constitution. Even if one assumes that the anti-bootlegging right is subject to the same duration as copyright, it raises other constitutional problems. For example, the Constitution's Copyright Clause grants Congress the authority to protect for limited times the *writings* of authors. Unfixed musical performances, whatever they may be, are certainly not writings in the constitutional meaning of that term. This raises a serious question whether Congress had the authority to incorporate the anti-bootlegging provisions into federal law at all. In *U.S. v. Moghadam*[41] the Court of Appeals for the Eleventh Circuit rejected a constitutional challenge, stating that the "Copyright Clause does not envision that Congress is positively forbidden from extending copyright protection under other constitutional clauses, such as the commerce clause, to works of authorship that may not meet the fixation requirement inherent in the term 'writings.'" In dicta, however, the decision stated that the apparently perpetual protection provided by statute might prove "fundamentally inconsistent with the 'Limited Times' requirement of the Copyright Clause." Because the criminal defendant had not raised that issue, the court reserved the question for another day. Despite the misgivings of the *Moghadam* court, other courts have confirmed the constitutionality of the civil provisions of the anti-bootlegging statute,[42] and its criminal provisions have passed muster as well.[43]

Constitutional problems aside, are the anti-bootlegging provisions the beginning of a full-range demise of the fixation principal? Although the anti-bootlegging provisions are limited to musical works, one may ask whether these provisions will be extended eventually to prohibit the unauthorized fixation of live performances covering the entire range of copyrightable subject matter (*i.e.*, literary and dramatic works).

---

[41] 175 F.3d 1269, 1280 (11th Cir. 1999).

[42] *See, e.g.*, *KISS Catalog v. Passport Int'l Prods.*, 350 F. Supp. 2d 823 (N.D. Cal. 2004), *on reconsideration*, 405 F. Supp. 2d 1169 (N.D. Cal. 2005) (holding on reconsideration that § 1101 is constitutional).

[43] *See, e.g.*, *United States v. Martignon*, 492 F.3d 140, 151 (2d Cir. 2007), (holding that 18 U.S.C. § 2319A does not "secure" an exclusive right within the meaning of the Copyright Clause, because it "does not create and bestow property rights upon authors or inventors, or allocate those rights among claimants to them," but instead is only a criminal prohibition). Because the law was not a "copyright" law, it could be upheld under the Commerce Clause. *Id.* at 152–53.

§ 2.05 WORKS NOT FIXED IN A TANGIBLE MEDIUM OF EXPRESSION: COMMON LAW COPYRIGHT

So far, the discussion has focused on works fixed in a tangible medium of expression and qualifying for federal copyright protection.[44] How, if at all, can one protect the creative effort of those works that are not fixed and thus do not qualify for protection under federal copyright law? Due to their inherently vague nature, oral works present difficult problems of proof of their existence and ownership. Apart from these difficult practical problems, there is little case law directly establishing state protection under a common law copyright theory.[45] Only one state court has suggested that protection could be effected by this means. In *Hemingway v. Random House, Inc.*,[46] A. E. Hochner, a friend of Hemingway, kept a meticulous record of Hemingway's reflections on a range of matters and published a book, *Papa Hemingway*, based largely on these oral musings. Although the New York Court of Appeals did not find common law copyright infringement on the part of Hochner's publisher, Random House, the court suggested that there could be situations in which an interlocutor utters statements protectable under state law; however, it must be clear from the circumstances that the speaker intended to create a property interest in his oral work. The speaker should, at least, mark off the utterance from common speech to demonstrate that he meant to adopt it as a unique statement and to control its publication. The court was apparently concerned about the problem of determining what constituted the work in question and whether an infringement or misuse of the work by third parties had taken place.

In *Falwell v. Penthouse International, Ltd.*,[47] the court once again suggested that common law copyright for oral statements is an available form of protection in the appropriate case even though it denied the Reverend Jerry Falwell's claim on this basis. Falwell had given an interview to a reporter from *Penthouse Magazine* that was published without his consent in the magazine. In rejecting Falwell's claim of common law copyright infringement, the court found that nowhere had the Reverend identified the subject matter of his claim by design or implication. In addition, the court expressed a fear of nuisance suits brought by celebrities claiming protection for their oral statements. The court did leave open the possibility, however, of common law copyright protection for oral expression under narrow

---

[44] Until the 1976 Copyright Act, the American law of copyright was based on the dichotomy between federal and state law. Unpublished works were the domain of state common law copyright. Once a work was published, federal protection began, and the state law or common law copyright was divested. Under the 1976 Act, federal protection begins when a work is fixed. 17 U.S.C. § 102(a). Thus, if common law copyright is still available at all, it would apply to works not fixed in a tangible medium, consisting of oral works and performances. Unlike the 1976 Act, many "authors' rights" laws around the world do not differentiate between fixed and unfixed works as a basis for copyright protection. Neither the Berne Convention, to which the United States acceded effective March 1, 1989, nor the Universal Copyright Convention, to which the U.S. has been a party since 1955, limits member states to protecting fixed works.

[45] One state, California, by statute, protects works of authorship not fixed in a tangible medium of expression. *See* Cal. Civ. Code § 980(a).

[46] 244 N.E.2d 250 (N.Y. 1968).

[47] 521 F. Supp. 1204 (W.D. Va. 1981).

circumstances, but failed to define the appropriate circumstances in which this protection would occur.

The reluctance of the courts to entertain suits under a common law copyright theory reveals the policy behind the fixation requirement. Unlike real and personal property, a copyright is an intangible property right whose boundaries do not have natural physical limits. The fixation requirement renders those boundaries somewhat more concrete. At least, when a work is embodied in a tangible medium of expression, one can point to something, enabling a court to determine whether infringement has taken place. It also simplifies market transactions because buyers and sellers are better able to specify what rights are being acquired. Thus, the fixation requirement serves a useful economic goal by facilitating the organization of a market for copyrighted works, and at the same time, keeping ownership rights within reasonable limits.[48] The lack of boundaries appears to influence the courts, as in *Hemingway* and *Falwell*, which generally deny the claims of common law copyright. The fixation requirement is possibly the clearest example of a boundary-setting device that demarcates and delimits the grant of copyright. But there are others, and one can find a number of "boundary-making" doctrines throughout the 1976 Act, including the intricate texture of the enumerated rights and their limitations, the idea/expression dichotomy, and the originality requirement.

Part II. ORIGINALITY AND AUTHORSHIP

§ 2.06 ORIGINAL AND CREATIVE AUTHORSHIP

[A] Generally

The Constitution limits copyright protection to "writings of *authors*." The Constitutional requirement is echoed in § 102(a) of the Act that "Copyright subsists in original works of *authorship*." Obviously, the meaning of the terms "authors" and "originality" is of fundamental importance in the law of copyright. The Supreme Court in *Burrow Giles Lithographic Co. v. Sarony*, defined "author" in the Constitutional sense to be "[h]e to whom anything owes its *origin*; *originator*, maker."[49] Thus, authorship is intimately connected to originality. One could say that the very essence of authorship is originality. Original authorship presumes independent creation, and one who has slavishly copied from another may not claim status as an author. In addition to independent creation, the courts have required that the author add, at the least, a minimal amount of creative authorship. In other words, the author must give us at least something that transcends the bare confines of the public domain. The requirement of authorship implies that the copyrighted work be created by human authorship, which would exclude works

---

[48] *See* Wendy S. Gordon, *An Inquiry into the Merits of Copyright: The Challenges of Consistency, Consent, and Encouragement Theory*, 41 Stan. L. Rev. 1343, 1378–84 (1989), for a stimulating elaboration of this idea.

[49] 111 U.S. 53, 58 (1884).

created entirely by automated or mechanical means, such as a computer generated product.[50]

Although the essence of copyright is originality, this key term is purposely left undefined by the Copyright Act. According to the House Report, the reason for this lack of explicit definition is the legislative intention to incorporate the standard for originality as established by courts under the 1909 Act.[51] As developed by the case law, there are two aspects to originality: independent creation and a modest quantum of creativity. With *Feist Publications, Inc. v. Rural Telephone Service Company, Inc.*, the Supreme Court declared that originality (independent creation plus a modicum of creativity), the "*sine qua non* of copyright," is a constitutional requirement for copyright protection.[52] The influence of *Feist* significantly impacts the law of copyright in two important ways. First, although the *Feist* case itself concerned the copyrightability of compilations of fact, the case affects all varieties of works of authorship when the issue of originality arises, particularly for categories of works often manifesting low degrees of authorship such as maps and computer software programs. Second, in constitutionalizing the originality requirement, *Feist* clearly constrains Congress' power to legislate under the Copyright and Patent Clause of the Constitution in protecting works that do not meet the constitutional requirement of originality — independent creation and the requisite quantum of creativity.[53]

[B] Independent Creation

An original work is one that is independently created, owing its origin to an author. Simply put, it is a work not copied from another. Courts have inferred the requirement of originality from the constitutional language that limits copyright to writings of authors.[54] It follows that one cannot be an author unless he originated something. This standard for originality should be compared to the much more rigorous patent standard of novelty. To qualify for a patent, an invention must be novel — not known or previously practiced.[55] As a corollary, a patentee may establish infringement by showing that the alleged infringing product or process is substantially similar to the patented invention.[56] In patent law, infringement will be found even if the third party had independently created the invention.

---

[50] The authorship issues related to computer generated works are discussed at *infra* § 3.07.

[51] *See* H.R. Rep. No. 94-1476, at 51 (1976).

[52] 499 U.S. 340 (1990). Justice O'Connor's opinion referred no fewer than thirteen times to the constitutional basis of the originality requirement.

[53] For a discussion of constitutional issues involving attempts by Congress under the Commerce Clause or the states to circumvent *Feist*, see Paul J. Heald, *The Vices of Originality*, 1991 Sup. Ct. Rev. 143, 168–177 (arguing that neither Congress under the Commerce Clause nor the states have the authority to circumvent *Feist* by special legislation to protect unoriginal works).

[54] According to H.R. Rep. No. 94-1476, at 51 (1976), this standard of originality does not include requirements of novelty, and there is no intention to enlarge the standard of copyright protection to require them.

[55] *See* 35 U.S.C. §§ 101, 102.

[56] *See* 35 U.S.C. § 271.

By contrast, all that is required for protection in copyright law is independent creation,[57] and not striking uniqueness, ingenuity, or novelty.[58] Thus, nothing prevents a valid claim of copyright on two or more substantially similar works so long as they were independently created. An action for copyright infringement reflects this principle by requiring the copyright owner to prove both substantial similarity and copying. Unlike patent infringement cases, proving substantial similarity alone will not be enough to prove copyright infringement; one must prove by direct or circumstantial evidence that the infringer *actually copied* another's work. In a famous passage, Judge Learned Hand phrased the issue as follows: "If by some magic a man who had never known it were to compose anew Keats's *Ode on a Grecian Urn*, he would be an "author" and, if he copyrighted it, others might not copy that poem, though they might of course copy Keats's [public domain poem]."[59]

[C] The Quantum of Originality: Creative Authorship

Even if a work is an independent creation, it must demonstrate a minimal amount of creative authorship. The standard is a *de minimis* one; almost any distinguishable variation of a prior work will constitute a sufficient quantity of originality. Thus, courts have found originality in such banal creations as the label on a box of cake[60] and plastic flowers.[61] Copyright, however, has been denied to fragmentary words or phrases,[62] slogans,[63] slight variations of musical compositions,[64] and paraphrases of standard business forms for not meeting the *de*

---

[57] *See* 17 U.S.C. § 101.

[58] *See Alfred Bell & Co. v. Catalda Fine Arts, Inc.*, 191 F.2d 99 (2d Cir. 1951).

[59] *Sheldon v. MetroGoldwyn Pictures Corp.*, 81 F.2d 49, 54 (2d Cir. 1936).

[60] *See, e.g.*, *Kitchens of Sara Lee, Inc. v. Nifty Foods Corp.*, 266 F.2d 541, 545 (2d Cir. 1959) (noting "[t]he pictures of the cakes used by plaintiff on its labels although possibly not achieving the quality of a Leonardo 'Still Life' nevertheless have sufficient commercial artistry to entitle them to protection against obvious copying . . . "). *But cf. Bailie v. Fisher*, 258 F.2d 425 (D.C. Cir. 1958) (holding that a standing cardboard star does not fall within the historical and ordinary conception of a work of art).

[61] *See, e.g.*, *Prestige Floral S.A. v. California Artificial Flower Co.*, 201 F. Supp. 287 (S.D.N.Y. 1962). *But cf. Gardenia Flowers, Inc. v. Joseph Markovits, Inc.*, 280 F. Supp. 776 (S.D.N.Y. 1968) (holding that plaintiff's artificial corsages lacked the creativity and originality necessary for a work of art under the 1909 Act).

[62] The Copyright Office reflected this view in one of its regulations under the 1909 Act. Words and short phrases, such as names, titles and slogans, familiar symbols or designs are not copyrightable. 37 C.F.R. § 202.1(a) (1959). *See Alberto-Culver Co. v. Andrea Dumon, Inc.*, 466 F.2d 705 (7th Cir. 1972) (holding that the phrase "most personal sort of deodorant" is not copyrightable); *see also* 37 C.F.R. § 202.1 (1982) (including "words and short phrases such as names, titles and slogans" under the category of "Materials not subject to copyright"); *but see* Nimmer on Copyright § 2.01[B] (2014) (containing arguments that even a short phrase, if sufficiently creative, might be entitled to copyright protection).). For the opposing view, see Justin Hughes, *Size Matters (or Should) in Copyright Law*, 74 Fordham L. Rev. 575 (2005).

[63] Slogans can be protected in certain circumstances under the law of unfair competition. *See generally* J. Thomas McCarthy, Trademarks and the Law of Unfair Competition § 7.23 (2008); *see also* Samuel W. Tannenbaum, *Uses of Titles for Copyrighted and Public Domain Works*, 6 Bull. Copyright Soc'y 64 (1959).

[64] *See, e.g.*, *Shapiro, Bernstein & Co. v. Miracle Record Co., Inc.*, 91 F. Supp. 473 (N.D. Ill. 1950); *McIntyre v. DoubleA Music Corp.*, 179 F. Supp. 160 (S.D. Cal. 1959); *but cf. Wihtol v. Wells*, 231 F.2d 550

minimis standard.[65]

In determining whether a work meets the quantum of originality, the work must be evaluated as a whole, not dissected as to its individual components. In *Atari Games Corp. v. Oman*, [66] the court held that the Copyright Office improperly denied registration to a videogame screen. The Office erred because it focused on the independent components of the screens, made up of simple geometric shapes. The Office should have evaluated the work as a whole because even simple geometric shapes, when selected and combined in a distinctive manner, may meet the modest standard for creative authorship.[67]

Why require a quantum of originality?[68] One justification is the idea of a *quid pro quo* for the copyright monopoly. We should reward with a copyright only an author who has contributed to our fund of culture. Judge Kaplan has phrased this idea as follows: "we can . . . conclude that to make the copyright turnstile revolve, the author should have to deposit more than a penny in the box, and some like measure ought to apply to infringement."[69]

Although the requirement of creative authorship entails a certain *de minimis* amount of originality, it embodies no conception of artistic merit or beauty. *Bleistein v. Donaldson Lithographing Co.*,[70] a celebrated case decided early in the century and involving the copyrightability of a circus poster, explicitly established that courts should not inject their own views on what constitutes artistic merit in deciding questions of copyrightability. Justice Holmes expressed this principle as follows:

> It would be a dangerous undertaking for persons trained only to the law to constitute themselves final judges of the worth of pictorial illustrations, outside of the narrowest and most obvious limits. At one extreme some works of genius would be sure to miss appreciation. Their very novelty would make them repulsive until the public had learned the new language in which their author spoke. . . . At the other end, copyright would be denied to pictures that appealed to a public less educated than the judge.[71]

(7th Cir. 1956) (holding that a composition based on a folk song was copyrightable); *See also* Joel L. Friedman, *Copyright and the Musical Arrangement: An Analysis of the Law and Problems Pertaining to This Specialized Form of Derivative Work*, 7 PEPP. L. REV. 125 (1979).

[65] *See, e.g., Donald v. Zack Meyer's T.V. Sales and Serv.*, 426 F.2d 1027, 1031 (5th Cir. 1970), *cert. denied*, 400 U.S. 992 (1971) (holding that the plaintiff's legal form was not entitled to protection, the court stated, "[w]e reward creativity and originality with a copyright but we do not accord copyright protection to a mere copycat").

[66] 888 F.2d 878 (D.C. Cir. 1989); *Atari Games Corp. v. Oman*, 979 F.2d 242 (D.C. Cir. 1992).

[67] *See Atari Games Corp.*, 979 F.2d at 244 (stating that the work would be copyrightable "if the requisite level of creativity is met by either the individual screens or the relationship of each screen to the others and/or the accompanying sound effects").

[68] For a discussion of psychological research on creativity and its relationship to copyright, *see* Gregory N. Mandel, *Creativity and the Law: To Promote the Creative Process: Intellectual Property and the Psychology of Creativity*, 86 Notre Dame L. Rev. 1999 (2011).

[69] BENJAMIN KAPLAN, AN UNHURRIED VIEW OF COPYRIGHT 46 (1967).

[70] 188 U.S. 239 (1903).

[71] *Id.* at 251–52.

Since *Bleistein*, both the courts and the Copyright Office, as best they can, have avoided aesthetic decisions in deciding questions of originality.[72]

The *Bleistein* case also considered a corollary question: Could copyright be claimed for a work intended for advertising purposes? Under an earlier view, copyright protection was denied to advertisements on the grounds that they lacked artistic merit. Justice Holmes unequivocally rejected the notion that a prohibition against copyrightablity should be based on the context in which the work is found. Most courts have followed Justice Holmes' statement that "[a] picture is none the less a picture and none the less a subject of copyright that it is used for an advertisement."[73] In sum, so long as the work contains the required original elements, courts will not look to the intended purpose of the work or the audience to whom it is directed.[74]

Part III. COMPILATIONS AND DERIVATIVE WORKS

§ 2.07 COMPILATIONS AND DERIVATIVE WORKS

Compilations and derivative works are specifically recognized by § 103[75] of the 1976 Act as copyrightable subject matter. A compilation or derivative work is copyrightable only if it constitutes "an original work of authorship" and falls within one or more of the seven protected categories of works of authorship set forth in § 102.[76] The terms "compilations" or "derivative works" are defined in § 101 and comprehend every copyrightable work that employs preexisting material or data of any kind. A "compilation" (including collective works)[77] results from a process of selecting, organizing, and arranging previously existing material of all kinds, regardless of whether the individual items have been subject to copyright. By contrast, a "derivative work" requires a process of recasting, transforming, or

---

[72] As Diane Leenheer Zimmerman has noted, "Lower court judges both understood the case as setting the threshold for copyrightability at a very low level, and appreciated the pragmatic virtues of this approach. . . . [W]ithin thirty years, an appellate court could list dozens of decisions and cite to major treatises all agreeing that *Bleistein* required only 'a low degree of originality and artistic or literary merit' to obtain copyright." Diane Leenheer Zimmerman, The Story of Bleistein v. Donaldson Lithographing Company: Originality as a Vehicle for Copyright Inclusivity, in Intellectual Property Stories 77, 101–02 (J. Ginsburg & R. Dreyfuss eds. 2005).

[73] *Id.* at 251.

[74] One exception to the *Bleistein* doctrine can be found in the Visual Artists Rights Act ("VARA"), codified in 17 U.S.C. § 106A, in which the prohibition against the intentional destruction for certain works of visual art is limited to works of "recognized stature." For a discussion of the VARA and moral rights, see *infra* § 8.28. Some scholars have questioned Bleistein's aesthetic non-discrimination principle see Christine Farley, *Judging Art*, 79 Tulane L. Rev. 805 (2005) and Diane Zimmerman, *It's an Original!(?): In Pursuit of Copyright's Elusive Essence*, 28 Colum. J.L. & Arts 187 (2005); Lisa P. Ramsey, *Intellectual Property Rights in Advertising*, 12 Mich. Telecomm. & Tech L. Rev. 189 (2006) (questioning the justification for extending copyright to advertising).

[75] 17 U.S.C. § 103.

[76] 17 U.S.C. § 102(a).

[77] "Collective works" are a species of compilation in which independent works, such as an anthology of poems, are assembled and organized. *See* 17 U.S.C. § 101.

adapting "one or more preexisting works."[78] The "preexisting work" must fall within the general subject matter of § 102 of the Act. Thus, compilations and derivative works are substantially based on preexisting material. Section 103 defines the criteria for the interrelationship between the preexisting material and the "new" material in a particular work specifying that copyright in a "new version" covers only the material added by the later author and does not affect the copyright or public domain status of the preexisting material.

§ 2.08 DERIVATIVE WORKS

[A] Originality in Derivative Works

Section 101 defines a derivative work as:

> . . . a work based upon one or more preexisting works, such as a translation, musical arrangement, dramatization, fictionalization, motion picture version, sound recording, art reproduction, abridgement, condensation, or any other form in which a work may be recast, transformed, or adapted. A work consisting of editorial revisions, annotations, elaborations, or other modifications which, as a whole, represent an original work of authorship, is a "derivative work.[79]

Most works to a certain degree borrow from others, but in the case of a derivative work, substantial copying has taken place. To avoid infringement, the derivative work author must either base his work on one in the public domain or obtain permission from the author of the preexisting copyrighted work.[80] Any recasting, reforming, abridgement, or editorial revision can be copyrighted as a derivative work so long as the standard of originality is met.[81]

Original authorship in a derivative work consists of modifying the preexisting work into a new work. For example, if a person translates Flaubert's *Madame Bovary*, his copyright extends to the original aspects of the translation, such as finding the proper word equivalents and patterning the syntax to read properly in English. The derivative work copyright extends only to those original elements added by the derivative work author, not to the underlying work. Copyright in the resulting derivative work is unrelated to any exclusive right in the preexisting material. It is independent of, and does not affect or enlarge the scope, duration, ownership, or subsistence of, any copyright protection in the preexisting material.[82]

---

[78] *Id.*

[79] 17 U.S.C. § 101.

[80] On the other hand, if a work borrows only the ideas of a preexisting work and not the *expression* of those ideas, it is not a derivative work because there has been no infringement of the preexisting work. *See Reyher v. Children's Television Workshop*, 533 F.2d 87 (2d Cir. 1976); Paul Goldstein, *Derivative Rights and Derivative Works in Copyright*, 30 J. Copyright Soc'y 209 (1983).

[81] *See Lee v. A.R.T. Co.*, 125 F.3d 580 (7th Cir. 1997) (holding defendant's "mundane" epoxy mounting of plaintiff's note cards onto decorative tiles did not create derivative works); *Norma Ribbon & Trimming, Inc. v. Little*, 51 F.3d 45 (5th Cir. 1995) (finding a design of artificial flowers did not contain sufficient derivative authorship above preexisting public domain versions).

[82] *See* 17 U.S.C. § 103(b)(2).

In the Flaubert example, anyone could go to the public domain source and make his own independently copyrighted work.

The above example involved a derivative work based on a public domain work, but a derivative work can be based on a copyrighted work as well. Take, for example, a motion picture version of a copyrighted dramatic work such as *Death of a Salesman*. In this instance, the derivative work copyright would cover the original elements added to the underlying copyrighted work, for example, the original dialogue, the camera angles, and the montage. If the play went into the public domain, anyone could freely reproduce it, perform it, or make a motion picture based on it so long as he did not copy the original elements of the copyrighted derivative work.

[B] Originality in Derivative Works: Reproductions of Works of Art

Artistic reproductions, because they are substantially based on a preexisting work, are listed in the Copyright Act as derivative works.[83] As for all works of authorship, derivative or otherwise, an art reproduction must meet the standard of originality. The nature and extent of that originality has been a subject of long-standing controversy.

In general, an artistic reproduction that merely makes an exact copy of a prior work would lack sufficient originality.[84] If the copy, however, entails the independent creative judgment of the artist in its production, those aspects will render the work original. In *Alfred Bell & Co. v. Catalda Fine Arts, Inc.*,[85] the plaintiff's meticulous reproductions (mezzotint engravings) of public domain paintings met the standard of originality for the purposes of copyright. The court held that the engravings were sufficiently original as to be entitled to copyright because the author contributed something more than a trivial variation on the preexisting work — something that was recognizably his own. As applied to the mezzotints, the court found original authorship in the creative efforts of the engravers and artists in selecting the colors and in their using the engraving process, which introduced variations on the original painting. Under the court's view, a modest grade of originality is all that is required for copyrightability. This is, in effect, little more than a prohibition against actual copying.

Recent cases, particularly in the Second and Seventh Circuits, appear to run counter to *Catalda*'s *de minimis* standard for originality as applied to identical reproductions of works of art. Some courts have declined to award a derivative work copyright protection for the labor involved in transferring a work from one medium into another. To provide copyright protection under these circumstances would, in effect, confer copyright on the medium itself rather than on the work. In

---

[83] Art reproductions are specifically included in the definition of pictorial, graphic, and sculptural works and are also given as an example of a derivative work. *See* 17 U.S.C. § 101.

[84] *But see* Terry S. Kogan, *Photographic Reproductions, Copyright, and the Slavish Copy*, Colum. J.L. & Arts 445 (2012) (arguing that copyright law is mistaken in concluding that photographic reproductions of artwork generally constitute unoriginal copies).

[85] 191 F.2d 99 (2d Cir. 1951).

L. Batlin & Son, Inc. v. Snyder,[86] the Second Circuit Court of Appeals refused to grant copyright protection to the plaintiff in creating an exact copy of the cast iron public domain Uncle Sam bank in plastic. The court held that the standard for originality was not met because the variations were merely trivial and that the physical skill and special training to convert the cast iron bank were insufficient to support copyright. The court declared that, "To extend copyrightability to minuscule variations would simply put a weapon for harassment in the hands of mischievous copiers intent on appropriating and monopolizing public domain work."[87]

Batlin was affirmed, if not extended, in *Durham Industries v. Tomy Corp.*,[88] another Second Circuit case involving the copyrightability of three-dimensional reproductions of the famous Walt Disney characters, Mickey Mouse, Donald Duck, and Pluto. The court held that the toys did not display sufficient originality because copying from one medium to another requires nothing more than physical as compared with artistic skill.

Cases dealing with copyright for artistic reproduction are hard to reconcile even within the same circuit. *Batlin* and *Tomy* should be compared with *Alva Studios, Inc. v. Winninger*,[89] which involved the copyrightability of a small-scale reproduction of Rodin's famous public domain sculpture, the *Hand of God*. Here the court held that the work was copyrightable, requiring great skill and originality to reproduce a scale reproduction with such exactitude. *Alva* differs from *Batlin* and *Tomy* in the complexity and exactitude required to produce the resulting reduction of the Rodin sculpture, and perhaps the cases can be reconciled by the proposition that a scale reproduction *without more* should not support copyright.[90]

These Second Circuit cases have imposed what seems to be a more rigorous standard of originality for artistic reproductions than for other works of authorship. A standard requiring artistic as opposed to physical skill may inevitably lead to judicial considerations of artistic merit. This would conflict with the traditional copyright principles that judges should stay away from such matters. In addition, these decisions create a paradox where greater protection would be conferred on sloppy, inaccurate copies as opposed to skillful, highly accurate ones. At the very least, *Batlin* and *Tomy* require a greater showing of creative authorship for artistic reproductions — a substantial variation on the public domain rather than the *de minimis* or trivial variation standard enunciated in *Catalda*.

---

86 536 F.2d 486 (2d Cir. 1976).

87 *Id.* at 492.

88 630 F.2d 905 (2d Cir. 1980).

89 177 F. Supp. 265 (S.D.N.Y. 1959).

90 Although there appears to be some discrepancy in how far the courts will go in conferring copyright on art reproductions, the historical tendency has been expansive. *Cf. Eden Toys v. Florelee Undergarment Co.*, 697 F.2d 27 (2d Cir. 1982) (holding that a gift wrap design based on sketches of Paddington Bear was copyrightable because the "cleaner look" of the gift wrap design satisfied the minimal requirements for originality under the Copyright Act).

In *Gracen v. Bradford Exchange*,[91] the Seventh Circuit Court of Appeals opted unequivocally for a more rigorous standard for copyright in derivative works involving reproductions of works of art. In *Gracen*, the court refused copyright to an artist's reproduction of a photograph of Judy Garland's character "Dorothy" from the Wizard of Oz for lack of substantial variation. According to Judge Posner, the threshold of originality, particularly for derivative works such as artistic reproductions, should be higher than for preexisting works, to prevent potential overlapping claims and harassment by claimants of derivative work copyrights. Judge Posner reasoned that without requiring a quantum of originality, it may be very difficult to determine whether a third party has copied from a public domain source or copied from the copyrighted work. Thus, we should require a sufficiently gross difference between the underlying and the derivative work to avoid litigation over whether a subsequent artist has copied the original or copied the copy.[92]

The *Gracen* court, by requiring a substantial variation for derivative works such as artistic reproductions, has imposed a *de facto* novelty standard for certain works of authorship. Its justification for the higher standard was based on the practicality of judicial administration in deciding claims of infringement. Specifically, an unduly low standard could result in judicial error when courts are asked to decide whether the second derivative work author copied the public domain work or the copyrighted derivative work. In addition to this evidentiary problem, a low standard for originality may impose other costs on the judicial system by encouraging infringement suits of dubious merit brought by overzealous owners of derivative works. Alternatively, the standard set forth in *Gracen* may impede production of highly competent artistic renderings, which cannot be protected by copyright.

The elevated standard of originality for derivative works as expressed in *Gracen* and has continued to find favor in the courts[93] despite disapproval particularly

---

[91] 698 F.2d 300 (7th Cir. 1983).

[92] As the court pointed out, the concept of originality serves an important legal function: to prevent overlapping claims when derivative works are based on public domain works (even though the derivative work at issue in *Gracen* was based on an underlying copyrighted work). Suppose Artist A produces a reproduction of the *Mona Lisa*, a painting in the public domain, which differs slightly from the original. B also makes a reproduction of the *Mona Lisa*. A, who has copyrighted his derivative work, sues B for infringement. B's defense is that he was copying the original, not A's reproduction. "[I]f the difference between A's reproduction and the original is slight, the difference between A's and B's reproductions will also be slight, so that if B had access to A's reproductions, the trier of fact will also be hard pressed to decide whether B was copying A or copying the *Mona Lisa* itself." *Id.* at 304. For similar reasoning applied to derivative works based on preexisting copyrighted works, see *Entertainment Research Group, Inc. v. Genesis Creative Group, Inc.*, 122 F.3d 1211, 1220 (9th Cir. 1997) (stating that if a derivative work copyright be granted too readily, "[t]he owner of the underlying copyrighted work would effectively be prevented from permitting others to copy her work since the original derivative copyright holder would have a *de facto* monopoly due to her considerable power to interfere with the creation of subsequent derivative works from the same underlying work."). The role of originality in such instances is elaborated in Douglas Lichtman, *Copyright as a Rule of Evidence*, 52 Duke L.J. 683, 705 (2003) ("An originality requirement, then, empowers courts to exclude from the copyright system a particularly messy class of cases: cases in which courts would not be able to use similarity as the basis for even a weak inference regarding the likelihood of impermissible copying.").

[93] *See, e.g.*, *Meshwerks, Inc. v. Toyota Motor Sales U.S.A., Inc.*, 528 F.3d 1258 (10th Cir. 2008) (rejecting a claim of copyright in digital models whose intent and result was merely to reproduce

among legal commentators. Its death knell may have arrived when the Seventh Circuit itself specifically rejected *Gracen's* formulation in *Schrock v. Learning Curve International, Inc.*[94] In Schrock, the Court of Appeals reversed summary judgment in favor of the defendant who argued that Schrock failed to meet the *Gracen* standard for originality for Schrock's photographs of "Thomas & Friends" train characters. In citing the Second Circuit's test in *Batlin*, the court ruled that the originality requirement for derivative works is no more demanding than the originality requirement for other works, stating, "The key inquiry is whether there is sufficient nontrivial expressive variation in the derivative work to make it distinguishable from the underlying work in some meaningful way."[95] In applying this principle to the photographs at issue, the court declared:

> If the photographer's rendition of a copyrighted work varies enough from the underlying work to enable the photograph to be distinguished from the underlying work . . . then the photograph contains sufficient incremental originality to qualify for copyright . . . Schrock's photos of the 'Thomas & Friends' toys are highly accurate product photos but contain minimally sufficient variation in angle, perspective, lighting, and dimension to be distinguishable from the underlying works; they are not 'slavish copies.[96]

In effect, the standard of originality is no different for derivative works as it is for any other work. The threshold is low, but a derivative must manifest more than a trivial variation on the public domain.

[C] Digital Processes and Creative Authorship: The Colorization Controversy

"Colorization" is a digital process whereby copyright owners have been able to inject new value into commercially dormant black and white films. Film purists and artists are outraged at what they believe is the mutilation of an artistic creation. Apart from the ethics of adding color to a film originally created in black and white by its originator, some have questioned whether a colorized film meets the standard of creative human authorship sufficient to constitute a valid derivative work.[97]

The process of colorization involves the use of a computer that scans a black and white film transferred on videotape for its spectrum of gray tones.[98] From these

---

faithfully the appearance of certain Toyota cars constituted copies of the existing cars and not creative works); *Entertainment Research Group, Inc. v. Genesis Creative Group, Inc.*, 122 F.3d 1211 (9th Cir. 1997) (rejecting a claim of copyright in eight-foot high costume designs based on advertising characters such as the Pillsbury Doughboy, Geoffrey Giraffe, and Cap'n Crunch).

[94] 586 F.3d 513 (7th Cir. 2009).

[95] *Id.* at 521.

[96] *Id.* at 522.

[97] For a discussion of the originality requirement in the context of new digital technologies, *see* Edward Lee, *Digital Originality*, 14 Vand. J. Ent. & Tech. L. 919 (2012).

[98] For an overview of the subject and a detailed explanation of the colorization process, see James Thomas Duggan & Neil V. Pennella, *The Case for Copyrights in "Colorized" Versions of Public Domain Feature Films*, 34 J. Copyright Soc'y 333 (1987).

gray tones, an individual versed in this technique must choose an appropriate color corresponding to the object, the decor, and the epoch portrayed in the film. The colorization process is time consuming and costly.

The copyright issue is whether colorizers have added the requisite amount of human creative authorship to a preexisting work to meet the standard of copyrightability for a derivative work. Colorizers argue that they use a computer as a painter uses a brush or a novelist uses a typewriter and that the arrangement and combination of colors constitutes the requisite amount of creative authorship for a copyrightable derivative work. They would view their work as analogous to a musical arrangement or a translation that modifies a preexisting work in adding original authorship.[99] The contrary view holds that colorizers are mere computer technicians whose choices are governed by a predetermined process made possible by a new form of computer technology,[100] and whatever human authorship the colorizer adds it is too trivial to meet the standard of originality.[101]

Colorization has not been tested in the courts, but the Copyright Office has decided that colorized films are entitled to copyright registration as derivative works if the colorized work manifests a sufficient modification of the preexisting work that is more than a trivial variation. The Copyright Office has developed a set of criteria to determine whether the colorized film meets the requisite standard for a derivative work. In effect, the regulation requires that numerous color selections must be made by human beings from an extensive color inventory, and the range and extent of colors added must represent more than a trivial variation. The colorization must modify the overall appearance of the motion picture. In addition, neither the removal of color from a motion picture nor mere variations of color will justify registration.[102]

§ 2.09 OTHER ISSUES IN THE SCOPE OF PROTECTION OF DERIVATIVE WORKS

[A] The Lawful Use Requirement

A derivative work copyright can only be obtained when the author legally used the material on which the derivative work was based. Section 103(a)[103] of the Copyright Act states that no copyright can be claimed for any part of a derivative or collective work that has used the preexisting material unlawfully. This prevents

[99] Proponents emphasize that the requisite amount of authorship is governed by a *de minimis* standard. *See, e.g.*, *Pantone, Inc. v. A. I. Friedman, Inc.*, 294 F. Supp. 545 (S.D.N.Y. 1968) (discussing a color chart in a "how-to" book on mixing colors); *Sargent v. American Greetings Corp.*, 588 F. Supp. 912 (N.D. Ohio 1984) (having a painting colorized by adding color to line drawings).

[100] Copyright does not extend to a process. *See* 17 U.S.C. § 102(b). For a discussion of § 102(b), see *infra* § 2.13.

[101] *See, e.g.*, *McIntyre v. Double-A Music Corp.*, 166 F. Supp. 681 (S.D. Cal. 1958) (citing cases at page 683 to hold that the transposition of music to another key or arrangement using common chords are not copyrightable).

[102] *See* 37 C.F.R. § 202 (1987).

[103] 17 U.S.C. § 103(a).

one who uses another's copyrighted work without the owner's consent from profiting from the unlawful use. In addition, this principle protects aspects of the work that were unlawfully derived from preexisting material. The effect of this section is to deny copyright to derivative works that unlawfully use preexisting material throughout the entire work. If one can separate the unlawful aspects from the other parts of a work that were created lawfully, those latter aspects could qualify for copyright. Thus, the owner of the copyright for an anthology of poetry, as the collective work author, could sue anyone who infringed the whole anthology, even if the infringer showed that one or more of the poems were used illegally. On the other hand, an unauthorized translation of a novel could not be copyrighted at all.[104] Likewise, an infringer who makes a movie out of a copyrighted novel would not be entitled to a copyright in any portion of the movie in which the infringing material appears. In *Pickett v. Prince*[105] a fan made a guitar in the shape of the symbol that serves as the name for the artist known as Prince. The court held that the unauthorized use of the symbol infringed Prince's copyright. Because the underlying work "pervaded" the derivative work, the guitar maker could not sustain independent copyright protection in his creation. Even in instances where the underlying work may represent only a small part of the value of the derivative work, because it underlies the whole, it will defeat copyright protection for the entire derivative work.

This feature of copyright law differs significantly with patent law, which allows the patentability of improvement patents even though the improvement would infringe the basic patent.[106] Under the "blocking patents" principle, the owner of the improvement patent cannot exploit the improvement without the consent of the owner of the basic patent. Likewise, the owner of the basic patent cannot make, use, or sell the improvement without negotiating with the owner of the improvement patent. This "blocking patent" situation results in a bargaining between the owner of the basic patent and the owner of the improvement patent. In this way, patent law tries to balance the rights of original creators and subsequent improvers. No such institution exists in copyright law, because the copyright doctrine prohibits the persons from adding onto the copyrighted material of the original creator without permission.[107]

How can one explain the lack of an "improvement copyright" in copyright law, the result of which allows the copyright owner wide control over all manifestations, alterations, transformations or improvements of the work? One explanation is copyright law's policy favoring the reputational interests of authors by requiring derivative work authors to license the underlying work. The law of derivative works illustrates the way in which "moral rights" are reflected in U.S. law.[108]

---

[104] *See* H.R. No. 1476, at 57–58 (1976).

[105] 207 F.3d 402 (7th Cir. 2000).

[106] The "blocking patents" situation is discussed in Robert P. Merges, *Intellectual Property Rights and Bargaining Breakdown: The Case of Blocking Patents*, 62 TENN. L. REV. 74 (1997).

[107] For an excellent overview of the "improvement issue" in intellectual property, see Mark A. Lemley, *The Economics of Improvement in Intellectual Property Law*, 75 TEX. L. REV. 989 (1997).

[108] "Moral rights" are discussed at *infra* § 8.28.

The author of a derivative work does not, in all instances, require consent of the copyright owner for the creation of a "lawful" derivative work. Most important, the unauthorized reproduction of work may be "lawful" under the doctrine of fair use. Thus, certain "transformative" uses of a copyrighted work, such as for the purposes of parody, have been declared lawful under the doctrine of fair use.[109]

[B] Use of Derivative Works in the Public Domain

Difficult conceptual problems arise when the derivative work goes into the public domain while the underlying work remains copyrighted. The problems are most complex when the original elements of the derivative work are inextricably intertwined with the preexisting work, such as a screenplay based on a novel or a translation of a novel from its original language.

In *Grove Press, Inc. v. Greenleaf Publishing Co.*,[110] an English translation of Jean Genet's novel, *Journal du Voleur*, entered the public domain for failure to comply with the *ad interim* provisions of the manufacturing clause.[111] The underlying French version of the novel, however, was protected by a valid copyright. Suit was brought by the copyright owner to enjoin reproduction and distribution of the public domain English translation. The court held that in copying the translation, the defendant had infringed the copyrighted aspects of the preexisting French language work. In theory, a third party could use the original aspects added by the translation to the underlying work. But these public domain aspects, the new matter of the translation, were so intertwined and fused with the underlying work that they could not be used without infringing the underlying work. Paradoxically, the effect of the court's ruling was to keep the public domain translation out of the public domain.[112]

Grove supports protection of the copyright owner, but undermines an equally important policy in copyright law: enriching the public domain. Arguably, the better result would have been to allow copying of the public domain translation. This would have deprived the copyright owner of royalties for that translation, but solely as to that one version in that medium only. The copyright owner could still license other translations of his work, while the public could have access to what

---

[109] "The defense of fair use" is discussed in *infra* Chapter 10. For the application of fair use defense in parody and other transformative use contexts, see *Campbell v. Acuff-Rose Music, Inc.*, 510 U.S. 569 (1994), and *Suntrust Bank v. Houghton Mifflin Co.* 268 F.3d 1257 (11th Cir. 2001).

[110] 247 F. Supp. 518 (E.D.N.Y. 1965).

[111] For a discussion of the *ad interim* provisions of the manufacturing clause under the 1909 Act, see *infra* § 4.17[B].

[112] The *Grove* reasoning was also applied in *Russell v. Price*, 612 F.2d 1123 (9th Cir. 1979), in which a derivative work film based on the Shaw play *Pygmalion* and prepared during the first term of the play's copyright entered the public domain because of failure to renew the copyright for the film. The defendant, who wanted to exploit the film, argued that because the copyright for the film had expired, the film was in the public domain free for all to use. The court disagreed. Only the original elements of the film entered the public domain, but the material used in the film from the underlying play was left unaffected. Because the film could not be used without using the play, the defendant would be liable for infringement. *See also Stewart v. Abend*, 495 U.S. 207 (1990) (noting author's grant of short story gave the defendant no right to exploit the picture *Rear Window*, based on the story, during the story's renewal term, since the author had died before the renewal term vested). *Stewart* is discussed *infra* § 6.10[B].

should properly belong in the public domain.

§ 2.10 COMPILATIONS: GENERALLY

Compilations are similar to derivative works because they too are substantially based on preexisting materials and data. A compilation is defined in the Act as: " a work formed by the collection and assembling of preexisting materials or of data that are selected, coordinated, or arranged in such a way that the resulting work as a whole constitutes an original work of authorship. The term "compilation" includes collective works."[113]

The compilation differs from the derivative work in one significant way. Unlike the derivative work author, the creator of a compilation does not recast, reform, or change the underlying materials but rather compiles (or assembles) them in his own manner. Thus, a compilation can include the selection, coordination, and arrangement of facts, data, or materials that are in the public domain. Examples of factual assemblage of this type are telephone books, case reporters, and catalogs of various kinds. The term "compilation" encompasses "collective works," defined as including works such as periodicals, anthologies, or encyclopedias, in which separate works are assembled into a collective whole. Instead of an assembly of facts or data, a collective work is made up of an assembly of independent works, such as an anthology of poems or articles in a monthly magazine.

To be copyrightable, the derivative work, compilation, or collective work must satisfy the standard of originality. In other words, the work must display a variation on the preexisting work, one that is more than trivial, and a variation that is sufficient to render the work distinguishable from the prior work in a meaningful way.[114]

§ 2.11 ORIGINALITY IN COMPILATIONS

[A] Originality in Compilations: An Overview

As discussed previously, compilations are works of authorship created by collecting, selecting, and assembling preexisting materials or data. The compiled materials may consist of individually copyrighted works, as in an anthology of contemporary short stories, or may only include public domain materials such as facts or data. Consider a compilation composed of factual matter such as a telephone book, a catalog of prices, or a list of potential customers, each element of

---

[113] 17 U.S.C. § 101 (compilation).

[114] For cases finding sufficient originality, see *Hesse v. Brunner*, 172 F. Supp. 284 (S.D.N.Y. 1959) (regarding an original photograph of a public domain building); and *Roth Greeting Cards v. United Card Co.*, 429 F.2d 1106 (9th Cir. 1970) (noting a greeting card considered as a whole, including text, arrangement of text, art work, and association between art and text, constitutes sufficient originality). Cases finding insufficient originality include: *Shapiro, Bernstein & Co. v. Jerry Vogel Music Co.*, 73 F. Supp. 165 (S.D.N.Y. 1947) (discussing a change in rhythm and a slight variation in the bass of the accompaniment of a song); *Eggers v. Sun Sales Corp.*, 263 F. 373 (2d Cir. 1920) (regarding new and original pagination for a public domain work); and *Carter v. Hawaii Trans. Co.*, 201 F. Supp. 301 (D. Hawaii 1961) (discussing the selection of cities to be included in public domain map).

which is in the public domain. Often, unearthing facts and putting them into a compilation requires skill and hard work. Copyright law, however, does not protect facts *per se*, or the talent that went into discovering them. Rather, copyright protects original works of authorship. One cannot author a fact because facts simply exist, even if they sometimes have to be discovered at great effort and expense. This principle is embodied in § 102(b) of the 1976 Act, which denies copyright to any "discovery, regardless of the form in which it is described. . . ."[115]

Copyright in a compilation covers the original elements an author has added to the assembled preexisting materials or data. These elements may vary widely in original authorship. Some compilations contain facts plus extensive authorial analysis and judgment in the selection and organization of the preexisting data; other compilations contain nothing more than an arrangement of facts, such as certain indexes. For all varieties of compilations, however, copyright in the compilation extends not to the preexisting materials or data themselves, but to the author's judgment in selecting and arranging the disparate materials or data and organizing them into a unified work. Other indicia of authorship would include analysis, description, and instruction accompanying the individual elements making up the compilation. Like any other work of authorship, the compilation must contain more than a trivial variation on what is in the public domain, but a compilation need not be novel or unique. It must be independently created and display a *de minimis* amount of creative, intellectual, or aesthetic labor. This fundamental principle about the requisite standard for copyright protection was raised to the level of a constitutional requirement in *Feist Publications, Inc. v. Rural Telephone Service Co.*[116]

[B] The *Feist* Case and the Demise of the Industrious Effort Doctrine

Compilations, particularly those that assemble public domain materials, reflect basic tensions in copyright policy. Modern copyright law has had difficulty with works that are low in original authorship even though the works themselves may be high in commercial value.[117] Consider the following situation. Suppose B, without doing independent research, appropriates the factual information contained in a compilation produced at great expense by A, such as a telephone book or other catalog. Suppose also that B has not taken the original elements added to the public domain, such as A's subjective arrangement or organization of the compilation. Can A be protected under copyright law from B's total appropriation of A's hard work in gathering the facts? Under traditional copyright law principles, facts *per se* are not protectable. Nevertheless, some courts have stretched copyright law to protect a compilation from similar "free riders" like B who have appropriated the fruits of another's labor. To limit protection to the expressive elements in this instance would seem to confer inadequate protection on

---

[115] 17 U.S.C. § 102(b).

[116] 499 U.S. 340 (1991).

[117] For an elaboration of this idea, see Jane C. Ginsburg, *Creation and Commercial Value: Copyright Protection of Works of Information*, 90 Colum. L. Rev. 1865 (1990).

a compilation containing little expression.[118] The sentiment favoring protection is understandable and may be justified on a natural law theory that people are entitled to the fruits of their labor. Moreover, uninhibited free riding may well undermine the incentive to create such informational works. Despite these equitable considerations, if carried to its logical conclusion, this expansive "sweat of the brow" approach to copyright would risk turning copyright into a general misappropriation law.

Although the "sweat of the brow" doctrine has enjoyed a persistent success through the years, the United States Supreme Court specifically rejected it in *Feist Publications, Inc. v. Rural Telephone Service Co.*[119] Here, the Court specifically discarded industrious effort as a standard for copyrightability separate from the effort's embodiment in the creative arrangement, selection, and coordination of the subject matter in the work.

In *Feist*, plaintiff Rural Telephone provided telephone service to several communities in northwest Kansas and published white pages containing an alphabetical listing of subscriber's names, towns, and telephone numbers. Defendant Feist also published telephone books and tried to license Rural's list of names but was refused. Feist used Rural's listings without permission, copying about 1,300 names and numbers from Rural's white pages, including four fictitious listings that Rural had inserted to detect copying.

The Supreme Court found that Rural's copyright in its telephone directory did not protect the names and numbers copied by Feist. In her opinion, Justice O'Connor used the bedrock constitutional principle that a protectable work must be original with the author. "Original" in the copyright sense means that the work was independently created and possesses at least some minimal degree of

---

[118] The expansive view is represented by *Leon v. Pacific Telephone & Telegraph Co.*, 91 F.2d 484 (9th Cir. 1937). In *Leon*, the plaintiff compiled a telephone directory with the names and telephone numbers arranged in alphabetical order. The defendant took the same names and numbers and rearranged them by the numerical order of the numbers, creating a reverse telephone book. *See also Rand McNally & Co. v. Fleet Management Sys., Inc.*, 600 F. Supp. 933, 941 (N.D. Ill. 1984); *National Bus. Lists, Inc. v. Dun & Bradstreet, Inc.*, 552 F. Supp. 89 (N.D. Ill. 1982). Other cases involving similar fact situations present a rationale closer to the traditional purpose of copyright law. *See Schroeder v. William Morrow & Co.*, 566 F.2d 3 (7th Cir. 1977) (finding infringement in a catalog of names and addresses where defendant copied the selection, order, and arrangement of the names); *Southern Bell Tel. & Telegraph Co. v. Associated Tel. Directory Publishers*, 756 F.2d 801, 811 (11th Cir. 1985).

[119] The commentary on *Feist* and the question of originality in copyright law are voluminous. *See* David Shipley, *Thin But not Anorexic: Copyright Protection for Compilations and Other Fact Works*, 15 J. INTELL. PROP. 91 (2007); Alan L. Durham, *Speaking of the World: Fact, Opinion, and the Originality Standard of Copyright*, 33 ARIZ. ST. L.J. 791 (2001); Russ VerSteeg, *Rethinking Originality*, 34 WM. & MARY L. REV. 801 (1993); *Symposium, Copyright Protection for Computer Databases, CD-ROMS and Factual Compilations* (pts. I, II) 17 U. DAYTON L. REV. 323, 331 (1992); Howard B. Abrams, *Originality and Creativity in Copyright Law*, 55 Law & Contemp. Probs. 3 (1992); Jane C. Ginsburg, *"No Sweat?," Copyright and Other Protection of Works of Information After Feist v. Rural Telephone*, 92 COLUM. L. REV. 338 (1992); Robert A. Gorman, *The* Feist *Case: Reflections on a Pathbreaking Copyright Decision*, 18 RUTGERS COMPUTER & TECH. L.J. 731 (1992); Marci A. Hamilton, *Justice O'Connor's Opinion in Feist Publications Inc. v. Rural Telephone Service Co., An Uncommon Though Characteristic Approach*, 38 J. COPYRIGHT SOC'Y 83 (1990); Paul J. Heald, *The Vices of Originality*, SUP. CT. REV. 143 (1991); Shira Perlmutter, *The Scope of Copyright in Telephone Directories: Keeping Listing Information in the Public Domain*, 38 J. COPYRIGHT SOC'Y 1 (1990).

creativity. Factual works may possess the requisite creativity, *e.g.*, where the author chooses which facts to include, in what order, and their arrangement for effective use. However, the protection extends only to those parts of the work original to the author and not to the facts themselves. In sum, protection of a factual work extends only to its *original* selection or arrangement. The *Feist* Court ruled that Rural's alphabetical arrangement of its telephone listings could not have been more obvious or banal, lacking the minimal modicum of creativity necessary to constitute original authorship. Thus, even though Feist took a substantial amount of factual information from Rural's directory, it did not take anything that amounted to original authorship. Accordingly, Feist's copying did not constitute copyright infringement.

Feist is unequivocal on one point: an alphabetical listing of telephone subscribers and their numbers cannot be protected as a compilation under copyright unless the selection, coordination, or arrangement of the facts is original. This in itself is a dramatic holding, and from a practical standpoint, has had a substantial impact on the numerous publishers of telephone books. In addition, its effect has been felt beyond the confines of the telephone book industry.

[C] Originality in Selection and Arrangement After *Feist*

[1] From the White Pages to the Yellow Pages

Feist does not, however, answer what kind of selection or arrangement is original and protectable authorship. Subsequent case law has filled in the gaps. A series of Yellow Pages cases reveal the difficulties in determining originality in compilations. For the most part, Yellow Pages directories require more organization and arrangement than the White Pages held uncopyrightable in *Feist*. Plaintiffs have, nevertheless, had difficulty in enforcing their rights. In *Key Publications, Inc. v. Chinatown Today Publishing Enterprises, Inc.*,[120] the Second Circuit upheld the copyright in a listing of businesses located in New York's Chinatown and of interest to the Chinese community. However, it found no infringement, even though defendant had copied 1,500 of the 9,000 entries found in plaintiff's directory, because defendant had used a different selection and arrangement of the material. The copied listings made up 75% of defendant's directory and represented 17% of plaintiff's. Thus, it makes no difference what percentage or how many facts are taken from plaintiff's work so long as the compiler does not appropriate the copyrightable selection and arrangement of the prior work. In *Bellsouth Advertising & Publication Corp. v. Donnelley Information Pub., Inc.*,[121] another Yellow Pages case, defendant copied into a computer both the directory's listings and the classification headings. The court did not find sufficient originality in the structure of the compilation headings to be protectable. Although more intricate than *Feist*'s alphabetical ordering of the White Pages, one could characterize plaintiff's Yellow Page classifications as obvious, typical, or commonplace. As the court stated:

---

[120] 945 F.2d 509 (2d Cir. 1991).

[121] 999 F.2d 1436 (11th Cir. 1993).

"[Bellsouth] can claim no copyright in the idea of dividing churches by denomination or attorneys by area of specialty."[122]

[2] Originality in Selection

A compilation may display sufficient originality for copyright purposes if the work as a whole constitutes either original selection or original arrangement. Thus, a work may be arranged in a commonplace way (*e.g.*, an alphabetical arrangement of a telephone book), but may nevertheless be copyrightable if the data is selected in an original way. An example of creative selection occurred in *Eckes v. Card Prices Update*,[123] in which a selection of 5,000 premium baseball cards from approximately 18,000 cards was held copyrightable. Here, the selection of data required creative rather than merely mechanical decisions of inclusion.[124]

The originality standard is met where the selection criteria are driven by subjective and evaluative considerations. This principle is illustrated in *CCC Information Services v. Maclean Hunter Market Reports, Inc.*[125] In *CCC*, the plaintiff published the Automobile Red Book of used car values in various versions, one of which could be found on a computer database. The Red Book prices were based on the professional judgment of the editors who made their valuations after consulting a variety of sources. Defendant CCC loaded major portions into its computer network and republished the information in various forms. The District Court ruled that the Red Book valuations were uncopyrightable because they were mere interpretations of factual information. The Court of Appeals disagreed. Here the valuations were neither reports of historical prices nor mechanical derivations of such prices. The fact that the valuations were expressed in numbers was immaterial to originality. They were the fruit of professional judgment and expertise of the editors after a review of multiple data sources. As such, the selection and arrangement of the data displayed sufficient originality to meet the low threshold of originality.[126]

---

[122] *Id.* at 1444.

[123] 736 F.2d 859 (2d Cir. 1984).

[124] Compare *Financial Info. v. Moody's Investors Serv.*, 751 F.2d 501 (2d Cir. 1984) (holding that a compilation of bond redemptions culled from bond tombstones in newspapers was not copyrightable. No selection was involved in the compilation and the actual gathering of information was purely mechanical). Discussed below.

[125] 44 F.3d 61 (2d Cir. 1994).

[126] *See also CDN Inc. v. Kapes*, 197 F.3d 1256 (9th Cir. 1999) (individual used coin prices were "compilations" rather than "ideas"); *but see New York Mercantile Exchange, Inc. v. Intercontinental Exchange, Inc.*, 497 F.3d 109 (2d Cir. 2007) (distinguishing *CCC* and holding NYMEX's futures contracts settlement prices were subject to the merger doctrine, in part because the incentive rationale for copyright did not apply to prices which NYMEX was required to make and report). For a spirited critique of both *CCC* and created facts cases see David Burk, *Method and Madness in Copyright Law*, 2007 Utah L. Rev. 587 (arguing that cases like CCC result in protecting the underlying processes that produce the protected output); and Alan Durham, *Speaking of the World: Fact, Opinion, and the Originality Standard of Copyright*, 33 Ariz. St. L.J. 791 (2001).

[3] Originality in Arrangement

Under *Feist*, a compilation may be copyrightable if the arrangement is original. For example, a baseball pitching performance chart, setting forth nine categories of past performance statistics has constituted originality in its arrangement.[127] By contrast, a directory that arranged cable systems alphabetically by state and within each state, as well as alphabetically by the name of the principal community served by the cable system, was found to be obvious and mechanical, thus failing to meet the standard of originality.[128] Unfortunately for enterprising compilers seeking copyright protection, the most useful ordering systems for compilations would not meet the *Feist* criteria for originality. Ironically, highly original systems of arrangement often are of limited value. For example, an alphabetical list of lawyers might be highly useful and valuable but uncopyrightable from the standpoint of arrangement. On the other hand, a list of local lawyers arranged according to the size of their libraries or the square footage in their waiting rooms may contain sufficient originality in arrangement for copyright protection. But who needs such a compilation? Accordingly, one might expect the issue of originality in compilations to arise with greater frequency over the selection rather than the arrangement of the facts or data.

[D] Computer Databases[129]

Quickly updated, easy-to-use, automated databases make information readily accessible, which was previously only obtained by laboriously thumbing through such sources as card catalogs, dictionaries, or legal encyclopedias. Automated databases are copyrightable as compilations,[130] and, as such, they present the same doctrinal problems of scope and protection as the traditional database. Rather than being fixed on pages of a book, automated data is fixed in electromagnetic media that require the intervention of a computer in order to communicate the content. Automated databases are different from hard copy dictionaries or encyclopedias because the collection of information contained in them are so easy to retrieve and manipulate with the use of an appropriate search engine. The problem, from the owner's standpoint, is that these automated compilations may be copied effortlessly and with low visibility, rendering them difficult to protect. Essentially, the legal issues concerning the protection of computer databases are similar to those related to protection of any other compilation, which, after *Feist*, must embody some creative authorship.

The difficult conceptual problems for compilations in copyright most often arise when a compilation manifests a low degree of authorship, *i.e.*, where the author has added little more than an arrangement of facts. Such compilations often occur in connection with an automated database.

---

[127] *See, e.g.*, *Kregos v. Associated Press*, 937 F.2d 700 (2d Cir. 1991).

[128] *See Warren Publ'g, Inc. v. Microdos Data Corp.*, 115 F.3d 1509 (11th Cir. 1997).

[129] For a discussion of this issue, see Jack B. Hicks, Note, *Copyright and Computer Databases: Is Traditional Compilation Law Adequate?*, 65 Tex. L. Rev. 993 (1987); and National Commission on New Technological Uses of Copyright Works ("CONTU"), Final Report 41 (1978).

[130] *See* 17 U.S.C. § 101 (compilation).

A good example of the difficult issues of originality for an automated database occurred in a pre-*Feist* case, *West Publishing Co. v. Mead Data Central Inc.*[131] The *Mead Data* case concerned the copyrightability of West's arrangement of legal decisions (the star pagination system) in its National Reporter System. Lexis had planned to add star pagination to the text of opinions stored in its legal database to enable viewers to use Lexis without having to consult West reporters for page citations. West contended that Lexis' wholesale appropriation of pagination from West's reporters infringed West's copyright in its compilation of cases. The court rejected Mead's argument that West was trying to protect the numbers on its pages. It found instead that Mead infringed the copyright in West's case arrangement, an important part of which was the internal page citations. The court distinguished taking the numbering system and isolated factual data from the wholesale taking of the plaintiff's arrangement of the data. In sum, the court concluded that a numbering system and its factual data are not copyrightable, but the overall arrangement of the actual data is.

Is *West* still viable after *Feist* with its requirement of original selection or arrangement of factual matter? Specifically, what is original about a numeric arrangement — consecutive numbering — of the pages in a given legal opinion or set of opinions? Unquestionably, West could prevent Mead from publishing a competing volume of the Supreme Court Reporter using West's system of pagination. But *West* goes much further than this, finding an infringement because Mead's database showed where a specific group of words are found on a certain page in the West reporters.

This holding is questionable in the post-*Feist* world. The two decisions can only be reconciled on the difficult premise that West's consecutive arrangement of pages in its reporter system manifests a greater degree of originality than Feist's uncopyrightable alphabetical arrangement of a telephone book. Litigation over West's copyrights on its pagination system has continued with conflicting results.[132] In *Matthew Bender & Co. v. West Pub. Co.*,[133] the Second Circuit Court of Appeals refused to follow *West*, holding that the pagination and case information related to court opinions published by West Publishing were not copyrightable and may be used by competing electronic publishers. The court viewed the Eighth Circuit decision as resting on the "sweat of the brow" doctrine, now defunct (after *Feist*). In other words, the earlier decision erroneously protected West's industrious collection rather than its original creation. Even worse for West, the same court, in a companion opinion, held that other aspects of West's editorial alterations to factual information failed to meet the standard of originality under *Feist*. These included: (1) the arrangement of prefatory information, such as parties, the court, and date of decision; (2) selection and arrangement of attorney information; (3) arrangement of information on subsequent procedural developments; and (4) selection of parallel and alternative citations.[134]

---

[131] 799 F.2d 1219 (8th Cir. 1986).

[132] *See Oasis Pub. Co. v. West Publ'g Co.*, 924 F. Supp. 918 (D. Minn. 1996) (upholding West's compilation copyrights).

[133] 158 F.3d 674 (2d Cir. 1998).

[134] *Id.* at 683–86.

Another database compilation with low authorship content was involved in *Financial Information, Inc. v. Moody's Investors Service, Inc.*[135] As compared with *West*, this case shows that (even before *Feist*) the courts would not protect individual facts despite a free-riding defendant. Financial Information, Inc. ("FII") mailed to subscribers the *Daily Bond Card*, consisting of index cards containing information about municipal bonds. The cards were a pure compilation of financial facts, and the information collected on them required little, if any, editorial skill. Moody's copied the information from these cards and incorporated it into *Moody's News Reports*. The District Court took an expansive view on the daily fact cards, stating, "[t]o accord copyright protection to the annual compilation but deny it to each daily component would negate the value of the protection accorded the yearly compilation."[136] In other words, why should the serial thief go free while the thief who waited to copy the final compilation is punished as an infringer? The Court of Appeals was troubled by this paradox, but rejected the District Court's decision in favor of the plaintiff and remanded the case to decide whether the data on the FII cards involved a modicum of selection, coordination, or arrangement by FII.

The decision in *FII* supports the basic principle for protection of compilations in copyright law as articulated in *Feist*. Facts *per se* are not protected under copyright law no matter how sympathetic one might be toward the author who expended the effort to compile them. A compilation should be entitled to copyright protection only if the author has added original authorship to public domain facts in the selection, coordination, and arrangement of the data.

[E] Protection of Databases Outside Copyright Law: Toward a *Sui Generis* Federal Right

Despite the fears of some database owners, the practical effect of the *Feist* decision on their economic lives has hardly been dramatic. Companies appear to routinely cross-license their data to one another as a matter of course. Even some users, such as direct mail marketers, who could, as a matter of law, copy white page phone numbers from directories, continue to pay in order to receive the data in more convenient formats, and to be assured current updates.

By contrast, compilers of other comprehensive databases, particularly computerized databases whose collections of information are easily accessed online, manipulated, and downloaded at minimal cost, may be profoundly affected. Moreover, due to their inherent structure, these databases have characteristics that would render them difficult to protect under copyright law. For example, suppose a user of WESTLAW or LEXIS was to download all the recent copyright cases dealing with the "fair use" doctrine and then distribute them to others. The company would have much difficulty in arguing that the user copied the "organization" of its database. In addition, because of its inclusiveness, it would be difficult to justify its protection on the basis of "selection." These difficulties have

---

135 751 F.2d 501 (2d Cir. 1984).

136 *Id.* at 506.

left owners of comprehensive computerized databases in a position of legal limbo and economic vulnerability.[137]

For some time, compilers of databases have looked to protection for their collections of information outside of copyright law. Some have explored contractual mechanisms for protecting their compilations.[138] Others have employed technological safeguards to prohibit or control access to their databases. In addition to contractual and technological mechanisms, much of the "extracopyright law" focus has centered on the protection of databases under a *sui generis* regime, or one based on principles in other legal realms such as tort or misappropriation law. Such protection would be founded on the Commerce Clause rather than art. 1 § 8, cl. 8 of the Constitution.[139] One open question is whether Congress has the authority to pass such legislation, in light of the *Feist* opinion's declaration that originality is a requirement under the Constitution.[140]

Some of the impetus for special protection in U.S. law came from developments abroad. In 1996, the European Union issued Directive 96/9/EC on Legal Protection of Databases,[141] instructing the fifteen member nations to harmonize their laws to grant copyright protection for databases. Defined as "a collection of independent works, data or other materials arranged in a systematic or methodical way and individually accessible by electronic means,"[142] databases are to be protected under an originality standard similar to that found in *Feist*.[143] The Directive, however, goes beyond copyright in providing a *sui generis* right against unauthorized "extraction" and "reutilization" of a "substantial part" of a database, irrespective of the work's eligibility for copyright.[144] Most troublesome from a U.S. perspective, protection for foreign databases is available only on the basis of reciprocal

---

[137] *See* Laura D'Andrea Tyson & Edward F. Sherry, Statutory Protection for Databases: Economic & Public Policy Issues, research paper prepared under contract to Reed-Elsevier, Inc. and the Thomson Corp., and presented as testimony on behalf of the Information Industry Association at the Oct. 23, 1997, Hearing on H.R. 2652, the "Collections of Information Antipiracy Act", held by the Subcommittee on Courts and Intellectual Property of the Committee on the Judiciary of the U.S. House of Representatives.

[138] *See ProCd v. Zeidenberg*, 86 F.3d 1447 (7th Cir. 1996). Moreover, efforts on the part of the National Conference of Commissioners on Uniform State Laws and the American Law Institute to revise the Uniform Commercial Code to include a new Article 2B, dealing specifically with the licensing of information, seem likely to promote the use of contractual mechanisms in the future.

[139] *See, e.g.*, H.R. 354, 106th Cong. 1st Sess., 1999; H.R. 3872, 108th Cong. (2nd Sess. 2004). A growing scholarly literature holds that whatever problems exist in the database market are better cured through selective application of tort principles of unfair competition rather than by comprehensive *sui generis* protection. *See* J. H. Reichman & Pamela Samuelson, *Intellectual Property Rights in Data?*, 50 Vand. L. Rev. 51 (1997). Critics question whether it truly represents a misappropriation approach because the bill created would apply not only against competitors but also against consumers.

[140] The issue has attracted much interest in the law reviews. For a comprehensive overview, see Paul J. Heald & Suzanna Sherry, *Implied Limits on the Legislative Power: The Intellectual Property Clause as an Absolute Constraint on Congress*, 2000 U. Ill. L. Rev. 119.

[141] O.J.E.C. No. L 777/20 (23.3.96). The directive can be found in Marshall Leaffer, International Treaties in Intellectual Property 881 (2d ed. 1997).

[142] *Id.* Art. 1.2.

[143] *See id.* Art. 3.

[144] *Id.* Art. 7.

protection in the foreign country.[145] Thus, the U.S. database owners are left without protection in the European Union until the United States adopts a similar law that would protect non-original databases. Whether such a law would actually benefit the public interest is highly debatable, particularly after a 2005 European Union evaluation of the Directive. This E.U. report concluded that there was little evidence regarding the Directive's effectiveness in creating growth in the production of European databases.[146]

In addition to the European Union, a proposal for an international system of *sui generis* database protection was on the agenda at a World Intellectual Property Organization ("WIPO") conference held in Geneva in December, 1996.[147]

The new treaty would have made such protection of databases an international legal norm. The proposal was tabled amid widespread skepticism from scientific and educational communities as well as by delegates to the conference from developing countries. WIPO has announced that it will continue to pursue an international database treaty.[148] Although the drive for some sort of database treaty continues, it is no longer on a fast track, and the United States is no longer taking a lead role in the process.

§ 2.12 COLLECTIVE WORKS

The Copyright Act defines a "collective work" as "a work, such as a periodical issue, anthology, or encyclopedia, in which a number of contributions, constituting separate and independent works in themselves, are assembled into a collective whole."[149] A collective work is a species of compilation that involves the selection, ordering, and arranging of a number of independent contributions. The House Report indicates that collective works do not include cases, "such as a composition consisting of words and music, a work published with illustrations or front matter, or three one act plays, where relatively few separate elements have been brought together."[150] In other words, a collective work exists only if each contribution can

---

[145] *Id.* Art. 11. For an overview of the issue, see Charles R. McManis, *Database Protection in the Digital Information Age*, 7 Roger Williams U. L. Rev. 7 (2001) (counseling against broad protection for databases driven by a desire for reciprocal protection in Europe); Jacqueline Lipton, *Balancing Private Rights and Public Policies: Reconceptualizing Property in Databases*, 18 Berk. L.J. 773 (2003) (suggesting *sui generis* protection founded on compulsory licensing and government supervision to protect the public interest).

[146] Commission of the European Communities, DG Internal Market and Services Working Paper, First Evaluation of Directive 96/9/EC on the Legal Protection of Databases (Dec. 12, 2005), *available at* http://ec.europa.eu/internal_market/copyright/docs/databases/evaluation_report_en.pdf. The paper, however, did not recommend that the Directive be abrogated because it did not impose significant administrative or other regulatory burdens on the database industry or any other industries that depend on having access to data and information.

[147] *See Basic Proposal for the Substantive Provisions of the Treaty on Intellectual Property in Respect of Databases*, Memorandum Prepared by the Chairman of the Committee of Experts, August 30, 1996.

[148] WIPO Doc. CRNR/DC/88, Dec. 20, 1996.

[149] 17 U.S.C. § 101 (collective work).

[150] H.R. Rep. No. 94-1476, at 122 (1976).

stand on its own, independent from the collective work, and have some value in its own right.[151]

In addition to the quantitative threshold, protectable collective works must manifest originality, as required for all compilations. Collective authorship consists of the selection and arrangement of the independent works chosen by the collective work author. Thus, an anthology of the complete short stories of O. Henry put in chronological order would no more meet the standard of originality than the alphabetical ordering of the white pages of a telephone book.[152] On the other hand, a selection and thematic ordering of twenty-five stories of the same author should meet the originality threshold for collective works to obtain protection under the Act.

Part IV. NON-COPYRIGHTABLE SUBJECT MATTER

§ 2.13 IDEAS AND SYSTEMS UNDER § 102(b)

[A] Generally

The Copyright Act has codified the longstanding, judicially evolved rule that copyright protects the expression of an idea but not the idea itself. Section 102(b) provides: "In no case does copyright protection for an original work of authorship extend to any idea, procedure, process, system, method of operation, concept, principle, or discovery, regardless of the form in which it is described, explained, illustrated, or embodied in such work."[153]

Once an author reveals his work to the public, he injects the idea into the public domain and must be content to maintain control only over the *form* in which the idea is expressed. Copyright extends only to the specific, concrete, expressive vehicle through which the creator's ideas appear, leaving the substance of the ideas outside the scope of the author's monopoly. This fundamental principle of copyright law cuts across the entire range of copyrightable subject matter. It is consistent with the purpose of copyright law, which is to encourage the creation of an optimal variety of artistic expression. To create new works, future authors must have access to a well-endowed public domain, the place where fundamental building materials — concepts, discoveries, and technological solutions — reside and are freely available for those wishing to embellish them with their own original expression.[154]

---

[151] *See Blum v. Kline*, 8 U.S.P.Q. 2d 1080 (S.D.N.Y. 1982) (holding that a photograph of a fashion model was not a collective work to which a photographer's efforts constituted an independent contribution).

[152] *See Silverstein v. Penguin Putnam, Inc.*, 368 F.3d 77 (2d Cir. 2004) (remanding for a determination as to whether plaintiff's selection of unpublished poems by Dorothy Parker was original), *on remand*, 522 F. Supp. 2d 579 (S.D.N.Y. 2007) ("Silverstein's choices were obvious ones that required no creative judgment.").

[153] 17 U.S.C. § 102(b).

[154] For an excellent overview of the idea-expression dichotomy in copyright, see Leslie A. Kurtz,

As a result, copyright law does not preclude others from using ideas or information revealed in an author's work. Copying another person's ideas or expression without attribution may constitute what is known as "plagiarism", a serious ethical violation and a punishable offense in the world of academia. Copyright law, however, allows the defendant to copy another's ideas, with or without attribution. Accordingly, a discoverer of a scientific principle or historical fact, or someone who unearths an unknown play by Shakespeare cannot claim copyright despite the effort and ingenuity expended. Ideas, discoveries, principles, and facts are freely accessible to the public, and to confer property status on them would hinder rather than promote "the progress of science and the useful arts," thereby undermining the constitutionally declared purpose of copyright. Any lower standard would intolerably burden future creative activity and the dissemination of knowledge, and might even conflict with the First Amendment. It has been said that copyright does not significantly interfere with the First Amendment because it protects only the form of expression contained in the copyrighted work and allows the author's ideas to circulate freely.[155] The Supreme Court has identified the idea/expression distinction as one of two major copyright doctrines that protect the values of the First Amendment, the other being "fair use".[156]

Once an abstract idea is disclosed to the public, it becomes a part of our common reservoir of knowledge, and it will not matter whether the originator has spent vast sums of money developing it, advertising it, or making it popular. It may, however, be possible to protect the private disclosure of an original idea, plan, or scheme to others under circumstances that suggest a confidential relationship or an implication of contract. But an action for the misappropriation of an idea must be sought under a state law cause of action such as breach of trust or contract, not under federal copyright law.[157]

As in the case of originality, the idea/expression distinction is left undefined in the Copyright Act. Its application is to be determined by standards developed in case law under the 1909 Act. The idea-expression issue often arises in a suit for copyright infringement. To prove infringement, the copyright owner must prove substantial similarity between his work and the defendant's. The plaintiff must show that the alleged infringer took not just an abstract idea from his work, but copied the *expression* of that idea.[158]

Speaking to the Ghost: Idea and Expression in Copyright, 47 U. Miami L. Rev. 1221 (1993).

[155] *See* Nimmer on Copyright § 1.10 (2014).

[156] *See Eldred v. Ashcroft*, 537 U.S. 186, 219 (2003); *Golan v. Holder*, 132 S. Ct. 873, 890 (2012).

[157] *See, e.g.*, *Desny v. Wilder*, 299 P.2d 257 (Cal. 1956) (discussing an alleged express promise by movie producer to pay for story). The California Supreme Court stated: "The person who can and does convey a valuable idea to a producer who commercially solicits the service or who voluntarily accepts it knowing that it is tendered for a price should likewise be entitled to recover." *Id.* at 734, 299 P.2d at 267. *See also Davies v. Krasna*, 245 Cal. App. 2d 535 (1966); *Donahue v. Ziv Television Programs, Inc.*, 245 Cal. App. 2d 593 (1966); *Minniear v. Tors*, 266 Cal. App. 2d 495 (1968). For an extensive discussion of protection under state law, see Nimmer on Copyright § 16.03 (2014).

[158] *See Nichols v. Universal Pictures Corp.*, 45 F.2d 119 (2d Cir. 1930); Edward Samuels, *The Idea-Expression Dichotomy in Copyright Law*, 56 Tenn. L. Rev. 321 (1989); Amy B. Cohen, *Copyright Law and the Myth of Objectivity: The Idea-Expression Dichotomy and the Inevitability of Artistic Value Judgments*, 66 Ind. L.J. 175 (1990).

Here, the court must determine whether the defendant borrowed the unprotectable elements of plaintiff's work. Often this determination overlaps the requirement of originality, because basic ideas, such as a basic plot device, common geometric shapes in a work of art, or many elements of computer programs, are readily accessible from many sources. Of course, not all ideas are unoriginal. But they often are, and the author has simply copied them from public sources. How broadly a court defines what constitutes the idea as compared to the expression depends on the nature of the subject matter at issue. Thus, ideas that form a musical work — basic melody, harmony, rhythm — differ substantially from those that are embodied in a literary work, such as general theme, plot structures, and character development.

The idea/expression dichotomy, which cuts across all copyrightable subject matter, is easy to state but difficult to apply in practice. To distinguish what constitutes idea, as opposed to expression, is a matter of degree, and where expression ends and idea begins is not an either/or proposition; it is more akin to a continuum. All works, whether literary, artistic, or musical, contain ideas. Expression begins at some point by the author's elaboration, execution, and embellishment in explaining, applying, and implementing those ideas. No copyright protection can be afforded to the depiction of a bee in a jeweled pin,[159] the portrayal of a whiskey bottle in a photograph,[160] a life-like presentation of a glass-in-glass sculpture of a jellyfish,[161] the notion of producing stuffed dinosaur toys,[162] or the idea of a realistic depiction a Puerto Rican tree frog.[163] In such instances, the range of protectable expression is constrained by the conventions of depicting a bee, a jellyfish, or a whiskey bottle, and when original expression is subtracted from the underlying idea, the plaintiff is left with "thin" copyright protection against virtually identical copying.

Separating an idea from its expression is an *ad hoc* process but a necessary one.[164] In every situation, regardless of the kind of work involved, the court must strike a balance between two conflicting interests. If the idea is defined too broadly, it will create a bottleneck, impeding the production of future works. On the other hand, if the idea is defined too narrowly, future authors will not have sufficient economic incentive to create new works. One court put it this way: "The guiding consideration . . . is the preservation of the balance between competition and protection reflected in the copyright laws."[165]

---

[159] *Herbert Rosenthal Jewelry Corp. v. Kalpakian*, 446 F.2d 738 (9th Cir. 1971).

[160] *Ets-Hokin v. Skyy Spirits, Inc.*, 323 F.3d 763 (9th Cir. 2003).

[161] *Sativa v. Lowry*, 323 F.3d 805 (9th Cir. 2003) (holding that allegedly protected elements of glass-in-glass jellyfish sculpture — "a vertically oriented, colorful, fanciful jellyfish with tendril-like tentacles and a rounded bell encased in an outer layer of rounded clear glass" — could not be protected under the idea-expression dichotomy; "Satava possesses a thin copyright that protects against only virtually identical copying.").

[162] *Aliotti v. R. Dakin & Co.*, 831 F.2d 898 (9th Cir. 1987).

[163] *Coquico, Inc. v. Rodriguez-Miranda*, 562 F.3d 62 (1st Cir. 2009).

[164] *Peter Pan Fabrics, Inc. v. Martin Weiner Corp.*, 274 F.2d 487, 489 (2d Cir. 1960).

[165] *Herbert Rosenthal Jewelry Corp.*, 446 F.2d at 742.

Because of these competitive market concerns, courts distinguish between different categories of ideas: those that undertake to advance the understanding of phenomena or the solution of problems, such as the symptoms of a disease, or the bookkeeping system of *Baker v. Selden*,[166] and those infused with the author's taste or opinion, like a comprehensive list of the best restaurants in New York, or a valuation of certain models of used cars.[167] The need to keep ideas free from private ownership is far greater for the first category — those that are directed to solving problems or explaining phenomena — as compared with the second category of "soft" ideas — those that reflect taste or opinion.[168] To confer copyright protection on the first category of ideas would unduly impede competition and the progress of science and the useful arts.

Because the idea-expression dichotomy is best examined in a specific context, the discussion now turns to four applications of the idea-expression principle: *Baker v. Selden* and the merger doctrine; the protection of graphical user interfaces and menu hierarchies in computer programs, the copyrightability of literary characters; and the protection of historical facts and research.

[B] Idea and Expression: The Doctrine of *Baker v. Selden*

[1] The Nature of Functional Works: Patent Policy and Copyright Law

Functional works, such as computer programs, architectural plans, and legal forms are those that carry out a specific task or achieve a certain result.[169] These works are found in all varieties of copyrightable subject matter. For example, although computer programs are literary works, and architectural blueprints are pictorial works, both are also functional works because they share a common task-oriented dimension. They differ from a poem or painting because their

---

[166] 101 U.S. 99 (1880).

[167] *See CCC Info. Sys., Inc. v. Maclean Hunter Mkt. Reports, Inc.*, 44 F.3d 61, 72 (2d Cir. 1994), *cert. denied*, 516 U.S. 817 (1995). The court found no merger of idea and expression for the valuations of used car prices in plaintiff's Red Book. In so ruling, the court distinguished between "building block" ideas, which are subject to the merger doctrine because they must be freed up to "assist the understanding of future thinkers," and "approximative statements of opinion," which are "infused with the author's taste or opinion." *Id.* at 72–73.

[168] *See American Dental Ass'n v. Delta Dental Plans Ass'n*, 126 F.3d 977 (7th Cir. 1997) (stating that Code on Dental Procedures and Nomenclatures that classifies all dental procedures into groups where each procedure receives a number, a short description, and a long description was a copyrightable work of authorship, not an uncopyrightable method or system under § 102(b)); *Kregos v. Associated Press*, 937 F.2d 700 (2d Cir. 1991) (holding baseball pitching performance chart, which set forth nine categories of past performance statistics for the day's starting pitchers to aid in predicting outcome of game, copyrightable).

[169] For example, recipes have been denied copyright protection under § 102(b) as a system, process, or method of operation. *Compare Publications Int'l, Ltd. v. Meredith Corp.*, 88 F.3d 473 (7th Cir. 1996) (finding recipes contained in a cookbook of yogurt dishes were not copyrightable as comprising lists of required ingredients and the directions for combining them to achieve the final products contained no expressive elaboration on the functional components), *with Barbour v. Head*, 178 F. Supp. 2d 758, 759 (S.D. Tex. 2001) (declining to grant summary judgment to defendants, in an amusing decision beginning with the line: "This case involves a rustled cowboy cookbook").

aesthetic aspect is only incidental to their primary purpose — to accomplish a given task. Because functional works often closely integrate idea and expression, they tend to conflict with copyright law's protection of original expression. This basic principle is embodied in § 102(b), which precludes copyright protection not only for ideas, but also for systems, processes, and methods of operation.[170] As Professor Goldstein points out, interests of utility will frequently compel expression in functional works "to hew closely to the underlying — and unprotectable — idea, procedure, process, system or method of operation that it expresses."[171]

When encountering a functional work, the courts will limit protection to avoid conferring a *de facto* monopoly over the unprotectable, utilitarian aspects of the work. Distinguishing between idea and expression is a difficult but necessary task because of the policies that differentiate copyright from patent law. Copyright law encourages the production of a broad range of artistic, literary, and musical works. Its standard of validity, based on originality, is relatively easy to meet, and a rigorous formal examination process is not required. Once obtained, a copyright confers a relatively thin but lengthy term of property rights (life of the author plus seventy years). Despite the lengthy term, the exclusionary force of the copyright grant is relatively weak because the consumer generally can turn to satisfactory substitutes for any given novel, film, or work of art, a multitude of which compete for the consumer's dollar. If satisfactory substitutes are available, the seller will enjoy no market power for the work. Thus, even though the copyright grant is long, it confers a legal rather than an economic monopoly.

The patent laws encourage protection of works in the realm of technology. The patent grant, however, is conferred only on those inventions that represent a substantial advance over the prior art.[172] Unlike a copyright, a patentable invention must demonstrate considerably more than originality and must meet the rigorous tests of novelty and nonobviousness.[173] Failure to meet these standards would result in conferring monopoly protection on an insubstantial advance over the public domain. Although of relatively short duration, the patent grant provides a more powerful set of exclusive rights.[174]

In contrast to copyright, the patent grant may confer a powerful economic monopoly in the absence of satisfactory substitutes that compete in the market for the patented product or process. Thus, the courts are justifiably concerned, given the risk of providing copyright protection of such long duration over subject matter failing to meet the more rigorous standards of patent law. The conflict between copyright and patent policy often arises when a work of utility contains expressive elements. In this situation, the courts must develop a principled approach by which the expressive elements of a work are rendered discrete from the work's underlying ideas and utilitarian aspects.

---

170 *See, e.g.*, *Brooks-Ngwenya v. Indianapolis Public Schools*, 564 F.3d 804 (7th Cir. 2009) (ideas for better educating students are not protectable); *Hutchins v. Zoll Medical Corp.*, 492 F.3d 1377 (Fed. Cir. 2007) (method of treating victims using CPR or instructing others how to use CPR was not protected).

171 Paul Goldstein, Copyright § 2.15 (3d ed. 2014).

172 See *supra* § 1.11, for a discussion of patents.

173 35 U.S.C. §§ 102, 103.

174 *See* 35 U.S.C. § 154 (twenty years from the date of application).

These principles concerning the protectability of functional works in copyright law were established in the leading case of *Baker v. Selden*.[175] In *Baker*, copyright protection was sought for a work entitled *Selden's Condensed Ledger of Bookkeeping Simplified*, which explained a new system of bookkeeping. Included in the work were a set of blank forms consisting of ruled lines and headings specially designed for use with the system. Those forms permitted the entire operations of a day or a week to be reported on a single page or on two pages facing each other. The defendant published a book with forms achieving the same result but with different arrangements of the columns and headings. The Supreme Court could have decided the case simply by finding; however, the Court reversed a judgment for the plaintiff, reasoning that the system could not be used absent the methods and diagrams in the book.[176] Thus, according to the Court, the ledger was actually a utilitarian object rather than an expressive work. Unless copyright was denied in this instance, a monopoly could in effect be granted over the underlying idea of the system. The Court stated that monopolies over systems or processes should be difficult to obtain, and the claimant should have to meet the rigorous examination for novelty and invention used by the Patent Office.[177] Moreover, a grant of the patent monopoly lasted a relatively short time as compared to the substantially longer term of copyright. In other words, we should not allow a creator of inherently patentable subject matter, *i.e.*, a system or process, to use copyright law to circumvent the patent system.

[2] The Use/Explanation Dichotomy and the Merger Doctrine

The Court's views on distinguishing patent from copyright law have become universally accepted. The *Baker* Court enunciated another rationale in denying copyrightability, known as the doctrine of *Baker v. Selden*, which may be summarized as follows: where the use of an idea requires the copying of the work itself, such copying will not constitute infringement. On the other hand, if the copying does not involve the use of the art but instead its explanation, then such copying will constitute an infringement. No one is exactly sure what the Court really meant by its use/explanation dichotomy. For that matter, the case is oracle-like and permeated with obscure language, so we can only speculate about what the Court actually had in mind.

Not all courts have followed the "use/explanation" doctrine of *Baker v. Selden*.[178] In *Harcourt, Brace & World, Inc. v. Graphic Controls Corp.*,[179] copyright was allowed for answer sheet forms that not only provided spaces for the correct

---

[175] 101 U.S. 99 (1879).

[176] *See id.* at 103.

[177] For a discussion of the general exclusion of games as systems from copyright, *see* Bruce E. Boyden, *Games and Other Uncopyrightable Systems*, 18 Geo. Mason L. Rev. 439 (2011).

[178] The Supreme Court stated in *Mazer v. Stein*, 347 U.S. 201, 218 (1954), "[w]e find nothing in the copyright statute to support the argument that the intended use or use in industry of an article eligible for copyright bars or invalidates its registration. We do not read such a limitation into the copyright law."

[179] 329 F. Supp. 517 (S.D.N.Y. 1971). *See also Continental Cas. Co. v. Beardsley*, 253 F.2d 702 (2d Cir. 1958) (holding blanket bond forms copyrightable).

answers, but also provided minimal information. Other courts have stated that the question of liability should turn on whether the defendant has copied the copyrightable elements of the work for which it originally received protection, no matter what kind of use is to be made of the copied material.

Another interpretation of the use/explanation dichotomy is known as the "merger doctrine." According to this view, the doctrine of *Baker v. Selden* implies that there are some instances where the use of a system or process necessitates the identical copying of the author's expression of the system or process. In other words, if the underlying idea (or system, process, or method of operation) can effectively be expressed in only one way, the idea and expression are said to have "merged." When this occurs, the work cannot receive protection under copyright law. To allow copyright protection in such an instance would undermine the notion that ideas are in short supply and their protection is not worth the social costs of the monopoly. It would also blur the distinction between copyright and patent law: "To give the author of a book an exclusive property in the art described therein, when no examination of its novelty has ever been officially made, would be a surprise and a fraud upon the public. That is the province of letters-patent, not of copyright."[180]

The merger doctrine has found support in Copyright Office regulations,[181] denying copyright to works designed for recording information that do not in themselves convey information. The case law also supports the doctrine as for example where verbatim copying of a contract form was allowed because it was for use rather than explanation.[182] Similarly, in *Kern River Gas Transmission Co. v. Coastal Corp.*,[183] the plaintiff's depiction of its proposed natural gas pipeline route on government survey maps was not copyrightable. The maps may have been original, but, according to the court, they expressed the idea of the location of the pipeline in the only effective way. Thus, when idea and expression are inseparable, they merge to preclude copyright protection.[184]

Some courts have extended the merger doctrine to works that may be expressed in more than one way but only in a limited number of ways. In the leading case, *Morrissey v. Procter & Gamble Co.*,[185] the court allowed verbatim copying of contest instructions, even though more than one form of expression was possible, because there existed only a limited number of possible forms of expression.[186]

---

[180] 101 U.S. at 102.

[181] *See* 37 C.F.R. §§ 202.1(b), (c) (1987). *See also Taylor Instrument Co. v. Fawley-Brost Co.*, 139 F.2d 98 (7th Cir. 1943) (holding chart for recording temperatures not copyrightable); *Aldrich v. Remington Rand, Inc.*, 52 F. Supp. 732 (N.D. Tex. 1942) (holding forms for keeping tax records not copyrightable).

[182] *See Crume v. Pacific Mut. Life Ins. Co.*, 140 F.2d 182 (7th Cir. 1944).

[183] 899 F.2d 1458 (5th Cir. 1990).

[184] One should compare *Kern* with *Mason v. Montgomery Data, Inc.*, 967 F.2d 135 (2d Cir. 1992) (finding no merger in real estate ownership maps based on public domain sources because presentation of factual subject matter — i.e. placement, size, dimensions of survey tracts, etc. — could be expressed in many different ways). *See also Herbert Rosenthal Jewelry Corp. v. Kalpakian*, 446 F.2d 738 (9th Cir. 1971) (noting plaintiff's jewel-encrusted pin, shaped like a bee, was not copyrightable because the jeweled bee-shaped pin was an idea that defendant could freely copy).

[185] 379 F.2d 675, 678 (1st Cir. 1967).

[186] Since *Morrissey*, the doctrine has been alluded to often in the case law. *See, e.g.*, *Ho v. Taflove*, 648

Does the "merger doctrine" have an empirical basis? As a factual matter, is there any system or method that can be performed by the use of only one particular form of written expression? Accordingly, some commentators have challenged this basic assumption of the merger doctrine.[187]

[3] Functionality and Standardization: Graphical User Interfaces, Menu Hierarchies, and the Merger Doctrine

The extent that copyright covers computer-generated screen displays, such as Windows, or Apple's graphical user interface ("GUI"), has led to some hard fought legal battles. These cases illustrate the complex nature of separating idea and expression in works of utility that contain expressive elements.[188]

Generally, the courts will allow protection for the artistic features of an interface while denying protection to clearly functional features, such as centered headings and underscored program names.[189] From a more controversial standpoint, courts have also denied protection to user interfaces and other features that have become industry standards, even though those features were completely arbitrary at the time they were adopted.[190] The graphical user interface is one aspect of the user interface that governs how people interact with the computer.[191] These displays contain attractive aesthetic features while facilitating efficient use and can become, over time, an industry standard. A computer programmer's design choices (not just for screen displays but for all aspects of the user interface) are often determined by many considerations, both aesthetic and utilitarian, such as mechanical specifications, compatibility requirements, and industry demands.[192] Generally categorized as audiovisual works for copyright purposes, graphical user interfaces combine color, graphics, and sound in facilitating communication between the user and a computer.

When judging infringement of certain screen displays, notably videogames, the courts have for the most part invoked the standards used for other audiovisual works, such as cartoons. Unlike videogame displays, a more significant portion of the GUI is dictated by functional considerations. Careful not to extend copyright

---

F.3d 489, 499 (7th Cir. 2011); *R.W. Beck, Inc. v. E3 Consulting, LLC*, 577 F.3d 1133, 1145 (10th Cir. 2009); *Veeck v. Southern Building Code Congress Intl, Inc.*, 293 F.3d 791 (5th Cir. 2002) (holding that the merger doctrine applied to privately drafted model building which rendered them unprotectable when enacted into law); *but see Merkos Llnyonei Chinuch, Inc. v. Otsar Sifrei Lubavitch, Inc.*, 312 F.3d 94 (2d Cir. 2002) (rejecting the merger claim where plaintiffs English Translation of a Hebrew prayer had been endorsed by the chief rabbi of a religious community).

[187] *See* Nimmer on Copyright § 2.18[C][2] (2014).

[188] *See Apple Computer, Inc. v. Microsoft Corp.*, 799 F. Supp. 1006 (N.D. Cal. 1992).

[189] *See Manufacturers Techs., Inc. v. Cams, Inc.*, 706 F. Supp. 984 (D. Conn. 1989) (denying protection to elements that represent a narrow range of possibilities); *Lotus Dev. v. Paperback Software Int'l*, 740 F. Supp. 37 (D. Mass. 1990) (conferring protection on spreadsheet program's command structure).

[190] Much of the case law focused on the copyrightability of Graphical User Interfaces and that of command and menu hierarchies.

[191] *See* Que's Computer User's Dictionary 634 (4th ed. 1993).

[192] *See Computer Assocs. Int'l, Inc., v. Altai, Inc.*, 982 F.2d 693, 709–10 (2d Cir. 1992).

over these functional elements, courts have required "bodily appropriation of expression" or "virtual identity" to establish infringement of a compilation copyright in the elements of a user interface.[193] Although courts will protect the more fanciful aspects of GUI, they are careful not to provide patent-like protection to basic ideas embodied in the interface, such as the use of windows to display multiple images on the screen or iconic representation of familiar office objects.[194] In short, GUIs have received thin copyright protection that amounts to a prohibition against verbatim copying. This heightened standard is justified by an interest in standardization and the fact that there is a limited range of expressions to achieve a useful screen display.

Closely related to the graphical user interface is the menu command hierarchy found in many programs such as spreadsheets, word processing, and database applications. Unlike GUIs, which often contain artistically imaginative elements, command hierarchies, such as "Copy," "Print," and "Quit," and more complicated menu command trees, present difficult questions under the idea/expression doctrine and § 102(b) of the Copyright Act. Again the courts have applied the "thin" copyright doctrine, protecting command hierarchies against all but verbatim copying, and, in special situations, have denied copyright to them upon their becoming the industry standard.

The copyrightability of computer command hierarchies arose in *Lotus Development Corp v. Borland International*.[195] In *Lotus*, the defendant copied the Lotus command hierarchy of the popular Lotus 1-2-3 spreadsheet program in its entirety. The question arose whether the command hierarchy was copyrightable subject matter under § 102(b) or was an uncopyrightable method of operation. The District Court had ruled that the Lotus menu command hierarchy, with its specific choice and arrangement of command terms, constituted copyrightable expression. The Court of Appeals disagreed. Because the Lotus menu command hierarchy provides the means by which users control and operate the Lotus program, the court viewed Lotus's command hierarchy as an uncopyrightable method of operation, much like the buttons on a VCR machine.

The most controversial aspect of the decision is the court's acknowledgement that the Lotus developers made some expressive choices in selecting and arranging the command terms, and yet the command hierarchy was not capable of protection. The court tied its conclusion to the issue of compatibility, expressing concern that users of Lotus 1-2-3 who wished to switch to other programs would have to learn how to perform the same operation in a different manner. The concurring opinion was troubled by the fact that the Lotus command structure has become the industry standard: if a monopoly were granted to Lotus, users who have learned and devised their own macros would be locked into Lotus much like a typist who has learned the QWERTY keyboard would be captive to one who enjoyed a monopoly over it.[196]

---

[193] *See MiTek Holdings, Inc. v. Arce Eng'g Co.*, 89 F.3d 1548 (11th Cir. 1996).

[194] *See Apple Computer, Inc. v. Microsoft Corp.*, 35 F.3d 1435 (9th Cir. 1994).

[195] 49 F.3d 807 (1st Cir. 1995). On January 19, 1996, the Supreme Court affirmed the First Circuit by a 4-4 vote. The effect of the Court's "nondecision" is that the result stands and is binding precedent in the First Circuit but whether it achieves broader acceptance remains to be seen.

[196] *See id.* at 819–21. A number of articles have discussed the issues in *Lotus*. *See, e.g.*, Loyd Weinreb,

Thus, as Lotus illustrates, what constitutes an idea, process, or system for a computer program's command hierarchy, or a computer's user interface (or any other work for that matter) is not self-defining. Inevitably, complicated competitive considerations, which may regulate an entire industry, loom large in determining the scope of protection for computer interfaces and programs. The ultimate determination may be stated as follows: if a third party were deprived of copying a particular feature, how serious would be the resulting social costs of the monopoly on consumer welfare?

The GUI and command hierarchy cases illustrate the complex and multilayered decisions involved in applying the idea/expression doctrine under § 102(b) of the Act, particularly when works of utility are concerned. Here, courts, in close cases, engage in a delicate balancing process in determining whether society should have access to certain technological solutions. In this context, it becomes clear that the terms idea and expression should not be taken at face value but as the conclusions in setting boundaries around what should be protectable and what should not. On the whole, courts will exclude protection of material that constitutes an essential building block of creative expression, or a method for solving a problem. In cases like *Lotus v. Borland*, § 102(b) becomes a way of injecting into copyright law the kinds of competition policy concerns that we typically associate with antitrust law. Courts, however, should be circumspect in overloading copyright cases with concepts borrowed from antitrust law. The risk is that this body of law, taken out of context, will be applied in a haphazard and incomplete fashion.

[4] The Merger Doctrine and *Scènes à Faire*

The merger doctrine has been applied primarily to works of utility, such as forms, rules, and computer programs. Under the merger doctrine, courts will not protect a copyrighted work from infringement if the idea underlying the work can be expressed only in one or few different ways, for fear that there may be a monopoly on the underlying idea. In such an instance, it is said that the work's idea and expression "merge." Under the related doctrine of *scènes à faire*, courts will not protect a copyrighted work from infringement if the expression embodied in the work necessarily flows from a commonplace idea. Generally, the courts have applied the *scènes à faire* doctrine to fictional works, such as novels and plays, whereby protection is denied to elements of these works, such as basic plots, incidents, and character traits.[197] Deemed as unprotectable ideas, *scènes à faire* are rudimentary, commonplace, and standard — the fundamental building blocks of the narrative art. Thus, a car chase, the kiss in a love scene, and the all-knowing butler are examples of hackneyed narrative devices that fall within the doctrine.[198]

Copyright for Functional Expression, 111 HARV. L. REV. 1149 (1998); Glynn S. Lunney, Lotus v. Borland: *Copyright in Computer Programs*, 70 TULANE L. REV. 2347 (1996); Marci A. Hamilton & Ted Sebety, *Computer Science Concepts in Copyright Cases: The Path to a Coherent Law*, 10 HARV. J.L. & TECH. 239 (1997).

[197] The *scènes à faire* doctrine was first adopted in *Cain v. Universal Pictures Co.* 47 F. Supp. 1013, 1017 (S.D. Cal. 1942). For an overview of the subject, see Leslie Kurtz, *Copyright: The scènes à faire Doctrine*, 41. FLA. L. REV. 79 (1989).

[198] As one court noted, absent the doctrine "[i]t would be difficult to write successful works of fiction without negotiating for dozens or hundreds of copyright licenses, even though such stereotyped

Courts have extended the *scènes à faire* doctrine beyond the narrative arts to include other varieties of works, such as a work of photography[199] and computer software.[200] When applied in such situations, the doctrine loses its precise meaning and becomes a complicated way of saying that the element in question either lacks originality or is deemed to be an unprotectable idea. In a series of computer software cases, the courts have expressed the *scènes à faire* doctrine in the same terms as they do for the merger doctrine. This usage is unfortunate, because the two doctrines, although related, serve different purposes. The merger doctrine is appropriately applied when a work of utility is involved, such as a computer program, a work of architecture, or a database. Alternatively, the *scènes à faire* is more suitable in a context where the narrative arts are involved. Nonetheless, courts have applied the *scènes à faire* doctrine to computer programs, excluding from protection those elements that have been dictated by external standards, such as hardware specifications, software standards, compatibility requirements, manufacturer design standards, and industry practices.[201]

[C] Fictional Literary Characters

The protection of fictional literary characters such as Sam Spade, James Bond, and Superman, presents a recurring question in copyright law and an interesting variation on the idea-expression dichotomy. First, some primary distinctions should be made. This discussion focuses on *literary* characters, those described in *words*, whether in a novel or a play, and not on cartoon or other pictorial characters that are copyrightable as part of a drawing, painting, or other visual work. Pictorial characters present less theoretical difficulties justifying copyright protection. The reason is the enormous difference between literary and graphic expression. The description of a character in prose leaves much to the imagination, whereas the impact of a graphic character is immediate, concrete, and unmediated.[202] Second, names of characters may be protected under unfair competition law[203] and possibly

---

characters are products not of the creative imagination but of simple observation of the human comedy." *Gaiman v. McFarlane*, 360 F.3d 644, 660 (7th Cir. 2004).

[199] *See, e.g.*, *Ets-Hokin v. Skyy Spirits Inc.*, 323 F.3d 763, 765 (9th Cir. 2003) (holding that a "product shot" of a blue vodka bottle met the minimal standards of originality but that protection was limited against identical copying only by the doctrines of merger and *scènes à faire*); *Taylor Corp. v. Seasons Greetings, LLC*, 315 F.3d 1039 (8th Cir. 2003) (stating that *scènes à faire* doctrine applied to stock elements found in all depictions of Christmas wreath cards as a defense against infringement).

[200] *See, e.g.*, *Bucklew v. Hawkins, Ash, Baptie & Co.*, 329 F.3d 923 (7th Cir. 2003) (holding that arbitrary formatting elements in software programs are not *scènes à faire* and are copyrightable).

[201] *See, e.g.*, *Gates Rubber Co. v. Bando Chemical Indus., Ltd.*, 9 F.3d 823, 838 (10th Cir. 1993); *Computer Mgmt. Assistance Co. v. Robert F. De Castro, Inc.*, 220 F.3d 396 (5th Cir. 2000).

[202] For protection of graphic characters, see *Walt Disney Prod. v. Air Pirates*, 345 F. Supp. 108 (N.D. Cal. 1972) (holding that Walt Disney characters, particularly Mickey Mouse, were protectable). *See also Halicki Films, LLC v. Sanderson Sales & Marketing*, 547 F.3d 1213 (9th Cir. 2008) (remanding for determination whether customized Ford Mustang "Eleanor" from movie *Gone in 60 Seconds* was a distinctive character that "displays consistent, widely-identifiable traits."); and *Gaiman v. McFarlane*, 360 F.3d 644, 660 (7th Cir. 2004) (making the distinction between literary and graphic characters).

[203] *See DC Comics, Inc. v. Filmation Assocs.*, 486 F. Supp. 1273 (S.D.N.Y. 1980). *See generally* Michael T. Helfand, *When Mickey Mouse Is as Strong as Superman: The Convergence of Intellectual Property Laws to Protect Fictional Literary and Pictorial Characters*, 44 Stan. L. Rev. 623 (1992);

trademark law, but not under copyright law. This leaves open the important question: what protection, if any, may be claimed for the delineation of a literary character, apart from the character's name and visual appearance?

Perhaps the most famous comment on the copyrightability of literary characters is that of Judge Learned Hand in *Nichols v. Universal Pictures Corp.*,[204]

> If *Twelfth Night* were copyrighted, it is quite possible that a second comer might so closely imitate Sir Toby Belch or Malvolio as to infringe. But it would not be enough to cast as one of the characters a riotous knight who keeps wassail to the discomfort of the household or a vain and foppish steward who becomes amorous towards his mistress. These would be no more than Shakespeare's ideas in the play, as little capable of monopoly as Einstein's *Doctrine of Relativity* or Darwin's theory of the *Origin of Species*. It follows that the less developed the characters, the less they can be copyrighted; that is the penalty an author must bear for marking them too indistinctly.[205]

Judge Hand suggests that there are two aspects of character protection: the infringed character must be sufficiently delineated and the infringing character must closely imitate the infringed character. Under this test, the line must be drawn between mere ideas sketching the general nature of the character and more fully developed characterization. In this sense, the protectability of the literary dimension of a character is no different from the protectability of other elements in literary works, such as the details of plot and setting.

Courts have differed on the principle involved in the protection of literary characters. In *Warner Bros. Pictures, Inc. v. Columbia Broadcasting System*,[206] the court suggested another test, stating that copyright might cover a fictional character if the character constitutes the story being told, rather than merely a chessman or vehicle in the telling of the story. This somewhat more restrictive view of copyright for literary characters arose out of a contractual dispute covering the rights to Dashiell Hammet's fictional detective Sam Spade. In this case, the Ninth Circuit Court of Appeals held that the contract assigning the motion picture, radio, and television rights to the book, *The Maltese Falcon*, did not cover a copyright in the character of Sam Spade because characters *per se* are not copyrightable. This holding goes far beyond Judge Hand's statement and would deny copyright

Francis M. Nevins, *Copyright + Character = Catastrophe*, 39 J. Copyright Soc'y 303 (1992); Leslie A. Kurtz, *The Independent Legal Lives of Fictional Characters*, 1986 Wis. L. Rev. 429; E. Fulton Brylawski, *Protection of Characters-Sam Spade Revisited*, 22 Bull. Copyright L. Soc'y 77 (1974).

204 45 F.2d 119 (2d Cir. 1930). In *Nichols*, the author of the play, *Abie's Irish Rose*, sued the producer of the movie, *The Cohens and the Kellys*. Both were comedies dealing with religious intermarriage. Judge Learned Hand held for the defendant on the grounds that the theme of the play fell in the realm of unprotected "ideas." *See also Warner Bros, Inc. v. American. Broad. Co., Inc.*, 654 F.2d 204 (2d Cir. 1981) (holding that the television comedy, *The Greatest American Hero*, did not infringe the copyright in cartoon strips and movies of *Superman* because the idea of a character with superhuman powers who battles the forces of evil is not copyrightable, although the expression of such an idea could be). For an excellent discussion of the protection of dramatic characters, see *Authors League Symposium on Copyright*, 29 J. Copyright Soc'y 611 (1982).

205 *Nichols*, 45 F.2d at 121.

206 216 F.2d 945 (9th Cir. 1954) (also known as the *Sam Spade* case).

protection, even against direct copying of a unique and developed character, unless the character really constitutes the story being told.

This Sam Spade standard would rarely be met, virtually excluding protection of literary characters. It has not been widely approved by either the bench or commentators.[207] The *Sam Spade* case may be distinguished as a contracts rather than a copyright case, with the statements on character rights mere dicta. Perhaps the better view is Judge Hand's, which presents the proper question concerning rights in fictional characters: has the infringer taken the expressive details of an adequately delineated character rather than the general abstract idea of a character?[208]

[D] Historical Research

Copyright protection has been denied to historical fact, whether part of a historical novel, biography, or news story. The discovery of a fact is simply not an original work of authorship.[209] The discoverer does not create facts; he finds and records them, making him an author neither in a constitutional nor in a statutory sense. As a corollary, copyright protection does not extend to the interpretation of historical fact. Suppose, for example, a researcher proposed a new theory about the true identity of Shakespeare, or why the Watergate break-in took place. Here again, protection is denied for much the same reasons. For one, an interpretation of fact is simply a fact derived from other facts. For another, an interpretation is very much like an abstract idea, and when published, it becomes part of the public domain.

Copyright for any nonfiction narrative, whether history, biography, or news story, covers the literal form of the author's expression. Thus, anyone may relate a writer's theory of Shakespeare's identity or of the Watergate break-in, but may not copy or closely paraphrase another's expression of the theory. Moreover, even literal copying may be allowed if the form of the expression is not original with the author, such as a purported actual conversation between the Watergate participants even if unearthed from the public domain sources at the author's great expense and labor.

Historical works, news stories, and biographies present much the same questions of copyrightability as encountered in compilations and collective works. As in all works using public domain materials, disparate or individual facts are freely appropriable by third parties, whereas their selection, patterning, and arrangement are protected under copyright.[210]

---

[207] *See* Nimmer on Copyright § 2.12 (2014).

[208] For an application of Hand's principle of delineation to a group of characters in the *Rocky I, II,* and *III* films, see *Anderson v. Stallone*, 11 U.S.P.Q.2d 1161 (C.D. Cal. 1989), finding defendant's script using the *Rocky* characters infringing because the *Rocky* characters were so highly developed and central to the three movies that they constituted the story being told.

[209] *See Rubin v. Boston Magazine Co.*, 645 F.2d 80 (1st Cir. 1981).

[210] Although historical facts in themselves, even newly discovered ones, may not be entitled to copyright, it may be argued that their selection and arrangement in a particular work provide sufficient originality to warrant protection. This problem displays the inherent tension in copyright law between

After *Feist v. Rural Telephone Service Co.*[211] and the demise of the "sweat of the brow" doctrine as a basis of copyright protection, the trend in the case law should weigh against protecting the industrious effort involved in unearthing historical fact. Pre-*Feist* cases manifested a tension between protection of the efforts of the researcher and the need to allow dissemination of historical knowledge. Some cases have come very close to allowing protection for the general body of historical research resulting from the labor of the researcher. For example, in *Toksvig v. Bruce Publishing Co.*,[212] the plaintiff had written a biography of Hans Christian Anderson, exhaustively researching Anderson's life from original Danish sources. The defendant based his biography on the plaintiff's work and other English language books. Although the court could have found infringement because of the defendant's literal copying, it suggested that the defendant was free to obtain the same material by going to the public domain sources, but could not make a substantial and unfair use of the plaintiff's work. Other cases following this view have analogized the *Toksvig* principle to the protection of compilations like city directories, where infringement has been found based on the defendant's copying of the entire directory.[213]

Despite some pronouncements in the case law that historical research in itself can be the basis of copyright, the recent trend in the case law, even before *Feist*, was to refuse copyright protection based on the industrious effort of the researcher. For example, in *Miller v. Universal Studios, Inc.*,[214] the plaintiff had spent some 2,500 hours in the preparation of a book involving a notorious Georgia kidnapping in which the victim was imprisoned in an underground coffin. The kidnapping victim and the reporter collaborated on the book. Universal Studios, after unsuccessful attempts to secure movie rights, nevertheless made a movie based entirely on the book. The District Court declared itself in favor of the copyrightability of research. Its justification was based on a rationale similar to the telephone directory compilation cases: to reward the effort and ingenuity involved

---

the underlying and competing policies of protecting the interests of an author who may have spent great time and effort on his product, and the benefit to the public in the wide dissemination of facts. *See generally* Robert C. Denicola, *Copyright in Collections of Facts: A Theory for the Protection of Nonfiction Literary Works*, 81 COLUM. L. REV. 516 (1981); Robert A. Gorman, *Copyright Protection for the Collection and Representation of Facts*, 76 HARV. L. REV. 1569 (1963); Robert A. Gorman, *Fact or Fancy? The Implications for Copyright*, 29 J. COPYRIGHT SOC'Y 560 (1982). The question of the copyrightability of research often arises when a second work, for example, a television movie, is based upon facts uncovered in an earlier work. *See, e.g.*, *Rosemont Enters., Inc. v. Random House, Inc.*, 366 F.2d 303 (2d Cir. 1966), *cert. denied*, 385 U.S. 1009 (1967) (regarding the life story of Howard Hughes); *Miller v. Universal City Studios, Inc.*, 650 F.2d 1365 (5th Cir. 1981) (discussing a kidnapped victim who was buried alive); *Hoehling v. Universal City Studios, Inc.*, 618 F.2d 972 (2d Cir. 1980) (involving the destruction of the Hindenberg). This decision is extensively criticized in Jane C. Ginsburg, *Sabotaging and Reconstructing History: A Comment on the Scope of Copyright Protection in Works of History After* Hoehling v. Universal Studios, 29 J. COPYRIGHT SOC'Y 647 (1982). *See also Nash v. CBS*, 899 F.2d 1537 (7th Cir. 1990) (regarding a novel version of the shooting of the gangster John Dillinger).

[211] 499 U.S. 340 (1991).

[212] 181 F.2d 664 (7th Cir. 1950).

[213] *See Miller v. Universal City Studios, Inc.*, 460 F. Supp. 984 (S.D. Fla. 1978).

[214] 650 F.2d 1365 (5th Cir. 1981).

in giving expression to facts and to the effort required to unearth the facts.[215]

The Court of Appeals reversed the District Court decision because it was unable to identify any appropriation of original expression. The court distinguished the telephone directory cases as constituting a category in themselves rather than extending their questionable logic to another setting.[216] According to the Fifth Circuit, copyright should be based only on the resulting writing and the original elements of authorship expressed in the work. The court could find "no rational basis for distinguishing between facts and the research involved in obtaining facts."[217] To hold that research is copyrightable is the same as holding that the facts discovered by research are entitled to copyright protection. Whether the material in question is considered to be historical fact depends largely on how the author characterizes the work. If the historian holds out the events as factual matter, they enter into the public domain despite their strangeness or the improbability of their occurrence. For example, in *Nash v. CBS*,[218] the plaintiff had a novel theory about the killing of the famous gangster, John Dillinger. In his work, *Dillinger: Dead or Alive?*, the author purported to show, among other things, that Dillinger was not killed in an assassination ambush when leaving a Chicago restaurant. Rather, the gangster, on learning of the trap, sent another person — a Dillinger lookalike — who was shot instead. This bizarre story, which was never legitimized by reputable historians, became the subject of a CBS television show and, subsequently, the basis of a suit for copyright infringement. The court found that the plaintiff portrayed his work as historical rather than fictional. As such, CBS had copied historical fact, but not its expression.[219] Thus, if Nash had characterized his work as historical fiction (as it most certainly was), CBS may well have been found to have infringed the work.[220]

§ 2.14 OTHER ISSUES ON NON-COPYRIGHTABLE SUBJECT MATTER

[A] Copyright in Immoral, Illegal, and Obscene Works and Other Works of Negative Utility

Should all forms of expression receive protection? What if the work can be demonstrated to have "negative social utility" in the eyes of the law, so that it could be successfully prosecuted as, for example, fraudulent, libelous, seditious, or obscene? In other words why should we not to extend copyright protection to works containing material that is outside the zone of speech protected by the First

---

215 *See generally* Kellogg, *The Problem of Fictional Facts: Idea and Expression in Copyright*, 47 U. Miami L. Rev. 221 (1993).

216 *See id.* at 1371.

217 *Id.* at 1372.

218 899 F.2d 1537 (7th Cir. 1990).

219 *See id.* at 1541.

220 Another interesting question concerning the idea/expression dichotomy is whether ratings are copyrightable. For a discussion of this topic, *see* James Grimmelman, *Three Theories of Copyright in Ratings*, 14 Vand. J. Ent. & Tech. L. 851 (2012).

Amendment? Copyright infringers have sometimes asserted as an affirmative defense that the plaintiff's work was obscene, immoral, or fraudulent. This form of the unclean hands defense, despite some older authority, has been rejected in more recent times.[221]

In *Mitchell Brothers Film Group v. Cinema Adult Theater*,[222] the court rejected an unclean hands defense by defendants who obtained and exhibited the pornographic motion picture *Behind the Green Door*. The court found no implied exception in the Copyright Act for obscene works and also found that the Copyright Clause of the Constitution is best served when read without restrictions on content imposed by governmental officials. The court feared that an obscenity determination based on community standards would fragment the law of copyright. As a result of these differing standards, copyright protection would vary from locality to locality and generation to generation. In place of a uniform copyright law that is national in scope, one community might allow piracy while another would enforce the copyright in the same work. Incorporating the obscenity standard would undermine the goal of a uniform copyright law.[223]

The question remains whether the Copyright Office could reject registration based on obscenity or fraudulent content.[224] The Copyright Office would have to imply this authority but has declined to do so, despite a Department of Justice opinion concluding that the Copyright Office has the discretion to reject registration on morality grounds.[225]

Unlike the Copyright Act, which is silent on matters of morality, the Federal Trademark Act expressly forbids registration for a trademark of immoral, deceptive, or scandalous matter.[226] The federal government, however, may be ill suited for such determinations of morality. The Trademark Office, for example, has made totally arbitrary decisions in appearance, denying registration to Booby Trap[227] as a mark for brassieres, while allowing Weekend Sex[228] for a magazine.

---

[221] *See, e.g.*, *Belcher v. Tarbox*, 486 F.2d 1087 (9th Cir. 1973) (noting racing forms are copyrightable); *Jartech Inc. v. Clancy*, 666 F.2d 403 (9th Cir. 1982) (finding that obscenity is not a defense to claim of copyright infringement). Some courts remain reluctant to extend copyright protection to such works. *See, e.g.*, *Devils Films, Inc. v. Nectar Video*, 29 F. Supp. 2d 174 (S.D.N.Y. 1998) (declining to order seizure of allegedly infringing films on grounds of obscenity).

[222] 604 F.2d 852 (5th Cir. 1979).

[223] Although *Mitchell Bros.* was based on the 1909 Act, its reasoning has been adopted by *Jartech Inc. v. Clancy*, 666 F.2d 403 (9th Cir.), *cert. denied*, 459 U.S. 826 (1982), under the 1976 Act.

[224] This subject is debated in Ann Bartow, Copyright Law and Pornography, 91 Or. L. Rev. 1 (2012) (arguing for that certain forms of pornographic works that are "harmful to the individual depicted" should be denied copyright registration by the Copyright Office) and Ariel E. Ronneburger, 91 Or. L. Rev. 39 (2012)(taking the position that exclusion from registration of pornographic works would be ineffective from a social policy standpoint and could potentially impede copyright protection for a number of other films and may ultimately encroach on First Amendment rights).

[225] *See* Op. Att'y Gen. 171 U.S.P.Q. (BNA) 329 (1958). *See, e.g.*, *Devils Films, Inc. v. Nectar Video*, 29 F. Supp. 2d 174 (S.D.N.Y. 1998) (declining to order seizure of allegedly infringing films on grounds of obscenity).

[226] 15 U.S.C. § 1052(a).

[227] *In re Runsdorf*, 171 U.S.P.Q. (BNA) 443 (TMTAB 1971).

[228] *In re Madsen*, 180 U.S.P.Q. (BNA) 334 (TMTAB 1973).

Fortunately, the Copyright Office has formally decided not to make such decisions.[229]

[B] Government Works

[1] Works of the United States Government

Section 105 of the Copyright Act provides: "Copyright protection under this title is not available for any work of the United States Government, but the United States Government is not precluded from receiving and holding copyrights transferred to it by assignment, bequest, or otherwise."

By this section, the United States Government cannot claim copyright in works prepared by employees of the government in the course of their official duties.[230] Thus, all reports, manuals, videotapes, musical or artistic works produced by a government employee pursuant to his official duties are in the public domain. According to the House Report, a government worker's official work product is similar to a work made for hire.[231] Accordingly, a government employee could claim copyright only in a work written at his or her own volition outside formal duties. Whether a work is deemed created pursuant to or independent of official duties will turn on a series of factual considerations varying from case to case.[232]

Section 105 does not preclude the U.S. government from owning copyright in a work when the copyright is obtained by a transfer. For example, the government can obtain copyright ownership by assignment, bequest, or otherwise. The question is how to treat a governmentally commissioned work — a work created at governmental insistence by an independent contractor pursuant to a contract in which the independent contractor agrees to assign the work to the government. According to the House Report, where the government commissions a work in this manner, as an alternative to having one of its employees do the same work, it should be unable to claim copyright through contract with the independent contractor.[233] Otherwise, the government would be able by subterfuge to circumvent the statute disallowing copyright in works of the government. On the other hand, if the commissioned work is not related to the specific duties of an employee of an agency, the Government can obtain the copyright by a contract for its assignment.[234]

---

[229] *See* Compendium II of Copyright Office Practices § 108.10.

[230] *See Wheaton v. Peters*, 33 U.S. 591 (1834); For background see Craig Joyce, The Story of Wheaton v. Peters: A Curious Chapter in the History of Judicature, in Intellectual Property Stories 36, 49–76 (J. Ginsburg & R. Dreyfuss, eds. 2005).

[231] *See* H.R. Rep. No. 94-1476, at 58 (1976).

[232] *See, e.g., Scherr v. Universal Match Co.*, 297 F. Supp. 107 (S.D.N.Y. 1967). For a discussion of the work made for hire doctrine, see *infra* § 5.02.

[233] H.R. Rep. No. 94-1476, at 59 (1976).

[234] *See Schnapper v. Foley*, 667 F.2d 102 (D.C. Cir. 1981). *Contra*: Professor Nimmer argues that such a contract should be void since the statute does not refer to commissioned works because Congress wished that independent contractors be allowed to retain copyright in their works. Interpreted in this way, any contract for assignment of a work created by an independent contractor would subvert the statute. Nimmer on Copyright § 5.13[C][3] (2014).

[2] Works of State Governments

The above rules apply to the federal government only; state and local governments have no § 105 constraints on their ownership in copyrighted works created by public officials as part of their official duties. There are, however, certain categories applicable to all governmental works, state or federal, which are inherently in the public domain. This category of inherently noncopyrightable works includes statutes, ordinances, regulations, and judicial opinions. Accordingly, in *Georgia v. The Harrison Co.*,[235] the State of Georgia could not claim copyright in its new code. The court held that the code was a public domain work, owned by the people of Georgia, who as citizens must have free access to the laws governing them.

The exclusion of copyright for judicial opinions and legislative enactments has been settled law since the nineteenth century. With the advent of the regulatory state and its abundance of administrative regulations, the question has arisen whether copyright should attach to statutory texts, such as a model code, drafted by private parties in an independent capacity and later enacted into law by a governmental authority. In *Veeck v. Southern Building Code Congress Int'l*,[236] the court held that, as a matter of law, a model building code drafted by Southern Building Code Congress International (SBCCI) entered the public domain on its adoption by two Texas towns. The court based its reasoning on more than a century of case law holding that enacted laws cannot be copyrighted.[237]

Moreover, because the building codes could only be expressed in one way, the court found that they constituted "facts" and were uncopyrightable under the merger doctrine.[238]

Veeck's holding, that privately formulated codes enter the public domain by their enactment into law, is firmly grounded in both law and policy.[239] An alternative holding would contradict the policy of favoring dissemination of statutory texts, particularly under a Copyright Act that no longer requires notice as a requirement of protection. If model codes enacted into law were protected by copyright, anyone who copied the statutory text without consent of the copyright owner would risk infringement, even though the user may have given no notice of a claim to copyright. Users of statutory texts should have an expectation that the public document is freely accessible and unprotected by copyright. Clearly, users have an interest in copyright-free codes, but do code writing organizations need copyright as an incentive to produce them? Experience indicates that, in the case of model codes,

---

[235] 548 F. Supp. 110 (N.D. Ga. 1982).

[236] 293 F.3d 791 (5th Cir. 2002).

[237] *Wheaton v. Peters*, 33 U.S. 591, 668 (1834); *Banks v. Manchester*, 128 U.S. 244 (1888).

[238] *See also Building Officials & Code Admins. Int'l v. Code Technology, Inc.*, 628 F.2d 730 (1st Cir. 1980) (vacating preliminary injunction; suggesting strongly that nonprofit organization's building code entered the public domain when enacted by Massachusetts). *But see Practice Management Info. Corp. v. American Medical Ass'n*, 121 F.3d 516 (9th Cir. 1997) (upholding trial court's ruling that AMA's medical procedure coding system did *not* enter public domain when adopted by agreement with federal health care agency as sole permissible system for use by applicants for Medicaid reimbursement).

[239] *But see* Shubha Ghosh, *Copyright as Privatization: The Case of Model Codes*, 78 Tul. L. Rev. 653 (2004) (arguing that the Fifth Circuit's focus on authorship was misguided and is potentially destructive to lawmaking through democratic process).

the copyright incentive does not play a significant role in their production. The savings from industry standardization, quality control, and self-regulation make the creation of model codes profitable for any trade organization, regardless of whether they enjoy copyright protection.

This is not to say, however, that all works affiliated with government should fit within the governmental exception. Unlike model codes, lesser works of government, such as tax maps and health care coding systems do not have the same built-in incentives to encourage their production. Costly to make and difficult to maintain, these labor-intensive works may be neglected in favor of more remunerative activities that do enjoy copyright protection. Thus, in *County of Suffolk v. First American Real Estate Solutions, Inc.*,[240] even though a New York statute directed each county to create tax maps, the court ruled that copyright protection for the maps might be necessary to ensure that they were adequately developed.[241]

---

[240] 261 F.3d 179 (2d Cir. 2001).

[241] Provisions of state law, however, may dictate public availability of potentially protectable works. *See, e.g., County of Santa Clara v. Superior Court*, 170 Cal. App. 4th 1301 (2009) (county is required to provide copies of its Geographic Information Systems (GIS) maps and may not claim copyright or require an end-user license agreement); *Seago v. Horry County*, 663 S.E.2d 38 (S.C. 2008) (county must provide copies of GIS maps on request, but may pass ordinance or require license agreement to restrict commercial dissemination); *Microdecisions, Inc. v. Skinner*, 889 So. 2d 871 (Fla. Dist. Ct. App. 2004) (tax maps produced by county employee within scope of his employment are public records and therefore not subject to copyright). For an analysis of these cases, see Justin Hughes, *Created Facts and the Flawed Ontology of Copyright Law*, 83 NOTRE DAME L. REV. 43 (2007).

Chapter 3

WORKS OF AUTHORSHIP: CATEGORIES OF COPYRIGHTABLE SUBJECT MATTER

§ 3.01 INTRODUCTION AND CHAPTER OVERVIEW

The types of works that may qualify for copyright protection are enumerated in eight broad, overlapping categories of copyrightable subject matter called "works of authorship." This chapter focuses on the categories of works that qualify for copyright protection, and, while doing so, elaborates on the general standards of copyrightability such as originality, fixation, and idea-expression treated in Chapter 2.

This chapter is divided into four parts. Part I examines the meaning of the term "works of authorship" and the importance of how a work is categorized. Parts II and III have a unifying theme: the difficulty copyright law has had in assimilating works of utility, *i.e.*, those works that combine the useful and the expressive, such as computer programs and works of applied art. Part II addresses literary works, focusing on the protection of computer programs. Part III concerns graphic, pictorial, and sculptural works. Most of the discussion emphasizes the scope of copyright protection for works of applied art. Part IV introduces the other categories of copyrightable subject matter, namely: musical works, sound recordings, dramatic works, choreographic works, pantomimes, and motion pictures.

Part I. WORKS OF AUTHORSHIP: OVERVIEW

§ 3.02 THE EIGHT CATEGORIES

[A] Generally

Section 102(a)[1] of the 1976 Act sets forth eight illustrative categories of works of authorship:

(1) literary works;

(2) musical works, including any accompanying words;

(3) dramatic works, including any accompanying music;

(4) pantomimes and choreographic works;

---

[1] 17 U.S.C. § 102(a).

(5) pictorial, graphic, and sculptural works;

(6) motion pictures and other audiovisual works;

(7) sound recordings; and

(8) architectural works.

Congress purposely chose the term "works of authorship" in § 102(a) of the 1976 Act rather than the more inclusive term "all the writings of an author" as is found in the 1909 Act.[2] By choosing the more restrictive term, Congress indicated its intention not to exhaust the full scope of its constitutional authority to protect all writings.[3] One reason for Congress' choice of terminology was to avoid an ambiguity inherent in the 1909 Act that conferred copyright on "all the writings of an author." This seemingly all-inclusive language, however, had been construed by the courts as conferring copyrightability on less than all writings.[4] Thus, Congress has made explicit in the 1976 Act what the courts had imposed on the 1909 Act by their restrictive interpretation of the term "writings."

The term "works of authorship" is purposely left undefined in the 1976 Act.[5] According to the House Report,[6] this omission was intended to provide for coverage that would be both extensive and flexible enough to accommodate new technologies and new ways in which authors find to express themselves, but still less extensive than the full scope of constitutional authority to protect all writings. In short, copyright protection will be extended not only to works clearly falling into the eight specified categories but to analogous works as well.

[B] Excluded Writings

The question remains, which writings of authors are excluded from protection under the less-than-comprehensive term "works of authorship"? The legislative history is not explicit on this point. In general, deciding whether a writing will be considered a work of authorship is a two-step process. First, one must determine whether the legislative history has expressly excluded it. Examples of express exclusion are industrial design[7] and typeface design,[8] which Congress has explicitly indicated are not to be considered works of authorship. Second, even absent

---

[2] 17 U.S.C. § 4 (1909 Act).

[3] *Writings* may be defined as "any physical rendering of the fruits of creative intellectual and aesthetic labor." *See Goldstein v. California*, 412 U.S. 546, 561 (1973).

[4] *See id.* at 567; *Capitol Records, Inc. v. Mercury Records Corp.*, 221 F.2d 657, 660 (2d Cir. 1955).

[5] For a new look at the concept of the work of authorship in copyright, see Michael J. Madison, *The End of the Work as We Know It*, 19 J. Intell. Prop. L. 325 (2012).

[6] H.R. Rep. No. 94-1476, at 51 (1976).

[7] For a discussion of industrial design, see *infra* § 3.12.

[8] "Typeface" is defined as a set of letters, numbers, or other symbolic characters whose forms are related to repeating design elements consistently applied in a notational system and are intended to be embodied in articles whose intrinsic utilitarian function is for use in composing text or other cognizable combinations of characters. The House Report indicates an intent to exclude typeface designs from protection despite their status as writings. H.R. Rep. 94-1476, at 55 (1976). *See Eltra v. Ringer*, 579 F.2d 294 (4th Cir. 1978) (finding that typefaces are not copyrightable as works of art). For a comprehensive overview, see Jacqueline Lipton, *To © or Not to ©? Copyright and Innovation in the Digital Typeface*

express exclusion, one must determine whether the writing has been *historically* excluded.

To make this determination, one must review the case law under the 1909 Act. For example, literary characters[9] and titles are writings in the constitutional meaning of the term, but are writings that have traditionally been excluded from protection under U.S. copyright law. Moreover, neither the current Copyright Act itself nor the legislature have expressly included them in the copyright realm. Thus, under the above two-step process, they would remain outside copyright protection until given explicit statutory recognition.

One could easily make a persuasive case for the protection of titles under copyright law. As writings, they fall within the scope of feasible copyrightable subject matter. Consisting of words and symbols, titles meet the definitional requirement of a literary work under § 102(a). The title of a work can be commercially valuable. Catchy and clever titles such as *Everything You Always Wanted to Know About Sex But Were Afraid to Ask* can have great market impact.

Although not specifically excluded from copyright protection by the 1976 Act or its Committee Reports, titles are regarded as uncopyrightable subject matter despite a declared legislative intent for flexibility in § 102(a).[10] Thus, even if titles are writings and look like literary works, they are excluded. The reason lies in their *de minimis* nature, as reflected in the Copyright Office Circular that lumps together titles, short words and phrases, and trademarks as uncopyrightable.[11] Title protection must be sought elsewhere, primarily under state or federal unfair competition law on a theory of "passing off."[12]

[C] Copyrightable Subject Matter: The 1909 and 1976 Acts Compared

The categories listed in § 102(a) of the 1976 Act are meant to be illustrative, rather than limitative.[13] By this approach, Congress wanted to avoid the definitional rigidities of the 1909 Act and give as much flexibility to the courts as possible to adapt the law to new technologies and media. This rigidity was reflected in § 5 of the 1909 Act, which set forth fourteen categories of works of authorship ostensibly to provide administrative categories for registration in the Copyright Office.[14] Although these categories were meant only for administrative convenience, courts tended not to find a work copyrightable unless it fit into one of

---

Industry, 43 U.C. Davis L. Rev. 143 (2009) (examining arguments for and against extending protection to digital typefaces).

[9] Literary characters *per se* are not copyrightable. For a discussion of literary characters, see § *supra* 2.13[C].

[10] *Arthur Retlaw & Assocs., Inc. v. Travenol Labs., Inc.*, 582 F. Supp. 1010, 1014 (N.D. Ill. 1984).

[11] *See* Copyright Office Circular No. 34. Copyright Office Compendium II § 202.021 (stating that " . . . words and short phrases such as names, titles, and slogans are not copyrightable.").

[12] *See, e.g.*, *Davis v. United Artists, Inc.*, 547 F. Supp. 722 (S.D.N.Y. 1982).

[13] As stated in the House Report: "the seven categories do not necessarily exhaust the scope of "original works of authorship" that the bill is intended to protect." H.R. Rep. No. 94-1476, at 53 (1976).

[14] 17 U.S.C. § 5 (a)–(n) (1909 Act).

the categories.[15] The list lacked logic and coherency. It was no more than a grab bag of specific categories, some of which were based on the material object embodying a work — such as books and periodicals — and others on broad subject matter categories such as sound recordings and motion pictures. More importantly, however, it was often difficult to determine whether a work fit into one or another of the classes. This determination could have important substantive consequences as to the form and location of notice, the manufacturing clause requirements, protection in unpublished form, and whether the work enjoyed the right of public performance for profit.

In comparison, the 1976 Act has conceptually streamlined the classification of copyrightable subject matter. The current Act is consistent in separating the work of authorship from the material object — the copy or phonorecord — in which it is embodied. For example, a literary work may be embodied in a book or recorded on tape; a musical work may be fixed on tape or written as sheet music; and a choreographic work may be written in specialized notation or filmed on tape. Regardless of the medium in which it is embodied, the work of authorship remains a literary or musical work under § 102(a).

The categories set forth in § 102(a) of the 1976 Act are not only broad but also overlapping. For example, a "literary work," defined in the Act as consisting of words and symbols, overlaps the dramatic work category; lyrics for a song can fit into either the literary work or musical work category; pantomimes and choreographic works can, in certain instances, double as dramatic works.

This overlapping aspect of copyrightable subject matter is reflected in the Register of Copyright's classification system for registration purposes[16] that has collapsed the eight statutory categories into four broader ones: Class TX (nondramatic literary works); Class PA (performing arts); Class VA (visual arts); Class SR (sound recordings). When reviewing the copyright application, the Register may determine whether the claim fits into one of the categories.

[D] Importance of How a Work Is Categorized

How a work is categorized can have important legal consequences, particularly as to the scope of the copyright owner's exclusive rights.[17] The exclusive rights are extensively covered in Chapter 8 of this treatise, but to provide a few examples: an owner of a copyright in a sound recording does not enjoy a performance right;[18] only non-dramatic musical works are subject to compulsory ("mechanical") license

---

[15] *See Capitol Records, Inc. v. Mercury Records Corp.*, 221 F.2d 657 (2d Cir. 1955).

[16] Copyright Office Regulations § 202.3 (registration of copyright).

[17] For arguments regarding various lesser-recognized or emerging types of works and their proper level of copyright protection, see Jerome H. Reichman & Ruth L. Okediji, *When Copyright Law and Science Collide: Empowering Digitally Integrated Research Methods on a Global Scale*, 96 Minn. L. Rev. 1362 (2012) (arguing that copyright law is a science-hostile environment and offering proposed solutions to the problems created by intellectual property law for digitally integrated scientific research); Megan M. Carpenter, *Drawing a Line in the Sand: Copyright Law and New Museums*, 13 Vand. J. Ent. & Tech. L. 463 (2011) (discussing the efforts by museums and galleries to enhance user experience and discussing the copyright implications of such a move).

[18] *See* 17 U.S.C. § 114.

for reproduction and distribution under § 115;[19] and a library's reproduction right under § 108(h) is much wider for literary and dramatic works than for other categories.[20] Thus, the classification of a work is more than just a formality.

Who decides whether a work fits into one category or another? Ultimately, a court makes this decision. The Copyright Office, however, has an influential role in determining into which category a work falls. Section 408(c)(1) of the Act[21] authorizes the Copyright Office to promulgate regulations specifying administrative classes for registration purposes. Despite that section's proviso that "[t]his administrative classification of works has no significance with respect to the subject matter of copyright or the exclusive rights provided by this title," the Office's administrative classification can, as a practical matter, have a significant influence on a court's determination on classification.[22]

Part II. LITERARY WORKS

§ 3.03 GENERALLY

Literary works are defined by the 1976 Act as, "works, other than audiovisual works, expressed in words, numbers, or other verbal or numerical symbols or indicia, regardless of the nature of the material objects, such as books, periodicals, manuscripts, phonorecords, film, tapes, disks, or cards, in which they are embodied."[23]

This category encompasses all works written in words or symbols of any kind, regardless of the material objects in which they are embodied. The word "literary," in this context, does not imply any benchmark of literary merit. A literary work can be a computer program, catalog, database, or a poem written on a piece of paper or recorded on cassette. Copyright in computer programs is one form of literary work that has caused much controversy in recent years.

Computer programs are now a fundamental part of copyright law, and issues concerning them are discussed at various points in this text.[24] The following two sections introduce the computer question in a historical overview and present the basic terminology of computer technology. These two sections are followed by an examination of the leading case of *Apple Computers, Inc. v. Franklin Computer Corp.*[25]

---

[19] 17 U.S.C. § 115.

[20] 17 U.S.C. § 108(h).

[21] 17 U.S.C. § 408(c)(1).

[22] *See Esquire, Inc. v. Ringer*, 591 F.2d 796, 802 (D.C. Cir. 1978).

[23] 17 U.S.C. § 101 (literary works).

[24] For a discussion of the videogame cases, see *supra* § 2.03[C]. For a discussion of limitations on the exclusive rights to a computer program, see *infra* § 3.06.

[25] 714 F.2d 1240 (3d Cir. 1983).

§ 3.04 COMPUTER PROGRAMS (SOFTWARE)

[A] Historical Background: CONTU

Formal recognition of computer programs as copyrightable subject matter did not come about until a 1980 amendment to the Copyright Act.[26] Under the original version of § 117, the 1976 Act kept the legal status quo of computer programs as it existed on December 31, 1977.[27] But it was widely accepted that computer programs were copyrightable as literary works. According to the House Report, the definition of literary works included, "computer databases, and computer programs, to the extent that they incorporate authorship in the programmer's expression of original ideas, as distinguished from the ideas themselves."[28]

Although copyrightability of computer programs was clearly favored by the legislative history of the 1976 Act, doubts remained after its passage because computer programs did not fit neatly into the more traditional forms of literary works. Because of this uncertainty, the complexity of the issues, and the economic stakes, Congress appointed the National Commission of New Technological Uses of Copyrighted Works ("CONTU") to study the computer program issue. Their final report in 1979 made specific recommendations to amend the Copyright Act, which were adopted in their entirety.[29] The revisions included a new definition of "computer program" in § 101 and § 117's Limitations on Exclusive Rights: Computer Programs.

Computer programs are now defined in § 101 as: "a set of statements or instructions to be used directly or indirectly in a computer in order to bring about a certain result."[30]

In addition, the Act now contains a revised § 117 setting forth the scope of exclusive rights in computer programs.[31] Thus, the Copyright Act, its legislative history, and, with little exception, the case law, have fully recognized computer programs as a mainstream form of copyrightable subject matter.[32]

---

[26] Act of December 12, 1980, Pub. L. No. 96-517, § 10(b), 94 Stat. 3028.

[27] As early as 1964, the Copyright Office registered the first computer program in the book category under the Office's Rule of Doubt (policy favoring the applicant when uncertainties about copyrightability arise), and continued this practice as long as the programs were deposited in humanly readable form.

[28] H.R. Rep. No. 94-1476, at 54 (1976).

[29] *See* Pub. L. No. 96-517, § 10, 94 Stat. 3015, 3028. One should note the minor deviation from the CONTU language in § 117. Nat'l Comm'n. on New Technological Uses of Copyrighted Works, Final Report 12 (1979).

[30] 17 U.S.C. § 101 (computer programs).

[31] 17 U.S.C. § 117. For a discussion of § 117, see *infra* § 8.10.

[32] For an overview of copyright law on computers since passage of the computer program amendments, see Peter Menell, *Envisioning Copyright Law's Digital Future*, 46 N.Y.L. Sch. L. Rev. 63 (2002); Arthur R. Miller, *Copyright Protection for Computer Programs, Databases, and Computer-Generated Works: Is There Anything New Since CONTU?*, 106 Harv. L. Rev. 977 (1993).

[B] Copyrightability of Programs: Initial Doubts

Computer programs have a different look and feel as compared to more traditional forms of copyrightable subject matter. Reservations on this basis concerning the wholesale inclusion of computer programs in copyright law were expressed in the dissenting and concurring comments of Commissioners Hershey and Nimmer to the CONTU *Final Report*. Hershey argued against protection because computer programs, unlike other forms of copyrightable subject matter such as sound recordings or motion pictures, do not communicate with people but are essentially mechanical, labor-saving devices which transmit electronic impulses to operate machines called computers.[33] Professor Nimmer, in his concurring opinion, wrote that full protection of computer programs under copyright law would strain the meaning of "writings" and "authors" under the Constitution, thereby broadening copyright law into a general misappropriation law and one that covers subject matter more appropriate for patent protection. Nimmer's solution for this over breadth was to grant copyright protection only to programs producing a copyrightable output. Thus, a program producing a videogame whose output is an audiovisual work, or one producing a database whose output is a compilation, would be copyrightable.[34] But a program that controlled the air conditioning in a building, a non-copyrightable output, would not be eligible for copyright protection. Neither Hershey's nor Nimmer's approach was adopted, and all programs are now copyrightable regardless of their nature or output.

To grasp the legal issues surrounding the scope of protection for computer programs requires a basic understanding of the technology involved.

§ 3.05 COMPUTER TECHNOLOGY

[A] Computer Hardware: The Basics[35]

Phenomenal progress in computer technology has dramatically altered the way in which we use, store, record, and transmit information.[36] The first room-sized computers of the late 1940s could do no more than today's personal desktop models, which are becoming smaller, faster, and cheaper all the time.

This technological progress is reflected in the key elements of computer hardware, which have gone through four generally acknowledged generations: vacuum tubes, transistors, printed circuits, and integrated circuits. With each change in the fundamental building blocks, the new technology has reduced the computer's energy requirements and price. For example, first generation vacuum tubes, unreliable and energy-inefficient, were replaced in the late 1940s by the second-generation transistor. Smaller and more efficient, the transistor marked the

---

[33] *See* CONTU Final Report, Dissent of Commissioner Hershey at 27–28.

[34] *See id.* at 26–27 (concurring opinion of Professor Nimmer).

[35] For an overview of the subject, see CONTU Final Report at 9–12.

[36] For a discussion of the implications for legal frameworks of changing technology, culture, and business environments in the digital era, see Olufunmilayo Arewa, *YouTube, UGC, and Digital Music: Competing Business and Cultural Models in the Internet Age*, 104 Nw. U. L. Rev. 431 (2010).

beginning of the semiconductor industry's use of silicon material. Next followed the printed circuits, replaced by today's fourth generation integrated circuits, which place all essential components and connectors in silicon material. The revolution continues, and one can expect newer, smaller, faster, more efficient configurations.

The integrated circuitry of a digital computer (the hardware), housed in the central processing unit ("CPU") of the computer, can do nothing without being instructed. The computer program, or software, as it is called in the industry, instructs the computer on how to carry out its logical functions to produce the intended result or perform a task, such as producing patterns for a videogame, arranging columns in a spreadsheet, or performing the "spell check" in a word processing program. The design of the program is based on an algorithm, a procedure for solving a given type of mathematical problem. The algorithm is sometimes called the "logic" of the program.

[B] Computer Software: Development Stages[37]

A program goes through various developmental stages before it is ready to instruct the CPU. The first task of the program designer is to express the logical structure of the program, which was traditionally done through an elaborate set of charts. Flow-charting has given way to other more expedient methods, but a basic recitation in English to define the program logic is a necessary first step. The program is then implemented by coding it first into human-readable language using English symbols, such as C, C++, and JAVA, so-called "high-level languages." The program is then rewritten into an intermediate-level language called Basic Assembly Language, which in turn is translated into machine language for execution by the computer. Both high-level language and Basic Assembly are written in "source code," and are intelligible to humans. The CPU, however, can only follow directions in machine language, called "object code," a binary code written in zeros and ones. Object code is unintelligible to a human reader. Because object code cannot be read by the human eye, many software proprietors, in order to impede copying, distribute their programs only in that form and never in source code.

Computer programs are fixed in a variety of devices (e.g., on paper, floppy disks, or semiconductor chips). One such device is ROM (Read Only Memory),[38] a semiconductor chip containing the computer programs permanently embedded into it in object code. ROMs are manufactured separately and then placed into the circuitry of the computer. As the name indicates, information stored in a ROM can only be read, not erased.

---

[37] For a discussion of the process, see Raymond T. Nimmer, Law Of Computer Technology § 1:8–1:9 (3d ed. 2005).

[38] Other kinds of memory chips, such as the widely used RAM (Random Access Memory), are more versatile than ROM because the computer can erase them and write new data or instructions into them.

[C] Application and Operating System Programs

Computer programs can be classified functionally as either application or operating system programs. Application programs perform precise tasks or solve specific problems, such as word processing, checkbook balancing, or game playing. Operating system programs generally manage the internal functions of the computer, or facilitate operations of applications programs, performing tasks common to any applications program. An operating system program, for example, might start the computer and activate its circuits, preparing it to accept instructions.

The discussion now turns to an application of these technological concerns in a leading case that examined the key aspects of copyright in computer software.[39]

§ 3.06 COMPUTER PROGRAMS IN THE COURTS: *APPLE COMPUTER, INC. v. FRANKLIN COMPUTER CORP.*

[A] *Apple Computer, Inc. v. Franklin Computer Corp.*: The Issues Involved

Computer programs have received expansive protection in the courts, as exemplified in the leading case of *Apple Computer, Inc. v. Franklin Computer Corp.*[40] In *Apple*, defendant Franklin copied Apple's operating system program to manufacture an Apple-compatible computer. With minor variation, Franklin copied the system identically from the ROMs in which it was embedded. Having the identical operating system permitted the defendant's Franklin ACE Computer to use the vast number of application programs written for the Apple II computer. On these facts, the court was confronted with three basic issues about the scope of protection for computer programs: (1) whether copyright can exist in a computer program expressed in object code; (2) whether copyright can exist in a computer program embedded in a ROM; and (3) whether copyright can exist in an operating system program. The first two questions had already been considered in other litigation ultimately favorable to the plaintiffs[41] the third issue involving the copyrightability of operating systems constituted the novel aspect of the case. The court answered all three issues affirmatively, both reaffirming and expanding the scope of protection for computer programs.

---

[39] For commentary on the subject, see Jacqueline Lipton, *IP Problem Child: Shifting Paradigms for Software Protection*, 58 Hastings L.J. 205 (2006) (arguing for the substantial scaling back of copyright protection for software); Peter S. Menell, *Tailoring Legal Protection for Computer Software*, 39 Stan. L. Rev. 1329 (1987); I.T. Hardy, *Six Copyright Theories for the Protection of Computer Object Programs*, 26 Ariz. L. Rev. 845 (1984); Pamela Samuelson, *CONTU Revisited: The Case Against Copyright Protection for Computer Programs in Machine Readable Form*, 1984 Duke L.J. 663; Note, *Copyright Protection of Computer Program Object Code*, 96 Harv. L. Rev. 1723 (1983).

[40] 714 F.2d 1240 (3d Cir. 1983).

[41] *See Williams Elec., Inc. v. Artic Int'l, Inc.*, 685 F.2d 870 (3d Cir. 1982); *Stern Elec., Inc. v. Kaufman*, 669 F.2d 852, 855–56 (2d Cir. 1982).

[B] Copyright in a Program Expressed in Object Code

The court had little trouble concluding that a work written in object code unintelligible to humans would qualify as a literary work.[42] Section 102(a) states that copyright protection extends to works fixed in any tangible means of expression "from which they can be perceived . . . with the aid of a machine or device," and does not require that they be intelligible to humans.[43] As to whether object code is a literary work, the court stated that the definition of "literary works" as those expressed in " . . . numbers, or other . . . numerical symbols or indicia . . . ,"[44] clearly encompasses the zeros and ones of a binary language object code.

[C] Copyrightability of a Program Embedded in a ROM

The defendant also argued that the embodiment of a program on a ROM precluded its protection because ROMs are utilitarian objects or machine parts. This argument had previously been rejected in the videogame cases,[45] and the court had no difficulty repeating that the statutory requirement of fixation was satisfied because the ROM computer chip constituted the material object in which the copyrighted work (*i.e.*, the program) was embedded.[46]

[D] Copyrightability of Operating Systems

The key issue in *Franklin* involved the copyrightability of the operating system programs, which Franklin claimed were *per se* uncopyrightable under *Baker v. Selden*[47] and its extension in *Morrissey v. Procter & Gamble Co.*[48] The defendant argued that there were a limited number of ways to write an operating system program that would run most Apple Computer software. This argument states the doctrine of "merger" in which a work is uncopyrightable if its idea and expression merge or are so closely related that one cannot be used without the other. Here, the Third Circuit found that the trial court had made insufficient findings as to whether idea and expression had merged and remanded the case on this issue.[49]

---

[42] The first case holding that computer software embedded in a ROM was copyrightable was *Tandy Corp. v. Personal Micro Computers, Inc.*, 524 F. Supp. 171 (N.D. Cal. 1981). The copyrightability of the object code embedded in a ROM was much in doubt under 1909 Act case law. *Data Cash Sys., Inc. v. JS & A Group, Inc.*, 480 F. Supp. 1063 (N.D. Ill. 1979), *aff'd on other grounds*, 628 F.2d 1038 (7th Cir. 1980) (finding program non-protectable because not intelligible to human readers). The court's holding was based on the early decision of *White-Smith Music Publ'g Co. v. Apollo Co.*, 209 U.S. 1 (1908), which held that a piano roll was not a copy of the musical composition because it was not in a form humans could perceive. *White* has been specifically discarded by the 1976 Act, leading to the protection of non-human-readable fixations. *See supra* § 2.04.

[43] 17 U.S.C. § 102(a).

[44] 17 U.S.C. § 101 (literary works).

[45] *See Williams Elec., Inc. v. Artic Int'l*, Inc., 685 F.2d 870, 876 (3d Cir. 1982).

[46] *Franklin Computer Corp.*, 714 F.2d at 1249.

[47] 101 U.S. 99 (1879). For a discussion of *Baker*, see *supra* § 2.13[B].

[48] 379 F.2d 675 (1st Cir. 1967).

[49] *Franklin Computer Corp.*, 714 F.2d at 1253.

The court, however, unequivocally upheld the copyrightability of computer programs, whether application or operating systems:

> Both types of programs instruct the computer to do something. Therefore, it should make no difference for purposes of Section 102(b) whether these instructions tell the computer to help prepare an income tax return (the task of an application program) or to translate a high level language program from source code into its binary language object code form (the task of the operating system . . .).[50]

Franklin has established the copyrightability of operating system programs and the illegality of copying the programmer's expression manifested in the program without license.[51] The pertinent question in forthcoming cases will be the scope of that protection and what constitutes infringement of a program. In that regard, the court did not define the difference between idea and expression as applied to computer programs. This distinction is not easy to show in the case of computer programs because they are essentially different from most other copyrighted works. The idea-expression doctrine as applied to a painting, a novel, or a piece of music has a long tradition developed over the years through case law. To separate idea from expression is sometimes a difficult task but one which is possible because of their inherent nature. These familiar forms communicate with people, and their design is dictated by aesthetics. On the other hand, computer programs are inherently functional and are designed to perform specialized tasks. In a novel, for example, the idea could be viewed as the general theme, whereas the copyrightable expression lies in the details, scenes, events, and characterizations.[52]

In the computer program context, one can equate idea with the accomplishment of a given task or function. Thus, if there are other ways to achieve the same result, there are alternative means of expression, and the doctrine of merger does not apply. Copyright should not be used to monopolize a result — the very essence of § 102(b). But stating this proposition does not answer the hard question: how broadly or narrowly does one define the result in the operating system context? Franklin wished to define the result as broadly as 100% Apple compatibility in order to use the vast library of application programs written for the Apple system. Assuming Apple compatibility is the uncopyrightable result and that total compatibility could only be achieved by identical copying, the doctrine of merger would apply. Thus, if one accepts *Franklin*'s definition of the result as Apple compatibliity, the Apple operating system is rendered totally uncopyrightable. The *Franklin* court, however, fell short of establishing 100% compatibility as the uncopyrightable "idea." In addition, it did not indicate either what degree of compatibility would be copyrightable or how this compatibility could be achieved. As the court stated

---

[50] *Id.* at 1251.

[51] The basic holdings in *Franklin* have been strengthened in *Apple Computer, Inc. v. Formula Int'l, Inc.*, 562 F. Supp. 775 (C.D. Cal. 1983) (finding the object code in ROM copyrightable); *NEC Corp. v. Intel Corp.*, 645 F. Supp. 590 (N.D. Cal. 1986) (holding microcode and microprograms copyrightable computer programs within the meaning of the Copyright Act and defining microprograms as "a set of statements used, directly or indirectly to bring about the result of interpreting the INTEL 8086 instruction set." *Id.* at 593).

[52] *See Reyher v. Children's Television Workshop*, 533 F.2d 87 (2d Cir. 1976).

"*Franklin* may wish to achieve total compatibility . . . but that is a commercial and competitive objective that does not enter into the somewhat metaphysical issue of whether particular ideas and expressions have merged."[53]

Now that computer programs are copyrightable regardless of their form or expressive content, the next set of issues, as suggested above, will be to determine the scope of their protection. This issue arises when the defendant (unlike in *Franklin*) has not engaged in verbatim copying of the program but has copied the sequence and organization of the program. The difficult question in this context is to determine when a programmer's protectable expression has been taken.[54]

Another currently debated scope-of-protection issue is whether a defendant can copy a plaintiff's program to develop a non-infringing, competing or compatible program. This process of reverse engineering, called "disassembly and decompilation," has been successfully defended as a fair use and has presented intricate problems of copyright and competitive policy.[55]

§ 3.07 COMPUTER-GENERATED WORKS[56]

Authors have always used machines such as quill pens, typewriters, and cameras while creating their works. Computers, the latest development in this line, are machines that organize information and do nothing unless instructed by a program. Some programs, word processing programs for example, are inert tools for creation, and a computer so programmed works much like a camera or typewriter, where virtually all choices are made by a human author. Other programs, however, contribute to creative authorship, such as those that compose music or graphic images with only the slightest human input.

Can computers be authors? Neither the Constitution nor the Copyright Act indicates that authors must be human. It is universally assumed, however, that the copyright monopoly was intended for human authors and that granting copyright to a machine would be an absurdity. The reason relates to the purpose of copyright (and all intellectual property law, for that matter), which is to provide incentives to create. Machines do not need these monopoly incentives; they just need electricity.

If a machine cannot be an author for copyright purposes, who is the author of a computer-generated work? The choice is between the user of the program and the programmer. CONTU found that the author was the one who employed the computer.[57] This is an overstatement because an author must demonstrate originality and a quantum of creativity that justifies the copyright. One who simply turns

---

[53] *Franklin Computer Corp.*, 714 F.2d at 1253.

[54] *See, e.g.*, *Whelan Assoc., Inc. v. Jaslow Dental Lab., Inc.*, 797 F.2d 1222 (3d Cir. 1986); *Computer Assoc. Int'l v. Altai, Inc.*, 982 F.2d 693 (2d Cir. 1992). For a discussion of these cases, see *infra* § 9.04[F].

[55] *See Sega Enter. v. Accolade, Inc.*, 977 F.2d 1510 (9th Cir. 1992), *infra* § 10.13, for a discussion of the issue.

[56] For an overview, see Pamela Samuelson, *Allocating Ownership Rights in Computer-Generated Works*, 47 U. Pitt. L. Rev. 1185 (1986).

[57] *See* CONTU Final Report at 43–46. *See also* Raymond T. Nimmer, The Law of Computer Technology § 1:9 (3d ed. 2005).

on a computer and inserts a program that composes music would be hard put to claim originality in the result. There must be some evidence of choice, selection, or intellectual labor constituting originality. The range of user originality is quite easy to find in the output generated through use of a word processing program. But at the other end of the continuum, for computer-generated works involving insignificant or no user discretion, copyright should be denied. As in any other legal determination, there will be different line-drawing processes within these extremes to determine whether the user of the program has supplied sufficient original authorship to the computer-generated work.[58]

The programmer is the other person who may have a claim to authorship in a computer-generated work. The right to the copyright in the program is clear, but does the same principle apply to what the program produces? Despite the significant intellectual effort put into creating the program, there are fundamental reasons why the programmer should not be allowed to claim the output. First, the programmer did not fix the work himself. He created the possibility of a work but did not embody it in the tangible medium of expression. The user is the one who did that, and copyright law confers authorship on the person who fixes the work. Second, for computer-generated works the output is randomly determined and unpredictable. Copyright should only be conferred upon an author who conceives as well as fixes a work. From the above, the raw output of a computer-generated work should be treated as fact, without ownership rights in anybody. In short, copyright protection should be conferred on the user of the program, not the programmer, but only when the user has added original authorship to the raw output.

§ 3.08 OTHER FORMS OF INTELLECTUAL PROPERTY PROTECTION FOR COMPUTER SOFTWARE

[A] Trade Secret Protection[59] for Computer Software

Copyright law is only one means of intellectual property law protection for computer software. Trade secret law and patent law also have important roles to play. Traditionally, trade secret protection has been the body of law that owners of computer programs have used to protect their creations.

A trade secret has been defined as: "any formula, pattern, device or compilation of information which is used in one's business, and which gives him an opportunity to obtain an advantage over competitors who do not know or use it."[60]

Providing a broader range of subject matter protection than copyright law, trade secret law has been the law of choice through the years for the computer software industry.[61]

---

[58] For an interesting view on the nature of authorship and randomly generated works, see Alan L. Durham, *The Random Muse: Authorship and Indeterminacy*, 44 Will. & Mary L. Rev. 569 (2002).

[59] For a discussion of trade secret law, see *supra* § 1.14[A].

[60] Restatement of Torts § 757, Comment b (1939).

[61] *See* Duncan M. Davidson, *Protecting Computer Software: A Comprehensive Analysis*, 1983 Ariz.

Trade secret protection is in some important ways more limited than copyright and patent law protection. Trade secrets are protected only as long as the subject matter has not become generally known in the industry.[62] Moreover, trade secrets are only protected against misappropriation by breach of a confidential relationship, not against discovery by innocent means such as reverse engineering.[63] These general standards place computer programs in a precarious position once the program is distributed to the public, where its design could be easily discovered by third parties. Thus, trade secret protection is of most value during a program's developmental stage, where it can be protected against improper disclosure by breach of confidence. Nevertheless, even for publicly distributed programs, the computer software industry has tried a variety of ingenious techniques designed to retain the trade secret status of the program either by licensing it to customers under an obligation of confidence or nondisclosure or by distributing the program only in machine-readable object code. Despite these techniques, any publicly distributed program is vulnerable to discovery by reverse engineering, and once it becomes generally known within the industry, the trade secret protection is lost.

[B] Patent Law Protection for Computer Software

Due to the uncertainties about the scope and protection of computer software, software developers have looked to patent law as an alternative mode of protection.

Patent law,[64] which confers a twenty-year monopoly on products and processes, is another possible source of intellectual property protection for computer software.[65] The advantage of patent protection is that, unlike copyright law, whose threshold of protection is originality, a patent protects its owner against all users and sellers of the patented invention (even independent discoverers).[66] In addition, unlike copyright law, patent law provides protection against reverse engineering in ways that copyright may not. The disadvantage of patent protection is its cost — the time and money it takes to obtain a patent — which makes patent law protection an inappropriate route for most computer software. The examination process may take years if there are complications, and the filing costs and legal fees can amount to thousands of dollars, even for an application ultimately denied protection. The Patent Office scrutinizes the application thoroughly to determine whether it meets the rigorous standards of patentability — namely, novelty and nonobviousness.[67] These hurdles are often difficult to overcome, ending in the abandonment of the application or its final rejection by the Patent Office.

St. L.J. 611; Glen T. MacGrady, *Protection of Computer Software — An Upgrade and Practical Synthesis*, 20 Hous. L. Rev. 1033 (1983).

[62] *See* Roger M. Milgrim, Trade Secrets § 2–74 (1988) (maintaining that absolute secrecy is not required).

[63] *See, e.g., Telex Corp. v. I.B.M. Corp.*, 510 F.2d 894 (10th Cir. 1975).

[64] For a discussion of patent law, see *supra* § 1.11.

[65] *See* 35 U.S.C § 101.

[66] *See* 35 U.S.C. § 271.

[67] 35 U.S.C. § 102.

Once issued, a software patent may already be obsolete from a technological standpoint, given the rapidly evolving nature of the field. Moreover, to obtain a patent, one must disclose the key elements of the program, thereby divulging any trade secrets that may be embodied in it. Thus, the decision to seek patent protection depends on the anticipated long market life and significant commercial value of the program. For example, a novel operating system program may be more appropriate for patent protection than an applications program for a videogame that has a relatively short market appeal.

Despite these drawbacks, software developers have achieved growing success in protecting their creations under patent. Once viewed as a type of mathematical algorithm (a class of non-patentable laws of nature), patents for software inventions had been treated with distinct hostility by the courts and the Patent and Trademark Office. This view persisted until the Supreme Court's (five to four) decision in *Diamond v. Diehr*[68] established that an invention is no less patentable because it makes use of computer software. *Diehr* involved the patentability of a process for curing raw synthetic rubber. The process used computer software to compute time, temperature, and pressure accurately so that rubber would retain its shape after molding was completed. The process employed a well-known mathematical formula for which no claim was made. The Court held that, "[a] claim drawn to subject matter otherwise statutory does not become nonstatutory simply because it uses a mathematical formula, computer program, or digital computer."[69]

In sum, software embodied in an otherwise patentable process or apparatus can qualify for patent protection so long as protection is not sought for a mathematical formula or method of calculation.[70] The case law after *Diehr* has expanded protection for computer programs[71] to allow increasingly broad claim coverage.[72] Following the trend in the case law, the U.S. Patent and Trademark Office issues yearly a greater number of software patents.[73] Considering the greater number and breadth of software patents issuing today, and the ever-increasing number of companies computerizing their manufacturing processes, patenting computer

[68] 450 U.S. 175 (1981).

[69] *Id.* at 187.

[70] *See In re Walter*, 618 F.2d 758 (C.C.P.A. 1980).

[71] *See, e.g.*, *In re Pardo*, 684 F.2d 912 (C.C.P.A. 1982); *In re Beauregard*, 53 F.3d 1583 (Fed. Cir. 1995) (upholding a claim as to a computer-readable medium that would provide protection for the actual disk or other medium on which the software is sold).

[72] *See, e.g.*, *Arrhythmia Research Tech., Inc. v. Corazonix Corp.*, 958 F.2d 1053 (Fed. Cir. 1992). It has also engendered much controversy. For differing views about the patentability of computer software, see, e.g., Pamela Samuelson, *Benson Revisited: The Case Against Patent Protection for Algorithms and Other Computer Program-Related Inventions*, 39 Emory L.J. 1025 (1990) (opposing patent protection and advocating *sui generis* protection); Samuel Oddi, *An Uneasier Case for Copyright Than for Patent Protection of Computer Programs*, 72 Neb. L. Rev. 351 (1993) (urging that a somewhat easier case can be made for patent protection of computer programs than under copyright or a *sui generis* system).

[73] Currently, it is estimated that 20,000 patents are issued in software-related patent classifications each year. *See* James Bessen and Robert Hunt, *An Empirical Look at Software Patents* (Federal Reserve Bank of Philadelphia, Working Paper No. 03-17R, 2004).

software has become an increasingly attractive method of protecting it.[74]

In response to the explosive growth of software patent filings, the Patent and Trademark Office has issued *Examination Guidelines for Computer-Related Inventions*.[75] The Guidelines abandon the various formalistic grounds for rejecting claims based on lack of subject matter. A claim containing a mathematical algorithm, for example, is non-statutory only if it represents, as a whole, an abstract idea rather than applied technology. In addition, expansive case law formulated by the Federal Circuit has extended protection to business methods that were once considered unpatentable subject matter.[76] The net effect of the Guidelines and liberal court decisions resulted in the issuance of more software patents and their immunity from challenge on subject matter grounds. This expansive attitude toward the patenting of all forms of computer software is on the wane. In *Biski v. Kappos*[77] the Supreme held that a patent on methods for hedging risks for commodities trading constituted an abstract idea ineligible for patent protection. Despite current trends, given the limited scope of copyright protection afforded to software, patent protection has become the preferred alternative for protecting the functional aspects of computer programs, at least for companies with enough money to pursue it. Whether the recent limitations on patent protection for software render patent protection less desirable remains to be seen.

[C] State Contract Law

Software developers have also looked to contract law to provide protection when copyright might fall short. Normally, contracts in the software field employ restrictive licensing provisions that prohibit disclosure and reverse engineering. From this standpoint, contract law may provide an effective alternative to copyright law. One drawback to contract protection is that contract rights run between the parties to the contract whereas copyright gives the copyright owner rights against the world. Nonetheless, the contract has proved to be an attractive alternative source of protection in the software world, especially for "custom" software designed for large computer systems.

Obviously, contract regimes are not as well adapted to situations in which standardized software products are sold in large numbers to individual consumers. In such situations, copyright law typically has established limits on the purchaser's use of the program. One contractual mechanism to circumvent the limits of copyright is known as the "shrink-wrap" license. Sometimes called "tear me open licenses," these form agreements are packaged with consumer software products,

---

[74] *See* Roger L. Cook, *The Software Industry Anticipates a Flood of Patent Litigation*, Nat'l L.J., Jan. 24, 1994, at S2.

[75] 61 Fed. Reg. 7478 (Feb. 28, 1996).

[76] For the outer reaches of patentable subject matter for computer software *see State Street Bank & Trust Co. v. Signature Financial Group, Inc.* 149 F.3d 1368 (Fed. Cir. 1998) which upheld as statutory subject matter claims directed to financial services software resulting in cost and tax savings by pooling investment funds into a single portfolio.

[77] Bilski v. Kappos, 561 U.S. 593 (2010).

Bilski was confirmed in another Supreme Court case involving software patentability. *See Alice Corp. v. CLS Bank Int'l*, 2014 U.S. LEXIS 4303 (June 19, 2014).

the restrictive terms of which the consumer is said to "accept" by his or her decision to open the package and to remove its contents. Under the terms of a typical "shrink wrap" license, certain activities that would otherwise be permissible or be considered a "fair use" are contractually prohibited. Although questions linger about the enforceability of such agreements, recent case law[78] suggests they may indeed have the legal effect that software manufacturers have claimed for them. Moreover, ongoing efforts to revise the Uniform Commercial Code to include a new Article 2B, covering the licensing of information, seem likely to promote the further use of such legal mechanisms.

[D] Protecting Technological Safeguards: The Digital Millennium Copyright Act

More and more informational products, including software, are being sold on the Internet. The terms of the online sale are agreed to by means of a "click-on" license, whereby the consumer clicks on a "virtual 'OK' button." For security purposes, electronic information vendors employ technological safeguards such as encryption and scrambling. These measures are designed to exclude those who have not agreed to the terms of the license and exercise control over the uses of the product once access has been established. These technological safeguards, however, can be overridden, avoided, or "hacked" by relatively sophisticated computer users. As a result, copyright owners were successful in persuading Congress to enact new federal statutory provisions at the end of 1998 (Digital Millennium Copyright Act ("DMCA") that imposes civil and criminal penalties on those whose who "circumvent" (or assist others in "circumventing")) technological protection measures applied to copyrighted works.[79] In addition, the Act imposes prohibitions on equipment or services that can be used to circumvent technological safeguards. In addition to meeting the needs of copyright owners, the DMCA, with its anti-circumvention provisions, enabled the United States to ratify the WIPO Treaties[80] concluded in 1996. These treaties require ratifying countries to take steps to provide "adequate legal protection and effective legal remedies" against circumvention.

---

[78] *See ProCD v. Zeidenberg*, 86 F.3d 1447 (7th Cir. 1996).

[79] The Digital Millennium Copyright Act, Pub. L. 105-304 (105th Cong. 2d Sess. 1998) is discussed at greater length at *infra* §§ 8.35–8.39.

[80] The WIPO Copyright Treaty and the WIPO Performances and Phonograms Treaty can be found in Marshall Leaffer, International Treaties in Intellectual Property (2d ed. 1997) at 388 (WCT) and 438 S (WPPT). They are discussed at greater length in this treatise at *infra* § 12.06.

§ 3.09 SEMICONDUCTOR CHIPS

[A] The Technological Background, the Economic Stakes, and the Legal Dilemma[81]

The controversy over the copyrightability of computer programs was resolved by protecting them under existing copyright law. A different solution was adopted by Congress with respect to another mini-marvel of the Information Age: semiconductor chip products or, more familiarly, "chips." Chips are small pieces of semiconductor material. As their name suggests, they are intermediate in function between conductors, which efficiently conduct electricity, and insulators, which do not appreciably conduct electricity. In essence, chips are tiny instances of complex electronic circuitry. The basic building block of a chip is an electronic switch, or "transistor," which controls or amplifies electronic signals. These transistors are connected, or "integrated," to form circuits that perform specific electronic functions. Hundreds of thousands of such sophisticated switching mechanisms can be compacted on a wafer, typically of silicon, no larger than a baby's fingernail. The two principal types of chips that result are indispensable to American industry: "memory" chips, which store information for use in computers, databases, and the like; and "microprocessors," which serve as the brains of computers, smart phones, microwave ovens, robots, automobile ignition systems, and a myriad of other modern devices.

To compact thousands of switching devices on this fingernail-size wafer is a complex and expensive task, often involving thousands of engineering hours and millions of dollars. The process generally begins by producing a series of drawings representing the electronic circuitry. From these drawings, a series of stencils, called masks, are produced. Each mask corresponds to one layer of the final chip, and is layered into the final chip by a chemical process. Creation of these masks is a costly and critical element of microchip production; copying them is the goal of the microchip pirate.

Although masks are expensive and time-consuming to produce, they are relatively cheap and can be copied quickly. The microchip pirate simply removes a chip's casing and photographs its individual layers. Having no research and development costs, the pirate is often able to undersell the original producer. This gross discrepancy between the cost of creation and the cost of reproduction has led microchip producers to seek the law's protection to ensure that they will receive an adequate return on their investment.

Traditional forms of intellectual property protection, however, have been unavailable for semiconductor chips for several reasons. First, trade secret protection is impractical. Relatively easy to reverse engineer, chips lose trade secret protection quickly following an unrestricted sale. Second, patent protection is largely unavailable. Despite their high production costs, chips have difficulty meeting the rigorous patent standard of inventiveness. Third, copyright law has not provided a source of protection. To the Copyright Office, which reflects the

---

[81] *See generally* H.R. Rep. No. 98-781, 98th Cong., 2d Sess. (1984).

current thinking, chips are uncopyrightable utilitarian objects. The Copyright Office has registered the schematic drawings of the electrical interconnections of the chip, but protection extends only to the drawings, not to the chip itself. The reason for this anomaly lies in § 113(b) of the Copyright Act,[82] which states that copyright in a pictorial, graphic, or sculptural work portraying a useful article does not extend to the manufacture of the article itself. For example, technical drawings for a motorcycle are protectable under copyright law, but the motorcycle they portray is not.[83]

[B] The Semiconductor Chip Act: Statutory Overview

Lack of significant protection for this important industry under traditional intellectual property law led to *sui generis* protection in the Semiconductor Chip Protection Act of 1984 ("SCPA"). Rather than classifying chips as "writings" protected by copyright or as "discoveries" more suitable for patent protection, Congress chose an intermediate course, codified in an entirely new Chapter 9 of Copyright Act entitled, "Protection of Semiconductor Chip Products."[84] A hybrid of patent and copyright law (but closer to copyright in nature), the SCPA provides protection upon registration or first commercial use,[85] whichever occurs first, and then lasts ten years from that date.[86] It confers exclusive rights on proprietors to reproduce such works and to make and sell chips embodying them. The SCPA exempts innocent infringers from liability for use or resale of unauthorized chips occurring before receiving notice of infringement. Importantly, it permits reverse engineering of mask works to teach, analyze, or evaluate the concept or technique embodied therein.[87]

Mask works must meet a copyright-like standard of originality. Protection is available for original mask works independently created, but it is not available for commonplace staple designs, or their trivial variations.[88] As in copyright law, protection does not extend to an idea, concept, principle, or discovery used in the mask work design. Procedures, processes, and methods of operation described or embodied in a mask work are not eligible for protection; for this, one must seek patent protection. To avoid forfeiture, registration in the Copyright Office must be sought within two years of commercial exploitation anywhere in the world.[89] The Copyright Office will issue registration if the formal elements of the application are present and the subject matter is apparent, but it will conduct no search for conflicting prior registrations. The effective date of registration is the date on

---

[82] 17 U.S.C. § 113(b). For a discussion of § 113(b), see *infra* § 8.07.

[83] Similarly, before the passage of the Architectural Works Protection Act of 1990, Architectural drawings of a building were protected under copyright but not the construction of a building based on the plans. The 1990 Act changed this rule and architectural works now receive full copyright protection not limited by § 113 (b) of the Copyright Act. For a discussion of architectural works, see *infra* § 3.16.

[84] Act of November 8, 1984, Pub. L. No. 98-620, 98 Stat. 3347; 17 U.S.C. § 900 *et seq.*

[85] 17 U.S.C. § 904.

[86] 17 U.S.C. § 905.

[87] 17 U.S.C. § 906.

[88] *See* 17 U.S.C. § 902(b)(1), (2).

[89] *See* 17 U.S.C. § 908(a).

which a complete and allowable registration is filed in the Copyright Office.[90]

Notice on mask works is permissive, but strongly recommended because it constitutes *prima facie* notice that the mask work is protected.[91] Notice consists of the symbol "M" in a circle, plus the name or recognized abbreviation of the mask owner.[92] A mask owner must affix notice in a way that gives reasonable notice of his claim.

The federal district courts are given exclusive jurisdiction over claims for infringement of a mask work. Registration or application for registration of the work is a prerequisite to bringing suit.[93] Remedies include injunction, damages, and profits. As in copyright law, the owner of the work may elect an award of statutory damages to a maximum of $250,000 for infringement of any one-mask work, in lieu of damages and profits.[94] The Act establishes a three-year statute of limitations.[95]

The SCPA has not generated a flood of litigation, which may attest to its efficacy. In fact, during its first two decades, the only reported case deciding the merits of an SCPA claim was *Brooktree v. Advanced Micro Devices, Inc.*[96] The court held that the copying of any material portion of a chip was an infringement, even if the rest of the chip was independently created. The potential scope of the SPCA was broadened considerably in *Altera Corp. v. Clear Logic, Inc.*[97] which held that the SCPA protects the overall architecture of a chip, such as the placement of large groups of transistors on the chip, and not just the specific layout of transistors within those groups.

Microprocessor Chips protected under the SCPA may contain, among other things, computer programs. Although the subject matter of protection under the SCPA is not the program as such, and although works other than programs (such as databases) commonly are represented in semiconductor chip form, many protected chips do in fact embody programs. In effect, for such programs the SCPA provides a third, overlapping form of legal protection in addition to whatever protection is provided by copyright and patent law.

---

90 *See* 17 U.S.C. § 908(e).

91 *See* 17 U.S.C. § 909(a).

92 *See* 17 U.S.C. § 909(b).

93 *See* 17 U.S.C. § 910(a), (b).

94 *See* 17 U.S.C. § 911.

95 17 U.S.C. § 911(d).

96 977 F.2d 1555 (Fed. Cir. 1992).

97 424 F.3d 1079 (9th Cir. 2005).

Part III. PICTORIAL, GRAPHIC, AND SCULPTURAL WORKS: THE UTILITARIAN OBJECT

§ 3.10 GENERALLY

Section 102(a)(5) of the 1976 Act provides protection to pictorial, graphic, and sculptural works, a category that, "include[s] two-dimensional and three-dimensional works of fine, graphic, and applied art, photographs, prints and art reproductions, maps, globes, charts, technical drawings, diagrams and models."[98]

The term "graphic, pictorial, and sculptural works" encompasses works of fine art as well as applied art and implies no criteria of aesthetic value or taste.[99] The aspect of this category that has engendered the most controversy is the role of copyright in protecting artistic creations embodying utilitarian objects. The following sections concentrate on this issue by examining the question of industrial design and architectural works.

§ 3.11 WORKS OF APPLIED ART AND THE DESIGN OF USEFUL OBJECTS

The designer's art fuses the functional with the aesthetic, producing objects of everyday life — telephones, lighting fixtures, automobiles, tableware — that are both beautiful and useful. Excellence comes at a price, and designers must recoup their investment to stay in business. They wish to protect their designs from free-riding imitators who are able to sell their imitations at a lower price than the originator's.

These objects of utility have presented a difficult issue for the law of copyright. The reason for this difficulty lies in their fusion of the utilitarian and the aesthetic. The goal of the law has been to grant protection to the aesthetic features of an object without unduly extending the monopoly to its functional or mechanical features. In other words, the Copyright Act denies protection to utilitarian aspects of industrial design to save consumers from paying more for unpatented utilitarian articles. It is often impossible, however, to separate in a rational way the aesthetic aspect of the article (the realm of copyright) from its utilitarian dimension (the realm of patent law). Drawing the line between protectable pictorial, graphic, and sculptural works and unprotectable utilitarian elements of industrial design has proven to be one of the most troublesome tasks of copyright law.

---

[98] 17 U.S.C. § 101 (pictorial, graphic, and sculptural works). For an alternative approach to copyright protection for photography and a discussion of her proposed "compositional-equivalence" test, see Teresa Bruce, *In the Language of the Pictures: How Copyright Law Fails to Adequately Account for Photography*, 115 W. Va. L. Rev. 93 (2012). For a discussion of the difficulties of applying copyright law to visual works, see Rebecca Tushnet, *Worth a Thousand Words: The Images of Copyright*, 125 Harv. L. Rev. 683 (2012).

[99] *See* H.R. Rep. No. 94-1476, at 55 (1976).

Until the leading case of *Mazer v. Stein*,[100] it was unclear whether copyright protection was available for works of art embodied in industrial objects or whether protection was limited to design patent laws.[101] The Copyright Office took the position that copyright protection was limited to works of artistic craftsmanship insofar as their form but not as to their mechanical or utilitarian aspects, as in jewelry, enamels, glassware, and tapestries.[102]

Mazer involved the copyrightability of male and female statuettes of Balinese dancers used for bases of table lamps. Petitioners, who had copied these lamp stands, argued against the validity of a copyright for a work of art made as part of a mass-produced good. The Supreme Court disagreed, however, upholding the Copyright Office's regulation allowing copyright for works embodied in useful objects as to their form but not as to their mechanical or utilitarian features. In addition, the Court also held that protection by design patent did not bar copyright protection.[103] The Court justified the overlapping forms of intellectual property protection because the copyright monopoly is of a different nature than the patent monopoly. It is less exclusive than the patent monopoly and protects originality rather than novelty or invention.

After *Mazer v. Stein*, the use to which a work of art was put became irrelevant, but the question remained whether the whole range of industrial design in useful articles could qualify for copyright. From Balinese dancers used as a lamp base, courts extended protection to an antique telephone shape used as a pencil sharpener[104] and a coin bank in the shape of a dog.[105] In addition to these mass-produced objects, graphic designs for textiles were also included within copyrightable subject matter.[106]

If a statuette of a Balinese dancer was copyrightable, why not an automobile, a toaster, or a modernistic lighting fixture? The difference between these useful objects and the *Mazer* statuettes is that their artistic aspects are of an abstract nature often fused with the functional attributes of the object. To deny copyright to these objects, however, would run contrary to the basic tenet of American copyright law, that individual perception of the beautiful is too varied a power to permit a narrow or rigid conception of art.[107] Despite this tradition, which prevented judges and bureaucrats from discriminating against art forms, the Copyright Office wished not to incorporate the entire range of mass-produced objects into copyright law. By regulation, the Copyright Office adopted the separability standard[108] that continues

---

[100] 347 U.S. 201 (1954).

[101] *See* Brown, *supra* note 96, at 1344.

[102] *See* 37 C.F.R. § 202.8(a) (1949).

[103] *Mazer*, 347 U.S. at 215.

[104] *See Ted Arnold Ltd. v. Silvercraft Co.*, 259 F. Supp. 733 (S.D.N.Y. 1966).

[105] *See Royalty Designs, Inc. v. Thrifticheck Serv. Corp.*, 204 F. Supp. 702 (S.D.N.Y. 1962).

[106] *See, e.g.*, *Peter Pan Fabrics, Inc. v. Martin Weiner Corp.*, 274 F.2d 487, 489 (2d Cir. 1960).

[107] *See Bleistein v. Donaldson Lith. Co.*, 188 U.S. 239, 243 (1903).

[108] 37 C.F.R. § 202.10(c) (1959):

> If the sole intrinsic function of an article is its utility, the fact that the article is unique and attractively shaped will not qualify it as a work of art. However, if the shape of a utilitarian

to be the focus of debate under the 1976 Act.[109]

§ 3.12 INDUSTRIAL DESIGN UNDER THE 1976 ACT

Section 101 provides that:

> The design of a useful article . . . shall be considered a pictorial, graphic, or sculptural work only if, and only to the extent that, such design incorporates pictorial, graphic, or sculptural features that can be identified separately from, and are capable of existing independently of, the utilitarian aspects of the article.[110]

As explained in the House Report, this section is designed to draw a line between copyrightable works of applied art and uncopyrightable industrial design.[111] The pertinent section of the House Report reads as follows:

> Unless the shape of an automobile, airplane, lady's dress, food processor, television set, or any other industrial product contains some element that, *physically or conceptually,* can be identified as separable from the utilitarian aspects of the article, the design would not be copyrighted under the bill. (Emphasis added).[112]

In effect, the House Report would deny protection to the overall design of the useful article even if aesthetic considerations govern some aspects of the article.

§ 3.13 PHYSICAL SEPARABILITY: *ESQURE v. RINGER*

In *Esquire, Inc. v. Ringer,*[113] the Court of Appeals for the District of Columbia held that the overall shape of certain outdoor lighting fixtures was ineligible for copyright as a work of art. The Register of Copyright had denied copyright to the fixtures, based on Office regulations that precluded registration of a design of a

---

article incorporates features, such as artistic sculpture, carving, or pictorial representation, which can be identified separately and are capable of existing independently as a work of art, such features will be eligible for registration.

[109] For comprehensive reviews of the subject, see Raymond M. Polakovic, *Should the Bauhaus Be in the Doghouse? Rethinking Conceptual Separability,* 64 U. Colo. L. Rev. 871 (1993); J. H. Reichman, *Design Protection and the Legislative Agenda,* 55 Law & Contemp. Probs. 281 (1992); Michael J. Lynch, *Copyright in Utilitarian Objects: Beneath Metaphysics,* 16 U. Dayton L. Rev. 647 (1991); Shira Perlmutter, *Conceptual Separability and Copyright in Designs of Useful Articles,* 37 J. Copyright Soc'y 339 (1990); Ralph S. Brown, *Design Protection: An Overview,* 34 UCLA L. Rev. 1341 (1987); Robert C. Denicola, *Applied Art and Industrial Design: A Suggested Approach to Copyright in Useful Articles,* 67 Minn. L. Rev. 707 (1983); J.H. Reichman, *Design Protection After the Copyright Act of 1976: A Comparative View of the Emerging Interim Models,* 31 J. Copyright Soc'y 267 (1984); J.H. Reichman, *Design Protection in Domestic and Foreign Copyright Law: From the Berne Revision of 1948 to the Copyright Act of 1976,* 1983 Duke L.J. 1143. For a discussion of fashion design in the United States and the application of copyright law, see Alexandra Manfredi, *Haute Copyright: Tailoring Copyright Protection in High-Profile Fashion Designs,* 21 Cardozo J. Int'l & Comp. L. 105 (2012).

[110] 17 U.S.C. § 101 (pictorial, graphic, and sculptural works).

[111] H.R. Rep. No. 94-1476, at 55 (1976).

[112] *Id.*

[113] 591 F.2d 796 (D.C. Cir. 1978).

utilitarian object when, "the fixtures . . . did not contain elements, either alone or in combination, which are capable of independent existence as a copyrightable pictorial, graphic, or sculptural work apart from the utilitarian aspect."[114]

Unlike the statuettes in *Mazer*, which could exist independently as a sculptural work when removed from the lamp mechanism, the modernistic abstract form of the lighting fixture was inextricably fused with its utilitarian function.

The *Esquire* court upheld the Register's interpretation of its regulations and the denial of copyright. Although a pre-1976 Act case, the court looked to the recently passed 1976 Act's provisions and its legislative history. Section 101 was considered to be a codification of 1909 Act practices and was deemed to reflect congressional understanding of the design problem.

In applying § 101 of the recently passed Copyright Act of 1976 and reviewing the House Report's analysis, the *Esquire* court denied copyright, finding no aspect of the lighting fixture physically separable from its overall configuration. In so doing, the court refused to apply the other aspect of the conceptual separability test suggested by the House Report. Instead, the court preferred to read the legislative history as a whole, which indicated an intent "to draw as clear a line as possible between copyrightable works of applied art and uncopyrighted works of industrial design."[115] The court focused on the phrase in the House Report that stated that, "the overall design or configuration of the utilitarian object, even if it is determined by aesthetic as well as functional considerations, is not eligible for copyright."[116]

In short, the *Esquire* court took a narrow view of the separability issue: first, holding that the overall design of an industrial object is never eligible for copyright and, second, that only those aspects removable from the object and that maintain an independent existence as a graphic, pictorial, or sculptural work qualify for copyright protection. Several courts have employed the *Esquire* approach, denying copyright protection to toy airplanes[117] and automobile hubcaps.[118]

Physical separability, as adopted by *Esquire*, has been largely rejected by both courts and commentators as being contrary to the intent of Congress. Professor Nimmer has pointed out that, from the simplest instance of a statuette on the hood of a car, there are very few objects that could pass the physical separability test. For example, even the *Mazer* statuettes could not exist independently if their utilitarian lamp bases were removed.[119] Another shortcoming in the *Esquire* approach lies in its holding that the overall configuration of a useful object cannot be protected. This approach leads to irrational results. Carried to its logical conclusion, a physical separability approach would protect the *Mazer* statuettes because they were only a part of the object's entire configuration, while it would deny protection to a statuette

---

[114] *Id.* at 798.

[115] *Id.* at 803, *quoting* H.R. Rep. No. 94-1476, 94th Cong., 2d Sess. 55 (1976).

[116] *Id.* at 804.

[117] *See Gay Toys, Inc. v. Buddy L. Corp.*, 522 F. Supp. 622 (E.D. Mich. 1981).

[118] *See Norris Indus., Inc. v. International Tel. & Tel. Corp.*, 212 U.S.P.Q. (BNA) 754 (N.D. Fla. 1981), *aff'd*, 696 F.2d 918 (11th Cir. 1983).

[119] Nimmer on Copyright § 2.08[B][3] (2014).

used as a receptacle for collecting coins. Finally, under the same reasoning, a fabric design could not be protected under copyright because the design, dyed into a textile, cannot be physically separated and exist independently of the material. For these reasons, other courts, particularly the Second Circuit, have looked to the House Report's statement that separability could be determined *physically or conceptually*.[120]

§ 3.14 CONCEPTUAL SEPARABILITY

Congress clearly intended that the concept of conceptual separability be distinct from that of physical separability. But to define conceptual separability in a useful and understandable manner so that it may be applied intelligibly as a legal standard in a court of law has proven to be one of the most elusive issues in copyright law. How is one to identify those artistic aspects that must be separated conceptually from the utilitarian aspects of the article? A series of Second Circuit cases reveal the difficulties and lack of agreement on how to resolve the issue.

One case decided early under the 1976 Act suggests that a copyright should be upheld whenever the decorative or aesthetically pleasing aspect of an article can be said to be "primary" and the utilitarian function can be said to be "secondary."[121] In *Kieselstein-Cord v. Accessories By Pearl, Inc.* the Second Circuit Court of Appeals applied the conceptual separability test to the highly ornamental surfaces of two belt buckles. To the court, the ornamental surfaces of these belt buckles were conceptually separable from their composite design because they were unrelated to the utilitarian function of the buckles. As evidence of this aesthetic appeal, some persons were wearing the buckles as jewelry other than at the waist, which indicated that "the primary ornamental aspect of the . . . buckles is conceptually separable from their subsidiary utilitarian function."[122] The court suggested that conceptual separability exists where an article would be marketed as an aesthetic object even if it had no useful function.[123]

In *Carol Barnhart Inc. v. Economy Cover Corp.*,[124] the Second Circuit appeared to return implicitly to a standard of physical separability. *Barnhart* involved the copyrightability of four human torso mannequins used for clothing display was at issue. The court found that the claimed artistic features, the life-size breast form and the width of the shoulders, were inextricably related to their utilitarian function, *i.e.*, the display of clothes. The case was distinguished from *Kieselstein* where, by comparison, the ornamental aspect of the belt buckle was unrelated to its utilitarian function. In other words, the artistic and aesthetic features, in *Kiesel-*

---

[120] H.R. Rep. No. 94-1476, 94th at 55 (1976). For the pertinent quote from the House Report, see *supra* § 3.12.

[121] *See Kieselstein-Cord v. Accessories by Pearl*, 632 F.2d 989, 993 (2d Cir. 1980).

[122] *Id.*

[123] Some case law has followed this likelihood-of-marketability approach to conceptual separability. *See, e.g.*, *Poe v. Missing Persons*, 745 F.2d 1238 (9th Cir. 1984). Nimmer has criticized this approach as discriminating against non-representational art, being too difficult to prove and too restrictive in result. Nimmer on Copyright § 2.08[B][3] (2014).

[124] 773 F.2d 411 (2d Cir. 1985).

stein, as opposed to the Barnhart forms, were added to an otherwise utilitarian article, and these features could stand on their own as a work of art. In other words, the belt buckle, could work perfectly without these artistic and aesthetic features. In this way, the reasoning in *Barnhart* is an application of physical rather than conceptual separability.[125]

Judge Newman, in dissent, was troubled by the outcome of the case and by its absence of a unifying test for conceptual separability. He proposed the following test, sometimes referred to as the "temporal displacement test": for design features to be conceptually separate from the utilitarian aspects of the useful article that embodies the design, the article must stimulate in the mind of the beholder a concept that is entirely separable from the utilitarian functions.[126] To the dissent, these *Barnhart* forms created in the observer's mind's eye not just a useful object but a work of art as well.[127]

Another panel of the Second Circuit took a different tack in denying the copyrightability of a design for a bicycle rack constructed of metal tubing bent to create a serpentine form. In *Brandir International, Inc. v. Cascade Pacific Lumber Co.*,[128] the court adopted a test proposed by Professor Denicola[129] to determine the fine line between protectable works of applied art and unprotectable industrial design: if the design elements reflect the merger of aesthetic and functional considerations, the artistic aspects are not conceptually separable. Alternatively, if the design elements reflect the designer's artistic judgment independent of functional considerations, there is conceptual separability. In reviewing the process followed by the designer, the court found that the form of the rack was significantly influenced by functional concerns so that the artistic elements were not conceptually separate from the utilitarian.[130] Thus, even though the rack may be admired for its aesthetic qualities alone, it remains nonetheless a product of industrial design. Here, according to the court, form and function were inextricably intertwined in the rack, and its form was dictated as much by utilitarian choices as by aesthetic concerns.

---

[125] Other courts have extended and refined the *Barnhart* majority's formulation of conceptual separability, gravitating to Professor Goldstein's two part test for conceptual separability: a pictorial, graphic, or sculptural work incorporated into the design of a useful article is conceptually separable (1) if it can stand on its own as a work of art traditionally conceived, and (2) if the useful article in which it is embodied would be equally useful without it. *See* Paul Goldstein, Copyright § 2.5.3 (3d ed. 2014). This two part test was adopted in *Pivot Point Int'l Inc. v. Charlene Prods. Inc.*, 170 F. Supp. 2d 828, 833 (N.D. Ill. 2001). In applying the Goldstein test and denying copyright protection to mannequin form, the court admitted that this two part standard differs little if any from the test of physical separabilty found in *Esquire v. Ringer*. The district court was overturned in *Pivot Point Int'l Inc. v. Charlene Prods. Inc.*, 372 F.3d 913 (7th Cir. 2004) (favoring Judge Newman's dissent in *Barnhart*).

[126] *Id.* at 422.

[127] *Id.* at 426.

[128] 834 F.2d 1142 (2d Cir. 1987).

[129] *Id.* at 1145. Professor Denicola is the author of an important article on the design issue that proposes the text adopted by the court. *See* Robert C. Denicola, *Applied Art and Industrial Design: A Suggested Approach to Copyright in Useful Articles*, 67 Minn. L. Rev. 707, 741 (1973).

[130] 834 F.2d at 1146.

Judge Winter, in dissent, would not have focused on the process used by the designer but rather on how the rack was perceived. Thus, the test (similar to Newman's temporal displacement test) should be whether the design of a useful object, however intertwined with its functional aspects, is perceived as an aesthetic concept not related to the article's function.[131] Judge Winter was particularly troubled that the majority's adaptation of the Denicola test would diminish the concept of conceptual separability to the vanishing point. By focusing on the process followed by a particular designer, cases would be decided on the fortuitous circumstances concerning the creation of the design.

The problem of industrial design will continue to plague the courts so long as they must apply some form of the separability test. Unfortunately, the courts have yet to achieve a consensus in formulating a test that separates the utilitarian from the artistic, does not discriminate between various art forms, and is phrased clearly enough so that the trier of fact can come to a reasoned judgment. This is perhaps an impossible task given the inherently illogical nature of the inquiry. One point of view (the majority in *Brandir*) would judge the separability as revealed in the design process and whether the designer was motivated by aesthetic choices. This test has the virtue of separating the aesthetic from the utilitarian, but at the same time, it will often necessitate a lengthy procedure replete with expert testimony. The alternate view (the dissents in *Brandir* and *Barnhart*) would judge separability from the standpoint of the ordinary observer — whether the design engenders an aesthetic reaction in the eye of the beholder. The advantage of this approach, advocated by Judges Newman and Winter, is that it presents the question of separability in a more administratively convenient form for the trier of fact.

With all the complexities of the separability test, it is easy to lose sight of the purpose of the inquiry, which is to avoid the anti-competitive effect in giving copyright protection over unpatented utilitarian articles. In other areas of the copyright law, this purpose is achieved by application of the merger doctrine, the idea/expression dichotomy, or the requirement of originality. Indeed, many industrial design cases could have been disposed on these grounds. This method of analysis in most cases would provide a more direct, reasoned, and transparent basis in drawing the line between aesthetic expression and utilitarian functionality.[132]

---

[131] *Id.* at 1151.

[132] This idea is developed in Paul Goldstein, Copyright § 2.5.3.1(c) (3d ed. 2014); *Superior Form Builders, Inc. v. Dan Chase Taxidermy Supply Co.*, 74 F.3d 488 (4th Cir. 1996) (using originality analysis in upholding the copyrightability of animal mannequins used by taxidermists to mount animal skins).

§ 3.15 OTHER FORMS OF PROTECTION FOR WORKS OF APPLIED ART: VESSEL HULL DESIGNS, DESIGN PATENT, AND PROPOSED DESIGN LEGISLATION[133]

[A] Design Patent

In addition to copyright law, industrial designers can protect their creations under design patent law.[134] Section 171 of the Patent Act[135] confers a design patent for a fourteen-year term, as measured from the date of the grant, to whomever invents a new (novel), original, and ornamental design for an article of manufacture. As for subject matter, design patents may be issued for the appearance of articles of manufacture for their shape, surface ornamentation, or both. Design patents have been issued for the appearance of a stadium grandstand,[136] the design of jets of water in a fountain,[137] and the shank of a drill bit.[138] A patentable design must be primarily ornamental, appealing to the aesthetic sense as a thing of beauty. If the design is dictated by functional considerations, it is ineligible for protection. Unlike copyright, the courts are directly involved in questions of aesthetics in determining the validity of design patents.[139]

Despite their seeming appropriateness, design patents are often not practical means for the protection of industrial design. The reasons are the time and expense required to obtain a design patent, the difficulty that many designs have in meeting the standards of patentability, and their marked tendency of being declared invalid when challenged in federal court.

By comparison with copyright, whose key standard is originality, the standards for obtaining a design patent, novelty and non-obviousness, are much more rigorous and difficult to meet. As for novelty, the design must differ from prior art and not merely modify it. Moreover, even if novel, the design must meet the standard of non-obviousness. Here the question presented is whether the design would be non-obvious to ordinary skilled designers in the field.[140] One can think of very few designs that could not plausibly be challenged on one or both of these

---

[133] This section focuses on three statutory forms of design protection. The form of useful objects, including aspects of architecture, can also be protected under trademark and unfair competition law. Generally, protection under federal trademark and unfair competition law extends to nonfunctional aspects of the work. In addition, secondary meaning must be shown in these nonfunctional aspects. For an overview, see Ralph S. Brown, *Design Protection: An Overview*, 34 UCLA L. Rev. 1341, 1357–95 (1987). For an excellent case reviewing the entire area and providing an integrated theory, see Judge Posner's opinion in *W.T. Rogers Co. v. Keene*, 778 F.2d 334 (7th Cir. 1985).

[134] *See generally* Donald S. Chisum, Patents § 1.04 (2014).

[135] 35 U.S.C. § 171.

[136] *See In re Hadden*, 20 F.2d 275 (D.C. Cir. 1927).

[137] *See In re Hruby*, 373 F.2d 997 (C.C.P.A. 1967).

[138] *See In re Zahn*, 617 F.2d 261 (C.C.P.A. 1980).

[139] *See, e.g., Blisscraft of Hollywood v. United Plastics Co.*, 294 F.2d 694 (2d Cir. 1961).

[140] *See In re Nalbandian*, 661 F.2d 1214 (C.C.P.A 1981).

grounds. As a result, design patents are often declared invalid when challenged in federal court.[141]

Whether an accused design infringes a patented design is determined from the perspective of the ordinary observer. Thus, a design patent is infringed by a second design if in the eyes of an ordinary observer the two designs are substantially the same. In other words infringement occurs if the resemblance deceives the ordinary observer, inducing him to purchase one supposing it to be the other.[142]

The costs of obtaining a design patent, including filing fees, issuance fees, and attorney's fees, are substantial, particularly when compared with copyright. The complicated application process requires hiring a patent attorney, one specifically admitted to practice before the Patent Office. The examination procedure takes time because the Patent Office conducts a search to determine novelty and non-obviousness.[143] A design patent can be more valuable to its owner than a copyright. Unlike a copyright, the design patent can be enforced against all persons creating a design substantially similar in appearance, even those persons who have not copied the design.

Copyright and design patent law have overlapping subject matter. Thus, the question arises whether a design patent can be obtained for a copyrighted work or whether a copyright can concurrently protect a design patent. In the leading case on the issue, *In re Yardley*,[144] the Court of Customs and Patent Appeals allowed a design patent to be issued on a watch design even though the applicant had previously registered a claim for copyright.

The effect of a design patent on the validity of a copyright was unclear before the 1976 Act.[145] The rationale was that the public act of filing for a patent dedicated the work to the public. The 1976 Act would appear to undermine this public domain rationale because a copyright subsists from the moment of creation and not just from the moment of publication.[146] Thus, both copyright and design patent protection could exist concurrently in the same object.

---

[141] For an overview and survey of design patent litigation, see Thomas B. Lindgren, *The Sanctity of the Design Patent: Illusion or Reality? Twenty Years of Design Patent Litigation Since Compco v. Day-Brite Lighting, Inc., and Sears Roebuck & Co. v. Stiffel Co.*, 10 Okla. City U. L. Rev. 195 (1985). Despite the hurdles in obtaining a design patent, between 4,000 and 5,000 design patents are issued each year on about double the number of applications. *See id.* at 205.

[142] *See Gorham Mfg. v. White*, 81 U.S. 511, 528 (1871). The ordinary observer test for design patent infringement was reconfirmed in *Egyptian Goddess Inc. v. Swisa Inc.*, 543 F.3d 665 (Fed. Cir. 2008). The court rejected prior Federal Circuit law known as the "point of novelty" test, which had required that the accused device appropriate the *novelty* in the patented device in distinguishing it from the prior art.

[143] Statistics show that the process takes on average two-and-a-half years for issuance of a design patent. *See* 1986 *PTO Annual Report* at 21.

[144] 493 F.2d 1389 (C.C.P.A. 1974).

[145] *Compare Korzybski v. Underwood & Underwood, Inc.*, 36 F.2d 727 (2d Cir. 1929) (finding design patent bars copyright), *with Zachary v. Western Publ'g Co.*, 75 Cal. App. 3d 911 (1977) (noting publication by government does not dedicate copyright to public domain).

[146] For a discussion of publication under copyright law, see *infra* §§ 4.02–4.07.

[B] Design Legislation

Because of the limited protection provided by design patent and copyright law, *sui generis* design protection legislation has been introduced in Congress virtually every year for the past thirty years.[147] Most proposals for industrial design legislation provide protection for original ornamental designs of a useful article, including both two-dimensional and three-dimensional aspects of shape and surface. Protection would be denied to the utilitarian features of a design as well as to staple commonplace designs.

Industrial design legislation is closer in spirit to copyright law than patent law. All recent proposals have used the less strict standard of originality, as opposed to the more rigorous novelty standard of patent law. Infringement of the design would be based on copyright principles, and evidence of copying would have to be shown to sustain the action.

Unlike copyright law, design legislation requires registration of the design. After the design is made public, its registration would have to take place within six months in order to avoid forfeiture. A governmental agency would examine registration applications for *prima facie* subject matter but would conduct no search for previously registered, confusingly similar designs. Protection would last for ten years, beginning from the date when the design was made public by exhibition, sale, or offer to sell. Most design legislation provides for flexible notice requirements, (*i.e.*, a "d" in a circle). Failure to affix notice would not forfeit protection but would significantly limit remedies against infringers.

Proposed design legislation has taken varying approaches to whether design patent, design protection, and copyright could exist concurrently in the same object. In other words, should these forms of intellectual property be mutually exclusive or cumulative? For example, some versions of design legislation would require a choice between design protection, copyright, and design patent.[148] Thus, copyright would terminate on registration of the design. Alternatively, issuance of a design patent would terminate protection under the design legislation. Other versions would allow concurrent copyright protection, but the design protection would cease on issuance of a design patent.[149]

---

147 *See, e.g.*, S. Rep. No. 100-791, 100th Cong., 1st Sess. (1987). *See generally* Gerard Magliocca, *Ornamental Design and Incremental Innovation*, 86 Marq. L. Rev. 845 (2003) (justifying the longstanding Congressional reluctance to recognize *sui generis* design protection). Industrial design is protected internationally in many countries as part of the Union of Paris for the Protection of Industrial Property. To enjoy protection under the Convention, an author or owner of a design must comply with national law, which varies from country to country. *See* Stephen P. Ladas, Patents, Trademarks, and Related Rights § 490 (1975).

148 *E.g.*, Title II of S. Rep. No. 94-22, 94th Cong. 2d Sess. (1976). *See* H.R. Rep. No. 94-1476 at 94-50 (1976).

149 *See, e.g.*, S. Rep. No. 100-791, 100th Cong. 2d Sess. §§ 1027–28 (1988).

[C] Protection of Design Under Trademark and Unfair Competition Law

Protection for ornamental designs of useful articles may also be available in appropriate circumstances under the Lanham Act — the law governing federal trademark and unfair competition law.[150] The Lanham Act has afforded protection, sometimes quite robust, to works of industrial design. To meet the standards of protection under the Act, the designer must show that the design in question is non-functional[151] and, most often, that the design has acquired secondary meaning. If these standards are met, the work is protected as long as the design is used and maintains origin-indicating significance.[152] Thus, when available, protection under federal trademark and unfair competition law circumvents the separability problem under copyright law and the demanding standards of patent law. This has led some to be concerned about how federal trademark and unfair competition law may be undermining the limits of protection embodied in patent and copyright law and policy.[153] The courts have tended to erect a more rigorous standard for the protection of product designs than for ornamental, non-utilitarian forms of design and trade dress, such as the decor of a restaurant or fanciful packaging. The leading case is *TrafFix Devices, Inc. v. Marketing Displays, Inc.*,[154] in which the Supreme Court held that the existence of expired utility patents on a product feature created a strong evidentiary inference of a design's functionality.

Compared to federal protection, state misappropriation and unfair competition law are much more difficult for an industrial designer to use in order to protect a creation. If the design is one that passes the separability test and qualifies for copyright, there will be significant problems under § 301 of the Copyright Act.[155] Alternatively, if the design fails to meet the relevant separability standard, protection could be afforded under state law. Once again the preemption doctrine presents a significant hurdle. The Supreme Court's opinion in *Bonito Boats, Inc. v. Thundercraft Boats, Inc.*[156] held that, under state law, unpatentable technologies (in this case boat hull designs) could not be given patent-like protection, even against direct slavish imitation. The Court relied on general preemption doctrine and on its view that intellectual property law should be designed to promote, rather than discourage, technological competition. Although *Bonito Boats* does not speak to copyright as such, its implications are clear for the availability of state law protection for designs of useful articles unprotected under federal law.

---

[150] For a fuller treatment of trademark law, see *supra* § 1.12[C].

[151] *See In re Morton-Norwich Prods., Inc.*, 671 F.2d 1332 (C.C.P.A. 1982) (finding that non-functional spray bottle shape can be registrable under the Lanham Act); *In re Weber-Stephen Prods. Co.*, 3 U.S.P.Q.2d 1659 (T.T.A.B. 1987) (finding barbecue grill configuration registrable under the Lanham Act.).

[152] *Specialized Seating, Inc. v. Greenwich Industries, L.P.*, 616 F.3d 722 (7th Cir. 2010) (holding that design of folding chairs was functional even though alternative designs were available and the trademark registration in the design had become "incontestable).

[153] *See, e.g.*, Jay Dratler, *Trademark Protection for Industrial Designs*, 1988 U. Ill. L. Rev. 887.

[154] 532 U.S. 23 (2001).

[155] Federal preemption under § 301 of the Copyright Act is discussed at *infra* Chapter 11.

[156] 489 U.S. 141 (1989). This case is discussed at *infra* § 11.04.

[D] The *Sui Generis* Protection of Vessel Hull Designs

In 1998, Congress conferred *sui generis* protection for original boat hull designs in Title V of the Digital Millennium Copyright Act. This new Chapter 13 of the Copyright Act, referred to as the Vessel Hull Design Protection Act ("VHDPA"), protects original boat hull designs for a ten-year term. Although limited in the scope of its subject matter, the Act constitutes the first federal design protection statute. Protection for vessel hulls is based on copyright's standard of originality,[157] as compared with the more rigorous novelty requirement of the design patent law.[158] One must wonder whether vessel hull protection is an aberration, forever limited to a small industry. Or will it become the model for other specialized design statutes protecting furniture, automobiles, lighting fixtures, or fashion design?[159] More importantly, is it a harbinger of an eventual design protection statute covering all useful articles, perennially on the congressional agenda since the passage of the 1976 Act?[160]

Congressional interest in providing *sui generis* protection of vessel hull designs was prompted by the Supreme Court's decision in *Bonito Boats, Inc. v. Thunder Craft Boats, Inc.*,[161] where the Court struck down, as preempted by federal patent law, a Florida statute that had protected the design of boat hulls against copying by means of plug-molding processes. The relevant section of the 1998 legislation was intended to address the concerns of boat manufacturers and design firms in the wake of that decision.

Only *original* boat hull designs qualify for protection under the Act, and protection is limited to those designs that make the "article attractive or distinctive

---

[157] *See* 17 U.S.C § 1301(b)(1) (defining originality as "the result of the designer's creative endeavor that provides a distinguishable variation over prior work pertaining to similar articles which is more than trivial and has not been copied from another source.").

[158] For the standard of protection for design patents, see 35 U.S.C. § 171.

[159] In the 110 Congress, bills were introduced to amend the VHDPA to provide protection for registered fashion design. *See* The Design Piracy Prohibition Act, H.R. 2033, 110 Cong., 1st Sess., 1957, 110th Cong,. 2d Sess. (2007). Digital technologies and automated production techniques have enabled the copying and the instant world-wide transmission of fashion design images, enabling knockoffs to hit the market within days. These bills would protect fashion designs for a 3-year period, using the VHDPA as a template. Protection would be extended to the "appearance as a whole of an article of apparel, including its ornamentation. Apparel would include clothing, gloves, handbags, belts, and eyeglass frames. For an excellent discussion of the issues concerning the protection of fashion design, see Kal Raustiala & Christopher Sprigman, *The Piracy Paradox: Innovation and Intellectual Property in Fashion Design*, 92 Va. L. Rev. 1687 (2006) (analyzing why the fashion industry prospers despite the lack of protection while maintaining that copying may promote innovation). See their more elaborate treatment in Kal. Raustiala & Christopher Sprigman, The Knockoff Economy: How Imitation Sparks Innovation (2012).

[160] To determine the efficacy of the statute will take some time. In November 2003, the U.S. Copyright Office issued a comprehensive report on the impact of the VHDPA. It found that in the five years since the VHDPA's enactment, 156 registrations were made and only one lawsuit was filed. It concluded that "it is too soon to tell whether the VHDPA has had [a] significant overall effect on the boat building industry." *See* U.S. Copyright Office & U.S. Patent and Trademark Office, The Vessel Hull Design Protection Act: Overview and Analysis 211 (2003), *available at* www.copyright.gov/reports/vhdpa-report.pdf.

[161] 489 U.S. 141 (1989). The case is discussed at *infra* § 11.04.

in appearance to the purchasing or using public."[162] Much like the copyright standard, a design is original if it results from the designer's creative endeavor, provides a distinguishable variation over prior similar works that is more than merely trivial, and was not copied from another source.[163] By contrast, an unoriginal design is not subject to protection, nor is a design that is staple, commonplace, familiar, standard, prevalent, ordinary, or dictated solely by a utilitarian function of the article that embodies it.[164]

As a prerequisite for protection, an application for registration must be filed within two years of the date the design was first made public.[165] The owner of a registered design would have the exclusive right to make, sell, import, or distribute for sale or any commercial use any hull embodying the design.[166] The Act exempts certain activities from liability for infringement, including the reproduction of a protected design "solely for the purpose of teaching, analyzing, or evaluating the appearance, concepts, or techniques embodied in the design, or the function of the useful article embodying the design."[167] In addition, a distributor who sold a vessel hull embodying a protected design would not be liable if he or she did not know the design was protected and copied.[168] Finally, as with copyright, no liability would attach to the making or distributing of an allegedly infringing boat that was independently designed. In other words, there would be no liability for one that was created without having copied the first boat hull.

To assert one's rights under the Act, notice is required for all publicly exhibited or distributed boat hulls. Proper notice must be located so as to give reasonable notice and include the words "Protected Design," the abbreviation "Prot'd Des," the letter "D" with a circle, or the symbol "D." Notice must also contain the name of the owner, through a recognizable abbreviation, and the year in which protection for the design commenced.[169] Omission of notice prevents the owner from recovering against a party who infringes before receiving notice of protection.[170]

Before Congress passed the VHDPA, boat hull designers were limited to protection under design patent. Now they can avail themselves of a more practical basis of protection, one that is obtained more easily, quickly, and at less cost than a design patent. Section 1329 prohibits dual protection under both design patent and the VHPA. The issuance of a design patent will terminate any protection of the design provided under the Act.

---

[162] 17 U.S.C. § 1301(a)(1).

[163] *See* 17 U.S.C. § 1301(b)(2).

[164] *See* 17 U.S.C. § 1302(1)–(4).

[165] *See* 17 U.S.C. § 1310.

[166] *See* 17 U.S.C. § 1308.

[167] *See* 17 U.S.C. § 1309(g).

[168] *See* 17 U.S.C. § 1309(b).

[169] *See* 17 U.S.C. § 1306(a).

[170] *See* 17 U.S.C. § 1307.

§ 3.16 ARCHITECTURAL WORKS[171]

[A] Generally

As works of applied art, architectural works present many of the same problems encountered in the discussion on industrial objects. There are two aspects to the copyrightability of architectural works: (1) the plans and models that represent the structure; and (2) the architectural structure itself. Both received protection under copyright law, but that protection was limited. Architectural works were viewed as useful objects, subject to the same constraints discussed previously. This changed with the passage of The Architectural Works Protection Act of 1990.[172] This legislation, designed to comply with Berne Convention obligations, conferred full protection on architectural structures and officially recognized that architectural works are the eighth category of copyrightable subject matter under § 102(a)(8).[173] The Act, however, does not apply to architectural structures constructed before the effective date of the Act, December 1, 1990. Thus, it is necessary to understand the pre-1990 law governing architectural plans and structures for the overwhelmingly greater number of buildings constructed before that date.

[B] Architectural Works Constructed Before December 1, 1990

[1] Architectural Structures

The scope of protection in a three-dimensional architectural structure is the same as the protection afforded to all pictorial, graphic, or sculptural works embodied in useful objects. After all, architectural structures are simply useful objects that fuse the aesthetic and the functional in a three-dimensional object. Thus, as is the case for the design of useful objects, copyright protection extended only to those elements in a building that were physically or conceptually separable from its overall design. For example, a gargoyle on a building would receive copyright protection but not the overall appearance of the building or the arrangement of the spaces and shapes within and outside the building.

This rule was not above criticism. The separability test as applied to architectural structures discriminates against the truly artistic output of the architect's craft. Thus, the overall configuration of a "modernist" Mies Van der Rohe building would be excluded from protection, whereas the crudest add-on surface ornamentation

---

[171] For a comprehensive overview, see Jane C. Ginsburg, *Copyright in the 101st Congress: Commentary on the Visual Artists' Rights Act and the Architectural Works Copyright Protection Act of 1990*, 14 Colum.-VLA J.L. & Arts 477 (1990); David E. Shipley, *Copyright Protection for Architectural Works*, 37 S.C. L. Rev. 393 (1986); Rafael Winick, *Copyright Protection for Architectural Works: Copyright Protection Act of 1990*, 41 Duke L.J. 1598 (1992).

[172] Pub. L. No. 101-650, 104 Stat. 5089, 5133 (1990). For a discussion of whether the Architectural Works Copyright Protection Act is necessary and whether copyright protection is needed as an incentive for architects, see David Shipley, *The Architectural Works Copyright Protection Act at Twenty: Has Full Protection Made a Difference?*, 18 J. Intell. Prop. 1 (2010).

[173] 17 U.S.C. § 102(a)(8).

would be copyrightable. In other words, a modernist building would run into the same separability problems as the unadorned lighting fixture in *Esquire v. Ringer*.[174] In sum, for a standing structure, infringement does not occur unless the copier has reproduced the building's "separable" pictorial, graphic, or sculptural features that are capable of existing independently of its utilitarian aspects.[175]

[2] Architectural Plans, Models, and Drawings

Under § 101's definition of pictorial, graphic, and sculptural works, diagrams, models, technical drawings, and architectural plans were included as copyrightable subject matter.[176] Unlike buildings, architectural plans, models, and drawings are not useful articles and are not subject to a "separability" limitation because their purpose is to "merely portray the appearance of the article or to convey information."[177]

Although not subject to the separability limitation, architectural plans did not receive first class citizenship under the original 1976 Act.[178] Architectural plans and models could be infringed by their reproduction as such, but the unauthorized construction of a building by using the plans was not an infringement of the plans. Thus, under the copyright law before the 1990 amendments, a structure was not a copy of a plan or model. If a lawful copy of an architectural plan were obtained, it could be used to construct the building that it portrayed so long as no copies of the plans were made. In short, copyright in architectural plans or models did not convey a right to control their use.[179] This rupture between the plan and the building it portrays is an exception to the normal rule that a substantially similar three-dimensional sculptural work can infringe a two-dimensional graphic or pictorial work.[180]

Imperial Homes Corp. v. Lamont[181] provides an example of this gap in protection for architectural plans and drawings. In *Imperial Homes*, defendants, the Lamonts, had visited one of Imperial's residences where they made detailed observations and measurements of its architecture. In addition, the Lamonts had obtained copies of the copyrighted advertising brochures containing floor plans. The court concluded that infringement could be found if they had copied in whole or in part the floor plans from the brochures in making their own architectural plans,

---

[174] 591 F.2d 796 (D.C. Cir. 1978).

[175] *See* 17 U.S.C. § 101 (pictorial, graphic, and sculptural works).

[176] *See* 17 U.S.C. § 101; *see also* H.R. Rep. No. 94-1476, at 53 (1976). As for the case law, see, for example, *Aitken, Hazen, Hoffman, Miller P.C. v. Empire Constr. Co.*, 542 F. Supp. 252 (D. Neb. 1982). The 1988 amendments to the 1976 Copyright Act were not intended to change the scope of copyright in either architectural plans or the structures they represent. *See* H.R. Rep. No. 100-609, at 49 (1988).

[177] 17 U.S.C. § 101 (useful article).

[178] *See* 17 U.S.C. § 113(b) (specifying that the body of law existing at the passage of the 1976 Act governs the scope of protection for architectural plans).

[179] The reason for this anomalous rule relates to the doctrine of *Baker v. Selden* that would allow copying for the purpose of use but not for the purpose of explanation. For a discussion of the doctrine of *Baker v. Selden*, see *supra* § 2.13[B].

[180] *See, e.g.*, *Ideal Toy Corp. v. Kenner Prods. Div.*, 443 F. Supp. 291 (S.D.N.Y. 1977).

[181] 458 F.2d 895 (5th Cir. 1972).

even if these same plans would give the copyright owner no claim over the features they detail.[182] As we will see, these limitations on copyright for architecture have been removed by the 1990 amendments.

[C] The Architectural Works Protection Act of 1990

[1] Scope of Protection

Under the 1990 amendments to the Copyright Act, architectural works are explicitly recognized as the eighth form of copyrightable subject matter under § 102(a).[183] Architectural works are defined as "the design of a building, architectural plans, or drawings." The work includes "the overall form as well as the arrangement and composition of spaces and elements in the design, but does not include individual standard features."[184] In other words, while individual standard features and architectural elements classifiable as ideas are not themselves copyrightable, an architect's original combination or arrangement of such features may be.[185] The term "building" is intended to cover habitable structures (and those used by people, *e.g.*, churches, gazebos, etc.) and would exclude three-dimensional non-habitable structures such as highways, bridges, and pedestrian walkways. In addition, any features, including external and interior architecture, which reflect the architect's creativity, will be covered by the amendments.[186]

The Act confers full protection on works of architecture. As the legislative history indicates, infringement of an architectural work may occur regardless of whether access to the three-dimensional work is obtained from a two-dimensional or three-dimensional depiction of it.[187] The Act applies only to buildings constructed on or after December 1, 1990. Buildings constructed on or after the effective date of the Act are no longer subject to the separability test applicable to pictorial, graphic, or sculptural works embodied in useful objects. The separability test as applied by the courts has engendered much confusion and controversy. One principal reason that Congress did not treat architectural works as pictorial, graphic, or sculptural works was to avoid entangling architectural works in this disagreement. As is the case with all categories of works of authorship, architectural works are subject to the limitations under § 102(b). Thus, protection for an architectural work will not extend to functional features of the building, including individual standard features, such as common windows, doors, and other staple building components.

---

[182] *See also Demetriades v. Kaufmann*, 680 F. Supp. 658 (S.D.N.Y. 1988) (finding unauthorized copying of architectural plans an infringement, but injunction against further construction of structure denied).

[183] 17 U.S.C. § 102(a)(8).

[184] 17 U.S.C. § 101 (architectural works).

[185] *See Oravec v. Sunny Isles Luxury Ventures, L.C.*, 527 F.3d 1218, 1225 (11th Cir. 2008).

[186] Does a building have to be a free standing structure? *See Yankee Candle Co., Inc. v. New England Candle Co.*, 14 F. Supp. 2d 154 (D. Mass. 1998) (holding that a candle store, "structure within a structure," within a shopping mall was not a protectable "building" under the Act).

[187] H.R. Rep. No. 101-735, at 19 (1990).

Determining the scope of protection for an architectural work involves a two-step process. First, one must examine the work to determine if there are original design elements, including the overall shape and interior architecture. Second, if such design elements are present, one must then determine whether the elements are functionally required. If these elements are not functionally required, the work will be protected without applying physical or conceptual separability tests.[188] Otherwise, architectural works will be subject to the standard of originality for all works of authorship, as developed by the case law. Because determinations of originality are generally made *ad hoc*, the courts have only began to create a body of law providing significant guidance on what constitutes originality for architectural works.[189] Ultimately, it remains to be seen whether protection of architectural works will encourage creativity in the field or whether it will discourage architects from incorporating certain stylistic ideas into their works for fear of litigation.

The 1990 amendments have also changed the relationship between the copyright in the architectural work and the copyright in the plans and drawings. As discussed above, under the original 1976 law, a defendant who had access to the plans or drawings could construct a building and escape liability if the plans and drawings were not copied. Now, infringement may lie even though access to the three-dimensional work is obtained from its two-dimensional or three-dimensional depiction.

The Act covers only those architectural works created on or after the date of enactment, December 1, 1990, and will include architectural works that are unconstructed and embodied in unpublished plans and drawings. As an incentive to construct these works, the legislation terminated protection on December 31, 2002, if the architectural work has not been constructed by that date. If the work was constructed by that date, its term of protection will not expire before December 31, 2047.[190] This provision excludes those works of architecture embodied in "constructed" buildings and published plans before December 1, 1990. But when is a building constructed for the purposes of the Act? The Second Circuit, in *Richard J. Zitz, Inc. v. Dos Santos Pereira*[191] has held that the Act should be interpreted to mean "substantially constructed" on the critical date. The important question is not whether the building was finished or habitable, but whether the structure was accessible to others who could readily see and copy it. In the court's view, the term "constructed" bears the same meaning as "publication" for purposes of copyright protection. Thus, as often is the case in copyright law, one cannot forget the statute

---

188 *See* H.R. Rep. No. 101-735, at 20–21 (1990). For examples in the developing case law, see *Attia v. Society of the New York Hospital*, 201 F.3d 50 (2d Cir. 1999) (holding that because plantiff's drawings, at least to the extent copied, consisted only of generalized ideas and concepts, defendant could not be liable for appropriating protected expression); *Sparaco v. Lawler, Matusky, Skelly, Engineers LLP*, 303 F.3d 460 (2d Cir. 2002); and *Scholz Design, Inc. v. Sard Custom Homes*, 681 F.3d (2d Cir. 2012) (rejecting the argument that plaintiff's drawings "were not entitled to copyright protection because they lacked sufficient detail to allow for construction of the homes depicted.").

189 For an application and discussion of the scope of protection for architectural works, see *Richmond Homes Management, Inc. v. Raintree, Inc.*, 862 F. Supp. 1517 (W.C. Va. 1994).

190 Pub. L. No. 101-650, Stat. 5089 (1990). *See* 17 U.S.C. § 303. Duration under § 303 is discussed at *infra* § 6.04[G].

191 232 F.3d 290 (2d Cir. 2000).

and the case law regarding works published before the effective date of the amendment to the Act.[192]

[2] Limitations on the Exclusive Rights of an Architectural Work

Owners of architectural works are granted the same exclusive rights as other copyright owners with three exceptions. First, state common laws and statutes relating to "local landmarks, historic preservation, zoning, or building codes will not be preempted by the Copyright Act.[193] Second, under § 120(a),[194] the owner cannot prevent the making, distributing, and displaying of pictures, photographs, or other pictorial representations of an architectural work visible from a public place. This would allow an author to publish a book on architecture using photographs of copyrighted architectural works without infringing the copyrights in the works. Absent this exception, a tourist who took pictures of a recently constructed building would risk infringement.

Section 120(a) has involved some difficult problems of interpretation when works of two and three-dimensional works of art, such as sculptures, are incorporated in, or closely connected with, an architectural work. This issue arose in *Leicester v. Warner Bros.*[195] in which a panel of the Ninth Circuit split into three separate decisions. Leicester, an artist known for large scale works of public art, designed a set of towers and a courtyard space for a Los Angeles office building (801 Tower) to fulfill the developer's obligation under local law to provide for a public artwork on the building site. The owner of the building licensed the towers for use in the movie *Batman Forever*. The appellate court affirmed the lower court's holding that the towers were part of the design of the building. The court found that standing by itself, plaintiff's work was a sculptural work; but in this context, it became part of the office building as a whole and was thus limited by § 102(a) in the control of its photography. To hold otherwise, § 120(a)'s exemption for pictorial representations of buildings would make no sense, given the underlying rationale of the limitation to allow the photography of publicly visible buildings.

The dissent maintained that the sculptural towers could be deemed conceptually separable from the building and could receive full protection as copyrighted work, unfettered by the § 120(a) limitation, and that the majority's absolute allowance of sculptures attached to buildings to be freely photographed, undermined Congress's desire to augment the rights of artists.[196] According to the dissent, a contrary holding would place a disincentive for artists to collaborate with architects, if the artist were to lose full copyright protection by placing their works of art in

[192] See *John G. Danielson, Inc. v. Winchester-Conant Properties*, 322 F.3d 26 (1st Cir. 2003), where the court held that displays of plans before neighborhood groups and public officials were not "publications" under the definition of § 101, nor was their inclusion in a cable broadcast of a public meeting. In addition, inclusion of an image of the plans in a videotape of a public meeting was not published under the authority of the copyright owner.

[193] 17 U.S.C. § 301(b)(4).

[194] 17 U.S.C. § 120(a) (added by Pub. L. No. 101-650, Stat 5089, 5133 (1990)).

[195] 232 F.3d 1212 (9th Cir. 2000).

[196] *Id.* at 1232.

connection with a building. Comparing the majority and dissent's opinions reveals that Congress was less than clear spelling out the contours of § 120(a) and further litigation is to be expected on this issue.

The third exception concerns the rights of an owner of a building embodying an architectural work to make changes and alterations to it. Under § 120(b),[197] the owner of a building embodying a protected architectural work may make alterations to the building and even destroy it, notwithstanding the exclusive rights of the copyright owner to prepare derivative works under § 106(2).[198] This provision poses interesting questions. Does a building owner's right of alteration include the right to make changes to drawings of the existing building (either from existing plans or from the building itself) that would otherwise constitute an infringement of copyright?[199] In addition, does the building owner's right of alteration include the right to build an addition that copies the design of the original? In both instances it would appear that the courts should imply a license in favor of the building owner, otherwise the alteration and destruction rights would be rendered meaningless. When viewed from a more global standpoint, the perceived necessity for a destruction and alteration right implies that the copyright model for architectural works is an awkward fit in the real world of architectural design and the environment in which the design exists.

§ 3.17 MAPS[200]

Maps have been recognized as copyrightable works since the first American copyright statute was enacted in 1790. Under the 1976 Act, maps are not explicitly included as copyrightable subject matter but qualify as pictorial, graphic, and sculptural works.[201] Although their copyrightability has never been in doubt, the element of originality required in maps involved controversy because some case law under the 1909 Act imposed a higher standard of originality for maps than for other varieties of copyrightable subject matter.

Maps are generally a rearrangement of factual matter, and the map maker must go either to public domain sources for this information or to the terrain itself.[202] Whether the creator of a map must directly observe the terrain to claim copyright in his creation has long been a controversial issue. In *Amsterdam v. Triangle Publications, Inc.*,[203] the court held that in order to meet the standard of

---

197 17 U.S.C. § 120(b) (added by Pub. L. No. 101-650, Stat. 5089, 5133 (1990)).

198 17 U.S.C. § 106(2).

199 *See Javelin Investments, LLC v. McGinnis*, 2007 U.S. Dist. LEXIS 21472 (S.D. Tex. Jan. 23, 2007) (holding that the building owner's right of alteration includes the right to make plans that copy the original).

200 For an overview of the subject placed in the context of copyrightability of factual works, see Robert A. Gorman, *Fact or Fancy? The Implications for Copyright*, 29 J. Copyright Soc'y 560 (1982); David B. Wolf, *Is There Any Copyright Protection for Maps After Feist*, 39 J. Copyright Soc'y 224 (1992).

201 *See* H.R. Rep. No. 94-1476, at 54 (1976).

202 Maps present the same issues as other factual compilations. For a discussion of compilations, see *supra* § 2.11.

203 93 F. Supp. 79 (E.D. Pa. 1950).

originality, the publisher of a map must engage in some direct observation, that is, some original work of surveying or calculation or investigating the terrain. By this approach, a mere rearrangement of public domain sources would not meet the standard. *Amsterdam* imposes a special kind of "sweat of the brow" requirement on the author, and, as such, this direct observation standard imposed a stricter standard of originality on maps than on other copyrightable works. With the demise of the "sweat of the brow" doctrine under *Feist Publications v. Rural Telephone Service Co.*,[204] the validity of the case law requiring direct observation is all the more doubtful.

Even before *Feist*, the recent case law has rejected the direct observation rule, treating the standard of originality for maps the same as for any other compilation or factual work. In *United States v. Hamilton*,[205] for instance, the court rejected the defendant's argument that the copied map was not subject to copyright since it was simply a synthesis of information already in the public domain. The court viewed maps as any other copyrightable work, requiring only that the work display something original, and held that arrangements and combinations of facts are copyrightable so long as they are not merely trivial variations of information within the public domain. The authorship elements of selection, design, and synthesis were enough to meet the standard. *Hamilton* puts the cartographer in the same position as any other author creating a pictorial, graphic, or sculptural work.[206] There seems to be little justification for discouraging creative arrangement in the cartographic arts by holding the cartographer to a higher standard of originality. Of course, some originality must be shown, and merely copying the outline of the United States and selecting the principal cities of North America from memory,[207] or changing the color, shading, and labeling of U.S. Census maps[208] will not constitute sufficient originality for the issuance of copyright registration.[209]

---

204 499 U.S. 340 (1991).

205 583 F.2d 448 (9th Cir. 1978).

206 Questions of originality and merger of idea and expression arise in map cases. *Compare Mason v. Montgomery Data, Inc.*, 967 F.2d 135 (5th Cir. 1992) (finding plaintiff's real estate ownership maps using information from public domain sources were capable of a variety of expression and were sufficiently original in their selection and arrangement of facts, as well as in their pictorial and graphic elements, to meet the *Feist* standard of originality), *with Kern River Gas Transmission Co. v. Costal Corp.*, 899 F.2d 1458 (5th Cir. 1990) (noting plaintiff's representation of a proposed national gas pipeline route on government survey maps was not copyrightable even though it may have been original, because it was the only effective way the idea of the location of the pipeline could be expressed).

207 *See Carter v. Hawaii Transp. Co.*, 201 F. Supp. 301 (D. Haw. 1961).

208 *See Darden v. Peters*, 488 F.3d 277 (4th Cir. 2007).

209 The same principles apply to more specialized maps, such as site plans for development. In *Sparaco v. Lawler, Matusky, Skelly, Engineers LLP*, 303 F.3d 460 (2d Cir. 2002), for example, the court held that, while a surveyor's use of standard cartographic symbols to represent existing physical features was not original, detailed plans for proposed physical improvements (such as creation of parking lots, drives, curbs, and walkways; placement of utilities; creation of fire lanes, fences, walls, and security gates; and landscaping) constituted protected expression. In so holding, the court distinguished an earlier case rejecting copyright in plans that conveyed only general ideas about how a site might be developed. *See Attia v. Society of the New York Hospital*, 201 F.3d 50 (2d Cir. 1999).

The same principles apply to more specialized maps, such as site plans for development. In *Sparaco v. Lawler, Matusky, Skelly, Engineers LLP*,[210] for example, the court held that, while a surveyor's use of standard cartographic symbols to represent existing physical features was not original, detailed plans for proposed physical improvements, such as creation of parking lots, drives, curbs, and walkways; placement of utilities; creation of fire lanes, fences, walls, and security gates; and landscaping, constituted protected expression. In so holding, the court distinguished an earlier case rejecting copyright in plans that conveyed only general ideas about how a site might be developed.[211]

Part IV. OTHER CATEGORIES OF COPYRIGHTABLE SUBJECT MATTER

§ 3.18 MUSICAL WORKS[212]

Although the 1976 Act does not define "musical works" because of a commonly understood definition for this category,[213] it does clarify one important point of controversy under the 1909 Act. Section 102(a)(2) specifies that the category of musical works encompasses both the words of a song and its instrumental component. A "musical work" can be embodied in various material objects such as musical notation written on paper or directly recorded on a phonorecord.[214]

Musical works, like other works of authorship, must display a quantum of originality and creativity, manifested in melody, harmony, or rhythm, individually or in some combination.[215] Much music is based on public domain sources, and issues regarding the standard of originality arise with relative frequency for arrangements of these public domain sources. The same issue arises when an action is brought by a copyright owner of a popular song.[216] Popular songs resemble one another — there are only a finite number of possibilities for this genre. But

---

210 303 F.3d 460 (2d Cir. 2002),

211 *see also Peter F. Gaito Architecture LLC v. Simone Development Corp.*, 602 F.3d 57 (2d Cir. 2010) (allegedly copied matter consisted solely of "generalized notions of where to place functional elements," and concepts and ideas "common to countless other urban high-rise residential developments.").

212 For a discussion of how, when, and why music first came within copyright's domain, see Michael W. Carroll, *The Struggle for Music Copyright*, 57 Fla. L. Rev. 907 (2005). For an analysis of how those who create and distribute music first began to consider that music as their property and when Western law began to support this belief, see Michael W. Carroll, *Whose Music Is It Anyway?: How We Came to View Musical Expression as a Form of Property*, 72 U. Cinn. L. Rev. 1405 (2004).

213 *See* H.R. Rep. No. 94-1476, at 53 (1976).

214 For deposit purposes, however, the Copyright Office will accept, in place of the written work, a recorded version of the musical work if it exists only in this form. *See* 37 C.F.R. § 202.20; Copyright Office Circular 50.

215 Rhythm, however, is the least likely aspect of music in which originality may be manifested. *See Northern Music Corp. v. King Record Distrib. Co.*, 105 F. Supp. 393 (S.D.N.Y 1952); Nimmer on Copyright § 2.05[D] (2014).

216 For an analysis of copyright protection and the song "Happy Birthday to You" and an argument that changes in copyright law are necessary because of the existence of a long, unitary term of copyright

originality, not novelty, is required, and the author need add very little to the public domain to meet the standard of originality. Similarly, musical arrangements, a form of derivative work, are copyrightable, so long as the arranger adds the requisite amount of original authorship.[217]

§ 3.19 SOUND RECORDINGS[218]

[A] Distinguishing the Sound Recording from Other Works of Authorship and the Phonorecord

"Sound recordings" as defined in § 101 are

> works that result from the fixation of a series of musical, spoken, or other sounds, but do not include the sounds accompanying a motion picture or other audio visual work, regardless of the nature of the material objects, such as disks, tapes, or other phonorecords, in which they are embodied.[219]

This statutory definition sets forth the basic features of a sound recording, and, in so doing, distinguishes this form of copyrightable subject matter from other works. Essentially, a sound recording is a captured performance. The performance captured in the sound recording may be a musical, literary, or dramatic work. These works of authorship should be distinguished from the copyright in the sound recording. This area of ambiguity exists because both the musical or literary work is also embodied in the same material object, the phonorecord. The distinction is of more than academic interest because the owner of a sound recording copyright enjoys different exclusive rights than the copyright owner of the musical or literary work captured in the sound recording. Most importantly, the copyright owner of a sound recording may not control its performance, while the copyright owner of a literary, musical, or dramatic work enjoys a full performance right.[220]

The sound recording must also be distinguished from the material object in which it is embodied. Sound recordings are embodied in phonorecords that, under the Copyright Act, include anything capturing sound, such as tapes, disks, or computer chips.[221] These distinctions are illustrated in the following example. Suppose CBS issues a CD of Copeland's *Third Symphony* performed by the New York Philharmonic. The musical copyright would be of the *Third Symphony*, and the sound recording copyright would be of the aural version of the work fixed in the material object, the compact disc. The sound recording copyright confers no

---

protection, see Robert Brauneis, *Copyright and the World's Most Popular Song*, 56 J. COPYRIGHT SOC'Y 335 (2009).

[217] *See Plymouth Music Co. v. Magnus Organ Corp.*, 456 F. Supp. 676 (S.D.N.Y. 1978).

[218] For an overview, see Sidney Diamond, *Sound Recordings, and Phonorecords: History and Current Law*, 1979 ILLINOIS L. FORUM 337 (1979).

[219] 17 U.S.C. § 101 (sound recordings).

[220] *See* 17 U.S.C. § 114. For a discussion of the less-than-full exclusive rights in sound recordings, see *infra* § 8.08. For an argument that the United States needs to implement a public performance royalty for sound recordings, see William Henslee, *"What's Wrong with U.S.?": Why the United States Should Have a Public Performance Right for Sound Recordings*, 13 VAND. J. ENT. & TECH. L. 739 (2011).

[221] 17 U.S.C. § 101 (phonorecords).

ownership right to either the material object — the CD — or to the underlying musical work.

[B] Originality in Sound Recordings

As with any copyrightable subject matter, sound recordings must meet the standard of originality. The source of originality in sound recordings may emanate from the performers whose performance is being captured or from the record producer who sets up the recording and processes, compiles, and edits the sounds. Performer originality consists of all the choices a performer makes in interpreting a tune, a story, or a literary work, such as tone, inflections of voice, or musical timing. Almost any conscious performance by a human being would add the degree of originality necessary for copyrightability in a sound recording.

Originality can also emanate from the producer who sets up the recording, even if no performer is involved in the rendition. One can think of such examples as a recording of sea sounds, bird calls, or motor traffic. Here the acts of capturing the performance, processing the sounds, and then compiling and editing them would supply the requisite originality. Of course, the author of the sound recording must add something of his own; a purely mechanical recording involving no authorial choice would fail for lack of originality.[222]

Sound recordings are by nature derivative works that often combine original contributions by several original authors. Determining who among these several authors owns the sound recording can present difficult legal and factual issues. The ownership of a sound recording is essentially a matter to be determined by the participants who create the recording. Absent a contractual provision to the contrary, and assuming originality by both a record producer and a performer, the sound recording would be owned jointly by the performer and record producer.[223] To avoid creating joint ownership, contract negotiations should be employed to resolve questions about who owns the copyright to the sound recording.

[C] No Federal Protection for Pre-1972 Sound Recordings

Sound recordings were formally recognized by federal law for the first time in the Sound Recording Act of 1971. The need for nationally uniform protection under copyright law was critically important to the recording industry at that time because pirates were inflicting substantial losses on the industry with unauthorized recordings. Bearing only a fraction of the production costs, they could often undersell the original producers who would, as a result, be unable to recoup their investments. Thus, the need for federal protection was apparent, despite a patchwork of state laws conferring common law protection for sound recordings before 1972.

Sound recordings were finally recognized in a systematic way by the Copyright Act of 1976, but the Act only applies to sound recordings fixed after 1972. Sound recordings fixed before 1972 are not subject to statutory protection under federal

---

[222] *See* H.R. Rep. No. 94-1476, at 57 (1976).

[223] For a discussion of the implications of joint ownership, see *infra* § 5.06.

copyright law. These pre-1972 sound recordings are not, however, as a group thrown into the public domain but are subject to continuing protection by state law.[224] Section 301(c) of the 1976 Act confers continuing protection on sound recordings first fixed before 1972, providing that "any rights and remedies under common law and statutes of any state shall not be annulled or limited . . . until February 15, 2047."[225] Thus, the plaintiff in any action for infringement of a sound recording fixed before 1972 must look to state copyright law, if any, for his remedies.

§ 3.20 DRAMATIC WORKS

Dramatic works are a separate category of copyrightable subject matter purposefully left undefined in the 1976 Act because of a generally accepted definition. For administrative reasons, the Copyright Office has defined a "dramatic work" as follows: "one that portrays a story by means of dialogue or acting and [that] is intended to be performed. It gives directions for performance or actually represents all or a substantial portion of the action as actually occurring, rather than merely being narrated or described."[226]

Whether a work is categorized as a dramatic work, rather than a nondramatic literary or musical work, can be of legal and practical importance. Under the 1976 Act, for example, exceptions for performance and display of works for non-profit or governmental entities apply only in certain instances to nondramatic literary and nondramatic musical works.[227] The compulsory license to make sound recordings under § 115 is limited to nondramatic musical works,[228] and the manufacturing clause pertains to works consisting preponderantly of nondramatic literary works in English.[229] In addition, performing rights societies, such as ASCAP and BMI, and licensing organizations, such as Harry Fox, limit their activities to nondramatic musical works.[230]

---

[224] *See Capitol Records, Inc. v. Naxos of Am., Inc.*, 372 F.3d 471 (2d Cir. 2004) (holding that the Common Law of the state of New York extends copyright protection to pre-1972 foreign-made sound recordings). For a comprehensive examination of the issue, see Copyright Office Report, *Federal Protection for Pre-1972 Sound Recordings* (Dec. 2011).

[225] 17 U.S.C. § 301(c).

[226] COMPENDIUM II OF COPYRIGHT OFFICE PRACTICES § 431.

[227] 17 U.S.C § 110(2).

[228] 17 U.S.C. § 115.

[229] 17 U.S.C. § 601.

[230] For a discussion of these organizations and the licensing of nondramatic musical works, see *infra* § 8.22.

§ 3.21 PANTOMIMES AND CHOREOGRAPHIC WORKS[231]

The 1976 Copyright Act has for the first time added pantomimes and choreographic works[232] to the categories of copyrightable subject matter in § 106. Along with musical and dramatic works, choreographic works and pantomimes are not defined in the Act. The House Report indicates that this absence of definition was purposeful because these categories have settled, generally accepted meanings.[233]

The only specific mention of choreographic works in the House Report states that the category does not include social dance steps and simple routines.[234] This statement appears to reiterate nothing more than the basic *de minimis* standard of originality as it would apply to a choreographic work.

The Copyright Office has defined choreography in its compendium of practices as: "the composition and arrangement of dance movements and patterns, usually intended to be accompanied by music. Dance is defined as static and kinetic successions of bodily movement in certain rhythmic and special relationships. Choreographic works need not tell a story in order to be protected by copyright."[235]

This definition gives choreography a broader scope of protection as compared to the 1909 Act, which protected choreography only as a dramatic work, that is, if it told a story. This narrow view of choreography under the 1909 Act left abstract forms of dance in a state of uncertain protection.[236] Because choreography now constitutes copyrightable subject matter in its own right, it would appear that a dramatic content requirement is no longer required.[237]

To meet the originality standard, the choreographer need only add something recognizably her own. This standard could be met even though the choreographer was heavily influenced by a style of dance such as that of Balanchine or Martha Graham. Artistic style *per se* is not copyrightable. Expression in choreography

---

[231] For a useful overview of the subject, see Martha M. Traylor, *Choreography, Pantomime and the Copyright Revision Act of 1976*, 16 New Eng. L. Rev. 227 (1981).

[232] Pantomimes as well as choreography were recognized for the first time in the 1976 Act. "Pantomimes" may be defined as, "the art of imitating or acting out situations, characters, or some other events with gestures and body movement. Mime is included in this category. Pantomimes need not tell a story or be presented before an audience to be protected by copyright." Compendium II of Copyright Office Practices § 460.01. Pantomimes are distinct from choreographic works as copyrightable subject matter. Many of the same concepts, however, are involved in the protection of these two art forms. The discussion in this section is limited to choreography, which has drawn the most commentary and case law.

[233] H.R. Rep. No. 94-1476, 94th Cong., at 53 (1976).

[234] *Id.* at 54. For a discussion of choreography and copyright protection, see Kathleen Abitabile & Jeanette Picerno, *Dance and the Choreographer's Dilemma: A Legal and Cultural Perspective on Copyright Protection for Choreographic Works*, 27 Campbell L. Rev. 39 (2004).

[235] Compendium II of Copyright Office Practices § 450.01.

[236] *See* Nimmer on Copyright § 2.07[B] (2014).

[237] *See Horgan v. MacMillan, Inc.*, 789 F.2d 157 (2d Cir. 1986). Some choreographic works, as well as pantomimes, qualified for protection under the 1909 Act and were registered by the Copyright Office as either a "dramatic work" or as a "book." These works will receive continued protection under the 1976 Act. A more difficult issue involves the status of choreographic works or pantomimes not published under the 1909 Act. No cases have treated this issue, but it would appear that these works would now be protected under the 1976 Act. *See* Nimmer on Copyright § 2.07[D] (2014).

involves the concrete details worked out by the choreographer, within the school or technique of dance movement, such as the sequencing and organization of the dance. For much the same reason that style is uncopyrightable, so too the invention of a new dance step is not copyrightable.

Choreography is usually fixed either in notation or in film. Two systems specific to dance, Laba notation and Benesh notation, are generally used. These systems of symbolic choreographic language are known by few choreographers. Film, despite certain limitations, is the most widely used method of fixing a choreographic work.

§ 3.22 MOTION PICTURES AND OTHER AUDIOVISUAL WORKS

Motion pictures and audiovisual works are accorded separate status as copyrightable subject matter under the 1976 Act. The broader category of audiovisual works is defined as:

> Works that consist of a series of related images that are intrinsically intended to be shown by the use of machines or devices such as projectors, viewers, or electronic equipment, together with accompanying sounds, if any, regardless of the nature of the material objects, such as films or tapes, in which the works are embodied.[238]

A work can qualify as an audiovisual work, even though it consists of individually copyrightable works, so long as it communicates related images. These images do not have to occur in sequential order. In *Stern Electronics, Inc. v. Kaufman*,[239] the Second Circuit Court of Appeals upheld copyright in the audiovisual display of a videogame even though the display was predetermined by a computer program embodied in a microchip memory device and the repetitive series of images were affected by the intervention of the player. In addition, the court held that the images did not have to be sequential to be copyrightable: "[t]he repetitive sequence of a substantial portion of the sights and sounds of the game qualifies for copyright protection as an audiovisual work."[240]

As is the case for all works of authorship, originality in an audiovisual work is determined by evaluating the work as a whole. In *Atari Games Corp. v. Oman*,[241] the District of Columbia Court of Appeals held that, even if the individual graphic elements of a videogame screen were not copyrightable, the audiovisual work as a whole would be copyrightable if the requisite level of creativity was satisfied by the

---

[238] 17 U.S.C. § 101 (audiovisual works).

[239] 669 F.2d 852 (2d Cir. 1982).

[240] *Id.* at 856. The notion of an audiovisual work was further broadened in *WGN Continental Broad. Co. v. United Video, Inc.*, 693 F.2d 622 (7th Cir. 1982), where the court held that copyright in a television news program included the teletext in the vertical blanking interval. The defendant, a satellite carrier, picked up WGN's news program but did not retransmit the teletext, instead substituting another service on the vertical blanking interval. The court held that the defendant was an infringer even though the teletext could not be viewed simultaneously with the television program. In effect, the plaintiff's news program was a two-channel program consistent with the expansive definition of an audiovisual work, as a series of related images that do not have to be seen in sequence.

[241] 979 F.2d 242 (D.C. Cir. 1992).

individual screens or the relationship of each screen to the others and/or the accompanying sound effects. In this way, an audiovisual work resembles a compilation of facts where the individual components may not be copyrightable, but their selection and arrangement may supply the minimal degree of creativity needed for the purposes of copyright.

Motion pictures are a subcategory of audiovisual works and are defined as: "works consisting of a series of related images which, when shown in succession, impart an impression of motion, together with accompanying sounds, if any."[242]

This definition clarifies a long-standing ambiguity in copyright about the status of motion picture sound tracks.[243] Now motion picture sound tracks are an integral part of the copyright in a motion picture.[244]

From the above definition, the essence of a motion picture is a series of related images that can be shown in successive order and give the impression of motion. As for any work, the motion picture must be fixed in a tangible medium of expression. Thus, mere live performances, such as telecasts of live sports events, are not covered unless simultaneously fixed in at least one copy.[245] Absent such a fixation, protection must be sought under the common law.[246]

---

[242] 17 U.S.C. § 101 (motion pictures).

[243] *See* H.R. Rep. No. 94-1476, at 56 (1976).

[244] The importance of categorization lies in the exclusive rights that vary according to the category. Thus, if the sound track was considered a sound recording instead of part of the motion picture copyright, it would not enjoy a performance right. For a discussion of the lack of a performance right in a sound recording, see *infra* § 8.24.

[245] *See* H.R. Rep. No. 94-1476, at 52 (1976).

[246] For a discussion of unfixed works protectable under common law copyright, see *supra* § 2.05.

Chapter 4

PUBLICATION, NOTICE, AND OTHER FORMALITIES

§ 4.01 INTRODUCTION AND CHAPTER OVERVIEW

An author's dissemination of his or her work to the public — i.e., publication — is a significant event from a copyright standpoint. Under the 1909 Act, a work of authorship enjoyed perpetual protection until it was published. At that moment, the work became subject to federal protection, which limited the duration of the copyright to two twenty-eight-year terms — a first term and a renewal term — for a total of fifty-six years. The 1909 Act also required the copyright owner to affix proper notice to each publicly distributed copy of the work. Non-compliance with the notice requirement could inject the work into the public domain. It was a trap for the unwary, and many an author inadvertently forfeited copyright in his work in this manner.

By having federal copyright begin when a work is created, the 1976 Act reduces, but does not eliminate, the role that publication plays in the overall scheme of copyright protection. For works publicly distributed on or after January 1, 1978, and before March 1, 1989, the 1976 Act retains the notice requirement. Failure to affix proper notice on a publicly distributed work between these two dates could inject the work into the public domain unless the copyright owner took certain affirmative steps within five years of the publication to "cure" the improper notice. Until the 1988 amendments to the Copyright Act, the United States was alone in the world in requiring compliance with notice formalities as a prerequisite for copyright protection. Insistence on this formality was a major impediment to United States entry into the Berne Copyright Convention, which requires, as a condition of membership, the protection of copyright without requiring compliance with formalities.[1]

With the passage of the Berne Convention Implementation Act of 1988 ("BCIA"), affixation of notice is no longer required on published copies or phonorecords of a work publicly distributed on or after March 1, 1989, the effective date of U.S. entry into the Berne Convention. Instead, affixation of notice is permissive, and omission of notice on publicly distributed copies will not inject a work into the public domain. By adopting permissive notice, the BCIA amendments removed a major stumbling block to United States' entry into the Berne Union, the major international copyright convention.

---

[1] *See* Berne Convention art. 5(2) (Paris text).

The Berne amendments operate prospectively. In so doing, they leave undisturbed copyrights that had been injected into the public domain for failure to comply with formalities such as proper notice, renewal registration, and manufacturing requirements. The desire to forge international trade agreements, and achieve reciprocal treatment of U.S. works in foreign countries, forced a rethinking of the status of these public domain copyrights.

The first break with traditional practice came about with legislation implementing the North American Free Trade Agreement ("NAFTA") in 1993 that restored copyrights in certain Mexican and Canadian films that had fallen into the public domain. One year later, the Uruguay Round Agreements Act, in more dramatic fashion, restored copyright in a much larger group of foreign public domain copyrights. Under the Act, copyright is automatically restored for works originating with a World Trade Organization ("WTO") or Berne country that had been ejected into the public domain for failure to comply with copyright formalities. These restored works will be given the remainder of the copyright term that they would have enjoyed if they had not entered the public domain.

Despite the abrogation of the notice requirement, the 1909 Act and the original provisions of the 1976 Act are still relevant to determining the status of a work. First, the 1976 Act as originally passed is not retroactive and does not revive a work of U.S. origin falling into the public domain under the 1909 Act. Second, the 1988 amendments to the 1976 Act are not retroactive either, and any work of U.S. origin falling into the public domain for failure to comply with the notice provisions of the 1976 Act in effect before March 1, 1989, will remain permanently in the public domain. Third, for a work publicly distributed on or after January 1, 1978, and before March 1, 1989, omission of notice can be overcome, and copyright in a work saved, if the copyright owner took certain steps to cure the omitted notice.[2]

The copyright practitioner has a complicated task in determining whether a work, published before March 1, 1989, is in the public domain. To do so, the practitioner must keep in mind three time frames:

(1) For works published before January 1, 1978, the harsh notice provisions of the 1909 Act will apply;

(2) For works published on January 1, 1978, and before March 1, 1989, the less strict notice provisions of the 1976 Act as originally enacted will apply; and

(3) For works published on or after March 1, 1989, the permissive notice provisions of the BCIA amendments will apply.

Finally, after establishing the date of first publication, the practitioner must determine if the copyright in a work has been restored under the Uruguay Round Agreements Act by ascertaining whether the work originates from a WTO or Berne

---

[2] The copyright owner must register a work within five years and make a reasonable effort to add notice to copies distributed to the public in the United States after discovery of notice. *See* 17 U.S.C. § 405(a). For a discussion of this provision, see *infra* § 4.11.

member country.[3]

This chapter is divided into three parts. Part I examines publication doctrine under the 1909 and 1976 Acts. Much of Part I examines the important role publication plays in copyright law. This part also demonstrates how the courts carved exceptions out of the publication doctrine to avoid forfeiture of copyright. Part II considers the notice requirement, focusing on what constitutes adequate notice and the consequences of publishing a work without affixing proper notice under the 1909 Act and the 1976 Act as originally enacted, as well as the effect of the BCIA amendments that have abrogated the notice requirement. Part III treats the now abrogated curiosity of American law known as the "manufacturing clause," which had required certain books written by American authors to be manufactured in the United States. Although no longer a part of the law, the manufacturing clause may still have a limited effect on previously distributed works not complying with its provisions.

Part I. PUBLICATION

§ 4.02 PUBLICATION: ITS ROLE IN COPYRIGHT LAW

[A] Generally

Under the Copyright Act of 1976, copyright protection begins on creation, that is, when an author has fixed a work in a tangible medium of expression.[4] At that moment, copyright protection begins as a matter of federal law and endures, generally, for the life of the author plus seventy years.[5] State common law copyright may still apply to works not fixed in a tangible medium, such as oral works, but the 1976 Act effectively federalizes copyright.[6] This is a fundamental change from the 1909 Act, which recognized a dual system of copyright in which the dividing line was publication. Under the 1909 Act, unpublished works were protected by state common law copyright, and so long as a work remained unpublished, common law copyright could theoretically endure forever. Once a work was published, state common law protection ended (divested) and federal protection began (invested).[7] To encourage authors to disclose their works to the public, the 1909 Act gave the advantages of federal protection but with limited duration. As measured from the moment of publication, federal copyright protection lasted for a maximum of fifty-six years: twenty-eight years for the initial term plus a twenty-eight-year renewal term.[8]

---

[3] The restoration provisions under § 104A of the Copyright Act are discussed at *infra* § 6.18 and § 6.19.

[4] *See* 17 U.S.C. § 102(a).

[5] *See* 17 U.S.C. § 302(a).

[6] *See* 17 U.S.C. § 301.

[7] For an excellent overview of the subject of publication, see Fulton E. Brylawski, *Publication: Its Role in Copyright Matters, Both Past and Present*, 31 J. Copyright L. Soc'y 507 (1984).

[8] *See* 17 U.S.C. § 24 (1909 Act).

[B] Historical Overview of the Publication Doctrine

Divestiture of common law rights on publication of a work is a doctrine that originated in England with *Millar v. Taylor*,[9] a case decided several decades after passage of the Statute of Anne,[10] the first English copyright statute. In *Millar*, the court of the King's Bench concluded that common law rights were perpetual, lost neither by publication nor by the expiration of copyright. According to the court, the Statute of Anne provided extra remedies during the term of copyright but did not abrogate common law rights.

Five years later, the House of Lords, in *Donaldson v. Becket*,[11] considered what effect the Statute of Anne had on common law rights. The House of Lords narrowly overruled *Millar v. Taylor*, holding that common law rights were divested on publication by operation of the Statute. Whether the House of Lords misconstrued the law is still a matter of historical controversy.[12]

The effect of publication on common law rights was first considered in the United States in *Wheaton v. Peters*,[13] in which the Supreme Court agreed with the House of Lords' view in *Donaldson*. Reviewing the history of the publication doctrine, the Court held that the copyright owner could not claim common law copyright protection in his published works. Thus, until the passage of the 1976 Act, the principle that publication divests common law rights was universally accepted.

[C] Justification of the Publication Doctrine

Why should the act of publication divest common law copyright? One can look to the Patent and Copyright Clause in the Constitution authorizing Congress to protect writings of authors only for "limited times."[14] The "limited times" provision attempts to promote the public interest by creating an environment for the optimum production and dissemination of works of authorship. On the one hand, we encourage production of works of authorship by providing a limited monopoly to the copyright owner. On the other hand, we encourage dissemination by allowing the public free access to these works upon expiration of the copyright term, when a work enters the public domain. Common law copyright for unpublished works, which could last in perpetuity, recognized the author's right to privacy in his work. This privacy interest prevailed over the public's access right until the author decided to exploit his work economically by publishing it. So, a bargain was struck: the author could enjoy the economic fruits of his labor and could have access to the

---

[9] 98 Eng. Rep. 201 (K.B. 1769).

[10] 8 Anne ch. 19 (1710).

[11] 4 Burr. 2408 (H.L. 1774).

[12] For an extensive examination of the English common law copyright and its American legacy, particularly regarding the interpretation of *Donaldson v. Becket* as construed by *Wheaton v. Peters*, see Howard B. Abrams, *The Historic Foundation of American Copyright Law: Exploding the Myth of Common Law Copyright*, 29 Wayne L. Rev. 1119 (1983).

[13] 33 U.S. 591 (1834).

[14] U.S. Const. art. I, § 8, cl. 8.

remedies conferred by federal copyright protection. In exchange, she would have to accept the limitations imposed on her monopoly by the eventual dedication of her work to the public domain.

Because it constituted the dividing line between common law and federal copyright, the concept of publication was perhaps the most important single concept under the 1909 Act. It was also criticized as the 1909 Act's major defect. As developed in case law, publication became a highly technical concept, often difficult to apply in a practical context. Although the 1976 Act removed the central role of publication in copyright law, the concept of publication remains of utmost importance for works published both before and after January 1, 1978, the effective date of the 1976 Act.

§ 4.03 "PUBLICATION" DEFINED

What constitutes "publication"?[15] This most important concept was purposely left undefined by the drafters of the 1909 Act, leaving the publication doctrine to develop, sometimes inconsistently, through the case law. The 1976 Act, however, has attempted to codify and clarify this decisional law, defining publication as:

> . . . the distribution of copies or phonorecords of a work to the public by sale or other transfer of ownership, or by rental, lease or lending. The offering to distribute copies or phonorecords to a group of persons for purposes of further distribution, public performance, or public display, constitutes publication. A public performance or display of a work does not of itself constitute publication.[16]

By this definition, publication occurs when the copyright owner voluntarily sells, leases, loans, or gives away the original or a tangible copy of the work to the general public. However, publication is not limited to situations in which tangible copies are conveyed to the public. Even if no sale or other disposition of the work has taken place, publication will occur if the work is offered to the public in any manner authorized by the copyright owner. Publication has been found, for instance, when the copyright owner has distributed the work to retail dealers for sale to the general public[17] or has placed material on a website available for downloading by the public.[18] Alternatively, publication does not occur by a public performance or

---

[15] For a general discussion of publication concepts under the 1909 Act, the Universal Copyright Convention, and the Berne Convention, *see* Nimmer on Copyright § 4.05 (2014). For an argument that the term "publication" needs to be redefined and for a proposed redefinition consistent with the current statutory definition, see Thomas F. Cotter, *Toward a Functional Definition of Publication in Copyright Law*, 92 Minn. L. Rev. 1724 (2008). For an empirical study of copyright publication, a discussion of whether accepted notions of copyright publication conform with legal doctrine, and an argument that commonly used definitions of publication be revised, see Deborah R. Gerhardt, *Copyright Publication: An Empirical Study*, 87 Notre Dame L. Rev. 135 (2011).

[16] 17 U.S.C. § 101.

[17] *See Data Cash Sys., Inc. v. JS & A Group, Inc.*, 628 F.2d 1038 (7th Cir. 1980).

[18] *Compare Getaped.com Inc. v. Cangemi*, F. Supp. 2d 398 (S.D.N.Y. 2002) (granting access to an internet website is not simply a "display" but involves the distribution of "copies" and is thus a publication) *with Einhorn v. Mergatroyd Prods.*, 426 F. Supp. 2d 189 (S.D.N.Y. 2006) (holding that posting a video to a website does not constitute "publication"). A number of other cases, however, have

display[19] of a work, so long as the public performance or display occurs without a sale, offer to sell, or other disposition of tangible copies of the work. In short, publication generally occurs in, but is not limited to, situations where the public has obtained a possessory right in the work.

Two other curiosities of the publication doctrine should be noted. One is that the copyright owner's subjective intent to publish is irrelevant. Thus, publication can take place even if the copyright owner does not realize that, as a matter of law, he is committing or consenting to acts that would publish the work. The second is that even *de minimis* distribution constitutes publication so long as the general public has obtained or is offered a possessory right in the work.[20] Publication may occur upon distribution of just one copy of the work.[21] Thus, to publish a work does not mean that the public's need is satisfied by sufficient public distribution of the work.

§ 4.04 PUBLICATION UNDER THE 1909 ACT: ITS CONTINUING IMPORTANCE

For works published before January 1, 1978, the provisions of the 1909 Act apply. Once a work enters the public domain (unless restored under the Uruguay Round Agreements Act),[22] it remains there irrevocably, unaffected either by the provisions of the 1976 Act, as originally passed, or the BCIA amendments that have abrogated the notice requirement. To decide whether a work has entered the public domain before January 1, 1978, one must look to the 1909 Act provisions governing publication and notice. Under the 1909 Act, every time a work was published, the copyright owner was required to affix proper copyright notice to each copy of the work.[23] Failure to do so could inject the work into the public domain. Thus, if in 1989, A brought an action for copyright infringement of a work published in 1970 without proper notice, B, the alleged infringer, could assert as a defense that the work was published without proper notice and was therefore in the public domain. Indeed, many authors and copyright owners have forfeited the copyright to their work through the harsh terms of the 1909 Act. Unless restored under the Uruguay

---

noted that the definition of "publication" is broader than the definition of "distribution," in that the former also includes "offering to distribute copies or phonorecords to a group of persons for purposes of further distribution, public performance or public display. *See Atlantic Recording Corp. v. Howell*, 554 F. Supp.2d. 976 (D. Ariz. 2008); *London-Sire Records, Inc. v. Doe*, 542 F. Supp. 2d 153 (D. Mass. 2008).

19 The statutory definition of "publication" excludes publication by display. This differs from the case law under the 1909 Act, which indicated that an unrestricted display could be considered a publication. *See, e.g., Letter Edged in Black Press, Inc. v. Public Bldg. Comm.*, 320 F. Supp. 1303 (N.D. Ill. 1970). For a discussion of publication by display under the 1909 Act, see *infra* § 4. 07[B].

20 When a work is offered to a limited class of the public, the courts have found no publication at all under the limited publication doctrine. *See infra* § 4.05[C].

21 *See Burke v. National Broad. Co., Inc.*, 598 F.2d 688 (1st Cir. 1979); *Stern v. Remick & Co.*, 175 F. 282 (S.D.N.Y. 1910).

22 Under the Uruguay Round Agreements Act, copyright is restored for works originating from Berne or World Trade Organization countries that were injected into the public domain for failure to comply with U.S. copyright formalities. *See* 17 U.S.C. § 104A. These restoration provisions are discussed at *infra* §§ 6.18–6.19.

23 17 U.S.C. § 10 (1909 Act): "Any person entitled thereto by this title may secure copyright for his work by publication thereof with notice of copyright required by this title."

Round Agreements Act,[24] these works remain in the public domain and are not retrievable by the 1976 Act.[25] Because of the large number of works published before January 1, 1978, today's copyright practitioner must be well aware of publication doctrine as it existed under the 1909 Act.

§ 4.05 TWO COURT-MADE EFFORTS TO AMELIORATE THE PUBLICATION REQUIREMENT'S HARSH EFFECT UNDER THE 1909 ACT

[A] Generally

By failing to comply with the formalities required under the 1909 Act, copyright owners often unwittingly injected their works into the public domain. This would typically occur when the author distributed his work to members of the public without affixing the requisite notice. The act of publication was said to have "divested" the author's common law rights, and because the author did not properly secure federal rights available through meeting the requisite formalities, federal copyright was not "invested." Divestment of common law rights without investment of federal rights resulted in the work's "dedication" to the public domain.

It is often said that "the law abhors a forfeiture"; the same is true for the law of copyright. Courts gradually developed doctrines to mitigate the harsh effects of the 1909 Act's mechanistic rules regarding publication without notice.

[B] Divestive and Investive Publication

To avoid forfeiture of copyright, some courts required a larger public distribution of a work for a publication to divest common law protection than to invest federal copyright. The leading statement of this doctrine was made in *American Visuals Corp. v. Holland*,[26] where Judge Frank concluded:

> [T]he courts apply different tests of publication depending on whether plaintiff is claiming protection because he did not publish and hence has a common law claim of infringement — in which case the distribution must be quite large to constitute "publication" — or whether he is claiming under the copyright statute — in which case the requirements for publication are quite narrow. In each case the courts appear so to treat the concept of publication as to prevent piracy.[27]

---

[24] Restoration of copyrights in certain foreign works that were injected into the public domain for noncompliance with U.S. formalities is discussed at *infra* §§ 6.18–6.19.

[25] 17 U.S.C. Trans. & Supp. Prov. § 103. See *infra* §§ 6.18–6.19, for a discussion of these copyright restoration provisions.

[26] 239 F.2d 740 (2d Cir. 1956).

[27] *Id.* at 744.

In short, it takes a greater degree of publication to divest common law copyright than to invest federal statutory copyright.[28]

The investive/divestive distinction can be considered *dictum*, never adopted as the law in a specific case. It is a difficult doctrine to apply in a systematic, non-arbitrary way because it leaves two basic questions unanswered: first, how extensive must a public distribution be for a divestive publication to take place? Second, how small must the distribution be for an investive publication? It comes as no surprise that these questions have never been properly answered in the case law. Accordingly, it is virtually impossible for an author to determine with any certainty whether common law rights have been divested and/or federal rights invested. The doctrine imposes another level of complexity on the already elusive determination of when publication has occurred.

Despite its dubious status as a rule of law, the *investive/divestive doctrine* may still be relevant in practice under the 1976 Act, and it may have important consequences in a given case, if adopted. First, if a work were published without proper notice and the publication were found to be divestive, federal protection would not invest, and the work would fall into the public domain. As a second possibility, if the publication were considered divestive, but copyright was secured by proper affixation of notice, federal protection would have begun. In this instance, the copyright would endure for an initial term of twenty-eight years plus a renewal term of another forty-seven years.[29] If, as a third possibility, a court found the publication was neither investive nor divestive, the work would be considered unpublished. The consequence is that for works unpublished on or after January 1, 1978, copyright duration would be determined under the 1976 Act, whose main term is life of the author plus seventy years.[30] Because of the important consequences involving duration and validity of copyright, copyright owners will try to invoke the investive/divestive distinction for years to come.

[C] Limited versus General Publication

Another court-made doctrine, ostensibly developed under the 1909 Act to avoid forfeiture of copyright, is the distinction between limited and general publication.[31] A limited publication is a non-divestive publication that communicates the contents of a work to a narrowly selected group for a limited purpose, without transferring the rights of diffusion, reproduction, distribution, or sale.[32] For example, a limited publication would occur where copies of manuscripts are distributed to trade members for criticism or review[33] or where copies of architectural plans are distributed to contractors for bidding purposes.[34] The essential point is this: a

---

28 *See American Vitagraph, Inc. v. Levy*, 659 F.2d 1023 (9th Cir. 1981); *Hirshon v. United Artists Corp.*, 243 F.2d 640 (D.C. Cir. 1957).

29 *See* 17 U.S.C. § 304.

30 *See* 17 U.S.C. § 302(a).

31 *See generally* NIMMER ON COPYRIGHT § 4.13 (2014).

32 *See White v. Kimmell*, 193 F.2d 744, 746 (9th Cir. 1952).

33 *See, e.g., Hemingway v. Random House, Inc.*, 244 N.E.2d 250 (N.Y. 1968).

34 *See Nucor Corp. v. Tennessee Forging Steel Serv., Inc.*, 476 F.2d 386 (8th Cir. 1973); *see also John*

limited publication is one in which circulation of the work is restricted *both* as to the persons who receive it and the purpose for its distribution. Otherwise it is considered a general (divestive) publication. Because it focuses on the copyright owner's purpose in publishing the work, the limited publication doctrine contradicts the general rule that a person's subjective intent is irrelevant in deciding whether a publication has taken place.

Despite noticeable exceptions, for the most part, the courts have pushed the limited publication doctrine to its farthest reaches to avoid a forfeiture of copyright. In *King v. Mister Maestro, Inc.*,[35] the court found a limited publication where advance copies of Martin Luther King's *I Have a Dream* speech were given to the press. The speech was later broadcast to millions of people. The advance copies of the text that were given to the press contained no copyright notice and were distributed with no apparent limitation. The court found this to be a limited publication because the tangible copies of the speech were given to a limited group, the press, and not to the general public. In addition, the copies were distributed to serve a limited purpose only, which was to assist the press in covering the event.

In a sequel decided twenty-five years later, *Estate of Martin Luther King, Jr., Inc. v. CBS, Inc.*,[36] Dr. King's address did not fare nearly so well. The District Court granted a summary judgment for CBS news in a suit over the use of the speech in a documentary. Refusing to be bound by the earlier case, the court declared that the speech was in the public domain due to its general publication without copyright notice. Calling the King speech "the poster child for general publication," the court held that, while performance itself may not be sufficient to constitute publication, performance coupled with such wide and unlimited reproduction as occurred in conjunction with the King speech can only be viewed as a general publication. In 1999, however, the Eleventh Circuit reversed, faulting the District Court for failing to give sufficient weight to the principle that a performance does not constitute a publication.[37]

The *King* case is questionable in its reasoning. Initially given the speech, the press could be viewed as a limited group for the purposes of the limited publication doctrine. It operated, however, as a conduit for the eventual dissemination of the speech to the general public. If the essential feature of a general publication is the public's possessory right in tangible copies of the work, it is hard to imagine a more general publication than the one that took place in this case. Despite its questionable reasoning, the *King* cases are of special interest because they show the lengths to which some courts have gone to stretch the definition of "limited publication" to avoid forfeiture of copyright, a trend that continues.[38] The bias

G. Danielson, Inc. v. Winchester-Conant Properties, Inc., 322 F.3d 26, 34–37 (1st Cir. 2003) (incorporating the "limited publication" doctrine into the 1976 Act and holding that the submission of architectural plans to municipality for approval did not constitute a distribution because the submission was for a limited purpose).

[35] 224 F. Supp. 101 (S.D.N.Y. 1963).

[36] 13 F. Supp. 2d 1347 (N.D. Ga. 1998).

[37] *Estate of Martin Luther King, Jr. Inc. v. CBS, Inc.*, 194 F.3d 1211 (11th Cir. 1999).

[38] *See, e.g.*, *Burke v. National Broad. Co.*, 598 F.2d 688 (1st Cir. 1979) (finding limited non-divestive publication where author authorized one copy of film to be made to be shown on German non-commercial

against forfeiture by general publication continued, for example, in *Academy of Motion Pictures Arts and Sciences v. Creative House Promotions, Inc.*[39] The Academy had distributed 158 copies of its famed Oscar statuette to award winners between 1929 and 1941, without notice of copyright and without any express restriction on the recipient's right to sell or dispose of their Oscars. In 1941, the Academy registered their claim to copyright, and from that time, all Oscars have borne notice of copyright. In 1976, the defendant commissioned a trophy sculptor to create a sculpture strikingly similar to the Oscar, which it sold to various corporate buyers. In an infringement suit, the District Court ruled that the Oscar had entered the public domain before 1941 because the Academy's divestive and general publication, without notice, triggered the loss of copyright. Although distributed to a limited group of persons (a highly select group of award winners), the Academy's distribution was not sufficiently limited as to purpose. The Academy asserted that its publication was limited and non-divestive because the Oscars were distributed to a select group of persons for a limited purpose. The Court of Appeals agreed with the Academy's limited publication theory, reversing the District Court.

Although no express restrictions on the use or distribution of the Oscar existed before 1941, the Ninth Circuit held that such restrictions were implied. First, neither the Academy nor any living Oscar recipient had ever offered to transfer an Oscar to the general public. Second, each Oscar was personalized with the name of the original winner. Third, the Academy never gave the recipients the permission to sell, distribute, or make other copies of their Oscars.

In contrast with the *King* and *Oscar* cases, courts will find a general publication when the general public is given tangible copies of a work. For example in *Public Affairs Associates, Inc. v. Rickover*,[40] involving copyright in speeches given by Admiral Rickover on various occasions, the acts of publication were unequivocal and indiscriminate. In this pre-1976 Act case, the Admiral made his speeches available to the press, sent them to individuals both on request and unsolicited, and gave printed copies to sponsors for further distribution. The general nature of the publication lay in the unrestricted ability of the public to obtain tangible copies of the speeches. Failure to affix notice on the speeches, coupled with their general publication, injected the speeches into the public domain. Although it may appear that the case stands for a rule that the subjective intent is determinative on whether a general publication has occurred, the court rejected this rationale for its decision.[41] Unlike the *King* and *Oscar* cases, the unrestricted distribution of the Admiral's speeches to the public rendered a claim of limited publication too difficult to sustain with any plausibility. One question that will continue to arise is whether, in distinguishing "general" and "limited" publication, any importance should be attached to the fact that copies of a work were given only to selected, identified individuals, with no copies being offered for sale to the public at large.[42]

---

television and for lecture purposes, even though there was no explicit prohibition on further distribution of the film).

[39] 944 F.2d 1446 (9th Cir. 1991).

[40] 284 F.2d 262 (D.C. Cir. 1960). *See also* NIMMER ON COPYRIGHT § 4.01 (2014).

[41] *Rickover*, 284 F.2d at 270.

[42] *See, e.g.*, *Warner Bros. Entertainment, Inc. v. X One X Prods.*, 644 F.3d 584 (8th Cir. 2011)

§ 4.06 THE IMPORTANCE OF PUBLICATION UNDER THE 1976 ACT

[A] Generally

For works published on or after January 1, 1978, publication remains a pivotal point in many aspects of the law of copyright. First, the act of publication necessitates compliance with formalities, including notice and deposit. For works publicly distributed on or after January 1, 1978 and before March 1, 1989, affixation of notice is permissive, but failure to affix notice on works published during that time frame can inject a work into the public domain. Second, the act of publication has important consequences in international copyright relations. Third, the act of publication can determine the duration of copyright. In addition to these contexts, the act of publication is significant in a number of other situations.[43]

[B] Publication and Compliance with Formalities

The act of publication is important in determining whether one must or should comply with certain formalities. Most importantly, for works published after January 1, 1978, and before March 1, 1989, notice showing the date of publication was required on all publicly distributed copies of the work.[44] Failure to affix proper notice on published copies of a work during that ten year and two month time frame can lead to a forfeiture of copyright.[45] With the passage of the BCIA amendments, notice is no longer required, although it is still highly recommended, for a work published on or after March 1, 1989.

Other than this modification brought about by the BCIA amendments, the other important consequences of publication remain unchanged. The basic deposit requirements are the same. For all works published in the United States, one must fulfill the deposit requirements of the Library of Congress within three months after publication.[46] Noncompliance can lead to criminal fines.[47] After having published a work, one must register a claim for copyright or lose certain

---

(publicity materials for motion pictures *Gone With the Wind* and *The Wizard of Oz* were "published" without notice; although some agreements with theaters required that movie posters and lobby cards be returned or destroyed, publication was not "limited" because restriction was not enforced and redistribution and sale was encouraged and permitted); *Soc'y of the Holy Transfiguration Monastery, Inc. v. Archbishop Gregory of Denver, Colo.*, 689 F.3d 29 (1st Cir. 2012) (distribution of copyrighted translations of ancient texts to selected congregations for purpose of soliciting editorial feedback was a "limited" publication, and any further distributions were unauthorized and therefore immaterial).

[43] *See* 17 U.S.C. § 203(a)(3) (termination of transfers covering publication rights); 17 U.S.C. § 108(b) (right of libraries to reproduce certain works depends on whether the work is published); 17 U.S.C. § 118(b), (d) (non-commercial compulsory broadcast performance license applies only for published musical and published pictorial, graphic and sculptural works).

[44] *See* 17 U.S.C. §§ 401(a), 402(a).

[45] *See* 17 U.S.C. § 405. For a discussion of forfeiture of copyright by omitting notice, see *infra* § 4.11.

[46] *See* 17 U.S.C. § 407(a). For a discussion of deposit requirements for the Library of Congress, see *infra* § 7.08.

[47] *See* 17 U.S.C. § 407(d).

advantages in an infringement suit.[48] For example, registration in the Copyright Office within five years of publication confers *prima facie* evidence of validity of the copyright.[49] Moreover, one can obtain statutory damages and attorney's fees for published works only if registration preceded the infringement or if the work was registered three months after publication.[50]

[C] Publication and International Copyright

The act of publication has great significance in international copyright relations. For both the Universal Copyright Convention and the Berne Convention, works first published in a member state or by a national of a member state must be given the same protection in every other member state as works first published in the member's own territory.[51]

[D] Publication: Durational Consequences

The date of publication determines the duration of copyright for certain categories of works. Under the 1976 Act, the term for anonymous and pseudonymous works and works made for hire is measured from the year of first publication.[52] The normal copyright term is the life of the author plus seventy years,[53] and, unless Copyright Office records reveal otherwise, the author may be presumed dead for at least seventy years, ninety-five years after publication.[54] For these and other reasons,[55] publication plays an important role for works published on or after January 1, 1978.[56]

§ 4.07 SPECIAL PUBLICATION CONTEXTS: 1909 AND 1976 ACTS COMPARED

[A] Performance as Publication

A performance is not a publication. No matter how large the audience or to whom it is directed, an oral dissemination of a musical or literary work does not

---

48 *See generally* 17 U.S.C. §§ 408–412. For a discussion of remedies, see *infra* §§ 9.09–9.15.

49 *See* 17 U.S.C. § 410(c).

50 *See* 17 U.S.C. § 412.

51 For a discussion of international copyright matters, see *infra* § 12. 02.

52 *See* 17 U.S.C. § 302(c). For a discussion of duration, see *infra* §§ 6.01–6.04.

53 *See* 17 U.S.C. § 302(a), (d).

54 *See* 17 U.S.C. § 302(c), (d), (e).

55 The rights of foreign authors under United States copyright law are dependent upon whether the work is published. *See* 17 U.S.C. §§ 104, 108. *See also* 17 U.S.C. §§ 118, 504(c)(2)(ii) (availability of public broadcasting license).

56 Another durational consequence of publication is found in 17 U.S.C. § 303, which extends the period of protection of a work unpublished as of January 1, 1978, if the work is published before 2003.

constitute a publication.[57] The Martin Luther King case[58] graphically illustrates this basic tenet of copyright law. Although Martin Luther King Jr. delivered his *I Have a Dream* speech to millions of people through the media, the court held that he did not publish the work by performing it.

That a performance is not a publication seems contradictory to the rationale of the *publication doctrine*. Publication enables an author to exploit his work economically. In return, the author must eventually dedicate his work to the public domain. From this standpoint, a performance should be a publication. Authors profit enormously from the performance of their works, even though no tangible copies of the work are distributed to the public. Nevertheless, the basic rule that a performance is not a publication is ingrained in 1909 Act case law and is now codified in the 1976 Act.[59] In addition, the 1976 Act explicitly provides that a public display is not a publication.[60]

[B] Publication by Display

By expressly providing that a public display is not a publication, the 1976 Act has clarified a matter of some uncertainty under the 1909 Act. What little case law exists on this topic indicates that a public display of a work of art in a gallery, museum, or other public place, even without an accompanying offer to sell, constitutes a publication if the public viewing the work were not restricted from copying it. In *Letter Edged in Black Press, Inc. v. Public Building Commission of Chicago*,[61] an unrestricted public display forfeited copyright in a Picasso sculpture. The plaintiff, Chicago's Public Building Commission, erected a monumental Picasso sculpture, built from a maquette that it publicly displayed without proper copyright notice. The court found that the maquette was an original tangible work of authorship and that the monumental sculpture was merely a large copy of it. When the maquette was displayed, there were no restrictions on its being photographed or copied in any way. This "unrestricted" display was found to be a general publication, not a limited one. As a result, the work was injected into the public domain.[62] Thus, the unrestricted display dedicated the work to the public domain.

Alternatively, a display would not constitute a publication if the public were admitted to view the work with an express or implied understanding that copying

---

[57] *See Ferris v. Frohman*, 223 U.S. 424 (1912) (finding public performance of a written drama not a publication).

[58] *King v. Mister Maestro, Inc.*, 224 F. Supp. 101 (S.D.N.Y. 1963).

[59] *See* 17 U.S.C. § 101.

[60] *See id.*

[61] 320 F. Supp. 1303 (N.D. Ill. 1970).

[62] The unrestricted display was only one of the ways in which the work was injected into the public domain. The Commission sent out pictures of the maquette without copyright notice for use in a publicity drive that appeared in national magazines. Souvenir booklets, containing drawings and photographs of the maquette, were distributed without copyright notice. The Art Institute of Chicago sold postcards of the maquette, again without notice of copyright.

was not allowed. In the leading case of *American Tobacco Co. v. Werckmeister*,[63] gallery guards strictly enforced a no copying policy for a painting on public display. In these circumstances, failure to affix copyright notice did not inject the work into the public domain, and only a limited publication took place.

[C] The Distribution of Phonorecords as Publication of the Sound Recording and the Musical Work

Under the 1976 Act, a publication of a sound recording publishes both the sound recording and the recorded musical work embodied on the phonorecord. This rule applies to works distributed on or after January 1, 1978. Until the Sound Recording Act of 1971, the 1909 Act took the opposite approach that publication of a sound recording did not publish the musical work. For example, suppose A in 1970 recorded and distributed records of his copyrighted song to the public in phonorecord form. This distribution would publish neither the sound recording nor the musical work no matter how wide the distribution or how many records were sold. Even if the phonorecord were distributed without notice, no forfeiture of copyright on the sound recording or musical work would occur because no publication had occurred.

What is the explanation for this deviation from the law and policy of the publication doctrine? A historical quirk may explain these inconsistencies. In *White-Smith Music Publishing Co. v. Apollo Co.*,[64] the Supreme Court held that a recordation of a musical composition by mechanical means in a piano roll (later extended by analogy to phonorecords) was not a copy of the musical composition. Thus, because a phonorecord was not a copy of the work embodied on it, its sale did not publish the musical work. The record industry relied on the *White-Smith* doctrine, and it became an industry practice to make and distribute recordings without registering the musical work or publishing the work in any other way. The *White-Smith* doctrine was overturned with the 1976 Act, and now all material objects, whether a copy or phonorecord, are treated alike for the purpose of the law. In short, sale of a phonorecord will now publish both the musical work and the sound recording.

The Sound Recording Act of 1971,[65] the first federal act to protect sound recordings, amended the 1909 Act to include phonorecords in the definition of "copies" to protect the copyright owners of musical works and sound recordings. But sound recordings were not treated the same as musical works under the amendment. As for the sound recording, the publication of a phonorecord divested common law rights, and the copyright owner was required to comply with the 1909 Act's notice requirements to avoid forfeiture of copyright. On the other hand, it was generally accepted that the musical composition, i.e., the words and the music, was unaffected by failure to affix notice on the phonorecord.[66] Doubts remained, however, on the effect that publication had on *the musical work* embodied in a

---

63 207 U.S. 284 (1907).

64 209 U.S. 1 (1908).

65 Sound Recording Amendment, Pub. L. No. 92-140, 85 Stat. 391 (1971).

66 *See Rosette v. Rainbo Record Mfg. Corp.*, 354 F. Supp. 1183 (S.D.N.Y. 1973).

phonorecord. This issue was critically important to the music industry because phonorecords were often published without notice. If publication of the phonorecord published both the sound recording and musical composition, many songs (perhaps thousands) would be in the public domain for lack of proper notice. Much to the horror of the music industry, a 1995 case, *La Cienega Music Co. v. ZZ Top*, took the dual publication position, thereby jeopardizing the copyright status of many musical works.[67] In response, Congress immediately enacted a statutory amendment to overturn the decision.[68] As a result, § 303(b) of the Copyright Act states the "distribution before January 1, 1978, of a phonorecord shall not for any purpose constitute a publication of the musical work embodied therein."[69] Thus, after the amendment, a publication of the sound recording on a phonorecord without notice would inject the sound recording into the public domain, whereas the musical work embodied on the same phonorecord would be unaffected for failure to comply with the notice requirement.

The 1976 Act has eliminated the *White-Smith* doctrine, and now the public distribution of a phonorecord publishes both the sound recording and the musical work embodied on it. The 1909 Act rules, however, remain important to determine the public domain status of works published before the effective date of the 1976 Act.

[D] Publication of a Derivative Work

Another unsettled issue under the 1909 Act was whether publication of a derivative work[70] constituted publication of the preexisting work on which it was based. For example, if A writes a screenplay and authorizes B to make a movie of it, does publication of the movie publish the underlying work? Arguably, publication of the movie should publish the screenplay. After all, a derivative work, by definition, is one that substantially reproduces the underlying work and, as such, is a copy of the preexisting work.[71] The issue continues to be important to this day. The 1909 Act required notice on all copies of a published work, and failure to affix notice injected the work into the public domain. Moreover, publication starts the renewal clock ticking. Thus, if publication of a derivative work publishes the underlying work, failure to renew the derivative work forfeits copyright in the underlying work. Unfortunately, the case law is in conflict on the consequences of publication of the derivative work. The issue has engendered a degree of controversy similar to the related issue concerning the publication of a sound recording embodied in a phonorecord.

The manner in which a publication of a derivative work publishes the underlying work is most easily understood when the derivative work and preexisting work are published in the same medium, such as a third edition of a textbook, or an enlargement of a photograph. Generally, the courts applying the 1909 Act have held

---

[67] 53 F.3d 950 (9th Cir. 1995).

[68] *See* Pub. L. No. 105-80, 111 Stat. 1534 (1997).

[69] 17 U.S.C. § 303(b).

[70] *See* 17 U.S.C. § 101 (derivative work). For a discussion of derivative works, see *supra* §§ 2.08–2.09.

[71] Professor Nimmer takes this position. *See* Nimmer on Copyright § 4.12[A] (2014).

that when the two works were in the same medium, publication of the derivative work published the preexisting work.[72] The derivative work was regarded as a copy of the preexisting work, and failure to affix notice on the derivative work injected the preexisting work into the public domain.

By contrast, when the derivative work was reproduced in a different medium, such as a screenplay into a film or a photograph of a three-dimensional work, the case law is in conflict. Some courts, applying the 1909 Act, have held that the publication of the derivative work did not publish the underlying work.[73]

These cases are hard to reconcile with the basic justification for the publication doctrine. Clearly, the owner of the underlying work has consented to the creation, publication, and distribution of the derivative work and has obtained an economic benefit from its exploitation. Moreover, if publication of the underlying work did not occur when the derivative work was published, an author could extend indefinite control over a derivative work through an unpublished preexisting work. For example, a copyright in a film that has gone into the public domain under the 1909 Act could be resurrected by an unpublished screenplay.[74] Perhaps the conflict in the case law can be explained as another attempt to avoid the forfeiture of copyright under the harsh provisions of the 1909 Act.

Under the 1976 Act, publication of the derivative work would appear to publish the preexisting work. This principle is not specifically stated in the 1976 Act but is implied in § 401(b)(2), which provides that "in the case of compilations or derivative works . . . the year contained in the year date of first publication of the compilation or derivative work is sufficient."

From the language of the statute it would appear that a publication of a derivative work with omitted notice could inject the underlying work into the public domain. Thus, copyright lawyers will continue to be confronted with cases turning on the consequences of events that took place before January 1, 1978. In addition, they will also have to take into account those acts that could have led to a dedicatory publication occurring between January 1, 1978 until March 1, 1989, when a dedicatory publication still remained a possibility.[75]

---

[72] *See First Am. Artificial Flowers, Inc. v. Joseph Markovits, Inc.*, 342 F. Supp. 178 (S.D.N.Y. 1972).

[73] *See Shoptalk, Ltd. v. Concorde-New Horizons Corp.*, 897 F. Supp. 144 (S.D.N.Y. 1995) (stating that publication of motion picture "The Little Shop of Horrors" did not publish the film's screenplay: subsequent non-renewal of film's copyright therefore did not affect the screenplay's duration of protection); *Key West Hand Print Fabrics, Inc. v. Serbin, Inc.*, 244 F. Supp. 287 (S.D. Fla. 1965) (finding that publication of photograph of plaintiff's fabric design in magazine did not inject fabric design into the public domain despite lack of notice); *O'Neill v. General Film Co.*, 171 A.D. 854 (N.Y. App. Div. 1916) (noting that publication of film based on play will divest common law rights in film only).

[74] *See Batjac Prods. Inc. v. Goodtimes Home Video Corp.*, 48 U.S.P.Q. 2d 1647 (9th Cir. 1998) (holding that unpublished screenplay fell into public domain for failure to renew in 1991 motion picture "McLintock!," a derivative work based on the screenplay; the preservation of "subsisting copyrights with the publication of derivative works," under § 7 of the 1909 Act, does not apply to common law copyrights in an unpublished work).

[75] 17 U.S.C. § 401(b)(2).

Part II. NOTICE

§ 4.08 GENERALLY: JUSTIFICATION FOR NOTICE REQUIREMENT

[A] The Background

In general, notice of copyright consists of affixing the name of the copyright owner, the date of first publication of the work, and a symbol (©, copr., or copyright) in a reasonably noticeable location on the work. Before the effective date of the Berne Convention Implementation Act of 1988 ("BCIA"), March 1, 1989, the 1976 Act, as did the preceding Acts, required notice of copyright for all publicly distributed copies of a work of authorship.[76] The notice requirement was unique to American law, the United States being the only major country where noncompliance with the affixation of notice on a work could lead to a forfeiture of copyright.[77] Our insistence on this formality (among other reasons) impeded U.S. entry into the Berne Convention, the preeminent international copyright convention, for over 100 years.[78] With the entry of the United States into the Berne Convention, notice of copyright is no longer required for works publicly distributed on or after March 1, 1989.

Why did we insist on notice in our law? According to the House Report accompanying the 1976 Act, notice serves several purposes. It places into the public domain works in which no one has an interest in maintaining copyright. It also informs the public of a claim for copyright. In addition, it identifies the copyright owner and shows the date of publication.[79]

It is doubtful that the value of these functions of notice outweighed its unfairness to authors or our inability to enter into the Berne Convention.[80] In addition to these basic objections, the notice on a work can often be misleading. Notice presumably informs a user of the copyright owner's identity. But this is not always the case. A copyrighted work may be transferred while copies of the work may continue to circulate for years containing the name of the previous copyright owner.

---

[76] 17 U.S.C. § 401(a). H.R. Rep. No. 94-1476, at 143 (1976).

[77] *See* Nimmer on Copyright § 7.02 (2014).

[78] The Berne Convention prohibits imposition of formalities as a prerequisite to protecting works by the nationals of other signatory states or works first or simultaneously published in such states. *See* Berne Convention art. 5(2) (Paris text, 1971). For a discussion of the Berne Convention, see *infra* § 12.04.

[79] H.R. Rep. No. 94-1476, at 143 (1976).

[80] For a comprehensive discussion of formalities and how to achieve an appropriate balance between the benefits of enforcing formalities versus forfeiting copyright protection, see Jane C. Ginsburg, *The U.S. Experience with Mandatory Copyright Formalities: A Love/Hate Relationship*, 33 Colum. J. L. & Arts 311 (2010).

[B] Abrogation of the Notice Requirement: The Berne Convention Implementation Act of 1988

As of March 1, 1989, notice is no longer required on a publicly distributed work, and omission of notice can no longer result in forfeiture of copyright.[81] Notice is permissive, a choice left to the copyright owner's discretion. But even for works distributed on or after March 1, 1989, notice of a claim for copyright is recommended and may be particularly useful in litigation where a defendant asserts a defense of innocent infringement. Under § 401(d), as amended by the BCIA, if reasonable notice is given as specified in the 1976 Act, then no weight shall be given to a defendant's interposition of a defense based on innocent infringement to mitigate actual or statutory damages.[82] In effect, although notice is permissive for works published after March 1, 1989, it is still encouraged by the 1976 Act because it cuts off the defense of innocent infringement. As a result, the copyright owner must continue to be concerned about the technical rules of proper notice, no longer to avoid forfeiture, but to enjoy the full extent of remedies allowed in a suit for copyright infringement. These rules of proper notice are discussed in *infra* § 4.10.

Despite the abrogation of the notice requirement for publicly distributed works after March 1, 1989, the notice provisions of both the 1976 Act and the 1909 Act are very much alive. The reason is that works that have entered the public domain under a previous statute are not revived by the subsequent legal regime, unless restored under the Uruguay Round Agreements Act.[83] Thus, a work falling into the public domain because of failure to affix notice under the 1909 Act is not revived by the less harsh provisions of the 1976 Act. Similarly, a work entering the public domain for omission of notice under the provisions of the 1976 Act is not revived by the permissive notice provisions of the BCIA amendments.[84] In short, the copyright practitioner must be conversant with the 1909 Act, the 1976 Act as originally enacted, the BCIA amendments, and be able to apply the appropriate statute.

---

[81] For a discussion of opt-in and opt-out systems of copyright in a world of instant authorship and an argument that an opt-in system founded on formalities would disincentivize authors motivated by the present copyright system, see Brad A. Greenberg, *More Than Just a Formality: Instant Authorship and Copyright's Opt-Out Future in the Digital Age*, 59 UCLA L. REV. 1028 (2012).

[82] *See* 17 U.S.C. § 401(d) ("If a notice of copyright . . . appears on the published copy or copies . . . , then no weight shall be given to . . . a defense based on innocent infringement . . . .").

[83] *See* 17 U.S.C. § 104A, which automatically restores copyright to works originating in Berne or WTO countries that lost copyright protection for failure to comply with U.S. formalities. For a discussion of the restoration provisions, see *infra* §§ 6.18–6.19.

[84] In only one narrow instance has Congress resurrected works from the public domain for failure to publish with notice. 17 U.S.C. § 104A, passed pursuant to requirements for entering the North American Free Trade Agreement, resurrects copyright in Mexican and Canadian motion pictures that had entered the public domain for failure to comply with the notice provisions of the 1976 Act as originally passed.

[C] Chart: Notice Provisions for Published Works Under the 1909, 1976, and Berne Convention Implementation Acts

FOR WORKS PUBLISHED BEFORE 1/1/78	FOR WORKS PUBLISHED ON OR AFTER 1/1/78 AND BEFORE 3/1/89	FOR WORKS PUBLISHED ON OR AFTER 3/1/89
Federal protection began on publication with proper notice. Publication without proper notice injected work into public domain. §§ 10, 19 (1909 Act).	Notice required for all published works. If work published without notice, copyright owner must comply with five-year cure provisions to avoid injecting work into public domain. § 405(a)	Notice is optional. §§ 401–404. Lack of notice may allow innocent infringer defense. §§ 401(d), 402(d).

§ 4.09 NOTICE REQUIREMENTS UNDER THE 1976 ACT BEFORE THE BERNE CONVENTION IMPLEMENTATION ACT OF 1988 AMENDMENTS

For works publicly distributed on or after January 1, 1978, and before March 1, 1989, the 1976 Act, while easing the harsh forfeiture provisions of the 1909 Act,[85] nevertheless forced the copyright owner to comply with notice formalities. Section 401(a) provided:

> Whenever a work protected under this title is published in the United States or elsewhere by authority of the copyright owner, a notice of copyright as provided by this section shall be placed on all publicly distributed copies from which the work can be visually perceived, either directly or with the aid of a machine or device.[86]

Certain important points arise from this statutory language. First, notice was not a permissive act but was a requirement for copyright protection[87] any time a work was published.[88] Second, the notice requirement was limited to published works in all copies visually perceived with the naked eye or with the aid of a machine

---

[85] The 1976 Act intended to avoid the "arbitrary and unjust forfeitures" resulting under the 1909 Act from "unintentional or relatively unimportant omissions or errors in the copyright notice." H.R. REP. NO. 94-1476, at 143 (1976).

[86] 17 U.S.C. § 401(a). The BCIA has changed the language "shall be placed on" to "may be placed on." *See* 17 U.S.C. § 401(a).

[87] Strict adherence to statutory formalities became the American viewpoint as early as 1824 in *Ewer v. Coxe*, 8 F. Cas. 917 (C.C.E.D. Pa. 1824). The most famous case holding that formalities be strictly observed was decided by the Supreme Court in 1834, *Wheaton v. Peters*, 33 U.S. (8 Pet.) 591 (1834). The *Wheaton* doctrine is extensively explored in Craig Joyce, *The Rise of the Supreme Court Reporter: An Institutional Perspective on Marshall Court Ascendancy*, 83 MICH. L. REV. 1291 (1985).

[88] *See* 17 U.S.C. § 101. Section 101 defines "publication" as:

> . . . the distribution of copies or phonorecords of a work to the public by sale or other transfer of ownership, or by rental, lease, or lending. The offering to distribute copies or phonorecords to a group of persons for purposes of further distribution, public performance, or public display, constitutes publication. A public performance or display of a work does not of itself constitute publication.

or device.[89] Third, notice had to be affixed to copies of a work whether published in the United States or abroad; it was not solely limited to United States publications.[90] Fourth, notice was required on all tangible copies published by or under the authority of the copyright owner;[91] the rules of notice did not apply to unauthorized publication of the work.[92] From these general considerations, the discussion now turns to the technical aspects of complying with the notice requirements.

Even though improper notice can no longer forfeit copyright for works publicly distributed on or after March 1, 1989, the rules of proper notice remain important because affixation of proper notice on copies or phonorecords deprives a defendant of the defense of innocent infringement in the mitigation of actual or statutory damages for causes of action arising after the effective date of the BCIA. Thus, a copyright practitioner should be concerned about the rules of proper notice regardless of when the work was published.[93]

§ 4.10 FORM AND POSITION OF NOTICE UNDER THE 1976 ACT

[A] Form of Notice on Copies

As specified by § 401(b), notice of copyright consists of three elements: (1) the symbol "©" or the abbreviation "Copr.," or the word "Copyright"; (2) the name of the owner of the copyright; and (3) the date of first publication. For example, a typical notice may look like this: © John Doe 1986. The three elements constituting notice may be placed in any order.

To inform copyright owners of the correct form of notice, the 1976 Act authorizes the Register of Copyrights to prescribe by regulation the proper form and position of notice for various kinds of works.[94] In questionable cases, the Register's regulations should be consulted, but, as the 1976 Act specifically provides, these regulations are not to be considered exhaustive.[95]

Requirements for proper notice can become ridiculously formalistic. For example, to constitute proper notice, must the "c" be surrounded by a circle (©), or will some other form of enclosure suffice, such as "c" in parentheses ((c))? The Copyright Office's final regulations reject anything but ©, "Copr.," or "Copyright" as specified in the 1976 Act.[96] One court, however, has disagreed, holding that "c"

---

[89] *See* 17 U.S.C. § 401(a).

[90] *See* H.R. Rep. No. 94-1476, at 144 (1976). The phrase, "or elsewhere," which does not appear in the present law, made the notice requirements applicable to copies or phonorecords distributed to the public anywhere in the world, regardless of where and when the work was first published.

[91] *See* 17 U.S.C. § 401(a).

[92] *See* 17 U.S.C. § 405(c); *Fantastic Fakes, Inc. v. Pickwick Int'l, Inc.*, 661 F.2d 479 (5th Cir. 1981).

[93] *See* 17 U.S.C. §§ 401(d), 402(d).

[94] 17 U.S.C. § 401(c). *See* H.R. Rep. No. 94-1476, at 144 (1976).

[95] 17 U.S.C. § 401(c).

[96] 17 U.S.C. § 401(b)(1). Use of the symbol "c" without a circle around it was said to be defective in Goldsmith v. Max, 1978-1981 Copyright Dec. ¶ 25,248 (S.D.N.Y. 1981).

surrounded by a hexagon constitutes adequate notice.[97]

What should the rule be regarding the copyright symbol? Flexibility should govern rather than technical rules about circles or parentheses, and decisions should be based on a reasonableness standard.[98] Moreover, the burden should be on the party asserting improper notice to show that the notice as given was inadequate to inform a reasonable person about a claim to copyright.[99]

[B] Form of Notice on Phonorecords for Sound Recordings

Further complicating an already technical subject, the 1976 Act sets forth a special form and position of notice for phonorecords of sound recordings.[100] For phonorecords, the Act requires the symbol ℗, the year of first publication, and the name of the owner of the copyright.[101] The notice has to be placed on the surface of the phonorecord or phonorecord label or container "to give reasonable notice of the claim of copyright."[102]

The form of notice required for phonorecords embodying a sound recording differs from that imposed for "copies."[103] For copies (all material objects other than phonorecords), the Act specifies three variations for the copyright symbol: ©, "Copr.," or "Copyright."[104] On the other hand, for a phonorecord embodying a sound recording, only one form is specified, the symbol ℗.[105]

What justifies the special form for phonorecords of sound recordings, the symbol ℗, rather than the universal © for all tangible embodiments of copyrighted works? The House Report provides two principal reasons: the first is to distinguish claims in the sound recording from the musical work, artistic work, or literary work embodied on it or contained on the phonorecord, album cover, or liner notes. Second, the symbol has been adopted as the international symbol by the phonogram convention.[106] These justifications hardly justify the added complexity needed to comply with copyright formalities under the 1976 Act.

---

[97] In *Videotronics, Inc. v. Bend Elec.*, 586 F. Supp. 478 (D. Nev. 1984), the court suggested that the letter "c" within a parenthesis instead of a circle might constitute a defective notice, but held that a hexagonal figure that completely surrounded the "c" was an adequate substitute for a circle as used on a video screen which was incapable of producing a perfect circle.

[98] *See* 17 U.S.C. § 401(c). H.R. Rep. No. 94-1476, at 144 (1976), notice "shall be affixed to the copies in such manner and location as to give reasonable notice of the claim of copyright." Subsection (c) follows " . . . the flexible approach. . . . "

[99] *See Quinto v. Legal Times of Washington, Inc.*, 506 F. Supp. 554 (D.D.C. 1981); 17 U.S.C. § 406(a).

[100] 17 U.S.C. § 402(b), (c).

[101] 17 U.S.C. § 402(b).

[102] 17 U.S.C. § 402(c).

[103] 17 U.S.C. § 401, 402.

[104] 17 U.S.C. § 401(b)(1).

[105] 17 U.S.C. § 402(b)(1).

[106] H.R. Rep. No. 94-1476, 94th Cong., 2d Sess. 145 (1976).

[C] Year Date

Proper notice must include the year date of first publication of the work[107] on all categories of copyrightable works with one exception. The "date may be omitted where a pictorial, graphic, or sculptural work with accompanying text matter, if any, is reproduced in or on greeting cards, postcards, stationery, jewelry, dolls, toys or any useful articles."[108]

Apart from this narrow exception, the date of first publication (not creation) must be placed on all copies or phonorecords to constitute proper notice.

[D] Name of Copyright Owner

To constitute proper notice, copies of a work have to include the name of the copyright owner.[109] The full name need not be affixed; an abbreviation by which the name can be recognized or an alternative designation of the owner is sufficient.[110] For a sound recording, when the producer of the sound recording is named on the phonorecord labels or containers and no other name appears with the symbol and year date, the producer's name shall be considered a part of the notice.[111]

[E] Location of the Notice

In contrast with the 1909 Act, the 1976 Act does not specify where on a particular work copyright notice must be affixed to constitute proper notice. The 1976 Act provides that notice shall be affixed in such a manner and location as to give reasonable notice of the claim of copyright.[112] The Register of Copyrights, pursuant to legislative authority, has issued regulations indicating where notice should be placed on various kinds of works to comply with reasonable notice requirements.[113]

---

[107] *See* 17 U.S.C. §§ 401(b)(2), 402(b)(2).

[108] 17 U.S.C. § 401(b)(2).

[109] *See* 17 U.S.C. §§ 401(b)(3), 402(b)(3).

[110] *See id.*

[111] *See* 17 U.S.C. § 402(b)(3).

[112] As stated in the House Report:

> A notice placed or affixed in accordance with the regulations would clearly meet the requirements but, since the Register's specifications are not to "be considered exhaustive," a notice placed or affixed in some other way might also comply with the law if it were found to "give reasonable notice" of the copyright claim.

H.R. Rep. No. 94-1476, at 144 (1976). *See* 37 C.F.R. § 201.20 (1987).

[113] The Copyright Office's regulations pertaining to methods of affixation and position of notice are found at 37 C.F.R. § 201.20 (1987). For explanatory comment, *see* 46 Fed. Reg. 58, 307-14 (1981).

§ 4.11 OMISSION OF NOTICE

[A] Generally

The notice provisions of the 1909 Act threatened the copyright owner with a possible loss of copyright for non-compliance.[114] Under the 1976 Act, for works published on or after January 1, 1978, and before March 1, 1989, non-compliance with notice formalities can forfeit copyright. But forfeiture is more difficult.[115] One can inject a work into the public domain under § 405 of the 1976 Act as originally enacted if notice was omitted from a substantial number of copies and if registration of the work is not made within five years of publication.[116] In addition to registration, a reasonable effort is required, upon discovering the omissions, to add notice to copies or phonorecords publicly distributed in the United States.[117] These provisions reveal that omission need not be fatal to the copyright so long as two further formalities were complied with, that is, registration of the work and an attempt to affix notice after discovery of the omission.

The BCIA amendments abrogated the notice requirement, but their effect was not retroactive. Thus, copyright owners, to save their work from falling into the public domain, were still required to use these cure provisions for omitted notice on works publicly distributed before March 1, 1989. Accordingly, a copyright owner had to avail himself of these savings provisions for all public distribution of the work even after the effective date of the BCIA. For example, suppose that a public distribution of a work with omitted notice took place on February 28, 1989, the last day before the effective date of the BCIA amendments. To save the work from forfeiture, the copyright owner had five years, until March 1, 1994, to cure omitted notice by registering the work and making a reasonable effort to add notice to works distributed after discovery of the omission.

As stated above, the BCIA amendments were prospective in effect and did not revive a work falling into the public domain for failure to apply notice after publication of the work. This conforms to the basic policy of the 1976 Act, which did not revive works in the public domain before 1978.[118] In 1993, pursuant to its responsibilities in joining the North American Free Trade Agreement ("NAFTA"), Congress enacted implementing legislation that would resurrect certain copyrights from the public domain. A new § 104A of the Copyright Act would restore copyrights in Mexican and Canadian motion pictures that had fallen into the United States public domain for failure to comply with the 1976 Act notice requirement. The legislation would allow the continued use for one year of copies

---

[114] *See* 37 C.F.R. § 202 (1987); *Original Appalachian Artworks, Inc. v. Toy Loft, Inc.*, 684 F.2d 821, 826 (11th Cir. 1982) (finding that copyright would have been forfeited had dolls been published in 1977). *See also* 17 U.S.C. § 10 (1909 Act).

[115] H.R. Rep. No. 94-1476, at 147 (1976), "Section 405(a) takes a middle-ground approach in an effort to encourage use of a copyright notice without causing unfair and unjustifiable forfeitures on technical grounds."

[116] 17 U.S.C. § 405(a).

[117] 17 U.S.C. § 405(a)(2).

[118] *See* 17 U.S.C. Trans. & Supp. Prov. § 103.

owned before the effective date of the amendment.[119]

The relatively modest restoration provisions of NAFTA were greatly extended the following year by the Uruguay Round Agreements Act.[120] On January 1, 1996, copyright was automatically restored in certain works of foreign origin that entered the public domain for failure to comply with U.S. copyright formalities such as notice and renewal registration. This legislation, however, does not revive works of *U.S.* origin from the public domain. Thus, despite, the BCIA's abrogation of formalities and the Uruguay Round's restoration provisions, a large number of works — those of U.S. origin — are unaffected by these dramatic changes in United States copyright law. Their public domain status will still be determined by compliance with notice and other formalities under prior U.S. law.

[B] Omission of Notice and Forfeiture of Copyright

For a work publicly distributed on or after January 1, 1978, and before March 1, 1989, omission of notice sufficient to forfeit copyright could only take place if the act of omission was authorized by the copyright owner.[121] Copyright is not affected if notice is somehow removed from published copies or phonorecords of the work without the authorization of the copyright owner.[122]

Moreover, even if the copyright owner authorized a third party to distribute his work, these notice provisions do not apply if notice was omitted pursuant to an express written agreement between the parties that the distributor comply with the notice provisions of the 1976 Copyright Act.[123]

Even if omission of notice has taken place by authority of the copyright owner, forfeiture cannot occur (and the cure provisions need not be used) unless notice had been omitted from "more than a relatively small number of copies or phonorecords."[124] The meaning of what constitutes "more than a relatively small number" of copies has led to some debate. By "small number," does the Act refer to a percentage of the total distribution or to some absolute number equivalent to a

---

[119] *See* Pub. L. No. 103-182, 107 Stat. 2115 (1993).

[120] *See* Pub. L. No. 103-465, 108 Stat. 4809 (1994). The Act's provisions are codified at 17 U.S.C. § 104A. For a discussion of restoration, see *infra* §§ 6.18–6.19.

[121] *See Beacon Looms, Inc. v. S. Lichtenberg & Co., Inc.*, 552 F. Supp. 1305 (S.D.N.Y. 1982). *But cf.* 17 U.S.C. §§ 405(a), (b).

[122] *See* 17 U.S.C. § 405(c). S. Rep. No. 94-473, at 131 (1975):

> Subsection (c) of section 405 involves the situation that arises when someone in the chain of distribution removes, destroys, or obliterates the notice. The courts dealing with this problem under the present law, especially in connection with copyright notices on the selvage of textile fabrics, have generally upheld the validity of a notice that was securely attached to the copies when they left the control of the copyright owner, even though removal of the notice at some later stage was likely. This conclusion is incorporated in subsection (c).

See, e.g., *Peter Pan Fabrics, Inc. v. Martin Weiner Corp.*, 274 F.2d 487 (2d Cir. 1960) (stating that at least in the case of a deliberate copyist, the absence of notice is a defense that the copyist must prove, and the burden is on him to show that notice could have been embodied in the design without impairing its market value).

[123] *See* 17 U.S.C. § 405(a)(3).

[124] 17 U.S.C. § 405(a)(1).

small amount? The House Report is silent on this issue except to say that the provision is intended to be less restrictive than the analogous provision in § 21 of the 1909 Act.[125]

Although the case law is not totally consistent, the percentage formula has generally been adopted. Thus, the omission of notice from nine percent of garments made from fabric designs was excused,[126] while the omission of notice from twenty-two to thirty-seven percent of 1,335 publicly distributed sculptural reproductions was deemed to constitute more than a relatively small number.[127] Most other courts have taken this percentage approach as well.[128]

[C] Omission of Notice: The Savings Provision

The 1976 Act includes a savings provision where notice has been omitted on more than a relatively small number of copies or phonorecords publicly distributed on or after January 1, 1978, and before March 1, 1989. Under § 405(a)(2) of the 1976 Act, the copyright owner must take the following two steps:

(1) register the work before or within five years after the publication is made, and

(2) make a reasonable effort to add notice to all copies or phonorecords publicly distributed in the United States after discovery of the omission.[129]

This important savings provision contains several ambiguities that the case law is just beginning to resolve.

The registration requirement in § 405(a)(2) is relatively straightforward. Registration can take place before or after the public distribution without notice, so long as it is accomplished within five years.[130] The effective date of registration is the day on which an application, deposit, and fee are received in the Copyright Office.[131] However, registration occurring after the five-year period will not save the copyright if notice has been omitted from more than a relatively small number of copies of the work.[132]

---

[125] H.R. Rep. No. 94-1476, at 147 (1976).

[126] *See Flora Kung, Inc. v. Items of California, Inc.*, 29 Pat. Trademark & Copyright J. (BNA) No. 721, at 515 (S.D.N.Y. Nov. 16, 1984).

[127] *See King v. Burnett*, 1981–1983 Copy. Dec. ¶ 25,489 at 17,913 (D.D.C. 1982).

[128] *See, e.g., Ford Motor Co. v. Summit Motor Prods., Inc.*, 930 F.2d 277 (3d Cir. 1991), *cert. denied*, 502 U.S. 939 (1991) (finding that four million copies without notice out of 100 million constituted a relatively small number).

[129] 17 U.S.C. § 405(a)(2).

[130] *See Original Appalachian Artworks, Inc. v. Toy Loft, Inc.*, 684 F.2d 821 (11th Cir. 1982) (finding that registration effectuated within five years of the date of first publication).

[131] *See* 17 U.S.C. § 410(d): "Where the three necessary elements [of application, deposit, and fee] are received at different times, the date of receipt of the last of them is controlling." *See* H.R. Rep. No. 94-1476, at 157 (1976).

[132] *See id.* at 147.

[D] Discovery of Omission

The second aspect of § 405(a)(2) requires a reasonable effort to add notice to all copies or phonorecords that are publicly distributed in the United States after the omission has been *discovered*.[133] In addition to what constitutes a reasonable effort to add notice, this section presents two difficult issues concerning the discovery of the omitted notice. First, can deliberate omissions of notice be cured under § 405(a)(3)? Second, at what point does discovery occur for the purposes of the cure provisions?

The first question, whether deliberate omissions can be cured at all, has spawned litigation despite a clear indication in the legislative history that they can be. According to the House Report, a work published without any copyright notice will be subject to statutory protection for at least five years whether the omission was partial or total, unintentional or deliberate.[134]

The Second Circuit, in *Hasbro Bradley, Inc. v. Sparkle Toys, Inc.*,[135] adopted the House Report's view that the cure provisions of § 405(a)(2) extend to deliberate as well as inadvertent omissions of notice. In this case, the plaintiff, a toy manufacturer, brought an action to enjoin an admitted copyist from distributing its *Transformer* brand robot toys in the United States. The defendant claimed that copyright was forfeited by the Japanese company, the assignor to Hasbro and the originator of the toys, in deliberately omitting notice from 213,000 of the toys sold in Asia. The defendant relied on *Beacon Looms, Inc. v. S. Lichtenberg & Co., Inc.*,[136] which held that a deliberate omission of notice cannot be cured because, under the words of the statute, such an omission cannot be "discovered."[137] The defendant reasoned that this would preclude a cure for a deliberate omission of notice. The court rejected this premise, stating that the assignor's deliberate omission of notice was indeed discovered by the assignee who was then attempting to cure the omission. The Second Circuit also relied on the drafters' desire to avoid murky questions of proof relating to subjective intent.

From a theoretical standpoint, the moment when an omission of notice is "discovered" for purposes of § 405 is relatively clear where unintentional omissions are concerned. In such cases the timing of the "discovery" simply presents a question of fact. The more difficult question and one the *Hasbro* court did not address is as follows: at what point does discovery occur for intentional omissions of notice. Courts and commentators have adopted differing approaches to the problem. One view holds that discovery occurs when a copyright owner finds out that someone else is copying his or her work.[138] By contrast, a second approach holds that discovery occurs automatically when a copy of the work is first published

---

[133] 17 U.S.C. § 405(a)(2). *See Original Appalachian Artworks, Inc. v. Toy Loft, Inc.*, 684 F.2d 821 (11th Cir. 1982) (finding that registration without "reasonable effort" will not excuse notice omission).

[134] H.R. Rep. No. 94-1476, at 147 (1976).

[135] 780 F.2d 189 (2d Cir. 1985).

[136] 552 F. Supp. 1305 (S.D.N.Y. 1982).

[137] 17 U.S.C. § 405(a)(2).

[138] *See O'Neill Devs., Inc. v. Galen Kilburn, Inc.*, 524 F. Supp. 710, 714 (N.D. Ga. 1981).

or publicly distributed.[139] Based on logic and common sense, this latter interpretation of the statute is clearly preferable. After all, how can one "discover" a deliberate omission?[140] Moreover, the first view has no basis in the language of § 405(a)(2) and would appear to negate the policy behind the notice requirement.[141]

[E] Reasonable Efforts to Cure Omitted Notice

In addition to registration, § 405(a)(2) requires that the copyright owner make a reasonable effort to add notice to all copies or phonorecords that are publicly distributed before March 1, 1989, in the United States after the omission has been discovered.[142] By this provision, the copyright owner does not have to make a reasonable effort to add notice to copies already possessed by members of the public.[143] On the other hand, the copyright owner has a clear duty to affix notice to copies still in his possession awaiting distribution.[144] Does the duty of reasonable effort to affix notice extend to copies distributed before discovery, no longer in the copyright owner's possession, but that have not yet reached the public? In other words, does the copyright owner have to make a reasonable effort to add notice to copies held by wholesalers or retailers?[145] Some sort of reasonable effort to add notice must be made by the copyright owner. From the language of the statute, copies held by retailers and wholesalers are still to be distributed to the public.

It is unclear what constitutes a reasonable effort in attempting to affix notice for those copies.[146] The reasonable effort requirement is a question of fact to be worked out under the circumstances of each case. But as one court states:

---

[139] *See* Nimmer on Copyright, § 7.13[B][3] (2014).

[140] *See Beacon Looms, Inc. v. S. Lichtenberg & Co., Inc.*, 552 F. Supp. 1305, 1310 (S.D.N.Y. 1982).

[141] Other courts have suggested a middle ground between the two prevailing interpretations. *See Charles Garnier, Paris v. Andin Int'l, Inc.*, 36 F.3d 1214 (1st Cir. 1994) (suggesting that the moment of discovery for a deliberate omission of notice would take place after publication when the copyright owner is appraised of the legal significance of a failure to provide notice).

[142] *See generally* Nimmer on Copyright § 7.13[B] (2014).

[143] *See, e.g.*, *Midway Mfg. Co. v. Artic Int'l, Inc.*, 704 F.2d 1009, 1013 (7th Cir. 1983) (finding that plaintiff did not lose copyright in videogames, even if published without notice in Japan, when copyright was registered within five years and all copies distributed in United States contained notice); *Hagendorf v. Brown*, 707 F.2d 1018, 1019 (9th Cir. 1983) (stating that publication without notice did not forfeit protection if registration occurred within five years of publication and no copies were distributed in United States after omission was discovered or, if distribution occurred, the author made a reasonable effort to add notice to copies distributed).

[144] *See Videotronics, Inc. v. Bend Elec.*, 586 F. Supp. 478 (D. Nev. 1984) (noting fact that notice was omitted from only 28 copies was irrelevant in view of "all copies" requirement).

[145] *See Shapiro & Son Bedspread Corp. v. Royal Mills Assocs.*, 568 F. Supp. 972 (S.D.N.Y. 1983), *rev'd on other grounds*, 764 F.2d 69 (2d Cir. 1985) (denying plaintiff's motion for preliminary injunction because it had not made reasonable efforts to replace defective notice with proper notice); *Beacon Looms, Inc. v. S. Lichtenberg & Co.*, 552 F. Supp. 1305, 1313 (S.D.N.Y. 1982).

[146] *See Beacon Looms, Inc. v. S. Lichtenberg & Co.*, 552 F. Supp. 1305 (S.D.N.Y. 1982) (holding that where some 900,000 units not bearing a copyright notice had been sold to retail dealers, the sending of only 50,000 labels bearing a notice to such dealers, without ascertaining the number of units still held in the dealers' inventories, failed to comply with the "reasonable effort" requirement).

> Implicit in the concept . . . is the expectation that an expenditure of time and money over and above that required in the normal course of business will be made.[147]

In short, until the courts have filled in more details, a prudent copyright owner should promptly supply retailers with a sufficient means to affix notice to the pertinent copies.

[F] Discovery of Omitted Notice After the Berne Convention Implementation Act

In the Berne Convention Implementation Act of 1988, the provisions of § 405(a) are preserved but apply only to works published before March 1, 1989. The transition from pre-Berne to post-Berne raises interesting questions. Clearly, a copyright owner would be required to make reasonable efforts to affix notice to a work distributed before Berne but whose omission is discovered after Berne. For example, if a work had been distributed with defective notice only in January and February of 1989 and the problem was discovered on March 15, after the effective date of the Act, the copyright owner would still be required to attempt to "cure" the defect for distributed copies to preserve its rights. But what if a distribution of copies with defective notice began in January 1989 and continued after March 1 and the defect in question was discovered (and corrected prospectively) only on January 1, 1990, ten months after the effective date of the BCIA? In this situation, is the copyright owner required to make "reasonable efforts" to add notice to the January and February copies only or for all copies made available to the public in the calendar year 1989?

The answer is not free from doubt. In *Charles Garnier, Paris v. Andin International, Inc.*,[148] the Court interpreted § 405(2) as requiring an attempt to "cure" the defect in all copies — even for those distributed post-BCIA when notice was no longer required. This interpretation appears inconsistent with the purpose of the notice provisions because it perpetuates the very formality that the BCIA sought to abolish. In addition, it would make little sense as a matter of copyright policy to generate uncertainty about the copyright status of works whose public distribution occurred both before and after the effective date of the BCIA.

[G] Omitted Notice and Innocent Infringement

As previously indicated, the most severe consequence of omission of notice for works publicly distributed on or after January 1, 1978, and before March 1, 1989, is that it may lead to an eventual forfeiture of copyright.[149] Omitted notice can lead to another adverse consequence that also applies to works distributed after March 1,

---

[147] *Videotronics, Inc. v. Bend Elec.*, 586 F. Supp. 478, 483 (D. Nev. 1984).

[148] 36 F.3d 1214 (1st Cir. 1994).

[149] Where copyright notice is required and its omission is not excused under 17 U.S.C. § 405(a), the legal consequence is forfeiture of the copyright and release of the work into the public domain. *See Shapiro & Son Bedspread Corp. v. Royal Mills Assoc.*, 568 F. Supp. 972 (S.D.N.Y. 1983).

1989. Section 405(b) limits remedies against innocent infringers misled by lack of notice.[150]

Section 405(b) applies only to innocent infringers who can prove they were misled by omission of notice from an authorized copy of the work. Once the infringer meets this burden, this section shields him against liability for actual damages and statutory damages and, although not specified, probably attorney's fees as well.[151]

This limitation lasts until the infringer is put on notice of the claim to copyright, as actual knowledge bars innocent infringement.[152] On the other hand, the court has the discretion to allow recovery for profits made by the infringing acts and to enjoin further infringements or, in the appropriate case, to allow the infringing acts to continue upon payment of a reasonable license fee.

Despite the concern for those who may have innocently relied on omission of notice from an authorized copy of the work, it seems contradictory that there can be any innocent infringement when copyright protection, on or after January 1, 1978, begins automatically on creation.[153] Further, as indicated by the House Report, persons who plan to undertake major enterprises based on copies of works lacking notice should check the records of the Copyright Office before starting a project.[154] In accordance with this view, one court has held that one cannot be an innocent infringer misled by lack of notice if a search of the Copyright Office records would have revealed the registration.[155]

§ 4.12 ERROR IN NAME AND DATE

[A] Generally

Under the 1909 Act, errors in name and date could inject copyright into the public domain.[156] By comparison, the 1976 Act specifies that an error in name will not affect the validity or ownership of copyright. However, certain errors in date for works publicly distributed on or after January 1, 1978, and before March 1, 1989, are considered omissions of notice subjecting the copyright owner to possible forfeiture. For errors in both name and date, innocent infringers can avoid liability if misled by these errors.[157] For works publicly distributed on or after March 1, 1989, errors in name or date will not affect validity or duration of copyright, but the copyright owner will not benefit from the evidentiary weight of proper notice

---

[150] *See* 17 U.S.C. § 405(b).

[151] 17 U.S.C. § 405(b). *See* Nimmer on Copyright § 14.10[D] (2014); S. Rep. No. 473, 94th Cong., 1st Sess. 131 (1975) (stating that courts have broad discretion to grant or limit damages, depending upon the specific situation).

[152] *See Aitken, Hazen, Hoffman, Miller, P.C. v. Empire Constr. Co.*, 542 F. Supp. 252 (D. Neb. 1982).

[153] *See* 17 U.S.C. § 102(a).

[154] H.R. Rep. No. 94-1476, at 148 (1976).

[155] *See Quinto v. Legal Times of Washington, Inc.*, 506 F. Supp. 554 (D.D.C. 1981).

[156] 17 U.S.C. § 10 (1909 Act). *See* 17 C.F.R. § 202.2 (1987).

[157] *See* 17 U.S.C. §§ 405(b) and 406(a).

provided in §§ 401(d) and 402(d), which deprive a defendant of an innocent infringement defense in mitigation of actual or statutory damages.

[B] Error in Name

When the name of the copyright owner is incorrect in the copyright notice, copyright validity or ownership is not affected.[158] However, § 406 provides a complete defense to a person, "who innocently begins an undertaking that infringes the copyright . . . if such person proves that he or she was misled by the notice and began the undertaking in good faith under a purported transfer . . . from the person named therein."[159]

What constitutes "an undertaking begun in good faith" was examined in *Quinto v. Legal Times of Washington, Inc.*[160] In *Quinto*, the defendant reprinted an article that had been published in the Harvard Law Review. The article did not bear copyright notice, although there was a blanket notice in the masthead of the publication. The defendant published the article verbatim after receiving general permission to do so from the editor of the student journal, but without inquiring further into the copyright status of the article and without trying to contact the author. The court concluded that the good faith defense was not available and, "that good faith in the context of this case entails not only honesty in fact but reasonableness as well."[161]

Accordingly, the defendant had a duty to inquire as to who owned the copyright.[162]

> Even if a person shows he or she was misled by the notice and began the undertaking in good faith under a transfer from the person named in the notice, the defense of good faith does not apply if before the undertaking was begun:
>
> (1) registration for the work had been made in the name of the owner of copyright; or
>
> (2) a document executed by the person named in the notice and showing the ownership of the copyright had been recorded.[163]

[C] Error in Date

Antedated and post-dated notices are governed by § 406(b).[164]

For works publicly distributed on or after January 1, 1978, and before March 1, 1989, bearing an antedated notice (stating a date of publication earlier than the

---

[158] 17 U.S.C. § 406(a) (the BCIA). *See Fantastic Fakes, Inc. v. Pickwick Int'l, Inc.*, 661 F.2d 479 (5th Cir. 1981).

[159] 17 U.S.C. § 406(a).

[160] 506 F. Supp. 554 (D.D.C. 1981).

[161] *Id.* at 562.

[162] *See id.* at 563.

[163] 17 U.S.C. §§ 406(a)(1) and (2).

[164] 17 U.S.C. § 406(b).

actual publication date), duration of copyright is measured from that date. On the other hand, if the year date in the notice was more than one year later than the year date of publication, such notice is deemed to be an omission of notice and is treated under the provisions of § 405. For example, if A publishes his work on February 28, 1989, but affixes at that time a notice date of 1991, the post-dated notice is treated as no notice at all, being more than one year later than the actual publication date for the work. Here the copyright owner must avail himself of the cure provisions of § 405 (registration within five years and reasonable attempt to add notice) or face forfeiture of copyright. For works published on or after March 1, 1989, neither antedated nor post-dated notice has any effect on duration or validity of copyright, but the provisions of §§ 401(d) and 402(d), concerning the evidentiary weight of proper notice, will not benefit the copyright owner.

[D] Omission of Name or Date

For works publicly distributed on or after January 1, 1978, and before March 1, 1989, complete omission of the name or date from copyright notice is treated as an omission of notice under § 405.[165] The 1976 Act contains no provision that the elements of notice must be directly contiguous or accompany one another.[166] However, if the elements of notice are too widely separated for their relationship to be reasonably apparent, this situation will be treated as an omission of notice.[167]

§ 4.13 SPECIAL NOTICE SUBSECTIONS

[A] Notice for Publications Containing Government Works

Works produced by the United States government are precluded from copyright protection and are in the public domain.[168] Often government documents are published commercially along with new matter added by the publisher, such as introductions, illustrations, and editing. Although copyrightable subject matter is added by the publisher, the great bulk of the work may consist of a public domain governmental work. Section 403 attempts to avoid the misleading nature of a notice of copyright in publications containing government works by requiring that when copies or phonorecords consist preponderantly of one or more works of the United States government, the copyright notice must identify that part of the work in which copyright is claimed.[169] For works published on or after January 1, 1978, and before March 1, 1989, failure to do so is treated as an omission of notice under § 405.[170] Section 403 has now been amended by the BCIA. For works published on or after March 1, 1989, an absence of an identifying statement will deprive the copyright owner of the evidentiary weight of proper notice under §§ 401(d) and

---

[165] 17 U.S.C. § 406(c).

[166] H.R. Rep. No. 94-1476, at 150 (1976).

[167] *Id.*

[168] *See* 17 U.S.C. § 105.

[169] 17 U.S.C. § 403.

[170] *See* H.R. Rep. No. 94-1476, at 146 (1976).

402(d) but will not invalidate copyright in the work.[171]

[B] Notice for Contribution to Collective Works

As discussed previously, the compiler of a collective work or other compilation may be entitled to copyright in that work irrespective of the copyright status of the work's constituent elements. Until March 1, 1989, the compiler (or the compiler's successor-in-interest) was required to use notice on published copies to safeguard that copyright. When both the preexisting work and the collective work share the same ownership and the same year of first publication, omission of notice for the smaller work scarcely matters in the practical sense. But what if the copyrights in the two works are owned by different persons, or the works were first published in different years, or the works differ in both respects? Under the 1909 Act, it was unclear what constituted proper notice for a contribution to a collective work. Generally, cases decided under the 1909 Act concluded that a properly affixed "general" or "masthead" copyright notice would be sufficient to secure or maintain copyright protection for all contributions contained in that work.[172] The case law, however, is hardly unanimous on this point.[173]

Section 404 of the 1976 Act has attempted to solve this traditionally troublesome problem.[174] The basic approach of this section is summarized in the House Report as follows:

> (1) to permit but not require a separate contribution to bear its own notice;
>
> (2) to make a single notice covering the entire collective work as a whole sufficient to satisfy the notice requirement for each contribution it contains; and
>
> (3) to protect the interests of the innocent infringer of copyright in a contribution that does not bear its own notice, who has dealt in good faith with the person named in the notice covering the collective work as a whole.[175]

Section 404 provides that for works publicly distributed before March 1, 1989, the copyright owner of an individual contribution need not affix notice to his individual work to protect the copyright from forfeiture, so long as notice is affixed by the owner of the collective work.[176] However, for works publicly distributed on or after January 1, 1978, and before March 1, 1989, the 1976 Act allows a defense of good faith infringement by a person misled by an improper name in the notice.[177]

---

[171] 17 U.S.C. § 403.

[172] *See Goodis v. United Artists Television, Inc.*, 425 F.2d 397 (2d Cir. 1970).

[173] *See Sanga Music, Inc. v. EMI Blackwood Music, Inc.*, 55 F.3d 756 (2d Cir. 1995) (invalidating copyright in song lyrics published in 1957, when magazine containing masthead notice in the name of publisher failed to print alongside lyrics a copyright notice bearing the name of the author of the lyrics).

[174] 17 U.S.C. § 404 (a) and (b).

[175] H.R. Rep. No. 94-1476, at 146 (1976).

[176] *See Quinto v. Legal Times of Washington, Inc.*, 506 F. Supp. 554 (D.D.C. 1981).

[177] *See* 17 U.S.C. § 406(a).

For works publicly distributed on or after March 1, 1989, there is no longer any obligation to affix notice to protect the validity of copyright in a separate contribution to a collective work. However, so long as a single notice appears in the name of the collective work owner, the owner of a contribution can benefit from the new §§ 401(d) and 402(d), which disallow the defense of innocent infringement in mitigation of actual or statutory damages.[178]

A special problem occurs where an advertisement is placed in a collective work by persons other than the owners of copyright in the collective work.[179] For example, suppose that an advertisement is placed in a magazine consisting of several articles written by outside authors. The general copyright notice in the collective work does not protect the advertisement as it did the authors of the individual contributions to the collective work. For works publicly distributed on or after January 1, 1978, and before March 1, 1989, the copyright in the advertisement is not protected by notice in the collective work, and if notice was not affixed to the advertisement, the work faces forfeiture of copyright by this omission of notice.[180] For works publicly distributed on or after March 1, 1989, copyright in the advertisement cannot be invalidated by this omission of notice, but the provisions of §§ 401(d) and 402(d), which disallow the defense of innocent infringement in mitigation of actual or statutory damages, will not benefit the copyright owner.

§ 4.14 NOTICE UNDER THE 1909 ACT

[A] Generally

The highly technical notice provisions of the 1909 Act, with all their pitfalls, often led to the inadvertent forfeiture of copyright.[181] These notice provisions are still important today. The reason they are still important is that neither the 1976 Act as originally enacted nor the BCIA amendments will revive a work that went into the public domain before January 1, 1978. With passage of the Uruguay Round Agreements Act, copyrighted works originating from Berne or WTO countries that were injected into the public domain for failure to comply with U.S. copyright formalities are automatically restored to copyright. Works of U.S. origin, however, will stay in the public domain.[182] Thus, determination of the status of a work published before January 1, 1978, requires looking to the provisions of the 1909 Act.[183]

The important notice provision under the 1909 Act is § 10, specifying that:

> [a]ny person entitled thereto by this title may secure copyright for his work by publication thereof with the notice of copyright required by this title;

---

[178] *See* 17 U.S.C. §§ 401(d) and 402(d). These sections allow no evidentiary weight to be given to a defense of innocent infringement when proper notice has been affixed to the work.

[179] *See* 17 U.S.C. § 404(a).

[180] *See* H.R. Rep. No. 94-1476, at 146 (1976).

[181] *See id.*

[182] *See* 17 U.S.C. § 104A. The restoration provisions are discussed at *infra* §§ 6.18–6.19.

[183] *See* 17 U.S.C. § 301(a).

> and such notice shall be affixed to each copy thereof published or offered for sale in the United States by authority of the copyright proprietor. . . . [184]

Section 10, by its use of the words "may secure copyright," appears to treat affixation of notice as discretionary for the protection of copyright. To the contrary, however, proper notice was required under the 1909 Act, and an omitted or defective notice on published copies of the work could inject it into the public domain.[185] Moreover, the savings provisions found in § 405(a)[186] of the 1976 Act are not available in the 1909 Act.[187]

[B] Form of Notice

Sections 19 through 21 of the 1909 Act[188] set forth the requirements for proper notice, consisting of the three common elements: the copyright symbol, the proprietor's name, and the year date of first publication. Despite this broad similarity, the requirements for proper notice under the 1909 Act differ from those under the 1976 Act.

As for the copyright symbol: "©," "Copr.," or "Copyright" was sufficient.[189] The 1909 Act did not recognize wide variations from these three recognized forms.[190] However, to promote a minimum of disfigurement for works of art,[191] the 1909 Act allowed a short form of notice for pictorial, graphic, and sculptural works. Here, an initial monogram or trade symbol accompanied by "©" constitutes proper notice.[192] However, if the symbol was not identified with the copyright owner, his name had to appear on some accessible portion of the work such as a margin, back or permanent base, or pedestal.[193] Although the 1976 Act does not provide a similar short form of notice, works published before January 1, 1978, may continue to affix the same short form of notice on copies published afterwards.[194]

---

[184] 17 U.S.C. § 10 (1909 Act).

[185] 17 U.S.C. § 10 (1909 Act). *See, e.g.*, *Original Appalachian Artworks, Inc. v. Toy Loft, Inc.*, 684 F.2d 821, 826 (11th Cir. 1982) (noting that copyright would have been forfeited had work been published in 1977); *Bessett v. Germain*, 18 F. Supp. 249 (D. Mass. 1937); *United Thrift Plan, Inc. v. National Thrift Plan, Inc.*, 34 F.2d 300 (E.D.N.Y. 1929).

[186] 17 U.S.C. § 405(a).

[187] *See* H.R. Rep. No. 94-1476, at 146 (1976).

[188] 17 U.S.C. §§ 19–21 (1909 Act).

[189] *See* 17 U.S.C. § 19 (1909 Act).

[190] *See Fleischer Studios, Inc. v. Ralph A. Freundlich, Inc.*, 73 F.2d 276 (2d Cir. 1934); *American Code Co. v. Bensinger*, 282 F. 829 (2d Cir. 1922).

[191] *Hearings on S. 6330 and H.R. 19-853 Before the Committees on Patents*, 59th Cong., 1st Sess. 97–100 (1906).

[192] *See* 17 U.S.C. § 19 (1909 Act); *Puddu v. Buonamici Statuary, Inc.*, 450 F.2d 401 (2d Cir. 1971); *Dan Kasoff, Inc. v. Palmer Jewelry Mfg. Co.*, 171 F. Supp. 603 (S.D.N.Y. 1959); *Hollywood Jewelry Mfg. Co. v. Dushkin*, 136 F. Supp. 738 (S.D.N.Y. 1955).

[193] *See* 17 U.S.C. § 19 (1909 Act).

[194] 17 U.S.C. Trans. & Supp. Prov. § 108.

[C] Location of Notice

The 1909 Act prescribed specific locations for notice on books, periodicals, and musical works.[195] If the copyright owner did not comply with these specific location provisions, the work could be injected into the public domain for lack of proper notice.[196] A reasonable notice standard applied for other kinds of works such as motion pictures and pictorial, graphic, or sculptural works.[197]

Often highly technical questions arose about the location of notice on repetitive designs such as gift wrapping or dress fabric. One early case required notice of copyright on each design.[198] Later case law loosened this formalistic approach. For example, in *H. M. Kolbe Co., Inc. v. Armgus Textile Co.*,[199] the court held that notice placed every sixteen inches on the selvage of the plaintiff's checkerboard rose design constituted proper notice. Similarly, in *Peter Pan Fabrics, Inc. v. Martin Weiner Corp.*,[200] a flexible approach was taken to notice of copyright placed on the selvage of a fabric design that would either be cut off from the fabric or rendered undetectable on a dress. Here, Learned Hand adopted a "commercial impairment test" in which, at least in the case of a deliberate copyist, the defendant has the burden to show that notice could have been embodied in the design without impairing its market value.

[D] Year Date

The requirements for affixing the year date are less specific under the 1909 Act than under the 1976 Act. The year date of first publication was required only for printed literary, musical, dramatic works,[201] and sound recordings.[202] For other works, such as motion pictures and pictorial works, the copyright symbol and copyright owner's name sufficed.[203]

[E] Omission of Notice

Section 21 of the 1909 Act provided:

> Where the copyright proprietor has sought to comply with the provisions of this title with respect to notice, the omission by accident or mistake of the

---

[195] 17 U.S.C. § 20 (1909 Act).

[196] *See, e.g.*, *United Thrift Plan v. National Thrift Plan*, 34 F.2d 300 (E.D.N.Y. 1929) (holding notice in proper form but on the last page of a ten-page booklet was equivalent to no notice at all).

[197] *See Coventry Ware, Inc. v. Reliance Picture Frame Co.*, 288 F.2d 193 (2d Cir. 1961); *Scarves by Vera, Inc. v. United Merchants and Mfrs., Inc.*, 173 F. Supp. 625 (S.D.N.Y. 1959); *Trifari, Krussman & Fishel, Inc. v. Charel Co., Inc.*, 134 F. Supp. 551 (S.D.N.Y. 1955).

[198] *See DeJonge & Co. v. Breaker de Kassler Co.*, 235 U.S. 33 (1914).

[199] 315 F.2d 70 (2d Cir. 1963).

[200] 274 F.2d 487 (2d Cir. 1960).

[201] 17 U.S.C. § 19 (1909 Act); *see Wildman v. New York Times Co.*, 42 F. Supp. 412 (S.D.N.Y. 1941).

[202] 17 U.S.C. § 19 (1909 Act).

[203] *See Advertisers Exch., Inc. v. Anderson*, 144 F.2d 907 (8th Cir. 1944); *Abli, Inc., v. Standard Brands Paint Co.*, 323 F. Supp. 1400 (C.D. Cal. 1970); *Florence Art Co. v. Quartite Creative Corp.*, 158 U.S.P.Q. 382 (N.D. Ill. 1968); *Leigh v. Gerber*, 86 F. Supp. 320 (S.D.N.Y. 1949).

prescribed notice from a particular copy or copies shall not invalidate the copyright or prevent recovery for infringement against any person who, after actual notice of the copyright, begins an undertaking to infringe it. . . . [204]

This provision appears to be similar to that of the original notice provisions of the 1976 Act,[205] but there are significant differences. Section 21 applied only to accident or mistakes due to some sort of mechanical failure[206] in affixing notice and not to inadvertence[207] or mistake of law.[208] In addition, the copyright owner must have omitted notice on a particular copy or copies; an omission of notice from all of the copies would not be excused by § 21.[209] How "few" are a "few"? The case law suggests a percentage test. The court in *American Greetings Corp. v. Kleinfarb Corp.*[210] indicated that § 21 applied where the copyright owner omitted notice from 500,000 of twenty-two million copies, or two percent of the total number of copies.

[F] U.S. Works First Published Outside the United States

The notice requirement is not just limited to works published in the United States. The 1976 Act, as originally enacted, requires that notice be placed on works published here or abroad.[211] The House Report justifies this requirement because of the great flow of works across national boundaries.[212] To protect economic and proprietary interests in this intellectual material, the notice requirement applied equally to works published abroad.[213] Thus even after the U.S. entered into the Berne Convention, notice is still required for all works — no matter the place of location.

---

[204] 17 U.S.C. § 21 (1909 Act).

[205] 17 U.S.C. § 405(a)(1).

[206] *See Leon B. Rosenblatt Textiles, Ltd. v. M. Lowenstein & Sons, Inc.*, 321 F. Supp. 186 (S.D.N.Y. 1970); *Florence Art Co., Inc. v. Quartite Creative Corp.*, 158 U.S.P.Q. 382 (N.D. Ill. 1968) (upholding copyright where mechanical difficulties led to partial obliteration of notice on some copies — § 21 not expressly invoked); *Strauss v. Penn Printing & Publishing Co.*, 220 F. 977 (E.D. Pa. 1915).

[207] *See Seiff v. Continental Auto Supply, Inc.*, 39 F. Supp. 683 (D. Minn. 1941); *Basevi v. Edward O'Toole Co.*, 26 F. Supp. 41 (S.D.N.Y. 1939). *But cf. Rexnord, Inc. v. Modern Handling Sys., Inc.*, 379 F. Supp. 1190, 1197 (D. Del. 1974) (stating that omission of notice " . . . must occur despite [the claimant's] efforts to the contrary; it must be, in short, inadvertent").

[208] *See Puddu v. Buonamici Statuary, Inc.*, 450 F.2d 401 (2d Cir. 1971); *Rexnord, Inc. v. Modern Handling Sys., Inc.*, 379 F. Supp. 1190 (D. Del. 1974); *Gardenia Flowers, Inc. v. Joseph Markovits, Inc.*, 280 F. Supp. 776 (S.D.N.Y. 1968); *Wildman v. New York Times Co.*, 42 F. Supp. 412 (S.D.N.Y. 1941).

[209] *See Data Cash Sys., Inc. v. JS & A Group, Inc.*, 628 F.2d 1038 (7th Cir. 1980); *Puddu v. Buonamici Statuary, Inc.*, 450 F.2d 401 (2d Cir. 1971); *Krafft v. Cohen*, 117 F.2d 579 (3d Cir. 1941); *J. A. Richards, Inc. v. New York Post, Inc.*, 23 F. Supp. 619 (S.D.N.Y. 1938).

[210] 400 F. Supp. 228, 231 (S.D.N.Y. 1975).

[211] 17 U.S.C. § 401(a). The use of the phrase "or elsewhere" indicates that the requirements of notice are applicable to foreign editions of works copyrighted in the United States. *See* H.R. Rep. No. 94-1476, at 144 (1976).

[212] H.R. Rep. No. 94-1476, at 144 (1976).

[213] *See Hasbro Bradley, Inc. v. Sparkle Toys, Inc.*, 780 F.2d 189 (2d Cir. 1985) (noting that U.S. law requires notice even on copies of the work distributed outside the United States).

Whether the copyright owner had to abide by the formalities of the 1909 Act for works published abroad has never been resolved, and the issue has provoked a split of authority in the case law.[214] The extent to which the foreign publication will affect the availability of copyright protection under the 1909 Act is important for two reasons. First, if proper notice is required for a work published abroad, one must take into account the foreign activity to determine whether a work has entered the public domain before 1978.[215] Second, for works published after 1978, the copyright owner has the option to choose the 1909 or 1976 Act's notice requirements.[216]

Despite the split in authority on this issue, the dominant view is that the 1909 Act's notice requirement did not apply outside the U.S. The leading case interpreting the 1909 Act's requirement for works published abroad is *Heim v. Universal Pictures Co.*[217] In *Heim*, the court took the position that publication abroad without notice did not place a work into the public domain in the United States. Justice Frank argued that because § 9 of the 1909 Act merely required that "notice be affixed to each copy published or offered for sale in the United States,"[218] its provisions apply only to U.S. publications.[219] The contrary view, asserting that notice was required for foreign publications, looked to the language of § 10 of the 1909 Act's first clause, which provides that, "[a]ny person entitled thereto by this title may secure copyright for his work by publication thereof with the notice of copyright required by this title. . . . "[220]

Thus, the language "under this title" could be construed as requiring notice as set forth in §§ 19 and 20.[221] Advocates of extraterritorial application of the notice requirement dismiss the second clause of § 10, stating that the phrase "such notice shall be affixed to each copy thereof published or offered for sale in the United States . . . " applies only to preservation of copyright for works on which

---

214 Common law copyright protection in the United States was lost upon publication of the work, even if publication occurred abroad. *See Hill & Range Songs, Inc. v. London Records, Inc.*, 142 N.Y.S. 2d 311 (1955); *see also McKay v. Barbour*, 199 Misc. 893 (N.Y. Sup. Ct. 1950). Publications occurring within the United States must bear the required notice under the 1909 Act to command statutory copyright protection.

215 *Data Cash Sys., Inc. v. JS & A Group, Inc.*, 628 F.2d 1038 (7th Cir. 1980); *Conner v. Mark I, Inc.*, 509 F. Supp. 1179 (N.D. Ill. 1981); *Excel Promotions Corp. v. Babylon Beacon, Inc.*, 207 U.S.P.Q. 616 (E.D.N.Y. 1979).

216 *See* 17 U.S.C. Trans. & Supp. Prov. § 108.

217 154 F.2d 480 (2d. Cir. 1946).

218 *Id.* at 486.

219 *See* 17 U.S.C. § 10 (1909 Act); *G. & C. Merriam Co. v. United Dictionary Co.*, 146 F. 354 (7th Cir. 1906). *Heim* was reconfirmed in *Twin Books Corp. v. Walt Disney Co.*, 83 F.3d 1162 (9th Cir. 1996) (finding "Bambi, A Life in the Woods" was not injected into the public domain for failure to apply notice in a 1923 German publication). *See also Société Civile Succession Richard Guino v. Renoir*, 549 F.3d 1182 (9th Cir. 2008) (holding sculptures published in France in 1917 with no notice were neither "in the public domain or copyrighted" in 1978, and were entitled to the life-plus-70-years term of § 303). For an extensive analysis, see Tyler Ochoa, *Copyright Protection for Works of Foreign Origin*, *in* The Internationalization of Law and Legal Education (Klabbers & Sellers eds., 2008).

220 17 U.S.C. § 10 (1909 Act).

221 17 U.S.C. §§ 19, 20 (1909 Act).

copyright has already been secured.[222]

This reading of the 1909 Act is not the dominant view and certainly not the better view in light of the presumption against the extraterritorial application of U.S. copyright law. Also, there is nothing in the legislative history of the 1909 Act indicating that Congress wished to vary from the exclusively territorial application of the U.S. copyright law.

Part III. THE MANUFACTURING CLAUSE

§ 4.15 THE DEMISE BUT CONTINUING IMPORTANCE OF THE MANUFACTURING CLAUSE

The manufacturing clause, a prominent feature of both the 1909 and 1976 Copyright Acts, prohibited importation into the United States of English language literary works by American authors unless the works were manufactured, printed, and bound in the United States or Canada.[223]

The manufacturing clause was in effect protectionist legislation, benefiting American printers at the expense of American authors. A unique and much criticized feature of American law since 1891,[224] the manufacturing clause has been a trap for unwary authors, a barrier to United States' participation in the Berne Union, and a violation of the General Agreement on Tariffs and Trade.[225] Fortunately, by its own terms, § 601 of the 1976 Act expired on July 1, 1986.[226]

Even though the manufacturing clause is currently dead, it cannot be totally ignored. It is of continuing, though limited, importance because of its effect on non-complying works under both the 1976 Act and the 1909 Act. The following sections outline the 1976 and 1909 Acts' versions of the manufacturing clause, examining first what it entailed and then turning to the effect of non-compliance with its provisions.

---

[222] NIMMER ON COPYRIGHT § 7.12[D][2][a] (2014).

[223] Under the 1976 Act, the work could be manufactured in Canada as well as the United States. *See* 17 U.S.C. § 601(a). Under the 1909 Act, only the United States could be the place of manufacture. *See* 17 U.S.C. § 16 (1909 Act).

[224] 26 Stat. 1106 (1891).

[225] General Agreement on Tariffs and Trade (GATT), 55 U.N.T.S. 194, T.I.A.S. No. 1700.

[226] Section 601 was originally to be repealed as of July 1, 1982, though the House Report suggests the even earlier date of January 1, 1981. *See* H.R. REP. NO. 94-1476, at 166 (1976). Section 602 was amended by Pub. L. No. 97-215, 96 Stat. 178 (1982), to extend the date of repeal to July 1, 1986. President Reagan vetoed the Act of July 13, 1982, but the veto was overridden by the House and the Senate, and § 601 expired on July 1, 1986.

§ 4.16 THE MANUFACTURING CLAUSE UNDER THE 1976 ACT

[A] Generally

The subject matter of the manufacturing clause extends to "copies of a work consisting preponderantly of nondramatic literary material that is in the English language."[227] Other varieties of copyrightable subject matter such as pictorial, graphic, and sculptural works were exempted from the provisions of the manufacturing clause. Importation of copies falling into these narrow confines is prohibited if these works were not manufactured[228] in the United States or Canada.

[B] The "Preponderantly" Requirement

Works were subject to the manufacturing requirement only if they consisted "preponderantly" of nondramatic literary material in English; the nondramatic literary material must have exceeded the exempted material in "importance." Thus, a book consisting of graphics, photographs, or illustrations with a short preface, brief captions, and an index in English would not meet the "preponderantly" standard.[229] But even if the English language portions of the book were extensive enough to meet the "preponderantly" test, only those aspects would be required to be manufactured in the United States. The manufacture of the pictorial portion of the book outside the United States or Canada would not be a violation of the manufacturing clause.

[C] Exceptions to the Manufacturing Provisions

The manufacturing clause was subject to several exceptions.[230] It applied only to American authors and domiciliaries on the date of importation or distribution of a work into the United States. Copies imported for personal use, use by federal or state government, educational, scholarly, or religious purposes, and works in Braille were exempt. In addition, two thousand copies of a non-complying work could be imported pursuant to certain formalities. Finally, individual authors who arranged for manufacture of the first publication abroad were exempt.

---

[227] 17 U.S.C. § 601(a).

[228] What constitutes "manufacture" is a highly technical question. Some of these complexities are reflected in The Compendium of Copyright Office Practices, Chs. 1210, 1211 (1984), which tries to define the meaning of the term in light of 17 U.S.C. § 601(c).

[229] *See generally* H.R. Rep. No. 94-1476, at 166–67 (1976). However, in *Stonehill Communications, Inc. v. Martuge*, 512 F. Supp. 349, 352 (S.D.N.Y. 1981), the court found the "importance" test suggested by the House Report too vague for practical application. The court adopted instead an objective or mechanical test such that " . . . a book 'consists of preponderantly nondram[a]tic literary material . . . in the English language' when more than half of its surface area, exclusive of margins, consists of English-language text."

[230] *See* 17 U.S.C. § 601(b).

[D] Effect of Non-Compliance Under the 1976 Act

Failure to comply with the manufacturing clause did not result in forfeiture of copyright. The sanctions imposed were less drastic but nonetheless serious. The non-complying copies could be seized, forfeited, and destroyed by the Department of the Treasury and the U.S. Postal Service.[231] In addition, violation constituted a complete defense in any civil or criminal action for infringement of the copyright owner's exclusive rights to reproduce and distribute his work.[232] To raise this defense the infringer had to prove: (1) that the copyright owner imported non-complying copies of the work, (2) that the infringing copies were manufactured in the United States or Canada, and (3) "that the infringement was commenced before the effective date of registration for an authorized edition of the work."[233] The defense extended not only to the nondramatic literary aspects of the work but also to aspects such as photographs or foreign language materials, if the same copyright owner owned both types of materials. Although the manufacturing clause has expired, its violation can arguably be used as a defense against a non-complying work publicly distributed between January 1, 1978, and July 1, 1986, the expiration date of the manufacturing clause. Thus, the possibility of a defense based on plaintiff's noncompliance remains until the copyright owner registers an American edition in compliance with the law.

§ 4.17 THE MANUFACTURING CLAUSE UNDER THE 1909 ACT

[A] Generally

The manufacturing clause under the 1909 Act was more restrictive than under the 1976 Copyright Act. Section 16 of the 1909 Act established the major requirements.[234] Under its terms, any printed book or periodical in the English language, as well as foreign language books of American authors, had to be manufactured in the United States. Canadian manufacture was prohibited under the 1909 Act as well. The manufacturing clause requirements encompassed not just the texts of books but the illustrations as well.

[B] *Ad Interim* Protection

Under the 1909 Act manufacturing clause, *ad interim* copyright protection could be obtained for English language books and periodicals manufactured abroad.[235] To secure *ad interim* protection, the claimant had to deposit and register the *ad interim* claim in the U.S. Copyright Office within six months of first publication abroad. Fifteen hundred copies of the work could then be imported into the United

---

[231] *See* 17 U.S.C. § 603(a).

[232] *See* 17 U.S.C. § 601(d).

[233] *See* 17 U.S.C. § 601(d)(3).

[234] 17 U.S.C. § 16 (1909 Act).

[235] *See generally* NIMMER ON COPYRIGHT § 7.23[F] (2014).

States within six months of foreign publication. *Ad interim* protection endured for five years, measured from the date of publication abroad. If, within the five-year period, an edition of the work was published in compliance with the manufacturing clause, the work could claim a twenty-eight-year copyright term, measured from the date of its first publication. According to some case law, failure to register within the six-month period and failure to publish the complying edition within the five-year period resulted in the loss of copyright protection.[236]

[C] Forfeiture by False Affidavit and General Non-Compliance

Under § 17 of the 1909 Act,[237] anyone depositing a work with the Copyright Office also had to submit an affidavit swearing that manufacturing clause requirements had been met. Section 18 provided that knowingly making a false affidavit forfeited copyright.[238] It was unclear, however, whether failure to comply with manufacturing clause requirements without making a knowingly false affidavit resulted in forfeiture of copyright.

Whether the work was injected into the public domain is a matter of controversy. The answer to this question is important because works going into the public domain are not revived by the 1976 Act or by the subsequent Berne Convention Implementation Act amendments. Although the case law is not clear on this issue, the better view is that non-compliance did not inject a work into the public domain.[239] Section 18 specifically provided for forfeiture when a knowingly false affidavit is submitted, whereas forfeiture is not mentioned as the result of general non-compliance with manufacturing requirements. This implies that forfeiture did not occur except where expressly stated.

---

[236] *See* H.R. Rep. No. 94-1476, at 164 (1976). The issue is whether failure to comply with manufacturing clause provisions and *ad interim* requirements places the work in the public domain or invalidates an author's copyright enforcement rights. *See Hoffenberg v. Kaminstein*, 396 F.2d 684 (D.C. Cir. 1968) (noting that failure to comply justified Copyright Office's refusal to register a work); *Bentley v. Tibbals*, 223 F. 247 (2d Cir. 1915).

[237] 17 U.S.C. § 17 (1909 Act).

[238] 17 U.S.C. § 18 (1909 Act).

[239] *See, e.g.*, *Hoffenberg v. Kaminstein*, 396 F.2d 684 (D.C. Cir. 1968); *but see Meccano, Ltd. v. Wagner*, 234 F. 912 (S.D. Ohio 1916). Professor Nimmer argues that copyright in a work would not be forfeited if non-compliance was not accompanied by a knowingly false affidavit in connection with a claim for registration. In this situation, copyright would have been suspended during the period of the 1909 Act, but would have been revived under the 1976 Act. Thus, non-compliance with the *ad interim* provisions under the 1909 Act is a moot issue today. *See* Nimmer on Copyright § 7.23[E] (2014).

Chapter 5

OWNERSHIP OF COPYRIGHT

§ 5.01 INTRODUCTION AND CHAPTER OVERVIEW

Chapter two of the 1976 Copyright Act concerns ownership and transfer of copyright. It begins with the proposition that copyright vests initially in the author or authors of a work. This key term, "author," is left undefined by the Act, but it is generally accepted that an author is the person who originates a work.[1] The author is most frequently the creator of a work, but this is not always the case. For example, an employer is considered the author of a work made for hire.

Initial ownership of copyright is easy to determine for works created by an individual author on his or her own motivation. Many works of authorship, however, are created pursuant to employment (works made for hire), and others are created by the collaborative efforts of several authors who may contribute their authorship at different times (joint works). Under the 1909 Act, these two situations presented difficult conceptual problems in determining the nature and scope of copyright ownership. The 1976 Act has done much to clarify some of the more unsatisfactory doctrines under the 1909 Act. However, even with this added clarity, important questions about copyright ownership are left open. For this reason, the case law developed under the 1909 Act is sometimes used to fill in those gaps left unattended by the 1976 Act. Moreover, rules that were developed under the 1909 Act and its case law are of utmost importance in determining the ownership status of works created before January 1, 1978, the effective date of the 1976 Act.[2]

This chapter, which is divided into two parts, concerns ownership of copyright. Part I examines how copyright ownership vests, focusing on two important situations in which ownership rights in works are created and allocated: works made for hire and joint works. Part II concerns the special nature of contracts transferring some or all of the bundle of rights which comprise copyright ownership. This part examines the doctrine of divisibility, how copyright assignments and licenses are drafted and construed, and the importance of recording documents in the Copyright Office.

---

[1] 17 U.S.C. § 201(a).

[2] For an overview of the extent to which the 1976 Act is retroactive, see Susan K. Beckett, *The Copyright Act of 1976: When Is It Effective?*, 24 Bull. Copyright Off. Soc'y 391 (1977).

Part I. INITIAL OWNERSHIP: WORKS MADE FOR HIRE AND JOINT WORKS

§ 5.02 WORKS MADE FOR HIRE

[A] Generally

In copyright law, certain works created as part of one's job responsibilities are called "works made for hire," and as such they are treated differently than works created by individual authors on their own motivation. For a work made for hire, initial ownership vests in the employer, who is considered the author of the work.[3] From a practical, economic standpoint, this category is significant. Works created in the course of employment constitute a large percentage of all copyrighted works.

Important legal consequences spring from categorizing a work as one made for hire. First, the employer/author has the entire right to the work; the employee-creator has no ownership rights whatsoever.[4] Second, a work made for hire is not subject to the termination provisions of the 1976 Act.[5] Third, the normal duration for a copyrighted work is the life of the author plus seventy years. Works made for hire, however, have copyright protection for 95 years from publication, or 120 years from creation, whichever is less.[6] Fourth, because the employer is the author of a work made for hire, the nationality and status of the employer can have important consequences. For example, if the employer is the United States government, copyright cannot be claimed at all.[7] In addition, if the employer is a foreign national, the manufacturing clause[8] will not apply, and questions of copyrightability may be determined in certain circumstances by the foreign employer/author's nationality or domicile.[9]

---

[3] *See* 17 U.S.C.§ 201(b):

> In the case of a work made for hire, the employer or other person for whom the work was prepared is considered the author for purposes of this title, and, unless the parties have expressly agreed otherwise in a written instrument signed by them, owns all of the rights comprised in the copyright.

[4] For an argument that the term "employee" according to "work made for hire" doctrine should be interpreted in a manner that best accomplishes the goals of the Constitution, see Assaf Jacob, *Tort Made for Hire — Reconsidering the* CCNV *Case*, 11 Yale J. L. & Tech. 96 (2009).

[5] Under the 1976 Act, an author can terminate a transfer of a copyright interest between the thirty-fifth and fortieth years under § 203 and for the 19-year extension of the renewal under § 304. These termination-of-transfer provisions do not apply to works made for hire. For a discussion of termination of transfer, see *infra* §§ 6.11–6.17.

[6] *See* 17 U.S.C. § 302(c). For works copyrighted before 1978, the employer-author of a work made for hire has the right to claim the second 28-year renewal term. For a discussion of copyright renewal, see *infra* §§ 6.05–6.10.

[7] *See* 17 U.S.C. § 105.

[8] For a discussion of the now-defunct manufacturing clause, which required works published in English to be manufactured in the United States, see *supra* §§ 4.15–4.17.

[9] *See* 17 U.S.C. § 104. For a discussion of foreign authors, see *infra* § 12.08.

[B] Works Made for Hire: An Overview of the Basic Standards

Section 101[10] defines a work made for hire as follows:

> (1) a work prepared by an employee within the scope of his or her employment; or (2) a work specially ordered or commissioned for use as a contribution to a collective work, as a part of a motion picture or other audiovisual work, as a translation, as a supplementary work, as a compilation, as an instructional text, as a test, as answer material for a test, or as an atlas, if the parties expressly agree in a written instrument signed by them that the work shall be considered a work made for hire.

Subdivision (1) of the basic definition concerns works that are created by an employee within the scope of employment. This subsection must be read in connection with § 201(b), which provides that "[t]he employer or other person for whom the work was prepared is considered the author for purposes of this title, and, unless the parties have expressly agreed otherwise in a written instrument signed by them, owns all of the rights comprised in the copyright."[11]

In other words, when a work is created by an employee within the scope of employment, it is presumed to be made for hire unless the parties agree otherwise in a written instrument. Thus, a graphic artist who works full time as an employee for an advertising agency will not own the copyright on his drawings made for a client of the firm — nor will she be considered the author of the work — unless she and the firm expressly agree otherwise in a written instrument signed by them that designates the employee as the owner of all rights comprised in the copyright. Only then will the presumption in favor of the employer be overcome and the actual creative employee be considered the author and owner of all rights in the work.

Subdivision (2) concerns specially commissioned works, those works that are created by independent contractors[12] — persons who are not salaried workers of the commissioning party. The Copyright Act imposes two requirements to create a work made for hire for specially commissioned works. First, subdivision (2) of the § 101 definition limits the creation of a work made for hire to nine enumerated categories of works.

As set forth in the Act, these nine categories are as follows:

(1) a contribution to a collective work;[13]

---

[10] Whether a work qualifies as a work made for hire will depend on several objective factors rather than on the intent of the parties to an employment relationship. The Act sets forth two mutually exclusive ways, in the two subdivisions of the statutory definition, by which a work made for hire is created. 17 U.S.C. § 101 (work made for hire).

[11] 17 U.S.C. § 201(b).

[12] An independent contractor may be defined as: "[o]ne who is entrusted to undertake a specific project but who is left free to do the assigned work and to choose the method for accomplishing it." Black's Law Dictionary 639 (9th ed. 2009).

[13] 17 U.S.C. § 101 of the Copyright Act defines a "collective work" as "a work, such as a periodical issue, anthology, or encyclopedia, in which a number of contributions, constituting separate and independent works in themselves, are assembled into a collective whole."

(2) a part of a motion picture or other audiovisual work;

(3) a translation;

(4) a supplementary work;[14]

(5) a compilation;

(6) an instructional text;

(7) a test;

(8) answer material for a test;

(9) an atlas.

Second, falling into one of these categories is not enough; to qualify as a work made for hire, the parties must "expressly agree in a written instrument signed by them that the work shall be considered a work made for hire."[15] In other words, even if a specially commissioned contribution to a collective work falls into one of the nine categories (*e.g.*, a compilation or an instructional text), a work made for hire is not created unless the hiring party and the independent contractor have explicitly stated their intention to do so in a signed writing. On the other hand, no contract, however explicit, is sufficient if the independent contractor's work product does not fall into one of the nine categories. Thus, if A commissions B to make a sculpture for his home, a work made for hire cannot be created even if the parties so agree in a written contract because B's creation does not fit into one of the nine categories.[16] In sum, subdivision (2) makes it more difficult to create a work made for hire for a work commissioned from an independent contractor than one created in the scope of employment.

The nature of the writing necessary to create a work made for hire differs from other written contracts in that it must be signed by *both* parties.[17] In addition, the writing must indicate unambiguously that the parties agree to a work made for hire.[18] Thus, a check endorsement legend that mentions only an "assignment" is insufficient to create a work made for hire. It is not clear whether a failure to specifically mention the words "work made for hire" will invalidate the writing. It would seem, however, if the intent of the parties was clear, a work made for hire

---

[14] Section 101 defines a work made for hire as:

> [a] work prepared for publication as a secondary adjunct to a work by another author for the purpose of introducing, concluding, illustrating, explaining, revising, commenting upon, or assisting in the use of the other work, such as forewords, afterwords, pictorial illustrations, maps, charts, tables, editorial notes, musical arrangements, answer material for tests, bibliographies, appendixes, and indexes. .

17 U.S.C. § 101

[15] 17 U.S.C. §101 (defining a work made for hire).

[16] Despite congressional intent to limit strictly the creation of works made for hire for commissioned works, a broad interpretation of supplementary and collective works would encompass a large percentage of work done by free-lance artists and writers. *See* Note, Walter R. Sadler, *Free Lance Artists, Works for Hire, and the Copyright Act of 1976*, 15 U.C. Davis L. Rev. 703, 708 (1982).

[17] *See Schiller & Schmidt, Inc. v. Nordisco Corp.*, 969 F.2d 410, 412 (7th Cir. 1992).

[18] *See Playboy Enters., Inc. v. Dumas*, 831 F. Supp. 295 (S.D.N.Y. 1993).

could nonetheless be created absent the magic words.[19]

At what point in time must the writing be executed to create a work made for hire? In other words, must there be a pre-creation writing for the purposes of the doctrine? Section 101(2) is silent on the issue and the courts are in conflict. One view is that parties must agree that the commissioned work is a work made for hire before the work is created, but agreement may be either oral or implied. Thus, the writing may date from after creation if it confirms the prior agreement, explicitly or implicitly.[20] The problem with this approach is that it introduces a degree of uncertainty in the determination of ownership of a copyrighted work.

With this drawback in mind, other courts have insisted that the writing requirement necessitates that the written memorandum precede the creation of the property to serve the purpose of identifying the non-creator owner unequivocally. The latter view also has the virtue that it encourages the creation of an unambiguous written record before the work is created; it protects against false claims of oral agreement, while rendering ownership rights clear and readily marketable.[21]

Under the 1909 Act, commissioned works were given substantially different treatment, clearly favoring the rights of employers — the commissioning party. Case law established a presumption that the commissioning party was the author of a work made for hire unless the parties intended the contrary. The 1976 Act has clearly reversed that presumption. The reason for this change, according to the legislative history, was to remedy an inequitable situation where the copyright on a work created by an independent contractor would presumptively fall into the hands of a commissioning party.[22]

§ 5.03 DISTINGUISHING BETWEEN EMPLOYERS AND INDEPENDENT CONTRACTORS

[A] Clarifying the Categories: *Community for Creative Non-Violence v. Reid*

On its surface, the statutory framework set forth in § 101 is relatively straightforward, one in which Congress intended to limit works made for hire to two bright-line categories. Despite this clarity of purpose, the courts differed significantly on the meaning of "employee" and "scope of employment" in subdivision (1) and "specially ordered or commissioned works" in subdivision (2). These key terms are undefined in the Act and undiscussed in the committee reports.

---

19 *But see Armento v. Laser Image, Inc.*, 950 F. Supp. 719, 731 (W.D.N.C. 1996) (requiring the explicit words).

20 *See Playboy Enters., Inc.*, 53 F.3d at 560 (holding that post-creation writing is acceptable).

21 *See Schiller & Schmidt, Inc.*, 969 F.2d at 412 (holding that the writing must precede the creation of the work).

22 *See* H.R. Rep. No. 94-1476, at 121 (1976).

Some courts refused to accept the intent of Congress, by blurring the distinction between the two subdivisions in the definition of a work made for hire. The issue that had divided the case law was whether the clause "employee within the scope of his or her employment" in subdivision (1) could encompass an independent contractor in some circumstances. One line of cases interpreted the term "employee" expansively, extending its meaning to employment relationships involving independent contractors.[23] In contrast, another line of cases narrowly interpreted "employee," limiting it, for example, to the master-servant relationship in agency law.[24]

The meaning of "employee" was resolved in *Community for Creative Non-Violence v. Reid*,[25] in which the Supreme Court read the statute literally. In so doing, it limited the definition of employee in subdivision (1) to the master-servant relationship. In *CCNV*, a charitable organization dedicated to eliminating homelessness claimed copyright ownership of a statue called "Third World America." CCNV had commissioned the sculptor, Reid, to create a sculpture dramatizing the plight of the homeless for a Christmas pageant in Washington, D.C. CCNV supplied the plans and sketches, ultimately executed by Reid. On that basis, CCNV claimed ownership of the copyright in the sculpture as an employer for hire.

The Supreme Court, in finding that the work could not be a work made for hire, reviewed the four bases for a work made for hire that had emerged in the case law: (1) a work made for hire comes into existence when the hiring party retains the right to control the work;[26] (2) a work made for hire comes into existence when the hiring party actually retains control in the creation of the work;[27] (3) the term "employee" applies only to those persons so defined under agency law;[28] and (4) the term "employee" only refers to formal salaried employees.[29] The Court rejected the first two tests: the right to control and actual control tests. Instead, it selected

[23] *See, e.g.*, *Aldon Accessories, Ltd. v. Spiegel, Inc.*, 738 F.2d 548 (2d Cir. 1984) (holding that an independent contractor can be considered an employee under subdivision (1) of the work made for hire definition if the hiring author directed and supervised the independent contractor). Courts in subsequent cases had difficulty applying *Aldon*'s supervision standard and produced inconsistent results. One point of controversy was whether the right to direct and supervise meant that the right had to be actually and actively exercised. Or was the right to supervise the independent contractor enough in itself to create a work made for hire? The cases were in conflict on this point. In *Peregrine v. Lauren Corp.*, 601 F. Supp. 828 (D. Colo. 1985), the court found a work made for hire where the commissioning party had the right to supervise the way in which a free-lance photographer did the work, though the court did not define the actual degree to which the employer exercised this right. Alternatively, in *Sygma Photo News, Inc. v. Globe Int'l, Inc.*, 616 F. Supp. 1153 (S.D.N.Y. 1985), official photographs of the British royal family taken at their insistence, and with their right to supervise and approve the photographs, were not works made for hire. Here, the court found that the royal family insufficiently exercised its right to supervise. Also adopting *Aldon* is *Evans Newton, Inc. v. Chi. Sys. Software*, 793 F.2d 889, 894 (7th Cir. 1986).

[24] *See* RESTATEMENT (SECOND) OF AGENCY § 220 (1958). *See, e.g.*, *Easter Seal Soc'y for Crippled Children (and Adults of Louisiana, Inc.) v. Playboy Enters.*, 815 F.2d 323 (5th Cir. 1987).

[25] 490 U.S. 730 (1989).

[26] *See Peregrine*, 601 F. Supp. 828 (D. Colo. 1985).

[27] *See Aldon Accessories Ltd.*, 738 F.2d at 551.

[28] *See Easter Seal Soc'y*, 815 F.2d at 335–36.

[29] *See Dumas v. Gommerman*, 865 F.2d 1093 (9th Cir. 1989).

the third alternative, holding that the words "employee" and "employment" describe the conventional master-servant relationship as understood by the common law of agency. In addition to complying with the legislative history, the court pointed out that this interpretation seems more consistent with the logic of the work made for hire provisins. Why have a subdivision (2) which limits the creation of a work made for hire to nine situations for a commissioned work if subdivision (1) can be read so broadly as to cover commissioned works as well?[30] The rationale is that the ambiguous words "employee," "employer," and "independent contractor" would be rendered more precise by tying their meanings to agency law. As a result, a more precise definition for these key terms will provide buyers and sellers with greater predictability in their dealings.

Thus, to determine if someone is an employee under the law of agency, the following factual matters must be considered:

> [R]ight to control the manner and means by which the product is accomplished . . . the skill required; the source of the instrumentalities and tools; the location of the work; the duration of the relationship between the parties; whether the hiring party has the right to assign additional projects to the hired party's discretion over when and how long to work; the method of payment; the hired party's role in hiring and paying assistants; whether the work is part of the regular business of the hiring party; whether the hiring party is in business; the provision of employee benefits; and the tax treatment of the hired party.[31]

Here, Reid had all the attributes of an independent contractor. He supplied his own tools, worked for a limited time on a specific project, hired his own assistants at his own discretion, and was paid a flat sum for his work. In addition, Reid neither received employee benefits nor contributed to the unemployment insurance of the worker's compensation club. Thus, Reid was not an employee for hire and, as an independent contractor, retained copyright in the work. However, the evidence indicated that the work might be a joint work if the commissioning party contributed sufficient authorship.

In applying these criteria, the Court held that Reid was not an employee of CCNV but an independent contractor. CCNV, as hiring party, did exercise actual control over details in the creation of the sculpture. The extent of control, however, is only one of the criteria to be applied in determining the work made for hire status. The court found that all the other circumstances favored Reid. Hired for only a short two-month period, the sculptor supplied his own tools, worked in his own studio, had total discretion in hiring and paying assistants, and received no employment benefits (or payment of taxes) from CCNV. In addition, CCNV was not in the business of creating sculptures. Thus, Reid was not an employee for hire but an independent contractor and owner of the copyright in the sculpture. The Court did remand the case to the District Court to determine whether a joint work was

---

[30] *See* H.R. Rep. No. 94-1476, at 121 (1976). See the excellent discussion of the legislative history in William F. Patry, Copyright Law and Practice 373–82 (1994) and Jessica D. Litman, *Copyright, Compromise, and Legislative History*, 72 Cornell L. Rev. 857, 900–01 (1987).

[31] *CCNV*, 490 U.S. at 751–52.

created. If this were the case, CCNV and Reid would be co-owners of the work.

[B] Who is an "Employee": Applying the *Restatement of Agency* Criteria After *CCNV*

If one of the objectives of the Supreme Court in *CCNV v. Reid* was to accomplish clear and predictable rules for works made for hire, it has fallen far short of the ideal. The *CCNV* approach has hardly eliminated problems in deciding who is an employee under the statute.[32] Multifactor tests, such as that of the *Restatement (Second) of Agency*, are often difficult to apply.[33] This should come as no surprise. Most of the thirteen *Restatement* factors enumerated in *CCNV* are intensely factual, and none of them are independently determinative. As expected, most courts since *CCNV* have weighed the factors variously, according to the totality of the parties' relationship.[34] Some factors, however, will be more important and will undoubtedly be considered in every case. These more salient factors may include: (1) the hiring party's right to control the manner and means of creation, (2) the skill required, (3) the provision of employee benefits, (4) the tax treatment of the hired party, and (5) whether the hiring party has the right to assign additional projects to the hired party.[35]

[C] *CCNV* in Perspective: Will It Help the Independent Contractor?

CCNV seems to be a substantial victory for freelance (independent contractor) authors. Now, the work made for hire category can only be created in certain narrow contexts (the nine categories) and only if the parties sign a written contract. The statute, however, does not delineate which parties are required to

---

[32] For a comprehensive overview of the issues involved in applying the common law agency test, see Robert Kreiss, *Scope of Employment and Being an Employee Under the Work-Made-for-Hire Provision of the Copyright Law: Applying the Common-Law Agency Tests*, 40 U. Kan. L. Rev. 119 (1991). For a discussion of how the common law rules of agency have been reconsidered and an argument that business owners need to adjust their practices in response, see Jon Garon & Elaine D. Ziff, *The Work-Made-for-Hire Doctrine Revisited: Startup and Technology Employees and the Use of Contracts in a Hiring Relationship*, 12 Minn. J.L. Sci. & Tech. 489 (2011).

[33] The unsettled state of the work made for hire doctrine has prompted calls for an amendment to the 1976 Copyright Act clarifying the meaning of the phrase, "a work prepared by an employee within the scope of his or her employment." One attempt would limit scope of employment situations to those in which the employee receives all employment benefits due under applicable state and federal law and the employer withholds taxes from such payments to the employee, remitting such taxes to the Internal Revenue Service. Under this provision, freelance authors would not be considered employees for hire. *See* S. 1253 101st Cong., 1st Sess. (1989).

[34] *See, e.g., Marco v. Accent Publ'g Co.*, 969 F.2d 1547, 1552 (3d Cir. 1992) (holding that a photographer was an independent contractor, while ignoring some factors and noting that some were "indeterminate" and should not be considered).

[35] Thus, not one of the thirteen factors mentioned in *CCNV* will be dispositive in determining the status of the work as a work made for hire. Some factors should always be given more weight because they will be more probative in revealing the true nature of the employment relationship. *See Carter v. Hemsley-Spear, Inc.*, 71 F.3d 77 (2d Cir. 1995); *Aymes v. Bonelli*, 980 F.2d 857 (2d Cir. 1992) (noting that some factors will often have little or no significance while others will be significant in almost every situation).

sign the written contract or when in the parties' relationship they must agree. In answer to this question, the Seventh Circuit held that the writing must be signed by both the hiring party and the hired party and that the writing must be executed before the work has been created.[36] Even if the agreement has to occur before creation of the work, must it be contemporaneous? For example, suppose a photographer and a magazine enter into a written agreement creating a work made for hire relationship concerning all future pictures the photographer takes for the magazine. If such a blanket agreement would not literally violate the statute, would it violate the spirit of the work made for hire provisions? Even though blanket contracts may be efficient in reducing transaction costs between the parties, they might well transgress the pro-author bias of the work made for hire provisions.

The Court in *CCNV* narrowed the basis by which the hiring party and an independent contractor may contractually create a work made for hire in favor of the hiring party. Unless a "specially ordered or commissioned work" falls within the nine enumerated categories specified in § 101 of the Act, the parties cannot by contract create a work made for hire relationship. But has *CCNV* really changed things from a practical standpoint? One result is that more employers have tried to circumvent the uncertainties of the work made for hire doctrine, with its fact-intensive definition of "employee." Employers have adopted a rule of thumb: when in doubt, insist on an assignment of copyright from the prospective employee. Although an assignment of copyright provides a somewhat shorter duration of copyright ownership than a work made for hire, it may satisfy the needs of most employers. The major drawback to an assignment of copyright when compared with a work made for hire is that an assignment (or any transfer of copyright) can be terminated between the thirty-fifth and fortieth years of the grant if the author or her heirs decide to do so.[37] Realistically, not many employers will be concerned about termination of their ownership rights after 35 years. Most works, including advertising jingles, commercial artwork, or computer software, have a much shorter economic life than that. From this point of view, are freelance authors really better off after *CCNV* now that employers, who usually have greater bargaining power, will mechanically insist on an assignment of copyright from their independent contractors?

§ 5.04 WORKS PREPARED WITHIN THE SCOPE OF EMPLOYMENT

Under the first prong of the statutory definition, a work made for hire is created if it is prepared by the "employee" but only if the work was prepared "within the scope of employment." *CCNV* and subsequent cases have focused on whether the creator of the copyrighted work is an "employee" for the purposes of the work made

---

[36] *Shiller & Schmidt, Inc. v. Nordisco Corp.*, 969 F.2d 410, 412 (7th Cir. 1992).

[37] *See* 17 U.S.C. § 203(a). An assignment of copyright will not confer absolute ownership rights on the assignee because the author can still terminate the transfer between the thirty-fifth and fortieth years of the grant. But despite this, some commissioning parties prefer the security of an assignment of copyright to the unpredictable nature of the work made for hire doctrine as construed in the courts. For a discussion of termination of transfer, see *infra* §§ 6.11–617.

for hire doctrine. A growing number of cases concern works clearly created by "employees," but the issue arises whether these works were made within the "scope of employment."

The fact that "scope of employment" issues are appearing with increasing frequency in the case law should come as no surprise given the nature of today's increasingly decentralized working environment, where the line between workplace and home has blurred. Indeed, many people must use their homes for work related to the job, and some enjoy working, or are even expected to work, after hours on projects related to their employment. Today's reality is that employers encourage these after hour activities and sometimes directly compensate them. Once again, the courts have looked to the *Restatement (Second) of Agency* to determine whether an employee has created a work "within the scope of employment." The *Restatement* employs a tripartite test:

> (1) whether the work was of the type the employee was hired to perform;
>
> (2) whether the creation of the work in question occurred "substantially within the authorized time and space limits" of the employee's job; and
>
> (3) whether the employee was "actuated, at least in part, by a purpose to serve" the employer's purpose.[38]

Avtec Sys. v. Peiffer,[39] illustrates an application of the tripartite test in determining scope of employment issues. In *Avtec*, the court held that a computer program developed after-hours at the employee's home was not created within the scope of employment. In applying the *Restatement* test, the court found that the first element was met. It was clearly the kind of work that the employee was hired to perform. The employer was unable to prove the second and third elements. As to the second element, the work had been created outside the time and space limits of the employment. In applying the third element, the court found that the employee had not been appreciably motivated by a desire to further the employer's corporate goals. By contrast, in *Cramer v. Crestar Fin. Corp.*,[40] the court found that the plaintiff had written the work within the scope of employment even if he did so at home, outside regular working hours, on his own initiative, and on his own equipment. Here, the court held that the first element was met — that the work was the kind the employee was hired to perform.

Whether the work is the type the employee was hired to perform has arisen in the academic context. Specifically, absent express agreement, are a professor's writings created in a university setting works made for hire for which ownership vests in the employer-university?[41] Nothing in the statute directly addresses this

---

[38] RESTATEMENT (SECOND) OF AGENCY § 228.

[39] 67 F.3d 293 (4th Cir. 1995).

[40] *Id.* at 294.

[41] This question has been discussed extensively in the literature. *See* Laura G. Lape, *Ownership of Copyrightable Works of University Professors: The Interplay Between the Copyright Act and University Copyright Policies*, 37 VILL. L. REV. 223 (1992); Russ VerSteeg, *Copyright and the Educational Process: The Right of Teacher Inception*, 75 IOWA L. REV. 381 (1990); Rochelle Cooper Dreyfuss, *The Creative Employee and the Copyright Act of 1976*, 54 U. CHI. L. REV. 590 (1987); Leonard D. DuBoff, *An*

question. Professors are expected to publish, and that is taken into account for their promotion, tenure, and level of salary. Moreover, most academics work on their projects at the office and use other university resources such as secretarial help and research assistants. But according to two law professors sitting on the federal bench, faculty writings are excluded from the work made for hire doctrine under a broad-based "teacher's exception."[42] In the opinion of Judge Posner, Congress did not wish to abolish the teacher's exception, which had been developed under the 1909 Act. To do so would wreak havoc on settled practices and understandings in academic institutions and would result in undermining conditions for academic publication.[43] Whatever one thinks of a blanket teacher's exception,[44] in close cases, the expectation of the parties and the customs of the industry should be taken into account in determining "scope of employment" issues.

§ 5.05 WORKS MADE FOR HIRE UNDER THE 1909 ACT

Section 26 of the 1909 Act recognized the work made for hire doctrine in providing that "the word 'author' shall include an employer in the case of works made for hire."[45] The 1909 Act did not define the key terms in this phrase, and the courts were forced to create their own standards for construing the statute. The case law clearly favored employers over creators in determining whether a work made for hire was created.

Under the 1909 Act, whether a work was created in the scope of employment or commissioned from an independent contractor, courts applied a presumption that ownership of the copyright vested in the employer as a work made for hire.[46] The presumption could be overcome by an agreement to the contrary.[47] Absent an agreement, the employee could rebut the presumption by showing a contrary intent of the parties.[48] For this purpose, the court would look to such evidentiary factors as industry custom, pattern of dealing, at whose expense and insistence the work was created, and the supervision and control of the work.[49] Of these factors, the most important was the supervision and control exercised by the employer. Actual supervision or control in the preparation of the work was not necessary, so long as

---

Academic's Copyright: Publish and Perish, 32 J. Copyright Soc'y 17 (1984); Todd F. Simon, *Faculty Writings: Are They "Works Made for Hire" Under the 1976 Copyright Act?*, 9 J.C. & U.L. 485 (1982–83).

[42] *Hays v. Sony Corp. of Am.*, 847 F.2d 412 (7th Cir. 1988) (supporting a teacher's exception); *Weinstein v. Univ. of Illinois*, 811 F.2d 1091 (7th Cir. 1987) (rejecting university's claim to copyright ownership for a work prepared by an academic in the course of employment and with university funds).

[43] *Hays*, 847 F.2d at 415.

[44] Some commentators are skeptical of a blanket exception. *See* William Patry, 1 Copyright Law and Practice 382 (1984) (suggesting that some academic writing should be considered as such (course syllabus) whereas others (an article written for tenure) written as the result of the author's volition should not be so considered).

[45] 17 U.S.C. § 26 (1909 Act).

[46] *See May v. Morganelli-Heumann & Assoc.*, 618 F.2d 1363 (9th Cir. 1980).

[47] *See Roth v. Pritikin*, 710 F.2d 934 (2d Cir. 1983).

[48] *See Meltzer v. Zoller*, 520 F. Supp. 847, 851 (D.N.J. 1981).

[49] *See Brattleboro Publ'g Co. v. Winmill Publ'g Corp.*, 369 F.2d 565 (2d Cir. 1966).

the commissioning party retained the right of supervision and control.[50] Even a person who simply commissioned another on a one-time basis for the limited purpose of creating a single work might be deemed an employer for work made for hire purposes.[51]

Twentieth Century Fox Film Corp. v. Entm't Distrib.,[52] which involved ownership of Dwight D. Eisenhower's account of World War II, illustrates how the 1909 Act's "insistence and expense" test is applied by a present day decision. In concluding that the General's memoires were a work made for hire, the court emphasized the fact that Eisenhower was persuaded by the publisher to take on the project. [As for the "expense," Doubleday, the publisher, paid Eisenhower a flat fee instead of royalties, covered all the expenses involved in the writing of the book, and was deeply involved in the writing of book, providing the General with extensive notes and comments throughout the process.] Thus, the two prongs of "the insistence and expense" test were clearly met under these facts.

As seen above, the concern with 1909 Act case law is of more than historical interest because the 1976 Act is not applied retroactively in determining copyright ownership. Such retroactivity would raise serious constitutional problems. The leading case regarding the non-retroactivity of the 1976 Act is *Roth v. Pritikin*,[53] where the plaintiff, a freelance author, delivered recipes for a successful diet book under an oral contract in October 1977 and received payment for her work. The book became a best seller. Roth argued that the 1976 Act should be applied retroactively and that, because the 1976 Act required a written contract to create a work made for hire, the pre-1978 oral contract was ineffective. The court held that transactions taking place before 1978 should be governed by the 1909 Act, which would give ownership to the commissioning parties, at whose insistence and expense the work was created, and to those who retained the right to supervise and control Roth's freelance work.[54]

The rationale for looking to the 1909 Act was based on constitutional principles. Divesting the commissioning parties of their ownership status under the new 1976 Act definition of "work made for hire" would raise serious constitutional due process issues under the Fifth and Fourteenth Amendments and would possibly violate the Fifth Amendment prohibition on the federal government's right to take public property for public use without just compensation.[55]

---

[50] *See Martha Graham Sch. & Dance Found., Inc.*, 380 F.3d 624 (2d Cir. 2004); *Murray v. Gelderman*, 566 F.2d 1307, 1310 (5th Cir. 1978).

[51] *See, e.g.*, *Estate of Hogarth v. Edgar Rice Burroughs, Inc.*, 342 F.3d 149 (2d Cir. 2003). For an example of a work that escaped the 1909 work made for hire presumption, see *Dolman v. Agee*, 157 F.3d 708 (9th Cir. 1998) (holding that songs written by composer while in employ of soundtrack company, but apparently for other purposes, were not composed within scope of employment or at employer's "instance and expense").

[52] 429 F.3d 869 (9th Cir. 2005).

[53] 710 F.2d 934 (2d Cir.1983)

[54] *Id.* at 937.

[55] *See id.* at 939; *see also* NIMMER ON COPYRIGHT § 1.11 (2014) (applying the 1976 Act to ownership would constitute a violation of the Due Process Clause of the Fifth and Fourteenth Amendments and a violation

§ 5.06 JOINT WORKS UNDER THE 1976 ACT

[A] Generally

Works of authorship are often created by two or more persons and are treated as joint works. Section 101 of the 1976 Copyright Act defines a "joint work" as "a work prepared by two or more authors with the intention that their contributions be merged into inseparable or interdependent parts of a unitary whole."[56]

The key terms in the definition, "inseparable" and "interdependent," are not defined. The House Report gives as examples of "inseparable," a novel or a painting, while examples of "interdependent" include a motion picture, opera, or words and music.[57] Whether a work entails interdependent or inseparable elements is irrelevant in determining whether a joint work has been created. What counts is that the authors intended their respective labors to be integrated into one work.

[B] Intent to Create a Joint Work

Even if the collaborating authors contribute copyrightable elements to the resulting work, a joint work is not created unless the authors intended, at the time of the writing, that their contributions become part of a joint work.[58] The intent requirement is stringent. In other words, collaboration alone is insufficient: there must be an intent to create a jointly authored and jointly owned work. The requirement of mutual intent is founded on the principle that the equal sharing of rights in a jointly authored work should be limited to collaborators who fully intend to be joint authors.[59] Although intent is the essential element of a joint work, it does not matter when the *fulfillment* of that intent takes place. Returning to the songwriting example, a joint work could be created if A's words were created in 1946 and B's music was created in 1978, with their integration into the final song taking place in 1988. Each composer's intent to create a joint work at the time of creation is the essential requirement. It is irrelevant that the composers were unknown to each other or had no idea which words or music would eventually be used. Nor do the authors have to have collaborated together at the same time and place so long as each author intended at the time of the creation that his or her contribution would be combined in some way with another's work.

---

of the Fifth Amendment limitation on the federal government's right to take private property for public use without just compensation).

[56] 17 U.S.C. § 101 (joint works).

[57] H.R. Rep. No. 94–1476, at 120 (1976). It appears that the House Report, in referring to "inseparable," means a work that has been recast, reformed, or adapted as opposed to an interdependent work, *i.e.*, one that is made of assembled parts, such as various collective works. *See* Nimmer on Copyright § 6.04 (2014). In any event, whether a work is transformed or assembled, the intent is the critical aspect for creating a joint work.

[58] *See* H.R. Rep. No. 94-1476, at 120 (1976).

[59] *See Thomson v. Larson*, 147 F.3d 195 (2d Cir. 1998) (finding plaintiff's copyrightable contributions to the musical "Rent" was insufficient to create a joint work because its co-author never intended the joint authorship relationship).

Alternatively, a joint work is not created if an author did not intend at the time of creation that his work be merged into an inseparable or interdependent work. By this principle, a joint work would not be created when, for example, A, the writer of the words, intended them to be nothing more than a poem but later decided that they should be integrated with music into a song. Nor would a joint work be created if a poet, a playwright, or a novelist were to show that he merely hoped that someday his work would be integrated into a song, an opera, or a motion picture without an explicit intention for this to occur.

Does the joint authorship of an underlying work confer any joint ownership rights in a new work created by one of the joint authors that is substantially based on the underlying work? Suppose that A and B create a joint work, for example, an article in a scientific journal. After a falling out between the two parties, A uses a substantial portion of the original article but adds substantial original authorship to the new article. Is B a joint author of the second article?[60] Here, joint ownership would not attach to the second work unless there was evidence that the authors intended their joint product to be forever indivisible. Without such evidence, a derivative work would be created, and B would not be a joint author of the resulting derivative work. A contrary rule, as one court stated, "would convert all derivative works based upon jointly authored works into joint works, regardless of whether there had been any joint labor on the subsequent version. If such were the law, it would eviscerate the independent copyright protection that attaches to a derivative work that is wholly independent of the protection afforded the preexisting work."[61]

In sum, what counts is the *primary intent* to create a joint work. The appropriate question to ask is whether each author created his work primarily for the purpose that it be integrated at some future time into a joint work. In many cases, deciding such nuances of intent is a difficult task, particularly if a court has to decide the primary intent of a deceased author who never explicitly indicated his intent during his lifetime. This task becomes all the more difficult in situations involving more than two authors, as in a movie or theater collaboration.[62] Nevertheless, much rides on this elusive concept of intent in determining whether a work is, on the one hand, a joint work, or, on the other hand, a derivative or collective work.

Childress v. Taylor[63] illustrates the elements that courts look to in determining whether the parties manifested the requisite intent to create a joint work. In *Childress*, the defendant Taylor contacted Childress to write a play based on the life of the legendary comedienne "Moms" Mabley. Although Taylor, a professional actress, wrote none of the script, she provided Childress with her research on "Moms" Mabley's life and suggested that certain scenes be included in the play. The relationship between the parties deteriorated before the rights between them

[60] *See, e.g.*, *Weissman v. Freeman*, 868 F.2d 1313 (2d Cir. 1989) (holding, under similar facts, that the second work was not a joint work).

[61] *Weissman*, 868 F.2d at 1317.

[62] For an excellent overview of these problems, see Susan Keller, *Collaboration in Theater: Problems and Copyright Solutions*, 33 UCLA L. Rev. 891 (1986).

[63] 945 F.2d 500 (2d Cir. 1991).

were specified by contract. Taylor then had another author modify the script and shortly thereafter, using this new version, performed the work publicly. In response to Childress's suit for copyright infringement, Taylor contended she was a joint author and shared with Childress the rights to the play.

The Second Circuit rejected Taylor's claim of joint authorship because her efforts lacked the two basic elements needed to create a joint work. First, Taylor, who supplied only certain ideas and research, did not contribute the requisite degree of authorship. Second, even if Taylor's contribution was independently copyrightable, a joint work was not created due to a lack of intent. The Court held that for a joint work to exist there must be "intent of both participants in the venture to regard themselves as authors."[64]

The court rejected the notion that the *dominant* author could have the requisite intent only if he or she "intends the legal consequences of co-authorship." Each author must have considered the idea of joint authorship, whether or not they fully appreciated the legal ramifications of the concept.

In *Childress*, nothing indicated that the putative joint authors ever regarded themselves as joint authors. Critical to the absence of intent was a lack of understanding on the question of recognition through billing and credit. Here, there was no evidence that Childress ever considered, or would even have agreed, that Childress and Taylor would be "billed" and "credited" as joint authors of the play. *Childress* shows how a court will set up a presumption against a finding of a joint work when a putative co-author has contributed only a relatively small amount to the work. In this situation, the court will require convincing evidence of intent to create a joint work. The court in *Childress* justified its interpretation by asserting that Congress could never have intended collaborators such as editors and research assistants to qualify as joint authors. Thus, the "relationship test," as it has come to be called, focuses on how the parties perceived their relationship,[65] and it has generally been accepted as the standard for determining joint work status. The problem is that Judge Newman's interpretation runs counter to the statutory definition of § 101 that the requisite intention is the authors' intent that "their works be merged into a unitary whole" and not that the parties somehow regarded themselves as joint authors.[66]

As the case law reveals, the intent requirement has engendered complicated and contentious litigation. The disputes over ownership rights can be reduced if the collaborators reduce their understandings to a writing that clearly states the intent of the parties as to the division of royalties and other aspects of the credit for and control of the work. Moreover, the agreement should track the language of the statute — that the parties regard themselves as joint authors and intend to merge

---

[64] *Id.* at 507.

[65] *Erickson v. Trinity Theatre, Inc.*, 13 F.3d 1061 (7th Cir. 1994); *Thomson v. Larson*, 147 F.3d 195 (2d Cir. 1998).

[66] *Childress* and its progeny have received substantial criticism in the law reviews. *See, e.g.*, Russ VerSteeg, *Intent, Originality, Creativity, and Joint Authorship*, 68 Brook. L. Rev. 123 (2002); Mary LaFrance, *Authorship, Dominance, and the Captive Collaborator: Preserving the Rights of Joint Authors*, 50 Emory L.J. 193 (2001); Roberta Rosenthal Kwall, *"Author's Stories:" Narrative's Implications for Moral Rights and Copyright's Joint Authorship Doctrine*, 75 S. Cal. L. Rev. 1 (2001).

their work into a jointly owned unitary whole. Agreeing to such terms in a signed writing will avoid many of the uncertainties regarding the intent to create a joint work. Absent an express agreement, the courts should look to the likely intentions of the contributors, based on their economic expectations. Depending on the relationship, they should imply a transfer of ownership in the form of a nonexclusive license, which does not require a writing, from one party to the other. Professor Goldstein argues that an implied contract approach would solve practical problems while avoiding the thick *Childress* gloss to the statutory definition of a joint work.[67]

[C] Joint Work Authorship: Copyrightability and Ownership of Individual Contributions

To create a joint authorship, each collaborator must have contributed sufficient original expression that could stand on its own as copyrightable subject matter. [68]In other words, a collaborating party must contribute more than general ideas, factual matter, or a description of what the work should do or look like. The Copyright Act itself does not indicate whether all the authors must make a copyrightable contribution to the collaborative effort. Despite this uncertainty, courts have unanimously denied joint authorship claims where an individual contribution is not itself copyrightable. Thus, a joint author must not only intend that his contribution be part of a joint work but must contribute more than *de minimis* authorship to the resulting work.[69] The contributions of the individual authors do not have to be equal in quantity and quality, and a joint work can be created even if the collaborative efforts of the authors are substantially unequal. Moreover, it is not required for the creation of a joint work that each collaborator actually fixes the work in a tangible medium of expression.[70]

The requirement that each collaborator in a joint work contribute copyrightable subject matter is consistent with the language of the statute and more generally with copyright policy. First, § 101's definition of a joint work as a work prepared by two or more authors implies that the contribution of each collaborator must be a copyrightable work of authorship under § 102(a). Second, this rule may prevent spurious claims by those who might otherwise try to share the fruits of the efforts of a sole author of a copyrightable work. Third, it may encourage those with non-copyrightable contributions to protect their rights through contract, because if they neglect to do so, the copyright will remain with the one or more persons who created the copyrightable material. Thus, the rule should tend to force the parties to specify their rights in a written contract, such as an assignment of the copyright or to establish a work made for hire in the appropriate situation. In sum, the

---

[67] *See* Paul Goldstein, Copyright § 4.2.1 (3d ed. 2014).

[68] For an argument that user-created avatars should be considered a joint work between the game provider and the user and that avatars should be considered a contribution to a collective work, see Tyler T. Ochoa, *Who Owns an Avatar? Copyright, Creativity, and Virtual Worlds*, 14 Vand. J. Ent. & Tech. L. 959 (2012).

[69] *See Donna v. Dodd, Mead & Co., Inc.*, 374 F. Supp. 429 (S.D.N.Y. 1974); *Erickson v. Trinity Theatre*, 13 F.3d 1061 (7th Cir. 1994).

[70] *See, Easter Seal Soc'y*, 815 F.2d at 335–36.

copyrightability standard should lead to greater judicial and administrative efficiency.[71]

In highly collaborative works, such as in the making of a feature film, the Ninth Circuit has redefined the meaning of "author" for the purpose of creating a joint work. In *Aalmmuhamed v. Lee*,[72] the court held that Jefri Aalmmuhamed, hired by Spike Lee as a consultant to assist in certain aspects in the making of the film "Malcom X," was not a joint author despite his substantial contribution to the film. Among other things, he reviewed the shooting script, made extensive script revisions, created at least two entire scenes with new characters, and translated Arabic into English. In affirming a grant of summary judgment, the court gave two basic reasons for its holding that plaintiff was not a co-author of the film even though he added substantial copyrightable material to the movie. First, the parties manifested no intention that Aalmmuhamed be considered a joint author, as defined by cases in the Second Circuit such as *Childress v. Taylor*. Second, and more controversially, the court instituted a new meaning to the term "author" in determining the existence of a joint work. Citing *Burrow-Giles Lithographing Co. v. Sarony*,[73] the court defined an author as the person to whom the work owes its origin, and "in a movie, this definition, absent a contract to the contrary, would generally limit authorship to someone at the top of the screen credits, sometimes the producer, sometimes the director, possibly the star, or the screenwriter — someone who has artistic control."[74] In the present situation, Aalmmuhamed did not fit into the above categories. In addition, he provided no evidence that, at any time, he had "superintendence" of the work or that he was the "inventive or master mind of the movie."[75]

Aalmmuhamed's test in determining the authorship of a joint work is a dramatic and ill-advised departure from copyright doctrine. Rather than examining the actual contributions of each putative author, the Court supplanted traditional rules in determining authorship by focusing on the relationship and status of the individuals that take part in a motion picture setting. Misconstruing *Burrow-Giles*, a case involving an individual author, the court fabricated a *de facto* work made for hire doctrine for special application to the movie industry. The problem is that outside the motion picture industry, how is a court to apply the test to other highly collaborative endeavors such as a software project involving a multitude of programmers? In other settings, who will be deemed the analog of the producer, star, or the one who "superintends" the work and was its "inventive master"? *Aalmmuhamed*'s formulation further complicates the rules for determining co-authorship and will burden the process of the copyright title search when, with the passage of time, the facts concerning authorship become more remote and less attainable.[76]

---

[71] *See Childress v. Taylor*, 945 F.2d 500 (2d Cir. 1991).

[72] 202 F.3d 1227 (9th Cir. 2000).

[73] 111 U.S. 53 (1884).

[74] 202 F.3d at 1233.

[75] *Id.* at 1235.

[76] *See generally* F. Jay Dougherty, *Not a Spike Lee Joint? Issues in the Authorship of Motion*

[D] Joint Works Created by Non-Collaborative Means

This definition of joint works — two or more authors who intend that their contributions be merged into inseparable or interdependent parts of a unitary whole — describes only one way in which a joint work is created. A joint work, however, can also result from other circumstances.[77] First, a joint work is created when a copyright owner transfers the copyright to more than one person. Second, a joint work arises when the copyright passes by will or intestacy to two or more persons. Third, a joint work occurs when the work is subject to state community property laws.[78]Fourth, a joint work is created when renewal rights or rights terminated under the termination of transfers provision vest in a class made up of two or more persons.[79] Thus, a joint work may be more broadly defined as one in which a copyright is owned in undivided shares by two or more persons, whether created by joint authorship or in some other way.

[E] Consequences of Joint Ownership

Whether a joint work is created by joint authorship or in some other way, the authors are co-owners of copyright in the work. As co-owners, the authors are deemed to be tenants-in-common,[80] a term borrowed from real property law, which means that each of the co-owners has an undivided ownership in the entire work.[81] As a result, each co-owner can use or license the whole work as he wishes, and the only obligation is a duty to account for profits to the other joint owner. What a joint owner cannot do is transfer all interest in the work — that is, assign the work or grant an exclusive license in it — without the written consent of the other co-owners.[82]

Consistent with real property law, a co-owner may not make or authorize a use of the work which would lead to the destruction of its value.[83] Although the principle is easy to state, it is less than clear what this means in practice.

Pictures Under U.S. Copyright Law, 49 UCLA L. Rev. 225 (2001) (discussing the principles of joint authorship in the motion picture context).

[77] *See* Nimmer on Copyright § 6.01 (2014).

[78] For an argument regarding whether state domestic relations laws that govern the allocation of copyright interests are preempted by federal law, see Llewellyn Joseph Gibbons, *Love's Labors Lost: Marry for Love, Copyright Work Made-for-Hire, and Alienate at Your Leisure*, 102 Ky. L.J. 223 (2012).

[79] *See infra* §§ 6.11–6.17, for a discussion of renewal rights and termination of transfers.

[80] Absent an agreement to the contrary between joint owners, their relationship is one of tenancy-in-common, not a joint tenancy. The basic difference between the two is that on the death of a co-tenant, the ownership right passes to his heirs, whereas in a joint tenancy, the right passes to the surviving joint tenant. *See* Nimmer on Copyright § 6.09 (2014); *Picture Music, Inc. v. Bourne, Inc.*, 314 F. Supp. 640 (S.D.N.Y. 1970), *aff'd*, 457 F.2d 1213 (2d Cir. 1972).

[81] Absent an agreement otherwise, joint authors share an equal percentage of ownership in the joint work. The joint authors share equally despite the degree of individual authorship contributed. *See, e.g.*, *Sweet Music, Inc. v. Melrose Music Corp.*, 189 F. Supp. 655 (S.D. Cal. 1960).

[82] *See* 17 U.S.C. § 204(a). For a discussion of the implications of a co-owner unilaterally resolving an act of copyright infringement by a third party by retroactively licensing the infringer, seemingly authorizing the prior infringement, see James Rothstein, *Unilateral Settlements and Retroactive Transfers: A Problem of Copyright Co-Ownership*, 157 U. Pa. L. Rev. 881 (2009).

[83] *See Shapiro, Bernstein & Co. v. Jerry Vogel Music Co.*, 73 F. Supp. 165 (S.D.N.Y. 1947).

Fortunately, the issue does not arise with frequency because a co-owner has no economic incentive to dissipate the value of the work.

The paradigm of joint authorship is a collaboration between songwriters:[84] A, who composes the music, and B, who composes the words. Assuming that A and B intend, at the time of the writing of their respective works, to create a joint work, either can use the work or grant a *nonexclusive* license (but not an exclusive license or assignment) to others. No consent is needed in granting these rights, but the joint authors must share the profits from any exploitation of the work.[85]

[F] Joint Works and Derivative Works Compared

Rights of ownership in a derivative or collective work vary substantially from joint ownership. For a derivative or collective work, the contributing author owns his own contribution only. There is no undivided interest in the whole work as in the case of joint ownership. The practical effect of this difference can be quite significant.

Consider the example of a musical work where a lyricist A composes the words to a song and musician B composes the music to a song. Assume that neither A nor B had the intention at the time of creation that their works be integrated into a joint work. If they eventually decide to do so, the resulting song would be considered a derivative work. As owner of the derivative work, each author would own nothing more than his original contribution — one the words, the other the music. Absent a specific contractual agreement, each author would have to obtain permission for every use of the song from the owner of the underlying work.

Other consequences result from joint ownership, as compared with ownership of a derivative or collective work. In the case of a joint work, the entire work passes to the heirs or devisees of each joint author, and the term of protection is life-plus-seventy-years, as measured from the life of the last living joint author.[86] By comparison, the owner of a derivative or collective work can convey no more than his individual contribution to his heirs or devisees, and the term of protection is measured from the life of each individual author. In the songwriting example, this would result in the heirs of A owning the words and the heirs of B owning the music.

---

[84] Joint works have arisen out of a variety of situations. *See, e.g.*, *Donna v. Dodd, Mead & Co., Inc.*, 374 F. Supp. 429 (S.D.N.Y. 1974) (involving photographer and writer of a text); *Meltzer v. Zoller*, 520 F. Supp. 847 (D.N.J. 1981) (regarding architect and home owner); *Community for Creative Non-Violence v. Reid*, 846 F.2d 1485 (D.C. Cir. 1988) (suggesting that a sculpture may have been a joint work of the sculptor and commissioning party because both parties contributed to it; the court remanded the case to determine whether the two parties' contributions were intended to be inseparable parts of a whole and whether each contribution was substantial enough to meet the test of originality and authorship).

[85] *See Oddo v. Ries*, 743 F.2d 630 (9th Cir. 1984).

[86] For a discussion of duration of copyright, see *infra* §§ 6.02–6.04.

§ 5.07 JOINT OWNERSHIP UNDER THE 1909 ACT

Section 24 of the 1909 Act[87] indirectly acknowledged the principle of joint ownership by allowing a renewal of copyright to be owned jointly by more than one person. The Act, however, did not specify how joint ownership could be created. The principles of joint authorship developed through case law culminating in the *12th Street Rag* doctrine, which the 1976 Act was designed to overrule.[88]

Until the *12th Street Rag* decision in 1955, the case law under the 1909 Act essentially reflected the codification of joint authorship principles in the 1976 Act. The key element in creating a joint work was the common design or intent of the authors to merge their contributions into an indivisible whole at the time of creation. This intent could be found even if the authors wrote their works at different times, did not work together, or did not even know one another.[89]

A major departure in the case law occurred in the *12th Street Rag* decision.[90] This controversial decision removed the requirement that the intent to create a joint work be shown at the time of creation. In *12th Street Rag*, a composer created an instrumental piano solo, never intending that it eventually be accompanied by words. The composer assigned his rights to a publisher who commissioned lyrics for the piano solo. Was the song a joint work? The court held that it was, even though the author did not intend to create a joint work.

The *12th Street Rag* holding greatly increased the potential number of joint works and departed from prior case law in two ways. First, the intent to create a joint work no longer had to be shown at the time of creation; it could be shown at anytime thereafter. Second, this intent could be supplied by the copyright owner, in this case the assignee, who might or might not necessarily be the author.

The *12th Street Rag* doctrine has been vigorously criticized.[91] The major objection is that it throws an element of uncertainty into determining ownership rights for derivative or collective works created under licenses given by a copyright owner before 1978.[92] The doctrine also has a tendency to extend the copyright term for works that may have fallen into the public domain.[93] For these and other reasons, the doctrine has been overruled by the 1976 Act.

---

[87] 17 U.S.C. § 24 (1909 Act).

[88] *See Shapiro, Bernstein & Co., Inc. v. Jerry Vogel Music Co.*, Inc. (*12th Street Rag* case), 221 F.2d 569 (2d Cir.), *modified on rehearing*, 223 F.2d 252 (2d Cir. 1955).

[89] *See Shapiro, Bernstein & Co., Inc. v. Jerry Vogel Music Co., Inc.* (*Melancholy Baby* case), 161 F.2d 406 (2d Cir. 1946), *cert. denied*, 331 U.S. 820 (1947).

[90] *Shapiro, Bernstein & Co.*, 221 F.2d at 569.

[91] *See, e.g.*, NIMMER ON COPYRIGHT §6 .06[B] (2014).

[92] For the difference in ownership between derivative and collective works, see *supra* §§ 2.08–2.12. For example, in a situation where A writes the music and B the words for a song, neither A nor B has any rights to the other's work absent agreement; whereas if a joint work is created, each can grant nonexclusive licenses to the whole work without the other's consent.

[93] For example, consider the songwriting example where A writes the words and B the music. Assume that the song is a derivative work. If the copyright term in the song ends, anyone could use A's words. But if the work is considered a joint work, the copyright term under § 302(b) of the 1976 Act endures for the life of the last surviving author plus 70 years.

The question remains: must a court today apply the *12th Street Rag* doctrine in construing ownership rights for transactions taking place before 1978? The 1909 Act case law is still important because nothing indicates that the 1976 Act is to be applied retroactively, and to do so in some instances would raise serious constitutional problems.[94] Unlike the relatively well-settled 1909 Act case law on works made for hire, the *12th Street Rag* case is more an aberration than a decision supported by the mainstream case law. Thus, a court could reasonably ignore the doctrine as being inconsistent with better-reasoned authority, the result being virtually identical to the 1976 Act conception of joint authorship.

§ 5.08 OWNERSHIP OF CONTRIBUTIONS TO COLLECTIVE WORKS

[A] Distinguishing Between Copyright in the Collective Work and Copyright in a Contribution to the Collective Work

A "collective work" is defined in § 101 of the Copyright Act as "[a] work, such as a periodical issue, anthology, or encyclopedia, in which a number of contributions, constituting separate and independent works in themselves, are assembled into a collective whole."[95] A collective work is, in effect, a species of compilation,[96] but unlike other types of compilations, it consists of separate and independent copyrighted works. The distinction is also made between a joint work, where the separate elements merge into a unified whole, and a collective work where they remain separate and distinct.[97]

Under the 1909 Act, there was much confusion about the relation between copyright in the collective work and copyright in the individual work. Section 201(c) of the 1976 Act is intended to clarify the confusion.[98]

It provides as follows:

> Copyright in each separate contribution to a collective work is distinct from copyright in the collective work as a whole and vests initially in the author of the contribution. In the absence of an express transfer of the copyright or of any rights under it, the owner of copyright in the collective work is presumed to have acquired only the privilege of reproducing and distrib-

---

[94] *See Roth v. Pritikin*, 710 F.2d 934 (2d Cir.1983). Retroactive application of the 1976 Act law for "works made for hire" may well violate the due process clause under the Fifth and Fourteenth Amendments and possibly the Fifth Amendment's limitation on the federal government's taking of private property for public use.

[95] 17 U.S.C. § 101 (collective work).

[96] *Id.* (compilation): A "compilation" is a work formed by the collection and assembling of preexisting materials or of data that are selected, coordinated, or arranged in such a way that the resulting work as a whole constitutes an original work of authorship. The term "compilation" includes collective works.

[97] *See* H.R. Rep. No. 94-1476, at 122 (1976).

[98] 17 U.S.C. § 201(c).

uting the contribution as part of that particular collective work, any revision of that collective work, and any later collective work in the same series.

The main thrust of § 201(c) is the distinction between the copyright in the contribution to the collective work and the copyright in the collective work. Collective work authorship is similar to authorship in a compilation and extends to the elements of compilation and editing that went into creating the collective work as a whole, including contributions written by employees of the collective work's author. For example, collective work authorship in an anthology of poetry would extend to the selection and arrangement of the poems and other editing, such as an introduction to the poems, but not to the poems themselves.

Section 201(c) stipulates that the individual contributors to the collective work retain the copyrights in their works, absent a written agreement stating the contrary.[99] In addition, the section sets up a presumption that the copyright owner in the collective work has the right to reproduce and distribute the contribution as part of that particular collective work, a revision of the collective work, or as part of any later collective work in the same series. Take, for example, an issue of a magazine that is comprised of several individually copyrighted articles. Absent a written agreement to the contrary, the magazine could not republish individually one of those copyrighted articles. The publisher of the magazine, however, does have the right to republish that entire issue, or a revision of it, without consent of the copyright owner of the article. In addition, the collective work author has no implied right to revise the individual contribution without the author's consent. This would give the copyright owner of a collective work in an encyclopedia, for example, the right to republish an article written by an independent contractor in a new edition of the encyclopedia. The owner of the collective work, however, could not revise the contribution itself, reprint it individually, or include it in another collective work, without the consent of the owner of the copyright in the individual contribution.

These rules involving collective works were designed to clarify a somewhat uncertain situation existing under the 1909 Act, as well as to improve the legal position of authors to contributions.[100] The legal presumptions set forth in § 201(c) require the copyright owner of the collective work — the encyclopedia, anthology, or symposia — to obtain written contracts for the right to reprint the contribution or for the transfer of its copyright.

[B] The Collective Works and the Revision Right in the Digital Environment

The "revision" right has raised difficult issues in the digital environment. In *Tasini v. The New York Times Company*,[101] a group of freelance authors brought suit against the *New York Times*, *Newsday*, and *Time* for placing their articles in three online databases. In upholding summary judgment in favor of the freelance

---

[99] *See, e.g.*, *Quinto v. Legal Times of Washington, Inc.*, 506 F. Supp. 554 (D.D.C. 1981).

[100] *See* H.R. Rep. No. 94-1476, 94th Cong., 2d Sess. 122 (1976).

[101] 533 U.S. 483 (2001).

authors, the Supreme Court rejected the publisher's contention that the use of the republishing of the articles in this fashion was a privileged "revision" of their collective works under § 201(c) of the Copyright Act and held instead that it was a separate exploitation of the constituent works. The Court emphasized that the key factor in determining whether a privileged revision has occurred is the manner in which the articles are "[p]resented to, and perceptible by, the user of the databases."[102] Unlike microfilm where the user encounters the article in the same position as he would in the newspaper, the user of the database obtains the article as a separate item within the search result. In short, the databases offered individual articles, disembodied from their original context. The Court agreed that the "transfer of a work between media" does not alter the character of that work for copyright purposes but "[i]n this case, media neutrality should protect the Authors' rights in the individual Articles to the extent those Articles are now presented individually, outside the collective work context, within the databases' new media."[103]

With *Tasini*, the freelancers have won a sweet but modest one-time windfall.[104] The reason for this limited victory is that publishers had already adapted their contractual negotiations, insisting on the transfer to them of all the pertinent rights. In the 1990s, with the "Tasini" issue looming in the background, the publishers became fully aware of the possible risk of liability and began insisting on "all rights" agreements designed to republish freelancer articles in all media, including electronic databases. The contracts are standard now, and with the continuing consolidation of media outlets, the publishers are in an increasingly powerful negotiating position. After all, media outlets for freelance articles have continued to consolidate so that the publishers are now virtual oligopolists. In other words the market is a buyer's market: "You want to write an article for us? Then you need to sign over the rights."[105] In sum, the case will have its effect only on a limited number of pre-1990 works written by freelance writers.

From a doctrinal standpoint, *Tasini* has clarified some issues in regard to the "revision" privilege by holding that as long as an individual work appears in its "original context," it is permissible as a reproduction or revision under § 201(c). So long as the context in which the work appears is similar, it should make no difference whether digital media is used for the purposes of reproduction and

---

[102] *Id.* at 499.

[103] *Id.* at 502.

[104] In 2005, the parties agreed to settle four consolidated class actions (including *Tasini*) by creating an $18 million fund to compensate freelancers (including but not limited to the named plaintiffs) for previous infringing uses. That settlement was threatened when the Second Circuit ruled that the district court could not assert subject-matter jurisdiction over unregistered copyrights, even for settlement purposes. *See In re Literary Works in Elec, Databases Copyright Litig.*, 509 F.3d 116 (2d Cir. 2007). In 2009, however, the Supreme Court granted certiorari to determine whether the registration requirement deprived the district court of jurisdiction. *See Reed Elsevier, Inc. v. Muchnick*, 129 S. Ct. 1523 (2009). For now, more than eight years after the Supreme Court's decision in *Tasini*, the freelancers have yet to receive a dime.

[105] For an example of model forms, see ALEXANDER LINDEY & MICHAEL LANDAU, LINDEY ON ENTERTAINMENT, PUBLISHING AND THE ARTS, Ch. 1, I, B, § 1:36 (2009). For an analysis of the current strategies that freelancers might use in a world of unequal bargaining power, see MAUREEN A. O'ROURKE, *Bargaining in the Shadow of Copyright Law After* Tasini, 53 CASE W. RES. L. REV. 605 (2003).

revision. How similar the context needs to be for the proper exercise of the revision privilege will be an issue for some time. In one case, the court held that the publication of the *National Geographic* digital archive of copyrighted photographs and past articles from the *National Geographic* magazine on CD-ROMs and DVDs, in which individual contributions were arranged and presented to the viewer in their original context, was a privileged "revision" of the original work under § 201(c). The court concluded that it was an "electronic replica" that was more analogous to microfilm than to the electronic databases in *Tasini*.[106]

In close cases, the courts should opt for a more expansive revision privilege encouraging the dissemination of the copyrighted work, unencumbered by the transaction costs of renegotiating rights with a multiplicity of authors.

§ 5.09 OWNERSHIP OF COPYRIGHT AS DISTINGUISHED FROM OWNERSHIP OF THE MATERIAL OBJECT: THE *PUSHMAN* DOCTRINE

Section 202 of the 1976 Act codifies a fundamental principle in copyright law: the distinction between ownership of the material object and ownership of the copyright. As discussed earlier, an outright sale of a material object, such as a book, canvas, or master tape recording of a musical work, does not transfer copyright.[107] One possible exception to this rule is the *Pushman* doctrine[108] under which an author or artist who has sold an unpublished work of art or a manuscript is presumed to have transferred his *common law*[109] copyright, unless the copyright has been specifically reserved. In *Pushman*, an artist sold an unpublished painting, which had not yet been divested of its common law copyright. As to who owned the copyright in the painting, the court held that the sale of the material object (i.e., the canvas) was presumed to have conveyed the common law copyright as well.

The legislative history[110] of § 202 indicates that this section was drafted in part to overturn the *Pushman* doctrine. But the demise of this doctrine began even

---

106 *See Faulkner v. Nat'l Geographic Enters. Inc.*, 409 F.3d 26 (2d Cir. 2005) (granting summary judgment in favor of publishers for the use of reelancer's photographs in CD-ROM versions). The *Faulkner* court rejected plaintiff's *res judicata* and collateral estoppel arguments based on a pre-*Tasini* case, *Greenburg v. Nat'l Geographic Soc'y*, 244 F.3d 1267 (11th Cir. 2001), holding that the use of freelancer's photographs in CD-ROM versions of National Geographic Magazine was not a privileged revision. The *Greenberg* case returned to the Eleventh Circuit. The court held that its prior decision had been overruled by the intervening Supreme Court decision in *Tasini*, and that *Faulkner* reached the correct result as to everything except the animated introduction. *See Greenburg v. Nat'l Geographic Soc'y* 533 F.3d 1244 (11th Cir. 2008).

107 For a discussion of this concept, see *supra* § 2.02.

108 *Pushman v. N.Y. Graphic Soc'y, Inc.*, 39 N.E.2d 249 (N.Y. 1942).

109 Recall that under the 1909 Act, before a work was published, it was protected by state common law copyright. Publication was the dividing line between state and federal protection. The *Pushman* doctrine applies only to the sale of an object embodying an unpublished work and is, therefore, protected by common law copyright. For a discussion of publication, see *supra* §§ 4.02–4.07.

110 H.R. Rep. No. 94-1476, at 124 (1976).

before the 1976 Act, when California[111] and New York[112] enacted statutes reversing the presumption that an unconditional sale of an unpublished work of art transferred copyright along with the material object. Despite these attempts to overrule it, the *Pushman* doctrine is not entirely dead. The reason is that the 1976 Act does not operate retroactively for transactions involving pre-January 1978 transfers of copyright. Thus, the *Pushman* doctrine is still alive, and one should scrutinize all pre-1978 transfers of a material object embodying a work then protected under common law copyright to determine the ownership rule in the pertinent state jurisdiction.[113]

Part II. TRANSFERS OF COPYRIGHT INTERESTS

§ 5.10 DIVISIBILITY OF COPYRIGHT

[A] Generally

Copyright in a work may be regarded as a bundle of rights that may be transferred in its entirety or individually. The 1976 Act in § 201(d)(2) explicitly recognizes the principle of the divisibility of copyright in providing:

> Any of the exclusive rights comprised in a copyright, including any subdivision of any of the rights specified by Section 106, may be transferred . . . and owned separately. The owner of any particular exclusive right is entitled, to the extent of that right, to all of the protection and remedies accorded to the copyright owner by this title.[114]

Divisibility of ownership applies to transfer of copyright ownership, defined in § 101 as follows:

> [A]n assignment, mortgage, exclusive license, or any other conveyance, alienation, or hypothecation of a copyright or of any of the exclusive rights comprised in a copyright, whether or not it is limited in time or place of effect, but not including a nonexclusive license.[115]

To be effective, transfers of copyright must be written and signed by the copyright owner.[116]

Section 201(d) recognizes the concept of divisibility of copyright, which allows the copyright owner to transfer less than the full ownership interest in the copyright.

---

[111] Cal. Civ. Code § 982(c) (West 1976).

[112] N.Y. Gen. Bus. Law §§ 223–24 (McKinney 1968).

[113] Even in New York and California — states that have abrogated the *Pushman* doctrine by statute — the doctrine may well be applicable to transactions taking place before the effective date of those statutes. Moreover, the statutes in New York and California apply to the sale of works of fine art. There remains the question of whether the *Pushman* doctrine is still viable in those states for works other than fine art even after the effective date of the abrogating statutes.

[114] 17 U.S.C. § 201(d)(2).

[115] 17 U.S.C. § 101 (defining the transfer of copyright ownership).

[116] *See* 17 U.S.C. § 204.

Section 201(d) explicitly provides that each of the exclusive rights set forth in § 106 — those of reproduction, adaptation, publication, performance, and display — may be infinitely subdivided, and each of these subdivided rights may be owned and enforced separately.[117] For example, A, a novelist, could grant an exclusive license in his writing to B to write a screenplay from the novel, another to C to write a play based on a chapter of the novel, and a third to D to perform the work in the State of Ohio during the month of July 1993.

[B] Consequences of Divisibility: Standing to Sue

All transferees of copyright are given standing to sue without having to join the copyright proprietor. In effect, each transferee enjoys all the rights of a copyright owner.[118] This right is particularly important to the exclusive licensee who can bring suit on his own behalf to protect his ownership interest in the copyright. By contrast, under the 1909 Act, the exclusive licensee was not considered an owner of copyright and was forced to join the copyright owner.[119] This requirement could be quite burdensome on the exclusive licensee whose rights were infringed, and it could result in the exclusive licensee's exclusion from the courts because of his or her inability to join a copyright owner as an indispensable party.[120] Now, under the 1976 Act, the exclusive licensee enjoys standing to sue and can therefore effectively protect his ownership interest.

[C] Does an Exclusive Licensee Have the Right to Sublicense the Copyrighted Work?

The 1976 Act has abrogated the doctrine of indivisibility, and as indicated above, one important consequence of indivisibility is that the owner of an exclusive license may sue in his or her own name for an infringement of the assigned right.[121] However, when it comes to the right of an exclusive licensee to sublicense the work, at least some courts have not pushed indivisibility to its farthest reaches. In *Garner v. Nike, Inc.*,[122] the Ninth Circuit held that an exclusive licensee does not have the right to transfer its rights without the consent of the licensor. The court declared that, under § 201(d)(2) of the Copyright Act, an exclusive licensee is entitled to the protection and remedies afforded by the Act but not to rights of ownership, as specified under § 101, such as the right to transfer. The court pointed

---

117 *See* H.R. Rep. No. 94-1476, at 123 (1976).

118 *See, e.g., Hubbard Broad., Inc. v. S. Satellite Sys.*, Inc., 777 F.2d 393 (8th Cir. 1985) (finding that exclusive license to local television broadcaster confers standing to sue); *Library Publ'ns, Inc. v. Med. Econ. Co.*, 714 F.2d 123 (3d Cir. 1983) (stating that exclusive license to newsstand dealer confers standing to sue).

119 The 1909 Act considered copyright to be an indivisible entity, and the copyright owner could not transfer ownership of the copyright in part. *See infra* § 5.11.

120 *See, e.g., Ilyin v. Avon Publ'ns, Inc.*, 144 F. Supp. 368, 374–75 (S.D.N.Y. 1956) (holding that the exclusive licensee was unable to join foreign copyright owners as an indispensable party).

121 For an argument that a license is a form of property interest and is not simply a "contract not to sue," see Christopher M. Newman, *A License Is Not a "Contract Not to Sue": Disentangling Property and Contract in the Law of Copyright Licenses*, 98 Iowa L. Rev. 1144 (2013).

122 279 F.3d 774 (9th Cir. 2002).

out that when enacting the 1976 Act, Congress was aware that, under the 1909 Act, licensees could not sublicense their right in an exclusive license.[123]Accordingly, the fact that Congress chose not to address this issue explicitly, coupled with the limiting language of 201(d)(2), indicated the state of the law was to remain unchanged. Moreover, placing the burden on the licensee to get the licensor's consent was said to assure that the licensor will be able to monitor the use of copyright.[124]

The court's rationale is dubious. After all, Congress explicitly abolished the 1909 Act doctrine of indivisibility, and § 101 defines an exclusive licensee as an owner of copyright. If an exclusive licensee may now sue on his own behalf for infringement of his ownership right, should not the right to sublicense follow from this? It would seem that, from a policy standpoint, the parties should be made to explicitly negotiate the right to sublicense. In sum, the *Gardner* rule complicates the exploitation of copyrighted works.[125]

§ 5.11 INDIVISIBILITY OF OWNERSHIP UNDER THE 1909 ACT

Under the 1909 Act, a copyright was perceived as an indivisible entity incapable of being broken up into smaller rights. This doctrine of indivisibility, as it was known, was justified mainly as protecting infringers against harassment from successive lawsuits. Only an assignee of the entire copyright could bring suit, whereas licensees could not; this effectively cut down on the number of persons who could sue.

Under the 1909 Act, the distinction between a license and an assignment[126] led to important consequences other than the inability to bring suit in one's own name. The most serious consequence of indivisibility involved the right to claim copyright. Under the 1909 Act, copyright could be secured only if notice appeared in the name of the copyright owner.[127] If no notice or improper notice, such as notice in a name other than the copyright owner, was given, the work could be injected into the public domain.

These requirements caused problems in many copyright industries, but their effect was particularly evident in magazine publishing. For example, assume that A, author of an unpublished and uncopyrighted article, granted to B magazine the right to publish the article in B magazine in 1970. If B magazine carried a copyright notice only in the magazine's name, A's copyright would be jeopardized. The reason for this problem is that B magazine was a licensee of A, not a copyright owner of A's

---

123 *Id.* at 779.

124 *Id.* at 780.

125 For a decision explicitly rejecting *Gardner*, see *In re* Golden Books Family Ent. Inc., 269 B.R. 311 (Bankr. D. Del 2001).

126 In general, a grant is an assignment if the grantee is given full rights; a grant is a license if the grantor retains some of those rights. *See* Harry G. Henn, *"Magazine Rights" — A Division of Indivisible Copyright*, 40 Cornell L.Q. 411, 430–31 (1955).

127 *See* 17 U.S.C. §§ 10, 19 (1909 Act).

article, and correct notice had to bear the name of the copyright owner. Thus, the general notice in the name of B magazine was incorrect, and the article was published without notice. The result was a possible injection of A's article into the public domain.[128]

These problems forced authors to use various means, artificial and inconvenient, to protect their works. By one method, the author would assign all rights to the publisher, who would agree to transfer the rights back to the owner after publication. Not many authors were aware of the notice requirement and its consequences, much less the complicated practices built up to avoid the problems created by the doctrine of indivisibility. In short, to circumvent problems created by indivisibility, authors tried to create ingenious methods, which sometimes, but not always, worked.[129]

Because of its unfairness to authors, indivisibility was one of the most criticized doctrines in copyright law.[130] It was dealt a severe blow in *Goodis v. United Artists Television, Inc.*,[131] which held that where a magazine purchases the right of first publication of an article, copyright notice in the magazine's name is sufficient to secure copyright for the author. Since *Goodis*, most courts have refused to forfeit copyright in a work containing the name of the licensee rather than the copyright owner.[132]

The result in *Goodis* foreshadowed the total abrogation of indivisibility in the 1976 Act. It also explains § 404 of the 1976 Act, which specifically provides that:

> [a] single notice applicable to the collective work as a whole is sufficient to satisfy [notice requirements]. . . with respect to the separate contributions it contains . . . regardless of the ownership of copyright in the contributions and whether or not they have been previously published.[133]

These notice provisions have freed the contributor to a collective work from having to worry about the loss of copyright through improper notice. In addition, the author no longer has to worry about setting up artificial means, such as the transfer arrangements described above, to avoid the problems of copyright indivisibility.

---

[128] *See Letter Edged in Black Press, Inc. v. Pub. Bldg. Comm'n of Chi.*, 320 F. Supp. 1303, 1312 (N.D. Ill. 1970).

[129] To avoid forfeiture, some courts would interpret the agreement as an assignment, instead of a license, in which the magazine acquired legal title to the contribution and the author retained beneficial title. *See* NIMMER ON COPYRIGHT § 10.01[C] (20210).

[130] *See* STAFF OF S. COMM. ON THE JUDICIARY, 86TH CONG., DIVISIBILITY OF COPYRIGHTS, STUDY NO. 11 (Comm. Print 1960).

[131] 425 F.2d 397 (2d Cir. 1970).

[132] *See, e.g.*, *Fantastic Fakes, Inc. v. Pickwick Int'l, Inc.*, 661 F.2d 479 (5th Cir. 1981). *But see Letter Edged in Black Press, Inc.*, 320 F. Supp. 1303 (distinguishing *Goodis* as applying to magazine publishing only).

[133] 17 U.S.C. § 404(a).

§ 5.12 DRAFTING AND CONSTRUING LICENSES

[A] In General

For the most part, transfers and nonexclusive licenses of copyright present no greater problem in legal drafting and interpretation than in any other specialized area of the law. No set form exists for drafting an assignment or license, but most agreements include provisions, among others, for: (1) royalties, (2) duration of the agreement, (3) its geographical scope, (4) the manner in which the work may be exploited, (5) termination circumstances, (6) the name to be carried on the notice of copyright, and (7) responsibilities for maintaining an infringement suit. Once in court, these provisions are no more or less difficult to construe than any other kind of legal writing.

A copyright owner may specify the terms under which others may use a copyrighted work. How the terms are described can affect the remedies available to the copyright holder if terms of the license are breached. A good example of this principle concerns "open-source" licenses. The free software movement has encouraged the use of "open-source" licenses, under which the source code of a computer program is publicly disclosed along with a nonexclusive license. Open source licenses that permit others to freely copy and adapt the source code, provided that the user publicly discloses its own source code under an open-source license as well. Until recently, a key question concerning such licenses was whether they could be enforced. In *Jacobson v. Katzer*,[134] the Court of Appeals for the Federal Circuit held that the terms of an open-source license were conditions that could be enforced by a copyright infringement action, rather than independent covenants that could only give rise to an action for breach of contract. In sum, the restrictions on use should be carefully drafted as conditions, the violation of which would fall outside the scope of the license and, therefore, subject the infringer to all remedies under the Copyright Act. Careless drafting of the license may leave the copyright holder with only unsatisfactory contractual remedies.

[B] The Problem of New Media

One issue of contract construction, however, has proved to be particularly challenging: the determination of the scope of media to which the transfer pertains. This problem results from the rapid and revolutionary change in communications media. Sometimes the parties fail to take into account a new medium. Other times, they are either unaware of the medium, or such medium was not in existence at the time the grant was executed.

To decide scope-of-media issues, courts generally search for the intent of the parties by analyzing the language of the agreement along with permissible extraneous evidence. The intent may be clear from a specifically worded contract or implied by other circumstances, including the general customs and expectations

---

[134] 535 F.3d 1373 (Fed. Cir. 2008). (On remand, the district court refused to issue a preliminary injunction, finding no evidence of imminent future harm. 89 U.S.P.Q.2d (BNA) 1441 (N.D. Cal. 2009)). For more on open-source licenses, see the Open Source Initiative at www.opensource.org.

of the author in the particular industry.[135] When the parties knew or should have known about a new medium, the courts adopt an interpretation most consistent with all the terms of the license, including presumptions in favor of authors and against drafters. For example, in *Manners v. Morosco*,[136] an exclusive licensing agreement that included the right "to produce, perform and represent" a play did not include the motion picture rights. This interpretation was consistent with the terms of the license mainly because the parties were aware of the new medium and failed to mention it in the agreement.[137] Here, the court applied a general principle of contract construction (i.e., the contract must be viewed as a whole — one part interpreted in connection with its other parts).[138]

In comparison with cases involving the right to exploit a work in existing media, a more difficult problem of interpretation is presented when a court has to decide whether new or undeveloped media fall within the grant. In this situation, the traditional quest for the intent of the parties will not work when the issue involves media of which they could not have been aware. This is not a new problem; technology changes more rapidly than our ability to describe it, even in the best-drafted contracts.[139]

When faced with this problem, courts have followed two approaches. A strict approach, which generally favors the licensor, would limit media use to the literal terms of the agreement (sometimes referred to as the unambiguous core meaning of the term). The second approach would apply a "reasonableness" standard in which media use would include all uses reasonably falling within the media described in the license. This approach generally favors the grantee and promotes a wider distribution of copyrighted works in new media.

Cohen v. Paramount Pictures Corp.[140] provides an example of the stricter approach to construing contractual language, one that would take a more literal reading of the contractual terms. In *Cohen*, the issue was whether a license conferring the right to exhibit a film "by means of television" included the right to distribute videocassettes of the films. When executed in 1969, the videocassette was not envisaged. The court sided with Cohen, the plaintiff-licensor, who wished to prevent distribution of the videocassettes. The court scrutinized the contractual terms of the Cohen-Paramount license and found that it lacked broad enough language to encompass distribution by videocassette. The court distinguished the other cases allowing distribution by the new media. In these cases, the language of the contract expressly conferred the right to exhibit films by methods yet to be invented. By contrast, the Cohen-Paramount license lacked such broad terms, while expressly reserving to the copyright owner all rights not expressly granted.

---

[135] *See, e.g., Goodis v. United Artists Television, Inc.*, 425 F.2d 397 (2d Cir. 1970).

[136] 252 U.S. 317 (1920).

[137] *See also Klein v. Beach*, 232 F. 240 (S.D.N.Y. 1916).

[138] *See* RESTATEMENT (SECOND) OF CONTRACTS § 202(2) (1981).

[139] *See L.C. Page & Co. v. Fox Film Corp.*, 83 F.2d 196 (2d Cir. 1936) (construing a grant of motion picture rights in 1923, before "talkies," to include the right to produce the film with sound).

[140] 845 F.2d 851 (9th Cir. 1988).

In its meticulous examination of the contractual language, the court claimed to be guided by the purpose of copyright law, which is to protect authors and encourage them to create. Thus, it would frustrate the purpose of the Act to construe the license as granting a right in a medium unknown at the time the parties entered into the agreement. The implication is that, in construing agreements, close questions concerning the rights granted should be resolved in favor of the grantor, to provide authors adequate incentives to create.[141] This incentive rationale for literal interpretation is hard to justify. The author of a new work may be motivated by the expectation of a certain return on her investment of time and effort, and this motivation will be based on known uses and not unforeseen ones. Thus, from an incentive standpoint, it makes little difference in whose favor the agreement is construed.

By comparison with *Cohen*, the court in *Bartsch v. Metro-Goldwyn-Mayer, Inc.*[142] placed the burden on the licensor to show that the terms of the license do not extend to the new medium. *Bartsch* concerned a 1930 assignment of a musical play in which the assignee was given the right "to project, transmit and otherwise reproduce the said work or any adaptation or version thereof, visually or audibly by the art of cinematography or any process analogous thereto."[143]

The assignee argued that this clause gave the right to broadcast the work by live telecast. The court did not agree because transmission of a work by cinematography is not analogous to its transmission by live telecast.[144] The *Bartsch* court did, however, discuss the principles of construction to be applied when dealing with media unknown to the parties and when the language of the contract is ambiguous. By general proposition, if the words are broad enough to cover the new use, it is fairer that the burden of framing and negotiating the exception should fall on the grantor.[145] In addition, the broader definition supports diffusion of copyrighted works, allowing the person in the best position to distribute the work through the new media to do so. Alternatively, the narrower definition might impede distribution of works in the new media by creating a deadlock between grantor and grantee. Thus, the expansive approach benefits the public by encouraging greater distribution of copyrighted works.[146]

---

[141] *See* William F. Patry, Copyright Law and Practice § 5:115 (2014) (arguing that "agreements should, wherever possible, be construed in favor of the copyright transferor," to reflect Congress's "policy judgment that copyright owners should retain all rights unless specifically transferred").

[142] 391 F.2d 150 (2d Cir. 1968).

[143] *Id.* at 151.

[144] The court did, however, allow the defendant's use of the work in live telecasts based on another provision in an assignment from Bartsch, which transferred the motion picture rights throughout the world. *Id.* at 153. Thus, the analysis used by the court in how it would construe transfers of copyright involving a scope of media problem is essentially *dictum*. It has been influential, however, and represents the current view. *See* Nimmer on Copyright § 10.10[B] (2014).

[145] *Bartsch*, 391 F.2d at 155.

[146] *Bartsch* was cited in *Platinum Record Co., Inc. v. Lucasfilm, Ltd.*, 566 F. Supp. 226 (D.N.J. 1983) (finding a license, which gave grantee rights to exhibit and distribute film containing copyrighted songs throughout the world by any means or methods now or hereafter known, covered the right to distribute videocassettes and discs of the film; such distribution was allowed even though plaintiff might have anticipated future developments in exhibiting motion pictures).

Bartsch should not be construed as adopting a default rule in favor of copyright licensees. Rather, new-use analysis should be grounded on neutral principles of contract construction rather than favoring a particular party to the dispute. In other words, the language of the contract should govern the interpretation. As Judge Leval states:

> If the contract is more reasonably read to convey one meaning, the party benefited by that reading should be able to rely on it; the party seeking exception or deviation from the meaning reasonably conveyed by the words of the contract should bear the burden of negotiating for language that would express the limitation or deviation. This principle favors neither licensors nor licensees. It follows simply from the words of the contract.[147]

§ 5.13 TRANSFERS OF COPYRIGHT: THE WRITING REQUIREMENT

[A] The 1976 Act

Under § 204(a) of the Copyright Act, when copyright ownership is transferred other than by operation of law, it is not *valid* "[u]nless an instrument of conveyance, or a note or memorandum of transfer, is in writing and signed by the owner of the rights conveyed."[148]

The writing requirement ensures that the copyright owner will not inadvertently give away his or her copyright. In addition, a writing serves as a guidepost to resolve disputes by rendering the ownership rights clear and definite. To serve these functions, the writing must be executed contemporaneously with the agreement.[149]

The writing requirement of § 204(a) applies to transfers of copyright. The term "transfers of copyright" include: an assignment, mortgage, exclusive license, or any other conveyance . . . of any of the exclusive rights . . . but not including a

---

[147] *Boosey & Hawkes Music Publ'g, Ltd. v. Walt Disney Co.*, 145 F.3d 481 (2d Cir. 1998) (finding that 1939 license agreement giving the Disney Co. a nonexclusive right to record in any manner, medium, or form, and license a musical work covers 1991 release in video format; if new use license depends on the foreseeability of new channels of distribution at the time of contracting, Disney offered unrefuted evidence that a nascent market for home viewing of movies existed in 1939). *See also Random House v. Rosetta Books, LLC*, 150 F. Supp. 2d 613, 622 (S.D.N.Y. 2001) (holding that a grant to publisher of rights "to print, publish and sell the work in book form" did not encompass the right to exploit work in the form of an electronic book: "in this case, the 'new use' — electronic digital signals sent over the internet — is a separate medium from the original use — printed words on paper"); and *Welles v. Turner Entm't Co.*, 503 F.3d 728 (9th Cir. 2007) (finding triable issue of fact of whether contracts by which RKO acquired "motion picture and television rights" in *Citizen Kane* screenplay included home video distribution).

[148] 17 U.S.C. § 204(a).

[149] *See Kongsberg Int'l, Inc. v. Rice*, 16 F.3d 355 (9th Cir. 1994) (finding that copyright owner's letter written three-and-one-half years after alleged oral agreement is not substantially contemporaneous with oral agreement); *but see Eden Toys, Inc. v. Florelee Undergarment Co.*, 697 F.2d 27, 36 (2d Cir. 1982) (stating that memorandum of transfer made within one year of oral agreement and during term of exclusive license validated agreement ab initio).

nonexclusive license.[150]

To determine whether a writing is necessary, one must distinguish between transfers that require a writing and nonexclusive licenses that do not. Nonexclusive licenses, that may be transferred orally, are those in which the grantor retains the right to license the same right to others.

The writing requirement is a flexible one. The statute does not specify prescribed forms for the writing transferring copyright except that it be signed by the copyright owner.[151] Although the "writing" may take many forms, it can be viewed as a simple, straightforward, and absolute requirement for a valid transfer (assignment or exclusive license) of copyright. Accordingly, courts have not relaxed the writing requirement to allow for industry practices (e.g., in the movie industry) where written contracts are uncommon.[152] Although a gratuitous implied license remains valid until it is revoked,[153] an implied license supported by consideration may be irrevocable.[154]

By contrast with transfers of copyright, nonexclusive licenses may be granted orally. The writing requirement § 204(a) is inapplicable because that provision of the Copyright Act only applies to transfers of ownership — assignments and exclusive licenses — not to nonexclusive licenses. Consistent with traditional contract law, nonexclusive licenses may also be implied from conduct or the relationship between the parties. For example, courts have implied a license arising out of a partnership relation.[155] In other instances, a nonexclusive license may be implied where a copy of the work is given to a hiring party who has commissioned the work. In general, an independent contractor grants an implied license when three elements are met. First, the licensee must request the creation of the work. Second, the licensor must make that work and deliver it to the licensee. Third, the licensor must intend that the licensee copy and distribute that work.[156]

As discussed above, nonexclusive licenses need not be in writing and may be granted orally or by implication. But what law determines whether an implied nonexclusive license exists? In *Foad Consulting Group, Inc. v. Musil Govan Azzalino*,[157] the court held that although the effect of an implied license may be based on federal law, state law determines the contract question of whether such a license was in fact granted. The state whose contract law is applied could make a

---

[150] 17 U.S.C. § 101 (defining the transfer of copyright ownership).

[151] Although not a requirement, it is recommended that the instrument be notarized. Under 17 U.S.C. § 204(b), proper notarization constitutes prima facie evidence of execution of the transfer.

[152] *See, e.g., Effects Assocs. Inc. v. Cohen*, 908 F.2d 555 (9th Cir. 1990).

[153] *See, e.g., Wilchombe v. Tee Vee Toons, Inc.*, 555 F.3d 949 (11th Cir. 2009).

[154] *See, e.g., Asset Mktg. Sys., Inc. v. Gagnon*, 542 F.3d 748 (9th Cir. 2008).

[155] *See, e.g., Oddo v. Ries*, 743 F.2d 630 (9th Cir. 1984) (stating that manuscript prepared pursuant to partnership duties impliedly gave other members of the partnership right to use manuscript).

[156] *Effects Assocs., Inc. v. Cohen*, 908 F.2d 555, 558 (9th Cir. 1990) (finding nonexclusive license implied where author created a work at defendant's request and delivered it intending that defendant copy and distribute it); *see also Asset Mktg. Sys., Inc. v. Gagnon*, 542 F.3d 748, 754–55 (9th Cir. 2008).

[157] 270 F.3d 821 (9th Cir. 2001).

difference in whether a court will find an implied license. For example, California has a liberal parol evidence rule,[158] permitting consideration of extrinsic evidence of the terms of a contract even though the meaning appears unambiguous. Other states, however, are much less generous in accepting extrinsic evidence.[159] To avoid choice of law problems, the parties should specify in the written licensing agreement the governing law for the purpose of construing the terms of a contract.[160]

[B] The Writing Requirement Under the 1909 Act

Under § 28 of the 1909 Act, a total transfer of copyright, such as an assignment, was required to be in writing.[161] Unlike the 1976 Act, however, there was no similar requirement for licenses, exclusive or nonexclusive. Thus, under the 1909 Act, an oral contract could convey an exclusive license to copyright, and an assignment of state common law copyright could be either oral or implied by conduct.[162] These rules are still important today to determine the status of grants executed before 1978, because it is doubtful that the current Act could be applied retroactively in such an instance without raising serious constitutional problems.[163]

§ 5.14 RECORDATION

[A] Generally: The Importance of Recordation

Section 205 of the Copyright Act of 1976[164] allows recordation in the Copyright Office of all documents of copyright ownership whether assignments, exclusive licenses, or nonexclusive licenses. To fully enjoy the benefits of the 1976 Act, an owner of a copyright interest should accompany the recordation with a registration of the underlying work.

For causes of action arising on or after March 1, 1989, recordation as a prerequisite to bringing a copyright infringement suit is no longer required. For causes of action that arose before March 1, 1989, recordation of a copyright interest was a prerequisite to bringing a suit for copyright infringement.[165]

---

[158] Cal. Code Civ. Proc. (West 1856).

[159] For example, Virginia. *See, e.g.*, *Anden Group v. Leesburg Joint Venture*, 377 S.E.2d 452 (Va. 1989).

[160] *See, e.g*, *Welles v. Turner Entm't. Co.*, 488 F.3d 1178 (9th Cir. 2007).

[161] 17 U.S.C. § 28 (1909 Act).

[162] *See, e.g.*, *Martha Graham Sch. and Dance Found., Inc. v. Martha Graham Ctr. for Contemporary Dance*, 380 F.3d 624, 643–44 (2d Cir. 2004) (holding that unpublished dances created by Martha Graham prior to 1956 were assigned to the Center she founded, based on written and oral testimony of board members and the conduct of the parties), *on appeal after remand*, 466 F.3d 97 (2d Cir. 2006) (affirming finding that unpublished dances created between 1956 and 1965 were likewise assigned to the Center).

[163] For a discussion of these constitutional problems, see *supra* § 5.05.

[164] 17 U.S.C. § 205.

[165] 17 U.S.C. § 205(d). For example, an owner of an exclusive license to perform a copyrighted work could not defend his rights in a court of law without recording his exclusive license in the Copyright Office. *See, e.g.*, , *Burns v. Rockwood Dist. Co.*, 481 F. Supp. 841 (N.D. Ill. 1979) (noting that recordation is a jurisdictional prerequisite to bringing an infringement action); *see also Swarovski, Ltd. v. Silver Deer*

Recordation of a copyright interest — particularly *prompt* recordation — provides important benefits for owners of a copyright interest. Although recordation is not required for bringing a suit for infringement, it is highly recommended for a couple reasons. First, recordation specifically identifying the work will give notice to the world of the terms set forth in the document.[166] Thus, even if a person did not have actual notice of the document, he is presumed to have had that information when a transfer is recorded. This important constructive notice aspect of recordation applies only if the underlying work is registered.[167] Second, recordation establishes priority of ownership between conflicting transfers of copyright as well as conflicts between a transfer and a nonexclusive license.[168]

[B] What Should Be Recorded?

Section 204(a) provides that a transfer of ownership may be accomplished by a signed "instrument of conveyance, *or* a note or memorandum of the transfer" (emphasis added). Section 205(d), however, in stating the actual recordation requirement, refers somewhat opaquely to "the instrument of transfer." In applying these provisions, the courts have held that either of the indicia of transfer named in § 204(a) will satisfy the § 205(d) requirement.[169] The note or memorandum of the transfer to be recorded need not have been created when the transfer itself occurred. If the agreement is oral and the creation of the note or memorandum is substantially contemporaneous with it, the writing will most likely pass muster.[170] A requirement strictly demanding a contemporaneous writing would offer no particular evidentiary advantage, so long as the eventual writing is signed by the owner of the rights conveyed.[171]

The document recorded need not reflect all the terms and conditions of the agreement pursuant to which the transfer took place. In practice, documents prepared especially for recordation often are "short form" instruments, which recite the names of the parties and the subject matter of the agreement but omit, for example, any description of the consideration in exchange for which the transfer was given. In order for recordation to yield any of the benefits described

---

Ltd., 537 F. Supp. 1201 (D. Colo. 1982) (stating that proper recordation for the purpose of bringing an infringement suit imposes no obligation to record each instrument of transfer in a chain of title; plaintiff need only record the immediate transfer to him to comply with § 205(d)). Recordation as a prerequisite to bringing an infringement suit was deemed to be a formality incompatible with membership in the Berne Convention and was abrogated by the Berne Convention Implementation Act of 1988. For a discussion of the Berne Convention, see *infra* §§ 12.04–12.05.

166 *See* 17 U.S.C. § 205(c).

167 *See* 17 U.S.C. § 205(c)(2).

168 *See* 17 U.S.C. § 205(d), (e) (before the 1988 amendments, these were 205(e) and (f), respectively).

169 *See, e.g.*, *Co-Opportunities, Inc. v. Nat'l. Broad. Co.*, 510 F. Supp. 43 (N.D. Cal. 1981).

170 *See Eden Toys, Inc. v. Floralee Undergarments Co.*, 697 F.2d 27 (2d Cir. 1982) (concluding that the memorandum of transfer made within one year of oral agreement and during term of exclusive license validated the agreement ab initio); *but see Konigsberg Int'l, Inc. v. Rice*, 16 F.3d 355 (9th Cir. 1994) (holding that the letter written 3-1/2 years after alleged oral agreement was not sufficient).

171 *Cf.* Uniform Commercial Code § 2-201 (1978) (no requirement of contemporaneous memorandum under Uniform Commercial Code statute of frauds).

below, however, it is essential that the document recorded refer to the titles of the specific works involved in any transfer.

In addition to documents evidencing a transfer, the Act permits recordation of "[a]ny . . . other document pertaining to a copyright"[172] if the document has a direct or indirect relationship to the existence, scope, duration, or identification of a copyright, or to the ownership, division, allocation, licensing, or exercise of rights under a copyright. The relationship may be past, present, future, or potential. Examples include contracts, mortgages, powers of attorney, wills, and division orders.

Besides bearing an original signature (or proper certification of the photocopy), the Copyright Office requires that every document filed in the office be complete on its own terms (i.e., lacking any reference to an external document not submitted as an attachment), be legible and capable of being reproduced in legible imaged copies, and be accompanied by the correct fee. While it is technically unnecessary that the document evidencing the transfer be notarized, § 204(b), notarization provides prima facie evidence of the execution of the transfer and is still clearly advisable. Recordation, while providing constructive notice of the matters asserted in the document filed, does *not* affect the legal sufficiency of the document. Thus, whether a transfer is valid is a question for the law of contracts, not the law of copyright. Recordation is not a magic cure-all for a defective document.[173]

[C] Recordation: Priority Between Conflicting Transfers (Assignments and Exclusive Licenses)

Section 205(d)[174] of the 1976 Act establishes priorities of ownership between conflicting transfers of copyright, including any combination of conflicting assignments and exclusive licenses. Consider the following hypothetical situation: suppose that A, a writer, assigns to B the copyright of his novel in December 1989 and then conveys the same rights to C in January 1990. The question is who owns the copyright. Under the terms of this section, the first transferee, B, will prevail if he records within one month after execution of the agreement (two months if the agreement was executed outside the country). When the one-month grace period terminates, it then becomes a race between the two transferees of record, and if the first transferee, B, is the last to record, he loses his ownership to the copyright in the novel.

These priority provisions apply only if the work was registered in addition to being recorded.[175] If the work has not been registered, these provisions will not apply, and the court will decide priority based on proof submitted by the parties.

---

[172] 17 U.S.C. § 205(e).

[173] Detailed information regarding the mechanics of recordation, including Copyright Office Circular 12 (*Recordation of Transfers and Other Documents*), is available at the Copyright Office website: www.loc.gov/copyright.

[174] 17 U.S.C. § 205(d).

[175] Section 205(d) incorporates § 205(c)'s requirements for constructive notice: that the recorded document so identifies the work, that its ownership status be revealed by a reasonable search, and that the work be registered.

Two exceptions attach to these priority rules. First, one cannot enjoy a priority if he has received a transfer in bad faith (*e.g.*, with actual knowledge about the prior transfer). The second exception involves a transfer given without valuable consideration, such as by gift or bequest. In these two situations, the later transferee will not prevail over the first even if the first transferee fails to record his transfer. In summary, later transferees, even if they record first, cannot prevail over a prior transferee if they receive an ownership right in bad faith or without valuable consideration.

[D] Priority Between a Transferee and a Non-Exclusive Licensee

Section 205(e)[176] concerns priority between a transferee and a nonexclusive licensee. Under this section, a nonexclusive licensee will prevail over a transferee (assignee or exclusive licensee), but only in certain circumstances. First, the nonexclusive license must be evidenced in a written instrument signed by the copyright owner, and the license must be taken before execution of the transfer. Second, even if the nonexclusive license were taken after the transfer, it would prevail if evidenced in a writing and taken in good faith before recordation of the transfer without notice of it. For example, suppose a playwright assigned his copyright in his play to B and one month later gave a nonexclusive license to C to perform the play. Here, the nonexclusive license would continue to be effective if B failed to record the work in the Copyright Office and if C took his nonexclusive license in good faith.

[E] Reliance on Copyright Office Records: Practical Limitations

In operation, the federal recordation scheme poses practical problems in reliance on Copyright Office records. Under § 205, constructive notice takes effect as of the time a submission complies fully with the statutory requirements. But documents forwarded to the Copyright Office for recordation are not indexed and made accessible to search for some months afterwards. In the interim, a recorded transfer may have legal priority, even though a subsequent transferee of rights in the same work would have no means of discovering its existence from the public record.

In addition to administrative lag time, search of the records is further complicated by § 205(d), which provides transferees with a one month grace period to record their documents for transfers executed in the United States or a two-month grace period for transfers executed outside the United States. This grace period exposes transferees to the risk that their interests will be subordinated to previous unrecorded transfers. Suppose on January 1, 2004, in the United States, A assigns copyright to B, who does not immediately record his interest. A, five days later, assigns the copyright to C who searches the Copyright Office records and records immediately. B will prevail over C if B records within the one-month grace period — before February 1, 2004. Even though C could not have discovered the

---

[176] 17 U.S.C. § 205(e).

transfer through a search of the Copyright Office records, his rights will be subordinated to those of B.

A similar problem occurs under § 205(e)(1), which gives a written and signed nonexclusive license priority over later transfers of ownership even though the license is unrecorded and would, therefore, not be subject to discovery by the latter transferee. This undiscoverable nonexclusive license could frustrate the economic expectations of a subsequent exclusive licensee who may have thought he was buying a much more valuable right. To insure against such an eventuality, the exclusive licensee should insist on a warranty and indemnity against the grantor (hopefully solvent) at the time the exclusive license is executed.

[F] Recordation Under the 1909 Act

The 1909 Act's recording provisions correspond to those in the 1976 Act, yet they bear some significant differences. Under § 30 of the 1909 Act, the first transferee in time would prevail over the later transferee unless the later transferee could show: (1) that he purchased the interest for valuable consideration and without notice of the earlier transfer, (2) that he recorded his interest, and (3) that the earlier transfer was not recorded within three months of its execution in the United States or six months of its execution abroad. The 1909 Act rules apply to transfers made before January 1, 1978. As a result, a prior transferee who complied with the three and six months priority provisions would be protected after January 1, 1978, even though he did not record within the 1976 Act's shorter grace periods of one and two months.

The 1909 rules concerning recordation of transfers diverge in a number of significant particulars from the somewhat parallel provisions of the 1976 Act. Most significant is the dissimilarity in the requirements imposed on the prior transferee to impart constructive notice on subsequent transferees. For the purpose of constructive notice, § 30 of the 1909 Act had no requirement that the copyright be registered, unlike its counterpoint provision, § 205(c) of the 1976 Act. Two other differences between the two sections are worth mentioning. Section 30 did not protect a subsequent transfer made in return for a promise to pay royalties,[177] and one court applied the three month and six month grace periods to both subsequent transfers and prior transfers.[178] As to the latter difference, the grace periods of section 205(c) of the 1976 Act apply only to prior transfers.

§ 5.15 INVOLUNTARY TRANSFERS

Section 201(e)[179] of the Copyright Act provides as follows:

> [W]hen an individual author's ownership of a copyright, or any of the exclusive rights under a copyright, has not previously been transferred voluntarily by that individual author, no action by any governmental body

---

177 *See, e.g.*, *Venus Music Corp. v. Mills Music, Inc.*, 261 F.2d 577, 579–80 (2d Cir. 1958).

178 *See Kenya Music, Inc. v. Warner Bros., Inc.*, 391 F. Supp. 1228, 1229 (S.D.N.Y. 1975).

179 17 U.S.C. § 201(e).

or other official or organization purporting to seize, expropriate, transfer, or exercise rights of ownership with respect to the copyright, or any of the exclusive rights under a copyright shall be given effect . . . except as provided under Title 11.

The purpose of this provision is to impede possible attempts by foreign governments (i.e., China) to seize copyright from a dissident writer and prohibit the distribution of the work in the United States.[180] Other *involuntary* transfers are exempt from § 201(e). These include bankruptcy proceedings and mortgage foreclosures to which the author in such instances has voluntarily consented.[181]

§ 5.16 ORPHAN WORKS: WORKS WHOSE COPYRIGHT OWNERS CANNOT BE FOUND

[A] The Orphan Works Dilemma

"Orphan works" are copyrighted works — books, music, records, films, etc. — whose owner cannot be located. Works can become "orphaned" for a number of reasons: the owner did not register the work, the owner sold rights in the work and did not register the transfer, the owner died and his heirs cannot be found, and the list goes on. As copyright has grown in duration and extent, these so-called orphan works problems have become more and more common. Under the 1976 Act, protection has become automatic, and the term of copyright, once tied to the affirmative act (and dates) of publication, registration, and renewal, has been extended twice. It was done so in 1978 and 1998, and was prospectively extended to life-of-the-author-plus-seventy-years. In 1989, Congress removed the condition that published works must contain a copyright notice. In 1992, it removed the last vestiges of the renewal registration requirement. In 1996, many foreign copyrights were restored from the public domain. These changes have exacerbated the myriad difficulties of finding copyright owners and clearing rights.

With rising public awareness of the risks of copyright infringement, the problem also has become more severe. Increasingly, the various gatekeepers under whose scrutiny works must pass on their way from the creator's desk or studio to the public (publishers for books, distributors or broadcasters for films, and so forth) have become reluctant about allowing unlicensed material of any kind to appear in the products they make available. The result has been heightened frustration on the part of individual scholars and artists, as well as nonprofit cultural institutions.[182]

---

[180] *See* H.R. Rep. No. 94-1476, at 123 (1976).

[181] *See id.* at 124. In addition, § 201(e) does not apply to involuntary bankruptcy provisions under Title 11 of the Federal Bankruptcy Act. *See, e.g.*, *Thompkins v. Lil'Joe Records, Inc.*, 476 F.3d 1294 (11th Cir. 2007) (rejecting a contract obligation to pay royalties that did not result in a reversion of copyright to author); *ITOFCA, Inc. v. Mega Trans Logistics, Inc.*, 322 F.3d 928 (7th Cir. 2003).

[182] *See* James Gibson, *Risk Aversion and Rights Accretion in Intellectual Property Law*, 116 Yale L.J. 882 (2007) (showing how risk averse users often seek licenses where none are needed and the effect on the market for licensing copyrighted works); Jennifer Rothman, *The Questionable Use of Custom in Intellectual Property*, 93 Va. L. Rev. 1899 (2007) (criticizing judicial reliance on industry clearance

[B] Orphan Works Legislation

In 2006, the U.S. Copyright Office published an exhaustive report on orphan works.[183] The Report concluded that the orphan works problem is real but difficult to quantify, and it recommended legislation to provide a meaningful solution to the problem. The bills that have been introduced into the House and Senate have adopted the recommendations of the Copyright Office.

Proposed legislation[184] follows a core concept: if the user has performed a reasonably diligent search for the copyright owner but is unable to locate that owner, then that user should enjoy a benefit of limitations on the remedies that a copyright owner could obtain against him if the owner showed up at a later date. If an owner does emerge, the user must pay "reasonable compensation" or face full liability. Under the proposed legislation, reasonable compensation will be mutually agreed upon by the owner and the user or, failing that, be decided by a court; but it must also reflect objective market values for the work and the use. Orphan works legislation, not surprisingly, has received wide support from user groups such as libraries and the academic community.[185] Certain publishers and authors groups are less than enthusiastic, viewing orphan works legislation as an affront to the traditional contours of copyright ownership. Should orphan works legislation be enacted, it will be the first significant modification of the Copyright Act specifically designed to compensate for the ever-lengthening reach of copyright protection.[186]

---

practices and other litigation avoidance measures in defining the scope of copyright).

[183] Register of Copyrights, U.S. Copyright Office, Report on Orphan Works (2006), *available at* www.copyright.gov/orphan/orphan-report-full.pdf.

[184] Orphan Works Act of 2008, H.R. 5889 (2008). The bill also directs the Register of Copyrights to: (1) undertake a certification process for the establishment of an electronic database to facilitate the search: for pictorial, graphic, and sculptural works that are subject to copyright protection; and (2) study and report to Congress on remedies for copyright infringement claims by an individual copyright owner or a related group of copyright owners seeking small amounts of monetary relief.

[185] For a discussion of the privileged status of libraries in copyright law and the way recent licensing trends undercut that privileged position, see William M. Cross, *Restoring the Public Library Ethos: Copyright, e-Licensing, and the Future of Librarianship*, 104 L. Libr. J. 313 (2012).

[186] Although no action has been taken legislatively to solve the orphan works problem, the Register of Copyright continues to list orphan works as one of her priorities. *See* M. Pallante, Priorities and Special Projects of the United States Copyright Office, October 2011–October 2013, at 7 (2011). With orphan works legislation languishing, what might eventually resolve the problem of orphan works may come in the form of a grandiose if not audacious effort known as the Google Book Search initiative. For a discussion of Google Books, see Chapter 10, § 10.17[D], *supra*.

Chapter 6

DURATION, RENEWAL, TERMINATION OF TRANSFERS, AND RESTORATION OF COPYRIGHT

§ 6.01 INTRODUCTION AND CHAPTER OVERVIEW

How long should a copyright last?[1] In a speech on copyright before the House of Commons in 1841, Lord Macaulay reflected on the length of the copyright term:

> It is good that authors should be remunerated; and the least exceptionable way of remunerating them is by a monopoly. Yet monopoly is an evil. For the sake of the good we must submit to the evil; but the evil ought not to last a day longer than is necessary for the purpose of securing the good.[2]

In much the same spirit, Article I, section 8 of the U.S. Constitution allows Congress to pass laws protecting writings of authors for "limited times" only.[3] Although copyright is "limited" in duration, it does last a long time: the basic term of copyright is measured by the life of the author plus 70 years. Is such a long duration of copyright consistent with the constitutional language, "to promote the progress of science and the useful arts"? Macaulay, who called copyright "a tax on readers to give bounty to writers,"[4] certainly would not have thought so. On an intuitive level, one might conclude that such a long term is not warranted to encourage the optimum production of advertising jingles, computer programs, and commercial art, all of which fall within the broad range of copyrightable subject matter.

The fact is that it is impossible to determine the minimum duration sufficient to encourage the optimum amount of investment for the enormous range and variety of works of authorship. But even if the length of protection exceeds the ideal from a consumer welfare standpoint, we need not fear the copyright monopoly with the same intensity as, for example, the patent monopoly.[5] Generally, a consumer has reasonable substitutes for most copyrighted works. By comparison, the exclusionary effect of the patent grant is much greater, even though its duration is shorter.

---

[1] For an overview of the subject, see Saul Cohen, *Duration*, 24 UCLA L. Rev. 1180 (1977).

[2] Thomas Babington Macaulay, Macaulay's Speeches and Poems 285 (A.C. Armstrong & Son 1874). Lord Macaulay gave his speech pursuant to a legislative proposal to extend the copyright term to the life of the author plus 60 years.

[3] U.S. Const. Art. I, § 8, cl. 8.

[4] *See* Macaulay, *supra* note 2.

[5] The patent monopoly is much more exclusive than that of copyright. It provides a 20-year monopoly (measured from the date of application) encompassing the right to make, use, and sell the patented invention. For a discussion, see *supra* § 1.11.

Quite often there are few satisfactory substitutes for many patented products or processes, such as a patent on a life-saving drug. Moreover, despite the length of the copyright term, and the burdens it imposes, the copyright monopoly is tempered by various limiting doctrines such as the requirement of originality, the idea-expression doctrine, and the privilege of fair use.[6] In sum, the copyright monopoly is long but relatively weak.

This chapter, which is divided into four parts, is concerned broadly with the duration of copyright. Part I treats duration under the 1976 Act, where the basic term is life of the author plus seventy years. The 1976 Act has retained the bifurcated two-term system of copyright for works published before January 1, 1978. For works published before January 1, 1964, the author was required to file for renewal in the Copyright Office during the 28th year of the first copyright term. For works published between January 1, 1964, and December 31, 1977, renewal is automatic, and a copyright owner is no longer required to file a renewal registration in the Copyright Office. Part II discusses renewal and the continuing importance of 1909 Act case law in construing questions relating to the second copyright term. Part III considers termination of transfers whereby an author or his designated successor(s) may terminate transfers and nonexclusive licenses in two situations. Section 304(c) of the 1976 Act[7] allows termination of the extended thirty-nine-year renewal term in certain circumstances, while § 203 of the 1976 Act[8] permits the termination of transfers and nonexclusive licenses for works enjoying a duration of life plus seventy years. Part IV examines the restoration of copyrights from the public domain under the Uruguay Round Agreements Act for copyrights originating from Berne or WTO countries that had been injected into the public domain for failure to comply with statutory formalities such as notice or renewal. These once dead copyrights (of foreign origin) are automatically restored for the remainder of the term of copyright that they would have enjoyed if they had not entered the public domain.

Part I. DURATION

§ 6.02 GENERALLY: THE 1909 AND 1976 ACTS COMPARED

For most works created after January 1, 1978, the copyright term is measured by the life of the author plus 70 years. The 1976 Act, as originally enacted, specified life plus 50 years. This basic term prevailed until 1998 when it was extended twenty more years to a life plus 70 term.[9] The 1976 Act is founded on a unitary term of duration, whose exact contours is determined by an event: the death of the author of the work. By comparison, the 1909 Act used a radically different system of

---

[6] For a discussion of originality and idea-expression, see *supra* § 2.13. For a discussion of fair use, see *infra* Chapter 10.

[7] 17 U.S.C. § 304(c).

[8] 17 U.S.C. § 203.

[9] *See* Sonny Bono Copyright Term Extension Act, Pub. L. No. 105-298, 112 Stat. 2827 (1998).

duration, measured by the date of publication[10] (or the date of registration of certain works in unpublished form),[11] and continued for 28 years, followed by a renewal term of 28, for a total of 56 years.[12] This change in the duration of copyright and its unitary term is the centerpiece of the 1976 Act. Was there a need for it?

The House Report[13] offers a series of justifications for the longer life-plus-fifty term, summarized as follows:

(1) The longer term is needed to ensure an author and his dependents a fair remuneration for his works, particularly since life expectancy is longer than it was when the 1909 Act was passed.

(2) A shorter term would discriminate against works whose value is not recognized until many years later, particularly in our era where new communications media have greatly increased the commercial life of works.

(3) The public will not be hurt by a longer term but rather will benefit from its effect on encouraging increased production and dissemination of works.

(4) Based on a certain moment (death), the life-plus-50 system is a more precise measure as compared with the 1909 Act's use of "publication" to determine duration of copyright.

(5) The life-plus-50 system replaces the 1909 Act's burdensome, expensive renewal system with all its pitfalls.

(6) Although authors lose perpetual protection under common law copyright, they are fairly compensated for this loss by a term of life-plus-50-years.

(7) Without a life-plus-50 system, entry into the Berne Convention, the major international copyright convention, would be impossible.[14]

These justifications address three major concerns: fairness to authors, administrative convenience, and entry into Berne. The fairness arguments are speculative and sometimes dubious. Although some authors will benefit from the longer term, it is uncertain whether the public will benefit accordingly. There are costs to any monopoly. The longer the monopoly, the greater the costs to the public, which will have less access to the copyrighted work and will have to pay higher prices for it. This point is not mentioned by the House Report. In general, the optimum term for copyright is a question of endless debate, and fairness to authors is only one aspect of the durational puzzle. The second group of arguments, based on administrative

---

[10] *See* 17 U.S.C. § 10 (1909 Act).

[11] As listed in the statute, these works are: a lecture or similar production; a dramatic, musical, or dramatic-musical composition; a motion-picture photoplay; a photograph; a work of art; or a plastic work or drawing. Statutory copyright protection was not available under the 1909 Act for unpublished books, periodicals, maps, reproductions of works of art, prints, labels, and sound recordings. For these works, publication was the only way in which to secure statutory copyright and set the 28-year clock ticking. *See* 17 U.S.C. § 12 (1909 Act); William S. Strauss, Copyright Office Study No. 29, Protection of Unpublished Works (1958).

[12] Thus, unlike the 1976 unitary term, the 1909 Act was based on a bifurcated term based on the act of publication. *See* 17 U.S.C. § 24 (1909 Act).

[13] H.R. Rep. No. 94-1476, at 134–35 (1976).

[14] *See* Berne Convention art. 7(1). Entry into the Berne Convention requires a life-plus-50-year term as a minimum term of copyright protection.

efficiency, is accurate for the most part. Abolishing the two-term copyright and replacing it with a single life-plus-fifty-years term simplifies administration even though, as a practical matter, the date of an author's death may sometimes be difficult to determine. The last justification, concerning entry into Berne, arguably provides the most persuasive reason for the current term of copyright. Without a life-plus-50 term, the United States could not have hoped to join the Berne Convention and, thus, the world copyright community.[15]

§ 6.03 THE COPYRIGHT TERM EXTENSION ACT OF 1998: ITS HISTORY AND JUSTIFICATION

[A] From Life-Plus-Fifty to Life-Plus-Seventy

In 1998, Congress amended the Copyright Act to extend the term of copyright 20 more years and lengthened the renewal term for 1909 Act works from 47 to 67 years.[16] Term extension came about despite a vigorous opposition from academics and a number of loosely allied groups. Opponents of term extension argued that the copyright term is long enough already, perhaps too long, for the true commercial life of most works. To these critics, a longer duration would undermine the function of the public domain. By extending the term of copyright, the public would not have access to these works of authorship, and future authors would be deprived of basic material with which to produce new works.

Despite these arguments, copyright owners, authors (and their heirs) prevailed in obtaining another 20 years of protection. Copyright term extension progressively gained momentum as copyright owners — in particular large companies, *e.g.*, Disney, Time-Warner — confronted the reality of losing copyright in their valuable creations, both here and abroad, as the public domain loomed for works published more than 75 years ago.[17] Advocates of a longer term could not base their arguments on the need to comply with the Berne Convention, which constituted the most powerful rationale for the life-plus-50 term. Berne requires nothing more. Rather, supporters made their case on national economic policy. They were persuasive in convincing Congress that extended duration would enrich United States authors and nurture a favorable balance of trade. After all, the United States is the world's largest exporter of copyrighted works, and some countries, particularly those in the European Union, are major consumers of these works.

Once in the public domain in the United States, these works would no longer be protected in the European Union, even though the basic term of protection there has now been harmonized to life plus 70 years. Much to the chagrin of U.S. Copyright owners, the European Union adopted "the rule of shorter term" as provided in § 7(8) of the Berne Convention.

---

[15] For a discussion of the Berne Convention and the United States' entry, effective March 1, 1989, see *infra* §§ 12.04–12.05.

[16] 17 U.S.C. § 304(a).

[17] See *infra* § 6.05[C] for duration of copyright regarding works published before 1978.

What is this "rule of the shorter term"? As a general proposition, the Berne Convention establishes that a member country must confer a term of protection for copyright governed by the legislation of the country where protection is claimed. There is, however, an exception to the basic nondiscrimination principle known as "the rule of the shorter term." Under Article 7(8) of the Berne Convention, countries are permitted, but not required, to adopt the "rule of the shorter term," which limits the duration of copyright in the protecting country to the term provided in the country of origin.[18] Thus, without term extension, a copyright of U.S. origin whose term would expire and enter the public domain in the U.S. would do so simultaneously in the European Union. Put concretely, the economic reality is simply this: copyrighted in 1928, Disney's Mickey Mouse would have entered into the public domain in 2004. As a result of the term extension, Mickey and others will be protected until 2024. Thus, adding another 20 years to U.S. protection would allow U.S. copyright owners the continuing exploitation of this important export market.

[B] The Constitutional Challenge: *Eldred v. Ashcroft* and Beyond

The Copyright Term Extension Act (CTEA) was a controversial issue among certain academics, public domain users, and advocates, most of whom rigorously questioned the wisdom and constitutionality of extending existing copyrights for another twenty years.[19] In *Eldred v. Ashcroft*,[20] the Supreme Court rejected the constitutional challenges to the term extension. These challenges were based on two fundamental grounds: first, that the CTEA violated the "limited times" provision as required by Article I, Section 8, Clause 8 of the United States Constitution, and second, that the term extension violated the First Amendment. As to the "limited times" argument, Justice Ginsberg, writing for the Court, stated that "text, history and precedent" confirm that the Copyright Clause empowers Congress to prescribe "limited times" for protection for all copyrights, present and future. The Court noted that "[h]istory reveals an unbroken congressional practice of granting term extensions so that all under copyright protection will be governed evenhandedly under the same regime,"[21] and that a "time span appropriately 'limited' as applied to future copyrights does not automatically cease to be 'limited' when applied to existing copyrights."[22] Justice Ginsberg then turned to whether Congress exercised its authority rationally. On this point, the Court deferred to Congress, which wanted to ensure that American authors would receive the same copyright protection in Europe as their European counterparts. Justice Ginsberg

---

[18] Berne Convention art. 7(8) (Paris text). For a discussion of Berne, see *infra* §§ 12.04–12.05.

[19] *See, e.g.*, Tyler Ochoa, *Patent and Copyright Term Extension and the Constitution: A Historical Perspective*, 49 J.Copyr. Soc'y 19 (2001) (concluding that the term extension cannot be justified under the Copyright clause of the constitution). *But see* Thomas Nachbar, *Constructing Copyright's Mythology*, 6 Green Bag 37 (2001) (taking a skeptical approach to term extension opponents' appeals to a romanticized vision of copyright).

[20] 537 U.S. 186 (2003).

[21] *Id.* at 200.

[22] *Id.* at 199.

also noted that, in passing the CTEA, Congress considered demographic, economic, and technological changes and the projections that longer terms would encourage investment in the restoration and public distribution of their works.

The court also rebuffed Eldred's argument that the CTEA is content-neutral regulation of speech that fails heightened judicial review under the First Amendment. On the First Amendment issue, the majority agreed with the government's position that the "speech-protective purposes and safeguards"[23] embodied in copyright law were sufficient to preclude any heightened scrutiny of copyright legislation. In that regard, the Court referred to the idea/expression dichotomy in § 102(b) and § 107's fair use doctrine as part of the definitional balance that retains a free marketplace of ideas while protecting the author's original expression. Significantly, the court added that "the D.C. Circuit spoke too broadly when it declared copyrights categorically immune from challenges under the First Amendment. But when, as in this case, Congress has not altered the traditional contours of copyright protection, further First Amendment scrutiny is unnecessary."[24]

The *Eldred* case illustrates the current Supreme Court's deferential attitude toward Congress in copyright matters.[25] One might question the policy of the CTEA, but it is up to Congress, in its traditional role, to evaluate the costs and benefits of its actions. Congress has wide latitude in determining what kind of "progress" it is trying to promote when it passes copyright legislation.[26] Looking further out, what will happen in anticipation of 2019, when the twenty-year extension will expire on the oldest currently protected works. For example, what if the European Union were to extend copyright another twenty years to life plus 90? After *Eldred*, there appears to be no basis for a constitutional challenge. Whether this means "limited times" amounts to "eternity minus one day" is a question that can be debated, but for the near future, the power of Congress to extend copyright duration, incrementally, seems unassailable.

Copyright extensions are troublesome because they impoverish the public domain and impede access to works whose owners have no real interest in them. As Justice Breyer noted in his dissent, the Congressional Research Service study prepared for the *Eldred* case "indicates that only about 2% of copyrights between 55 and 75 years old retain any commercial value."[27] The practical problem is that the costs of identifying, much less finding and then negotiating, a license would discourage many a person from trying to get access to such works. To liberate those works that no longer have value to the copyright owner, and ameliorate the dead weight loss that term extensions impose, some have proposed a nominal

---

[23] *Id.* at 219.

[24] *Id.* at 221 (citations omitted).

[25] *See generally* Marshall Leaffer, *Life After* Eldred: *The Supreme Court and the Future of Copyright*, 30 WM. MITCHELL L. REV. 1597 (2004).

[26] For a vigorous defense of judicial deference as reflected in *Eldred*, see Paul M. Schwartz & Michael Treanor, Eldred *and* Lochner: *Copyright Term Extension and Intellectual Property as Constitutional Property*, 112 YALE L J. 2331 (2003).

[27] *Id.* at 248.

copyright maintenance fee.[28] By this means, copyright owners would be encouraged to reveal which of their works have value and which do not.[29]

§ 6.04 THE MECHANICS OF DURATION UNDER THE 1976 ACT

[A] All Terms Run to the End of the Calendar Year

Under § 305 of the 1976 Act,[30] all copyright terms run to the end of the calendar year in which they would otherwise expire. This provision applies to all important time-limit formalities, such as renewals and terminations of transfers. Expiration of the term at the end of the calendar year provides an administrative convenience to both the Copyright Office and the copyright owner. For example, suppose that A copyrighted his work on April 10, 1972. Instead of the renewal deadline[31] falling on April 10, 2000, as it would have under the 1909 Act, the deadline extends to December 31, 2000.

[B] The Basic Term: Life of the Author Plus Seventy Years

Copyright in works created after January 1, 1978, subsists for the life of the author plus seventy years.[32] The basic term is relatively easy to apply. Assume that A creates works in 1980, 1985, and 1990, and dies in 2000. All of these works will enter into the public domain on the same date, after December 31, 2070, because all of A's copyrights will be measured by his life plus seventy years. That all of A's works enter the public domain at the same time simplifies copyright administration.

[C] Anonymous and Pseudonymous Works and Works Made for Hire

Anonymous works, pseudonymous works, and works made for hire constitute a major exception to the basic term of copyright. Under § 302(c),[33] the term for these works is ninety-five years from the first publication, or 120 years from creation,

---

[28] *See* Public Domain Enhancement Act, H.R. 2601, 108th Cong. § 3(c) (2003). The PDEA would require a copyright holder to pay a $1 renewal fee 50 years after the work is first published and every 10 years after until the end of the copyright term. *See also* William Landes & Richard A. Posner, *Infinitely Renewable Copyright*, 70 U. Chi. L. Rev. 471 (2001) (arguing for a system of renewable copyrights with a relatively short initial term).

[29] Others argue that as a work moves further into its copyright term the ambit of permissible fair use should increase. *See* Joseph P. Liu, *Copyright and Time: A Proposal*, 101 Mich. L. Rev. 409 (2003); Justin Hughes, *Fair Use Across Time* 50 UCLA L. Rev. 775 (2003); *see also* Kenneth D. Crews, *Looking Ahead and Shaping the Future: Provoking Change in Copyright Law*, 49 J. Copyr. Soc'y 549 (2001) (proposing variable durations for different varieties of works and for different exclusive rights).

[30] 17 U.S.C. § 305.

[31] Even though renewal is automatic, filing for renewal in the Copyright Office provides important benefits. *See infra* § 6.09.

[32] *See* 17 U.S.C. § 302(a).

[33] 17 U.S.C. § 302(c).

whichever is shorter. Thus, if A creates a work in 1978 in the course of employment (*i.e.*, a work made for hire) and publishes it in 1980, the work will go into the public domain after 2075. As compared with the basic copyright term, the term for anonymous works, pseudonymous works, and works made for hire is much less precise from an administrative standpoint. This alternative term of copyright is measured by creation or publication events, which are sometimes difficult to determine with any precision.

[D] Joint Works

The life-plus-70-years term also applies to joint works, but with an important difference. Under § 302(b),[34] copyright is measured from the last surviving author's death plus 70 years. For example, suppose A and B create a joint work in 1980. A dies in 1990 and B dies in 2000. The copyright will enter the public domain after 2070, 70 years after B's death (the last surviving author). Because of this provision, joint works have a chance of lasting much longer than works of individual authors, particularly if one of the joint authors is young.

[E] Duration of Sound Recordings: The Special Status of Sound Recordings Fixed Before February 15, 1972

Sound recordings were not recognized as copyrightable subject matter by federal copyright law until February 15, 1972.[35] Before that date, a sound recording author had to look to state law for protection of his creation against infringement. The 1976 Act has not changed the pre-1972 status of sound recordings. Section 301(c) provides that "any rights or remedies [for pre-1972 sound recordings] under the common law or statutes of any State shall not be annulled or limited by this title until February 15, 2047."[36]

Section 301(c) leaves sound recordings created before 1972 in a netherworld of uncertain state law protection.

Aside from their peculiar status before 1972, sound recordings are treated the same as any other work. Thus, sound recordings created between February 15, 1972, and December 31, 1977, will have a 20-year first term and a 67-year renewal term. For sound recordings created after 1977, however, the basic life-plus-70-years term will apply.[37]

---

[34] 17 U.S.C. § 302(b).

[35] Act of Oct. 15, 1971, Pub. L. No. 92-140, 85 Stat. 391 (1971).

[36] *See* 17 U.S.C. § 301(c).

[37] However, when an anonymous work, pseudonymous work, or work made for hire is created, the 95/120 year term applies. *See* 17 U.S.C. § 302(c).

[F] Death Records

The year date of an author's death is the critical measure in computing the length of copyright. Because of its importance, § 302(d)[38] requires that the Register of Copyrights keep a public record containing information about the death of authors of copyrighted works. This section allows anyone having an interest in a copyright to file a statement in the Copyright Office that an author is living or dead. Section 302(e)[39] also creates a presumption of death, taking effect 95 years after publication or 120 years after creation, whichever is less. Any person who obtains a certified report from the Copyright Office that there is no indication that the author of the work is living, or had died less than 70 years before, is entitled to a presumption that the author has been dead for at least 70 years. Good faith reliance on this presumption is a complete defense to copyright infringement.[40]

[G] Works Created But Not Published or Copyrighted Before January 1, 1978

Section 303[41] provides that all works created, but not copyrighted or published before 1978, will be treated under the basic term of copyright set forth in § 302,[42] and their copyrights will not expire before 2003. But if these works are published before this expiration date, copyright protection will last through December 31, 2047. In passing the 1976 Act, Congress was aware of the many unpublished works written by authors who had died more than 50 years earlier. To apply the life-plus-50 duration to these works would result in their immediate placement into the public domain on January 1, 1978. For reasons of fundamental fairness, Congress decided to provide these works with another 25 years of protection, until 2003. As an inducement to publish such works before January 1, 2003, Congress has extended copyright for another forty-five years.

These unpublished and uncopyrighted works typically include letters, diaries, and other manuscripts never sold, exhibited, or reproduced for public distribution. Suppose, that A owns a copyright on a letter sent to B in 1911, which has never been published. A dies in 1927. The copyright on the letter would have continued through December 31, 2002, instead of going into the public domain, after 70 years after death, in 1998. But if the copyright owner had published the letter before 2003, he or she would receive another 45 years of protection — through December 31, 2047.

The number of unpublished works that were in existence on December 31, 2002, is difficult to know, but it was probably substantial. Failure to have published these works before 2003 forfeited copyright protection, depriving the copyright owner of an extra 45 years of protection. In short, December 31, 2002, is a significant date

---

[38] 17 U.S.C. § 302(d).

[39] 17 U.S.C. § 302(e).

[40] *See id.*

[41] 17 U.S.C. § 303.

[42] Life of the author plus 70 years. *See* 17 U.S.C. § 302.

for the public domain, even though the extent of unpublished and uncopyrighted works falling into the public domain on the critical date is impossible to quantify.

Part II. RENEWAL

§ 6.05 WORKS PUBLISHED OR COPYRIGHTED BEFORE JANUARY 1, 1978: AN OVERVIEW

[A] Generally

For works published before 1978, the 1976 Act continues the bifurcated durational structure of the 1909 Act. The 1909 Act set up statutory copyright protection for two consecutive terms: a first term of 28 years, measured from the date of publication, and a second or renewal term of 28 years, for a total of 56 years.[43] The renewal term reverted to the author automatically if he properly filed for renewal registration during the 28 year. Failure to comply with renewal formalities resulted in the forfeiture of copyright to the public domain. Indeed, many works entered the public domain through an author's ignorance of the formalities. Paradoxically, renewal formalities, designed to protect an author and his family, often operated to deprive an author of his work. With the passage of the Uruguay Round Agreements, copyright was restored in works for the remainder of the term of copyright if the work entered the public domain for failure to comply with formalities such as renewal. But these provisions apply only to works whose origin is a Berne or WTO country. Copyright was not restored for failure to renew in works whose origin is the United States.

[B] The Renewal Registration Requirement Under the 1976 Act

The 1976 Act has progressively modified the nature and effect of the renewal system in three significant ways. First, as originally enacted, the 1976 Act retained the bifurcated durational system for works copyrighted before 1978, with one major difference: the second term of copyright was lengthened from 28 to 47 years.[44] The second change occurred in 1992, with legislation establishing automatic renewal of all works.[45] Before these amendments, renewal registration had to be filed in the Copyright Office during the 28 year of the first term of copyright for all works still in their first terms on January 1, 1978. Failure to comply with this formality injected the work into the public domain. The Automatic Renewal Amendment abrogates the registration requirement. Now, for works first published between 1964 and 1977 (inclusive), an author will enjoy a full (now 95 years after the 1998 amendments to the Copyright Act) copyright term, without having to file for renewal during the 28 year. The Automatic Renewal Amendment,

---

[43] 17 U.S.C. § 24 (1909 Act).

[44] *See* 17 U.S.C. § 304(a). It is now 67 years after the 1998 amendments.

[45] Pub. L. No. 102-307, 106 Stat. 264 (1992).

however, does not revive a first term copyright, published before 1964, that went into the public domain for failure to file a renewal registration.

The third major change occurred with the Uruguay Round Agreements Act passed at the end of 1994. Under its provisions, copyright in certain foreign works that entered the public domain for failure to comply with formalities such as renewal registration were restored on January 1, 1996.

The term of protection for restored works is the same term the work would have enjoyed if it had not lost U.S. copyright protection. For example, a 1940 Italian movie, which had lost protection for failure to renew in 1967, will endure until December 31, 2035. The restoration provisions do not revive *all* works that fell into the public domain for failure to renew. They only apply to certain foreign works whose source country is a member of the WTO or an adherent of the Berne Convention. By contrast, the Uruguay Round amendments do not revive copyright in a work whose country of origin is the United States.[46] Thus, the renewal requirement remains an important consideration in determining whether a work of U.S. origin — a large number of works — is in the public domain.

[C] Works in Their Second Term as of January 1, 1978

The second kind of subsisting copyright is found in works in their renewal terms between December 31, 1976, and December 31, 1977. As originally enacted, the 1976 Act added an extra 19 years to the second term, extending copyright to a total term of 75 years. In other words, the second term lasted 47 years, that is, 19 years longer than the 28 year renewal term of the 1909 Act. Extension of the term was automatic, and the copyright owner needed to do nothing to receive the extra 19 years added to the renewal term of copyright. For example, suppose that a work was copyrighted in 1922 and renewal was properly claimed in 1950. Under the 1976 Act as originally enacted, the copyrighted work, subsisting on January 1, 1978, now enjoyed a second term of copyright that lasted forty-seven years, expiring after December 31, 1997.[47]

With the passage of the Copyright Term Extension Act in 1998, 20 years are added to the 47-year renewal term. With the renewal term extended to 67 years, the term of copyright for 1909 Act works now totals 95 years. The Act applies only to works still protected by copyright on its effective date of October 27, 1998. It

---

[46] A work eligible for restoration under 17 U.S.C. § 104A(h)(6)(D) must have entered the public domain for failure to comply with U.S. copyright formalities. In addition, it must have at least one author or rightholder who at the time the work was created was a national or domiciliary of a WTO or Berne country and it must not have been published in the United States during the 30-day period following publication in such eligible country. Restoration of copyright is discussed in *infra* §§ 6.18–6.19.

[47] A special status is given to older copyrights that were extended in duration by a series of congressional enactments in 1962. *See* U.S. Copyright Office, Circular 15t Extension of Copyright Terms (2005). Congress believed that passage of a new Copyright Act was imminent and thought it was unfair to allow these works to fall into the public domain. To avoid this result, Congress, from 1962 until the passage of the 1976 Act, extended the term of these copyrights every year. As for other copyrights subsisting as of January 1, 1978, these specially extended copyrights automatically receive a 75 year term. For example, a work that was copyrighted on April 10, 1915, and renewed by April 10, 1943, would have expired in 1971, but was kept alive by yearly congressional enactments. It received a 75 year term, which would have lasted through December 31, 1990.

does not restore copyright to works that fell into the public domain at the end of 1997. In other words, the Act does not extend the copyrights for works first published between 1904 and 1922, even though they were published less than 95 years ago. These works, as in the example given above, will stay in the public domain.

[D] Summary Chart: Duration Under the 1976 Act

	Date of Protection	Nature of Term	Length of Term
Works created on or after 1/1/78	When work was fixed in a tangible medium of expression	Unitary	Basic Term: Life of the author plus 70 years Alternative term for anonymous or pseudonymous works, or works made for hire: 95 years from publication or 120 years from creation, whichever is shorter
Works created but not published before 1/1/78	Federal protection began on 1/1/78	Unitary	Same as above at least through 12/31/2002 if the work remained unpublished as of that date or until 12/31/2047 if the work was published before 1/12/2003
Works published between 1964 and 1977	When work was published with notice	Dual term	28-year first term Automatic renewal term of 67 years (renewal registration is optional but incentives attach to renewal registration)
Works published between 1923 and 1963	When work was published with notice	Dual term	28-year first term Renewal term of 67 years, but only if renewal was properly obtained
Works published before 1923	N/A	N/A	Work is now in the public domain

§ 6.06 RENEWAL: COPYRIGHTS IN THE FIRST TERM AS OF 1978

[A] Generally: The Continuation of the Renewal System Under the 1976 Act

Section 24 of the 1909 Act, now incorporated into § 304(a) of the 1976 Act, establishes a bifurcated copyright term. The first term lasts 28 years, followed by a 67 year second or renewal term, which automatically reverts to the author and his family. The original rationale of the renewal term was a paternalistic one: to protect authors and their families against unremunerative transfers, which may have been given under economic duress or without knowledge of a work's potential value. Thus, authors have been given a special status in copyright law, as persons who should be helped out of bad deals they may have been stuck with.

Renewal procedures are straightforward. To claim renewal, one must file for renewal in the Copyright Office during the 28 year of the first copyright term.[48] A renewal application can be filed by anyone on behalf of someone else, but it has to be filed in the name of one entitled to the renewal term.[49] Timely filing was required to obtain the term, and failure to do so dedicated the work to the public domain. Through inadvertence or ignorance, many authors forfeited their works to the public domain by failing to comply with renewal formalities.[50]

As originally conceived, the renewal system proved to be neither fair to authors nor easy to administer. Despite its obvious drawbacks, § 304(a)[51] of the 1976 Act has incorporated the renewal system, faults included, as it existed under the prior law.[52] Congress has done so perhaps less for paternalistic reasons than to avoid the unfairness of changing rules on which authors and copyright owners have relied.[53] Today's practitioner must, therefore, understand the renewal system under the 1909 Act.

Understanding the renewal system under the 1909 Act, and the case law interpreting it, is important for determining the validity of works that would currently be in their second renewal term. First, for works whose origin is the United States,[54] the 1976 Act does not revive copyrights entering the public domain before 1978, and failure to renew was frequently the way works entered the public domain under the 1909 Act. Thus, the renewal provisions of the 1909 Act become

---

[48] 17 U.S.C. § 24 (1909 Act).

[49] *See* Nimmer on Copyright § 9.05[D] (2014).

[50] *See* Barbara A. Ringer, Copyright Office Study No. 31, Renewal of Copyright (Arthur Fisher ed. 1963).

[51] 17 U.S.C. § 304(a).

[52] By incorporating the language of § 24 of the 1909 Act, the present Copyright Act has adopted some of the most obscure language in a notoriously obscure piece of legislation.

[53] *See* H.R. Rep. No. 94-1476, at 139 (1976).

[54] The Uruguay Round Agreements Act has restored copyright in certain foreign works that were injected into the public domain for failure to comply with U.S. copyright formalities such as notice and renewal. Works of U.S. origin, however, that were ejected into the public domain for failure to renew, remain there. See *infra* §§ 6.18–6.19 for a discussion of copyright restoration.

important for evaluating whether a work has gone into the public domain. Second, one must look to the 1909 Act and its case law to determine the ownership status of a copyrighted work because the 1976 Act will not be applied retroactively for such matters.[55]

[B] Renewal Claimants

Section 24 of the 1909 Act and § 304(a)[56] of the 1976 Act provide that the renewal term vests in the author of the work.[57] As for joint works,[58] the renewal right vests in the joint authors, and renewal by one joint author or statutory successor is deemed a renewal for all the other joint authors.[59]

If an author is not living at the vesting of the renewal term, §§ 24 and 304(a) designate other classes of persons who can claim copyright. Both sections provide that if the author is not living, the widow, widower, *or* children will own the renewal term. Despite the use of the disjunctive, the Supreme Court in *DeSylva v. Ballentine*[60] constructed this language to mean that renewal rights vested in the widow or widower *and* children of an author, who would take as a class.

To illustrate, suppose an author dies before the vesting of the renewal term in his work, leaving a widow and one child. Here, widow and child would each take a 50% share as joint owners of the copyright. But what if the author left a widow with more than one child? In the previous example, if the author left two children instead of one, would each survivor take a 331/3% share, or would the widow take 50%, with each child taking a 25% share? The case law under the 1909 Act indicates the equal share solution.[61] Once it is decided who owns what shares in the copyright, all the owners are considered tenants-in-common.

If neither the author's widow nor any children are alive, the rights vest in the author's executor, to be distributed to the legatees under his will.[62] Absent a will, renewal rights vest in the author's next of kin, determined by the laws of intestacy

---

[55] *See Roth v. Pritikin*, 710 F.2d 934 (2d Cir. 1983) (noting that the 1976 Act definition of work made for hire will not be applied retroactively to transactions occurring under the 1909 Act).

[56] 17 U.S.C. § 24 (1909 Act) has been completely incorporated into 17 U.S.C. § 304(a) of the 1976 Act. *See* H.R. Rep. No. 94–1476, at 139 (1976).

[57] This would include vesting of the renewal term in the employer of a work made for hire. For a discussion of works made for hire, see *supra* § 5.02.

[58] A joint work is a work prepared by two or more authors with the intention that their contributions be merged into inseparable or interdependent parts of a unitary whole. *See* 17 U.S.C. § 101 (joint works). For a discussion of joint works, see *supra* § 5.06.

[59] *See* Nimmer on Copyright § 9.05[E] (2015).

[60] 351 U.S. 570 (1956).

[61] *See Bartok v. Boosey & Hawkes, Inc.*, 523 F.2d 941 (2d Cir. 1975). Whether the courts will adopt the 1909 Act's equal share solution is an open question. A court might be persuaded to look to the termination of transfer provisions under the 1976 Act, which provide that the widow would take a one-half interest and the children would apportion the other half *per stripes*. For a discussion of these provisions, see *infra* § 6.12.

[62] *See* 17 U.S.C. § 304(a).

in the state where the author is domiciled at death.[63]

The definitions of "widow" and "children" are no longer a matter of state law, as they were under the 1909 Act.[64] Section 101 of the 1976 Act now provides a statutory definition for these terms.[65] The term "children" now includes the author's illegitimate[66] and adopted children, and the term "widow(er)" includes the author's surviving spouse under the law of the author's domicile at death, whether or not the spouse has later remarried.[67]

§ 6.07 EXCEPTIONS TO THE AUTHOR'S RIGHT TO THE RENEWAL TERM

[A] Generally

Section 304(a) of the 1976 Act sets forth four exceptions to the rule that the author and his family are proper claimants for the renewal term. The copyright owner, rather than the author or his family, can claim the renewal term for the following: (1) posthumous works, (2) periodical, cyclopedic, or other composite works, (3) works copyrighted by a corporate body, and (4) works copyrighted by an employer as a work made for hire. The language in § 304(a) is identical to that of the 1909 Act.[68] Accordingly, one must look to the case law developed under the 1909 Act to construe these terms.

[B] Posthumous Works

To most people, the term "posthumous work" would mean any work published after the author's death. This dictionary definition of "posthumous" has not been adopted in § 304(a) of the 1976 Act. According to the House Report,[69] a posthumous work is to be defined more narrowly, as in *Bartok v. Boosey & Hawkes, Inc.*[70] This case concerned Bartok's *Concerto for Orchestra*, created toward the end of his life and assigned to his publisher before his death. Both the publisher and Bartok's son claimed the renewal rights to the work on expiration of the initial term of copyright in 1974.

The court held that this was not a posthumous work under § 24 of the 1909 Act. Although the work was published after Bartok's death, the court held that a posthumous work was a work for which no copyright assignment or other contract for exploitation of the work has occurred during the author's lifetime and which is

---

[63] *See DeSylva v. Ballentine*, 351 U.S. 570, 580–81 (1956).

[64] *See id.*

[65] 17 U.S.C. § 101 (children).

[66] *See Stone v. Williams*, 970 F.2d 1043 (2d Cir. 1992) (stating that "children" are to be determined by state law).

[67] *See* 17 U.S.C. § 101 (widow).

[68] 17 U.S.C. § 24 (1909 Act).

[69] H.R. Rep. No. 94-1476, at 139 (1976).

[70] 523 F.2d 941 (2d Cir. 1975).

unpublished before the author's death. Although the work was unpublished, Bartok had assigned rights to it before his death. Therefore, it was not a posthumous work as the court construed this term. Accordingly, the renewal term could be claimed by Bartok's son rather than the proprietor of the initial term.

Although this usage of "posthumous" deviates from the dictionary meaning of the term, the definition of "posthumous work" is consistent with the congressional purpose of the renewal term. It favors the author's family versus transferees and protects the author's family from unremunerative transfers given by the author.

[C] Composite Works and Corporate Works

The proprietor owns the renewal term for composite and corporate works. A composite work is one in which several authors have contributed individual work. It is much like a collective work,[71] except that it does not encompass anthologies of a single author. The composite work author can claim renewal for the entire work, but each individual author has a claim to the renewal rights in his individual contribution.[72]

For a work copyrighted by a corporate body (other than as an assignee or licensee of the individual author), renewal vests not in the author but in the corporate body. What this arcane category encompasses is not entirely clear, and it would appear to overlap the category of works made for hire. It has been applied in very few cases without satisfactory elucidation of its basis as an independent ground for a claim to the renewal term.[73] The Copyright Office discourages renewal registration on this basis except in certain narrow circumstances but has not clarified what those cases are or how they differ from the work made for hire category.[74]

[D] Employer of a Work Made for Hire

The fourth situation in which renewal may be claimed by the proprietor occurs in the case of an employer of a work made for hire. Although the 1976 Act has significantly modified the definition of a "work made for hire," this significant change in the law will not be applied retroactively.[75] Thus, for works published before 1978 in their first renewal term, one must apply the work made for hire doctrine developed under the 1909 Act.

Epoch Producing Corp. v. Killiam Shows, Inc.[76] demonstrates some of the difficulties involved in this retroactive application to determine who, if anyone,

---

[71] *See* 17 U.S.C. § 101 (collective work).

[72] *See* COMPENDIUM II OF COPYRIGHT OFFICE PRACTICES § 1310 (1984) (hereinafter "COMPENDIUM II").

[73] *See Schmid Bros., Inc. v. W. Goebel Porzellanfabrik, K.G.*, 589 F. Supp. 497, 505 (E.D.N.Y. 1984).

[74] *See* COMPENDIUM II, *supra* note 79, at § 1317.06(c) (giving an example of works to which stockholders of a corporation have contributed indistinguishable parts).

[75] *See Roth v. Pritikin*, 710 F.2d 934, 939 (2d Cir. 1983), (remarking that retroactive application of the 1976 Act's definition of "work made for hire" to pre-1978 transactions would raise a due process violation and be a taking of property without just compensation).

[76] 522 F.2d 737 (2d Cir. 1975).

owns the renewal term in a copyrighted work. Plaintiff Epoch, in a suit for infringement, asserted ownership as an employer for hire of D.W. Griffith's *Birth of a Nation* and argued that it had the right to claim the renewal term in the work. Epoch had renewed the work in 1942 and brought its suit for infringement against Killiam in 1969. The defendant argued that Epoch had no right to claim the renewal term because it did not qualify as an employer for hire. Thus, according to the defendant, the work had entered the public domain because the proper party had not renewed it.

The court agreed that, under the circumstances, no work for hire was created and that, unlike an original registration of copyright, a renewal registration carried no presumption of validity.[77] In addition, nowhere did the author, D.W. Griffith, explicitly state his intent to convey the renewal right.[78] Thus, the work had entered the public domain after the first 28 year term of copyright. This case is instructive because it reveals the problems of both proof and legal standards that may arise when today's courts apply the 1909 Act to transactions of the distant past.

§ 6.08 TRANSFERS OF THE RENEWAL TERM: *FISHER v. WITMARK*

The stated congressional purpose of the two-term copyright protection was to protect authors against unremunerative transfers. This paternalistic goal, however, was undermined by 1909 Act case law. In *Fred Fisher Music Co. v. M. Witmark & Sons*,[79] the Supreme Court held that an assignment by an author of the renewal term, before that right had vested, was binding on the author. It soon became industry practice to require an assignment of the author's renewal rights in the initial contract. In order to sell their works, authors were pressured into conveying their renewal rights in the second copyright term.

There was one limitation on an author's power to assign the renewal term before its expiration. The author had to survive until the renewal term vested.[80] In *Miller Music Corp. v. Charles N. Daniels*, Inc.,[81] the Supreme Court held that, when an assigning author died before the renewal vested, the right to the second term would vest in the statutory successors under § 24 of the 1909 Act. To circumvent this risk, assignees of renewal rights sought to bind all the potential statutory successors,

---

[77] *Id.* at 745.

[78] *Id.* at 747.

[79] 318 U.S. 643 (1943).

[80] It was not clear exactly when the renewal vested. The issue was never decided under the 1909 Act, and the 1976 Act did not fill the gap. There are three possibilities for the vesting date: anytime during the 28th year; when renewal is registered, *see, e.g.*, *Frederick Music Co. v. Sickler*, 708 F. Supp. 587 (S.D.N.Y. 1989); and at the beginning of the renewal term, *see, e.g.*, *Marascalco v. Fantasy, Inc.*, 953 F.2d 469 (9th Cir. 1991). *See generally* Nimmer on Copyright § 9.05[C] (2014). The Copyright Renewal Act of 1992 (Pub. L. No. 102-302, 106 Stat. 264 (1992)) has resolved the issue of the vesting date for copyrights originally secured between January 1, 1964 and December 31, 1977. Under the automatic renewal provisions, renewal vests on either of two dates: when the registration is filed, or if no registration is filed, at the beginning of the renewal term. 17 U.S.C. 304(a)(2)(A)(i) and (2)(B)(i). Automatic renewal is discussed at *infra* § 6.09.

[81] 362 U.S. 373 (1963).

such as the author's spouse, by written contract. Again, contrary to the paternalistic objective of the renewal term, courts upheld these agreements so long as they were supported by adequate consideration and were written in express language granting rights in the renewal term.[82] In sum, *Fred Fisher* and its progeny undermined the basic policy of the renewal grant, which was to protect the unequal bargaining position of many authors.

Although no renewal application need be filed after December 31, 2005,[83] the problems arising in *Fred Fisher*, as well as in *Epoch* and *DeSylva*, will arise well into the 21st century so long as ownership of renewal rights must be determined.

§ 6.09 AUTOMATIC RENEWAL FOR COPYRIGHTS ORIGINALLY SECURED BETWEEN JANUARY 1, 1964 AND DECEMBER 31, 1977

[A] Generally

The 1976 Act substantially decreased the historic importance of statutory formalities. This movement gathered further momentum with the United States' entry into the Berne Convention. One of the fundamental provisions of Berne is that the enjoyment and exercise of rights shall not be subject to any formality.[84] To many, the renewal requirement in United States law appeared inconsistent with Berne obligations. At the same time, the practical justification for retaining renewal formalities seemed increasingly dubious.

Originally, the renewal provisions were designed to allow authors to reclaim copyright and to provide certainty about copyright ownership. The renewal requirements, rather than achieving these laudatory goals, caused the opposite effect: they proved to be unfair to authors and bred legal uncertainty. First, as to fairness, renewal requirements dispossessed authors of their works. They erected a trap for many authors who failed to file for timely renewal in a procedurally correct way, thereby injecting their works into the public domain.

Second, the renewal provisions generated uncertainty about copyright ownership. Much of this uncertainty can be traced to the confusion over when the renewal term "vested" under applicable statutory principles.

The problem here is obvious. Suppose that an author granted an assignment of renewal rights and that renewal was timely claimed (*i.e.*, during the 28 year), and suppose further that the author died before the renewal term began. Who owned the rights to the renewal term: the author's statutory beneficiaries or the grantee of the renewal term? Under the case law, the answer depended upon *when* the renewal term had vested. Some courts held that the renewal vested on the date of

---

[82] *See* NIMMER ON COPYRIGHT § 9.06[C] (2014).

[83] Works published in 1977 will be the last group of works for which a renewal application will be required. For these works, a renewal application will have to be filed in 2005 to claim the renewal term of 67 years.

[84] Berne Convention for the Protection of Literary and Artistic Works art. 5(2), S. Treaty Doc. No. 99–27, 1161 U.N.T.S.3.

the renewal registration, which could occur at any time during the 28 year. Other courts held that the author had to survive until the beginning of the renewal term.[85]

Congress enacted the Copyright Renewal Act of 1992[86] to remedy the various difficulties of the prior, mandatory, renewal system.

[B] How Automatic Renewal Works

[1] Permissive Renewal

For works whose copyright was secured between January 1, 1964, and December 31, 1977, renewal was awarded automatically at the end of the first term.

These works will enjoy the 67-year renewal term without having to file a renewal registration. An author may still file for renewal, and will want to do so because of certain advantages that flow from a renewal registration, but compliance with renewal formalities is permissive and will not affect the validity of the work. On the other hand, pre-1964 works are not affected by the automatic renewal amendment. The amendment does not alter the public domain status for pre-1964 works that have failed to comply with the renewal requirements.

From a practical standpoint, this means that the first works to have been automatically renewed were those whose renewal term began on January 1, 1993. The last works to be renewed were those whose first terms ended in 2005. Thus, after 2005, an actual renewal process no longer exists. But as discussed below, issues involving the renewal process are very much alive.

[2] Clarifying the Vesting Problem

Under the Renewal Act, if a renewal application was filed during the twenty-eighth year by the person entitled to the renewal (*i.e., the author or the author's statutory heirs*), the renewal term vested at the beginning of the twenty-ninth year in that person even though that person died before the renewal term began — thereby validating any preexisting assignments of the renewal term.[87]Alternatively, if no application was made, the renewal term vested in whoever was the appropriate renewal claimant on December 31st of the initial term's 28 year.[88]

---

[85] *Compare Frederick Music Co. v. Sickler*, 708 F. Supp. 587 (S.D.N.Y. 1989) (stating that renewal vests when the first qualified claim is filed), *with Marascalco v. Fantasy, Inc.*, 953 F.2d 469 (9th Cir. 1991) (noting that § 304(a) requires an author to survive until the start of the renewal term in order for the renewal copyright interest to vest in his assignees).

[86] 102 Pub. L. No. 102-307, 106 Stat. 264 (1992).

[87] *See, e.g., Roger Miller Music, Inc. v. Sony/ATV Publishing, LLC*, 672 F.3d 434 (6th Cir. 2012) (where author's assignee filed for renewal in author's name in January and April 1992, and author died in October 1992, renewal terms vested in assignee on January 1, 1993, rather than in author's heirs). Alternatively, if no application was made, the renewal term vested in whoever was the appropriate renewal claimant on December 31st of the initial term's 28th year. 17 U.S.C. § 304(a)(2).

[88] *See* 17 U.S.C. 304(a)(2)(B) (as amended by 102 Pub. L. No. 307, 106 Stat. 264 (1992)).

For example, suppose that the composer of a musical work secured copyright in 1977. The renewal term will have begun automatically on January 1, 2006. The renewal term will vest in the author if she or he applied for renewal in 2005 or lived to December 31, 2005. If the author died before January 1, 2006, without having registered, the renewal term will have vested in those of the author's widow(er) or children alive when any of them obtained a 28-year registration. If no registration is obtained, renewal will have vested in those who are alive on December 31, 2005. If none of the statutory beneficiaries were alive, the renewal term will have vested in the author's executor.

[C] Continuing Incentives to Register

The opportunity to "lock in" an early vesting date is an obvious reason why renewal claimants should have preferred actual over automatic renewal where they had the choice. In addition, the Act provided three powerful incentives for a timely renewal filing. Thanks to automatic renewal, the owner of the renewal term no longer lost his or her copyright for failure to comply with renewal formalities. But the owner may not be able to enjoy the economic benefits of copyright ownership without having filed a timely claim for renewal.

The first major incentive in the 1992 Renewal Act concerns derivative works prepared under an authorization granted during the original term of copyright. If a timely renewal was filed, first-term grants of renewal rights may be nullified. Thus, the principles of *Stewart v. Abend*[89] still apply, but only if a renewal registration was obtained during the 28 year of publication. If no registration was filed, a derivative work made pursuant to the grant can still be exploited, but no new derivative work can be made after the new term had begun. For example, suppose an author of a play secures copyright in the play and grants motion picture and renewal rights to a film company. If the renewal right vests in the author, he is bound by the grant, and the film company will own the renewal rights. On the other hand, if the author dies before renewal vests, the author's statutory beneficiaries can prevent the motion picture from being exploited, but only if renewal registration was timely claimed. Without a timely renewal registration, an authorized film, translation, or other derivative work prepared under the grant can continue to be exploited under the terms of grant.

The second benefit of timely registration concerns the evidentiary weight accorded the registration. If registration was made during the last year of the first term, the certificate of renewal registration constitutes prima facie evidence as to the validity of the facts stated in the certificate. The evidentiary weight to be given to the certificates for registration made after the end of that one-year period is within the discretion of the court.

A third incentive to register concerns the remedies available to those who have registered their renewals. Remedies for copyright infringement are narrowed for authors who failed to file a timely renewal registration. Failure to file for renewal disallows statutory and actual damages, attorney's fees, and seizure and forfeiture

---

[89] 495 U.S. 207 (1990) (discussed at *infra* § 6.10).

for all infringements that commence before registration.[90] Registration at any time during the second term made the above remedies available for acts taking place after registration.

§ 6.10 THE RENEWAL TERM AND DERIVATIVE WORKS[91]

[A] Generally

When an author has licensed another, during the first copyright term, to create a derivative work, to what extent can the owner of the copyright in the derivative work continue to exploit the work in the second copyright term? The issue arises as follows: suppose R has licensed E, during the first copyright term, to create a motion picture of R's novel. E's motion picture is a derivative work based on the underlying work (*i.e.*, the novel). Can E's motion picture, a derivative work, continue to be exploited without R's consent during the renewal term?

This situation involves a conflict between the rationale of the renewal term and the theory of derivative rights. On the one hand, the renewal term creates an entirely new right, one that reverts automatically to the author and his family, unencumbered by assignments and licenses granted during the initial term. This suggests that a license to prepare a derivative work would terminate at the end of the initial term, as would the right to exploit the derivative work prepared under that license.

On the other hand, a derivative work may be individually copyrighted, and the derivative work author will own the copyright in the original elements added to the underlying work. Some derivative works surpass the underlying works in their creative and commercial value. Thus, to impede exploitation of the derivative work after the first term has expired may be both unfair to derivative work authors and costly to the public, who may be deprived of access to the work.

Until the Supreme Court case of *Stewart v. Abend*,[92] the case law was very much in conflict on the issue of the right to continued exploitation of a derivative work after expiration of the first copyright term. One line of cases implied that the derivative work could not be exploited without the consent of the copyright owner of the underlying work.[93] The opposite approach would permit continued exploitation of a derivative work in the second copyright term absent authorization of the owner of the renewal term.[94]

---

[90] *See* 17 U.S.C. §§ 504, 505, 509.

[91] For a detailed overview, see Peter Jaszi, *When Works Collide: Derivative Motion Pictures, Underlying Rights, and the Public Interest*, 28 UCLA L. Rev. 715 (1981); Carol A. Ellingson, *The Copyright Exception for Derivative Works and the Scope of Utilization*, 56 Ind. L.J. 1 (1980).

[92] 495 U.S. 207 (1990).

[93] *See Ricordi & Co. v. Paramount Pictures, Inc.*, 189 F.2d 469 (2d Cir. 1951); *see also Fitch v. Shubert*, 20 F. Supp. 314 (S.D.N.Y. 1937); *Grove Press, Inc. v. Greenleaf Publ'g. Co.*, 247 F. Supp. 518 (E.D.N.Y. 1965); *supra* § 2.09[B].

[94] The leading case is *Rohauer v. Killiam Shows*, 551 F.2d 484 (2d Cir. 1977). In *Rohauer*, a movie, *Son of the Sheik*, based on a preexisting novel, could continue to be exploited even though the author died before vesting of the renewal term, and successors to the renewal term assigned their rights to a third

This latter approach views the derivative work as an independent work — a "new property" — in its own right and in its entirety, unattached to the underlying work.[95] Because it runs counter to the principle that derivative work authors own only the original elements added to the underlying work, this "new property rights" theory of derivative works received harsh criticism by commentators,[96] and even subsequent Second Circuit cases challenged its authority.[97] But it was not until 1990, with *Stewart v. Abend*, that the Supreme Court reconciled this conflict about the effect of expiration of the first term of copyright on the continuing right to exploit a derivative work made pursuant to a first-term grant.

[B] *Stewart v. Abend:* Demise of the New Property Theory of Derivative Works

In *Stewart v. Abend*,[98] the Supreme Court explicitly rejected the new property rights theory of derivative works, holding that the assignment of renewal rights by an author does not defeat the right of the author's statutory successor(s) to those rights if the author dies before the renewal right vests. In other words, when the grant of rights in the preexisting work lapses, the right to use parts of it in the derivative work ceases, and its continued use will infringe the preexisting work.

Stewart involved the film rights to a short story, "It Had to Be Murder," first published in 1942. The author, Cornell Woolrich, assigned the film rights to the short story to a production company and agreed to renew the copyright and assign the rights to the second term. Actor Jimmy Stewart and director Alfred Hitchcock acquired these rights and released the film version, *Rear Window*, in 1954. Woolrich died in 1968 before he could renew his copyright. In 1969, the executor of Woolrich's estate renewed the copyright and assigned the renewal term to Abend,

---

party. Defendant's right to continued exploitation of the derivative work was limited to the version created under the grant and the court gave no right to make second generation derivative works. In so holding, the court was heavily influenced by the policy behind the not-yet-effective termination of transfer provisions of the 1976 Act, which would have allowed the author to recover interests transferred for the last 19 years (now 39 years) of the renewal term (17 U.S.C. § 304(c)), and allowed termination of all transfers at the end of their 35th year (17 U.S.C. (§ 203)). Under these provisions, a grant may be terminated, but the continued exploitation of a derivative work prepared under the grants is allowed. See the discussion of termination of transfers in *supra* § 6.11.

[95] Professor Nimmer called this the "new property rights" theory of the derivative work. *See* Nimmer on Copyright § 3.07[A] (2014).

[96] *See* Malcolm L. Mimms, Jr., *Reversion and Derivative Works Under the Copyright Acts of 1909 and 1976*, 25 N.Y.L. Sch. L. Rev. 595 (1980); Nimmer on Copyright § 3.07[A] (2014); Ralph S. Brown, *The Widening Gyre: Are Derivative Works Getting Out of Hand?*, 3 Cardozo Arts & Ent. L.J. 2 (1984).

[97] *See Russell v. Price*, 612 F.2d 1123 (9th Cir. 1979). Although a derivative work film based on the Shaw play, *Pygmalion*, prepared during the first term of the play's copyright, had entered the public domain for failure to renew, defendant could not exploit the public domain because to do so would infringe the underlying work (the play), which was not in the public domain. Only the original elements of the film entered the public domain, but the material used in the film from the underlying play was left unaffected. Thus, because the film could not be used without using the play, defendant would be liable for infringement. *See also Filmvideo Releasing Corp. v. Hastings*, 668 F.2d 91 (2d Cir. 1981) (finding the entry into public domain of derivative work motion picture for failure to renew had no effect on valid copyright in underlying stories).

[98] 495 U.S. 207 (1990).

who was acquiring the renewal copyrights to a number of stories based on films. On the re-release of the film in various media, Abend sued for copyright infringement, claiming that the right to use the film version terminated when Woolrich died before renewing his copyright.

The Supreme Court agreed with the plaintiff, holding that the derivative work film could not be exploited without the permission of the owner of the underlying work. Justice O'Connor, writing for the majority, based her decision on a general principle: one may exploit only such copyrighted material as one owns or is authorized to use. Under this basic principle, a derivative work author cannot escape his obligations to the owner of the renewal copyright merely because he created a new version under an assignment or license that ended with the first copyright term. By implication, it would not change matters even if the derivative work author had contributed as much or more than the author of the underlying work. The Court also rejected the defendant's assertion that the termination of transfer provisions of the 1976 Act, allowing continued exploitation of a derivative work created before termination, manifested congressional intent to alter the delicate balance between the rights of authors of preexisting and derivative works.

[C] *Stewart v. Abend* Reassessed

Simply stated, *Stewart* denies continued exploitation during the renewal term of a derivative work prepared during the initial term, unless rights during the renewal term were properly obtained. It gives primacy to authors of preexisting works at the expense of derivative work authors. Of course, the derivative work author owns the original elements added to the underlying work and can continue to use them as he wishes, unless this use would infringe the underlying work. This traditional principle, however, presents intractable problems for the continued exploitation of certain works, such as an opera based on a play, a film based on a novel, or a translation. In these kinds of derivative works, the new elements are so inextricably fused with the underlying work that one cannot be used without the other. In such instances, the practical effect will be to deny the derivative work author the right to his own original authorship.

Given the extensive number of movies, plays, television programs, sound recordings, etc., that are based on preexisting works in which copyright was secured before 1978, *Stewart* changes the way licenses for these derivative works are negotiated. For example, suppose a short story published in 1977 is made into a movie in 1999 under a grant conveying the renewal term, and the author dies before the renewal terms vests. If the statutory beneficiaries comply with renewal formalities, all rights to the continued exploitation of the film terminate.

For the most part, continued use of the derivative work will have to be renegotiated, and the new terms will be subject to the bargaining process. But this renegotiation process may often involve heavy transaction costs, thereby diminishing the value of both the preexisting and derivative works. Moreover, some derivative work owners may be faced with a tough decision: either pay the price of a new license or assignment (including the costs of negotiation) or stop using the derivative work. An inability to meet the new contract price may prevent the dissemination of some valuable derivative works, ultimately depriving the consumer of access to these works. Even so, one might conclude that at least the practical effect is beneficial to a worthy group of persons: the heirs of authors of preexisting works. One might view *Stewart* as a ruling that transfers wealth from derivative work authors to heirs of authors of preexisting works. But it is uncertain that the heirs of authors will really benefit from the "windfall" they apparently gain from *Stewart*. Instead, the heirs of authors may obtain less than they anticipated if future derivative work authors, to avert the risks and uncertainties of renegotiation, avoid using pre-1978 works on which to base their derivative works. Thus, the unintended effect of *Stewart* may well be to reduce the value of pre-1978 works, harming the very heirs of the authors it appears to champion.

Part III. TERMINATION OF TRANSFERS

§ 6.11 TERMINATION GENERALLY

[A] Sections 304(c), 304(d) and 203 Distinguished.[99]

The termination of transfer provisions initiated by the 1976 Act allow authors and their statutory successors the right to terminate copyright grants after a designated period of time.[100] This unwaivable right serves much the same purpose as the renewal term of the 1909 Act. The purpose of the provisions is paternalistic, protecting authors from unremunerative transfers that may be given because of an author's "unequal bargaining position . . . resulting in part from the impossibility of determining a work's value until it has been exploited."[101] These termination provisions allow an author and her family a second chance to reap the benefits from the author's works but avoid the objectionable features of the two-term copyright durational mechanism of the 1909 Act.

Despite Congress's paternalistic intentions, the termination provisions are in many ways a poor substitute for the renewal opportunity that was largely thwarted by the Supreme Court's decision in *Fisher v. Witmark*.[102] Whereas the renewal term *automatically* vested in the author or the author's heirs (unless assigned), termination requires that the author or the author's heirs take a series of formal steps in order to recapture the copyright. In practice it can be quite difficult to

---

[99] For an overview, see Frank R. Curtis, *Caveat Emptor in Copyright: A Practical Guide to the Termination of Transfer Provisions of the New Copyright Act*, 25 Bull. Copyright Soc'y 19 (1977); Harold See, *Copyright Ownership of Joint Works and Terminations of Transfers*, 30 U. Kan. L. Rev. 517 (1982); Marc R. Stein, *Termination of Transfers and Licenses Under the New Copyright Act: Thorny Problems for the Copyright Bar*, 24 UCLA L. Rev. 1141, 1152 (1977).

[100] For a discussion of the rights and policy regarding termination rights and a discussion of how renegotiation of the original agreement is used to avoid the termination rights, see Lydia Pallas Loren, *Renegotiating the Copyright Deal in the Shadow of the "Inalienable" Right to Terminate*, 62 Fla. L. Rev. 1329 (2010).

[101] H.R. Rep. No. 94-1476, at 124 (1976). For a discussion of entitlements theory and how termination alters parties' bargaining positions, see Matthew V.H. Noller, *Darkness on the Edge of Town: How Entitlements Theory Can Shine a Light on Termination of Transfers in Sound Recordings*, 46 Ga. L. Rev. 763 (2012).

[102] Discussed at § 6.08.

identify the grant(s) to be terminated, to determine whether the work is made for hire, to calculate the proper termination window(s), and to complete all the steps necessary to terminate.[103]

Termination provisions cover two distinctly different situations: those made under § 304(c) and (d) and those terminations made pursuant to § 203. Sections 304(c) and (d)[104] apply to works in their second renewal term as of January 1, 1978. Section 304(c) allows the author and statutory successors to terminate transfers made *before 1978* in order to recover the thirty-nine years of the extended renewal term. The 1976 Act, as originally enacted, lengthened the renewal term an extra nineteen years. In 1998, Congress added another twenty years to the renewal term, which now totals 39 years.[105] Section 304(d) was added by the 1998 amendments, extending the term of subsisting copyrights another 20 years. This section accords a termination right for this 20-year extension to authors or successors who did not exercise their original termination rights under § 304(c).

The other termination of transfer provision, § 203,[106] applies to transfers made *on or after January 1, 1978*. These two provisions, those under § 304 and those under § 203, give the author and her family the right to terminate, but only if the procedures established by statute and regulation are followed. In other words, termination is not automatic, and if the author or her family neglect to take the necessary steps within the statutory time period, the transfer will continue in accordance with the original contract.[107]

[B] "Agreements to the Contrary"

For both § 304 and § 203, the right to terminate cannot be waived, and the parties may terminate a grant "notwithstanding any agreement to the contrary, including an agreement to make a will or to make a further grant."[108]

---

[103] *See e.g. Siegel v. Warner Bros. Entertainment.*, Inc., 542 F. Supp. 2d 1098 (C.D. Cal. 2008). (holding that the Siegels had, under Section 304(c) of the Copyright Act, successfully terminated the first grant of rights in Superman — resulting in a recapture of a one-half share of rights to the first Superman comic story and entitling them to an accounting of profits attributable to that story as exploited in new comics, films and other works by the defendants after 1999, the effective date of the termination. The court, however, limited its ruling by denying profits arising from exploitation of pre-1999 Superman derivative works and profits attributable to DC's famous Superman related trademarks. The court also held that a black-and-white depiction of the iconic cover of Action Comics #1 was not subject to termination because it was published outside of the statutory timeframe for serving a termination notice.) For a critical analysis of changes in the law regarding termination of transfers and suggestions on how to restore clarity in this area of the law, see Peter S. Menell & David Nimmer, *Pooh-Poohing Copyright Law's "Inalienable" Termination Right*, 57 J. Copyright Soc'y 799 (2010).

[104] 17 U.S.C. § 304(c)–(d).

[105] For example, suppose that the second 28-year term would have expired in 1990. Section 304(c) extends the renewal term for another 39 years until 2029.

[106] 17 U.S.C. § 203.

[107] *See* 17 U.S.C. §§ 203(a)(5), 304(c)(5).

[108] 17 U.S.C. §§ 203(a)(5), 304(c)(5). For an argument that Congress should enact new legislation expressly authorizing authors to make a nonwaivable, irrevocable dedication of their works for the use and benefit of the public, see Timothy K. Armstrong, *Shrinking the Commons: Termination of Copyright Licenses and Transfers for the Benefit of the Public*, 47 Harv. J. Legis. 359 (2010).

In addition to nonwaivability, the right to terminate cannot be assigned in advance of the termination date. The Act provides that a "further grant, or agreement to make a further grant, of any right covered by a terminated grant is valid only if it is made after the effective date of the termination." Thus, the termination provisions avoid the problem created by 1909 Act case law, whereby renewal rights may be assigned before their vesting.

Unlike the 1909 practice, third parties can no longer buy future interests in a speculative manner and deprive the original grantee of the opportunity to negotiate future transfers.[109]

Despite the statutory language hostile to the waiver of termination rights, difficult issues arise when rights are renegotiated in anticipation of termination. In particular, the question arises whether termination rights may be effectively alienated before their "vesting," so as to frustrate the expectations of the successors designated in § 304. Obviously, the general answer is "no." Section 304(c)(5) states that "[t]ermination of the grant may be effected *notwithstanding any agreement to the contrary*, including an agreement to make a will or to make any future grant" (emphasis added). But what, exactly, is an "agreement to the contrary"?[110] This provision came about as a reaction to the *Fred Fisher*[111] decision to prevent the author from waiving termination rights. But can an author and a publisher voluntarily agree to terminate an existing agreement, otherwise subject to termination under § 304(c), and enter into a new agreement, even if the effect is to postpone or eliminate a future termination opportunity?

Congress apparently thought the answer was "yes." The House Report expressly states that "§ 203 would not prevent the parties to a transfer or license from voluntarily agreeing at any time to terminate an existing grant and negotiating a new one, thereby causing another 35-year period to start running."[112] What Congress did not anticipate, however, was that voluntary termination and renegotiation after 1978 of a grant made before 1978 could eliminate the future termination rights altogether. In this instance, § 304(d) would not apply, because the new grant was made after 1978, and that section only applies to agreements executed before 1978. Nor would § 203(a)(5) apply because the new grant was not made by the "author," but by the author's heirs. The question is whether a contractual revocation of the right to terminate is "an agreement to the contrary" under § 304(c)(5) or an ordinary contract freely negotiated by the parties.

Three cases illustrate the thorny factual issues involved. In both *Milne v. Stephen Slesinger, Inc.*[113] (which involved rights in *Winnie-the-Pooh*) and *Penguin Group (USA) Inc. v. Steinbeck*,[114] the courts held that a post-1978 renegotiation of a pre-1978 agreement was a new agreement to which neither § 304 nor § 203 applied. The courts reasoned, in similar fashion, that the purposes of termination

---

109 See H.R. Rep. No. 94-1476, at 125 (1976).

110 17 U.S.C. § 304(c)(5).

111 For a discussion of renewal rights revocations see *supra* § 6.08.

112 *See* H.R. Rep. No. 94-1476, at 127 (1976).

113 430 F.3d 1036 (9th Cir. 2005).

114 537 F.3d 193 (2d Cir. 2008).

had been served because the author's son (in *Milne*) or widow (in *Steinbeck*) had used the threat of termination to negotiate a more favorable deal. Accordingly, they held that a renegotiated agreement was not an "agreement to the contrary," even though it had the effect of eliminating the later-enacted § 304(d) rights of the author's heirs (Milne's granddaughter and Steinbeck's two sons), who were not parties to the renegotiated agreements. In *Milne*, the court noted that although the "statute does not define the phrase 'agreement to the contrary,' it does provide two examples of agreements that would constitute an 'agreement to the contrary': 'an agreement to make a will' and 'an agreement to make any future grant.'" Here, the agreement did not fall into either category and could not be considered an agreement to the contrary.[115]

By contrast, in *Classic Media, Inc. v. Mewborn*,[116] the court held that the daughter of author Eric Knight could terminate a 1976 agreement granting rights in her father's story *Lassie Come Home*, notwithstanding a 1978 agreement confirming and modifying the 1976 agreement. The court distinguished *Milne*, noting that Milne had used the threat of termination to negotiate a more favorable deal. By contrast, the court concluded that Mewborn did not "intend to relinquish a known termination right" and did not receive any additional consideration. Mewborn's predicament was quite different than those of Milne and Steinbeck. In those situations, the beneficiaries had bargaining power. In addition, the transfer of rights was more lucrative for the author's heirs, and the agreements were freely and intelligently entered into by the parties.[117]

§ 6.12 TERMINATION OF THE EXTENDED RENEWAL TERM UNDER §§ 304(c) AND 304(d)

[A] Termination of the Extended Renewal Term

The Copyright Act allows the termination of the extended renewal term under two separate time frames. Section 304(c) gives authors or successors the right to terminate a grant and recapture the full 39 years of the extended renewal term. Initially, § 304(c) permitted the author or successor to terminate the extended 19-year term. With the term extension amendments of 1998, 20 more years were added for a total of 39 years. Second, § 304(d), added by the term extensions amendments of 1998, allows authors or successors the right to terminate the extended 20-year term — the "second bite at the termination apple" — even if they did not exercise their rights to recapture the initial 19 years of the extended term. Authors may terminate the grant and recapture the last 20 years of the extended renewal term. Thus, § 304(c) and (d) ensure that any windfall resulting from extension should go first to authors rather than be given to the owner of the

---

[115] 430 F.3d at 1043.

[116] 532 F.3d 978 (9th Cir. 2008).

[117] For another example of invalid "an agreement to the contrary" under § 304 see *Marvel Characters, Inc. v. Simon*, 310 F.3d 280 (2d Cir. 2002) (holding that an agreement made after a work's creation stipulating that the work was created as a work made for hire constitutes an "agreement to the contrary" under § 304(c)(5), which can be disavowed pursuant to the statute).

existing renewal rights. The termination provisions of § 304(d) can be used only if the termination rights under 304(c) expired before the effective date of the 1998 term extension amendments.

The grants covered by § 304(c) and (d) should not be confused with an author or family making advance assignments of the renewal term. These transfers of the renewal term are still binding. The provisions in § 304(c) and (d) concern only recovery of the 39 years of the extended renewal term for grants executed before 1978.

How the two phases of termination function is best illustrated by an example. Suppose that a novel was copyrighted by an author in 1935, who, in 1963, before the 1976 Act became effective, assigned her expectancy in the renewal term of the copyright to a movie studio. Assume that the author survives the vesting of the renewal term. Here, the author and her heirs would have no rights in the copyright during the renewal term that would expire after 1991. Under § 304(c), however, the author and his or her heirs could recuperate the extended renewal term for a maximum of nineteen years so long as they followed the notice of termination procedures. Assume that they do so. Now, under the 1998 amendments to the Act, they would receive another twenty years of protection, and, in our example, the copyright in the work would enter the public domain after 2030.

What if the author or his or her heirs failed to accomplish timely notice in terminating the grant? They would, of course, miss out on the first "windfall" of nineteen years. Fortunately for them, the term extension amendments of 1998 created another "windfall." Here, § 304(d) provides them with a second opportunity — the so-called "second bite at the apple" — to terminate the grant, beginning 2010, if they abide by the statutory notice procedures. In that event, the author and heirs will enjoy a maximum of twenty years in the work until it enters the public domain after 2030.

Schematically, the copyright terms referred to, in the above example, look like this:

1935:	1963:	1991:	2010:	2030:
Work is published.	copyright renewed.	Second term ends.	First termination period ends.	Copyright ends.
28-year first term begins.	28-year second or renewal term begins.	19-year first termination period begins. § 304(c)	20-year second termination period begins. § 304(d)	Work enters public domain.
FIRST TERM	67-YEAR RENEWAL TERM			

[B] The Mechanics of § 304(c) and 304(d)

The intricate mechanics of § 304(c) and 304(d) termination can be broken down into six questions:

(1) *What grants are covered?*

(a) Grants executed before January 1, 1978, by the author or his successors who could claim the renewal term of any transfer covering renewal rights, including exclusive and nonexclusive licenses.[118]

(b) Exceptions are works made for hire and dispositions by will.

(2) *Who can terminate?*[119]

(a) The author or a majority of authors of a joint work.

(b) If the author is dead:

(i) If the author dies without children, leaving only a widow or widower, then the widow or widower owns the entire termination interest.

(ii) If the author leaves surviving children, without a widow or widower, then the children take the entire interest.

(iii) If both a widow(er) and children are surviving, the widow(er) takes a 50% share and the children take the other 50%. The rights of the children and grandchildren are exercised *per stirpes*. This means that the children take the share that their parents would have taken. Suppose, for example, the author's widow and two of his three children are living and a third is deceased:[120]

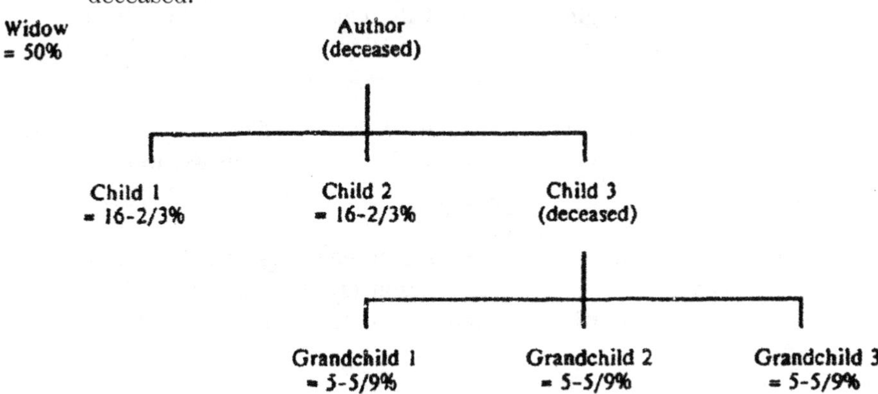

In this example, the widow will take 50% and the children will take 50%. The share of each child will be $16^{2/3}$%, but if Child 3 is

[118] *See* 17 U.S.C. § 304(c).

[119] See 17 U.S.C. § 304(c)(1), (2).

[120] *See* H.R. Rep. No. 94-1476, at 125 (1976).

dead, leaving three children, each of the three grandchildren will get $5^{5/9}$%. Because a majority interest is needed to terminate a right, the widow must be joined by one of the children to terminate. If neither Child 1 nor Child 2 joins, then the widow must obtain a *majority* consent of the third child's children to terminate the right. The result is consistent with the principle that the interest of a deceased child can be exercised only by majority action of his or her surviving children.[121] One grandchild will not be enough, even though it would look as if the ownership would constitute $55^{5/9}$%.

(iv) If the author's widow or widower, children, and grandchildren are not living, the author's executor, administrator, personal representative, or trustee shall own the author's entire termination interest.[122]

(c) When a grant is given by one other than the author, all surviving grantors are required to terminate.

(3) *When may termination take place?*[123]

(a) Section 304(c) concerns the additional nineteen years added to the renewal term by the original provisions of the 1976 Act.

Section 304(c) termination may be effected during the five-year period beginning at the end of 56 years from the date copyright was originally secured, or beginning on January 1, 1978, whichever is later.

(b) Section 304(d) concerns the additional twenty years provided by the 1998 term extension amendments. Section 304(d) can be used only if the termination rights under § 304(c) expired before the effective date of the 1998 term extension amendments and if the termination right provided in § 304(c) were not exercised.

Section 304(d) termination may be effected during the five-year period beginning at the end of 75 years from the date copyright was originally secured.[124]

(4) *How may termination be effected?*[125]

(a) By serving written notice on the grantee or his successor in title. If the grant was executed by a person or persons other than the author, all of those who executed the grant and are surviving must sign the notice.

---

121 *See id.*

122 As amended in 1998 by the Sonny Bono Copyright Term Extension Act. *See* § 304(c)(2)(D). The 1976 Act, as originally enacted, said nothing about who, if anyone, could exercise termination rights if the widow or widower and children or grandchildren were not alive when termination arose.

123 *See* 17 U.S.C. § 304(c)(3), 304(d)(2).

124 *See* 17 U.S.C. § 304(d)(2).

125 *See* 17 U.S.C. § 304(c)(4).

(b) Notice must comply with Copyright Office regulations.[126]

(c) A copy of the notice must be recorded in the Copyright Office before the effective date of termination.

(5) *What is the effect of termination?*[127]

(a) All rights revert to those having the right to terminate.

(b) The exception is that derivative works prepared before termination may continue to be exploited under the terms of the grant.

(c) No new derivative works may be prepared after the termination date.

(d) Termination rights vest on the date notice is served.

(6) *Who can make further grants?*[128]

(a) Owners are tenants-in-common who can authorize further grants if signed by the same number and proportion as are required to terminate. The right granted is effective for all owners, even non-signers.

§ 6.13 TERMINATION FORMALITIES

The 1976 Act sets forth the general formalities for termination of transfer, and the Copyright Office has issued the form, content, and manner of service for proper notice of termination.[129] There remain, however, several open questions that will have to be answered by case law. For example, the 1976 Act states that "termination shall be effected by serving an advance notice in writing upon the grantee or grantee's successor in title."[130] The meaning of "successor in title" is nowhere indicated in the Act.

This and other issues concerning § 304(c) terminations were examined in *Burroughs v. Metro-Goldwyn-Mayer, Inc.*,[131] which involved an attempt to terminate a 1931 nonexclusive license to film rights with use of certain *Tarzan* characters. The nonexclusive license in question was given by a family-owned corporation, ERB, Inc., to MGM's predecessor in title. The author's heirs served notice of termination on the family-owned corporation, but not on MGM, in 1977, before the effective date of the 1976 Act. The plaintiffs contended that the *Tarzan* grant was effectively terminated and that a 1981 remake of *Tarzan* by MGM infringed their rights. The District Court held that the character, Tarzan, was sufficiently delineated to be a copyrightable interest and as such could be terminated.[132] The

---

126 *See* 37 C.F.R. § 201.10.

127 *See* 17 U.S.C. § 304(c)(6).

128 *See* 17 U.S.C. § 304(c)(6)(C), (D).

129 *See* 37 C.F.R. § 201.10.

130 *See* 17 U.S.C. § 304(c)(4).

131 519 F. Supp. 388 (S.D.N.Y. 1981), *aff'd*, 683 F.2d 610 (2d Cir. 1982).

132 *Id.*

termination was ineffective, however, because it was premature (the Act was not yet in effect in 1977) and because it was served on the family-owned corporation (the original grantee) and not on the "current successor in title," MGM, as it should have been.

On appeal, the Second Circuit affirmed the decision, but on different grounds, stating that the Copyright Office regulations require that notice of termination be accompanied by a short statement as to the grants covered. The plaintiffs failed to list five titles of works in their notice of termination. The court concluded that this omission rendered the termination ineffective because the grant gave the right to use the Tarzan character for each of these titles. Thus, the grant remained intact because, to be effective, a notice of termination must clearly identify the grant to which the notice applies.[133]

Burroughs still leaves open the question of whether a notice of termination, to be effective, must be served on the grantee, the grantee's successor in title, or both. The Act provides that the notice must be served on the grantee *or* the grantee's successor in title.[134] Does use of the disjunctive in the statutory language mean that the terminating party has the choice? Judge Newman, in a concurring opinion,[135] suggested that notice was ineffective because it was not served on MGM. To allow the notice to be served on the family-owned corporation would be like allowing the heirs to serve notice on themselves. In the circumstances of this case, the heirs should have at least served notice on a realistic grantee, which was MGM.

Clearly, an obligation to serve all nonexclusive licensees of an original grantee would place an enormous burden on the author, particularly if the author's grantee has conveyed a large number of nonexclusive licenses. On the other hand, to allow notice on the original grantee would undermine a basic policy of the notice provisions, which is to provide adequate notice for the person whose interest is being terminated. One intermediate solution, supporting both the interest of the author and his grantee, would require the author to serve notice on the original grantee and his exclusive licensees, but not on nonexclusive licensees. Such a requirement would impose the minimum amount of hardship for all concerned.[136]

§ 6.14 TERMINATION OF TRANSFER UNDER § 203[137]

Terminations of transfers under § 203 provisions apply to grants made after 1977. Because the first terminations under § 203 will take place beginning in 2013 for grants given in 1978, they are not of such immediate practical importance as terminations covering the last thirty-nine years of the renewal term under § 304(c). The practical effect of § 203 termination provisions, however, will be felt where parties to transfers of copyright take these provisions into account in drafting their

---

133 *See* 37 C.F.R. § 201.10(b)(ii).

134 17 U.S.C. §§ 203(a)(4), 304(c)(4).

135 *Burroughs v. Metro-Goldwyn-Mayer, Inc.*, 683 F.2d 610, 635 (2d Cir. 1982) (Newman, J., concurring).

136 *See* Nimmer on Copyright § 11.06[B] (2014).

137 *See* 17 U.S.C. § 203.

agreements. As was the case with § 304(c) terminations, a termination of transfer under § 203 requires the author or his successors to affirmatively follow procedures set forth in the Act. If the termination right is not exercised, the grant will last the entire term unless otherwise stated in the contract. In addition, the right to terminate cannot be contracted away, including an agreement to make a will or to make a future grant.[138]

Section 203 is similar, but not identical, to the termination provisions of § 304(c).[139] The same questions, however, should be considered in analyzing § 203 terminations as were considered for § 304(c) terminations:

(1) *What grants are covered?*[140]

(a) Grants by the author of any copyright interest, including exclusive and nonexclusive licenses.

(b) Grants made on or after January 1, 1978, for works created before or after 1978.

(c) Grants not covered are of works made for hire and dispositions by will.

(2) *Who can terminate?*[141]

(a) The author or, for joint works, a majority of authors who executed the grant.

(b) If the author is deceased, a majority of owners of his termination interest.[142]

(c) If the author's widow or widower, children, and grandchildren are not living, the author's executor, administrator, personal representative, or trustee shall own the author's entire termination interest.[143]

(3) *When may termination take place?*[144]

(a) The termination right may be exercised during a five-year period starting at the end of thirty-five years from the date of execution of the grant.

(b) There is an exception if the grant was of a right of publication, in which case the five-year period begins at the earlier of thirty-five years after publication, or forty years after the grant was made.

(4) *How may termination be effected?*[145]

---

[138] *See* 17 U.S.C. § 304(c)(5).

[139] For a discussion of the differences, see *infra* § 6.16.

[140] *See* 17 U.S.C. § 203(a).

[141] *See* 17 U.S.C. § 203(a)(1), (2).

[142] *See supra* § 6.12.

[143] *See* 17 U.S.C. § 203(a)(2).

[144] *See* 17 U.S.C. § 203(a)(3).

[145] *See* 17 U.S.C. § 203(a)(4).

(a) By serving a written notice no less than two nor more than ten years before termination is to occur.

(b) Notice must comply with Copyright Office regulations.[146]

(c) A copy of the notice must be recorded in the Copyright Office before the effective date of termination.

(5) *What is the effect of termination?*[147]

(a) All rights revert to those having the right to terminate.

(b) The exception is for derivative works prepared before termination, which may continue to be exploited under the terms of the grant.[148]

(c) No new derivative works may be prepared after the date of termination.

(6) *Who can make further grants?*[149]

(a) Further grants are valid if signed by the same number and proportion of owners as are required for termination. All owners are bound, even nonsigners.[150]

§ 6.15 SECTIONS 304(c) AND 203 COMPARED

Although the two termination provisions are essentially the same in both their goals and procedures, they do contain significant differences. The following discussion summarizes these differences.

(1) *Grants covered.*

(a) The grants covered by § 304(c) and 304(d) are different from those covered in § 203. Sections 304(c) and (d) apply only to grants executed before January 1, 1978, while § 203 applies only to grants executed on or after January 1, 1978.

(b) Sections 304(c) and 304(d) apply to grants given by the author or renewal beneficiary under the second provision of § 304(a). Section 203 applies only to grants given by the author.

(c) Sections 304(c) and 304(d) apply to grants covering the renewal term for copyrighted works. Section 203 applies to any interest in copyright.

(2) *Who may terminate?*

Persons who may qualify to terminate the extended renewal term under § 304(c)(1)(2) are slightly different than those who can terminate under § 203(a)(1)(2) for post-1977 grants.

---

[146] *See* 37 C.F.R. § 201.10.

[147] *See* 17 U.S.C. § 203(b)(3).

[148] *See* 17 U.S.C. § 203(b)(1). See discussion of § 304(c) and *Mills Music, Inc. v. Snyder*, 469 U.S. 153 (1985) in *supra* § 6.14.

[149] *See* 17 U.S.C. § 203(b).

[150] *See* 17 U.S.C. § 203(b)(3).

(3) *When may termination take place?*

For § 304(c), termination may be effected during a five-year period beginning at the end of 56 years from the date copyright was originally secured. Under § 304(d), termination may be effected during a five-year period beginning at the end of 75 years from the date copyright was originally secured. For § 203, termination takes place during the five years beginning at the end of 35 years from the grant, or, if the grant covers the right of publication, 35 years from the date of publication or forty years from the grant, whichever is less.

(4) *How may termination be effected?*

The same for both sections.

(5) *What is the effect of termination?*

The same for both sections.

(6) *Who is entitled to make further grants?*

Owners of a reverted right are tenants-in-common under § 304(c)(6) and can deal separately with the right, except when the right is shared, further grants require majority action as to that shared. Under § 203(b), no tenancy-in-common exists, and for further grants, the same number and proportion as for termination are required.

§ 6.16 SOME WORKS ENJOY NO TERMINATION RIGHT, AND OTHER WORKS HAVE BOTH TERMINATION AND RENEWAL RIGHTS

The following two subsections present several situations revealing how some works will have neither termination nor renewal rights, while other works will enjoy rights of both termination and renewal. These situations provide a good review of termination and renewal principles and their possible interplay. They also indicate that the drafters of the termination provisions may not have taken into account certain anomalies arising out of gaps in the termination and renewal provisions, which could have been avoided by careful drafting.

[A] Certain Grants Subject to No Termination

Some works will not enjoy termination rights at all. Section 304(c) applies only to grants covering *subsisting copyrights* made before January 1, 1978, whereas § 203 applies only to grants made after that date. In addition, § 203 termination will apply only to grants made by the *author*. Thus, grants of common law rights are excluded from termination, that is, a grant made before 1977 for an unpublished work. For example, suppose that in 1977 a publisher buys the rights for a forthcoming novel and the work is not completed until 1980. The grant cannot be terminated because § 304(c) applies to subsisting copyrights only, whereas § 203 applies to post-1977 grants. In addition, the copyright term will simply be the basic life-plus-seventy-years term. No renewal term will revert to the author because renewal applies only to works copyrighted before 1978.

A second example involves a novel completed and published in 1977. Suppose the author dies in 1980 and the author's widow assigns the copyright in 1981 to a third party. No termination can be effected because § 203 applies only to an *author's* grant. Furthermore, although copyright did subsist in the work at the time of the grant, § 304(c) cannot be invoked because that section applies to grants made before 1978. The widow will, however, enjoy a renewal right after 2005 at the end of the first twenty-eight-year term.

If, however, in the above example, the work was created in 1977 but not published, and the widow assigns the copyright in 1980, the widow would have neither a termination right nor a right to the renewal term. Again, the reason is that the § 203 termination applies to grants made by the author, whereas § 304(c) applies to subsisting copyrights. There will be no renewal rights because renewal applies only to works in their first or second term of copyright. In this example, however, the work was not yet copyrighted as of January 1, 1978.

[B] Grants Subject to Both Termination and Renewal

The interplay between §§ 304(a) and 203 will permit some works to enjoy both a renewal term and a right of termination. For example, assume that A copyrights a work in 1962 and, in 1978, assigns to B his renewal interest, which will vest in 1990. If A does not live until the vesting of renewal, the term will simply revert to his widow and family. But if A lives until the vesting of the renewal (1989), B will enjoy the rights to the sixty-seven-year renewal term — until 2057. But here the author or his family can terminate the transfer pursuant to § 203, beginning in 2013 (35 years after the 1978 grant), thus cutting short B's renewal term by forty-four years.

§ 6.17 TERMINATION OF TRANSFERS AND DERIVATIVE WORKS EXCEPTION

A derivative work prepared under a grant can continue to be used under its terms even after termination of the grant.[151] Continued exploitation is limited to the specific derivative work made under the grant and does not extend to preparation of other derivative works based on the copyright covered by the terminated grant.

The derivative work exception has raised some difficult issues, unanswered either by the statute or the legislative history. One such question relates to derivative work rights that are assigned to intermediaries who then license derivative rights to third parties. When the time comes, the author can terminate the assignment to the intermediary. Under the terms of the Act, the derivative rights licensee can continue his or her use of the derivative work (on payment of royalties). The problem is that neither statute nor legislative history makes clear whether the licensee is to pay royalties to the intermediary or to the author.

---

[151] *See* 17 U.S.C. §§ 203(1), 304(c)(6)(A).

In *Mills Music, Inc. v. Snyder*,[152] the Supreme Court held that the intermediary publisher and not the author is entitled to receive royalties paid by the licensees for the continued use of the derivative work. In *Mills*, Ted Snyder, author of the song *Who's Sorry Now*, had assigned the renewal term to Mills Music. As owner of the renewal term to the song, Mills Music had sublicensed the song to more than 400 record companies, each of which had prepared separate derivative works and paid royalties. The author's family served on Mills Music notice of termination covering the nineteen-year extended renewal term and demanded that royalties revert to them. The Supreme Court, reversing a decision in favor of Snyder, held that the use of the term "grant" three times in § 304(c)(6)(A) revealed a legislative intent to cover not only the original grant but the sublicense made under that grant as well.[153] The Court acknowledged that the principal purpose of § 304 was to benefit authors but recognized that this was not its sole rationale. Its other purpose was to enable continued public accessibility to derivative works after termination. The Court concluded that upholding the status quo did justice to both policies.[154]

Justice White, in a dissenting opinion, sharply criticized the majority's reading of the statutory language and legislative history of § 304(c). He concluded that a middleman assignee's right to receive continued royalties had nothing to do with continued public access to a work, but would undermine the other policy of the 1976 Act, which is to benefit authors.[155] Moreover, a rule benefiting authors in this instance would not disturb any system of economic incentives that the 1976 Copyright Act was intended to provide because neither author nor middleman assignee acted in reliance on § 304(c) when they entered into their contractual relations. In other words, from a policy standpoint, if someone should obtain an extra nineteen-year windfall (now thirty-nine year windfall), it should be the author who was the intended beneficiary of the renewal term.[156] Displeasure with *Mills Music* has led to legislative efforts, so far unsuccessful, to overturn the opinion.[157]

As important as *Mills Music* may be for the point it decides, however, its reach is limited to that point. In *Mills Music* and similar situations, an author's termination is not wholly ineffective as to middlemen and their licensees. For example, after termination, Mills itself had no authority to authorize the preparation of any *additional* derivative works. If a license already issued by Mills to a record company had authorized the preparation of several derivative works, only one of which had been prepared at the time of the Snyders' termination, the remaining, unexercised portion of the license would have constituted part of the "terminated grant." Moreover, a middleman's right to continued royalties remains limited, even after *Mills Music*, by the terms of the grant, and will not extend to

---

152 469 U.S. 153 (1985).

153 *Id.* at 170–72.

154 *Id.* at 177.

155 *Id.* at 186 (White, J., dissenting). For other criticism of the majority opinion's rationale, see Howard B. Abrams, *Who's Sorry Now? Termination Rights and the Derivative Works Exception*, 62 U. Det. L. Rev. 181 (1985).

156 *See* H.R. Rep. No. 94-1476, at 140 (1976).

157 *See, e.g.*, H.R. 3163, 99th Cong. (1985).

uses beyond its scope.[158]

There is one further hurdle to be surmounted by a middleman seeking to benefit from the Derivative Works Exception after *Mills Music*: the derivative work must manifest sufficient originality to constitute an independently copyrightable work. *Woods v. Bourne Co.*[159] concerned the termination of a grant involving the famous song *Red Red Robin*. The defendant claimed that its piano-vocal version was a derivative work lawfully prepared under the grant of copyright and that it could continue to claim royalties for both the sale of the sheet music and public performance of the song. The Second Circuit held that for the Derivative Works Exception to apply, the derivative work in question must contain at least some substantial variation from the underlying work. In *Woods*, the piano-vocal arrangements had been prepared in a mechanical way, and when compared to the "lead sheet," displayed nothing more than trivial changes, thus failing to meet the standard of originality.

Part IV. RESTORATION OF COPYRIGHT IN WORKS PREVIOUSLY IN THE PUBLIC DOMAIN

§ 6.18 RETROACTIVITY UNDER ARTICLE 18 OF THE BERNE CONVENTION AND THE CONSTITUTIONAL DILEMMA

When the United States adhered to the Berne Convention, it took a minimalist position about the necessity of changing United States law to comply with the requirements of Berne. In so doing, it sidestepped Article 18 of Berne. Known as the "retroactivity" provision, Article 18 invites (if it does not actually require) new member nations on accession to protect all works from other member countries whose copyrights have not yet expired in their countries of origin.[160] This would include restoration of copyright protection for foreign works that had fallen into the public domain in the United States for failure to comply with formalities, such as notice and renewal. Aside from Berne requirements, it was thought that restoration of copyright for foreign works would facilitate efforts to secure effective protection of U.S. works in foreign markets. At least, restoration of copyright would improve the position of the U.S. in future negotiations to extend the rights of U.S. authors in Berne member countries. Despite these cogent arguments supporting restoration of copyright in the public domain, Congress determined that no special

---

[158] *See, e.g.*, *Fred Ahlert Music Corp. v. Warner Chappell Music, Inc.*, 155 F.3d 17 (2d Cir. 1998) (holding that the terms of the grant limited the use of the song to the sale and distribution of phonograph records, and excluded the use of the song in a motion picture soundtrack).

[159] 60 F.3d 978 (2d Cir. 1995).

[160] Berne Convention art. 18 (Paris Text). The pertinent subsections 1 and 4 read:

> (1) This Convention shall apply to all works that, at the moment of its coming into force, have not yet fallen into the public domain in the country of origin through expiry of the term of protection. . . . (4) The preceding provisions shall also apply in the case of new accessions to the Union. . . .

legislation was necessary to implement Article 18 of the Berne Convention. The issue was thought to merit further study, particularly the question whether Congress had the constitutional authority to revive public domain copyrights.

The constitutional issue presents itself on two fronts: the limited times language of the Patent and Copyright Clause[161] and the Due Process Clause of the Fifth Amendment.[162] Restoring a dead copyright would not appear to violate the limited times provision, which prohibits *perpetual* copyrights. Thus, so long as the copyright will eventually expire, the limited times provision would not appear to require that copyright protection be confined to a single and uninterrupted term. The second constitutional concern, the "Takings" Clause of the Fifth Amendment, offers the more challenging question. One could legitimately ask: would a resurrection of copyright impair the Due Process rights of those who have used a work in reliance on its public domain status? To avoid the reliance issue and its Due Process implications, Congress took these concerns into account. In both the NAFTA and Uruguay Round restoration provisions, Congress exculpated past uses of a restored work. In addition, it provided a one-year grace period for certain other uses to allow those who had relied on the public domain status to adjust to the new realities.[163]

§ 6.19 RESTORATION OF COPYRIGHT IN CERTAIN FOREIGN PUBLIC DOMAIN WORKS UNDER SECTION 104A: FROM NAFTA TO THE URUGUAY ROUND AGREEMENTS ACT

[A] The North American Free Trade Agreement Act

The North American Free Trade Agreement ("NAFTA") Act[164] implemented the first provisions to restore copyright protection for foreign works. The NAFTA amendments restored copyright in certain Mexican and Canadian motion pictures, and works that were included in them, that had fallen into the public domain for failure to comply with the notice formality. To reclaim copyright from the public domain, copyright owners of eligible works had to file a statement of intent with the Copyright Office between January 1 and December 31, 1994.[165] A restored copyright will endure for the remainder of the copyright term that the work would

---

[161] U.S. CONST. Art. I, § 8 cl. 8.

[162] U.S. CONST. amend. V.

[163] The constitutionality of the § 104A restoration provisions were upheld in *Luck's Music Library v. Gonzales*, 407 F.3d 1262 (D.C. Cir. 2005). *But see Golan v. Gonzales*, 501 F.3d 1179 (10th Cir. 2007) (holding that copyright restoration did not violate the Copyright Clause because Congress had a "rational basis" for the legislation — namely, to bring the U.S. into compliance within Article 18 of the Berne Convention; but also holding that copyright restoration "altered the traditional contours of copyright protection," rendering it vulnerable to a First Amendment challenge); *Golan v. Holder*, 611 F. Supp. 2d 1165 (D. Colo. 2009) (holding that § 104A burdened substantially more speech than was necessary to comply with Article 18, because Congress could have enacted a permanent exception for reliance parties).

[164] North American Free Trade Agreement, U.S.–Can.–Mex., Dec. 17, 1992, 32 I.L.M. 289 (1993).

[165] *See* 17 U.S.C. § 104A(b).

have enjoyed if it had proper notice affixed.

However interesting they are from a theoretical standpoint, the restoration provisions of NAFTA are narrow in scope. For one, they apply only to Mexican and Canadian motion pictures, not to audiovisual works generally. Moreover, for works published on or after January 1, 1978, and before March 1, 1989, the NAFTA amendments apply only to works that entered the public domain for failure to affix proper notice. Thus, works in the public domain before 1978 or those that entered the public domain for failure to comply with other formalities (*e.g.*, renewal registration) are not revived.

[B] The Uruguay Round Agreements Act

[1] Requirements for Restoration

One year after the NAFTA amendments, the Uruguay Round Agreements Act[166] restored copyrights for certain foreign works in the public domain in a much more dramatic fashion. This legislation, which implemented the negotiations completed under the Uruguay Round of the General Agreement on Tariffs and Trade ("GATT"),[167] rewrote § 104A of the Copyright Act. Effective January 1, 1996,[168] copyright was automatically restored in certain foreign works that had lost U.S copyright protection because of noncompliance with formalities or because the work did not originate in a country with which the United States had copyright relations. To ensure that the legislation did not result in such restorations being "takings" of property under the Fifth Amendment, it included provisions to protect the interests of parties who had relied on the loss of copyright protection for such works. These users of public domain works are called "reliance parties."[169]

Restorable works must meet three requirements.[170] First, they must enjoy copyright protection in their source country to be eligible for restoration.[171] Thus,

---

166 Pub. L. No. 103-465, 108 Stat. 4809 (1994).

167 United States obligations under the new World Trade Organization are based on the Uruguay Round negotiations pursuant to the General Agreement on Tariffs and Trade ("GATT"). One result of the negotiations was the Agreement on Trade Related Aspects of Intellectual Property ("TRIPS"), which is the basis for the amendments to the Copyright Act retroactively restoring copyright. Article 9 of TRIPS stipulates that "members shall comply with Articles 1–21 and the Appendix of the Berne Convention." *See* the Dunkel Draft from the GATT Secretariat, Annex III 57, 59 (William S. Hein, 1992). Thus, compliance with the retroactivity provisions of the Berne Convention Article 18 is required. See *supra* § 4.11 for a discussion of retroactivity under Berne. GATT, now renamed the World Trade Organization, is discussed at *infra* § 12.13.

168 The restoration provisions of the Uruguay Round Agreements Act were not clear about the date on which copyright is restored for works previously in the public domain — whether that date is January 1, 1995, January 1, 1996, or perhaps some date in between. The issue was resolved in the Copyright Clarification Act of 1997. (*See* § 104A(h)(2)(A) as amended that stipulated January 1, 1996 as the effective date of restoration. On that date, all qualifying works became protected under U.S. law. Of course, should additional works qualify in the future (because, for example their source countries join the Berne Union or the World Trade Organization for the first time), they will be protected as well.

169 *See* 17 U.S.C. § 104A(h)(4).

170 For a case discussing the restoration requirements, see *Cordon Art B.V. v. Walker*, 41 U.S.P.Q. 2d 1224 (S.D. Cal. 1996) (restoring copyrights in the United States for reproductions of drawings of Dutch

a work that lies in the public domain in the source country,[172] for whatever reason, will not be restored in the United States.

A second requirement for restoration concerns the identity and nationality of the author or rightholder of the work. For restoration to take place, at least one author or rightholder must have been a national or domiciliary of an eligible country at the time the work was created, and, if the work was published, it must have been first published in an eligible country and not published in the United States during the 30-day period following publication in such eligible country.[173] An eligible country is one, other than the United States, that is a World Trade Organization ("WTO") member, adheres to the Berne Convention, or is subject to a presidential proclamation.[174] Thus, the Uruguay Round restoration provisions do not affect public domain status of works of U.S. authors who forfeited copyright for failure to comply with formalities. Similarly, even works of foreign authors, who first published their works in the United States, will also remain in the public domain.

As a third requirement for restoration, the work in question must have fallen into the public domain under U.S. law for any of the following reasons: failure to comply with any of the formalities such as copyright notice, registration, renewal, or the manufacturing requirement; the lack of copyright relations between the U.S. and the source country; or that the work in question was a sound recording published before February 15, 1972.[175] If these three requirements are met, copyright will be restored for the remainder of the term of copyright as if the work had not gone into the public domain.

Ownership rights of restored works will vest initially in the author or rightholder[176] as determined by the law of the source country.[177] Subsequent transfers will determine ownership status. The term of protection for restored works is the same term the work would have enjoyed if it had not lost copyright protection.[178]

For example, a 1942 French film that entered the public domain in 1970 for failure to renew would enjoy the remainder of its original, ninety-five-year term, enduring until December 31, 2037. Similarly, a Chinese work from 1980, before China joined the Berne Convention, will have a term of protection measured by its

---

artist Escher, despite the absence of copyright notices on either original drawings or derivative works from those drawings; the court adopted January 1, 1996 as the effective date of restoration under the Act).

[171] *See* 17 U.S.C. § 104A(h)(6)(B) (defining "source country").

[172] *See* 17 U.S.C. § 104A(h)(8).

[173] *See* 17 U.S.C. § 104A(h)(6)(D).

[174] See 17 U.S.C. § 104A(h)(3).

[175] *See* 17 U.S.C. § 104A(h)(6)(C).

[176] In general, under § 104A(b), ownership of a restored work vests initially in the "author"; where sound recordings are concerned, they may belong, alternatively, to the "rightholder." (The latter term, defined in § 104A(h)(7), is included because, in some countries, a "sound recording" does not have an "author.")

[177] *See Alameda Films S.A. de C.V. v. Authors Rights Restoration Corp.*, 331 F.3d 472 (5th Cir. 2003) (holding that under Mexican law, film production companies were "authors" of movies entitled to restored U.S. copyrights).

[178] *See* 17 U.S.C. § 104A(a)(1)(B).

author's life-plus-50-years. In other words, copyright protection for restored works will resume for the remainder of the original term as if it had run without interruption.

[2] The Special Case of Reliance Parties

A work protected by a restored copyright is treated like any other copyrighted work. The owner of copyright in a restored work can proceed in all respects like any other copyright owner and is entitled to all the same remedies in cases of copyright infringement.[179] To avoid unfairness and possible constitutional problems, the Act accommodates those persons who have relied on the absence of copyright protection. These so called "reliance parties" are persons who owned copies of the relevant works, or were engaged in exploiting those works, before the country of that work became an eligible country.[180] Having made extensive use of such works, reliance parties are given special consideration.[181] A reliance party must have engaged in an ongoing series of acts, and cessation of that activity for an appreciable period of time will deprive one of reliance party status.[182]

Reliance parties are prospectively liable for unauthorized use of a restored work, but only on receipt of notice of restoration.[183] Effective notice may be given to reliance parties in either of two ways. The copyright owner of a restored work may, within 24 months after the date of restoration of copyright, file a notice with the Copyright Office. The Copyright Office will periodically publish these filed notices, which will constitute constructive notice of restoration. Alternatively, the copyright owner can serve a reliance party with actual notice indicating an intent to enforce the restored copyright. In either instance, a reliance party may continue the performance, distribution, or display of the work for twelve months from the earliest notice.[184] Copies of the work made before the date of restoration of copyright may be sold or otherwise disposed of without the authorization of the restored work's copyright owner only during the twelve-month period commencing on the date of receipt of actual notice or of publication in the Federal Register of the notice of intent, whichever occurs first.[185]

The rules are still more complicated for one class of "reliance parties" — those who, before the date of enactment of the URAA, used a then-public domain work as the basis for a new "derivative work" containing additional copyrightable content. In an effort to preserve the value of adaptations made in good faith, the URAA

---

[179] *See* 17 U.S.C. § 104A(d).

[180] *See Cordon Holding, B.V. v. Northwest Publ. Corp*, 63 U.S.P.Q.2d. (BNA) 1013 (S.D.N.Y. 2002) ("[W]here the source country is an 'eligible country' before the date of the enactment of the statute [December 8, 1994], the allegedly infringing acts must have begun prior to that date.").

[181] 17 U.S.C. § 104A(h).

[182] *See, e.g.*, *Troll Co. v. Uneeda Doll Co.*, 483 F.3d 150 (2d Cir. 2007) (holding that the defendant was not a reliance party where it had ceased production before restoration and reentered market after restoration).

[183] *See* 17 U.S.C. § 104A(e)(1); *Hoepker v. Kruger*, 200 F. Supp. 2d 340, 347 (S.D.N.Y. 2002) (granting a motion to dismiss where the plaintiff failed to file or serve the requisite notice).

[184] *See* 17 U.S.C. § 104A(d)(2).

[185] *See* 17 U.S.C. § 109(a).

provides that, if the reliance party pays the restored copyright owner "reasonable" compensation, it "may continue to exploit that derivative work for the duration of the restored copyright."[186] If the parties are unable to agree, 104A(d)(3)(B) provides a mechanism for judicial determination of what constitutes reasonable compensation, based on "harm to the actual or potential market for or value of the restored work . . . as well as . . . the relative contributions of expression of the author of the restored work and the reliance party to the derivative work."[187]

How courts will make the value-laden assessments of "reasonable compensation" based on "relative contributions" in the just-recited formula is a matter which will take some time to sort out. What types of "continued exploitation" will be permitted? One court suggested that this might include, at the very least, the right to display and reproduce the derivative work, and arguably "might include the right to create new derivative works."[188] In addition to questions concerning continued exploitation, how substantial a change must the "reliance party" have made in order to qualify for the special treatment accorded derivative works? Presumably, the standard is the same one applied in determining the copyrightability of derivative works in general, whatever that may be. In *Dam Things From Denmark v. Russ Berrie & Co.*,[189] involving two competing lines of novelty "troll" figures, described by the court as "short, pudgy, plastic dolls with big grins and wild hair," the Court of Appeals vacated a preliminary injunction and remanded with instructions to reconsider "whether the infringing works are derivatives of the restored work."[190] In particular, it directed the trial court to focus on the subtle but important difference between the "substantial similarity" standard for infringement and the "minimal creativity" standard for assessing whether a revision qualifies as a derivative work. "The fact that the two companies' dolls have the 'same aesthetic appeal' or 'are very similar in appearance' does not rule out the applicability of the safe harbor for derivative works."[191]

[C] The Constitutionality of Restoration: *Golan v. Holder* [192]

Ever since the restoration provisions came into being in 1996, users who previously relied on the public domain questioned the constitutionality of restoring to life hitherto dead copyrights.[193]The controversial nature of the issue and a split

---

[186] 17 U.S.C. § 104A(d)(3)(A).

[187] 17 U.S.C § 104A(3)(B).

[188] *See, e.g.*, *Hoepker v. Kruger*, 200 F. Supp. 2d. 340, 347 (S.D.N.Y. 2002).

[189] 290 F.3d 548 (3d Cir. 2002).

[190] *Id.* at 563.

[191] *Id.* at 565.

[192] For a discussion of the Tenth Circuit's decision in *Golan*, see Elizabeth Townsend Gard, *Copyright Law v. Trade Policy: Understanding the* Golan *Battle Within the Tenth Circuit*, 34 Colum. J.L. & Arts 131 (2011).

[193] The constitutionality of the § 104A restoration provisions were upheld in *Luck's Music Library v. Gonzales*, 407 F.3d 1262 (D.C. Cir. 2005). *But see Golan v. Gonzales*, 501 F.3d 1179 (10th Cir. 2007) (holding that copyright restoration did not violate the Copyright Clause because Congress had a "rational basis" for the legislation — namely, to bring the U.S. into compliance within Article 18 of the Berne Convention; but also holding that copyright restoration "altered the traditional contours of

in the Circuits prompted the Supreme Court to grant certiorari in *Golan v. Holder* to decide two questions concerning the constitutionality of § 514 of the Uruguay Round Agreements Act (§104A of the Copyright Act): First, whether the Progress Clause of the United States Constitution prohibits Congress from taking works out of the Public Domain, and second, whether restoration violates the First Amendment of the United States Constitution.

In an opinion reminiscent of *Eldred v. Ashcroft* involving the constitutionality of term extension,[194] Justice Ginsberg, writing for the majority, concluded that Congress has the authority to restore the copyrights. Justice Ginsburg, writing for the majority, stated that "[n]either the Copyright and Patent Clause nor the First Amendment, we hold, makes the public domain, in any and all cases, a territory that works may never exit." Further, the Supreme Court explained that the law merely "places foreign works on an equal footing with their U.S. counterparts."

Regarding the Copyright and Patent Clause, which authorizes Congress "to promote the progress of science and useful arts, by securing for limited times to authors and inventors the exclusive right to their respective writings and discoveries," the majority differed with petitioners that the clause requires federal legislation to promote the creation of new works. Observing that it had rejected a nearly identical argument in *Eldred*, the Supreme Court explained that Congress is empowered to determine the intellectual property regimes that overall will serve the general purpose of the clause. In addition to providing incentives for the creation of new works, "the dissemination of existing and future works" serves its purpose.

As to petitioners' First Amendment objections, Justice Ginsberg concluded that free speech interests are effectively protected by the fair use doctrine and the idea/expression dichotomy — the "built-in First Amendment accommodations" of copyright.

In dissent, Justice Breyer, joined by Justice Alito, argued that in enacting § 514 of the URAA, Congress had exceeded its authority "under any plausible reading of the Copyright Clause," because the clause does not authorize Congress to enact a statute that fails to provide incentives for creation of new works. Characterizing the issue as whether "the clause empower[s] Congress to enact a statute that withdraws works from the public domain, brings about higher prices and costs, and in doing so seriously restricts dissemination, particularly to those who need it for scholarly, educational, or cultural purposes — all without providing any additional incentive for the production of new material," the dissent answered "no."

Even though the majority in *Golan* treats both term extension and restoration as functionally similar for the purposes of the Constitution, the two concepts do

copyright protection," rendering it vulnerable to a First Amendment challenge); *Golan v. Holder*, 611 F. Supp. 2d 1165 (D. Colo. 2009) (holding that § 104A burdened substantially more speech than was necessary to comply with Article 18, because Congress could have enacted a permanent exception for reliance parties). For a reading of copyright through the lens of the "traditional contours of copyright," a phrase invoked by the Tenth Circuit in *Golan*, see W. Ron Gard & Elizabeth Townsend Gard, *The Present (User-Generated Crisis) is the Past (1909 Copyright Act): An Essay Theorizing the "Traditional Contours of Copyright,"* 28 CARDOZO ARTS & ENT. L.J. (2011).

[194] For a discussion of Eldred v. Ashcroft, *see* § 6.03 infra.

have significant differences. Both term extension and restoration provide added protection to works already created that would have or have already entered the public domain. Unlike term extension, however, restoration of copyright not only plays havoc with users' expectations regarding the public domain, but it also complicates the economic lives of those whose businesses were built around works that were once in the public domain.

Chapter 7

COPYRIGHT REGISTRATION AND DEPOSIT

§ 7.01 INTRODUCTION AND CHAPTER OVERVIEW

Copyright registration (and the important role it plays) is a unique feature of American law. The act of registration does not create a copyright; copyright begins when an author fixes his work in a tangible medium of expression. Registration, however, can be critically important to the copyright owner because it can preserve copyright,[1] and for works that originated in the United States, it is a prerequisite for bringing an infringement suit. In order to register a claim for copyright, the applicant is required to deposit a specified number of copies of the work with the Register. The deposit serves two purposes: it identifies the work and satisfies the mandatory deposit requirement for the Library of Congress. Both registration and deposit, covered in §§ 401 through 412[2] of the Act, are administered by the Copyright Office.

This chapter, which is divided into two parts, presents a brief overview of copyright registration and the deposit requirements for the Library of Congress. Part I examines the mechanics and the importance of registering a claim of copyright in the Copyright Office. Part II reviews the mandatory deposit requirements designed to enrich the collection of the Library of Congress and the interplay of the deposit requirement with registration of a claim for copyright. In both parts of this chapter, the central role played by the Copyright Office is emphasized.

Part I. REGISTRATION

§ 7.02 THE COPYRIGHT OFFICE

The first federal copyright statute, enacted in 1790, provided for registration of each work to be made not in a central office, but rather in the office of the clerk of the federal judicial district where the author resided. In addition, within six months

---

[1] *See* 17 U.S.C. § 405(a)(2). For works publicly distributed before March 1, 1989, copyright can be invalidated by omitting notice from more than a relatively small number of copies or phonorecords publicly distributed unless, "registration for the work has been made before or is made within five years after the publication without notice, and a reasonable effort is made to add notice to all copies or phonorecords that are distributed to the public in the United States after the omission has been discovered." For works publicly distributed after March 1, 1989, notice is permissive, and omission of notice can no longer forfeit copyright. *See* 17 U.S.C. § 401(a). For a discussion of this provision, see *supra* § 4.11.

[2] 17 U.S.C. §§ 401–12.

after publication of the work, the author was required to deposit a copy thereof with the Department of State. While the place of deposit was changed a number of times in the early years, the place of registration remained the same until 1870, when Congress revised the law to centralize both registration and deposit in the Library of Congress.

The impetus for the 1870 Act derived largely from the unusual vision of Ainsworth Rand Spofford, the sixth Librarian of Congress. Appointed by President Lincoln in 1864, Spofford saw the potential for creating, in effect, a national library, by obtaining for the Library of Congress virtually the entire cultural output of the United States — books, periodicals, music, works of art, and other works — through a centralized copyright deposit system. With the adoption of Spofford's proposal in 1870, the Library began its transformation into the largest library in the world, an institution with over 3,600 employees in three large buildings containing approximately 650 miles of shelving and holding more than 140 million items in its collections.[3]

Ever since it was created in 1897 to administer copyright registrations and deposits, the Copyright Office has remained a separate department of the Library of Congress.[4] In addition to its principal administrative function, the registration of copyright, the Copyright Office promotes the overall policies of the Library of Congress. Its chief officer, the Register of Copyrights, is appointed by the Librarian of Congress and is the Assistant Librarian of Congress for Copyright Services.[5]

From modest beginnings at the end of nineteenth century, the Copyright Office, located in Washington, D.C., is now a significant governmental institution. Housed in the James Madison Building on Capitol Hill, the Copyright Office, has over 475 employees. In fiscal year 2009, the Office registered over 382,000 claims to copyright. While not all of the copies deposited to make these registrations can be retained permanently due to space limitations, more than half are used by the Library to enrich its collections or to carry out other functions, such as its gift programs and exchanges with other libraries and learned institutions. In addition to these responsibilities, the Copyright Office provides assistance to visiting members of the public seeking information about particular works, and answers more than 350,000 letters, emails, and telephone inquiries annually.[6]

---

[3] For a historical overview of the Copyright Office see United States Copyright Office: A Brief Introduction and History, at http://www.copyright.gov/circs/circ1a.html: The latest available on-line Annual Report of the Register of Copyrights covers FY 2011. For updates, see www.copyright.gov/reports/.

[4] *See* Compendium II of Copyright Office Practices § 104. The placement of the Copyright Office in the Library of Congress, and therefore in the legislative branch, when Congress revised the law to centralize both registration and deposit in the same institution; it is a historical anomaly. By contrast, the Patent and Trademark Offices are placed in the executive branch, under the Department of Commerce. The important administrative and regulatory role of the U.S. Copyright Office is unique in the world. Concerns about coordinating the formation and administration of U.S. intellectual property law, particularly in the international sphere, has prompted serious consideration to reform and restructure the Copyright Office, integrating its operations along with the Patent and Trademark Office, in the executive branch.

[5] *See* 17 U.S.C. § 701(a).

[6] For the Copyright Office budget, see Library of Congress Fiscal 2014 Budget Justification at

The Office plays an important role in advising Congress on national and international copyright policy.[7] The Register of Copyrights is one of the principal advisors to Congress and the various agencies of the federal government, including the Department of State, on international copyright matters. To carry out these duties, the Copyright Office has assembled a staff of attorneys and other experts with special competence in copyright and actively solicits the input of authors, publishers, librarians, and other users of copyrighted works.

In conjunction with its registration activities, the Copyright Office keeps elaborate records. The Copyright Office Card Catalog, one of the largest in the world, contains the record of almost 30 million copyright registrations (including renewals), totaling more than 50 million catalog entries.[8] The Copyright Card Catalog and post-1977 automated files provide an index to United States copyright registrations from 1870 to the present.[9] These records are open for public inspection. In addition, the Office keeps an Assignment and Related Documents Index pertaining to the recordation of assignments, licenses, and other ownership interests in a copyright. For persons not wishing to do their own research, the Certifications and Document section of the Copyright Office, will search, for a fee, the records and issue a report concerning the copyright status or ownership of a work.[10] Reproduction of deposit copies,[11] obtained for a fee pursuant to regulations established by the Copyright Office,[12] are available in three situations: when requested by the claimant, when requested by an attorney for litigation purposes, or when ordered by a court for litigation.[13]

---

http://lcweb2.loc.gov/master/libn/about/reports-and-budgets/documents/budgets/fy2014.pdf.

[7] For example, Title I of the Digital Millennium Copyright Act (DMCA), Pub. L. No. 105-304, 112 Stat. 2860 (1998) requires the U.S. Copyright Office to perform two joint studies with the National Telecommunications and Information Administration of the Department of Commerce (NTIA). One deals with encryption research (*see* 17 U.S.C. § 1201(g)(5)). The other (required by § 104 of DMCA) concerns the effect of technological developments on § 109 (first sale doctrine) and § 117 (exemption allowing owners of copies of computer programs to reproduce and adapt them for use on a computer). Along with the two joint studies, § 403 of DMCA directs the Copyright Office to consult with affected parties and make recommendation to Congress on how to promote distance education through digital technologies. In addition to the above studies, the DMCA gives the Copyright Office (in collaboration with NTIA) a prominent administrative role in an on-going rule-making proceeding to evaluate the impact of the prohibition against the act of circumventing access control measures proscribed by the Act. This periodic rule making will determine the applicability of exemptions for users of a work adversely affected by the prohibition in making non-infringing uses. *See* 17 U.S.C. § 1201(a)(1)(B)–(E). The DMCA is discussed at *infra* § 8.35.

[8] *See* 17 U.S.C. § 705.

[9] *See* Copyright Office Circular R23.

[10] *See* Copyright Office Circular R22.

[11] One must deposit the required number of copies or, in some instances, identifying material to register a claim for copyright. For a discussion of the deposit requirement, see *infra* §§ 7.10–7.15.

[12] *See* 17 U.S.C. § 706; 37 C.F.R. §§ 201.1–201.2 (1987); *see also* Copyright Office Circulars R6, R96.

[13] *See* 37 C.F.R. § 201.2(d) (1987).

§ 7.03 WHY A REGISTRATION SYSTEM?

Copyright registration is a unique aspect of American law. No other country has anything quite like our elaborate system, carefully administered by a government agency. Is there a need for a system of copyright registration?[14] If copyright protection begins on creation, what purpose is served by registration?

Registration has been justified on the basis that it provides benefits to both users and owners.[15] It protects owners against the unauthorized use of their works by establishing priority of authorship, and it confers prima facie evidence of the validity of the copyright and the facts stated in the certificate.[16] Generally, a registration system produces a more efficient, readier market for copyrighted works. It facilitates transfers, assignments, and licenses of copyrighted works because prospective transferees have more confidence in the validity of a registered copyright. In this way, the Copyright Office registry aids prospective purchasers in determining the status of a work and provides them information about what may be available on the market.[17]

Despite these benefits, the system has been criticized as not working according to its ideal. Fundamentally, a registration system is only as good as the information reflected in the records. Unfortunately, a search of Copyright Office records may often be unrewarding or even misleading. The absence of any mention of a work in the records does not mean it is unprotected. The reason is that copyright registration is essentially voluntary, and many copyright owners choose not to register. The only exception to voluntary registration was for works copyrighted before 1978 (published with notice). For pre-1978 copyrights, the 1976 Act required that the copyright owner file a renewal registration to claim the second term. In 1992, the Act was amended to make the renewal term automatic for pre-1978 copyrights for works published after 1963 and before 1978. Renewal registration is now voluntary.[18] Renewal registration, however, was only required for published works. For works unpublished before 1978, protection was perpetual without the need to register one's claim in the Copyright Office. Moreover, works created after 1978 are no longer subject to a renewal term, and for these works copyright registration is purely voluntary. In short, searches of the Copyright Office records are rarely conclusive.

---

[14] In British copyright law, the registration system was abrogated by The Act of 1911. In 1908, Britain had provisionally entered the Berne Convention, which required that the works of an author of a member state must be protected without formality. It was believed that the registration system was such a formality. *See* Benjamin Kaplan, Copyright Office Study No. 17, Registration of Copyright (1958). *See also* Berne Convention Art. 5(2) (Paris text) ("The enjoyment and the exercise of these rights shall not be subject to any formality. . . .").

[15] For a comprehensive overview of the advantages and disadvantages of a registration system, see Kaplan, *supra* note 13.

[16] *See* 17 U.S.C. § 410(c).

[17] *See* Arthur J. Levine & Jeffrey L. Squires, *Notice, Deposit and Registration: The Importance of Being Formal*, 24 UCLA L. Rev. 1232, 1254 (1977).

[18] *See* 17 U.S.C. § 304(a). Incentives still remain for renewal registration. For a discussion of automatic renewal, see *supra* § 6.09.

Copyright Office records can be unreliable because the information contained in them may be inaccurate or incomplete or both.[19] To understand why, one must look at how the Office gathers, accepts, and catalogs this information, which ultimately finds its way into its records. Except for obvious discrepancies, the Copyright Office accepts as true all information provided by the applicant for registration and does not make factual findings on matters external to the Copyright Office.[20] Consistent with this general policy, the Office will record [21] virtually any instrument involving an interest in the copyright without evaluating its legal sufficiency.[22] Added to these problems of reliability, the work may not yet have been catalogued, or the work may have been registered under a different title as part of a larger work. Whether these inadequacies of the system undermine its justification is debatable, but one must keep them in mind whenever using Copyright Office records.

§ 7.04 REGISTRATION OF COPYRIGHT: AN OVERVIEW

Copyright protection begins not with registration, but when an author creates a work by fixing it in a tangible medium of expression.[23] Registration is a legal formality, and an important one, but in only two instances can it be viewed as a condition of copyright itself. First, works copyrighted (published with notice) before January 1, 1964, must have been registered and renewed during the 28th year to maintain copyright protection.[24] Second, under §§ 405 and 406 of the 1976 Act,[25] copyright registration is a required step in preserving a copyright when copyright notice has been omitted from more than a relatively small number of publicly distributed copies of the work.[26] This aspect of registration is no longer required for works publicly distributed on or after March 1, 1989, the effective date of the BCIA amendments.[27] After that date, notice is permissive, and copyright can no longer be forfeited by omitting notice.

Other than in these two instances, registration is permissive, voluntary, and can be effected at any time during the term of copyright.[28] Although permissive, registration confers important advantages on the registrant, and early registration is rewarded. Generally, the advantages of registration are: (1) it establishes a public

---

[19] To promote accuracy and completeness in Copyright Office records, the 1976 Copyright Act authorizes the Register to establish procedures by which claimants may correct or supplement information in a registration. *See* 17 U.S.C. § 408(d); 37 C.F.R. § 201.5 (1987). No such statutory procedures existed under the 1909 Act.

[20] *See* Compendium II of Copyright Office Practices § 108.05.

[21] For a discussion of recordation of ownership interests in copyright and its significance in establishing priorities among conflicting transfers, see *supra* § 5.12.

[22] *See* Compendium II of Copyright Office Practices § 1603.01.

[23] *See* 17 U.S.C. § 102(a).

[24] *See* 17 U.S.C. § 304(a). For works published on or after January 1, 1964 and before January 1, 1978, (for works whose 28th year began January 1, 1993), renewal is automatic and copyright cannot be lost for failure to register and renew. See *supra* § 6.09 for a discussion of automatic renewal.

[25] *See* 17 U.S.C. §§ 405, 406.

[26] *See* 17 U.S.C. § 405(a).

[27] *See* 17 U.S.C. § 401(a).

[28] *See* 17 U.S.C. § 408(a).

record of the claim of copyright; (2) it secures the right to file an infringement suit for works whose country of origin is the United States;[29] (3) it establishes prima facie validity of the copyright;[30] (4) it makes available a broader range of remedies in an infringement suit, allowing recovery of statutory damages and attorney's fees;[31] and (5) only if registration is made, will recordation of a document in the Copyright Office give constructive notice of the facts stated in the recorded document.[32] These substantial advantages provide a strong inducement to register, particularly because registration is relatively inexpensive and involves no examination for basic validity of the copyright, in contrast to the procedure for obtaining a patent.

§ 7.05 REGISTRATION PROCEDURES

[A] Generally

Any copyright owner, including an owner of an exclusive license to a work, may register a claim for copyright. The claimant must send three elements in the same envelope to the Register of Copyrights.[33] These are (1) a properly completed application form; (2) a nonrefundable fee[34] for each application; and (3) a deposit copy of the work to be registered. Copyright registration is effective on the date of receipt in the Copyright Office of all the required elements in acceptable form, no matter how long it takes for the actual registration to issue from the Copyright Office.[35]

[B] Expediting and Streamlining the Process: Special Handling and Pre-Registration Procedures

Because of its importance in the litigation process, copyright owners facing potential or actual infringement are in need of an expedited process for obtaining registration. For persons needing a rapid issuance of a certificate, the Copyright Office has instituted a procedure called "special handling" to expedite the registration process. Special handling will be granted only in cases involving

---

[29] *See* 17 U.S.C. § 411. Before March 1, 1989, all persons were required to register a claim for copyright before they could bring a suit for copyright infringement. After March 1, 1989, registration as a prerequisite for bringing an infringement suit will no longer be required of works whose country of origin is a Berne Convention country. *See* 17 U.S.C. §§ 101 (Berne Convention Works), 104(b).

[30] *See* 17 U.S.C. § 410(c).

[31] *See* 17 U.S.C. § 412.

[32] *See* 17 U.S.C. § 205(c).

[33] *See* 17 U.S.C. §§ 408, 409.

[34] As of August 1, 2009, the basic fee for copyright registration is $35 for an electronic filing The registration fee for form CO is $50 and the registration fee for paper fillings of Forms PA, SR, TX, VA, SE, are $65. The introduction of the dual fee structure reflects the reduced cost of processing electronic claims and to provide incentive for using the online filing system. *See* 74 Fed. Reg. 32805. For the current fee schedules, visit: http://www.copyright.gov/docs/fees.html. For explanations of copyright fees for such services as recordation, searches, and special handling, see Copyright Office Circular 4 ("Copyright Fees"), *available at* http://www.copyright.gov/circs/circ04.pdf.

[35] *See* 17 U.S.C. § 410(d).

pending or prospective litigation, customs matters, or contract or publishing deadlines that necessitate the expedited process.[36]

In addition to special handling, Congress has turned its attention to other ways of accelerating and streamlining the registration process. To this end, 2005 amendments to the Copyright Act allow preregistration of a work that is being prepared for commercial distribution and has not been published. The provisions of § 412 sometimes made it difficult for motion-picture companies to recover statutory damages or attorney's fees, because a motion picture could not be registered as a published work until it had been released, and it was impractical to register a motion picture as an unpublished work until the film was edited for release. Congress responded to these concerns in 2005 by requiring the Copyright Office to establish a procedure for "preregistration" of an unpublished work "being prepared for commercial distribution," for any "class of works that the Register determines has had a history of infringement prior to authorized commercial distribution."[37] Preregistration allows a copyright owner to file suit for infringement before formal registration is made; however, a copyright owner who preregisters a work is required to register the completed work within three months after first publication, or within one month of learning of the alleged infringement (if the infringement commenced no later than two months after first publication), or else the action must be dismissed.[38] Statutory damages may be recovered for infringement of a preregistered work if these time limits are met. The work must be of a class that the Register determines suffers a history of precommercial distribution infringement.[39]

[C] Copyright Application Forms and Deposit Copies

In recent years, the Copyright Office has transitioned to a primarily online registration system from a primarily paper-based system. The preferred method of registration is through the Electronic Copyright Office (eCO) system at the Copyright Office's website. In most cases a hard-copy deposit must still be submitted, except for certain works that are published only in electronic form or are unpublished. The eCO system reduces processing time and is less expensive.[40]

To register a claim for copyright using hard copy forms, only the official forms printed by the Copyright Office can be used; photocopies are not allowed. For example, form TX[41] is designated for published and unpublished non-dramatic literary works (books, computer programs, etc.), and form SR is designated for

---

[36] The fee for a special handling request is $760, plus a $50 additional fee for each claim using the same document registration filing fee. For a complete list of special handling fees, see Copyright Office Circular 10 ("*Special Handling*") and, Copyright Office Circular 4 ("Copyright Fees"). Circulars are available online at www.copyright.gov/circs/.

[37] 17 U.S.C. § 408(f)(1)–(2).

[38] 17 U.S.C. § 408(f)(4).

[39] *See* 17 U.S.C. § 408(f).

[40] As of 2014, the fee for online registration is $35 and the fee for processing traditional paper forms is $65.

[41] Copyright Office registration forms are downloadable in Adobe Acrobat at http://www.copyright.gov/forms/.

published and unpublished sound recordings.[42] The forms are basically self-explanatory and relatively easy to complete.

The second and third elements of registration, the deposit copies and the application fee, must accompany the application form.[43] The deposit copies must comply with the statutory requirements and regulations established by the Copyright Office.[44] The Register of Copyrights has exempted certain categories of works from the deposit requirement, allowing identifying material to be sent instead.[45]

[D] Examination of a Claim to Copyright

Under § 410(a),[46] the Register of Copyright shall register, after examination, a claim to copyright if, "the material deposited constitutes copyrightable subject matter and that the other legal and formal requirements . . . have been met."[47]

Alternatively, the Register of Copyright is given the authority to refuse registration when the claim is invalid and most courts defer to the Register's decision in refusing the claim.[48] The examination is carried out by the Examining Division of the Copyright Office, which limits its inquiry to the material deposited and the application for registration.[49] The examiner scrutinizes the application for obvious discrepancies, but does not try to verify the facts set forth in it.[50] The examination conducted by the Copyright Office has little in common with the Patent Office's search of the prior art or the Trademark Office's search of registered marks confusingly similar to the applicant's. Unlike the Patent and Trademark Office, the Copyright Office does not institute interference proceedings to determine who has the priority between two conflicting applications.[51]

---

[42] The other forms are VA, for pictorial, graphic, and sculptural works; PA, for the performing arts; SE, for serials; and GR/CP, an adjunct application for copyright registration covering a group of contributions to a periodical. *See* Copyright Office Circular Rlc.

[43] *See* 17 U.S.C. § 409

[44] *See* 37 C.F.R. § 202.20 (1987).

[45] *See, e.g.*, 37 C.F.R. § 202.21 (1987) (allowing in certain cases identifying material instead of an actual copy of the work). For a discussion of the deposit requirement, see *infra* §§ 7.10–7.15.

[46] 17 U.S.C. § 410(a).

[47] *Id.* The Copyright Office has adopted a long-standing principle that all copyrightable elements embodied in the work are covered by a single registration. *See* 37 C.F.R. § 202.3(b)(2)(3). For example, the Office will accept registration on a single form to cover all copyrightable expressions in a computer program including screen displays. However, if a screen display is claimed in the registration of a computer program, deposit must include a reproduction of the screen display. *See* 37 C.F.R. § 202.20(c)(2)(vii)(C) (1989). Most courts have followed the Copyright Office approach. They have held that the program code and the screen display are integrally related and form one work, even though the nature of authorship on screens may be different from computer program code authorship. In sum, copyright in a computer program extends to screen displays as well, and infringement of one will infringe the other. *See Whelan Assoc., Inc. v. Jaslow Dental Lab., Inc.*, 797 F.2d 1222 (3d Cir. 1986). *But see Digital Commc'ns Assoc., Inc. v. Softklone Distrib. Corp.*, 659 F. Supp. 449 (N.D. Ga. 1987).

[48] *See, e.g., Norris Indus., Inc. v. Int'l Tel. & Tel. Corp.*, 696 F.2d 918 (11th Cir. 1983).

[49] *See* Compendium II of Copyright Office Practices § 108.

[50] *See id.* at § 108.05.

[51] The Copyright Office has adopted a principle of interpretation, known as the "Rule of Doubt,"

§ 7.06 THE IMPORTANCE OF REGISTRATION

[A] Prerequisite to Bringing Suit for Infringement

The 1976 Act, as originally enacted, required registration of a claim for copyright as a prerequisite for bringing a suit for infringement. Effective March 1, 1989,[52] registration as a prerequisite for bringing an infringement suit is required only for works whose country of origin is the United States. In general, a work that is first published in the United States is considered a work whose country of origin is the United States. For these works, the copyright owner must register in order to bring a suit for infringement. Absent registration, a federal court should dismiss the case. The only exception to the registration requirement for works of U.S. origin applies to an action brought for a violation of the rights of attribution and integrity for works of visual arts under § 106A of the Copyright Act.[53] Apart from this exception, registration, which cannot be waived by the parties, is required to bring a suit for infringement. This rule applies regardless of the remedy sought, whether money damages, injunction, or impoundment.[54] Once registration has taken place, suit can be brought for all infringing acts occurring before or after registration.

Although registration is required to bring an action for infringement for works of U.S. origin, is it a jurisdictional requirement? The courts were split on the issue until the Supreme Court in *Reed Elsevier v. Muchnick*[55] ruled that the Copyright Act's registration requirement does not restrict a federal court's subject matter jurisdiction. In *Reed Elsevier*, the United States Supreme Court overturned a Second Circuit Court of Appeals decision which held that the district court lacked jurisdiction to certify either the class or the settlement in a case involving holders of registered and unregistered copyrights.[56]The ramifications of this opinion are unclear but it clearly does not abrogate the registration requirement of § 411(a). It

---

which is consistent with the passive role it takes in the examination process. Under the Rule of Doubt, the Office

> will register the claim even though there is a reasonable doubt about the ultimate action which might be taken under the same circumstances by an appropriate "court" with respect to whether the material deposited for registration constitutes copyrightable subject matter or the other legal and formal requirements of the statute have been met.

Id. at § 108.07.

[52] *See* 17 U.S.C. § 411(a).

[53] 17 U.S.C. § 411(a).

[54] *See* H.R. Rep. No. 94-1476, at 157 (1976).

[55] 559 U.S. 154 (2010). The decision of the Supreme Court originated from its decision in *The New York Times Co. v. Tasini*, 533 U.S. 483 (2001), that freelance authors had right a right to negotiate separate licenses when their works were incorporated into online databases. For a discussion of *Tasini*, see § 5.08[B] *infra*.

[56] In 2005, the parties agreed to settle four consolidated class actions (including *Tasini*) by creating an $18 million fund to compensate freelancers (including but not limited to the named plaintiffs) for previous infringing uses. That settlement was threatened when the Second Circuit ruled that the district court could not assert subject-matter jurisdiction over unregistered copyrights, even for settlement purposes. *See In re Literary Works in Electronic Databases Copyright Litigation*, 509 F.3d 116 (2d Cir. 2007).

would allow a district court to include unregistered copyrights in a settlement/class action lawsuit. On the other hand, a court would deny holders of those unregistered copyrights the right to bring the lawsuit themselves without complying with the registration requirement. Thus, the ruling allows, but does not require, a district court to certify a class containing members who have not fulfilled the registration requirement, enabling the court to create equitable exceptions to registration requirement as circumstances may call for. At its essence, *Reed Elsevier* negates any argument that a plaintiff's failure to obtain federal registration before bringing suit will divest the court of subject matter jurisdiction, but as a practical matter, it does not change the basic registration requirement except in limited circumstances.

The courts, however, are split on the issue of when registration has been made in compliance with the § 411(a) registration requirement. The problem is the differing approaches in construing by what, exactly, is meant by "has been made?" Some courts treat the submission of an application, accompanied by payment of the required fee and deposit of the requisite copies, as sufficient compliance,[57] whereas others hold that the prerequisite is not satisfied until the Copyright Office has acted on the application.[58] The dispute turns, in part, on § 410(d), which provides that the effective date of a copyright registration is the date on which the application and supporting materials are received by the Copyright Office, rather than the later date on which the application is determined to be acceptable for registration. Many of the courts adhering to the latter position, however, allow the plaintiff to file an amended complaint once the registration in fact issues, thus curing the jurisdictional problem.[59] While others adhering to the former position have taken an even more generous approach. For example, in *Positive Black Talk, Inc. v. Cash Money Records, Inc.*,[60] the Fifth Circuit Court of Appeals ruled that the jurisdictional defect was cured when the Copyright Office received the complete application four days after action was filed, despite the fact that the plaintiff never filed an amended or supplemental pleading. This difference in these two positions could have a practical significance if, for example, the statute of limitations expires before the amended complaint is filed.[61]

Alternatively, for a work whose country of origin is a Berne Convention country, registration is not required for bringing an infringement suit. In general, a Berne Convention work is one which is first published in a Berne member country.[62] The

---

[57] *See, e.g.*, *Apple Barrel Prods., Inc. v. Beard*, 730 F.2d 384 (5th Cir. 1984); *Prunte v. Universal Music Group*, 484 F. Supp. 2d 32 (D.D.C. 2007).

[58] *See, e.g.*, *LaResolana Architects v. Clay Realtors Angel Fire*, 416 F.3d 1195 (10th Cir. 2005) (collecting cases); *M.G.B. Homes, Inc. v. Ameron Homes, Inc.*, 903 F.2d 1486 (11th Cir. 1990); *Walton v. United States*, 80 Fed. Cl. 251 (2008).

[59] *See, e.g.*, *M.G.B. Homes*, 903 F.2d at 1489; *but see Walton*, 80 Fed. Cl. at 265–66 (noting that the amended complaint does not cure a lack of jurisdiction at time complaint was filed, but is treated as a new complaint).

[60] 394 F.3d 357 (5th Cir. 2004).

[61] *See Int'l Trade Mgmt., Inc. v. United States*, 553 F. Supp. 402 (Cl. Ct. 1982).

[62] A Berne Convention work is defined as:

> [i]n the case of an unpublished work, one or more of the authors is a national of a nation

important consideration for determining what is a Berne Convention work is the situs of the publication, not the nationality of the author.[63]

Even for Berne works, registration, though not required, is strongly encouraged by the 1976 Act. First, for all works regardless of their country of origin, registration within five years of its publication confers prima facie validity of originality and ownership. Second, and even more important, under § 412 of the Act, registration is a prerequisite to statutory damages and attorney's fees.[64] Third, recordation of a document in the Copyright Office gives all persons constructive notice of the facts stated in the recorded document but only if the work is registered.[65] In short, prompt registration for all works, whether originating from Berne countries or not, can be critically important in effectively enforcing one's rights in a suit for infringement.

The rule that a copyright owner must register a claim for copyright before bringing suit applies across the board except in one situation concerning live transmissions. Section 411(c) provides that "a work consisting of sounds and images, or both, the first fixation of which is made simultaneously with its transmission."[66] The copyright owner must comply with regulations issued by the Copyright Act and satisfy two statutory conditions: (1) serve notice upon the infringer, not less than 48 hours before such fixation, identifying the work and specific time and source of its first transmission (2) "makes registration for the work if required by subsection (a) within three months after its first transmission."[67]

[B] Registration as *Prima Facie* Evidence of Validity

Under § 410(c),[68] a certificate of registration constitutes prima facie evidence of the validity of the copyright and the facts stated in the certificate. A copyright registration reorders the burden of proof, creating a rebuttable presumption of

---

adhering to the Berne Convention, or in the case of a published work, one or more of the authors is a national of a nation adhering to the Berne Convention on the date of first publication.

The work must either be first published in a Berne country or published simultaneously in a non-Berne and a Berne country. *See* 17 U.S.C. § 101. For a discussion of the Berne Convention, see *infra* §§ 12.04–12.05.

[63] *Compare Moberg v. 33T LLC*, 666 F. Supp. 2d 415 (D. Del. 2009) (assuming Swedish author's photos were "published" when posted on German website, they were not simultaneously "published" in the U.S. and were therefore not "United States works" for purposes of § 411(a)) *with Kernal Records Oy v. Mosley*, 794 F. Supp. 2d 1355 (S.D. Fla. 2011) (sound recording created by a Norwegian citizen and first published on an Australian website was simultaneously published in the United States and other nations and was therefore a "United States work" for which registration was required).

[64] *See* 17 U.S.C. § 412. Section 412 appears ripe for repeal despite arguments that its repeal (as well as the repeal of the registration requirement in § 411) would adversely affect the Library of Congress' acquisition of deposits. *See, e.g.*, Copyright Reform Bill of 1993, H.R. 897, 103d Cong. (1993).

[65] *See* 17 U.S.C. § 205(c). For a discussion of recordation, see *supra* § 5.12.

[66] 17 U.S.C. § 411(c).

[67] *Id.*

[68] 17 U.S.C. § 410(c). This section applies to all works whether originating from the United States or a Berne Convention country.

validity of the copyright claimed in the registration.[69] The prima facie validity effect applies only if the registration takes place within five years of publication of the work.[70] This can be especially valuable to a plaintiff seeking a preliminary injunction because the registration confers prima facie validity of the work's originality and ownership.

If registration is accomplished after five years, the court has the discretion to decide what evidentiary weight the registration will receive.[71]

[C] Registration as a Prerequisite for Obtaining Statutory Damages and Attorney's Fees

Early registration is also rewarded by § 412,[72] which allows recovery of statutory damages, costs, and attorney's fees if registration has taken place before the infringing acts occurred. For infringing acts that take place before registration, statutory damages and attorney's fees cannot be recovered in the following two situations: (1) for infringement of an unpublished work;[73] and (2) for infringement of copyright that began after first publication of the work, unless registration was made within three months of its first publication.[74] From a practical standpoint, § 412 provides a powerful inducement for early registration because in some instances, statutory damages[75] may be the only viable remedy for the copyright owner. Registration is still required to obtain statutory damages for works originating from Berne Convention countries, even though registration is no longer a prerequisite for bringing an infringement suit for these works on or after March 1, 1989.[76]

---

[69] *See* H.R. Rep. No. 94-1476, at 156 (1976).

[70] *See* 17 U.S.C. § 410(c).

[71] *Id.*

[72] 17 U.S.C. § 412.

[73] *See* 17 U.S.C. § 412(1).

[74] *See* 17 U.S.C. § 412(2). A third exception is found in § 411(b), which involves an infringement of a work consisting of sounds, images, or both, the first fixation of which is made simultaneously with its transmission and registration of which is accomplished within three months after its first transmission.

[75] Statutory damages can be chosen as an alternative to actual damages and profits. They can be the only viable measure of damages when the plaintiff may have difficulty in proving actual damages and profits. *See* 17 U.S.C. § 504(c). For a detailed discussion of statutory damages, see *infra* § 9.13.

[76] Legislation has proposed the elimination of §§ 411(a) (requiring registration as a prerequisite for bringing suit) and 412 (requiring registration as prerequisite to obtaining statutory damages and attorney's fees). Advocates of this legislation maintain that the registration requirement is an anachronism that discriminates against U.S. authors. Moreover, the incentives to register provided by §§ 411(a) and 412 do not in fact serve any other practical purpose such as enriching the collections of the Library of Congress. In addition, the § 412 requirement discriminates against small copyright owners who either do not know of the benefits of prompt registration or do not have the time or money to register within the short grace period provided. *See, e.g.*, Copyright Reform Bill of 1993, H.R. 897, 103d Cong. (1993).

[D] The Interplay of Registration and Recordation

For causes of action arising on or after March 1, 1989, the BCIA amendments have totally abrogated the recordation of a transfer of copyright ownership as a requirement to bring a suit for infringement.[77] Recordation, however, is still required under § 205(c)[78] to give constructive notice of the facts stated in the recorded document. This constructive notice provision applies only if *registration* is made for the work. The constructive notice effect of recordation is particularly important if there arises a conflict between two transfers of an interest in copyright. Priority will be given to the transfer executed first, but only if it is recorded within one month of its execution in the United States (two months in a foreign country), and recordation is made in the manner required to give constructive notice. Otherwise the later transfer will prevail if it is first properly recorded and the transfer was taken in good faith.[79]

These constructive notice provisions strongly encourage prompt registration and recordation.

§ 7.07 REGISTRATION OF DERIVATIVE WORKS AND INDIVIDUAL COMPONENTS OF COLLECTIVE WORKS

[A] The Importance of Registration

For works of U.S. origin, registration is required to bring an action for copyright infringement and is necessary to confer subject matter jurisdiction.[80] Once the registration has been accomplished, the copyright owner can recover for infringements that occurred both before and after the registration. The Copyright Act however, does not answer the question of who can rely on a registration certificate for the purposes of bringing an infringement suit, an issue that has presented special difficulties in the case of collective and derivative works. It is an important question because a failure to register properly and in a timely manner will not confer certain rights or remedies for infringement of copyright such as prima facie validity, statutory damages, and attorney's fees. As the following discussion will show, to enjoy the full rights and remedies provided by the Copyright Act, owners of a derivative work and its individual components of collective works should individually register their works within three months of publication as specified by § 412 of the Act.

---

[77] Before passage of the Berne amendments, 17 U.S.C. § 205(d) required recordation of a transfer of an interest in copyright in order to bring an infringement suit. This section has been abrogated for causes of action arising after March 1, 1989, but will be required for causes of action arising before that date. For a discussion of recordation, see *supra* § 5.12.

[78] 17 U.S.C. § 205(c).

[79] *See* 17 U.S.C. § 205(d).

[80] *See, e.g., Well-Made Toy Mfg. Corp. v. Goffa Int'l Corp.*, 354 F.3d 112 (2d Cir. 2003).

[B] Derivative Works and the Registration Requirement

In general, the courts have held that registration in the underlying work, or in the collective work, will not support an action for infringement brought on behalf of an unregistered derivative work or an individual component of a collective work. To illustrate the general rule in the derivative work context, the courts have held that a registered copyright in a 20-inch doll did not confer subject matter jurisdiction for a suit for infringement of plaintiff's 48-inch doll based on the underlying work.[81] Similarly, the registration of a copyrighted song did not extend to a later unregistered adaptation of that song by the writer.[82]

The rule that a registration of the underlying work will not support an action for infringement of an unregistered derivative work will in some instances make little practical difference. For the most part, an infringer who copies protectible expression from the derivative work will unavoidably copy protected expression from the underlying work as well. If the action were brought for infringement of the derivative work, an amendment of the complaint to claim infringement of the underlying work should remedy the absence of registration in the derivative work. On the other hand, if the materials copied from the derivative work consisted of the newly added components, registration of the underlying work would not support an action for infringement of the derivative work.

[C] Registration of Collective Works and Their Individual Components

Similar to the rules regarding underlying works and derivative works, the courts have held that registration in a collective work is inadequate to support a suit for infringement of a constituent element of that collective work. In *Morris v. Business Concepts, Inc.*,[83] the Second Circuit held that a registration in a magazine would not support suit for infringement in an unregistered article published in the magazine. The court ruled that the magazine, which held an exclusive license to publish the article, may not be considered a copyright owner capable of satisfying § 411(a)'s registration requirement for the author of the article. The Court relied on Copyright Office practice for the proposition that a collective work registration does not apply to the separate, contributed works unless all rights in those works have been transferred to the collective work owner.[84] Following the Copyright Office pronouncement, courts have held that registration of the collective work could support an action for infringement in the

---

[81] *Id.*

[82] *Murray Hill Publ'ns, Inc. v. ABC Commc'ns, Inc.*, 264 F.3d 622 (6th Cir. 2001) (holding that subject matter jurisdiction for a copyright claim over an unregistered derivative work may not be satisfied by the registration of the underlying work). For a case holding that the registration of the underlying work extends to derivative work, see *Montgomery v. Noga*, 168 F.3d 1282 (11th Cir. 1999) (holding that the registration of a computer program would support an action for infringement of a later unregistered program that incorporated 70% of the underlying registered work).

[83] 283 F.3d 502 (2d Cir. 2002).

[84] *See* Copyright Office Circular 62 ("Copyright Registration for Serials on Form SE").

constituent part when both entities are owned by the same party.[85] This rule is consistent with the Copyright Act, which provides in § 504(c) that, for the purpose of assessing statutory damages, "all the parts of a compilation or derivative work constitute one work."[86]

§ 7.08 REFUSAL OF REGISTRATION: § 411(a)

What happens when the claimant is refused registration but wishes to bring suit for infringement? Section 411(a)[87] takes into account the situation in which the applicant has delivered the application, deposit, and fee in proper form but registration has been refused. If the application for registration is denied, the applicant may seek judicial review under the Administrative Procedure Act, pursuant to § 701(e) of the Copyright Act.[88] Alternatively, § 411(a) allows the rejected applicant to file an action for infringement, so long as the Register of Copyrights is given notice and an opportunity to intervene.[89] The Register has the discretion to become a party to the suit on the issue of registrability. Even if the Register does not make an appearance within 60 days of service, the court is not precluded from determining questions of registerability.[90]

What if, for no good reason, the Copyright Office simply fails to act on an application, one way or the other? It has been held that, unlike the situation that prevailed under the 1909 Act, the availability of judicial review as specified above renders a writ of mandamus under 28 U.S.C. § 1361 no longer available to compel registration.[91]

As discussed above, section 411(a) applies only when the applicant has complied with all the formal requirements of registration; that is, when the application, deposit, and fee are delivered in proper form. Ordinarily, however, judicial review cannot occur until there is a final agency action, including the exhaustion of available administrative appeal procedures. For example, in *Proulx v. Hennepin Technical Centers*,[92] the applicant refused to deposit a complete copy of his 137-hour set of videotaped lectures, as required by Copyright Office regulations, depositing identifying material instead. Plaintiff also failed to respond to the Register's request

---

[85] *See Xoom, Inc. v. Imageline, Inc.*, 323 F.3d 279, 284 (4th Cir. 2003); *Medforms, Inc. v. Healthcare Mgmt. Solutions, Inc.*, 290 F.3d 98 (2d Cir. 2002).

[86] 17 U.S.C. § 504(c).

[87] 17 U.S.C. § 411(a).

[88] 17 U.S.C. § 701(e); *see, e.g.*, *Darden v. Peters*, 488 F.3d 277 (4th Cir. 2007) (reviewing denial for abuse of discretion).

[89] *See, e.g.*, *Paul Morelli Design, Inc. v. Tiffany and Co.*, 200 F. Supp. 2d 482 (E.D. Pa. 2002) (giving "some deference" to Register's decision, rather than abuse of discretion or *de novo* review); *Brooks-Ngwenya v. Indianapolis Pub. Sch.*, 564 F.3d 804 (7th Cir. 2009) (holding that although the notice rule is mandatory, failure to notify does not deprive the court of jurisdiction). This is an intentional change from 1909 Act law, which required the applicant to bring an action against the Register of Copyrights to compel issuance of a certificate before an infringement suit could be brought. *Id.*

[90] *Paul Morelli Design, Inc.*, 200 F. Supp. 2d 482 (E.D. Pa. 2002).

[91] *See Nova Stylings, Inc. v. Ladd*, 695 F.2d 1179 (9th Cir. 1983).

[92] *Proulx v. Hennepin Technical Ctrs.*, 1981 U.S. Dist. LEXIS 17634 (D. Minn. Dec. 7, 1981).

for clarification as to certain inconsistencies in his application and deposit. The court held that registration had not been refused by the Copyright Office within the meaning of § 411(a): "The term 'refused' as used in Section 411(a) contemplates a final decision by the Copyright Office on the merits of the registerability of the plaintiff's submission."[93] In this case, the plaintiff failed to exhaust his administrative remedies since he did not respond properly to the Register's requests or obtain a final refusal to register before proceeding with his claim in federal court.

§ 7.09 REGISTRATION UNDER THE 1909 ACT: THE "PROMPT" DEPOSIT AND REGISTRATION REQUIREMENT

Under the 1909 Act, federal statutory copyright began not on registration but when the work was published with proper notice.[94] Section 13 of the 1909 Act[95] provided that once a work was copyrighted by publication with notice, "there shall be promptly deposited" the required copies and the claim for registration. The question has arisen whether failure to comply with this apparent requirement for prompt deposit would inject a work into the public domain. The meaning of the term *promptly* under the 1909 Act is still important to determining whether a failure to promptly deposit ejected a work into the public domain. If so, the work cannot be retrieved from the public domain because all works that have entered the public domain before 1978 remain there, unaffected by the 1976 Act.[96]

The case law under the 1909 Act has undermined the meaning of the "promptly" requirement. The process began with *Washingtonian Publishing Co. v. Pearson.*[97] In *Washingtonian*, plaintiff had published with proper notice an issue of the *Washingtonian* magazine. Fourteen months later, copies were deposited in the Copyright Office, and a certificate of registration was secured. Defendant argued that although prompt deposit is not a prerequisite to copyright, no action could be brought for an infringement occurring before the tardy deposit. The Supreme Court disagreed, holding that an infringement action can be brought for acts committed before and after registration.

The *Washingtonian* reasoning was pushed one step further in *Shapiro, Bernstein & Co. v. Jerry Vogel Music Co.*,[98] excusing a 27-year delay in deposit and registration. *Shapiro* effectively removed any meaning from the word "prompt," except when deposit is specifically requested from the Register of Copyright.[99] Only then may copyright be forfeited in a work. But for the purpose of bringing an

---

[93] *Id.* at ¶17,249.

[94] There was one minor exception under § 13 of the 1909 Act for certain works "not produced for sale," (*i.e.*, unpublished works). *See* NIMMER ON COPYRIGHT § 7.16[A][2][c][i] (2014).

[95] 17 U.S.C. § 13 (1909 Act).

[96] *See* 17 U.S.C. § 103 (Trans. & Supp. Prov., 1976 Act).

[97] 306 U.S. 30 (1939).

[98] 161 F.2d 406 (2d Cir. 1946).

[99] *See* 17 U.S.C. § 14 (1909) (stating that noncompliance within three months of the Register's demand for a deposit of copies results in a forfeiture of the copyright).

infringement suit under the 1909 Act, deposit and registration could be made any time during the first term of copyright.

§ 7.10 SUMMARY CHART: REGISTRATION PROVISIONS FOR PUBLISHED WORKS UNDER THE 1909, 1976, AND BERNE CONVENTION IMPLEMENTATION ACTS

DATE OF PUBLICATION	Work published before 1978	Work published on or after 1/1/78 and before 3/1/89	Work published on or after 3/1/89
NATURE OF REQUIREMENT	Optional until last year of first term, § 24 (1909 Act), but now mandatory for works published before 1964.	Optional. § 408.	Optional. § 408.
PREREQUISITE TO BRING SUIT FOR INFRINGEMENT OF COPYRIGHT?	Yes, during both terms of copyright.	Yes. § 411.	Yes for U.S. works, except for actions brought under § 106A(a). § 411. No for non-U.S. Berne works. § 411.
INCENTIVES TO REGISTER	Prerequisite to suit (see above).	Prerequisite to suit (see above). Also, except for actions under §§ 106A(a) or 411(b), statutory damages and attorneys' fees are not available unless work was registered before infringement began, or work is infringed during first three months of publication and registration is made within three months after first publication. § 412.	Same as for works published between 1/1/78 and 3/1/89 for both U.S. and non-U.S. Berne works. § 412.

Part II. DEPOSIT

§ 7.11 GENERALLY

The deposit of copies of copyrighted works serves two purposes. The first is to provide copies of the work for the collections of the Library of Congress. The second is to identify the work for the conjunction with copyright registration. These two deposit requirements are intertwined because a single deposit of copies for registration will satisfy both purposes.[100]

§ 7.12 MANDATORY DEPOSIT FOR THE LIBRARY OF CONGRESS

With some exceptions, the deposit for the Library of Congress is mandatory and applies to all types of works.[101] These mandatory deposit requirements, designed to build up the collection of our national library, the Library of Congress, have been a feature of American law since 1790. The Register of Copyrights has been given the authority to establish regulations specifying the mechanics of the deposit requirement.[102]

Section 407 outlines the basic procedure. Within three months after a work is published with notice of copyright in the United States, the owner of the copyright, or the owner of the exclusive right of publication, must deposit two copies or phonorecords of the work in the Copyright Office.[103] Works excluded from the deposit requirement are unpublished works,[104] published works not having notice, works published in foreign countries, and certain other categories exempted by the Register of Copyright.[105] Generally, though, once a work is published in the United States, even if it was first published abroad, deposit is mandatory.[106]

§ 7.13 FAILURE TO COMPLY WITH DEPOSIT REQUIREMENTS

Failure to comply with deposit requirements will not forfeit copyright. Rather, mandatory deposit requirements are enforced by a graduated series of fines. For failure to deposit within three months of publication, the Register of Copyright may impose an initial fine of no more than $250 plus the cost of acquiring the requested

---

[100] Since 1870, a single deposit has been accepted for both Library of Congress and registration purposes. *See* Elizabeth K. Dunne, Copyright Office Study No. 20, Deposit of Copyrighted Works (1960).

[101] *See* 17 U.S.C. § 407.

[102] *See* 17 U.S.C. § 407(c).

[103] *See* 17 U.S.C. § 407(a)(1),(2).

[104] Once registration is sought for an unpublished work, the claimant must comply with deposit requirements. *See* 17 U.S.C. § 408.

[105] *See* 37 C.F.R. §§ 202.19–202.21 (1987).

[106] The deposit requirement has withstood constitutional challenges on First and Fifth Amendment grounds. *See Ladd v. Law and Tech. Press*, 762 F.2d 809 (9th Cir. 1985).

copies and an additional fine of $2,500 for willful refusal to comply with a demand for deposit.[107] By comparison, the 1909 Act treated deposit and registration as a unit and failure to comply with prompt deposit after a demand by the Register of Copyrights would not only subject the claimant to a fine, but would void copyright as well.[108] The deposit provisions of the 1909 Act should be kept in mind, despite the changes made by the 1976 Act, because the current Act will not revive a work going into the public domain before January 1, 1978.

§ 7.14 MECHANICS OF DEPOSIT

Section 407 of the 1976 Act requires that deposit of a work consist of, "(1) two complete copies of the best edition; or (2) if the work is a sound recording, two complete phonorecords of the best edition, together with any printed or other visually perceptible material published with such phonorecords."[109]

The key term is "best edition," which means that the Library of Congress is entitled to receive the copies of phonorecords best suiting its needs.[110] In concrete terms, the best edition is the one of the highest quality relative to other published editions of the work.[111]

Many deposits are not suitable for the Library of Congress' collections, and the Register of Copyright has exempted certain categories of works from the deposit requirement.[112] For example, three-dimensional sculptural works, most advertising material, and individual contributions to collective works are exempt. One should consult the regulations for the entire list of exemptions.[113]

Even if the work is not specifically exempted, a person may apply for special relief from deposit requirements.[114] Special relief is most often given when an undue burden or cost would be imposed on the copyright owner if the deposit requirement for a nonexempt work were required. The grant of special relief is discretionary with the Copyright Office, which balances the needs of the Library of Congress with the hardship to the copyright owner.

---

[107] *See* 17 U.S.C. § 407(d)(3).

[108] *See* 17 U.S.C. § 13 (1909).

[109] *See* 17 U.S.C. § 407(a)(1), (2).

[110] *See* 17 U.S.C. § 101 (defining "best edition").

[111] *See* 37 C.F.R. § 202.19(b)(iii) (1987).

[112] *See* 17 U.S.C. § 407(c)(1), (2).

[113] *See* 37 C.F.R. §§ 202.20–202.21 (1987).

[114] *See id.* at § 202.20.

§ 7.15 MANDATORY DEPOSIT UNDER § 407 AND THE DEPOSIT REQUIREMENT FOR REGISTRATION UNDER § 408 COMPARED

Even though closely related and largely overlapping, deposit requirements for the Library of Congress, § 407, should be distinguished from deposit requirements for registration purposes, § 408. Deposit for the Library of Congress is mandatory, whether one registers or not. An applicant for registration need only supply one deposit copy to meet the requirements for registration and the mandatory deposit for the Library of Congress. An applicant for registration can satisfy both requirements in a single deposit. The reverse is not true. If registration is made after deposit for the Library of Congress, another deposit copy is required. For practical reasons, most parties choose to register and deposit at the same time, accompanying the deposit with the application and the fee.[115]

Because they serve somewhat different purposes, mandatory deposit with the Library of Congress and deposit for registration with the Copyright Office are not entirely identical. Because deposit for registration serves an identifying function, one copy is generally required for registration of works not subject to the mandatory deposit with the Library of Congress. First, one copy of an individual contribution to a collective work must be deposited for registration, but is not mandatory for the Library of Congress. Second, registration requires deposit of one complete copy or phonorecord of any unpublished work, whereas unpublished works are completely exempt from deposit with the Library of Congress.[116] Third, works published outside the United States are exempt from the mandatory deposit, but not deposit for registration purposes.[117] With these exceptions, the mandatory deposit provisions of the Library of Congress are virtually identical to the deposit requirements for registration purposes.[118]

---

[115] *See* 37 C.F.R. § 202.19(f) (1987).

[116] *See* 17 U.S.C. § 408(b)(1).

[117] *See* 17 U.S.C. § 408(b)(3).

[118] Deposit requirements for both the Library of Congress and the Copyright Office may be modified in special cases. The Register of Copyrights has the authority to issue regulations covering the deposit requirements for registration in order to meet the practical needs of the parties, the Library of Congress, and the Copyright Office. Thus, under the regulations, one deposit copy is required instead of two, and identifying material instead of actual work can be deposited, if such works are cumbersome or very valuable. *See* 37 C.F.R. § 202.19 (1987).

§ 7.16 SUMMARY CHART: DEPOSIT PROVISIONS FOR PUBLISHED WORKS UNDER THE 1909, 1976, AND BERNE CONVENTION IMPLEMENTATION ACTS

DATE OF PUBLICATION	Work published before 1978	Work published on or after 1/1/78 and before 3/1/89	Work published after 3/1/89
PREREQUISITE TO BRING SUIT FOR INFRINGEMENT OF COPYRIGHT?	Yes. § 13 (1909 Act).	Yes. § 411(a).	Yes for works of U.S. origin. No for U.S. Berne works. § 411(a).
SANCTIONS FOR FAILURE TO DEPOSIT?	Yes. § 14 (1909 Act).	Yes. § 407(d).	Yes for both U.S. works and non-U.S. Berne works. § 407(d).

§ 7.17 THE FUTURE OF THE COPYRIGHT OFFICE

The placement of the Copyright Office in the Library of Congress, and therefore in the legislative branch, is a historical anomaly. Some commentators have even suggested that this anomaly renders regulations promulgated by the Register of Copyrights constitutionally suspect.[119] It is extremely unlikely, however, that the Supreme Court would invalidate an arrangement that has stood for more than a century; and the only court to address the issue upheld the Register's authority on the ground that the Register is appointed by the Librarian of Congress, who in turn is appointed by the President with the advice and consent of the Senate under Article II.[120]

During the Clinton Administration, the increased influence of international trade consideration in the formulation of U.S. intellectual property law and policy prompted serious consideration of reforming the structure of the Copyright Office and its companion agency, the U.S. Patent and Trademark Office. In 1999, the PTO, which has been part of the Commerce Department since 1925, was reorganized. Previously, the PTO was led by a single Commissioner of Patents. Now there are separate Commissioners of Patent and Trademarks under the supervision of the Under Secretary for Intellectual Property and the Director of the United States Patent and Trademark Office. In creating the position of Under Secretary for Intellectual Property, Congress at least implicitly raised the question of whether the Copyright Office should be consolidated with the PTO.

What are the pluses and minuses of the basic suggestion that the United States should have a single agency which is: (1) responsible for all of patent, trademark, and copyright law, and (2) lodged in a department of the executive branch rather

---

[119] *See* E. Fulton Brlylawski, *The Copyright Office: A Constitutional Confrontation*, 44 Geo. Wash. L. Rev. 1 (1975); Jeanane Marie Jiles, *Copyright Protection in the New Millennium: Amending the Digital Millennium Copyright Act Prevent Constitutional Challenges*, 52 Admin. L. Rev. 443 (2000).

[120] *See Eltra Corp. v. Ringer*, 579 F.2d 294 (4th Cir. 1978).

than under the supervision of a Congressional agency? One way to approach the issue is to ask the following questions: If you were designing, from scratch, a system for the administration of U.S. intellectual property law, what would it look like? How important is it that the various bodies of I.P. law be coordinated by a single federal agency? Should such an agency, if created, report to the legislative branch, which at least in theory makes U.S. law, or to the Commerce Department, which increasingly helps negotiate revisions in intellectual property law through the treaty making process conducted under the authority of the President? Is there anything special about copyright law that justifies the current administrative regime?

One response might be that copyrights traditionally have been treated differently from patents and trademarks in international law. While copyrights are governed by the Berne Convention, patents and trademarks fall under the Paris Convention for the protection of Industrial Property. Moreover, because the Berne Convention prohibits mandatory formalities, most countries lack any kind of registration system for copyrights, even though it is common to require government examination and registration for patents and trademarks. The fact alone makes the existence of any Copyright Office having important regulatory responsibilities unusual in the international sphere.

The question of consolidation arose in part because TRIPS broke with tradition in addressing copyrights in the same agreement with patents and trademarks. The spirit of consolidation can also be detected in the Prioritizing Resources and Organization for Intellectual Property (PRO-IP) Act of 2008,[121] which created an Intellectual Property Enforcement Coordinator (or "IP Czar") whose principal duty is to chair an interagency intellectual property enforcement committee consisting of representatives from the Copyright Office and various agencies, including the PTO, the Department of Justice, and the U.S. Trade Representative. The committee was charged by Congress to create and implement a Joint Strategic Plan for, among other things, "reducing counterfeiting and infringement in the domestic and international supply chain" and "disrupting and eliminating domestic and international counterfeiting and infringement networks."[122]

It remains to be seen whether the creation of the IP Czar will lead to substantive changes in the administration of copyright and other intellectual property laws. For now, however, despite the PRO-IP Act, the push for formal consolidation has subsided, and both inertia and tradition suggest that the Copyright Office will remain where it is for the foreseeable future.

---

[121] Prioritizing Resources and Organization for Intellectual Property Act of 2008, Pub. L. No. 110-403, 122 Stat. 4256 (2008).

[122] See Strategic Plan 2008–2013, http://www.copyright.gov/reports/s-plan2008/index.html and 2013 Joint Strategic Plan on Intellectual Property Enforcement, at http://www.whitehouse.gov/sites/default/files/omb/IPEC/2013-us-ipec-joint-strategic-plan.pdf.

Chapter 8

THE EXCLUSIVE RIGHTS AND THEIR LIMITATIONS

§ 8.01 INTRODUCTION AND CHAPTER OVERVIEW

The six exclusive rights of reproduction, adaptation, distribution, performance, display, and the digital sound recording transmission right create the boundaries of copyright ownership,[1] and their violation constitutes copyright infringement. Each exclusive right is subject to a series of limitations set forth in §§ 107–122 of the Copyright Act. Describing these limitations is a complex, detailed task, and the length of this chapter reflects the nature of the subject.

This chapter is split into six parts and, after an introduction to the subject, concentrates individually on each exclusive right and its limitations. Part I presents an overview of the subject, focusing on the structure of the exclusive rights and their limitations. It introduces the concept of the compulsory license, whereby access to a copyrighted work can be obtained without negotiation with the copyright owner so long as the user meets the statutory terms and royalties. Compulsory licenses constitute a developing but controversial trend in copyright law, and their justification and administration are examined in the first part of this chapter. Part II concerns the reproduction and adaptation rights and the various limitations on them. Part III continues with the distribution right, devoting most of the discussion to the major limitation on the distribution right called the "first sale doctrine." Part IV covers the performance and display rights whose limitations, such as the compulsory license for cable television, are among the most complicated in the Copyright Act. Part V examines the moral right, given explicit recognition for the first time in the Visual Artists Rights Act of 1990. Part VI reviews what may be called "rights beyond" traditional copyright law. This part examines the regulation of digital audio recording devices in the Audio Home Recording Act of 1992 and the protection of rights management mechanisms and anticircumvention measures in the Digital Millennium Copyright Act of 1998.

---

[1] For a proposed analytic approach to determine ownership of a tangible copy of copyrighted work, see Brian W. Carver, *Why License Agreements Do Not Control Copy Ownership: First Sales and Essential Copies*, 25 Berkeley Tech. L.J. 1887 (2010).

Part I. EXCLUSIVE RIGHTS, LIMITATIONS, AND COMPULSORY LICENSES

§ 8.02 INTRODUCTION TO THE EXCLUSIVE RIGHTS AND THEIR LIMITATIONS

A copyright consists of a bundle of exclusive rights that empower the copyright owner to exclude others from certain uses of his work. The exclusive rights of reproduction, adaptation, distribution, performance, display, and the digital sound recording transmission right enumerated in § 106[2] define the boundaries of copyright ownership, and their violation constitutes copyright infringement.[3] In short, they are the essence of copyright ownership. Exclusive rights can be subdivided infinitely, and each can be owned and enforced separately.[4] For example, the copyright owner of a novel may grant exclusive licenses for the reproduction, distribution, and performance rights to different parties, each of whom can sue for infringement in his own right.[5]

The exclusive rights are cumulative and, to a certain extent, they overlap. The same act may simultaneously infringe both the reproduction and adaptation rights. For example, by making an unauthorized translation of a copyrighted work, an infringer has reproduced the work and has also adapted it in the translation. Other than this reproduction/adaptation rights overlap, it takes separate acts to infringe the other exclusive rights. If the infringer in the above example sold copies of the translation and authorized readings of it, the distribution and performance rights of the copyright owner would also be infringed.

The exclusive rights of the copyright owner are subject to important limitations set forth in §§ 107 through 122.[6] Although the most complex set of limitations are set forth in these sections, limitations first begin to appear in § 106.[7] First, not all copyrightable subject matter as defined under § 102[8] enjoys the same degree of copyright protection. Neither graphic, pictorial, sculptural works, nor sound recordings enjoy the same full range of exclusive rights as do literary, musical, and dramatic works. For example, the copyright owner of a sound recording cannot control the right of performance (except for certain digital audio transmissions) and display of the work. In addition, graphic, pictorial, and sculptural works do not enjoy a performance right. Second, § 106 limits the exclusive rights of performance and display to *public* performance and display. Accordingly, copyright owners have

---

[2] 17 U.S.C. § 106.

[3] *See* 17 U.S.C. § 501(a) ("Anyone who violates any of the exclusive rights . . . is an infringer of the copyright."). For an argument for a limited right of first online publication, see Jake Linford, *A Second Look at the Right of First Publication*, 58 J. Copyright Soc'y 585 (2011).

[4] *See* 17 U.S.C. § 201(d)(2). For a discussion of ownership matters, see *supra* §§ 5.08–5.09.

[5] For discussion of transfers of copyright ownership, see *supra* § 5.13.

[6] 17 U.S.C. §§ 107–122.

[7] 17 U.S.C. § 106.

[8] 17 U.S.C. § 102.

no control over private performances or displays of their work.[9]

The longest and most complicated sections of the 1976 Act that pertain to these limitations vary in concreteness and detail. The fair use provision of § 107, for example, is a broad limitation covering all varieties and uses of copyrighted works, whereas § 111, the cable television provision, constructs a relatively concrete and intricate system of regulation for a specific industry. The compulsory licenses, found in sections 111, 112, 113, 114, 115, 118, 119, and 122, were once regulated by a now defunct administrative body called the Copyright Royalty Tribunal ("CRT"). In 1993, Congress abolished the CRT, reassigning its functions to Copyright Arbitration Royalty Panels ("CARPs") convened by the Librarian of Congress on recommendation of the Register of Copyrights. In 2004, Congress abolished the CARP system, replacing it with three full-time Copyright Royalty Judges ("CRJs") who comprise the Copyright Royalty Board ("CRB").[10] The following section introduces seven compulsory licenses and their administration.

§ 8.03 THE COMPULSORY LICENSES AND THEIR ADMINISTRATION

[A] What is a Compulsory License?

To use a copyrighted work, one must normally obtain a license, the terms of which are determined through negotiation with the copyright owner. If A, for example, wishes to reproduce B's copyrighted painting in a poster, he or she must obtain authorization from B, and the terms of the ensuing agreement will depend on market conditions. In seven instances, however, the Copyright Act supersedes the normal market mechanism for distributing copyrighted works and allows the prospective user the right to obtain a compulsory license under which he can use the work without the copyright owner's permission. So long as the licensee complies with the statutory procedure and pays the established royalties, the compulsory license applies.

The seven compulsory licenses, including the now repealed (in 1993) jukebox licenses, will be discussed in more detail at various points in this chapter. By way of introduction, they are:

(1) The Cable License of § 111,[11] which establishes a compulsory license for secondary transmissions by cable television systems;

(2) The Ephemeral Recordings License (§ 112(e)), which establishes a statutory license for ephemeral recordings used to facilitate the digital transmissions permitted under § 114;

---

[9] For a discussion of the meaning of *public* performance and display, see *infra* § 8.17.

[10] *See* Library of Congress, Copyright Royalty Board: Background (providing basic information and biographies on the three judges entrusted with "determining and adjusting the rates and terms of the statutory licenses and determining the distribution of royalties from the statutory license royalty pools that the Library of Congress administers."). http://www.loc.gov/crb/background

[11] 17 U.S.C. § 111.

(3) The Mechanical License and the Digital Audio Transmission License of § 115,[12] which establishes a compulsory license for production and distribution of phonorecords of non dramatic musical works, and their delivery by digital audio transmission;[13]

(4) The Digital Performance Right in Sound Recordings License Recordings of § 114,[14] which establishes a statutory license for some operators of non-interactive digital transmission services;

(5) The Public Broadcasting License of § 118,[15] which establishes a compulsory license for the use of certain copyrighted works by noncommercial broadcasting entities;

(6) The General Satellite Retransmission License of § 119,[16] which establishes a compulsory license for satellite retransmissions to the public for private viewing;

(7) The Local-to-Local Satellite Retransmission License (§ 122), which establishes a statutory license for satellite retransmissions of local television stations' broadcasts into their local markets.

In addition, the Audio Home Recording Act of 1992 establishes immunity from liability for copyright infringement for manufacturers and importers of digital audio recording equipment in connection with the imposition of a duty to pay statutory "royalties" into a fund for the benefit of copyright owners. Failure to pay these royalties does not, however, subject the manufacturer or importer to an infringement action, but only to an action for statutorily prescribed penalties.[17]

[B] Are the Compulsory Licenses Justifiable?

If the compulsory licenses are a major departure from the ordinary way of obtaining the right to use a copyrighted work, how did they come about and are they justifiable?[18]

The compulsory licenses are essentially products of political compromise where certain user interest groups have carved out for themselves an exception to the way in which a license is normally negotiated.[19] The cable television compulsory

---

[12] 17 U.S.C. § 115.

[13] 17 U.S.C. § 115. For an argument that the compulsory license for making phonorecords of nondramatic musical works should be repealed because it is no longer a useful way to foster the creation of intellectual works, see Howard B. Abrams, *Copyright's First Compulsory License*, 26 SANTA CLARA COMPUTER & HIGH TECH L.J. 215 (2010).

[14] 17 U.S.C. § 114.

[15] 17 U.S.C. § 118.

[16] 17 U.S.C. § 119.

[17] The Audio Home Recording Act of 1992, 17 U.S.C. §§ 1001–10 (adding Chapter 10 to Title 17 of the U.S. Code). AHRA is discussed at § 8.31 *infra*.

[18] For an overview of the compulsory licenses, see Paul Goldstein, *Preempted State Doctrines, Involuntary Transfers and Compulsory Licenses: Testing the Limits of Copyright*, 24 UCLA L. REV. 1107, 1127–39 (1977).

[19] For the nature of the political compromise leading to the compulsory licenses, see Barbara A. Ringer, *Copyright and the Future of Authorship*, 101 LIBR. L.J. 229 (1976).

license provides an excellent example of this political compromise. As embodied in § 111, it reflects the intense negotiations between powerful interest groups, copyright owners, and the cable television industry, resulting in a complicated system of regulation.[20]

What justifications are there for these compulsory licenses, which have been attacked as undermining the fundamental rights of authors?[21] Supporters of compulsory licensing justify this preemption of an author's control over the use and distribution of a work on economic grounds. The argument is that the compulsory license serves both owners and users by reducing the transaction costs involved in licensing works through the private market system. Thus, the cable systems and copyright owners are spared the costs of hiring lawyers who would individually negotiate a license on their behalf. Without the compulsory license mechanism, these transaction costs could be so high that negotiations would not take place at all, impoverishing owners, users, and the public. Instead, the cable systems, mechanical licensees, and the public broadcasting system know exactly what they must pay and what procedures they must follow to use a copyrighted work. In sum, they avoid transaction costs and uncertainties of the marketplace and facilitate dissemination of copyrighted works.

[C] Administering the Compulsory Licenses; From the Copyright Royalty Tribunal[22] to Copyright Arbitration Panels

To administer the compulsory licenses, Congress initially created the now defunct Copyright Royalty Tribunal ("CRT")[23] as an independent agency functioning within the legislative branch of the government.[24] The president nominated members of the agency for staggered seven-year terms.[25] The Copyright Royalty Tribunal served two functions.[26] The first was to set the statutory royalty rates for the compulsory licenses.[27] The second was to settle disputes concerning the distribution of monies collected for cable television and

---

[20] For a background, overview, and critique of the cable television compulsory license, recommending its elimination and return to normal market mechanisms, see David Ladd et al., *Copyright, Cable, the Compulsory License: A Second Chance*, 3 COMM. & L. 3(1981).

[21] *See* Barbara A. Ringer, *Copyright in the 1980's*, 23 BULL. COPYRIGHT SOC'Y 299 (1976).

[22] For an overview and background, see Fulton E. Brylawski, *The Copyright Royalty Tribunal*, 24 UCLA L. REV. 1265 (1977).

[23] *See* 17 U.S.C. §§ 801–10.

[24] The Tribunal had the authority to create its own rules of procedure if consistent with the Administrative Procedure Act. *See* 17 U.S.C. § 803(a).

[25] *See* 17 U.S.C. § 802. There was no requirement that the appointed members have any copyright experience.

[26] *See* Barbara A. Ringer, *The Unfinished Business of Copyright Revision*, 24 UCLA L. REV. 951, 974 (1977).

[27] The Tribunal had the authority to raise rates periodically. It had been criticized as being too pro-copyright owner in its rate-making activities rather than balancing the rights of creators and users. Generally, the Tribunal tried to approximate the actual market value of the works. By its actions, jukebox royalties were raised from $8.00 to $64.00 and the mechanical royalty rate was raised from 2.75¢ to 6.60¢.

jukebox performances.[28] Although the statue provided relatively clear direction for the Tribunal's ratemaking activities, it gave little indication of how the Tribunal should distribute royalties. As a result of this vagueness, the Tribunal's activities became embroiled in a constant stream of litigation and criticism.[29] Legislative hearings pointed out in detail the inadequacies[30] of the system, and sunset bills[31] were constantly proposed to phase out aspects of the compulsory licenses. From an international copyright perspective, the jukebox license, even after its amendment by the Berne Convention Implementation Act ("BCIA"), had come under particularly vigorous attack as impeding American efforts to join the Berne Union, the preeminent international copyright convention.[32]

The CRT came under intense criticism during its fifteen-year life. Its decisions on the distribution of royalties never operated smoothly and provoked protracted litigation. To the critics (invariably author groups), whatever advantages were derived from the compulsory licenses were outweighed by the costly and wasteful system of regulation, which they claimed was not only unfair to authors but economically unsound. As for the argument that compulsory licenses reduced transaction costs, critics of compulsory licenses maintained that there are private clearinghouse mechanisms, such as ASCAP and BMI to accomplish the same result at a fraction of the administrative cost and without government intervention.[33] Rather than abolishing the compulsory licenses, Congress responded to the shortcomings of the regulatory system. This ever-increasing dissatisfaction with the CRT led to its elimination in 1993.

With the Copyright Royalty Tribunal Act of 1993, Congress closed down an entrenched administrative agency and radically changed the regulatory landscape of compulsory licenses. In place of the CRT, the Act created a more flexible

---

[28] The Copyright Royalty Tribunal did not distribute royalties for the mechanical license or for noncommercial broadcasting. For these licenses, the parties involved arrange the distribution for themselves. For a discussion of these compulsory licenses, see *infra* § 8.07.

[29] The United States Courts of Appeals reviewed Tribunal decisions. *See* 17 U.S.C. § 810. The following cases are representative of this litigation: *Nat'l Ass'n of Broadcasters v. Copyright Royalty Tribunal*, 809 F.2d 172 (2d Cir. 1986) (cable television); *Christian Broad. Network, Inc. v. Copyright Royalty Tribunal*, 720 F.2d 1295 (D.C. Cir. 1983) (cable television); *Amusement & Music Operators Ass'n v. Copyright Royalty Tribunal*, 676 F.2d 1144 (7th Cir. 1982); *Recording Indus. Ass'n of America v. Copyright Royalty Tribunal*, 662 F.2d 1 (D.C. Cir. 1981) (mechanical license).

[30] The first systematic review of the Tribunal by the General Accounting Office revealed serious deficiencies in the system. Among other things, the Tribunal had vague criteria by which to act, the royalty funds were distributed inefficiently because of legal challenges, and the commissioners had little copyright experience. *See Hearings Before the Subcomm. on Courts of the House Comm. on the Judiciary, Civil Liberties, and the Administration of Justice*, 96th Cong., (1981); *see also Oversight Hearing on the Copyright Royalty Tribunal and Copyright Office Before the Subcomm. on Courts, Civil Liberties, and the Administration of Justice of the H. Comm. on the Judiciary*, 99th Cong. (1985).

[31] *See, e.g.*, H.R. REP. NO. 99-2752 (1985).

[32] The other compulsory licenses appear compatible with Berne. *See* Ralph Oman, *The Compulsory License Redux: Will It Survive in a Changing Marketplace?*, 5 CARDOZO ARTS & ENT. L.J. 37, 49 (1986). For a discussion of U.S. entry into the Berne Union, see *infra* § 12.05.

[33] *See generally* Paul Goldstein, *The Private Consumption of Public Goods: A Comment on Williams and Wilkins Co. v. United States*, 21 BULL. COPYRIGHT SOC'Y 204, 210–11 (1974). For a discussion of these Performing Rights Societies, see *infra* § 8.23.

alternative, Copyright Royalty Arbitration Panels ("CARPs"). These expert panels convened from time to time by order of the Librarian of Congress, on advice of the Register of Copyrights, to reconsider particular rates or to resolve disputes over the distribution of royalties. The goal of this system was to reduce the cost of administering the compulsory licenses and to shift these costs to the parties involved.[34] Unfortunately, after more than a decade of practice, the CARP system was hardly an improvement over its much maligned predecessor, the CRT. Participants in the system pointed out three shortcomings.[35] First, CARP proceedings were very costly to administer. In addition to the high hourly fee paid to arbitrators, the proceedings required considerable amounts of time and Copyright Office personnel. Second, because of their ad hoc nature, CARP proceedings lacked stability, predictability, continuity, and reliability. Third, comprised of arbitrators often having limited knowledge of copyright, CARP lacked institutional expertise, burdening the Copyright Office with the task of correcting errors made in CARP proceedings. In 2004, Congress abolished the CARP system, replacing it with the Copyright Royalty Board — three full-time copyright royalty judges appointed by the Librarian of Congress.[36]

[D] The Current System (For Now): the Copyright Royalty Board

Desiring to replace the CARP system with a more stable, professional, and less costly mechanism to determine statutory royalties, Congress passed the Copyright Royalty and Distribution Act of 2004.[37] The Act deleted all provisions relating to CARPs and created a new chapter 8 of the Copyright Act,[38] entitled "Proceedings by Copyright Royalty Judges." The legislation replaced the occasional three-member Copyright Royalty Arbitration Panels with three full-time Copyright Royalty Judges ("CRJs"), appointed for six-year terms by the Librarian of Congress and known collectively as the Copyright Royalty Board ("CRB"). The legislation also gave additional authority to the Register of Copyrights to reduce costs, put limits on the scope of discovery in the proceedings, and allow the judges to issue subpoenas.

CRJs must have at least seven years of legal experience, and the chief judge must have at least five years of experience in adjudications, arbitrations, or court trials. One of the other two judges must have "significant knowledge" of copyright law, and the other must have "significant knowledge" of economics.[39] The three

---

[34] *See* H.R. Rep. No. 103–286, at 2956 (1993).

[35] *Copyright Royalty and Distribution Act of 2003: Hearing on H.R. 1417 before the Subcomm. on Courts, the Internet, and Intellectual Prop. of the H. Comm. on the Judiciary*, 108th Cong. (2003) (statement of Marybeth Peters, Register of Copyrights and Associate Librarian, Library of Congress).

[36] *See* Copyright Royalty and Distribution Reform Act of 2004, Pub. L. No. 108-419, 118 Stat. 2341 (2004).

[37] *See, e.g.*, Copyright Royalty and Distribution Reform Act of 2004, Pub. L. No. 108–419 (2004); *see also*, Copyright Royalty Judges Program Technical Corrections Act, Pub. L. No. 109–303 (2006).

[38] 17 U.S.C. §§ 801–05.

[39] 17 U.S.C. § 802(a)(1).

CRJs serve staggered six-year terms.[40] The role of the CRJs is limited to fact finding and rate determinations; the judges are required to request a decision from the Register of Copyrights on any "novel material question of substantive law."[41] The Register may also review and comment on the CRJs' resolution of any "material question of substantive law" (without regard to novelty), and the Register's interpretations of substantive law are binding on the CRJs in any subsequent proceedings.[42] CRB decisions are subject to judicial review in the U.S. Court of Appeals for the D.C. Circuit.[43] The standard of review applicable to such review is different from the previous CARP system. Under the 1993 amendments, decisions of the Librarian of Congress taken on the basis of a determination by a CARP could be set aside or modified only if the court found "on the basis of the record before the Librarian, . . . the Librarian acted in an arbitrary manner." Under the 2004 amendments, the CRJs' decisions are now subject to review under the Administrative Procedure Act, which provides that a court should allow an agency determination to stand unless it is "arbitrary, capricious, an abuse of discretion, or otherwise not in accordance with law."[44]

The Copyright Royalty Tribunal Act of 1993 indicated that compulsory licensing was here to stay despite its vigorous denunciation in certain quarters.[45] Whether administered by the CRT, CARPs, or the CRB, the compulsory licenses reflect political reality and have become an integral aspect of the way the system functions. Economic relationships and certain copyright industries are organized around the compulsory licenses. Rather than witnessing their demise, we may even see more compulsory licenses created as a result of political expediency.[46] In addition to compulsory licenses, other forms of comprehensive regulatory schemes, such as that embodied in the Audio Home Recording Act[47] and the Digital Performance Right in Sound Recordings Act,[48] may become more common in subsequent years.

---

[40] 17 U.S.C. § 802(c).

[41] 17 U.S.C. § 802(f)(1)(B).

[42] 17 U.S.C. § 802(f)(1)(D).

[43] 17 U.S.C. § 802(d)(1).

[44] 5 U.S.C. § 706(2)(A).

[45] For a transactional view and criticism of compulsory licenses in copyright, see Andre Francon, *The Future of Copyright*, 132 RIDA 2 (1987).

[46] Compulsory license solutions have been proposed for off-the-air videotaping and audio taping. *See*, *e.g.*, S. 31, 98th Cong., (1983) (video); S. 1739, 99th Cong., (1985) (audio). For performance rights in sound recording, *see* H.R. 1805, 97th Cong. (1981).

[47] The Audio Home Recording Act of 1992, 102 P.L. 563, 106 Stat. 4237 (1992), discussed at *infra* § 8.30.

[48] Digital Performance Right in Sound Recordings Act of 1995 Pub. L. No. 104-39, 109 Stat. 336 (1995), discussed at *infra* § 8.26.

Part II. THE REPRODUCTION AND ADAPTATION RIGHTS AND THEIR LIMITATIONS

§ 8.04 THE REPRODUCTION RIGHT: GENERALLY

[A] Fixation in a Copy or Phonorecord: Material and Temporal Requirements

The exclusive right to reproduce a copyrighted work in copies or phonorecords[49] may be regarded as the most fundamental right granted by the copyright law. To reproduce a work is to fix it in a tangible and relatively permanent form in a material object — a copy or a phonorecord — as specified in § 101. The Copyright Act defines "copies or phonorecords" as material objects that must meet two requirements. First, the material object must be one in which a work is fixed by any method now known or later developed. Second, the material object must be one from which the work can be "perceived, reproduced or otherwise communicated, either directly or with the aid of a machine or device."[50] Thus, one can infringe the reproduction right by reproducing the work on the hard disk of a computer, a CD, or on microfiche, all of which could be perceived by the use of the appropriate device.

In *Cartoon Network LP v. CSC Holdings, Inc.*,[51] the Second Circuit interpreted the meaning of fixation under the statutory definition. This case involved a cable television provider's "remote storage" DVR system, which allowed customers to make copies of TV programs and store them on hard drives at Cablevision's premises for later viewing. The court based its ruling in favor of defendant cable company in applying the definition of "fixed" in § 101, namely that a work is "fixed in a tangible medium of expression" when its "embodiment in a copy or phonorecord . . . is sufficiently permanent or stable for it to be perceived, reproduced or otherwise communicated for more than a transitory duration."[52] The court held that copying a data stream of copyrighted works into a RAM "buffer"[53] of a computer server, which held data for approximately 1.2 seconds before being overwritten, was not sufficiently "fixed" to constitute reproduction. Unfortunately the court's rationale is based on a misreading of the language of the Act. It assumes that the phrase "for a period of more than transitory duration" modifies the words "permanent or stable" when in fact it modifies the preceding phrase "permit it to be perceived, reproduced or otherwise communicated." In other words, it is the perception, reproduction, or other communication of the work, and not its embodiment, that must last for more than a transitory duration. This is certainly the case for the cable company's remote storage system. Their system

---

49 *See* 17 U.S.C. § 106(1).

50 17 U.S.C. § 102(a).

51 536 F.3d 121 (2d Cir. 2008).

52 17 U.S.C. § 101.

53 A buffer is an area in memory that holds data being sent to, or received from a disk.

fixed the copies in a sufficiently permanent state in one buffer (*i.e.*, the 1.2 seconds) for them to be reproduced in another buffer for more than a transitory duration, allowing viewers to watch the entire recorded program.

[B] The Reproduction Right and the Digital Challenge: The RAM Copy Doctrine

Even the most ordinary access to information by a computer, such as reading, viewing, or hearing a work involves the making of copies of a work. When a computer user opens an image or word processing file, it places the contents of the file in temporary storage — in its Random-Access Memory ("RAM") — so that it may be viewed on the computer screen. Such RAM storage is temporary for two reasons. First, it is often quickly replaced with new material. Second, it is "volatile" because material stored in RAM generally disappears when one turns off the computer.[54] How should the law treat these "copies stored" temporarily in RAM?

Some courts have held that the temporary storage of a copyrighted work in RAM reproduces — fixes — the work under the law of copyright. The leading case for this proposition is *MAI Systems Corp. v. Peak Computer Inc.*[55] In *MAI*, the court held that the loading of the plaintiff's copyrighted software into RAM constitutes a fixation and qualifies as a copy under the Copyright Act. Permanence and stability requirements were met even though the text will vanish forever when the computer is turned off at the end of the work session unless, of course, it is first stored in some other way — for example, on a disk. The *MAI* case involved a service firm, Peak, that maintained and repaired its clients' computers, including those manufactured by MAI. To correct problems in the MAI computers, Peak's technicians frequently made use of the diagnostic software built into the machines, which automatically loaded into the computer's RAM every time the computer was turned on. The court accepted MAI's argument that it licensed the software only to the purchasers of the machines and that the service firm's copying of the software into the machine's RAM constituted infringement.

Whether loading a work in RAM memory constitutes fixation has generated spirited controversy. Critics of the *MAI* decision maintain that it is inconsistent with both the prior case law[56] and the intent of Congress.[57] In fact, the House Report, in discussing the definition of fixation in § 101, states, "the definition of 'fixation' would exclude from the concept purely evanescent or transient reproductions such as those projected briefly on a screen, shown electronically on

---

[54] For a description of the process, see NAT'L RESEARCH COUNCIL COMM. ON INTELLECTUAL PROPERTY RIGHTS AND THE EMERGING INFORMATION STRUCTURE, THE DIGITAL DILEMMA: INTELLECTUAL PROPERTY IN THE INFORMATION AGE 28–31 (2000).

[55] 991 F.2d 511 (9th Cir. 1993). *See also Stenograph L.L.C. v. Bossard Assocs. Inc.*, 144 F.3d 96, 101–102 (D.C. Cir. 1998); *Triad Sys. Corp. v. Se. Express Sys.*, 64 F.3d 1330 (9th Cir. 1995); *Sony Computer Entm't, Inc. v. Connectix Corp.*, 203 F.3d 596 (9th Cir. 2000). Other courts have implicitly rejected the proposition that temporary storage in RAM constitutes a reproduction. *See, e.g.*, *Hogan Sys. Inc. v. Cybersource Int'l*, 158 F.3d 319 (5th Cir. 1998).

[56] *See Apple Computer v. Formula Int'l*, 594 F. Supp. 617, 621–22 (C.D. Cal. 1984) (indicating that copies stored in RAM, unlike those loaded in ROM, were only temporary).

[57] *See* H.R. REP. NO. 94-1476, at 5253 (1976).

a television or other cathode ray tube, or captured momentarily in the 'memory' of a computer." Most commentators have found fault with the decision. Some would argue that loading software (much less email or chat room messages) into RAM is no more a fixation than skywriting, or a poem written on sand or on the frost of a windowpane.[58] Others base their disapprobation less on doctrinal concerns than on their fear that *MAI*'s interpretation of the fixation requirement will ultimately suppress freedom in browsing the Internet.[59]

In 1998, Congress addressed the issue that arose in the *MAI* case in the Digital Millennium Copyright Act. The DMCA amended § 117 of the Copyright Act by creating a defense to services that temporarily reproduce computer programs in the course of maintaining and repairing computer systems. If the owner of the hardware authorizes the repair or maintenance and the copy is made "solely by virtue of the activation of the machine that lawfully contains an authorized copy of the computer program,"[60] no infringement will occur despite lack of authorization from the owner of copyright in the software. Although Congress intended to abrogate the *MAI* case, the legislation is narrowly drafted to specifically cover computer repair services.

Thus, the RAM controversy will continue outside the realm of computer repair services unless the courts take the cue from the new legislation and generalize its application beyond the terms of the amended § 117 of the Copyright Act. The United States might take as its model the European Union, which has directed its member states to exempt from the copyright owner's exclusive reproduction right "certain acts of temporary reproduction, which are transient and incidental reproductions, forming an integral and essential part of a technological process and carried out for the sole purpose of enabling . . . a lawful use of a work" and which "have no separate economic value on their own."[61]

---

[58] For an elaboration of these and other issues concerning RAM fixation, see R. Anthony Reese, *The Public Display Right, The Copyrights Acts' Neglected Solution to the Controversy Over Ram "Copies,"* 2001 U. Ill. L. Rev. 83; Ira L. Brandiss, *Writing in Frost on a Window Pane: E-Mail and Chatting on RAM and Copyright Fixation*, 43 J. Copyright Soc. U.S.A. 237 (1996); Niva Elkin Koren, *Copyright Law and Social Dialogue on the Information Superhighway: The Case Against Copyright Liability of Internet Providers*, 13 Cardozo Arts & Ent.L.J. 345, 381–82 (1995); Mark A. Lemley, *Intellectual Licenses and Shrinkwrap Licenses*, 68 S. Cal. L. Rev. 1239, 1280 (1995).

[59] This idea is developed in Jessica Litman, *The Exclusive Right to Read*, 13 Cardozo Arts & Ent. L.J. 29 (1994) (arguing that Congress never intended the Copyright Act to control such activity). Despite such criticism, past administrations have enthusiastically endorsed *MAI*. *See* Information Infrastructure Task Force, Intellectual Property and the National Information Infrastructure: The Report of the Working Group on Intellectual Property Rights(1995).

[60] *See* § 117(c) as amended by the DMCA, Pub. L. 105–298, 112 Stat. 2860 (1998).

[61] Directive 2001/29/EC of the European Parliament and of the Council of 22 May 2001 (harmonizing of certain aspects of copyright and related rights in the information society).

[C] The Reproduction Right in Relation to the Other Exclusive Rights

It takes little to infringe the reproduction right. One unauthorized fixation can infringe the reproduction right even though the copy made is not sold or otherwise distributed to others.[62] As with all the other exclusive rights, it is possible to infringe the reproduction right without infringing any other exclusive rights. Typically, however, the distribution right is infringed along with the reproduction right. This occurs because reproducing the work without distributing it (usually by sale) rarely is of interest from a financial standpoint. The distribution of the copy is what constitutes the out-of-pocket loss to the copyright owner. Nonetheless, the reproduction right stands on its own and protects even against private, nondistributed reproductions of copyrighted works.[63]

One should distinguish reproduction from the broader concept of copying. Reproduction takes place when a work is copied in a material object, as when an artist puts paint on a canvas or a singer records a work on a phonorecord. Copying, a broader concept, can take place without a fixation, such as by a performance or a display.

§ 8.05 THE RIGHT TO PREPARE DERIVATIVE WORKS[64]

[A] The Adaptation Right: Generally

In its earlier form, protection under copyright law was limited to reproducing the work in the same medium. With time, copyright law has increasingly expanded its protection to cover a wide range of derivative media. Today, the adaptation right is infringed when a third party makes an unauthorized derivative work[65] in which a preexisting copyrighted work is recast, reformed, or adapted. Thus, if a third party makes a translation, abridgement, musical arrangement, motion picture version, or dramatization without the consent of the copyright owner, the exclusive right to make derivative works is infringed.[66] The exclusive right to prepare derivative works enables the copyright owner to exploit markets other than the one

---

62 17 U.S.C. § 101.

63 *See Sega Enters., Ltd. v. Accolade, Inc.*, 977 F.2d 1510 (9th Cir. 1993) (copying for the purposes of reverse engineering plaintiff's software violates the reproduction right unless privileged by the fair use doctrine); *Walker v. Univ. Books*, 602 F.2d 859, 864 (9th Cir. 1979) ("[T]he fact that an allegedly infringing copy of a protected work may itself be only an inchoate representation of some final product to be marketed commercially does not in itself negate the possibility of infringement."); *Walt Disney Prods. v. Filmation Assocs.*, 628 F. Supp. 871 (C.D. Cal. 1986) (finding that defendant's reproduction of copyrighted works in the course of producing a finished film infringed the reproduction right, even though the works copied were never distributed to the public).

64 *See* 17 U.S.C. § 106(2).

65 For a discussion of derivative works, see *supra* §§ 2.08–2.12.

66 For an argument that current copyright protection under the derivative works right is too broad and for proposed limitations to it, see Christina Bohannan, *Taming the Derivative Works Right: A Modest Proposal for Reducing Overbreadth and Vagueness in Copyright*, 12 Vand. J. Ent. & Tech. L. 669 (2010).

in which the work was first published. These derivative markets can often be more valuable than the market of first publication. Frequently, motion picture rights to a successful novel or merchandising rights for characters in that motion picture can earn far greater returns than the novel on which they are based. The justification for providing the copyright owner exclusive rights to prepare derivative works is twofold: (1) but for the underlying work, more lucrative derivative works based on that work would have never been possible, and (2) it is unfair to affect the sanctity of an author's original work with a substantially similar derivative work that does not qualify as fair use, without first obtaining the author's/copyright owner's consent.[67] Through the adaptation right, American law has expanded the concept of "copying" to cover much broader ground than suggested by the ordinary meaning of that word. In one sense, to recast or transform — to adapt the work — is to "copy" it. A derivative work author, however, often does much more than mere copying. By transforming another's work, the derivative work author may add his own substantial authorship to the underlying work. As a result, some derivative works greatly outstrip the value of the underlying work, but without recognition of the adaptation right, the copyright owner would have recourse only against verbatim forms of copying in the same medium.

[B] The Adaptation Right and Cross Media Infringement

The issue of infringement of § 106(2), the derivative work right, often arises in instances where a work is adapted to different media. Derivative right cases can run the gamut from those in which the infringing work completely incorporates the underlying work to those in which the underlying work is imperceptible, the question being always whether the second work is based upon the first. At one end of the spectrum, the underlying work is easily recognized, as in a translation or an abridgment of a novel or where a three-dimensional sculptural work is incorporated in a two-dimensional graphic work or in a photograph.

How far the concept of cross-media infringement can be pushed raises interesting conceptual problems regarding the scope of the derivative right.[68] In the middle are more difficult cases involving, for example, the stage dramatization of a novel.[69] In another case, still photographs were found to infringe the copyright on the choreography for a ballet.[70] Finally, at the other end of the spectrum, the underlying work may not appear at all in the derivative work. For example, in one case, infringement was found in the publication of a manual providing answers to

---

[67] For an excellent overview of the subject, see Paul Goldstein, *Derivative Rights and Derivative Works in Copyright*, 30 J. Copyright Soc'y 209 (1983). *See also* Michael Abramowicz, *A Theory of Copyright's Derivative Right and Related Doctrines*, 90 Minn. L. Rev. (2005) (pointing out that the derivative right may enhance social welfare, even placing aside the potentially destructiveness of copyright races); David Bambauer, *Faulty Math: The Economics of Legalizing the Grey Album*, 59 Ala. L. Rev. 345 (2008) (arguing that from an economic perspective, a separate derivative is unjustified).

[68] *See, e.g., Grove Press, Inc. v. Greenleaf Publ'g Co.*, 247 F. Supp. 518 (E.D.N.Y. 1965) (translation).

[69] *See, e.g., Metro-Goldwyn-Mayer, Inc. v. Showcase Atlanta Coop. Prods., Inc.*, 479 F. Supp. 351 (N.D. Ga. 1979).

[70] *See Horgan v. Macmillan, Inc.*, 789 F.2d 157 (2d Cir. 1986).

questions presented in a well-known physics book.[71] Of course, the critical question is the point along this continuum at which courts should draw the line in protecting the work under § 106(2). But cases like the above seem to stretch the derivative work concept too far, transforming copyright law into a general law of misappropriation. Even though one might agree that infringement extends beyond verbatim copying, there are limits. To violate the adaptation right, the infringing work must at least transform, recast, or adapt a portion of the copyrighted work in some form.

[C] Infringement of the Adaptation Right: Fixation and Computer Enhancements

The derivative right is broader than the reproduction right in that reproduction requires fixation in copies or phonorecords, whereas defendant's derivative work need not be fixed for purposes of infringement.[72] Thus, a performance, such as a ballet, pantomime, or some other improvised performance, could violate the adaptation right even though the infringing acts were not embodied in some stable medium.[73]

Cases involving computer enhancements have presented difficult issues in resolving the right to make derivative works and the use of computer programs that "interoperate" with, and thus enhance, existing software and hardware systems. Although they may not reproduce the codes of those systems, these new programs necessarily refer to the existing works and depend on them for the "interoperative" work's own functionality. For example, in *Lewis Galoob Toys, Inc. v. Nintendo of America, Inc.*,[74] defendant Galoob manufactured a device called "Game Genie," which altered the performance characteristics of Nintendo's copyrighted videogame. Game Genie could increase the number of lives of the player's character, increase the speed of the character's moves, and allow the character to float over obstacles. These alterations, occurring in the computer's processor, remained unfixed, did not modify the data in the game cartridge, and produced effects that were only temporary. The court found no violation of § 106(2) because the game itself was not recast, transformed, or adapted, and the Game Genie did not incorporate a portion of the copyrighted work in any form.

Cases like *Galoob* are troublesome from both a doctrinal and policy standpoint. The works that alter the original do not fall under the traditional definition of derivative works in the Act. Moreover, these enhancing works do not replace the need for the original, unlike the examples of derivative works listed in the statute

---

[71] *See, e.g., Addison-Wesley Publ'g Co. v. Brown*, 223 F. Supp. 219 (E.D.N.Y. 1963).

[72] *See* H.R. REP. NO. 94-1476, at 62 (1976).

[73] *See Lewis Galoob Toys, Inc. v. Nintendo of Am. Inc.*, 964 F.2d 965, 967 (9th Cir. 1992). The court noted that "[a] derivative work must be fixed to be protected under the Act . . . but not to infringe" but left some ambiguity on the matter by stating that an infringing "derivative work must incorporate a protected work in some concrete or permanent 'form.'" The requirement for permanence and concreteness as suggested in *Galoob* was reconfirmed in *Micro Star v. Formgen, Inc.*, 154 F.3d 1107, 1111 (9th Cir. 1998).

[74] 964 F.2d 965 (9th Cir. 1992).

(*e.g.*, a translation or art reproduction).[75] Because they cannot stand on their own, some might argue that they do not harm the original author.

Despite these arguments, some courts have found enhancing, nonreplacing works to be infringing derivative works. In *Micro Star v. Formgen, Inc.*,[76] the Court of Appeals for the Ninth Circuit found that a computer enhancement constituted an infringing derivative work. In *Formgen*, the defendant published a CD-ROM containing a number of user-created "game levels" for the popular "Duke Nukem 3D" computer game. The copyrighted game software consisted of a game engine, a source art library, and "MAP" files of instructions that told the game engine what images to take from the source library and how to organize them to make the screen display for a particular level of play. The MAP files themselves contained none of the copyrighted art images. Instead, they consisted of a series of instructions indicating where the art images were to be placed, much like a "paint by numbers" system. The defendant published user-created game levels consisting of MAP files that created new levels of play.

The issue in *Micro Star* was whether the audiovisual displays generated when the copyrighted game was run with the defendant's MAP files constituted infringing derivative works. In finding for the plaintiff, the court noted that, unlike *Galoob*, the defendant's MAP files were much more than an advanced version of the copyrighted game because they described in exact detail the audiovisual display, much like sheet music describes the way a copyrighted melody sounds. The court also rejected defendant's argument that the MAP files did not incorporate any of Duke Nukem's protected expression, noting that "the copyright owner holds the right to create sequels"[77] and the stories contained in the MAP files constituted telling of new tales involving Duke Nukem.[78]

[D] The Adaptation Right and Authorial Control

Concern for authorial control and reputation has led some courts to extend unduly the statutory definition of the derivative right. For example, in *Mirage Editions, Inc. v. Albuquerque A.R.T. Co.*,[79] the defendant cut out photographs of works of art from a commemorative book and transferred them to individual ceramic tiles. The court found this to be an infringement of the derivative right,

---

[75] This argument is nicely elaborated in Christian H. Nadan, *A Proposal to Recognize Component Works: How a Teddy Bears on the Competing Ends of Copyright Law*, 78 CAL. L. REV. 1633 (1990).

[76] 154 F.3d 1107 (9th Cir. 1988).

[77] *Id.* at 1112.

[78] For another "enhancement" case finding infringement, see *Worlds of Wonder v. Vector Intercontinental, Inc.*, 653 F. Supp. 135 (N.D. Ohio 1986); *Worlds of Wonder v. Vertel Learning Sys.*, 658 F. Supp. 351 (N.D. Tex. 1986) (finding that defendant manufacturer's cassette inserted into a toy bear created an audiovisual work that was substantially similar to plaintiff's work, and modification of the toy in this manner created a derivative work). The videogame cases have also found infringement of the derivative work right when computer chips have been used to alter an audiovisual display. *See, e.g.*, *Midway Mfg. Co. v. Artic Int'l, Inc.*, 547 F. Supp. 999 (N.D. Ill. 1982), *aff'd*, 704 F.2d 1009 (7th Cir. 1983) (holding that a "speed-up kit" in modifying plaintiff's audiovisual display created an illegal derivative work). The videogame cases are discussed at *supra* § 2.03[C].

[79] 856 F.2d 1341 (9th Cir. 1988).

chiefly because the defendant's work supplanted the demand for the underlying work. From these facts, it is difficult to understand how the derivative right was infringed for two reasons. First, § 106(2) of the Copyright Act provides that a work subject to the derivative right "be recast, transformed, or adapted." Here, the defendant merely took copies that he lawfully owned and remounted them. He did so without recasting, transforming, or adapting the copyrighted work in any significant way.[80] Second, for the derivative right to be infringed, the defendant must have created a derivative work, but to create a derivative work, the defendant must have added copyrightable expression to the underlying work. The defendant's contribution, gluing prints onto backing and then a tile, should no more constitute copyrightable authorship than reframing a drawing or covering it with transparent plexiglass. Thus, *Mirage* establishes a dual standard for the protection of derivative works. Under this formulation, a derivative work is copyrightable only if it manifests original authorship, but even an unoriginal derivative work may constitute infringement.

Other courts have rejected the *Mirage* "double standard." In *Lee v. A.R.T. Co.*,[81] defendant bought postcards containing original art and sent them to the mounting service used in *Mirage*, which trimmed the cards and glued them onto ceramic tiles. The court held that the defendant did not recast, adapt or transform the work under the statutory definition of the derivative work because no intellectual effort or creativity was necessary to transfer the notecard to the tile. The court noted that if "[plaintiff was] right about what counts as a derivative work, then the United States had established through the backdoor an extraordinarily broad version of author's moral rights under which artists may block any modification of their works of which they disapprove."[82] Moreover, the court pointed out that "no European version of *droit moral* goes so far."[83]

The adaptation right overlaps the reproduction and performance rights, and, with few exceptions, infringement of the adaptation right infringes the reproduction right, performance right, or both. Thus, if a person writes a play based on a novel without permission from the copyright owner, and if the play substantially embodies the copyrighted work, the copyright owner could bring an action for infringement of both the adaptation and reproduction rights. If the play were then performed, the performance right in the novel would also be infringed.

Although the adaptation right overlaps the reproduction right, it is not merely superfluous, but can constitute a valuable and separate exclusive right for the copyright owner. In one significant instance, it is possible to infringe the adaptation right without infringing simultaneously the reproduction or performance rights.[84]

---

80 *Mirage* was affirmed in *Munoz v. Albuquerque A.R.T. Co.*, 38 F.3d 1218 (9th Cir. 1994).

81 125 F.3d 580 (7th Cir. 1997).

82 *Id.* at 582.

83 *Id. See also Precious Moments, Inc. v. La Infantil, Inc.*, 971 F. Supp. 66 (1997) (reading the originality requirement out of the definition of "derivative work" to infer that *Mirage* opens the door for the most trivial of modifications to generate an infringing work.) *See* Laura Heymann, *The Trademark/Copyright Divide*, 60 SMU L. Rev. 55 (2007) (pointing out that objections to derivative uses are efforts to prevent undesirable associations with the copyrighted work).

84 *See generally* Nimmer on Copyright § 8.09[A] (2014).

This could occur when the copyright owner has licensed another to reproduce or perform the work but has not specifically licensed the right to make a derivative work. For example, suppose A has licensed B to reproduce (make copies of) and perform his copyrighted play, and B, as a matter of convenience, abridges the play (sells copies of it in the abridged form) and performs it in its new version. If the contract were silent on the right to abridge (*i.e.*, adapt), a court might find an infringement of the adaptation right even though the licensee has infringed neither the performance nor the reproduction rights.[85] Thus, a prospective user of a copyrighted work should negotiate, in the appropriate situation, a license to adapt, as well as the rights to reproduce and perform, the work.[86]

§ 8.06 LIBRARY PHOTOCOPYING UNDER § 108[87]

Section 108 details the circumstances in which libraries and archives may reproduce and distribute copies of works without infringing copyright. In general, § 108 allows library photocopying for scholarly purposes, unless it is systematic and is a substitute for purchase or subscription. Section 108 sets forth the requirements for exemption, but § 107 fair use is still available for those acts exceeding the exemption. To avoid the uncertainties of general fair use doctrine and be mindful of the result in *Williams & Wilkins*, Congress has singled out library photocopying for separate treatment under § 108 of the 1976 Act.[88]

To qualify for the exemption, the library collection must be open to the public or to researchers in a specialized field in addition to researchers affiliated with the library. Two other initial criteria must be met to qualify for the § 108 exception.[89] First, the copy reproduced must be a single copy. Second, it must be made without any purpose of direct or indirect commercial advantage. Before passage of the Berne Convention Implementation Act of 1988, libraries were also required to include a notice of copyright on behalf of the copyright owner. After March 1, 1989, it is no longer an infringement of copyright for a library to distribute a reproduction of a work not containing a notice of copyright.[90]

---

[85] The leading case is *Gilliam v. Am. Broad. Co., Inc.*, 538 F.2d 14 (2d Cir. 1976), where ABC obtained a license to broadcast *Monty Python* programs in their entirety except for minor editing to insert commercials. ABC substantially abridged the programs, cutting twenty-four of ninety minutes from them. The court held that the unauthorized editing of the underlying work constituted an infringement of the copyright.

[86] There are common sense limits, and courts have recognized that licenses are entitled to some degree of latitude in arranging the licensed work for presentation to the public consistent with the licensee's style or standards. *See Stratchborneo v. Arc Music Corp.*, 357 F. Supp. 1393 (S.D.N.Y. 1973); *Gilliam v. Am. Broad. Co., Inc.*, 538 F.2d 14 (2d Cir. 1976).

[87] *See* James M. Treece, *Library Photocopying*, 24 UCLA L. Rev. 1025 (1977); 17 U.S.C. § 108.

[88] *But see* U.S. Copyright Office, Report of the Register of Copyrights: Library Reproduction of Copyrighted Works (17 U.S.C. § 108) 93–104 (1983) (maintaining that copying beyond the § 108 exemption cannot be defended on general fair use grounds of § 107).

[89] 17 U.S.C. § 108(a).

[90] *See* 17 U.S.C. § 108(a). Repeal of the notice provision does not condone removal or obliteration of notice from a copy of a work before it is reproduced by a library. *See* S. Rep. No. 100–352, 100th Cong., 2d Sess. (1988).

In addition to the right to distribute photocopies to scholars, qualifying libraries can make three copies or phonorecords of a work for preservation or security if "(1) the copy or phonorecord reproduced is currently in the library collection and (2) such copy or phonorecord reproduced in digital format is not made available to the public in that format outside the premises of the library or archives."[91]

Section 108 takes into account the controversial issue posed by *Williams & Wilkins*,[92] that of reproducing single copies for distribution to users. Under this section, a library can distribute both small amounts of a work and copies of the entire work if certain conditions are met. For small amounts of a work or an article in a periodical, the copy can be made in response to user request if the copy becomes the property of the user and the library has no reason to believe that the copy will be used for anything other than private scholarship.[93] In addition, the library must prominently display at its copy order desk and in its order form a warning of copyright.[94] The above provisions apply to user copies of an entire work if the library first determines after reasonable investigation that the work cannot be obtained at a fair price.

Sections 108(g) and (h) impose limitations on copying. Section 108(g) permits the library to distribute isolated, unrelated single copies to users on separate occasions, but prohibits a library from distributing related or concerted reproductions of multiple copies of the same materials. Section 108(g)(2) further prohibits a library from engaging "in the systematic reproduction or distribution of single or multiple copies . . . of" copyrighted works. This subsection allows interlibrary arrangements as well, except when these arrangements involve a distribution "in such aggregate quantities as to substitute for a subscription to or purchase of such work."[95] Finally, § 108(h)[96] limits reproduction and distribution under all of § 108 to books and periodicals, not to musical, pictorial, graphic, or sculptural works, or to motion pictures or other audiovisual works other than those dealing with news.[97] Since § 108 became part of the Copyright Act, technological trends in the digital environment have permanently changed the role and functioning of libraries. Libraries now acquire access to works in digital form and in multiple formats. Reproduction of copyrighted works in the library setting transcends the photocopy machine, the central focus of the current § 108. In addition to their reproduction of works, the role of libraries in the preservation of works is also challenged in the digital setting. For example, should libraries be able to preserve copyrighted works

---

[91] *See* 17 U.S.C. § 108(b)(1), (2). These provisions, regarding digital formats, increase the number of copies that can be made from one to three, and were added by the Digital Millennium Copyright Act, Pub. L. 105–304, 112 Stat. 2860 § 404 (1998).

[92] *Williams & Wilkins Co. v. United States*, 487 F.2d 1345 (1973), *aff'd by an equally divided court*, 420 U.S. 376 (1975).

[93] *See* 17 U.S.C. § 108(d).

[94] *See id.*

[95] 17 U.S.C. § 108(g).

[96] 17 U.S.C. § 108(h).

[97] 17 U.S.C. § 108(i) requires the Register of Copyrights to issue a report every five years on library photocopying. The first report was issued in 1983, offering various statutory and nonstatutory recommendations. *See* U.S. Copyright Office, Report of the Register of Copyrights: Library Reproduction of Copyrighted Works (17 U.S.C. § 108) (1983).

by digital means and then allow access to these works by users and other libraries? These are only a few of the questions facing libraries on a daily basis. Unfortunately, nothing in the current § 108 takes such uses into account. These issues are governed by various licensing agreements that libraries negotiate with a multiplicity of parties. Currently, typical licensing agreements concerning digital content are perceived as curtailing the library's role in the preservation and distribution of copyrighted works. Because of the complex issues involved, Congress may have to amend § 108 to facilitate the needs of copyright owners and the public so that libraries may preserve and distribute digital content.[98]

§ 8.07 LIMITATIONS TO THE REPRODUCTION AND ADAPTATION RIGHTS: EPHEMERAL RECORDINGS, § 112[99]

Ephemeral recordings are copies or phonorecords of a work made for transmission[100] by a broadcasting organization legally entitled to transmit the work. The right to make ephemeral recordings is a narrow limitation on the exclusive reproduction right created to accommodate the needs of the broadcasting industry. A broadcaster may have a right to perform or display a work but may not have the right to make copies of it. Under this section, a broadcaster who has obtained a license to perform the work (or fits under an exception to do so) may make an ephemeral recording of the work.[101]

---

[98] In 2004, the Copyright Office and the Office of Strategic Planning Initiatives assembled a group of experts to study the possible revision of § 108. Its report was issued in 2007. The Section 108 Study Group Report is available at http://www.section108.gov. The report recommends that § 108 be extended to cover certain museums and that the rules governing interlibrary loans be restructured to meet the needs of the digital age. The Study Group's recommendations are examined by one of its key members. *See* Laura N. Gasaway, *Amending the Copyright Act for Libraries and Society: The Section 108 Study Group*, 70 Alb. L. Rev. 1331 (2007). For a discussion about whether libraries can (and, if not, should be able to) lend e-books to their customers without violating the exclusive right of distribution of the copyright owners, see Gregory K. Laughlin, *Digitization and Democracy: The Conflict Between the Amazon Kindle Licensing Agreement and the Role of Libraries in a Free Society*, 40 U. Balt. L. Rev. 3 (2010). For other commentary exploring challenges for libraries in the digital age, see Rebecca Tushnet, *My Library: Copyright and the Role of Institutions in a Peer-to-Peer World*, 53 UCLA L. Rev. 977 (2006); and Roberta Kwall, *Library Reproduction Rights for Preservation and Replacement in the Digital Era: An Author's Perspective on § 108*, Colum. J.L. & Arts 343 (2006).

[99] 17 U.S.C. § 112.

[100] Section 101 defines "transmit" as follows: "To 'transmit' a performance or display is to communicate it by any device or process whereby images or sounds are received beyond the place from which they are sent as in a television, radio, or cable transmission."

[101] With the Digital Millennium Copyright Act ("DMCA"), Pub. L. No. 105-304, 112 Stat. 2860 (1998), codified at 17 U.S.C. § 112(A)(1) the ephemeral recording exemption extends explicitly to broadcasters the same privilege for digital broadcasts (*see* 17 U.S.C. § 114(f)) that they already enjoy for analog broadcasts. The Act clarifies the relationship between the ephemeral recording exemption in the Digital Performance Right in Sound Recordings Act of 1995 ("DPRSRA"), Pub. L. No. 104-39, 109 Stat. 336 (1995). For a discussion of DPRSRA, see *infra* § 8.26. The DMCA also addressed the relationship between the ephemeral recording exemption and the anticircumvention provisions of 17 U.S.C. § 1201. Section 112(a)(2) addresses the concerns that if use of copy protection technologies becomes widespread, a transmitting organization might be prevented from engaging in its traditional activities of assembling transmission programs and making ephemeral recordings allowed by § 112. Under § 112(b)(1), trans-

Section 112 may be briefly summarized as follows:

1) *Licensed Broadcasters*: Under § 112(a),[102] a licensed broadcaster may make one copy of a work, provided that the copy is retained and used solely by the organization that made it and is used for the organization's own transmissions within its local service area. No further copies or phonorecords can be made of it. In addition, unless the copy is preserved exclusively for archival purposes, it must be destroyed within six months.

(2) *Government and Nonprofit*: § 112(b)[103] provides a wider privilege for governmental bodies and nonprofit organizations entitled to transmit a performance or display of a work under § 110(2),[104] or to make sound recordings under § 114(a).[105] These entities may make up to thirty copies or phonorecords of the transmission embodying the performance or display, provided that no further copies are made. All copies must be destroyed within seven years of the first transmission. However, one copy may be kept for archival purposes.

(3) *Governmental and Nonprofit Religious Broadcasts*: § 112(c)[106] covers religious broadcasts. It allows a governmental or nonprofit organization to make one copy of a transmitted nondramatic musical religious work if there is no charge for the copy and the broadcaster is under a license or transfer of the copyright. All copies, except one for archival purposes, must be destroyed within one year of the first transmission.

(4) *Handicapped Audiences*: § 112(d)[107] grants the right to governmental or nonprofit organizations to make ephemeral recordings for transmissions to handicapped audiences as authorized under § 110(8).[108]

(5) *Statutory License for Sound Recordings*: § 112(e), added by the Digital Millennium Copyright Act of 1998, creates a statutory license for the making of an ephemeral recording of a sound recording by certain transmitting organizations. This statutory license is intended primarily to benefit entities that transmit performances of sound recordings to business establishments pursuant to the limitation on exclusive rights set forth in § 114.[109] The § 112(e) statutory license is also available to a transmitting entity with a statutory license under § 114(f). This enables the transmitter to make more than the one phonorecord it is entitled to make under § 112(a). For example, a webcaster might make several copies of a

mitting organizations are permitted to engage in activities that otherwise would violate 17 U.S.C. § 1201(a)(1) in certain limited circumstances if necessary to exercise the privilege to make ephemeral recordings.

[102] 17 U.S.C. § 112(a).

[103] 17 U.S.C. § 112(b).

[104] *See* 17 U.S.C. § 110(2) (exempting transmitted performances and displays in certain instructional settings). *See infra* § 8.18[B].

[105] 17 U.S.C. § 114(a).

[106] 17 U.S.C. § 112(c).

[107] 17 U.S.C. § 112(d).

[108] 17 U.S.C. § 110(8).

[109] 17 U.S.C. § 114(d)(1)(C)(iv). For a discussion of the compulsory license for digital audio transmission of sound recordings, see *infra* § 8.26.

sound recording to use on various servers. In addition, ephemeral recordings of sound recordings made by certain transmitters may embody copyrighted musical compositions, so long as the conditions set forth in § 112(a) are met.

Section 112(e) also establishes the procedures for determining rates and terms of the statutory license.[110] If interested parties do not arrive at negotiated rates and terms during the voluntary negotiation proceedings, the Copyright Royalty Judges shall determine reasonable rates and the terms of the license.[111]

(6) *Ephemeral Recordings as Derivative Works*: § 112(f)[112] states that ephemeral recordings are not copyrightable as derivative works unless the copyright owner gives consent.

§ 8.08 LIMITATIONS TO THE REPRODUCTION AND ADAPTATION RIGHTS: REPRODUCTION OF PICTORIAL, GRAPHIC, AND SCULPTURAL WORKS IN USEFUL ARTICLES, § 113

Section 113(a)[113] reconfirms the general rule under 1909 Act case law[114] that copyright in a pictorial, graphic, or sculptural work is not affected when the work is used as the design for a useful object. In other words, a work may be protected under copyright law regardless of whether it is embodied in a useful or purely aesthetic object. Thus, a statuette on the hood of a car, a gargoyle on a building, and a lamp base resembling a Balinese dancer are all copyrightable works of art. That they are embodied in a useful object — car, building, or lamp — has no bearing on their copyrightability.

Section 113(b),[115] however, limits the reproduction right of useful objects. It provides that "the owner of copyright in a work that portrays a useful article as such, [is not afforded] any greater or lesser rights with respect to the making, distribution, or display of the useful article so portrayed" than under the law as it developed under the 1909 Act. This codifies and reconfirms the basic rule that a drawing or model of a lighting fixture, a building, or an automobile is copyrightable as such, but the copyright does not give the artist the exclusive right to make the lighting fixture, building, or automobile. In sum, a copyright in a pictorial, graphic, or sculptural work portraying a useful object does not extend to the manufacture of the useful object.[116]

---

[110] 17 U.S.C. § 112(e)(4), (5).

[111] 17 U.S.C. § 112(e)(4).

[112] 17 U.S.C. § 112(f).

[113] 17 U.S.C. § 113(a).

[114] *Mazer v. Stein*, 347 U.S. 201 (1954). For a discussion of the copyrightability of the design of useful objects, see *supra* §§ 3.10–3.14.

[115] 17 U.S.C. § 113(b).

[116] *See* H.R. Rep. No. 94-1476, at 105 (1976).

Section 113(c)[117] further limits the reproduction right of a work embodied in a useful object. Under this subsection, the copyright owner cannot prevent the making, distribution, or display of pictures or photographs of such articles in connection with advertisements, commentaries, or news reports relating to the useful object.

§ 8.09 LIMITATIONS TO THE REPRODUCTION AND ADAPTATION RIGHTS: SOUND RECORDINGS, § 114[118]

[A] The Independent Fixation Limitation

Section 114 limits the exclusive rights of reproduction, adaptation, and performance in sound recordings, illustrating that sound recordings receive much less protection under copyright as compared with other copyrightable subject matter, in particular musical works.[119] Under § 114(b),[120] infringement of copyright in a sound recording occurs by either (1) reproducing it by mechanical means or (2) rearranging, remixing, or altering it in some way by mechanical means.[121] Alternatively, one does not infringe the copyright in a sound recording by making an independent fixation, despite the extent to which the new recording imitates the preexisting sound recording. To illustrate, suppose a sound recording were made of the New York Philharmonic's rendition of Beethoven's *Fifth Symphony*. Under the limitation set forth in § 114(b), another orchestra could legally imitate the New York Philharmonic's performance down to the last detail so long as the orchestra hired its own musicians and made an independent recording of the subsequent live performance.

The limitation of § 114(b) relates to the copyright in the sound recording. One should not confuse the rights in a sound recording with the rights in the musical work embodied on the same phonorecord.[122] This confusion arises from a failure to distinguish two forms of copyrightable subject matter, the musical work and the sound recording, both of which are embodied on the same material object, the phonorecord. For example, suppose record company A is the owner of the copyright of a sound recording of Irving Berlin's *White Christmas*. Under § 114(b),

---

[117] 17 U.S.C. § 113(c).

[118] "Sound recordings" are works that result from the fixation of a series of musical, spoken, or other sounds, but not including the sounds accompanying a motion picture or other audiovisual work, regardless of the nature of the material objects, such as disks, tapes, or other phonorecords, in which they are embodied. 17 U.S.C. § 101.

[119] Sound recordings enjoy a much more limited scope of protection than, for example, musical works. A sound recording does not enjoy a performance right as does a musical work. *See* 17 U.S.C. §§ 106(4), 114(a). For a discussion of the lack of protection given to performance rights in sound recordings, see *infra* § 8.25.

[120] 17 U.S.C. § 114(b).

[121] Infringement by "mechanical means" takes place where the actual sounds in a sound recording are reproduced by repressing, transcribing, recapturing off the air, or reproducing them by other technology. *See* H.R. Rep. No . 94-1476, at 106 (1976).

[122] *See* 17 U.S.C. § 114(c).

record company B can imitate, without permission, the style and sound of A's recording down to its smallest detail without infringing A's reproduction right or adaptation right in the sound recording. Even though the copyright in the *sound recording* cannot be infringed in this manner, B could still infringe the copyright, specifically the reproduction and adaptation rights, in the musical composition *White Christmas* by making the unauthorized recording.[123] The point is that one should always distinguish between the copyright in the sound recording and that in the musical work.

[B] Sampling

The adaptation right in a sound recording "is limited to the right to prepare a derivative work in which the actual sounds fixed in the sound recording are rearranged, remixed, or otherwise altered in sequence or quality." § 114(b). In limiting the adaptation right in this manner, did Congress intend that any such electronic manipulation would *automatically* infringe the copyright owner's § 106(2) exclusive right to prepare derivative works? The question arises in the context of digital "sampling."

Digital sampling is a frequently used technique in the recording industry that is particularly prevalent in rap and hip-hop music. A recording artist copies or "samples" a short segment of an existing sound recording, electronically manipulates the sample, and incorporates it into a new sound recording. Generally, record producers license the right to use samples from the owners of copyright, in particular sound recordings (as well as the musical compositions rendered in those recordings). But sometimes, for a variety of reasons, sampling occurs without authorization. Does unlicensed sampling violate the right to prepare derivative works?

While some courts have shown little sympathy for unauthorized sampling,[124] other courts have granted summary judgment for the defendant on grounds that the amount sampled was *de minimis* and the two works were not "substantially similar" as a matter of law. For example, in *Newton v. Diamond*,[125] the court ruled that use of a portion of a composition requires no license if it is so meager and fragmentary that the average audience — the ordinary observer — would not recognize the appropriation. Other courts have taken a harsh, if not a bright line prohibition against digital sampling. In *Bridgeport Music, Inc. v. Dimension Films*,[126] the court reversed a lower court decision holding which involved a sample

---

[123] The same conceptual difficulty in distinguishing between copyright in a sound recording and copyright in a musical work will arise again for performance rights, which musical works enjoy, but which sound recordings, except in limited circumstances, do not.

[124] *See, e.g., Grand Upright Music Ltd. v. Warner Bros. Records*, 780 F. Supp. 182 (S.D.N.Y. 1991) (granting motion for preliminary injunction); *Jarvis v. A&M Records*, 827 F. Supp. 282 (D.N.J. 1993) (denying defendants' motion for summary judgment in relevant part).

[125] 349 F.3d 591 (9th Cir. 2003).

[126] 410 F.3d 792 (6th Cir. 2005). For commentary on *Bridgeport* of a critical nature see, Andre Smith, *Other People's Property: Hip-Hip's Inherent Clashes with Property Laws and its Ascendance as Global Counter Culture*, 7 Va. Sports & Ent. L.J. 59 (2007); Olufunmilayo B. Arewa, *From J.C. Bach to Hip-Hop: Musical Borrowing, Copyright and Cultural Context*, 84 N.C. L. Rev. 545 (2006); Julie Cromer, *Harry*

of a recording of a three-note guitar riff from plaintiff's work that lasted two seconds. The Court of Appeals found that this was an infringement of the copyright in the sound recording even though the defendant's sampling from the sound recording was insufficiently discernable to constitute substantial similarity.

Bridgeport is a departure from sound copyright law and policy. Although the statute is silent on the issue, the *Bridgeport* court improperly departed from the basic copyright doctrine by rejecting the doctrine of substantial similarity in the sampling context. The doctrine of substantial similarity should not be given such short shrift. One function of substantial similarity is to determine whether the defendant's copying has co-opted plaintiff's market for the work. But if the works are dissimilar, no market has been supplanted by defendant's use of the work, and the sampling should not constitute an improper appropriation of the copyrighted work.

§ 8.10 LIMITATIONS TO THE REPRODUCTION AND ADAPTATION RIGHTS: THE COMPULSORY LICENSE FOR MAKING AND DISTRIBUTING PHONORECORDS (THE MECHANICAL LICENSE), § 115[127]

[A] The Traditional "Mechanical License"

[1] Generally

Section 115, known as the "mechanical license," places substantial limits on the reproduction, adaptation, and distribution rights of musical copyright owners.[128] It sets up a compulsory licensing system for the making and distribution of phonorecords of nondramatic musical works. The mechanical license, which first appeared in the 1909 Act,[129] was adopted out of a fear of monopoly control of recorded music by powerful turn-of-the-century music companies.[130] Although times have changed in the music industry, the compulsory license is still a mainstay of the 1976 Copyright Act.[131]

Potter and the Three-Second Crime: Are We Vanishing the De Minimis Defense From Copyright Law? 36 N.M. L. Rev. 261 (2006). For a defense of *Bridgeport* see Tracy L. Reilly, *Debunking the Top Three Myths Of Digital Sampling: An Endorsement of the Bridgeport Music Court's Attempt to Afford "Sound" Copyright Protection to Sound Recordings*, 31 Colum. J.L. & Arts 355 (2008).

[127] For an overview of the mechanical license, see Fredrick F. Greenman, Jr. & Alvin Deutsch, *The Copyright Royalty Tribunal and the Statutory Mechanical Royalty: History and Prospect*, 1 Cardozo Arts & Ent. L.J. 1 (1982).

[128] 17 U.S.C. § 115.

[129] 17 U.S.C. § 1(e) (1909 Act).

[130] *See* H.R. Rep. No. 2222, at 6 (1909).

[131] For an overview of the various rights and exemptions involving the reproduction and distribution of music, including the mechanical recording right, see Lydia Pallas Loren, *Untangling the Web of Musical Copyrights*, 53 Case W. Res. L. Rev. 673 (2003) (analyzing the exceedingly complex, fragmented, and "non-functional" state of musical copyright with suggestions for reform).

[2] How the Compulsory License Works

Once a phonorecord of a nondramatic musical work is distributed to the public, any other person can make a sound recording of the work for sale to the public. Section 115 gives the musical copyright owner the right to make the first distribution to the public. Thereafter, the compulsory license provisions are triggered, and the musical work is fair game for anyone else wishing to make independent recordings of the work — "covers" — to sell to the public.[132] To illustrate, suppose A composes a song and licenses B to gather musicians and singers for a recording. Once B's recording is distributed to the public in cassette or record, C can make his own recording of the song under the terms of the compulsory license. To obtain the compulsory license, C must follow the procedures set forth in the 1976 Act[133] and pay the statutory royalty to the copyright owner on each record distributed under the license. The royalty rate has been adjusted periodically, originally by the CRT. After abolition of the CRT, a different regulatory mechanism was devised using CARPs, a system that was based on voluntary negotiations between interested parties, immune from the antitrust laws. Under § 115(c) of the Act, the Librarian of Congress is directed to review the royalty rates periodically by instituting voluntary negotiations involving those affected by the compulsory license (*e.g.*, owners of nondramatic musical works). If no agreement could be reached by voluntary negotiation, the Librarian of Congress would convene a CARP to determine the statutory rate for the compulsory license. In 2004, the ad hoc CARP system was replaced by the Copyright Royalty Board, which now determines royalty rates for statutory licenses once every five years.[134]

[3] Where the Compulsory License Does Not Apply

The compulsory license applies only to nondramatic[135] musical works; it cannot be obtained for a recording of an opera, motion picture sound track, a ballet score, or a medley of tunes from a Broadway show. To use a *dramatic* musical work, one

---

[132] When a second musician makes his own recording subject to the compulsory license, the second musician is said to "cover" the song. Thus, the compulsory license provision is sometimes known as the "cover" license.

[133] 17 U.S.C. § 115(b)(1).

[134] The royalty rate started out as 2.75 cents per record or 0.5 cent per minute of playing time, whichever was greater. Since 1986, the royalty has been the larger of 5 cents or 0.95 cent per minute of playing time or fraction thereof. *See* 37 C.F.R. § 307 (1986). For every phonorecord made and distributed on or after January 1, 2006, and before January 1, 2012, the royalty rate payable for each work embodied in the phonorecord is either 9.1 cents or 1.75 cents per minute of playing time or fraction thereof, whichever is larger. For a list of the current and future rates for the mechanical license, see Copyright Office, Copyright Royalty Rates Section 115, the Mechanical License, *available at* www.copyright.gov/carp/m200a.html. Section 115(c)(3) adds to the obligation to pay royalties on records sold to the public the further requirement to pay a proportionate royalty for every rental of a record made with the authority of the copyright owner. This section was added pursuant to the Record Rental Amendment of 1984, now codified in 17 U.S.C. § 109(b). To date, there has been no activity under this provision, the record companies preferring an outright prohibition of rentals rather than obtaining royalties under the licensing system. For a discussion of the Record Rental Amendment, see *infra* § 8.15[A]. For the problems of determining Record Rental Royalties and their interplay with 17 U.S.C. § 115(c)(3), see Nimmer on Copyright § 8.04[H] (2014).

[135] For a discussion of the distinction between non-dramatic and dramatic rights, see *infra* § 8.23[C].

must first negotiate with the copyright owner. Second, a person can obtain the compulsory license only if her primary purpose is to distribute the work to the public for private use.[136] This excludes recordings intended primarily for jukeboxes and background music. Third, the compulsory license can be obtained only if the original sound recording was lawfully made; that is, a first distribution was made or authorized by the copyright owner.

The compulsory license allows a person to make his own sound recording of a musical work by assembling his own musicians for an independent recording ("cover"). This provision precludes someone from reproducing the sound recording of another and using the compulsory license as his defense.[137] When making the recording, the compulsory licensee may arrange the work to conform it to his style of performance.[138] The privilege, however, is a limited one; it does not extend to changes in the basic melody or fundamental character of the work. And if the privilege is exceeded, the licensee has infringed the copyright owner's adaptation right.[139] Thus, a substantially modified arrangement will be protected as a derivative work only with the copyright owner's consent. This narrow privilege places the licensee in a delicate position because how much change is too much remains an open question. The general rule is that the changes must be minimal, designed only to conform the musical work to the range and style of the licensee's performers.[140] In short, a licensee must be faithful to the work as presented by the copyright owner and cannot distort it in any way to enjoy the statutory privilege of a compulsory "mechanical" license.

[4] Procedures

Obtaining the compulsory license requires compliance with the procedures set forth in the statute plus the regulations promulgated by the Register of Copyrights. The process begins with a notice of intention to obtain the compulsory license.[141] The notice must be served on the copyright owner, or in the Copyright Office, if the copyright owner's address is unknown. The notice must be filed before distribution of the phonorecords or within thirty days of making the new recording. A compulsory license will not be issued if there is failure to comply with notice, and noncompliance constitutes infringement.[142]

---

136 *See* 17 U.S.C. § 115(a)(1).

137 *See id.* "A person is not entitled to a compulsory license of copyrighted musical works for the purpose of making an unauthorized duplication of a musical sound recording originally developed and produced by another." H.R. REP. NO. 94-1476, at 108 (1976) (citing *Duchess Music Corp. v. Stern*, 458 F.2d 1305 (9th Cir. 1972).

138 Even though the authorized recording contains words and music, the courts have allowed a purely instrumental work under the compulsory license. *See Edward B. Marks Music Corp. v. Foullon*, 171 F.2d 905 (2d Cir. 1949).

139 *See* 17 U.S.C. § 115(a)(2).

140 *See Stratchborneo v. Arc Music Corp.*, 357 F. Supp. 1393 (S.D.N.Y. 1973); NIMMER ON COPYRIGHT § 8.04[F] (2014).

141 *See* 17 U.S.C. § 115(b)(1).

142 *See* 17 U.S.C. § 115(b)(2).

The compulsory licensee must pay monthly statutory royalties, known in the trade as "mechanical royalties." In practice, the royalty rate works as a ceiling price for a privately negotiated agreement. The 1976 Act does not prevent the parties from negotiating the terms of the license privately. Indeed, most parties find a privately negotiated agreement more convenient, and they usually work through an agent, such as the Harry Fox Agency,[143] which specializes in licensing mechanical rights. This company, founded by a person of the same name, represents virtually every major publisher and many copyright owners in licensing mechanical reproductions of copyrighted music. For this purpose, the Agency has a form document that provides the terms of the license, including any departure from the statutory rate. The Harry Fox Agency also plays a key role in other reproductive uses of musical works that are not covered under the compulsory license in § 115. These include the right to reproduce the work in dramatic musical uses and the right to synchronize musical works with motion pictures and other audiovisual works.

[B] The Compulsory License for Digital Sound Recording Delivery

[1] Generally

Effective January 1, 1996, The Digital Performance Right in Sound Recordings Act of 1995,[144] ("DPRSRA") broadened the mechanical compulsory license to include a right to distribute recordings by digital transmission. The Act reflects the way in which digital age technology has blurred the distinction between performance and distribution. Specifically, the possibility that interactive digital audio transmission technology will be used to deliver copies of sound recordings to consumers' orders has been a growing concern of the record industry for some time. We think of the traditional "mechanical license" under § 115 as a mechanism by which record producers can secure the rights to make versions of musical compositions previously recorded under a consensual license from the copyright owner and to distribute them for private use. The DPRSRA amendments to § 115 extend the compulsory license by permitting record companies to obtain compulsory mechanical licenses for songs that will be recorded and then distributed by digital transmission. It also provides a method for determining the licensing fee for recordings distributed in this way.

To understand the role of the compulsory license, one should distinguish between two types of commerce that can take place via the "celestial jukebox." In addition to § 115 amendments, DPRSRA amended § 114 to address issues involving the transmission of sound recordings that can be heard in "real time" by consumers, some of whom may also engage in simultaneous and perhaps unlawful home recording.[145] By contrast, the § 115 amendments relate to a quite different technological possibility. Here, the concern is that firms engaged in the digital

---

[143] *See generally* Ralph Oman, *Source Licensing: The Latest Skirmish in an Old Battle*, 11 Colum.-VLA J.L. & Arts 251 (1987).

[144] Pub. L. No. 104-39, 109 Stat. 336 (1995). For an overview of the Act, see Lionel Sobel, *A New Music Law for the Age of Digital Technology*, 17 Ent. L.J. 3 (1995).

[145] Section 114 amendments are discussed *infra* § 8.26.

"delivery" of sound recordings could make use of facilities such as the World Wide Web to provide customers with high-speed feeds of digital data intended to be downloaded for later playback. This mode of distribution is already rendering obsolete the traditional record store.

[2] The Terms and Operation of the Compulsory License

The DPRSRA distinguishes between digital performances and digital distributions by creating a new type of digital transmission called a "digital phonorecord delivery." The Act attempts to distinguish "digital phonorecord delivery" — one that results in a reproduction — from performances in real time noninteractive subscription transmission where no reproduction is made.[146]

The Act confirms that the compulsory license does not impair any existing rights of the owners of copyrights to nondramatic musical works. It does so by expressly providing that a company making "digital phonorecord delivery" is infringing copyright unless: (I) the digital phonorecord delivery has been authorized by the copyright owner in the sound recording; and (II) the owner of the copyright in the sound recording or the entity making the digital phonorecord delivery has obtained a compulsory license under the section or has otherwise been authorized by the copyright owner of the musical work to distribute or authorize the distribution, by means of a digital phonorecord delivery, of each musical work embodied in the sound recording.[147]

In addition to the conditions for triggering the compulsory license, one who makes a digital phonorecord delivery must pay the required royalty rates established through voluntary negotiations or through the administrative assessment, which, until 2005, was carried out within the CARP system.[148] The distributor of a sound recording who uses the compulsory license must contain any information encoded in the recording concerning its title, the recording artist, and the songwriter.[149]

The Act takes into account the special problem of contributory infringement in the digital environment. This was a particular concern of record companies and other sound recording copyright owners who feared exposure to liability through the acts of third parties making unauthorized "digital phonorecord deliveries." Here, the Act exempts the sound recording copyright owner from secondary

---

[146] 17 U.S.C. § 115(d) defines "digital phonorecord delivery" as

> each individual delivery of a phonorecord by digital transmission of a sound recording which results in a specifically identifiable reproduction by or for any transmission recipient of a phonorecord of that sound recording, regardless of whether the digital transmission is also a public performance of the sound recording or any nondramatic musical work embodied therein.

[147] 17 U.S.C. § 115(c)(3)(H).

[148] DPRSRA specifies the procedure for settling the practical aspects of the statutory licenses. Section 115(c)(3)(B)-(F) provides that, under the umbrella of a limited antitrust exemption, affected parties may voluntarily negotiate terms and rates. After several delays, groups representing songwriters, music publishers and the recording industry reached an agreement which was embodied in a notice of proposed rulemaking published by the Copyright Office on November 18, 1997.

[149] *See* 17 U.S.C. § 115(c)(3)(G).

liability for these unauthorized deliveries if it did not license the distribution of the phonorecord of the nondramatic musical work.

To illustrate how the § 115 compulsory license operates, suppose C, a composer of a musical work, authorizes A to perform and sell copies to the public of his song in 1990. From that time on, B may resort to the compulsory license to bring together musicians for a recording of his own version of the song. He must, of course, pay the compulsory fee for the traditional "mechanical license" to C for copies sold. Suppose that D wishes to invoke the compulsory license for "digital phonorecord delivery." D must pay the statutory fee to C for the use of the music. He may use A's or B's sound recording, but he must obtain their consent to do so. Alternatively, if D is unable to obtain a license from A and B, he may wish to gather together his own musicians to record a new rendition of the song for the purpose of eventual digital phonorecord delivery. Here D must pay statutory license fees to C, the composer, but nothing to A or B, the sound recording copyright holders. Suppose A and B consent to the use of their sound recording for digital delivery to consumers. In this instance, D will be able to avail himself of the compulsory license but only if all digitally encoded information about the work is transmitted along with the work.[150]

§ 8.11 LIMITATIONS TO THE REPRODUCTION AND ADAPTATION RIGHTS: COMPUTER USES, § 117[151]

A specially appointed presidential commission, CONTU[152] drafted a 1980 amendment to the 1976 Act § 117[153] to meet the needs of the users and producers of computer software. The original version of § 117 served as a holding measure until CONTU had an opportunity to examine the issue. Once CONTU issued its final report, Congress quickly adopted CONTU's proposed amendment virtually in its entirety.

Section 117 creates a limited exception to the reproduction and adaptation rights by allowing the *owner* (not a licensee) of a copy of a computer program to copy it or adapt it if (1) the new copy or adaptation is created as an *essential*[154] step toward

---

[150] *Id.*

[151] For an excellent overview of the subject, see Robert A. Kreiss, *Section 117 of the Copyright Act*, 1991 B.Y.U. L. Rev. 1497. See also Raymond T. Nimmer, The Law of Computer Technology §§ 1:111–1:115 (3d ed. 2005), covering all aspects of computer law.

[152] National Commission on New Technological Uses of Copyrighted Works ("CONTU"). The Commission was established to study the issue of computer uses of copyrighted works. Its recommendations for an amended § 117, as part of its *Final Report of the Commission on New Technological Uses of Copyrighted Works* (1979) (hereinafter "CONTU Final Report"), were adopted in their entirety. The one major change in the final version of § 117 from CONTU's version is Congress's substitution of the word "owner" for "rightful possessor." CONTU's version would have conferred on licensees the same rights as an owner. The legislative history does not reveal the purpose of the change. *See Midway Mfg. Co. v. Artic Int'l, Inc.*, 704 F.2d 1009 (7th Cir. 1983).

[153] 17 U.S.C. § 117. *See* Pub. L. No. 96-517, 94 Stat. 3015, 3028 (1980).

[154] 17 U.S.C. § 117(a)(1). *See* Raymond T. Nimmer, The Law of Computer Technology § 1:114 (3d ed. 2005). *But see Apple Computer, Inc. v. Formula Int'l, Inc.*, 594 F. Supp. 617 (C.D. Cal. 1984) (stating that the defendant owner of diskette program was not permitted to put a program on a silicon chip, and that

using the program in a computer or (2) the copy or adaptation is for archival purposes and "all archival copies are destroyed in the event that continued possession of the computer program should cease to be rightful."[155]

In *Krause v. Titleserve*,[156] the court took an expansive view of the meaning of the two key terms — "owner" and "essential steps" — in § 117(a)(2). First, the court held that the former employer of the plaintiff, which still had a lawful copy of the computer program in its possession, had sufficient incidents of ownership to be considered an "owner" of that copy, even if it lacked formal title. In so holding, the court opined that the license terms conditioned ownership of the copyright only, and not ownership of the particular copy. The problem is that CONTU, which was instrumental in drafting § 117, had proposed an exception in favor of the "rightful possessor" of a copy of a computer program, but Congress changed the draft so that the exception applies only to an "owner" of a copy. Because many software providers purport only to "license" their software to users rather than "sell" it, this literal interpretation would defeat the purpose of § 117. Thus, the court took a pragmatic approach by imposing its judicial gloss despite the language of § 117. The court then held that fixing bugs, updating client information, incorporating the program into its new Windows-based system, and adding functional capabilities to the program were all "essential steps" in utilizing the program. The court rejected the view that "essential" included "the addition of features so that a program better serves the needs of the customer for which it was created."[157]

In addition, § 117(b)[158] stipulates that any exact copies prepared in accordance with § 117(a) may be leased, sold, or otherwise transferred, along with the copy from which the copies were prepared, only as part of the lease, sale, or other transfer of all rights in the program. An adaptation of the program can be transferred only with the authorization of the copyright owner.

Section 117 was amended in 1998 to ensure that independent service organizations do not inadvertently become liable for copyright infringement merely because they have turned on a computer to service its hardware.[159] Section 117(c) was a response to the decision in *MAI Systems Corp. v. Peak Computer, Inc.*[160] in which an independent service organization that leased software from the plaintiff infringed copyright in the program by loading the copyrighted software into the RAM of the customer's computer. In a controversial decision, the court held that the loading of the program into the RAM memory violated the copyright owner's exclusive right to reproduce the copyrighted work under § 106(1) of the Copyright Act.[161] The *MAI* court ruled that § 117 only exempted "owners" of software, not "licensees." Section 117(c) effectively overrules *MAI* by allowing an owner to make

---

the use was for convenience and not for an essential use, i.e., indispensable and necessary).

155 17 U.S.C. § 117(a)(2).

156 402 F.3d 119, 124 (2d Cir. 2005).

157 *Id.* at 128.

158 17 U.S.C. § 117(b).

159 *See* Title III of Digital Millennium Copyright Act, Pub. L. 105-304, 112 Stat. 2860 § 301 (1998).

160 991 F.2d 511 (9th Cir. 1993). *See supra* § 8.04[B].

161 What constitutes a "fixation" and the controversy spawned by *MAI* is discussed at *supra* § 2.03.

or authorize the making of a copy of a computer program under certain conditions for repair or maintenance of the computer hardware.

Section 117(c) allows the making of a copy (1) if the copy is made "solely [on] activation of a machine that lawfully contains an authorized copy of the computer program, for . . . maintenance or repair of that machine," (2) if the new copy is used for no other purpose and is destroyed on completion of the maintenance and repair,[162] and (3) if "any computer program . . . that is not necessary for that machine to be activated . . . is not accessed or used other than to make such new copy by virtue of the activation of the machine."[163] Most important, the exception applies only to *RAM* copies made during *hardware* maintenance, not software maintenance.

Section 117 supports the needs of users but is also designed to protect the rights of creators. The above provisions apply only to a rightful owner of a copy of a program for use in his own computer.[164] Thus, the program owner's right to make archival copies ceases once the original copy is resold, and the previous owner must destroy an archival copy unless it is an exact copy of the program, which may then be transferred to the new owner instead of being destroyed. The reason for this rule is to prevent the owner of a copy from profiting from a sale of the copy and at the same time keeping an archival copy for continued use.

Special needs of the software medium dictate § 117 exceptions to the reproduction and adaptation rights. The first, the adaptation of a program, is often necessary because program languages are not standardized.[165] The second, the right to make archival copies of a program, recognizes the fragility of the medium supported by the long-standing practice of computer users of making backup copies as a precaution against mechanical or electronic failure. The privilege to make these backup copies applies only when the program faces a legitimate threat of mechanical failure and does not apply where no substantial risk is present.[166] Similarly, the repair and maintenance exception of § 117(c) recognizes the practical needs of the computer repair industry. It does so by providing that a person who merely turns on someone else's computer for the purpose of servicing it is not guilty of copyright infringement.

---

[162] *See Storage Tech. Corp. v. Custom Hardware Eng'g & Consulting, Inc.*, 421 F.3d 1307 (Fed. Cir. 2005) (noting that under § 117(c), temporary RAM copies may be erased at the maintenance contract, rather than every time a repair is made).

[163] 17 U.S.C. § 117(c)(2).

[164] *See* Nimmer on Copyright § 8.08[A] (2014); *Apple Computer, Inc. v. Formula Int'l, Inc.*, 594 F. Supp. 617 (C.D. Cal. 1984).

[165] *See* CONTU Final Report, *supra* note 152, at 13–14.

[166] See *Micro-Sparc Inc. v. Amtype Corp.*, 592 F. Supp. 33 (D. Mass. 1984); *see also Atari, Inc. v. JS & A Group, Inc.*, 747 F.2d 1422 (Fed. Cir. 1984) (holding the right to prepare an archival copy does not apply to programs distributed in a read only memory (ROM) because these chips were not susceptible to risks of *mechanical or electrical* failure). *But see Vault Corp. v. Quaid Software Ltd.*, 847 F.2d 255, 267 (5th Cir. 1988) (holding that an owner of a program is entitled to make an archival copy of that program to guard against *all* types of risks, including physical and human mishap as well as mechanical and electrical failure).

While providing access to the copyrighted work, § 117 protects the rights of the copyright owner by strictly limiting reproduction and adaptation to the peculiarities of the medium. In effect, one might view § 117 as setting forth explicitly what would certainly have constituted a fair use[167] of a copyrighted computer program absent the § 117 exception. Thus, the possibility exists that fair use under § 107 may be applied to computer uses that transcend the limited exception to the reproduction right set forth in § 117.[168]

§ 8.12 LIMITATIONS TO THE REPRODUCTION AND ADAPTATION RIGHTS: ARCHITECTURAL WORKS, § 120

Section 120(a) of the Copyright Act provides that once an architectural work has been constructed and is publicly visible, "no right exists to prevent the making, distributing, or public display of pictures, paintings, photographs, or other pictorial representations of the work."[169] Thus, photographers will not only be able to take pictures of publicly visible buildings but will be able to commercialize their photos as well in posters, postcards, and slides.

Section 120(b) imposes another limitation to the adaptation right. Under this section "the owners of a building embodying an architectural work may, without the consent of the author or copyright owner of the architectural work, make or authorize the making of alterations to such building, and destroy or authorize the destruction of such building." Unfortunately, § 120 leaves open several thorny questions. For example, does the building owner's right of alteration include the right to build an addition that copies the design of the original? Here, the courts should imply a license in favor of the building owner, but the issue is not settled. Such issues suggest that the copyright model for an architectural work, because of its inherent utilitarian character, fits awkwardly in the real world of architectural design and the environment in which the design exists.

The exercise of a building owner's right to alter a building may conflict with a visual artist's "moral right" of integrity, protected under § 106A and § 113(d)(2) of the Act. Section 113(d)(2) specifies that if the building embodies a work of visual art as defined in § 101, the owner of the building may be subject to liability for distortion, mutilation, or other modification of the work by reason of its removal unless the work was installed before June 1, 1991, the effective date of the Visual Artists Rights Act. To avoid liability for a work installed after the effective date of the Act, the owner of the building and the author are required to specify, in a written instrument, that the work may be subject to distortion, mutilation, or modification upon its removal.[170]

---

167 For a discussion of fair use, see *infra* chapter 10.

168 *See, e.g.*, *Sega Enters., Ltd. v. Accolade, Inc.*, 977 F.2d 1510, 1520 (9th Cir. 1992) (holding that § 117 does not protect a user who disassembles object code, converts it from source code, and makes printouts and photocopies of the version in source code). See *infra* § 10.13 for a discussion of *Sega*.

169 17 U.S.C. § 120(a).

170 17 U.S.C. § 120(b). See *infra* § 8.29 for a discussion of the Visual Artists Rights Act of 1990.

§ 8.13 LIMITATIONS TO THE REPRODUCTION AND ADAPTATION RIGHTS: REPRODUCTION FOR THE BLIND OR OTHER PEOPLE WITH DISABILITIES, § 121

Section 121[171] carves out a narrow exception to the reproduction and adaptation rights for nonprofit and governmental organizations whose main purpose is to promote access to information by blind or other disabled individuals. Section 121(a) provides that "it is not an infringement of copyright for an authorized entity to reproduce or to distribute copies or phonorecords of a previously published, nondramatic literary work if such copies or phonorecords are reproduced or distributed in specialized formats exclusively for use by blind or other persons with disabilities."[172]

Section 121(c) defines the exemption's three operative terms. First, an "authorized entity" is "a nonprofit organization or governmental agency that has a primary mission to provide specialized services relating to training, education, or adaptive reading or information access needs of blind or other persons with disabilities."[173] Second, "blind or other persons with disabilities" are persons eligible or who qualify under the 1931 "Act to provide books for the adult blind." Third, "specialized formats" are "braille, audio, or digital text which is exclusively for use by blind or other persons with disabilities."

Section 121(c)[174] sets forth the formats in which copies and phonorecords must exist, as well as certain notice requirements that they must contain. First, the copies and phonorecords must exist in specialized formats for the blind or other persons with disabilities. Second, these copies and phonorecords must bear "a notice that any further reproduction or distribution in a format other than a specialized format is an infringement." Third, they must also include "a copyright notice identifying the copyright owner and the date of the original publication." In addition to these limitations, the provisions of § 121 do not apply to standardized, secure, or norm-referenced tests and related testing material, or computer programs except when portions of the above are in conventional human language that are displayed to users in the ordinary use of computer programs.[175]

---

[171] 17 U.S.C. § 121(a); Pub. L. No. 104–97, § 316, 110 Stat. 2394 (1996).

[172] 17 U.S.C. § 121(a).

[173] 17 U.S.C. § 121(c).

[174] *Id.*

[175] 17 U.S.C. § 121(b)(2).

Part III. THE DISTRIBUTION RIGHT AND ITS LIMITATIONS

§ 8.14 THE DISTRIBUTION RIGHT: GENERALLY

Section 106(3)[176] creates the exclusive right "to distribute copies or phonorecords of the copyrighted work to the public by sale or other transfer of ownership, or by rental, lease, or lending."

The distribution right gives the copyright owner the right to control the first public distribution of the work. This first public distribution may take place by sale, rental, lease, or lending.[177] It differs from the other rights in § 106, which involve copying in one way or another. Rather than the right to copy, the distribution right involves the right to transfer physical copies or phonorecords of the work. Thus, an unauthorized public performance does not infringe the distribution right for two reasons: first a performance is not a publication, and second, a performance does not transfer physical copies of the work. On the other hand, a public distribution can occur when only one member of the public receives a copyrighted work.[178] Courts have historically read § 106(3) to require that for the public distribution right to be infringed, copies or phonorecords must actually be distributed. In *Hotaling v. Church of Jesus Christ of Latter-Day Saints*,[179] the Court of Appeals for the Fourth Circuit departed from that rule. It held that "a library distributes a published work within the meaning of the Copyright Act . . . when it places an unauthorized copy of the work in its collection, includes the copy in its catalog or index system, and makes the copy available to the public."[180] The *Hotaling* court rejected the defendant's argument that a physical copy of the work must have changed hands to infringe the distribution right. In so doing, the court implicitly adopted the concept of a "making available" right, a norm found in the 1996 WIPO Treaties[181] to which the United States has adhered.

The Internet has presented a special challenge to adapt § 106(3) to electronic distributions of a work. District courts have struggled to determine whether the requirement to prove actual dissemination or whether merely making a work available should apply to cases involving online file sharing. Some courts agreeing with *Hotaling* have held that merely making a work *available* to the public, such as making a work accessible for downloading over the Internet, constitutes a distribution,[182] particularly when other circumstantial evidence supports an inference of

---

[176] 17 U.S.C. § 106(3).

[177] *See* H.R. Rep. No. 94-1476, at 62 (1976).

[178] *See Ford Motor Co. v. Summit Motor Prods., Inc.*, 930 F.2d 277 (3d Cir. 1991) (finding that gratuitous transfer of even a single copy may be enough to violate the right: "damages may be limited, or even non-existent, but the liability for infringement remains").

[179] 118 F.3d 199 (4th Cir. 1997).

[180] *Id.* at 201.

[181] WIPO Copyright Treaty Art. 6(1); WIPO Performances and Phonograms Treaty Art. 8(1).

[182] *See, e.g.*, *A&M Records, Inc. v. Napster, Inc.*, 239 F.3d 1004, 1014 (9th Cir. 2001) ("Napster users

actual distribution.[183] By contrast, others take the view that merely making a copy of a work available on a peer-to-peer network does not constitute a distribution.[184]

One can sympathize with efforts to read a making available right into 106(3). In principal, the copyright owner should be able to control uses that harm the market value of a work such as placing the copyright owner's work on a website without consent. The language of the Copyright Act, however, indicates a more restrictive reading than a full-fledged "making available" right, one that is limited to an *actual* distribution as opposed to an *offer* to distribute the copyrighted work. . . . Section 106(3) follows the first sentence in the Copyright Act's definition of publication in § 101: "the distribution of copies or phonorecords of the copyrighted work to the public by sale or other transfer of ownership, or by rental, lease or lending."[185] Section 106(3), however, does not include, as does the definition of publication, the "*offering* to distribute copies or phonorecords to a group of persons for purposes of further distribution, public performance or public display, constitutes publication."[186] Rather than having courts artificially engraft a "making available" right into the Act, a legislative fix would be a more constitutionally appropriate way to proceed.

The important factor here is that the work is made available to the public. Thus, one who downloads a copyrighted article from the Internet and emails it to a family member or small circle of friends may have violated the reproduction right but would not have made a distribution to the "public" under the statutory definition.[187] On the other hand, sending a single private email to a stranger might well constitute a public distribution of its contents.

The distribution right is frequently infringed simultaneously with the reproduction right but can also be infringed alone. Infringement of the distribution right alone commonly occurs in the music industry when unlawfully made audio or video tapes are acquired by a retailer and sold to the public. Although the retail seller may not have copied the work in any way and may not have known that the works were made unlawfully, he nevertheless infringes the distribution right by their sale. The seller's innocent intent is not a valid defense to an action for copyright infringement, which allows the copyright owner to proceed against any member in the chain of distribution.[188]

---

who upload file names to the search index for others to copy violate plaintiff's distribution rights."); *London-Sire Records, Inc. v. Doe*, 542 F. Supp. 2d 153 (D. Mass. 2008).

[183] *Capitol Records, Inc. v. Thomas*, 579 F. Supp. 2d 1210, 1225 (D. Minn. 2008); *Atlantic Recording Corp. v. Howell*, 554 F. Supp. 2d 976, 981, 983–84 (D. Ariz. 2008); *London-Sire Records*, at 169.

[184] *See, e.g., Thomas*, at 1216–19; *Howell*, at 981–84; *In re Napster, Inc. Copyright Litig.*, 377 F. Supp. 2d 796, 802–05 (N.D. Cal. 2005).

[185] 17 U.S.C. § 106(3).

[186] 17 U.S.C. § 101 (publication).

[187] *See* 17 U.S.C. § 101 (to perform or display a work publicly).

[188] *See Costello Publ'ns Co. v. Rotelle*, 670 F.2d 1035, 1044 (D.C. Cir. 1981).

§ 8.15 LIMITATIONS ON THE DISTRIBUTION RIGHT: THE FIRST SALE DOCTRINE

[A] Generally

Section 109(a)[189] creates a basic exception to the distribution right known as the "first sale doctrine," which limits the copyright owner's control over copies of the work to their first sale or transfer. Section 109(a) provides:

> Notwithstanding the provisions of section 106(3), the owner of a particular copy or phonorecord lawfully made under this title, or any person authorized by such owner, is entitled, without the authority of the copyright owner, to sell or otherwise dispose of the possession of that copy or phonorecord.

The first-sale doctrine thus attempts to strike a balance between assuring a sufficient reward to the copyright owner and permitting unimpeded circulation of copies of the work.

The first-sale doctrine was first established by the Supreme Court in *Bobbs-Merrill Co. v. Straus*.[190] In this pre-1909 Act case, a book publisher inserted into its books a notice purporting to prohibit resale for less than $1. The Court held that the exclusive right to "vend" a copyrighted work did not include the right to impose conditions on future resale. The doctrine was later codified in § 27 of the 1909 Act, and then in § 109(a) of the 1976 Act.

The elements of the first sale doctrine can be summarized as follows: (1) the copy was lawfully made with the authorization of the copyright owner; (2) the copy was initially transferred under the copyright owner's authority; (3) the defendant is a lawful owner of the copy in question; and (4) the defendant's use implicates the distribution right only, not the reproduction right.

To elaborate on these elements of the first sale doctrine, once the work is lawfully sold[191] or even transferred gratuitously,[192] the copyright owner's interest in the material object, the copy or phonorecord, is exhausted; the owner of that copy can then dispose of it as he sees fit.[193]

---

[189] 17 U.S.C. § 109(a).

[190] 210 U.S. 339 (1908)

[191] The first sale doctrine applies to sales of copies or phonorecords of copyrighted work, not to a lease of the copyrighted work. To avoid the first sale doctrine, owners have tried to characterize a transaction as a lease rather than a sale by means of a contractual provision, often in the context of a click wrap or shrink wrap license. *See, e.g., Adobe Sys. Inc. v. One Stop Micro, Inc.*, 84 F. Supp. 2d 1086 (N.D. Cal. 2000) (holding that an agreement providing for distribution of computer software to educational users was a licensing agreement, not subject to the Copyright Act's first sale doctrine). Whether such contractual provisions are valid and not preempted by § 301 of the Copyright Act is discussed *infra* § 11.07[B].

[192] *See Walt Disney Prods. v. Basmajian*, 600 F. Supp. 439 (S.D.N.Y. 1984).

[193] The doctrine traces its origin to *Bobbs-Merrill Co. v. Strauss*, 210 U.S. 339 (1908), in which the Supreme Court construed the exclusive right to vend under the pre-1909 Act as limited to the initial sale but not to resales.

The first sale doctrine entitles the owner of a copy to dispose of it physically. Thus, one who buys a copy of a book is entitled to resell it, rent it out, give it away, rebind it, or destroy it. This same owner, however, would infringe copyright by reproducing it or performing it publicly without the consent of the copyright owner.[194] Alternatively, under § 109(d), the first sale doctrine is not triggered when the copyright owner has rented, leased or loaned the copy without actually transferring ownership of it.[195] By contrast, any transfer of ownership, even a gratuitous transfer, brings the doctrine into play.[196] Courts have held that transfers of copies that imply a shift in ownership can qualify, and even involuntary transfers,[197] such as a judicial sale.[198] The copies sold in bankruptcy[199] with the copyright owner's consent constitute a first sale.

The first sale doctrine can be modified by the parties,[200] but any agreement would be enforced under contract law rather than copyright law.[201] Is there anything in the first sale doctrine or in copyright law generally that would prevent the original owners of copies or phonorecords from imposing supplementary restraints on their distribution after sale by way of contract? Obviously, such restraints are highly desirable in certain circumstances if they can be enforced. The issue has arisen in the context of software licenses. The second-hand trade in genuine (as distinct from counterfeit) software products is a "big little business," and it is coming under increasing legal fire from major software vendors. Typically, these enterprising resellers invoke "first sale," asserting that the firms and individuals from whom they bought their wares were themselves lawful purchasers. The manufacturers respond that the copies in question were never sold, merely "licensed." As evidence, they point to various terms in the "shrink-wrap" agreements that accompany these software products when they are made available by or under the authority of their copyright owners, including "end user license agreements" ("EULAs").[202]

---

194 *See* 17 U.S.C. § 202; *see also* H.R. Rep. No. 94-1476, at 79 (1976).

195 17 U.S.C. § 109(d) ("The privileges prescribed by subsections (a) and (c) do not . . . extend to any person who has acquired possession of the copyright or phonorecord from the copyright owner, by rental, lease, loan, or otherwise, without, acquiring ownership of it.").

196 *See UMG Recordings, Inc. V. Augusto*, 628 F.3d 1175 (9th Cir. 2011) (resale of free promotional CDs on eBay was permitted under first sale doctrine; label on CDs with alleged resale restriction did not create a license).

197 *See United States v. Wise*, 550 F.2d 1180 (9th Cir. 1977) (transfer of possession of a film print without time limitation can qualify).

198 *See Platt & Munk Co. v. Republic Graphics, Inc.*, 315 F.2d 847, 854 (2d Cir. 1963)

199 See *Bryant v. Gordon*, 483 F. Supp. 2d 605 (N.D. Ill. 2007) (first-sale doctrine applies to copies sold in bankruptcy, where copyright owner had notice and did not object). *But see Denbicare U.S.A., Inc. v. Toys R Us, Inc.*, 84 F.3d 1143, 1150 (9th Cir. 1996) (stating in d*icta* that a bankruptcy trustee's sale of copies without authorization of the copyright owner would be an infringement).

200 *See United States v. Wise*, 550 F.2d 1180 (9th Cir.1977).

201 *See* H.R. Rep. No. 94-1476, at 79 (1976). For an excellent article discussing the techniques used to modify the first sale doctrine by restrictive notices, see Mark A. Fischer, *Reserving All Rights Beyond Copyright: Non-Statutory Restrictive Notices*, 34 J. Copyright Soc'y 249 (1987).

202 Different courts have taken dramatically different approaches to sorting out this conundrum. *Vernor v. Autodesk, Inc.*, 621 F.3d 1102 (9th Cir. 2010 (holding that "a software user is a licensee rather than an owner of a copy where the copyright owner (1) specifies that the user is granted a license; (2)

The rationale of the first sale doctrine is to prevent the copyright owner from restraining the free alienability of goods. Without a first sale doctrine, a possessor of a copy or phonorecord of a copyrighted work would have to negotiate with the copyright owner every time he wished to dispose of his copy or phonorecord. This principle sometimes clashes with the copyright owner's reproduction and adaptation rights, forcing the court to make delicate distinctions. In *C.M. Paula Co. v. Logan*,[203] the defendant bought the plaintiff's greeting cards, transferred the designs on the cards to ceramic plaques, and sold the plaques commercially. The court held that neither the reproduction nor adaptation right was infringed and that the sale of the plaques was immunized by the first sale doctrine.[204] The defendant was not reproducing the work but simply disposing of it physically: "[e]ach ceramic plaque sold by defendant with a Paula print affixed thereto requires the purchase and use of an individual piece of artwork marketed by the plaintiff."[205]As for infringement of the adaptation right, the court found no adaptation, rearrangement, or compilation sufficient to violate the right. Using similar reasoning, other courts have found no infringement of the distribution right where individuals have lawfully purchased copies of paper-bound books and rebound them in hard covers, even when combined with other works.[206] The case law reveals that courts in close cases will often side with the defendant when the rights of the copyright owner encroach on the right of an owner to dispose of physical copies of the work.[207]

The above freedom of disposition of physical copies of the work applies only where the book is lawfully made.[208] Any resale or other disposition of a pirated copy would constitute an infringing act, even if the defendant had no knowledge of the piracy. Accordingly, a retail record store that has unknowingly sold pirated copies

significantly restricts the user's ability to transfer the software; and (3) imposes notable use restrictions.). For more on these agreements from the standpoint of copyright preemption, see *infra* § 11.07 [B].

203 355 F. Supp. 189 (N.D. Tex. 1973).

204 The first sale doctrine was incorporated into the 1909 Act in 17 U.S.C. § 27 (1909 Act).

205 *C.M. Paula*, 355 F. Supp. at 191.

206 *See Fawcett Publ'ns, Inc. v. Eliot Publ'g Co.*, 46 F. Supp. 717 (S.D.N.Y. 1942). *But see Nat'l Geographic Soc'y v. Classified Geographic*, 27 F. Supp. 655 (D. Mass. 1939) (finding that defendant infringed the adaptation right by taking individual articles from *National Geographic Magazine* and reassembling them with his own index).

207 *See also Lee v. A.R.T. Co.*, 125 F.3d 580 (7th Cir. 1997) (finding that adaptation right not infringed where defendant transferred artworks from notecards and lithographs to individual ceramic tiles); *Precious Moments, Inc. v. La Infantil, Inc.*, 971 F. Supp. 66 (D.C.P.R. 1997). *But see Mirage Editions, Inc. v. Albuquerque A.R.T. Co.*, 856 F.2d 1341 (9th Cir. 1988) (holding that adaptation right infringed where defendant transferred artworks from a commemorative book to individual ceramic tiles because, by borrowing and mounting the preexisting copyrighted art images, defendant prepared derivative works whose sales supplanted purchasers' demand for the underlying works). See discussion of these cases at *supra* § 8.05.

208 According to the House Report, the burden of proving whether a particular copy was lawfully made or acquired should rest on the defendant. *See* H.R. Rep. No. 1476, at 80-81 (1976). This indicates a legislative intention to overturn the rule developed by 1909 Act case law that copyright owners in civil cases, and the government in criminal cases, had the burden of proving absence of a first sale. *See United States v. Atherton*, 561 F.2d 747, 749 (9th Cir. 1977) (holding that there was a sale of motion picture prints). Due process considerations may prevent imposing the burden of proof on a criminal defendant. *See, e.g., United States v. Moore*, 604 F.2d 1228 (9th Cir. 1979).

of a popular album is an infringer of copyright. Lack of knowledge that one is infringing is not a defense to an action for an infringement of the distribution right.

As codified in § 109(a), the first sale doctrine applies only to copies "lawfully made under this title." May a copy that was *not* lawfully made ever be resold without violating the distribution right? In *Christopher Phelps & Assoc. v. Galloway*,[209] the plaintiff sought an injunction against future lease or sale of a house found to be infringing. The Fourth Circuit rejected this request, initially holding that once a judgment for damages was satisfied, the house became a lawfully made copy for purposes of the first sale doctrine. On rehearing, however, the court removed this language, holding instead that an injunction should not issue because it would encumber real property unrelated to the infringement such as a swimming pool, a fence, or underground aspects of the property. The court drew an analogy to the law of conversion in which satisfaction of a judgment for damages gives the defendant good legal title.[210] Should this holding be extended to infringing copies of other copyrighted works? Or is there something special about architectural works that justifies a departure from the "plain language" of the statute? Not too much should be read into *Christopher Phelps* except for the following proposition: Whether to grant the injunction remains in the equitable discretion of the court.[211] One can easily understand why the court ruled as it did in the architectural work context. An injunction would have been inconsistent with the Copyright Act's prohibition against punitive damages.

[B] Should the First Sale Doctrine Be Extended to Digital Transmissions?

In today's world, copies of copyrighted works, music, films, and computer software, are bought with increasing frequency by downloading them through the Internet. Can a lawful owner of a copy of such a work be allowed, consistent with the first sale doctrine, to distribute the copy to others, and if so, under what circumstances?[212] Digital transmissions of copyrighted works over the Internet do not comfortably fit within the constraints of the first sale doctrine. The principal reason is that the first sale doctrine is restricted to the transfer of physical copies of the work and provides no defense to infringements of the reproduction right. Unlike transactions where a tangible copy changes hands, an Internet transmission results in a reproduction of the work through the electronic transmission of a new copy of the work to its recipient. In other words, the sender retains the source copy unless deleted from the hard disk by human or

---

[209] 477 F.3d 128 (4th Cir. 2007).

[210] *Christopher Phelps & Assoc. v. Galloway*, 492 F.3d 532 (4th Cir. 2007).

[211] *eBay Inc. v. MercExchange, LLC*, 547 U.S. 388, 393 (2006) ("[T]he decision whether to grant or deny injunctive relief rests within the equitable discretion of the district courts, and that such discretion must be exercised consistent with traditional principles of equity, in patent disputes no less than in other cases governed by such standards.").

[212] So far the courts have not been sympathetic with a digital first sale doctrine. See *Capitol Records LLC v. ReDigi, Inc.*, 934 F. Supp. 2d 640 (S.D.N.Y. 2013)(holding that the digital creation of a copy of a sound recording in order to facilitate its transfer from one computer to another resulted in a copy that was not "lawfully made" and thus rendered the first sale doctrine inapplicable).

technological intervention; by sending a copy to the recipient, the sender infringes both the reproduction and distribution rights.

The question remains whether the first sale doctrine should be retooled to reflect the realities of the digital age and be made to apply to digital transmissions. Some have argued for a statutory change or a rule permitting the transfer of an electronic work to a single party so long as the sender deletes the copy of the work within a reasonable time.[213] Whether this would be wise from a policy standpoint is another question. The crux of the matter is that physical copies are inherently different from information in digital formats, and the economic effect of this difference is significant. Physical copies degrade over time, whereas digital information does not. Moreover, works in a digital form can be reproduced flawlessly and be disseminated globally at little cost and with low visibility. Thus, a digital first sale right would affect the market for the original to a greater degree than transfers of physical copies. The Copyright Office report sums it up: "The tangible nature of a copy is a defining element of the first sale doctrine and critical to its rationale."[214]

§ 8.16 MODIFICATIONS AND EXCEPTIONS TO THE FIRST SALE DOCTRINE

[A] Record Rental[215]

The Record Rental Amendment of 1984[216] prohibits an owner of a phonorecord that embodies a sound recording or musical work from renting it to the public for direct or indirect commercial advantage. This exception to the first sale doctrine was directed against the increasing number of record stores renting records, cassettes, and compact disks to their customers. The purpose of these rentals was to facilitate home copying, thereby displacing sales that could have been made by the copyright owner.[217] Thus, instead of buying a compact disc for $15.99, the client would rent the disc and purchase a blank tape for a fraction of the price. This practice was perceived as a major threat to the record-producing industry, and § 109(b) was added as an amendment to the 1976 Copyright Act in 1984.[218]

---

[213] *See, e.g.*, Mark A. Lemley, *Dealing with Overlapping Copyrights on the Internet*, 22 U. Dayton L. Rev. 547, 584 (1997); Joseph P. Liu, *Owning Digital Copies: Copyright Law and the Incidents of Copy Ownership*, 42 Wm. & Mary L. Rev. 1245 (2001).

[214] U.S. Copyright Office, Digital Millennium Copyright Act: Section 104 Report, Executive Summary (2001), *available at* www.copyright.gov/reports/studies/dmca/dmca_executive.html/ (recommending no legislative change to § 109(a) to encompass digital first sale right).

[215] *See* 17 U.S.C. § 109(b). For an overview of the subject, see David H. Horowitz, *The Record Rental Amendment of 1984: A Case Study in the Effort to Adapt Copyright Law to New Technology*, 12 Colum.-VLA J.L. & Arts 31 (1987).

[216] Pub. L. No. 98-450, 98 Stat. 1727 (1984).

[217] *See* H.R. Rep. No. 98-987, at 2 (1984).

[218] Nonretroactivity and sunset provisions were attached to § 109(b), codified in Pub. L. No. 98-450, 98 Stat. 1727 § 4. The effective date of the Act is October 4, 1984. *Id.* at § 4(a). Records bought before that date still enjoyed the first sale exemption under § 109(a). *Id.* at § 4(b). The Act also contained a five-year sunset provision. *Id.* at § 4(c). Rentals of records made after October 3, 1989, were to be once again

Section 109(b) constitutes a limited exception to the first sale doctrine. It applies to rentals of phonorecords[219] of a sound recording containing a musical work only[220] and not to a resale or other transfer of a phonorecord. Note that this legislation applies only to sound recordings of musical works and not to sound recordings of literary works.[221] Nor does it apply to motion pictures or other audiovisual works. In addition, it is limited to rentals by commercial establishments, whereas nonprofit rentals by libraries and educational institutions are specifically excluded from its provisions.

Copyright owners have long wished to benefit from lucrative secondary markets from which they were barred by the first sale doctrine. Authors, who earn their living by selling tangible copies of their works, such as textbook writers, would naturally like a percentage of sales in the organized used book market. They feel disfavored by copyright law, which appears more generous to authors who rely on the performance right for remuneration, such as composers of music. A musical copyright owner does benefit from the reproduction right, but even more from the performance right, which is not limited by the first sale doctrine. To the musical copyright owner, every performance of his work represents a possible source of revenue.[222]

[B] Software Rental

Until the Record Rental Amendment was enacted, most efforts to carve out exceptions to the first sale doctrine were unsuccessful. The record producers achieved their goal because they were able to point out a real threat to their survival made plausible by the ease with which records can be copied. As predicted, it was only a matter of time before other industry groups[223] would persuade Congress to protect them as well by creating a similar exception to the first sale doctrine.[224] So far only the software industry has successfully made their case for an exception to § 109(a). The arguments for a software rental exception were similar to those made by the record industry. Here the focus was on businesses

---

exempt under § 109(a). The purpose of the sunset provision was to give Congress a chance to evaluate the Record Rental Amendment. *See* H.R. Rep. No. 98-987, at 6 (1984). On November 5, 1988, President Reagan signed into law (Pub. L. No. 100-617) a bill (S. 2201) extending the Record Rental Amendment of 1984 for an additional eight years. In 1993, as a part of the North American Free Trade amendments, the sunset provisions were completely repealed. *See* Pub. L. No. 103-182, Title III, § 332, 107 Stat. 2114 (1993).

[219] *See* 17 U.S.C. § 101 (defining "phonorecords").

[220] It would appear that the amendment applies only to musical works, which would exclude rentals of literary works on tape as rented by the various book on tape companies. *See* Nimmer on Copyright § 8.12[B][a] (2014).

[221] *See Brilliance Audio, Inc. v. Haights Cross Comms., Inc.*, 474 F.3d 365 (6th Cir. 2007).

[222] For a discussion of the performance right as it relates to the musical copyright owner, see *infra* § 8.24.

[223] *See* Ralph Oman, *1976 Copyright Revision Revisited*, 34 J. Copyright L. Soc'y 29 (1987) (noting that the movie industry would like their own exception to the first sale doctrine).

[224] *See, e.g.*, H.R. Rep. No. 1029, 98th Cong., 2d Sess. (1984) (repealing the first sale doctrine for video cassettes embodying copyrighted works). *See also* State Resale Royalty Act, *infra* § 8.15[E]; Public Lending Right, *infra* § 8.15[F].

specializing in the rental of such popular programs as Microsoft Office. Software owners claimed that an organized rental industry would facilitate unauthorized private copying, threatening the economic health of the industry.[225]

The Copyright Software Rental Amendments Act of 1990[226] amended § 109(b) to prohibit the rental of computer software for direct or indirect commercial advantage.[227] The Software Rental Amendments are limited to the *rental* of a program. Otherwise, the owner of a copy of a program is as free to transfer that copy as any other owner of a copy of a work, such as a book, painting, or phonorecord. Unauthorized software rental constitutes copyright infringement.[228] As with the Record Rental Amendment, no criminal liability lies.[229] The restrictions on software rental are not absolute. First, the amendments do not apply to the lending of a copy by a nonprofit library for nonprofit purposes, provided the library has affixed an appropriate copyright warning.[230] Second, these provisions exempt from their scope "a computer program embodied in or used in conduction with a limited purpose computer that is designed for playing videogames and may be designed for other purposes."[231] This odd provision overturns the decision in *Red Baron-Franklin Park, Inc. v. Taito Corp.*[232] In *Red Baron*, the court held that the first sale doctrine did not allow the operator of a video arcade, who had acquired videogame circuit boards overseas, to perform the game publicly without the copyright owner's consent. Section 109(e) permits the owner of a copy of a lawfully made videogame to perform or display that game publicly on coin-operated equipment. This exemption is apparently designed to favor American video arcade owners at the expense of "foreign" (*i.e.*, Japanese) copyright owners of videogame software.[233]

[C] Importation of Copies and Phonorecords

Section 602(a)(1) states that the unauthorized "importation into the United States . . . of copies or phonorecords of a work that have been acquired outside the United States, is an infringement of the exclusive right to distribute copies or phonorecords under § 106." Since unlawful importation into the United States is also an infringement of 106(3), this provision might seem redundant to the distribution right, but on closer inspection it is not. Section 601(a) bolsters the rights of copyright owners because it provides the opportunity to stop goods before they enter the stream of commerce. In addition, by incorporating both piratical

---

225 *See* Cong. Rec. S17, 577 (1990) (remarks of Sen. Orrin Hatch).

226 Pub. L. No. 101-650, 104 Stat. 5089 (1990).

227 17 U.S.C. § 109(b)(1)(A).

228 Case law holds that the work must be registered as a computer program, and not in some other category, such as a "work of visual art." *See Action Tapes, Inc. v. Mattson*, 462 F.3d 1010 (8th Cir. 2006).

229 17 U.S.C. § 109(b)(4).

230 *See* 17 U.S.C. § 109(b)(2)(A).

231 17 U.S.C. §§ 109(b)(1)(B)(ii), 109(e).

232 883 F.2d 275 (4th Cir. 1989).

233 For an analysis of new opportunities for video game businesses to enforce their intellectual property rights, see Andrew W. Eichner, *Game Over, Insert Coin to Continue: Entering a New Era of Video Game Intellectual Property Enforcement*, 53 IDEA 101 (2013).

copies as well as gray market goods within its terms, § 602(a)(1) relieves copyright owners of the need to assert ineffectual contract remedies against domestic or foreign licenses for violation of territorial licenses.

Amendments in 2008[234] extended the scope of § 602 to include unlawful exportation into the United States. Section 602(a)(2) provides:

> Importation into the United States or exportation from the United States, without the authority of the owner of copyright under this title, of copies or phonorecords, the making of which either constituted an infringement of copyright, or which would have constituted an infringement of copyright if this title had been applicable, is an infringement of the exclusive right to distribute copies or phonorecords under section 106, actionable under sections 501 and 506.

The provisions on importation in § 602(a)(2) are redundant because § 602(a)(1) already prohibited importation. What is new is infringement by exportation and the express reference to criminal penalties for unauthorized importation and exportation. Three narrow statutory exceptions apply to the importation and exportation prohibitions: copies or phonorecords imported or exported by or for the use of the U.S. government or the government of any state or political subdivision (except for audiovisual works or works for use in schools); a single copy or phonorecord of a work imported or exported in a person's personal baggage for private use; and no more than five copies or phonorecords of a work (or one copy of an audiovisual work for archival purposes only) imported (but not exported) by a scholarly, educational, or religious organization for library lending or archival purposes.[235]

[D] Imported Copies Legally Obtained Abroad: The Gray Market

Gray market dealers typically buy goods in foreign countries at a significant discount from U.S. prices. They import these goods into the United States and sell them to discount retailers who are then able to undersell authorized U.S. dealers. The gray market exists because of various economic factors, particularly rapid fluctuations in foreign currencies. These fluctuations result in price differentials that may exceed tariff, freight, and related importation costs.

The distribution of genuine products outside a manufacturer's authorized channels is big business. Gray market importation has been estimated to be at various times between five to seven billion dollars.[236] Gray market goods are disruptive to the authorized distribution network. Gray marketers typically incur lower overhead costs than competing authorized dealers because they take a free ride on the advertising provided by the domestic suppliers and rarely service the warranties accompanying the goods. The result is that gray market goods are able

---

[234] Prioritizing Resources and Organization for Intellectual Property Act of 2008 (PRO- IP Act), Pub. L. 110-403, § 1(a), 122 Stat. 4256 (2008).

[235] *See* § 602(a)(3)(A)(B)(C).

[236] *See* Doris R. Perl, Comment, *The Use of Copyright Law to Block the Importation of Gray-Market Goods: The Black and White of It All*, 23 Loy. L.A. L. Rev. 645, 646 (1990).

to undersell those of authorized distributors. On the other hand, consumer advocates point out that the public should be able to purchase cheaper genuine goods and that these goods often do not have a warranty or service dimension at all.

Authorized dealers have attacked the importation of gray market goods under trademark law and, with increasing success, under copyright law.[237] Section 602 of the Copyright Act covers unlawful importation in two situations. Section 602(b) deals with piratical copies — those made abroad without the copyright owner's consent. From a legal standpoint, one can always prevent piratical copies from entering the United States. The issue is one of enforcement.

By contrast, subsection (a) has generated difficult legal issues. It covers situations where the copyright owner has authorized the production of the goods.[238]

On its face, § 602(a), barring unauthorized importation, would appear to clash with the first sale doctrine, which permits the resale of "lawfully made" copies. The issue is whether § 602(a) creates an affirmative right to bar all unauthorized importation, or does § 109(a) limit the reach of § 602(a), thus permitting the resale of at least some "lawfully made" imported copies? Discount sellers and other importers of gray goods have argued that § 602 derives its authority from § 106(3) distribution and is therefore subject to the first sale doctrine limitation of § 109(a) in the resale of goods domestically.

After much conflict in the case law, the Supreme Court, in *Quality King Distributors, Inc. v. L'Anza Research International, Inc.*,[239] confronted the issue of whether goods imported from abroad are subject to the first sale defense. The Court held that where a product is lawfully manufactured in the United States for export and subject to a valid first sale, its subsequent reimportation is permissible under § 109 and thus does not fall within the prohibition of § 602(a). The Court reasoned that § 602(a) does not categorically prohibit the unauthorized importation of copyrighted materials but instead provides that such importation is an infringement of the exclusive right to distribute copies under § 106(3). As such, the importation right is limited by the provisions of §§ 107 through 122, which includes § 109(a), the first sale doctrine. Here, defendant was entitled to the first sale defense because the product labels bought abroad were lawfully made under U.S. law.

Limited to its facts, *Quality King* involved copies that were lawfully manufactured in the United States, exported, and then later imported into the

---

[237] A major drawback to the use of trademark law against the gray market has been U.S. Customs Office refusal to prohibit importation of gray market goods so long as the trademark and goods are legitimate and subject to the common control of the trademark owner. *See K Mart Corp. v. Cartier, Inc.*, 486 U.S. 281 (1988). By contrast, courts have not imposed these limitations in their application of copyright law. *See Parfums Givenchy, Inc. v. Drug Emporium, Inc.*, 38 F.3d 477, 485 (9th Cir. 1994) (finding rationale for the parent-subsidiary exception to the import protection of the Lanham (Trademark) Act inapplicable to copyright law).

[238] 17 U.S.C. § 602(a).

[239] 523 U.S. 135 (1998).

United States by a third party. In fact, the Court makes this distinction, indicating that the importation of goods made outside the United States could perhaps be barred under § 602(a), since such goods would not be "lawfully made under this title" under § 109. In other words, gray market copies manufactured outside the United States might be lawfully made, either by the copyright owner or a licensee, but they would not be lawfully made under Title 17. Rather, they would be lawfully made under the copyright laws of the other country; and the first sale doctrine would therefore not limit the § 602 importation restriction right for such copies.[240] The distinction that the Court makes, based on the place of manufacture, might be somewhat artificial. But it did keep § 602(a) from being completely subsumed by the first sale doctrine, a position more consistent with the congressional intent behind this section of the Act.[241]

In 2013, the Supreme Court in *Kirtsaeng v. John Wiley & Sons, Inc.*,[242] held that the phrase "lawfully made under this title" does not mean copies lawfully made in the *United States* but applies to works made abroad if they have been imported with the authority of the copyright holder. In *Kirtsaeng*, defendant had obtained copies of textbooks manufactured abroad, reselling them in the United States through commercial websites such as eBay. In holding that §602(a)(1) implies no geographical limitation, the Court pointed out that the owners of works manufactured abroad have the power to prohibit resale (or public displays) that would threaten the conventional practices of libraries, museums, and others. It would give manufacturers unexpected powers over a very broad array of imported goods that are copyright-protected or contained in copyrighted works; these powers might include the power of copyright owners to suppress the importation of cars, microwaves, and the like containing copyrighted software.

In a vigorous dissent, Justice Ginsberg declared that the majority opinion was irrelevant and ignores Congressional intent by eviscerating §601(a)(1)'s goal to provide copyright owners the ability to segment different markets through variable pricing. According to the dissent, "the court's parade of horribles . . . is largely imaginary"[243] and that practical realities restrained copyright holders from asserting overreaching claims.[244]

What will the future bring after *Kirtsaeng*? Will consumers benefit from lower priced foreign produced gray goods imported into the United States? It is hardly certain that consumers will so benefit. In reaction to the decision, copyright owners

---

240 *See Omega S.A. v. Costco Wholesale Group*, 541 F.3d 982 (9th Cir. 2008).

241 Other courts have agreed with Quality King. The leading case before Quality King is *Columbia Broadcasting System v. Scorpio Music Distributors, Inc* 569 F. Supp. 47 (E.D. Pa. 1983), *aff'd mem.*, 738 F.2d 424 (3d Cir. 1984). *See also, e.g., Parfums Givenchy, Inc. v. Drug Emporium, Inc.*, 38 F.3d 477 (9th Cir. 1994); *BMG Music v. Perez*, 952 F.2d 318 (9th Cir. 1991); *Hearst Corp. v. Stark*, 639 F. Supp. 970 (N.D. Cal. 1986) (rejecting First Amendment defense for the importation of out-of-print books); *Nintendo of Am., Inc. v. Elcon Indus., Inc.*, 564 F. Supp. 937 (E.D. Mich. 1982) (holding that copyright owners' exclusive licensing agreements with authors did not violate antitrust laws). *But see Cosmair, Inc. v. Dynamite Enters., Inc.*, 226 U.S.P.Q. 344 (S.D. Fla. 1985) (questioning the *Scorpio* decision's reasoning).

242 133 S. Ct. 1351 (2013).

243 Id. at 1374.

244 Id. at 1390.

such as John Wiley may try to sell their products at a single world price or they might try to differentiate their works so that they will be appropriate only for sale in the foreign market. Alternatively, copyright owners may try to use contract law through a series of license agreements to avoid the transfer of title. Ultimately, the Court's decision may encourage copyright owners to distribute their works in intangible form rather than in copies or phonorecords disseminated in encrypted form by Internet streaming. In sum, *Kirtsaeng*, will impose undue costs on copyright owners while disadvantaging both foreign and domestic consumers of copyrighted works.

[E] The Right to Dispose of Copies or Phonorecords of a Restored Work

Pursuant to the Uruguay Round Agreements Act of 1994,[245] copyright is automatically restored in certain foreign works that fell into the public domain for failure to comply with U.S. copyright formalities. These restored copyrights will endure for the remainder of the term of copyright as if they had not fallen into the public domain. Restored copyrights will enjoy the same rights as any other. Once copyright is restored in these works, it is illegal for third parties to make further copies of the work without a license (permission) from the copyright owner.

But what about copies that were made before restoration (*i.e.*, January 1, 1996)? Section 109(a) would allow owners of such copies to sell or otherwise dispose of them without authorization of the owner of the restored copyright. This right to dispose of copies, however, is limited to a twelve-month period beginning on "(1) the date of publication in the Federal Register of the notice of intent filed with the Copyright Office under section 104A(d)(2)(A), or (2) the date of receipt of actual notice served under section 104A(d)(2)(B)."[246]

[F] The Resale Royalty Right (*Droit de Suite*)[247]

The resale royalty right (*droit de suite*) is a European concept, not as yet recognized in United States copyright law.[248]

The "resale royalty right" is the right of an artist to recover a percentage of the resale value from a work of art, and as such, runs counter to the basic policy of the first sale doctrine in U.S. law. Whether to adopt a resale royalty on a national basis remains a subject of continuing debate.[249] Those favoring *droit de suite* maintain

---

[245] Pub. L. No. 103-465, 108 Stat. 4809 (1994).

[246] 17 U.S.C. § 104A(d)(2)(A), (B). Restoration of copyright in certain foreign works is discussed at *supra* §§ 6.18–6.19.

[247] *See generally* John Henry Merryman, Law, Ethics and the Visual Arts 213–28 (2d ed. 1987); Shira Perlmutter, *Resale Royalties for Artists: An Analysis of the Register of Copyrights Report*, 16 Colum.-VLA J.L. & Arts 395 (1992).

[248] The European Union has harmonized the resale right among member countries. *See* Directive 2001/84/EC of the European Parliament and of the Council of 27 September 2001 on the Resale Right for the Benefit of the Author of an Original Work of Art, 2001 O.J. (L 272), pp. 0032–36.

[249] *See* U.S. Copyright Office, Droit de Suite: The Artists Resale Royalty (1992), summarized at 16 Colum.-VLA J.L. & Arts 381 (1992).

that a resale royalty is needed for fine artists who, unlike other authors, create one-of-a-kind works and do not have the opportunity to exploit the work in multiples. One can think of examples where an artist sells a unique work for a pittance and the work is soon sold for many times more. To advocates of the resale royalty right, fairness to artists calls for an equitable sharing of the resale price.[250]

Critics of the resale royalty argue that it is both unfair to buyers and harms artists. The reason is that investment in art is a highly risky endeavor. More often than not, contemporary art works sell at a loss rather than a profit. Even recognized artists can have periods where they produce works that decrease in value. But the resale royalty is a one-way street, and the artist whose work declines in value is not expected to compensate disappointed buyers. Moreover, art works increase in value for many reasons, some of which have little to do with the artist. The resale royalty, however, fails to take into account the value added by other persons and institutions in the art world such as critics, museums, collectors, dealers, and auction houses. Finally, its critics maintain that the resale royalty will hurt the very group it purports to help. In essence the resale royalty operates as a five percent sales tax, and, like any tax, reduces the demand for the product. Thus, many artists may receive no actual benefit because a buyer will negotiate a lower price on the initial sale, anticipating the reduced value of the art object he or she is buying.[251]

Despite the controversial nature of the resale royalty, the State of California has adopted a version of it, but it is the only common law jurisdiction to have done so.[252] Effective January 1, 1977, the California Act covers fine art only, defined as "an original painting, sculpture, drawing or an original work of art in glass." Whenever a work of fine art is either sold by a California resident or sold in California, the seller must pay the artist a five percent royalty on a sale of $1,000 or more. The Act does not apply to sales of less than $1,000, those made 20 years after the artist's death, or to certain resales by an art dealer to a purchaser within 10 years of the initial sale.

The California Act has also been criticized as benefiting too few artists and hurting the California art market.[253] Moreover, because the Resale Royalty Act applies only to sales transacted in California or by California residents, buyers simply avoid the California art market. As a result, unless a uniform national act is passed, the California art market may well suffer.

Some critics call for a uniform national act because conflicts would arise if another state passed a Resale Royalty Act. For example, if New York passed a similar statute and a California resident sold a painting in New York, would two resale royalties be imposed on the seller? In addition, the California Act may

---

[250] *See generally* Monroe E. Price, *Government Policy and Economic Security for Artists: The Case of the* Droit de Suite, 77 Yale L.J. 1333 (1968).

[251] For a summary of the arguments, pro and con, see Marshall Leaffer, *Of Moral Rights and Resale Royalties: The Kennedy Bill*, 7 Cardozo L. & Ent. J. 234 (1991), and John Henry Merryman, *The Wrath of Robert Rauschenberg*, 40 J. Copyright Soc'y 241 (1993).

[252] The California Resale Royalties Act, Cal. Civ. Code § 986 (1977) (amended 1983).

[253] For a general critique, see Stephen Weil, *Resale Royalties: Nobody Benefits*, ArtNews.

violate the dormant Commerce Clause because it attempts to regulate transactions taking place wholly outside the state. The statute does so by requiring a royalty payment so long as the piece's seller is a California resident, regardless of where the transaction takes place, and even if the auction house, the artist, and the buyer are not based in California.[254] Because of this type of conflict, some have proposed national uniform legislation as a solution.[255] Finally, whether the California Act is preempted by the federal Copyright Act remains an open question, despite a pre-1976 Act case, *Morseburg v. Balyon*,[256] which found no preemptive effect under the 1909 Act.[257]

[G] The Public Lending Right[258]

The public lending right is another example of a European pro-author entitlement which would contradict the first sale doctrine if adopted in the United States. Such a right entitles an author of a book to royalties any time a book is borrowed from a public library. The rationale is that the authors should be able to benefit from organized borrowing of their books from libraries, much as a musical copyright owner can capture the performance right in a work. Like the resale royalty right and the Record Rental Amendment, it would be an exemption to the § 109(a) first sale doctrine, in which a copyright owner's right over physical copies of the work is exhausted on their sale. Contrary to this fundamental doctrine in American law, the public lending right has never been close to adoption in the United States.[259]

The public lending right is found in a number of countries and the concept appears to be slowly gathering support in the United States.

The United Kingdom's Public Lending Right Act of 1979 illustrates how the public lending right works. The Act applies to books only, not phonorecords or video cassettes, and only to British citizens or nationals of the European community whose homes are in the United Kingdom. For an author to benefit, her book must be at least thirty-two pages, and it must be registered with the Register of Public Lending Right. Thereafter, the author is entitled to a modest statutory royalty based on samples conducted to determine how often the book has been checked out. The right is transferable and endures for the term of copyright.

---

[254] Estate of Graham v. Sotheby's, Inc., 860 F. Supp. 2d 1117 (C.D. Cal. 2013).

[255] *See e.g.* H.R. 4103: American Royalties Too Act of 2014, 113th Cong. 2d Sess. (Feb. 26 2014).

[256] 621 F.2d 972 (9th Cir. 1980).

[257] For a discussion of preemption and how it relates to the Resale Royalty Act, see *infra* § 11.08[D].

[258] *See generally* William Cornish & David Llewelyn, Intellectual Property: Patents, Copyright, Trademarks and Allied Rights 526–29 (2003); Ernest Seemann, *A Look at the Public Lending Right*, 30 Copyright L. Symp. (ASCAP) 71 (1983).

[259] *See* 17 U.S.C. § 109(a). For a discussion of the first sale doctrine, see *supra* § 8.14.

Part IV. THE PERFORMANCE AND DISPLAY RIGHTS AND THEIR LIMITATIONS

§ 8.17 THE PERFORMANCE RIGHT: GENERALLY

Section 106(4) of the Copyright Act provides that the owner of the copyright in "literary, musical, dramatic, and choreographic works, pantomimes . . . and other . . . audiovisual works" has the exclusive right "to perform the copyrighted work publicly."

Not all categories of copyrightable subject matter under § 102 enjoy a performance right. Pictorial, graphic, and sculptural works are excluded, as are sound recordings. As defined in § 101, "[t]o 'perform' a work means to recite, render, play, dance, or act it, either directly or by means of any device or process."

So defined, a performance includes not only the initial rendition but any further act by which that rendition is transmitted to the public.[260] Thus, one performs by reciting a poem, singing a song, playing a cassette on a VCR, or simply turning on a radio. Likewise, a broadcaster performs whenever he transmits a live performance or one captured on a phonorecord. Modern technologies have provided endless opportunities to perform copyrighted works. Because of an infinite number of situations where performances take place, the right to perform can be the most valuable exclusive right for the copyright owner.[261]

There are substantial limitations, however, on the performance right. First, the copyright owner can control only *public* performances of his work. Second, the 1976 Act specifically limits the performance right in §§ 107–122 through an elaborate set of exemptions and compulsory licenses.

§ 8.18 WHAT IS A PUBLIC PERFORMANCE OR DISPLAY?

[A] Generally

The exclusive right to perform is limited to public performances. Clearly, the 1976 Copyright Act was not designed to keep people from singing in their bathtubs or playing their favorite records during dinner in their homes. These are essentially private performances that cannot be controlled by copyright owners. What distinguishes a public from a private performance is set forth in two clauses of § 101

Under the first clause, "publicly" means:

> (1) to perform . . . it at a place open to the public or at any place where a substantial number of persons outside of a normal circle of a family and its social acquaintances is gathered; or

---

[260] *See* H.R. Rep. No. 94-1476, at 63 (1976).

[261] For the view that the performance right imposes a multiplicity of claims on the public and significant costs on society, see Sara Stadler, *Performances Values*, 83 Notre Dame L. Rev. 697 (2008).

> (2) to transmit or otherwise communicate a performance . . . of the work to a place specified by clause (1) or to the public, by means of any device or process, whether the members of the public capable of receiving the performance . . . receive it in the same place or in separate places and at the same time or at different times.[262]

A public performance is one that takes place in a public setting or before a public group. Thus, one can rent a movie and show it in one's house to neighbors and friends without infringing the performance right. Showing the film is "performing" it, but the performance is a private, not a public, one. Alternately, if the movie were shown in a semipublic place such as a club, factory, or summer camp, rather than at home, a public, and therefore infringing (if performed without a license), performance would occur.[263]

Under the second clause, a public performance takes place when a work is transmitted. As defined in the Act, a work is transmitted when it is communicated by a "process whereby images or sounds are received beyond the place from which they are sent."[264] This clause allows the copyright owner to control transmission of the work, such as by radio or television, even though the recipients are not gathered in a single place or do not receive it at the same time. The same principles apply for transmissions to limited segments of the public, such as occupants of hotel rooms or subscribers to a cable television service.[265]

[B] Performances in Places Open to the Public

The various aspects of what constitutes a "public" performance are nicely illustrated in *Columbia Pictures Industries, Inc. v. Redd Horne, Inc.*[266] In *Redd Horne*, defendant operators of video-cassette stores provided television sets in private screening rooms where up to four people could rent and watch a movie of their choice. While the viewers were in the room, the movie was transmitted from a central location in the store. The videocassettes were clearly being "performed," but was the performance "public"? In finding there was a public performance, the court read the definition of "public" in the statute disjunctively, holding that if a place is public, the size and composition of the audience is irrelevant. Alternatively, if a place is not public, the size and composition of the audience will be determinative.[267] Here, the performance was public because the place where the showing took place was open to the public, even though the actual viewing audience was restricted to a small group of family or social acquaintances. Because the performance was public under this part of the definition, the court found it unnecessary to examine the second part — the size and composition of the audience.[268] Moreover, the performances were also public under subsection (2)

---

[262] 17 U.S.C. § 101.

[263] *See* H.R. Rep. No. 94-1476, at 64 (1976).

[264] 17 U.S.C. § 101.

[265] *See* H.R. Rep. No. 94-1476, at 64–65 (1976).

[266] 749 F.2d 154 (3d Cir. 1984).

[267] *Redd Horne*, 749 F.2d at 158.

[268] As for the size and composition of the audience, the court suggested that it was public in nature,

because they were transmitted, and it made no difference that the recipients were not located in the same place or watching at the same time.[269]

[C] The Size and Composition of a Public Audience

As indicated in *Redd Horne*, when a performance is not open to the public, the court must then analyze the size and composition of the audience to determine whether a performance is public. In the language of the statute, a performance is public, "[a]t any place where a *substantial* number of persons outside of a normal circle of a family and its social acquaintances is gathered."[270]

But how many persons constitute a "substantial" number? The House Report provides little help on this question, except to specify that performances at routine meetings of businesses and governmental personnel do not represent the gathering of a substantial number of persons.[271] A group of 20 persons at a private party or wedding reception would probably not be substantial enough to render a performance public. But what about a gathering of 200 persons? There is no definite point between twenty and 200 at which to draw the line. In general, the larger and more diverse the gathering, the more likely a performance will be deemed public by a court.[272]

[D] Transmission of a Work to the Public

[1] Early Interpretations Under the 1976 Act

Under the Copyright Act, a public performance occurs in a transmission of a work to the public "whether the members of the public . . . receive it in the same place or in separate places and the same time or at different times."[273] According to the 1967 House Report,

> This language makes doubly clear that] a performance made available by transmission to the public at large is "public" even though the recipients are not gathered in a single place, and even if there is no direct proof that any of the potential recipients was operating his receiving apparatus at the time of the transmission. The same principles apply whenever the potential recipients of the transmission represent a limited segment of the public, such as the occupants of hotel rooms . . . .; they are also applicable where the transmission is capable of reaching different recipients at different

---

because the showcasing operation was really no different from an exhibition of a film at a conventional theater. *Id.* at 159.

[269] *Id.*; *see also Columbia Pictures Indus., Inc. v. Aveco, Inc.*, 612 F. Supp. 315 (N.D. Pa. 1985), *aff'd*, 800 F.2d 59 (3d Cir. 1986). The court affirmed the reasoning in *Redd Horne* on similar facts, where customers were given tapes to play for themselves in screening rooms with a twenty-person capacity.

[270] 17 U.S.C. § 101 (emphasis added).

[271] H.R. Rep. No. 94-1476, at 64 (1976).

[272] *See* David E. Shipley, *Copyright Law and Your Neighborhood Bar and Grill: Recent Developments in Performances and the Section 110(5) Exemption*, 29 Ariz. L. Rev. 475, 499 (1987).

[273] 17 U.S.C. § 101

times, as in the case of sounds or images stored in an information system and capable of being performed or displayed at the initiative of individual members of the public.[274]

One can characterize a viewing room in a video store as a public place, but can the same be said for individual rooms in a hotel? For example, suppose a hotel equips each room with a radio, television, or video player. Are public performances taking place each time someone plays these machines? This situation is distinguishable from *Redd Horne*, since hotel rooms are living quarters and not rented for the sole purpose of watching movies. They are more akin to renting a movie in the privacy of one's home. The House Report specifically exempts these performances from control by the copyright owner.[275] Thus, so long as the recipients constitute a normal circle of family and social acquaintances, a public performance does not take place. One case affirmed the House Report, holding that a hotel is not publicly performing works when it merely installs a videodisc player in each private room.[276]

On the other hand, what if a hotel equips their guest rooms with a centrally located console containing DVDs, enabling guests to view the motion picture whenever they like by selecting the movie on their television screens? Consistent with *Redd Horne*,[277] a strong argument could be made that public performance has been infringed whether or not the transmission took place into only one room at a time.[278] The definition of "perform a work publicly" in the Copyright Act would cover these multiple, sequential performances of a single copy of a motion picture to different members of the public even though they may be to individual rooms in the same hotel. Here, the guests are "members of the public" whose relationship with the hotel and its movie transmission system is essentially commercial regardless of where the viewing place is located.

[2] Performances by Transmission and Emerging Digital Technologies: *ABC, Inc. v. Aereo, Inc.*

From transmissions by hotels and other institutions, as illustrated in *Redd Horne* and the hotel cases, methods of disseminating content has seen a revolution with the explosion of interactive and cloud computing services. The new technologies have played havoc with traditional notions of copyright law and have disrupted entrenched business models for conveying information. The problem is as always to strike the proper balance between the rights of copyright owners, users, and disseminators without suppressing the development of new technologies. This task not easily accomplished. The questions is: When an individual copy of a work is transmitted to a viewer's computer or iPhone, does a public performance occur? Should the potential audience be considered in determining whether the transmis-

---

[274] H.R. REP. NO. 83, 90th Cong., 1st Sess. 29 (1967)

[275] H.R. REP. NO. 94-1476, at 91-2 (1976).

[276] *See Columbia Pictures Indus., Inc. v. Prof'l Real Estate Investors, Inc.*, 866 F.2d 278 (9th Cir. 1989).

[277] *Redd Horne*, 749 F.2d 154 at 157.

[278] See *On Command Video Corp. v. Columbia Pictures Indus.*, 777 F. Supp. 787 (N.D. Cal. 1991).

sion is public or private, and if the potential audience is only one subscriber, is it a private performance?

In *American Broadcasting Companies, Inc. v. Aereo, Inc.*,[279] the Supreme Court examined these questions in the context of a service that captured television signals, digitized them, and transmitted them individually to its subscribers. The Aereo system assigned to each user a miniature antenna that was used to create a personal copy of the selected program. When selected for viewing on a TV, computer, or mobile device, the copy of the program could not be viewed by any other Aereo user. Television producers, broadcasters, and other copyright owners sought a preliminary injunction arguing that Aereo was infringing the right to perform their works publicly by transmitting their works to the public. Aereo had argued successfully in the Second Circuit that the subscriber to the system controlled the antenna.[280] Accordingly, Aereo maintained that it had engaged in no volitional acts would sustain the broadcasters' direct copyright infringement.[281]

In rejecting Aereo's position, the Supreme Court pointed out that Aereo is not simply an equipment provider but performs and transmits a work in a way substantially similar to those of cable TV companies who publicly perform, and must have broadcasters' prior consent for use of, their programming. The Court emphasized the statutory history reflected in the 1976 Act to conclude that Aereo performed the copyrighted work.

> Congress enacted new language that erased the Court's line between broadcaster and viewer, in respect to "perform[ing]" a work. The amended statute clarifies that to "perform" an audiovisual work means "to show its images in any sequence or to make the sounds accompanying it audible." § 101. Under this new language, *both* the broadcaster *and* the viewer of a television program "perform," because they both show the program's images and make audible the program's sounds. See H.R. Rep., at 63 ("[A] broadcasting network is performing when it transmits [a singer's performance of a song] . . . and any individual is performing whenever he or she . . . communicates the performance by turning on a receiving set").[282]

After finding that Aereo "performed," the Court turned to the issue of whether Aereo "publicly" preformed. The Court rejected Aereo's logic that each subscriber's transmission was a distinct performance that went to only one subscriber and not to the public. The Court concluded that the transmission clause expressly states that a public performance can be received by members of the public at different

---

[279] 134 S. Ct. 2498 (2014).

[280] *See WNET v. Aereo, Inc.*, 712 F.3d 676 (2d Cir. 2013).

[281] The Second Circuit felt bound by its previous decision in *Cartoon Network LP, LLP v. Cablevision Systems Corp.*, 536 F.3d 121 (2d Cir. 2008), where a cable television provider's "remote storage" DVR system allowed customers to make copies of TV programs and store them on hard drives at Cablevision's premises for later viewing. The Court of Appeals for the Second Circuit rejected plaintiff's argument that the transmission constituted a public performance, reasoning that because members of the public capable of receiving the performance were limited to one customer's household, each transmission should be treated as a separate private performance.

[282] Am. Broad. Companies, Inc. v. Aereo, Inc., 134 S. Ct. 2498, 2506 (2014).

times.[283] In effect the *Aereo* decision confirms that "transmissions" and "performance" under the Copyright Act are separate and distinct. The decision stands for the principal that there should no distinction between individual versus common source of the work being transmitted. To do so would eliminate all asynchronous transmissions irrespective of their origin and would exclude every instance of on-demand performances, a result at odds with congressional intent and the copyright owner's vital economic interests.

Are other emerging technologies threatened by *Aereo*? One might conclude that cloud computing is endangered because providers are infringing when any two users shared and played a song. To avoid liability because of its customers' actions, the cloud computing company would have to monitor the content of all its customers, a costly task that could result in undermining the development of this burgeoning industry. It is hard to predict what affect the *Aereo* decision will have other technologies such as cloud computing. The Court emphasized that its opinion should be limited to entities that communicate contemporaneously perceptible images and sounds of a work, but should not be extended to " '[q]uestions involving cloud computing, [remote storage] DVRs and other novel issues not before the court.' "[284] Despite these disclaimers, the impact of the *Aereo* decision and how it will be applied in other contexts is hard to predict. *Aereo* will no doubt have unforeseen ramifications as digital technologies continue their relentless growth.

§ 8.19 NONPROFIT AND OTHER EXEMPTIONS TO THE PERFORMANCE RIGHT, § 110

[A] Generally

Under the 1909 Act, the copyright owner of a musical or nondramatic literary work could only control public for-profit performances of his work.[285] The rationale for encouraging nonprofit performances was to allow easy access to musical and nondramatic literary works, promoting their performance by nonprofit entities such as schools and churches. The 1976 Act rejected the for-profit requirement. The House Report explains that this limitation was dropped because the line between profit and nonprofit organizations became too difficult to draw.[286] In addition, many nonprofit organizations are financially able to pay copyright royalties. The 1976 Act has not completely abandoned the nonprofit exception to the performance right. Rather, it contains a specific set of exceptions to the public

---

283 *Id.* at 2510.

284 *Id.* at 2511 (*quoting Sony Corp. of America v. Universal City Studios, Inc.*, 464 U.S. 417, 431 (1984)).

285 *See* 17 U.S.C. § 1(c), (e) (1909 Act). For an examination of the "for-profit" restrictions on rights enclosed in the 1909 Act, see Lydia Pallas Loren, *The Evolving Role of "For Profit" Use in Copyright Law: Lessons from the 1909 Act*, 26 Santa Clara Computer & High Tech. L.J. 255 (2010).

286 H.R. Rep. No. 94-1476, at 63 (1976). Under 1909 Act case law, the term "for-profit" was broadly construed. For example, in *Associated Music Publishers, Inc. v. Debs Mem'l Radio Fund, Inc.*, 141 F.2d 852 (2d Cir. 1944), a nonprofit radio station was held to be performing for-profit because it paid for one-third of its air time by accepting commercial advertising, even though it played plaintiff's song on the noncommercial portion of its program.

performance right. Many of these provisions are based on the nonprofit nature of the performance. In short, the 1976 Act accomplishes by specific exemption what the 1909 Act did through its broad nonprofit exception.

Section 110 is the vehicle by which certain nonprofit performances are exempted. The following sections summarize their key features.

[B] Face to Face Teaching, § 110(1)

Section 110(1)[287] exempts performances of copyrighted works given by instructors or pupils in face-to-face, live teaching situations. All varieties of copyrightable subject matter are included under this exemption, unless the person responsible for the performance had reason to know that the copy used was made illegally. The educational institution must be nonprofit,[288] and the performance must occur in a place devoted to teaching.[289]

This exception, for instance, would allow a high school teacher to have the school band play music from Lerner and Loewe's *My Fair Lady* in a classroom before a music appreciation class without obtaining the consent of the copyright owner. This is a typical situation where the exemption applies to an in-class performance in a classroom limited to members of the class. On the other hand, the high school band could not, under this exemption, play the same music in a concert for the entertainment of parents. The latter performance may be exempt under another clause of § 110,[290] but not under § 110(1), which applies to face-to-face teaching situations only.

[C] Transmissions of Instructional Activities, § 110(2)

Section 110(1) exempts the use of copyrighted materials in traditional face-to-face teaching situations. In today's teaching environment, however, an ever greater amount of instruction takes place through distance learning by means of a transmission. With this in mind, Congress added § 110(2) to accommodate the need for exempted performances and displays in distance-learning situations. As originally enacted, § 110(2) was limited in scope. It exempted performances and displays of nondramatic literary or musical works in a transmission if three conditions were met. First, the transmission had to be a regular part of the systematic instructional activities of a governmental body or nonprofit educational institution. Second, the performance and display had to be "directly related and of material assistance to the teaching content of the transmission." Third, the transmitted performance had to be made primarily for reception in classrooms or similar places normally devoted to instruction. This third limitation was not wide enough to encompass certain forms of distance education — a phenomenon of rapid

---

[287] 17 U.S.C. § 110(1).

[288] This would exclude profit-making institutions such as dance studios and language schools. *See* H.R. Rep. No. 94-1476, at 82 (1976).

[289] The performance must be confined to an audience made up of members of the class. Excluded from the scope of § 110(1) would be, for example, a play or concert given by students before the entire student body. *See id.*

[290] *See* 17 U.S.C. § 110(4).

increase in the late nineties where individual students sitting at computer terminals were instructed in the privacy of their homes. In addition, § 110(2) did not exempt the acts of reproduction and public distribution that inevitably occur when works are transmitted over digital networks.

The limited nature of the original § 110(2) led to calls for amendment by the teaching industries. The result was a compromise piece of legislation, the TEACH Act,[291] as it is popularly called, which broadened § 110(2) significantly by permitting performances and displays of copyrighted works in digital "distance learning" on the Internet.[292] Section 110(2)(A) requires that the performance or display be "made by, at the direction of, or under the actual supervision of an instructor as an integral part of a class session offered as a regular part of the systematic mediated instructional activities of a governmental body or an accredited nonprofit educational institution."[293]

The amended § 110(2) extends the exemption beyond nondramatic literary and musical works to the full range of copyrighted works for "reasonable and limited performances and displays." Instructional activities exempted in § 110(2) now include digital as well as analog transmissions. This subsection also recognizes a limited right to reproduce and distribute transient copies created as part of the automated process of digital transmissions. In this regard, the TEACH Act amended § 112,[294] permitting institutions to upload copyrighted works onto servers for later transmission to students consistent with § 110. It thus enables asynchronous Internet-based distance education. It also allows the conversion of print or other analog versions of works into digital format if no digital version of the work is available, or if the available digital version contains technological protections preventing its use.[295]

For digital transmission, § 110(2) imposes two requirements on the institution or transmitting body: (1) apply technological measures that "reasonably prevent" the recipients' retention of the work in accessible form for longer than the class

---

[291] Pub. L. 107-273, 13301, 116 Stat. 1910 (2002). For an overview and background of the TEACH Act, see Laura N. Gasaway, *Impasse: Distance Learning and Copyright*, 62 OHIO ST. L.J. 195 (2001).

[292] The issue of updating § 110(2) for the digital age was hotly (and inconclusively) debated in the months leading up to the final enactment of the Digital Millennium Copyright Act ("DMCA"). In the end, Congress settled on the time-honored option of commissioning a study and, in § 403 of the DMCA, directed the Copyright Office to investigate and report in six months' time. *See* U.S. COPYRIGHT OFFICE, REPORT ON COPYRIGHT AND DIGITAL DISTANCE EDUCATION (1999), *available at* www.copyright.gov/reports/de_rprt.pdf. Eventually, Congress adopted some of the Copyright Office's suggestions and rejected others. Some three years after the Report was issued, President Bush on November 2, 2002, signed the Technology, Education and Copyright Harmonization Act ("TEACH Act").

[293] 17 U.S.C. § 110(2). The term "mediated instructional activities" refers to activities that use a work as an integral part of the classroom experience, controlled by the instructor and analogous to the type of performance or display that would take place in a live class session. For an explanation of "mediated activities," see H.R. REP. NO. 107-687, at 10 (2002). ("The term does not refer to activities that use . . . such works as textbooks, course packs, or other material . . . which are typically purchased or acquired by the students in higher education for their independent use and retention or are typically purchased or acquired for elementary or secondary students for their possession and independent use.").

[294] *See* 17 U.S.C. § 112(f)(2).

[295] *Id.*

session[296] and prevent further unauthorized distribution by the recipient to others;[297] and (2) do not engage in conduct that would interfere with technological measures used by the copyright owner to prevent retention or unauthorized further dissemination.[298] It is not clear, however, what degree of technological rigor distance-learning institutions must employ. It would appear that reasonable measures under the circumstances should be the standard.

The § 110(2) exemption is limited to performances and displays of lawfully acquired copies of the work. Participants in authorized distance education transmissions are protected against liability for infringement based on the transient or temporary reproductions that may occur as part of the transmissions. Finally, § 110(2) requires the Undersecretary of Commerce for Intellectual Property, after consulting with the Copyright Office, to submit a report on technological protections for digitized copyrighted works.

[D] Religious Services, § 110(3)

Section 110(3)[299] exempts the performance of nondramatic literary or musical works of any nature, and dramatic-musical works of a religious nature, "in the course of services at a place of worship or other religious assembly." The purpose of the exemption for dramatic-musical works of a religious nature was "to exempt certain performances of sacred music, dramatic in nature, such as oratorios, cantatas, musical settings of a mass, choral services and the like."[300] This exemption, however, does not cover performances of works such as secular operas or motion pictures even though they have an underlying religious theme and are performed during religious services.[301]

The religious services exemption imposes two conditions. First, the performance must take place "in the course of services." This would exclude performances that are for social, educational, fundraising, or entertainment purposes even though they occur in a place of worship. Second, performances must occur at "a place of worship or other religious assembly," which would include such locations as auditoriums, outdoor theatres, and the like. The House specifies that performances originating in a place of worship that are *transmitted* to homes or listeners will not qualify for the exemption. Thus, the exemption would not extend to religious broadcasts to the public at large. In addition, one court has held that the religious services exemption does not apply if the services are also broadcast on the radio.[302]

[296] 17 U.S.C. § 110(2)(D)(ii)(I)(aa).

[297] 17 U.S.C. § 110(2)(D)(ii)(I)(bb).

[298] 17 U.S.C. § 110(2)(D)(II).

[299] 17 U.S.C. § 110(3).

[300] H.R. Rep. No. 94-1476, at 84 (1976).

[301] *See id.*

[302] *Id.* at 84–85. *See Simpleville Music v. Mizell*, 451 F. Supp. 2d 1293 (M.D. Ala. 2006).

[E] Exemption for Certain Non Profit Performances, § 110(4)[303]

Section 110(4) contains a general exception to the performance right that covers some of the same provisions as the for-profit limitation of the 1909 Act. This exemption excludes transmissions and is limited to performances given directly by live performers, the playing of phonorecords, or by a receiving apparatus.[304]

The performance must be given without any purpose of direct or indirect commercial advantage. To construe this provision, the House Report indicates that one must look to the case law under the 1909 Act.[305] This case law reveals that a public performance associated with a profit-making activity was a for-profit performance even if no admission was charged. In the leading case of *Herbert v. Shanley Co.*,[306] the Supreme Court held that an orchestra's performance of music for the clientele of a restaurant was a for-profit performance even though the customers were not asked to pay a music charge. The Court's rationale was that the restaurant was profiting from the performance because the music provided an attractive environment for its clientele. They were paying not just for a meal but for an entire service that was reflected in the price of the check. By incorporating 1909 Act case law, § 110(4) will not apply to performances that are connected with the profit-making aspect of an enterprise.[307]

In addition to prohibiting direct or indirect commercial advantage, § 110(4) precludes payment of any fee or compensation to performers, promoters, or organizers for the performance in question. The exemption is lost only if the above persons are paid for the performance. It is not affected if the performers receive a salary for duties encompassing the performance.[308] For example, a performance by a school orchestra conducted by a music teacher who is paid an annual salary is exempt, but a performance by that same school orchestra conducted by a bandleader hired for the one performance is not.

Even if all of the above conditions are met, the § 110(4) exemption will not apply if there is a direct or indirect admission charge.[309] Admission may be charged, however, if the proceeds, after deducting reasonable production costs, are used exclusively for an educational, religious, or charitable purpose.[310] For performances charging an admission, this section provides the copyright owner with a veto power over the performance if notice is served under the terms of § 110(4)(B).

---

[303] 17 U.S.C. § 110(4).

[304] *See* H.R. Rep. No. 94-1476, at 85 (1976).

[305] *Id.*

[306] 242 U.S. 591 (1917). *See also Associated Music Publishers, Inc. v. Debs Mem'l Radio Fund, Inc.*, 141 F.2d 852 (2d Cir. 1944).

[307] *See MCA, Inc. v. Parks*, 796 F.2d 200, 204 (6th Cir. 1986); *Quackenbush Music, Ltd. v. Wood*, 381 F. Supp. 904, (M.D. Tenn. 1974).

[308] *See* H.R. Rep. No. 94-1476, at 85 (1976).

[309] 17 U.S.C. § 110(4)(A).

[310] 17 U.S.C. § 110(4)(B).

To illustrate, assume that a high school orchestra plans to hold a concert using tunes by the Beatles and charges a $5.00 admission, and that the proceeds after deducting costs will be used for educational purposes. Section 110(4) gives the copyright owner the right to decide the conditions under which the work is performed, if at all. The copyright owner must serve written notice at least seven days before the date of the performance stating the reasons for this objection to the admission charge.[311] According to the House Report, the veto power was given to copyright owners so they would not be compelled to make involuntary donations to fundraising activities for causes to which they are opposed.[312]

This veto power given to the copyright owner raises some perplexing questions.[313] First, the 1976 Act does not explicitly impose an affirmative duty on the user to inform the copyright owner of the forthcoming performance so that he can serve notice within the seven-day limit. Should there be a duty to notify? One might argue that the 1976 Act implies that at least a reasonable attempt is required to notify the copyright owner about the performance. This would be consistent with the purpose of the provision, which is to prevent authors from being identified with causes which they do not support. Second, assuming that the copyright owner finds out about the performance and notice of objection is duly filed,[314] the copyright owner must state a reason for objecting to the performance. Would *any* reason suffice? It would appear so. But if any reason may be given, the requirement to provide a reason is rendered meaningless.

[F] Incidental Public Reception and the Multiple Performance Doctrine, § 110(5)

[1] From the 1909 Act to the Fairness in Music Licensing Act of 1998

Section 110(5), known as the "*Aiken* Exemption," and § 111, the compulsory license for cable television, respond to a long-standing controversy about how to treat secondary transmissions (rebroadcasts) of copyrighted works under the 1909 Act. The possibilities of rebroadcasting a copyrighted work can take place in an endless number of settings, ranging from the local barbershop that plays the radio for its clientele, to the cable system that picks up a primary signal and retransmits it to millions of persons. Both are secondary transmitters engaging in a rebroadcast of a primary broadcast. The basic question is whether a rebroadcast of the primary transmission is a public performance. If so, should a copyright owner be entitled to enforce the performance right for every rebroadcast of a work, or should the right be limited to the first transmission in some other way?

This question has been resolved in the elaborate and convoluted compulsory licensing systems of § 111 (cable systems) and § 119 (satellite retransmission).

---

311 *See* 17 U.S.C. § 110(4)(B)(ii).

312 H.R. Rep. No. 94-1976, at 86 (1976).

313 *See* Nimmer on Copyright § 8.15[E](5)(b) (2014).

314 Notice must comply with the formalities set forth in Copyright Office regulations. 17 U.S.C. § 110(4)(B)(iii).

These statutory regimes reflect political compromises that industry groups mediated though the legislative process. In addition to these industry groups, the issue has created much tension between retransmitters of broadcasts, such as small business establishments, and the performing rights societies, such as ASCAP, BMI, and SESAC. The following discussion traces the history of this aspect of the multiple-performance doctrine, from its 1909 Act background, to the original § 110(5) (the *Aiken* exemption) and its vague contours, and finally to the amended § 110(C) that widens the exemption for the incidental reception of copyrighted works over the public airwaves.

[2] The Multiple Performance Doctrine: The 1909 Act Background

Under the 1909 Act, the case law developed incoherently in its approach to secondary transmissions. In *Buck v. Jewell-LaSalle Realty Co.*,[315] the Supreme Court held that a hotel equipped with a master radio was performing when it simultaneously rebroadcast music from a local radio station into private hotel rooms. Plaintiff was the owner of a copyrighted song broadcast repeatedly by a local radio station without authorization from the copyright owner. Suit was brought against the radio station and the hotel for the rebroadcast. The Court established the multiple performance doctrine, whereby a single rendition of a work can be performed more than once as it is retransmitted from a receiving apparatus.[316]

The issue of secondary transmissions arose again in the 1960s with the development of cable television systems. Despite the *Jewell-LaSalle* multiple-performance doctrine, the Supreme Court in two cases refused to hold that cable systems were performing by retransmitting television signals.[317] First came *Fortnightly Corp. v. United Artists Television, Inc.*,[318] in which the Court reasoned that the cable system was not a broadcaster (*i.e.*, performer) but rather like a viewer because it did no more than enhance the viewer's capacity to receive the original broadcaster's signals. The Court viewed *Jewell-LaSalle* as antiquated authority and limited it to its specific facts, that is, where the original broadcast was unauthorized by the copyright owner. Several years later, the issue arose again in *Teleprompter Corp. v. Columbia Broadcasting System, Inc.*[319] In this case, the cable system was bringing in distant signals otherwise not available to viewers in the service area. Ignoring *Jewell-LaSalle* completely, the Court again found that cable television served essentially a viewer function, regardless of the distance

[315] 283 U.S. 191 (1931).

[316] The Court also found a public performance, making the analogy to cases where an orchestra plays live music in a restaurant for the entertainment of its clientele. *Buck*, 283 U.S. at 201.

[317] Cable television systems receive the signals of television broadcasting stations, amplify them, and then transmit these signals by cable or microwave and ultimately send the signals by wire to their paying customers. Once commonly referred to as "CATV" (community antenna television), cable television was originally used to facilitate transmission of television signals to areas with hilly terrain or cities where normal, direct reception was inadequate. Since these early days, cable systems have greatly expanded their operations and now originate programming as well as retransmit the programs of other creators. *See United States v. Sw. Cable Co.*, 392 U.S. 157 (1968).

[318] 392 U.S. 390 (1968).

[319] 415 U.S. 394 (1974).

between the broadcaster and the viewer.[320]

In 1975, one year after *Teleprompter*, the Supreme Court decided *Twentieth Century Music Corp. v. Aiken*,[321] which extended the reasoning of the cable television decisions to a fact situation much like *Jewell-LaSalle*. Defendant owned and operated a small fast-food shop (640 square feet) where he installed a radio and four small ceiling speakers that were played during business hours to entertain customers and employees. Plaintiff brought suit against Aiken, claiming infringement of the performance right for playing the copyright owner's music without a license. The Supreme Court held that, like the cable television systems, Aiken was not a broadcaster/performer, but fell into the category of viewer/listener. Although *Jewell-LaSalle* was not explicitly overruled, it was limited to its specific facts. The Court maintained that to hold Aiken liable would result in a regime of copyright that would be both unenforceable and inequitable. It would be unenforceable from a practical standpoint because of the infinite number of performances in cafes, bars, beauty shops, and like places. It would be inequitable for two reasons: first, Aiken would have no sure way of protecting himself against infringement except by keeping the radio off; second, it would be inequitable because

> to hold that all in Aiken's position "performed" . . . would be to authorize the sale of an untold number of licenses for what is basically a single public rendition of a copyrighted work. The exaction of such multiple tribute would go far beyond what is required for the economic protection of copyright owners. . . .[322]

This dual rationale is the basis behind the *Aiken* exemption in section 110(5) of the 1976 Act.

[3] Incidental Public Reception under the 1976 Act as Originally Passed, § 110(5)

The 1976 Act completely overturned the Supreme Court's narrow construction of "performance" as found in *Aiken* and the cable television cases. Instead, the Act broadly defines the term "perform," returning to the traditional interpretation of *Jewell-LaSalle*, in which any further transmission of a copyrighted work is considered to be a performance. Thus, under this definition, the playing of a radio or television before a public group is a public performance and an infringing one, if done without consent of the copyright owner. The 1976 Act, however, did not turn all bars, beauty parlors, and cafes into infringers of copyright whenever they play a radio or television for their customers. These *de minimis* performances are exempted in section 110(5),[323] known as the "*Aiken* exemption,"[324] which provided:

---

320 *Teleprompter*, 415 U.S. at 408.

321 422 U.S. 151 (1975).

322 *Aiken*, 422 U.S. at 162–63.

323 Many, though not all, of the clauses discussed in § 110 are the counterparts of the 1909 Act's for-profit limitation. Section 110(5) is a notable departure from the nonprofit origin of this section.

324 Cable television systems are also performing under the Act but are now subjected to a complicated compulsory licensing provision in § 111. *See infra* § 8.19[D].

communication of a transmission embodying a performance or display of a work by the public reception of the transmission on a single receiving apparatus of a kind commonly used in private homes [is not an infringement of copyright], unless —

(A) a direct charge is made to see or hear the transmission; or

(B) the transmission thus received is further transmitted to the public.

Section 110(5), as originally enacted, exempted from copyright liability works performed by the use of standard radio and television sets in small commercial establishments when the works were played for the enjoyment of customers. The rationale behind this exemption was that retransmitted public performances of this type are a *de minimis* invasion of the copyright owner's interest. Accordingly, such establishments should not be forced to obtain a license from the copyright owner. The exemption was intended to be a limited one; it applied to transmissions only, excluding performances of recorded music or a videotape in a small commercial establishment. Thus, the local bar that played a record on the phonograph or a videotape of a movie on the television is not covered by the exemption. Moreover, there could be no admission charge to listen to the performance. Finally, the performance could not be further transmitted to the public.

The exemption was further limited by the fact situation in the *Aiken* case itself. According to the House Report, the *Aiken* fact situation (standard radio attached to four ceiling speakers) represented the outer limit of the exemption.[325] Liability would be imposed where the proprietor of the establishment has installed a commercial sound system or has converted a standard receiving apparatus into the equivalent of a commercial system. The House Report set forth factors to consider whether the exemption has been exceeded. These would include "the size, physical arrangement, and noise level of areas within [the] establishment . . . and the extent to which the receiving apparatus is altered or augmented."[326] Moreover, as stated in the Conference Report, the exemption does not apply if "the commercial establishment is of sufficient size to justify . . . a subscription to [a] commercial background music service."[327]

From this legislative history, it comes as no surprise that the *Aiken* exemption created litigation. At what point does a sound system become so sophisticated as to become a commercial sound system? How should one apply the criteria listed in the House Report as to the physical environment justifying the exemption? When is a commercial establishment large enough to justify a subscription to a commercial background music service? The courts have had to grapple with these imponderables.

---

325 H.R. Rep. No. 94-1476, at 87 (1976).

326 *Id.*

327 H.R. Conf. Rep. No. 94-1733, at 75 (1976).

[4] The § 110(5) Exemption in the Courts: Ambiguity and Uncertainty

As a result of a certain vagueness in its terms and a convoluted legislative history, the § 110(5) exemption generated much more litigation than any other clause in § 110. The case law has generally not exempted commercial establishments that have sophisticated sound systems and are significantly larger than the 640-square-foot *Aiken* restaurant. Courts looked to the legislative history, indicating that the *Aiken* exemption should be limited to smaller commercial establishments that could not justify a subscription to a background commercial music service. Typical is *Sailor Music v. Gap Stores, Inc.*,[328] where plaintiff sued to enjoin a chain of clothing stores (The Gap) from retransmitting radio broadcasts to their customers in two of their New York City stores. The Second Circuit upheld the injunction and found that the commercial sound systems in the large public areas within the stores greatly exceeded the outer limits of the *Aiken* fact situation. In addition, the Gap Stores were large enough to justify a subscription to a commercial music service. *Sailor* has been reconfirmed in other cases.[329]

Even though the House Report indicated that the *Aiken* fact situation was the outer limit, courts took a more flexible approach, applying the exemption even where some physical aspects of the *Aiken* fact situation are exceeded. Despite the legislative history, some courts held that the defendant's ability to pay for background music is not relevant in determining whether the § 110 exemption has been exceeded. Moreover, the term "single receiving apparatus" was construed to mean one apparatus at a particular location even though a chain may have an apparatus at each of its several hundred stores. Thus, a chain of stores was able to avail itself of the exemption so long as each individual store used homestyle equipment.[330] Nor have the courts been insistent about requiring a maximum square footage to qualify for the *Aiken* exemption. Rather, the focus is on the quality of the sound system used and not on the square footage of the establishment using it.[331] For example, in *Springsteen v. Plaza Roller Dome, Inc.*,[332] a Putt-Putt miniature golf course had a radio receiver and six speakers mounted to light poles

---

[328] 516 F. Supp. 923 (S.D.N.Y.), *aff'd*, 668 F.2d 84 (2d Cir. 1981), *cert. denied*, 456 U.S. 945 (1982).

[329] *See Broad. Music, Inc. v. U.S. Shoe Corp.*, 678 F.2d 816 (9th Cir. 1982); *Rodgers v. Eighty-Four Lumber Co.*, 617 F. Supp. 1021 (W.D. Pa. 1985) (involving public area larger than 10,000 square feet having eight interior and exterior speakers); *Lamminations Music v. P & X Markets, Inc.*, 1985 U.S. Dist. LEXIS 20429 (N.D. Cal. Apr. 24, 1985) (regarding supermarkets of 10,000 to 14,500 square feet equipped with sophisticated commercial sound system); *ESPN, Inc. v. Edinburg Cmty. Hotel*, 623 F. Supp. 647 (S.D. Tex. 1985) (discussing satellite dish antennae used to retransmit to individual rooms in a hotel, rather than a "single receiving apparatus of a kind commonly used in private homes").

[330] *See, e.g., Edison Bros. Stores Inc. v. Broad. Music, Inc.*, 954 F.2d 1419 (8th Cir. 1992); *Broad. Music, Inc. v. Claire's Boutiques, Inc.*, 949 F.2d 1482 (7th Cir. 1991). *But see Am. Broad. Cos. v. Flying J, Inc.*, 2007 U.S. Dist. LEXIS 13252 (S.D.N.Y. Feb. 22, 2007) (involving a chain of truck stops that received satellite TV signals but also utilized a device that switched to prerecorded substitute advertisements whenever it detected broadcast commercials in the satellite TV signal. The district court held that substituting commercials in this manner violated the public performance right in the broadcast programming because the commercial-switching device was not one "commonly used in private homes").

[331] *See Edison Bros. Stores Inc. v. Broad. Music, Inc.*, 954 F.2d 1419, 1424 (8th Cir. 1992).

[332] 602 F. Supp. 1113 (M.D.N.C. 1985).

over a 7,500-square-foot playing area. The court exempted the performances under § 110(5) and distinguished this fact situation from *Sailor*. As compared with that case, the noise level in an outside Putt-Putt course was much greater, and the quality of the sound system was much poorer. In addition, the operation was not of sufficient size to justify, as a practical matter, a subscription to a commercial background music service.

[5] The Fairness in Music Licensing Act of 1998

[a] The § 110(5)(B) Business Exemption

Passed in 1998 as Title II of the Copyright Term Extension Act, the Fairness in Music Licensing Act amended § 110(5), with the strong support of retailers and restaurant owners. These groups had, for a long time, militated for a more extensive privilege for playing radio or television background music in their establishments. Section 110(5)(B) retains key features of the original provision. To enjoy this privilege, the business or restaurant cannot charge an admission and cannot retransmit the transmission beyond the store or restaurant. Section 110(5)(B) provides that business establishments having an area of less than 2,000 square feet, and restaurants having less than 3,750 square feet, incur no infringement liability when providing radio or television background music for their customers. In addition, even establishments larger than 2,000 square feet for a business or larger than 3,750 square feet for a restaurant are exempt so long as they conform to certain limitations regarding the number of loudspeakers and television screen size. Specifically, these establishments, regardless of size, will be exempt if they have six or fewer external speakers or four televisions measuring fifty-five inches or less.

Although § 110(5)(B) substantially broadens the kinds of music performances that need not be licensed, it does not exempt all music performances. Some large stores, restaurants, and bars will still need to have public performance licenses because they use more than the specified number of speakers or television sets. And restaurants and bars of all sizes, even those smaller than 2,000 or 3,750 square feet, will still need public performance licenses if they host live music or use tape or CD players, rather than exempt radio and television receivers.

The 1998 amendments did more than just broaden the original exemption. Restaurant owners also succeeded in creating a statutory process by which to challenge the royalty rates charged by performing rights societies like ASCAP and BMI for the use of music in such establishments. Now, individual proprietors who own or operate fewer than seven nonpublicly traded establishments may challenge as unreasonable the licensing rates offered by a performing rights society.[333] This procedure is highly detailed and specifically sets forth the terms concerning the details of the procedure. A proceeding is launched when an individual proprietor files an action in the applicable district court and serves a copy of the application on the performing rights society. The proceeding must commence in the applicable

---

333 *See* 17 U.S.C. § 513.

court within ninety days after service of the copy.[334] Moreover, instead of having to litigate the issue in the Southern District of New York (as specified by the ASCAP consent decree), an individual proprietor can now bring an action in federal district court in the seat of the federal circuit where the proprietor's establishment is located.[335] Proceedings must be concluded within six months after commencement.[336]

Although the Fairness in Music Licensing Act greatly favors users, it provides copyright owners one benefit. If an establishment asserts a § 110(5) exemption defense in an infringement suit, without having reasonable grounds for believing that its activities were exempt, the copyright owner is entitled to recover two times the amount of the licensing fee the establishment should have paid, in addition to any other damages that may be awarded.[337] Because § 110(5) is now so detailed, there should be few if any "good faith" disputes over the circumstances under which the exemption is available.

[b] Section 110(5) and U.S. Obligations under the Berne Convention

At the time that the United States joined the Berne Convention, courts had consistently held that § 110(5) was not available to businesses financially capable of paying reasonable licensing fees for the use of music even though some courts, as discussed above, expanded the scope of the exemption in a way that violated the spirit, if not the letter, of Berne. By contrast, the 1998 Fairness in Music Licensing Act ("FIMLA") of § 110(5)(B) went much further in violating Berne obligations than the expansive case law decided under the old regime. The reality is that the Berne Convention allows only narrow exemptions to the author's exclusive right to authorize public performance. Under Berne, only in rare instances may third parties use a broadcast without a license and without remuneration to the author. Specifically, Article 11*bis*(1)(iii) of the Berne Convention establishes the exclusive right to "authorize the public communication by loudspeaker or any other analogous instrument transmitting by signs, sounds, or images, the broadcast of the work."[338] Violations of Berne are subject to enforcement through the World Trade Organization (WTO) whose TRIPS Agreement incorporates Articles 1–21 (except for Article 6*bis*) of the Berne Convention.

Article 13 of the TRIPS Agreement, however, does tolerate some qualifications to the exclusive rights of the copyright owner, allowing countries to adopt exceptions to the rights of copyright owners so long as they meet a three-step test. Under Article 13, permissible exceptions are limited to "certain special cases which do not conflict with a normal exploitation of the work and do not reasonably

[334] *See* 17 U.S.C. § 513(1).

[335] *See* 17 U.S.C. § 513(2).

[336] *See* 17 U.S.C. § 513(6).

[337] See 17 U.S.C. § 504(d).

[338] Berne Convention art. 11*bis*(1)(iii), (Paris Text), reprinted in MARSHALL LEAFFER, INTERNATIONAL TREATIES ON INTELLECTUAL PROPERTY 366 (2d ed. 1997).

prejudice the legitimate interests of the rights holder."[339] It was clear to many that § 110(5)(B) transgressed the United States' multilateral trading obligations under the WTO. The broadly drafted "business exception" violated basic tenets of the Berne Convention and largely exceeded the limited exceptions under Article 13. Not long after passage of the FIMLA, it came as no surprise that the European Union commenced sanction proceedings against the United States before the WTO, asserting that both exemptions in § 110(5) violated the TRIPS agreement.[340]

On June 15, 2000, the WTO dispute resolution panel announced its decision that the FIMLA, the original "homestyle exception" of § 110(5)(A) was consistent with Articles 11*bis*(1)(ii) and 11*bis*(1)(iii) of the Berne Convention, whereas § 110(5)(B) of the FIMLA, the "business exception," violated the terms of Berne and failed to meet the three-step test of TRIPS' Article 13.[341] First, it found that the broadly defined business exception greatly exceeded the "certain special cases" allowed under the first prong of Article 13. In addition, the Panel ruled that § 110(B) conflicted with "the normal exploitation of the work" and unreasonably "prejudiced the legitimate interests of the rights holder" by impeding the ways that rights holders normally extract economic value from the right to the work. As a result, § 110(5)(B) deprived musical copyright owners of significant tangible commercial gains that they would have earned absent the exception. The panel also intimated strongly that the United States could not bring itself into compliance merely by reinstating the pre-FIMLA "home-type apparatus" provisions of old § 110(5). Although the remnant of that provision now found in § 110(5)(A) of the Copyright Act was determined to be TRIPS-compatible, this was only because the WTO panel (somewhat dubiously) concluded that § 110(5)(A) no longer applied to nondramatic musical works — for which there is the greatest demand, and hence, the greatest potential licensing revenue. The Panel gave the United States until July 27, 2001, to comply with its ruling to avoid sanctions.[342]

[G] Agricultural and Horticultural Fairs, § 110(6)

Performances of nondramatic musical works by a governmental body or nonprofit agricultural or horticultural organization are exempted by § 110(6).[343] The performance must take place during an agricultural or horticultural fair and must be conducted by nonprofit agricultural or horticultural organizations. This section removes vicarious liability of the organization, which sponsored the fair, for infringing performances given by concessionaires, businesses, or other persons. These direct infringers, however, remain personally liable.

---

[339] Trade Related Aspects of Intellectual Property Rights (TRIPS Agreement), art. 13, reprinted in Marshall Leaffer, International Treaties on Intellectual Property 593 (2d ed. 1997).

[340] For a comprehensive background and analysis of the issue, see Laurence R. Helfer, *World Music on a U.S. Stage: A Berne/TRIPs and Economic Analysis of the Fairness in Music Licensing Act*, 80 B.U. L. Rev. 93 (2000).

[341] *Panel Report, United States — Section 110(5) of the U.S. Copyright Act:*, WT/DS/160/R (June 15, 2000).

[342] As of 2010, the United States has not complied with the Panel's decision despite damages and retaliatory measures.

[343] 17 U.S.C. § 110(6).

[H] Retail Sales of Sheet Music and Phonorecords, § 110(7)

Section 110(7)[344] provides a limited exemption to vending establishments, allowing performance of nondramatic musical works for the sole purpose of promoting the retail sale of copies or phonorecords "or other audiovisual devices utilized in such performance of the work."[345] The performance must take place at the store location or in the immediate vicinity of the sale and may not be transmitted to another location and must occur in a vending establishment open to the public without any direct or indirect admission charge. The purpose of § 110(7) is to allow retail stores the privilege of playing music recordings to promote the sale of records without having to obtain a performance license. By the 1998 amendment, the exemption of § 110(7) has been expanded so that stores that play music recordings or music videos to promote the sale of home video, cassette, or CD players, do not have to obtain performance licenses to do so, even if those stores do not sell recordings or music videos.

[I] Exemption for Transmissions of Nondramatic Literary Works to the Handicapped, § 110(8)

Section 110(8)[346] exempts transmissions of performances of a nondramatic literary work designed for the blind or the handicapped who are unable to read. Performances for the deaf are also included in this provision. The performance must be made without any purpose of direct or indirect commercial advantage and must be transmitted through a governmental body or noncommercial educational broadcast station, an authorized radio subcarrier, or a cable system.

[J] Transmissions of Dramatic Works to the Handicapped, § 110(9)

Section 110(9)[347] applies to transmissions designed for the blind and those unable to read printed material because of their handicaps. As in the preceding exemption, there can be no direct or indirect commercial advantage. The transmission must be made through an authorized radio subcarrier and, unlike § 110(8), can be of a dramatic literary work. The performance, however, may only take place on a single occasion and must be of a work published at least ten years before the date of performance.

[K] Veterans and Fraternal Organizations, § 110(10)

A 1982 amendment to the Copyright Act added the fraternal organizations exemption under § 110(10).[348] One purpose of this amendment was to allow these organizations an exemption in circumstances which would otherwise violate

---

[344] 17 U.S.C. § 110(7).

[345] Language added by Pub. L. 105-298, 112 Stat. 2827 (1998).

[346] 17 U.S.C. § 110(8).

[347] 17 U.S.C. § 110(9).

[348] Although of minor significance from an economic standpoint, § 110(10) is viewed by some as a

§ 110(4). This section exempts performances of nondramatic literary and musical works performed during a social function of a veterans or fraternal organization. The event must be one that is not open to the general public, although guests of the organization may be invited. An admission fee may be charged, but whatever proceeds are left after deducting costs must be used for charitable purposes. Social functions of college fraternities and sororities are not included in § 110(10) unless they are held solely to raise funds for a specific charitable purpose.

[L] Muting and Skipping of Motion Picture Content for Private Home Viewing

Section 110(11) exempts from infringement "the making imperceptible, by or at the direction of a member of a private household, of limited portions of audio or video content of a motion picture, during a performance in or transmitted to that household for private home viewing."[349] Section 110(11) is intended to create a safe harbor from both copyright and trademark infringement liability for movie filtering technology that skips or mutes scenes deemed offensive, but does not create a fixed copy of the altered version of the motion picture. The exemption is lost if the technology mutes or skips more than a limited portion of a film or if the technology reproduces the film in a tangible medium.

On its way to passage, this 2005 amendment to the Copyright Act engendered substantial controversy. Industry groups brought suit against the makers of the technology, claiming that it infringed the adaptation right of motion picture copyright owners. Some critics of the exemption wondered whether it was needed at all, given that parents could simply choose not to play movies bearing offensive material. Others argued that the exemption was unnecessary because muting and skipping for private viewing without creating a fixed copy was clearly legal under existing law.[350] Still others pointed out that § 110(11) is not limited to profanity, sex, or violence but can be used to censor any content contrary to the author's artistic vision. Despite the pending litigation against the skipping and muting technology, Congress decided to preempt the issue rather than wait for a judicial pronouncement. In short, alarm at the ever increasing sex, violence, and profanity in commercial movies won the day rather than continued reflection on the need or wisdom for a targeted exemption.

Whatever one thinks about its need or wisdom, § 110(11) will surely raise troublesome questions. For example, would the safe harbor apply to the skipping or muting of entire advertisements? Probably not because the exemption is limited to the making "imperceptible . . . limited portions of audio or visual content of a motion picture," and a product or service that would allow the skipping of an *entire*

---

continuing erosion of the rights of authors by special interest groups. *See* Alvin Deutsch, *Politics and Poker Music Faces the Odds*, 34 J. Copyright L. Soc'y 38 (1986).

[349] 17 U.S.C. § 110(11).

[350] *See, e.g., Family Movie Act of 2004: Hearing on H.R. 4586 Before the H. Subcomm. on Courts, the Internet and Intellectual Property*, 108th Cong., 2d Sess. (2004) (statement of Marybeth Peters, Register of Copyrights, U.S. Copyright Office) (noting that the legislation is not needed because it seems relatively clear that such conduct is not prohibited under existing law).

advertisement (or an entire copyrighted work) would appear to be beyond the scope of § 110(11).[351]

§ 8.20 SECONDARY TRANSMISSIONS, § 111

[A] Generally

Section 111 primarily involves the complex compulsory licensing system for retransmission of over-the-air broadcast signals by cable television systems, which pick up broadcasts of programs originated by others and retransmit them to paying subscribers. Because of two key Supreme Court decisions before the 1976 Act, the cable television industry did not have to pay royalties for its retransmission of over-the-air broadcast signals.[352] The cable television conflict became the most hotly debated issue during the revision process, leading to the longest and most complex section in the Copyright Act. The resulting compulsory license represents a delicately woven compromise among industry groups, which overturns the earlier Supreme Court decisions. Under § 111, a cable television system is subjected to full copyright liability for its retransmissions unless it complies with the terms of the compulsory license, such as reporting requirements and the payment of royalties. The royalty rate, initially set forth in the 1976 Act, is to be periodically adjusted by the Copyright Royalty Judges.[353]

[B] Overall Structure of § 111

One can best make sense of this complicated section by keeping in mind its overall structure:

Subsection (a)[354]exempts four kinds of secondary transmissions from infringement of the performance right under § 106(4).

Subsection (b)[355] imposes full liability on secondary transmissions intended for limited audiences such as pay cable and background music services.

Subsection (c)[356] sets up the compulsory license for cable television systems.

Subsection (d)[357] specifies the operation of the compulsory license and defines the responsibility of the Librarian of Congress and Register of Copyrights in the collection and distribution of fees.

Subsection (e)[358] treats certain aspects of off-shore cable systems.

---

[351] *See* 151 Cong. Rec. S495 (daily ed. Jan. 25, 2005) (statement of Sen. Orrin Hatch).

[352] *See Fortnightly Corp. v. United Artists Television, Inc.*, 392 U.S. 390 (1968); *Teleprompter Corp. v. CBS, Inc.*, 415 U.S. 394 (1974). For a discussion of these cases, see *supra* § 8.19.

[353] *See* 17 U.S.C. § 803(b)(1)(A).

[354] 17 U.S.C. § 111(a).

[355] 17 U.S.C. § 111(b).

[356] 17 U.S.C. § 111(c).

[357] 17 U.S.C. § 111(d).

[358] 17 U.S.C. § 111(e).

Subsection (f)[359] provides technical definitions of cable matters not found in § 101.

The following discussion primarily concentrates on subsections (a)-(d).

[C] General Exemptions, § 111(a)

[1] Clause (1): Retransmissions to Private Lodgings

Certain secondary transmissions are given a general exemption under clause (1) of § 111(a). The first exemption covers the same situation as *Buck v. Jewell-LaSalle.*[360] It places beyond copyright liability transmissions consisting "entirely of the relaying, by the management of a hotel, apartment house, or similar establishment" of a broadcast to the private lodging of guests or residents who are not charged directly for the secondary transmission.[361] This exemption is limited to a simple relay of the transmission, and the retransmitter cannot adapt or change the signal in any way, such as by cutting out advertisements or running new commercials.[362] Moreover, the term "private lodgings" is limited to private rooms or rooms used for private parties and does not include dining rooms, meeting halls, or any places that are outside of a normal circle of a family and its social acquaintances.[363] Finally, the House Report specifies that placing an ordinary radio or television set in a private hotel room does not constitute an infringement.

[2] Clause (2): Instructional Transmissions

Section 111(a)(2) reconfirms that instructional transmissions under § 110(2) are exempt.[364]

[3] Clause (3): The Passive Carrier Exemption[365]

Section 111(a)(3), known as the "passive carrier exemption," exempts from copyright liability, carriers, such as AT&T, who merely provide wires and cables for the use of others.[366] The carrier is exempt so long as it neither controls the content nor chooses the recipients of the secondary transmission.[367]

---

359 17 U.S.C. § 111(f).

360 283 U.S. 191 (1931). *See supra* § 8.19[C].

361 17 U.S.C. § 111(a)(1).

362 *See* H.R. REP. NO. 94-1476, at 91 (1976).

363 *See id.*

364 17 U.S.C. § 110(2).

365 For an overview, see Stephen R. Barnett, *From New Technology to Moral Rights: Passive Carriers, Teletext, and Deletion as Copyright Infringement — the* WGN *Case*, 31 J. COPYRIGHT L. SOC'Y 427 (1984).

366 *See* H.R. Rep. No. 94-1476, at 92 (1976).

367 *Compare E. Microwave, Inc. v. Doubleday Sports, Inc.*, 691 F.2d 125 (2d Cir. 1982) (exempting microwave and satellite rebroadcasts of Mets baseball games), *with WGN Cont'l Broad. Co. v. United Video, Inc.*, 693 F.2d 622 (7th Cir. 1982) (finding the exemption did not apply to a carrier who deleted material from vertical blanking interval of broadcast signal).

[4] Clause (4): The Secondary Transmitter Exemption

Section 111(a)(4) exempts secondary transmitters, operating on a nonprofit basis, who provide translators or boosters to improve reception.

Even if the retransmission falls into one of the exempt categories outlined above, under § 111(b)[368] copyright infringement will occur if the primary transmission is intended not for the public at large, but rather for a controlled group. These transmissions include services such as background music services, pay television, or closed circuit broadcasts to theaters. The secondary transmission, even to a controlled group, is not actionable if the primary transmission is made by a broadcast station licensed by the Federal Communications Commission ("FCC"), the retransmission is required by the FCC, and the transmission is not changed in any manner.

[D] The Compulsory License for Cable Systems, § 111(c)

Section 111(c) establishes the general contours of the compulsory license, which is conditioned on the reporting requirements and the payment of royalties set forth in § 111(d). As a rule of thumb, any public performance that falls outside the scope of § 111 exemptions and limitations will constitute copyright infringement unless it qualifies under some other exemption or limitation under copyright law.

The compulsory license applies only to the retransmission of over-the-air broadcast signals and is inapplicable to the secondary transmission of a nonbroadcast primary transmission. This means that a cable system can retransmit only programs originating from a broadcast station licensed by the FCC, such as the local CBS affiliate. It cannot, however, retransmit a nonbroadcast program such as one originating with another cable television system.

In retransmitting the broadcast signal, the cable television system cannot willfully change in any way the content of the primary broadcast.[369] For such deletions, full copyright liability is imposed on the cable television system.[370] In addition, a secondary transmission to the public will infringe the performance right in a copyrighted work embodied in the primary transmission "if the primary transmission is not made for reception by the public at large but is controlled and limited to reception by particular members of the public."[371] Examples of such infringing retransmissions — those not intended for the general public — would include background music services, such as MUZAK, closed circuit broadcasts to theatres, pay television, or pay cable.[372]

---

[368] 17 U.S.C. § 111(b). *See* H.R. Rep. No. 94-1476, at 92 (1976).

[369] One exemption allows changes in commercial advertisements made by those engaged in television commercial advertising market research with the prior consent of the original advertiser. *See* 17 U.S.C. § 111(c)(3).

[370] *See WGN Cont'l Broad. Co. v. United Video, Inc.*, 693 F.2d 622 (7th Cir. 1982) (showing § 111 exemption exceeded by deletion of teletext).

[371] *See* 17 U.S.C. § 111(b).

[372] H.R. Rep. No. 94-1476, at 92 (1976).

The compulsory licensing system generally does not apply to foreign broadcasts unless carried by a broadcast station licensed by the FCC. Thus, a cable television system would be subjected to full copyright liability if it retransmitted a British television station's programming. An exemption is made for Canadian signals and Mexican signals licensed by a governmental authority.[373] To retransmit a Canadian signal, the cable system must be located within limited geographic zones in the United States.[374]

Mexican signals can also be imported pursuant to the compulsory license, but the limitation to the qualifying signal is based on technology rather than geography.[375] The above limitations on Canadian and Mexican signals do not apply to a cable system authorized by the FCC before April 15, 1976, to carry these foreign signals. For such cable systems, the compulsory license is available.[376]

[E] Reporting Requirements and Royalty Fees for Cable Systems, § 111(d)

Section 111(d) is a complicated provision setting up the reporting and royalty fee requirements for cable system operators. Failure to comply subjects the cable system to full copyright liability. The cable system must file information in the Copyright Office regarding its subscribers and accounts and must list all signals it regularly carries.[377] The cable system must also file a semiannual statement of account, which includes the royalty fees and various other information concerning the signals carried during that time period. The Register of Copyright collects the royalty fees and then deposits them with the treasury after deducting reasonable costs incurred by the Copyright Office.[378] Every person claiming to be entitled to royalties must file a claim with the Register of Copyrights during the month of July.[379] The Librarian of Congress, on recommendation with the Register of Copyrights, is responsible for distributing the royalties and determines whether a controversy exists.[380] If no controversy exists, the funds are distributed to the appropriate copyright owners after deducting reasonable operating expenses.

---

373 *See* 17 U.S.C. § 111(c)(1).

374 This applies to areas located within 150 miles from the U.S.-Canadian border, or south from the border to the 42nd parallel of latitude, whichever is greater. *See* 17 U.S.C. § 111(c)(4). Detroit and Pittsburgh could receive the Canadian signals, whereas New York City and Chicago, outside the geographic boundaries, could not.

375 The signal cannot be made "by means other than direct interception of a free space radio wave emitted by such broadcast television station." *See* 17 U.S.C. § 111(c)(4).

376 *See* 17 U.S.C. § 111(c)(4).

377 *See* 37 C.F.R. § 201.11.

378 *See* 17 U.S.C. § 111(d)(2).

379 *See* 17 U.S.C. § 111(d)(4).

380 *See id.*

[F] The Computation and Distribution of Royalty Fees

The compulsory license entitles the cable system to retransmit all licensed signals, but the royalty fee is based on the retransmission of distant non-network programs. Why are local programming and distant networks excluded from the royalty determination? As for local programming, Congress believed that its retransmission did not harm the copyright owner who would be compensated for his work within the local markets. As for distant network programming, Congress determined that its retransmission did little harm because copyright owners were adequately remunerated in their contracts with the networks. On the other hand, Congress found that retransmission of distant non-network programming harmed the copyright owner who would no longer be able to license his work in the community where the work was retransmitted.[381]

The royalty fee to be paid is based on the cable system's use of distant non-network programming and a percentage applied against the cable system's gross receipt base.[382] The computation involves a two-step process. The first step is to determine how many distant non-network programs the cable system has retransmitted. The House Report describes the process as follows:

> First, a value called a "distant signal equivalent" is assigned to all "distant" signals. Distant signals are defined as signals retransmitted by a cable system . . . outside the local service area of the primary transmitter. Different values are assigned to independent, network and educational stations because of the different amounts of viewing of non-network programming carried by such stations. For example, the viewing of non-network programs on network stations is considered to approximate 25 percent. These values are then combined and a scale of percentages is applied to the cumulative total.[383]

Once the total distant signal equivalent ("d.s.e.") is determined for the semiannual accounting period, a schedule of percentages is multiplied against the cable system's gross receipts base[384] for each d.s.e. unit used. Under current rates, the cable system would have to pay 956 one-thousandths of one percent of its gross receipts for the first d.s.e. For the second, third, and fourth d.s.e., the percentage falls to 630 one-thousandths of one percent of its gross receipts for each unit used. For the fifth and each additional unit, the percentage falls to 296 one-thousandths of one percent of the gross receipts.[385]

For example, suppose the cable system has a gross receipts base of $10 million and has used two d.s.e. units, the computation would look like this:

---

[381] *See* H.R. Rep. No. 94-1476, at 90 (1976).

[382] *See* 17 U.S.C. § 111(d)(2).

[383] H.R. Rep. No. 94-1476, at 90 (1976).

[384] Smaller cable systems are required to pay a lesser percentage of their gross receipts base for each d.s.e. used but are subject to a minimum payment. *See* 17 U.S.C. § 111(d)(2)(C)–(D); H.R. Rep. No. 94-1476, at 96 (1976).

[385] For current rates, see 37 C.F.R. § 256.2.

For the 1st d.s.e.:.956 of 1% of $10,000,000 =	$95,600
For the 2nd d.s.e.:.630 of 1% of $10,000,000 =	$63,000
Total amount owed by the cable system =	$158,600

The Register of Copyrights then distributes the royalties to copyright owners whose works were part of non-network distant signal retransmission. The Act does not delineate exactly what process should be used to determine the distribution, leaving it instead to the Register of Copyrights to decide these matters. Copyright owners must file their claims each July,[386] and gain immunity from the antitrust laws[387] to facilitate agreement among themselves on the division of royalties. By August 1,[388] the Register of Copyrights must determine whether there is a controversy among claimants. If no controversy exists, distribution takes place immediately. However, if a controversy does exist, the Register must seek a Copyright Royalty Board judgment to determine the distribution of royalties. Before it was abolished in 1993, the Copyright Tribunal handled the collection and distribution functions. With the number of groups involved and the stakes high,[389] the process generated great controversy, and every Tribunal distribution decision was challenged, leading to endless litigation. The courts, however, in the end have invariably upheld the Tribunal's findings and procedures.[390] Unfortunately, the regulatory system envisaged by the Copyright Royalty Tribunal Reform Act of 1993 failed to produce a significantly smoother, more efficient mechanism for the determination and distribution of royalties, and was ripe for reform. The Copyright Royalty and Distribution Reform Act of 2004 established the three-judge Copyright Royalty Board, which now presides over royalty distribution controversies.

[G] Afterthoughts: Is § 111 an Anachronism?

Much has changed since Congress laid down the framework for the cable television compulsory license in 1976. The technological and regulatory environment, on which § 111 is premised, has largely disappeared. This has led some to question whether § 111 should be repealed or at least seriously modified.

When § 111 was being formulated in the mid-1970s, the cable industry was strictly regulated by the FCC. First, a cable system in one of the top fifty television markets was limited to the number of distant signals it could import. Second, a local station could require a cable system to delete syndicated programming from

---

386 *See* 17 U.S.C. § 11(d)(4)(A).

387 *See id.*

388 *See* 17 U.S.C. § 111(d)(4)(B).

389 In 1984, more than $86.9 million in cable royalties were received by the Copyright Office. *See* Ralph Oman, *The Compulsory License Redux: Will It Survive in a Changing Marketplace?*, 5 CARDOZO ARTS & ENT. L.J. 37, 44 (1986).

390 *See, e.g.*, *Nat'l Ass'n of Broadcasters v. Copyright Royalty Tribunal*, 809 F.2d 172 (2d Cir. 1986); *Christian Broad. Network, Inc. v. Copyright Royalty Tribunal*, 720 F.2d 1295 (D.C. Cir. 1983); *Nat'l Ass'n of Broadcasters v. Copyright Royalty Tribunal*, 675 F.2d 367 (D.C. Cir. 1982).

imported signals if the local station had an exclusive right to the program. These FCC regulations resulted in protecting the dominant position of networks and independent stations from the threat of a fledgling cable industry, which was immune from copyright liability under the *Fortnightly* and *Teleprompter* cases.[391] With this FCC regulatory framework in mind, Congress drafted § 111 establishing liability for cable television in return for the compulsory license. In sum, the cable provisions were designed to interrelate with FCC regulations, reflecting a delicate and intricate political compromise.

In 1980, the FCC repealed both the distant signal and program exclusivity rules. In just two years after the effective date of the 1976 Act, the regulatory environment on which the mosaic of § 111 was based, ceased to exist.

Technological change has also brought into question the basis of § 111. Cable television is hardly the fledgling industry that needs the protective support of the compulsory license. The industry has expanded enormously in the last few years, challenging the once overwhelmingly dominant networks. Developing satellite technology has given cable television an almost unlimited ability to retransmit signals at increasingly lower costs. As a result, the television marketplace is now one of abundance in which cable has to compete with other new technologies such as direct broadcast satellites, low-power television, and video disks. Despite these new competing technologies, § 111 favors the cable industry.

These basic changes in the regulatory and technological environment of the cable industry call for a reexamination of § 111 that, short of outright repeal, will probably lead to a more market-oriented system while eliminating the burdensome administrative apparatus used to administer the system.

§ 8.21 SATELLITE RETRANSMISSIONS

[A] Satellite Retransmissions for Private Home Viewing: § 119 Statutory License

With the Satellite Home Viewer Act of 1988,[392] Congress again met the challenge of a new technology by establishing a fifth compulsory license. Effective January 1, 1989, the Act established a temporary compulsory license for satellite carrier television transmission to the public for private home viewing. This compulsory license concerns the retransmission of television programming by companies who have rented space on a satellite for this purpose. Satellite carrier companies generally retransmit scrambled signals containing television programming to persons owning backyard satellite dishes. The satellite carrier charges the dish owner a subscription fee, which includes a descrambling device. This lucrative business has raised some difficult questions under the 1976 Copyright Act.

---

[391] For a discussion of these cases, see *supra* § 8.18.

[392] Pub. L. No. 100-667 (1988).

Satellite carriers, by retransmitting from satellite to earth, are essentially engaging in secondary transmissions of copyrighted works. As defined by the 1976 Act, the secondary transmission of a copyrighted work constitutes a public performance[393] and is an infringement of copyright without the copyright owner's consent. Although admitting that they are publicly performing works, satellite carriers have argued that they are essentially cable systems, subject to the cable compulsory license, or that they are exempt from liability by falling under the passive carrier exemption.

Does this activity fall into the cable compulsory license? The problem is that satellite carriers are not cable systems as defined in the 1976 Act. Under § 111(f) of the 1976 Act, a cable system is defined as "a facility located in any State, Territory, Trust Territory, or possession."[394] Satellite carriers, however, do not limit their activities to these enumerated locations but carry out their operations on orbiting satellites.

In addition, satellite carriers do not comply with the terms of the passive carrier exemption. Section 111(a)(3)[395] of the 1976 Act exempts liability for secondary transmissions of copyrighted works where the carrier has no direct or indirect control over the content or selection of the primary transmission. Most satellite carriers, however, are hardly passive. They scramble the signals, market descramblers, and package programming. As such, their activities greatly exceed those of passive carriers under the 1976 Act. Thus, secondary transmissions of satellite carriers do not fall within the cable compulsory license and would appear to be an infringement of a copyright owner's public performance right.

The congressional response to this legal uncertainty was a compulsory license for satellite retransmissions. It was felt that the compulsory license would meet the needs of the industry, compensate copyright owners, and enable continued access to television programming by the growing satellite dish-owning public, particularly those living in rural areas not adequately served by other means.[396]

The response was the Satellite Home Viewer Act of 1988, creating a new statutory license, specifically tailored for satellite systems, in § 119 of the Copyright Act. The statutory licensing provisions of § 119 were initially modeled on those of § 111, but with a few innovations. One of those innovations has since been generalized. According to the 1988 legislation, the procedures for distributing the royalties were to be determined by the Copyright Royalty Tribunal, which was

---

393 17 U.S.C. § 101 (public performance).

394 17 U.S.C. § 111(f). *See Pacific & S. Co., Inc. v. Satellite Broad. Networks, Inc.*, 694 F. Supp. 1565 (N.D. Ga. 1988).

395 17 U.S.C. § 111(a)(3).

396 The compulsory license subject to a sunset provision has been extended five times. The latest extension stipulates a sunset date of December 31, 2014. Satellite Television Extension and Localism Act of 2010 (STELLA), Pub.L. No. 111–175 (2010). The Act expands the definition of "unserved households" for purposes of importing distant network signals; and it lifts an injunction previously entered against satellite provider DISH Network, on the condition that it provide local-to-local retransmission into all 210 Designated Market Areas in the United States. *See also DISH Network, Inc. v. FCC*, 636 F.3d 1139 (9th Cir. 2011) (requirement under STELA that satellite providers carry public broadcasting channels in HD as a condition of the statutory license does not violate the First Amendment).

required to initiate voluntary negotiations among satellite carriers, distributors, and copyright owners. If voluntary negotiations did not work, the Tribunal was required to institute arbitration proceedings to determine a reasonable royalty rate. In 1993 the functions formerly assigned to the Copyright Royalty Tribunal were transferred to ad hoc Copyright Arbitration Royalty Panels ("CARPs"), with the Librarian of Congress responsible for making final determinations based on the CARPs' decisions; and since 2005, the CARPs in turn were replaced with three full-time Copyright Royalty Judges ("CRJs") known collectively as the Copyright Royalty Board ("CRB").

Section 119 covers the retransmission of copyrighted works included in primary transmissions made both by so-called "superstations" (broadcasting outlets which originate significant amounts of programming in the expectation that their signals will be retransmitted nationally) and by conventional network affiliates outside of their local markets.[397] In addition, in 1999 Congress added a new, permanent, royalty-free statutory license in § 122 for retransmission of copyrighted works included in a primary transmission by a television broadcast station into its local market (so-called "local-to-local" satellite retransmissions).[398]

As amended in 2004, § 119 treats satellite retransmissions of superstation programming and network programming in substantially different ways. Satellite retransmissions of superstation programming are subject to relatively few significant conditions other than payment of royalties. In particular, as of 2005, superstations may be retransmitted for viewing in "commercial establishments" as well as for private home viewing. By contrast, satellite retransmissions of distant network programming qualify for the statutory license only if they are made "to the public for private home viewing" and they are subject to a number of additional conditions.[399]

Under § 119, as amended, distant analog network programming may be retransmitted to satellite subscribers under the following circumstances:

> *Unserved Households.* For people who reside in areas in which there is no off-air reception (so-called "unserved households"),[400] satellite carriers may retransmit distant analog network programming (1) to subscribers who are legally receiving such programming as of January 1, 2005, even if local network programming was, is, or becomes available by satellite; (2) to new subscribers, if the local network affiliate's programming is not available by satellite; or (3) if the local network affiliate waives its right to prohibit importation of a distant network signal.[401]
>
> *Grandfathered Subscribers.* For subscribers in served households who were "grandfathered" under the 1999 legislation, satellite carriers may continue to retransmit distant analog network programming if the sub-

[397] *See* 17 U.S.C. § 119(d)(9) (defining the term "superstation").

[398] 17 U.S.C. § 122.

[399] *See* 17 U.S.C. § 119(b).

[400] For a definition of "unserved" households, see 17 U.S.C. § 119(d)(10).

[401] 17 U.S.C. § 119(a)(4).

scriber was actually receiving such programming as of October 1, 2004.[402] However, when a local analog network signal becomes available by satellite under § 122, subscribers must either elect to receive the local network signal or have their distant network programming terminated within 60 days.[403]

Significantly Viewed Stations. As of 2005, satellite operators may retransmit into local markets any superstation or distant network signal that is "significantly viewed" in that market on the same basis as cable operators (royalty-free, but with retransmission consent), provided that the subscriber also receives the local network affiliate signal (if there is a local affiliate of that network) or a waiver is obtained from the local network affiliate.[404]

Anticipating the transition to digital high-definition broadcasting, in 2004 Congress further amended § 119 to permit distant digital network signals to be retransmitted to satellite subscribers in areas where the local affiliates are not yet broadcasting in digital format (so-called "digital white areas") under the following circumstances:

Analog Unserved Households. Satellite operators may retransmit distant digital network programming to subscribers who reside in analog "unserved households" under the same conditions as distant analog network programming; except that if the satellite operator provides local analog network programming to such households under § 122, then the satellite operator may provide to the same or later time-zone distant digital network programming after April 30, 2006 (for the top 100 markets) or after July 15, 2007 (all other markets) only if the subscriber also takes the local affiliate's analog programming. Subscribers will have to drop the distant digital programming when the local affiliate goes digital if the local affiliate's digital signal can be received by the subscriber off-air.[405]

Off-Air Digital Signal Not Available. Satellite operators may retransmit distant digital network programming to subscribers who can receive a local analog signal off-air (and are therefore not an "unserved household"), but cannot receive a local digital signal of sufficient strength off-air. However, if the satellite operator provides local digital network programming by satellite, it may not retransmit distant digital network programming to such subscribers unless they cannot receive the local digital network satellite signal, or unless they qualify under the grandfather provisions below.[406]

Digital Grandfather Provisions. Satellite operators may continue to retransmit distant digital network programming to subscribers who lawfully

---

[402] 17 U.S.C. § 119(a)(4)(A)(ii).

[403] 17 U.S.C. § 119(a)(4)(A)(i)(I)(aa); 47 U.S.C. § 339(a)(2)(A).

[404] 17 U.S.C. § 119(a)(2)(3)(C).

[405] 47 U.S.C. § 339(a)(2)(D).

[406] 47 U.S.C. § 339(a)(2)(D)(i).

receive such programming after the 2004 amendments but before the local digital network signal becomes available by satellite, provided the subscriber also subscribes to the local digital network programming when it becomes available. Satellite operators may also continue to retransmit distant digital network programming to subscribers who lawfully received such programming before the 2004 amendments, even after the local digital network signal becomes available.[407]

Significantly Viewed Stations. Satellite operators may retransmit "significantly viewed" distant digital signals into local markets on the same basis as distant analog signals, provided that the subscriber also receives the local network affiliate signal in digital format (if there is a local affiliate of that network) or a waiver is obtained from the local network affiliate.[408]

The purpose of these limitations is to prevent satellite TV operators from importing distant network affiliate signals into local markets, where they might compete unfairly with local over-the-air broadcasters. Not surprisingly, the limitation concerning "unserved households" has raised problems of definition.[409]

[B] Satellite Retransmissions Within Local Markets: § 122

The Satellite Home Viewer Improvement Act of 1999 added § 122[410] to the Copyright Act, granting direct satellite carriers a royalty-free statutory license to retransmit local signals to customers in the same local market. The law was intended to create parity and to enhance competition between satellite and cable industries. The local-to-local statutory license should be distinguished from the § 119 statutory license under which a satellite carrier is permitted to retransmit distant signals to subscribers residing in unserved households.

To make use of the local-to-local license, the secondary transmission must be made by the satellite carrier to the public.[411] In addition, a satellite carrier must be in compliance with FCC rules, regulations, and authorizations[412] and is prohibited from making a direct or indirect charge for the secondary transmission of the local broadcast to subscribers or to distributors that have contracted with the satellite

---

407 47 U.S.C. § 339(a)(2)(D)(ii).

408 17 U.S.C. § 119(a)(3).

409 *See, e.g.*, *ABC, Inc. v. PrimeTime 24*, 184 F.3d 348 (4th Cir. 1999) (§ 119 embodies an objective signal strength rule rather than a subjective reception quality rule); *CBS, Inc. v. PrimeTime 24 Joint Venture*, 245 F.3d 1217 (11th Cir. 2001) (same); *EchoStar Satellite LLC v. FCC*, 457 F.3d 31 (D.C. Cir. 2006) (upholding FCC order adopting new model for predicting signal strength). The stakes in the resolution of these problems were high, as significant remedies are available against satellite broadcasters who persistently disregard the limitation. *See CBS Broad., Inc. v. EchoStar Commc'n Corp.*, 450 F.3d 505 (11th Cir. 2006) (upholding finding that satellite carrier was guilty of "willful and repeated violations" of § 119, and remanding for entry of mandatory nationwide permanent injunction against use of the statutory license).

410 Pub. L. No. 106-113, 113 Stat. 1501A-524 (1999),

411 17 U.S.C. § 122(a)(1).

412 17 U.S.C. § 122(a)(2).

carrier for transmission to the public.[413] Because cable and other terrestrial multichannel delivery systems, for the most part, do not pay any copyright royalty for local retransmission of broadcast stations, the local-to-local license does not require payment of copyright royalties by satellite carriers. A satellite carrier, however, is liable for copyright infringement to a local television station holding the copyright if it willfully alters the programming contained in a local broadcast,[414] retransmits a television broadcast station to a subscriber located outside the local market of the station,[415] or fails to comply with the provision's reporting requirements, including FCC rules, regulations, and authorizations.[416]

§ 8.22 THE JUKEBOX LICENSE

[A] The Rise and Fall of the Compulsory Jukebox License

Before passage of the 1976 Act, jukebox operators enjoyed a highly controversial[417] blanket exemption from copyright liability. With the 1976 Act, as originally enacted, the jukebox industry lost its total exemption but was able, through political compromise, to carve out for itself a compulsory licensing system with favorable terms. This jukebox compulsory license was deemed to be incompatible with the requirements of the Berne Convention and thus an impediment to U.S. entry into the Convention.[418] Accordingly, the Berne Convention Implementation Act of 1988[419] added § 116(A) to the 1976 Copyright Act, modifying the original compulsory license and replacing it with a voluntarily negotiated system.[420]

The original compulsory license was still relevant. It was to be used during an interim period and, more importantly, if copyright owners and jukebox operators were unable to negotiate a license, readopted. With the Copyright Royalty Tribunal Reform Act of 1993, the compulsory license was repealed, ending a historical peculiarity of American copyright law.

---

[413] 17 U.S.C. § 122(a)(3).

[414] 17 U.S.C. § 122(e).

[415] 17 U.S.C. § 122(f).

[416] 17 U.S.C. § 122(h).

[417] Under § 1(e) of the 1909 Act, the jukebox industry enjoyed a blanket exemption from copyright liability, which was widely condemned as an anachronistic, historical accident, and totally unjustified. *See* H.R. Rep. No. 94-1476, at 112 (1976).

[418] *See* Berne Convention art. 11(1). For a discussion of the Berne Convention and U.S. entry, see *infra* §§ 12.04–12.05.

[419] Pub. L. No. 100-568 (1988).

[420] *See* 17 U.S.C. § 116(A).

[B] The Jukebox Licensing Procedure: A Voluntarily Negotiated License

The revised § 116 creates a voluntary negotiated license covering music played by jukeboxes. Before the 1988 and 1993 amendments to the Copyright Act, a jukebox compulsory license existed whose terms were established entirely by the original provisions of the 1976 Act. With the repeal of the original compulsory licensing system, the current jukebox licensing system is based on voluntary negotiations. Under these provisions, copyright owners of nondramatic musical works[421] and operators of coin-operated phonorecord players are authorized to negotiate and agree on the terms, rates, and distributions of the royalty payments for performances of these works.[422] The purpose of these provisions is to allow negotiations between the performing rights societies (ASCAP, BMI, SESAC)[423] and the Amusement Music Operators of America ("AMOA"). These negotiations are to be immune from antitrust liability.[424]

§ 8.23 PERFORMING RIGHTS SOCIETIES

[A] Why They Are Needed: Capturing the Valuable But Elusive Performance Right

Every day, musical works are publicly performed thousands of times. Each time a musical work is played on the air or before live groups, the event becomes a possible source of revenue for the copyright owner. The performance right is unquestionably the most important of the exclusive rights for composers and publishers of music.[425] The problem is that musical works are performed so extensively and in such widely diverse settings, that individual copyright owners are unable to enforce their performance right on their own. Unauthorized performances frequently occur because it is too costly for the copyright owners to police their rights and too costly for the users to obtain a license.[426]

The performing-rights society is the means by which music composers and publishers police, license, and otherwise administer the potentially valuable but elusive performance right.[427] Their membership consists of musical copyright owners who have pooled their copyrights and have authorized the performing-rights society both to represent them in licensing these works to users and in policing unauthorized performances. In addition, the performing-rights society collects royalties and distributes them to the membership. In short, the

---

[421] For a discussion of what constitutes a non-dramatic musical work, see *infra* § 8.23[C].

[422] *See* 17 U.S.C. § 116(b)(2).

[423] For a discussion of the role of the performing rights societies, see *infra* § 8.23.

[424] *See* 17 U.S.C. § 116(b)(2).

[425] *See* 17 U.S.C. § 106(4).

[426] For a recent review of the difficulties music users and copyright owners face regarding licensing, see *Buffalo Broad. Co. v. ASCAP*, 546 F. Supp. 274 (S.D.N.Y. 1982), *rev'd*, 744 F.2d 917 (2d Cir. 1984), *cert. denied*, 469 U.S. 1211 (1985).

[427] The performing rights societies are recognized in the 1976 Act in § 116(e).

performing-rights society is a middleman that organizes the market for performance rights, enabling both copyright owners and users to reduce the transaction costs associated with the enforcement and licensing of the performance right. Today, almost every domestic musical composition is in the repertory of ASCAP or BMI, the two largest performing rights societies. The first performing-rights society, the American Society of Composers, Authors, and Publishers ("ASCAP"), was founded in 1914.[428] It remains the largest of the performing rights societies,[429] followed in size by Broadcast Music, Inc. ("BMI") and several smaller organizations.[430]

[B] How They Operate: The ASCAP Model[431]

The ASCAP system provides a prime example of how a performing rights society operates. ASCAP membership consists of music writers and publishers who sign an agreement encompassing three major terms. First, the member grants ASCAP the nonexclusive right to license nondramatic public performance of his works. This provision allows each member to license a work outside the ASCAP system. Second, ASCAP is given the right to bring suit in the name of the member and to police the performance right. Third, the agreement binds the member to ASCAP's method of distributing royalties.

ASCAP simplifies the licensing of its members' performance rights by charging users one fee for the right to use the entire repertory. This agreement is called a "blanket license" under which the user must pay one fee for the three million musical compositions that ASCAP controls. Thus, a television network, radio station, or background music company need not license an individual performance right to play a certain song on a certain date.

Although a single fee is charged, the fee schedule varies greatly between industry groups. Generally, the wealthier are required to pay more.[432] Accordingly, a major television network will be charged more for its blanket license than a small local radio station. License fees generate over $125 million annually.

---

428 See I. Fred Koenigsberg, *Performing Rights in Music and Performing Rights Organizations, Revisited*, 50 J. Copr. Soc'y 355 (2003), for a description of the current operation of ASCAP.

429 The organization grows constantly. As of 1988, ASCAP had approximately 29,400 writer members and 12,007 publisher members. *See* Bernard Korman & I. Fred Koenigsberg, *Performing Rights in Music and Performing Rights Societies*, 33 J. Copyright Soc'y 332, 352 (1987). As of 2002, ASCAP had 90,000 writers and 44,000 publishers. *See* Sidney Shemel & William M. Krasilovsky, This Business of Music 136 (9th ed. 2003). In addition, ASCAP adds about 100,000 titles annually. *Id.* at 136.

430 The most important of these smaller groups is the privately owned SESAC, originally known as the Society of European Stage, Authors and Composers. See *ACEMLA v. Copyright Royalty Tribunal*, 763 F.2d 101 (2d Cir. 1985), for a discussion of these smaller organizations.

431 For various discussions of the ASCAP model, see Nimmer on Copyright § 8.19 (2014), and Sidney Shemel & William M. Krasilovsky, This Business of Music ch. 14 (9th ed. 2003). Other performing rights societies, such as BMI and SESAC, differ in certain significant details.

432 That the ASCAP fee schedule discriminates in price has been a bone of contention between the Society and industry groups, such as the major television networks, leading to an endless series of antitrust litigation. *See infra* § 8.23[D].

After deducting operating expenses, ASCAP apportions and distributes the collected royalties to its members. Publishers and writers are paid according to how much and by whom the musical work is performed. ASCAP obtains this information largely by sampling techniques — for example, by taping radio programs on a random basis.[433] These results are subjected to a weighted formula, which determines the actual monetary distribution. Thus, a copyright owner of a popular song earns more when it is played on national television than on a local radio station. In short, the copyright owner of a hit song stands to gain handsomely from the performance right royalties.

[C] Dramatic (Grand Rights) and Non Dramatic (Small Rights)[434] Performing Rights

Performing-rights societies license nondramatic or "small" rights, whereas dramatic or "grand" rights remain under the control of the copyright owner. Distinguishing between a dramatic as opposed to a nondramatic performance is not always easy. Generally, a performance is nondramatic when it is removed from a dramatic context and unrelated to a larger plot structure. Alternatively, a dramatic performance occurs when it is used to develop a story line. The entire drama need not be developed to render a performance dramatic, so long as the performance takes place within a dramatic context and carries forth a plot. The distinctions between dramatic and nondramatic performances are easy to make at the extremes but difficult to distinguish at the margins.[435]

Under this definition of "dramatic," a performance need not necessarily depict a plot in which the song originally occurred.[436] Thus, when a nightclub singer performs the song "I've Grown Accustomed to Her Face" from the musical *My Fair Lady*, unrelated to a larger dramatic context, a nondramatic performance has taken place. On the other hand, if this same singer performed a significant portion of the musical, singing the songs in sequence or using more songs to carry forth a story line, a dramatic performance has occurred. Because an ASCAP or BMI license does not cover dramatic rights (grand rights), the performer would have to negotiate a license directly from the copyright owner to avoid infringement.

Dramatic performances are treated differently from nondramatic ones in law and in practice for practical reasons. Nondramatic performances number in the millions daily and would be impossible to police without a performing rights society. Dramatic performances, by contrast, occur with much less frequency and are more amenable to individually negotiated licenses. They present potentially

---

[433] ASCAP also polices live performances as well, developing information by field representatives who locate users, by advertisements in local media, and by copyright owners who alert ASCAP of use of their works. *See* Korman & Koenigsberg, *supra* note 429, at 364.

[434] For a discussion of the difference between dramatic and nondramatic works, see Korman & Koenigsberg, *supra* note 429.

[435] *See Robert Stigwood Group, Ltd. v. Sperber*, 457 F.2d 50 (2d Cir. 1972); *Rice v. Am. Program Bureau*, 446 F.2d 685 (2d Cir. 1971); *Leeds Music Ltd. v. Robin*, 358 F. Supp. 650 (S.D. Ohio 1973).

[436] *See* Nimmer on Copyright § 12.06[C] (2014). Note also that under this definition, any musical work used in a dramatic context is a dramatic performance, even those that were originally composed to be played non-dramatically.

greater awards to copyright owners since they are performed before paying audiences and present greater problems of artistic control. Because dramatic performances are advertised, they are more easily policed by the copyright owner.[437]

[D] Synchronization Rights

A synchronization right is the right to use music in timed relations with other visual elements in a film, video, television show, commercial, or other audiovisual production. In other words, it is the right to use the music as a soundtrack with visual images. Synchronization licenses are obtained from the publisher (or composer, if there is no publisher) or the music library. Suppose you are producing a movie or a commercial and, rather than commission an original soundtrack, you would prefer to use preexisting compositions to supply a musical background. In the parlance of the entertainment industry, you need to obtain "synchronization rights" (or simply, "synch rights") to any copyrighted music you have chosen. The fact that synchronization rights are not mentioned in § 106 does not excuse you from the duty to license them. Generally, these rights are considered to be an emanation of the § 106(1) right, but they also relate to § 106(4) because any exhibition or transmission of an audiovisual work to which music has been synchronized necessarily will entail a performance of that music. ASCAP, BMI, and SESAC do not engage in "synch" licensing, and such licenses must be obtained directly from the copyright owner. A spirited debate exists about whether synchronization licenses are necessary and/or sufficient to produce karaoke products that display lyrics in conjunction with recorded music.[438]

[E] Digital Network Transmissions

The advent of new interactive technologies for the delivery of copyrighted content "on demand" over the Internet has enormous practical implications for the owners of copyrighted works. Important questions are raised, for example, as to whether the delivery of a digital file over the Internet constitutes a "public performance" within the meaning of § 106(4). The 1995 "White Paper" on *Intellectual Property and the National Information Infrastructure* has this to say (at p. 71):

> When a copy of a work is transmitted over wires, fiber optics, satellite signals or other modes in digital form so that it may be captured in a user's computer, without the capability of simultaneously "rendering" or "showing," it has rather clearly not been performed. Thus, for example, a file

---

[437] *See* Korman, *supra* note 429, at 335.

[438] *Compare Leadsinger, Inc. v. BMG Music Publ'g*, 512 F.3d 522 (9th Cir. 2008) (display of lyrics makes product an audiovisual work, making it ineligible for § 115 compulsory license and necessitating a synch license), *ABKCO Music, Inc. v. Stellar Records, Inc.*, 96 F.3d 60 (2d Cir. 1996) (§ 115 compulsory license was not sufficient without lyric reprint license), *with EMI Entm't World v. Priddis Music*, 505 F. Supp. 2d 1217 (D. Utah 2007) (karaoke products that display only lyrics without other images are not audiovisual works and require only a § 115 compulsory license and a lyric reprint license), *and Bourne Co. v. Walt Disney Co.*, 1992 U.S. Dist. LEXIS 11731 (S.D.N.Y. 1992) (right to display lyrics on videocassettes was qualitatively different from right to synchronize song with visual images).

> comprising the digitized version of a motion picture might be transferred from a copyright owner to an end user via the Internet without the public performance right being implicated. When, however, the motion picture is "rendered' — by showing its images in sequence — so that users with the requisite hardware and software might watch it *with or without copying the performance*, then under the current law, a "performance" has occurred.

Notably, the just-quoted passage contains no citations to authority and clearly overstates what constitutes the performance right. For example, it would be hard to argue that an email containing copyrighted material is a "public performance" if it is sent from one friend to another.

The Digital Millennium Copyright Act of 1998 did nothing to clarify the answers to these questions. Assuming, however, that some form of permission from copyright owners is necessary before their works can be transmitted commercially using these new technologies, why is it important to know whether such transmissions constitute performances (as distinct from reproduction and/or distributions) of those works? The answer is that different mechanisms exist for licensing different § 106 rights, and the identification of the right implicated by a particular use may determine both the nature of the license the user must obtain and the source from which he or she must obtain it.

In the case of musical works, for example, it seems relatively clear that "streaming" technologies like RealAudio, which permit recorded audio files to be transmitted over the Internet and listened to in "real time," facilitate public performances that must be licensed from ASCAP or BMI. But do such performances also implicate the reproduction and distribution rights? The Harry Fox Agency, which handles "mechanical license" for musical works, has taken the position that they do.[439]

And what about Internet music services like Apple's iTunes that allow users to download digital music files for later playback? Again, it seems that such services implicate the reproduction and distribution rights, and are therefore subject to the compulsory license for musical works in § 115, or require mechanical licenses from the Harry Fox Agency. But do such "digital phonorecord deliveries" also constitute "public performances" within the meaning of 106(4)? Despite the position taken by the ASCAP and BMI White Paper that they are public performances, the Second Circuit has rejected this contention, holding that a digital download is not a "performance" because "[t]he downloaded songs are not performed in any perceptible manner during the transfers."[440]

In addition, there is the limited public performance right in sound recordings — as distinguished from the musical works discussed to this point — to consider.[441] Such licenses currently are being handled by another titan of the music world, the

---

[439] *See Rogers & Hammerstein Org. v. UMG Recordings, Inc.*, 60 U.S.P.Q.2d (BNA) 1354 (S.D.N.Y. 2001) (holding that temporary reproductions made to facilitate "streaming" must be separately licensed and are not covered by the § 115 compulsory license or the Harry Fox mechanical license).

[440] *United States v. ASCAP*, 627 F.3d 64, 73 (2d Cir. 2010).

[441] See 17 U.S.C §§ 106(6) and 114.

Recording Industry Association of American, and are highly controversial. Thus, the "turf" of the Internet music industry is a crowded place, occupied by three potential tiers of licensing for the would-be music distributor to deal with. Despite the industry catchphrase of "one-stop shopping," such convenience does not now exist, at least in this particular corner of the copyright world. The result is that Internet music distributors must weave their way through a complicated terrain fraught with risk.

Two examples will suffice to give a taste of the controversy. A tentative agreement among the National Music Publishers Association (NMPA), the Harry Fox Agency, and the RIAA of October 2001 drew fire for its apparent premise that would-be providers of "streaming" audio on the Internet also must license "mechanical" rights (for temporary server reproduction, etc.).[442] In addition, the Register of Copyrights has recommended to Congress that the § 115 compulsory license be eliminated and that the Copyright Act be amended to provide that any license to publicly perform a musical work by means of digital audio transmission must include the nonexclusive right to reproduce and distribute copies of the work to facilitate such streaming.[443]

[F] Antitrust Problems

Almost from the outset, the performing rights societies have been under attack through the antitrust laws by both the federal government and various industry groups. Much of the practices engaged in by the performing rights societies came about through consent decrees worked out over a twenty-year period between ASCAP and the Department of Justice.[444] Some of the more salient provisions are that (1) ASCAP cannot acquire exclusive licenses of its members' performance rights. Individual members can negotiate licenses themselves and receive royalties from them; (2) ASCAP must offer a per-program license along with its blanket license on an economically meaningful basis; and (3) ASCAP is prohibited from discriminating against similarly situated licensees.[445]

The performing rights societies continue to be challenged on antitrust grounds by national[446] and local broadcasters.[447] The major focus of the attack has been the

---

[442] *See* Initial Comments, Effect of the RIAA/NMPA/HFA Agreement on Inquiry into Digital Phonorecord Deliveries (2002), *available at* www.copyright.gov/carp/dpd/comments.html.

[443] *See Music Licensing Reform: Hearing Before the H. Subcomm. on Courts, the Internet and Intellectual Property* (2005) (statement of Marybeth Peters, Register of Copyrights, U.S. Copyright Office), *available at* www.copyright.gov/docs/regstat062105.html.

[444] The first consent decree was entered into in 1941 between the Department of Justice and ASCAP. BMI is covered by its own consent decree. For a discussion of the two consent decrees, see *Broad. Music, Inc. v. Moor-Law, Inc.*, 484 F. Supp. 357 (D. Del. 1980). The decrees can be found at 1950–51 Trade Cas. ¶ 62,595 (S.D.N.Y. 1950) (ASCAP), and 1966 Trade Cas. ¶ 71,941 (S.D.N.Y. 1966) (BMI). *See also* W. Michael Garner, United States v. ASCAP: *The Licensing Provisions of the Amended Final Judgment of 1950*, 23 Bull. Copyright Soc'y 119 (1976); Ralph Oman, *Source Licensing: The Latest Skirmish in an Old Battle*, 11 Colum.-VLA J.L. & Arts, 251, 254–56 (1987).

[445] For a discussion of the provisions, see *Broad. Music, Inc. v. Columbia Broad. Sys., Inc.*, 441 U.S. 1 (1979). See also *F.E.L. Publ'n, Ltd. v. Catholic Bishops of Chi.*, 506 F. Supp. 1127 (N.D. Ill. 1981).

[446] *See Columbia Broad. Sys., Inc. v. Am. Soc'y of Composers, Authors and Publishers*, 620 F.2d 930 (2d Cir. 1980).

blanket license, by which a single fee is charged for use of the entire repertory, based on a flat sum or on the users' revenues. The fee is unrelated to the frequency of use of the musical works. Actions under § 1 of the Sherman Act[448] brought by national and local broadcasters alleging price fixing and restraint of trade have largely failed.[449]

§ 8.24 THE COMPULSORY LICENSE FOR PUBLIC BROADCASTING, § 118[450]

Section 118 sets up a compulsory license for noncommercial broadcasting entities.[451] Under § 118(d), a public broadcasting entity may include in a broadcast the performance and display of *published* nondramatic musical works and published pictorial, graphic, and sculptural works. The section also allows for the reproduction and distribution of copies of the above programs and for simultaneous off-the-air videotaping of a transmission by nonprofit institutions or governmental bodies for face-to-face teaching purposes. Unlike the three other compulsory licenses, § 118 specifies neither the terms nor the royalties to be assessed for use of the works. Section 118 encourages voluntary agreements between public broadcasters and copyright owners (who are given an exemption from the antitrust laws) to facilitate negotiations between the parties. The agreement must then be filed in the Copyright Office.[452]

§ 8.25 PERFORMANCE RIGHTS IN SOUND RECORDINGS (*NEIGHBORING RIGHTS*)[453]

Unlike a number of European countries,[454] American copyright law under §§ 106(4) and 114(a) specifically excludes a performance right in sound recordings. For the first time, in the Digital Audio Performance Right in Sound Recordings Act

---

[447] *See Buffalo Broad. Co., Inc. v. Am. Soc'y of Composers, Authors and Publishers*, 744 F.2d 917 (2d Cir. 1984). After losing in the courts, the independent television networks have lobbied for legislation that would prohibit the blanket license. *See, e.g.*, H.R. Rep. No. 3521, 99th Cong., 1st Sess. (1985). These bills, known as source licensing legislation, generally provide that an owner of an audiovisual work may not convey public performance rights in a work to a non-network television station without simultaneously conveying the performance right to the music in the audiovisual work. For an overview of source licensing legislation, see Alvin Deutsch, *The Buffalo Shuffle*, 4 Entm't & Sports Law (1985), and Ralph Oman, *Source Licensing: The Latest Skirmish in an Old Battle*, 11 Colum.-VLA J.L. & Arts 251 (1987).

[448] 26 Stat. 209 (1980) (codified as amended at 15 U.S.C. §§ 1–7 (1980)).

[449] The leading case is *Broad. Music, Inc. v. Columbia Broad. Sys., Inc.*, 441 U.S. 1 (1979), holding that the blanket license does not constitute a per se violation of the antitrust laws. *See* Alan J. Hartnick, *The Network Blanket License Triumphant: The Fourth Round of the ASCAP-BMI/CBS Litigation*, 2 Comm. & L. 49 (1980).

[450] For an overview, see Harriet L. Oler, *Legislating Copyright Protection for Works Used in Public Broad.*, 25 Bull. Copyright Soc'y 118 (1977).

[451] 17 U.S.C. § 118(g) defines a public broadcasting entity as a noncommercial, educational broadcasting station as defined by the FCC. Moreover, any nonprofit institution or organization is eligible if it is engaged in the activities described in § 118(d)(2).

[452] *See* 17 U.S.C. § 118(b)(3).

[453] Often, dissemination of a work of authorship to reach its widest possible clientele can only be

of 1995,[455] American copyright law has recognized a performance in sound recordings involving certain "digital audio transmissions." Except in this limited circumstance, however, most performances of sound recordings are still excluded from protection. Thus, when a radio station plays a popular song, only the copyright owner of the musical work, and not the copyright owner of the sound recording of that work, may claim royalties for the performance of the musical composition. Alternatively, the owners of the sound recording, whether they are the record manufacturers or the performers, have no claim. The copyright owner of the song receives all the performance royalties even though the song's success may be due to interpretive musicians or to the artists and technicians who capture the performance in a sound recording. Many have pointed out the illogic of the system, as well as its unfairness.[456]

Despite a strong sentiment expressed by those favoring the performance right,[457] for the first time, Congress is coming close to amending the Copyright Act to grant a blanket performance right to sound recordings.[458] Powerful broadcasting groups such as the National Association of Broadcasters ("NAB") have vigorously opposed legislation conferring performance rights as a tax every time a record is played on the air, driving marginal stations out of business. Not only would the broadcaster have to buy a license from a performing rights society like ASCAP for the right to perform the musical work, but he or she would also have to negotiate a license to play the sound recording.[459] In addition, drafting an adequate and

---

accomplished by intermediaries who get the work to the public in a pleasing, efficient, and accessible form. Plays are presented by actors on the stage and songs are interpreted by musical artists. These performances may be captured on a CD and later broadcasted by radio or television. Legal protection conferred on those who facilitate the dissemination of copyrighted works is known as rights neighboring on copyright or in its shortened version "neighboring rights." It is generally understood that there are three kinds of neighboring rights: the rights of performing artists in their performances, the rights of broadcasting organizations, and the rights of producers of phonograms. For an overview of the subject, see WIPO, Introduction to Intellectual Property Theory and Practice (1998), and Steven Stewart, International Copyright and Neighboring Rights (1983).

[454] *See, e.g.*, France, Law No. 85-660 of July 3, 1985; United Kingdom, Performers Protection Acts 1958/72. Performance rights in sound recording are subject to the *International Convention for the Protection of Performers, Producers of Phonograms and Broadcasting Organizations*. Called the "Rome Convention" and signed at Rome in 1961, some twenty-three countries are members. The convention is based on national treatment setting forth minimum terms of protection for contracting states. For a discussion of the Rome Convention, see *infra* § 12.06[A].

[455] Digital Performance Right in Sound Recordings Act of 1995, Pub. L. 104-39 (1995).

[456] *See* Steven J. D'Onofrio, *In Support of Performance Rights in Sound Recordings*, 29 UCLA L. Rev. 168 (1981). Pursuant to § 114(d), the Register of Copyrights submitted a report recommending an amendment to the section to include a performance right for sound recordings. *See also* Staff of H. Comm. on the Jud., 95th Cong., 2d Sess., Performance Rights in Sound Recordings (Comm. Print No. 15, 1976).

[457] *See* H.R. 1805, 97th Cong., 2d Sess. (1981) (Commercial Use of Sound Recordings Amendments).

[458] *See* H.R. 848, 111th Cong. (2009) (Performance Rights Act).

[459] For a comprehensive critique of performance rights in sound recordings, see Robert L. Bard & Lewis S. Kurlantzick, *A Public Performance Right in Recordings: How to Alter the Copyright System Without Improving It*, 43 Geo. Wash. L. Rev. 152 (1974), who find no convincing argument for such legislation. They argue that performance right legislation will not redress alleged injustices to performers but that the benefits will be divided according to the relative bargaining positions of the parties. As a result, composers, rather than record companies or performers, will be the most likely

effective statute taking into account the various interests involved is a difficult task from both a political and practical standpoint. Legislative proposals have provided for a compulsory license, administered by the Copyright Royalty Board, (and previously by the Copyright Royalty Tribunal or the Register of Copyrights and Copyright Arbitration Royalty Panels), to use a sound recording. By this performance right legislation, performers and record companies would equally share the royalties obtained from broadcasters, jukebox box owners, and anyone else performing a work.[460]

Clearly, legislation of this kind that revises and restructures industry practices and expectations is not easily accomplished. What did take place was recognition for the first time, in 1995, of a performance right for certain digital audio performances. This amendment to § 114 resulted from recognition of digital age challenges and a subtle change in the political dynamics of the controversy.

§ 8.26 THE DIGITAL PERFORMANCE RIGHT IN SOUND RECORDINGS

[A] Introduction

Enacted in 1995, the Digital Performance Right in Sound Recordings Act ("DPRSRA")[461] added a (sixth) exclusive right to the Copyright Act. Section 106(6) confers the exclusive right "in the case of sound recordings to perform the copyrighted work publicly by means of a digital audio transmission."[462] Subject to a dazzling series of limitations, this performance right reflects a number of political tradeoffs reflected in its complex regulatory scheme.

Sound recordings have never enjoyed a general right of public performance under § 106(4) of the Copyright Act. Indeed, until 1972, sound recordings were completely excluded from federal protection, even against acts of piracy. At the outset, federal protection of sound recordings was limited to protection against piracy and did not include a public performance right.[463] Viewed in this manner, the DPRSRA was a delayed legislative response to the dissatisfaction long expressed by the recording industry about the 1971 compromise that brought sound recordings within copyright. At the same time, the DPRSRA is a reaction to recent technological developments — in particular, the transmission of digital audio by terrestrial means (such as cable and wireless relay), via direct broadcast satellites or, ultimately, over the Internet. These technologies share the potential to transmit large amounts of commercial-free audio to subscribers. Moreover, they may do so interactively by permitting a subscriber to order precisely the music he

---

beneficiaries, contrary to the aims of performance right legislation.

[460] *See id.*

[461] Digital Perfomance Right in Sound Recordings Act of 1995, Pub. L. No. 104-39, 109 Stat. 336 (1995). For an overview, see Lionel Sobel, *A New Music Law for the Age of Digital Technology*, 17 Ent. L.J. 3 (1995).

[462] 17 U.S.C. § 106(6).

[463] *See supra* § 3.19.

or she wants to hear at any time whether it is a single cut or an entire album.[464]

In providing for the first time a limited performance right in sound recordings, Congress has given tangible recognition that particular new technologies seriously threaten the traditional market for pre-recorded music. The fear was that if a consumer can order up a high-quality transmission of any piece of music at any time, why should he ever pay for a tape or CD? Even more troublesome, a digital service subscriber with consumer home audio equipment could easily download a digital transmission to a home recording format to replay at leisure or even resell.

The DPRSRA reveals the tangled and ever-evolving nature of interest group politics of copyright industries. For years, the over-the-air broadcasting industry has been the strongest and most effective opponent of the performance right in sound recordings. That industry, however, had its own reason not to oppose the DPRSRA. After all, the DPRSRA imposed licensing costs on digital audio subscription services, potentially the broadcasters' most significant future commercial competitors.

Further complicating the political dynamics, other players in the legislative drama led to the enactment of DPRSRA. Since 1971, musical copyright owners (and the organizations which represent them, like ASCAP, BMI, and SESAC) also have been skeptical about the desirability of performance rights in sound recordings. Those interests already receive performance royalties for the compositions incorporated in recordings, and they have reasoned that if broadcasters and others have to pay an additional license fee to recording companies, this may mean a smaller share of the licensing dollar for composers. Thus, the 1995 Act was shaped to protect the interests of copyright owners as well as the performing rights organizations.

In the end, the compromise that became DPRSRA also embraced language intended to assure that the rights created by the Act would not be abused in ways that could stifle the development of the new business model represented by interactive subscription-based audio transmission services. And finally, the Act attempted to provide legal infrastructure for another potential new business model — the on-demand digital "delivery" of sound recordings by means of transmission — and to assure that the rights of all parties will be observed when and if it emerges. This ambitious program inevitably resulted in a complex piece of legislation.

[B] Highlights of the DPRSRA

[1] The Digital Audio Transmission Right of § 106(6)

The DPRSRA adds another exclusive right to § 106 of the Copyright Act, effectively prohibiting the unlicensed digital transmissions of sound recordings. This exclusive right, however, is subject to special exemptions and limitations

[464] For a description of the technology and some of the ways in which it has been (or could be deployed), *see generally* COPYRIGHT IMPLICATIONS OF DIGITAL AUDIO TRANSMISSION SERVICES: A REPORT OF THE REGISTER OF COPYRIGHTS (1991). For a far-reaching speculation on the significance of the technology, see PAUL GOLDSTEIN, COPYRIGHT'S HIGHWAY: FROM GUTENBERG TO THE CELESTIAL JUKEBOX 202–04 (2003).

beyond those, such as fair use, that apply to all of the § 106 and § 106A rights. These limitations are specified in subsection (d) of § 114 ("Scope of exclusive rights in sound recordings,") entitled "Limitations on exclusive right."

[2] The § 114 Amendments: Exemptions to the Right

exemptions to the right embodied in § 114(d)(1) focus on those aspects of the digital broadcasting that have the greatest potential to affect future performance rights markets in the new transmission environment. The greatest concerns about the new digital audio technology were rooted in its potential for interactivity, whereby an individual could hear a song at any time by dialing up a "celestial jukebox," and in so doing would be less likely to buy a phonorecord, either in a record store or by download. Significantly, no interactive services are made exempt by § 114(d)(1). Thus, the most important exemption provided in § 114(d)(1) is for *non-interactive, non-subscription* services. These exemptions break down as follows. First, broadcasters of "free" content (i.e., advertising-supported radio and television programming) may continue to perform sound recordings without license as they do today, even if they should choose to convert their operations to digital technology. Second, various secondary transmissions of exempt primary transmissions (as well as program "feeds" directed to exempt broadcasters) are also exempt. Third, transmissions within business establishments and to those establishments (for use in the ordinary course of business) are exempted. This later exemption allows for commercial use of recordings as background music and permits background music services such as MUZAK to be carried on by digital means.

[3] Compulsory Licensing Provisions

Congress enacted the DPRSRA, creating a performance right in sound recordings limited to digital transmissions. Under that legislation three categories of digital transmissions were taken into account. First, broadcast transmissions (FCC licensed terrestrial broadcast stations) were exempted from the performance right. Second, subscription transmissions were generally subject to a statutory license. Third, on-demand (interactive) transmissions were subject to the full exclusive right under § 106(6).

To use the compulsory license, services that digitally perform sound recordings and are not interactive must comply with four requirements: (1) they must not use a signal that causes the receiver to change from one program channel to another;[465] (2) they must include the information encoded in the sound recording being transmitted, if technically feasible;[466] (3) they must not publish an advance program schedule or prior announcement of titles of upcoming sound recordings;[467] and (4) they must not exceed the "sound recording performance complement."[468] The rates

[465] 17 U.S.C. § 114(d)(2)(A)(ii).

[466] 17 U.S.C. § 114(d)(2)(A)(iii).

[467] 17 U.S.C. § 114(d)(2)(B)(iii).

[468] 17 U.S.C. § 114(d)(2)(C)(i). See 17 U.S.C. § 114(j)(13) for the definition of "sound recording performance complement," which limits the number of related selections (*e.g.*, same artist, same album) of sound recordings that can be played during a three-hour period.

are determined by voluntary industry negotiation. If no voluntary agreement is possible, the royalties are set by administrative assessment.[469]

The original provisions, set forth in § 114, concerned "conventional" transmissions, but what about the growing number of entities that have been making digital transmissions of sound recordings over the Internet using the latest streaming audio technologies? This activity did not fall squarely within any of the four categories in the original Act. In 1998, with the Digital Millennium Copyright Act, Congress addressed this "gap" in protection by amending § 114 to take into account digital transmissions of sound recordings over the Internet by the use of streaming audio technologies. In amending § 114, the DPRSRA expands the statutory license for subscription transmissions to include webcasting as a new category of "eligible nonsubscription transmissions."[470]

The webcasting provisions of DPRSRA have created a number of controversies concerning their scope and coverage. One such debate concerned the practice of some radio stations simultaneously streaming their signal on the Web. These "Simulcasting" Broadcasters claimed that such activity should be exempt from the provisions of DPRSRA, as was their over-the-air broadcasting. The Copyright Office, sustained by the courts, disagreed with the broadcasters, concluding that a transmission by an FCC-licensed broadcaster of its AM or FM radio broadcast over the Internet is not exempt from the limited public performance right.[471] Thus, over-the-air broadcasters who wish to webcast must pay the statutory fee.

Another controversy concerns the amount of royalty rates to be assessed against small and noncommercial webcasters. As originally contemplated by § 114, no special provision was made for the wide variety of entities that stream their broadcasts over the Internet. Section 114 provides that the statutory license is to be accomplished through voluntary negotiation at five-year intervals, with a CARP (now replaced by the Copyright Royalty Board) to be employed if no agreement is reached.[472] The recording industry advocated a per-listener, per-song basis for royalty computation, which, according to small and noncommercial webcasters, would put them out of business. After a series of CARP proceedings that were clearly unsatisfactory to small webcasters, Congress came to their aid. The Small Webcaster Settlement Act of 2002[473] ratified an eleventh-hour industry agreement, whereby small webcasters are subject to an alternative arrangement based on "a percentage of revenue or expenses, or both, and [to] include a minimum fee."[474] The terms of the Act were not permanent. Once again, Congress passed a bill, the Small Webcaster Settlement Act of 2008,[475] that allows small webcasters to adopt

---

[469] Until 2005, this role was carried by CARPs. The CARP system was replaced by Copyright Royalty Judges. *See supra* § 8.03[C].

[470] An "eligible nonsubscription transmission" is defined as a non-interactive, non-subscription digital audio transmission not exempt under § 114(d)(1). *See* 17 U.S.C. § 114(j)(6).

[471] *See Boneville Int'l Corp. v. Peters*, 347 F.3d 485 (3d Cir. 2003).

[472] 17 U.S.C. § 114(f).

[473] Pub. L. 107-321, 116 Stat. 2780 (2002).

[474] 17 U.S.C. § 114(f)(5)(A).

[475] Pub. L. No. 110-435 (2008); Webcaster Settlement Act of 2009, Pub. L. No. 111-36 (2009)

alternative rates negotiated by SoundExchange[476] and other webcasters. Consequently, future negotiations over royalty rates will continue, and Congress may be disposed to intervene once again.[477]

As indicated above, of somewhat less concern to sound recording copyright owners were those digital transmission services that offer non-interactive programming by subscription, much like the digital audio equivalent of cable television. Here § 114(d)(2), (e), and (f) erect a scheme whereby so-called "voluntary negotiation proceedings" between representatives of various groups of copyright owners and transmitting entities are supposed to be convened at five-year intervals to determine reasonable royalty rates. The compulsory license, however, is potentially available to otherwise qualifying subscription services only under certain relatively stringent conditions designed to minimize the impact of such services on other commercial distribution channels for recorded music.

[4] Protective Provisions

Additional protective provisions are built into the DRPSRA as a result of political compromise. Section 114(g) provides that in limited circumstances, performers, both featured and nonfeatured, who render words or music, will share in the royalties derived from licensing of the digital performance right. Section 114(h) provides means by which would-be entrants into the digital audio transmission marketplace can avoid being blocked by existing participants and arrangements. In addition, § 114(i) of the DPRSRA specifies that digital audio transmission services must license performing rights in the underlying music as well as in the sound recording itself.

§ 8.27 THE RIGHT OF PUBLIC DISPLAY, § 106(5)

Section 106(5) specifically recognizes the right of public display for the first time in American copyright law. The display right applies to all categories of copyrightable subject matter except for sound recordings and architectural works. Under § 101, "to display a work means to show a copy of it, either directly or by means of a film, slide, television image, or any other device or process or, in the case of a motion picture or other audiovisual work, to show individual images nonsequentially."[478]

Thus, a series of still photographs of a dancer or a pantomimist would not infringe the performance right but may infringe the display right in the choreographic work or the pantomime. Similarly, a television program that uses a work of visual art as part of a set decoration would not violate the performance right but

(extending the period in which SoundExchange may negotiate with webcasters regarding music royalties).

[476] SoundExchange is a nonprofit performance rights organization that collects royalties on the behalf of sound recording copyright owners and featured artists for noninteractive digital transmissions, including satellite and Internet radio.

[477] The determination of royalty rates for transmissions after December 31, 2004, is to be governed by the statutory rules that bind all webcasters. *See* § 114(f)(5)(F).

[478] 17 U.S.C. § 101 (display).

could well infringe the display right if the work is visible for such time so as to meet the standard of substantial similarity.[479]

Like the performance right, the right of display is limited to *public* displays. The definition of "public" is the same for both performances and displays.[480] Section 101 defines a display as public if it takes place, "at a place open to the public or at any place where a substantial number of persons outside of a normal circle of a family and its social acquaintances is gathered."[481]

Moreover, a display is public, as is a performance, when the display of a copy of the work is transmitted to the public "whether members of the public . . . receive it in the same place or in separate places and at the same time or at different times."[482] A public display can take place by means of television, or by the Internet, where a copy of a work is transmitted to private homes. The Internet, in particular, provides an unprecedented ability to display publicly copyrighted works. Generally, the public display takes place when an Internet service provider transmits to the public a copyrighted work residing on its own server. But does a public display occur when a service provider engages in "inline linking" and "framing"[483] of another person's website? In *Perfect 10, Inc. v. Google, Inc.*,[484] the Ninth Circuit Court of Appeals held that the "owner of a computer that does not store and serve the electronic information to a user is not displaying that information even if such owner in-line links to or frames the electronic information."[485] Plaintiff, Perfect 10, operated a commercial website featuring images of nude models. It brought suit against Google's use of a web-crawler program that generated thumbnails on its website in response to a search term request. If the user clicked on a thumbnail, it displayed a full but framed image. Google did not store or physically transmit the full images, only their thumbnails. As to the framing of the inline linked images, the court reasoned that because Google's computers do not store the images, Google does not maintain a copy of the images on its servers. Rather Google simply provided HTML instructions through which images stored on third party computers were located and accessed. Accordingly, such activity may raise contributory

---

[479] *See Ringgold v. Black Entm't Television, Inc.*, 126 F.3d 70 (2d Cir. 1997) (finding use of a poster reproducing a work of art as part of the background (set decoration) in a television episode violated display right, even thought the aggregate duration of its use in nine sequences totaled only 26.75 seconds); *but see Gottlieb Dev. LLC v. Paramount Pictures Corp.*, 590 F. Supp. 2d 625 (S.D.N.Y. 2008) (appearance of copyrighted pinball machine "Silver Slugger" in the background of the movie *What Women Want* was *de minimis* use as a matter of law).

[480] For a discussion of what constitutes a public performance or display, see *supra* § 8.17.

[481] 17 U.S.C. § 101.

[482] *Id.*; *see, e.g., Playboy Enters. v. Frena*, 839 F. Supp. 1552 (M.D. Fla. 1993) (finding the display right violated where subscribers to a computer bulletin board uploaded photographs from Playboy and defendant bulletin board operator allowed subscribers to download them).

[483] "Framing" is a technique whereby the current website includes its own banner ads and other content as a "frame" around images or text from a third-party site. An "inline link" works in the same way, in that the code tells the site to go to another site and display the image from that third-party site. The website does not copy the image or text from the third-party site, but rather has code that tells the site to go to another URL (uniform resource locator) and display that image.

[484] 508 F.3d 1146 (9th Cir. 2007).

[485] *Id.*

infringement issues but does not constitute direct infringement. By contrast, the Ninth Circuit ruled that Perfect 10 made a prima facie case that Google's communication of its thumbnail images, stored on Google's servers, directly infringed Perfect 10's display right.[486]

§ 8.28 LIMITATIONS ON THE DISPLAY RIGHT

[A] Public Display of an Owned Copy, § 109(c)[487]

Under § 109(c), an owner of a lawfully made copy may "display that copy publicly, either directly or by the projection of no more than one image at a time, to viewers present at the place where the copy is located."[488]

This limitation to the display right is the counterpart of the § 109(a)[489] first sale doctrine. Like the first sale doctrine, it applies only in favor of a person who owns a lawfully made copy of the work. Such a person has the privilege, notwithstanding the copyright owner's display right, to publicly display the lawfully owned copy. The display can take place directly or by protection, so long as no more than one image at a time is displayed and the viewers are present at the place where the copy is located.

Thus, if a museum has bought a work of art from a contemporary artist, it can display the work publicly even though it does not own the copyright on the work. This exemption to the display right applies only if the museum owns the work. The museum could not display or authorize others to display a work on loan from the copyright owner without his permission. Once title to the work passes, the owner of the work has not only the right to display it publicly but may even charge admission for the public to see the work. Absent an agreement to the contrary, § 109(c) gives the copyright owner no right to participate economically in the public display, despite the number of persons who see the work and how much they are charged.[490] Moreover, the owner of a copy of a work can display it directly or

---

486 In another part of the opinion, the court concluded that Google's use of the thumbnails was a fair use. For a discussion of the fair use defense, see *infra* § 10.11. See also *Kelly v. Arriba Soft Corp.*, 280 F.3d 934 (9th Cir. 2002). In *Kelly*, the Ninth Circuit Court of Appeals held that the defendant Arriba Soft infringed a professional photographer's display rights by providing links to websites bearing the photographs and framing them in Arriba Soft's own website. According to the court, "[b]y allowing the public to view Kelly's copyrighted works while visiting Arriba's website, Arriba created a public display of Kelly's works." After reconsideration, however, the court vacated this portion of the opinion because the "linking and framing" issue had not been raised in the court below. *See Kelly v. Arriba Soft Corp.*, 336 F.3d 811 (9th Cir. 2003). The court did confirm that Arriba Soft's display of thumbnails on its site constituted a fair use.

487 17 U.S.C. § 109(c).

488 *Id.*

489 For a discussion of the first sale doctrine, see *supra* § 8.14.

490 For a discussion of the display right as limited by § 109(a), see Thomas A. Goetzl & Stuart A. Sutton, *Copyright and the Visual Artist's Display Right: A New Doctrinal Analysis*, 9 Colum.-VLA J.L. & Arts 15 (1984). The authors argue that the § 109(c) limitation is unfair to artists considering the profits made on these works by museums, galleries, and corporations who display these works publicly before massive paying audiences, sometimes over a million persons (e.g., the Picasso exhibit in 1980). *See id.* at

indirectly by, for example, an opaque projector, so long as the display occurs at a place where the copy is located. The exemption, however, would not apply if the image of the work were transmitted to members of the public at another location.[491]

Even if the viewing public is located at the same place, § 109(c) will not exempt a display when "more than one image at a time" is projected to viewers. This provision is intended to give copyright owners control over computer uses of their work because such use may indirectly affect the market for the reproduction and distribution of copies of the work. To illustrate, § 109(c) would not exempt a display in which every person in a lecture hall were provided with a screen at a computer terminal to view the copyrighted work. Here the "one image at a time" limitation would be superseded, and permission of the copyright would have to be obtained for the display.[492] Similarly, a transmission of a copyrighted work from one computer terminal to another would violate the display right and fall outside the § 109(c) exemption, whether or not the transmission of the image took place simultaneously or at different times, or whether the computers or terminals are located in the same physical space.[493]

[B] Other Exemptions to the Display Right

Many, but not all of the exemptions for performances outlined in § 110 apply with equal force to displays:

(1) the face to face teaching exemption, § 110(1);

(2) the instructional broadcast exemption, § 110(2);

(3) the religious services exemption, § 110(3); and

(4) certain public receptions of transmission (the *Aiken* exemption), § 110(5).[494]

In addition, displays are equally exempt under § 111's provisions concerning secondary transmissions by cable television systems. Finally, § 118 exempts performance displays of copyrighted works made in connection with certain activities of public broadcasting stations.[495]

---

32. The authors argue for a compulsory licensing system, privately administered to replace the § 109(c) limitation.

[491] *See* 17 U.S.C. § 109(c).

[492] *See* H.R. Rep. No. 94-1476, at 80 (1976).

[493] The same rules apply to secondary transmissions except for those that are exempt under § 111(a) and § 110(5).

[494] The following § 110 exemptions do not cover the display right, but the performance right only: § 110(4), the not-for-profit performance exemption; § 110(6), the agricultural fair exemption; § 110(7), the record vending establishment exemption; § 110(8), transmissions to the blind and handicapped; § 110(9), transmissions to the blind and handicapped of a dramatic literary work; and § 110(10), the fraternal order exemption.

[495] 17 U.S.C. § 118(d). See *supra* § 8.23 for a discussion of the exemption.

Part V. BEYOND CONVENTIONAL COPYRIGHT PROTECTION: THE MORAL RIGHT

§ 8.29 THE MORAL RIGHT[496]

[A] Generally

The 1976 Act's protection of authors' exclusive rights is based on the economic principle that the consumer benefits by the incentives given to authors to produce copyrighted works. By comparison, a number of other countries[497] and signatories of the Berne Convention recognize the moral right of the author, which treats the author's work not just as an economic interest,[498] but as an inalienable, natural right and an extension of the artist's personality.[499] Although the scope of the moral right varies from country to country, it is a composite right consisting generally of fundamental components:

(1) The right of integrity — the right that the work not be mutilated or distorted; and

---

[496] For an overview of the moral right, see Nimmer on Copyright § 8D (2014); Russel J. DaSilva, Droit Moral *and the Amoral Copyright: A Comparison of Artists' Rights in France and the United States*, 28 Bull. Copyright Soc'y 1 (1980); Andre Francon & Jane C. Ginsburg, *Authors' Rights in France: The Moral Right of the Creator of a Commissioned Work to Compel the Commissioning Party to Complete the Work*, 9 Colum.-Vla J.L. & Arts 381 (1985); Roberta Rosenthal Kwall, *Copyright and the Moral Right: Is an American Marriage Possible?*, 38 Vand. L. Rev. 1 (1985); John Henry Merryman, *The Refrigerator of Bernard Buffet*, 27 Hastings L.J. 1023 (1976). For an argument that moral rights law actually serves to endanger art in the name of protecting it, see Amy M. Adler, *Against Moral Rights*, 97 Cal. L. Rev. 263 (2009).

[497] The most famous moral rights law is that of France. *See* Law of March 11, 1957 on Literary and Artistic Property. Although moral rights have found their greatest strength in Western European countries, there are some thirty-five countries around the world including those in Africa, Asia, and Latin America that recognize moral rights. *See* Kwall, *supra* note 496, at 98 (listing countries in the appendix). For a look at the range of moral rights available in India, see Arathi Ashok, *Moral Rights — TRIPS and Beyond: The Indian Slant*, 59 J. Copyright Soc'y 697 (2012).

[498] Two concepts are embodied under French *droit d'auteur.* The first is *droit patrimoniaux*, analogous to our copyright, which recognizes the author's economic stake in his work, lasts 70 years after death, and is freely alienable. The second component is *droit moral*, nonpecuniary in nature, made up of a collection of prerogatives to preserve the integrity of a work and an artistic personality. *See* Claude Sarraute, *Current Theory on the Moral Right of Authors and Artists Under French Law*, 16 Am. J. Comp. L. 465 (1968).

[499] Colorization of black and white films has generated a debate over recognition of the moral right in the United States. Copyright owners of black and white films have recently begun adapting these films to color by a computer process. Copyright owners colorize films to reach audiences that prefer movies in color. Authors and others (who had originally assigned the copyrights to their works to these current owners or waived them as works made for hire) have vigorously opposed colorization as a mutilation of an artist's work. Copyright owners, however, claim they have a legal right to do what they want with the films to protect their investment. *See* Roger L. Mayer et al., *Colorization: The Arguments For*, 17 J. Arts Mgmt. & L. 64 (1987); Woody Allen et al., *Colorization: The Arguments Against*, 17 J. Arts Mgmt. & L. 79 (1987). Unless special legislation is passed, the critics of colorization have lost the battle. The Copyright Office will register colorized films as derivative works. *See supra* § 2.08[C].

(2) The right of paternity — the right to be acknowledged as an author of the work.

In addition to these two components, most formulations would include the right of disclosure — the right to decide when and in what form the work will be presented to the public. Some formulations would also include the right of withdrawal — the right to withdraw the work from publication or to make modifications to it, and the right to prevent excessive criticism.[500] *Droit de Suite*, or the resale royalty right, is sometimes considered an aspect of the moral right but is in reality more in the nature of an economic right.[501]

Although American copyright law has never adopted an integrated version of the moral right, the concept has made its way incrementally into the law in three ways. First, an author's integrity and attribution rights have been protected piecemeal by various bodies of state and federal law. Second, about a dozen states have passed statutes explicitly recognizing the moral rights of visual artists. Third, in the Visual Artists Rights Act of 1990, federal law has followed the lead of state law by protecting the integrity and attribution rights of visual artists.

[B] Analogs of the Moral Right in State and Federal Law[502]

Although American copyright law has never adopted an integrated version of the moral right, some case law has come very close to achieving the same result in protecting certain aspects of the author's integrity and paternity rights. The leading case is *Gilliam v. American Broadcasting Cos., Inc.*,[503] where plaintiff's right to prevent distortion of his work was protected under both the copyright and unfair competition laws. In *Gilliam*, defendant ABC obtained a license to broadcast several taped shows created by *Monty Python*, the famous British comedy group. The license provided that shows were to be broadcast in their entirety except for minor editing to adapt the programs for commercials. ABC, however, cut twenty-four minutes from each ninety-minute program. The court held that this truncation violated the terms of the license and constituted an infringement of plaintiff's adaptation right by creating an unauthorized derivative work. In addition, the court found a violation under § 43(a) of the Lanham Act[504] because the abridged version constituted a false designation of origin under the terms of the Act by deforming the work and presenting plaintiff as an author of a work not his own, subjecting him to criticism for a work he did not do. Thus, both copyright and unfair competition laws were invoked to protect the plaintiff's business and personal reputations, providing de facto protection of artistic interests akin to the

---

[500] For an evaluation of recent moral rights models in light of comments by American supernatural fiction authors, see Jacqueline D. Lipton, Ph.D., *Moral Rights and Supernatural Fiction: Authorial Dignity and the New Moral Rights Agendas*, 21 Fordham Intell. Proper. Media & Ent. L.J. 537 (2011).

[501] For a discussion of the resale royalty right now in existence in California, see *supra* § 8.15[F].

[502] *See* James M. Treece, *American Law Analogues of the Author's "Moral Right"*, 16 Am. J. Comp. L. 487 (1968).

[503] 538 F.2d 14 (2d Cir. 1976).

[504] 60 Stat. 427, 15 U.S.C. § 125(a) (1946).

moral rights of integrity and paternity.[505] In addition to copyright and unfair competition laws,[506] American authors have turned to contract,[507] defamation,[508] and privacy[509] laws to protect other aspects of their artistic personality and reputation.

As illustrated by *Gilliam*, the courts have used § 43(a) of the Lanham Act to provide de facto protection to paternity rights though a cause of action for "passing off." In the classical passing off situation, one author places another author's name on the work, as did ABC when it misrepresented the origin of the truncated version of the *Monty Python* show. Alternatively, the courts have also extended § 43(a) to situations of "reverse passing off," where one author takes credit for another author's work-in effect, a civil action for plagiarism. For example, the doctrine has been applied where a plaintiff's name was replaced with another's in the credits and advertisements for a motion picture.[510]

Despite its recognition in the law, the scope of reverse passing off was substantially reduced in *Dastar Corp. v. Twentieth Century Fox Film Corp.*,[511] where the Supreme Court held that the phrase "designation of origin" refers only to the source of tangible goods and not to the originator of ideas or creative works contained in those goods. Specifically, the court ruled that the defendant did not violate § 43(a) by editing, repackaging, and selling plaintiff's public domain work television series, *Crusade in Europe*, without crediting plaintiff or any of its production employees. "To hold otherwise would be akin to finding that § 43(a) created a species of perpetual . . . copyright, which Congress may not do."[512] In sum, *Dastar* allows copying and distribution without attribution of works whose copyright has expired.[513] In so doing, *Dastar* appears to undermine the argument that the United States complies with its Berne obligations by providing de facto protection of the attribution right.[514]

---

505 The court noted that a cause of action to redress a distortion of an artistic work "finds its roots in the continental concept of *droit moral* or moral right." *Gilliam*, 538 F.2d at 24.

506 Section 43(a) of the Lanham Act (false designation of origin) provided the most creative incorporation of moral right principles of paternity and integrity in American law. *See, e.g.*, *Geisel v. Poynter Prods. Inc.*, 283 F. Supp. 261 (S.D.N.Y. 1968); *Rich v. RCA Corp.*, 390 F. Supp. 530 (S.D.N.Y. 1975).

507 In addition to *Gilliam*, see, for example, *Granz v. Harris*, 198 F.2d 585 (2d Cir. 1952).

508 *See, e.g.*, *Edison v. Viva Int'l, Ltd.*, 421 N.Y.S. 2d 203 (1979) (sustaining action for libel for publication of author's article in substantially different version).

509 *See, e.g.*, *Zim v. W. Publ'g Co.*, 573 F.2d 1318 (5th Cir. 1978) (stating cause of action under invasion of privacy for publication of unauthorized versions of author's work).

510 *See Smith v. Montoro*, 648 F.2d 602 (9th Cir. 1981); *see also Lamothe v. Atl. Recording Corp.*, 847 F.2d 1403 (9th Cir. 1988) (holding that the omission of the names of two of the work's coauthors from a record album cover and sheet music featuring their works violated § 43(a)).

511 539 U.S. 23 (2003).

512 *Id.* at 37.

513 *Dastar* has influenced other courts to deny "reverse passing off" attribution claims. *See, e.g.*, *Keane v. Fox Television Stations, Inc.*, 297 F. Supp. 2d 921 (S.D. Tex. 2004); *Tao of Sys. Integration, Inc. v. Analytical Servs. & Materials, Inc.*, 299 F. Supp. 2d 565 (E. D. Va. 2004); *Williams v. UMG Recordings*, 281 F. Supp. 2d 1177 (C.D. Cal. 2003).

514 For commentary on *Dastar*, see Justin Hughes, *American Moral Rights and Fixing Dastar*, 2007

Before Congress passed the Visual Artists Rights Act, several states had adopted their own version of a moral right for visual artists.

[C] State Art Preservation Acts

A number of states, such as California, New York, Massachusetts, and Louisiana,[515] have incorporated the moral rights in statutes generally known as "state art preservation statutes." These state moral rights statutes, except for that of Massachusetts,[516] are limited in their application to works of fine art. The California and New York statutes provide two differing models of moral rights protection. The California Art Preservation Act[517] prohibits intentional physical defacement, mutilation, alteration, or destruction of a work of *fine* art.[518] The artist can waive the right, but only in a written instrument. The right passes to his heirs upon his death and terminates seventy years after the artist's death. The Statute of Limitations for bringing an action is three years.

New York has passed a somewhat different version of a Moral Rights Act. The New York Artists' Authorship Rights Act[519] prevents unauthorized public display, publication, or reproduction of an altered, defaced, or mutilated work where such display would reasonably damage the artist's reputation. By precluding mutilation of a work, the California and New York Acts are similar, but their underlying moral right rationale is somewhat different. California emphasizes a broad personal interest in the integrity of the work. The prohibited act is the destruction of a work of fine art in the interest of cultural preservation. By contrast, the New York Act, in prohibiting the *display* of a mutilated work, focuses on the artist's reputational interest. In other words, one violates the California Act by defacing a work of art, whereas one violates the New York Act by displaying the defaced artwork.[520] In one way, New York goes a step further into moral rights protection than California: it recognizes not only a right to integrity, but a paternity right as well. The New York Act provides that "the artist shall retain at all times the right to claim

---

UTAH L. REV. 659 (concluding that misattribution of someone else's work survives *Dastar*); D. Lastowka, *Digital Attribution: Copyright and the Right to Credit*, 87 B.U. L. REV. 41 (2007); Tom W. Bell, *Misunderstanding* Dastar: *How the Supreme Court Copyright Preemption*, 65 MD. L. REV. 206 (2006); Mary LaFrance, *When You Wish Upon a* Dastar: *Creative Provenance and the Lanham Act*, 23 CARDOZO ARTS & ENT. L.J. 197 (2005).

515 LA. REV. STAT. ANN. § 51:2152.

516 The Massachusetts law generally follows the California model except that it has broadened the definition of fine art to include: "any original work of visual or graphic art of any media which shall include, but not be limited to, any painting, print drawing, sculpture, craft, object, photograph, audio or video tape, film, hologram, or any combination thereof, of recognized quality." MASS. GEN. LAWS ANN. Ch. 231 § 85S(b).

517 CAL. CIV. CODE § 987.

518 Fine art is defined as, "an original painting, sculpture, or drawing, or an original work of art in glass of recognized quality, but shall not include work prepared under contract for commercial use by its purchaser." CAL. CIV. CODE § 987.

519 Effective January 1, 1984. *See* N.Y. ARTS & CULT. AFF. L. §§ 14.51–14.59.

520 *See, e.g.*, *Wojnarowicz v. Am. Family Ass'n*, 745 F. Supp. 130 (S.D.N.Y. 1990) (finding the unauthorized publication of 14 photographically reproduced fragments extracted from plaintiff's works constituted actionable mutilation reasonably likely to damage reputation and violate the New York act).

authorship."[521] These state moral rights acts present serious questions of federal preemption nder § 301 of the Copyright Act and the Visual Artists Rights Act of 1990.[522]

§ 8.30 COPYRIGHT PROTECTION OF MORAL RIGHTS: THE VISUAL ARTISTS RIGHTS ACT OF 1990 ("VARA")

[A] Generally

The United States became a party to the Berne Convention on March 1, 1989, without passing special legislation designed to comply with Article 6*bis*[523] of Berne, which requires member nations to protect authors' rights of attribution and integrity.[524] Congress justified its decision not to adopt specific moral rights legislation, claiming that the United States already gives de facto recognition to moral rights when the entirety of American law is considered. But serious doubts lingered about whether U.S. obligations under Berne had really been met, without specific recognition of moral rights. The proponents of specific legislation quickly prevailed. Congress responded by passing the Visual Artists Rights Act of 1990 ("VARA").[525] Ironically, VARA falls short of conforming to the requirements of the Berne Convention. Most significantly, VARA specifies that protection last no longer than the life of the author, whereas Berne requires that moral rights should be protected at least for term of the related economic rights — which in the United States is the life of author plus seventy years.[526] Apart from its obvious Berne

---

521 N.Y. Arts & Cul. Aff. L. §§ 14.51–14.59.

522 For a discussion of federal preemption of these acts, see *infra* § 11.8[D].

523 In the U.C.C. and the Berne Convention, *bis* indicates a statutory article added to the original text and "sandwiched in" so as not to affect the original numbering scheme (much as §§ 106A and 116A were added to the 1976 Copyright Act subsequent to its enactment). The designations *ter* and *quater* indicate the addition of further articles in the same fashion.

524 Berne Convention for the Protection of Artistic and Literary Property, July 24, 1971 (Paris) art. 6*bis*, which reads:

> (1) Independently of the author's economic rights and even after the transfer of the said rights, the author shall have the right to claim authorship of the work and to object to any distortion, mutilation or other modification of, or other derogatory action in relation to, the said work, which would be prejudicial to his honor or reputation.
>
> (2) The rights granted to the author in accordance with the preceding paragraph shall, after his death, be maintained, at least until the expiry of the economic rights, and shall be exercisable by the persons or institutions authorized by the legislation of the country where protection is claimed. However, those countries whose legislation, at the moment of their ratification of or accession to this Act, does not provide for the protection after the death of the author of all the rights set out in the preceding paragraph may provide that some of these rights may, after his death, cease to be maintained.
>
> (3) The means of redress for safeguarding the rights granted by this Article shall be governed by the legislation of the country where protection is claimed.

525 Pub. L. No. 101-650, 104 Stat. 5128 (1990).

526 § 106A(d)(1).

shortcomings,[527] VARA adds a new § 106A that confers the rights of attribution and integrity in certain works of visual art.[528]

[B] Summary of the Provisions of VARA

[1] Works Protected

The Visual Artists Rights Act is limited in its subject matter and scope and is essentially confined to the protection of works of fine art.[529] Qualifying works include those that exist in a single copy, such as original paintings, drawings, prints, sculptures, or works existing in signed and consecutively numbered editions of no more than 200 copies. Thus, a unique original painting does not have to be signed and numbered, but if the artist makes two copies of the painting, both copies must be signed and consecutively numbered. In addition to paintings and sculpture, still photographic images are covered if produced for "exhibition purposes only, existing in single copy that is signed by the author, or in limited editions of 200 copies or fewer, that are signed and consecutively numbered by the author."[530] This provision results in excluding most photographic works taken by most amateur photographers, whose initial purpose for snapping the shutter was not done for inclusion in an exhibit.[531]

Under VARA, the courts will inevitably have to make judgments about art, a particularly tricky task when dealing with the outer reaches of the avant-garde. The legislative history recognized this challenge, directing the courts to use common sense and generally accepted standards of the artistic community in determining if a particular work falls within the definition of a "work of visual art." In addition, whether a work meets the definitional requirements should not depend on the medium or materials used.[532]

So far, the courts have taken a restrained vision of what constitutes a work of art under the terms of VARA. For example in *Phillips v. Pembroke Real Estate, Inc.*,[533] the court held that § 106A does not encompass site-specific art — a work that comprises two or more physical objects that must be presented together as the artist intended to retain its meaning and integrity. The plaintiff had created multiple pieces of sculpture and stoneworks that were integrated into a park, which

---

527 Another of these shortcomings that would run afoul of Berne's ban on formalities as a condition of protection (Berne, Art. 5(2)), is the statute's requirement that an edition of the work must be signed by the author and consecutively numbered. *See* 17 U.S.C. § 101 (work of visual art).

528 For an argument that the Visual Artists Rights Act of 1990 (VARA) also benefits the purchasing and viewing public, see Xiyin Tang, *The Artist as Brand: Toward a Trademark Conception of Moral Rights*, 122 YALE L.J. 218 (2012).

529 For an analysis of whether tattoos fit under the Copyright Act and whether tattoo artists could be given the rights provided under the Visual Artists Rights Act, see Christine Lesicko, *Tattoes as Visual Art: How Body Art Fits into the Visual Artists Rights Act*, 53 IDEA 29 (2013).

530 17 U.S.C. § 101 (Work of Visual Art).

531 According to the legislative history, this provision would exclude photographs for use by newspapers, magazines, and for other non-exhibition purposes. *See* H.R. REP. NO. 101-514, at 11 (1990).

532 *Id.*

533 459 F.3d 128 (1st Cir. 2006).

were removed and relocated on the park redesign. The court took a pragmatic approach to the question of site-specific art stating "there is no basis for [plaintiff's] claim that VARA establishes two different regulatory regimes: one for free standing works of art . . . and one for site-specific art that can never be moved and must always be displayed."[534]

A "work of visual art" under VARA refers solely to the physical embodiment of a qualifying work of art. To illustrate, suppose an artist creates a work of sculpture. Section 106 protects the physical embodiment of the sculptural work against acts that would violate its attribution and integrity interests. Thus, a museum would be liable under VARA if it failed to identify the creator of the work or if it intentionally destroyed the work. By contrast, the museum would not be liable if it made an unauthorized reproduction or adaptation of the work in a bulletin and failed to identify the artist. The museum may well have infringed the artist's reproduction or adaptation right, but not the right of attribution under VARA, because the unauthorized act of reproduction or adaptation did not concern the physical object itself.

The limited scope of VARA is illustrated by the large categories of works of visual art not covered under the definition of visual art. The following are excluded from protection as defined by § 101 of the Act:

> (A)(i) any poster, map, globe, chart, technical drawing, diagram, model,[535] applied art, motion picture or other audiovisual work, book, magazine, newspaper, periodical, data base, electronic information service, electronic publication, or similar publication;
>
> (ii) any mechanizing item or advertising, promotional,[536] descriptive, covering, or packaging material or container;
>
> (iii) any portion or part of any item described in clause (i) or (ii).

Even if a work meets the criteria, it does not qualify as a work of visual art if it is a work made for hire.[537]

---

534 *Id.* at 143.

535 *See Flack v. Friends of Queen Catherine, Inc.*, 139 F. Supp. 2d 526 (S.D.N.Y. 2001) (finding that a thirty-five foot clay model made for a later contemplated bronze statue is a work of art in its own right as is customarily recognized in the artistic community).

536 *See Pollara v. Seymour*, 344 F.3d 265 (2d Cir. 2003) (finding that a mural by a professional artist, intended solely to promote a charitable event, did not qualify as a work of visual art under the Act).

537 *See* 17 U.S.C. § 101 (work of visual art); *see also Carter v. Helmsley-Spear, Inc.*, 71 F.3d 77 (2d Cir. 1995) (finding that large walk-through sculpture occupying most of a building's lobby was a qualifying work under the Act, but as a work made for hire, it was not protectable against alteration, defacement, and mutilation in its removal from the building).

[2] The Rights of Attribution and Integrity

[a] The Attribution Right

The attribution right promotes the interests of artists by encouraging full and accurate information about their works of art. The right of attribution includes the artist's right: (a) to claim authorship of the work; (b) to prevent the use of her name as the author of any work of visual art that she did not create; and (c) to prevent the use of her name as the author of the work in the event of a distortion, mutilation, or other modification of the work that would be prejudicial to her honor or reputation.

[b] The Integrity Right

Subject to limitations described below, the right of integrity encompasses the right: (a) to prevent any intentional distortion, mutilation, or other modification of the work that would be prejudicial to the artist's honor or reputation; and (b) to prevent any destruction of a work of "recognized stature" by an intentional or grossly negligent act.

What constitutes a work of "recognized stature" is not defined in the Act. The case law has defined the term as describing a work that is (1) meritorious, and (2) acknowledged as such by art experts and other members of the artistic community or by some cross-section of society.[538] To prove "recognized stature," plaintiffs, for the most part, will need to call expert witnesses to testify before the trier of fact. For example, in *Martin v. City of Indianapolis*,[539] a work of monumental sculpture which won a best of show award and received acclaim from critics, favorable write-ups in newspaper articles, and other expressions of community appreciation met the criteria for a work of recognized stature. The statutory standard of "recognized stature" continues to plague the courts. One open question is whether a work of "recognized stature" must be one that has been on public display. The courts have treated the issue inconsistently. The better view, one more coherent with the spirit of VARA, is that a public display should be only one factor in making the ultimate determination on the issue of "recognized stature."[540]

---

[538] 17 U.S.C. § 106A(a). *See Carter v. Helmsley-Spear*, 861 F. Supp. 303 (S.D.N.Y. 1994) (holding that removal of a sculptural work incorporated into the lobby of a New York office building would violate VARA).

[539] 192 F.3d 608 (7th Cir. 1999).

[540] *See, e.g., Pollara v. Seymour*, 150 F. Supp. 2d 393, 397–98 (N.D.N.Y. 2001) (holding that a public display of a work of art is not required in order for it to qualify as "a work of recognized stature"). *But see Scott v. Dixon*, 309 F. Supp. 2d 395 (E.D.N.Y. 2004) (holding that a sculpture which was kept at all times in its owner's backyard and was not visible to the public is not "a work of recognized stature" under VARA).

[3] Exceptions to the Attribution and Integrity Rights

[a] The Attribution Right

Section 106A(c)(3) provides that the attribution right does not pertain to works of visual art reproduced in commercial media, such as motion pictures and magazines. Thus, if a work is depicted in a poster, newspaper, or motion picture, and the artist's name is erroneously given, the attribution right cannot be enforced against such use of the work. In addition to the commercial media exception, the attribution right does not apply to works commissioned as a work made for hire.

[b] The Integrity Right

[i] General Exemptions

Mirroring the same exception for the attribution right, § 106A(c)(3) exempts the use of works of visual art in commercial media from liability for distortion or destruction. Likewise, works made for hire are insulated from liability under § 106A(a)(3).

Other general exemptions to the integrity right concern the caring and handling of works of visual art. A work is not destroyed, distorted, mutilated, or otherwise objectionably modified, for purposes of the integrity right, if the modification is the result of the passage of time or the inherent nature of the materials. Likewise, the integrity right is not violated when a modification is the result of conservation measures or of public presentation, including lighting or placement, unless the modification is caused by gross negligence. Finally, the integrity and attribution rights do not apply to reproductions or other uses of protected works in forms not themselves protected by VARA.[541]

[ii] Works Incorporated Into Buildings

Frequently, works of fine art are incorporated in the structure of buildings, and when a building is repaired or altered, the integrity of the work of art is jeopardized. VARA tries to strike a balance between the practical economic concerns of building owners and the moral rights of artists. The Act amends § 113 to establish conditions under which a work of art incorporated as a part of a building may be removed from the building. If the work cannot be removed without being mutilated or destroyed, the owner of the building, nonetheless, may accomplish such removal if the artist consented to the installation before June 1, 1991, or if thereafter, she consented to the possibility of mutilation or destruction in a signed instrument. If the work can be removed without mutilation or destruction, the work automatically is subject to the artist's attribution and integrity rights unless the owner has tried and failed in a diligent, good faith attempt to notify[542] the artist or her successor-in-interest. If, in such an instance,

---

[541] 17 U.S.C. § 106A(c).

[542] Section 113(d)(3) directs the Register of Copyrights to establish a system of records and procedures to meet the notice requirement on behalf of building owners and artists.

notice succeeds, the artist has ninety days to remove the work or pay for its removal; and that fixation of the work then becomes the artist's property.[543]

[iii] Scope and Exercise of Rights: Transfer and Waiver

The author of a work of visual art enjoys the rights provided in § 106A. The author may exercise these rights whether or not she has assigned ownership of the copyright to another. In addition, the author can exercise these rights even though the work does not qualify for protection under the national origin provisions of § 104 of the Copyright Act. Persons who jointly create a work of visual art are co-owners of the § 106A rights.[544]

The artist's attribution and integrity rights cannot be transferred. They can, however, be waived, but only if the waiver is expressly given in writing, through an instrument signed by the artist, and only as to works and uses specified in that instrument.[545]

[iv] Duration of Rights

With respect to works of visual art created on or after June 1, 1991, the effective date of the Act, the § 106A rights endure for the life of the artist (for joint works, the life of the last-surviving artist). The artist's other § 106 rights (e.g., reproduction, adaptation, etc.) are unaffected and endure for the normal life plus a seventy-year term.[546]

If the work of visual art was created before June 1, 1991, the Act creates, in certain circumstances, what can only be described as a peculiar situation. Provided that the artist has not parted with title to the copy(ies) of the work, she receives the life plus seventy years term for both the § 106A rights. Under this provision, it is irrelevant whether the artist has parted with title to the work. By contrast, no § 106A rights arise at all if the work was created before June 1, 1991, and the artist has sold the copy or copies to others.[547]

[v] Infringement and Preemption of State Law

The Act subjects violators of the attribution and integrity rights in works of visual art to the normal liabilities for infringement, but not to criminal penalties.[548]

The preemption provisions of VARA are limited in scope, allowing a continuing role for state art preservation statutes. The statute amends § 301 by preempting any legal or equitable rights at state law that are equivalent to those created by the Act's provisions. Nothing in the Act, however, annuls or limits any rights or

[543] *See* 17 U.S.C. § 113(d).

[544] 17 U.S.C. § 106A(b).

[545] 17 U.S.C. § 106A(e).

[546] 17 U.S.C. § 106A(d).

[547] 17 U.S.C. § 106A(d).

[548] *See* 17 U.S.C. §§ 501, 506.

remedies under the common law or statutes of any state with respect to (a) causes of action arising from undertakings commenced before the Act's effective date, or (b) activities violating state-created rights that are not equivalent to those created by § 106A.[549]

[C] VARA Applied: *Carter v. Helmsley-Spear*

Carter v. Helmsley-Spear illustrates several of the key issues in the practical application of VARA, particularly those involving works of art erected in buildings. In *Carter*, the plaintiffs were professional sculptors who contracted with the defendants, an owner and manager of a commercial building, to design, create, and install sculptures and other permanent installations in the lobby of a building. The artists were granted a high degree of creative freedom in planning and executing their work. The contract also specified that the artists were to receive design credit and their own copyright in the work but were to share the proceeds of any resulting exploitation of the work with the building owner. The artists were paid weekly, received health and insurance benefits, and had taxes withheld from their weekly payments for the first two years of engagement. No fixed completion date for the project was specified. In 1994, the owners of the building became insolvent and filed for bankruptcy. Defendant Helmsley-Spear, the new manager of the property, ordered the artists to leave the premises and expressed an intention to remove or materially alter the work. The work in question, a large walk-through sculpture, occupied most of the lobby and sprawled over the building with hundreds of separate components. Plaintiffs filed an action, and the District Court eventually granted a permanent injunction, prohibiting acts of destruction.

The Second Circuit reversed and vacated the judgment, concluding that the work was one "for hire" and was thus excluded from protection under § 106A. Before turning to the "work made for hire" issue, the court focused on whether, and to what degree, this sprawling "walk through sculpture," with its multiplicity of components, qualified for protection under the statute. It determined that the installation (thematically consistent, and interrelated) was a single work to be analyzed under VARA as a whole rather than separate works individually. In addition, the court ruled that the work was one of "fine art," not "applied art," therefore qualifying for moral rights protection. Even though parts of the installation were affixed to utilitarian objects, the court noted that VARA does not bar protection of works of visual art that incorporate elements of applied art. Despite its status as a qualifying work, the court held that the sculpture was a work made for hire and was not entitled to moral rights protection under VARA.[550]

---

[549] 17 U.S.C. § 301(f). The extent to which VARA preempts state law is unclear. The issue has been treated infrequently, inconsistently, and superficially by the courts *See, e.g.*, *Soho Int'l Arts Condo. v. N.Y.*, 2003 U.S. Dist. LEXIS 10221 (S.D.N.Y. June 17, 2003) (holding New York Act is preempted). *But see Phillips v. Pembroke Real Estate, Inc.*, 288 F. Supp. 2d 89 (D. Mass. 2003) (granting a preliminary injunction under the Massachusetts Art Preservation Act without discussing preemption).

[550] The court applied the 13 factors listed by the *Supreme Court in Comty. for Creative Non-Violence v. Reid*, 490 U.S. 730 (1989). Most prominent among them favoring the "for hire" status were the provision of employee benefits such as life, health and liability insurance, paid vacations, unemployment insurance, and workers compensation funds, the payment of payroll and social security taxes. In

Even though the defendants prevailed (albeit narrowly), *Carter* reveals the tension that VARA creates between protection of moral rights and the practical economic concerns of property owners. In the future, building owners will avoid the nightmare scenario illustrated by *Carter* by insisting on waiver as a precondition to any contract or commission. After all, VARA rights are waivable by the artist at any time. But for those buildings that contain irremovable works of art, future buyers will factor in VARA costs in the price they are willing to pay to bear the statutory burden.

[D] Beyond Moral Rights for Visual Artists?

The VARA is an attempt to accommodate moral rights with federal copyright law. One striking aspect of the Act is its limited scope: its narrow class of qualifying art, its waiver provisions, and its duration limited to life of the author. In addition, the Act protects only works of "recognized stature," a subject matter limitation that, by requiring judges to make aesthetic judgments, would appear to contradict a basic principle of copyright law. But whatever one thinks of the VARA, it is doubtful that it complies with our obligations under Berne and the WIPO Copyright Treaty ("WCT"). Article 1(4) of the WCT provides that "Contracting Parties shall comply with Articles 1 to 21 and the Appendix of the Berne Convention"[551] — presumably including Article 6*bis* on moral rights. On March 6, 2002, the United States became a signatory to the WCT. By joining the WCT, the United States would appear to have voluntarily recommitted itself to the protection of moral rights, an obligation that it assumed when it entered Berne on March 1, 1989, and has arguably yet to fulfill.

For these reasons, some would consider VARA as only a first step in a more expansive recognition of moral rights, encompassing the full range of literary, musical, and audiovisual works. Legitimate concerns about fulfilling international obligations aside, a more comprehensive engrafting of moral rights into American copyright law will be met with serious resistance. At one level, some works are simply not appropriate for moral rights, such as computer programs, databases, and other functional works. These kinds of works that have little or no artistic, personal, or cultural heritage are ill suited for moral rights protection.

But even for works with an artistic and cultural dimension, moral rights protection is inappropriate for other reasons. Moral rights protection will inherently clash with the way many works are created in cultural and entertainment industries such as moviemaking, publishing, and broadcasting. These intensely collaborative endeavors are exploited through subsidiary markets. For example, motion pictures are abridged for television; textbooks are revised and translated; and music is synchronized, adapted, and broadcast in a multiplicity of forms. These lucrative derivative markets, which attract significant investment into the entertainment and cultural industries, are regulated by contractual agreement. But an expansive moral rights concept, presenting a constant threat of legal

---

addition, each employee was paid a weekly salary. For a discussion of the "work made for hire doctrine," see *supra* § 5.02.

[551] *See* WIPO Copyright Treaty, art. 1(4) reprinted in Marshall Leaffer, International Treaties in Intellectual Property 391 (2d ed. 1997).

challenge brought by any one or more collaborators, would tend to undermine the economic expectations and the delicate allocation of rights achieved through private negotiation between authors, users, and labor unions. The result may be less financial support for such collaborate artistic endeavors, ultimately harming the public interest.[552]

Part VI. RIGHTS BEYOND COPYRIGHT IN THE DIGITAL AGE: THE AUDIO HOME RECORDING ACT OF 1992 AND THE DIGITAL MILLENNIUM COPYRIGHT ACT OF 1998

§ 8.31 THE AUDIO HOME RECORDING ACT OF 1992

[A] The Challenge of Digital Recording Technology

By the mid-eighties, the recording industry decided to shift its marketing emphasis from analog formats, such as vinyl disks and magnetic tapes, to a digital format of compact disks. Soon after the public began gravitating to this new format, an even newer technology originating in Japan offered a powerful new threat to the industry. This technology, called the digital audio recording technologies ("DART"), differed from analog recording methods. Unlike analog recording methods, DART would allow the ordinary consumer to make near perfect copies of prerecorded music. While the first generation of digital audio tape ("DAT") received tepid consumer acceptance, a digital recording mini-disc format called DCC (3.5 inch), introduced in 1990, was thought to have great promise for the revival of a languishing electronics industry. In addition, mini-disks, unlike conventional compact disks, can be used to make copies from all media such as records, tapes, or disks. The record industry feared that these new recording technologies, once readily available, would encourage a new surge of home audiotaping and undermine the robust market for CDs. The record industry focused its efforts on ways of legally controlling this new technology.

Whether copyright liability should extend to home audiotaping has been a matter of controversy since Congress first recognized protection of sound recordings in 1971.[553] In some ways, audiotaping is a much more serious threat to

[552] For an elaboration of these criticisms, see Robert A. Gorman, *Federal Moral Rights Legislation: The Need for Caution*, 14 Nova L. Rev. 421 (1990). Others have advocated a federal enactment of comprehensive moral rights. *See, e.g.*, Roberta Rosenthal Kwall, *Inspiration and Innovation: The Intrinsic Dimension of the Artistic Soul*, 81 Notre Dame L. Rev. 1945 (2006); Roberta Rosenthal Kwall, *The Attribution Right in the United States: Caught in the Crossfire Between Copyright and Section 43(a)*, 77 Wash. L. Rev. 985 (2002); Ilhyung Lee, *Toward an American Moral Rights in Copyright Law* 58 Wash. & Lee L. Rev. 795 (2001).

[553] The Supreme Court in the *Betamax* case (*Sony Corp. of Am. v. Universal City Studios*, 464 U.S. 417 (1984)) did not abate the controversy by ruling that private home taping of copyrighted works for time-shifting purposes constituted fair use. It rejected the Court of Appeals' suggestion that a continuing royalty be imposed upon VCR and tape manufacturers based on the sale of VCRs and blank tape. In its

copyright owners than off-the-air videotaping. Unlike the use of video machines to copy shows off the air, people copy prerecorded sound recordings not just to listen to the music at a more convenient moment, but to avoid buying a record, tape, or disc at full price. For many years, the music industry has maintained that audio recording has greatly decreased sales of prerecorded music.

Industrial relations in the audio field took a more conciliatory path than those involved with videotaping. To clarify the legal status of digital audio recording and avoid wasteful litigation, the music and electronics industries entered into negotiations to fashion a compromise that would promote the new technology without harming the record companies. Concluded in 1991, the agreement between these powerful industry groups was transformed into the Audio Home Recording Act of 1992.[554] Breaking new ground in American copyright law, the Act reflects a carefully wrought compromise and ambitious, if not *sui generis*, legislative undertaking. In addition to erecting another compulsory license, it creates, for the first time in American copyright law, a cause of action apart from copyright infringement. Moreover, for the first time, copyright legislation has placed legal restraints on a technology per se rather than on certain uses of that technology.

[B] Provisions of the Audio Home Recording Act of 1992

The Act, which is now codified as Chapter 10 of the Copyright Act, prohibits legal actions for copyright infringement based on the manufacture, importation, or distribution of a digital audio recording device for private noncommercial audio recording.[555] To protect the record industry, the Act requires digital recording machines to be equipped with the Serial Copy Management System ("SCMS") that blocks second-generation digital copying — making copies from copies.[556] Original works may be copied without limit. The Act also requires manufacturers and importers of digital hardware and blank digital software to pay compensatory royalties to music creators and copyright owners.[557] In sum, the Act accomplishes two goals: first, it allows manufacturers to sell digital audio recording technology to the consumer, who can use it for home taping within certain limits. Second, it establishes funds to compensate copyright owners likely to be injured by the DART technology.

Subchapter C of the Act[558] establishes procedures to collect and distribute the royalty payments, based on sales of digital audio recording devices and the audio recording media (the blank tapes or disks). The provisions of the Act are limited to digital audio recording devices such as DCC and DAT as mentioned above. Other audio recording technologies, such as analog audio recording products, diction machines, and personal computers, are excluded.

---

narrow ruling, the *Betamax* case left in abeyance the legality of audio copying of prerecorded musical works. For a discussion of *Betamax*, see *infra* § 10.11[B].

554 102 Pub. L. No. 102-563, 106 Stat. 4237 (1992).

555 *See* 17 U.S.C. § 1008.

556 *See* 17 U.S.C. § 1002(a).

557 *See* Subchapter C, 17 U.S.C. §§ 1003–07.

558 *Id.*

To compensate copyright owners, the royalty pool is derived from manufacturers and importers, who must pay 2% of the transfer price for digital devices and 3% of the transfer price of the tape or disc.[559] Only one payment is due for any digital recording device, blank tape, or disk, and only the first person to distribute the item must pay the royalty. The royalty pool is based on artists' prior year sales or air time of their musical works or sound recordings and is pre-allocated: two thirds of the fund is reserved for the Sound Recordings Fund and the rest earmarked for the Musical Works Fund.[560]

The Register of Copyright will administer the royalty system. Royalty-paying parties will file notices, send reports, and make payments to the Register. Interested parties will file claims with the Register of Copyrights. If the Register decides that no controversy exists, it will then distribute the money yearly. If the Register finds the existence of a controversy, the Register must convene a copyright arbitration royalty panel to determine the distribution of royalty fees.[561]

The Act establishes civil remedies for violations of the royalty or SCMS provisions. Any interested party injured by a violation of audio recording provisions can bring an action in federal district court.[562]

The Act authorizes a full battery of remedies, including injunctive relief, damages, costs, and attorney's fees for failure to observe the serial copying requirements or to pay the required royalties.[563] Penalties increase for repeat offenders.[564] Liability under the Act is limited to serial copying and royalty requirements. Accordingly, no action can be brought under the Act for copyright infringement for noncommercial home taping by consumers using digital recording equipment and media. In addition, no action for contributory infringement may be based on the manufacture, importation, or distribution of such equipment or media.[565]

[C] The Audio Home Recording Act and Digital Hardware Devices

Despite the promise of DAT as a new digital platform, the technology failed in the marketplace. Sales of DAT equipment were hardly flourishing, and recording companies issued only small numbers of prerecorded DAT tapes. Some consumer marketing experts contend that this failure can be attributed to the incremental increased cost attributable to the statutory royalty. Another possible explanation is that there were two competing DAT formats, and consumers were reluctant to invest in either until a single standard emerged. Finally, with the rise of the

---

[559] The royalty rate on recorders is subject to a per unit cap of $8 and a per unit minimum fee of $1. For machines that have two or more digital recorders, the cap is $12. *See* 17 U.S.C. § 1004(a)(3).

[560] *See* 17 U.S.C. § 1006 (b)(1), (2).

[561] See 17 U.S.C. § 1007(c).

[562] *See* 17 U.S.C. § 1009(b).

[563] *See* 17 U.S.C. § 1009(d).

[564] *See* 17 U.S.C. § 1009(d)(2).

[565] *See* 17 U.S.C. § 1008.

Internet, DAT was largely supplanted by computer-based digital technologies, such as MP3, which made possible the authorized and unauthorized distribution of music over the Internet in the form of compressed digital files. Inexpensive portable MP3 players and mobile phones equipped with MP3 players can be loaded with thousands of musical work files previously downloaded from the Internet to a personal computer, thus allowing their playback anywhere and anytime.

In 1998, Diamond Multimedia introduced the Rio, a portable hard drive capable of storing approximately one hour of music. With the advent of such portable devices, consumer interest in downloading music files and extracting files ("ripping") from CDs increased substantially. No longer did the consumer have to sit at a computer to listen to music on computer speakers or headphones. Even before the Rio, the first of such devices, had come to market, several recording industry associations sued its manufacturer for, among other things, violating the Audio Home Recording Act ("AHRA") because it did not use a Serial Copyright Management system, and for failing to pay the statutory royalties on the sales of its device. In June 1999, the Ninth Circuit Court of Appeals in *Recording Industry Ass'n of America v. Diamond Multimedia Systems, Inc.*,[566] concluded that computers do not constitute "digital audio recording devices" within the meaning of the statute; and because players like the Rio merely allow consumers to "space-shift" digital music files for personal use,[567] it is consistent with both the letter and the spirit of the AHRA to exempt them from its coverage. By excluding computers from its terms, the court severely limited the scope of the AHRA and frustrated its advocates, who viewed the 1992 legislation as a model for regulating future digital recording devices. The AHRA is limited to moribund, if not entirely obsolete, digital technology.

§ 8.32 COPYRIGHT PROTECTION SYSTEMS AND COPYRIGHT MANAGEMENT INFORMATION UNDER THE DIGITAL MILLENNIUM COPYRIGHT ACT: THE BACKGROUND

From the piano rolls in the beginning of the century to the VCRs of the 1980s and today's digital networks, copyright laws have struggled to keep pace with emerging technologies. The Digital Millennium Copyright Act ("DMCA") of 1998[568] is Congress' first attempt to resolve issues presented by the digital challenge. It is a complex piece of legislation consisting of five titles.[569] Title I, the focus of this

---

[566] 180 F.3d 1072 (9th Cir. 1999).

[567] For a new approach to personal use, using the principle of copyright exhaustion, see Aaron Perzanowski & Jason Schultz, *Copyright Exhaustion and the Personal Use Dilemma*, 96 MINN. L. REV. 2067 (2012).

[568] P.L. 105-304, 112 Stat. 2860 (1998).

[569] Title I implements the WIPO treaties. Title II limits the copyright infringement of on-line service providers and internet service providers under certain circumstances. *See infra* § 9.21. Title III clarifies copyright law by allowing the lawful owner or lessee of a computer program to authorize someone to turn on her computer for the purpose of maintenance and repair without infringing the copyright owner's reproduction right in the program. The issue is discussed at *supra* § 8.10. Title IV addresses the issues of ephemeral recordings, distance education, and digital preservation for libraries and archives. Title V

section, implements two World Intellectual Property Organization ("WIPO") treaties: the WIPO Copyright Treaty and the WIPO Performances and Phonogram Treaty, adopted at the WIPO Diplomatic Conference in 1996. Those treaties require member nations to protect digitally transmitted works in two ways: (1) to provide legal remedies against the circumvention of technological measures designed to block access to copyrighted works; and (2) to prohibit the interference with copyright management information digitally encoded in copyrighted works, including information about copyright ownership and licensing terms. Title I of the DMCA adds a chapter 12 to the Copyright Act that includes the norms adopted by the WIPO treaties, but in some cases it goes even further. The DMCA exceeds the mandates of the WIPO treaties by outlawing products that enable users to circumvent protection measures and by imposing criminal penalties for violations of the Act.

The Administration's proposals that led to the passage of the DMCA engendered much controversy. They were criticized as trying to regulate conduct that has traditionally fallen outside the regulatory scope of copyright law. In this regard, chapter 12 of the Copyright Act may be termed "paracopyright" legislation, which may be defined as an uncharted new domain of legislative provisions designed to strengthen copyright protection by regulating conduct which has traditionally fallen outside the regulatory scope of intellectual property law. What troubled these critics was that the broadly sketched legislation, particularly the anticircumvention measures, could result in chilling expressive activity, obstructing encryption research, preventing reverse engineering in the production of software, and jeopardizing education and research. Moreover, it was feared that the administration's proposals would allow copyright owners to lock up public domain materials and frustrate the fair use rights of information consumers.[570] By contrast, copyright owners greatly favored a legal regime that would better enable them to enjoy the benefits of making a work public while minimizing the traditional costs associated with public distribution of a work.

With its passage at the end of 1998, the DMCA represents a victory for copyright owners. In its final form, however, Congress fashioned a series of exceptions to the anticircumvention provisions to assuage the concerns of the critics.

---

creates a *sui generis* protection for boat hull designs.

[570] The issues are explored in Symposium, *A Right to Read Anonomously: A Closer Look at Copyright Management in Cyberspace*, 28 Conn. L. Rev. 981 (1996) (focusing on the threat to privacy posed by "copyright management systems"); and Julie E. Cohen, *Lochner in Cyberspace: The New Economic Orthodoxy of "Rights Management,"* 97 Mich. L. Rev. 462 (1998) (taking a skeptical view of certain copyright/cyberspace economic reasoning). For a particularly apocalyptic view of the post DMCA world, see David Aviad Deuel, *Circumspection of the Rule of Anticircumvention Under the Digital Millennium Copyright Act* (2003) (unpublished SJD diss., Indiana University Maurer School of Law) (on file with law library at Indiana University Maurer School of Law — Bloomington).

§ 8.33 SECTION 1201: THE PROHIBITION AGAINST MANUFACTURE AND USE OF DEVICES TO DEFEAT COPYRIGHT PROTECTION SYSTEMS

In the 1980s, when personal computers first became widely available, manufacturers of computer software became concerned that it would be impossible to combat widespread copying with infringement lawsuits alone. As a result, many software manufacturers tried to prevent copying through technological means, including encryption and password protection. These measures were largely unsuccessful for three reasons. First, hackers were able to defeat each new technological measure almost as soon as it was released. Second, some courts held that it was lawful to sell products that helped consumers to circumvent such measures, because consumers had a right under § 117 to make a backup or archival copy of a program.[571] Third, technological measures often rendered software inconvenient to use, which harmed the software in the marketplace. By the end of the decade, many software manufacturers had decided that copy-protection measures were simply not worth the effort.

The commercial development of the Internet revived interest in technological protection measures. In August 1995, the "White Paper" on Intellectual Property and the National Information Infrastructure[572] proposed that "[t]he public will . . . have access to more copyright works via the NII if they are not vulnerable to the defeat of protection systems" and called for a ban on the importation, manufacture, and sale of devices (and device components) "the primary purpose or effect of which" is to defeat such systems.[573]

The administration carried a similar proposal to the WIPO Diplomatic Conference in December 1996, where, after heated debate, a compromise was struck, under which the new treaties called for national legislation to "provide adequate legal protection and effective legal remedies against the circumvention of effective technological measures that are used by authors in connection with the exercise of their rights."[574] Obviously, this formulation leaves a great deal to the discretion of national legislatures.

Section 1201 contains three new causes of action: a prohibition on the circumvention of technological measures that control access to a copyrighted work in § 1201(a)(1); a prohibition on trafficking in technology that helps circumvent such access — control measures in § 1201(a)(2); and a prohibition on trafficking in technology that helps circumvent copy-protection measures in § 1201(b).

---

571 *See, e.g.*, *Vault Corp. v. Quaid. Software, Ltd.*, 847 F.2d 255, 267 (5th Cir. 1988).

572 Bruce A. Lehman, Information Infrastructure Taskforce, Intellectual Property and the National Information Infrastructure, The Report of the Working Group on Intellectual Property Rights (1995). "The National Information Infrastructure" (NII) refers to current state of communications in the United States. The convergence of computer and communications technologies has made possible the development and rapid growth of the (NII) and created new challenges for copyright law.

573 *Id.* at 230.

574 WIPO Copyright Treaty, Dec. 20, 1996, art. 11.

Section 1201 prohibits the conduct of circumvention and the manufacture or trafficking of technologies that are designed to circumvent technological safeguards, known collectively as "technological protection measures" or "TPMs."[575] Section 1201 distinguishes between TPMs that block unauthorized access to works and those that control the unauthorized exercise of one or more of the exclusive rights to copyright. The former are "gatekeeper" technologies that must be bypassed (lawfully or otherwise) if a user is to read, see, hear, or otherwise perceive a work to which they have been applied. The latter are technologies, usually the same technologies, that limit the further uses of copyrighted works — reproduction, adaptation, distribution, public performance, and public display — after which access has been obtained.

A violation of § 1201 involves the "circumvention" of an "effective" technological measure that controls access to a work or copying of a work. To "circumvent a technological measure" is defined broadly as "to descramble a scrambled work, to decrypt an encrypted work, or otherwise avoid, bypass, remove, deactivate, or impair a technological measure."[576] What kinds of technological safeguards are these provisions designed to protect against circumvention? The legislation applies only to "effective" safeguards. The House Commerce Committee Report on the DMCA states that "effective" measures would include those "based on encryption, scrambling, authentication, or some other measure that requires the use of a 'key' provided by a copyright owner."[577] The requisite threshold of effectiveness is quite low, so that even simple "password"-based systems are included.[578]

The key to liability under § 1201 is the circumvention or the marketing of a prohibited device, not whether the circumventing act resulted in the infringement of copyright. Violations of the anticircumvention provisions are not copyright infringement. The act of circumvention, whether by conduct or device, is an independent violation separately actionable under § 1201 and subject to the remedies, civil and criminal, codified in § 1203.[579] The difference between traditional copyright and the paracopyright status of § 1201 is highlighted in § 1201(c)(1), which provides that nothing in § 1201 affects defenses to copyright infringement, including fair use.[580]

---

575 For a catalogue of such measures, see Eric Schlachter, *The Intellectual Property Renaissance in Cyberspace: Why Copyright Law Could be Unimportant on the Internet*, 12 Berkeley Tech. L.J. 15 (1997).

576 17 U.S.C. § 1201(a)(3).

577 H.R. Rep. No. 105-551, at 39–40 (1998).

578 *But cf. I.M.S. Inquiry Mgmt. Sys., Ltd. v. Berkshire Info. Sys.*, 307 F. Supp. 2d 521 (S.D.N.Y. 2004) (holding that anticircumvention provisions of the DMCA, which require avoiding, bypassing, descrambling, or impairing a technological measure, do not apply to the unauthorized use of a password).

579 *See supra* § 8.03.

580 17 U.S.C. § 1201(c)(1).

§ 8.34 TECHNOLOGICAL CONTROLS ON ACCESS: CIRCUMVENTION BY CONDUCT

In its prohibitions against circumventing access controls, § 1201 makes the distinction between conduct that circumvents and the sale of devices that circumvent. Section 1201(a)(1)(A) applies to conduct that circumvents a technological protection measure. Its terms are broad and direct: "[n]o person shall circumvent a technological measure that effectively controls access to a work protected under this title." Unlike the sale of device provisions, the conduct provisions went into effect on October 28, 2000, two years after the passage of the DMCA. This interval was designed to give the Librarian of Congress time to conduct a rulemaking proceeding to evaluate the impact of the prohibition against the circumvention of the access control measures set forth in the Act. After this initial rulemaking, subsequent rulemaking proceedings are to take place every three years. The Librarian has exercised his rulemaking authority with restraint, issuing in 2000 and 2003 a set of narrow exemptions to § 1201(a)(1)(A).[581]

In his rulemaking capacity, the Librarian of Congress decides whether users of a copyrighted work are likely to be adversely affected in their ability to make noninfringing uses of a particular class of copyrighted works, and for that reason should be exempted from the prohibition.[582] The factors that the Librarian must take into account in his rulemaking capacity resemble those that courts must apply in determining fair use in § 107. In making this determination, the Librarian must consider various factors, including the availability for use of copyrighted works and works for nonprofit archival, preservation, and educational purposes; the impact that the prohibition has on comment, criticism, news reporting, teaching, scholarship, or research; and the effect of circumvention on the market for, or value of, copyrighted works.[583]

---

[581] For the first two rulemakings, see U.S. Copyright Office, Exemption to Prohibition on Circumvention of Copyright Protection Systems for Access Control Technologies, 65 Fed. Reg. 64, 556, 64574 (Oct. 27, 2000) (codified at 37 C.F.R. 201) (exempting two classes of works: (1) compilations consisting of lists of websites blocked by filtering software applications; and (2) literary works, including computer programs and databases, protected by access control mechanisms that fail to permit access because of malfunction, damage or obsoleteness); The Copyright Office has concluded four other rulemakings since 2000. *See e.g.* C.F.R. 201.40 (2013-07-01) for the latest rulemaking. computer programs in cell phones, "for the sole purpose of lawfully connecting to a wireless telephone communication network"; and sound recordings and audiovisual works distributed on CDs that contain access-control measures that create or exploit security flaws on personal computers, solely for the purpose of investigating, testing or correcting such flaws. *Id.*

[582] 17 U.S.C. § 1201(a)(1)(B)–(E).

[583] 17 U.S.C. § 1201(a)(1)(A).

§ 8.35 TECHNOLOGICAL CONTROLS ON ACCESS: CIRCUMVENTION BY TECHNOLOGY OR DEVICE

[A] Technologies and Devices Covered by § 1201(a)(2)

Section 1201(a)(2) prohibits the manufacturing of or making available technologies, products, and services used to defeat technological measures controlling access.[584] These prohibitions are aimed at any device, technology, or service that

> (A) is primarily designed or produced for the purpose of circumventing a technological measure that effectively controls access to a work protected under this title; (B) has only limited commercially significant purpose or use other than to circumvent a technological measure that effectively controls access . . . ; or (C) is marketed . . . for use in circumventing a technological measure that effectively controls access to a work protected under this title.[585]

Section 1201(a)(2) proscribes the manufacture of devices such as "black boxes" or software, such as hacking programs, or the provision of services that circumvent access controls.[586] Unlike the prohibition on acts of circumvention, which takes effect in two years from the effective date of the Act, the prohibition on the manufacture and distribution of circumvention devices took effect on October 28, 1998.[587]

Section 1201(a)(2) is limited in its prohibitions to the design or production of devices or technologies that have only a limited commercially significant purpose other than to circumvent a technological measure. This standard is similar to the test for contributory infringement formulated in *Sony Corp. of America v. Universal City Studios, Inc.*[588] If applied too broadly, § 1201(a)(2) can render illegal a device or software program that could be used in a variety of ways, such as a general purpose computer. Clearly, Congress did not wish the anticircumvention provisions to cast such a wide net. Thus, multipurpose devices or technologies would be excluded from the reach of § 1201(a)(2).

---

[584] 17 U.S.C. § 1201(a)(2).

[585] 17 U.S.C. § 1201(a)(2)(A)–(C), (b)(1)(A)–(C).

[586] *See, e.g., Universal City Studios, Inc. v. Corley*, 273 F.3d 429 (2d Cir. 2001) (holding that a program DeCSS posted on a website that allowed users to copy movies by unscrambling code that protected contents DVD circumvented a technological measure that effectively controlled access to plaintiff's copyrighted movies).

[587] 17 U.S.C. § 1201(c)(1)–(2).

[588] 464 U.S. 417, 442 (1984). The *Sony* case is discussed at *infra* § 9.8[B].

[B] The Developing Case Law

[1] Constitutional Issues

The anticircumvention provisions of the DMCA left open many controversial issues about its scope and application. Is there a continuing role for the application of fair use within the context of § 1201?[589] Does the DMCA violate the First Amendment?[590] A number of these fundamental issues were addressed in *Universal City Studios, Inc. v. Reimerdes*,[591] later recaptioned in *Universal City Studios, Inc. v. Corley*.[592] This litigation concerned a suit by a group of motion picture companies against the posting on a website of a computer program called DeCSS that unscrambled the code (CSS) protecting the contents on a DVD. At trial, the court found that the CSS code that protects the DVD was a technological measure that effectively controlled access to plaintiffs' copyrighted movies and that defendant's program was primarily intended to circumvent that measure. The Second Circuit affirmed the trial court on substantially the same grounds, concentrating on the defendant's constitutional challenges to § 1201(a)(2)(A). As a threshold issue, the court recognized that executable computer code is entitled to First Amendment protection to the extent that it conveys information comprehensible to a human being. The DMCA, however, proscribes the use of circumvention software not for its communicative effect, but rather for its ability to circumvent technical measures that prevent unauthorized access to a copyrighted work. In this perspective, the court held that § 1201(a)(2)(A) is a content neutral regulation with an incidental effect on speech, and whatever burdens it places on speech are proportionate with the necessity to further the government's legitimate interests.[593] As for defendant's assertion of fair use, the court observed that there was "no authority for the proposition that fair use . . . guarantees copying by the optimal method," and that nothing in the DMCA prevented users from making a fair use of movies, such as quoting dialogue from movies or even pointing a video camera at a monitor playing a DVD.[594] Following *Corley*, the anticircumvention provisions of the DMCA were sustained, in a criminal cause of action, against the argument that they transgressed the Fifth Amendment and First Amendment, and that Congress exceeded its authority under the Intellectual Property Clause in enacting them.[595]

---

589 For a discussion of fair use, see *infra* Chapter 10. For a discussion of the Copyright Office's recent protections of fair uses under the DMCA and possible solutions if rulemaking proceedings overwhelm its time and resources, see Elizabeth F. Jackson, *The Copyright Office's Protection of Fair Uses Under the DMCA: Why the Rulemaking Proceedings Might Be Unsustainable and Solutions for their Survival*, 58 J. Copyright Soc'y 521 (2011). For a proposed solution to the unpredictable fair use doctrine and a discussion of the lack of protection provided under the doctrine in anticircumvention contexts, see Gideon Parchomovsky & Kevin A. Goldman, *Fair Use Harbors*, 93 Va. L. Rev. 1483 (2007).

590 For a discussion of the DMCA's chilling effects on speech and a proposed change to protect online speech better, see Wendy Seltzer, *Free Speech Unmoored in Copyright's Safe Harbor: Chilling Effects of the DMCA on the First Amendment*, 18 J. Intell. Prop. L. 1 (2010).

591 111 F. Supp. 2d 294 (S.D.N.Y. 2000).

592 273 F.3d 429 (2d Cir. 2001).

593 *Id.* at 455.

594 *Id.* at 458–59.

595 *See United States v. Elcom, Ltd.*, 203 F. Supp. 2d 1111 (N.D. Cal. 2002) (upholding criminal

[2] The Anticircumvention Provisions and the Protection of Durable Goods Markets

Anticircumvention provisions of § 1201 have not engendered a vast amount of litigation. Initially, the cases brought under this section have involved copyright industries that one might characterize as the kind Congress contemplated in passing the DMCA. These cases have involved an authentication code that protected access to a video game from unauthorized persons,[596] the sale of software that bypassed a secret handshake authentication sequence required for accessing audio and video files encoded in a certain sequence,[597] the posting of a computer program on the Internet that circumvented an encryption system that protected against the copying of video disks,[598] and the marketing of software that removed copying and distribution restrictions from digitally formatted e-books.[599]

These cases have a common feature: a content provider's technological measure to prevent access to a copyrighted work, such as video games, music files, videos, and books. Computer programs also enjoy copyright protection and are often embedded in countless consumer products, ranging from automobiles to refrigerators. With increasing incidence, spare parts manufacturers, to make their products operable, must use the proprietary software written for the original manufacturer's device. For example, automobile manufacturers might install inexpensive microchips programmed with copyrighted software that would lock out unauthorized brake shoes, air filters, or other replacement parts, thereby jeopardizing the multibillion dollar independent automotive aftermarket industry. The question has arisen whether companies can use the DMCA to block the use of such software in order to quash aftermarket competition.[600]

In *Chamberlain Group, Inc. v. Skylink Technologies, Inc.*,[601] the plaintiff, Chamberlain, manufactured a garage door system which used a "rolling code" technology to defeat signal grabbers by constantly changing the sequence of numbers that unlock the system. The defendant began selling a universal replacement transmitter that worked with plaintiff's system, as well as a number of other brands of garage door openers. Chamberlain sued alleging, *inter alia*, that defendant violated § 1201(a)(2) by manufacturing a device primarily designed to circumvent a technological measure that effectively controlled access to the copyrighted work. In affirming summary judgment for defendant, the Court of Appeals for the Federal Circuit rejected plaintiff's broad reading of the DMCA — one that would override all preexisting consumer expectations about the use of products containing copyright embedded software. As a preliminary matter, the

---

indictment against Russian computer programmer and his employer who created a program designed to circumvent technological measures used in the Adobe eBook Reader to prevent unauthorized access).

[596] *Sony Computer Entm't Am., Inc. v. Gamemasters*, 87 F. Supp. 2d 976 (N.D. Cal. 1999).

[597] *RealNetworks, Inc. v. Streambox, Inc.*, 2000 U.S. Dist. LEXIS 1889 (W.D. Wash. Jan. 18, 2000).

[598] *Universal City Studios, Inc. v. Corley*, 273 F.3d 429 (2d Cir. 2001).

[599] *United States v. Elcom*, 203 F. Supp. 2d 1111 (N.D. Cal. 2002).

[600] For a review of the issue, see Jacqueline Lipton, *The Law of Unintended Consequences: The Digital Millenium Copyright Act and Interoperability*, 62 Wash. & Lee L. Rev. 487 (2005).

[601] 381 F.3d 1178 (Fed. Cir. 2004).

court emphasized that, unlike the patent and copyright laws, "[t]he anti-circumvention provisions convey no additional property rights in and of themselves; they simply provide property owners with new ways to protect their property."[602] The court interpreted § 1201(a)(2) as "prohibit[ing] only forms of access that bear a reasonable relationship to the protections that the Copyright Act otherwise affords copyright owners,"[603] and that trafficking in circumvention devices violates § 1201(a)(2) only if the circumvention enables access that "infringes or facilitates infringing a right protected by the Copyright Act."[604] Here, the plaintiff failed to show the nexus between access and protection. The plaintiff "neither alleged copyright infringement nor explained how the access provided [by defendant's] transmitter facilitates the infringement of any right the Copyright Act protects."[605]

In the court's view, circumvention of an access control measure must, to be actionable, result in or facilitate infringement of a conventional copyright interest. From a policy standpoint, this interpretation of § 1201(a)(2) is sensible and consistent with congressional intent. The anticircumvention provisions were designed to provide copyright owners with additional legal protection against digital pirates, but not to allow original parts manufacturers the means by which to regulate the multibillion dollar aftermarket industry.[606] The problem with this interpretation is that it deviates from the plain meaning of § 1201. Read literally, the DMCA has created a de facto new property right, one that proscribes the hacking of any digital fortress erected by a company. With such major ambiguities in the statute, Congress may well have to amend the anticircumvention provisions so that they do not effectively repeal longstanding principles of property law.

§ 8.36 CIRCUMVENTION OF TECHNOLOGICAL MEASURES PROTECTING RIGHTS OF A COPYRIGHT OWNER

Section 1201(b) concerns the circumvention of technological measures protecting a "right of a copyright owner," as compared with "access" to a work, the focus of 1201(a). Like § 1201(a), § 1201(b) prohibits the sale of devices that circumvent technological protection measures. Unlike § 1201(a), it does not proscribe circumventing conduct even though the copyrighted work may be subject to technological controls that impede its reproduction, performance, or display. The rationale for the distinction is that, unlike access, a copyright owner's rights are limited by exemptions and defenses, such as fair use, and those users should be able to exercise their privileges within the boundaries of traditional copyright law. One defect with this rationale is that § 1201(b) bars the use of circumvention tools or

---

[602] *Id.* at 1193–94.

[603] *Id.* at 1202.

[604] *Id.*

[605] *Id.* at 1204.

[606] In addition to *Chamberlain*, see *Lexmark Int'l Inc. v. Static Control Components, Inc.*, 387 F.3d., 387 F.3d. 522 (6th Cir. 2004) (holding that a device that circumvented a software-implemented device that prevented printer toner cartridges from being refilled by the manufacturer's competitors was not actionable under § 1201(a)(2)).

services. Thus, users unskilled in disencryption methods will be unable to exercise their fair use or any of the other privileges they may have under copyright. In short, for most consumers the absence of a ban on the circumvention of rights control measures is of little practical importance.

Even for those consumers who are capable of circumventing "copying" control measures, they may be risking a violation of § 1201(a) which prohibits conduct that circumvents "access" controls. Section 1201(b) attempts to make a distinction between the circumvention of technological measures that control access and those that control rights of the copyright owner. The reality is not so straightforward. The statute does not define "access," and there is nothing in the law or technology to bar copyright owners from imposing "persistent" access controls (i.e., measures that not only regulate a consumer's initial access to purchased copies of works, but also effectively control the subsequent utilization of those works by requiring new permission for "access" each time the work is consulted). In practice, copyright owners employ technological protection systems that incorporate both an access control and a rights control, and these merged control measures are entitled to the legal protection given to both access control and rights control. In other words, the "access/use" distinction tends to collapse in a merged control setting, undermining congressional intent to balance the rights of copyright owners with the public's interest in noninfringing use.[607]

§ 8.37 EXCEPTIONS TO THE PROHIBITION ON CIRCUMVENTION

Congress recognized legitimate reasons for engaging in circumvention. Accordingly, the DMCA provides for six specific exceptions to the prohibition on circumvention and circumvention devices. Despite the number and range of the exceptions, the broad language of § 1201 may well render illegal all uses not specifically excepted.

Exemption for Nonprofit Libraries, Archives, and Educational Institutions: Section 1201(d) provides an exemption for nonprofit libraries, archives, and educational institutions to gain access to commercially exploited copyrighted works solely to make a good faith determination of whether to acquire the work. The library must be open to the public or to nonaffiliated researchers. The exemption applies only if a qualifying institution cannot obtain a copy of the work by other means, presumably in a nonencrypted form. The copy of the work may not be retained longer than necessary to make such good faith determination and may not be used for any other purpose.

Law Enforcement and Intelligence Activities: Section 1201(e) allows circumvention for any lawfully authorized investigative, protective, or intelligence activity by or at the direction of a federal, state, or local law enforcement agency, or of an intelligence agency of the United States. Section 1201(e) allows the circumvention of both access and copy controls and permits the production and distribution of

---

[607] The issue is examined in Symposium, *The Law and Technology of Digital Rights Management: Will Merging Access Controls and Rights Controls Undermine the Structure of Anticircumvention Law?*, 18 Berkeley Tech. L.J. 619 (2003).

circumvention devices. It would appear that the exemption's extension to private contractors would include device manufacturers if the production of such a device were considered a security activity.

Reverse Engineering: Section 1201(f) allows an owner of a lawfully obtained computer program to circumvent technological measures that block access for the purpose of analyzing those elements necessary to achieve interoperability of an independently created computer program. The exemption covers the circumvention of both access and copy controls and permits the development of devices or technologies to circumvent access and copy controls if necessary to accomplish operability. The reverse engineering privilege is allowed only if the elements essential to interoperability could not previously have been "readily available" to the person engaging in the circumvention, and to the extent any such acts of identification and analysis do not otherwise constitute infringement. Thus, the reverse engineering exception is available only if a program's interface specifications are not accessible by other means. Thus, a copyright owner of the computer program could preclude reverse engineering by publishing the program's interface specifications. Under § 1201(f)(3), information obtained by reverse engineering may be revealed to third parties, but only for the purpose of achieving interoperability and only if it does not constitute copyright infringement.

Encryption Research Exception: Section 1201(g) allows circumvention when conducting good faith encryption research. The purpose of the exception is to advance the state of knowledge in the field of encryption technology and to assist in the development of encryption products.[608] The conditions of good faith acts of disencryption mirror the conditions of the reverse engineering exemption. These require: the lawful possession of the encrypted copy and that the act of circumvention is necessary to conduct encryption research. In addition, one must make reasonable efforts to obtain authorization before the circumvention, and not engage in copyright infringement or violation of applicable law. Section 1201(g)(3) lists several factors to be considered in determining whether a person qualifies for the exemption. These include whether the encryption research was disseminated and was reasonably calculated to advance the state of knowledge; whether the person is engaged in a legitimate course of study, is employed, or is appropriately trained or experienced in the field of encryption research; whether the person provides the copyright owner of the work with notice of the findings of the research and the time when such notice is provided.

Exception Regarding Minors: Section 1201(h) provides that in applying § 1201(a) to the manufacture of a component or part, a court may consider the necessity for the component's intended and actual incorporation in a device or technology that does not violate the provisions of Title 17, and whose sole purpose is to assist parents in preventing access of minors to objectionable material on the Internet.

Protection of Personally Identifying Information: Section 1201(i) permits circumvention to identify and disable technological means that collect or disseminate personally identifying information about the online activities of the user and that is not a violation of any other law. This exception is applicable only if the user

[608] *See* Conf. Rep. No. 105-796, at 96 (1998).

is not provided with adequate notice of such collection or dissemination and is not given the capability to prevent or restrict such collection or dissemination. In addition, the act of circumvention must have the sole effect of identifying and disabling the measure's information and collection capacity and have no other effect on the availability of access to the work.

Security Testing Exception: Section 1201(j) permits circumvention conducted for security testing if it is conducted for the sole purpose of performing permitted acts of security testing. Security testing is defined as obtaining access, with proper authorization, to a computer, computer system, or computer network for the sole purpose of testing, investigating, or correcting a potential or actual security flaw, or vulnerability or processing problem. Two factors must be weighed to determine if the exemption applies: (1) whether the information derived from the testing was used solely to promote the security of the computer or computer system's owner or operator or was shared directly with its developer; and (2) whether the information was used in a way that does facilitate copyright infringement or violation of applicable law. Section 1201(j)(4) exempts the production and distribution of otherwise lawful technological means that have the sole purpose of performing the defined acts of security testing.[609]

---

[609] 17 U.S.C. § 1201(j)(1).

§ 8.38 THE BASIC PROVISIONS OF § 1201: A SCHEMATIC DIAGRAM

The following is a summary of the basic provisions of § 1201:

Section 1201: Circumvention of Technological Protection Measures (TPMs)		
	CIRCUMVENTION BY CONDUCT	CIRCUMVENTION BY DEVICE
TPMs that control Access to a Work	§ 1201(a)(1)(A) "No person shall circumvent a technological measure that effectively controls access to a work protected under this title."	§ 1201(a)(2): "No person shall manufacture, import, offer to the public, provide or otherwise traffic in any technology . . . that — (A) is primarily designed . . . for the purpose of circumventing a technological measure that effectively controls access to a work protected under this title."
TPMs that protect rights of the copyright owner		§ 1201(b)(1): "No person shall manufacture, import, offer to the public, provide, or otherwise traffic in any technology . . . that — (A) is primarily designed . . . for the purpose of circumventing . . . a technological measure that effectively protects a right of a copyright owner [to a work protected] under this title. . . ."

§ 8.39 THE PROTECTION OF COPYRIGHT MANAGEMENT INFORMATION ("CMI")

[A] The Integrity of Copyright Management Information

Digital technology, with its ability to encode significant amounts of data, can greatly facilitate the clearing of rights. All pertinent information, such as name and address, telephone number, fax number, email address, and licensing rates can be encoded into the work and displayed to a potential customer. For works available over digital networks, embedded links to the copyright owner can make electronic licensing even more convenient, significantly reducing the transaction costs associated with copyright licensing.

Consistent with the WIPO treaties,[610] the DMCA prohibits tampering with CMI and creates liability for any person who provides or distributes false CMI.[611] In addition, the Act prohibits the intentional removal or alteration of CMI and its knowing distribution in altered form. To be covered by the Act, the CMI must be "conveyed in connection with copies or phonorecords of a work or performances or displays of a work, including in digital form." Thus, the express language of § 1202(c) ("including in digital form") indicates that it covers analog as well as digital uses of CMI.[612]

The term CMI includes all identifying information involving the title and other information identifying the work, the name of the author or performer, the terms and conditions for the use of the work, and other identifying numbers or symbols referring to such information or links to such information. A digital watermark also qualifies as CMI.[613] The Register of Copyrights may prescribe by regulation other information to be included as CMI.[614] Information concerning users of works is explicitly excluded. In contrast to the strict liability created by the anticircumvention protections, the CMI protections require that violators either intend or know their actions will induce, enable, facilitate, or conceal infringement.[615]

---

[610] Article 12 of the WIPO Copyright Treaty (WTC) provides in relevant part:

> Contracting Parties shall provide adequate and effective legal remedies against any person knowingly performing any of the following acts knowing, or with respect to civil remedies having reasonable grounds to know, that it will induce, enable, facilitate or conceal an infringement of any right covered by this Treaty or the Berne Convention:
>
> (i) to remove or alter any electronic rights management information without authority;
>
> (ii) to distribute, import for distribution, broadcast or communicate to the public, without authority, works or copies of works knowing that electronic rights management information has been removed or altered without authority.

Article 19 of the WIPO Performances and Phonograms Treaty contains nearly identical language.

[611] *See* 17 U.S.C. § 1202(a).

[612] The plain language of § 1202(c) ("including in digital form") indicates that it covers analog as well as digital uses of CMI. *See Murphy v. Millennium Radio Group, LLC*, 650 F.3d 295 (3d Cir. 2011). In so holding, the Third Circuit expressly rejected two lower court decisions that had held that § 1202 was limited to CMI that functioned as a component of an automated copyright protection or management system." *See e.g., IQ Group, Ltd. v. Wiesner Publ'g, LLC*, 409 F. Supp. 2d 587 (D.N.J. 2006). *See also Textile Secrets Int'l v. Ya-Ya Brand, Inc.*, 524 F. Supp. 2d 1184 (C.D. Cal. 2007) (§ 1202 does not apply to "circumstances that have no relation to the Internet, electronic commerce, automated copyright protection or management systems . . . or other technological measures or processes.").

[613] *See e.g., IQ Group, Ltd.*, 409 F. Supp. 2d at 587.

[614] *See* 17 U.S.C. § 1202(c)(1)–(8).

[615] *See* 17 U.S.C. § 1202(b)(3); *Gordon v. Nextel Commc'ns and Mullen Adver., Inc.*, 345 F.3d 922, 926–27 (6th Cir. 2003) (holding that § 1202 was not violated where defendant's agent believed that the allegedly infringing artwork had been cleared for use in television commercials, not knowing that copyright management information had been removed without the authority of the copyright owner).

[B] Exemptions and Limitations

Law Enforcement and Intelligence Activities: Section 1202(d) makes an exception for the lawfully authorized investigative, protective, information security, or intelligence activities of an officer, agent, or employee of the United States, a state, or a political subdivision thereof. The term "information security" means activities carried out in order to identify and address the vulnerabilities of a government computer, computer system, or computer network.

Certain Limitations on Liability for Broadcasters: Analog broadcasters who do not intend or otherwise further copyright infringement are not required to comply with the CMI provisions if it is not technologically feasible to avoid the violation or if avoiding the violation would "create an undue financial hardship."[616]

For digital broadcasters, the DMCA contemplates voluntary cross-industry standards for the placement of CMI in transmitted works. Digital broadcasters are required to comply with the Act unless the CMI does not conform to such standards. Until such standards are met, the DMCA exempts digital broadcasters if transmission of CMI would perceptibly degrade the digital signal or if it would conflict with an applicable government regulation or industry-wide standard. To qualify for either exemption, the digital broadcaster must not intend to induce, enable, facilitate, or conceal infringement.[617]

§ 8.40 CIVIL REMEDIES AND CRIMINAL PENALTIES

The DMCA creates civil remedies[618] and criminal penalties[619] for violations of §§ 1201 and 1202. A civil action may be brought in the appropriate U.S. District Court. The court has wide discretion to grant injunctions and award damages, costs, and attorney's fees.[620] In addition, the court may also order impounding, remedial modification, or destruction of devices used in the violation, and treble damage awards may be assessed against repeat offenders.[621] The court, in its discretion, may decide whether to reduce damage awards against innocent violators. For nonprofit libraries, archives, or educational institutions, however, the court must remit damages if it finds that the qualifying entity had no reason to know of the violation.[622]

The DMCA provides for substantial criminal penalties for the violations of §§ 1201 or 1202. In particular, willful violations of §§ 1201 or 1202 for purposes of commercial advantage or private financial gain are punished up to $500,000 in fines or imprisonment for up to five years.[623] Repeat offenders are punishable by up to

[616] 17 U.S.C. § 1202(e).

[617] *See* 17 U.S.C. § 1202(e)(2).

[618] *See* 17 U.S.C. § 1203.

[619] *See* 17 U.S.C. § 1204.

[620] *See* 17 U.S.C. § 1203(b).

[621] See 17 U.S.C. § 1203(c)(4).

[622] *See* 17 U.S.C. § 1203(c)(5).

[623] *See* 17 U.S.C. § 1204(a)(1).

$1,000,000 in fines or imprisonment for up to ten years.[624] The Act requires that the action be brought within five years after the cause of action arose.[625] Criminal penalties do not apply to nonprofit libraries, archives, and educational institutions.[626]

---

624 *See* 17 U.S.C. § 1204(a)(2).

625 *See* 17 U.S.C. § 1204(c).

626 *See* 17 U.S.C. § 1204(b).

Chapter 9

INFRINGEMENT AND REMEDIES

§ 9.01 INTRODUCTION AND CHAPTER OVERVIEW

Copyright infringement occurs when a third party violates one or more of the copyright owner's exclusive rights as enumerated in § 106 of the 1976 Act.[1] Thus, to infringe, the defendant must have reproduced, adapted, distributed, publicly performed, or publicly displayed the copyrighted work in an unprivileged way. Alternatively, if defendant's use of the work does not fall within these enumerated rights (e.g., a private performance), infringement has not occurred. The exclusive rights create the boundaries between an infringement and an allowable use of a copyrighted work.

This chapter is divided into four parts. Part I treats the substantive law of infringement, focusing on the infringement of the reproduction right or, as it is sometimes called, "the right to make copies." Part II covers third party liability (contributory infringement and vicarious liability), including the liability of online service providers under the Digital Millennium Copyright Act of 1998. Part III turns to the remedies, legal and equitable, provided in a suit for copyright infringement. Part IV examines the suit for copyright infringement in the procedural context, discussing jurisdiction, pleading, proof, and standing issues.

Part I. INFRINGEMENT: SUBSTANTIVE ISSUES

§ 9.02 THE ELEMENTS: OWNERSHIP, COPYING, AND IMPROPER APPROPRIATION[2]

To sustain an action for infringement, the copyright owner must prove:

(1) ownership of a valid copyright in the work,

(2) copying by the defendant, and

(3) that the defendant's copying constitutes an improper appropriation.

To prove ownership, the plaintiff must show originality, copyrightable subject

---

[1] 17 U.S.C. § 106.

[2] For an in-depth discussion of harm in the realm of copyright law and an argument that the First Amendment requires that real harm be done to the copyright holder's incentives in order to impose liability, see Christina Bohannan, *Copyright Infringement and Harmless Speech*, 61 Hastings L.J. 1083 (2010).

matter, compliance with statutory formalities, and the necessary citizenship status. If the plaintiff is not the author, he must produce the proper transfer documents or show a relationship that supports the claim for copyright. For most ownership questions, copyright registration constitutes prima facie evidence of ownership.[3]

In addition to ownership, the plaintiff must prove that the defendant *copied* the work. *Copying*[4] is a term of art, an umbrella term embodying two basic issues governing the ultimate determination that the plaintiff's exclusive rights have been violated. First, the plaintiff must prove that the defendant *actually* copied the copyrighted work in creating his own, and second, that defendant's copying amounted to an improper appropriation. Copyright law prohibits copying but does not prohibit independent creation.

The first issue, the requirement of actual copying, is fundamental to copyright law and is dictated by the requirement of originality.[5] A work is copyrightable if original and independently created, even though it is identical to another copyrighted work. In marked contrast to patent law, the creator of an original work cannot be an infringer.[6] Independently created, virtually identical works are more than a theoretical possibility and occur with some frequency in fabric designs, popular music, and factual works, where common public domain sources are often used.[7]

Even if the defendant has copied the plaintiff's work, infringement has not occurred unless defendant's copying constituted an improper appropriation. Here the question is whether the defendant took a sufficient amount of the copyright owner's original expression in creating what is termed a "substantially similar" work. The requirement of substantial similarity is a complicated issue because copyrighted works are invariably composed of original expression intermingled with public domain materials such as facts, ideas, and other uncopyrightable materials. In determining substantial similarity, the courts have struggled to develop a legal standard that protects the interests of copyright owners while not unduly extending copyright protection beyond its statutory scope.

---

[3] *See* 17 U.S.C. § 401(c).

[4] The term "copying" is a misnomer. The reproduction, adaptation, and even performance rights involve copying in one way or another. But the term "copying" covers unlawful distribution and display as well, which are hardly acts of copying as one might use the term in ordinary language.

[5] An original work of authorship for copyright purposes is one that is independently created, (i.e., not copied from another source) where the author has added more than a *de minimis* amount to the public domain. For a discussion of originality, see *supra* § 2.06.

[6] Striking similarity between two works can create a presumption against independent creation that forces the defendant to prove independent creation.

[7] *See, e.g.*, *Jewel Music Publ'g Co. v. Leo Feist, Inc.*, 62 F. Supp. 596, 599 (S.D.N.Y. 1945); *Arnstein v. Edward B. Marks Music Corp.*, 82 F.2d 275, 277 (2d Cir. 1936).

§ 9.03 CIRCUMSTANTIAL PROOF OF COPYING: ACCESS AND PROBATIVE SIMILARITY

One can prove copying by direct or by circumstantial evidence. Direct evidence of copying is rarely available, for obvious reasons. First, seldom will a defendant admit to copying a work. Second, copying is often carried out secretly or accomplished by nonphysical means (*e.g.*, from memory). As a result, few plaintiffs are able to produce a witness who can testify that he saw the defendant physically copying the work. These practical limitations on direct proof of copying do not stop the plaintiff from establishing copying by circumstantial evidence. The circumstantial case is made by proving: (1) access (i.e., a reasonable opportunity to copy) and (2) probative similarity (i.e., similarities between the works probative of copying).

[A] Access

To prove access, plaintiff must show that defendant had a reasonable opportunity to view or copy the work. Generally, the evidence must be sufficient for the trier of fact to infer a reasonable probability of access. On the other hand, a mere possibility of access based on conjecture or speculation is not enough to make the circumstantial case. Accordingly, access has been inferred where the work was in possession of a third party that had done business with both plaintiff and defendant,[8] or where the work was available to employees in defendant corporation's files, one of whom eventually produced a substantially similar work,[9] or where evidence exists that the same person or persons who created plaintiff's work also created the defendant's work.[10] Alternatively, evidence of access was insufficient to support a claim for infringement where nothing more could be shown other than that the work was available in defendant's city of residence.[11] In other words, a court will not infer access from speculative proofs.[12]

Access to a famous, widely-disseminated work may also be inferred where facts suggest that defendant had a reasonable opportunity to view or copy it. In *Bright Tunes Music Corp. v. Harrisongs Music, Ltd.*,[13] plaintiff claimed that George

---

8 *See Kamar Int'l., Inc. v. Russ Berrie & Co.*, 657 F.2d 1059 (9th Cir. 1981).

9 *See Meta-Film Assocs., Inc. v. MCA, Inc.*, 586 F. Supp. 1346 (C.D. Cal. 1984); *Smith v. Little, Brown & Co.*, 245 F. Supp. 451 (S.D.N.Y. 1965), *aff'd*, 360 F.2d 928 (2d Cir. 1966); *Stanley v. Columbia Broad. Sys., Inc.*, 221 P.2d 73 (Cal. 1950). The key aspect of these cases is a close relationship linking the intermediary and the alleged copier, not just a showing that they shared the same employer. *Morrissey v. Proctor & Gamble Co.*, 379 F.2d 675 (1st Cir. 1967).

10 *Taylor Corp. v. Four Seasons Greetings, LLC*, 315 F.3d 1039 (8th Cir. 2003).

11 *See Ferguson v. Nat'l Broad. Co.*, 584 F.2d 111 (5th Cir. 1978).

12 *See, e.g., Jones v. Blige*, 558 F.3d 485 (6th Cir. 2009) (affirming summary judgment for defendants; demo CD was received by employee at Universal Music, where Blige had recording contract, but no evidence of any connection between employee and Blige's work); *Armour v. Knowles*, 512 F.3d 147 (5th Cir. 2007) (affirming summary judgment for defendant where the only evidence of access was the mailing of a demo tape to a "mysterious and unidentified" alleged associate of defendant); *Jorgensen v. Epic/Sony Records*, 351 F.3d 46, 48 (2d Cir. 2003) ("[E]vidence of corporate receipt of unsolicited work is insufficient to raise a triable issue of access where there is no evidence of any connection between the individual recipients of the protected work and the [individual] alleged infringers.").

13 420 F. Supp. 177 (S.D.N.Y. 1976).

Harrison's "My Sweet Lord" infringed their popular song, "He's So Fine," which had been played extensively on the radio, becoming No. 1 on the billboard charts in the United States and a top hit in England. Harrison denied having copied the song, asserting independent creation. The court found, however, that defendant had access to the copyrighted work because of its popularity as a hit in the United States and abroad. And even though defendant may have unintentionally copied it through subconscious processes, unintentional copying does not constitute a defense against an action for copyright infringement.[14] *Bright Tunes* provides a good example of a situation where defendant's lack of access is simply not plausible.

Another presumption of access, given the facts, arises when the two works are so strikingly similar that independent creation is not a reasonable possibility. To infer access in this situation, plaintiff must show similarities that could only be explained by copying rather than by coincidence, independent creation, or use of a prior common source.[15] The nature of the copyrighted work is the essential factor in making the circumstantial case in this situation. For example, where complex works are virtually identical, access may be presumed, and courts have taken the view that similarity can be so striking as to constitute proof of access sufficient to withstand summary judgment.[16] Moreover, a plaintiff may prove access when the works are so strikingly similar to each other and no earlier work, commonly in the public domain, could have supplied the motivation for defendant's work.[17]

Alternatively, when the works are trite or commonplace and resemble available public sources,[18] the fact that they are similar does not support the inference that the work was copied, and other proof of access showing a reasonable opportunity to view the work will be required.[19]

In *Selle v. Gibb*,[20] the question was whether the Bee Gees' international hit song "How Deep Is Your Love" was so strikingly similar to defendant's prior song that proof of access could be inferred. The court held that even striking similarity is not

---

[14] *Bright Tunes Music*, 420 F. Supp. at 181. Although innocent intent is not a defense to copyright infringement, it can affect the extent of damages (particularly statutory damages) plaintiff can recover. *See infra* § 9.13[B].

[15] *See Stratchborneo v. Arc Music Corp.*, 357 F. Supp. 1393, 1403 (S.D.N.Y. 1973).

[16] *See Repp v. Webber*, 132 F.3d 882 (2d Cir. 1997); *Ass'n of Am. Med. Colleges v. Mikaelian*, 571 F. Supp. 144, 150–51 (E.D. Pa. 1983), *aff'd mem.*, 734 F.2d 3 (3d Cir. 1984).

[17] *See Ty, Inc. v. GMA Accessories, Inc.*, 132 F.3d 1167 (7th Cir. 1997) (determining that striking similarity to plaintiff's well known Beanie Babies proved access, despite defendant's denial of access).

[18] *See, e.g.*, *Mag Jewelry Co. v. Cherokee, Inc.*, 496 F.3d 108, 119 (1st Cir. 2007) ("There are only so many ways one can depict an angel. . . . [W]here the simplicity of the design makes independent creation highly plausible, similarity alone could not establish access and, in turn, copying."); *Ferguson v. Nat'l Broad. Co.*, 584 F.2d 111, 113 (5th Cir. 1978) (finding evidence of striking similarity insufficient for summary judgment).

[19] One such similarity is the presence of similar errors. For example, in *Eckes v. Card Prices Update*, 736 F.2d 859, 863–64 (2d Cir. 1984), there were numerous common errors in defendant's and plaintiff's baseball card price guides, sufficient to support inference of copying. *See also Coll. Entrance Book Co. v. Amsco Book Co.*, 119 F.2d 874 (2d Cir. 1941); NIMMER ON COPYRIGHT § 13.02[C] (2014); PAUL GOLDSTEIN, COPYRIGHT § 9.2.1.1 (3d ed. 2014).

[20] 741 F.2d 896 (7th Cir. 1984).

enough to infer access unless there is some evidence making it reasonably possible that plaintiff's work was available to the infringer. Here, the reasonable possibility did not exist. The Bee Gees' song was created in France, whereas plaintiff's song was limited to play in the Chicago area. Moreover, the songs did not involve the kind of striking similarity sufficient to overcome the need to show reasonable opportunity to copy. The material here was relatively trite and commonplace, lacking the complexities that would negate an explanation of independent creation.[21]

[B] Probative Similarity

If the defendant had access to the plaintiff's work and the defendant's work appears to have made use of the plaintiff's work, there is a high probability that the defendant copied. The issue is not whether the defendant copied a sufficient amount to constitute infringement. Rather, the issue is whether the defendant copied rather than independently created his work. The inquiry focuses on whether there are similarities between the works that are probative of copying. Here, even the presence of uncopyrightable features of the protected work may be sufficient for this purpose.

Unfortunately, the courts have used confusing terminology when applying the various issues in infringement litigation. Some courts (especially in the Ninth Circuit) use the term "substantial similarity" to refer both to the kind of similarity used to establish indirect proof of copying and the kind required to show improper appropriation (i.e., illegal copying). One explanation for this terminological confusion is that in many cases the same proofs of similarity are used for both purposes. But the type of similarity needed to prove indirect copying is not necessarily the same as that needed to prove improper appropriation. For example, suppose that the plaintiff is able to prove certain common errors between his work and the defendant's. These common errors may well be probative for an indirect proof of copying. In themselves, however, these common errors may be inadequate to prove that the defendant appropriated enough of the plaintiff's work to constitute an improper appropriation. Thus, the term "probative similarity" should be used for similarities referring to indirect copying, and the term "substantial similarity" should be employed when improper appropriation is at issue.[22]

The issue of indirect copying turns on probabilities: is it more likely than not that the defendant copied from the plaintiff's work? To prove copying, probative similarity and access are inversely related. Under this notion, the degree of

---

[21] On the same issue, see *Scott v. WKJG, Inc.*, 376 F.2d 467 (7th Cir. 1967). No access was proven where defendant's allegedly infringing play contained no verbatim passages, plaintiff's play was performed a few times, and no copies were distributed to the public.

[22] The term "probative similarity" is taken from Alan Latman, *"Probative Similarity" as Proof of Copying: Toward Dispelling Some Myths in Copyright Infringement*, 90 Colum. L. Rev. 1187 (1990). Professor Latman's article examines how similarities between the works are used in the litigation process. In this regard, he demonstrates that the term "substantial similarity" is misused by the courts to cover both similarity that is probative of copying and similarity that is necessary to prove improper appropriation. For Court of Appeals decisions adopting this terminology, see, *e.g.*, *Johnson v. Gordon*, 409 F.3d 12 (1st Cir. 2005); *Bridgmon v. Array Sys. Corp.*, 325 F.3d 572 (5th Cir. 2003) (note 8); *Dam Things from Denmark v. Russ Berrie & Co., Inc.*, 290 F.3d 548, 562 (3d Cir. 2002).

similarity required to establish an inference of access is inversely related to the quantum of direct evidence presented to establish access. Where the case for access is weak, the court will require a correspondingly greater degree of similarity to establish copying. Conversely, where the proof of access is strong, the courts will require a lesser degree of probative similarity. Of course, there are limits. No amount of proof of access will suffice to show copying if there are no similarities.[23]

Although it appears that access and probative similarity are inversely related issues, the courts are often less than explicit in revealing their analytical process on the copying issue. If the similarities between the two works are obvious, many courts do not bother to discuss similarity, focusing entirely on access. Alternatively, if evidence of access is absent, the courts will insist that the similarities be so striking as to preclude the possibility that the plaintiff and defendant independently arrived at the same result.[24] Once a sufficient circumstantial case is made, the burden shifts to the defendant to disprove copying by showing independent creation[25] or use of a common source.[26]

§ 9.04 IMPROPER APPROPRIATION

[A] The Requirement of Substantial Similarity

In an action for copyright infringement, plaintiff must prove that defendant copied plaintiff's copyrighted work and that defendant's copying amounted to an unlawful or improper appropriation.[27]

To prove improper appropriation, plaintiff must show that defendant copied a sufficient amount of the protectable elements of the plaintiff's copyrighted work as to render the two works substantially similar.[28] It makes no difference how strong the proof of access is if the works are not substantially similar. Moreover, not every taking or use of another's copyrighted work amounts to substantial similarity. A third party may freely copy the ideas embodied in a work but cannot copy the author's expression beyond what the law allows. And even if some of the expression

---

23 *See Arnstein v. Porter*, 154 F.2d 464, 468 (2d Cir. 1946).

24 *See id.*

25 *See Original Appalachian Artworks, Inc. v. Toy Loft, Inc.*, 684 F.2d 821 (11th Cir. 1982).

26 Defendant can assert other defenses as well, such as plaintiff's authority to use the work. *See Oboler v. Goldin*, 714 F.2d 211, 212 (2d Cir. 1983).

27 For an overview of the issue in various contexts, see Gary L. Francione, *Facing the Nation: The Standards for Copyright Infringement and Fair Use of Factual Works*, 134 U. Pa. L. Rev. 519 (1986); Steven B. McKnight, *Substantial Similarity Between Video Games: An Old Copyright Problem in a New Medium*, 36 Vand. L. Rev. 1277 (1983); David May, *So Long as Time Is Music: When Musical Compositions Are Substantially Similar*, 60 S. Cal. L. Rev. 785 (1987); John Pinheiro & Gerard Lacroix, *Protecting the "Look and Feel" of Computer Software*, 1 High Tech L.J. 411 (1986).

28 For an argument that the requirement of "substantial similarity" should be given more attention as a factor of copyright infringement, see Shyamkrishna Balganesh, *The Normativity of Copying in Copyright Law*, 62 Duke L.J. 203 (2012). For a proposal of a better system to use to prove "substantial similarity" in copyright infringement, see Mark A. Lemley, *Our Bizarre System of Proving Copyright Infringement*, 57 J. Copyright Soc'y 719 (2010).

is copied, there must be a substantial, material taking to constitute infringement. Thus, to say that the works are substantially similar is to say that the defendant has copied a substantial and material amount of plaintiff's protected expression.

[B] Verbatim Similarity and Pattern Similarity Compared[29]

A defendant can produce a substantially similar work in two ways. One is by verbatim copying; the other is by taking the overall pattern and arrangement of the work. These methods are not mutually exclusive. Defendant can produce a work that contains both identical copying and comprehensive pattern copying as well.

[C] Verbatim Similarity

The defendant need not copy the entire work to be guilty of infringement. But if one can infringe by copying less than the entire work, how much of a taking is too much? No arbitrary rule can be formulated, and each case is decided on its own facts using both quantitative and qualitative criteria.[30] Copying a single sentence of a work could theoretically constitute an infringement, depending on the sentence taken.[31]

In general, a wider taking is tolerated for copyrighted works that are made up of essentially public domain materials, such as compilations of facts and directories. For these types of works, near identity will be required to show infringement because idea and expression are difficult to distinguish. On the other hand, less appropriation would constitute infringement for wholly creative works such as poetry or a novel.[32]

---

[29] The terms "verbatim similarity" and "pattern similarity" are used here as a shorthand to conceptualize broadly the two general types of similarity. Professor Nimmer has adopted a more complicated terminology for these two kinds of similarity: "fragmented literal similarity" and "non-fragmented comprehensive similarity." *See* Nimmer on Copyright § 13.03[A][2] (2014). Nimmer's terminology is being accepted in the case law. *See, e.g.*, *Walker v. Time-Life Films, Inc.*, 784 F.2d 44 (2d Cir. 1986); *Smith v. Weinstein*, 578 F. Supp. 1297 (S.D.N.Y. 1984).

[30] The question is how much of plaintiff's work defendant has taken, not how much of defendant's work the taking constitutes.

[31] Infringement can be found even if only a small amount of a copyrighted work is taken, if the part taken is qualitatively significant. *See Horgan v. MacMillan, Inc.*, 789 F.2d 157 (2d Cir. 1986). In music infringement cases, copying two bars of plaintiff's work has constituted an infringement. *See Robertson v. Batten, Barton, Durstine & Osborne, Inc.*, 146 F. Supp. 795 (S.D. Cal. 1956). But copying much more than that may not be actionable if qualitatively insignificant. *See Marks v. Leo Feist, Inc.*, 290 F. 959 (2d Cir. 1923).

[32] *Compare Triangle Publ'ns, Inc. v. Sports Eye, Inc.*, 415 F. Supp. 682 (E.D. Pa. 1976) (finding that defendant took nothing more than public domain facts, not their arrangement), *with Schroeder v. William Morrow & Co.*, 566 F.2d 3 (7th Cir. 1977) (holding that defendant infringed plaintiff's gardening directory by taking the selection, ordering, and arrangement of compilation of names and addresses).

[D] Pattern Similarity

The second way one can create a substantially similar work is by taking the overall pattern of the copyrighted work, even if plaintiff cannot show any instance of verbatim or literal copying. As one court summed it up:

> [A]n infringement is not confined to literal and exact repetition or reproduction; it includes also the various modes in which the matter of any work may be adopted, imitated, transferred or reproduced, with more or less colorable alterations to disguise the piracy.[33]

What justification is there for the proscription against pattern copying? If infringement were limited to exact copying, a clever plagiarist could avoid a copyright violation by carefully paraphrasing the work. Moreover, absent a concept of infringement by pattern similarity, works could be freely copied in a different medium, such as a novel to film, without copying any specific language or dialogue.[34] In sum, without the proscription against pattern copying, the incentive to create works of authorship would be greatly undermined.

Pattern copying presents greater practical and theoretical problems for a plaintiff trying to prove substantial similarity than does verbatim copying. The difficulty lies in defining the line between use of expression and use of an idea. In attempting to draw that line, we are trying to reach equilibrium between the optimum incentive to create works of authorship and the optimum dissemination of information. It is a difficult line to draw. On the one hand, copyright law should protect against the clever paraphrase in order to encourage creation; on the other hand, it should not impede the use of ideas and facts revealed in the copyrighted work.[35] Thus, the ultimate issue in determining infringement by pattern copying becomes whether defendant has appropriated the author's copyrightable expression rather than the abstract ideas revealed in the work.

[E] Determining Pattern Similarity: The Learned Hand Abstractions Test

In *Nichols v. Universal Pictures Corp.*,[36] Judge Learned Hand made a famous attempt to draw the line between taking idea and taking expression. In *Nichols*, plaintiff-author of the play *Abie's Irish Rose* sued defendant for its motion picture *The Cohens and the Kelleys*. The issue was whether the play and the movie were substantially similar, given the obvious similarity of the storylines of the two shows. Meticulously comparing the plots, the court concluded that "the only matter common to the two is a quarrel between a Jewish and an Irish father, the marriage

---

[33] *Universal Pictures Co., Inc. v. Harold Lloyd Corp.*, 162 F.2d 354, 360 (9th Cir. 1947).

[34] Copying in a different medium is not a defense to infringement. Substantial similarity can exist across media. *See, e.g.*, *Horgan v. Macmillan, Inc.*, 789 F.2d 157 (2d Cir. 1986) (stating photographs can infringe choreography); *Filmvideo Releasing Corp. v. Hastings*, 668 F.2d 91 (2d Cir. 1981) (noting that dolls can infringe cartoon characters); *Roy Export Co. Establishment v. Columbia Broad. Sys., Inc.*, 672 F.2d 1095 (2d Cir. 1982) (noting that movies can infringe books).

[35] For a discussion of the idea-expression dichotomy, see *supra* § 2.13, and 17 U.S.C. § 102(b).

[36] 45 F.2d 119 (2d Cir. 1930).

of their children, the birth of grandchildren and a reconciliation."[37] To determine how much and what constitutes substantial similarity, Judge Hand formulated what has become well known as his "abstractions" test:

> Upon any work, and especially upon a play, a great number of patterns of increasing generality will fit equally well, as more and more of the incident is left out. The last may perhaps be no more than the most general statement of what the play is about, and at times might consist only of its title; but there is a point in this series of abstractions where they are no longer protected, since otherwise the playwright could prevent the use of his "ideas," to which, apart from their expression, his property is never extended.[38]

The abstractions test provides insight into how to separate copyrightable expression from noninfringing public domain ideas to determine substantial similarity.[39] The test may be viewed as a continuum with pure idea at one end and pure expression at the other. As the idea travels along the continuum, it gathers concrete detail and becomes more complex. No longer a vague set of generalities, it cannot be summed up in a few words. A taking at this point is a taking of the author's expression.

Although the abstractions test is a useful conceptualization of the problem, it does not clearly indicate where on the continuum an undue amount of plaintiff's expression has been taken. Perhaps all that can be said is that there comes a point where defendant's use of the general theme combines with similarities in details, scenes, sequences of events, characterization, and interplay of characters to constitute infringement.[40]

[F] Applying the Abstractions Test to Computer Programs: From *Whelan Associates* to *Computer Associates* (*Altai*)

The above approach to substantial similarity works relatively well when dealing with traditional literary works such as plays and novels (i.e., works that tell a story). It has been applied less easily to visual works, music, factual works, and more recently to computer programs.[41] Now that computer programs are

---

[37] *Id.* at 122.

[38] *Id.* at 121.

[39] Closely related to the abstractions test is the *scènes à faire* doctrine. *Scènes à faire* are incidents, characters, or settings that are common to a standard treatment of a topic, such as incidents or sequences of events and stock characters. If *scènes à faire* are the only similarities between two works, a court will not find substantial similarity between the two works. *Scènes à faire* are placed in the realm of unprotectable ideas and are not copyrightable. See *Schwarz v. Universal Pictures Co.*, 85 F. Supp. 270, 275 (S.D. Cal. 1945), where the term *scènes à faire* originated, and *Hoehling v. Universal City Studios, Inc.*, 618 F.2d 972, 979 (2d Cir. 1980) (finding that certain standard devices are used in all historical writing and are not copyrightable). For an excellent overview, see Leslie A. Kurtz, *Copyright: The Scènes à Faire Doctrine*, 41 Fla. L. Rev. 79 (1989).

[40] *See Reyher v. Children's Television Workshop*, 533 F.2d 87, 91 (2d Cir. 1976); Zechariah Chafee, Jr., *Reflections on the Law of Copyright*, 45 Colum. L. Rev. 503, 513 (1945).

[41] For a discussion of the special issues that arise in copyright infringement cases involving musical expression and a suggestion of how to deal with these problems, see Margit Livingston & Joseph

copyrightable subject matter and are protected against verbatim copying,[42] the difficult question is to what extent programs are protected against nonliteral copying. The question is whether copyright protection will extend beyond the written code itself to the structure of the program and its user interface.[43] The problem of nonliteral copying arises because different lines of computer code can use the same program structure or create similar user interfaces. To determine how far computer programs should be protected against nonliteral copying should ultimately depend on whether the particular approach encourages the optimal production and dissemination of computer programs. Inadequate protection will undermine the incentive to create computer programs, whereas too much protection will unduly impede their dissemination and deprive creators of basic material on which they build their own works.

In these "second generation"[44] computer software copyright cases, the courts have been less than unanimous in developing a conceptual framework to determine the proper scope of protection of computer programs in their nonliteral elements. In *Whelan Associates, Inc. v. Jaslow Dental Laboratory, Inc.*,[45] the Third Circuit became the first Circuit Court of Appeals to confront the issue of nonliteral copying in the computer domain. The heart of inquiry is a definitional one: how does one separate idea from expression in a computer program? In answer to this question, the *Whelan* court defined a program's idea broadly as its purpose or function. The court held that defendant's computer program for managing dental laboratories infringed plaintiff's similarly oriented program. In that regard, copyright protection extended beyond the program's literal codes to its overall structure, sequence, and organization that is not necessitated by the purpose or the functioning of the program.[46] The court reasoned that computer programs are a variety of literary work, a class that includes plays and novels. Like other literary works, such as a play or novel whose overall structure, plots, and themes are protected by the law, so too should a computer program's structure, sequence, and organization receive analogous protection.[47]

Urbinato, *Copyright Infringement of Music: Determining Whether What Sounds Alike is Alike*, 15 VAND. J. ENT. & TECH. L. 227 (2013). For a discussion of how copyright law should be modified to better regulate digital remix, see Steven Hetcher, *The Kids are Alright: Applying a Fault Liability Standard to Amateur Digital Remix*, 62 FLA. L. REV. 1275 (2010); see also Rebecca Tushnet, *I Put You There: User-Generated Content and Anticircumvention*, 12 VAND. J. ENT. & TECH. L. 889 (2010) (arguing that there should be an exemption for noncommercial remix video).

[42] *See supra* § 3.04; *Apple Computer, Inc. v. Franklin Computer Corp.*, 714 F.2d 1240, 1248 (3d Cir. 1983).

[43] The user interface includes the option menus, labels, key strokes to implement choices or commands, and text describing what the choices accomplish. *See* RAYMOND T. NIMMER, THE LAW OF COMPUTER TECHNOLOGY: RIGHT, LICENSES, AND LIABILITIES 1–72 (3d ed. 2004). *See, e.g.*, *Lotus Dev. Corp. v. Borland Int'l, Inc.*, 831 F. Supp. 223 (D. Mass. 1993); *Apple Computer Inc. v. Microsoft Corp.*, 821 F. Supp. 616 (N.D. Cal. 1993); *Lotus Dev. Corp. v. Paperback Software Int'l*, 740 F. Supp. 37 (D. Mass. 1990).

[44] The term "second generation" was adopted in Peter Menell, *An Analysis of the Scope of Copyright Protection for Application Programs*, 41 STAN. L. REV. 1045, 1048 (1989) (noting that the first generation cases focused on whether the literal elements could be protected).

[45] 797 F.2d 1222 (3d Cir. 1986).

[46] *Whelan Assocs.*, 797 F.2d at 1234.

[47] The court found that substantial similarity existed between the formats and structures, file

The literary analogy should not be pushed too far when computer software is at issue. Unlike books and articles, computer programs are inherently utilitarian, fusing idea, expression, process, and function. Separating idea from expression in such functional works entails a different process than a traditional work of literature. The term "idea" is a loaded term in the copyright lexicon, one that the *Whelan* court took too literally. As Professor Samuelson states, "the term 'idea' in copyright parlance is not confined in its meaning to 'abstract generalized conceptions' such as the general purpose or function of a program; rather, it is a metaphor used in copyright law to describe the unprotectable elements in a copyrighted work."[48] As such, the *Whelan* test has been criticized as taking an overly narrow view of the meaning of "idea" in copyright law. The case suggests that a computer program contains one idea and that everything else in the work is expression unless it is necessary to implement the idea. As a result, *Whelan* ignores § 102(b), which would exclude "processes, procedures, systems, and methods of operation" from copyright protection, even when they are embodied within a copyrighted work. The problem is that the program's structure may be viewed as a process, system, or method of operation more akin to idea than expression. By taking this bright line approach, *Whelan* appears to reject the traditional abstractions test adopted by Learned Hand in *Nichols*. The abstractions test is a fact-intensive inquiry that tries to determine at each level of abstraction whether there was sufficient expression to confer copyright protection on the work as a whole. The *Whelan* "structure, sequence, organization" test differs considerably from this case-by-case process, resulting in an over inclusive protection of computer programs.

Since *Whelan*, courts have continued to be challenged in determining what degree of nonliteral copying constitutes an infringement of a computer program.[49] As a general trend, most courts have either rejected or modified the *Whelan* "structure, sequence, organization" formulation. They have, for the most part, returned to some form of the Hand "abstractions test" in determining how far nonliteral aspects of a program should be protected.[50] The most important of these

---

structures, screen outputs, and file subroutines. *Id.*

48 Pamela Samuelson, *Computer Program, User Interfaces, and Section 102(b) of the Copyright Act of 1976: A Critique of Lotus v. Paperback*, 55 Law & Contemp. Probs. 311 (1992). *See* Paul Goldstein, *Infringement of Copyright in Computer Programs*, 47 U. Pitt. L. Rev 1119, 1126 (1986) ("Clearly the [*Whelan*] court construed the copyright concept of 'idea' too literally and failed to recognize that, in the copyright lexicon, 'idea' is no more than a metaphor for elements generally belonging in the public domain.").

49 *See Dynamic Solutions, Inc. v. Planning & Control, Inc.*, No. 86 Civ. 1886–CSH,1987 U.S. Dist. LEXIS 596 (S.D.N.Y. Feb. 2, 1987) (holding, on hearing for preliminary injunction, operations management programs were substantially similar due to literal and structural similarities that were not functionally mandated).

50 *See, e.g.*, *Plains Cotton Coop. Ass'n v. Goodpasture Computer Serv., Inc.*, 807 F.2d 1256 (5th Cir. 1987); *Lotus Dev. Corp. v. Paperback Software Int'l*, 740 F. Supp. 37 (D. Mass. 1990) (announcing a three-step test for determining that non-literal elements merited protection under copyright law: (1) defining the "idea," (2) determining whether idea and expression have merged, and (3) ascertaining whether any remaining protectable expression was a substantial part of the allegedly copyrightable work. Applying this test, Judge Keeton concluded the user interface was protected by copyright); *Lotus Dev. Corp. v. Borland Int'l, Inc.*, 799 F. Supp. 203 (D. Mass. 1992) (finding that component parts of Lotus interface program were protected, modifying the three-part test to explicitly include the language of

cases rejecting the *Whelan* approach is *Computer Associates v. Altai, Inc.*[51] In *Altai*, both plaintiff and defendant marketed a computer program that performed similar functions on IBM mainframe computers. Although defendant's first version of the program had directly used significant parts of the code structure, the second version contained no program code in common with plaintiff's software. Defendant conceded liability for copyright infringement for the first version of the program while denying that the second version infringed plaintiff's copyright. The similarity between the programs, however, raised the question of how far copyright should go to protect the nonliteral elements of a program.

In rejecting the *Whelan* bright line approach, *Altai* adopted a practical inquiry based on the Learned Hand abstractions test. The *Altai* inquiry involves three stages of analysis entitled *abstraction, filtration, comparison.* First, one must abstract the program into various layers of generality. Here, in a manner similar to reverse engineering, a court should dissect the copyrighted program's structure and isolate each level of abstraction in it. Second, the merger doctrine can be used to filter out those elements of the program dictated by efficiency or by factors external to the program itself (*e.g.*, mechanical specifications, compatibility requirements) or those taken from the public domain. When abstraction and filtration are accomplished, the third step involves comparing the remaining elements with the corresponding elements of defendant's work. In *Altai*, the court agreed with the district court that the programs were not substantially similar. The court found that defendant's program contained protectable elements similar to plaintiff's program. These similarities, however, were not sufficiently material to the overall program to uphold a finding of infringement.

Although its exact contours are unclear, *Altai* clearly narrows the scope of protection for nonliteral components of computer programs. The tripartite test seems appropriate because it provides a practical framework for distinguishing protectable from unprotectable expression.[52] Its weakness is that it provides little substantive guidance apart from its analytical framework superimposed on a vague and contradictory body of case law. Over time, however, the court's abstraction-filtration-comparison test may provide a useful framework to decide future cases.[53]

102(b)); *Brown Bag Software v. Symantec Corp.*, 960 F.2d 1465 (9th Cir.), *cert. denied*, 506 U.S. 869 (1992); *Apple Computer, Inc. v. Microsoft Corp.*, 799 F. Supp. 1006 (N.D. Cal. 1992) (finding that defendant did not infringe the Apple user interface and rejecting the *Whelan* approach by examining the user interface in light of the doctrines of merger, *scènes à faire*, originality, and § 102(b)).

[51] 982 F.2d 693 (2d Cir. 1992).

[52] Not all commentators support *Altai*'s approach. *See* Arthur R. Miller, *Copyright Protection for Computer Programs, Databases, and Computer-Generated Works: Is Anything New Since CONTU?*, 106 Harv. L. Rev. 977, 1001–11 (1993) (arguing that *Altai* merely refines the idea-expression framework begun in *Whelan*, rather than making a complete break with *Whelan*).

[53] For a thoughtful application of *Altai*'s three-part test, *see Oracle America, Inc. v. Google, Inc.*, 103 U.S.P.Q.2d (BNA) 1023 (N.D. Cal. 2012).

[G] *De Minimis* Copying

The legal maxim of *de minimis non curat lex* — the law does not concern itself with trifles — applies to copyright actions as it does to other areas of the law. Actionable copying is copying that is sufficiently significant to meet the threshold of substantial similarity. By contrast, *de minimis* copying, that is, copying that is so trivial and insignificant that no liability can result, is the converse of substantial similarity. To determine whether copyright is *de minimis*, the courts will look at the amount copied and how prominent a role it plays in defendant's work. Thus, a background with an out-of-focus and fleeting display of a dental illustration in a television commercial was held to be *de minimis*.[54] Alternatively, the twenty-six second, plainly observable display of a poster of an artistic work, which was used as a set decoration for a television program, was not a *de minimis* use of the copyrighted work.[55] Music sampling cases have also involved the *de minimis* doctrine. A hip-hop band's sampling of a three note sequence from a copyrighted musical composition was *de minimis* because an average audience would not discern, from the use of the sample, plaintiff's authorship of the musical work.[56] On the other hand, defendant's unauthorized use of three words and some music from plaintiff's copyrighted song constituted actionable copying.[57] Cases applying the *de minimis* doctrine reveal no bright line rule specifying what quantum of similarity is permitted before the threshold of substantial similarity is met. As one court put it in holding that a six note sequence exceeded the *de minimis* threshold: "the ear of the court must yield to the ears of the jurors."[58]

§ 9.05 IMPROPER APPROPRIATION IN THE LITIGATION PROCESS

[A] Generally

Deciding whether defendant has improperly appropriated plaintiff's copyrighted work in creating a "substantially similar" work presents special difficulties in the litigation process. The problem is how to frame this issue in practical form so that the trier of fact can analyze the question properly. Substantial similarity is a question of fact, but it is a complex question of ultimate fact, much like a determination of negligence. For such complex determinations, courts may present a single question to the trier of fact or break it down into separate issues. First, has defendant copied plaintiff's copyrightable expression? Second, will audiences for the two works find the elements present in defendant's work to be similar to the plaintiff's work? Although the proper method of analyzing substantial similarity is still a point of controversy, the courts have generally adopted some form of the "ordinary observer or audience test." The ordinary observer or audience test is

---

[54] *Gordon v. Nextel Commun's*, 345 F.3d 922 (6th Cir. 2003).

[55] *Ringgold v. Black Entm't Television, Inc.*, 126 F.3d 70 (2d Cir. 1997).

[56] *Newton v. Diamond*, 349 F.3d 591 (9th Cir. 2003).

[57] *Grand Upright Music Ltd. v. Warner Bros. Records, Inc.*, 780 F. Supp. 182 (S.D.N.Y. 1991).

[58] *Baxter v. MCA, Inc.*, 812 F.2d 421, 425 (9th Cir. 1987).

based on the view that the purpose of copyright law is to provide creators with a financial incentive to create, for the ultimate benefit of the public.[59]

[B] The Ordinary Observer or Audience Test

The ordinary observer or audience test is based on the subjective reactions of lay observers.[60] For example, suppose the infringement issue concerns the substantial similarity of two songs. Under the ordinary observer or audience test, the trier of fact would be asked whether defendant took from plaintiff's work so much of what is pleasing to the ears of lay listeners, who comprise the audience for whom such popular music is composed. That is, did defendant wrongfully appropriate something that belonged to the plaintiff?[61]

Under the ordinary observer or audience test, neither expert testimony, detailed analysis, nor dissection are a proper basis for determining whether works are substantially similar.[62] Rather, the trier of fact is to fall back on an immediate, visceral reaction to the two works and should consider their total concept and feel. If fabric designs are involved, the ultimate question to be asked is whether the ordinary observer tends to see the works as the same.[63] For instance, Learned Hand would find infringement of two dress designs if "the ordinary observer, unless he set out to detect the disparities, would be disposed to overlook them and regard their aesthetic appeal as the same."[64] In the same manner, courts have found infringement when the defendant's work has the same "total concept and feel" as the plaintiff's.[65] Similarly, for infringement of a novel by a movie, an ordinary person who has recently read the novel and viewed the movie should detect the piracy without resorting to critical analysis by experts. The reaction of the public to the matter should be both spontaneous and immediate.[66]

Courts have varied in their application of the audience test. Some have used it as the sole measure of infringement, holding that substantial similarity poses just one question: would an average lay observer recognize the alleged copy as having been appropriated from the copyrighted work?[67] The lay observer test was designed for cases where the lay audience purchases the product at issue, and where that same

---

[59] *Dawson v. Hinshaw Music, Inc.*, 905 F.2d 731, 733 (4th Cir. 1990).

[60] For a discussion of the "reasonable" observer standard and a proposal for the use of an openly subjective standard in its place, see Irina D. Manta, *Reasonable Copyright*, 53 B.C.L. Rev. 1303 (2012).

[61] *See Arnstein v. Porter*, 154 F.2d 464, 468 (2d Cir. 1946). The term "average lay observer" is not the exclusive term. Other interchangeable terms are the "ordinary reasonable person," and "ordinary lay observer." *See Brubaker v. King*, 505 F.2d 534 (7th Cir. 1974); *Int'l Luggage Registry v. Avery Prods. Corp.*, 541 F.2d 830, 831 (9th Cir. 1976).

[62] *See Roth Greeting Cards v. United Card Co.*, 429 F.2d 1106, 1110 (9th Cir. 1970); *Bevan v. Columbia Broad. Sys., Inc.*, 329 F. Supp. 601 (S.D.N.Y. 1971).

[63] *See Novelty Textile Mills, Inc. v. Joanne Fabrics Corp.*, 558 F.2d 1090 (2d Cir. 1977).

[64] *Peter Pan Fabrics, Inc. v. Martin Weiner Corp.*, 274 F.2d 487, 489 (2d Cir. 1960).

[65] *See Roth Greeting Cards v. United Card Co.*, 429 F.2d 1106, 1110 (9th Cir. 1970).

[66] *See Harold Lloyd Corp. v. Witwer*, 65 F.2d 1 (9th Cir. 1993).

[67] *See Ideal Toy Corp. v. Fab-Lu Ltd.*, 266 F. Supp. 755, 756 (S.D.N.Y. 1965), *aff'd*, 360 F.2d 1021 (2d Cir. 1966); *Ideal Toy Corp. v. Kenner Prods. Div. of Gen. Mills Fun Group, Inc.*, 443 F. Supp. 291, 303 n.11 (S.D.N.Y. 1977).

audience's untutored judgment gauges the effect of the defendant's work on the plaintiff's market. Obviously, not all copyrighted works are sold to the same audiences, such as technical drawings, architectural plans, or software programs. In cases where the target audience has specialized expertise, the courts have found it appropriate to consider similarity from the specialist's perspective. The goal is to determine who the intended audience is for the work. In most cases, the intended audience will be the lay observer who occupies a place in copyright law much like the "ordinary reasonable person" in tort law. In other cases, where the audience for the work possesses specialized expertise relevant to the purchasing decision, the courts have made the determination from the perspective of the intended audience. Here, expert testimony will often be necessary to educate the trier of fact about those elements to which the specialist will look. Courts, however, will deviate from the lay observer standard only when necessary. To warrant departure from the lay observer test, "specialized expertise" must transcend mere differences in taste and must involve knowledge that the lay public lacks.[68]

Using the ordinary observer test alone has the advantage of simplicity, but may lead the trier of fact to overlook important issues regarding substantial similarity.[69] Although it may be appropriate for determining whether two fabric designs or popular songs are substantially similar, the ordinary observer test may be less well-suited when more complex works are involved, such as those adapted into different media.[70] For infringement of software programs, the test is particularly meaningless.[71]

The ordinary observer test has its shortcomings. Because it looks at the totality of the works (*e.g.*, "total concept and feel") and eschews dissection and use of expert testimony, it is ultimately concerned with surface illusion and the appearance of copying, not its reality. This can lead the trier of fact to find infringement in works independently created, while overlooking situations where a wholesale appropriation has taken place. For example, expression of an author's work in a different medium often hides the resemblances that should be taken into account. The ordinary observer test based on "total concept and feel" is essentially impressionistic and visceral. In sum, an audience's impression of infringement is not the same as actual infringement. Without self-consciously analyzing the similarities and differences between two works, the audience will overlook the similarities between them, particularly for infringement in a different medium.[72] As a result, by relying solely on the ordinary observer test, the trier of fact may fail to analyze properly whether a work was independently created.

---

[68] *See, e.g., Kohus v. Mariol*, 328 F.3d 848 (6th Cir. 2003) (holding that the issue of substantial similarity involving technical drawings, whose intended audience was not the lay public, necessitate the use of expert guidance).

[69] For an excellent discussion of the limitations of the ordinary observer test, see Amy B. Cohen, *Masking Copyright Decisionmaking: The Meaninglessness of Substantial Similarity*, 20 U.C. Davis L. Rev. 719, 733 (1987).

[70] *See Bevan v. Columbia Broad. Sys., Inc.*, 329 F. Supp. 601, 604 n.3 (S.D.N.Y. 1971) (finding infringement where novel adapted into film).

[71] *See Whelan Assocs., Inc. v. Jaslow Dental Lab., Inc.*, 797 F.2d 1222 (3d Cir. 1986), *cert. denied*, 479 U.S. 1031 (1987).

[72] Nimmer on Copyright § 13.03[E][2] (20149).

An equally serious criticism is that under an ordinary observer test, the trier of fact may not distinguish between the copying of ideas and the copying of expression. An ordinary observer test alone does not provide the analytical basis necessary to distinguish between similarity derived from copying expression and similarity due to copying non-copyrightable materials. For these reasons, courts have generally looked to a framework that uses the ordinary observer test, but that also avoids its obvious limitations. The current approach is a two-step process known generally as the "bifurcated test."

[C] Bifurcated Tests: *Arnstein* and *Krofft*

In *Arnstein v. Porter*,[73] the court used a bifurcated approach to evaluate whether the works at issue were substantially similar. In this two-step approach, the trier of fact was first to decide whether defendant copied plaintiff's work. If copying was proved, the trier of fact was then to proceed to the second step: whether the copying amounted to an improper appropriation.

The bifurcated submission of issues first articulated in *Arnstein* avoids certain drawbacks of a simple audience test, allowing the trier of fact to examine the works in different ways for different purposes. On the first issue, the trier of fact examines each work in detail, dissecting them as to their protectable and unprotectable aspects. Most importantly, expert testimony can be used in this "copying" step. If copying has been proved, the second issue that of unlawful appropriation, is proved by using the ordinary observer or audience test.

For example, in *Arnstein*, which involved the alleged infringement of several of Cole Porter's musical compositions, the court articulated the ordinary observer test as follows: "whether defendant took from plaintiff's works so much of what is pleasing to the ears of lay listeners, who comprise the audience for whom such popular music is composed, that defendant wrongfully appropriated something which belongs to plaintiff."[74]

In applying the test, the trier of fact is to rely on the subjective reaction of a lay observer. To that end, most courts use the terms "ordinary observer test" and "audience test" interchangeably. But as the *Arnstein* quote reveals, the term "audience" suggests something specific: that substantial similarity should be judged not only by spectator reactions, but by a specific audience composed of people who possess specialized tastes, skills, or knowledge as compared with the average lay observer or the general public. It is not always clear whether courts make the distinction, but some do so by assessing the overall effect of the works on the intended audience.[75]

---

[73] 154 F.2d 464 (2d Cir. 1946).

[74] *Id.* at 473.

[75] *See* La Resolana Architects, P.A. v. Reno, Inc., 555 F.3d 1171, 1180–81(10th Cir. 2009) (architectural works); *Clarion Textile Corp. v. Slifka*, 223 F. Supp. 950 (S.D.N.Y. 1961) (dress design); *Arnstein v. Porter*, 154 F.2d 464 (2d Cir. 1946) (musical compositions); *Clarke v. G. A. Kayser & Sons, Inc.*, 472 F. Supp. 481 (W.D. Pa. 1979), *aff'd mem.*, 631 F.2d 725 (3d Cir. 1980) (children's audience for baseball gloves). *See generally* Michael F. Sitzer, *Copyright Infringement Actions: The Proper Role for Audience Reactions in Determining Substantial Similarity*, 54 S. Cal. L. Rev. 385 (1981) (advocating need for

In *Sid & Marty Krofft Television Prods., Inc. v. McDonald's Corp.*,[76] the Ninth Circuit modified *Arnstein* and proposed its own two-step test to determine substantial similarity. As set forth in *Krofft*, the first step is an extrinsic test where the trier of fact compares the works for similarity of ideas. This first step is similar to the "copying" stage of *Arnstein*, and the process is one of analytical dissection aided by expert testimony. If substantial similarity of ideas is found, the court proceeds to the second step, called the "intrinsic test." Here, the trier of fact must respond to the works as an ordinary observer, without analytic dissection or use of expert testimony, to determine whether defendant took enough of what is pleasing to the audience to be held liable.[77]

The *Krofft* test has been criticized as unduly reducing the role of the court when deciding questions of substantial similarity.[78] According to this view, the problem lies in *Krofft*'s *extrinsic* first step, in which plaintiff must prove by any appropriate means that defendant has copied the ideas in the work. Once the plaintiff meets this burden, the case proceeds to the jury to determine the copying of expression under an *ordinary observer test*. *Krofft*'s extrinsic test (copying of ideas) improperly frames the inquiry. Similarity in ideas may be probative of copying but does not prove that defendant took plaintiff's protected expression. Thus, if all defendants took were plaintiff's ideas — factual matter, a discovery, method of operation, or a marketing plan — she cannot be liable for copyright infringement. For this reason, decisions since *Krofft* have broadened their inquiry under the extrinsic test, comparing the two works to determine the extent to which defendant's work incorporated the expressive elements contained in plaintiff's.[79] As for the second step in the *Krofft* analysis, the intrinsic test, the trend in the Ninth Circuit appears to be to incorporate the more traditional "audience test" in addition to *Krofft*'s "total concept and feel" formulation.[80]

As compared with *Arnstein*, it would appear that the changes in the *Krofft* test for infringement renders plaintiff's task more difficult in getting a case to the jury in the Ninth Circuit. In general, plaintiffs have had a harder time in overcoming defendant's motion for summary judgment in an *Arnstein* jurisdiction. Under the first step in *Arnstein*, plaintiff has a greater burden in getting the case to the jury because the court may consider both the copying of expression as well as the copying of ideas — that is, a comparison of both protectable and non-protectable material. Thus, the *Arnstein* approach gives the court greater control over the litigation than the originally articulated *Krofft* approach did and provides the ability to dispose of cases before trial as a matter of law.

Whatever their merits, the *Krofft* and *Arnstein* bifurcated tests are probably impossible to apply as intended. It is unrealistic to require juries to first dissect a work to determine whether copying has occurred (*Arnstein*) or whether there are

---

clear recognition of the audience test as opposed to a general lay observer test in determining substantial similarity).

[76] 562 F.2d 1157 (9th Cir. 1977).

[77] *Krofft*, 562 F.2d at 1165.

[78] *See* Nimmer on Copyright § 13.03[E][3][b] (2014).

[79] *See Shaw v. Lindheim*, 919 F.2d 1353 (9th Cir. 1990).

[80] *See id.* at 1358.

similarities in the ideas between the works (*Krofft*). After dissecting the works and listening to expert testimony under the first step of *Arnstein* or *Krofft*, the jury is then asked to forget what they have just heard and apply the second step to determine improper appropriation (*Arnstein*) or copying of expression (*Krofft*). These bifurcated tests require that juries postpone making an immediate overall assessment of the works at issue.[81] The ideal jury in an action for copyright infringement must have a conveniently short, collective memory in order to keep each submission separate and distinct. Such a jury panel probably does not exist.

In addition to its method of determining improper appropriation, a court must exercise control over the judicial process granting summary judgment in copyright infringement litigation.[82] Much has changed since *Arnstein v. Porter*, where Judge Jerome Frank observed that summary judgment should be granted in copyright cases only in the face of outlandish claims as to which there is not the "slightest doubt about the facts."[83] In reality, courts these days often decline to follow *Arnstein* in this manner. Although summary judgment in favor of copyright plaintiffs remains highly unusual, grants of summary judgment for defendants are relatively commonplace, if far from routine.[84] This is so because a judge who is better able to separate original expression from non-original elements of the work will more readily understand that not all copying is infringement.[85]

§ 9.06 IMPROPER APPROPRIATION AND JUDICIAL CONTROL OVER THE LITIGATION PROCESS

Many students (like many attorneys and their clients) urgently desire a simple, even mathematical, test for infringement: x number of bars of music, or x number of pages from a novel, equals infringement. Alas, no such bright line rule exists or is possible. To quote Judge Learned Hand, "wherever it is drawn [any such line] will seem arbitrary,"[86] and thus "the test for infringement of a copyright is of necessity vague."[87]

The inability to be specific is the reason that Congress chose not to define infringement in the statute, but instead to leave the matter to *ad hoc* determination by the courts. There are an almost inexhaustible variety of contexts in which the

---

[81] For a discussion of this point, see Julie J. Bisceglia, *Summary Judgment on Substantial Similarity in Copyright Actions*, 16 HASTINGS COMM. & ENT. L.J. 51, 82 (1993).

[82] *See* Daniel Wanat, *Copyright Law: Infringement of Musical Works and the Appropriateness of Summary Judgment Under theFederal Rules of Civil Procedure, Rule 56(C)*, 39 U MEM. L. REV. 1037 (2009).

[83] *Arnstein*, 154 F.2d at 468.

[84] Courts have held that where the works in question are attached to the complaint, a court may properly determine lack of substantial similarity as a matter of law. *See Peters v. West*, 692 F.3d 629 (7th Cir. 2012); *Peter F. Gaito Architecture, LLC v. Simone Development Corp.*, 602 F.3d 57 (2d Cir. 2010).

[85] *See, e.g.*, *Intervest Construction, Inc. v. Canterbury Estate Homes, Inc.*, 554 F.3d 914, 920 (11th Cir. 2008); *Johnson v. Gordon*, 409 F.3d 12 (1st Cir. 2005); *Strombach v. New Line Cinema*, 384 F.3d 283 (6th Cir. 2004); *Schoolhouse, Inc. v. Anderson*, 275 F.3d 726 (8th Cir. 2002).

[86] *Nichols v. Universal Pictures Co.*, 45 F.2d 119, 122 (2d Cir. 1930).

[87] *Peter Pan Fabrics, Inc. v. Martin Weiner Corp.*, 274 F.2d 487, 489 (2d Cir. 1960).

determination of substantial similarity will vary. Take literary works, for example. The category of literary works includes great works of fiction, biographies, short stories, plays, telephone directories, databases, computer programs, restaurant guides, treatises like this one, class notes like those you take, and a thousand other permutations of literary "writings." Clearly, no one test could feasibly be drafted that would fit each of these types of works equally well.

Additionally, the types of infringement may vary considerably. In the most easily understood instance, the defendant copies substantially word-for-word an impermissibly large portion of the plaintiff's work. Alternatively, the defendant's copying may appear not as a particular segment taken substantially intact from the plaintiff's work, but rather as a relatively larger portion of the accused work which duplicates the fundamental structure of the accusing work, including perhaps the latter's selection and arrangement of contents. Such takings might be described as offending on the basis of this "pattern" similarity. Whether the taking is large or small, the defendant cannot be allowed to escape liability simply by the device of disguising the piracy; copyright "cannot be limited literally to the text, lest a plagiarist would escape by immaterial variation."[88]

Ultimately, whether the work is fine literature or the result of careful historical research, and whether the defendant has copied literally from the text or taken portions from a number of parts of the text, infringement must be evaluated on a case-by-case basis. One is forced to conclude that the inquiry into improper appropriation, both at trial and on appeal, remains one of the most contentious and least precisely delineated exercises in all of copyright law.

In reality, it may not be possible to formulate one all-purpose method of administering the substantial similarity issue in the litigation process. The range of copyrighted works and the particular interests involved call for a flexible approach to the issue of substantial similarity and the way it is submitted to the jury. Accordingly, the court should be able to adapt its test of substantial similarity to the medium involved, the variety of copyrightable subject matter, and the scope of protection. For example, a single ordinary observer test may be all that is needed in less complicated fabric design or popular music cases. For more complicated literary works, as well as graphic, pictorial, and sculptural works, experts may play a useful role in determining whether copying has taken place and in separating protectable and non-protectable aspects of the work.[89] In either event, the court must exercise control over the litigation process in deciding whether the trier of fact should be allowed to evaluate piracy from an ordinary observer standpoint. In other situations, however, neither the ordinary observer nor the bifurcated test may be appropriate, particularly when complex, difficult media, such as computer programs are involved. In these instances, the court should adopt a single substantial

---

[88] *Nichols v. Universal Pictures Co.*, 45 F.2d 119, 121 (2d Cir. 1930).

[89] *See, e.g., Boisson v. Banian, Ltd.*, 273 F.3d 262 (2d Cir. 2001) (holding that where plaintiff's work (quilt design) contains protectible as well as unprotectible elements, a more refined analysis is required to determine substantial similarity so that the ordinary observer must be more discerning); *Tufenkian Import/Export Ventures, Inc. v. Einstein Moomjy, Inc.*, 338 F.3d 127 (2d Cir. 2003) (infringing similarities are not rendered noninfringing because the works at issue (carpet designs) have a different concept and feel).

similarity test admitting both lay and expert testimony, a trend that is developing in the case law.[90]

Part II. THIRD PARTY LIABILITY (CONTRIBUTORY INFRINGEMENT AND VICARIOUS LIABILITY) INCLUDING THE LIABILITY OF ONLINE SERVICE PROVIDERS UNDER THE DIGITAL MILLENNIUM COPYRIGHT ACT

§ 9.07 RELATED DEFENDANTS: CONTRIBUTORY INFRINGEMENT AND VICARIOUS LIABILITY

[A] Generally

Although not expressly recognized in the 1976 Act, a person can be liable as a related defendant for the infringing activity of another.[91] This general principle is derived from § 106,[92] which grants the copyright owner the exclusive right to *authorize* others to exploit the exclusive rights of ownership.[93] Through this provision, the principle of related defendants is recognized in the 1976 Copyright Act. As used in the following subsections, the term "related defendants" refers to all situations where one can be held liable for the acts of another, including vicarious liability and liability for contributory infringement. It is not coincidental that these terms come from the law of torts, because copyright infringement is a tort. The major focus in the following subsections is on contributory infringement, whereby one can be held liable for actively aiding another to infringe copyright.

Fact situations involving the liability of related defendants vary widely but generally have the following attributes: (1) Contributory infringement: A will be held liable for B's infringing acts if A has actively induced the infringement, or, with knowledge of the infringement, A has supplied the means to infringe; (2) Vicarious liability: A will be held liable for the infringing acts of B if A supervises or has the power to supervise the acts of infringement and benefits or stands to benefit financially from the infringing acts.[94]

---

[90] *See Whelan Assocs., Inc. v. Jaslow Dental Lab., Inc.*, 797 F.2d 1222 (3d Cir. 1986), *cert. denied*, 479 U.S. 1031 (1987); *E.F. Johnson Co. v. Uniden Corp. of Am.*, 623 F. Supp. 1485 (D. Minn. 1985).

[91] For a discussion of the harmful effects of the current de facto open-ended secondary liability standard and an argument for a clear, predictable standard, see Lital Helman, *Pull Too Hard and the Rope May Break: On the Secondary Liability of Technology Providers for Copyright Infringement*, 19 Tex. Intell. Prop. L.J. 111 (2010).

[92] 17 U.S.C. § 106.

[93] *See* H.R. Rep. No. 94-1476, at 159 (1976).

[94] For an analysis of third party liability from an economic standpoint, see Douglas Lichtman & William Landes, *Indirect Liability for Copyright Infringement: An Economic Perspective*, 16 Harv. J. L. & Tech. 395 (2003).

[B] Contributory Infringement: Causing, Contributing or Inducing the Direct Infringer

The doctrine of contributory infringement originates in tort law and stems from the principle that one who directly contributes to another's infringement should be held accountable. In other words, the common law doctrine is applicable under copyright law. That is, one who knowingly participates in or furthers a tortious act is jointly and severally liable with the principal tortfeasor. The easiest cases to find liability for contributory infringement are those in which the related defendant has actual knowledge of and comes the closest to directly participating in the infringement. The case law reveals several basic patterns involving related defendants as contributory infringers. In one pattern, liability is based on defendant's active inducement of, and all but direct participation in, the infringement. For example, in *Elektra Records Co. v. Gem Electronic Distributors, Inc.*,[95] defendant stores sold blank tapes and, for a fee, loaned shoppers pre-recorded tapes containing the copyrighted musical works. The clientele would then duplicate the tapes on a system provided for them on the store premises. The court granted a preliminary injunction against the defendants for their all but direct participation in the infringing acts. Although the court's legal basis for granting the relief requested is not altogether clear, the case well illustrates the contributory infringement principle. In effect, defendant controlled the acts of the infringer by supplying all the means necessary to infringe. The only thing defendant did not do was carry out the actual acts of copying. In addition, defendant had or should have had knowledge of the infringing acts and had a direct financial stake in the infringement.

When the defendant's knowledge and control over infringing activity is less pronounced, the case for liability is correspondingly weaker. For example, in *Perfect 10, Inc. v. VISA Int'l Service Assoc.*,[96] the Ninth Circuit Court of Appeals ruled that credit card companies cannot be held liable for contributory infringement or vicarious copyright infringement when their customers purchase infringing material on line. The court reasoned that credit cards, unlike location services such as Google, Amazon, or Napster, do not make a material contribution to the infringing activity, and if users could not use credit cards, they could pay by other means. The majority declined to embrace a rule that would include peripherally involved third parties such as computer display companies, storage device companies, and certain software companies.[97]

The most complex contributory infringement cases arise when the defendant has done nothing more than supply materials or equipment to the direct infringer. When the equipment or materials can be used both for infringing and non-infringing purposes such as a photocopy machine, a DVD recorder, or software

---

[95] 360 F. Supp. 821 (E.D.N.Y. 1973).

[96] 494 F.3d 788 (9th Cir. 2007).

[97] In a lengthy dissent, Judge Kozinski flatly disagreed with the majority: "But why is locating infringing images more central to infringement than paying for them? If infringing images can't be found, there can be no infringement; but if infringing images can't be paid for, there can be no infringement either." *Id.* at 812–14.

that can be used to copy musical works, the policy considerations are particularly difficult to resolve. The courts have found infringement in situations when the defendant has induced the infringed.[98] In others, liability has been established when the defendant has actively contributed to the infringement.[99] In *Sony Corp. v. Universal City Studios, Inc.* (the *Betamax* case),[100] the Supreme Court held that the manufacturer of the Betamax machine ("VCR") was not liable as a contributory infringer for the off-the-air taping carried out by an individual owner of a Betamax machine.

In its decision, the Supreme Court borrowed a principle from patent law[101] that manufacturers of staple articles of commerce, suitable for substantial non-infringing uses, cannot be held as contributory infringers. Otherwise, a finding of contributory infringement would give the plaintiff effective control over the use of the item, placing it within the plaintiff's copyright monopoly. The Supreme Court identified two types of substantial non-infringing uses of which the Betamax was capable: (1) the videotaping of televised programs for later viewing which was then authorized by their producers; and (2) the unauthorized videotaping of copyrighted programs by consumers in their homes for later viewing, which the Supreme Court held was a fair use.[102] After *Sony*, the seller or manufacturer of copying equipment, such as typewriters, photocopying machines, and VCRs, will not be liable as a contributory infringer even if some buyers will predictably use the machine to infringe copyright.

In addition to the staple article of commerce aspect, the *Betamax* case differs significantly from mainstream contributory infringement cases, such as *Elektra Records*.[103] In the *Betamax* case, Sony had knowledge of possible infringing uses of the machine, but there was much less certainty in that knowledge. In addition, Sony did not control the copying process to the same degree as did the defendant in *Elektra Records*; Sony's participation was less direct, and, although it supplied the means to copy, it did not supply the copyrighted work. In this more attenuated case of contributory infringement, it is understandable that the Court did not wish to suppress the development of a worthwhile copying technology. The staple article doctrine, which places limits on liability for contributory infringement, seemed the appropriate analysis for the case.[104]

---

[98] See *A&M Records v. Napster, Inc.*, 239 F.3d 1004 (9th Cir. 2001).

[99] See *Metro-Goldwyn-Mayer Studios, v. Grokster, Ltd.*, 125 S. Ct. 2764 (2005).

[100] 464 U.S. 417 (1984).

[101] 35 U.S.C. § 271(a).

[102] The fair use issue is discussed at *infra* § 10.11.

[103] *Elektra Records Co. v. Gem Elec. Distribs., Inc.*, 360 F. Supp. 821 (E.D.N.Y. 1973).

[104] For an analysis of the Court's decision in *Flava Works v. myVidster* and a discussion regarding whether embedding or inline linking to a copyright-infringing video on another website infringes copyright, see Barry Sookman, *Understanding Flava Works v. myVidster: Does Inline Linking Infringe Copyright?*, 59 J. COPYRIGHT SOC'Y 723 (2012).

[C] Applying *Sony*: Third Party Liability and Peer-to-Peer Filing Sharing

[1] The P2P Challenge

Digital file compression formats such as MP3,[105] coupled with Internet peer-to-peer file sharing technology ("P2P"), have made it difficult to hold direct infringers liable for copyright infringement.[106] This technology, which is used by millions of music lovers to download songs, is reviled by the entertainment industry, which fears, with some justification, that the unauthorized massive downloading and sharing of music and films presents a major threat to the profitability of their endeavors. New technology of this sort is a double-edged sword. The widespread equation of P2P with piracy obscures the fact that the same technology can be applied in a constructive manner to all varieties of content distribution, such as academic and scientific information and public domain film, music, and literature. The legal challenge presented by P2P is daunting. Is it possible to develop rules that would stamp out the illegal uses of peer-to-peer without dampening the development of its exceedingly valuable uses? In trying to reconcile *Sony*'s "staple article" rule with traditional copyright doctrine, the Supreme Court and two courts of appeal, in finding the distributors of P2P software liable as third party infringers, have reconfirmed *Sony* but have yet to come up with a satisfactory solution to the problem.[107]

---

[105] MP3 technology allows individual computer users to copy an audio compact disc directly on their hard drive by compressing the information into the MP3 format with almost no deterioration in sound quality, regardless of the numbers of copies made. The compressed format of MP3 files has enabled users to rapidly transmit digital audio files from one computer to another by e-mail or to download files available through the Internet. This technology has converged with Internet peer-to-peer ("P2P") file sharing technology (which allows the transmission and retention of digital audio files between and among users) and has created a massive problem for the record industry. For a description of MP3 technology, see *Recording Indus. Ass'n of Am. v. Diamond Multimedia Sys., Inc.*, 180 F.3d 1072, 1074 (9th Cir. 1999).

[106] In a flood of litigation, RIAA has systematically sued as of today sued more than 30,000 individual downloaders. See the 2008 report RIAA v. THE PEOPLE: FIVE YEARS LATER, of the Electronic Frontier Foundation available at http://www.eff.org/wp/riaa-v-people-years-later. The effectiveness of this strategy is a matter of ongoing debate. For justification of the RIAA litigation initiative see Justin Hughes, *On the Logic of Suing One's Customers and the Dilemma of Infringement-Business Models*, 22 CARDOZO ARTS & ENT.L.J. 725 (2005) (questioning the received wisdom about suing one's customers); Matthew Sag, *Piracy: Twelve Year-Olds, Grandmothers, and Other Good Targets for the Recording Industry's File Sharing Litigation*, 4 N.W.J. TECH. & INTELL. PROP. 133 (2006) (arguing that the RIAA litigation is a rational response to file-sharing). Others are skeptical about the efficacy of litigation to change social norms. See the 2008 Report of the Electronic Frontier Foundation, and D. Opderbeck, *Peer-to-Peer Networks, Technological Evolution, and Intellectual Property Reverse Private Attorney General Litigation*, 20 BERK. TECH. L.J. 1685 (2005).

[107] The scholarly literature discussing the peer-to-peer problem is substantial. For differing views, see Mark A. Lemley & R. Antony Reese, *Reducing Digital Copyright Infringement without Restricting Innovation*, 56 STAN. L. REV. 1345 (2004); WILLIAM R. FISCHER, PROMISES TO KEEP: TECHNOLOGY, LAW, AND THE FUTURE OF ENTERTAINMENT 199-258 (Stanford University Press 2004) (proposing legalization of peer-to-peer file sharing coupled with a tax levy on hardware and internet service to replace lost revenue); Neil Netanel, *Impose a Noncommercial Use Levy to Allow Free Peer-to-Peer File Sharing*, 17 HARV. J.L. & TECH. 1 (2003) (proposing legalization of peer-to-peer file sharing with a tax levy to make up for lost revenue); Raymond Shih Ray Ku, *The Creative Destruction of Copyright: Napster and the New*

[2] From *Napster* to *Aimster*: Differing Views on the *Sony* Rule

In *A&M Records v. Napster*,[108] the Court of Appeals of the Ninth Circuit applied the principles of third party liability to the peer-to-peer sharing of music on the Internet. Napster distributed free software from its website that allowed its users to connect directly to one another via the Internet. Napster's software enabled users to make MP3 files stored on personal computer hard drives available for copying by other Napster users. Napster did not keep files on its centralized indexing system, but it facilitated the sharing of music files by others. The direct infringers were the individual users who uploaded and downloaded the music, but the court found that Napster was liable for contributory infringement in its operation of a centralized indexing system listing all files available for Napster users. Napster's liability for contributory infringement was based on its knowledge of, and material contribution to, the infringing activities of its users. The court acknowledged that the Napster service itself might be capable, currently and in the future, of commercially non-infringing uses, but "Napster's actual, specific knowledge of direct infringement renders *Sony*'s holding of limited assistance to Napster."[109] In sum, the uploading and downloading that infringed both the rights of reproduction and distribution were done with the knowledge and participation of the Napster service.[110]

In contrast to the *Napster* court, the meaning of the *Sony* rule was the focus in *In re Aimster Copyright Litigation*.[111] The Aimster system had been used to exchange music and other files over the AOL Instant Messaging system, as well as over the Internet. In upholding an injunction against Aimster, the Seventh Circuit held that the content providers were likely to succeed on their contributory infringement claim. The court, however, disagreed with the suggestion in *Napster* that actual knowledge of specific uses is a sufficient condition for deeming a facilitator a contributory infringer.[112] Rather, the court opted for a revised *Sony* test that would permit a service provider to avoid liability if it demonstrates actual, not merely potential, non-infringing uses of its service.[113]

Once non-infringing uses are shown, the test would then require a cost-benefit analysis to determine how burdensome it would be to eliminate or reduce the non-infringing uses. Aimster introduced no evidence showing that its file sharing system was actually used in a non-infringing way, and it did not show that it would

---

Economics of Digital Technology, 69 U. Chi. L. Rev. 263 (2002).

[108] 239 F.3d 1004 (9th Cir. 2001).

[109] *Id.* at 1020.

[110] The court also found Napster liable for vicarious liability: Napster had the ability to supervise and control the infringing conduct through its file index and received financial benefit from the infringing activity of its customers. *Id.* at 1024.

[111] 334 F.3d 643 (7th Cir. 2003).

[112] The court noted that they agreed with Professor Goldstein that "the Ninth Circuit erred in *A& M v. Napster*, 239 F.3d 1004, 1020 (9th Cir. 2001), in suggesting that actual knowledge of specific infringing uses is a sufficient condition for determining whether a facilitator is a contributory infringer." *Id.* at 649. *See* Goldstein on Copyright, § 8.3.1.

[113] *Id.* at 649.

be disproportionately costly to police its system.

[3] *Metro-Goldwyn-Mayer Studios, Inc. v. Grokster, Ltd.:* Active Inducement of Infringement

With the obvious disarray in the Circuit Courts on P2P file sharing, the Supreme Court in *Metro-Goldwin-Mayer Studios, Inc. v. Grokster, Ltd.*[114] turned its attention to the issue. In a "unanimous" opinion,[115] the court ruled that distributors of the file-sharing companies (Grokster and StreamCast) may be liable for copyright infringement if their products encourage consumers to illegally swap copyrighted works. In its opinion, the court preserved the *Sony* principle but rested its decision on the common law rationale of active inducement to infringe copyright.

The file-sharing software in *Grokster* differed significantly from that found in the *Napster* and *Aimster* cases. Unlike Napster and its centralized index of files, the Grokster and StreamCast software created a completely decentralized system whereby each user maintained an index of files that the user was willing to share with others. Once defendants distributed their "free" software, they had no capacity to control the user's conduct. In applying the *Sony* doctrine, the Ninth Circuit sustained a motion for summary judgment and established that the software was capable of substantial non-infringing uses, while refusing to find that Grokster had constructive knowledge or actual knowledge of specific infringement.[116]

In a bluntly worded opinion that remanded the case for trial, the Supreme Court held that the appeals court had misapplied the *Sony* decision by focusing only on the technology, without regard to the business model that the technology served. According to the Court, "[o]ne who distributes a device with the object of promoting its use to infringe copyright, as shown by clear expression or other affirmative steps taken to foster infringement, is liable for the resulting acts of infringement by third parties."[117]

The court found ample evidence of such intent. First, the defendants sought, through promotion and marketing, to attract the business of former Napster users. Second, neither company tried to develop filtering tools or other ways to limit infringement by users of their software. Third, defendants, who derived their profits from selling advertising space rather than the software itself, needed a maximum number of users.[118]

---

[114] 125 S. Ct. 2764 (2005).

[115] The court held unanimously in favor of petitioner, but with two concurring opinions, at least six justices were divided on the issues concerning the application of the *Sony* rule.

[116] 380 F.3d 1154 (9th Cir. 2004).

[117] *Grokster*, 125 S. Ct. at 2770.

[118] *Id.* at 2781–82. For commentary of the element "intent" in Grokster and copyright in general see Timothy Holbrook, *The Intent Element of Induced Infringement*, 22 Santa Clara Computer & High Tech. L.J. 399 (2006); and Timothy Wu, *Copyright Paradox*, 2005 Supreme Court Rev. 229.

[4] The Future of P2P and the *Sony* Doctrine[119]

The *Grokster* decision provides copyright owners with an important new avenue for protecting their rights where they can show that purveyors of technology are purposely seeking to profit on the infringing acts of users. In cases in which active inducement is pleaded, relevant discovery will likely transcend product design to encompass corporate decision making and corporate strategy. Alternatively, distributors of new technologies may take some comfort knowing that the *Grokster* court did not revisit the *Sony* safe harbor, which remains intact. But the decision's emphasis on finding the "intent" of a company could mire new technologies in litigious limbo, where every e-mail message, marketing plan, or other information is fair game as proof in a future lawsuit.

In refusing to revisit *Sony*, *Grokster* did nothing to clear up the ambiguities of the *Sony* rule, particularly the elusiveness of *Sony*'s stable article of commerce doctrine borrowed from patent law. Moreover, *Grokster* provides no guidance on the critical issue of how to determine when a non-infringing use would be deemed "substantial" or "commercially significant." *Grokster* reflects the inherent vagueness of the *Sony* rule. How else can one explain why at least six of the justices were divided on issues concerning the relative balance of infringing and non-infringing use that may keep the technology within the *Sony* safe harbor? This is hardly a recipe for legal certainty and predictability.

New technologies are infinitely variable in their effect on legal rights. Compare P2P technology as it is currently used with the Sony Betamax machine of the early 1980s. The Betamax machine was, for the most part, put to legal uses. The evidence of damage to copyright owners, and the evidence of damage from home time shifting, was minimal and speculative at best. In contrast, the peer-to-peer file sharing is overwhelmingly illegal and has imposed real and substantial damage on the music industry. In her concurring opinion in *Grokster*, Justice Ginsberg maintained that there was insufficient evidence that the software at issue was capable of substantial or commercially significant non-infringing uses.[120]

Whatever the future contours of the law, the P2P programs are too widespread and too decentralized for control though litigation. The music industry will be forced to create a new business model for the distribution of music and may try to impose technological measures to impede copying of music.[121]

---

119 For an argument that courts should return to the *Sony* standard to assess vicarious liability issues concerning ISPs, see Veronica Corsaro, *From Betamax to YouTube: How Sony Corporation of America v. Universal City Studios, Inc. Could Still Be a Standard for New Technology*, 64 FED. COMM. L.J. 449 (2012).

120 *Id.* at 2783.

121 *See* Peter Yu, *P2P and the Future of Private Copying* 76 U. COLO. L. REV. 653 (2005) (concluding that law alone cannot provide a stable resolution to the P2P dilemma). For the international implications of Grokster see Graeme Austin, *Importing Kazaa — Exporting Grokster*, 22 SANTA CLARA COMPUTER & HIGH TECH. L.J. 577 (2006).

[D] Vicarious Liability: The Right to Supervise and a Financial Interest

The concept of vicarious liability in copyright law was developed in the Second Circuit as an outgrowth of agency principles involving the concept of *respondeat superior*. In the copyright context, the issue of vicarious liability arises in cases where the defendant has the right or power to supervise the acts of the direct infringer and has a financial stake in the infringing acts, even though the defendant had no knowledge of, or did not directly participate in, the infringing acts.[122]

In *Shapiro, Bernstein & Co. v. H.L. Green Co.*,[123] the defendant retailer was held liable as a related defendant for the infringing acts of its lessee, who had sold pirated records. Liability was found even though the retailer had no knowledge of the infringement because "[w]hen the right and ability to supervise coalesce with an obvious and direct financial interest," liability should be imposed on the financial beneficiary despite lack of knowledge of the infringement.[124] Under the same reasoning, owners of dance halls have been held liable for infringing performances given on their premises by musical groups.[125]

The rationale of vicarious liability was examined in *Fonovisa, Inc. v. Cherry Auction, Inc.*,[126] where an operator of a flea market was held vicariously liable for its vendors' sales of counterfeit records. Unlike the landlord in *H.L. Green* who received a ten or twelve percent commission from its vendors, the flea market owner was paid a daily rental fee by the vendors, an admission fee by the public, as well as parking fees and receipts from the concession stands. Thus, the defendant reaped substantial benefits from the public's fees, profiting from a public drawn to the site to buy the counterfeit recordings. In short, although the result in some vicarious liability cases may be harsh, particularly where the defendant has no actual knowledge of the infringing activity, it may be justified on basic equitable principles: those who benefit financially from the infringement should compensate the copyright owner.

Liability in cases such as *Shapiro* and *Fonovisa* is not based on the doctrine of master-servant (*respondeat superior*) or even the presence of an employment

---

[122] *See id.*; *see also Gershwin Publ'g Corp. v. Columbia Artists Mgt., Inc.*, 443 F.2d 1159 (2d Cir. 1971). Defendant C.A.M.I. formed and sponsored a community concert association that put on a concert at which there occurred unauthorized performances of copyrighted music. Although C.A.M.I. had no formal power to control the local association or the artist for whom it served as agent, the court found C.A.M.I. vicariously liable for being in a position to police the activity, and for deriving substantial financial benefit from the performances; moreover, C.A.M.I. knew that copyrighted music was to be played at the concert and that no one would secure a copyright license.

[123] 316 F.2d 304 (2d Cir. 1963).

[124] *H.L. Green*, 316 F.2d at 307; *see also Screen Gems-Columbia Music, Inc. v. Mark-Fi Records, Inc.*, 327 F. Supp. 788 (S.D.N.Y. 1971), *rev'd on other grounds*, 453 F.2d 552 (2d Cir. 1972) (advertising agency defendant held liable for aiding a client in selling pirated copyrighted music. Liability was based on the ad agency's participation in the commercial exploitation, even though it had not actually engaged in the copying.)

[125] *See, e.g.*, *Dreamland Ball Room v. Shapiro, Bernstein & Co.*, 36 F.2d 354 (7th Cir. 1929); *Famous Music Corp. v. Bay State Harness Horse Racing & Breeding Ass'n, Inc.*, 554 F.2d 1213 (1st Cir. 1977).

[126] 76 F.3d 259 (9th Cir. 1996).

relationship. The rationale is based instead on the right or power to control the infringing acts while financially benefiting from them. Thus, not every landlord whose lessee engages in infringing acts will be liable as a related defendant for contributory infringement. Landlords are not liable due to their status. Instead, courts have required some proof that a landlord exercised some control over the leased premises and had a financial interest in the infringing activity to find liability on a theory of vicarious liability.[127] Similarly, a sponsor of radio programs will not be liable vicariously unless one could show the right to supervise or control the infringing performance.[128] On the other hand, lack of knowledge by the related defendant is not a defense to infringement, although it can affect the extent of the remedies provided.[129]

§ 9.08 LIABILITY FOR THE ACTIVITIES OF ONLINE SERVICES

[A] Background to the Passage of Title II of the Digital Millennium Copyright Act

Online service providers ("OSP") provide Internet access, e-mail, chat rooms, web page hosting, and various other transmission, routing, and connection services.[130] OSPs, such as America Online, Worldnet, or their smaller local counterparts, have long been concerned about potential liability resulting from the infringing acts of their users. As a theoretical possibility, OSPs could be held directly or vicariously liable for third party activity that they neither knew about nor sanctioned. For example, a message posted to a Usenet group is often copied by thousands of servers owned by different persons who engage in disseminating such messages. If the Usenet message includes copyrightable material posted without the consent of the copyright owner, the owner of each server may well be liable for direct copyright infringement by allowing the message to be copied on its server. Some of these parties may also be liable under theories of vicarious and contributory infringement. The issues have been litigated in a series of cases that left the contours of liability of OSPs for their acts and those of their users in a state of uncertainty.[131] Other common activities of OSPs create risks of liability under copyright law but have yet to be tested in the courts. One such risk arises out of "caching," in which the OSP makes a temporary copy of popular Internet material

---

[127] *See Robert Stigwood Group, Ltd. v. Hurwitz*, 462 F.2d 910 (2d Cir. 1972).

[128] *See Bevan v. Columbia Broad. Sys., Inc.*, 329 F. Supp. 601 (S.D.N.Y. 1971).

[129] *See Fourth Floor Music, Inc. v. Der Place, Inc.*, 572 F. Supp. 41 (D. Neb. 1983). *See also* 17 U.S.C. § 504(c)(2).

[130] For a discussion of graduated response (a law enforcement program developed between ISPs, rights holders, and sometimes an independent administrative body to address copyright infringement claims) as an important starting point to achieve a better balanced system of copyright law, see Daniel Lieberman, *A Homerun for Three Strikes Law: Graduated Response and Its Bid to Save Copyright*, 59 J. Copyright Soc'y 223 (2012).

[131] The Act repudiates the position taken in *Playboy Enters., Inc. v. Frena*, 839 F. Supp. 1552 (M.D. Fla. 1993), in favor of that articulated in *Religious Tech. Ctr. v. Netcom On-Line Comm. Servs., Inc.*, 907 F. Supp. 1361 (N.D. Cal. 1995).

in order to make access to frequently used websites quicker.[132]

The possibility that OSPs could be held directly or vicariously liable for third party activity about which they neither knew nor sanctioned led to a legislative solution to the issue. Title II of the Digital Millennium Copyright Act, codified in § 512 of the Copyright Act, addressed the concerns of OSPs by limiting their liability for copyright infringement in several key circumstances. These exemptions from liability add to any defense that an OSP might have under copyright or any other law. The Act creates safe harbors for specified OSP activity. If the activity falls within the safe harbor, it is exempted from liability. If not, the question of liability will be determined by traditional copyright analysis. Overall, the Act provides greater certainty for OSPs, immunizing them from inadvertent liability that may arise from the peculiar nature of the Internet.

[B] Who are Online Service Providers?

Section 512 (k) defines an online service provider as "an entity offering the transmission, routing, or providing the connections for digital online communications, between or among points specified by a user, or material of the user's choosing, without modification to the content of the material as sent or received."[133]

The statutory definition of "service provider" is written broadly and has been interpreted broadly by the courts. For example, the online auction site eBay,[134] as well as websites that permitted users to post and access real estate listings,[135] and one that verified the age of visitors to participating adult websites have all qualified as service providers.[136] Once an entity qualifies as a service provider, it is eligible to enjoy the exemptions from liability provided by the DMCA.

[C] Eligibility for the OSP Exemption: Threshold Conditions

To qualify for any of the exemptions, an OSP must meet two general conditions. First, it must adopt, implement, and inform its subscribers and account holders of its policy providing for termination of users who are repeat infringers.[137] Second,

---

[132] Specifically, by caching, the OSP makes a temporary copy of popular Internet material requested by a user so that the copy can be delivered to the subsequent user, rather than obtaining the material from the original website for each subsequent user. "Caching" is provided a "safe harbor" under the Act if certain conditions are met. *See* 17 U.S.C. § 512(b).

[133] 17 U.S.C. § 512(k).

[134] *Hendrickson v. eBay, Inc.*, 165 F. Supp. 2d 1082 (C.D. Cal. 2001).

[135] *ALS Scan, Inc. v. RemarQ Cmtys., Inc.* 239 F.3d 619 (4th Cir. 2001).

[136] *Perfect 10, Inc. v. Cybernet Ventures, Inc.*, 167 F. Supp. 2d 1114 (C.D. Cal. 2001). *See also In re Aimster Copyright Litigation*, 334 F.3d 643 (7th Cir. 2003) ("Although the Act was not passed with Napster-type services in mind, the definition of Internet service provider is broad . . . [and] Aimster fits it.").

[137] *See* 17 U.S.C. § 512(I)(1)(A). *See Perfect 10, Inc. v. CCBill LLC*, 481 F.3d 751 (9th 2007) (ruling that "a service provider implements a policy if it has a working notification system, a procedure for dealing with DMCA-compliant notifications, and if it does not actively prevent copyright owners from collecting

the OSP must have adopted standard technical measures used by copyright owners to identify and protect copyrighted works.[138]

To qualify for the exemptions, an OSP does not need to monitor its service or affirmatively seek out information about copyright infringement on its service, except to accommodate technical measures described above. In addition, the Act provides that an OSP does not have to access, remove, or block material to qualify for the exemptions, if such action is prohibited by law.[139]

The Act erects a number of safe harbors if certain conditions are met. If the OSP's activity qualifies for any of the safe harbors, the OSP is not liable for monetary relief for claims of copyright infringement founded on that activity. In addition, qualifying for a safe harbor will limit injunctive relief against the OSP. In deciding whether to grant injunctive relief, the court must take a number of factors into consideration, including burden on the OSP system, technical feasibility, and interference with non-infringing material if such relief is granted.[140]

The provisions of § 512 expressly limit the potential liability of service providers in four activities:

(1) Transitory digital network communications;

(2) System caching;

(3) Information residing on systems networks at the direction of users; and

(4) Information location tools.

[D] Safe Harbors

[1] Transitory Digital Network Communications: § 512 (a)

As long as someone other than the service provider initiated a transmission and chose its recipient, and the service provider does not interfere with its content, no liability can attach to the service provider in connection with that transmission. This includes liability for transitory reproductions, so long as they are not "maintained on the system or network . . . for a longer period than is reasonably necessary for the transmission, routing, or provision of connections."[141] As it turns out, the "intermediate or transient storage" exempted under § 512(a) can be relatively long-lived. In a challenge to America Online's invocation of this "safe harbor" from liability, a science fiction writer seeking to hold the company responsible for unauthorized exchanges of his works on the Usenet system pointed out that AOL may maintain Usenet messages on its servers for as long as fourteen days.

information needed to issue such notifications") 481 F.3d at 758.

[138] *See* 17 U.S.C. § 512(I)(1)(B).

[139] 17 U.S.C. § 512(m).

[140] *See* 17 U.S.C. § 512(j).

[141] 17 U.S.C. § 512(a)(4).

Reviewing the legislative history of the provision, however, the court found that § 512(a) was satisfied.[142]

[2] System Caching: § 512(b)

Service providers are not liable for the "intermediate and temporary storage of material" posted online by another person, as long as the storage is carried out through an automatic technical process and the service provider complies with industry standards for refreshing, reloading, and updating the material and does not interfere with password protections and other security measures. The service provider must also comply with the "notice-and-take-down" provisions of subsection (c) if the material has been removed or disabled on the originating website. The distinction between subsection (a) and subsection (b) is that the former applies to the pass-through and storage of directed transmissions, such as e-mail, while the latter applies to the temporary local storage of the contents of frequently visited websites, to speed or simplify user access.[143]

[3] Information Residing on Systems or Networks at Direction of Users: § 512(c)

This subsection limits the liability of service providers who provide "hosting" services by allocating server space to customers or clients who wish to make information available to others, typically by way of the Internet. Web-hosting activities pose a range of potential copyright concerns for service providers, including potential liability for direct infringement of the reproduction and distribution rights and for contributory infringement or vicarious liability by assisting or abetting the online activities of customers. Section 512(c) cuts across these various doctrines of infringement to provide a qualified defense against any and all financial liability and some, though not all, forms of injunctive relief.

The Act limits liability based on the material being stored or referred to if the OSP meets the following conditions:

(1) the OSP does not actually know that the material is infringing;

(2) the OSP is not aware of information from which the infringing nature of the material is apparent;

(3) if the OSP acquires such knowledge or awareness, the OSP acts expeditiously to remove or block access to the material;

---

142 *See Ellison v. Robertson*, 189 F. Supp. 2d 1051, 1068–70 (C.D. Cal. 2002) (holding that the statute was designed to codify the rule in *Netcom*, where Usenet messages had been maintained for 11 days). Although the Ninth Circuit reversed *Ellison* on other grounds, it specifically approved this portion of the district court's opinion, see *Ellison v. Robertson*, 357 F.3d 1072, 1081 (9th Cir. 2004).

143 As Internet technology evolves, the phenomenon of caching and the scope of the exemption are likely to become more controversial. In *Field v. Google Inc.*, 412 F. Supp. 2d 1106 (D. Nev. 2006), the court upheld the Google search engine's use of caching on a number of grounds, including § 512(b) and fair use. Subsequently, in *Perfect 10 v. Amazon.com, Inc.*, 508 F.3d 1146 (9th Cir. 2007), Google was absolved of secondary liability for enabling local caching by users — on the ground that a local cache was a fair use, without reaching the § 512(b) issue — but the court remanded for further fact-finding to determine whether Google was secondarily liable for caching and linking to full-size infringing images stored on third-party websites.

(4) the OSP does not obtain a financial benefit directly attributable to the infringing material while having the right and ability to control the material; and

(5) the OSP complies with the "notice and takedown" provisions of the Act. These provisions, specified in the Act, allow copyright owners to notify an OSP of allegedly infringing material of the OSP's system. They require the OSP to remove or block access to such material after receiving notice.[144]

[a] Actual Knowledge, Red Flag Knowledge

If the OSP has actual knowledge or is aware of facts or circumstances from which infringing material is stored on its system, the OSP is required to act expeditiously in taking steps to remove or disable the material. The § 512(c)(1) safe harbor is only available when the infringement occurs "by reason of storage at the direction of a user of material that resides on a system or network controlled or operated by or for the service provider." Courts have interpreted the storage provision as encompassing more than the specific act of storage. It includes as well related conduct necessary to give users access to the stored material.

The safe harbor of § 512(c) may be lost if a service provider had actual knowledge of infringing material. Actual knowledge of the infringement differs from liability for contributory infringement in two ways. First, for contributory infringement, the defendant need only know of the infringing conduct. By contrast, for liability under § 512(c), the OSP must also know that the conduct is *infringing*.[145] Second, as is the case for contributory liability, the defendant under § 512(c) may be informed of the infringing activity by the copyright owner. Unlike contributory infringement, the copyright owner must inform the OSP of the infringing activity pursuant to the "notice and takedown" regime discussed below.

Section 512(c)(1)(A)(ii) requires that service providers not be "aware of facts or circumstances from which infringing activity is apparent." A service provider will not fall into the § 512(c) safe harbor if it can be shown that there were "red flags." These are facts that the service provider should have been aware of indicating infringing activity. An OSP need not monitor its service or affirmatively seek facts indicating infringing activity. However, if the OSP becomes aware of a "red flag" from which infringing conduct is obvious, it must take action expeditiously or lose the safe harbor. In *Viacom International, Inc. v. YouTube*,[146] the court distinguished between actual and red flag knowledge. The key difference is that red flag knowledge of infringing conduct requires more than a general awareness that infringements are taking place. Rather, red flag liability turns on whether the provider was subjectively aware of facts that would have made the specific infringement objectively obvious to a reasonable person. In sum, "the red flag provision, because it incorporates an objective standard, is not swallowed up by the actual knowledge provision . . . Both provisions do independent work, and both

[144] The Notice and Takedown Provisions are specified in 17 U.S.C. § 512(c)(1), (d).

[145] See e.g. UMG Recordings, Inc. v. Veoh Networks, Inc., 718 F.3d 1006, 1021 (9th Cir. 2013).

[146] 676 F.3d 19 (9th Cir. 2012).

apply only to specific instances of infringement."[147]

[b] Notice and Takedown

Qualification as a service provider is just the beginning of a successful effort to limit liability. Companies engaged in web hosting also must have "adopted and reasonably implemented" and informed subscribers of, a policy that provides for the termination in appropriate circumstances of subscribers who are repeat infringers.[148] The "notice-and-takedown" provisions require that every service provider designate an agent to receive notices of alleged infringement from copyright owners, by filing with the U.S. Copyright Office *and* by posting the agent's name and address (including an email address) on a publicly accessible website.[149] The function of this agent is to receive notices of claimed infringement from copyright owners, and the statute goes to some lengths to detail the elements that such a notice must contain, including requirements that (subject to various penalties for misrepresentation) it:

- be sworn and physically or virtually signed;
- be based on a good faith belief that the allegedly infringing material is being used without permission (although not, apparently, that the use is in fact an infringement, rather than, say, a "fair use");
- identify the work allegedly infringed; and
- identify the infringing material and provide "information reasonably sufficient to permit the service provider to locate the material."[150]

An OSP must comply with the notice and takedown provisions to enjoy the benefits of the Act. These provisions permit the copyright owner to notify an OSP of allegedly infringing material on the OSP's system. After receiving such notice, the OSP must remove or block access to such material. To exercise these provisions, the OSP must designate, both to the Copyright Office and on its service, information about contacting a designated agent for notice purposes.

After receiving proper notice, a service provider must "respond [e]xpeditiously to remove, or disable access to, the material that is claimed to be infringing."[151] The person whose material is at issue may then serve a "counter notification," including a sworn statement that he or she believes in good faith that the material was removed or disabled as a result of mistake or misidentification."[152] If the person does so, the service provider must pass this notification along to the copyright owner, which has ten working days in which to seek judicial relief. If the owner does not do so, the service provider must restore the material. If the service provider complies with this procedure in good faith, § 512(g) immunizes the se[rvice provider] against claims by the subscribers

[147] *Id.* at 31.

[148] 17 U.S.C. § 512(i)(

[149] *See* 17 U.S.C

[150] *See* 17 U

[151] *See* 17

[152] 17 U.S

whose material is "taken down." The "notice-and-takedown" procedure has come under some criticism from consumer advocates who charge that copyright owners are abusing the procedure by sending § 512(c) notices to request removal of material that is merely embarrassing or unflattering, rather than infringing.[153]

Copyright owners have a strong motivation to provide notices that comply with the statutory requirements. A service provider is entitled to ignore any notice that is not in "substantial" compliance; and if it does, its receipt of the non-complying notice cannot be used against it in a subsequent effort to prove its "knowledge" of a customer's activities as an element of liability for contributory infringement.[154] A service provider may also choose to ignore even a fully compliant notice; but if it does, it loses the limitation on liability that § 512 provides, and its exposure to liability for contributory infringement may be considerably enhanced by the receipt of the notice. The timing of the notice also has been the subject of litigation. One court considered the issue of blanket notices.[155] It held that a blanket notice that all DVDs of a motion picture were infringing was adequate for purposes of § 512(c) for all copies then available on the service provider's website. But the notice was not sufficient for other copies of the same movie that were posted several months later. In effect, imposing on a service provider a continuing duty to monitor its site for infringing activity was contrary to the intent of Congress in enacting § 512.

The Act imposes affirmative obligations on the OSPs that have removed or blocked material on their systems at the copyright owner's request. On receiving notice, the OSP must take additional steps to protect the user's rights. This includes prompt notification to the user that the OSP has blocked or removed material. In response, the user may send a "counter notification" of the material stating that the removal and block resulted from mistake or misidentification.[156] If the counter notification complies with the statutory requirements, an OSP must then provide a copy of it to the copyright owner that sent the original notice. Unless the copyright owner then notifies the OSP that he has filed a court action to restrain the infringement, the OSP must replace or unblock the material within ten or fourteen business days of receiving the counter notification.[157]

---

153 For a critique … eaching take-down notices, see HEINS & BECKLES, WILL FAIR USE SURVIVE? FREE EXPRESSION IN THE … OPYRIGHT CONTROL (2005) (a report from the Free Expression Project of the Brennan Center for … t NYU School of Law), *available at* http://www.fepproject.org/ policyreports/WillFairUseSu…

154 What constitutes substan… ce with the notice requirements was litigated in *ALS Scan, Inc. v. RemarQ Communities, I*… 619 (4th Cir. 2001) (stripping the safe harbor from defendant). For a criticism of the cas… ybka, *ALS Scan, Inc. v. RemarQ Communities, Inc.: Notice and ISPs' Liability For Third* … *Infringement*, 11 DEPAUL-LCA J. ART. & ENT. L. 479 (2001).

155 See *Hendrickson v. Amazon.com, In*… d 914 (C.D. Cal. 2003).

156 The Act provides for liability to the OS… wner for knowing material misrepre- …tations both against copyright owners in givin… in proving counter notification. *See* … S.C. § 512(f). For a discussion of the problem … "blight" in copyright law and an … nt that section 512(f) of the DMCA should … John Tehranian, *Curbing* … *ht*, 14 VAND. J. ENT. & TECH. L. 993 (2012).

157 17 U.S.C. § 512(g)(2).

apply only to specific instances of infringement."[147]

[b] Notice and Takedown

Qualification as a service provider is just the beginning of a successful effort to limit liability. Companies engaged in web hosting also must have "adopted and reasonably implemented" and informed subscribers of, a policy that provides for the termination in appropriate circumstances of subscribers who are repeat infringers.[148] The "notice-and-takedown" provisions require that every service provider designate an agent to receive notices of alleged infringement from copyright owners, by filing with the U.S. Copyright Office *and* by posting the agent's name and address (including an email address) on a publicly accessible website.[149] The function of this agent is to receive notices of claimed infringement from copyright owners, and the statute goes to some lengths to detail the elements that such a notice must contain, including requirements that (subject to various penalties for misrepresentation) it:

- be sworn and physically or virtually signed;
- be based on a good faith belief that the allegedly infringing material is being used without permission (although not, apparently, that the use is in fact an infringement, rather than, say, a "fair use");
- identify the work allegedly infringed; and
- identify the infringing material and provide "information reasonably sufficient to permit the service provider to locate the material."[150]

An OSP must comply with the notice and takedown provisions to enjoy the benefits of the Act. These provisions permit the copyright owner to notify an OSP of allegedly infringing material on the OSP's system. After receiving such notice, the OSP must remove or block access to such material. To exercise these provisions, the OSP must designate, both to the Copyright Office and on its service, information about contacting a designated agent for notice purposes.

After receiving proper notice, a service provider must "respond expeditiously to remove, or disable access to, the material that is claimed to be infringing."[151] The person whose material is at issue may then serve a "counter notification," including a sworn statement that he or she believes in good faith "that the material was removed or disabled as a result of mistake or misidentification."[152] If the person does so, the service provider must pass this counter-notification along to the copyright owner, which has ten working days in which to seek judicial relief. If the owner does not do so, the service provider has four working days in which to restore the material. If the service provider complies with this procedure in good faith, § 512(g) immunizes the service provider against claims by the subscribers

---

147 *Id.* at 31.

148 17 U.S.C. § 512(i)(1)(A).

149 *See* 17 U.S.C. § 512(c)(2).

150 *See* 17 U.S.C. § 512(c)(3).

151 *See* 17 U.S.C. § 512(c)(1)(C).

152 17 U.S.C. § 512(g)(3)(C).

whose material is "taken down." The "notice-and-takedown" procedure has come under some criticism from consumer advocates who charge that copyright owners are abusing the procedure by sending § 512(c) notices to request removal of material that is merely embarrassing or unflattering, rather than infringing.[153]

Copyright owners have a strong motivation to provide notices that comply with the statutory requirements. A service provider is entitled to ignore any notice that is not in "substantial" compliance; and if it does, its receipt of the non-complying notice cannot be used against it in a subsequent effort to prove its "knowledge" of a customer's activities as an element of liability for contributory infringement.[154] A service provider may also choose to ignore even a fully compliant notice; but if it does, it loses the limitation on liability that § 512 provides, and its exposure to liability for contributory infringement may be considerably enhanced by the receipt of the notice. The timing of the notice also has been the subject of litigation. One court considered the issue of blanket notices.[155] It held that a blanket notice that all DVDs of a motion picture were infringing was adequate for purposes of § 512(c) for all copies then available on the service provider's website. But the notice was not sufficient for other copies of the same movie that were posted several months later. In effect, imposing on a service provider a continuing duty to monitor its site for infringing activity was contrary to the intent of Congress in enacting § 512.

The Act imposes affirmative obligations on the OSPs that have removed or blocked material on their systems at the copyright owner's request. On receiving notice, the OSP must take additional steps to protect the user's rights. This includes prompt notification to the user that the OSP has blocked or removed material. In response, the user may send a "counter notification" of the material stating that the removal and block resulted from mistake or misidentification.[156] If the counter notification complies with the statutory requirements, an OSP must then provide a copy of it to the copyright owner that sent the original notice. Unless the copyright owner then notifies the OSP that he has filed a court action to restrain the infringement, the OSP must replace or unblock the material within ten or fourteen business days of receiving the counter notification.[157]

---

153 For a critique of overreaching take-down notices, see HEINS & BECKLES, WILL FAIR USE SURVIVE? FREE EXPRESSION IN THE AGE OF COPYRIGHT CONTROL (2005) (a report from the Free Expression Project of the Brennan Center for Justice at NYU School of Law), *available at* http://www.fepproject.org/policyreports/WillFairUseSurvive.pdf.

154 What constitutes substantial compliance with the notice requirements was litigated in *ALS Scan, Inc. v. RemarQ Communities, Inc.*, 239 F.3d 619 (4th Cir. 2001) (stripping the safe harbor from defendant). For a criticism of the case, see Laura Rybka, *ALS Scan, Inc. v. RemarQ Communities, Inc.: Notice and ISPs' Liability For Third Party Copyright Infringement*, 11 DEPAUL-LCA J. ART. & ENT. L. 479 (2001).

155 *See Hendrickson v. Amazon.com, Inc.*, 298 F. Supp. 2d 914 (C.D. Cal. 2003).

156 The Act provides for liability to the OSP and copyright owner for knowing material misrepresentations both against copyright owners in giving notice and users in proving counter notification. *See* 17 U.S.C. § 512(f). For a discussion of the problem of overreach or "copyblight" in copyright law and an argument that section 512(f) of the DMCA should be strengthened, see John Tehranian, *Curbing Copyblight*, 14 VAND. J. ENT. & TECH. L. 993 (2012).

157 *See* 17 U.S.C. § 512(g)(2).

[4] Information Location Tools: § 512(d)

Service providers are not liable for referring or linking users to an online location containing infringing material, or for providing the means to locate infringing material, such as a directory, index, or search engine. All of the same conditions and limitations applicable to subsection (c), including the "notice-and-takedown" provisions, apply to subsection (d) as well.[158]

[E] Subpoena to Identify Infringers: § 512(h)

Section 512(h) of the Act allows any copyright owner who has served notice on a service provider to obtain an automatic *ex parte* court order requiring the service provider to identify the individual subscriber whose material or conduct was the subject of the original notice, and requiring the service provider to make this disclosure "expeditiously . . . notwithstanding any other provision of law." The copyright owner need not bring a suit for infringement if it files three items: (1) a proposed subpoena; (2) a copy of the notice and takedown; and (3) a sworn declaration that the information is being obtained solely to pursue rights protected "under this title." The issue is whether § 512(h) can be used only to identify subscribers who have posted infringing material or if it can also be used to identify subscribers who have used the OSP as a conduit. This provision was construed in *In re Verizon Internet Services, Inc.*,[159] in which the RIAA availed itself of § 512(h) to unearth individuals who were engaged in allegedly infringing peer-to-peer file sharing. Verizon refused to identify subscribers, taking the position that § 512(h) did not to apply to situations where the OSP was a mere conduit for arguably infringing transmissions. The Court of Appeals held that the subpoena power could not be used to obtain information from an OSP like Verizon in its activity as a mere conduit for allegedly infringing material. Admitting some sympathy with the plight of the RIAA, the court reasoned that § 512(h), in referring to § 512(c)(3), applies only to an OSP in its role in the *storage* of material on its website but not in its capacity of transmitting data.[160]

The ruling against the RIAA's use of the subpoena provision to sue infringers represented a setback for the record industry's attempts to suppress peer-to-peer file sharing. Despite this setback, the RIAA pursued its strategy of suing individual infringers by using a somewhat more difficult process — a procedure based on their numerical addresses.[161]

---

[158] *See, e.g.*, *Perfect 10 v. Amazon.com, Inc.*, 508 F.3d 1146 (9th Cir. 2007) (remanding for further fact-finding on this issue).

[159] 351 F.3d 1229 (D.C. Cir. 2003).

[160] *Id.* at 1237.

[161] *See generally* Alice Kao, *RIAA v. Verizon: Applying the Subpoena Provision of the DMCA*, 19 Berkeley Tech. L.J. 405 (2004).

Part III. REMEDIES

§ 9.09 INJUNCTIVE AND OTHER COERCIVE RELIEF

[A] In General

Under § 502(a) of the Copyright Act, a District Court may grant both temporary and final injunctive relief "on such terms as it may deem reasonable to prevent or restrain infringement of a copyright." Often, a copyright owner may need immediate relief against current or threatened infringing activity in order to avoid irreparable harm. Temporary relief may include a temporary restraining order, a preliminary injunction, and/or an impoundment order. Although the grant of preliminary relief is conferred at the court's discretion, such relief has been granted generously in copyright cases when the plaintiff is able to make a showing of irreparable harm and has acted expediently in requesting the injunctive remedy. A copyright owner who has obtained either a preliminary or a permanent injunction can enforce it against a defendant located anywhere in the United States.[162]

[B] Preliminary Injunctions

Section 502(a)[163] of the 1976 Act allows a court to grant, at its discretion, both preliminary (temporary) and permanent (final) injunctions. In general, the test in the Second Circuit for granting injunctions may be stated as follows:

> There must be a showing of possible irreparable injury [to the copyright] owner and either (1) probable success on the merits, or (2) sufficiently serious questions going to the merits to make them a fair ground for litigation and a balance of hardships tipping decidedly toward the party requesting the preliminary relief.[164]

The tests for preliminary injunctions vary depending on the circuit involved, but the threshold question in granting a preliminary injunction is the proof of irreparable harm. Accordingly, preliminary injunctions are normally granted where delay would deprive plaintiff of relief and cause him irreparable harm. In applying this factor, all courts appear to vary their general practice in considering applications for pretrial relief in copyright cases. In a copyright infringement action, however, if a plaintiff can demonstrate probable success on the merits — a prima facie case of infringement — a court generally will hold that irreparable injury can be presumed and need not be proved by a detailed showing. This presumption may be rebuttable, but to rebut it would, in practice, require an extraordinary showing. Typically, the need for an expedited procedure occurs in situations where the

---

162 *See* 17 U.S.C. § 502(b); H.R. Rep. No. 94-1476, at 160 (1976).

163 17 U.S.C. § 502(a).

164 *Paramount Pictures Corp. v. Carol Publ'g Group*, 11 F. Supp. 2d 329(2d Cir. 1998), *aff'd* 181 F.3d 83 (2d Cir. 1999); *Ass'n of Am. Med. Colls. v. Carey*, 482 F. Supp. 1358, 1364 (N.D.N.Y. 1980); *Caulfield v. Bd. of Educ.*, 583 F.2d 605, 610 (2d Cir. 1978).

plaintiff's work has a short commercial life. For example, the issue of preliminary injunction arises in fabric design cases where delay until final relief would effectively deny relief.[165]

The standards for the application of a preliminary injunction vary from circuit to circuit. For example the Ninth Circuit requires that "a plaintiff seeking preliminary injunctive relief must demonstrate 'either a likelihood of success on the merits and the possibility of irreparable injury . . . or that serious questions going to the merits were raised and that the balance of hardships tips sharply in its favor.' "[166] Unlike the Second and Ninth Circuits, a majority of the circuits employ the standard four-part preliminary injunction test familiar from other areas of the law. They consider the following: (a) the significance of the threat of irreparable harm to the plaintiff if the injunction is not granted; (b) the balance between this harm and the injury that granting the injunction would inflict on the defendant; (c) the probability that the plaintiff will succeed on the merits; and (d) promotion of the public interest.[167] One should not, however, overstate the significance of inter-circuit differences over the choice of standard. Even in jurisdictions that follow the four-part test, some of the factors tend to be differentially inflected — in favor of plaintiffs — where copyright infringement is at stake. As one court stated, if the balance of harm were given too much weight, "a knowing infringer would be permitted to construct its business around its infringement."[168]

Alternatively, when damages alone would be adequate, a preliminary injunction will not be issued. Although a showing of irreparable harm is normally required, courts have held that such harm may be presumed when the plaintiff makes out a prima facie case of infringement.[169] In some instances, special considerations may cut against a presumption of irreparable injury. Suppose, for example, that the plaintiff had known of the defendant's infringing uses for an extended period but had taken no legal steps until the present filing to bring them to an end.[170] There are other situations in which the presumption can be considered to have been rebutted as, for example, where the plaintiff has not been harmed, where any harm is *de minimis*, or where the defendant acted with innocent intent, relying on lack of copyright notice.[171] As a backdrop to granting a preliminary injunction, all circuits will take into account the "public interest." On the whole, "public interest" concerns will not figure prominently in decisions about preliminary injunctive relief

---

[165] *See Novelty Textile Mills, Inc. v. Joanne Fabrics Corp.*, 558 F.2d 1090 (2d Cir. 1977).

[166] *Cadence Design Sys., Inc. v. Avant! Corp.*, 125 F.3d 824, 826 (9th Cir. 1997) (quoting *Sega Enters. Ltd. v. Accolade, Inc.*, 977 F.2d 1510, 1517 (9th Cir. 1992)).

[167] *See Lakedreams v. Taylor*, 932 F.2d 1103 (5th Cir. 1991).

[168] *Apple Computer, Inc. v. Franklin Computer Corp.*, 714 F.2d 1240, 1255 (3d Cir. 1983).

[169] *See Educ. Testing Serv. v. Katzman*, 793 F.2d 533, 543–44 (3d Cir. 1986); *Hasbro Bradley, Inc. v. Sparkle Toys, Inc.*, 780 F.2d 189, 192 (2d Cir. 1985); *Apple Computer, Inc. v. Franklin Computer Corp.*, 714 F.2d 1240, 1254 (3d Cir. 1983).

[170] *See Bourne Co. v. Tower Records*, 976 F.2d 99 (2d Cir. 1992) (denying an injunction for Disney's use of songs from movie "Pinocchio" in videocassette trailer advertisements). And, for a closer case, see *Feiner & Co., Inc. v. Turner Entm't Co.*, 98 F.3d 33 (2d. Cir. 1996) (holding delay in suing is "suggestive of a lack of irreparable harm").

[171] *See Belushi v. Woodward*, 598 F. Supp. 36, 37 (D.D.C 1984) (denying injunction where one photograph in the defendant's book infringed the plaintiff's copyright).

in copyright cases, even in jurisdictions which retain it as a nominal element of the four-part test. As one circuit has stated the matter:

> Since Congress has elected to grant certain exclusive rights to the owner of a copyright in a protected work, it is virtually axiomatic that the public interest can only be served by upholding copyright protections and, correspondingly, preventing the misappropriation of the skills, creative energies, and resources which are invested in the protected work.[172]

Sometimes, however, even in the Second and Ninth Circuits, a version of the "public interest" factor, closely linked to considerations of copyright policy, may come into play.[173] For example, a district court in the Seventh Circuit denied a preliminary injunction in part because doing so would have prevented the defendants from completing their land development, putting contractors and construction workers out of a job.[174] Other instances where preliminary injunctions should be granted more sparingly for reasons of the public interest are those that involve the dissemination of expression through new technologies. For example, the trial court in the *Betamax* case, *Universal City Studios, Inc. v. Sony Corp. of America*,[175] denied the plaintiffs' request for a preliminary injunction stating that "[t]his is a doubtful case [and a]n injunction would deprive the public of a new technology capable of noninfringing uses."

[C] Permanent Injunctions

Even if plaintiff does not receive a preliminary injunction, a permanent injunction may be issued if there is the probability of continuing infringement. A permanent injunction is not issued as a matter of course, and the plaintiff must show a threat of further infringement to receive this remedy.[176] A final injunction must conform to the Federal Rule of Civil Procedure that the order "be specific in terms" and "describe in reasonable detail . . . the act or acts sought to be restrained."[177]

Historically, courts have freely granted final injunctions on a finding of copyright infringement. This liberal attitude in the granting of final injunctions relates to the difficulty in determining the value of a copyright and the avoidance of the costly process in proving actual damages and profits. The expansive view in the granting of final injunctions was placed in question by the Supreme Court in *eBay, Inc. v. MercExchange, LLC*.[178] In *eBay*, the court held that patent injunctions are to be granted in the trial court's discretion in evaluating the traditional four factors before granting an injunction. The court rejected the general rule unique to patent

[172] *Apple Computer, Inc.*, 714 F.2d at 1254.

[173] *See, e.g.*, *Silverstein v. Penguin Putnam, Inc.*, 368 F.3d 77 (2d Cir. 2004) (holding that even if plaintiff's selection of poems by Dorothy Parker was original, it would be an abuse of discretion to grant an injunction against publication of a book of Parker's complete poems that infringed that selection).

[174] *See Ocean Atl. v. DRH Cambridge Homes*, 2003 U.S. Dist. LEXIS 16737 (N.D. Ill. 2003).

[175] 480 F. Supp. 429, 464 (C.D. Cal. 1979), *rev'd*, 659 F.2d 963 (9th Cir. 1981), *rev'd*, 464 U.S. 417 (1984).

[176] *See Shapiro, Bernstein & Co. v. 4636 S. Vermont Ave., Inc.*, 367 F.2d 236 (9th Cir. 1966).

[177] Fed. R. Civ. P. 65(d).

[178] 126 S. Ct. 1837 (2006).

disputes "that a permanent injunction will issue once infringement and validity have been adjudged."[179] The court also observed that the rule in patent cases should be extended in copyright actions as well.[180] *eBay* has been applied in lower courts that have required a showing that the plaintiff: (1) has suffered an irreparable injury; (2) has suffered an irreparable injury; (3) that the remedies available at law, such as monetary damages, are inadequate; and (4) that the public interest would be disserved by a permanent injunction.[181] The Supreme Court's opinion in *eBay* reconfirms the basic notion that injunctive relief is a discretionary, equitable remedy tailored to meet the specific remedial needs of the situation. It should not be granted where there is little chance that the defendant will infringe in the future. In addition, thorny issues arise in a partially infringing work. Here, the Court should limit its order to the expunging, where possible, of the copyrighted material.

Obviously, a permanent injunction can prohibit future infringements of existing works already registered in the Copyright Office. May it also enjoin the defendant's offending activities with respect to works not yet registered, or even created? Under the terms of the statute, the grant of equitable power should be limited to those in suit and not to works yet to be created. This view comports with the language of the § 502(a) that empowers a court to issue injunctions "on such terms as it may deem reasonable to prevent or restrain infringement of *a copyright*."[182]

Generally, it would appear to be an abuse of discretion to deny a permanent injunction where liability has been established and there is a threat of continuing infringement. But where substantial public injury would result from an injunction, the courts could follow cases in other areas of property law and award damages or even a continuing royalty.[183] In its *Betamax* opinion, the Ninth Circuit noted the possible utility of continuing royalties in resolving the difficult dilemmas presented by new technologies.[184] And another federal appellate court took this approach, concluding on remand: "In assessing the appropriateness of any injunctive relief, we urge the [district] court to consider alternatives, such as mandatory license

---

179 *Id.* at 393–94.

180 *Id.* at 392.

181 *See Christopher Phelps & Assocs., LLP v. Galloway*, 492 F.3d 532, 543 (4th Cir. 2007).

182 17 U.S. C. § 502(a) (emphasis added); *See Pac. & S. Co. v. Duncan*, 744 F.2d 1490 (11th Cir. 1984) (videotaping of future news broadcasts by clipping service enjoined); *Walt Disney Co. v. Powell*, 897 F.2d 565 (D.C. Cir. 1990) (holding that in view of "history of continuing infringement and a significant threat of future infringement," trial court properly enjoined future infringement of works owned by plaintiff but not in suit).

183 Nimmer on Copyright § 14.06[B] (2014).

184 *Universal City Studios, Inc. v. Sony Corp. of Am.*, 659 F.2d 963, 976 (9th Cir. 1981), *rev'd on other grounds*, 464 U.S. 417 (1984); see also a similar proposal surfaced again in the same circuit in *Abend v. MCA, Inc.*, 863 F.2d 1465, 1479 (9th Cir. 1988) (denying *permanent* injunction after finding of infringement, on theory that withdrawal of film *Rear Window* would cause public injury as well as injustice to film's owners, and award of damages would vindicate plaintiff's interests), *aff'd on other grounds sub nom., Stewart v. Abend*, 495 U.S. 207 (1990) (carefully describing Court of Appeals' discussion of remedies as "not relevant to the issue on which we granted *certiorari*").

fees, in lieu of foreclosing the public's computer-aided access to this educational and entertaining work."[185]

[D] Impounding and Disposition of Infringing Articles

In addition to temporary and/or permanent injunctive relief, equitable remedies available to the successful plaintiff under the Copyright Act include impoundment and eventual disposition of the defendant's infringing copies and the equipment used to produce them, up to and including possible confiscation and destruction. Under § 503(a)[186] of the 1976 Act, the court may order the impounding of all copies and phonorecords claimed to have been used to violate the copyright owner's exclusive rights. This remedy extends as well to, "[a]ll plates, molds, matrices, masters, tapes, film negatives, or other articles by means of which such copies or phonorecords may be reproduced."[187]

It may also be applied against items that, though reproduced and acquired lawfully, have been used for infringing purposes such as rentals, performances, and displays.[188] Impounding orders are not issued ex parte, and defendant has a right to an adversarial hearing.[189] An ex parte impounding order may violate the Fifth Amendment guarantee against the taking of property without due process of law and may constitute a suppression of speech under the First Amendment.[190] Unlike many of the other remedies, impoundment has not generated much case law.[191]

In addition to the possibility of impoundment during the pendency of the action, § 503(b) provides that, as part of its final judgment or decree, a court may order "the destruction or other reasonable disposition" of both the infringing articles and the equipment used to produce them. What is "other reasonable disposition"?[192] Under § 101(d) of the 1909 Act, a court could order only that the infringing articles and equipment be delivered up for destruction. As the House Report points out, current § 503(b) permits the court to order that such products and devices be "sold, delivered to the plaintiff, or disposed of in some other way that would avoid needless waste and best serve the ends of justice."[193] In addition, a time-honored

---

[185] *Greenberg v. Nat'l Geographic Soc'y*, 244 F.3d 1267, 1275 (11th Cir. 2001).

[186] 17 U.S.C. § 503(a).

[187] *Id.*

[188] *See* H.R. Rep. No. 94-1476, at 160 (1976).

[189] *See WPOW, Inc. v. MRLJ Enters.*, 584 F. Supp. 132 (D.D.C. 1984).

[190] *See* Nimmer on Copyright § 14.07 (2014).

[191] Some interesting examples include: *Playboy Enters., Inc. v. Sanfilippio*, 46 U.S.P.Q.2d (BNA) 1350 (S.D. Cal. 1998) (ordering a pretrial seizure of 7,745 computer files containing infringing photographs); *Richard J. Zitz, Inc. v. Pereira*, 965 F. Supp. 350 (E.D.N.Y. 1997) (holding that § 503, while contemplating impoundment of movable articles by which copies or phonorecords may be reproduced, as well as the copies or phonorecords themselves, did not authorize seizure of house claimed to be infringing "copy" of plaintiff's architectural designs); and *Devils Films, Inc. v. Nectar Video, Inc.*, 29 F. Supp. 2d 174 (S.D.N.Y. 1998) (declining in view of strong public policy against obscenity) [declining to order U.S. Marshal to seize unlicensed copies of plaintiff's copyrighted "hard core" films].

[192] *See* 17 U.S.C. § 503(b).

[193] *See, e.g., Electra Entm't Group v. Crawford*, 226 F.R.D. 388 (C.D. Cal 2005) (ordering the destruction of computer files on the defendant's hard drive); *M.S.R. Imports, Inc. v. R.E. Greenspan*, 220

variant on the § 503(b) order requiring the destruction of infringing materials is the "turnover" order, under which the defendant must surrender the articles in question to the plaintiff. Such orders may raise delicate questions of fairness.[194] Although destruction of the article is available as a remedy, it is not the favored solution. More often the court will choose other dispositions, such as ordering the articles sold or delivered to plaintiff, to avoid needless waste while serving the ends of justice.[195]

§ 9.10 DAMAGES AND PROFITS: GENERALLY

According to § 504, a copyright infringer is liable for either:

(1) the copyright owner's actual damages and any additional profits of the infringer, or

(2) statutory damages.[196]

This provision generously allows the plaintiff to recover either actual damages and profits, or statutory damages. Plaintiff may choose the category of recovery at any time before final judgment.[197]

§ 9.11 ACTUAL DAMAGES AND PROFITS

Although the 1976 Act allows recovery of both damages and profits, a plaintiff can only recover profits that are not taken into account when computing actual damages.[198] In other words, double recovery is not allowed. Most often a plaintiff will have to choose between actual damages or profits because they represent the same harm, but the possibility of recovering both damages and profits remains. For example, assume that the plaintiff has created a decorative poster that defendant has infringed. Plaintiff can recover either the lost sales he would have made as actual damages or defendant's profits from the sale of the infringing posters. If defendant's profits were $10,000, plaintiff could recover the entire amount but could not recover for the diminution of sales in the same market because this would constitute a double counting (i.e., two recoveries for the same harm). On the other hand, if plaintiff could show that the infringing posters were of inferior quality and

---

U.S.P.Q. (BNA) 361 (E.D. Pa. 1983) (suggesting that the infringing toy wagons be donated to charity for distribution to poor children).

[194] For example, in *Feiner & Co., Inc. v. Turner Entm't Co.*, 47 U.S.P.Q.2d (BNA) 1539 (S.D.N.Y. 1998), the plaintiff held a court-ordered license of certain Laurel and Hardy screenplay copyrights, due to expire in 2001. The defendant was required to hand over copies of its compilation film, *The Laughing 20's*, despite the fact that it included noninfringing as well as infringing materials: "It is only correct," the judge reasoned, "that the infringer . . . suffer the loss of the inextricable material." At the same time, however, the defendant was permitted to retain a master copy of its film, for "use after [the plaintiff's] license expires."

[195] *See* H.R. Rep. No. 94-1476, at 160 (1976).

[196] 17 U.S.C. § 504(c)(1).

[197] *See id.*

[198] *See* 17 U.S.C. § 504(b); H.R. Rep. No. 94-1476, at 161 (1976). The 1976 Act departs from the 1909 Act under which a copyright holder could receive a cumulative award of his own damages and the infringer's profits. *See Thomas Wilson & Co. v. Irving J. Dorfman Co.*, 433 F.2d 409, 413 (2d Cir. 1970).

damaged plaintiff's future ability to sell his own, or that he lost a major client because of the infringement not reflected in defendant's sales, the diminution of market value amount could be recovered as damages because it was not reflected in defendant's profits.[199]

Actual damages are based on the extent to which the market value of a copyrighted work has been injured or destroyed. Both damages and profits must be proved without employing undue speculation. In a copyright cause of action, a trial court is entitled to reject a proffered measure of damages if it is too vague or speculative.[200] Although damages or profits must be proved without speculation, some courts have made plaintiff's task easier, holding that once the fact of damage is proved, the extent of the harm does not have to be proved to exact certainty.[201]

With ever greater frequency, U.S. copyright owners are damaged by activities occurring in foreign jurisdictions. As a result, the question has arisen whether plaintiff can recover for harm occurring outside the United States. The general rule is that the Copyright Act does not apply extraterritorially, and whatever harm plaintiff suffers must be recovered in the foreign jurisdiction and its legal system. The Ninth Circuit, however, has carved out an exception to this, allowing the recovery of exterritorial profits, but not actual damages, flowing from exploitation abroad of domestic acts of infringement.[202]

§ 9.12 RECOVERY OF PROFITS

[A] Advantages to Claiming Lost Profits

Because actual damages are difficult to prove, most plaintiffs concentrate on recovering defendant's profits. Plaintiff is aided by § 504(b) of the 1976 Act, which provides that "[i]n establishing the infringer's profits, the copyright owner is required to present proof only of infringer's gross revenue."[203]

The defendant then has the burden of proving deductible expenses and elements of profit due to factors other than the infringed work.[204] Which costs can be deducted, how to allocate the costs incurred by the infringing activity, and which profits should be attributable to the infringement have presented difficult problems in infringement litigation.[205]

---

199 *See Abeshouse v. Ultragraphics, Inc.*, 754 F.2d 467 (2d Cir. 1985) (recognizing the possibility of cumulative damages in addition to profits). In the actual case, plaintiff's proof was not sufficient on this issue to obtain an award.

200 *See Stevens Linen Assocs., Inc. v. Mastercraft Corp.*, 656 F.2d 11, 14 (2d Cir. 1981).

201 *See Deltak, Inc. v. Advanced Sys., Inc.*, 574 F. Supp. 400, 411 (N.D. Ill. 1983).

202 *L.A. News Serv. v. Reuters Television Int'l, Ltd.*, 340 F.3d 926 (9th Cir. 2003).

203 17 U.S.C. § 504(b).

204 *See* H.R. Rep. No. 94-1476, at 161 (1976).

205 For a critique of the disgorgement of profits remedy in copyright law, see Dane S. Ciolino, *Reconsidering Restitution with Copyright*, 48 Emory L.J. 1 (1999).

[B] Costs Defendant May Deduct

Because the 1976 Act does not specify which expenses defendant can deduct, one has to look to the body of case law for answers. The case law has held that almost all expenses proven with reasonable certainty are deductible if related to producing and selling the infringing work. These expenses normally encompass taxes, royalties to writers, advertising costs, overhead, and material developed to produce the infringing work.[206]

Infringers of a motion picture, popular song, or work of graphic art are often simultaneously engaged in noninfringing activities that share costs with the infringing activity. The general rule is that defendant can deduct only those costs related to the infringing activity. Deciphering which costs are related to the infringement and which are related to the noninfringing aspects of defendant's business poses both practical and theoretical difficulties. For example, one puzzling question of cost allocation is how to treat overhead. In general, overhead can be deducted if defendant proves that it actually contributed to the infringement. Alternatively, defendant cannot deduct overhead if he would have incurred these costs absent the infringement.[207] Mathematical certainty in overhead cost deduction is often impossible, and a proportional allocation of overhead expenses to the infringing activity will be accepted if reasonable.[208] Uncertainty about any deduction is resolved in favor of the plaintiff, since defendant has the burden of proof on all cost deduction issues.

[C] Apportionment of Profits to Infringing Activity

Plaintiff can only recover those profits attributable to the infringement.[209] This apportionment issue arises in two situations. One occurs when infringing materials become commingled with noninfringing materials, for example, when one infringing song is placed on an album containing ten songs. Another related pattern occurs when factors other than the use of defendant's work are responsible for some of the profits, for example, if the success of an infringing song is due to the efforts of a famous singer.

Defendant has the burden of proof on this issue of apportionment but can effectively reduce plaintiff's recovery by showing that its profits are attributable to other factors than the use of plaintiff's work. To illustrate, suppose that plaintiff's novel is made into a motion picture but has been changed drastically in the process. Suppose also that the movie has become a great success, much more so than the novel, partly because of the changed storyline taken from the novel, but also because of famous stars who play the key roles. Proof that defendant's success was attributable to aspects other than the copyrighted work can drastically reduce the percentage of recoverable profits. This example is similar to a leading case on the

---

[206] *See, e.g.*, *Cream Records, Inc. v. Jos. Schlitz Brewing Co.*, 754 F.2d 826 (9th Cir. 1985) (advertising expenses); *Kamar Int'l v. Russ Berrie & Co.*, 752 F.2d 1326 (9th Cir. 1984) (overhead expenses).

[207] *See Taylor v. Meirick*, 712 F.2d 1112 (7th Cir. 1983).

[208] *See Frank Music Corp. v. Metro-Goldwyn-Mayer, Inc.*, 772 F.2d 505, 516 (9th Cir. 1985).

[209] *See* 17 U.S.C. § 504(b).

issue, *Sheldon v. Metro-Goldwyn Pictures Corp.*,[210] where the Supreme Court allowed a twenty percent recovery of defendant's profits from the motion picture *Letty Lynton* as attributable to plaintiff's copyrighted play. The motion picture's success was in large part due to aspects unrelated to the copyrighted work, such as the famous movie stars and the MGM screenplay. Despite the virtually impossible task of exact apportionment, *Sheldon* stands for the principle that, when there is a reasonable basis for apportionment, the court should attempt to apportion, even though error in the process might favor the plaintiff. Of course, mathematical exactness can never be achieved, but to grant plaintiff all the profits would impose an undue penalty on the defendant.[211]

[D] Indirect Profits

Under § 504, plaintiff is entitled to recover any profits attributable to the infringement. Copyright owners can recover not only for direct sales, adaptations, displays, and performances of the copyrighted work, but can also recover profits that the infringer made indirectly from the exploitation of the copyrighted work. *Frank Music Corp. v. Metro-Goldwyn-Mayer, Inc.*[212] illustrates the issues concerning indirect damages. In *Frank*, the plaintiff music publisher alleged that MGM infringed its copyright to several songs from the musical *Kismet* by including them in a Las Vegas show without prior authorization. After concluding that MGM had indeed infringed the songs' copyrights, the court held that the publisher could recover indirect damages, such as profits from the hotel's casino that had been boosted by the show's promotional value.

The indirect profit issue arises typically in instances where the copyrighted work is used without authorization in an advertisement. The reason why indirect rather than direct profits are at issue is that advertisements are not sold and earn no profits in their own right, but they may increase the sales of a product.[213] Suppose plaintiff's copyrighted song is used in a commercial to sell a new household cleaning product. One may conjecture that the use of the song may have done wonders for sales, but conjecture is not enough; the plaintiff must prove a causal nexus between the use of the song and increased sales. Because of their inherently speculative nature, courts have required proof of a reasonably sufficient causal link between the infringing acts and indirect profits, those earned through the sale of noninfringing goods.[214] To quote Judge Posner, "[i]f General Motors were to steal your copyright and put it in a sales brochure, you could not just put a copy of General Motors' corporate income tax return in the record and rest your

[210] 309 U.S. 390 (1940).

[211] *See also ABKCO Music, Inc. v. Harrisongs Music, Ltd.*, 508 F. Supp. 798 (S.D.N.Y. 1981), *aff'd*, 722 F.2d 988 (2d Cir. 1983) (awarding 70% of profits for infringing song reproduced on the flip side of a record); *MCA Inc. v. Wilson*, 677 F.2d 180 (2d Cir. 1981) (assessing for use of song in musical show, 5% of the profits for infringement).

[212] 772 F.2d 505 (9th Cir 1985).

[213] *See, e.g., Cream Records, Inc. v. Joseph Schlitz Brewing Co.*, 754 F.2d 826 (9th Cir. 1985) (awarding plaintiff 1/10th of 1% of profits of sales of the advertised malt liquor).

[214] *See, e.g., Mackie v. Rieser*, 296 F.3d 909 (9th Cir. 2002); *Andreas v. Volkswagen of Am., Inc.*, 210 F. Supp. 2d 1078 (N.D. Iowa 2002).

case for an award of infringer's profits."[215] In one case a student artist's work, besides being reproduced "downside-up," was used without her authorization in a Mercedes-Benz advertising brochure. Her claim for infringer's profits, based on the gross revenues of the Daimler-Chrysler Corporation, did not survive summary judgment because she had failed "to introduce any evidence from which the fact finder could reasonably calculate [the] alleged indirect profits."[216]

§ 9.13 STATUTORY DAMAGES

[A] Overview of the Statutory Damage Remedy

Section 504 of the Copyright Act entitles a prevailing plaintiff, who complies with the Act's registration requirements,[217] to recover statutory damages instead of actual damages and profits. Unique to copyright law, statutory damages cannot be recovered for patent, trademark, and trade secret infringement.[218] The award of statutory damages may be assessed "for all infringements involved in the action, with respect to any one work, for which any one infringer is liable individually, or for which any two or more infringers are liable jointly and severally. Recovery of statutory damages is entirely at the copyright owner's election, and the parties have a right to a jury trial for the assessment of statutory damages.[219] The choice of statutory damages provides a powerful tool in the hands of the plaintiff who can choose this remedy at any time before final judgment is rendered.

Both statutory damages and attorney's fees have important practical significance in the litigation process. Often essential in acquiring legal representation, they provide attorneys with some reasonable prospect of being paid. The statutory damage remedy eliminates the need to prove profits, thereby avoiding the use of expensive time consuming modes of proof and the use of expert witnesses. Statutory damages expedite the litigation process, and induce settlement, particularly in cases of obvious and willful infringement. In short, the possibility of a statutory recovery discourages willful infringers from dragging out the litigation process. Unfortunately, those who would benefit most from statutory damages are often deprived of the remedy due to the requirement of timely registration.[220] Typically, these persons include photographers, freelance journalists, and artists who have a high output but do not have the means from a

---

[215] *Taylor v. Meirick*, 712 F.2d 1112, 1122 (7th Cir. 1983).

[216] *Rainey v. Wayne State Univ.*, 26 F. Supp. 2d 963, 970 (E.D. Mich. 1998).

[217] *See* 17 U.S.C. § 412.

[218] Why there is no corresponding recovery of statutory damages for patents, trademark, and trade secrets, is a matter of debate. One suggestion is that the lack of such of a rule may be attributable both to lower average cost of detection and to the greater magnitude of the harm caused by a single act of infringement in these other bodies of law. *See* Roger D. Blair & Thomas R. Cotter, *Economic Analysis of Damage Rules in Intellectual Property Law*, 39 Wm. & Mary L. Rev. 1585, 1658, (1999).

[219] *See Feltner v. Columbia Pictures Television, Inc.*, 523 U.S. 340 (1998) (holding that a jury trial on the issue of statutory damages is constitutionally mandated by the Seventh Amendment to the U.S. Constitution). *Feltner* is discussed *infra* § 9.17[E].

[220] *See* 17 U.S.C. § 412.

practical standpoint to consistently register their claims for copyright as required by the Act.

Before passage of the 1976 Act, the courts were in disarray over the proper role and scope of statutory damages. Some courts held that statutory damages could not be recovered if damages and profits had been proved, whereas others held the opposite. The 1976 Act resolved this confusion by providing the copyright owner with the option to obtain statutory damages instead of damages and profits.

Although the 1976 Act resolved a number of problems regarding statutory damages, two issues continue to trouble the courts in their assessment. These are (1) what factors should a court evaluate in calculating an award within the statutory minima and maxima and (2) how should a court ascertain the number of copyrighted works that have been infringed for purposes of multiplying the statutory award?

[B] Computing Statutory Damages: Statutory Maxima and Minima

Section 504(c) sets forth three basic measures for statutory damages:

(1) Where the infringement is neither willful nor innocent, section 504(c)(1) authorizes an award of statutory damages "in a sum not less than $750 or more than $30,000 as the court considers just."

(2) Section 504(c)(2) provides that "where the copyright owner sustains the burden of proving, and the court finds, that infringement was committed willfully, the court may at its discretion increase the award of statutory damages to a sum of not more than $150,000."

(3) The third situation involves innocent infringement. If the court finds that the infringer was not aware or had no reason to know that his acts constituted an infringement of copyright, the court may reduce the statutory damage award "to a sum of not less than $200." This might arise in situations where the infringer has an arguable case for fair use.

The decision to opt for statutory damages resides with the plaintiff, but the amount of those damages is within the court's discretion.[221] For most infringements, the court may award no less than $750 or more than $30,000.[222] But if the copyright owner can prove willful infringement, the amount can be increased at the court's discretion up to $150,000.[223]

The Copyright Act does not define willfulness for the purpose of assessing statutory damages. In determining willfulness, the courts will look to defendant's state of mind. They have found willful infringement cases where the defendant knew or had reason to know or recklessly disregarded the fact that its conduct constituted copyright infringement.[224] Willfulness is manifested in situations where

---

[221] *See* 17 U.S.C. § 504(c).

[222] *See* 17 U.S.C. § 504(c)(1).

[223] *See* 17 U.S.C. § 504(c)(2).

[224] *See, e.g., N.A.S. Import Corp. v. Chenson Enters. Inc.*, 968 F.2d 250 (2d Cir. 1992) (finding

defendant ignored the plaintiff's written notices of copyright protection. Often willfulness is found where defendant is a known recidivist in the infringement of copyrighted works.[225]

At the other end of the continuum, § 504(c)(2) mitigates the harshness of statutory damages by decreasing the statutory floor for innocent infringers. As stated in the House Report to the 1976 Act, the innocent infringement provision is designed in part to "protect against unwarranted liability in cases of occasional or isolated innocent infringement."[226] It is debatable whether this provision offers adequate insulation for the innocent infringer against unwarranted liability. The reason is that the infringer must sustain the burden of proving not only that it was unaware that its acts constituted copyright infringement but also that it had no reason to believe that they constituted infringement.[227] As an exception to the right to recover statutory damages, the 1976 Act specifically disallows them where employees of nonprofit educational institutions, libraries, archives, or public broadcasting entities, acting within the scope of their employment, infringe a copyrighted work, having reasonable grounds for believing their acts constituted fair use under § 107.[228] In this situation, statutory damages cannot be recovered.

[C] Multiple Works

A plaintiff can only recover a single minimum or maximum statutory damage recovery regardless of how many times a defendant has infringed the work or whether the infringing acts were separate, simultaneous, or occurred sequentially.[229] Although only one award can be recovered in spite of the number of infringements, the extent of the single award will be affected by the number of infringements, as well as by other factors, including the market value of the work, the revenue loss caused by the infringement, the gravity of the infringement, and the defendant's fault.[230]

---

willfulness where defendant's product was identical to plaintiff's and where defendant continued infringing after receiving demand letter from plaintiff's lawyer). On the other hand, willfulness was narrowly interpreted where a fair use defense was asserted in *Princeton Univ. Press v. Mich. Document Servs., Inc.*, 99 F.3d 1381 (6th Cir. 1996) (holding that reckless disregard for plaintiff's rights were not proved because fair use is an unsettled area of the law). The contrary view was expressed in *Twin Peaks Prods. v. Publ'ns Int'l, Ltd.*, 996 F.2d 1366, 1381–82 (2d Cir. 1993) (finding willful infringement despite the fact that defendant believed its use was covered by fair use defense and received advice of counsel to that effect).

[225] *See Davis v. The Gap, Inc.*, 246 F.3d 152, 172 (2d Cir. 2001).

[226] H.R. Rep. No. 94-1476, at 163 (1976).

[227] *See* 17 U.S.C. § 504(c)(2). Note that a defendant cannot assert a defense of innocent infringement in mitigation of actual or statutory damages when proper notice of copyright appears on published copies or phonorecords of the work to which defendant had access. *See* 17 U.S.C. §§ 401(d), 402(d). For a discussion of this notice provision, see *supra* § 4.10[D] and [E].

[228] *See* 17 U.S.C. § 504(c)(2).

[229] *See* H.R. Rep. No. 94-1476, at 162 (1976).

[230] *See N.A.S. Imp. Corp. v. Chenson Enters., Inc.*, 968 F.2d 250, 252 (2d Cir. 1992).

Alternatively, where the suit involves infringement of more than one work, at least minimum statutory damages must be awarded for each work infringed.[231] For example, if defendant's musical review infringes three copyrighted tunes, the copyright owner can recover at least $2,250 ($750 * 3) or up to $90,000 ($30,000 * 3) for the infringement.[232]

What constitutes a "work" for the purposes of computing the award of statutory damages is relatively easy to determine when an individual work, such as a novel, song, or painting, is involved. Difficulties arise when a work incorporates several separable works, such as an anthology of poetry or a collection of an author's paintings. In general, a separate statutory award can be obtained for each individual element that can stand alone in the marketplace. For example, in *Columbia Pictures Television, Inc. v Krypton Broadcasting, Inc.*,[233] defendant's television stations broadcast 440 infringing episodes of several television shows. In awarding plaintiff an 8.8 million dollar statutory damage award, the court held that each episode of the television series constituted an individual work because each had an independent value. The court was influenced by the fact that the individual episodes were broadcast over the course of years, repeated in different orders, and watched by viewers in different amounts.

Is each constituent element of a compilation or collective work to be treated as a separate work for the purposes of statutory damages? Section 504(c)(1) provides that, for purposes of statutory damage awards, "all the parts of a compilation or derivative work constitute one work." In applying this provision, the courts have read the statute literally in refusing multiple awards. For example, if defendant has copied a CD containing ten copyrighted songs, statutory damages will not be calculated on the basis of the ten individual works contained in the collective work. In *U.M.G. Recordings, Inc. v. MP3.Com, Inc.*,[234] the court rejected a statutory award calculated on a per-song basis, despite plaintiff's argument that each track that appeared on the CD represented independent economic value. In another case, the court held that the copyright owner of a compilation, who also owned the rights to the compilation's individual works, could recover only one statutory award.[235]

[D] Multiple Plaintiffs and Defendants

The copyright owner can recover minimum to maximum statutory damages for each copyrighted work infringed, but multiple copyright owners cannot recover statutory damages in separate actions for infringement of their exclusive rights.[236]

---

[231] *Id.*

[232] The award could be reduced to 3 * $200 for innocent infringement (*see* 17 U.S.C. § 504(c)(2)) or increased to 3 * $150,000 for willful infringement.

[233] 106 F.3d 284 (9th Cir. 1997).

[234] 92 F. Supp. 2d 349 (S.D.N.Y. 2000) (holding that plaintiff could only recover on a per-CD basis not a per-song basis because all parts of a compilation must be treated as a single work for purposes of computing statutory damages).

[235] *Xoom, Inc. v. Imageline, Inc.*, 323 F.3d 279 (4th Cir. 2003).

[236] *See* H.R. Rep. No. 94-1476, at 162 (1976) ("[A]lthough the minimum and maximum amounts are to

The one-recovery limitation prevents statutory damages from becoming inordinately extensive where exclusive rights may be divided infinitely under the 1976 Act. For example, suppose defendant has infringed a work of art by reproducing and displaying it. Under the 1976 Act, exclusive rights are infinitely divisible, and each respective owner of the reproduction and display rights has standing to bring suit. Even though A may own the reproduction rights and B may own the display rights, only one recovery of statutory damages will be allowed for the infringing acts.

When multiple defendants are involved, whether plaintiff can recover a full amount from each depends on their status as related defendants. Related defendants,[237] such as two or more persons who in concert infringe copyright, are jointly and severally liable. As a result, only one statutory damage recovery can be obtained against any one or all of them.[238] Alternatively, if the defendants are unrelated, as for example, where two record companies independent of each other produce infringing versions of the same copyrighted song, plaintiff may recover two statutory damage awards.[239]

[E] The Timing of the Election to Recover Statutory Damages

As stated above, the plaintiff may elect to recover statutory damages, instead of actual damages and defendant's profits. The Copyright Act generously allows plaintiff to make this election, regardless of the adequacy of the evidence offered on actual damages or profits, any time before final judgment is rendered.[240] Otherwise, a plaintiff who does not expressly make such an election before judgment is limited to actual damages and profits.[241]

Can a plaintiff who is unsatisfied with the jury award choose to elect statutory damages? Some courts have allowed plaintiffs to choose statutory damages by plaintiffs disappointed by a jury award of actual damages and profits.[242] The validity of this case law is now in doubt after 1998, when the Supreme Court held that there is a constitutional right to a jury trial on the issue of statutory damages. In so ruling, the court specifically indicated that it was unlikely that "Congress intended that a jury, having already made a determination of actual damages,

---

be multiplied where multiple 'works' are involved in the suit, the same is not true with respect to multiple copyrights, multiple owners, multiple exclusive rights, or multiple registrations. This point is especially important since, under a scheme of divisible copyright, it is possible to have the rights of a number of owners of separate 'copyrights' in a single 'work' infringed by one act of the defendant.").

[237] For a discussion of related defendants, see *supra* § 9.07.

[238] *Louis Vuitton Malletier S.A. v. Akanoc Solutions, Inc.* 658 F.3d 936 (9th Cir. 2011).

[239] *See* H.R. Rep. No. 94-1476, at 162 (1976).

[240] *See Reader's Digest Ass'n Inc., v. Conservative Digest, Inc.* 642 F. Supp. 144 (D.D.C. 1986).

[241] Case law indicates that even if plaintiff does not elect statutory damages before entry of judgment, when judgment is vacated on appeal, the plaintiff can make that election on remand. *See Oboler v. Goldin*, 714 F.2d 211 (2d Cir. 1983).

[242] *Branch v. Ogilvy & Mather, Inc.*, 772 F. Supp. 1359 (S.D.N.Y. 1991) (awarding $10,000 in statutory damages plus $116,000 in attorney's fees in a case where a jury had awarded $1 in nominal damages).

should be reconvened to make a determination of statutory damages."[243] Subsequent case law[244] has held that in cases where defendant has requested a trial by jury, the plaintiff's last opportunity to elect statutory damages occurs when the case is submitted to the jury.[245]

§ 9.14 COSTS AND ATTORNEY'S FEES

Costs and attorney's fees are available in a suit for copyright infringement and are entirely at the court's discretion.[246] The copyright must be registered to recover attorney's fees (not costs) and to recover statutory damages.[247]

Reasonable attorney's fees may be given to the "prevailing party." This term of art, undefined in the 1976 Act, merits explanation. The prevailing party can be either plaintiff or defendant, and is the party who was successful at the conclusion of all proceedings, not just trial on the merits. Unlike patent law, which limits attorney's fees to exceptional cases,[248] courts in copyright cases have routinely awarded attorney's fees to prevailing plaintiffs, even though willful infringement has not been proved. In determining the amount of "reasonable" attorney's fees, courts may consider the counsel's skill and reputation, the actual fee charged, the amount of work expended, the monetary recovery allowed, and the result achieved at trial.[249]

When the prevailing party was the defendant, however, courts tended to allow recovery of attorney's fees only if the plaintiff brought the action frivolously or in bad faith.[250] Defendant did not have to show subjective bad faith on plaintiff's part, although a showing that plaintiff actually knew of the invalidity of the claims would be a strong indication of bad faith.[251]

Why allow recovery of attorney's fees more readily to the prevailing plaintiff than to the prevailing defendant? When the plaintiff prevails, attorney's fees theoretically work as a deterrent against future infringement. But when the defendant is the prevailing party, this policy no longer applies and the courts must look instead to the fault, if any, of the plaintiff in bringing the action in bad faith. Thus, stronger policy considerations merit recovery of attorney's fees for prevailing plaintiffs.

---

[243] *Feltner v. Columbia Pictures Television, Inc.* 118 S. Ct. 1279, 1284 n.5 (1998).

[244] *Alexander v. Chesapeake, Potomac, and Tidewater Books, Inc.*, 60 F. Supp. 2d 544, 546 (E.D. Va. 1999).

[245] Nimmer suggests that one device might be to instruct the jury on both statutory and actual damages, and allow plaintiff to elect the greater figure after the verdict is returned. *See* NIMMER ON COPYRIGHT § 14.04[A], 14-45 (2014).

[246] *See* 17 U.S.C. § 505.

[247] *See* 17 U.S.C. § 412. *See also supra* § 7.06.

[248] *See* 35 U.S.C. § 285.

[249] *See Quinto v. Legal Times of Wash., Inc.*, 511 F. Supp. 579 (D.D.C. 1981); *Moorish Vanguard Concert v. Brown*, 498 F. Supp. 830 (E.D. Pa. 1980).

[250] *See Jartech, Inc. v. Clancy*, 666 F.2d 403 (9th Cir. 1982). For an overview of the dual standard in awarding attorney's fees, see Robert S. LaPlante, *Awarding Attorney's Fees in Copyright Infringement Cases: The Sensible Use of a Dual Standard*, 51 ALB. L. REV. 239 (1987).

[251] *See Hughes v. Novi Am., Inc.*, 724 F.2d 122 (Fed. Cir. 1984).

In *Fogerty v. Fantasy Inc.*,[252] the U.S. Supreme Court overruled the case law supporting the favored treatment of plaintiffs on the issue of attorney's fees. The Court held that Congress intended no such disparity between plaintiffs and defendants when, in the 1976 Act, it permitted judges to award a reasonable attorney's fee to the prevailing party. *Fogerty* reverses the accepted rule in the Second, Seventh, Ninth, and D.C. Circuits in which attorney's fees were awarded to the prevailing plaintiff as a matter of course. In addition to abrogating the double standard for plaintiffs and defendants, the Court rejected the notion that attorney's fees should be automatic for any prevailing party. According to the Court, if Congress meant reimbursement to be automatic, it would not have used the words "may award" in the 1976 Act. Rather, the award of attorney's fees is in the court's discretion.

Writing for the Court, Justice Rehnquist declared that the policies underlying federal copyright law were served not only by vigorous prosecution of copyright claims but also by vigorous defense against them.[253] Because the boundaries of the copyright monopoly should be demarcated as clearly as possible, the law should encourage defendants to litigate meritorious defenses as vigorously as it should encourage plaintiffs to advance their claims for infringement. Thus, a system that favors plaintiffs in awarding attorney's fees distorts this boundary-making function of copyright litigation and, as such, conflicts with the underlying goals of copyright law.

Although *Fogerty* settled a longstanding conflict in copyright law, it did not specify what standard the courts should use in applying their discretion to award attorney's fees. Probably, the factors supporting an award of attorney's fees will include the frivolousness, motivation, and objective unreasonableness of the suit.[254] It will probably take some time for the district courts to elaborate on the factors to be considered in exercising their discretion. Since *Fogerty*, a disagreement has arisen over the appropriateness of awarding fees to a prevailing defendant when the plaintiff's claim was not "objectively unreasonable."[255] Whatever elements the courts use, *Fogerty* will probably reduce the incentive to bring suits for infringement. The number of copyright infringement claims might diminish somewhat now that prevailing defendants may also recover attorney's fees and the fact that any attorney's fees recoveries by plaintiffs or defendants will be awarded non-automatically and only at the court's discretion.[256] The effect of this ruling may well

---

252 510 U.S. 517 (1994).

253 *Id.* at 528.

254 *See, e.g.*, *Lieb v. Topstone Inds. Inc.*, 788 F.2d 151, 156 (3d Cir. 1986) (discussing the various factors).

255 *Compare Virgin Records Am., Inc. v. Thompson*, 512 F.3d 724 (5th Cir. 2008) (affirming denial of attorneys' fees where dismissed action was neither frivolous nor objectively unreasonable), *Fogerty v. MGM Group Holdings, Inc.*, 379 F.3d 348 (6th Cir. 2004) (reversing award of attorneys' fees where plaintiff's claims were not objectively unreasonable), *and Matthew Bender & Co., Inc. v. W. Publ'g Co.*, 240 F.3d 116 (2d Cir. 2001) ("[I]mposition of a fee award against a copyright holder with an objectively reasonable litigation position *generally* will not promote the purposes of the Copyright Act.") (emphasis added), *with Bridgeport Music, Inc. v. WB Music Corp.*, 520 F.3d 588 (6th Cir. 2008) (affirming award of attorneys fees despite fact that plaintiff's legal theory was objectively reasonable).

256 Whatever the actual statistics may be, defendants have obtained handsome awards in post —

be significant in two important circuits for copyright matters, the Second and Ninth, that had traditionally awarded attorney's fees automatically to prevailing plaintiffs.

Full costs may also be awarded at the court's discretion[257] against any party except the United States or one of its officers. Full costs are generally not assessed unless some degree of fault or bad faith is shown. Costs recovered have included amounts for filing fees, marshal's fees, transcripts, service of process, depositions, photocopying, and postage.[258]

The 1976 Act does not recognize punitive damages, and courts have awarded them rarely.[259] However, the assessment of costs and attorney's fees, as well as statutory damages ($150,000 for willful infringement), can serve much the same deterrent purpose as punitive damages in an infringement action. For example, in *Feltner*, the Supreme Court stated that "[s]tatutory damages may serve purposes traditionally associated with legal relief, such as compensation and punishment."[260] It is, however, the conventional wisdom that punitive damages, as such, are not available under the Copyright Act.[261] The conventional wisdom aside, one could argue that certain awards in statutory damages, such as the 8.8 million dollar assessment in *Krypton*,[262] serve the same purpose as punitive damages.[263]

Fogerty actions. *See, e.g., Assessment Tech. of WI, Inc. v. WIREdata, Inc.*, 361 F.3d 434 (granting $91,765.28 to prevailing defendant); *InvesSys, Inc. v. McGraw-Hill Cos., Ltd.*, 369 F.3d 16 (1st Cir. 2004) (granting $200,000 to prevailing defendant); *Compaq Computer Corp. v. Ergonome, Inc.*, 387 F.3d 403 (5th Cir. 2004) (granting $2,765,026.90 to prevailing defendant, based in part on finding that the plaintiff's attorneys would have received a contingent fee of 120 times that had their client's $800 million claim prevailed — perhaps a good reason not to high-ball the prayer for relief in a copyright complaint). Incidentally, the fees (and costs) ultimately awarded to Fogerty himself, following remand of the case to the trial court, amounted to almost $1.35 million. 94 F.3d 553 (9th Cir. 1996).

257 *See* 17 U.S.C. § 505. Under the 1909 Act, recovery of full costs was mandatory. *See also* 17 U.S.C. § 116 (1909 Act). *See* NIMMER ON COPYRIGHT § 14.09 (2014).

258 *See Quinto v. Legal Times of Wash., Inc.*, 511 F. Supp. 579 (D.D.C. 1981).

259 The Second Circuit Court of Appeals in *Oboler v. Goldin*, 714 F.2d 211 (2d Cir. 1983), specifically rejected use of punitive damages in statutory copyright infringements. *But see Aitkin v. Empire Constr. Co.*, 542 F. Supp. 252, 268 (D. Neb. 1982) (holding that defendant's outrageous conduct merited treble damage remedy).

260 *Feltner v. Columbia Pictures Television, Inc.*, 523 U.S. 340, 352 (1998).

261 *See, e.g., On Davis v. The Gap, Inc.*, 246 F.3d 152, 172 (2d Cir. 2001); *Bucklew v. Hawkins, Ash, Baptie & Co.*, 329 F.3d 923, 933–34 (7th Cir. 2003). Notwithstanding some dicta to the contrary, this conventional wisdom has been reaffirmed. *See Viacom Int'l, Inc. v. YouTube, Inc.*, 540 F. Supp. 2d 461 (S.D.N.Y. 2008) (disapproving contrary suggestions in *Blanch v. Koons*, 329 F. Supp. 2d 568 (S.D.N.Y. 2004), *aff'd on other grounds*, 467 F.3d 244 (2d Cir. 2006), and *TVT Island Records v. Island Def Jam Music Group*, 262 F. Supp. 2d 185 (S.D.N.Y. 2003), *rev'd on other grounds*, 412 F.3d 82 (2d Cir. 2005)); *accord Calio v. Sofa Express, Inc.*, 368 F. Supp. 2d 1290 (M.D. Fla. 2005). Punitive damages, however, may be available in state-law actions for infringement of common-law copyright in pre-Feb. 15, 1972 sound recordings. *See Bridgeport Music, Inc. v. Justin Combs Publ'g*, 507 F.3d 470 (6th Cir. 2007) (holding award of $3.5 million in punitive damages unconstitutionally excessive under Due Process Clause).

262 *See supra* 9.15[C].

263 *See UMG Recordings, Inc. v. MP3.com, Inc.*, 56 U.S.P.Q.2d (BNA) 1374 (S.D.N.Y. 2000). After a three — day trial, the court found MP3 to have willfully infringed Universal's musical copyrights and imposed statutory damages of $25,000 per CD. Judgment was eventually entered for a total of $53.4 million. 2000 U.S. Dist. LEXIS 17907. Under the proper circumstances, statutory damages can be large. *See also* John Tehranian, *Infringement Nation: Copyright Reform and the Law/Norm Gap*, 2007 UTAH

§ 9.15 CRIMINAL PENALTIES

[A] Generally

In addition to the remedies available to the copyright owner in a civil action, the government may subject the defendant to criminal penalties if the defendant willfully infringed copyright for commercial advantage, private financial gain, or when other proscribed effects result.[264] In addition, the Copyright Act imposes criminal liability on persons who fraudulently place a false notice on any article, fraudulently remove or alter the notice of copyright appearing on a copyrighted work, or knowingly make a false representation of a material fact in an application for copyright registration. Criminal actions are subject to a five-year statute of limitations.

As a reaction to the increasing piracy of copyrighted works, criminal liability for willful copyright infringement has correspondingly seen a progressive amplification in scope and severity. Although willful copyright infringement is carried out in diverse circumstances, criminal copyright actions have usually been brought against large-scale, systematic pirates of sound recordings and motion pictures. In general, the government has not had a successful record of curbing criminal infringement actions, largely because of the burden of proof required in a criminal suit. In *United States v. Atherton*,[265] involving motion picture video tape piracy, the court held that the government was required to prove the following five elements: (1) infringement of copyright (2) of a work that has not been subject to a first sale (3) done willfully (4) with knowledge that the copyrighted work has not been the subject of a first sale and (5) for profit. The difficult element has proved to be whether a criminal defendant knew that the tapes were *not* the subject of a first sale.[266] Unlike the civil preponderance-of-the-evidence standard, the prosecution must prove each element beyond a reasonable doubt. This heavy burden has impeded many criminal prosecutions.

The remedies provided by § 506 of the 1976 Act exhaust criminal relief for copyright violation, and the government has been prevented from using other provisions of federal criminal laws against copyright infringers. For example, in *Dowling v. United States*,[267] criminal suit was brought under the National Stolen Property Act[268] against a bootlegger of Elvis Presley recordings, who had reproduced and distributed copies of Presley's vocals. The Supreme Court limited recovery under the above Act to claims of conversion and fraud involving physical

---

L. Rev 537. (illustrating how a hypothetical professor can easily rack up $4.5 billion in statutory damages, even without downloading any music).

[264] *See generally* Geraldine Szott Moohr, *The Crime of Copyright Infringement: An Inquiry Based on Morality, Harm, and Criminal Theory*, 83 B.U. L. Rev. 731 (2003).

[265] 561 F.2d 747 (9th Cir. 1977).

[266] *See United States v. Wise*, 550 F.2d 1180 (9th Cir. 1977). Of course, if the government produces evidence that defendant oversaw reproduction of copies, there is no need to prove lack of first sale. *See United States v. Sachs*, 801 F.2d 839 (6th Cir. 1986). For a discussion of the first sale doctrine, see *supra* § 8.14.

[267] 473 U.S. 207 (1985).

[268] 18 U.S.C. § 2314.

goods, and not conversion of *intangible* property, such as a copyright. After *Dowling*, it appears that federal prosecutors must use the remedies provided under § 506 to bring suit for criminal copyright infringement.

[B] Willful Infringement for Commercial Advantage and Private Financial Gain

Under § 506(a)(1)(A) of the 1976 Act and 18 U.S.C. § 2319,[269] anyone "who infringes a copyright willfully and for purpose of commercial advantage . . . or private financial gain" is subject to felony or misdemeanor punishment. The felony provisions were overhauled in 1992. With the 1992 amendments, the felony copyright statute was for the first time generic in protection of copyrighted works rather than focused on particular categories such as sound recordings, motion pictures, or audiovisual works. Although all copyrighted works are included within the criminal provision, the principal motivation of the amendments was to deter the multibillion dollar business of computer software copyright infringement.[270]

Under § 506(a)(1)(A), felony liability will arise where, during any 180-day period, at least ten copies or phonorecords of one or more copyrighted works having a retail value of more than $2,500 are reproduced or distributed without the authorization of the copyright owner. The maximum penalty for such a violation is imprisonment for not more than five years or a fine,[271] or both. Second or subsequent offenses will result in a maximum of ten years imprisonment. Where the requisite number of copies is not made within the specified time periods, or the infringing acts are other than reproduction or distribution, misdemeanor liability will lie.

[C] Criminal Liability Without a Profit Motive: No Electronic Theft Act

In 1997, Congress enacted the "No Electronic Theft" legislation to close a perceived "loophole" in the criminal statutes by making willful copyright infringement a crime even if undertaken without a profit motive on the infringer's part.[272] Section 506 (a)(1)(B) and 18 U.S.C. § 2319 provide a sliding scale of criminal penalties (with jail terms up to six years) for infringers who reproduce or distribute copies of a work that have a total retail value of $1,000 or more during any six month period. The 1997 amendments provide that the penalties apply to (among other things) infringements by "electronic means."

The decision in *U.S. v. La Macchia*[273] provided the impetus for the "No Electronic Theft" legislation. In *La Macchia*, the court quashed the prosecution of

---

[269] 17 U.S.C. § 506(a)(1)(A); 18 U.S.C. § 2319.

[270] *See* Act of October 28, 1992 Pub. L. No. 102-561, 106 Stat. 4233; H.R. Rep. No. 102-997 (1992).

[271] Fines are set forth in 18 U.S.C. § 3571(b) (individuals — up to $250,000 for repeat offenders), or 18 U.S.C. § 3571(c) (organizations — up to $500,000).

[272] For an overview and the developing case law under the No Electronic Theft Act, see Eric Goldman, *Warez Trading and Criminal Copyright Infringement*, 51 J. Copyright Soc'y 395 (2004).

[273] 871 F. Supp. 535 (D.C. Mass. 1994).

a computer bulletin board operator who provided free unauthorized copies of commercial software programs to his subscribers on the grounds that his activity lacked the then-essential element of commercial gain. As stated above, § 506(a)(1)(A) applies only to commercial infringers who make ten copies or more in any given six-month period. By contrast, § 506(a)(1)(B) enables the prosecution of an infringer who has made even a single copy of a program which met the requisite value. Thus, besides providing a means to reach noncommercial actors, this subsection of the Act offers an alternative route for the prosecution of commercial infringers as well.

[D] Criminal Liability for the Unauthorized Distribution of Prerelease Commercial Works

In 2005, Congress updated the No Electronic Theft Act provisions, adding to § 506 a new category of criminal infringement for the unauthorized distribution of a work that has not yet been released to the public. Congress wished to target the activity of those who place files on the Internet for free download, including the latest movies, music, software, and games. Section 506(a)(1)(C) of the Copyright Act criminalizes "the distribution of a work being prepared for commercial distribution, by making it available on a computer network accessible to members of the public, if such person knew or should have known that the work was intended for commercial distribution." Persons who violate this subsection are subject to substantial penalties or fine or imprisonment, or both.[274] In conjunction with the 2005 amendments, Congress initiated a preregistration feature to expedite and streamline the registration process for certain categories of works that were particularly vulnerable to infringement before their release to the public.[275]

[E] Other Criminal Penalties and Offenses

The remainder of § 506 of the Copyright Act provides additional criminal penalties. Under § 506(b), forfeiture, destruction, or other disposition of infringing copies and equipment used in their manufacture are mandatory. The final three subsections of § 506 impose criminal sanctions for the fraudulent intent to place copyright notice on any article with knowledge of its falsehood,[276] for removing or altering copyright notice with fraudulent intent,[277] and for knowingly making a false representation of a material fact in an application for copyright registration.[278] These violations carry a maximum penalty of not more than $2,500.

---

[274] *See* 18 U.S. C. § 2319(d) (imposing a maximum three-year imprisonment for violation; five years if the violation was committed for commercial advantage or financial gain for violations; and six years for subsequent offenses). *See also* 18 U.S.C. § 3571 (setting forth fines).

[275] *See* 17 U.S.C. § 408(f)(1)–(2); prerelease registration is discussed at *supra* § 7.05[B].

[276] 17 U.S.C. § 506(c). For an overview of the problems associated with fraudulently claiming copyright on public domain works and the virtual lack of criminal enforcement see Jason Massone, *Copyfraud*, 81 N.Y.U .L. Rev. 1026 (2006) (advocating civil penalties falsely claiming copyright).

[277] 17 U.S.C. § 506(d).

[278] 17 U.S.C. § 506(e).

[F] Criminal Penalties for Unauthorized Recording of Motion Pictures in Theaters

Movie studios complain that all too frequently an unauthorized version of a film is available online even before or shortly after it is commercially released. Part of the problem can be traced to the illegal camcording of movies at movie theaters. Quickly stamped onto DVDs, these camcorded movies are illegally distributed to millions of people worldwide through "peer-to-peer" and other electronic networks. To deter the illegal camcording, in 2005, Congress enacted the Artists and Theft Prevention Act (ART Act).[279] The ART Act amended the federal criminal code to prohibit the unauthorized knowing use or attempted use of a video camera or similar device to transmit or make a copy of a motion picture or other copyrighted audiovisual work from a performance of such work in a movie theater. The Act sets forth penalties for such violations, including imprisonment for no more than three years for a first offense.[280] Possession of a recording device in a movie theater is evidence in any proceeding to determine whether that person committed such an offense, but shall not, by itself, be sufficient to support a conviction for such offense. Thus, persons who innocently carry a camcorder into a theater in a pocket or bag should not face prosecution.

Part IV. INFRINGEMENT: PROCEDURAL MATTERS

§ 9.16 JURISDICTION

[A] "Arising Under" Jurisdiction

28 U.S.C. § 1338(a)[281] gives federal courts exclusive jurisdiction for actions arising under the Copyright Act. When does a case "arise under" the 1976 Copyright Act? According to Judge Friendly's well-known synthesis of the issue:

> An action "arises under" the Copyright Act if and only if the complaint is for a remedy expressly granted by the Act, *e.g.*, a suit for infringement or for the statutory royalties for record reproduction . . . or asserts a claim requiring construction of the Act . . . or, at the very least and perhaps more doubtfully, presents a case where a distinctive policy of the Act requires that federal principles control the disposition of the claim. The general interest that copyrights, like all other forms of property, should be enjoyed by their true owner is not enough to meet this last test.[282]

---

[279] 18 U.S.C. § 2319B.

[280] 18 U.S.C. § 2319B(a).

[281] The section reads: "The district courts shall have original jurisdiction of any civil action arising under any Act of Congress relating to patents . . . copyrights and trademarks. Such jurisdiction shall be exclusive of the courts of the states in patent . . . and copyright cases."

[282] *T.B. Harms Co. v. Eliscu*, 339 F.2d 823, 828 (2d Cir. 1964). In *Schoenberg v. Shapolsky Publishers, Inc.*, 971 F.2d 926, 932–33 (2d Cir. 1992), the Second Circuit departed from the tripartite *Harms* test. The court held that to determine whether a lawsuit arises under the Copyright Act, the court must first determine whether the infringement claim is only "incidental" to the "claim seeking a determination of

To determine that an action arises under the 1976 Copyright Act requires distinguishing between an action based primarily on a right conferred by the 1976 Copyright Act and an action incidentally involving issues of copyright law. A suit for statutory copyright infringement is the classic example of an action expressly conferred by copyright, where federal jurisdiction is exclusive.

By comparison, an action brought to enforce an assignment of copyright is essentially an action under contract law.[283] Here, state court jurisdiction would be exclusive, even though the state court may have to interpret aspects of copyright law to determine whether to enforce the assignment. Similarly, an action brought to enforce royalties under a licensing agreement would lie essentially in the domain of state law,[284] as would a will conveying a copyright and an action to foreclose a statutory copyright mortgage.[285]

Even where the action does not involve statutory copyright infringement, exclusive jurisdiction will be conferred if the complaint necessitates construction or application of provisions of the 1976 Copyright Act. Examples are claims as to the extent of royalties under the compulsory licensing provisions,[286] ownership of copyright under the recording priorities, or whether a work constitutes a work made for hire.[287] Actions involving federal preemption of state law also belong on the list.[288] Each of these issues concerns a distinct policy of the 1976 Act, thus requiring that federal principles be controlling.

[B] Supplemental Jurisdiction

Often a complaint will include both nonfederal as well as federal claims. Under 28 U.S.C. § 1338(a), the federal court must determine whether it has jurisdiction to decide the case under the copyright laws. In addition to copyright claims, the complaint may allege state law claims, such as breach of contract, fraud, and a variety of counts of unfair competition. The question is whether once jurisdiction is conferred on the copyright claim, will the district court decide the state law claims as well? At first glance, a policy encouraging the conservation of judicial resources would suggest that all the claims should be handled in one trial. Resolution of all

---

ownership or contractual rights under the contract." Second, the court must next determine whether the complaint alleges a breach of a condition or of a contract covenant. If a breach of a condition is alleged, then the district court has subject matter jurisdiction. If the breach of covenant is so material as to create a right of rescission, then the asserted claim arises under the Copyright Act. Whatever the merits of the *Schoenberg* test, it was abrogated only eight years later. In *Bassett v. Mashantucket Pequot Tribe*, 204 F.3d 343 (2d Cir. 2000), the Second Circuit concluded that the *Schoenberg* test, with its references to the "essence" of the claim and to "claims incidental" to a contract, was "unworkable," and reverted instead to the three-part *Harms* test. The distinction between covenants and conditions may, however, still be important in deciding whether injunctive relief is appropriate. *See Sun Microsystems, Inc. v. Microsoft Corp.*, 188 F.3d 1115 (9th Cir. 1999).

[283] *See* Nimmer on Copyright § 12.01[A] (2014).

[284] *See Bevan v. Columbia Broad. Sys., Inc.*, 329 F. Supp. 601 (S.D.N.Y. 1971) (noting the failure to pay royalties); *see also Wolfe v. United Artists Corp.*, 583 F. Supp. 52 (E.D. Pa. 1983).

[285] *See Republic Pictures Corp. v. Security-First Nat'l Bank of L.A.*, 197 F.2d 767 (9th Cir. 1952).

[286] *See T.B. Harms Co. v. Eliscu*, 339 F.2d 823 (2d Cir. 1964).

[287] *See Royalty Control Corp. v. Sanco, Inc.*, 175 U.S.P.Q. (BNA) 641 (N.D. Cal. 1972).

[288] *See Morseburg v. Balyon*, 201 U.S.P.Q. (BNA) 518 (C.D.Cal. 1978).

the claims, federal and state, before one tribunal may be desirable, but federal law limits the district courts' power to do so in all situations. Under 28 U.S.C. § 1338(b), a district court has the power to decide the nonfederal claim if three jurisdictional requirements are met: (1) the basis of the nonfederal claim must be "unfair competition," and the federal claim to which it is attached must be both (2) substantial and (3) related.[289]

The first two requirements, that the state claims be "substantial" and constitute "unfair competition" have not presented much controversy. As for the "substantiality" of the federal claim, the courts will deny jurisdiction over the state cause of action if the federal claim is denied on a pretrial motion.[290] As for the requirement that the state claim constitute "unfair competition," the courts have broadly construed that term to include claims of passing off, misappropriation, misrepresentation, conversion, trade secret misappropriation, and breach of contract.[291]

By contrast, the "related" requirement has posed the greatest problems of interpretation. Two views exist on the meaning of "related" for the purpose of pendent jurisdiction. The more restrictive view holds that the two claims are related only if they rest on substantially identical facts.[292] The more liberal view, which appears to be the current trend, holds that the two claims are related if they have the same "factual nucleus," even though they might not derive from identical facts.[293]

Section 1338(b) was largely rendered redundant by the passage in 1990 of a federal statute, 28 U.S.C. § 1367, which was intended to codify the judge-made doctrines of "pendent jurisdiction" and "ancillary jurisdiction" under a new heading: "supplemental jurisdiction." Section 1367(a) provides that federal courts may exercise jurisdiction over state law claims if they arise from the same "case or controversy" as claims otherwise within their jurisdiction. There has not been much judicial discussion of the relationship between § 1338 and § 1367, but at least one decision suggests that, with regard to state law "unfair competition" claims, the two statutes, though varying in language, are coextensive in effect.[294] But § 1367(a) also permits supplemental jurisdiction in copyright cases over state law claims that could not be characterized as dealing with "unfair competition" such as trade secret, breach of contract, and tortious interference.[295] In addition, § 1367(a)

---

[289] *See Conopco, Inc. v. May Dep't Stores Co.*, 46 F.3d 1556 (Fed. Cir. 1994) (stating that § 1338(b) is a codification of the doctrine of pendant jurisdiction as it applies to patent, trademark, and copyright causes of action).

[290] *See, e.g.*, *Scholz Homes, Inc. v. Maddox*, 379 F.2d 84, 87 (6th Cir. 1967).

[291] *See, e.g.*, *Lone Ranger Television v. Program Radio Corp.*, 740 F.2d 718, 724 (9th Cir. 1984) (stating that a conversion claim lies within the ambit of unfair competition).

[292] *See Hurn v. Oursler*, 289 U.S. 238 (1933).

[293] *See, e.g.*, *Friedman, Eisenstein, Raemer & Schwartz v. Afterman*, 599 F. Supp. 902 (N.D. Ill. 1984).

[294] *See Historical Truth Prod's v. Sony Pictures Entm't, Inc.*, 39 U.S.P.Q.2d (BNA) 1807 (S.D.N.Y. 1995).

[295] *See, e.g.*, *King v. Ames*, 179 F.3d 370 (5th Cir. 1999) (negligence and breach of contract); *Architectronics, Inc. v. Control Sys., Inc.*, 935 F. Supp. 425 (S.D.N.Y. 1996).

expressly provides that "supplemental jurisdiction shall include claims that involve the joinder or intervention of additional parties."

Of course, pendant or supplemental jurisdiction is discretionary rather than compulsory, and all courts will draw the line before the point of abuse. In such instances, when "state issues substantially predominate, . . . in terms of proof, of the scope of the issues raised, [and] of the comprehensiveness of the remedies sought," the federal courts will decline to exercise pendent jurisdiction because the state claims "constitute the real body of [the] case, to which the federal claim is only an appendage."[296] Section 1367(c) echoes this analysis (in its subsection (2)), and also codifies other grounds, previously identified in the pendent jurisdiction case law, on which jurisdiction may be declined. It provides that the district courts may decline to exercise supplemental jurisdiction over a claim under subsection (a) if the following are met:

(1) the claim raises a novel or complex issue of State law;

(2) the claim substantially predominates over the claim or claims over which the district court has original jurisdiction;

(3) the district court has dismissed all claims over which it has original jurisdiction; or

(4) in exceptional circumstances, there are other compelling reasons for declining jurisdiction.

What happens if the federal copyright claim is dismissed on motion prior to trial — the situation addressed in § 1367(c)(3)? The usual course is to dismiss the state claims as well, without prejudice to re-filing in state court.[297]

The above discussion has focused on supplemental jurisdiction where a complaint includes both nonfederal as well as federal claims. But what about situations where a copyright infringement claim is joined in a federal district court with a nonfrivolous patent claim arising under 28 U.S.C. § 1338? Here, appellate jurisdiction lies exclusively in the Court of Appeals for the Federal Circuit for any and all counts.[298]

---

[296] *Mr. Vee Prods., Inc. v. LeBlanc*, 491 F. Supp. 493, 496 (S.D.N.Y. 1980) (quoting *United Mine Workers v. Gibbs*, 383 U.S. 715, 726–27 (1966)).

[297] *See, e.g., Sem-torq, Inc. v. K-Mart Corp.*, 936 F.2d 851 (6th Cir. 1991); *AGV Prods., Inc. v. Metro-Goldwyn-Mayer, Inc.*, 115 F. Supp. 2d 378 (S.D.N.Y. 2000). *But see Batiste v. Island Records, Inc.*, 179 F.3d 217, 227 (5th Cir. 1999) ("Although we have stated that our 'general rule' is to decline to exercise jurisdiction over pendent state law claims when all federal claims are dismissed or otherwise eliminated from a case prior to trial, this rule is neither mandatory nor absolute.")

[298] *See* 28 U.S.C. § 1295(a)(1) (requiring exclusive appellate jurisdiction in the Federal Circuit for cases in which District Court's jurisdiction was based in whole or in part on a patent claim under § 1338); *see also Abbott Labs. v. Brennan*, 952 F.2d 1346, 1349–50 (Fed. Cir. 1991) (holding that where the patent count, pleaded below, was not on appeal, and appeal issues involved only state law claims or nonpatent federal claims, the Federal Circuit has appellate jurisdiction). "The path of appeal is determined by the basis of jurisdiction in the district court and is not controlled by its decision or by the substance of the issues that are appealed."). *But see Holmes Group, Inc v. Vornado Air Circulation Sys., Inc.*, 535 U.S. 826 (2002) (holding that the Federal Circuit does not have appellate jurisdiction where patent infringement is asserted in a counterclaim only); *Denibcare U.S.A., Inc. v. Toys R Us, Inc.*, 84 F.3d 1143,

[C] Personal Jurisdiction

A copyright is an intangible, incorporeal right, and as such, it has no *situs* other than the domicile of its proprietor and cannot be the subject of *in rem* jurisdiction. Thus, an action for copyright infringement must rest on *in personam* jurisdiction. Fed. R. Civ. P. 4(k)(1)(A) permits jurisdiction over a defendant "who could be subjected to the jurisdiction of a court . . . in the state in which the district court is located." This rule thus incorporates the limits imposed on state courts by the Due Process Clause of the Fourteenth Amendment — the familiar "minimum" analysis that law students encounter in civil procedure.[299] Service of process may be made using a state "long arm" statute or any other means specified in Fed. R. Civ. P. 4(e)–(j).

In copyright cases, personal jurisdiction is typically based on the defendant's business activity in the state or the commission of an act of infringement in the state. The growth of the Internet has given the law of personal jurisdiction some fascinating new twists — and, as one might expect, some of them have come in copyright cases. For a sufficient basis of asserting personal jurisdiction, the courts have required that the defendant do more than make an infringing work available on the Internet. Such a limitation is necessary to avoid subjecting a defendant to jurisdiction in every forum in the country. In *ALS Scan, Inc. v. Digital Service Consultants, Inc.*,[300] the court formulated a tripartite test that would establish Internet activities in copyright cases subject to personal jurisdiction: (1) when a person directs electronic activity into the state, (2) with the manifested intent of engaging in business or other interactions within the state, and (3) that activity creates, in a person within the State, a potential cause of action cognizable in the state's courts.[301] In practice, whether a sufficient basis for personal jurisdiction can be found often turns on the degree the defendant has targeted, in a commercial manner, the residents of the forum state. Thus, the more the defendant's Internet activities facilitate the formation of contracts with residents of the forum state, or transmit the infringing material to them, the more likely personal jurisdiction will be found. Alternatively, courts have found that passive (non-interactive) websites, those that simply advertise or post information, are not subject to the long-arm statutes of foreign states.[302]

1148 (9th Cir. 1996) (where all patent claims were dismissed before trial, regional circuit had jurisdiction over partial final judgment on copyright claim).

[299] In general, the defendant must have purposeful minimum contacts with the forum; that the exercise of jurisdiction be reasonable, and that plaintiff's claim be related to defendant's contacts. *See Burger King Corp. v. Rudzewicz*, 471 U.S. 462, 472–78 (1985).

[300] 293 F.3d 707 (4th Cir. 2002).

[301] *Id.* at 714.

[302] *Compare ALS Scan, Inc. v. Digital Serv. Consultants, Inc*, 293 F.3d 707 (4th Cir. 2002) (holding that Georgia-based Internet service provider was not subject to personal jurisdiction in Maryland by enabling a website owner to publish photographs on the Internet); *Metro-Goldwyn-Mayer Studios, Inc. v. Grokster, Ltd.*, 243 F. Supp. 2d 1073 (C.D. Cal. 2003) (holding that defendant which provided its file sharing software and entered into licensing agreements with approximately two million California residents, was subject to personal jurisdiction under California long-arm statute); *Mink v. AAAA Development LLC*, 190 F.3d 333 (5th Cir. 1999) (holding that corporate defendant's website was insufficient to establish personal jurisdiction); The *Winfield Collection, Ltd. v. McCauley*, 105 F. Supp.

§ 9.17 PLEADING, PROOF, JURY TRIALS

[A] Pleading

Like every other pleading that an attorney prepares, the complaint in a copyright infringement action requires thoughtful consideration and usually a little practice if it is to be done properly. For purposes of satisfying Rule 8 of the Federal Rules of Civil Procedure, the courts have held that a properly pleaded copyright infringement claim must allege: "(1) which specific works are the subject of the copyright claim, (2) that plaintiff owns the copyright in those works, (3) that the copyrights have been registered in accordance with the statute, and (4) by what acts during what time the defendant infringed the copyright."[303] Other courts, taking note of Supreme Court authority rejecting "heightened pleading" requirements in other contexts, have held that "complaints simply alleging present ownership by plaintiff, registration in compliance with the applicable statute, and infringement by defendant have been held sufficient under the rules."[304]

[B] Burden of Proof

The plaintiff in a copyright action is responsible for proving:

(1) his or her *ownership* of the pertinent exclusive right(s) in the accusing work and

(2) a *prima facie case of infringement* of the right(s) in suit by the defendant.

Once a prima facie case has been established by the plaintiff, the defendant bears the burden of rebutting the case, including any of the limitations found in §§ 107–121, which act as affirmative defenses. As to ownership, the principal

---

2d 746 (E.D. Mich. 2000) (holding that eBay sales of Texas defendant's allegedly infringing craft items to Michigan residents were insufficient for personal jurisdiction), *with Bird v. Parsons*, 289 F.3d 865 (6th Cir. 2002) (holding that interactive national website through which thousands of Ohioans registered domain names was sufficient basis for personal jurisdiction; copyright claim dismissed on the merits); *Grokster*, 243 F. Supp. 2d 1073 (holding that the court had personal jurisdiction over defendant, "a company organized under the laws of the island-nation of Vanuatu and doing business principally in Australia," which distributed file-sharing software over Internet website, based on effects on California plaintiffs); *Sefton v. Jew*, 201 F. Supp. 2d 730 (W.D. Tex. 2001) (holding that the corporation that entered into contracts over the Internet with Texas subscribers was subject to personal jurisdiction in Texas, but the trial court did not have jurisdiction over individual corporate officer, a California resident).

[303] *See Elektra Entertainment Group, Inc. v. Barker*, 551 F. Supp. 2d 234, 238 (S.D.N.Y. 2008). Under the Supreme Court's opinion in *Bell Atl. Corp. v. Twombly*, 127 S. Ct. 1955 (2007), however, additional facts may be required when necessary to render the claim plausible. *See Barker* at 237; *Phillips v. Murdock*, 543 F. Supp. 2d 1219 (D. Haw. 2008) (dismissing claim based solely on statements in defendant's advertisements as impermissible speculation). *But see CoStar Realty Info., Inc. v. Field*, 612 F. Supp. 2d 660 (D. Md. 2009) (plaintiff need only allege that it owns a valid copyright and that the defendant copied original expression). *See also* Fed. R. Civ. P. Form 19 ("Complaint for Copyright Infringement and Unfair Competition"), as amended in 2007. The answer must, of course, plead any affirmative defenses on which the defendant intends to rely. Fed. R. Civ. P. 8(c).

[304] *Mid Am. Title Co. v. Kirk*, 991 F.2d 417, 421 n.8 (7th Cir. 1993); *Perfect 10, Inc. v. Cybernet Ventures, Inc.*, 167 F. Supp. 2d 1114, 1120 (C.D. Cal. 2001); *see also Capitol Records, Inc. v. Wings Digital Corp.*, 218 F. Supp. 2d 280, 284 (E.D.N.Y. 2002) ("[P]laintiffs are not required to state with particularity specific infringing acts or the times of such acts").

matters to be proved include:

(1) the copyrightability of the work;

(2) its authorship by the plaintiff;

(3) the plaintiff's citizenship status;

(4) compliance with any statutory formalities; and

(5) the basis of the plaintiff's claim to ownership if he or she obtained title to the right in a suit subsequent to registration of the copyright.

Under the 1976 Act, the plaintiff's task for the first four elements is radically simplified by § 401(c):

> In any judicial proceedings the certificate of a registration made before or within five years after first publication of the work shall constitute prima facie evidence of the validity of the copyright and of the facts stated in the certificate. The evidentiary weight to be accorded the certificate of a registration made thereafter shall be within the discretion of the court.

And even where a work has been registered more than five years after publication, a court has discretion to give its contents prima facie weight.[305]

As to the fifth element, ownership, problems in identifying the copyright owner may arise when the suit concerns a right or rights in a previously registered work so that the certificate of registration does not reflect the title. In such circumstances, courts hold that the plaintiff "must tender additional evidence in order to make a prima facie showing of proprietorship (present ownership) of the copyright.[306]

It is clear, however, that the presumption of validity created by § 410(c) may be rebutted "[w]here other evidence in the record casts doubt on the question."[307]

As stated, the plaintiff also has the burden of demonstrating that there has been an infringement of his or her interest in the copyright by the defendant. The specific components of the required showing — copying and improper appropriation — are discussed earlier in this chapter. Even if the plaintiff establishes the elements of a prima facie case, the defendant may rebut by introducing evidence that the allegedly infringing work was independently created or was derived from a source in common with the plaintiff's work. If such evidence is introduced, "the plaintiff has the burden of proving that the defendant in fact copied the protected material."[308] The defendant may also try to show that the use was authorized by the plaintiff or

---

305 *Thimbleberries, Inc. v. C&F Enters., Inc.*, 142 F. Supp. 2d 1132, 1137 (D. Minn. 2001).

306 *Peer Int'l Corp. v. Latin Am. Music Corp.*, 161 F. Supp. 2d 38, 45 (D.P.R. 2001); *see Broadcast Music, Inc. v. Moor-Law, Inc.*, 484 F. Supp. 357, 363 (D. Del 1980) (copies of plaintiff's assignment filed in court).

307 *Fonar Corp. v. Domenick*, 105 F.3d 99, 104 (2d Cir. 1997), quoting *Durham Indus., Inc. v. Tomy Corp.*, 630 F.2d 905, 908 (2d Cir. 1980); *see also Ets-Hokin v. Skyy Spirits, Inc.*, 225 F.3d 1068, 1076 (9th Cir. 2000) ("To rebut the presumption, an infringement defendant must simply offer some evidence or proof to dispute or deny the plaintiff's prima facie case of infringement.").

308 *Peel & Co., Inc. v. The Rug Market*, 238 F.3d 391, 395 (5th Cir. 2001). (citing *Miller v. Universal City Studios, Inc.*, 650 F.2d 1365, 1375 (5th Cir. 1981)).

was otherwise privileged (for example, under the doctrine of "fair use"). In attempting to make such showings, the defendant has the burden of proof.[309]

[C] Venue

Copyright actions present no special venue problems, at least at a theoretical level. Under 28 U.S.C. § 1400(a), they may be instituted "in the district in which the defendant or his agent resides or may be found." Because "may be found" has been interpreted to refer to personal jurisdiction, "[i]f personal jurisdiction in a copyright case may be exercised over a corporation in a district, then venue also is proper in that district."[310] By the same token, federal trial courts will entertain motions for change of venue under § 1404(a) in copyright cases, based on factors including the convenience of parties and witnesses, access to documents and witnesses, the locus of operative facts, and other considerations.[311]

[D] Cases Involving Both Patents and Copyright

Under 28 U.S.C. § 1295(a)(1) exclusive appellate jurisdiction resides in the Court of Appeals for Federal Circuit for cases in which District Court's jurisdiction was based in whole or in part on a patent claim arising under 28 U.S.C. § 1338. Likewise, in cases where a copyright infringement claim is joined in the District Court with a non-frivolous patent claim (or a compulsory counterclaim) arising under § 1338, appellate jurisdiction lies exclusively in the Court of Appeals for the Federal Circuit for any or all of the counts.[312]

---

309 *See Bourne v. Walt Disney Co.*, 68 F.3d 621, 631 (2d Cir. 1995) (authorization); *Campbell v. Acuff-Rose Music, Inc.*, 510 U.S. 569, 590 (1994) (fair use).

310 *Metro-Goldwyn-Mayer Studios, Inc. v. Grokster, Ltd.*, 243 F. Supp. 2d 1073 (C.D. Cal. 2003).

311 For an example of a successful transfer motion, see *Hogan v. DC Comics*, 48 F. Supp. 2d 298 (N.D.N.Y. 1998) (granting a change of venue to the Southern District).

312 *Atari, Inc. v. JS & A Group, Inc.*, 747 F.2d 1422, 1428, 1440 (Fed. Cir. 1984) (asserting appellate jurisdiction where copyright claim was joined to patent claim below, and refusing to rule upon situations in which, e.g., patent claim was withdrawn or frivolous); *Hughes v. Novi American, Inc.*, 724 F.2d 122, 123 (Fed. Cir. 1984) (holding that the Federal Circuit has jurisdiction of copyright and patent claims on appeal because District Court's jurisdiction was based in part on patent claim under 28 U.S.C. § 1338(a)); *Abbott Labs. v. Brennan*, 952 F.2d 1346, 1349–50 (Fed. Cir. 1991) (holding that where patent count pleaded below was not on appeal, and appeal issues involved only state law claims or nonpatent federal claims, Federal Circuit has appellate jurisdiction. *But see Holmes Group, Inc v. Vornado Air Circulation Sys., Inc.*, 535 U.S. 826 (2002) (Federal Circuit does not have appellate jurisdiction where patent infringement is asserted in a counterclaim only); *Denbicare U.S.A., Inc. v. Toys R Us, Inc.*, 84 F.3d 1143, 1148 (9th Cir. 1996) (holding that where all patent claims were dismissed before trial, regional circuit had jurisdiction over partial final judgment on copyright claim).

[E] Jury Trial

[1] Right to Trial by Jury: Legal, Equitable, and Mixed Relief

Most often, the parties to an action for copyright infringement do not request trial by jury. In any particular case, however, one or more of the parties may desire to have the matter tried by jury. The parties may agree to a jury trial. But if they do, the determinative factor whether a party has a right to a trial by jury will depend on whether the relief is legal, equitable, or a mixture of the two.

If the remedies are entirely legal in character, that is, compensatory damages or profits, either party has a right to trial by jury. Alternatively, if the remedy is wholly equitable in character (for example an injunction), the relief granted will lie entirely within the inherent powers of the court and may be awarded by the judge alone. In this instance, neither party can claim a right to a jury trial. But what if the relief sought involves both legal and equitable remedies (*e.g.*, an injunction and accounting for profits)? Here, the rule is clear: the entire matter must be tried by a jury if either party so requests.

[2] The Special Problem of Statutory Damages

When the relief involves statutory damages, the rules involving a right to a jury trial are relatively unclear by comparison. Statutory damages, as the name suggests, are a creature of statute. Unfortunately, § 504(c) of the Copyright Act fails to describe statutory damages as "equitable" or "legal" or to provide explicitly whether they are to be awarded by the judge or jury.

This issue was subject to a longstanding debate until the Supreme Court, in *Feltner v. Columbia Pictures Television, Inc.*[313] held that the Seventh Amendment to the Constitution provides a right to a jury trial on all issues pertinent to the award of statutory damages including the amount itself.

In *Feltner*, plaintiff Columbia terminated agreements licensing several television series to stations owned by defendant Feltner after the stations' royalty payments became delinquent. When the stations continued to broadcast the programs, Columbia sued, prevailed on partial summary judgment on its claims of copyright infringement, and then exercised its option under § 504(c) to recover statutory damages in lieu of actual damages and profits.

The District Court denied Feltner's request for a jury trial, and, after a bench trial, awarded Columbia $8,800,000, plus costs and attorney's fees. The Ninth Circuit affirmed, holding that neither § 504(c) nor the Seventh Amendment provided a right to jury trial on statutory damages.[314] In reversing and remanding on the issue of the right to trial by jury for statutory damages, the Supreme Court did not resort to the Copyright Act but to the Constitution and to history. In

---

[313] 523 U.S. 340 (1998).

[314] *Columbia Pictures Television v. Krypton Broad., Inc.*, 106 F.3d 284 (9th Cir. 1997), *rev'd & remanded*, 523 U.S. 340 (1998).

essence, if a party so demands, a jury must determine the actual amount of statutory damages under § 504(c) "to preserve 'the substance of the common-law right of trial by jury.' "[315]

The *Feltner* decision imposes a special responsibility on the courts in instructing the jury on the complicated issues involving statutory damages. Applied to its fullest extent, *Feltner* would have the jury decide the range of the award within the normal $750 to $30,000 range and whether willfulness or lack of awareness exists in assessing the raising or lowering of the normal limits.[316] Other jury issues would involve the determination of the number of infringements including the number of works in the suit. After *Feltner*, there was some question how trial courts would exercise their role. Would they more readily grant summary judgment, determining such questions as "willfulness" as a matter of law, or would they be more inclined to deny summary judgment, thereby sending everything to the jury?

§ 9.18 PARTIES TO SUIT: PLAINTIFF'S STANDING

Under § 501(b) of the 1976 Act,[317] the legal or beneficial owner of an exclusive right has standing to sue for infringement.[318] The standards by which "legal" ownership may be proven are relatively plain and straightforward in most instances. But determining who qualifies as a "beneficial owner" for the purposes of § 501(b) is not always easy. The term is not defined by the Copyright Act, and the courts, in applying this provision of the Act, have looked generally to the law of trusts to flesh out the terms of the Act.[319] Courts have held that an assignee may be a beneficial owner where he receives royalties in exchange for an assignment of rights.[320] In addition, the owner of an exclusive right may bring suit on his own behalf without having to join the licensor of the right in the action. By comparison, the nonexclusive licensee has no standing to bring suit.[321]

An assignee of copyright has standing to bring an infringement action. But who has standing to sue if the copyright is transferred after a cause of action has accrued? The general rule is that if it is not expressly included in the assignment, the assignee will not be able to prosecute the accrued cause of action.[322] It has been

---

[315] *Feltner*, 523 U.S. at 354.

[316] *See* 17 U.S.C. § 504(c)(2). *See BMG Music v. Gonzalez*, 430 F.3d 888 (7th Cir. 2005) (holding that a jury trial is not required if copyright owner seeks only the minimum award of $750 per work infringed).

[317] 17 U.S.C. § 501(b).

[318] 17 U.S.C. § 205(d). Related to standing is the concept of indispensable parties. Section 501(b) requires that the plaintiff serve written notice on any person whose interest is likely to be affected by a decision in the case. It is unclear under what conditions joinder should be required or permitted. *See* NIMMER ON COPYRIGHT § 12.02 (2014).

[319] *See, e.g., A. Brod, Inc. v. S.K. & I Co.*, 998 F. Supp. 314 (S.D.N.Y. 1998).

[320] *See, e.g., Batiste v. Island Records, Inc.*, 179 F.3d 217 (5th Cir. 1999); *Cortner v. Israel*, 732 F.2d 267 (2d Cir. 1984).

[321] Neither the 1976 Act nor the 1909 Act confers upon nonexclusive licensees standing to sue. *See, e.g., Sybersound Records, Inc. v. UAV Corp.*, 517 F.3d 1137 (9th Cir. 2008) (holding that because co-owner of copyright could only grant a nonexclusive license, licensee of co-owner did not have standing to sue competitors who allegedly lacked licenses).

[322] *ABKCO Music, Inc. v. Harrisongs Music, Ltd.*, 944 F.2d 971 (2d Cir. 1991).

held, however, that a party can cure a standing defect with a second assignment that explicitly transfers causes of action for infringement prior to the initial assignment.[323] On the other hand, a third-party who has been assigned the bare right to sue for infringement has no interest in the legal dissemination of the copyrighted material. As one court put it, "only parties with a legally recognized interest in copyright as delineated in § 106 (legal owners) and parties who stand to benefit from the legal dissemination of copyrighted material (beneficial owners) have the right to sue for infringement under . . . the Copyright Act."[324]

As to the joinder of parties in an infringement action, under § 501(b), the court *may* require the plaintiff to serve a written notice of the action, together with a copy of the complaint, "upon any person shown, by the records of the Copyright Office or otherwise, to have or claim an interest in the copyright," and *must* require such service "upon any person whose interest is likely to be affected by a decision in the case." While the court must permit the intervention of such persons, it has discretion as to whether to require their joinder. That discretion will ordinarily be exercised in accordance with Rule 19 of Federal Rules of Civil Procedure, which requires the joinder of "necessary" parties if joinder is possible, but otherwise permits the court to proceed unless nothing can be accomplished without the absent party.[325]

§ 9.19 STANDING TO SUE FEDERAL AND STATE GOVERNMENTS

[A] Federal Government

A copyright owner has a statutory right to sue the U.S. government in the U.S. Court of Federal Claims.[326] Also, employees of the U.S. government are personally liable for their infringing acts, even if carried out in the scope of their employment.[327]

---

323 *Intimo, Inc. v. Briefly Stated, Inc.*, 948 F. Supp. 315 (S.D.N.Y. 1996).

324 Righthaven LLC v. Wolf, 813 F. Supp. 2d 1265, 1273 (D.Colo. 2011).

325 *See, e.g.*, *ABKCO Music, Inc. v. LaVere*, 217 F.3d 684 (9th Cir. 2000) (holding that the beneficial owner of copyright was not an indispensable party where there was no evidence that interests diverged from or would not be adequately protected by legal owner); *Bassett v. Mashantucket Pequot Tribe*, 204 F.3d 343 (2d Cir. 2000) (holding that the Indian tribe was not an indispensable party in infringement suit against Museum located on reservation).

326 *See* 28 U.S.C. § 1498(b); *O'Rourke v. Smithsonian Institution Press*, 399 F.3d 113 (2d Cir. 2005) (holding that the Smithsonian is part of the "United States" within the meaning of § 1498(b)). *But see Blueport Co. v. United States*, 533 F.3d 1374 (Fed. Cir. 2008) (holding that claims for violations of the anticircumvention provisions of the DMCA do not fall within the waiver of sovereign immunity in § 1498(b)).

327 *See Towle v. Ross*, 32 F. Supp. 125 (D. Or. 1940).

[B] State Government: The Eleventh Amendment Issue

As discussed elsewhere, the federal government has waived its immunity against liability for infringement and may be sued in the Court of Federal Claims.[328] The situation concerning state governments is more complex.

Whether an action for infringement could be brought against a state government consistent with the Eleventh Amendment's doctrine of sovereign immunity[329] was an ongoing issue of debate until Congress tried to resolve the controversy by legislation in 1990. The Copyright Remedy Clarification Act of 1990 amended the Copyright Act to make states, state instrumentalities, and state officers or employees acting in their official capacity liable for copyright infringement "in the same manner and to the same extent as any non-governmental entity."[330] In addition, the amendments added a new § 511(a) to the Copyright Act, providing that no state entity, or state officer or employee acting in an official capacity, shall be immune "under the Eleventh Amendment of the Constitution of the United States or under any other doctrine of sovereign immunity, from suit in Federal court by any person, including any governmental or non-governmental entity for violation of any of the exclusive rights of copyright."[331] The abrogation of state sovereignty represents the resolution of a continuing clash between two constitutional principles, the Copyright Clause and the Eleventh Amendment to the Constitution, which insulates the states from suit in federal court.[332] Before the 1990 amendments, the trend in the case law favored state immunity from suit for damages, allowing the states to freely ignore the rights of copyright owners.[333] As intensive users of copyrighted works, the states represented a real and ever present possibility for systematic abuse. This threat led to the explicit abrogation of sovereign immunity for state governmental entities.[334]

The constitutionality of § 511(a) was thrown seriously in doubt by a 1995 decision of the Supreme Court that, on first blush, had little to do with the law of

---

[328] 28 U.S.C. § 1498(b).

[329] The Eleventh Amendment of the Constitution states: "The judicial power of the United States shall not be construed to extend to any suit in law or equity, commenced or prosecuted against one of the United States by Citizens of another State, or by Citizens or Subjects of any Foreign State."

[330] 17 U.S.C. § 501(a). *See* The Copyright Remedy Clarification Act of 1990, Pub. L. No. 101-553, 104 Stat. 2749 (1990).

[331] Section 511(b) of the Copyright Act, added by the 1990 amendments, makes legal and equitable remedies available against the states for infringing acts of states and their employees.

[332] 28 U.S.C. § 1338(a) confers exclusive jurisdiction of the federal courts over cases arising under the copyright law.

[333] *See BV Eng'g v. Univ. of Cal.*, 657 F. Supp. 1246 (C.D. Cal. 1987) (holding that unless Congress has expressly abrogated the immunity or the states have waived it, the states cannot be sued in federal court); *Richard Anderson Photography v. Radford Univ.*, 633 F. Supp. 1154 (W.D. Va. 1986); *Mihalek Corp. v. Michigan*, 595 F. Supp. 903 (E.D. Mich. 1984). For a leading Supreme Court case, see *Atascadero Hosp. v. Scanlon*, 473 U.S. 234, 239 (1985) (finding that a state may be subjected to damage suits in federal courts only if the state has expressly waived immunity or Congress has expressed its unequivocal intent to abrogate immunity).

[334] For an overview of the issue, see John C. Beiter, *Copyright Infringement and the Eleventh Amendment: A Doctrine of Unfair Use*, 40 VAND. L. REV. 225 (1987).

copyright. In *Seminole Tribe of Florida v. Florida*,[335] the Court held that Congress lacks the power under the Indian Commerce Clause of the U.S. Constitution to subject states to suit in federal court for violations of federally created rights. The ruling appears to mean that state sovereign immunity under the Eleventh Amendment trumps congressional power under Article I. This result casts doubts on the validity of recent statutory reforms, including § 511 of the Copyright Act, that made states liable for violations of federal intellectual property.

Of course, *Seminole Tribe* was not a copyright case, or even an intellectual property case. In 1999, however, the Supreme Court extended its reasoning to patent and trademark law. In *Florida Prepaid Postsecondary Education Expense Board v. College Savings Bank*,[336] the court concluded that congressional efforts to abrogate state sovereign immunity for patent and trademark infringement were unavailing, casting even greater doubt on the validity of § 511. A year later the Fifth Circuit Court of Appeals in *Chavez v. Arte Publico Press* closed the circle, concluding that Congress lacked the power to abrogate the states' sovereign immunity in copyright infringement cases.[337]

With the virtual invalidation of § 511 on the grounds of constitutionality, copyright owners are left with much weaker remedies against state government officials for their acts of infringement. True, an individual may be able to obtain injunctive relief against the state to prohibit a state official's continuing violation of federal law, but he or she could no longer recover damages for the harm incurred, by far the most effective remedy from both a compensatory and deterrent standpoint.[338] Congress has considered passing legislation to provide state courts with concurrent jurisdiction in copyright infringement actions to restrain state officials from infringing copyright with impunity.[339]

---

[335] 517 U.S. 44 (1995).

[336] 527 U.S. 627 (1999).

[337] 204 F.3d 601 (5th Cir. 2000).

[338] *But see Nat'l Ass'n of Bds. of Pharmacy v. Bd. of Regents of the Univ. Sys. of Ga.*, 86 U.S.P.Q.2d (BNA) 1683, 1700-01 (M.D. Ga. 2008) (holding that an *ex parte Young* action is not available where plaintiff could not allege an ongoing violation). In addition, some courts have held that actions for damages may be maintained against state officials in their individual capacity, unless it can be shown that the judgment would inevitably be paid out of the public purse. *Id.* at 1701; *Mktg. Info. Masters, Inc. v. Bd. of Trustees of the Cal. State Univ. Sys.*, 552 F. Supp. 2d 1088, 1095–96 (S.D. Cal. 2008). State officials are entitled to qualified immunity unless their actions violated "clearly established law." *See Nat'l Ass'n of Bds. of Pharmacy*, 86 U.S.P.Q.2d (BNA) at 1702–04.

[339] For a particularly aggressive approach at remedying the problems created by *Florida Prepaid* cases, see Sen. Patrick Leahy's Bill, S. 1835, 106th Cong. (1999) (supplying extensive historical and technical "findings" to overcome the perceived deficiency in prior legislation and providing that no state can acquire federal intellectual property rights unless it "opts into" the federal system by agreeing to waive sovereign immunity from suits that arise under federal IP laws or that seek a declaration with respect to federal IP rights).

Chapter 10

FAIR USE AND OTHER DEFENSES TO COPYRIGHT INFRINGEMENT

§ 10.01 INTRODUCTION AND CHAPTER OVERVIEW

The doctrine of fair use is a judicially created defense to copyright infringement that allows a third party to use a copyrighted work in a reasonable manner without the copyright owner's consent. Although codified in the 1976 Act, the doctrine of fair use has retained its nature as an equitable rule of reason to be applied where a finding of infringement would either be unfair or undermine "the Progress of Science and the useful Arts." The current Act sets forth fair use in § 107, which contains a preamble, gives examples of fair use contexts, and provides four broad criteria that must all be applied to determine whether a use is "fair."

This chapter contains five parts. Part I discusses fair use from a historical perspective and then focuses on § 107. Part II covers the four fair use factors in § 107 and the way in which the Court applies these broad criteria in making a fair use determination. Part III focuses on special situations where particularly difficult use issues have arisen, such as copying with the digital new technologies and the ever troublesome problem of the use of another's work in a parody. This part discusses how the fair use doctrine interrelates with First Amendment rights and values and concludes with a proposed synthesis of fair use. Part IV considers the troubled future of the fair use doctrine in light of the challenges it faces in a digital world. Part V reviews the other affirmative defenses to an action for infringement, such as statute of limitations, copyright misuse, and laches and estoppel.

Part I. FAIR USE: THE BACKGROUND

§ 10.02 GENERALLY

The judicially created doctrine of fair use is by far the most important defense to an action for copyright infringement. It has been defined as a "privilege in others than the owner of a copyright to use the copyrighted material in a reasonable manner without consent, notwithstanding the monopoly granted to the owner."[1]

The defense of fair use becomes relevant only after the plaintiff has made out a prima facie case for copyright infringement by showing copying of the original work and substantial similarity between the works. Once this occurs, the defendant bears

---

[1] *Rosemont Enters., Inc. v. Random House, Inc.*, 366 F.2d 303, 306 (2d Cir. 1966) (citing H. Ball, Copyright and Literary Property 260 (1944)).

the evidentiary burdens of production and persuasion that the infringing use of the copyrighted work was privileged as a fair use.[2]

Fair use is a mixed question of law and fact. If a reasonable trier of fact could reach only one conclusion, a court may conclude as a matter of law that the challenged use of the copyrighted work qualifies as a fair use.[3]

Although first articulated in case law in the mid-19th century,[4] fair use was not given its first statutory recognition until the 1976 Act.[5] The 1976 Act, however, does not try to define the doctrine. Instead, in § 107, Congress codified past practice by incorporating an incoherent body of case law into the 1976 Act.[6] As a result, the fair use defense continues to defy precise definition and remains an ad hoc equitable rule of reason where finding an infringement would undermine the ultimate purpose of copyright law. As one court stated, "[t]he doctrine of fair use . . . permits courts to avoid rigid application of the copyright statute when, on occasion, it would stifle the very creativity which that law is designed to foster."[7] The tradeoff for this flexibility is an elusive legal doctrine, reputed to be the most troublesome in copyright law.[8]

§ 10.03 HISTORICAL ORIGIN OF THE DOCTRINE OF FAIR USE: *FOLSOM v. MARSH*

The doctrine of fair use was first articulated in 1841 in *Folsom v. Marsh*,[9] yet it is surprising how little has changed since that time. In *Folsom*, defendant had taken 353 pages of plaintiff's multivolume work on George Washington to produce his own biography of the first president. Defendant did not copy the prior work verbatim but reproduced Washington's letters as they appeared in plaintiff's work, adding only transitional matter. On these facts, Justice Story found infringement, and set forth criteria to be evaluated in deciding questions of fair use: "In short, we must

---

[2] For a discussion of how liability for intermediaries affects the fair use privileges of individuals, see Joseph P. Liu, *Toward a Defense of Fair Use Enablement, or How U.S. Copyright Law Is Hurting My Daughter*, 57 J. Copyright Soc'y 423 (2010).

[3] *See Harper & Row, Publishers, Inc. v. Nation Enters.*, 471 U.S. 539 (1985); *Hustler Magazine, Inc. v. Moral Majority, Inc.*, 796 F.2d 1148, 1150 (9th Cir. 1986).

[4] *See Folsom v. Marsh*, 9 F. Cas. 342 (C.C.D. Mass. 1841) (No. 4901).

[5] 17 U.S.C. § 107.

[6] For a discussion of the four criteria used in determining fair use, see *infra* § 10.06.

[7] *Iowa State Univ. Research Found., Inc. v. Am. Broad. Cos.*, 621 F.2d 57, 60 (2d Cir. 1980).

[8] *See Dellar v. Samuel Goldwyn, Inc.*, 104 F.2d 661, 662 (2d Cir. 1939); for a more positive view of fair use, see Pamela Samuelson, *Unbundling Fair Uses*, 77 Fordam L. Rev. 2537 (2009) (arguing that fair use is more coherent and more predictable than many commentators have perceived once one recognizes that fair use cases tend to fall into common patterns). For a discussion of the developments of fair use since 2004 and how James Madison's separation of powers metaphor applies in a preliminary way to copyright, see Michael J. Madison, *Madisonian Fair Use*, 30 Cardozo Arts & Ent. L.J. 39 (2012). For a discussion of the Second Circuit's invention of the concept of "fair use markets" and for an argument that fair use is possible even when licensing revenues are available, see Wendy J. Gordon, *Fair Use Markets: On Weighing Potential License Fees*, 79 Geo. Wash. L. Rev. 1814 (2011).

[9] 9 F. Cas. 342 (C.C.D. Mass. 1841) (No. 4901). For an in-depth discussion of *Folsom v. Marsh* and fair use doctrine, see Matthew Sag, *The Pre-History of Fair Use*, 76 Brooklyn L. Rev. 1371 (2011).

often . . . look to the nature and objects of the selections made, the quantity and value of the materials used, and the degree in which the use may prejudice the sale, or diminish the profits, or supersede the objects, of the original work. . . . "[10]

The factors identified by Justice Story in determining fair use are strikingly similar to those incorporated in § 107 of the 1976 Act.[11] Despite the great changes that have come about in American society, due in part to new media and new reproductive technologies, the doctrine of fair use remains rooted in the 19th century, when information was transmitted almost exclusively by the printed word.

§ 10.04 SECTION 107 OF THE 1976 ACT: GENERALLY

The doctrine of fair use is codified in § 107 of the 1976 Act. The statute, however, does not provide a tight definition of the doctrine. Instead, it sets forth in its preamble the kinds of uses that usually prompt the defense, followed by four criteria that must *all* be applied to determine whether the defense succeeds. The legislative history of § 107 indicates no intent to freeze the doctrine, but rather to allow its continuing development through the case law and its adaptation to changing times and technology.[12]

§ 10.05 THE PREAMBLE TO § 107

[A] In General

At the threshold, parties asserting the defense of fair use should show that they are engaged in an activity enumerated in the preamble to § 107.[13] The preamble reads as follows:

> Notwithstanding the provisions of Section 106, the fair use of a copyrighted work, including such use by reproduction in copies or phonorecords or by any other means specified by that section, for purposes such as criticism, comment, news reporting, teaching (including multiple copies for classroom use), scholarship, or research, is not an infringement of copyright.

The examples listed are broad and overlapping. They are meant to be illustrative, not exhaustive, allowing for other contexts in which the fair use defense might arise.[14] For example, the preamble does not specifically mention parody, but the categories of criticism and comment are broad enough to include parody. Even if parody did not fall into the illustrative categories, one could nevertheless argue that it constitutes a context in which fair use should operate.[15]

---

[10] *Folsom*, 9 F. Cas. at 348.

[11] In fact, they are virtually the same as those stated in § 107 of the 1976 Act. *See infra* § 10.06.

[12] H.R. Rep. No. 94-1476, at 66 (1976).

[13] *See Ass'n of Am. Med. Colls. v. Mikaelian*, 571 F. Supp. 144 (E.D. Pa. 1983), *aff'd*, 734 F.2d 3 (3d Cir. 1984).

[14] *See* 17 U.S.C. § 101. The terms "including" and "such as" are illustrative, not limitative.

[15] See *infra* § 10.14 for a discussion of parody.

[B] Analyzing the Preamble: Productive/Transformative Uses

Is there a common theme to the diverse uses enumerated in the preamble? One might argue that they are *productive* uses of a copyrighted work. Productive uses build on the works of others by adding their own socially valuable creative element. Indeed, the uses listed in the preamble conveniently fit into the productive use concept, with the possible exception of "multiple copies for classroom use" to employ the copyrighted work in a different manner or for a different purpose from the original. The concept of productive use reappeared with renewed vigor and a new name — *transformative use* — in an article written by Judge Pierre Leval. Typically, a fair use is one that has *transformed* the original, and, in so doing, adds value by creating "new information, new aesthetics, new insights and understandings."[16] Thus, critics, reporters, and biographers copy not for copying's sake, convenience, or pleasure, but to produce separate works of authorship. Their use of the copyrighted work is productive or, in the current parlance, "transformative." On the other hand, a nonproductive use (*reproductive use*) occurs when a user copies the material to use it for the same intrinsic purpose for which the copyright owner intended it to be used, for example, when A copies B's download of a popular song from a peer to peer website rather than buying it. In sum, productive uses increase the number of original works of authorship, whereas reproductive uses merely increase the number of copies of a work to the detriment of the author, whose profits fall and whose incentive to create new works correspondingly diminishes.

The transformative use doctrine supports the underlying goal of copyright law by increasing our fund of knowledge and information. Accordingly, a transformative use should be impeded only when it is so excessive as to undermine the incentive to produce copyrighted works.[17] On the other hand, non-productive (reproductive) use merely appropriates without creating anything of social value. Because productive uses confer public benefits whereas reproductive uses do not, some would assert that the fair use privilege should be limited to such productive uses.[18] The courts, however, have differed on whether the concept of

---

[16] *See* Leon E. Seltzer, Exemptions and Fair Use in Copyright Law 24 (1978) (arguing statement that a fair use is a productive use). Instead of "productive use" some courts have adopted the term "transformative" use. The concept is the same. *See* Pierre N. Leval, *Toward a Fair Use Standard*, 103 Harv. L. Rev. 1105, 1111 (1990) (stating that a use is "transformative" if it is productive and employs the quoted matter in a different manner or for a different purpose from the original; it adds value to the original). For an application of Judge Leval's transformative use doctrine, see *Campbell v. Acuff-Rose Music, Inc.*, 510 U.S. 569, 579 (1994) ("[T]he goal of copyright, to promote science and the arts, is generally furthered by the creation of transformative works."). *See also* Judge Leval's opinion in *Am. Geophysical Union v. Texaco, Inc.*, 802 F. Supp. 1 (S.D.N.Y. 1992) (finding that reproduction of single copies from plaintiff's journals, even for research purposes, is not a transformative use and thus not a fair use). For a comprehensive discussion of the development of the fair use doctrine and the rise to prominence of the transformative use paradigm, see Neil Weinstock Netanel, *Making Sense of Fair Use*, 15 Lewis & Clark L. Rev. 715 (2011).

[17] *See, e.g.*, *Twin Peaks Prods., Inc. v. Publ'ns, Int'l, Ltd.*, 996 F.2d 1366 (2d Cir. 1993) (finding defendant's detailed report of the plots of a popular television program went far beyond merely identifying their basic outline for the transformative purposes of comment or criticism).

[18] *See Sony Corp. of Am. v. Universal City Studios, Inc.*, 464 U.S. 417, 475 (1984) (Blackmun, J.,

transformative use should be limited to instances where the copyrighted work has been altered or to other situations where the copyrighted work is used in an entirely different context than the copyrighted work. Some courts have taken the latter, more expansive view. For example, in *Blanch v. Koons*,[19] the court held that "appropriation artist" Jeff Koons' use of a photographic image of a woman's feet was transformative because it used the image of the feet in a manner that was not the intent of the original photograph, in a way that was not merely a change of artistic media or venue.

Of course, a doctrine such as transformative use with its inherently vague contours lends itself to misapplication and can undermine § 106(2)'s derivative right. A case in point is *Bill Graham Archives v. Dorling Kindersley Ltd*,[20] where the court in dubious fashion ruled that it was a fair use — a transformative use — for defendant to reproduce seven of plaintiff's copyrighted images of the Grateful Dead reduced in scale to fit the pages of a coffee table book on the band. Defendant, who could have negotiated a license with the copyright owner, added little if any original authorship to the copyrighted work consistent with the productive use doctrine.

The transformative use doctrine is appealing because it appears to be consistent with the underlying goals of copyright law while adding coherence to an amorphous fair use doctrine. Unfortunately, there seems to be little consensus in the case law whether the transformative use must truly alter the copyrighted work itself or whether the concept encompasses other uses of the copyrighted work.[21] While some courts insist on a substantial alteration of the copyrighted work,[22] the trend appears to construe the transformative use concept expansively. For example, in *Perfect 10 v. Google*,[23] the court excused the identical reproduction of plaintiff's work in thumbnails as being transformative in nature because they served an entirely different function than the copyrighted work. In the same case, the transformative use concept was also applied to the making of temporary cache copies of a copyrighted work in a computer because this mechanical process facilitated access to the Internet.[24]

Despite its seductive charm and approbation in the case law, the transformative use doctrine is neither supported by the language of the statute or the legislative history. There are sound reasons not to limit fair use to uses that transform or alter the copyrighted work. To do so would exclude some uses that are consistent with the law and policy of fair use. Most important, a narrowly conceived reading of fair use would run at cross-purposes to the language of the preamble such as the making of multiple copies for classroom use and copying in the furtherance of

---

dissenting); *Dow Jones & Co., Inc. v. Board of Trade*, 546 F. Supp. 113 (S.D.N.Y 1982).

[19] 467 F.3d 244 (2d Cir. 2006).

[20] 448 F.3d 605 (2d Cir. 2006).

[21] For a criticism of the productive/transformative use concept, see Paul Goldstein, Copyright § 12.2.2(c) (3d ed. 2014).

[22] *Leadsinger, Inc. v. BMG Music Publ'g*, 512 F.3d 522 (9th Cir. 2008).

[23] 508 F.3d 1146 (9th Cir. 2007).

[24] *Id.*

scholarship or research. Such copying is hardly "transformative," yet it clearly advances "the Progress of Science and the useful Arts." In addition, an underlying theory of fair use must support non-transformative but meritorious uses consistent with the public interest in the dissemination of information.

The transformative use theory of fair use has its obvious limits and was specifically rejected in *Sony Corp. of America v. Universal City Studios* (the *Betamax* case),[25] where private, noncommercial taping of "free" television programming for time-shifting purposes[26] was found to be a fair use. The use made by the defendant did not fall into any of those listed in the preamble to § 107. It was clearly not a transformative use, but merely copying for the sake of convenience. Rather than limiting fair use to transformative use, the Supreme Court viewed fair use in much broader terms, as an equitable rule of reason to be determined case-by-case. In upholding the fair use defense, the Court focused on the economic impact of the use on the incentives to produce copyrighted works: whether the use was commercial or nonprofit. The Court found no harm to the market from defendant's private noncommercial use of the copyrighted material on "free" television broadcasts. In sum, the *Betamax* case shows that one can successfully assert fair use even if the use does not fall squarely within those listed in the preamble, and even if it is far from being a productive use that transforms the copyrighted work. Generally, however, the defense of fair use is much easier to prove when defendant has made a productive use, rather than an ordinary or reproductive use, of the copyright owner's work.[27]

[C] Economic Analysis of Fair Use: Of Transactions Costs and Complementary Use

The application of fair use in *Betamax* (and fair use in general) has been explained and justified in economic terms as a legal means of avoiding market failure. Copyright law establishes a system of property rights that strikes a balance between rules that encourage optimal incentives to create original works and rules that facilitate the optimal dissemination of those same works. Fair use helps to establish this balance and is appropriate in situations where the transaction costs in negotiating a license between a user and a copyright owner would impede a mutually beneficial exchange between the copyright owner and the user of the work.[28] Forced to negotiate a license with the copyright owner,

---

[25] 464 U.S. 417 (1984). The Supreme Court reversed the Ninth Circuit Court of Appeals, which rejected the fair use defense and had based its decision on a productive use theory of fair use. *See Universal City Studios, Inc. v. Sony Corp. of Am.*, 659 F.2d 963, 970 (9th Cir. 1981).

[26] To "time-shift" means to copy a television program for viewing at a later, more convenient time.

[27] *See Pac. & S. Co., v. Duncan*, 744 F.2d 1490 (11th Cir. 1984).

[28] For the pioneering elaboration of these ideas, see Wendy Gordon, *Fair Use as Market Failure: A Structural and Economic Analysis of the* Betamax *Case and Its Predecessors*, 82 Colum. L. Rev. 1600 (1982). *See also* William Landes & Richard Posner, *An Economic Analysis of Copyright Law*, 18 J. Legal Stud. 325 (1989) (remarking that fair use arises where "costs of a voluntary exchange are so high relative to the benefits that no such exchange is feasible between a user of a copyrighted work and its owner"). For a more recent analysis of the economics of fair use and *Sony*, see Glynn S. Lunney, Jr., *Fair Use and Market Failure:* Sony *Revisited*, 82 B.U. L. Rev. 975 (2002), and Wendy Gordon, *The "Market Failure" and Intellectual Property: A Response to Professor Lunney*, 82 B.U. L. Rev. 1031 (2002).

researchers engaging in private photocopying or television viewers who wish to see their favorite show at a later time would forgo their activity rather than absorbing the search and negotiation costs. The same could be said of a school teacher who wishes to make copies of a work for his or her students. Although nonproductive, these uses are socially desirable and disseminate the copyrighted work without undermining its economic value.

One can apply the same transaction cost analysis in justifying the legality of certain productive uses of copyrighted works. For example, it is generally acknowledged that a book reviewer has a fair use privilege to quote brief passages from a book. Absent fair use, the costs of negotiating a voluntary exchange may be so high relative to the potential benefits that the reviewer may decide to abandon the project. Moreover, the copyright owner would license the reviewer at no charge and benefit from the free advertising that the review would bring. One might say that the review is a complement of copyrighted work rather than a substitute for the copyrighted original.[29] At the least, a book review operates in an entirely different market, does not displace the need for the original work, and may even expand the demand for the book. Thus, the fair use doctrine avoids the costs of transactions in situations where the outcome would be the same, even if negotiations had taken place, and where the benefits of the use greatly outweigh the potential harm to the market for the copyrighted work.

Adherence to the economic approach has tended to narrow the scope of fair use, limiting the defense to situations where market failure is present and economic harm to the copyrighted work is absent. As such, the market approach to fair use has been criticized as failing to comprehend basic principles of copyright law and fair use,[30] those that embody cultural values as well as economic ones. More specifically, critics of the economic approach point out that a more commodious fair use doctrine, based on the "public interest," may be important in assuring the continued creation of new works incorporating preexisting materials — and in promoting the wide dissemination of works to end users. In other words, "fair use" serves the cultural interests of both creators and consumers — two groups that are, in any event, becoming more and more difficult to distinguish in the new technological environment.

§ 10.06 THE FOUR CRITERIA

Whether or not the use falls into one of the enumerated categories of the preamble to § 107, one must apply the four factors set forth in the second part of the section to determine whether the use is fair. The four factors that follow the preamble are the heart of the fair use determination. Section 107 states as follows:

> In determining whether the use made of a work in any particular case is a fair use the factors to be considered shall include —

---

[29] *See Ty, Inc. v. Publ'ns Int'l Ltd.*, 292 F.3d 512, 518 (7th Cir. 2002).

[30] *See* Alfred C. Yen, *When Authors Won't Sell: Parody, Fair Use, and Efficiency in Copyright Law*, 62 U. Colo. L. Rev. 79 (1991); Anastasia P. Winslow, *Rapping on a Revolving Door: An Economic Analysis of Parody and Campbell v. Acuff-Rose Music, Inc.*, 69 S. Cal. L. Rev. 767 (1996).

(1) the purpose and character of the use, including whether such use is of a commercial nature or is for nonprofit educational purposes;

(2) the nature of the copyrighted work;

(3) the amount and substantiality of the portion used in relation to the copyrighted work as a whole; and

(4) the effect of the use upon the potential market for or value of the copyrighted work.

According to the legislative history, the four factors represent a codification of fair use.[31] One might ask why Congress would wish to codify the common law of fair use, with all its disarray and its questionable applicability to a world of new technologies and nonprint media. The goal was not merely to incorporate the past but also to allow for a flexible and dynamic future. The House Report states:

> Beyond a very broad statutory explanation of what fair use is and some of the criteria applicable to it, the courts must be free to adapt the doctrine to particular situations on a case-by-case basis. Section 107 is intended to restate the present judicial doctrine of fair use, not to change, narrow, or enlarge it in any way.[32]

Despite Congress' intention to codify fair use, § 107 is, in some important ways, a departure from past practice. First, the major criteria in determining fair use are made explicit for the first time. Second, and more important, is that the court must consider *all* four enumerated factors in determining fair use. The inquiry, however, need not be limited only to those factors. The language "shall include" indicates that the court can, in its discretion, consider other factors as well,[33] such as lack of good faith[34] and industry custom or practice.[35]

Practical application of § 107's four factors has not led to predictable results. In a given case, one may find majority and dissenting opinions disagreeing completely on the application of each factor.[36] This is hardly surprising. The factors are broadly stated, overlapping, and vague, and the legislative history provides little insight as to their meaning, what weight to give them, or how they interrelate. Most post-1976 Act cases dealing with fair use apply the four criteria in mechanical fashion.[37]

---

[31] H.R. Rep. No. 94-1476, at 66 (1976). One can trace the four-factor approach back to *Folsom v. Marsh* in 1841, 9 F. Cas. 342 (C.C.D. Mass. 1841) (No. 4901). In fact, the factors in § 107 differ from that early case only by the addition of the second factor, the nature of the copyrighted work.

[32] H.R. Rep. No. 94-1476, at 66 (1976).

[33] Section 101 defines "including" and "such as" as illustrative, not limitative.

[34] *See Roy Export Co. Establishment v. Columbia Broad. Sys., Inc.*, 503 F. Supp. 1137 (S.D.N.Y. 1980), *aff'd*, 672 F.2d 1095 (2d Cir. 1982).

[35] *See Use Triangle Publ'ns, Inc. v. Knight-Ridder Newspapers, Inc.*, 626 F.2d 1171 (5th Cir. 1980).

[36] *Compare, e.g.*, Justice O'Connor's majority opinion in *Harper & Row, Publishers, Inc. v. Nation Enters.*, 471 U.S. 539 (1985), *with* Justice Brennan's dissent in that case.

[37] For a criticism of the standard mechanical application the process, see Judge Posner's opinion in *Ty, Inc. v. Publ'ns Int'l, Ltd*, 292 F.3d 512, 522 (7th Cir. 2002) ("The important point is simply that . . . the four factors are a checklist of things to be considered rather than a formula for decision; and likewise the list of statutory purposes. . . . Because the factors and purposes are not exhaustive, Ty can get nowhere in defending the judgment by arguing that some or even all of them lean against the defense

Invariably, each factor is examined in sequence, the court focusing on one or more of the factors — often the fourth factor of market effect — in coming to a "reasoned" judgment.[38]

Part II. THE FOUR FACTORS INDIVIDUALLY EXAMINED

§ 10.07 FIRST FACTOR: THE PURPOSE AND CHARACTER OF THE USE

Like the preamble, the first factor in § 107 focuses on the nature and purpose of the use. In applying the first criteria, the courts invariably examine whether a defendant's use of a copyrighted work constitutes a productive or transformative use as discussed in § 10.05. In fact, transformative use considerations launch or even dominate the analysis in determining the nature and purpose of the use. The first criteria provides, however, further guidance about the meaning of fair use by emphasizing the distinction between commercial and nonprofit educational use. A nonprofit educational use is more likely to be a fair use because it is less inclined to harm the market for the copyrighted work than would a commercial use.[39] The focus on the economic impact of the use shows this factor's obvious connection with the fourth factor, the effect of the use on the potential market for the copyrighted work.

A commercial use is one that earns a profit and, as such, does not lose its commercial character even though it is ultimately intended for education, news reporting, or any of the other purposes set forth in the preamble to § 107.[40] As one court stated, "[t]he fair-use doctrine is not a license for corporate theft, empowering a court to ignore a copyright whenever it determines the underlying work contains material of possible public importance."[41] Thus, a claim of "news reporting" may sometimes be just a pretext for copying a work. In *Murphy v. Millennium Radio Group, LLC*,[42] the court held that it was not fair use for a radio station to post a

---

of fair use. The question is whether . . . the use of the photos is a fair use because it is the only way to prepare a collectors' guide.").

[38] For an empirical study of fair use cases see Barton Beebe, *An Empirical Study of U.S. Copyright Fair Use Opinions, 1978–2005*, 156 U. Pa. L. Rev. 549 (2008) (concluding that courts rely primarily on the first and fourth factors).

[39] *See Encyclopedia Britannica Educ. Corp. v. Crooks*, 542 F. Supp. 1156 (W.D.N.Y. 1982); *Wihtol v. Crow*, 309 F.2d 777 (8th Cir. 1962); *Sony Corp. of Am. v. Universal City Studios, Inc.*, 464 U.S. 417 (1984).

[40] *See Ass'n of Am. Med. Colls. v. Mikaelian*, 571 F. Supp. 144 (E.D. Pa. 1983), *aff'd*, 734 F.2d 3 (3d Cir. 1984). In *Mikaelian*, defendant copied test questions from the Medical College Admissions Test for use in booklets designed for a test preparation course. The court found a commercial rather than a nonprofit educational use. "Educational purpose" was defined as the free dissemination of information. Defendant's course cost $485, hardly free, and was profitmaking. *See also Twin Peaks Prod., Inc. v. Publ'ns, Int'l, Ltd.*, 996 F.2d 1366 (2d Cir. 1993) (holding that a companion book to the television show, *Twin Peaks*, that meticulously summarized the plot of the eight shows was commercial use).

[41] *Iowa State Univ. Research Found., Inc. v. Am. Broad. Cos.*, 621 F.2d 57, 61 (2d Cir. 1980).

[42] 650 F.3d 295 (3rd Cir. 2011); *See also Balsley v. LFP, Inc.*, 691 F.3d 747 (6th Cir. 2012) (reprinting

photo of two of its anchors receiving a "Best of New Jersey" award, without any accompanying commentary, and to invite users to alter the image using photo-manipulation software, without paying the photographer.

In short, users should not be able to profit from a copyrighted work without paying the copyright owner.[43]

Generally, if a challenged use of a copyrighted work is for commercial gain, a presumption against fair use arises.[44] A commercial purpose will not conclusively negate a finding of fair use, but "a court should not strain to apply the fair use defense when it is being invoked by a profit-making defendant."[45] Conversely, a clear nonprofit educational use would constitute an important indication of fair use.[46] In addition, the fact that a work is used in judicial proceedings will also weigh in favor of fair use.[47]

In considering the first factor, courts have examined purposes other than whether the use is a commercial or nonprofit educational use. For example, a use made in bad faith is less likely to be a fair use because fair use presupposes good faith and fair dealing.[48] A use made in bad faith has been found where the defendant has knowingly exploited a stolen manuscript or engaged in verbatim copying without any effort to obtain permission from the copyright owner or to cite the copyright owner as the source of the material.[49] Bad faith may weigh against a finding a fair use but is not dispositive if there are other factors favoring fair use.[50]

Alternatively, in *Hustler Magazine, Inc. v. Moral Majority, Inc.*,[51] fair use was sustained for a defendant who had used a copyrighted work to defend himself against personal attack. *Hustler* magazine had published an advertisement that parodied the Reverend Jerry Falwell by portraying his first sexual encounter as an incestuous one with his mother in an outhouse. Outraged, Falwell reproduced almost a million copies of the advertisement and sent them to his followers for

wet t-shirt photo of TV newswoman in *Hustler* magazine's "Hot News Babes" feature was not a fair use); *Monge v. Maya Magazines, Inc.*, 688 F.3d 1164 (9th Cir. 2012) (publishing photos of celebrity pop singer's clandestine wedding in celebrity gossip magazine was not a fair use).

43 *See Harper & Row, Publishers, Inc. v. Nation Enters.*, 471 U.S. 539 (1985).

44 *See Sony Corp. of Am. v. Universal City Studios, Inc.*, 464 U.S. 417, 451 (1984) ("If the intended use is for commercial gain, that [meaningful] likelihood [of future harm] may be presumed.").

45 *Ass'n of Am. Med. Colls. v. Mikaelian*, 571 F. Supp. 144, 153 (E.D. Pa. 1983).

46 *See* H.R. Rep. No. 94-1476, at 66-67 (1976).

47 *See, e.g., Bond v. Blum*, 317 F.3d 385 (4th Cir. 2003) (holding that it was a fair use to copy the entirety of plaintiff's autobiographical manuscript relevant in a custody proceeding).

48 *See Time, Inc. v. Bernard Geis Assocs.*, 293 F. Supp. 130, 146 (S.D.N.Y. 1968); *see also Harper & Row, Publishers, Inc. v. Nation Enters.*, 471 U.S. 539 (1985).

49 *See Marcus v. Rowley*, 695 F.2d 1171 (9th Cir. 1983); *see also Harper & Row, Publishers, Inc. v. Nation Enters.*, 471 U.S. 539 (1985); *Iowa State Univ. Research Found., Inc. v. Am. Broad. Cos.*, 621 F.2d 57 (2d Cir. 1980); *Roy Export Co. Establishment v. Columbia Broad. Sys. Inc.*, 503 F. Supp. 1137 (S.D.N.Y. 1980), *aff'd*, 672 F.2d 1095 (2d Cir. 1982).

50 *See, e.g., NXIVM Corp. v. Ross Inst.*, 364 F.3d 471 (2d Cir. 2004) (finding bad faith where defendants knew access to plaintiff's work was unauthorized, but nonetheless holding that the use of selected excerpts for the purpose of criticism was a fair use).

51 796 F.2d 1148 (9th Cir. 1986).

fundraising purposes. Despite the commercial purpose and the verbatim copying, the court found the purpose of the copying reasonable as comment to rebut the derogatory nature of *Hustler*'s ad.[52] *Hustler* shows that a use can be fair even though it is commercial when other equitable considerations can be shown.

Whether commercial use, nonprofit educational use, or use made in good faith, a court must still consider the three remaining factors before coming to its conclusion on the fair use issue.

§ 10.08 SECOND FACTOR: NATURE OF THE COPYRIGHTED WORK

The second factor reflects the view that to support the public interest, greater access should be allowed to some kinds of works than others. Because the ultimate goal of copyright law is to increase our fund of information, the fair use privilege is more extensive for works of information such as scientific, biographical, or historical works than for works of entertainment.[53] Thus, the second factor would allow wider use of a treatise on physics than a DVD of a rock concert. Similarly, if a work is unavailable or out of print, the need for public access and dissemination is greater, and, thus, the permissible scope of fair use is broader.[54] On the other hand, the fair use privilege may not be available at all for certain kinds of works particularly susceptible to harm from mass reproduction. For this reason the House Report would preclude all copying for studying or teaching from consumables such as workbooks, exercises, standardized tests, and answer sheets.[55] Any substantial amount of copying of the above materials in teaching situations would destroy the only available market for these works.[56]

Even if a work of information is involved, the fair use privilege narrows for an unpublished work.[57] The author's right to control the publication of the work may

---

[52] *See* H.R. Rep. No. 94-1476, at 73 (1976): "When a copyrighted work contains unfair, inaccurate, or derogatory information concerning an individual or institution, the individual or institution may copy and reproduce such parts of the work as are necessary to permit understandable comment on the statements made in the work."

[53] *See Sony Corp. of Am. v. Universal City Studios, Inc.*, 464 U.S. 417 (1984). For a discussion of fair use doctrine in the context of various different types of works, see Peter Decherney, *Communicating Fair Use: Norms, Myths, and the Avant-Garde*, 25 Law & Lit. 50 (2013) (discussing fair use myths in the area of American avant-garde and experimental filmmakers from the 1960s to the 1990s); Kate O'Neill, *The Content of Their Characters: J.D. Salinger, Holden Caulfield, Fredrik Colting*, 59 J. Copyright Soc'y 291 (2012) (analyzing the merits of J.D. Salinger's case against Fredrik Colting for copyright infringement); Michael Donaldson, *Refuge from the Storm: A Fair Use Safe Harbor for Non-Fiction Works*, 59 J. Copyright Soc'y 477 (2012) (analyzing the various aspects of the de facto safe harbor created by the courts for those seeking the protection of fair use when creating non-fiction works).

[54] *See* S. Rep. No. 94-473, at 64 (1975); H.R. Rep. No. 94-1476, at 67 (1976).

[55] H.R. Rep. No. 94-1476, at 69, 71 (1976). *See Ass'n of Am. Med. Colls. v. Mikaelian*, 571 F. Supp. 144, 153 (E.D. Pa. 1983).

[56] The same reason is given for a narrow fair use privilege in the case of newsletters as compared with mass circulation periodicals or scientific journals. *See* H.R. Rep. No. 94-1476, at 74 (1976).

[57] For a discussion of fair use in the context of unpublished works and an argument in favor of transformative fair use, see Robert E. Spoo, *"Ah, you publishing scoundrel!": A Hauntological Reading of Privacy, Moral Rights, and the Fair Use of Unpublished Works*, 25 Law & Lit. 85 (2013).

outweigh an extensive fair use privilege. This proved to be the critical factor in *Harper & Row, Publishers, Inc. v. Nation Enterprises.*[58] In *Harper & Row*, the *Nation* magazine obtained, through an undisclosed source, a stolen, as-yet unpublished manuscript of former President Gerald Ford's autobiography, which it hurriedly printed. The article scooped *Time* magazine's planned excerpt from the book, *A Time To Heal*, and *Time* cancelled its contract as a result. The Supreme Court rejected the *Nation*'s fair use defense. Despite the newsworthiness of the subject matter, and the *Nation*'s use of only 300 words verbatim from a 200,000 word manuscript, the Court concluded that, "the unpublished nature of a work is '[a] key, though not necessarily determinative, factor,' tending to negate a defense of fair use."[59]

Harper & Row spawned a number of controversial decisions involving fair use of unpublished works, mainly unpublished letters in serious biographies. That an unpublished work is less amenable to fair use was strongly reaffirmed in *Salinger v. Random House, Inc.*,[60] which involved copyrighted letters of the writer J.D. Salinger used by Ian Hamilton in his biography of the writer. The letters, although unpublished, were available to scholars in major libraries, and Hamilton incorporated substantial portions of them in his biography. Although publicly accessible, Salinger's letters did not lose their unpublished character because of that fact.[61] Enjoining publication of the biography, the court emphasized the unpublished nature of the letters as the principal factor in denying the fair use defense. It interpreted *Harper & Row* as holding that unpublished works normally enjoy complete protection against any copying. Thus, a biographer who copies more than minimal amounts of protected unpublished material should be enjoined.[62] A holding contrary to *Salinger* occurred two years later in *Wright v. Warner Books, Inc.*[63] Here, the court affirmed a summary judgment for the author and publisher of a biography of Richard Wright that had quoted and paraphrased a modest amount from his letters and journals. The court refused to lump all unpublished materials in one category for fair use analysis. In so doing, the court applied fair use in the traditional way by balancing the competing interests and weighing the enumerated fair use factors set forth in § 107.

These contradictory decisions left the protection of unpublished works in a confused state, making it a risky proposition for authors and publishers to use unpublished source materials. A remarkable outpouring of interest in the topic provoked much commentary and led to congressional hearings on proposed amendments to the Copyright Act. This ferment culminated in an amendment to § 107 of the Copyright Act[64] adding the following language at the end of that section: "The fact that a work is unpublished shall not itself bar a finding of fair use

---

58 471 U.S. 539 (1985).

59 *Harper & Row*, 471 U.S. at 554, (citing S. REP. No. 94-473, at 65 (1975)).

60 650 F. Supp. 413 (S.D.N.Y. 1986), *rev'd*, 811 F.2d 90 (2d Cir. 1987).

61 See *supra* §§ 4.02–4.07 for a discussion of publication.

62 *Salinger* was reconfirmed in dicta in *New Era Publ'ns Int'l v. Henry Holt & Co.*, 873 F.2d 576 (2d Cir. 1989).

63 953 F.2d 731 (2d Cir. 1991).

64 102 Pub. L. No. 492; 106 Stat. 3145 (1992).

if such finding is made upon consideration of all the above factors."[65]

The amendment applies to all unpublished works whether created before or after the date of the enactment. The purpose of this amendment, as indicated in the legislative history, is unambiguous: to ensure that courts do not erect a per se rule barring any fair use of unpublished works. In addition, each claim of fair use of an unpublished work should involve a careful consideration of all four statutory factors as well as any other factors the court deems relevant.[66] The House Report also approved of the statement in *Harper & Row* describing the unpublished nature of the work as a "key though not necessarily determinative factor tending to negate a defense of fair use."[67] It remains to be seen how much guidance this language will provide in a given case or to a publisher wishing to use an unpublished letter. The unpublished nature of the work will continue to be an important factor weighing against fair use but will not itself prohibit the use of work.[68]

§ 10.09 THIRD FACTOR: THE AMOUNT AND SUBSTANTIALITY OF THE PORTION USED IN RELATION TO THE COPYRIGHTED WORK AS A WHOLE

One must distinguish this third factor from the question of substantial similarity[69] because the fair use defense arises only *after* infringement is proved. This factor properly focuses on whether the defendant has taken more than is necessary to satisfy the specific fair use purpose. Self-defense in tort produces a helpful analogy. In tort law, the scope of the self-defense defense depends on necessity and proportionality: did the defendant need to defend himself, and was his reaction commensurate with the threat? Excessive force abrogates the privilege. Similarly, excessive copying not commensurate with the purpose of the use loses the privilege of fair use. This principle is often expressed in parody cases where the issue of fair use invariably focuses on whether the defendant has taken more of the copyright owner's work than is necessary to conjure up the original.[70]

The corollary principle is that verbatim copying invariably exceeds the purpose of the use. For example, a literary critic or biographer may need to quote liberally from plaintiff's work but may exceed fair use by quoting more than is necessary to make the biographical or critical point.[71] Thus, a literary critic, in evaluating an

---

[65] 17 U.S.C. § 107.

[66] *See* H.R. Rep. No. 836, at 9 (1992).

[67] 471 U.S. 539, 554 (1985); H.R. Rep. No. 836, at 9 (1992).

[68] For an assessment of the amendment, see Lynn I. Miller, *Fair Use, Biographers, and Unpublished Works: Life After H.R. 4412*, 40 J. Copyright Soc'y 349 (1993), and William M. Landes, *Copyright Protection of Letters, Diaries, and Other Unpublished Works: An Economic Approach*, 21 J. Legal Stud. 79 (1992).

[69] For a discussion of substantial similarity in proving copyright infringement, see *supra* § 9.04.

[70] *See infra* § 10.14 for a discussion of parody.

[71] *See Craft v. Kobler*, 667 F. Supp. 120 (S.D.N.Y. 1987) (rejecting fair use where the biographer of the musician Igor Stravinsky used excerpts from copyrighted material written by the composer and his assistant, Robert Craft). Even though the takings were a tiny part of the two-million-word Craft-

author's style, would not be allowed to quote two pages of a copyrighted work when two paragraphs would be adequate to support the critic's argument.

Questions of amount and substantiality of use have a qualitative, as well as quantitative, dimension.[72] Even small takings can exceed fair use when the essence of the work is taken. Accordingly, in *Harper & Row*, the verbatim copying of only 300 words out of 200,000 words of plaintiff's book was considered excessive because these words constituted the heart of the work.[73]

The third fair use factor has an obvious connection with the fourth — the harm to the market for the copyrighted work. Fair use is less likely when an entire work is reproduced because excessive copying may displace the need for the original and destroy its market.[74]

§ 10.10 FOURTH FACTOR: THE EFFECT OF THE USE UPON THE POTENTIAL MARKET FOR, OR VALUE OF, THE COPYRIGHTED WORK

The case law frequently states that this factor is the single most important element of fair use. The reason is easy to understand. If the market for the copyright owner's work is harmed, the incentives for creativity that the copyright monopoly is designed to encourage will not work. The fourth factor is related in one way or another to the other three factors, but perhaps most closely to the first factor where presumption of harm arises from commercial use of the copyrighted work.[75]

At one level, the market effect factor is circular in its reasoning: whether a use will affect the potential market for or value of the copyrighted work necessarily turns on whether the use will be proscribed. Thus, to avoid this circularity, a reviewing court must isolate those uses of a work most directly threatening to the incentives for creativity which copyright tries to protect. These incentives are most threatened when the infringing use tends to diminish the potential sale of the work, tends to interfere with its marketability, or fulfills the demand for the original.[76] Generally, copying that is complementary to, rather than a substitute for, the copyrighted work does not harm the market for the copyrighted work and is more easily regarded as fair use.[77] For example, in *Kelly v. Arriba Soft Corp.*,[78] defendant

Stravinsky writings, they were, from a qualitative standpoint, considered too numerous to justify defendant's biographical purpose. *See also Burnett v. Twentieth Century Fox Film Corp.*, 491 F. Supp. 2d 962 (C.D. Cal. 2007) (dismissing claim against animated TV series the *Family Guy* for 18-second scene featuring Carol Burnett's "Charwoman" character and lewd jokes, on fair use grounds).

[72] *See Meeropol v. Nizer*, 560 F.2d 1061 (2d Cir. 1977) (defendant's popular book on the Rosenberg trial used verbatim portions of 28 copyrighted letters, a total of 1957 words. The court considered this to be substantial despite constituting less than one percent of defendant's book, particularly since the words were featured prominently in promotional literature advertising the book).

[73] 471 U.S. 539, 569.

[74] *See Fisher v. Dees*, 794 F.2d 432, 437 (9th Cir. 1986).

[75] *See Sony Corp. of Am. v. Universal City Studios, Inc.*, 464 U.S. 417 (1984).

[76] *See Hustler Magazine, Inc. v. Moral Majority, Inc.*, 796 F.2d 1148 (9th Cir. 1986).

[77] *Ty, Inc. v. Publ'ns Int'l Ltd.*, 292 F.3d 512 (7th Cir. 2002) (holding that a publisher who placed photographs of Beanie Baby dolls in its collector guide engaged in a fair use).

Arriba operated an Internet website featuring a search engine that displayed its results as thumbnail pictures, some of which were plaintiff's copyrighted photographs. The Ninth Circuit sustained Arriba's fair use defense for the reproduction and display of plaintiff's copyrighted photographs as thumbnails. The court pointed out that Arriba's use of plaintiff's images did not supersede the need for the full-sized originals because the thumbnails served an entirely different function than Kelly's original images. It also improved access to the images on the Internet, directing users to the copyright owner's website where they could view or purchase the copyrighted work. Kelly was affirmed in *Perfect 10, Inc. v. Google, Inc.*,[79] where the court ruled that thumbnails of Perfect 10's copyrighted images are protected under fair use because they are both smaller in scale and serve an entirely different purpose than plaintiff's copyrighted images. The court determined that Perfect 10 did not produce sufficient evidence that the thumbnails harmed a potential market for the copyrighted work — such as the use of small images on cell phones.

Potential harm to the market, not actual harm, is the issue.[80] As for market effect, the court will consider not only the extent of market harm caused by the particular actions of the defendant, but also whether the widespread conduct of the kind that the defendant has engaged in would result in a substantially adverse impact on the potential market for the original.[81] Thus, actual harm need not be shown, although proof of quantifiable harm, such as a lost contract, is the best evidence of harm to the market for the work. The existence of a well-established licensing market can be determinative on the presence of market harm. For example, the existence of well-established markets for lyric reprint licenses and synchronization licenses has led two courts of appeals to conclude that making and selling karaoke products that display lyrics in conjunction with sound recordings of musical works is not a fair use.[82] Not only actual, but potential markets are taken into account. Thus, the fact that the copyright owner does not actually market copies of the work does not matter under the potential market language of § 107(4).[83] To prove potential market effect, plaintiff need only show a meaningful

---

[78] 336 F.3d 311 (9th Cir. 2003).

[79] 508 F.3d 1146 (9th Cir. 2007).

[80] *See, e.g., Meeropol v. Nizer*, 560 F.2d 1061 (2d Cir. 1977) (noting the fact that copyrighted letters had been out of print for 20 years did not necessarily mean they had no future market potential that could be injured). *See also Craft v. Kobler*, 667 F. Supp. 120 (S.D.N.Y. 1987) (finding harm to the potential market despite the fact that plaintiff's work was out of print).

[81] *See, e.g., L.A. News Serv. v. CBS Broad.*, Inc., 305 F.3d 924, 941 (9th Cir. 2002).

[82] *See, e.g., Leadsinger, Inc. v. BMG Music Publ'g*, 512 F.3d 522 (9th Cir. 2008); *Zomba Enters., Inc. v. Panorama Records, Inc.*, 491 F.3d 574 (6th Cir. 2007). *See also Elvis Presley Enters., Inc. v. Passport Video*, 349 F.3d 622 (9th Cir. 2003) (holding that 16-hour video documentary "The Definitive Elvis," that contained clips of every film and television appearance by Elvis, was not a fair use).

[83] *See Harper & Row, Publishers, Inc. v. Nation Enters.*, 471 U.S. 539 (1985); *see also WallData, Inc. v. L.A. County Sheriff's Dept.*, 447 F.3d 769 (9th Cir. 2006) (defendant installed the plaintiff's software on over 6,000 computers, but claimed that there was no harm to the plaintiff's market because, at any one time, there were never more than 3,663 copies in use (the number of licenses it had paid for). The court rejected this argument, because the plaintiff could not independently verify whether the defendant had complied with the claimed limitation; *Clean Flicks of Colo., LLC v. Soderbergh*, 433 F. Supp. 2d 1236 (D. Colo. 2006), where the declaratory judgment plaintiff claimed that, even though it was making and distributing edited copies of motion pictures for "family viewing," there was no harm to the copyright

likelihood of future harm by a preponderance of the evidence.

Part III. SPECIAL APPLICATIONS OF FAIR USE ANALYSIS: NEW TECHNOLOGIES, PARODY, AND THE FIRST AMENDMENT

§ 10.11 FAIR USE AND THE NEW REPRODUCTIVE TECHNOLOGIES: VIDEOTAPING, PHOTOCOPYING, INTERNET FILE SHARING

[A] Copyright and the New Reproductive Technologies: Generally

The doctrine of fair use originated in the nineteenth century when printed matter was virtually the only non-oral way to disseminate information. At that time, copying was done with pen in hand except for the few who had access to a printing press. With today's new reproductive technologies, anyone can reproduce and transmit a copyrighted work simply and inexpensively. The photocopying machine and videocassette recorder come to mind immediately. These devices, however, are only a small part of the radical changes that will take place in the way we receive and transmit information. In the future, the printed word may well become obsolete.[84] Despite these vast technological changes, the doctrine of fair use has changed little from its first judicial recognition in the nineteenth century.

Copying with the new technologies does not comport with the doctrine of fair use as traditionally formulated. For one, the doctrine has normally been invoked in *productive use* contexts where one author builds on the work of another. Second, fair use is normally denied when an entire work has been copied. By comparison, one who photocopies a chapter of a book or videotapes a film off the air is hardly a productive user but is reproducing an entire work for the same purpose and in the same medium as the original. Nonetheless, as the following sections on videotaping and photocopying will show, courts have rendered decisions that appear to contravene traditional fair use principles. As will be seen, they have employed fair use doctrine where the harm to plaintiff's market appears to be *de minimis* and a finding of infringement would suppress a useful new technology.

---

owner's market because it had bought an authorized copy for each copy that it made. The District Court said that this argument had "superficial appeal, but [that] it ignores the intrinsic value of the right to control the content of the copyrighted work."

[84] *See* David Ladd, *A Pavan for Print: Accommodating Copyright to the Tele-Technologies*, 29 J. Copyright Soc'y 246 (1982); *see also* I. Pool, Technologies of Freedom (1983).

[B] Videotaping: The *Betamax* Case

In the *Betamax* case,[85] plaintiff brought suit against the manufacturer of a video cassette recorder as a contributory infringer for supplying the means to the principal infringer, the home user, to infringe plaintiff's copyrighted works played on the public airwaves. Plaintiff asked for an injunction against Sony as well as profits and damages. In a narrow five-to-four decision, the Supreme Court held that off-the-air taping from the public airwaves for private (time-shifting) purposes constituted a fair use of the copyrighted work. For the majority, Justice Stevens reasoned that for this noncommercial use, harm to the market is not presumed and plaintiffs were not able to prove sufficiently future or potential harm from the time-shifting.[86] In dissent, Justice Blackmun argued that Congress intended to limit fair use to productive use contexts and that extensive reproduction use, as made by defendants, was an infringement unless specifically exempted.[87]

Off-the-air taping, even for noncommercial, educational purposes, cannot sustain a fair use defense if the economic harm to plaintiff is direct and apparent. Before *Betamax*, the most significant off-the-air taping case was *Encyclopedia Britannica Educational Corp. v. Crooks*.[88] In *Crooks*, defendant, a nonprofit corporation, had videotaped copyrighted films from television and distributed them to public school districts for educational purposes. The District Court issued a preliminary injunction despite defendant's claim that public education would be disrupted if the practice were enjoined. In refusing the fair use defense, the court emphasized that the substantiality of the copying and the harmful effect on plaintiff's market outweighed the noncommercial educational purpose of the copying.[89]

At first blush, the degree of the harm to plaintiff's market can account for the different results in *Betamax* and *Crooks*. But the cases have other distinguishing features. In *Crooks*, the court pointed out that defendants could have conveniently entered into a licensing agreement with plaintiffs.[90] In *Betamax*, however, the copier had no convenient, cost-justified way to negotiate a license.[91] Moreover, in *Betamax*, plaintiffs sued not only the direct copier, but also Sony, the manufacturer of the VCR, as a contributory infringer. The goal of the plaintiffs was not to resolve a dispute between two parties but rather to impose a court-ordered system of regulation on a new and valuable technology. Although the Court based its decision on different grounds, it may have been influenced by the general proposition that the judiciary is better at resolving disputes between parties in a single proceeding than at redistributing wealth, a function best left to the legislature. Many of these same difficult issues can be found in cases dealing with the equally complicated subject of photocopying.

---

[85] *Sony Corp. of Am. v. Universal City Studios, Inc.*, 464 U.S. 417 (1984).

[86] *Id.* at 456.

[87] *Id.* at 480–81.

[88] 542 F. Supp. 1156 (W.D.N.Y. 1982).

[89] *Id.* at 1179.

[90] *Id.* at 1176.

[91] This idea is discussed in Wendy J. Gordon, *Fair Use as Market Failure: A Structural and Economic Analysis of the* Betamax *Case and its Predecessors*, 82 Colum. L. Rev. 1600 (1982).

[C] Photocopying: *Williams & Wilkins*

It might seem old hat now, but the photocopying machine allows access to and dissemination of copyrighted works in ways that were once not thought possible. They have posed a dilemma for copyright law: how can a court, applying fair use in piecemeal litigation, balance the rights of copyright owners, the public interest in access to information, and the future of a new technology? In *Williams & Wilkins Co. v. United States*,[92] the Court of Claims held that the photocopying of an entire article from a specialized low circulation medical journal constituted fair use. The defendant, through its National Institutes of Health ("NIH") and the National Library of Medicine ("NLM"), photocopied and distributed articles to those requesting them. Generally, the defendant limited requests to no more than one article per journal, no more than 50 pages, and no more than a single copy of an article per request. The plaintiff, a publisher of limited circulation medical and scientific journals, claimed injury because relatively few lost subscriptions could make the difference between a profit and loss. Even though the NIH had photocopied millions of pages, the court found this activity a fair use because the plaintiff failed to prove future harm adequately. The small and speculative future harm to the plaintiff was outweighed by the certain harm to medical science if the photocopying was stopped. Thus, the public interest in medical science prevailed over the possible damage to the copyright owner.[93]

Since *Williams & Wilkins*, the pendulum seems to have swung against fair use in cases of systematic library photocopying. In *American Geophysical Union v. Texaco*,[94] the Second Circuit Court of Appeals held that a profit-seeking company's photocopying for research purposes of scientific journal articles is not a fair use. Like many companies, Texaco's corporate library subscribed to a number of scientific and technical journals. Texaco scientists, on learning of a journal article, would have it photocopied and kept for research purposes. As a defense to a class action brought by journal publishers, Texaco asserted that this practice was a fair use.[95] The court rejected the fair use defense. Even though Texaco was not gaining direct or immediate commercial advantage, its use was for archival purposes, which filled the same need for which additional subscriptions are normally sold, or for which photocopying licenses may be obtained. Texaco's photocopying, despite its research purpose, was not a "transformative" use. Rather, it was a superseding use because the company's systematic photocopying of articles in their entirety added nothing new or different to the original copyrighted work.

Texaco also argued that scientific research would be impaired without a fair use privilege for its photocopying. A contrary decision would burden the company with oppressive transaction costs every time a scientist wished to copy a journal article.

---

92 487 F.2d 1345 (1973), *aff'd by an equally divided court*, 420 U.S. 376 (1975).

93 For a critique of the court's reasoning, see David Ladd, *The Harm of the Concept of Harm in Copyright*, 30 J. COPYRIGHT SOC'Y 421 (1983).

94 37 F.3d 881 (2d Cir. 1994).

95 Texaco's defense under § 108 of the Act was rejected. First, § 108 is applicable only if the reproduction is made without commercial purpose. Here, the photocopying was made by a profit-seeking company for profit-motivated research. Second, § 108 permits the making of "no more than one copy" per customer. Texaco exceeded this limitation.

The court was unpersuaded, pointing out that much has changed since *Williams & Wilkins*.[96] The court found that Texaco's fears were illusory because the Copyright Clearance Center, which did not exist in the days of *Williams & Wilkins*, now provides an efficient licensing mechanism that would avoid administrative difficulty, wasteful delay, and inordinate expense in negotiating licenses with individual copyright owners.

Following much the same reasoning as Texaco, a divided en banc panel of the Sixth Circuit, in *Princeton University Press v. Michigan Document Services*,[97] concluded that copying excerpts of copyrighted books and providing compiled course materials to students by a copying service is not fair use. Defendant Michigan Document Services ("MDS") is a commercial copy shop that devotes a substantial portion of its business to creating "coursepacks" ordered by professors at the University of Michigan for use by their students. MDS did so for years without seeking permission from copyright owners. [Publishers whose works were affected brought suit against MDS.] In rejecting the defense of fair use, the court found that the first fair use factor, the purpose of the challenged use by the publishers, was not the students' use, but was commercial, driven by MDS's motive for profit. As commercial use, MDS bore the burden of rebutting the presumption that the unauthorized copying adversely affected the market for the copyrighted work. The court repudiated MDS's argument that it should consider only the adverse effect in terms of lost book sales rather than the impact on the market for licensing fees. Thus, the court found that the fourth factor clearly favored the plaintiff. Similarly, the court found the second and third weighed against fair use. As for the second factor (nature of the copyrighted work), the court noted that the works were creative material or expression that narrows the scope of fair use. As for the third factor, the substantiality of the copied material, the court found that the length and value of the portion weighed against a finding of fair use.

[D] Internet File Sharing: *A & M Records, Inc. v. Napster, Inc.*[98]

File compressing digital formats, such as "MP3,"[99] coupled with peer-to-peer networks, have facilitated the copying of massive amounts of music on the Internet. The Napster system, if not the first, was certainly the most famous of the peer-to-peer file sharing networks, permitting its users to exchange MP3 file audio recordings stored on individuals' hard drives. These functions were made possible by Napster software, provided free of charge on its website, that allowed a user to search the availability of a song and enabled its download onto the user's hard drive. Napster network servers continuously updated the links to millions of MP3 files that were indexed and displayed on the Napster website. Efficiently run and easy to use, the Napster system quickly attracted a vast following of avid users

---

[96] *See Williams & Wilkins*, 487 F.2d at 1356 (fearing that medicine and medical research would be seriously hurt if NIH and NLM were forbidden from engaging in photocopying).

[97] 99 F.3d 1381 (6th Cir. 1996).

[98] 239 F.3d 1004 (9th Cir. 2001).

[99] For a definition and description of MP3, see Douglass A. Downing et al., Dictionary of Computer and Internet Terms 329 (8th ed. 2003).

who could access and copy an almost unlimited quantity of digitally encoded sound recordings.

Members of the music industry brought suit against Napster, alleging contributory and vicarious infringement by facilitating the direct infringement of its users. Napster contended that its users did not directly infringe plaintiffs' copyrights because the users engaged in a fair use of the material. Napster argued that its software, like the Betamax VCR in *Sony*, was capable of substantial non-infringing uses. Among these uses, Napster contended that they included sampling, where users make temporary copies of a work before purchasing, and permissive distribution of recordings by both new and established artists. Referring to the successful "time shifting argument" in *Sony*, Napster also contended their users engaged in "space-shifting," where users access a sound recording through the Napster system that they already own in audio CD format. According to Napster, "space shifting" was as legitimate a use under fair use principles as was "time shifting" in the *Sony* case.

In rejecting Napster's fair use defense, the Ninth Circuit Court of Appeals applied the four factors and found in favor for the plaintiff on all. As for the first factor, the purpose and character of the use, the court concluded that the use was not transformative and was essentially commercial because users get something for free where they would ordinarily have to buy. The second and third factors cut against a finding of fair use because the copyrighted works were creative in nature and the defendants engaged in wholesale copying. The fourth factor, the effect on the market, weighed against a finding of fair use. The activity of the Napster users had a deleterious effect on the present and future market for music as well as the present market for CDs.

The court then focused on two specific uses that Napster had maintained were fair uses—sampling and "space-shifting." As for sampling, Napster argued that its users downloaded MP3 files to determine whether they wanted to purchase the CD. The court rejected this argument, concluding that the more music sampled, the less music purchased. Moreover, sampling had a harmful effect on the nascent market for downloaded music. Napster's "space shifting" argument, that users were downloading MP3 files to listen to music they already owned on audio CD, was also rejected as a fair use. Unlike the time shifters in *Sony*, who copy for private use in their homes, or those who copy CDs they own into a portable MP3 player,[100] the Napster software made copyrighted music potentially available to millions of other individuals, not just to the original owner of the CD.

The court had little difficulty in rebuffing Napster's fair use defense as well as finding Napster liable for contributory and vicarious infringement. But *Napster* was only the first challenge the music industry faced in the peer-to-peer wars. Much more troublesome are second-generation software such as Grokster and KaZaa, that, unlike Napster, do not use a central server with a directory of files

---

100 *See Recording Indus. Ass'n of Am. v. Diamond Multimedia Sys. Inc.*, 180 F.3d 1072, 1079 (9th Cir. 1999) ("Rio [a portable MP3 player] merely makes copies in order to render portable, or 'space shift,' those files that already reside on a user's hard drive . . . [s]uch copying is paradigmatic noncommercial personal use.").

available for download.[101] *Napster* and the peer-to-peer cases reveal that something significantly different has emerged concerning the use of copyrighted works in digital networks. Not long ago, one could assert as a general principle that private copying for personal use was presumptively fair, or at least, nonthreatening to the market for the copyrighted work. Today, this general principle is no longer appropriate because digital networks have blurred irrevocably the distinction between private and public uses.

[E] Walking the Fair Use Tightrope: Case by Case Litigation Versus Industry-Wide Resolution[102]

Can the results in *Betamax*, *Williams & Wilkins*, *Crooks*, *Texaco*, *MDS*, and *Napster* be reconciled? From these cases one finds two divergent tendencies. One general tendency is revealed in *Betamax* and *Williams & Wilkins*: when confronted with disputes involving the new technologies, courts will use restraint in evoking industry-wide solutions best left to legislatures. One detects fear that a finding of infringement will suppress a new and useful technology. As a result, copyright owners will not fare well when their rights are pitted against a new technological development. In sum, courts are less willing to impose liability when the costs imposed on the public by limiting the use of a copyrighted work are not offset by a correspondingly greater incentive for authors to produce. Accordingly, in *Betamax* and *Williams & Wilkins*, the courts were persuaded that judgment against defendants would deprive the public of videotaping and photocopying without greatly encouraging copyright owners to create more copyrighted works.

By comparison, *Crooks*, *Texaco*, *MDS*, and *Napster* reflect the tendency found in current fair use decisions. In these cases, the courts emphasized the direct harm suffered by the plaintiff, the commercial nature of the defendant's use, the nonproductive (nontransformative) nature of the defendant's use, and the relatively low transaction costs in obtaining a license for the use of the copyrighted work. Thus, a decision for the plaintiffs would not unduly impede access and dissemination of copyrighted works in these educational and corporate settings.

Reviewing the several cases involving the new technologies leaves the impression that the litigation process is not capable of solving the issues raised. The reason goes further than the unwieldy and unpredictable doctrine of fair use and is linked to the nature of the litigation process. Court cases are brought to decide grievances between parties at a particular point in time. But in complicated new technology cases, the process breaks down. In these cases, a decision can have far reaching ramifications and can result in one court imposing a de facto system of regulation on an entire industry. For example, in *Betamax*, the Supreme Court was bound by the record developed at trial in the mid-seventies but was called upon to reconcile changing technology with the law as it existed at the time of the appeal

---

[101] Other peer-to-peer cases are discussed at *infra* § 9.07[C].

[102] For a discussion of the type of judicial interpretation required in copyright fair use cases and how judicial interpretation currently falls short, see Rebecca Tushnet, *Judges as Bad Reviewers: Fair Use and Epistemological Humility*, 25 Law & Lit. 20 (2013).

some 10 years later.[103] Other mechanisms, both public and private, seem better able to resolve the challenge of the new reproductive technologies than piecemeal litigation. In short, legislatures, not courts, are much better at finding industry-wide solutions that orchestrate the interests of all concerned rather than just the interests of the parties to a single dispute.

Congress has taken the industry-wide approach to both new and perennial fair use dilemmas in several ways. One method is by an outright exemption of the use from copyright infringement.[104] This approach is evident in the library photocopying provisions of § 108, discussed in subsection § 10.12[A], below. Another method is by the use of voluntary guidelines detailing proper uses of copyrighted works.[105] This approach is discussed in subsection [B], involving classroom photocopying. In addition to legislative efforts, private collecting agencies, such as the Copyright Clearance Center, may provide an efficient mechanism to enforce the rights of copyright owners.

§ 10.12 AVOIDING FAIR USE DETERMINATIONS: INDUSTRY-WIDE RESOLUTION OF THE PHOTOCOPYING DILEMMA

[A] Library Photocopying Under § 108[106]

To avoid the uncertainties of general fair use doctrine and be mindful of the result in *Williams & Wilkins*, Congress has singled out library photocopying for separate treatment under § 108 of the 1976 Act.[107] This provision details the circumstances in which libraries and archives may reproduce and distribute copies of works without infringing copyright. In general, § 108 allows library photocopying for scholarly purposes, unless it is systematic and is a substitute for purchase or subscription. Section 108 sets forth the requirements for exemption, but § 107 is still available for those acts exceeding the exemption.[108]

---

[103] This idea is expressed in Douglas G. Baird, *Changing Technology and Unchanging Doctrine: Sony Corporation v. Universal Studios, Inc.*, 1984 Sup. Ct. Rev. 237.

[104] These specific exemptions and limitations are generally found in 17 U.S.C. §§ 108–122. An exemption is sometimes combined with a compulsory license.

[105] For an analysis of best practices statements, which in the fair use context establish voluntary guidelines of what should constitute a fair use, see Jennifer E. Rothman, *Best Intentions: Reconsidering Best Practices Statements in the Context of Fair Use and Copyright Law*, 57 J. Copyright Soc'y 371 (2010); *see also* Peter Jaszi, *Getting to Best Practices: A Personal Voyage Around Fair Use*, 57 J. Copyright Soc'y 315 (2010). For a discussion of the effects of the Documentary Filmmakers' Statement for Best Practices in Fair Use and specifically about its influence in teaching documentary filmmakers abut the fair use doctrine, see Michael C. Donaldson, *Fair Use: What a Difference a Decade Makes*, 57 J. Copyright Soc'y 331 (2010).

[106] Section 108 is discussed in fuller detail in this treatise in Chapter 8, § 8.05. *See* James M. Treece, *Library Photocopying*, 24 UCLA L. Rev. 1025 (1977).

[107] 17 U.S.C. § 108.

[108] *But see* U.S. Copyright Office, Report of the Register of Copyrights: Library Reproduction of Copyrighted Works (17 U.S.C. § 108) 93–104 (1983) (maintaining that copying beyond the § 108 exemption cannot be defended on general fair use grounds of § 107).

[B] Multiple Copies for Classroom Use

Classroom teachers have always needed to duplicate materials for their students, and most have probably done so without considering copyright law. Congress recognized that need: "multiple copies for classroom use" is listed in the preamble to § 107, and nonprofit educational use is explicitly mentioned in the first factor for determining fair use.[109] Although classroom use could be considered a classic fair use context, the case law has been less than accommodating. In *Wihtol v. Crow*,[110] for example, a high school teacher distributed about 48 duplicate copies of an arrangement he made of plaintiff's copyrighted song. Despite the nonprofit educational use, the court rejected the teacher's defense of fair use.[111]

To remedy the uncertainty and vagueness of the law, Congress wished to give special treatment to teachers who make multiple copies of a copyrighted work for classroom use. The help, however, fell short of the blanket exemption for which the educators lobbied.[112] Instead, educators, authors, and publisher groups produced an Agreement on Guidelines for Classroom Copying in Not-For-Profit Educational Institutions (hereinafter the "Guidelines"),[113] indicating the minimum threshold for fair use. The Guidelines are not part of the 1976 Act but are included in the House Report. They are presented as providing a minimum standard for copying, and exceeding them can still be defended as fair use under § 107.[114]

The Guidelines apply to not-for-profit educational institutions and are limited to books and periodicals. Part I of the Guidelines sets forth what a teacher can copy for his own scholarly or educational use. Part II deals with the more controversial making of multiple copies for classroom use. Multiple copying for classroom use must meet four basic criteria: (1) brevity, (2) spontaneity, (3) cumulative effect, and (4) a notice of copyright. The Guidelines further specify in detail the meaning of the above criteria. For example, the Guidelines describe "brevity" as "[e]ither a complete article, story or essay of less than 2,500 words or an excerpt from any prose work of not more than 1,000 words or 10% of the work. . . . "[115]

As for spontaneity, the decision to use the work and the moment of its use are to be so close in time that it would be impossible to ask for permission. As for cumulative effect, the copying must be for only one course in the school in which the copies are made. From this brief overview, one might conclude that much classroom copying exceeds fair use. The Guidelines, however, provide *minimum*

---

[109] 17 U.S.C. § 107.

[110] 309 F.2d 777 (8th Cir. 1962).

[111] *See also MacMillan Co. v. King*, 223 F. 862 (D. Mass. 1914).

[112] *See* H.R. Rep. No. at 66–67; *see also* 17 U.S.C. § 504(c)(2) (providing that teachers and other nonprofit users of copyrighted materials cannot be sued for statutory damages).

[113] H.R. Rep. No. 94-1476, at 68–70 (1976); *see also* Guidelines for Educational Uses of Music, H.R. Rep. No. 94-1476, at 70–74; 1981 Guidelines for Off-Air Taping of Copyrighted Works for Educational Use, H.R. Rep. No. 97-495, 97th Cong., 2d Sess. (1982).

[114] H.R. Rep. No. 94-1476, at 72 (1976).

[115] *Id.* at 68.

thresholds, and copying exceeding them can be justified under traditional fair use analysis.[116]

The Guidelines have become an issue in one litigated case, *Marcus v. Rowley*,[117] which provides an instructive example of how easy it is to violate the Guidelines and what is not educational fair use. In *Marcus*, defendant copied eleven of twenty-four pages from plaintiff's cake decorating booklet for use in her food service career classes. Before turning to the Guidelines, the court rejected the fair use defense under § 107. The court found that defendant's work was used for the same purpose as plaintiff's and that defendant showed bad faith in making no attempt to secure permission for the use. In addition, the use made was qualitatively and quantitatively a substantial copy. These aspects dictated against a finding of fair use despite the informational nature of plaintiff's work and lack of specific evidence on the market effect of the use. Moreover, defendant's copying violated all aspects of the Guidelines. Copying clearly exceeded the brevity factor. As for spontaneity, defendant had enough time to request permission to use the work. Defendant's use of the work in several classes failed the cumulative effect criterion as well. Finally, the requirement that each copy bear a copyright notice in the owner's name was also violated.[118]

[C] A Private Collecting Agency: The Copyright Clearance Center

An exclusive copyright, whether for reproduction or performance purposes, is only as good as the ability to enforce it. Massive unauthorized reproductions of copyrighted works take place at ever-increasing rates at such locations as corporate and law libraries. In principle, each of these unauthorized reproductions represents a lost royalty. In reality, however, policing the reproduction right, even if possible, would be prohibitively expensive if not impossible for the copyright owner. The Copyright Clearance Center ("CCC"), a nonprofit organization, was founded in 1978 to serve as a middleman between publishers and users. It functions as a clearinghouse that licenses the right to photocopy for a fee and distributes the collected revenues to copyright owners whose works were copied.

The CCC recovers licensing fees in two distinct ways. The first, the Transactional Reporting System, works on an individualized basis and depends on self-reporting by users. The first page of a covered journal article or other work informs the user of the licensing fee set by the publisher and instructs the user

---

[116] For a proposal of a new model for evaluating educational fair use, the administrative agency, see David A. Simon, *Teaching Without Infringement: A New Model for Educational Fair Use*, 20 Fordham Intell. Prop. Media & Ent. L.J. 453 (2010). For a discussion of fair use in the context of academic scholarship, see Deborah Gerhardt & Madelyn Wessel, *Fair Use and Fairness on Campus*, 11 N.C.J.L. & Tech. 461 (2010).

[117] 695 F.2d 1171 (9th Cir. 1983).

[118] Another development on the teacher photocopying front occurred when several publishing houses and the Association of American Publishers sued New York University faculty members and an off-campus copying center for infringement due to classroom photocopying practices. *See Addison-Wesley Publ'g Co. v. N.Y. Univ.*, No. 82 Civ. 833 (ADS), * (S.D.N.Y. May 31, 1983). The copying center consented to a stipulated judgment and the university professors agreed to observe the Guidelines.

how to forward the fee to the CCC. After deducting for costs, the CCC distributes royalties to the copyright owners. The second collecting method, the Annual Authorization Service ("AAS"), was designed to reduce the compliance costs associated with the Transactional Reporting System. Under AAS, a representative sample is taken from the users' photocopy machines, from which a statistical model estimates the fees owed. To cut monitoring costs further, the CCC has offered to users an alternative statistical method that avoids individual monitoring of photocopy machines. The CCC has developed statistical models of copying in some twenty industries (e.g., chemical companies). From this statistical model, a user's annual fee is determined based on the amount of copying in a particular industry and the average prices charged by publishers. Users are then free to copy all works registered with the CCC, without limitation on the number of copies made.[119]

§ 10.13 REVERSE ENGINEERING OF COMPUTER SOFTWARE: *SEGA ENTERPRISES LTD. v. ACCOLADE, INC.*

To what extent should software developers be permitted to manipulate their competitors' products to discover the ideas on which those products are based? For example, can a third party reproduce the copyrighted work, not to displace the need for the original, but for the purpose of analyzing the copyrighted work and unearthing its ideas from its expression, so that the third party may create a noninfringing or compatible work? Whether such intermediate copying constitutes a fair use has become a controversial issue in the context of computer software copyright. This need to make intermediate copies for purposes of analysis arises from the inherent nature of computer software.

There are basically three ways in which one can understand a computer program: one can read about the program, read the program itself, or observe the program by running it. Of these methods, reading the program is superior for gaining a complete understanding of it. This can be accomplished, however, only if access to the program is available in a humanly readable form. The problem is that, in most cases, software owners distribute their products only in object code, a form of machine language (a series of 0s and 1s) largely unintelligible to human beings. Thus, to obtain access to the ideas embodied in the program written in object code, a programmer must first translate it into source code, a humanly intelligible language. This entails a process of reverse engineering called "disassembly or decompilation"[120] that takes the finished program apart, translates it, and works

---

[119] *See generally* http://www.copyright.com/ (website for the Copyright Clearance Center) and Stanley M. Besen & Sheila Nararaj Kirby, Compensating Creators of Intellectual Property: Collectives That Collect (1989).

[120] The distinction is sometimes made between decompilation and disassembly. Decompilation is a procedure by which a high level representation of a program is derived from a machine language program. Disassembly is a procedure for translating the machine language program into an assembly language program. Despite this distinction, the terms are often used interchangeably. Whatever technique is used, the legal issues are identical. *See generally* Office of Technology Assessment, Finding a Balance: Computer Software, Intellectual Property, and the Challenge of Technological Change 7,

backward to see how it operates. Once the object code is translated into source code, a skilled programmer can then analyze it to develop noninfringing, compatible or competing software. The problem is that copyright infringement may occur at several stages of the process. Disassembly or decompilation involves reproducing the copyrighted work, presumably an infringement of copyright, even though the ultimate goal of this "intermediate" copying is to produce a noninfringing work.[121]

In *Sega Enterprises, Ltd. v. Accolade, Inc.*,[122] the Ninth Circuit Court of Appeals held that disassembly or decompilation of a computer program to produce a compatible, noninfringing program is a fair use. In this case, the defendant Accolade, an independent developer of videogame cartridges, purchased Sega game cartridges, disassembled them, and by reverse engineering techniques, produced a game cartridge that could be played in the Sega game platforms. The court held that Accolade's copying infringed Sega's copyright, finding that the plain language of the statute proscribed *intermediate* copying because the Copyright Act does not distinguish between when and for what purpose the defendant has made its unauthorized copies.[123] The court, however, sustained Accolade's intermediate copying for disassembly purposes as a fair use, finding it to be a necessary step in its examination of the unprotected ideas and functional concepts embodied in the code.

In applying the four factors, only the third, the amount and substantiality of the use, weighed in Sega's favor.[124] Both the first factor, the purpose and character of the use, and the closely related fourth factor, market effect, favored the defendant. The court admitted that commercial purpose weighs against fair use, but Accolade's use, though commercial, was intermediate only, and any commercial exploitation resulting from it was indirect. Moreover, Accolade's copying was productive in nature, enabling the copier to produce independently designed works. As for market effect, Accolade's use did not usurp the market for the copyrighted work. Rather, it permitted the company to produce its own works and to compete with works of the same kind. The court added that Sega's attempt to monopolize the market by making it impossible for others to compete runs counter to the statutory purpose of promoting creative expression.[125]

The court focused on the second factor, the nature of the copyrighted work, recognizing the unique qualities of computer software. Because Sega's videogames

---

147–50 (1992) (discussing the various reverse engineering techniques and providing concrete illustrations of high level language, machine language, and disassembled versions of a program).

[121] For a comprehensive overview of the reverse engineering issue (covering the entirety of intellectual property), see Pamela Samuelson & Suzanne Scotchmer, *The Law and Economics of Reverse Engineering*, 111 YALE L.J. 1575 (2002).

[122] 977 F.2d 1510 (9th Cir. 1993); *see also* a case based on a similar fact situation, *Atari Games Corp. v. Nintendo of Am.*, 975 F.2d 832, 842 (Fed. Cir. 1992) (finding that decompilation of a computer program to produce a compatible game cartridge might be fair use, but that defendant's program was "substantially similar" to plaintiff's).

[123] *See, e.g.*, *Walker v. Univ. Books*, 602 F.2d 859, 864 (9th Cir. 1979); *Walt Disney Prods. v. Filmation Assocs.*, 628 F. Supp. 871, 875–76 (C.D. Cal. 1986).

[124] *Sega*, 977 F.2d at 1527 (citing *Sony* for the proposition that even copying the whole work did not preclude a finding of fair use).

[125] *Id.* at 1523–24.

contained unprotected aspects that could not be examined without copying, the court determined that the games were afforded a lower degree of protection than more traditional literary works. If defendant's reverse engineering through disassembly or decompilation were illegal, the copyright owner would have a de facto monopoly over the functional aspects of the work.[126] To be a fair use, however, the disassembly and translation of object code into source code had to be the only means of access to the program's unprotected elements. Here, there were no viable alternatives to gaining this access short of disassembly.

As applied in *Sega*, the fair use privilege recognizes the unique attributes of computer software. By restraining the copyright owner from acquiring patent-like protection over the work, the case is consistent with the rationale of § 102(b)[127] that places ideas, processes, and methods of operation in the public domain. Without a fair use privilege for reverse engineering of computer software, the copyright owner could put an idea, process, or method of operation into an unintelligible format and assert copyright infringement against those who try to understand that idea. Thus, *Sega* allows effective access to the ideas underlying the program and prevents software owners from extending their property rights beyond the boundaries provided by copyright law. For these reasons, the court was reluctant to hinder a customary industry practice in a rapidly changing field of technology — particularly a practice that reduces development costs, accelerates innovation, and thereby facilitates competitive entry.[128]

Although *Sega* clearly established that reverse engineering of software would qualify as fair use under certain circumstances, the decision left several questions unanswered. *Sega* seemed to indicate that reverse engineering would be considered fair use only to the extent that it was necessary to identify and understand the unprotected elements of a copyrighted software program. The court, however, gave no guidance as to how literally this requirement was to be interpreted. The problem is that reverse engineering frequently is imprecise and may involve false starts and blind alleys. Would such acts be considered "strictly necessary" to the analysis of a competitor's software? In addition, what about the situation where alternative methods of analysis are available? Would the fair use defense apply only to the method which entailed the least amount of copying? And what if, during the reverse engineering process, some or all of the original program is used to test the validity of the information obtained to that point? Would such use still constitute fair use? *Sega* clearly does not stand for the proposition that decompilation and disassembly are privileged so long as they are done to explore the operation of a product that uses the copyrighted software.[129] But to what extent legitimate users can engage in

---

[126] *Id.* at 1526.

[127] 17 U.S.C. § 102(b). *See supra* § 2.13[B][1].

[128] For a criticism of *Sega*, see Arthur R. Miller, *Copyright Protection for Computer Programs, Databases, and Computer-Generated Works: Is There Anything New Since CONTU?*, 106 Harv. L. Rev. 977, 1014–34 (1993) (noting the law imposes no duty on authors to provide access to copyrighted works; permitting copyright owners to control intermediate copying is desirable because it increases protection against potentially infringing final products).

[129] *See DSC Communs. Corp. v. Pulse Commc'ns*, Inc., 170 F.3d 1354 (Fed. Cir. 1999) (declining to extend *Sega* to copying for the purpose of determining how the copyrighted system works and merely to demonstrate the interchangeability of its interface cards with those made by plaintiff).

acts of reverse engineering has not been specified by the case law.

In *Sony Computer Entertainment, Inc. v. Connectix Corp.*,[130] the Ninth Circuit attempted to answer some of these open questions. The court read *Sega* expansively, permitting extensive intermediate copying in the reverse engineering context even where other, more limited methods existed for gaining access to plaintiff's unprotectible ideas. Connectix's engineers, in the process of emulating and debugging, admittedly made copies of Sony's BIOS every time they booted up their computer. The court held that once the necessity of the defendant's method was established, the number of times that method was applied was not relevant. Because the defendant in *Connectix* had to make at least one copy of the Sony code to study it, it was permitted to make and use hundreds of subsequent copies to make the disassembly process more expedient. In addition, the court held that the new game platform was transformative because the defendant created its own new expression rather than just repackaging the plaintiff's code. In its finding of fair use, the Ninth Circuit was particularly influenced by the fact that the financial loss to Sony accrued not to its copyrighted works, but to the hardware used to access those works. As the court stated, "Sony understandably seeks control over the market for devices that play games Sony produces or licenses. The copyright law, however, does not confer such a monopoly."[131]

While U.S. law has employed fair use to accommodate reverse engineering, the European Union has approached the issue from a more comprehensive standpoint. Its 1991 Directive[132] allows reverse engineering of computer software if reproduction of the program is "indispensable to obtain the information necessary to achieve the interoperability of an independently created computer program."[133] Under the Directive, the acts of reverse engineering (decompilation and disassembly) are limited to persons in rightful possession of the program and for the purpose of obtaining information necessary to achieve interoperability, but only if that information is not available elsewhere.

The Directive was the combined result of considerable lobbying, of political considerations reflective of the state of software development in Europe, and of civil law traditions. Nonetheless, it includes a number of considerations that U.S. courts might want to weigh in attempting to distinguish, under fair use analysis, between chiselers and those who seek to promote the progress of science. In particular, the limitation on decompilation to those parts of the copyrighted work necessary to achieve interoperability arguably strikes the proper balance of interests. It recognizes the rights of copyright owners and the legitimate needs of users who are truly seeking information as opposed to those who are seeking a pretext to free ride on the creativity of others.

---

130 203 F.3d 596 (9th Cir. 2000).

131 *Id.* at 607.

132 Council Directive 91/250/EEC of 14 May 1991 on the Legal Protection of Computer Programs, O.J. (L 122) 42, *reprinted in* MARSHALL LEAFFER, INTERNATIONAL TREATIES ON INTELLECTUAL PROPERTY, 926 (2d. ed. 1997).

133 *Id.* at art. 6.

§ 10.14 THE PROBLEM OF PARODY

[A] Generally

A *parody*[134] is an imitation of a serious piece of literature, music, or composition for humorous or satirical effect. A "parodist" is a critic or commentator who exposes the mediocre and pretentious in art and society, forcing us to examine a serious text from a comic standpoint.

Parody, by its very nature, makes use of another's work, sometimes extensively, and because the purpose of this use is satire and ridicule, there is a tension between the parodist and the copyright owner. As a result, some copyright owners are less than eager to see their work ridiculed and will not license their work for this purpose. Consequently, the parodist must rely on the defense of fair use where substantial use has been made of a copyrighted work and where biting criticism and ridicule may have offended the sensibilities of a copyright owner.

Whether parody, for these reasons, is entitled to a wider fair use privilege than other uses has been the subject of a long, on-going debate.[135] In one sense, a true parody is not just an ordinary taking because it is a transformative use, a form of criticism or comment, and as such, a use specifically enumerated in the preamble to § 107. Moreover, the fair use defense is particularly important for the health of this genre because a copyright owner will seldom license a work to be satirized or ridiculed. One could say that the parody defense to copyright infringement exists precisely to make possible a use that generally cannot be bought.[136]

[B] Parody and the Four Factors: *Campbell v. Acuff-Rose*

The four factors listed in § 107 are applied to parody just as to any other fair use issue and follow a consistent pattern. For most parodies, application of the first two factors does not favor a finding of fair use because most parodies are commercial[137] in purpose, and the nature of the copyrighted work of which they make use is usually a work of entertainment, not one of information. The close questions usually relate to the third and fourth factors, that of amount and substantiality of the use and the market effect.

In *Campbell v. Acuff-Rose Music, Inc.*,[138] the Supreme Court held that a commercial parody may qualify as a fair use. To decide the question of fair use, the

---

[134] The term "satire" is often used synonymously with "parody."

[135] *See Berlin v. E.C. Publ'ns, Inc.*, 329 F.2d 541 (2d Cir. 1964). *But cf. Walt Disney Prods. v. Air Pirates*, 581 F.2d 751 (9th Cir. 1978).

[136] *See Maxtone-Graham v. Burtchaell*, 803 F.2d 1253 (2d Cir. 1986). *But see Original Appalachian Artworks, Inc. v. Topps Chewing Gum, Inc.*, 642 F. Supp. 1031 (N.D. Ga. 1986) (finding bad faith was on part of defendant who asked for a license to use plaintiff's children's dolls (Cabbage Patch Kids) and was rejected).

[137] The *Sony* presumption of market harm for commercial use should be relaxed for parodies that are invariably commercial. *See* David Goldberg, *Copyright Law*, N.Y.L.J., (1986). *But see Original Appalachian Artworks, Inc. v. Topps Chewing Gum, Inc.*, 642 F. Supp. 1031 (N.D. Ga. 1986), (applying the Sony presumption and rejecting the fair use defense primarily for that reason).

[138] 510 U.S. 569 (1994).

court must subject the parody to an overall balancing process in which the parody's "transformative" character is more important than its commercial purpose. In this case, Acuff-Rose owned the copyright to Roy Orbison's 1964 hit song "Oh, Pretty Woman." The rap group 2 Live Crew wrote and recorded a satirical version of the song also called "Pretty Woman" and in 1989 requested a license that Acuff-Rose refused to grant. 2 Live Crew released its satirical version of the Orbison classic anyway. Their version made use of the same drum beat from the original and its distinctive bass line, repeating it eight times throughout the song, while substituting its own words such as "big, hairy woman," "bald-headed woman," and "two-timin' woman" in place of Orbison's more genteel lyrics.

The Sixth Circuit found that 2 Live Crew had infringed Acuff-Rose's "Oh Pretty Woman."[139] Relying on the *Sony* presumption, in which all unauthorized commercial (for profit) uses of copyrighted works are presumptively unfair and have a harmful effect on the market for the work, the court disallowed the fair use defense. The Supreme Court rejected the *Sony* presumption, at least when a parody is at issue, opting for a balancing process that would apply all four fair use factors. As for the first factor, the purpose and character of the use, the Court held that the most important inquiry is not whether the use is commercial but whether it is "transformative." The focus should be on whether the work alters the original with "new expression, meaning, and message."[140] The more transformative the new work, the less will be the significance of the other factors, like commercialism, that weigh against a finding of fair use. After striking another blow against the *Sony* presumption, the Court then turned to an issue that has plagued the courts in determining whether a parody is a fair use: how much can parody take from the original?

[C] How Much Can the Parody Take from the Original?

The third fair use factor, the amount and substantiality of the taking — how much a parody can copy from the original — remains the most controversial issue in determining fair use in the context of parody. The issue arises because the best parodies must take extensively from the original to create the humorous effect. A tension is created with the rights of copyright owners because extensive copying on the part of the parodist may supplant the need for the original. Should there be a wider privilege to take from the original to satisfy the needs of this art form? The issue was not resolved in *Acuff-Rose*. The Court repeated a familiar principle: "the parody must be able to 'conjure up' at least enough of [the] original to make the object of its critical wit recognized."[141] The Court added that the amount necessary to conjure up the original will depend on the persuasiveness of a parodist's justification for the particular copying done and will vary with the purpose and character of the use. Other than articulating these general principles, the Court

---

139 *Acuff-Rose Music, Inc. v. Campbell*, 972 F.2d 1429 (6th Cir. 1992).

140 *Acuff-Rose*, 510 U.S. at 579 (citing Pierre Leval, *Toward a Fair Use Standard*, 103 HARV. L. REV. 1105, 1111 (1990)).

141 *Acuff-Rose*, 510 U.S. at 588.

refused to decide whether excessive copying of the music had actually taken place and remanded the case on this issue.[142]

There are some statements in the case law[143] suggesting a wider privilege for parody, but generally courts have not given the parodist *carte blanche* to take indiscriminately from the copyrighted work. In short, the right to make the best parody is balanced against the rights of the copyright owner. The legal standard applied is that the parodist should be allowed to appropriate no greater amount of the original work than is necessary to recall or "conjure up" the object of his satire.[144] As a corollary, near-verbatim copying will rarely, if ever, be a fair use.

The "conjure up" test was reaffirmed but applied strictly in *Walt Disney v. Air Pirates*,[145] suggesting that the parodist can take only that which is *minimally* necessary to conjure up the original. In *Air Pirates*, defendants prepared two magazines of cartoons entitled the *Air Pirates Funnies*, an underground counter-culture comic book that made use of Disney characters by placing them in bawdy situations. The court rejected fair use of the Disney characters as the taking exceeded what was necessary to conjure up the original. The court suggested that the conjure up standard will vary from case to case and that a lesser taking was necessary for widely recognizable graphic images of the Disney characters than if the subject of the parody was a less concrete literary work such as a speech: "By copying the images in their entirety, defendants took more than was necessary to place firmly in the reader's mind the parodied work and those specific attributes that are to be satirized."[146]

Other courts, notably the Second Circuit, apply the "conjure up" test, allowing a greater taking than that minimally necessary if the parody builds on the original and contributes something new for humorous effect or commentary.[147] On the whole, determining "amount and substantiality" is a question of reasonability and proportionality. As the Supreme Court indicates, "[o]nce enough has been taken to assure identification, how much more is reasonable will depend . . . [1] on the extent to which the [work's] *overriding purpose and character is to parody* the original or, in contrast, [2] the likelihood that the parody may serve as *a market substitute* for the original."[148]

---

142 *Id.*

143 *See, e.g.*, *Berlin v. E.C. Publ'ns, Inc.*, 329 F.2d 541, 545 (2d Cir. 1964).

144 *See id.*; *see also Sun Trust Bank v. Houghton Mifflin Co.*, 268 F.3d 1257, 1273 (11th Cir. 2001) ("A [parody] does not necessarily become infringing the moment it does more than simply conjure up another. . . . ").

145 581 F.2d 751 (9th Cir. 1978).

146 *Walt Disney*, 581 F.2d at 758.

147 *See Elsmere Music, Inc. v. Nat'l Broad. Co.*, 623 F.2d 252, 253n.1 (2d Cir. 1980).

148 *Campbell v. Acuff-Rose Music*, Inc., 510 U.S. at 588 (emphasis added).

[D] Parody and the Fourth Fair-Use Factor: Market Effect

The fourth factor, the market effect of the use, will be decided in favor of the parodist absent near-verbatim copying.[149] The parody will usually not fulfill the demand for the original, and rarely could plaintiff argue that the market for this type of derivative work has been co-opted by the use.[150]

Thus, no presumption or inference of market harm is applicable unless the parody simply duplicates the original in its entirety for commercial purposes. However, when the second use is transformative, market substitution is less certain and market harm is not so readily inferred.[151] In determining market effect, it is not the impact of the parody as criticism but the economic effect of the use in fulfilling the demand for the original that is the issue.[152] Because of its devastating criticism, an effective parody may actually diminish the demand for the original. This is not the kind of market effect that justifies a denial of fair use.[153] The real issue for the fair use determination is whether the parody fulfills the demand for the original, that is, whether consumers are likely to purchase the parody rather than the original because it serves the same purpose as the original.

[E] Does the Parody Have to Target the Copyrighted Work?

Whether a parody, to qualify for fair use, has to target the copyrighted work itself or whether it may use the copyrighted work for some other humorous purpose has been a point of controversy for some time.[154] The Second Circuit Court of Appeals, which has examined this question in greater depth than any other court, has vacillated on this basic issue, but the trend is to require that the parody comments in some way on the original.[155] The Supreme Court confirmed

---

149 *See Benny v. Loew's, Inc.*, 239 F.2d 532 (9th Cir. 1956).

150 *See Pillsbury Co. v. Milky Way Prods., Inc.*, 215 U.S.P.Q. (BNA) 124 (N.D. Ga. 1981) (finding fair use and no market harm for defendant's pornographic depiction in *Screw Magazine* of characters resembling plaintiff's *Poppin'* and *Poppin' Fresh* figures).

151 *See Campbell v. Acuff-Rose Music, Inc.*, 510 U.S. at 590.

152 *See Fisher v. Dees*, 794 F.2d 432 (9th Cir. 1986). The court held that a song parody, "When Sunny Sniffs Glue," based on the original song, "When Sunny Gets Blue," was a fair use, primarily because it did not supplant the need for the original. *Cf. Original Appalachian Artworks, Inc. v. Topps Chewing Gum, Inc.*, 642 F. Supp. 1031 (N.D. Ga. 1986) (discussing how defendant sold stickers resembling plaintiff's popular children's dolls, Cabbage Patch Kids, but which were much more grotesque in style; the district court rejected the fair use defense because of the commercial nature of defendant's use, emphasizing the *Sony* presumption of potential market harm, which could also be shown from the fact that the products competed for the same children's market. In addition, the court found defendant's principal purpose was to earn a profit rather than to engage in social commentary).

153 *See Campbell v. Acuff-Rose Music, Inc.*, 510 U.S. at 591–92 ("[W]hen a lethal parody . . . kills demand for the original, it does not produce a harm cognizable under the Copyright Act").

154 *Compare Metro-Goldwyn-Mayer, Inc. v. Showcase Atlanta Coop. Prods. Inc.*, 479 F. Supp. 351 (N.D. Ga. 1979) (finding the musical stage version of *Gone With The Wind*, although comic, did not constitute a parody), *with Fisher v. Dees*, 794 F.2d 432, 436 (9th Cir. 1986).

155 *See Berlin v. E.C. Publ'ns, Inc.*, 329 F.2d 541, 542 (2d Cir. 1964) (finding *Mad Magazine*'s lyrics to be sung to the tunes of Irving Berlin and others a fair use even though the object of the humor was not the songs themselves but the "idiotic world we live in today"); *Elsmere Music, Inc. v. Nat'l Broad. Co.*, 623 F.2d 252 (2d Cir. 1980) (finding the primary question is whether the use is a valid satire or

this view in *Acuff-Rose*, which sided with the traditional definition of "parody" as a literary or artistic work that imitates the characteristic style of an author or a work for comic-effect ridicule.[156] It rejected the contrary view that would allow use of the original work for humorous effect even though the original was not the object of ridicule or satire.

That a parody need be aimed at least partially at the original is justified by the principal purpose of granting to a parody a fair-use privilege — to criticize another text through satirical ridicule. When the original is used for general comic purposes or to criticize other targets, the same pressing need to encroach on the original does not exist. In other words, if the copyrighted song is not at least in part an object of the parody, there is no need to conjure it up. Thus, parody must do more than merely achieve comic effect but must make some critical comment or statement about the original work.[157] Otherwise, the parodist has simply created a derivative work based on the original and should be required to obtain permission from the copyright owner to use the work.[158]

---

parody, not whether it is a parody of the song itself). *But see MCA, Inc. v. Wilson*, 677 F.2d 180 (2d Cir. 1981) (holding risque version of the Andrews Sisters' classic, "The Boogie Woogie Bugle Boy of Company B," entitled "Cunnilingus Champion of Company C," not a fair use). Generally, pornographic parodies have not received a fair use privilege. *See, e.g., Dallas Cowboys Cheerleaders v. Scoreboard Posters, Inc.*, 600 F.2d 1184 (5th Cir. 1979); *Pillsbury Co. v. Milky Way Prods., Inc.*, 215 U.S.P.Q. (BNA) 124 (N.D. Ga. 1981); *Walt Disney Prods. v. Mature Pictures Corp.*, 389 F. Supp. 1397 (S.D.N.Y. 1975); *Walt Disney Prods. v. Air Pirates*, 581 F.2d 751 (9th Cir. 1978).

[156] *Campbell v. Acuff-Rose Music, Inc.*, 510 U.S. at 578; *see also Rogers v. Koons*, 960 F.2d 301 (2d Cir. 1992) (holding a three-dimensional wood sculpture in unnatural color scheme based on black and white photographs of puppies, was not a fair use; although it may be a satirical critique of the "materialist" society in which we live, there was no parody of the photograph itself).

[157] Since *Campbell*, the lower courts have had several opportunities to consider what is and is not parody. *Compare Dr. Seuss Enter., L.P. v. Penguin Books U.S.A. Inc.*, 924 F. Supp. 1559 (S.D. Cal. 1996), *aff'd*, 109 F.3d 1394 (9th Cir. 1997) (holding that the use of Dr. Seuss rhymes, illustrations, and book packaging to take a fresh look at the O.J. Simpson murder trial did not attempt to comment on the text or themes of *The Cat in the Hat*), *with Mattel, Inc. v. Walking Mountain Prods.*, 353 F.3d 792 (9th Cir. 2003) (affirming summary judgment that seventy-eight photographs featuring naked Barbie dolls being menaced by kitchen appliances, baked in enchiladas, and in various other absurd positions, was a fair use). For a critique of *Dr. Seuss*, see Tyler Ochoa, *Dr. Seuss, the Juice and Fair Use: How the Grinch Silenced a Parody*, 45 J. Copyright Soc'y 546 (1998).

[158] *See* Julie Bisceglia, *Parody & Copyright Protection: Turning the Balancing Act into a Juggling Act*, 34 Copyright L. Symp. (ASCAP) 1, 26 (1987); *see also* Richard A. Posner, *When Is Parody Fair Use?*, 21 J. Legal Stud. 67 (1992) (stating that parody is fair use when used to target the original, not when it is used as a weapon for humorous effect or to ridicule society at large). For criticism of this view, see Tyler T. Ochoa, *Dr. Seuss, the Juice and Fair Use: How the Grinch Silenced a Parody*, 45 J. Copyright Soc'y 546, 610 (1998) ("Drawing a distinction between 'weapon' and 'target' parody would . . . allow the copyright holder to censor satirical opinions with which he or she disagrees); Robert P. Merges, *Notes of Market Failure and the Parody Defense in Copyright Law*, 21 Aipla Q.J. 305, 311 (1993) (arguing that Posner's assumption "seems wrong, at least in those cases where the target of the parody is a set of values or cultural assumptions deeply cherished by the copyright holder or at least widely shared by a segment of public loyal to her").

§ 10.15 FAIR USE AND THE FIRST AMENDMENT

[A] Generally: No Irreconcilable Tension

A few courts[159] and many commentators[160] have referred to a tension between copyright and the First Amendment that "Congress shall make no law . . . abridging the freedom of speech. . . . "[161] Copyright appears to encroach on the freedom of speech and First Amendment values because it prohibits the right to reproduce the expression of others. Does this produce an irreconcilable tension between the two constitutional provisions: the Patent and Copyright Clause and the First Amendment?

Despite the amount of space devoted to this subject in law reviews, only one court has ever held that the First Amendment prevents the enforcement of copyright.[162] It has now been universally accepted that copyright's idea-expression dichotomy supplies the necessary definitional balance, allowing access to and dissemination of ideas and facts while protecting the author's expression.[163] Moreover, the defense of fair use can be invoked where rigid application of the Copyright Act would unreasonably prevent the dissemination of information.[164] Viewed in this way, copyright law optimizes First Amendment values by encouraging production of works of authorship without prohibiting the free communication of facts and ideas embodied in these works. Copyright law does not impede the flow of information per se, and is not an obstacle to the free flow of ideas, but provides positive incentives to encourage the flow.[165] As one court phrased it, "[t]he judgment of the Constitution is that free expression is enriched by protecting the creations of authors from exploitation by others. . . . The First Amendment is not a license to trammel on legally recognized rights of intellectual property."[166]

---

[159] *See, e.g.*, *Triangle Publ'ns, Inc. v. Knight-Ridder Newspapers, Inc.*, 626 F.2d 1171 (5th Cir. 1980); *Schnapper v. Foley*, 471 F. Supp. 426 (D.D.C. 1979); *Maxtone-Graham v. Burtchaell*, 631 F. Supp. 1432 (S.D.N.Y. 1986).

[160] To mention a few: Neil Netanel, Copyright's Paradox (2008); Rebecca Tushnet, *Copyright as a Model for Free Speech Law: What Copyright Has in Common with Anti-Pornography Laws, Campaign Finance Reform, and Telecommunications Regulation*, 42 B.C. L. Rev. 1 (2000); Rebecca Tushnet, *Copy This Essay: How Fair Use Doctrine Harms Free Speech and How Copying Serves It*, 114 Yale L.J. 535 (2004); Robert C. Denicola, *Copyright and Free Speech: Constitutional Limitations on the Protection of Expression*, 67 Calif. L. Rev. 283 (1979); Paul Goldstein, *Copyright and the First Amendment*, 70 Colum. L. Rev. 983 (1970); Melville B. Nimmer, *Does Copyright Abridge the First Amendment Guarantees of Free Speech and Press?*, 17 UCLA L. Rev. 1180 (1970); Lyman Ray Patterson, *Private Copyright and Public Communication: Free Speech Endangered*, 28 Vand. L. Rev. 1161 (1975).

[161] U.S. Const. amend. I.

[162] *Triangle Publ'ns, Inc. v. Knight-Ridder Newspapers, Inc.*, 626 F.2d 1171 (5th Cir. 1980); *see also Schnapper v. Foley*, 471 F. Supp. 426 (D.D.C. 1979).

[163] *See Sid & Marty Krofft Television Prods., Inc. v. McDonald's Corp.*, 562 F.2d 1157 (9th Cir. 1977).

[164] *See Consumers Union of U.S., Inc. v. General Signal Corp.*, 724 F.2d 1044, 1046 (2d Cir. 1983).

[165] *See, e.g.*, *Pac. & S. Co., Inc. v. Duncan*, 744 F.2d 1490 (11th Cir. 1984).

[166] *Dallas Cowboys Cheerleaders, Inc. v. Scoreboard Posters, Inc.*, 600 F.2d 1184, 1187–88 (5th Cir. 1979).

Accordingly, if plaintiff can demonstrate a substantial likelihood of copyright infringement, a court in its discretion can grant a preliminary injunction barring publication of the infringing work despite the First Amendment preclusion of prior restraints on speech.[167]

[B] The Merger of Idea and Expression

One may agree that no inherent irreconcilable conflict exists between copyright law and the First Amendment. But could there be certain situations in which the First Amendment would mandate copying beyond the furthest reaches of fair use? In *Triangle Publications, Inc. v. Knight-Ridder Newspapers, Inc.*,[168] defendant publisher of the *Miami Herald* used the cover of *T.V. Guide* in its comparative advertisement campaign to promote its own television supplement. The District Court held that the defendant's use of the *T.V. Guide* cover was not a fair use but found it privileged under the commercial speech branch of the First Amendment.[169] The Court of Appeals affirmed the result but not the lower court's First Amendment rationale. It held that defendant's use of the cover was a fair use, primarily because it did not affect the market for the work.[170]

A concurring opinion in *Knight-Ridder* suggested that there might be situations in which the First Amendment would have a role to play but not in the current case. Professor Nimmer, who has written extensively on the subject, would agree, but only where idea and expression are so inextricably wedded that one could not use the idea in the copyright without using its expression.[171] To Nimmer, it is difficult to come up with appropriate examples of the merger of idea and expression that would necessitate use of a copyrighted work beyond the fair use privilege. He does, however, cite the example of a news photo that would have to be reproduced and displayed in its entirety to express the idea embodied in it.[172] His rationale: how else could the idea of horror or revulsion in a picture of a rioting crowd, an assassinated political leader, or a natural disaster be conveyed?

---

[167] *See id.* at 1188; *Salinger v. Random House, Inc.*, 811 F.2d 90 (2d Cir. 1987) (enjoining publication of a biography of the writer J.D. Salinger); *see also Craft v. Kobler*, 667 F. Supp. 120 (S.D.N.Y. 1987) (enjoining a forthcoming biography of Igor Stravinsky, the composer, because the appropriations of copyrighted material were too extensive and important and their justification too slight to support an overall claim of fair use).

[168] 626 F.2d at 1171 (5th Cir. 1980).

[169] *Triangle Publications v. Knight-Ridder Newspapers, Inc.*, 445 F. Supp. 875 (S.D. Fla. 1978).

[170] *Knight-Ridder*, 626 F.2d at 1178.

[171] Nimmer on Copyright § 1.10[A] (2014).

[172] This situation approximates *Time, Inc. v. Bernard Geis Assocs.*, 293 F. Supp. 130 (S.D.N.Y. 1968), in which the court allowed extensive verbatim copying for commercial purposes of the Zapruder film taken of the Kennedy assassination. Frames of the film were closely rendered in drawings for a *Life* magazine article on the assassination. The court justified the taking on fair use grounds stating that, "the public interest in having the fullest information available on the murder of President Kennedy outweighed the copyright owner's interest in the work." See also *Rosemont Enters., Inc. v. Random House, Inc.*, 366 F.2d 303 (2d Cir. 1966), *cert. denied*, 385 U.S. 1009 (1967), where the court sustained a fair use defense on public interest grounds despite defendant's substantial use of copyrighted magazine articles. It is not clear in either *Rosemont* or *Time* whether the court has adopted the public interest as a separate fair use factor. Instead, reference to the public interest appears to incorporate First Amendment values into the fair use determination.

According to Nimmer, other than in this narrow news photo exception, there are few, if any, instances where First Amendment values would conflict with copyright.

The merger of idea and expression as a First Amendment defense was asserted by the defendant in the *Nation* case but was ultimately rejected by the Supreme Court.[173] According to the *Nation* magazine, not only the facts contained in the Ford memoirs but the precise manner in which he expressed them were newsworthy. The Supreme Court disagreed in the *Nation*'s case, finding that quoted portions of the unpublished manuscript were excessive and were not protected under fair use. As for the First Amendment, the Court reasoned that copyright's idea-expression dichotomy provided the proper definitional balance between copyright and the First Amendment, and even public figures who write newsworthy memoirs should be able to enjoy the market for their original expression. The Court stated, "in our haste to disseminate news, it should not be forgotten that the Framers intended copyright itself to be the engine of free expression. By establishing a marketable right to the use of one's expression, copyright supplies the economic incentive to create and disseminate ideas."[174]

As the Supreme Court noted, there should be no public figure exception to copyright protection,[175] otherwise public figures would have less incentive to record their impressions. In short, the Copyright Act and the First Amendment are mutually supportive.

§ 10.16 FAIR USE: A SYNTHESIS[176]

After almost 150 years, the doctrine of fair use remains as elusive as ever.[177] But despite its amorphous codification in § 107, and a conflicting body of case law, certain general principles do surface. The fair use determination supports the underlying goals of copyright law: to create conditions for the optimum amount of production and dissemination of works of authorship.[178] In applying fair use, a court ultimately must decide whether the interest in dissemination outweighs possible

---

173 *See Harper & Row, Publishers, Inc. v. Nation Enters.*, 471 U.S. 539 (1985).

174 *Id.* at 558.

175 *Id.* at 559.

176 For other attempts to synthesize the doctrine, see Stephen Fried, *Fair Use and the New Act*, 22 N.Y.L. Sch. L. Rev. 497 (1977); Wendy J. Gordon, *Fair Use as Market Failure: A Structural and Economic Analysis of the* Betamax *Case and its Predecessors*, 82 Colum. L. Rev. 1600 (1982); Note, *Toward A Unified Theory of Copyright Infringement for an Advanced Technological Era*, 96 Harv. L. Rev. 450 (1982); Leo J. Raskind, *A Functional Interpretation of Fair Use*, 31 J. Copyright Soc'y 601 (1984); *but see* Paul Goldstein, *Fair Use in Context*, 31 Colum. J. Law & Arts 433 (2008) (cautioning against global theories that purport to synthesize fair use).

177 This has led to a number of proposals to revise fair use in major ways. *See e.g.* Michael Carroll, *Fixing Fair Use*, 85 N. Car. L. Rev. 1087 (2007) (proposing a "Fair Use Board" in the Copyright Office that could offer ex ante certainty by declaring a petitioner's proposed use to be fair); Gideon Parchomovsky & Kevin A. Goldman, *Fair Use Harbors*, 93 Va. L. Rev. 1483 (2007) (advocating a series of statutory safe harbors to ameliorate the costs associated by ambiguous fair use standards).

178 For an analysis of copyright law's transformation over the past few decades and an argument that hyper enforcement of copyright law hinders creativity, see Patricia Aufderheide & Peter Jaszi, Reclaiming Fair Use: How to Put Balance Back in Copyright (2011).

harm to the economic incentives to produce copyrighted works. Courts, in determining fair use issues, if not always explicitly, appear to concentrate on two dimensions[179] more than others: (1) the public benefit of the defendant's use, whether the use is productive or reproductive; and (2) the harm to the market for the copyrighted work, whether the use is commercial or noncommercial. The analysis is illustrated by the following chart:

Extent of Commercial Exploitation			
		Noncommercial	Commercial
Public Benefit of the Use	Productive/Transformative	Strongest case for Fair Use	Hard cases, e.g., Parody
Reproductive	Hard Cases, e.g., *Betamax* case	Weakest case for Fair Use	

The easiest cases to justify on fair use grounds are those where defendant has made a productive, noncommercial use[180] of plaintiff's work, as for example, where a scholar writing an article for a learned journal quotes from plaintiff's copyrighted work. Here defendant's use is consistent with the ultimate public interest goal of copyright law, which is to encourage the optimal amount of production and dissemination of works of authorship. Access is given to plaintiff's work to enable another to build on it and to produce another work of authorship. The public benefits, and because the market for the work is not harmed, the incentives to produce works of authorship are not suppressed. Alternatively, the easiest case against fair use occurs when a nonproductive (reproductive) commercial use is made of a work. Here, ordinary infringement has occurred and fair use cannot be justified.

The more difficult fair use issues arise when defendant has made a reproductive but noncommercial use of plaintiff's work. The interplay of fair use and the new technologies often involves this issue, as for example, in the *Betamax*[181] case. In these situations, other factors must be considered. Fair use will often be found in the interest of dissemination of the copyrighted work, particularly when the copyright owner would gain little from prohibiting access to the work and it would be impractical for the defendants to negotiate for the use of a work.[182]Moreover, implicit in these cases is an awareness of effects of the ruling on a new technology.

---

[179] The term "dimensions" is used here rather than "factors" although the dimensions loosely relate to factors one and four of § 107 respectively.

[180] *See supra* § 10.05.

[181] *Sony Corp. of Am. v. Universal City Studios, Inc.*, 464 U.S. 417 (1984).

[182] *See* Wendy J. Gordon, *Fair Use as Market Failure: A Structural and Economic Analysis of the* Betamax *Case and its Predecessors*, 82 COLUM. L. REV. 1600 (1982) (justifying application of fair use doctrine in situations where the copier would be unable to reach an agreement with the copyright owner and no corresponding reward to the copyright owner would offset disallowing access to the work). For an analysis of the market failure rationale in the age of "frictionless," low transaction cost, digital networks, see Robert P. Merges, *The End of Friction? Property Rights and Contract in the Newtonian World of On-line Commerce*, 12 BERKELEY TECH. L.J. 115 (1997). *See also* Douglas G. Baird, *Changing Technology and Unchanging Doctrine: Sony Corporation v. Universal Studios, Inc.*, 1984 SUP. CT. REV. 237 (1984).

When defendant's use is productive but commercial, another difficult issue in fair use analysis arises. Here the courts will look to the nature of the copyrighted work and the amount and substantiality of the use, as was done in the *Nation*[183] case. Parody often presents this mix of productive and commercial use, and the critical issue is how much of plaintiff's work is needed to be used to conjure up the original for the purposes of parody. Thus, if a parody builds on but does not supplant the original through excessive use, the public is benefited. It has received a net increase in information available, a new work of authorship, and the possible harm to the economic incentives for future creation does not significantly offset the use.[184]

Part IV. THE FUTURE OF FAIR USE[185]

§ 10.17 FAIR USE IN THE DIGITAL NETWORK ENVIRONMENT

[A] The Background

As the preceding discussion has shown, fair use remains perhaps more than ever the most troublesome doctrine in copyright law. Nothing more illustrates this reality than the considerable doubt, if not outright disagreement, about how the fair use doctrine should operate in a digital network environment.[186] Academic and scholarly "users" insist that the change in technology ought not to affect the scope of their statutory privilege under § 107, and that the traditional "balance" of rights and privileges in copyright should be maintained in the digital world.[187] With equal verve, copyright owners assert that fair use should continue to be a legal factor in the digital environment but that its need, and thus its significance, should recede over time.

Hardly technical, this disagreement represents profoundly differing views about the dissemination and protection of information. The "user" community maintains that the fair use doctrine is not merely a matter of economics. Instead, it serves an

---

[183] *Harper & Row, Publishers, Inc. v. Nation Enters.*, 471 U.S. 539, 558 (1985).

[184] *See supra* § 10.14.

[185] I am deeply indebted to Professor Peter Jaszi for his insights on the future of fair use in a digitized world. *See* Marshall Leaffer, *The Uncertain Future of Fair Use in a Global Information Marketplace*, 62 Ohio St. L.J. 849 (2001). For a discussion of how legal futurist discourse concerning fair use focuses on the failure of fair use and an argument that such practice will likely result in self-fulfillment, see Barton Beebe, *Fair Use and Legal Futurism*, 25 Law & Lit. 10 (2013). For a discussion of the shortcomings of fair use doctrine and an argument for the implementation of a system of new user privileges to supplement fair use, see Phil Weiser & Gideon Parchomovsky, *Beyond Fair Use*, 96 Cornell L. Rev. 91 (2011).

[186] For an argument that courts should recognize a specific fair use known as technological fair use and that the four fair use factors should be tailored accordingly, see Edward Lee, *Technological Fair Use*, 83 S. Cal. L. Rev. 797 (2010).

[187] For a more complete articulation of this position, see the website of the Digital Future Coalition: www.dfc.org.

independent function, by facilitating the productive uses of copyrighted material that might not occur if subject to licensing. Alternatively, "content providers" regard fair use largely as a historic artifact of the print marketplace, in which the transaction costs associated with clearing rights sometimes exceeded the value of the proposed use.

Whatever the merits of these respective positions, we are entering an age where the dissemination of informational works is radically changing. In the new information environment where licensing of works may amount to a few clicks on a computer, the range of cognizable fair use claims would therefore be drastically restricted. In truth, the significance of fair use can be expected to diminish as the line between "private" and "public" uses of information blurs and information commerce conducted through digital networks increases.[188]

[B] Fair Use and Technological Safeguards

The protection of copyright management systems ("CMS") explicitly recognized by the Digital Millennium Copyright Act raises a critical issue concerning fair use: to what extent does the implementation of new technological safeguards against copying threaten important "access" values embodied in the fair use doctrine?

With the explosion in digital technology, copyright owners have been attempting to create technological barriers to prevent unauthorized use of materials available over digital networks. A totally secure system would yield manifest benefits to copyright owners. If works can be circulated safely over digital networks accessible only to authorized users, copyright owners would profit from an efficient distribution mechanism without the risk of "piracy" or "leakage" of their content. Several promising technologies for achieving this goal, including various forms of encryption and "stenography" (or digital watermarking), already exist. Moreover, new technologies may soon make copying virtually impossible without the permission of the copyright owner.[189] The trade-off, often forgotten, is the effect that technological safeguards or anti-copying devices may have on fair use. After all, such safeguards or devices, when effective, operate to prohibit *all* copying, including copying that may be fair use.

Even non-mandatory technological safeguards could, in the digital environment, negate the exercise of certain rights of the public historically protected by copyright law. What role would fair use play in a world where copyrighted content as well as pubic domain material is under electronic lock and key, with access available only subject to electronically mediated terms and conditions? Thus, where content made available over digital networks is concerned, systems of technological

---

[188] This is the position of the 1995 "White Paper," which concluded that "it may be that technological means of tracking transactions and licensing will lead to reduced application and scope of the fair use doctrine." Information Infrastructure Task Force, Intellectual Property and the National Information Infrastructure: The Report of the Working Group on Intellectual Property Rights 82 (1985) (citing *Texaco* case).

[189] *See* John Bigness, *Taking Aim at Digital Piracy; Intel Leads Group Designing Standard*, Chi. Trib., Feb. 20, 1998, at C1. For background, see Mark Stefik, *Shifting the Possible: How Trusted Systems and Digital Property Rights Challenge Us to Rethink Digital Publishing*, 12 Berkeley Tech. L.J. 137 (1997).

safeguards at least have the *capacity* to annul the intricate balances of copyright law, and to impose in their stead a far more rigorous regime of de facto protection.

[C] Fair Use and The Digital Millennium Copyright Act

"Anticircumvention" provisions have played a prominent role in public debate ever since the release of the "White Paper" in 1995. Culminating with the passage of the Digital Millennium Copyright Act ("DMCA"), anticircumvention provisions are now codified in a new § 1201 — part of a new chapter of the Copyright Act. These statutory provisions embody the following three elements: (1) prohibitions against "circumventing" technological protection measures to gain unauthorized access to protected works; (2) prohibitions against the manufacture, sale, or importation of hardware and software which is designed to aid in circumvention; and (3) civil and criminal penalties for violations of (1) and (2).

Most important, both the prohibitions and the penalties are independent of copyright law: consumers could be liable even if their circumvention was done in aid of the exercise of the fair use privilege or another exemption. Similarly, suppliers of hardware and software could be liable even if their productions had a "substantial non-infringing use."[190]

During the heated debate, critics expressed their fear that broadly drafted anticircumvention legislation would result in suppressing the flow of information needed by the scientific and educational communities. In particular, their concerns included the application of the law's provisions to various multi-purpose computers and home electronic devices, as well as to software programs. The effect of these legislative efforts would be to obstruct encryption research, prevent legitimate reverse engineering, and chill expressive activities. Moreover, opponents of the administration's approach were troubled that, as drafted, the legislation could imperil education and research by allowing copyright owners to lock up public domain materials and by undermining the fair use rights of information consumers.[191]

These concerns were partially met by the final version of the DMCA, which specifically exempts many of the activities that critics felt were jeopardized by the earlier administration proposals. For example, the Act allows circumvention of the technological measures for the purpose of reverse engineering to achieve interoperability of an independently created computer program. Also included are exceptions for encryption research and security testing.[192] In addition, the DMCA does include a fair use preservation clause. But this "fair use preservation" clause would come into play only when, despite technological safeguards, an information consumer had somehow gained unauthorized *access* to a protected work. Unless consumers are able to avoid technological protection measures to gain *access* to

---

[190] The quote is from the Supreme Court's decision in the *Betamax* case, *Sony Corp. of Am. v. Universal City Studios, Inc.*, 464 U.S. 417, 440 (1984).

[191] *See* the September 1997 letter concerning H.R. 2281 from 62 law professors to the House Judiciary Subcommittee on Courts and Intellectual Property, *available at* www.ari.net/dfc/legislat/profltr.htm.

[192] *See* 17 U.S.C. § 1201(c)–(j). The DMCA is discussed in fuller detail *supra* § 8.36.

safeguarded content, where appropriate, they will be deprived of exercising their various copyright-based use privileges.

The question remains whether the net effect of these broad-brush legal sanctions against circumvention and network-based distribution of copyrighted works tempered by enumerated exceptions will properly reconcile the rights of owners and the privileges of users, the role traditionally played by the doctrine of fair use. For the time being, the case law has affirmed the constitutionality of the DMCA against the claim that its anticircumvention provisions impermissibly burden fair use.[193] The prospect remains that courts may invent a new exceptional "para fair use" doctrine rooted in the constitutional values of free expression and specially applicable to "paracopyright."[194] Alternatively, Congress could restore fair use by amending § 1201(c) of the Act by insulating circumvention (or distributing tools to circumvent) if such circumvention does not result in an infringement of copyright.[195]

[D] Mass Digitization and Fair Use: The Google Book Search Project[196]

Since its debut at the Frankfort Book Fair in 2004, Google has made continued efforts to scan, archive, and digitize the contents of all books in major libraries with which it has concluded licensing agreements, including those of the University of Michigan, Harvard University, the New York Public library, and Oxford's Bodleian library.[197] The goal is to provide a searchable online database accessible to the public, containing all existing printed works. The general public will have access to view public domain works in their entirety. For copyrighted works, however, search results will be limited to snippets containing the search term, which Google continuously argued, is fair use.

---

[193] *Universal City Studios, Inc. v. Corley*, 273 F.3d 429 (2nd Cir. 2001). See *supra* § 8.34[B][1] for a discussion of *Corley* and the DMCA.

[194] What has been termed "paracopyright" legislation is the new and independent set of regulations, such as the anticircumvention provisions of the DMCA, on activities related to the use of copyrighted works, in addition to those of copyright law itself. The DMCA as paracopyright is discussed *supra* §§ 8.31–8.32.

[195] *See* Digital Media Consumers' Rights Act of 2003, H.R. 107, 108th Cong. § 5(b) (2003) (attempting to restore fair use within the confines of the DMCA).

[196] For a discussion and a preliminary estimate of the economic impact of mass digitization projects, see Hannibal Travis, *Estimating the Economic Impact of Mass Digitization Projects on Copyright Holders: Evidence from the Google Book Search Litigation*, 57 J. Copyright Soc'y 907 (2010).

[197] For commentary on the Google Book Search Project and its ramifications see Randal C. Picker, *The Google Book Search Settlement: A New Orphan Works Monopoly*, 5 Competition L. & E con. 383 (2009); Frank Pasquale, *Copyright in an Era of Information Overload: Toward the Privileging of Categorizers*, 60 Vand. L. Rev. 135 (2007); Oren Bracha, *Standing Copyright on its Head: the Googlization of Everything and the Many Faces of Property*, 85 Tex. L. Rev. 1799 (2007); Siva Vaidyanathan, the Googlization of Everything and the Future of Copyright, 40 U.C. Davis L. Rev. 1207 (2007); Hannibal Travis, *Google Book Search and Fair Use: iTunes for Authors or Napster for Books*, 61 U. Miami L. Rev 87 (2006); Steven Hetcher, *The Half-Fairness of Google's Plan to Make the World's Collection of Books Searchable*, 13 Mich. Telecomm. & Tech. L. Rev. (2006).

The Google initiative has unsurprisingly engendered much controversy and resistance among author groups in particular. In 2005, Google was sued in a class action by the Author's Guild, and the American Association of Publishers brought another action. In 2008, Google negotiated a settlement to the two lawsuits.[198] The change did not mollify the Authors Guild. In 2011, after comments from numerous sources, including the Antitrust Division of the U.S. Department of Justice, the U.S. District Court for the Southern District of New York rejected the proposed settlement as not being "fair, adequate, and reasonable" with respect to the rights of the members of the relevant class.[199] In her statement before Congress, the Register of Copyrights criticized the settlement as a privately formulated compulsory license that compromises the rights of copyright owners of out-of-print books and encroaches on the responsibility of Congress to make copyright policy.[200]

After much legal jockeying concerning the plaintiff's class action, the district court was directed to decide the key issue in the dispute — whether Google's mass digitization of millions of books as part of its Google Book Search project (including scanning, indexing, and displaying "snippets" from most books in response to search queries) constitutes a fair use of the copyrighted works.[201]

Some nine years after the initial launch of the Google Book Search project, the district court in 2013 held that the use of the full text of millions of books for its online search function was a transformative use, and, thus, Google's mass digitization of those books without authorization from copyright owners constituted a fair use. The Court said that the book scanning amounted to fair use because it was "highly transformative" because it did not harm the market for the original work. The Court argued that "Google Books provides significant public benefits," describing it as "an essential research tool" and noting that the scanning service has expanded literary access for the blind and helped preserve the text of old books from physical decay. The court also rejected the theory that Google was depriving authors of income, noting that the company does not sell the scans or make whole copies of books available, instead, that Google Books served to help readers discover new books and amounted to new income for authors. The Court found that

---

198 Under the settlement Google would have paid $45 million to copyright owners for books already scanned , and an additional $35 million to create a Book Rights registry — a collective licensing organization for authors and publishers. The complex 385-page amended (2009) settlement agreement is available at www.googlebooksettlement.com/agreement.html. For a discussion of the Google Books Settlement and an analysis of how the settlement should be characterized, see James Grimmelman, *The Elephantine Google Books Settlement*, 58 J. Copyright Soc'y 497 (2011). For an overview of the Google Book Settlement, see Pamela Samuelson, *The Google Book Settlement as Copyright Reform*, 2011 Wis. L. Rev. 479 (2011). For a comprehensive discussion of the Google Books Settlement and the surrounding legal and historical issues, see Jonathan Band, *The Long and Winding Road to the Google Books Settlement*, 9 J. Marshall Rev. Intell. Prop. L. 227 (2010). For a discussion of the settlement reached by Google books and the four ways that it differed from the "fair use" outcome that was predicted, see Matthew Sag, *The Google Book Settlement and the Fair Use Counterfactual*, 55 N.Y.L. Sch. L. Rev. 19 (2010).

199 *Authors Guild v. Google Inc.*, 770 F. Supp. 2d 666 (S.D.N.Y. 2011).

200 *The Register of Copyrights Hearing Before the H. Comm. on the Judiciary*, 111th Cong. 1st Sess. (2009) (statement of Marybeth Peters).

201 *Authors Guild v. Google, Inc.*, 721 F 3d 132 (2d Cir. 2013).

Google Books should actually enhance the market for individual books, as users who find "snippets" on Google Books may want to buy the entire work; in essence Google Books is acting as free advertising for the book.[202] This decision, which will certainly not be the last word on the matter, declares that fair use permits mass digitization of books for purposes that advance the arts and sciences, such as search, preservation, and access for the print-disabled.[203]

§ 10.18 FAIR USE IN COMPARATIVE PERSPECTIVE

Ultimately, the fate of the fair use doctrine in the United States may be determined even more by outside influences than internal politics. The fact remains, where limitations and exceptions on copyright are concerned, the United States does things differently from most of the rest of the world. In an era when "harmonization" has become the watchword in international copyright, will the United States continue to enjoy its unique position?

United States law contains both specific exemptions from copyright like those contained in §§ 108 and 110 of the Act, and a general, residuary provision of fair use under § 107, designed to reach the specific cases of worthy, unauthorized uses that do not fall comfortably within any of the exemptions. Elsewhere, particularly in civil-law countries, the situation is different. For example, the concept of fair use as such does not exist in German copyright law. In sections of the German statute on limitations of copyright, one can find the functional equivalent in certain exceptions specifically embodied in the German Act.[204] These specific exemptions include the making of single copies for strictly private use, reproducing small parts of works for instructional purposes, a narrowly restricted quotation privilege, copying in judicial opinions, reproduction of works in news reports, and certain reproductions of works of art in exhibition or auction catalogues. In addition, German law provides that other unlicensed private and educational uses of protected works may be permissible if the copyright owner's so-called "right of remuneration" is recognized. For example, home taping of broadcasts is exempt from liability for copyright infringement. A levy on equipment and blank media, however, creates a fund to remunerate copyright owners and creators through collective organizations. Treated similarly are exceptions and limitations that apply to photocopying, the creation of religious and instructional anthologies, and free, noncommercial performances.

Despite certain differences in conception, doctrines such as free utilization under German law may lead to similar results as one would find under the fair-use doctrine in U.S. law. For example, the German courts have given some leeway to forms of artistic expression, such as parody, that incorporate other protected works, while

---

[202] *Authors Guild v. Google, Inc.*, 954 F. Supp. 2d 282 (S.D.N.Y. 2013).

[203] In a parallel case upholding fair use for mass digitization see *Authors Guild, Inc. v. HathiTrust*, 902 F. Supp. 2d 445 (2d Cir. 2012) (holding project to systematically digitize copyrighted books to allow scholars to identify works more efficiently, to preserve universities" collections and to provide print-disabled individuals with access to library collections was protected by fair use doctrine)

[204] Adolf Dietz, *'Germany,' in* Paul Edward Geller & Lionel Bentley, eds.in 2 GER, International Copyright Law and Practice § 8[2][a](2013).

only partially transforming them, so that they remain clearly recognizable in the allegedly infringing work.[205]

Questions of form aside, how different in functional terms is the German system of specific exemptions from U.S. style fair use? Overall, the use privileges secured by fair use *are* significantly broader than their German counterparts. The U.S. conception of fair use is by its nature a dynamic rather than a static doctrine. As patterns of exploitation and consumption for copyrighted works change, courts can adapt the fair use doctrine to new circumstances as they have tried to do, for example, with respect to photocopiers, videocassette recorders, and software. Thus, the doctrine has the capacity to retain its relevance without the need for legislative enactment. By contrast, parliamentary action will be required to keep the German law abreast of current developments. Many civil law countries take the same general approach to limitations and exceptions as Germany does.

As for fair use, the United States presently stands alone in the world intellectual property community. Even countries of the common law tradition rely heavily these days on enumerated statutory exemptions. Although they typically recognize a general affirmative defense of "fair dealing," they do not give it the scope that the fair use doctrine enjoys in the United States.[206]

§ 10.19 INTERNATIONAL TREATIES AND THE FUTURE OF FAIR USE

[A] The Berne Convention Challenge: The Tripartite Test of Article 9(2)

Whether the United States will be able to maintain its unique position on the issue of limitations and exceptions may depend on how the governing instruments in the field of international intellectual property law are interpreted. Article 9(2) of the Berne Convention (Paris Act)[207] provides the following standard for granting exceptions to the reproduction right:

> It shall be a matter for legislation in the countries of the Union to permit the reproduction of [literary and artistic] works in certain special cases, provided that such reproduction does not conflict with a normal exploitation of the work and does not unreasonably prejudice the legitimate interests of the author.

This so-called "three-part test" had at its time of adoption (1967 Stockholm Conference that produced the 1971 Act) a very specific purpose. It was intended to provide a general formulation,[208] suitable for enactment into the national laws of

---

[205] *Id.*

[206] *See, e.g.*, William R. Cornish, *United Kingdom, in* Edward Paul Geller & Lionel Bentley, Eds., 2 UK International Copyright Law and Practice § 8[2][a], (2013).

[207] The United States, like a large majority of other Berne Countries, is a party to the 1971 Paris Act.

[208] Before 1967, the various Acts of the Berne Convention had addressed the question of limitations and exceptions to copyright in piecemeal fashion only, either through requiring member states to permit

Berne's member countries, which would balance public and private interests in the use of copyrighted works in resolving the problem of photocopying (or reprography).[209] The test's open-ended quality, however, clearly promised controversy to come — both in its application to national laws creating exceptions to the reproduction right for technologies other than photocopying and in relation to the supple U.S. doctrine of fair use.

Under the terms of the Berne Convention, every would-be party is the final arbiter whether its laws meet treaty requirements. When the United States became a party to the Convention in 1989, the question of whether various judicial applications of fair use could be viewed as fully consistent with Article 9(2) was averted.[210]

Subsequently, however, serious doubts have been raised about the conformity of U.S. fair use law with the three-part test, especially where the doctrine is applied to new technologies. The international law challenge to fair use may be of negligible significance where analog means of distribution and reproduction are concerned, but some would argue that a different calculus should apply in the digital environment. After all, Article 9(2) was adopted a quarter-century ago, a response to the media, marketing conditions, and technological challenges of the day.[211]

[B] The TRIPS Challenge: Article 13 of the Agreement

Whether U.S. fair use case law complies with the three-part test has generated mounting concern in light of the successful U.S. led effort in negotiating the World Trade Organization's incorporation of the TRIPS Agreement. A major goal of the negotiation was to stem the potential proliferation of exceptions and limitations in the laws of nations with poor records of copyright enforcement. Article 13 of the GATT/TRIPS agreement reflects the basic norm: "Members shall confine limitations or exceptions to exclusive rights to certain special cases which do not conflict with a normal exploitation of the work and do not unreasonably prejudice the legitimate interests of the author."

Article 13 is a reformulation of Berne's Article 9(2) but with two significant differences. First, unlike Article 9(2), the TRIPS formulation of the three-part test applies to *all exclusive rights*. Second, the TRIPS test is *restrictive in intent* (i.e., Article 9(2) merely permits nations to provide for limitations on copyright in certain circumstances). It leaves open the possibility that other limitations may be

---

certain unauthorized uses (such as brief quotations in news reports) of works protected under the Convention, or through provisions permitting those states to craft other particular exceptions under their national laws (e.g., for certain educational uses).

[209] *See* Stephen Stewart, International Copyright and Neighboring Rights 316 (2d. ed. 1989).

[210] *See generally* The Ad Hoc Working Group, *Final Report of the Ad Hoc Working Group on U.S. Adherence to the Berne Convention*, 10 Colum.-VLA J.L. & Arts 513 (1986). Some concern was expressed at the time as to whether the doctrine of *Sony Corp. of Am. v. Universal City Studios, Inc.* (the *Betamax* case) gave sufficient recognition to the "legitimate interests of the author." *See* Ralph Oman, *The United States and the Berne Union: An Extended Courtship*, 3 J.L. & Tech. 71, 104–05 (1988) (noting the use of systems of "equitable remuneration" in connection with home taping in European countries).

[211] *See* Geller, *Legal Transplants in International Copyright*, 13 UCLA Pac. Basin L.J. 199, 215 (1994).

allowable on the basis of other treaty provisions. By contrast, Article 13 expressly restricts allowable limitations and exceptions to those which comply with its standards.

Apart from these differences in formulation, the TRIPS agreement, unlike the Berne Convention, has teeth. The dispute-resolution mechanisms of the World Trade Organization stand ready to entertain allegations that the national laws of WTO countries are out of compliance with Article 13. This consideration, as one observer has noted, will become increasingly important as protected works and sound recordings are transmitted on advanced computer networks, "and unauthorized copying by the recipient — arguably justified under a private copying exemption — is challenged by copyright owners as incompatible with . . . 'normal exploitation.' "[212]

For the most part, fair use endures. But given the tendency of current thought on the world stage, the doctrine as we know it faces an uncertain future.[213]

Part V. OTHER AFFIRMATIVE COPYRIGHT DEFENSES

§ 10.20 GENERALLY

Clearly, fair use is a major defense to actions for copyright infringement, but it is only one means by which a defendant may prevail. There are a number of others. The plaintiff will lose if she fails to establish jurisdiction or to prove by a preponderance of the evidence the two key elements of infringement: ownership and impermissible copying. Issues covered elsewhere in this book may be relevant here as well. For example, the defendant might be able to show an assignment or licensing of rights by the plaintiff, perhaps even joint ownership.[214] Or, the term of protection for the plaintiff's rights could have expired.[215] The statutory formalities might also, in certain circumstances, prove a fatal pitfall in the path to recovery.[216] The plaintiff's rights under the Copyright Act could be subject to an exemption or compulsory license contained in §§ 108–120.[217] Or the claim might fall victim to any of a host of traditional defenses, including laches, estoppel, acquiescence, or res

---

[212] Eric Smith, *Impact of the TRIPS Agreement on Specific Disciplines: Copyrightable Literary and Artistic Works*, 29 Vand. J. Transnat'l L. 559, 578n.36. (1996).

[213] Another battle over U.S. fair use and its relationship with international norms was fought at the December 1996 WIPO Diplomatic Conference. As part of the Conference's consideration of various new international agreements in the fields of copyright and neighboring rights — with special reference to the digital information environment — the issue of limitations and exceptions, including those in the nature of fair use, received considerable attention. *See* Pamela Samuelson, *The U.S. Digital Agenda at WIPO*, 37 Va. J. Int'l L. 369 (1997); Neil Netanel, *The Next Round: The Impact of the WIPO Copyright Treaty on TRIPS Dispute Resolution*, 37 Va. J. Int'l L. 441 (1997).

[214] *See supra* §§ 5.06, 5.10.

[215] *See supra* § 6.04.

[216] *See supra* § 4.11.

[217] *See supra* § 8.03.

judicata.[218] For example, estoppel may be asserted where the plaintiff has induced or aided the defendant to infringe, and acquiescence where the infringing acts are tolerated over a significant period of time. The following section examines the other legal and equitable defenses, focusing on statute of limitations, abandonment, misuse of copyright, and fraud on the Copyright Office.

§ 10.21 LEGAL AND EQUITABLE DEFENSES

[A] Statute of Limitations

Copyright infringement is a tort, but a tort with its own statutory provision for limitation of actions. Under § 507 of the Copyright Act, the limitation period for criminal actions is five years from the date on which "the cause of action arose."[219] In civil actions, the limitation period is three years and runs from the date on which "the claim accrued."[220] If there is any practical consequence attached to the differing terminology of the two subsections, it has yet to surface in the case law.

Law students will recall their first-year torts course, where they read a series of entertaining cases involving doctors who left sponges or other such paraphernalia inside their patients when sewing them up after surgery. When does the patient's claim "accrue," thus triggering the statute of limitations? As in other areas of the law, pinpointing exactly when a cause of action accrues under a statute of limitations can present a thorny problem. Obviously, the answer is twofold: (a) the statute begins to run when the victim learns of the tortious wrong or could have learned of it through the exercise of reasonable diligence; and, in any event, (b) the statute is tolled by the tortfeasor's own acts if he or she fraudulently conceals the wrong. The same principles apply to civil actions for copyright infringement.

One particular conflict in the courts concerns the treatment of a series of infringing acts, where some of the acts occurred more than three years before the civil action was brought. One line of cases would allow recovery for those acts within the statutory period while barring those more than three years old. Alternatively, some courts would characterize the defendant's acts of copyright infringement as a "continuing wrong." *Taylor v. Meirick*,[221] is the leading case supporting the "continuing wrong" doctrine.

In *Taylor*, the defendant made and began selling nearly exact copies of the plaintiff's copyrighted maps in 1976. The resulting infringement action was not filed, however, until 1980. The unauthorized copies were still being peddled by the defendant himself, or by others with his encouragement, as late as 1979. Was the defendant liable for the infringing acts that occurred in 1976, or had the statute of limitations on those claims run? Judge Posner, in a precise and interesting opinion, held that the plaintiff might still recover. First, "[t]he initial copying was not a separate and completed wrong but simply the first step in a course of wrongful

---

[218] *See, e.g., New Era Publ'ns Int'l, APS v. Henry Holt & Co.*, 873 F.2d 576.

[219] 17 U.S.C. § 507(a).

[220] 17 U.S.C. § 507(b).

[221] 712 F.2d 1112 (7th Cir. 1983).

conduct that continued till the last copy of the infringing map was sold."[222] Alternatively, the plaintiff was unaware of the initial copying until late 1979, and the defendant deliberately threw him off the scent by replacing the plaintiff's copyright notice with his own. Thus, the statute of limitations was tolled as to the defendant's 1976 infringements until the plaintiff discovered them in 1979, and he had three years from that point forward in which to bring suit. *Taylor*'s "continuing infringement" theory has been distinguished or rejected elsewhere,[223] but there seems to be general agreement that the statute of limitations is properly tolled in cases of fraudulent concealment, coercion, and duress.

The statute of limitations typically applies to infringement claims, but some courts have extended it as well to claims seeking declarations of copyright ownership. For example in one case, plaintiffs claiming to be co-authors were time-barred three years after accrual of their claim "from seeking a declaration of copyright co-ownership rights and any remedies that would flow from such a declaration."[224] In another, a claim of sole ownership of sound recordings was time-barred; claim accrued when recordings were made, or at the latest, when copies were sold without payment of royalties.[225] If the statute of limitations is applied to questions of ownership, when does a claim for a declaratory judgment, as for example, of co-ownership accrue? Does the analogy to "adverse possession" in real property law counsel a discovery rule in these situations? The courts have taken varying positions on this issue.[226]

One other issue regarding the statute of limitations merits attention. What happens if the plaintiff files the complaint in the action within three years after the infringement but fails to register the copyright in the work or record the transfer of interest on which he relies until the § 507(b) period has expired? The probable answer is that later attention to these jurisdictional prerequisites relates back, so that the complaint is not time-barred.[227]

---

[222] *Id.* at 1119.

[223] Some courts would allow recovery for those acts within the statutory period while barring those more than three years old. *See Rosette v. Rainbo Record Mfg. Corp.*, 354 F. Supp. 1183 (S.D.N.Y. 1973), *aff'd*, 546 F.2d 461 (2d Cir. 1976); *Makedwe Publ'g Co. v. Johnson*, 37 F.3d 180 (5th Cir. 1994); *Stone v. Williams*, 970 F.2d 1043 (2d Cir. 1992); *Roley v. New World Pictures, Ltd.*, 19 F.3d 479 (9th Cir. 1994). To these courts, each act of infringement is a distinct harm giving rise to an independent claim for relief. Thus, recovery will be allowed only for those acts occurring within three years of suit, and disallowed for earlier infringing acts. *See, e.g., Kregos v. Associated Press*, 3 F.3d 656 (2d Cir. 1993); *Roley v. New World Pictures, Ltd.*, 19 F.3d 479 (9th Cir. 1994).

[224] *See, e.g., Merchant v. Levy*, 92 F.3d 51, 55–56 (2d Cir. 1996).

[225] *See Santa-Rosa v. Combo Records*, 471 F.3d 224 (1st Cir. 2006). *But see Pritchett v. Pound*, 473 F.3d 217 (5th Cir. 2006) (action for declaratory judgment not barred where party seeks no affirmative relief and only asserts ownership as a defense).

[226] *See Gaiman v. McFarlane*, 360 F.3d 644 (7th Cir. 2004) (neither publication nor registration of alleged joint work with copyright notice in name of one author only was sufficient to place alleged co-author on notice of adverse claim and commence running of three-year limitations period); *Ritchie v. Williams*, 395 F.3d 283 (6th Cir. 2005) (claim based on alleged assignment was time-barred where claim had been expressly repudiated more than three years before suit filed). *But see Advance Magazine Publishers, Inc. v. Leach*, 466 F. Supp. 2d 628 (D. Md. 2006) (doctrine of adverse possession does not apply to copyright).

[227] *See Co-Opportunities, Inc. v. Nat'l Broad. Co.*, 510 F. Supp. 43 (N.D. Cal. 1981).

[B] Laches and Estoppel

To prevail in a laches defense, the infringer must show that the copyright owner failed to assert his or her rights in a timely manner, was negligent in failing to act promptly, and that this failure prejudiced the infringer. Unlike the statute of limitations, which specifies an explicit time bar, laches stipulates no definite period of repose. For many years, the courts were divided on the issue whether laches applies to actions that are brought within the three-year statute of limited under § 507(b).[228]

Finally, in 2014, in *Petrella v. Metro-Goldwyn-Mayer*,[229] the Supreme Court resolved the conflict, holding that laches cannot be invoked to preclude adjudication of a claim for damages brought within the three-year statute of limitations window. The Court stated, however, that laches may still have "a role to play, in extraordinary circumstances, to bar the specific relief requested by the plaintiff."[230] In sum, "a plaintiff's delay can always be brought to bear at the remedial stage."[231]

The operative period of laches in copyright cases runs from the time the plaintiff knew or should have known about an actual or impending infringement, not an adverse claim of ownership.[232] Generally, the courts have required a showing that the delay caused a prejudice to defendant, who has taken actions or suffered consequences that would not have occurred had the copyright owner brought the suit promptly.[233] In addition to claims for copyright infringement, laches may also be asserted as a defense to claims of ownership interests in copyrighted works.[234]

Copyright decisions have recognized the closely related defense of estoppel. Four elements must be present to establish the defense of estoppel: (1) the plaintiff must know that the defendant is engaging in infringing conduct; (2) the plaintiff has intended that its conduct shall be acted on or that the defendant has a right to believe that it is so intended; (3) the defendant must be ignorant of the true facts;

---

[228] *Compare Peter Letterese & Assocs. v. World Inst. of Scientology Enters., Int'l*, 533 F.3d 1287 (11th Cir. 2008) (laches can only bar claims for damages, and not for prospective relief), *with Danjaq LLC v. Sony Corp.*, 263 F.3d 942, 954 (9th Cir. 2001) (laches held to bar claim of co-ownership in James Bond character, even though brought within statutory period), *and Chirco v. Crosswinds Cmtys., Inc.*, 474 F.3d 227 (6th Cir. 2007) (applying laches to bar destruction of infringing building).

[229] 134 S. Ct. 1962 (2014) (owner of the renewal rights in the screenplay for the movie "Raging Bull" informed MGM of its infringing use of the screenplay in 1998 but did not sue MGM until 2009; in rejecting the defense of laches, the Supreme Court ruled that the infringement of the work between 2006 and 2009 was actionable under "a separate accrual" rule that views each successive violation of copyright as a new infringing act within its own statute of limitations).

[230] *Id.* at 1977–78.

[231] *Id.* at 1978.

[232] *Kling v. Hallmark Cards, Inc.*, 225 F.3d 1030 (9th Cir. 2000) (noting that there was nothing in the record to suggest that a reasonably diligent plaintiff would have known about the infringing video cassette distribution until the plaintiff's 1994 video store visit).

[233] *Danjaq LLC v. Sony Corp.*, 263 F.3d 942, 955 (9th Cir. 2001).

[234] *Petrella v. Metro-Goldwyn-Mayer, Inc.*, 134 S. Ct. 1962, 1968–69 (2014).

and (4) the defendant must rely on the plantiff's conduct to its injury.[235] Thus, the defense is available if the plaintiff has aided in the acts of infringement, or has declared that he does not view defendant's conduct as infringing, or that he has no copyright in the work at issue.

In general, the defense is difficult to assert because it is based on two ingredients that coalesce infrequently: plaintiff's acquiescence to infringing conduct and defendant's lack of awareness of plaintiff's rights. Once the defense is proven, plaintiff's acquiescence to defendant's infringing acts may constitute a defense against past infringement, and if it continued for a sufficient amount of time, may provide a defense for acts occurring after the acquiescence has ended.[236]

[C] Abandonment or Forfeiture of Copyright

The plaintiff's assertion of copyright ownership can be countered, and the claim of infringement defeated, where the plaintiff (or the plaintiff's predecessor) has abandoned or forfeited the copyright. The nomenclature employed in the cases sometimes is less than precise, but abandonment must not be confused with forfeiture. Forfeiture usually occurred, in the older cases, as a consequence of publication without proper notice.[237] The copyright owner's intent was irrelevant; the forfeiture occurred by operation of law.

Abandonment, on the other hand, requires *intent* by the copyright owner to surrender rights in the work and normally is proved by an *overt act* evidencing such intent (for example, a statement relinquishing any copyright interest in a work or an act destroying the only existing copy of the work).[238] To say that this defense succeeds infrequently would be an understatement. Very occasionally, however, it has been asserted successfully. In *Stuff v. E.C. Comics*,[239] involving the "Alfred E. Newman" character adopted as a sort of mascot (but, as it turns out, not originated) by *Mad* magazine; the court concluded that the original artist's long acquiescence in the widespread use of his drawing amounted to a forfeiture.

[D] Misuse of Copyright

[1] The Misuse Doctrine: Its Patent Law Origins

An emerging and potentially important defense in copyright actions is "misuse." The courts seem to view this new defense as a close cousin of "unclean hands," the traditional equitable defense allowed in cases of serious plaintiff misconduct, such

---

235 *See HGI Assocs., Inc. v. Wetmore Printing Co.*, 427 F.3d 867, 875 (11th Cir. 2005); *Carson v. Dynegy, Inc.*, 344 F.3d 446, 454–55 (5th Cir. 2003).

236 *Hayden v. Chalfant Press*, Inc., 177 F. Supp. 303 (S.D. Cal. 1959).

237 *See Donald Frederick Evans v. Continental Homes, Inc.*, 785 F.2d 897 (11th Cir. 1986).

238 *See, e.g.*, *Seshadri v. Kasraian*, 130 F.3d 798 (7th Cir. 1997); *Pac. & S. Co., Inc. v. Duncan*, 572 F. Supp. 1186 (N.D. Ga. 1983), *aff'd in part and rev'd in part*, 744 F.2d 1490 (11th Cir. 1984); *Paramount Pictures Corp. v. Carol Publ'g Group*, 11 F. Supp. 2d 329 (S.D.N.Y. 1998), *aff'd*, 181 F.3d 83 (2d Cir. 1999) ("Star Trek" television series and motion pictures).

239 342 F.2d 143 (2d Cir. 1965).

as falsifying evidence or other fraudulent practices.[240]

The pedigree of the copyright misuse defense, however, lies not in equity generally, but in the specialized doctrine of patent misuse created by the courts to restrain anti-competitive abuses of the patent monopoly.[241] It began as an affirmative defense to a suit for patent infringement based on failure to pay royalties due under a patent licensing agreement. In patent law, the misuse defense was developed as a means to prevent patent owners from using the market power in their patents to restrain competition in other unpatented products through tie-ins and other restrictive licensing arrangements.

Although it is based on principles of free competition, the misuse doctrine has an identity distinct from antitrust laws. A defendant in an infringement action is shielded from suit if misuse can be shown, even though the acts of misuse neither constitute competitive injury nor indicate that the plaintiff was individually harmed by the defendant's misuse. Because of its vague contours that overlap antitrust law, the patent misuse doctrine has received sharp criticism from commentators and industry groups who contend that it discourages pro-competitive licensing practices, while reducing the incentive to innovate. In 1988, legislation greatly weakened the patent misuse defense by prohibiting a finding of patent misuse "unless . . . the patent owner has market power for the patent or patented product on which the license or sale is conditioned."[242]

[2] Copyright Misuse: The Developing Case Law

Whereas the misuse defense has had a rich and troubled tradition in patent law, it has not, until recently, been given recognition in copyright law. Copyright and patent law serve parallel public interests, seeking to increase the store of human knowledge and expression by rewarding authors and inventors for their creative efforts — but without, in the process, conferring monopoly power over property not directly subject to the copyright or patent. The Fourth Circuit, in *Lasercomb Am., Inc. v. Reynolds*,[243] has stated the rationale for recognition of a "misuse of copyright" defense in the following terms, adapted from the patent misuse context:

> The grant to the [author] of the special privilege of a [copyright] carries out a public policy adopted by the Constitution and laws of the United States, "to promote the Progress of Science and useful Arts, by securing for limited Times to [Authors] . . . the exclusive Right . . . " to their ["original works"]. United States Constitution, art. I, § 8, cl. 8 [17 U.S.C.A. § 102]. But

---

[240] *See Rohauer v. Killiam Shows, Inc.*, 379 F. Supp. 723 (S.D.N.Y. 1974), *rev'd on other grounds*, 551 F.2d 484 (2d Cir. 1977).

[241] *See Morton Salt Co. v. Suppiger*, 314 U.S. 488 (1942).

[242] 35 U.S.C. § 271(d). For a discussion of whether courts should depart from standard antitrust law and apply misuse doctrine to combat harms to competition and innovation, see Thomas F. Cotter, *IP Misuse and Innovation Harm*, 96 Iowa L. Rev. 52 (2011). For an argument that legal protections for fair use can be more practical by basing copyright misuse defense in First Amendment speech principles instead of in antitrust principles, see David S. Olson, *First Amendment-Based Copyright Misuse*, 52 Wm. & Mary L. Rev. 537 (2010). For a discussion of U.S. antitrust and IP law and innovation competition, see Herbert Hovenkamp, *Innovation and the Domain of Competition Policy*, 60 Ala. L. Rev. 103 (2009).

[243] 911 F.2d 970 (4th Cir. 1990).

> the public policy that includes [original works] within the granted monopoly excludes from it all that is not embraced in the [original expression]. It equally forbids the use of the [copyright] to secure an exclusive right or limited monopoly not granted by the [Copyright] Office and that it is contrary to public policy to grant.[244]

Lasercomb itself involved unauthorized copying and marketing of copyrighted computer software licensed by the plaintiffs to the defendants for use in the control of manufacturing processes. The plaintiffs satisfactorily proved their prima facie case, but the defendants prevailed because the language of the license agreement improperly prohibited licensees' use of their own ingenuity to create software implementing the idea expressed in the plaintiffs' software. This, the court held, was an attempt by the plaintiffs to use their copyright in a manner adverse to the underlying purposes of copyright law itself — in short, a misuse of copyright.

How widely this relatively new affirmative defense will be accepted remains to be seen. But its potential scope is broad, and the body of caselaw[245] and scholarly commentary has grown in its favor.[246] Prior authority had suggested that copyright misuse might arise only in connection with violation of the antitrust laws.[247] The *Lasercomb* court, however, observed as follows:

> [W]hile it is true that the attempted use of a copyright to violate antitrust law probably would give rise to a misuse of copyright defense, the converse is not necessarily true — a misuse need not be a violation of antitrust law in order to comprise an equitable defense to an infringement action. The question is not whether the copyright is being used in a manner violative of antitrust law (such as whether the licensing agreement is "reasonable"), but whether the copyright is being used in a manner violative of the public policy embodied in the grant of a copyright.[248]

Recent cases have continued a trend favoring the defense in appropriate circumstances, even if the conduct does not rise to the level of an antitrust

---

[244] *Lasercomb*, 911 F.2d at 976 (quoting from *Morton Salt*, 314 U.S. at 492).

[245] *See, e.g.*, *Assessment Techs. of WI, LLC v. WIREdata, Inc.*, 350 F.3d 640, 647 (7th Cir. 2003) ("The argument for applying copyright misuse beyond the bounds of antitrust, besides the fact that confined to antitrust the doctrine would be redundant, is that for a copyright owner to use an infringement suit to obtain property protection, here in data, that copyright law clearly does not confer, hoping to force a settlement or even achieve an outright victory over an opponent that may lack the resources or the legal sophistication to resist effectively, is an abuse of process.").

[246] *See, e.g.*, Dan L. Burk, *Anticircumvention Misuse*, 50 UCLA L. Rev. 1095 (2003) (arguing in favor of the misuse defense involving the abuse of the anticircumvention provisions of the DMCA).

[247] The case law is in conflict regarding whether the defense of copyright misuse may be asserted as an affirmative defense if the alleged acts must also violate the antitrust laws. *Compare F.E.L. Publ'ns, Ltd. v. Catholic Bishop of Chicago*, 754 F.2d 216 (7th Cir. 1985), *and Blendingwell Music, Inc. v. Moor-Law, Inc.*, 612 F. Supp. 474 (D. Del. 1985) (approving of defense), *with Columbia Pictures Indus. v. Redd Horne, Inc.*, 749 F.2d 154 (3d Cir. 1984). *See also Lasercomb Am. v. Reynolds*, 911 F.2d 970 (4th Cir. 1990) (noting that copyright misuse need not be a violation of the antitrust law). For a criticism of the copyright misuse defense, see Marshall A. Leaffer, *Engineering Competitive Policy and Copyright Misuse*, 19 U. Dayton L. Rev. 1087 (1994).

[248] *Lasercomb*, 911 F.2d at 978.

violation.[249] For example, in *Practice Management Information Corp. v. American Medical Association*, the court sustained the defense of copyright misuse in the AMA's licensing of their medical procedure coding system, a detailed numerical code to enable physicians to identify particular medical problems with precision. The AMA licensed the medical procedure coding system to the Federal Health Care Financing Administration in exchange for an agency agreement not to use any competing system of nomenclature and to require its use in the Administration's programs. The agency then required use of the AMA system by applicants for Medicaid reimbursement. In this action for declaratory judgment, the court held that Practice Management, who wished to publish AMA's copyrighted code without license, was not required to prove antitrust violation to prevail on a misuse theory.

[3] Copyright Misuse Reconsidered

It is somewhat a paradox that the misuse defense has engrafted into copyright law after Congress has virtually terminated the misuse defense as a viable doctrine in patent law. There are even fewer reasons to extend misuse principles to copyright law because of a fundamental difference between patent and copyright grants. The rationale for the misuse defense is weaker in copyright law because the exclusionary force of the monopoly is less than in patent law. A copyright, even more so than a patent, is a legal rather than an economic monopoly. Of course, persons may create copyrighted works hoping to charge super-competitive prices for their works, but this can only result if consumers are willing to pay the super-competitive price instead of seeking satisfactory substitutes. If these substitutes are available, the seller of the work will enjoy no economic power in the market for the work. Generally, copyrighted works are highly substitutable. Many different songs, films, or computer programs may compete at any one time for the consumer's dollars. Although copyright law may prohibit copying, this constraint in itself does not necessarily lead to market power.[250] As a result, the copyright grant will, with much less frequency, confer the degree of market power that the patent grant confers and that the patent misuse cases presuppose. For this reason, claims that the copyright owner has sought to extend his copyright beyond its proper scope should generally be rejected by the courts. Thus, courts have properly looked to antitrust law as the sole regulator of anticompetitive conduct, avoiding the uncharted if not unprincipled misuse doctrine.[251]

---

[249] 121 F.3d 516 (9th Cir. 1997). Other recent cases favoring a *sui generis* defense of misuse are: *Alcatel U.S.A., Inc. v. DGI Techns., Inc.*, 166 F.3d 772 (5th Cir. 1999) (holding that the licensing of a operating system software on condition that it be used only in conjunction with the licensor's hardware, constituted copyright misuse, despite defendant's failure to prove the relevant market in his antitrust claim) and *DSC Communications Corp. v. DGI Techs.*, 81 F.3d 597 (5th Cir. 1996) (deciding that plaintiff's copyright claims arguably prevented defendant from developing competing microprocessor card).

[250] There are exceptions to this general proposition that copyright does not confer an economic monopoly. For example, the Windows operating system enjoys significant market power, if not monopoly power in computer operating systems. *See United States v. Microsoft Corp.*, 253 F.3d 34 (D.C. Cir. 2001) (noting that Microsoft violated § 2 of the Sherman Act by engaging in various exclusionary acts by imposing conditions on original equipment manufacturers, restricting them to the use of Windows in order to exclude a rival web browser, Netscape Navigator, from the market).

[251] For a statement of this proposition, see *USM Corp. v. SPS Tech., Inc.*, 694 F.2d, 505, 512 (7th Cir

[E] Fraud on the Copyright Office

Another "coming" defense — which, like misuse of copyright, has roots both in the traditional equitable doctrine of unclean hands and in patent law — is "fraud on the Copyright Office." The gist of the defense is that the plaintiff, in the application for registration of the work in suit, willfully misstated or failed to state facts that, if known to the Copyright Office, would have constituted reason for rejecting the application. The penalty imposed by the courts is, at the least, a determination that the registration is invalid and incapable of supporting an infringement action. Indeed, the better view may be that, as a result of the claimant's actions, the copyright itself is void, thus precluding the possibility of reregistration and subsequent enforcement.

Whimsicality, Inc. v. Rubie's Costume Co., Inc. illustrates the "unclean hands" nature of the defense and the serious consequences when found.[252] In *Whimsicality*, the plaintiff, a designer and manufacturer of high-quality costumes for children and adults, succeeded in registering six of its creations — the Pumpkin, Bee, Penguin, Spider, Hippo Ballerina, and Tyrannosaurus Rex — not as mere utilitarian wearing apparel, but rather as "soft sculptures." Concluding that no reasonable observer could in fact believe the works to be soft sculptures and that the plaintiff had purposely deceived the Copyright Office as to the character of the works, the court held the copyrights invalid and thus incapable of enforcement. In fact, the Office knowingly registers costumes as "soft sculptures" when such works contain original aspects, and, subsequent to decision in the case, it filed an affidavit stating that it had not been defrauded in this instance. The court, however, refused further consideration of the matter. The result in *Whimsicality* presumably would have been different under an amendment made in 2008, which states that a registration certificate is valid, even if it contains inaccurate information, unless the information was both knowingly inaccurate and material to the Copyright Office's registration decision. In such cases, "the court shall request the Register of Copyrights to advise the court whether the inaccurate information, if known, would have caused the Register of Copyrights to refuse registration."[253]

A party asserting fraud on the Copyright Office must meet a "heavy burden": "[I]t must establish that the application for copyright registration is factually inaccurate, that the inaccuracies were willful or deliberate, and that the Copyright Office relied on those misrepresentations."[254] In other words, if the certificate would have been issued in any event, the defense will be denied. In addition, some courts have also required allegations of fraud on the Copyright Office to comply with the heightened pleading requirements that the Federal Rules impose for fraud claims under Rule 9(b).[255]

Given the changes made in the law of registration by the Berne Convention Implementation Act of 1988, one might ask whether "fraud on the Copyright

---

1982). *But see Assessment Techs. of WI, LLC v. WIREdata, Inc.* 350 F.3d 640, 647 (7th Cir. 2003).

[252] 891 F.2d 452 (2d Cir. 1989).

[253] 17 U.S.C. § 411(b)(1).

[254] *Lennon v. Seaman*, 84 F. Supp. 2d 522, 525 (S.D.N.Y. 2000) (citation omitted).

[255] *Id.* at n.2.

Office" survives as a defense with respect to Berne-era registrations. The likely answer is that it does. The BCIA itself is silent regarding the defense or any intention on the part of Congress to abolish it, and the BCIA's legislative history at one point mentions the doctrine approvingly.[256]

[F] Innocent Intent

In general, infringement with innocent intent is *not* a defense to a finding of liability. Outside of one narrowly drawn provision in the Act, infringement of copyright is a strict liability rule, where intent of the copier is not relevant in determining the fact of liability. The one exception to the general rule is found in § 406(a), which provides a complete defense to copyright infringement to the person who has relied in good faith on an error in name on the notice on certain copies or phonorecords publicly distributed before the Berne Convention Implementation Act.[257]

The customary explanation for excluding innocence as a defense to copyright infringement is that, as between the copyright owner and the infringer, the infringer is better placed to avoid the error. The rule is particularly harsh when applied against a person who reasonably believes that the copyrighted work is in the public domain or a publisher that has relied on a putative author's misrepresentations about the originality of a work. In one situation, the Copyright Act moderates the harshness of the "no innocent defense" rule: Section 405(b) of the Act provides that an innocent infringer who can show that it was misled by the omission of notice on copies publicly distributed before the effective date of the Berne Convention Implementation Act (March 1, 1989) will not be liable for actual or statutory damages.[258]

---

256 *See* H.R. Rep. No. 100-609, at 46 (1988) (registering a work consisting preponderantly of U.S. Government materials, where such work lacks an appropriate notice and is therefore without notice by operation of § 403, will constitute fraud on the Copyright Office).

257 17 U.S.C. § 406(a). Under 17 U.S.C. § 406(a)(1)–(2), the defense is not allowed if (1) registration of the work had been made in name of the copyright owner, or (2) a document executed by the notice and showing the ownership of the copyright had been recorded.

258 *See* 17 U.S.C. §§ 401(d), 402(d), 405(b), 504(c)(2).

Chapter 11

COPYRIGHT LAW IN A FEDERAL SYSTEM: PREEMPTION OF STATE LAW

§ 11.01 INTRODUCTION AND CHAPTER OVERVIEW

An extensive system of state law protection of intangibles has always coexisted with federal intellectual property law. State trade secret, common law copyright, and unfair competition laws overlap federal patent, trademark, and copyright laws both in the subject matter involved and in the rights protected. The coexistence, however, has not always been harmonious, and the overlapping forms of intellectual property protection have created tensions within the federal system. The vehicle for regulating these tensions is the Supremacy Clause of the Constitution,[1] which dictates that a federal statute preempts (i.e., displaces) state law when the state law "stands as an obstacle to the accomplishment and execution of the full purposes and objectives of Congress."[2] As applied to forms of intellectual property protection, the issue under the Supremacy Clause is not whether states have the power to protect intellectual property, but rather under what circumstances does state protection unduly interfere with the objectives and policies of federal protection? Deciding this difficult question has often led to irreconcilable results and conflicting doctrine as, for example, in copyright law, where the preemption doctrine was in disarray under the 1909 Act. One objective of Congress in promulgating the new Copyright Act in 1976 was to clarify the preemption doctrine. Unfortunately, the 1976 Act has done little, if anything, to solve the problem.

Some of the confusion under the 1909 Act[3] was caused by the bifurcated nature of copyright law, where the dividing line between state and federal copyright

---

[1] U.S. Const., art. VI, cl. 2 reads:

> This Constitution, and the Laws of the United States . . . shall be the supreme Law of the Land; and the Judges in every State shall be bound thereby, any Thing in the Constitution or Laws of any State to the Contrary notwithstanding.

[2] *Hines v. Davidowitz*, 312 U.S. 52, 67 (1941). *See also Synercom Tech., Inc. v. Univ. Computing Co.*, 474 F. Supp. 37, 42 (N.D. Tex. 1979). Traditionally, courts have found that a state law is preempted in two situations. First, when Congress has so occupied the field in question that state legislation is foreclosed. Courts have found federal occupation in the express terms of the federal legislation or by implication. *See, e.g., Ray v. Atlantic Richfield Co.* 435 U.S. 151 (1978) (finding clear congressional decision for national uniformity of standards). Second, state law will be preempted when it conflicts with the basic objectives of a federal statute. *See, e.g., Pac. Gas & Elec. Co. v. State Energy Resources Conservation Comm'n*, 461 U.S. 190, 203–04 (1983). Generally, courts have been reluctant to preempt state law unless there is an express congressional intent to do so or in instances where there is a high degree of federal-state conflict. *See, e.g., Maryland v. Louisiana*, 451 U.S. 725, 746 (1981).

[3] Ch. 320, 35 Stat. 1075, revised by 17 U.S.C. §§ 101–914 (1982 and Supp. III 1985).

protection was publication.[4] State common law copyright protected unpublished works, and federal copyright began when a work was published. But even after a work was published, it was never quite clear how far the states could go to protect writings of authors.[5]

Effective January 1, 1978, the Copyright Act of 1976 eliminated the dual system, replacing it with a single national system whereby virtually all works of authorship, whether published or unpublished, were made exclusively the subject of federal law. Partly in anticipation of conflicts between federal and state law, and partly to avoid the uncertainties of the pre-1976 preemption doctrine, § 301 of the 1976 Act sets forth specific criteria for preemption. Under the 1976 Act, state law is specifically preempted under § 301[6] when two conditions are met: first, the state law must protect the same rights conferred in § 106,[7] and second, the state law must protect the same subject matter enumerated in §§ 102 and 103.[8]

Although § 301 was intended to clarify the preemption doctrine as it applied to copyright law, it has instead superimposed another set of problems on this already complicated and confusing subject.[9]

To understand § 301, it is important to consider preemption doctrine as it developed before the 1976 Act. Part I of this chapter provides the pre-1976 background to the preemption issue. Its three sections trace the development of state copyright protection and the way in which the Supreme Court used preemption doctrine in trying to harmonize state law. The court did this not just with federal copyright law, but also with federal law in related areas of intellectual property, particularly federal patent law. Much of the controversy has concerned the misappropriation doctrine, a broad, amorphous, and basically equitable concept, used by courts to protect intangible property that failed to meet federal intellectual property standards. Part II examines preemption under § 301 of the 1976 Copyright Act. Most of the discussion is devoted to the meaning of "rights equivalent," one of the two elements that must be found for preemption to take place. The conclusion reached is that Congress largely failed to provide a bright line guide to preemption, and as a consequence, one must look to traditional preemption doctrine much as it was before the 1976 Act.

---

[4] For a discussion of publication doctrine, see *supra* § 4.02.

[5] U.S. Const., art. I, § 8, cl. 8.

[6] 17 U.S.C. § 301.

[7] 17 U.S.C. § 106.

[8] 17 U.S.C. §§ 102, 103.

[9] For a comprehensive overview of the preemption case law see Joseph P. Bauer, *Addressing the Incoherency of the Preemption Provisions of the Copyright Act of 1976*, 10 Vand. J. Enter. & Tech. L. (2007) (advocating a broader interpretation of § 301).

Part I. PREEMPTION BEFORE THE 1976 ACT

§ 11.02 THE MISAPPROPRIATION DOCTRINE AND OTHER STATE ATTEMPTS TO PROTECT INTELLECTUAL PROPERTY: THE 1909 ACT BACKGROUND[10]

[A] Two Divergent Tendencies

Federal intellectual property protection constitutes a relatively well-defined body of law, despite the intangible nature of its subject matter. In general, federal law, as exemplified by the copyright and patent statutes, attempts to balance the property rights of creators against the public's right of access to the intangible creation. Copyright law strikes this balance by protecting only certain categories of works. It also imposes limits on that protection, such as the fair use doctrine, the idea-expression dichotomy, and the limited duration of a copyright. Patent law[11] also balances access with incentive to create but in a significantly different way from copyright law. In return for disclosure of the invention, the patentee is given a highly exclusive monopoly right. That right, much more limited in duration than a copyright, lasts no more than 17 years. Further, the monopoly right is much more difficult to acquire than copyright because of the rigorous standards of patentability.

Through the years, two general attitudes have been expressed about how expansive state law should be in protecting valuable intangibles we call intellectual property. The expansive view would permit an active role for state law in filling gaps in protection left by federal law. This view would allow the state to actively regulate intellectual property, except in clear instances of conflict with federal law. The opposing minimal view would treat common law protection for intellectual property with much suspicion because of its tendency to take information out of the public domain. This view favors federal intellectual property law and the public domain over an active regime of state regulation of intellectual property.[12]

[B] The Classic Statement: The *INS* Case

Courts have wavered between these two divergent views, which found their classic statement in the eloquent majority and dissenting opinions in *International News Service v. Associated Press*.[13] In this pre-*Erie* case,[14] a majority of the

---

[10] For an excellent overview, see Howard B. Abrams, *Copyright, Misappropriation and Preemption: Constitutional and Statutory Limits of State Law Protection*, 1983 SUP. CT. REV. 509 (1983); NIMMER ON COPYRIGHT § 1.01 (2014); PAUL GOLDSTEIN, COPYRIGHT §§ 17–17.34 (3d ed. 2014).

[11] For a general discussion of patent law, see *supra* § 1.11.

[12] The power of the states to regulate matters of copyright dates back to the first copyright case in the Supreme Court, *Wheaton v. Peters*, 33 U.S. 591 (1834), where the Court acknowledged state protection of published works. This dichotomous system of copyright protection lasted until the 1976 Act unified copyright law under a single federal system.

[13] 248 U.S. 215 (1918).

[14] In *Erie R.R. v. Tompkins*, 304 U.S. 64 (1938), the Supreme Court held that the federal courts must

Supreme Court recognized broad common law[15] power to regulate intangible interests by upholding the misappropriation doctrine as a vehicle for protecting intellectual property. The Court forbade the International News Service ("INS"), a rival news organization, from copying the Associated Press' ("AP") hot news stories and publishing them on the west coast before AP was able to do so. "Passing off" — unfair competition in the traditional sense of the term — was not involved; the INS was not trying to deceive consumers about the origin of these stories. INS simply took valuable information without permission or payment. The news stories themselves may not have qualified for copyright protection, having been published without notice, or perhaps not demonstrating sufficient originality. Nonetheless, the Supreme Court held that INS' acts constituted a "misappropriation" because "he who has fairly paid the price should have the beneficial use of the property."[16] The misappropriation doctrine is based on a natural rights theory, which recognizes the right of an individual to the fruits of his labor.

Justice Brandeis, in dissent, eloquently stated the case for a narrower field of protection:

> [T]he fact that a product of the mind has cost its producer money and labor, and has a value for which others are willing to pay, is not sufficient to ensure to it this legal attribute of property. The general rule of law is, that the noblest of human productions — knowledge, truths ascertained, conceptions, and ideas — become, after voluntary communication to others, free as the air to common use. Upon these incorporeal productions the attribute of property is continued after such communication only in certain classes of cases where public policy has seemed to demand it.[17]

The sentiment expressed by Brandeis reflects a hostile attitude toward expansive state protection of intangibles. To Brandeis, any protection conferred on intellectual property should be limited and, except in narrow circumstances, should be a matter of federal statutory law.

The far-reaching equitable doctrine recognized in the *INS* case, known as the "misappropriation doctrine," provided broad, though vaguely defined, protection against the taking of intangible values.[18] Because state misappropriation laws

---

apply state substantive law on non-federal questions.

[15] *INS* was a diversity case that based its decision on federal common law. A major issue in the case was whether the misappropriation doctrine under federal common law impinged on federal statutory protection of intellectual property law. The *INS* case has also been read to permit state law to operate in the intellectual property field despite federal statutory patent and copyright law. If it were not read in this way, it would be only an historical curiosity because a general federal common law no longer exists after *Erie*. Indeed, the argument has been made that the *INS* case is no longer authoritative because it was decided before *Erie* had abolished federal common law. *See, e.g.*, *DeCosta v. Columbia Broad. Sys., Inc.*, 520 F.2d 499 (1st Cir. 1975). Other courts have based their decisions on the *INS* case despite its pre-*Erie* status. *See Board of Trade v. Dow Jones & Co., Inc.*, 439 N.E.2d 526 (Ill. App. Ct. 1982).

[16] *INS*, 248 U.S. at 240.

[17] *Id.* at 250.

[18] The elusive doctrine has been defined as follows:

> 1. Plaintiff has created an intangible product through extensive time, labor, skill, and money.
> 2. The free riding defendant, a competitor, makes use of that product and gains a special

overlapped federal patent and copyright law, it was inevitable that the preemption issue would rise again.

Beginning in the 1930s, the pendulum began to swing against permitting broad state protection of intangibles,[19] but the culmination of this anti-state sentiment occurred in 1964 when the Supreme Court confronted the preemption issue in the *Sears* and *Compco* cases. These two Supreme Court cases, decided the same day, appeared to drastically narrow the scope of state law protection of intellectual property.

§ 11.03 PREEMPTION REBORN: *SEARS* AND *COMPCO*[20]

In *Sears, Roebuck & Co. v. Stiffel Co.*[21] and *Compco Corp. v. Day-Brite Lighting, Inc.*,[22] the Supreme Court reasserted preemption under the Supremacy Clause, invalidating state law protection of intangible property rights. With these two cases, the Court seemed to declare the end of the misappropriation doctrine and other state law causes of action protecting intellectual property. In sum, the pendulum appeared to have swung in the direction of the Brandeis dissent in *INS*.

In *Sears* and *Compco*, plaintiffs brought actions under the Illinois unfair competition law for copying product shapes, pole lamps in *Sears*, and fluorescent lighting fixtures in *Compco*. Neither product shape qualified for either mechanical or design patent protection, and neither manufacturer had sought copyright protection. The Supreme Court invalidated Illinois' unfair competition law, finding that the state law was preempted because it conflicted with federal copyright and patent law. The Court appeared to reject the misappropriation doctrine and any similar state regulation providing intellectual property rights beyond those granted by federal law. The key language in *Compco* is as follows: "[W]hen an article is

---

advantage because the defendant is not burdened with the same costs of production. 3. Plaintiff suffers commercial damage.

See Associated Press v. All Headline News, 608 F. Supp. 2d 454, 461 (S.D.N.Y. 2009) (holding that a distributor of breaking news on the Internet is subject to a "hot news [misappropriate claim] under New York [state] law . . . "); *Synercom Tech., Inc. v. Univ. Computing Co.*, 474 F. Supp. 37, 39 (N.D. Tex. 1979); J. Thomas McCarthy, Trademarks and Unfair Competition § 10.51 (4th ed. 2009. Some courts do not require a competitive relationship but rather have focused on the unjust enrichment aspect of the defendant's actions. *See, e.g., Metropolitan Opera Ass'n v. Wagner-Nichols Recorder Corp.*, 199 Misc. 786, 795–796 (N.Y. Sup. Ct. 1950), *aff'd*, 279 A.D. 632 (N.Y. App. Div.1951) (upholding misappropriation where defendant transcribed radio broadcasts of plaintiff's operatic performances and sold them to the retail market). *See also Standard & Poor's Corp. v. Commodity Exch., Inc.*, 683 F.2d 704 (2d Cir. 1982) (upholding injunction preventing the Commodity Exchange from creating a market for futures contracts based on Standard & Poor's 500 Index (S&P 500)).

[19] See, for example, *Cheney Bros. v. Doris Silk Corp.*, 35 F.2d 279 (2d Cir. 1929), where Learned Hand refused to extend the *INS* rationale to protect dress designers. *See also R.C.A. Mfg. Co. v. Whiteman*, 114 F.2d 86 (2d Cir. 1940) (upholding the restrictive legend on a phonograph record cannot prevent subsequent broadcast of the record).

[20] For an overview, see J. Thomas McCarthy, Trademarks and Unfair Competition §§ 10.21–10.72 (4th ed. 2009).

[21] 376 U.S. 225 (1964).

[22] 376 U.S. 234 (1964).

unprotected by a patent or a copyright, state law may not forbid others to copy that article."[23]

Similar to the Brandeis dissent in the *INS* case, these decisions reflect a strong policy favoring competitive copying unencumbered by state law, unless the subject matter is protected by federal intellectual property law.

§ 11.04 THE AFTERMATH OF *SEARS* AND *COMPCO*[24]

Lower courts applied *Sears* and *Compco* inconsistently. Some adopted the broadest preemptive reading of these cases.[25] Other courts, however, struggled to reconcile *Sears* and *Compco* with the seeming inequity of allowing imitators to take a free ride on another's intellectual creation, simply because the creation was not protected by copyright or other federal intellectual property law. These courts often relied on trivial differences to distinguish *Sears* and *Compco* from the case at bar.[26] Given the uncertainty of state law protection following *Sears* and *Compco*, plaintiffs looked elsewhere to protect intangible values from imitation. One result was a heightened interest in § 43(a)[27] of the Lanham Act, a federal unfair competition law, which circumvented the preemption problem because it was federal law.[28]

In *Goldstein v. California*,[29] the broad preemptive thrust of *Sears* and *Compco* was substantially narrowed when the Supreme Court held that states have concurrent power with the federal government to protect works of authorship. *Goldstein* involved a criminal statute prohibiting the copying of musical recordings without permission. At the time the cause of action arose, sound recordings were not protected under federal copyright law, and record piracy was rife. The criminal statute in *Goldstein* attempted to protect an important state industry threatened by this widespread piracy. The issue in *Goldstein* was whether the California anti-piracy statute was preempted by federal law.

---

[23] *Compco*, 376 U.S. at 237.

[24] For an overview, see Ralph S. Brown, Jr., *Publication and Preemption in Copyright Law: Elegiac Reflections on Goldstein v. California*, 22 UCLA L. Rev. 1022 (1975).

[25] *See Columbia Broad. Sys., Inc. v. DeCosta*, 377 F.2d 315 (1st Cir. 1967).

[26] During this time, there were several state efforts to protect record producers against the unauthorized duplication of tapes and records. Until the Sound Recording Act of 1971, the (1909 Act) did not recognize sound recordings as copyrightable subject matter. Record producers looked to state remedies. *See, e.g., Tape Indus. Ass'n of Am. v. Younger*, 316 F. Supp. 340 (C.D. Cal. 1970); *Capitol Records, Inc. v. Erickson*, 2 Cal. App. 3d 526 (1969), *cert. denied*, 398 U.S. 960 (1970) (reasoning that tape duplication is not "copying" within the meaning of *Sears-Compco*, but rather misappropriation of the owner's labors). The distinction between copying and misappropriation is clearly a fiction. When one misappropriates, one is merely reproducing another's work. *See also Pottstown Daily News Publ'g Co. v. Pottstown Broad. Co.*, 247 F. Supp. 578 (E.D. Pa. 1965); *Capitol Records, Inc. v. Greatest Records, Inc.*, 43 Misc. 2d 878 (N.Y. Sup. Ct. 1964) (upholding New York State's power to protect sound recordings as unpublished works).

[27] 15 U.S.C. § 1025(a).

[28] *See, e.g., Truck Equip. Serv. Co. v. Freuhauf Corp.*, 536 F.2d 1210 (8th Cir.), *cert. denied*, 429 U.S. 861 (1976).

[29] 412 U.S. 546 (1973).

The Court analyzed the preemption issue on two different levels. The first level involved whether the Copyright Clause of the Constitution totally precluded the states from legislating in that area. The second level concerned whether federal copyright law implicitly preempted the California anti-piracy statute. The Court found no broad-based preemption under the Copyright Clause of the Constitution. First, nothing in the Constitution explicitly indicated that Congress had been granted exclusive power to protect writings of authors.[30] Second, the power given to Congress to protect writings of authors was not a matter of such national interest that state legislation in the field would inevitably lead to conflicts with federal law.[31]

The Court also held that the California statute was not preempted under the Supremacy Clause; it found no conflict between federal copyright policy and California's protection of sound recordings.[32] The opinion distinguished *Sears* and *Compco* as cases involving patent policy where the requirement for uniform national protection of limited duration is greater than in copyright.[33] As for any conflict with copyright policy, the Court stated:

> No comparable conflict between state law and federal law arises in the case of recordings of musical performances. In regard to this category of "Writings", Congress has drawn no balance; rather, it has left the area unattended, and no reason exists why the State should not be free to act.[34]

One year later, the Supreme Court, in *Kewanee Oil Co. v. Bicron Corp.*,[35] took a similar position on the power of the states to protect trade secrets, further narrowing the preemption doctrine as articulated in *Sears* and *Compco*. In *Kewanee*, the plaintiff had developed a process for a new synthetic crystal for use in detecting ionizing radiation. The process was potentially patentable, but the plaintiff decided not to seek patent protection; instead, it tried to enforce its rights to the process under Ohio's trade secret law. The Court found that state trade secret law was not preempted by federal patent law because the state law neither clashed with the objectives of federal patent law nor obstructed congressional purposes.[36] Thus *Goldstein* and *Kewanee* erased the bright line presumption favoring preemption as set forth in *Sears* and *Compco*. The new approach focused on whether state and federal law could exist harmoniously in the same field, and whether Congress had a clearly stated policy in favor of preemption. In short, by 1974, the pendulum had swung toward the expansionist view, giving the states a wide ambit in which to regulate matters of intellectual property, at least in those areas not directly occupied by federal law or those that clearly stand as an obstacle to federal policy.[37]

---

[30] *Goldstein*, 412 U.S. at 557.

[31] *Id.* at 559.

[32] *Id.* at 561.

[33] *Id.* at 567.

[34] *Id.* at 570.

[35] 416 U.S. 470 (1974).

[36] *Id.* at 491.

[37] *See also Zacchini v. Scripps-Howard Broad. Co.*, 433 U.S. 562 (1977).

This principle was reconfirmed by the Supreme Court in its 1989 *Bonito Boats v. Thunder Craft Boats*[38] opinion. Here, the Court applied the policy of the *Sears-Compco* decisions in determining the preemptive scope of federal patent law. The Court held that, under the Supremacy Clause, the Patent Act preempted a Florida "plug molding statute," which prevented the duplication of industrial product designs by a direct molding process. In a unanimous decision, the Court held that the statute, in effect, created a state mini-patent law. As a result, the "plug molding" statute improperly restricted competition in prohibiting the free imitation of designs in general circulation, unprotected by federal patent law. The Supreme Court's decision in *Bonito Boats* shows that the preemptive thrust of *Sears-Compco* is still alive and will be used to preclude state law protection for the designs of useful articles.[39] In sum, although its contours are not entirely clear, *Bonito Boats* appears to be limited to state law that provides patent-like protection to design and utilitarian aspects of products rather than applying to the full range of state intellectual property law.[40]

Part II. PREEMPTION UNDER § 301 OF THE 1976 ACT[41]

§ 11.05 SECTION 301: GENERALLY

The uncertainty left by inconsistent case law led Congress to attempt to clarify the preemption doctrine in the 1976 Copyright Act. Section 301 abolishes common law copyright and sets forth explicit criteria to resolve preemption issues. Section 301 reads:

> (a) On and after January 1, 1978, all legal or equitable rights that are equivalent to any of the exclusive rights within the general scope of copyright as specified by section 106 in works of authorship that are fixed in a tangible medium of expression and come within the subject matter of copyright as specified by sections 102 and 103, whether created before or after that date and whether published or unpublished, are governed

---

[38] 489 U.S. 141 (1989).

[39] Title V of the Digital Millennium Copyright Act, Pub. L. 105-304, 112 Stat. 2860 (1998), referred to as "Vessel Hull Design Protection Act," provides a new *sui generis* protection for original boat hull designs for a 10-year term by adding a new chapter 13 to the Copyright Act. The provisions are codified in 17 U.S.C. §§ 1301–1330. The legislation addresses the concerns of the boat manufacturers and circumvents the *Bonito Boats* preemption issue by providing federal protection.

[40] For a penetrating analysis of *Bonito Boats*, see John Shepard Wiley Jr., Bonito Boats: *Uniformed but Mandatory Innovation Policy*, 1989 Sup. Ct. Rev. 283 (1990) (criticizing the opinion's vague scope and lack of credible justification); David E. Shipley, *Refusing to Rock the Boat: The* Sears/Compco *Preemption Doctrine Applied to Bonito Boats v. Thunder Craft*, 25 Wake Forest L. Rev. 385 (1990) (approving of the opinion because it more precisely defines the sweep of preemption analysis than *Goldstein* and *Kewanee*).

[41] For an overview of the subject, see Ralph S. Brown, Jr., *Unification: A Cheerful Requiem for Common Law Copyright*, 24 UCLA L. Rev. 1070 (1977); Henry David Fetter, *Copyright Revision and the Preemption of State "Misappropriation" Law: A Study in Judicial and Congressional Interaction*, 27 Copyright L. Symp. (ASCAP) 1 (1982); Paul Goldstein, *Preempted State Doctrines,Involuntary Transfers and Compulsory Licenses: Testing the Limits of Copyright*, 24 UCLA L. Rev. 1107 (1977).

exclusively by this title. Thereafter, no person is entitled to any such right or equivalent right in any such work under the common law or statutes of any State.

(b) Nothing in this title annuls or limits any rights or remedies under the common law or statutes of any State with respect to —

(1) subject matter that does not come within the subject matter of copyright as specified by sections 102 and 103, including works of authorship not fixed in any tangible medium of expression; or

(2) any cause of action arising from undertakings commenced before January 1, 1978; or

(3) activities violating legal or equitable rights that are not equivalent to any of the exclusive rights within the general scope of copyright as specified by section 106.[42]

This section effectively abolishes the 1909 Act's dual system of federal and state copyright protection whose dividing line was publication. In place of the bifurcated system, § 301 creates a single system of federal protection for all published and unpublished works once the work of authorship is fixed in a tangible medium of expression. By doing away with the 1909 Act's dual system, Congress attempted to create a more unified, simplified, and effective copyright law to protect the writings of authors.

In addition to abolishing common law copyright, § 301(a) establishes specific criteria for preemption to prevent state law from unduly intruding into the field of copyright law. It sets forth three conditions, all of which must be met for state law to be preempted: (1) the right protected by state law must be equivalent to any of the exclusive rights within the general scope of copyright as specified by § 106; (2) the right must be in a work of authorship fixed in a tangible medium of expression; and (3) the work of authorship must come within the subject matter of copyright specified in §§ 102 and 103.

Both conditions must be met for preemption to occur. For example, assume that a state passed a law prohibiting the unauthorized copying of computer software. To decide whether the state law will be preempted, under the first prong, one must determine whether the law provides a right equivalent to copyright. Here, the right granted by unauthorized copying is equivalent to the reproduction right of § 106(1). The first prong being met, one must also meet the second requirement for preemption to take place: does the state law cover the same subject matter as that covered by federal copyright? The state law clearly covers the subject matter under § 102(1) because computer software is a literary work. Thus, having met the dual requirements of § 301 — rights equivalent and subject matter — the state law is preempted.

The above hypothetical provides a straightforward example of how the preemption provision should work. As stated in the House Report, the purpose of § 301 is

---

[42] 17 U.S.C. § 301.

to avoid ambiguity and uncertainty in a murky area of the law. The preemption principles set forth in § 301 are:

> [I]ntended to be stated in the clearest and most unequivocal language possible, so as to foreclose any conceivable misinterpretation of its unqualified intention that Congress shall act preemptively, and to avoid the development of any vague borderline areas between State and Federal protection.[43]

Despite the intended goal, § 301 has fallen far short of creating bright line criteria for matters of preemption. The problem is that neither the statute nor the legislative history answers puzzling questions about the meaning of rights equivalent and when such rights come within the subject matter of copyright. Because of the ambiguities left by § 301, in difficult cases, one must return, ironically enough, to traditional preemption doctrine expressed in the Supreme Court's inconsistent interpretations of the Supremacy Clause.[44] As always, the ultimate determination is whether the state law improperly interferes with the policies of federal copyright law.

§ 11.06 RIGHTS EQUIVALENT: THE LANGUAGE OF THE STATUTE AND THE LEGISLATIVE HISTORY

[A] Rights Equivalent: The Peculiar Structure of § 301

The major difficulty in construing § 301 has proven to be the first prong of the preemption test. There are several basic reasons for this difficulty. First, and most important, the Act does not define "equivalency," a meaningless term that lends itself to varied interpretations. Second, the legislative history concerning § 301, rather than clarifying congressional intent, actually obfuscates the issue of what constitutes a right equivalent. In addition to those basic deficiencies, § 301 is peculiarly drafted. The problem lies in § 301(b)(3),[45] which sets forth generally what is *not* preempted. This section preserves, for state control, activities relating to violations of "legal or equitable rights that are not equivalent to any of the exclusive rights within the general scope of copyright as specified by section 106."[46] The language of this section is almost, but not quite, the mirror image of § 301(a). What is the purpose of this apparently redundant provision, and what does it add in defining the scope of rights equivalent? To understand the puzzling redundancy, it is helpful to consider the legislative history of § 301.

---

[43] H.R. Rep. No. 94-1476, 94th Cong., 2d Sess. 130 (1976).

[44] *See, e.g.*, *Goldstein v. California*, 412 U.S. 546 (1973).

[45] 17 U.S.C. § 301(b)(3).

[46] *Id.*

[B] The Legislative Odyssey of § 301

As originally drafted, § 301(b)(3) listed examples of claims involving non-equivalent rights not preempted by the Copyright Act. By 1975, the section, as drafted and amended, read as follows:

> (b) Nothing in this title annuls or limits any rights or remedies under the common law or statutes of any State with respect to:
>
> . . . .
>
> (3) activities violating legal or equitable rights that are not equivalent to any of the exclusive rights within the general scope of copyright as specified by section 106, *including rights against misappropriation not equivalent to any of such exclusive rights, breaches of contract, breaches of trust, trespass, conversion, invasion of privacy, defamation, and deceptive trade practices such as passing off and false representation.*[47]

On the eve of passage, the examples listed in clause (3) were deleted from § 301(b)(3), leaving the section as it now reads. The italicized language was deleted because the Justice Department objected to the inclusion of misappropriation, fearing that states' misappropriation laws would be construed so broadly as to render the preemption section meaningless. The following dialogue ensued between Congressman Seiberling, who offered the amendment deleting the examples, and Congressman Railsback, the ranking Republican on the House Subcommittee reporting out the bill:

> MR. RAILSBACK: Mr. Chairman, may I ask the gentleman from Ohio, for the purpose of clarifying the amendment that by striking the word misappropriation, the gentleman in no way is attempting to change the existing state of the law, that is as it may exist in certain States that have recognized the right of recovery relating to misappropriation; is that correct?
>
> MR. SEIBERLING: That is correct. All I am trying to do is prevent the citing of them as examples in a statute. We are, in effect, adopting a rather amorphous body of State law and codifying it, in effect. Rather I am trying to have this bill leave the State law alone and make it clear we are merely dealing with copyright laws, laws applicable to copyrights.
>
> MR. RAILSBACK: Mr. Chairman, I personally have no objection to the gentleman's amendment in view of that clarification and I know of no objections from this side.
>
> . . . .
>
> MR. KASTENMEIER: Mr. Chairman, I too have examined the gentleman's amendment and was familiar with the position of the Department of Justice. Unfortunately, the Justice Department did not make its position known to the committee until the last day of markup.

---

[47] S. REP. NO. 94-22, 94th Cong., 2d Sess. (1976) (emphasis added); H.R. REP. NO. 94-1476, at 276 (1976).

MR. SEIBERLING: I understand.

MR. KASTENMEIER: However, Mr. Chairman, I think that the amendment the gentleman is offering is consistent with the position of the Justice Department and accept it on this side as well.[48]

This amendment was accepted just before passage of the bill, giving little time to consider its effect. Considering the 21 years of meticulous revision process, it is unfortunate that such an important amendment was added to the 1976 Act in this haphazard way. But how should this curious legislative history be treated? More specifically, how should a court take into account the deleted examples and the above exchange concerning them?

§ 11.07 RIGHTS EQUIVALENT: THE CASE LAW APPLYING § 301

[A] The Extra Elements Approach

To interpret a legislative provision, courts normally turn to the legislative history and the various drafts of the statute, but that process will not work here. The legislative history as reflected in the above exchange is simply too ambiguous to be helpful in determining whether a right equivalent has been provided by state law. The exchange on the House floor does not explain why all the examples were deleted, nor does it shed much light on the continuing scope of the misappropriation doctrine. As a result, most courts have ignored the legislative history and instead focused on what the state law cause of action does, whether labeled misappropriation, *quantum meruit*, or conversion.[49]

Overall, a right granted by state law is regarded as equivalent and preempted when the state law provides an infringement action for the acts of reproduction, adaptation, performance, and display, as set forth in § 106. Alternatively, a state cause of action is not preempted when it differs in nature from the rights and remedies conferred by copyright law and when it requires elements other than those set forth in § 106. As one court phrased it, the question is whether the state protected rights "are *qualitatively* different from the rights of reproduction, performance, distribution or display."[50] Thus, if the rights and remedies provided by state law are qualitatively different from those enumerated in § 106, preemption will not take place.[51] For example, if A violates a relationship of trust and appropriates B's trade secret, A has committed an act of reproduction under § 106. However, preemption will not occur because the crux of the cause of action involves the breach of trust, quite unlike anything covered in § 106 of the Copyright Act.

---

48 122 Cong. Rec. H32015 (Sept. 22, 1976).

49 *See Peckarsky v. Am. Broad. Co.*, 603 F. Supp. 688 (D.D.C. 1984); *see also Mitchell v. Penton Indus. Pub. Co.*, 486 F. Supp. 22 (N.D. Ohio 1979) (finding plaintiff's broad misappropriation claim preempted).

50 *Schuchart & Assocs. v. Solo Serve Corp.*, 540 F. Supp. 928, 943 (W.D. Tex. 1982) (*citing Harper & Row, Publishers, Inc. v. Nation Enters.*, 501 F. Supp. 848, 852 (S.D.N.Y. 1980)) (emphasis added).

51 *See* NIMMER ON COPYRIGHT § 1.01 (2014).

The courts have generally used this mode of analysis and for the most part have decided against preemption when the state law confers an important element in addition to the exclusive rights of § 106.[52] On the whole, the legitimate claims brought under the various causes of action deleted from § 301(b)(3)[53] pass muster when they truly constitute breaches of trust[54] or express contract,[55] conversion,[56] passing off[57] or defamation,[58] or infringe privacy[59] or publicity rights.[60]

In deciding whether a cause of action is preempted, a court must look beyond the label to determine whether, in fact, a right conferred by state law qualitatively differs from the exclusive rights of § 106 of the 1976 Copyright Act.[61] For example, a defamation action involves a claim vindicating one's relationship with society; a passing off action involves a deception about the origin of goods or services; and a privacy action involves the right to be let alone. Each of these actions include

---

[52] *See* Robert A. Gorman, *Fact or Fancy? The Implications for Copyright*, 29 J. Copyright Soc'y 560, 608 (1982).

[53] *See supra* § 11.06[B].

[54] *See Warrington Assocs., Inc. v. Real-Time Eng'g Sys., Inc.*, 522 F. Supp. 367 (N.D. Ill. 1981) (finding a trade secret claim not preempted).

[55] *See Smith v. Weinstein*, 578 F. Supp. 1297, 1307 (S.D.N.Y. 1984); *see also Werlin v. Reader's Digest Ass'n, Inc.*, 528 F. Supp. 451 (S.D.N.Y. 1981); *Wrench LLC v. Taco Bell Corp.*, 256 F.3d 446 (6th Cir. 2001) (holding that an implied in fact contract was not preempted because the plaintiff's expectation of payment made the claim qualitatively different from a copyright claim). See also, *Forest Park Pictures v. Universal Television Network, Inc.*, 683 F.3d 424 (2d Cir. 2012) ((implied-in-fact contract claim not preempted); *Grosso v. Miramax Film Corp.*, 383 F.3d 965 (9th Cir. 2004), *amended* 400 F.3d 658 (2005) (same); *and Montz v. Pilgrim Films & Television, Inc.*, 649 F.3d 975 (9th Cir. 2011) (en banc) (claims for breach of implied contract and breach of confidence not preempted).

[56] *See, e.g., Oddo v. Ries*, 743 F.2d 630, 635 (9th Cir. 1984) (regarding conversion and breach of fiduciary duty). A claim of conversion will escape preemption only if it contains the extra element of unlawful interference with the physical object embodying the work at issue. *See, e.g., Tire Engineering & Dist., LLC v. Shandong Linglong Rubber Co.*, 682 F.3d 292 (4th Cir. 2012).

[57] *See Warner Bros., Inc. v. Am. Broad. Co.*, 720 F.2d 231 (2d Cir. 1983); *see also* H.R. Rep. No. 94-1476, at 132 (1976).

[58] *See Allied Artists Pictures Corp. v. Rhodes*, 496 F. Supp. 408 (S.D. Ohio 1980), *aff'd*, 679 F.2d 656 (6th Cir. 1982).

[59] *See* H.R. Rep. No. 94-1476, at 132 (1976).

[60] The courts finding no preemption include *Downing v. Abercrombie & Fitch*, 265 F.3d 994 (9th Cir. 2001) (no federal preemption of a claim for infringement of the right of publicity of models by defendant's unauthorized use and reproduction of their photos in defendant's commercial Internet Web site); *Brown v. Ames*, 201 F.3d 654 (5th Cir. 2000) (holding that use of names and likenesses to market performers' musical performances on an infringing sound recording was not preempted); *Landham v. Lewis Galoob Toys, Inc.*, 227 F.3d 619 (6th Cir. 2000) (an actor's right of publicity claim against marketer of action figure of actor's movie character was not preempted); *Wendt v. Host Int'l Inc.*, 125 F.3d 806 (9th Cir. 1997) (holding that actors in a film could assert a right or publicity claim for the unpermitted use of their names to promote the unauthorized distribution of the film); *Toney v. L'oreal U.S.A., Inc.*, 406 F.3d 905 (7th Cir. 2005) (holding that federal copyright law did not preempt state law right of publicity claim where model's likeness was embodied in a photograph). Courts will, however, find preemption when the asserted state publicity rights would unduly interfere with the exclusive rights of the copyright owner. *See Laws v. Sony Music Entertainment, Inc.*, 448 F.3d 1134 (9th Cir. 2006) (holding the Copyright Act preempts a vocalist's claims for the unauthorized use of her voice in a sound recording).

[61] *See generally* Nimmer on Copyright § 1.01[B] (2014). As one Court phrased it, "Plaintiff cannot merely rephrase the same claim citing contract law and thereby obtain relief equivalent to that which he has failed to obtain under copyright law." *Smith v. Weinstein*, 578 F. Supp. 1297, 1307 (S.D.N.Y. 1984).

elements substantially different from copyright and unlike anything covered under the five exclusive rights enumerated in § 106. On the other hand, an action for *quantum meruit* or commercial immorality does not essentially involve anything different from the rights granted under federal copyright law, and thus should be preempted under § 301.

Mayer v. Josiah Wedgwood & Sons, Ltd.,[62] provides an example of how a court looked beyond the language of the pleading to determine whether the state law cause of action was equivalent to or qualitatively different from those provided under § 106. In *Mayer*, the plaintiff designed and published, but did not copyright, a snowflake design. Her complaint alleged that the Wedgwood Company misappropriated the design for use on a Christmas tree ornament. In 1979, Mayer had contacted Wedgwood about using the design on Christmas plates, but her proposal was rejected. Years later, the design suddenly appeared on Wedgwood's Christmas ornaments. Plaintiff demanded remuneration and brought an action under state law for conversion and unfair competition. The design itself was apparently in the public domain and not copyrightable under federal law, so the plaintiff had to seek redress under state law.

Was the cause of action preempted by § 301? The court found equivalent subject matter under §§ 102 and 103 and considered the second prong of the preemption test — whether the rights asserted were the same as those protected by § 106. Using this analysis, the court in *Mayer* found no extra element that would qualitatively distinguish plaintiff's conversion and misappropriation claims from the rights specifically addressed by federal copyright law.[63] Because the conversion claim was a functional equivalent of the reproduction and distribution rights outlined in § 106, the court did not state the extra element needed to avoid preemption. Similarly, plaintiff's misappropriation claim, based on commercial immorality, added no extra qualitative element.[64] In effect, the plaintiff was merely alleging that defendant had acted intentionally and improperly. According to the court, such an allegation, if proved, might alter the scope of the action but not its nature.[65] In sum, the nature of the plaintiff's conversion and misappropriation claims were both the same once the court looked behind the language used: they were simply claims of copyright infringement asserted under state law, and as such, were preempted by § 301.[66]

Other courts have not adopted the *Mayer* approach; instead, they appear to accept almost any colorable additional element claimed that would save plaintiff's state claim from preemption. For example, in *Schuchart & Associates v. Solo Serve*

---

[62] 601 F. Supp. 1523 (S.D.N.Y. 1985).

[63] *Id.* at 1535.

[64] *Id.* at 1536.

[65] *Id.* at 1534.

[66] Plaintiff also asserted both breach of confidentiality and unjust enrichment, which could possibly not be equivalent to a copyright claim. Because the design was in the public domain, plaintiff had lost her property interest in it. Accordingly, defendant was not unjustly enriched. The breach of confidentiality claim failed as well. The publication of the design removed the secrecy that a breach of confidentiality requires. *Id.* at 1536.

Corp.,[67] plaintiff alleged that its architectural drawings were used without permission by defendants in a construction project. One of the claims[68] in the complaint was for unjust enrichment — *quantum meruit*. The court found the cause of action in *quantum meruit* fundamentally different from a copyright claim because plaintiffs did not seek damages analogous to actual damages in a copyright action under § 504(b) of the 1976 Act but asked instead for the value of services rendered to defendants.[69]

This approach, as exemplified by the holding in *Schuchart*, seems to be too permissive because almost any state law claim can be worded so that it differs from a copyright claim. The question should be whether the extra element changes the nature of the cause of action under state law and makes it into something qualitatively different from a copyright claim.[70]

[B] Preemption of State Contract Law

State contract law poses the most challenging preemption issues under § 301(a). The terms of a contract may prohibit or regulate, in some way, the acts of reproduction, adaptation, distribution, performance, or display of a work. However, contract law, in addition to these acts, requires proof of a bargained-for exchange, an element not required in an action for copyright infringement. The preemption of state contract law arose in *National Car Rental Systems, Inc. v. Computer Associates International, Inc.*[71] In this case, National had entered into a contract with Computer Associates to create programs to analyze National's data. The contract stipulated that National would use the programs only to process its own data but not data of third parties. Computer Associates asserted that National had breached the license agreement by allowing third parties to use the programs. In response, National claimed that federal copyright law preempts the limitation on the uses to which a licensee may put a licensed work. The court rejected the preemption argument because the contractual restriction on the use of the programs constituted an extra element that made the cause of action qualitatively different from one for copyright.

In *ProCD v. Zeidenberg*,[72] the court went one step further than *National Car*, suggesting that no contractual provision would ever be preempted under copyright law. The case is all the more remarkable, not only for its position on preemption, but its ringing endorsement of shrink-wrap licenses in the preemption context. In

---

67 540 F. Supp. 928 (W.D. Tex. 1982).

68 Plaintiff's misappropriation claim, however, was preempted.

69 *Schuchart*, 540 F. Supp. at 945. *See* 17 U.S.C. § 504(b).

70 For a creative (and, so far, successful) attempt to avoid preemption by pleading "fraud," *see Bean v. McDougal Littell*, 538 F. Supp. 2d 1196 (D. Ariz. 2008) and *Shuptrine v. McDougal Littell*, 535 F. Supp. 2d 892 (E.D. Tenn. 2008), in which the plaintiffs alleged that the defendant publisher deliberately sought a license to print a small number of copies, knowing that its actual use would greatly exceed that number, in order to obtain access to the work at a lower cost. Other courts, however, have held that state-law fraud claims are merely improper attempts to obtain punitive damages, which are not available under the Copyright Act. *See, e.g.*, *Bucklew v. Hawkins, Ash, Baptie & Co.*, 329 F.3d 923, 933–34 (7th Cir. 2004).

71 991 F.2d 426 (8th Cir. 1993).

72 86 F.3d 1447 (7th Cir. 1996).

ProCD, plaintiff produced a comprehensive national directory of residential and business listings on CD-ROM discs. Each disc contained both telephone listings and a software program used to access, retrieve, and download data. The sale of the product included a license agreement contained in the user guide that limited access to the data for personal use only. Defendant downloaded the data, added some of his own, and eventually made his database available to users on the Internet. He had about 20,000 hits a day. Plaintiff sued for both copyright infringement and breach of contract. The District Court sided with defendant on all grounds.

The Court of Appeals for the Seventh Circuit reversed the lower court on both the contract and preemption issues. It accepted the District Court's ruling (based on *Feist*) that ProCD's telephone listing database could not be copyrighted because of lack of originality. It could, however, be protected under contract law. The court held that as a general proposition, shrink-wrap licenses are enforceable unless, as with any other contract, their terms violated a rule of positive law or were found to be unconscionable.

The court also reversed the District Court on the preemption issue. In so doing, it held that the rights created by contract are not equivalent to any of the exclusive rights within the general scope of copyright. Just as § 301(a) does not itself interfere with private transactions in intellectual property, so, too, it does not prevent states from respecting those transactions. The court reasoned that

> A copyright is a right against the world. Contracts, by contrast, generally, affect only their parties; strangers may do as they please, so contracts do not create exclusive rights. Someone who found a copy of [plaintiff's software product] on the street would not be affected by the shrink-wrap license. . . .[73]

The reasoning of *ProCD* was reaffirmed by a divided panel of the Court of Appeals of the Federal Circuit. *Bowers v. Baystate Technologies, Inc.*[74] concerned a contractual provision in a shrink-wrap license forbidding the reverse engineering of software. The court held that the Copyright Act neither preempts nor narrows the contract claim. As for the preemption issue, the Federal Circuit held the anti-reverse engineering clause does not require preemption as long as a state clause of action requires an extra element, beyond mere copying, preparation of derivative works, performance, and display. It also claimed that the contract claim did not conflict with the exemption from the anti-circumvention prohibition for certain acts of reverse engineering in § 1201(f) of the Copyright Act.[75] The dissent, in criticizing what appeared to be the majority's blanket rule in favor of shrink-wrap license, argued as follows: "If state law provided that a copyright holder could bar fair use of the copyrighted material by placing a black dot on each copy of the work offered for sale, there would be no question but that state law would be preempted."[76] Although agreeing with the majority that the state could permit parties

---

[73] *Id.* at 1447.

[74] 320 F.3d 1317 (Fed. Cir. 2002).

[75] *Id.* at 1325; 17 U.S.C. § 1201(f).

[76] *Id.* at 1335.

to contract away a fair use defense in a freely negotiated agreement, the dissent thought that shrink-wrap contracts were of different quality. In this situation, "state law thus gives the copyright owner the ability to eliminate the fair use defense and every instance at its option."[77]

ProCD and *Bowers* appear to take an extreme "freedom of contract" perspective that would find no contract susceptible to preemption. In so doing, these cases undermining the carefully wrought balance that copyright law provides between the incentive to create and the dissemination of information. After *ProCD*, why couldn't a publisher use a contract (shrink-wrap or otherwise) to eliminate fair use, the first sale doctrine, and other limitations on copyright? If this is the case, a publisher could forbid the reproduction of any part of a book without written permission, the sale of one's copy, or the reading of a book more than once.[78]

To avoid these extreme results that would undermine the very basis of copyright policy, courts should take a more flexible approach, evaluating state law on a case-by-case basis. Unfortunately, the Copyright Act gives little guidance about what contractual provisions are preempted.[79] These problems cannot be resolved by a mechanical application of some version of the extra elements test. Ultimately, the decision must answer the fundamental question posed under Supremacy Clause analysis: does the state law stand as an obstacle to achieving the general goals of federal law because it upsets the balance struck by Congress embodied in the Copyright Act?[80]

[C] Reconciling § 301(a) and the Supremacy Clause

As explained above, courts generally apply the extra elements approach when deciding whether the state cause of action is qualitatively different from copyright and, thus, not preempted by federal copyright law. This approach simply states a conclusion. When is a right provided by state law qualitatively different, and how different in nature must it be to escape preemption? In all but the simplest cases, the extra elements test cannot be applied with any certainty.

---

[77] *Id.*

[78] The academic literature has been hostile to freedom of contract view in ProCD and Bowers, *see* Christina Bohannan, *Copyright Preemption of Contracts*, 67 Md. L. Rev. 616 (2008); Viva R. Moffat, *Super-Copyright Policymaking*, 41 U.C. Davis L. Rev. 45 (2007); Thomas Bell, *Codifying Copyright's Misuse Defense*, 2007 Utah L. Rev. 573; Pamela Samuelson, *Forward: The Digital Content Symposium*, 12 Berkeley Tech. L.J. 1, 5 (1997); Niva Elkin-Koren, *Copyright Policy and the Limits of Freedom of Contract*, 12 Berkeley Tech. L.J. 93, (1997) ("[I]f the standard of assent necessary to form contractual relationships is minimal, then no unlicensed access to works will be possible. The outcome will be very similar to the effect of a right in rem."). *But see* Maureen O'Rourke, *Copyright Preemption After the* ProCD *Case: A Market-Based Approach*, 12 Berkeley Tech. L.J. 53, 91 (1997) (arguing that absent congressional clarification about which copyright rules are immutable, courts should continue to inform their decisions on market principles and analogy to other areas of the law).

[79] One exception can be found in § 203, which provides the author with a non-waivable right to terminate a transfer.

[80] *See* Mark A. Lemley, *Beyond Preemption: The Law and Policy of Intellectual Property Licensing*, 87 Cal. L. Rev. 111, 142 (1999) ("[Courts must] attempt to figure out whether each particular provision in the Copyright Act is merely a default rule that the parties are free to ignore, or whether it instead reflects a part of the balance of interests in federal policy that should not be upset.").

When a court concludes that a state cause of action contains extra elements and qualitative differences, it is expressing an overall judgment that the purpose and effect of the state legislation or case law does not unduly interfere with federal copyright law. Both the purpose and effect of the state statute must be scrutinized to determine whether the state cause of action is equivalent to the federal. The reason that both purpose and effect must be considered is to avoid a preemptive effect either too broad or too narrow. If a court were to look just at the stated purpose of the state law, many state laws, covering essentially the same ground as federal copyright law, would escape preemption because a state legislature can always indicate a non-copyright purpose for its legislation. On the other hand, if a court were to consider only the effect of the state law, preemption would cut too wide a path. State trade secret, defamation, publicity, and contract law all provide similar relief to copyright law, but it was not Congress' intention that these state causes of action be displaced. A court must strike a balance between these two extremes, and in difficult cases, this determination takes reasoned judgment.[81]

Thus, the basic question of preemption cannot be avoided: does the state cause of action interfere with the objectives and policies of federal copyright law? This, of course, is a traditional restatement of the preemption doctrine under the Supremacy Clause of the Constitution. Although § 301 of the 1976 Act was drafted in part to simplify preemption analysis, this result did not occur, and the courts are forced to base their analysis on basic constitutional doctrine with little additional guidance from Congress.

§ 11.08 THE NECESSARY RETURN TO TRADITIONAL PREEMPTION ANALYSIS: FOUR EXAMPLES

[A] State Anti-Blind-Bidding Statutes

State anti-blind-bidding statutes provide an excellent example of the futility of a mechanical application of § 301. These statutes exist in eighteen states and typically require suppliers of motion pictures to screen their films in the state before any negotiations can be completed or bids taken. In effect, they prohibit the practice of blind bidding, whereby a motion picture producer (the copyright owner) requires theater operators to bid on a picture without a prior trade screening within the state. Motion picture producers have argued that the 1976 Copyright Act preempts these statutes because they interfere with distribution and performance rights and generally impede the objectives and policies of the 1976 Copyright Act. The Circuit Courts have disagreed on the preemption question but

[81] Professor Gorman has proposed that the economic purpose of the state law should determine what constitutes a right equivalent. He would find preemption of a state cause of action that provides relief for the same economic harm as does copyright law (i.e., harm from copying in its various forms). On the other hand, state causes of action, such as those for privacy and defamation, which provide recovery against personal harm and reputation are different in economic focus than copyright and should survive preemption. *See* Robert A. Gorman, *Fact or Fancy? The Implications for Copyright*, 29 J. Copyright Soc'y 560, 608–10 (1982).

have analyzed it both under § 301 and under general Supremacy Clause principles.[82]

The following sections discuss other situations where the preemption issue cannot be determined by a mechanical application of § 301 or by a single-minded search for extra elements and qualitative differences.

[B] State Law Conferring Broader or Narrower Rights

Is a state law preempted if it creates a right either broader or narrower than the exclusive rights enumerated in § 106? The basic problem in addressing this question is that neither the statute nor the legislative history defines "equivalency," a term hopelessly ambiguous absent some indication of which features must be similar and can diverge.[83] As a result, one must ultimately retreat to the basic policy that motivated the equivalency test and reexamine the essential question: whether the state law improperly interferes with the goals and policies of the 1976 Copyright Act. For example, § 106(4), the performance right, covers public performances only; a private performance is not an infringing act.[84] If a state were to pass a law providing a private performance right for musical works, a right broader than § 106(4), would the state law be preempted as "equivalent to any of the exclusive rights within the general scope of copyright as specified by Section 106?"[85] One could argue that the state law should be preempted because a private performance right falls within the general scope of § 106(4), the right to perform the work publicly. But this argument simply states a conclusion; it provides no principled reason why a state law extending protection to private performances should be preempted or not.

A better method is to interpret equivalency according to the basic goal Congress intended to accomplish by § 301. According to this analytical method, it would seem that the broader private performance right conferred by the hypothetical state law would interfere with the basic goals of copyright law and would therefore be preempted. Otherwise, the states could greatly enlarge the range of copyright law by conferring a private performance right despite Congress' intention to limit copyright owners' control to public performances only.

---

[82] *See Associated Film Distrib. Corp. v. Thornburgh*, 520 F. Supp. 971 (E.D. Pa. 1981), *rev'd and remanded*, 683 F.2d 808 (3d Cir. 1982), *on remand*, 614 F. Supp. 1100 (E.D. Pa. 1985). The court initially found the state statute preempted as impeding the basic objectives of the Copyright Act. Summary judgment on the issue of preemption was overturned on appeal and the case was remanded to determine at trial whether in fact the statute interfered with federal law. After a trial on the merits the court decided against preemption. *See also Allied Artists Pictures Corp. v. Rhodes*, 496 F. Supp. 408 (S.D. Ohio 1980), *aff'd in part and remanded in part*, 679 F.2d 656 (6th Cir. 1982) (holding that state anti-blind-bidding statute did not frustrate the basic objectives of the Copyright Act).

[83] To take a simple example suggested by Professor William Richman, consider the comparison of these three items: a black dog, a yellow dog, and a black cat. If the relevant feature is color, items one and three are equivalent and item two is not. On the other hand, if the relevant feature is species, items one and two are equivalent and item three is not.

[84] 17 U.S.C. § 106(4). For a discussion of the performance right as it applies to private performances, see *supra* § 8.17.

[85] 17 U.S.C. § 301(a).

[C] Are Rights Equivalent to Those Provided Under §§ 107-121?

A related question involving the meaning of rights equivalent is whether this term applies to §§ 107–120, as well as to § 106. The problem is that § 301 limits its application of rights equivalent to those provided in § 106 and refers to no other sections of the 1976 Act. Once again, neither the statute nor the legislative history provides any help in deciding this question. Because preemption analysis should concern the ultimate question of whether state law unduly interferes with the objectives of copyright law, the entire range of limitations on exclusive rights outlined in §§ 107–120 should be considered in determining whether the state law confers rights equivalent.

For example, would a state law be preempted if it gave motion picture copyright owners the right to prohibit the rental of their movies by video stores that legally obtained copies of the films? This state law would conflict with § 109(a) of the 1976 Act, known as the "first sale doctrine," which gives the owner of a copy or phonorecord the right to sell, rent, or otherwise dispose of the possession of that copy.[86] Here a strong argument could be made for preemption because the state law would effectively annul the first sale doctrine of § 109, the promotion of the free alienability of goods. Similarly, a state law that would change the terms of the various compulsory licenses[87] would be preempted under the same reasoning, as would a state attempt to place a fee on the right of broadcasters to make ephemeral recordings under § 112.[88]

[D] The California Resale Royalty Act

California's Resale Royalty Act,[89] which allows artists a percentage of the resale price of their works, poses many of the same preemption questions as moral rights legislation. The preemption issue has already been litigated in a 1909 Act case, *Morseburg v. Baylon*,[90] where the court applied traditional preemption analysis to find that the Resale Royalty Act was not preempted by the 1909 Copyright Act. The court found the restrictions the Resale Royalty Act placed upon the first sale doctrine and the distribution rights were not serious enough interferences with the purposes and objectives of federal copyright to warrant preemption.

Morseburg, however, did not definitively settle the preemption issue because the case was decided under the 1909 Act. Whether the California Resale Royalty Act

---

[86] 17 U.S.C. § 109(a) reads as follows:

> Notwithstanding the provisions of section 106(3), the owner of a particular copy or phonorecord lawfully made under this title, or any person authorized by such owner, is entitled, without the authority of the copyright owner, to sell or otherwise dispose of the possession of that copy or phonorecord.

[87] For example, a state would be preempted from raising the royalty to be paid for the mechanical license. *See* 17 U.S.C. § 115. For a discussion of the mechanical license, see *supra* § 8.09.

[88] 17 U.S.C. § 112. For a discussion of ephemeral recordings, see *supra* § 8.06.

[89] Cal. Civ. Code § 986 (1983). For a discussion of the California Resale Royalty Act, see *supra* § 8.54[F].

[90] 621 F.2d 972 (9th Cir. 1980).

will fare as well if the preemption issue is litigated again under the 1976 Act is an open question. Here, the problem is that the right granted by state law is similar to, though narrower than, the distribution right under § 106(3). In addition, California law also modifies the effect of the first sale doctrine in § 109(a) of the 1976 Act. One could plausibly argue that the Resale Royalty Act does nothing more than restrict the first sale doctrine of § 109(a) and modify the distribution right of § 106(3).[91] But even if this is so, the Resale Royalty Act unduly interferes with basic copyright policy under §§ 109(a) and 106(3), whose purpose is to promote the free alienability of material objects embodying the copyrighted work. Moreover, the interference would become even greater if other states passed resale royalty acts whereby more than one resale royalty would be imposed on the same sale. This possibility for conflict among state laws that may impede the distribution of copyrighted works indicates a basic conflict with federal copyright principles.

[E] State Misappropriation Law and the "Partial Preemption Doctrine": *NBA v. Motorola*

Preemption, particularly in a misappropriation context, continues to be the subject of lively discussion in the courts. Witness the Second Circuit's recent decision in *National Basketball Ass'n v. Motorola Inc.*[92] There, the court ruled that the National Basketball Association could not bar Motorola and Sports Team Analysis and Tracking Systems ("STATS") from transmitting NBA scores and other information (to its site on America Online) through a paging device manufactured by Motorola. The NBA's suit had alleged, *inter alia*, federal copyright infringement and unfair competition and misappropriation under New York state law. The trial court dismissed all but the misappropriation claim, as to which it entered an injunction in the NBA's favor. The Court of Appeals framed the issue as follows: "The crux of the dispute concerns the extent to which a state law 'hot-news' misappropriation claim based on [*INS v. AP*] survives preemption by the federal Copyright Act and whether the NBA's claim fits within the surviving *INS*-type claims."[93] The court then reversed as to the District Court injunction.

Preemption analysis necessarily involved, as its predicate, a consideration of the federal copyright claim. The Second Circuit agreed with the District Court on the copyright issue. Although broadcasts of NBA games constitute copyrightable expression, sports events themselves are not protectable works of "authorship" in any common sense of the word. The Second Circuit, however, rejected the "partial preemption doctrine" articulated by the District Court. That doctrine would hold that federal copyright law preempts state claims based on the misappropriation of broadcasts as such, but not those based on takings of the underlying facts. The Second Circuit found no principled basis for the distinction. By allowing state law to vest exclusive rights in material that Congress intended to be in the public domain, the partial preemption doctrine would render the preemption intended by Congress unworkable.

---

[91] For a discussion of the first sale doctrine and the distribution right, see *supra* § 8.14.

[92] 105 F.3d 841 (2d Cir. 1997).

[93] *Id.* at 843.

The Court of Appeals indicated, however, that certain forms of commercial misappropriation *can* survive preemption if an "extra element" test is met — if, that is, the claim contains an element not equivalent to the exclusive rights granted by copyright law. Despite its rejection of the partial preemption doctrine, the Second Circuit ruled that a "hot-news" claim under New York misappropriation law, based on the *INS* case, is not necessarily preempted. According to the court, the "extra elements" in a nonpreempted hot-news claim (i.e., the elements beyond those required to prove a claim for copyright infringement) are as follows:

(i) the time-sensitive value of the factual information;

(ii) free-riding by a defendant; and

(iii) a threat to the very existence of the plaintiff's product or service posed by the defendant's free-riding.

Applying these standards, the Second Circuit found the misappropriation claim in *NBA* to be preempted: the defendants themselves assembled the information in question, and the plaintiff had failed to demonstrate that anyone would access the STATS site on AOL as a substitute for attending the games or watching the broadcasts.

Although the *NBA* court reconfirmed the continuing existence of state misappropriation doctrine, it did not do much to clarify its scope nor the extent of the "hot-news" exception to copyright preemption of state misappropriation laws. The court did not answer fundamental questions: to escape preemption, how "hot" or time-sensitive must the information be or how similar must the plaintiff's and defendant's products be? It would seem that the misappropriation doctrine as articulated by *NBA* will operate in a narrow band. Most importantly, because the defendant must prove freeriding is a threat to the very existence of a competitive product, it is hard to imagine that many plaintiffs will succeed in making out an *INS/NBA* claim.[94]

Misappropriation may be on the verge of making something of a comeback as a federal law doctrine. Arguably, one way to provide compiled databases with limited protection against predatory competition, in the aftermath of *Feist*,[95] might be to refine and standardize misappropriation doctrine as it applies to factual compilations.[96] How could this be done, short of federal legislation premised on Congress' power under the Commerce Clause? Legislation "to prevent the misappropriation of collections of information" was introduced in Congress. Critics of this kind of

---

[94] *See Associated Press v. All Headline News*, 608 F. Supp. 2d 454 (S.D.N.Y. 2009) (holding that a distributor of breaking news on the Internet is subject to a "hot news [misappropriate claim] under New York [state] law and is not preempted by . . . copyright").

[95] *Feist Publ'ns v. Rural Tel. Serv. Co.*, 499 U.S. 340 (1991).

[96] *See* J.H. Reichman & Pamela Samuelson, *Intellectual Property Rights in Data*, 50 VAND. L. REV. 51, 141 (1997). *See, e.g.*, The Collection of Information Antipiracy Act, H.R. 2252, 106th Cong. 2d Sess., 1998. The caption of the Bill — "A bill . . . to prevent misappropriation of collections of information" — refers to a growing scholarly literature that holds that whatever problems exist in the database market are better cured through selective application of tort principles of unfair competition rather than by comprehensive *sui generis* protection. *Sui generis* protection of databases is discussed at *supra* § 2.11[E].

legislation pointed out that, although the word "misappropriation" appeared in its caption, the substance of the rights provided had little to do with the *INS* approach to regulating predatory commercial competition. It seemed instead to represent yet another attempt to create *sui generis* intellectual property protection for noncopyrightable factual compilations.[97]

§ 11.09 SUBJECT MATTER: THE SECOND REQUIREMENT FOR PREEMPTION OF STATE LAW

The second prong of the preemption test requires that the subject matter covered by the state law come within the subject matter of copyright, as specified in §§ 102 and 103. This test involves two special problems of interpretation. First, can a work be protected under state law but for some reason be uncopyrightable? Examples would include a work that fails to meet the standard of originality or has fallen into the public domain or constitutes uncopyrightable subject matter (idea, fact, process) under § 102(b). Second, can state law protect subject matter that Congress has considered, but decided not to protect, such as typeface design, literary characters, or industrial design?

[A] Non-Original Works and Works in the Public Domain or Excluded by § 102(b)

According to the House Report,[98] states cannot protect a work within §§ 102 or 103 that fails to achieve copyright protection because it is minimal or lacking in originality or because it has fallen into the public domain. Otherwise, the states could confer unlimited protection on that which was unfit for even limited protection under federal law. Thus, a state law that protects a work of art that fails to meet the federal standard of originality or is injected into the public domain for failure to meet notice formalities would be preempted by § 301 or by general principles of the Supremacy Clause of the Constitution.

A similar question is whether state law can protect facts, ideas, systems, or processes because these are excluded from copyrightable subject matter under § 102(b). For example, suppose a state misappropriation law protects the taking of facts and ideas presented in an autobiography of a president. One might argue that the subject matter test is not met because copyright protects the arrangements of facts, not the facts themselves. As for ideas, copyright protects the expression of an idea, not the idea itself. Despite these arguments, preemption is appropriate because the entire work in question falls within the general category of copyrightable subject matter — it is a copyrightable literary work, even though it contains uncopyrightable portions that are the object of the state law protection. Preemption is proper; otherwise, state law protection would create "vague borderline areas between State and Federal protection" and circumvent one of the central purposes of the 1976 Act, the establishment of comprehensive federal

[97] For details, see the website of the Association of Research Libraries: www.cni.arl.org.

[98] H.R. Rep. No. 94-1476, 94th Cong., 2d Sess. 131 (1976).

standards.[99] In addition to these arguments favoring federal preemption of state protection of facts, such protection may also be suspect under the First Amendment.[100]

[B] Subject Matter Which Congress Could Have, But Did Not, Include

Congress chose not to include certain categories of subject matter in §§ 102 and 103 of the 1976 Act. Examples include typeface designs, literary characters, and industrial design. If a state were to pass a law protecting typeface design, or one protecting the design of useful articles, would such a law be preempted by federal copyright law as constituting works of authorship coming within §§ 102 or 103? To answer this question, one must first determine whether typeface or industrial design fall within the general categories of copyrightable subject matter. The initial response is that they fall generally within pictorial, graphic, and sculptural works as such terms are used in § 102.[101]

But does Congress' specific exclusion of these items indicate that the states are free to occupy the field? This is another area where courts must turn again to general preemption analysis based on the Supremacy Clause, that is, they must decide whether the state law conflicts with basic copyright policy. In the examples cited above, a strong argument could be made that a state law conferring protection would improperly interfere with the objectives of federal copyright law. Congress has apparently decided as a matter of policy that these forms of writings should not be given monopoly protection and should be in the public domain instead.[102] One cannot argue, as in *Goldstein v. California*,[103] that Congress left

---

99 *Harper & Row, Publishers, Inc. v. Nation Enters.*, 723 F.2d 195, 200 (2d Cir. 1983), *rev'd on other grounds*, 471 U.S. 539 (1985). *See Katz, Dochtermann & Epstein, Inc. v. Home Box Office*, 50 U.S.P.Q.2d (BNA) 1957 (S.D.N.Y. 1999) (holding that both the copyrightable expression, and the uncopyrightable idea that underlies it, fall within "the subject matter of copyright" for preemption purposes). The majority of appellate decisions agree with this proposition. In *Ho v. Taflove*, 648 F.3d 489, 501 (7th Cir. 2011), (holding that the subject-matter element of preemption was met, because "Congress sought to ensure that a state will not provide copyright-like protections in materials that should remain uncopyrighted or uncopyrightable" (internal quotes omitted). *See also, e.g., Barclay's Capital, Inc. v. Theflyonthewall.com, Inc.*, 650 F.3d 876, 892–93 (2d Cir. 2011); *Montz v. Pilgrim Films & Television, Inc.*, 649 F.3d 975, 979–80 (9th Cir. 2011) (en banc); and *R.W. Beck, Inc. v. E3 Consulting, LLC*, 577 F.3d 1133, 1146–47 (10th Cir. 2009).

100 Courts and commentators do not always adhere to the above analysis. *See, e.g.*, Paul Goldstein, *Preempted State Doctrines, Involuntary Transfers and Compulsory Licenses: Testing the Limi* § 301(b)(*1ts of Copyright*, 24 UCLA L. Rev. 1107, 1119 (1977). In *Bromhall v. Rorvik*, 478 F. Supp. 361 (E.D. Pa. 1979), the court upheld claims for the misappropriation of plaintiff's ideas regarding the cloning of rabbits that were expressed in plaintiff's thesis and later used in defendant's work on human cloning. The state law claims were not preempted because copyright protection under § 102(b) extends only to the expression of an idea, not the idea itself. *See also, Dunlap v. G & L Holding Group Inc.*, 381 F.3d 1285 (11th Cir. 2004), (concluding "that the subject matter of copyright, in terms of preemption, includes only those elements that are substantively qualified for copyright protection." *Id.* at 1295

101 *See* H.R. Rep. No. 94-1476, 94th Cong., 2d Sess. 55 (1976).

102 *See* Second Supplementary Report of the Register of Copyright on the General Revision of the U.S. Copyright Law: 1975 Revision Bill Ch. 1 (draft ed. 1975).

103 412 U.S. 546 (1973).

these forms of subject matter unattended so that state law could fill the void. Each was specifically considered by Congress, which decided that characters, typeface, and industrial design should not receive protection and should rest in the public domain.[104]

§ 11.10 NON-PREEMPTED WORKS

Section 301 leaves certain works outside its preemptive effect. First, this section, consistent with the Constitution, applies only to works fixed in a tangible medium of expression.[105] Unfixed works, such as purely oral works, improvised music, spontaneous speeches, and other unfixed performances, are not covered, and state law governing such works would not be preempted. Second, § 301 does not apply to any cause of action arising before January 1, 1978.[106] Third, for sound recordings fixed before February 15, 1972, rights and remedies under the common law are not affected until February 15, 2067.[107] Fourth, nothing in § 301 affects rights and remedies under any other federal statute.[108] From a practical standpoint, this last aspect is the most significant. Examples of federal statutes covering the same terrain as copyright and exempted from preemption provisions are the Federal Communications Act,[109] the Patent Act,[110] and, most particularly, the Lanham Act.[111]

This latter federal statute involves federal trademark protection and provides for the registration of words, names, symbols, and devices.

---

[104] For two cases refusing to register typeface designs, see *Eltra Corp. v. Ringer*, 579 F.2d 294 (4th Cir. 1978) (upholding Register's refusal to register typefaces as works of art) and *Leonard Storch Enters., Inc. v. Mergenthaler Linotype Co.*, 1980 U.S. Dist. LEXIS 16069 (E.D.N.Y. Aug. 8, 1980) (denying protection of typeface under state unfair competition law but holding that typeface was not preempted because typeface designs are uncopyrightable).

[105] 17 U.S.C. § 301(b)(1).

[106] 17 U.S.C. § 301(b)(2).

[107] 17 U.S.C. § 301(c). *See Capitol Records, Inc. v. Naxos of Am., Inc.*, 372 F.3d 471 (2d Cir. 2004) (holding that the common law of the state of New York extends copyright protection to pre-1972 foreign-made sound recordings that are not subject to copyright protection under the U.S. Copyright Act).

[108] 17 U.S.C. § 301(d).

[109] 47 U.S.C. §§ 151–611.

[110] 35 U.S.C. §§ 1–140 (1952).

[111] 15 U.S.C. §§ 1051–1127.

§ 11.11 OTHER PREEMPTION PROVISIONS OF THE COPYRIGHT ACT

[A] The Visual Artists Rights Act of 1990: § 301(f)

Section 301(f)[112] preempts state laws that give rights equivalent to § 106A's rights of attribution and integrity falling within the subject matter covered by that section's protection of works of visual art. The same two conditions, as are found in § 301(a), must be met for preemption of state law. First, the subject matter of state law must be a work of visual art as defined in § 101, which is limited to painting, graphic arts, and sculpture. According to the legislative history, Congress did not intend to preempt state art preservation acts that confer protection on such subject matter as audiovisual works or photographs that are not included in § 101's definition of a "work of visual art."[113] For example, the Massachusetts statute[114] includes movies and television productions and to that extent would not be preempted by § 301(f). Second, § 301(f)(2) will preempt state law only if it is equivalent to § 106A's rights of attribution or integrity. Thus, a state law that includes some extra element not included in § 106A, such as an affirmative obligation to attribute authorship of a work of visual art, will not be preempted.[115] Similarly, § 301(f)(2)(C) will not preempt a state statute that extends protection beyond the life of the author. Unlike the rights conferred under § 106, which last the life of the author plus 70 years, the rights under the Visual Artists Rights Act expire on the death of the author. Thus, the state provision conferring a *post mortem* right will become operative when federal protection under § 106A ends (i.e., when the author dies).

[B] The Architectural Works Protection Act of 1990: § 301(b)(4)

The Architectural Works Copyright Protection Act, enacted on the same date as the Visual Artists Rights Act of 1990, also takes preemption into account to avoid any preemptive effect the law may have on state law concerning landmarks, historic preservation, zoning, or building codes. Section 301(b)(4) provides:

> (b) Nothing in this title annuls or limits any rights or remedies under the common law or statutes of any State with respect to:
>
> . . . .
>
> (4) state and local landmarks, historic preservation, zoning, or building codes relating to architectural works protected under section 102(a)(8).[116]

---

112 17 U.S.C. § 301(f).

113 *See* H.R. REP. NO. 101-514, 101st Cong. 2d Sess. 21 (1990).

114 Mass. Gen. Laws Ann. ch. 231 § 855 (West Supp. 1986).

115 Section 106A grants the author the right to claim authorship of the work and prevent the use of his or her name as the author of the work of visual art in the event of a mutilation or other modification of the work that would be prejudicial to his or her honor or reputation. *See* 17 U.S.C. § 106A(a).

116 17 U.S.C. § 301(b)(4).

Chapter 12

AN OVERVIEW OF INTERNATIONAL COPYRIGHT

§ 12.01 INTRODUCTION AND CHAPTER OVERVIEW

In our information age, the international dimension of copyright law grows in importance each day. Satellite communications, broadband, and other developing technologies permit access to copyrighted works worldwide as never before. Copyrighted works can be copied cheaply and disseminated quickly, unimpeded by time, space, or national boundaries. The result of these developments, particularly when coupled with systematic piracy in certain foreign countries, is that copyright owners have less and less control over their creations. As the world's largest user and producer of copyrighted works, the United States has a special interest in an orderly and responsive international regime of copyright protection. This recognition is reflected in the United States' adherence (effective March 1, 1989) to the Berne Convention, the oldest and preeminent multinational copyright treaty.

This chapter, which is divided into four parts, provides a brief overview of international copyright matters. Part I examines the international copyright conventions. The major focus is on the provisions of the Berne Convention and the changes in American law that permitted the United States to adhere to this important international arrangement.

Part II treats the broad-based protection of foreign authors that is conferred by § 104 of the 1976 Copyright Act. It also discusses issues involving extraterritorial application of U.S. law, choice of forum, and conflicts of law in international copyright. Part II ends with a discussion of the enforcement of foreign judgments in copyright matters.

Part III provides an outline of various trade regulation laws affecting copyright. The first topic in Part III concerns the regulation of importation under §§ 602 and 603 of the 1976 Copyright Act, which designates the Customs Service as the agency to police importation of infringing articles. The second topic concerns § 337 of the Tariff Act, administered by the International Trade Commission, which prohibits unfair methods of competition in the importation of goods into the United States. The third topic in Part III reviews forms of international trade regulation, Generalized System of Preferences, and the Caribbean Basin Recovery Act, designed to encourage countries to provide adequate protection of U.S. intellectual property interests. Part IV focuses on international and regional trade agreements as they concern copyright law. It addresses the Trade Related Aspects of Intellectual Property ("TRIPS") agreement arising out of the Uruguay Round of the General Agreement on Tariffs and Trade ("GATT"). This part also discusses regional trade agreements, namely the European Union and the North American

Free Trade Agreement ("NAFTA"). Multilateral and regional trade agreements are the newest development in international copyright relations and may prove to be a powerful force for change on the international stage.

Part I. THE MAJOR INTERNATIONAL TREATIES INVOLVING COPYRIGHT

§ 12.02 GENERALLY

Worldwide copyright does not exist. The principal treaties, the Berne Union[1] and the Universal Copyright Convention ("U.C.C."), do not automatically protect an author's works throughout the world under a supranational copyright law. No matter what the international agreement, protection against infringement in any given country depends on the national laws of that country. Thus, an author who wishes to protect his work abroad must comply with the pertinent national laws.

Falling short of establishing an international copyright, the U.C.C. and particularly the Berne Union have simplified the requirements for obtaining foreign copyright protection. This has been accomplished by establishing convention *minima*, that is, minimum rights that may be claimed in all member countries, regardless of any other national legislation. The difference between the two major international conventions is the substantiality of the conventions' *minima*.[2]

From 1891 until its entry into the U.C.C. in 1955, the United States relied on a series of bilateral agreements[3] to protect its copyright interests internationally. These piecemeal arrangements became increasingly inadequate in an ever-shrinking world of new communication technologies, which recognize no national boundaries. By the 1950s, when the United States emerged as the major exporter of copyrighted works, the need for American participation in a truly integrated system of international copyright became readily apparent. The gap was filled by the United States' entry into the U.C.C.

---

[1] Convention concerning the creation of an International Union for the Protection of Literary and Artistic Works (Sept. 9, 1886, revised in 1908, 1928, 1948, 1967, 1971), hereinafter cited as the "Berne Convention."

[2] For an excellent comparison of the characteristics of the Berne Convention and the U.C.C., see the text of a speech made by Lewis Flacks, Policy Planning Adviser for the U.S. Register of Copyrights, contained in *Out of UNESCO and into Berne: Has the United States Participation in the Berne Convention for International Copyright Protection Become Essential?*, 4 Cardozo Arts & Ent. L.J. 216, 216–26 (1985).

[3] *See* Nimmer on Copyright § 5.05[B][2][c] (2014). For a list of the bilateral agreements in force, see Copyright Office Circular 38(a).

§ 12.03 THE UNIVERSAL COPYRIGHT CONVENTION ("U.C.C.")

[A] Generally

The United States was the motivating force behind the formation of the U.C.C. At that time, the Copyright Act of 1909 was in force, and its features[4] precluded United States entry into the Berne Convention, the major international copyright convention. The U.C.C. was negotiated as a stop-gap measure to protect U.S. copyright interests temporarily, and as a bridge to eventual U.S. entry into Berne.[5] The U.C.C. turned out to be more than a temporary measure. It took more than 30 years and major revisions of American copyright law before the United States was able to adhere to the Berne Convention. Although the U.C.C. has now been supplanted by the United States' adherence to the Berne Convention, it is still important for American copyright interests because a number of countries are members of the U.C.C. but are not members of Berne.[6]

The Universal Copyright Convention took effect in the United States on September 16, 1955. A revision of the Convention occurred in Paris in 1971 and became effective in 1974. The U.C.C. is administered by UNESCO, and because the United States has withdrawn from this United Nations agency,[7] some have questioned our continued reliance on this Convention to provide effective protection for U.S. copyright interests.[8]

[B] Basic Provisions of the U.C.C.

The basis of the U.C.C. is "national treatment,"[9] which requires all member countries to accord to foreign works eligible under the U.C.C. the same protection granted its own nationals. Additionally, the U.C.C. specifies certain minimum legal

---

[4] Most important of the features impeding entry into Berne was duration of copyright and required compliance with formalities imposed by American copyright law. For a discussion of Berne and its convention *minima*, see *infra* § 12.04.

[5] Evidence of U.S. intent to eventually enter the Berne Union can be found in the House Report on the 1976 Act. *See* H.R. Rep. No. 94-1476, 94th Cong., 2d Sess. 135 (1976). *See* Barbara A. Ringer, *The Universal Copyright Convention and its Future*, reprinted in The Copyright Act of 1976: Dealing with the New Realities 339 (1977). For the text of the U.C.C., see Marshall A. Leaffer, International Treaties on Intellectual Property 397 (2d. ed. 1997).

[6] As of January 1, 1989, some 26 countries are members of the U.C.C. but are not Berne adherents. These include certain developing countries in Africa and several Latin American countries.

[7] The U.S. gave the requisite one-year notice of intent to withdraw from the United Nations Educational, Scientific, and Cultural Organization (UNESCO), which administers the U.C.C., on December 29, 1983. *See U.S. Notifies UNESCO of Intent to Withdraw*, 84 U.S. Dept. of State Bull. No. 2083, 41 (1984).

[8] A country does not have to be a member of UNESCO to participate in the U.C.C., but without membership, the United States would not be able to influence the future direction and policy on international copyright matters within the organization that administers the U.C.C. *See* S. Rep. No. 100-352, 100th Cong., 2d Sess. 4 (1988).

[9] *See* Nimmer on Copyright § 17.04[B] n.6 (2014).

obligations for each contracting state. Its more important elements can be summarized as follows.

[1] General Obligations

The contracting states must provide for adequate and effective protection of the rights of authors and other copyright proprietors.[10]

[2] Basis of Protection

The published works of nationals of a contracting state must receive the same protection as the contracting state accords to works of its nationals first published in its own territory. The same applies for unpublished works.[11] The convention is not retroactive, and those works in the public domain of a contracting state remain there.

[3] Formalities

Formalities such as notice, registration, and manufacture, which may be part of a contracting state's copyright law, are satisfied for a foreign U.C.C. work

> if from the time of first publication all the copies of the work . . . bear the symbol ©; accompanied by the name of the copyright proprietor and the year of first publication placed in such manner and location as to give reasonable notice of claim of copyright.[12]

A member state may, however, require additional formalities, such as deposit, registration, and manufacturing requirements, for works first published within its territory by foreign nationals or by its own nationals, wherever they may be published. Thus, pursuant to this provision, formalities are not excused for works first published in the United States by either a U.S. citizen or a foreign national. In addition, a work first published abroad by a U.S. citizen was always subject to formalities under U.S. law.

[4] Minimum Term of Protection

Member states must grant a minimum copyright term of 25 years from publication, or life of the author plus 25 years.[13]

[5] Exclusive Rights

Contracting states must grant exclusive translation rights to foreign authors of other member states for at least seven years. After this term expires, a compulsory licensing arrangement can be instituted.[14]

---

[10] *See* U.C.C. art. 1 (Paris Act).

[11] *See* U.C.C. art. 2 (Paris Act).

[12] *See* U.C.C. art. 3 (Paris Act).

[13] *See* U.C.C. art. 4 (Paris Act).

[14] *See* U.C.C. art. 5 (Paris Act).

[6] Berne Safeguard Clause

The U.C.C. contains a Berne Safeguard Clause, which prohibits a Berne Convention country from denouncing Berne and relying on the U.C.C. in its copyright relations with members of the Berne Convention.[15] This provision came about through the efforts of Berne Union members who feared the U.C.C. was a step backwards and wanted to prevent Berne principles from being undermined by the adherence of its members to the U.C.C.. Thus, the United States, now a member of Berne, cannot look to the U.C.C. for protection of any work originating from a Berne country, even though that country may also adhere to the U.C.C..

[C] The Paris Revision of the U.C.C.

The U.C.C. was revised in Paris in 1971 in response to demands by developing countries.[16] The revision, effective in 1974, allows developing countries to obtain compulsory licenses under certain conditions to translate copyrighted works for teaching, scholarship, and research purposes. It also allows reproduction of copyrighted works for use in systematic instructional activities.

The Paris revision strengthened Convention *minima* for adequate and effective protection by adding basic rights that ensure an author's economic interest. These included the rights of reproduction, public performance, and broadcasting, three rights that are to be interpreted broadly. However, protection of the author's moral rights[17] was specifically excluded. In addition, the Berne Safeguard Clause was suspended, permitting developing countries to withdraw from Berne and adhere to the U.C.C..[18]

---

[15] *See* U.C.C. art. 15; Appendix Declaration (Paris Act).

[16] The United Nations General Assembly designates "developing countries" by a nation's cultural, social, and economic development; for example, Algeria, Barbados, Cambodia, Dahomey, and Ecuador are considered "developing countries." *See* Heinz Dawid, *Basic Principles of International Copyright*, 21 Bull. Copyright Soc'y 1 (1973). *See also* U.C.C. art. 5*bis* (Paris Act).

[17] Many countries recognize an artist's moral or personal right in his work to prevent mutilation, alteration, and false suggestion even after the work is legally transferred. In contrast, American copyright law is rooted in economic rights and once copyright of the work is transferred, the author can no longer control use of the work. For a discussion of moral rights and their lack of express recognition under American law, see *supra* § 8.28.

[18] The Berne Safeguard Clause prohibits a Berne Convention country from denouncing Berne and relying on the U.C.C. in its copyright relations with members of the Berne Convention. The Paris revisions reflected the desire of developing nations to reduce their treaty obligations, granting wider translation and instructional privileges in the U.C.C., plus more latitude in withdrawing from Berne without abandoning protections previously accorded their authors. *See also* "Appendix Declaration Relating to Article XVII" of the U.C.C. as revised at Paris, July 10, 1974.

§ 12.04 THE BERNE CONVENTION

[A] Generally

Until its adherence on March 1, 1989, the United States was the only major western country[19] that was not a member of the International Union for the Protection of Literary and Artistic Works (known as the Berne Union or Berne Convention), the oldest multilateral copyright convention. The Berne Union was first established in 1886 in Berne, Switzerland, and has been revised six times. The current text, the one to which the United States and most other countries have adhered, is that of Paris, 1971.[20] The Berne Convention is administered by the World Intellectual Property Organization ("WIPO"), an intergovernmental organization with headquarters in Geneva, Switzerland.[21]

[B] Berne Convention: Summary of Its Basic Provisions

The substantive provisions of Berne are found in the first 20 Articles, followed by administrative provisions and an Appendix incorporating special provisions for developing countries. These substantive provisions include both specific and general obligations imposed on its membership. Other rules are optional with the member country. Similar to the U.C.C., the Berne Union is based on national treatment and compliance with Convention *minima*. However, as the following summary will reveal, the Berne Union has established Convention *minima* more substantial than those found in the U.C.C..

[1] Subject Matter

Under Article 2(1), the scope of subject matter is broad, encompassing "literary and artistic works [which] shall include every production in the literary and artistic domain whatever may be the mode or form of its expression."[22]

This article provides an illustrative list of such works as choreography, painting, and architecture. Compilations and derivative works are to be given protection as well.[23] The Convention expressly excludes from obligatory protection "news of the day or . . . miscellaneous facts having the character of mere items of press

---

[19] As of January 1, 1989, the other notable non-adherents to Berne were the Soviet Union and China. Since that time, both China and Russia have become parties to the Berne Convention. For the text of the Berne Convention, see Marshall A. Leaffer, International Treaties on Intellectual Property 357 (2d. ed. 1997).

[20] The Berne Convention, signed Sept. 9, 1886, was supplemented by the Additional Act and Declaration signed at Paris, May 4, 1896. The Convention was revised at Berlin, Nov. 13, 1908; Rome, June 2, 1928; Brussels, June 26, 1948; Stockholm, July 14, 1967 (but not ratified); Paris, July 24, 1971.

[21] WIPO is a specialized agency within the United Nations system. Its central role is to conduct studies and provide services designed to facilitate protection of intellectual property. Its Director General is chief of the Berne Union.

[22] Protection of unfixed works is left to the discretion of each member state. Berne Convention art. 2(2) (Paris text).

[23] *See* Berne Convention art. 2(3), (5) (Paris text).

information."[24] Protection of industrial design is optional and is left to national law.[25]

[2] Basis of Protection

The Berne Convention requires that protection be given to published or unpublished works of an author who is a national of a member state. Berne protection is also required for a work of a non-national of a member state if the work is first published in a member state or simultaneously published in a non-member and member state. Under the Paris and Brussels texts of Berne, a work is published simultaneously if it is published in a member country within 30 days of its first publication in a non-member country.[26]

Even before the United States' entry into Berne, American authors were able to enjoy Berne privileges by simultaneously publishing their works in a Berne country. For example, American authors often published their works in Canada within 30 days of publication in the United States. Because Canada adhered to the Paris text of Berne, American authors benefited from Berne despite the United States' non-adherence. This technique of obtaining the benefits of Berne has become known as the "back door to Berne."

Simultaneous publication did not prove to be the panacea it may have appeared on first glance.[27] First, it could be costly, rendering the less wealthy author unable to avail himself of the privilege. Second, seeking protection under the simultaneous publication privilege was not altogether certain in conferring the benefits of Berne. This uncertainty lies in the meaning of "publication" under the Berne Convention. One view is that the term "publication" in the Berne context means that the author must supply enough copies to satisfy the public's need for the work. Under this definition of publication, an American author would have to do much more than send a couple of copies of a book to a Canadian distributor to meet Berne publication requirements, even though this act would constitute publication under U.S. law.[28] Apart from these difficulties, an author taking the "back door" route had to verify that the country chosen adhered to a text of Berne that allowed the 30-day publication privilege. For those countries adhering to the Rome text only, simultaneous publication means that publication must take place on the same day in the two countries, a task impossible to fulfill for many authors.[29]

[3] Preclusion of Formalities

Berne requires that the work be protected without formalities outside the country of origin. Thus, if a work originates from a member country, it must be protected in all Berne countries without being subjected to any formalities as a

---

[24] Berne Convention art. 2(8) (Paris text).

[25] *See* Berne Convention art. 2(7) (Paris text).

[26] Berne Convention art. 3(2) (Paris text).

[27] For a detailed overview, see Nimmer on Copyright § 17.04[D] (2014).

[28] See 17 U.S.C. § 101 (publication) for a discussion of publication.

[29] Berne Convention art. 4(3) (Rome text).

prerequisite to copyright protection.[30] The Berne Convention does not govern protection of works in their countries of origin. This means that formalities can be imposed on a work in its country of origin.

[4] Minimum Term of Protection

The Berne Convention has established a minimum term of protection of life plus 50 years or an alternative of 50 years from publication for anonymous or pseudonymous works.[31] As is generally the case for all Berne provisions, the member country can grant a term of protection in excess of the minimum term.[32]

[5] Exclusive Rights

The Berne Convention requires that certain exclusive rights be protected under national law. These rights, on the whole, are quite similar to the array of economic rights found in § 106 of the 1976 Copyright Act.[33] Berne, in some ways, is not as comprehensive as American law. For example, Berne is silent on distribution and display rights, both of which are specifically provided for under American law. Berne also recognizes certain limitations on the exclusive rights, such as a fair use[34] privilege, and a possible limitation of the right of recording of musical works, such as the right found in § 115 of the 1976 Act. In addition to these exclusive economic rights, Berne also requires that the author's moral right be recognized and endure beyond the life of the author.[35] This concept is alien to U.S. copyright law but may have received *de facto* recognition when considered in the entire context of American unfair competition and defamation law.[36] Finally, in 1990, with the Visual Artists Rights Act, the United States for the first time gave explicit, but hardly complete, recognition to a moral right.[37]

---

30 *See* Berne Convention art. 5(2) (Paris text).

31 Berne Convention art. 7(1), (3) (Paris text).

32 *See* Berne Convention art. 7(6) (Paris text).

33 *See* Berne Convention arts. 8(1) (translation right); 9(1) (reproduction); 11(1) (public performance); 12 (adaptation) (Paris text).

34 Berne Convention arts. 9(2), 10, 10*bis* (Paris text).

35 *See* Berne Convention art. 6*bis* (providing in part):

> (1) Independently of an author's economic rights and even after the transfer of said rights, the author shall have the right to claim authorship of the work and to object to any distortion, mutilation or other modification of, or other derogatory action in relation to, the said work, which would be prejudicial to his honor or reputation.
>
> (2) The rights granted to the author in accordance with the preceding paragraph shall, after his death, be maintained, at least until the expiry of the economic rights. . . .).

36 For a discussion of the moral right and its American analogs, see *supra* § 8.28.

37 The Act confers a right of integrity and paternity on certain works in the visual arts. *See supra* § 8.28.

§ 12.05 U.S. ENTRY INTO BERNE

[A] Generally

Before its entry into Berne on March 1, 1989, the United States was the only major Western country that was not a party to the Convention.[38] Because the United States has been for some time the world's largest exporter of copyrighted works,[39] it had a strong interest in joining the world's largest, preeminent copyright convention, particularly because Berne, by then, encompassed 85 nations, including America's major trading partners. By the late 1980s, the impetus for joining Berne was greater than ever because the United States had withdrawn from UNESCO, the United Nations organization that administers the U.C.C.. As a result, it was felt that the United States could no longer influence the policy within UNESCO even though its withdrawal does not preclude its membership in the U.C.C.. With the increase of organized international piracy of copyrighted works of American authors, it had often been pointed out how critically important it was for the United States to have a major role in influencing the direction of international copyright matters.[40] The entry of the United States into Berne appeared to be the logical solution to its current isolation in the world copyright system.

Major changes have taken place in American copyright law since the initial refusal of the United States to enter Berne at the outset in 1886.[41] The United States had taken a more international orientation in joining the U.C.C., thereby recognizing the principle of national treatment.[42] More importantly, the provisions of the 1976 Act eliminated many of the impediments to Berne adherence. The 1976 Act, however, still fell far short of compliance with certain substantial and explicit Convention *minima* required for Berne membership, and major amendments to the 1976 Act were needed to make membership possible.[43] The necessary changes to U.S. copyright law finally occurred with the passage of the Berne Convention Implementation Act that enabled U.S. entry into Berne after a delay of 103 years.

---

[38] *See* S. Rep. No. 100-352, 100th Cong., 2d Sess. 2 (1988).

[39] Export value of American motion pictures now exceeds the value of our steel imports. *See* U.S. Adherence to the Berne Convention Hearings Before the Subcomm. on Patents, Copyrights and Trademarks of the Senate Comm. on the Judiciary, 99th Cong., 1st and 2d Sess. 5 (1987).

[40] *See* S. Rep. No. 100-352, 100th Cong., 2d Sess. 4 (1988).

[41] United States' refusal to enter Berne in 1886 was the result of rivalries between American and British publishing houses over the national treatment doctrine and the extension of protection to non-resident foreigners.

[42] The national treatment principle requires that persons entitled to Convention benefits enjoy in each member nation the advantages accorded to nationals of the forum country.

[43] At the request of the U.S. State Department, individuals with significant experience in copyright formed an Ad Hoc Working Group on U.S. Adherence to the Berne Convention to consider possible U.S. adherence to Berne. The final report addresses items of conflict, including notice and registration. For the complete, detailed text, see The Ad Hoc Working Group, Final Report of the Ad Hoc Working Group on U.S. Adherence to the Berne Convention, reprinted in 10 Colum.-VLA J.L. & Arts 513 (1986) [hereinafter referred to as the "Ad Hoc Working Group"].

[B] The Berne Convention Implementation Act of 1988

On March 1, 1989, with the passage of the Berne Convention Implementation Act of 1988,[44] the United States officially entered the Berne Convention. Section 2(1) of the Implementation Act declares that the Berne Convention is not self-executing under U.S. law.[45] This means that rights and responsibilities dealing with copyright matters will be resolved under the domestic law, state and federal, of the United States. Thus, because the Berne Convention is not self-executing, special implementing legislation was needed, modifying the current Copyright Act to comply with the general and specific obligations of Berne adherence.

In drafting the implementing legislation, Congress took what has been termed as a minimalist approach. As used here, the term *minimalist* means that only the essential changes necessary to comply with Convention obligations would be made to American law.[46] An example of this minimalist approach can be found in the treatment of moral rights, which are specifically recognized in Article 6*bis* of the Berne Convention. Congress believed that the protection afforded by the entirety of American copyright, unfair competition, defamation, privacy, and contract law served to prevent improper alterations of an author's work, and were thus sufficient to meet the needs of Berne adherence.[47] The major aspects of the implementing legislation and amendments to the 1976 Act are summarized in the following sections.

[1] Formalities

Article 5(2) of the Berne Convention provides that the enjoyment and exercise of an author's rights shall not be subject to any formality. Thus, to enter Berne, the United States had to eliminate certain formalities, such as notice and registration requirements, contained in the 1976 Act. Under American law, omission of notice[48] could lead to forfeiture of copyright and registration,[49] a prerequisite for bringing suit for infringement and obtaining certain remedies. These requirements were contrary to Berne because they affect the "enjoyment and exercise of rights under copyright."[50]

The most significant change to American copyright law brought about by the Berne Convention Implementation Act of 1988 amendments is the abrogation of required notice for publicly distributed works on or after March 1, 1989. For these publicly distributed works, notice of copyright is permissive, and omission of notice can no longer forfeit copyright.[51] Although notice is no longer required for publicly

---

[44] Pub. L. No. 100-568 (1988).

[45] *Id.* at § 2(1).

[46] *See* 134 Cong. Rec. S14552 (daily ed. Oct. 5, 1988) (statement of Sen. Patrick J. Leahy).

[47] For a discussion of moral rights, see *supra* § 8.28. *See also* Nimmer on Copyright § 8D.01 (2014), for a discussion of the moral right as recognized in Article 6*bis* of the Berne Convention.

[48] *See* 17 U.S.C. § 405. For a discussion of notice, see *supra* §§ 4.08–4.14.

[49] *See* 17 U.S.C. §§ 401, 411. For a discussion of registration, see *supra* §§ 7.02–7.08.

[50] Berne Convention art. 5(2) (Paris text).

[51] *See* 17 U.S.C. § 401(a).

distributed works, it is still highly recommended. In fact, the Berne amendments encourage the affixation of proper notice. For causes of action arising on or after March 1, 1989, proper notice on a work will preclude a defendant from asserting a defense of innocent infringement in mitigation of actual or statutory damages.[52] The new permissive notice provisions are not retroactive, and a work publicly distributed before the effective date of the BCIA will be governed by the prior provisions and is still subject to possible forfeiture.[53]

Before the Berne amendments, recordation of an interest in a copyright was a condition prerequisite to bringing a suit for copyright infringement. Now, for causes of action arising on or after March 1, 1989, recordation is no longer a prerequisite.[54] However, recordation remains, even on or after March 1, 1989, a highly recommended procedure for the owner of an interest in a copyright. One reason recordation is recommended is because it is still important in determining the priority between conflicting transfers.

Opinions differed as to whether registration as a prerequisite for bringing an infringement suit was a formality incompatible with Berne. The Berne amendments took a compromise approach to this issue. Instead of flatly repealing § 411, the legislation adopted a two-tier approach to registration. For works originating from a Berne country, the Berne amendments have abrogated the registration requirement as a precondition to bringing suit. Alternatively, registration will still be required to bring suit when a work is first published (or simultaneously published) in the United States or for an unpublished work when all the authors are nationals, domiciliaries, or permanent residents of the United States.[55]

Although registration is no longer required for Berne works, the incentives to register continue, unaffected by the Berne amendments. First, the *prima facie* evidentiary value of the certificate of registration, which shifts the burden of proof to the benefit of the copyright owner in an infringement suit, is unchanged. Second, registration remains a prerequisite for obtaining statutory damages and attorney's fees. Moreover, statutory damages for infringement of copyrighted works have been doubled, thereby further encouraging registration of copyright.

In sum, as to formalities, the Berne amendments (with the exception of permissive notice) have done little to weaken the necessity of complying with formalities, and in some cases, have increased the rewards of such compliance. Although the Berne amendments have modified the formalities of notice, recordation, and registration, a copyright owner, in order to effectively protect and enforce his rights, is greatly encouraged to place proper notice on his work, register it, and record his ownership interest in the Copyright Office.

---

[52] *See* 17 U.S.C. §§ 401(d), 402(d).

[53] *See* 17 U.S.C. § 405(a), (b), (f).

[54] *See* 17 U.S.C. § 205. For a discussion of recordation, see *supra* § 5.14.

[55] *See* 17 U.S.C. § 411. *See also* 17 U.S.C. § 101 (defining country of origin of a Berne Convention work). In addition, registration will be required to bring an infringement suit when a work is published in a foreign nation that does not adhere to the Berne Convention and all the authors are nationals, domiciliaries, or permanent residents of, or in the case of an audiovisual work, legal entities with headquarters in, the United States. For a discussion of copyright registration, see *supra* § 7.06.

[2] Architectural Works

The Berne Convention includes architectural works and works of applied art as part of minimum subject matter protection.[56]

Traditionally, the "useful articles" doctrine of American copyright law has restricted the protection of architectural designs. Even so, consistent with the "minimalist" approach, which characterized United States adherence to the Berne Convention in 1988, no changes were then made in the domestic law relating to architectural works. As was the case for moral rights, however, Berne adherence has had a delayed effect on U.S. copyright law. After a 1989 Copyright Office study recommended change, Congress passed legislation establishing protection of architectural works.[57]

[3] Jukebox Compulsory License[58]

This compulsory license, contained in § 116 of the 1976 Act as originally enacted, clearly contravened the requirements of the Berne Convention. The relevant Berne provision, Article 11, prescribes an exclusive right to authorize the public performance of a musical work. The jukebox license under the original § 116 was a limitation on the copyright owner's performance right in a nondramatic musical work because it allowed the public performance of such works without the copyright owner's consent and for a non-negotiated compensation.[59] To harmonize the jukebox license with Berne requirements, the BCIA enacted a new § 116A to replace the compulsory license with a voluntarily negotiated one, but if the parties were not able to formulate a negotiated license, then the previous compulsory licensing system was to be reinstituted. All vestiges of the compulsory license were repealed by legislation in 1993. Section 116 as originally enacted is now replaced by a renumbered § 116A.[60]

[4] Works in the Public Domain: Retroactivity

Retroactivity of protection was one of the most controversial issues raised in the discussions leading to Berne adherence. Article 18 of Berne provides that "(t)his Convention shall apply to all works which, at the moment of its coming into force, have not yet fallen into the public domain in the country of origin through the expiry of protection." This would appear to mean that, under the treaty, the only reason a country may use for not protecting a member country's work is the expiration of its copyright in either the country of origin or the forum country. But Article 18 also provides that "the respective countries of the Union shall determine, each insofar as it is concerned, the conditions of application of this principle."[61] Whatever may be

---

[56] Berne Convention art. 2(1) (Paris text).

[57] *See* Pub. L. No. 101-650 (Title VII), 104 Stat. 5089 (1990): H.R. Rep. No. 101-735, 101st Cong., 2d Sess. (1990). For a discussion of copyright in architectural works, see *supra* § 3.16.

[58] For a discussion of the jukebox license, see *supra* § 8.21.

[59] 17 U.S.C. § 116.

[60] 17 U.S.C. § 116A.

[61] Berne Convention art. 18(3) (Paris text).

the proper interpretation of Article 18, Congress did nothing to protect works in the public domain as of March 1, 1989. Section 12 of the BCIA provides that no retroactive protection is provided for any work that is in the public domain in the United States.[62] Thus, the obligations of the United States under the Berne Convention will apply to works that are protected in the United States on the effective date of the BCIA. In addition, § 13(b) provides that the Berne Convention Implementation Act does not apply to causes of action arising before its effective date.[63] Although steadfast against retroactivity for Berne adherence, the United States in 1993 allowed for retroactivity pursuant to negotiations leading to the completion of NAFTA. To implement its obligations under NAFTA, the United States agreed to retroactive protection for Mexican and Canadian motion pictures that had fallen into the public domain for failure to comply with the notice provisions of the 1976 Act.[64]

In more dramatic fashion, the Uruguay Round Agreements Act, passed at the end of 1994, greatly expanded the relatively modest NAFTA restoration provisions. This legislation, the purpose of which is to implement United States obligations under the new World Trade Organization, restored copyright in certain foreign works that had fallen into the public domain for failure to comply with U.S. copyright formalities.[65] Thus, after many years of resistance, the concept of "retroactivity" has become firmly entrenched in U.S. law. This change in fundamental attitude shows once again the increasing influence of international norms on U.S. copyright law, the globalization of markets for copyrighted works, and the need to ensure full and reciprocal treatment of U.S. works in foreign countries.

[5] Copyright Infringement Remedies

Unrelated to Berne compatibility, the Berne amendments doubled the amount of statutory damages that can be recovered in lieu of actual damages and profits in copyright infringement actions.[66] Doubling the statutory damages enhances the incentives to register a work because statutory damages cannot be sought without a registration, even for works whose origin is a Berne country.

[C] Benefits to American Authors and Copyright Owners from Berne Membership

One immediate benefit of entry into Berne is that American authors and copyright owners no longer have to rely on the costly and risky use of the back-door Berne procedure to protect their works in some 24 Berne countries with which the United States has had no other copyright relations. For the most part,

---

[62] Berne Convention Implementation Act of 1988 § 12, Pub. L. No. 100-568 (1988).

[63] Berne Convention Implementation Act of 1988 § 13(b), Pub. L. No. 100-568 (1988).

[64] *See* 17 U.S.C. § 104A.

[65] *See* 17 U.S.C. § 104A. Section 104A restores copyright in works of foreign origin — i.e., works from Berne or WTO countries — but leaves works of U.S. origin in the public domain. Copyright restoration is discussed in *supra* §§ 6.18–6.19.

[66] *See* 17 U.S.C. § 504(c) (as amended by the BCIA). For a discussion of statutory damages, see *supra* § 9.13.

however, the tangible benefits that Berne membership will bring to American copyright owners may not be felt immediately. They will manifest themselves over the long term due to the United States' more effective influence over the direction of international copyright policy.[67]

§ 12.06 UPDATING THE BERNE CONVENTION: WIPO COPYRIGHT TREATIES

[A] From the Berne Protocol to the New WIPO Treaties

Over its 100-year plus life, the Berne Convention has undergone several major revisions, the most recent being the Paris Act of 1971. The revision process, requiring the development of consensus among the differing interests of Berne members, has become increasingly difficult, if not impossible, to carry out. As an alternative, WIPO initiated in 1991 a series of meetings designed to lead to a protocol or protocols to the Berne Convention — that is, new supplementary agreements dealing with issues unresolved in the Convention itself.to which states would then be free to adhere, or not, as they chose, without the necessity of revising the Convention as a whole. Beginning in 1995, the United States and a number of European countries pressed for the expansion of the ongoing discussions of new treaties to include a new so-called "digital agenda."

In December 1996, two new treaties, "The WIPO Copyright Treaty" and "The WIPO Performances and Phonograms Treaty," were concluded pursuant to a WIPO Diplomatic Conference.

[B] Overview of the WIPO Copyright Treaty and the WIPO Performances and Phonograms Treaty

The WIPO Copyright Treaty provides for the protection of computer programs as literary works and for copyright in original (as distinct from non-original) compilations of data.[68] It obligates ratifying states to recognize a general right of distribution and a rental right limited to computer programs, movies, and "works embodied in phonograms," and it is itself subject to a number of significant exceptions. It also bars ratifying states from taking advantage of Berne Convention provisions which otherwise would permit them to allow lesser terms of protection to phonograms than to other copyrighted works. The WIPO Performances and Phonograms Treaty break significant new ground.[69] In particular, performers fare better under the new treaty than under TRIPS. Not only are they afforded more extensive economic rights, but the text provides explicitly for the basic moral rights of the performer "as regards . . . live aural performances fixed in phonograms."

---

[67] Entry enabled the United States to have copyright relations with some 24 new countries. *See* S. Rep. No. 100-352, 100th Cong., 2d Sess. 3 (1988).

[68] For the text of the WIPO Copyright Treaty, see Marshall A. Leaffer, International Treaties on Intellectual Property 388 (2d. ed. 1997).

[69] For the text of the WIPO Performances and Phonograms Treaty, see *id.* at 438 (2d. ed. 1997).

With respect to digital issues, the relevant provisions of the two treaties approved in December 1996 are substantially identical. The relevant obligations in the final acts of the treaties include a duty to recognize a right of "communication to the public," along with a limited mandate for the protection of "copyright management information" against tampering, and another relating to "circumvention" of technological safeguards.[70]

On October 27, 1998, President Clinton signed into law the Digital Millennium Copyright Act ("DMCA"), legislation designed to implement the two WIPO treaties that emerged from Geneva in 1996.[71] The DMCA included provisions on "anti-circumvention" and "copyright management information" (but not moral rights of performers). In the United States, the Senate gave its advice and consent to the treaties on October 21, 1998. Some four years later, the two treaties came into force early in 2002, having acquired the requisite 30 ratifications.

[C] U.S. Participation in the New Order

Events and developments described in this chapter, of which the new WIPO treaties are only the most recent, suggest that the character of the international copyright regime continues to undergo significant change. A system that traditionally has emphasized national treatment, supplemented by a relatively few and easily satisfied treaty *minima*, is moving closer to one with an emphasis on true harmonization of national laws.

Moreover, thanks to TRIPS and its dispute-resolution procedures, there now exists a procedure that will yield authoritative interpretations of international norms and conclusive adjudications of the compliance of particular countries with those norms. Although the United States itself was the first to initiate such a procedure with the WTO,[72] it is inevitable that, sooner or later (and probably sooner), the United States will find itself the target rather than the initiator — perhaps concerning the compatibility of one or more of the remaining peculiar features of U.S. copyright law, such as our broadly conceived and generously applied doctrine of "fair use" (treated in detail in Chapter 9).

From the perspective of some in the United States, relinquishing the historical peculiarities of U.S. domestic copyright laws may be a small price to pay for the benefits that international harmonization at a consistently high level of protection may offer U.S. works in the global marketplace. Others, having different interests to protect, may find the price too high to accept without strenuous protest. One thing seems certain: the globalization of copyright law in an interconnected world will continue to be a subject of lively debate and high-powered maneuvering in a wide variety of forums, both domestic and international.

---

70 For a detailed discussion of the Diplomatic Conference and its outcome, see Pamela Samuelson, *The U.S. Digital Agenda at WIPO*, 37 Va. J. Int'l L. 369 (1997), and *Big Media Beaten Back*, WIRED 5.03, at 61 (1997).

71 P.L. 105-304, 112 Stat. 2860(1998). The DMCA is discussed at *supra* § 8.31.

72 *See Record Firms See More Gold in Oldies in Wake of U.S.-Japan Copyright Pact*, J. Commerce, Jan. 28, 1997, at 3A.

§ 12.07 OTHER COPYRIGHT-RELATED CONVENTIONS

[A] Convention for the Protection of Producers of Phonograms Against Unauthorized Duplication of Their Phonograms (The Geneva Phonograms Convention)

Signed in Geneva in 1971 and effective in 1974 in the United States, this Convention was created to provide international protection for sound recordings.[73] Each member nation agrees to protect nationals of other member nations against the unauthorized manufacture, importation, and distribution of copies of sound recordings. The Convention is based on national protection and has minimum requirements for participation. For example, one requirement is a 25-year minimum term as measured from fixation (i.e., embodied in tangible form in a phonorecord, cassette, disc, etc.) or first publication. Another requirement is a notice requirement, identical to U.S. law,[74] which is deemed to satisfy all other formalities. Compulsory licenses are limited and are allowed only for teaching or scientific research.

The 1971 Geneva Convention should be distinguished from the Rome Convention of 1961, entitled the International Convention for the Protection of Performers, Producers of Phonograms and Broadcasting Organizations.[75] The Rome Convention, unlike later phonogram conventions, protects performances embodied in sound recordings. The United States, which does not protect performance rights in sound recordings, has not ratified the Rome Convention.[76]

[B] Brussels Satellite Convention

In 1984, the United States ratified the Convention relating to the Distribution of Programme-Carrying Signals Transmitted by Satellite, known as the "Brussels Satellite Convention."[77] Established in 1974, its purpose is to combat the misappropriation of satellite signals on an international level. The need for a special international agreement covering satellite transmission was apparent from its inadequate treatment in the major international copyright conventions. Although the U.C.C. (art. IV*bis*) and the Berne Convention (art. 11*bis*) provide for the exclusive right to broadcast, it is unclear whether "broadcasting" in these Conventions covers satellite transmissions. To fill this void, the Brussels Satellite Convention was conceived.

---

[73] For the text of the Geneva Phonograms Convention, see MARSHALL A. LEAFFER, INTERNATIONAL TREATIES ON INTELLECTUAL PROPERTY 451 (2d. ed. 1997).

[74] *See* 17 U.S.C. § 402.

[75] For an overview, see Robert Dittrich, *The Practical Application of the Rome Convention*, 26 BULL. COPYRIGHT SOC'Y 287 (1979).

[76] For a discussion of performance rights in sound recordings, see *supra* § 8.24.

[77] The United States signed the treaty in 1974 but did not ratify it until 1984. For the text of the Brussels Satellite Convention, see MARSHALL A. LEAFFER, INTERNATIONAL TREATIES ON INTELLECTUAL PROPERTY 457 (2d. ed. 1997).

The Convention creates no new rights for programs transmitted by satellite. Implementation of the treaty is left to the contracting states, who agree to provide adequate protection against satellite signal piracy.[78] The United States viewed its copyright and communication laws as adequate in this regard; thus, unlike adherence to the Berne Convention, there was no perceived need for specific implementing legislation to join the Brussels Convention.

The Convention focuses on the unauthorized distribution of signals, not their unauthorized reception. Thus, the private reception of signals for private use does not violate the Brussels Convention. Moreover, the signal is the object of protection, not the content of the material sent by the signal. Accordingly, the Convention is designed to protect the emitter or carrier, not the copyright owner of the program material.

[C] Copyright in the Americas: Buenos Aires Convention

The United States and 17 Latin American nations adhere to the Buenos Aires Convention, which took effect in 1911.[79] Article 3, the basic provision of the Convention, requires that once copyright is obtained for a work in one member country, protection is given by all member countries without further formalities, provided that there appears in the work a statement that property rights are reserved. Usually this statement appears as *All Rights Reserved* or similar language. The U.S. Copyright Office, however, takes the position that Buenos Aires works have no special status under American law, that works must satisfy all formalities imposed on national authors, and that use of the words "all rights reserved" is insufficient notice of copyright.[80] Today, virtually all of the countries of the Americas are members of Berne or the U.C.C. or both — each of which is more effective than the Buenos Aires Convention. Nonetheless, publishers, by force of habit, continue to affix on the title page of a work the Buenos Aires notice "All Rights Reserved" that, if nothing more, has a nice ring to it. One might question whether the Buenos Aires Convention serves any practical purpose because virtually all the countries in the Americas are members of the U.C.C.. The U.C.C. provides much the same protection as does the Buenos Aires Convention, its terms are clearer, and the number of adherents is much greater than under the Buenos Aires Convention.

---

[78] Satellite signal piracy is also referred to as "signal poaching" or the unauthorized use of program-carrying satellite signals. *See generally* Heather Dembert, *Securing Authors' Rights in Satellite Transmissions: U.S. Efforts to Extend Copyright Protection Abroad*, 24 Colum. J. Transnat'l L. 73 n.2 (1985).

[79] The Buenos Aires Convention was not the first inter-American treaty governing copyright in which the United States participated. The first was the Mexico City Treaty of 1902, which governed copyright relations between the U.S. and El Salvador, until that country's adherence to the U.C.C. in 1979. For an overview, see Alfred L. Rinaldo, Jr. *The Scope of Copyright Protection in the United States Under Existing Inter-American Relations: Abrogation of the Need for U.S. Protection Under the Buenos Aires Convention by Reliance Upon the U.C.C.*, 22 Bull. Copyright Soc'y 417 (1975).

[80] *See* Compendium II of Copyright Office Practices §§ 1005.01(b), 1104.02.

Part II. FOREIGN AUTHORS AND CONFLICTS OF LAW IN INTERNATIONAL COPYRIGHT

§ 12.08 FOREIGN AUTHORS

[A] Unpublished Works

Nationals and domiciliaries of foreign nations may protect their works in the United States as an American citizen can, if the foreign author meets the conditions set forth in § 104 of the 1976 Act.[81] These conditions vary depending on whether the work is published or unpublished. The rule for unpublished works of foreign authors is simple and all inclusive: All works qualifying for statutory copyright are protected from the moment of creation, no matter what the nationality or domicile of the author. So long as the work has not gone into the public domain, an unpublished work of a foreign author is protected in the United States no differently than that of an American author.[82]

[B] Published Works: The Five Bases for Protection in § 104(b)[83]

Section 104(b) of the 1976 Copyright Act sets forth five broad, overlapping categories for published works, under which the foreign author must fall to be eligible for protection in the United States like any other citizen.

First, one or more of the authors must be a national or domiciliary of the United States or a country with which the United States has copyright relations under a treaty, or the author may be a stateless person.[84]

The term "domicile," as used in § 104, consists of two elements: (1) residence in the United States, and (2) an intent to remain in the United States. Mere residency without the requisite intent is insufficient for status as a domiciliary in the United States. The resident must manifest the requisite intent by establishing ties such as declarations, marriage, payment of taxes, voting, or establishing a home.

Even foreign authors not domiciled in the United States may claim copyright under United States law if on the date of publication the author is a domiciliary or national of a treaty nation. Treaty nations are those adhering to the Berne Union, the Universal Copyright Convention ("U.C.C."),[85] the Buenos Aires Convention,[86] or countries with which the United States has bilateral arrangements, such as

---

[81] 17 U.S.C. § 104.

[82] *See* 17 U.S.C. § 104(a); *see also* Nimmer on Copyright § 5.05 (2014).

[83] 17 U.S.C. § 104(b) (as amended by the BCIA).

[84] *See* 17 U.S.C. § 104(b)(1).

[85] Universal Copyright Convention, Sept. 6, 1952, 6 U.S.T. 2731, T.I.A.S. No. 3324, 753 U.N.T.S. 368, *amended by* Universal Copyright Convention, July 24, 1971, 25 U.S.T. 1341, T.I.A.S. No. 7868.

[86] Pan American Copyright Convention (Buenos Aires), Aug. 11, 1910, 38 Stat. 1785, T.S. No. 593, 155 I.N.T.S. 1979.

China, Romania, Thailand, and the Philippines.[87]

Second, if the work is first published in the United States or in a country that is a party to the U.C.C., it will receive non-discriminatory protection under U.S. law.[88]

When a work is first published in a U.C.C. country, the publication must have occurred no earlier than September 15, 1955, the date on which the United States became a member of the U.C.C.. If the work was published before that date, it is irrevocably in the public domain, unless it can be protected on some other basis.

Third, a published work of a foreign author receives protection if it was published by the United Nations, any of its specialized agencies, or by the Organization of American States.[89]

Fourth, to be eligible for protection, the work must be a Berne Convention work.[90] A work is a Berne Convention work if it is unpublished and one or more of the authors is a national of a nation adhering to the Berne Convention.[91] For published works, a work is a Berne work if first published in a Berne country.[92] Because the United States has adhered to the Paris text of the Berne Convention, a work that is first published simultaneously in a nation adhering to Berne and one not adhering to Berne will be protected under U.S. law. Under the Paris revision of Berne, a work is considered to have been simultaneously published in two or more nations if the dates of publication are within 30 days of one another.[93] If the basis of protection is publication in a Berne member country, the publication must have taken place after the United States' effective entry into the Convention, on March 1, 1989.

Fifth, the work is protected if covered by a presidential proclamation extending protection to works originating in a specific country that extends protection to U.S. works on substantially the same basis given to its own works.[94]

---

[87] The texts of these agreements are reprinted in the appendices in Nimmer on Copyright (2014). *See also International Copyright Relations of the United States*, U.S. Copyright Office Circular R38(a). What constitutes a valid bilateral arrangement is not free from doubt. For example, in 1946, the United States signed a Friendship, Commerce and Navigation Treaty ("FCN") with the Republic of China committing both countries to honor each other's copyrights. In 1948, with the Chinese Revolution, the Nationalist government was overthrown and established itself in Taiwan. In 1978, the President signed a memorandum recognizing the People's Republic of China and terminating diplomatic relations with Taiwan. *New York Chinese TV Programs, Inc. v. U.E., Inc.*, 954 F.2d 847 (2d. Cir. 1992), raised the question whether Taiwanese works still enjoy protection in this country under the 1946 Treaty. The court held that the Treaty should be recognized because of the deference we owe to the political branches of the government in treaty matters. Although the U.S. may not have diplomatic relations with a country, it does honor its treaty obligations.

[88] *See* 17 U.S.C. § 104(b)(2).

[89] *See* 17 U.S.C. § 104(b)(3).

[90] *See* 17 U.S.C. § 104(b)(4) (as amended by the BCIA).

[91] *See* 17 U.S.C. § 101 (as amended by the BCIA).

[92] *See id.*

[93] *See* 17 U.S.C. § 101 (defining a Berne Convention work).

[94] *See* 17 U.S.C. § 104(b)(5). Presidential proclamations issued under the 1909 Act remain in force today. *See* 17 U.S.C. Trans. & Supp. Prov. § 104.

§ 12.09 THE EXTRATERRITORIAL APPLICATION OF U.S. LAW TO FOREIGN INFRINGING ACTS

When acts of infringement occur abroad, the copyright laws of the United States do not apply. The courts, however, will relax this principle when the infringing acts committed abroad result in infringement taking place in the United States. Thus, U.S. copyright law was applied to defendant's sales in Germany to a German exporter of bottled water bearing allegedly infringing labels that were destined for U.S. distribution.[95] But what about the other side of the coin? Will U.S. copyright law be applied to infringing acts begun in the U.S. whose purpose is to infringe copyright in a foreign country? Here, the courts will apply U.S. copyright law so long as some of the infringing *acts* occurred in the United States.

On the other hand, United States copyright law will not reach acts of infringement that take place entirely abroad, even though these acts were *authorized* in the United States. In *Subafilms Ltd. v. MGM-Pathe Communications Co.*,[96] the Beatles, through Subafilms, Ltd., entered into a 1966 joint venture with Hearst Corporation to produce the animated movie *Yellow Submarine*. Hearst, as agent for the joint venture, negotiated an agreement with United Artists ("UA") to finance and distribute the film to movie theaters and later to television. In 1987, UA's successor authorized its subsidiary to distribute its film domestically and another company to distribute the picture internationally, in the home video market. Subafilms brought suit, claiming that both the domestic and foreign distribution exceeded the 1967 agreement and constituted copyright infringement.

An *en banc* panel of the Ninth Circuit Court of Appeals vacated an earlier panel decision, holding that extraterritorial acts authorized in the United States were actionable under U.S. copyright law. The court reasoned that the words "to authorize"[97] in the 1976 Act were meant to codify the doctrine of "contributory infringement" as a form of third party liability, not to establish a direct cause of action for illegal authorization. Thus, if no cause of action existed against the primary infringer, then neither did a cause exist against the authorizer of the act. Because U.S. copyright laws have no effect outside the United States, an extraterritorial primary infringement cannot serve as grounds on which to base the authorizing contributory infringement.

Subafilms contended that the U.S. copyright laws extend to extraterritorial acts of infringement when such acts result in adverse effects within the United States and failure to apply the copyright law extraterritorially would have a disastrous effect on the American film industry. Subafilms had argued that the securities laws and the Sherman Act had been applied to extraterritorial conduct where adverse affects are felt in the U.S. Despite authority in analogous bodies of law, the court would not overturn 80 years of consistent jurisprudence on the extraterritorial

---

[95] *See, e.g.*, *G.B. Marketing U.S.A. Inc. v. Gerolsteiner Brunnen GmbH & Co.*, 782 F. Supp. 763 (W.D.N.Y. 1991); *see also Update Art, Inc. v. Modiin Publ'g, Ltd.*, 843 F.2d 67 (2d Cir. 1988) (awarding damages from Israeli newspaper's unauthorized publication of a photograph of U.S. citizen's "Ronbo" poster later reproduced in the U.S.).

[96] 24 F.3d 1088 (9th Cir. 1994).

[97] *See* 17 U.S.C. § 106.

reach of the copyright law without further guidance from Congress.[98]

In *Subafilms*, the allegedly infringing conduct consisted solely of authorization given within the United States for foreign distribution of infringing cassettes. Instead, what if infringing cassettes were made in the United States and distributed abroad? Could extraterritorial damages that flowed from these acts of domestic infringement be recovered? This issue has not been addressed often, but the acts of domestic infringement leading to foreign exploitation support extraterritoriality. Thus, once acts of domestic infringement are found, one court has held that the copyright owner is entitled to recover profits, but not actual damages, "flowing" from the exploitation abroad of defendant's domestic infringement.[99]

§ 12.10 CHOICE OF FORUM AND CHOICE LAW IN INTERNATIONAL COPYRIGHT

[A] Choice of Forum and the Application of Foreign Copyright Law by U.S. Courts

As a general principle, copyright law is territorial in nature and, as such, is considered effective only within the borders of an individual country. But when an act of infringement occurs in a foreign country, a U.S. court may, nevertheless, have jurisdiction to hear the case. To understand why, one must make a distinction between jurisdiction to adjudicate — choice of forum — and the choice of law to be applied. The federal courts may have jurisdiction if the claim of copyright infringement is considered a transitory cause of action, even if the cause of action arose in the foreign jurisdiction. 28 U.S.C. § 1332(a)(2) confers jurisdiction in a federal court if the requirements of diversity of citizenship (citizens of a state and citizens or subjects of a foreign state) and jurisdictional amount ($75,000) are met. Even though U.S. law may not apply, a U.S. court might retain jurisdiction over an action for copyright infringement, and in so doing, apply the copyright law of the foreign jurisdiction. For example, in *London Film Productions Ltd. v. Intercontinental Communications, Inc.*,[100] a British plaintiff sued a New York corporation for alleged acts of infringement occurring in Chile and other Latin American countries. The court declared that it was competent to pass on the issues of the case and apply foreign law. Moreover, no principles of comity, such as the need to pass on the validity of acts of foreign officials, made it inappropriate for the U.S. court to adjudicate the controversy.

---

[98] For a critique of *Subafilms*, see Marshall Leaffer, *The Extraterritorial Application of U.S. Trademark and Copyright Law*, in 3 International Intellectual Property Law and Policy, 33-1 (H. Hansen, ed. 1998). For a case taking a view contrary to *Subafilms*, see *Curb v. MCA Records, Inc.*, 898 F. Supp. 586, 594–95 (M.D. Tenn. 1995) ("Under this [*Subafilms*] view, a phone call to Nebraska results in liability; the same phone call to France results in riches. In a global marketplace, it is literally a distinction without a difference").

[99] *See Los Angeles News Serv. v. Reuters Television Int'l.*, 340 F.3d 926 (9th Cir. 2003) (allowing profits, but not actual damages, from overseas infringing uses of videotape illegally reproduced in the United States where the predicate act of infringement in the United States enabled further reproduction abroad).

[100] 580 F. Supp. 47 (S.D.N.Y. 1984).

Even when personal jurisdiction can be exercised over the parties, a U.S. court may refuse to act, on the ground of *forum non conveniens*. Generally, a motion to dismiss under a *forum non conveniens* doctrine is decided in two steps. The court must determine whether there exists an alternative forum with jurisdiction to hear the case. If so, the court must then decide whether the balance of convenience tilts strongly in favor of trial in the foreign forum. Here, the court must consider the relevant private interests of the litigants such as the access to proof, availability of witnesses, and other factors that make the trial less costly in the venue at issue. Thus, one court held that New York is a *forum non conveniens* in a dispute about ownership between two British citizens, governed by British contract law, with events taking place in the United Kingdom.[101]

Normally, a district court has wide discretion on whether to dismiss an action under the doctrine of *forum non conveniens*. But in *Boosey & Hawkes Music Publishers, Ltd. v. Walt Disney & Co.*,[102] the Second Circuit overturned the trial court's application of the doctrine. There, plaintiff claimed that Disney had exceeded its authority under a grant from Igor Stravinsky when it distributed videocassettes of *Fantasia* — including sequences synchronized to "The Rite of Spring" — in at least 18 countries other than the United States. In reversing the trial court's *forum non conveniens* dismissal (which had been based, among other things, on the difficulty of ascertaining and applying foreign law), the court indicated that reluctance to apply foreign law is one factor favoring dismissal. Nonetheless, countervailing considerations suggested that New York was the appropriate venue: defendant is a U.S. corporation, the 1939 agreement was substantially negotiated and signed in New York, and the agreement was governed by New York law.

[B] Choice of Law Rules in International Copyright Conflicts

[1] Choice of Law Rules and National Treatment

The rights conferred by international conventions are territorially limited whereby national law decides both substance and procedure.[103] Thus, an American author who wishes to enforce her copyrighted work in France will be subject to French law. Because the United States and France are members of the major international conventions (i.e., Berne, U.C.C.), the American author must be afforded national treatment. What this means in practical terms is that a work originating in the United States is entitled to protection in France to the same degree as if it had been created by a French citizen.[104]

---

[101] *See Murray v. British Broad. Corp.*, 81 F.3d 287 (2d Cir. 1996).

[102] 145 F.3d 481 (2d Cir. 1998).

[103] For an overview of the conflicts issues in copyright and in intellectual property law generally, see Graeme B. Dinwoodie, *International Intellectual Property Litigation: A Vehicle for Resurgent Comparativist Thought*, 49 Am. J. Comp. L. 429 (2001).

[104] One exception to the principle of national treatment is the doctrine of the shorter term (Article 7(8) Berne Convention). This doctrine provides that a Berne Union country can grant works, originating in other Union states, a shorter term of protection than the country provides for equivalent domestic

The national treatment principle under the Berne Convention has little bearing on the choice of law in international copyright conflicts. The national treatment principle, embodied not only in the Berne Convention but in all other copyright treaties, is a rule of nondiscrimination. It assures that foreign intellectual property owners will enjoy in the protecting country the same treatment that the protecting country provides its own nationals. A choice of law issue may arise when parties or events in a copyright action are located in more than one national jurisdiction. When this occurs, a court must determine whose substantive law will govern the rights and obligations of the parties. The Berne Convention gives little direction on choice of law issues. The treaty provides that the law of the country where protection is claimed defines what rights are protected, the scope of protection, and the available remedies. Berne, however, does not supply a choice of law rule for determining the applicable law. The choice of law to be made will be a function of the largely unwritten rules prevailing in the particular forum.[105]

Similar to Berne, the U.S. Copyright Act provides no guidance on choice of law rules. Given the lack of statutory direction, the courts have found it necessary to fill the interstices of the Act by developing a de facto federal common law on the conflicts issue.

[2] Choice of Laws Regarding Issues of Ownership and Infringement

Conflicts of law in copyright cases often involve issues regarding the applicable law in determining ownership and infringement.[106] As for ownership, copyright is regarded as a form of property, and the usual rule is that the interests of the parties in the property are determined by the law of the state with the most significant relationship to the property and the parties.[107] Under this doctrine, the "country of origin" is the appropriate country for purposes of choice of law concerning ownership.[108] By contrast, the governing conflicts principle is usually the lex loci delicti (where the infringing activity occurred), the doctrine generally applicable to torts.

Conflict of law rules regarding ownership and infringement issues is illustrated by *Itar-Tass Russian News Agency v. Russian Kurier, Inc.*[109] In *Itar-Tass*, defendant Russian Kurier published a weekly Russian-language newspaper in New

---

works. But it may do so only if the term of protection of the work's country of origin is less than that provided in the county where protection is claimed. See *supra* § 6.04, for a discussion of the doctrine.

[105] *See* Berne Convention Article 5(2). For an overview, see Jane C. Ginsburg, *Ownership of Electronic Rights and the Private International Law of Copyright*, 22 Colum.-VLA J.L. & Arts 165 (1998).

[106] These issues are examined comprehensively in Paul Edward Geller, *Conflicts of Laws in Copyright Cases: Infringement and Ownership Issues*, 51 J. Copyright Law Soc'y, U.S.A. 315 (2004). *See also* Raquel Xalabarder, *Choice of Law and Jurisdiction in the Digital Age*, 8 Ann. Surv. Int'l & Comp. L. 79 (2002).

[107] *See* Restatement (Second) of Conflict of Laws § 222. In fact, the Restatement recognizes the applicability of this principle to intangibles as a "literary idea."

[108] *See* 17 U.S.C. § 104. *See* also Berne Convention Article 5(4) (country of origin).

[109] 153 F.3d 82 (2d Cir. 1998).

York that contained original articles from the Russian press. Russian publishers and newspapers sued Russian Kurier for copyright infringement. Since U.S. law permits suits only by owners of an exclusive right under copyright,[110] it must first be determined whether any of the plaintiffs own an exclusive right. The court held that the choice of law rule for ownership questions is to be determined by the law of the state with the "most significant relationship" to the property and the parties. Here, ownership is to be decided under Russian law, because the works at issue were created by Russian nationals and first published in Russia. Under Russian law, Itar-Tass, a press agency, was deemed to be the owner of the copyright interests in the articles written by its employees. Alternatively, the newspaper plaintiffs owned no exclusive right in the works copied because they were specifically denied benefits under the Russian version of the work made for hire doctrine. The infringement issue was easier to decide. The court held that the place of the tort, the United States, determines the applicable law. Thus, Itar-Tass and the other publisher plaintiffs were entitled to injunctive relief and damages for copyright infringement.

The *Itar-Tass* decision illustrates the difference between national treatment and choice of law rules. It reveals that courts will have to apply principles of foreign law in instances where they have jurisdiction over the case. In addition, *Itar-Tass* reveals that the application of foreign law, particularly on the question of ownership, may lead to a result different from one based on U.S. law. True, copyright laws around the world are converging toward universal norms, but the laws themselves are hardly uniform and may sometimes vary significantly.

[3] Choice of Law Rules Governing Contracts and Choice of Law Clauses

As a general principle, the law that a court will apply is that of the country in which the rights are claimed. Difficult conflicts of law issues, however, may arise when a work of foreign origin is exploited in the forum country pursuant to a contract executed in the country of origin. Sometimes the parties in their contract will choose the pertinent law (choice of law clause) to be applied. Normally, the law chosen by the parties is the applicable law unless the law so chosen offends the public policy of the forum state. If the parties have not stipulated their choice of law, the court must make this decision. In this situation, the court would apply the traditional choice of law rule, that is, the law where the contract was executed. But a strong public policy may override this traditional rule.

[4] The Public Policy of the Forum and its Effect on Choice of Law Rules: *Huston v. La Cinq*

Litigation over issues involving moral rights laws has created a tension between choice of law rules and the overriding public policy of the forum country. In contrast to the United States, moral rights in France are both inalienable and perpetual. Thus, a film director who has transferred all economic interest in a work still preserves the right to oppose violations of the work's integrity and paternity. This discrepancy between U.S. and French law arose in the choice of law context where

[110] *See* 17 U.S.C. § 501(b).

the heirs of the American director, John Huston, sought to prevent the broadcast on French television of a colorized version of his film, *The Asphalt Jungle*. The heirs brought suit in France and asked the French court to apply the French moral rights law to prohibit this distortion of the work. In *Huston v. la Cinq*,[111] the intermediate court applied American law and determined that the heirs had no standing to bring the action under their moral rights theory. In choosing American law, the court applied the prevailing choice of law rule that recognizes the rules of the country of origin on authorship status and copyright ownership. The French Supreme Court reversed, applying French law that would allow heirs of an author to defend the work's right of integrity. The court abandoned the traditional choice of laws analysis because of the imperative nature of moral rights protection.

The *Huston* case highlights the need to develop a uniform set of principles governing the conflicts of laws arising from the ever growing international exploitation of copyrighted works. Moral rights law is not the only area in which a court may consider overturning a traditional choice of law rule for public policy reasons. Many countries are much more paternalistic in their view of contracts concerning the use and ownership of copyright. For example, some countries specify in their copyright laws the number of years in which a grant may be given, the percentage of profits that an author must receive, and other such protective provisions. Suppose a U.S. work is exploited in a country that explicitly stipulates certain contractual provisions that are more favorable to the copyright owner than those of contract. In this situation, should the public policy of the forum override the traditional choice of law rule and entitle the U.S. author to the benefits of local law? Unfortunately, there are no convenient answers to these issues. Ultimately, a new international agreement may be required to harmonize the law concerning copyright, contracts, and the conflicts of law.[112]

§ 12.11 RECOGNITION AND ENFORCEMENT OF FOREIGN JUDGMENTS

The development of the Internet and e-commerce on a global scale has led to more and more transnational litigation and rendering of judgments in a variety of jurisdictions. Suppose a monetary judgment is rendered in France against a U.S. company. Under what circumstances is the French judgment enforceable in state court, for example New York, where defendant is domiciled? As a general rule, foreign judgments are enforced on the basis of reciprocity or participation in a treaty.[113] Unfortunately, the situation is hardly uniform, and some countries such as the United States have not entered into bilateral treaties or multilateral international conventions concerning the recognition and enforcement of foreign judg-

---

[111] *Huston v. la Cinq*, Judgment of May 28, 1991. For an excellent analysis of the case, see Jane C. Ginsburg & Pierre Sirinelli, *Authors and Exploitations in International Private Law: The French Supreme Court and the Huston Film Colorization Controversy*, 15 Colum.-VLA J.L. & Arts 135 (1991).

[112] *See* Paul Edward Geller, *Harmonizing Copyright-Contract Conflicts Analysis*, 25 Copyright 49 (1989).

[113] Between two different States in the United States, enforcement is based on "full faith and credit," a Constitutional concept which compels a State to give another State's Judgment an effect as if it were local. *See* U.S. Const. art. IV, § 1.

ments.[114] In the United States, foreign judgments are enforced on the basis of comity, and those judgments will be enforced without proof of diplomatic reciprocity. Enforcement of judgments issued by foreign courts in the United States is governed by state law.

Despite the recognition of foreign judgments under principles of comity, there are limitations for their mechanical enforcement. The general principle of international law applicable in such cases is that a foreign state claims and exercises the right to examine judgments for four causes: (1) to determine if the court had jurisdiction; (2) to determine whether the defendant was properly served; (3) to determine if the proceedings were vitiated by fraud; and (4) to establish that the judgment is not contrary to the public policy of the foreign country.[115]

The public policy exception to the recognition of foreign judgments is illustrated *in Louis Féraud Int'l. v. Viewfinder, Inc.*[116] Féraud and Balmain, French fashion designers, sued defendant in France alleging copyright infringement of their dress designs by defendant's photographs that were published on the internet. Plaintiff obtained a default judgment issued by the Tribunal de grande instance de Paris after defendant failed to answer the complaint or to appear in the foreign proceeding. Plaintiffs sought to enforce a substantial money judgment under New York's Uniform money Judgment Recognition Act.[117] The district court refused to enforce the French judgment because the judgment was repugnant to the public policy of New York as a violation of defendant's First Amendment fair use rights.[118] The Second Circuit reversed finding that the district court was required to undertake a full fair use analysis and determine whether French law provided similar protection before ruling that the judgment was repugnant to public policy. The court appeared to concede, however, that if on remand the use would be fair under U.S. law then the judgment could not be enforced. The court added that the "public policy" inquiry rarely results in refusal to enforce a judgment unless it is inherently vicious, wicked, or immoral, and shocking to the moral sense."[119] Furthermore, "it is well established that more divergence from American procedure does not render a foreign judgment enforceable."[120] Apparently, lack of a fair use equivalent in the jurisdiction would fall within these criteria.

---

[114] There are a number of international agreements in force to which the U.S. is a party on the subject of enforcement of arbitral awards. *See* Convention on the Recognition and Enforcement of Foreign Arbitral Awards, 21 U.S.T. 2517; TIAS 6997; 330 UNTS 3; Inter-American Convention on International Commercial Arbitration, 14 I.L.M. 336 (1975).

[115] Unif. Foreign-Country Money Judgments Recognition Act, 13 U.L.A. § 4; Restatement (Second) of Conflicts of Laws § 117 Cmt. C.

[116] 489 F.3d 474 (2d Cir. 2007).

[117] N.Y. C.P.L.R. §§ 5302, 5303.

[118] N.Y. C.P.L.R. §§ 5304(b).

[119] *Louis Féraud Int'l.*, 489 F.3d 474 at 479

[120] *Id.*

Part III. TRADE REGULATION AFFECTING INTERNATIONAL COPYRIGHT MATTERS

§ 12.12 INFRINGING IMPORTATION OF COPIES OR PHONORECORDS

[A] Sections 602 and 603 of the 1976 Copyright Act

International commercial counterfeiting is a big business and an ever expanding one. As a result, §§ 602 and 603[121] of the 1976 Copyright Act, which prohibit the importation of infringing copies or phonorecords acquired abroad, have become more important than ever to U.S. copyright owners. The United States Customs Service, an arm of the Department of the Treasury, may seize and "forfeit" the imported infringing articles.[122] Regulations implementing the provisions of § 602 have been issued by the Customs Service.

Unlawful importation of copyrighted works can be attacked both by private actions as well as by Customs Office enforcement. Although private enforcement is available, customs enforcement is clearly the more effective remedy against the importation of unlawful goods. In general, customs enforcement is less expensive and time-consuming. By preventing the goods from entering into the stream of commerce, Customs enforcement provides a global, one-stop remedy against unlawful importation. By comparison, a private action works in a less effective, piecemeal fashion. Private injunctive remedies prevent the sale of the goods, not their original importation. In a private action, an injunction applies only to the individual distributors, but not to others who were not parties to the suit. As a result, some unlawful goods are more likely to elude interdiction and will continue to be sold to the public.

To benefit from § 602 and its regulations, the copyright owner must record his registered copyright with the U.S. Customs Service. Each application must be accompanied by a registration certificate issued by the U.S. Copyright Office, five copies of any copyrighted work, and the required filing fee. Once the copyright is recorded, Customs Service officers are issued a copyright notice accompanied by identifying documents and information about suspected infringing copies or phonorecords.[123]

The Customs Office may hold articles suspected of being "pirated" (i.e., infringing) copies of copyrighted works, and officials will notify the importer, who is given 30 days to file a denial that the articles are piratical.[124] If the importer does not file the denial within 30 days, the articles are deemed piratical and are subject

---

[121] 17 U.S.C. §§ 602, 603.

[122] *See* 17 U.S.C. § 603(c).

[123] *See* 19 C.F.R. § 133.33.

[124] 19 C.F.R. § 133.43(a). For a definition of "pirated goods," see 19 C.F.R. § 133.42.

to seizure and forfeiture.[125]

Customs service regulations set forth a procedure used to substantiate the claims of the parties.[126] The copyright owner must file a bond to compensate the importer for any loss he may wrongly suffer,[127] and the copyright owner has the burden of proving that the articles are piratical.[128] The ultimate decision is made by the Commissioner of Customs and is based on evidence submitted by the parties. If the copyright owner wins, the articles are forfeited (i.e., destroyed or sent back to the country of origin); if the importer's position is upheld, the bond is forfeited to him.

Although Customs can be effective in excluding infringing goods at the border, it is not above reproach. Customs has been criticized for its confidentiality restrictions that prevent the service from giving intellectual property owners sufficient information to facilitate judicial action against manufacturers, importers, and distributors. Newly proposed regulations would endow the agency with authority to expedite the release of such data.[129]

[B] Section 337 of the Tariff Act of 1930: The U.S. International Trade Commission[130]

Section 337 of the Tariff Act of 1930[131] provides for relief against unfair methods of competition and unfair acts in the importation of articles into, or their sale thereafter in, the United States. The acts protected against include any patent, trademark, copyright, and mask work infringement that occurs in connection with the importation of goods into the United States. The burden varies, depending on whether the copyright or mask work is registered or unregistered. For registered copyright and mask works, a complainant must show that an industry in the United States relating to the articles protected by the copyright or mask work exists or is in the process of being established. Under the statute, an industry exists, for the articles at issue, if there is in the United States: "(A) significant investment in plant and equipment; (B) significant employment of labor or capital; or (C) substantial investment in its exploitation, including engineering, research and development, or licensing."[132] For unregistered copyright or mask works, a complainant has an extra burden in having to prove injury to a U.S. industry.[133] The U.S. International

---

125 *See id.*

126 *See* 19 C.F.R. § 133.43(b)(2).

127 *See id.*

128 *See* 19 C.F.R. § 133.43(c)(1).

129 *See* 19 C.F.R. § 133.43(b)(2).

130 For an overview, see R.V. Lupo, *International Trade Commission Section 337 Proceedings and Their Applicability to Copyright Ownership*, 32 J. COPYRIGHT SOC'Y 193 (1985).

131 19 U.S.C. § 1337.

132 19 U.S.C. § 1337(a)(3).

133 The Omnibus Trade and Competitiveness Act of 1988 has amended § 337 of the Tariff Act, which had required that the plaintiff prove that imports would destroy or injure a U.S. industry, an industry that was efficient and economically operated. *See* Trade and Competitiveness Act, Pub. L. No. 100-418, § 1342, 102 Stat. 1107, 1212–16 (1988) (codified as 19 U.S.C. § 1337(a) (1988)). The Omnibus Act also made

Trade Commission ("USITC") administers the statute and is required to make its determination based on an administrative hearing similar to federal court litigation. Under the Commission's rules, the complaint must contain a detailed statement of facts that consists of more than mere allegations.[134] Within 30 days after receipt of a complaint, the Commission must decide whether to go forward with an investigation.[135] If there is a positive decision by the USITC, the matter is assigned to an administrative law judge ("ALJ"), who is in charge of the investigation.[136] The Commission may issue temporary exclusion orders prohibiting the entry of merchandise during the pendency of an investigation.

Section 337 cases are litigated before an ALJ who conducts the litigation similar to a federal court judge. If the ALJ finds a violation and no appeal is made to the USITC, an *in rem* order excluding the infringing articles from the United States may be issued. This is known as an exclusion order and is often a more effective remedy than an injunction, which would require personal jurisdiction over foreign manufacturers or exporters. In addition, articles subject to an exclusion order can be seized and forfeited in certain clear instances of bad faith shown by the owner or importer of the articles.[137]

The exclusion order does not take effect immediately. The President has 60 days to review it for possible veto. At the end of 60 days, the order becomes effective, although review of the Commission's determination is available by the Court of Appeals for the Federal Circuit. Unlike private litigation, the plaintiff does not have to bear the cost of service and enforcement.

The 1988 Omnibus Act's revision of § 337 triggered a European Community complaint under the General Agreement on Tariffs and Trade, and a GATT panel subsequently found § 337 to violate GATT standards.[138] From a GATT perspective, § 337 was discriminatorily applied and thus constituted a barrier to free trade.[139] Congress finally addressed these concerns in the Uruguay Round Agreements Act, passed in 1994 to implement the new World Trade Organization agreement ("GATT").[140]

---

a number of procedural improvements to § 337 practice as well as changes relating to preliminary relief, cease and desist orders, fines, and default judgments. *See* H.R. Conf. Rep. No. 100-576, 100th Cong., 2d Sess. 632–39, *reprinted in* 1988 U.S. Code, Cong. & Admin. News 1665–72.

[134] *See* 19 C.F.R. § 210.20.

[135] *See id.* at § 210.12.

[136] *See id.* at § 210.24.

[137] Those instances are when "the owner, importer or consignee previously attempted to import the article into the United States" or the article was previously denied entry into the United States by a previous exclusion order. 19 U.S.C. § 1337(i).

[138] *See* § 337 of the Tariff Act of 1930, Report by the Panel Adopted on 7 November 1989 (L/6439), General Agreement on Tariffs and Trade: Basic Instruments and Selected Documents 345, 396 (36th Supp. 1990).

[139] For background, see *ABA Delegates Adopt Resolution Supporting Amendment of Section 377*, BNA Int'l Trade Reporter, Aug. 13, 1993.

[140] Congress took a minimalist approach in changing § 337. 19 U.S.C. § 1337 now requires that the ITC make its determinations at the earliest practicable times. Counterclaims by respondents are also allowed as well as termination or arbitration by mutual agreement of the parties. 19 U.S.C. § 1337(c). Bonding procedures under § 337(e), (f), and (g) are amended to make them more analogous to District

[C] Broad Based Trade Legislation

A major U.S. export, and a bright spot in an otherwise dismal balance of trade, intellectual property rights have become a major focus in U.S. trade negotiations.[141] Unfortunately, organized and systematic piracy of U.S. intellectual property has become a major industry in some countries. Alarm over this ever-increasing piracy and concern about the balance of trade has led to the passage of new and amended federal legislation. The major thrust of this legislation is to use economic reward and punishment to encourage other countries to provide adequate protection to American intellectual property owners.

The Generalized System of Preferences ("GSP"), enacted in 1974 and revised with amendments as part of the International Trade and Investment Act of 1984,[142] is one such legislative attempt to encourage proper protection of American interests. To reward protection within the foreign country, the GSP confers duty-free treatment on specific categories of goods exported to the United States by certain developing countries. To punish improper treatment of American intellectual property rights, the GSP contains both discretionary and mandatory sanctions. The most harsh mandatory provision of the GSP dictates that countries shall automatically lose their duty-free benefits for acts of nationalization and seizure of U.S. patents, trademarks, and copyrights. The President may allow certain countries benefits if they provide "adequate and effective protection"[143] for U.S. intellectual property. Information on trade losses is provided by the U.S. Trade Representative in an annual report.

Instituted in 1983, the Caribbean Basin Economic Recovery Act is similar to the GSP,[144] and it confers duty-free status on certain products exported by Caribbean countries. To obtain this favored status, a country must accord adequate protection of U.S. intellectual property. The legislation includes both mandatory and discretionary criteria for inclusion in the program.

The 1988 amendments to the Trade Act of 1974 have continued the trend toward increased sanctions against foreign countries that deny adequate and effective protection for intellectual property. The United States Trade Representative ("USTR") is required to identify "priority" nations that deny this protection. These "priority" countries would then become the target of unfair trade investigation. If the foreign country's acts are found to deny adequate protection, the USTR must recommend trade sanctions to the President, who is required to meet certain deadlines in taking the necessary action. These sanctions can include cessation of trade concessions, the imposition of duties, and withdrawal of designation under the Generalized System of Preferences.[145]

Court procedures. Finally, the District Courts handling actions involving parties who are also parties to an ITC proceeding must grant a motion to stay the District Court proceeding until the ITC determinations become final. *See* 28 U.S.C. § 1659.

141 *See* S. Rep. No. 100-352, 100th Cong., 2d Sess. 2 (1988).

142 Pub. L. No. 98-573, 98 Stat. 3000 (1984).

143 *See* 19 U.S.C. § 2462(c)(5).

144 Pub. L. No. 98-67, 97 Stat. 384 (1983).

145 *See* 19 U.S.C. §§ 2411–2416 (as amended by the Omnibus Trade and Competitiveness Act of 1988).

The 1988 amendments have created a new "Super 301" and special 301 procedures. Super 301 proceedings are initiated by the USTR against countries deemed to be particularly serious offenders of established norms.[146] One device that the USTR has used to exercise leverage over countries providing inadequate intellectual property protection is to place the country on a "watch list," and a country so designed will be considered a candidate for serious scrutiny.[147] The watch list procedure has enjoyed some success. For example, Taiwan, after being placed on the "watch list," enacted a new cable TV law and entered into a bilateral copyright agreement with the United States.[148] Some countries, such as Brazil and Thailand, have proved to be less responsive to the carrot-and-stick approach of Super 301. Both were designated as priority countries in May 1993. Since that time, Thailand has undertaken strong anti-piracy measures and has drafted a new copyright law. Many countries, most in the developing world and the former Soviet Union, have been placed on the watch list. Some have reacted in a positive way from a U.S. perspective, while others have persisted in their objectionable activity and have had sanctions imposed on them.[149]

Part IV. MULTILATERAL AND REGIONAL APPROACHES TO INTERNATIONAL COPYRIGHT PROTECTION

§ 12.13 BEYOND THE INTERNATIONAL TREATIES: A WTO SOLUTION

[A] The Shortcoming of the International Treaties

The 1988 amendments to the Trade Act have provided U.S. negotiators with a strong bargaining chip in bilateral dealings with developing countries. These efforts, however, have their inherent limitations: The problem of organized piracy is simply too large, and too diverse, for one country, even one as powerful as the

---

[146] The Uruguay Round Agreements Act, passed at the end of 1994, further strengthened the USTR's ability to identify offending countries. *See* 19 U.S.C. § 2242(d), (amended to provide that a country may be identified for "special 301" treatment if it denies market access to products protected by intellectual property law, notwithstanding its compliance with the GATT, TRIPS agreement).

[147] For the activities of the USTR in matters of Intellectual property and Special 301 hearing one should consult the USTR, *available at* http://www.ustr.gov/sites/default/files/05012013%202013%20Special%20301%20Report.pdf In the 2013 Report, the following countries were put on a Priority Watch List: Algeria, Argentina, Chile China, Indonesia, Pakistan, Russia, Thailand, Venezuela.

[148] *See* Office of the USTR Notice, 58 Fed. Reg. 31788, June 4, 1993.

[149] For example, the United States withdrew the Ukraine's benefits under the Generalized System of Preferences (GSP) program in August 2001 and imposed $75 million worth of sanctions on Ukrainian imports on January 23, 2002. These sanctions remained in effect for the repeated failure of the Government of Ukraine to enact and enforce adequate optical disc media licensing legislation to comply with the June 2000 U.S.-Ukraine Joint Action Plan to Combat Optical Media Piracy. *See* http://www.ustr.gov/archive/Document_Library/Reports_Publications/2004/2004_Special_301/Special_301_Report_Priority_Foreign_Country.html.

United States, to solve the problem acting alone. The reluctance of developing countries to enforce copyright adequately is related to economic realities in the third world. For developing countries, there is little to gain from costly efforts to enforce copyright. After all, third world countries are consumers of these new technologies and need access to them for economic progress. Thus, developing countries have little incentive to pass substantive laws in the areas of software or mask works. Clearly, a more comprehensive multilateral approach was needed to combat organized piracy in developing countries. For this purpose, industry groups and governmental agencies turned to the General Agreement on Tariffs and Trade (GATT) as the mechanism to resolve this worldwide problem.[150]

The shortcomings of the traditional international conventions prompted the search for a new multilateral mechanism. Although the international conventions have served an important function, they have failed, from a U.S. perspective, in certain significant ways. For one, they have lagged in providing adequate substantive coverage of new technological developments. But even more important, they contain no flexible dispute resolution mechanisms when member states neglect to meet their treaty obligations. By the early 1980s, the United States and other Western countries began to look for an innovative solution to the piracy dilemma and the shortcomings of the conventions. In this context, the GATT offered itself as the international institution best equipped to provide the needed remedy.

[B] From the GATT to the World Trade Organization

The GATT, renamed and reformulated as of January 1, 1995, the World Trade Organization (or WTO), is the most important international agreement regulating trade among nations. It was formed after the Second World War through negotiations between the United States and the United Kingdom and came into effect on January 1, 1948. At the outset, the GATT was conceived as an ancillary tariff agreement to work within a broadly designed institution to be called the International Trade Organization. Its goal was to engage its member countries in multilateral trade negotiations for the encouragement of free trade. Intended to be no more than interim measures, the GATT provisions were to be incorporated into the larger organization. The International Trade Commission never materialized, but the GATT has remained in place since the late 1940s. Despite its ambiguous origins and incoherent organizational structure, the GATT has been surprisingly successful.[151] Through the years, GATT has undergone periodic multilateral negotiations called "Rounds." The latest and most ambitious of these rounds, the Uruguay Round, placed intellectual property prominently on its agenda.

One might ask how the protection of intellectual property relates to the concept of free trade. The answer is that inadequate protection of intellectual property undermines the goal of free trade because it leads to trade distortions. Absent

---

[150] For a background on the international protection of intellectual property leading to a GATT solution, see Marshall A. Leaffer, *Protecting United States Intellectual Property Abroad: Toward a New Multilateralism*, 76 Iowa L. Rev. 273 (1991).

[151] *See generally* Robert Hudec, The GATT Legal System and World Trade Diplomacy 9–10, 45–46 (1975).

sufficient protection, creators can no longer recover the cost of their investment in research and development, resulting in lower production, fewer trading opportunities, and higher costs to the consumer. Despite the obvious need for its successful completion, until the last minute, it appeared that the negotiations might fail. But on December 15, 1993, the Uruguay Round was successfully concluded, incorporating within its framework the standards set forth in TRIPS.

The culmination of the Uruguay Round negotiations, taking eight years to finish, was a sweeping world trade agreement. In addition to the intellectual property provisions, the trade pact slashes tariffs globally by roughly 40% and tightens rules on investment and trade in services. As of January 1, 1995, the 47-year-old GATT no longer exists. In its place, the new World Trade Organization (WTO) oversees the trade agreement.[152]

[C] Intellectual Property Under the WTO: The TRIPS Agreement

In its substantive features, the TRIPS agreement covers all phases of intellectual property. TRIPS provides both national treatment and very detailed rules for minimum standards of protection for intellectual property rights. TRIPS also provides for Most Favored Nation (MFN) treatment with limited exceptions. MFN requires that any advantage, favor, privilege, or immunity granted by a party to the nationals of any other country shall be accorded immediately and unconditionally to the nationals of all other World Trade Organization ("WTO") members. In addition, TRIPS provides for transitional implementation: one year for developed countries, up to five years for developing countries, and extendable 10-year periods for the least developed countries.[153]

As for its substantive aspects concerning copyright law, TRIPS has taken a "Berne plus" approach to protection. The agreement incorporates by reference essentially the minimum standard contained in Articles 1-21 of the 1971 Berne Convention. At the insistence of the United States, the one exclusion is Article 6*bis* of Berne conferring moral rights. In certain of its other provisions, TRIPS goes further than Berne by explicitly requiring protection for computer programs and other compilations of data.[154] Even more than its substantive aspects, TRIPS enforcement provisions are perhaps its principal innovative feature. They require contracting parties to provide civil and administrative procedures and remedies for the enforcement of intellectual property rights. These enforcement provisions

---

[152] The provisions of the Uruguay Round were named "The Dunkel Draft" after Arthur Dunkel, the ex-director of GATT. *See* "The Dunkel Draft" from the GATT Secretariat, collected and edited by the Institute for International Legal Information, (W.S. Hein 1992). For the text of the TRIPS Agreement, see Marshall A. Leaffer, International Treaties on Intellectual Property 595 (2d. ed. 1997). On December 8, 1994, President Clinton signed the Uruguay Round Agreements Act, whose provisions implement the standards set forth in TRIPS. In addition to patent and trademark provisions, the Act dictates important changes in United States copyright law. See *supra* §§ 6.18–6.19 for a discussion of restoration of public domain copyrights, and *supra* § 2.03[B] for a discussion of the anti-bootleg provisions.

[153] *See* TRIPS, Articles 65, 66.

[154] *See* TRIPS, Article 10.

include preliminary measures for prohibiting the importation of infringing goods as well as criminal penalties for willful infringement.

But what happens if a member does not comply with the substantive or enforcement provisions? Here is where the WTO dispute settlement procedures are triggered. The WTO provides for consultations between the parties to resolve the dispute. If the consultations fail, a disputant may refer the matter to the Contracting Parties, who, through a panel, make recommendations to the disputants. If these settlement procedures fail, the Contracting Parties may suspend the application of concessions or other obligations to the offending party required under the WTO.[155] These dispute settlement features of the WTO distinguish it from the supposedly "toothless" quality of the international conventions.[156]

[D] TRIPS and the Berne Convention

One initial critique of the initiative to incorporate intellectual property standards into the GATT framework grew out of a fear that to do so would undermine the continuing effectiveness of existing multilateral intellectual property treaties, including the Berne Convention.[157]

That concern is addressed in the TRIPS Agreement itself, which calls upon the newly-created Council for Trade-Related Aspects of Intellectual Property Rights to consult and cooperate with the World Intellectual Property Organization ("WIPO"), which functions as the Secretariat of the Berne Convention (and other international intellectual property agreements).

Exactly how all this will play out will take some time. To a certain extent, WIPO's own initiative to create new treaties to supplement the Berne Convention, discussed below, can be seen as representing a continuing concern over the new arrangements. How the norms of TRIPS will interact with those of the treaties

---

[155] For Example, in 2009, the Dispute Resolution Body of the WTO adopted the panel report WT/DS362/R, 26 January 2009 on the United States' complaint against China's measures affecting the protection and enforcement of intellectual property rights. The U.S. complained that China's copyright law did not provide appropriate protection for all works in compliance with international copyright law. It also maintained violated TRIPs in not providing adequate border measures, and not imposing adequate criminal penalties for copyright infringement. The Dispute Resolution Body adopted the U.S. position in part.

[156] For an overview of the process, see Rochelle Cooper Dreyfuss & Andreas F. Lowenfeld, *Two Achievements of the Uruguay Round: Putting TRIPS and Dispute Settlement Together*, 37 Va. J. Int'l L. 275 (1997). For commentary on Dreyfuss and Lowenfeld, and other reflections on dispute resolution, see J.H. Reichman, *Enforcing the Enforcement Procedures of the TRIPS Agreement*, 37 Va. J. Int'l Law. 335 (1997). *See also* Frederick Abbott, *WTO Dispute Settlement and the Agreement on Trade Related Aspects of Intellectual Property Rights*, in International Trade Law and the GATT-WTO Dispute Settlement System (E.U. Petersman ed. 1996); Ruth Okediji, *TRIPS Dispute Settlement and the Sources of (International) Copyright Law*, 49 J. Copyright Soc'y 585 (2001).

[157] *See generally* Marshall Leaffer, *Protecting American Intellectual Property Abroad: Toward a New Multilateralism*, 74 Iowa L. Rev. 723 (1991); Peter Jaszi, *A Garland of Reflections on Three International Copyright Topics*, 8 Cardozo L. & Ent. L.J. 47, 67–72 (1989); GATT or WIPO? New Ways in the International Protection of Intellectual Property (Symposium at Ringberg Castle, July 13–16, 1989) (F.K. Beier & G. Schricker, eds., IIC Studies 1989).

administered by WIPO, and how WIPO itself will interact with the World Trade Organization and the TRIPS Council, remains to be seen.[158]

§ 12.14 REGIONAL INTEGRATION AND COPYRIGHT LAW: THE EUROPEAN UNION AND NAFTA

[A] The European Union ("EU")

The original treaties of the European Union did not specifically address intellectual property within the member states. What regulation there was of intellectual property arose under the general provisions of the Treaty of Rome, such as those covering the free movement of goods (article 30), services (article 59), and the rules preventing the distortion of competition (articles 85 and 86). But differences in intellectual property among the member states distort trade by raising transaction costs, contrary to the community policy of economic integration. Thus, even though the Community was not ready for uniform intellectual property laws, it began a serious effort toward harmonization.[159] In 1988, the Commission issued a Green Paper on Copyright in which it began its efforts to harmonize the Community's copyright laws.[160] Five specific copyright issues were covered: piracy, audio-visual home copying, distribution and rental rights, computer programs, and databases. Several of these issues are the subject of EU directives, to which the member states are obligated to conform their laws.

The first of these issues to receive final action was rights in computer software, with a Council directive requiring EU countries to extend specific statutory copyright protection to software.[161] The directive establishes the scope of protection for computer software and allows a limited reverse engineering right (decompilation for purposes of interoperability).[162] In 1992, the EU completed its second copyright directive covering rental rights.[163] This directive requires each member state to enact legislation protecting the rental right for works protected under copyright and neighboring rights regimes. It also allows states to adopt schemes of compulsory licensing or collective administration whereby owners of

---

[158] *See* Neil Netanel, *The Next Round: The Impact of the WIPO Copyright Treaty on TRIPS Dispute Resolution*, 37 VA. J. INT'L L. 441 (1997) (arguing that the recently enacted WIPO Copyright Treaty will become a point of reference in interpreting the relatively open-ended copyright norms of TRIPS).

[159] *See* Beryl R. Jones, *An Introduction to the European Economic Community and Intellectual Properties*, 18 BROOKLYN J. INT'L L. 665 (1992).

[160] GREEN PAPER ON COPYRIGHT AND THE CHALLENGE OF TECHNOLOGY — COPYRIGHT ISSUES REQUIRING IMMEDIATE ACTION, COM(88) 172 final.

[161] The Council Directive 91/250 on computer programs is reprinted in MARSHALL LEAFFER, INTERNATIONAL TREATIES IN INTELLECTUAL PROPERTY 926 (2d ed. 1997).

[162] One should compare the European resolution of the reverse engineering dilemma with that of the position taken in Sega Enterprises, Ltd. v. Accolade, Inc., 977 F.2d 1510 (9th Cir. 1992), which found that disassembly and decompilation of a computer program necessary to create a compatible or non-infringing program was a fair use. The European directive, by contrast, provides a narrower privilege. It would allow such reverse engineering only to create an interoperable (compatible) program.

[163] Directive 92/100 on rental rights, lending rights, and on certain rights related to copyright is reprinted in MARSHALL LEAFFER, INTERNATIONAL TREATIES IN INTELLECTUAL PROPERTY 917 (2d ed. 1997).

rental rights would receive "equitable remuneration." The United States does not recognize a rental right for audiovisual works or sound recordings, and the directive is silent on whether the EU countries must extend "national treatment" to works of U.S. origin. As indicated above, this very question has been vigorously debated in discussions relating to the Berne Protocol.[164]

Other successful efforts at harmonization include a directive that requires member states to extend the copyright term to life-plus-70-years as opposed to life-plus-50-years[165] and the controversial "database directive" that establishes a two-tier system of protection for databases.[166] Under the latter directive, those databases manifesting intellectual creation receive full copyright protection, whereas others that represent capital investment without true authorship (like the white pages in *Feist*), receive a 15-year period of protection against unfair extraction. Other E.U. initiatives include the Design Directive[167] and Design Regulation,[168] which harmonize design protection within the European Union and provide a means for a "Community Design" to have a unitary character throughout the European Union. Another initiative is the Directive on the Resale Royalty Rights, which harmonizes *droit de suite* throughout the European Union.[169] Two post-2000 directives focus on issues of the digital age and implement the WIPO Copyright Treaty and the WIPO Performances and Phonograms Treaty. The Information Society Directive[170] requires the member states to institute legislation to protect copyright management information and to prohibit the circumvention of technological measures that protect access to copyrighted works. The Directive on Electronic Commerce[171] provides limited liability for certain activities of online service providers.

European legislation in the field of copyright is affecting copyright policy in the United States with increasing frequency. For example, one principal reason that the U.S. term was lengthened to life plus 70 was the adoption of that term in the

---

164 *See supra* § 12.13[D].

165 Directive 93/98/EC of the European Parliament and of the Council of 29 October 1993 harmonizing the term of copyright is reprinted in Marshall Leaffer, International Treaties in Intellectual Property 896 (2d ed. 1997).

166 Directive 96/9/EC of the European Parliament and of the Council of 11 March 1996 on the legal protection of databases is reprinted in Marshall Leaffer, International Treaties in Intellectual Property 881 (2d ed. 1997). For a discussion of *sui generis* protection and legislative proposals, see *infra* § 2.11[E].

167 Directive 98/71/EC of the European Parliament and of the Council of 13 October 1998 on the legal protection of designs.

168 Council Regulation (EC) No 6/2002 of 12 December 2001 on Community designs. The regulation makes provision for Community both a registered and unregistered community design. For general information on the Community Design consult the FAQ located at www.oami.eu.int/en/design/faq.htm#40.

169 Directive 2001/84/EC of the European Parliament and of the Council of 27 September 2001 on the resale right for the benefit of the author of an original work of art.

170 Directive 2001/29/EC of the European Parliament and of the Council of 22 May 2001 on the harmonisation of certain aspects of copyright and related rights in the information society.

171 Directive 2000/31/EC of the European Parliament and of the Council of 8 June 2000 on certain legal aspects of information society services, in particular electronic commerce, in the internal market.

European Union and concern that United States works would no longer be protected in Europe after they entered the public domain in the United States.[172] Similarly, concern that U.S. database owners will be uncompensated for the exploitation of their creations in Europe may soon result in the protection of "non-original" databases in the United States. The hard reality is that the European Union "database directive" provides a right of remuneration to foreign database proprietors on a reciprocal basis.

These reciprocity issues relate to a pervasive ongoing tension between the United States and the European Union concerning the principle of "national treatment."[173] Recently, the United States has become alarmed at the increasing trend toward reciprocity among European countries. For example, when France developed a mechanism to collect and distribute royalties to compensate copyright owners for home audio and video recording, it specified that foreign copyright owners could not share in the returns unless their national laws accorded equivalent rights to French copyright owners. The question of "national treatment" remains one of the thorniest issues in the domain of international copyright.

[B] The North American Free Trade Agreement ("NAFTA")

NAFTA is an agreement creating a free trade area for the North American market. Based partially on the United States' current free trade agreement with Canada, NAFTA was entered into on December 17, 1993, and took effect on January 1, 1994. Similar to all free trade agreements, NAFTA's goal is to assure relatively free access to the markets of the member states by eliminating tariff and non-tariff barriers that impede trade between its members. Because inadequate protection of intellectual property can constitute a trade barrier, NAFTA has included provisions to harmonize Canadian, Mexican, and United States standards covering the entire range of intellectual property.[174]

The intellectual property provisions of the treaty are based on national treatment. Under this principle, each party to the treaty must accord to nationals of another party treatment no less favorable than it accords to its own nationals. As for copyright, the treaty requires the protection of computer programs as literary works, the protection of databases as compilations, and rental rights for sound recordings and software. It also places limits on compulsory licensing and requires recognition of rights against unauthorized importation of copies of protected works. Perhaps the most significant aspect of NAFTA is its emphasis on effective enforcement of intellectual property rights. In that regard, it requires signatories to make pretrial injunctive relief available in intellectual property cases. This requirement is designed to overturn the reluctance of Mexican courts to confer such preliminary relief. To comply with NAFTA's requirements, both Canada and

---

[172] See the discussion of the rationale for a life-plus-70 term at *infra* § 6.04.

[173] 46 BNA PTCJ 6 (May 6, 1993).

[174] The intellectual property provisions are included in Chapter 17 of the Treaty. For the text, see Marshall Leaffer, International Treaties in Intellectual Property 644 (2d. ed. 1997).

Mexico had to make major amendments to their intellectual property laws.[175] As for the United States, NAFTA implementation requires less significant legislative change, except that the United States had to restore the copyrights of certain Mexican and Canadian motion pictures previously in the public domain.[176]

What role do these regional agreements play in the multilateral system of trade in intellectual property? One might argue that regionalism, which these agreements represent, threatens to fragment and undermine the multilateral trading system. The threat is real as, for example, the conflict between the United States and the European Union over national treatment and reciprocity has shown. On the other hand, true multilateral agreements are difficult to negotiate and take years to complete. Once achieved, they become snapshots in time and may already be obsolete in some ways — another example of how legal change adapts slowly to technological change.

This gap, however, is particularly dramatic when a world body confronts a technologically driven body of law such as copyright or some other aspect of intellectual property law. By comparison, regional agreements can be concluded more quickly and produce more dramatic legal change. NAFTA, for example, goes further than TRIPS in many of its provisions. This is hardly surprising. An agreement among three countries (NAFTA) as opposed to more than a hundred (TRIPS) involves less intricate political compromise. Once concluded, regional agreements may actually enhance the multilateral system. Ideally, an agreement like NAFTA can operate as a beacon for change to spur the multilateral system toward quicker action and perhaps encourage the completion of side agreements within the multinational framework. Of course, it will take some time to evaluate what effect, salutary or otherwise, these regional agreements will have on the larger system. But they are clearly here to stay, and we can probably expect to find a larger role for them as time passes.

---

175 *See* Cristina Del Valle, *Intellectual Property Provisions of NAFTA* 4 No. 11 J. Proprietary Rts. 8 (1992).

176 *See* 17 U.S.C. § 104A. The Uruguay Round Agreements Act, passed at the end of 1994, amended § 104A to include much more substantial coverage of the restoration of public domain copyrights of foreign origin.

TABLE OF CASES

[References are to pages.]

A

[References are to pages.]

C

D

[References are to pages.]

E

[References are to pages.]

F

G

H

[References are to pages.]

I

J

K

[References are to pages.]

L

M

[References are to pages.]

N

[References are to pages.]

O

P

[References are to pages.]

[References are to pages.]

[References are to pages.]

T

U

V

W

[References are to pages.]

X

Y

Z

INDEX

[References are to sections.]

A

B

[References are to sections.]

C

[References are to sections.]

[References are to sections.]

[References are to sections.]

D

[References are to sections.]

[References are to sections.]

E

[References are to sections.]

[References are to sections.]

[References are to sections.]

[References are to sections.]

[References are to sections.]

[References are to sections.]

[References are to sections.]

[References are to sections.]

[References are to sections.]

[References are to sections.]

[References are to sections.]

[References are to sections.]

T

[References are to sections.]